The Measurement of
Durable Goods Prices

A National Bureau
of Economic Research
Monograph

The Measurement
of Durable
Goods Prices

Robert J. Gordon

University of Chicago Press

Chicago and London

ROBERT J. GORDON is the Stanley G. Harris Professor in the Social
Sciences at Northwestern University.

The University of Chicago Press, Chicago 60637
The University of Chicago Press, Ltd., London
© 1990 by the University of Chicago
All rights reserved. Published 1990
Printed in the United States of America
99 98 97 96 95 94 93 92 91 90 5 4 3 2 1

Library of Congress Cataloging-in-Publication Data

Gordon, Robert J. (Robert James), 1940–
    The measurement of durable goods prices/Robert J. Gordon.
        p. cm.—(A National Bureau of Economic Research monograph)
    Includes bibliographical references.
    ISBN 0-226-30455-8 (alk. paper)
    1. Price indexes. 2. Prices. I. Title. II. Series.
HB231.G57 1990
338.5′28—dc20   89-29895
                                                                      CIP

Relation of the Directors to the
Work and Publications of the
National Bureau of Economic Research

1. The object of the National Bureau of Economic Research is to ascertain and to present to the public important economic facts and their interpretation in a scientific and impartial manner. The Board of Directors is charged with the responsibility of ensuring that the work of the National Bureau is carried on in strict conformity with this object.

2. The President of the National Bureau shall submit to the Board of Directors, or to its Executive Committee, for their formal adoption all specific proposals for research to be instituted.

3. No research report shall be published by the National Bureau until the President has sent each member of the Board a notice that a manuscript is recommended for publication and that in the President's opinion it is suitable for publication in accordance with the principles of the National Bureau. Such notification will include an abstract or summary of the manuscript's content and a response form for use by those Directors who desire a copy of the manuscript for review. Each manuscript shall contain a summary drawing attention to the nature and treatment of the problem studied, the character of the data and their utilization in the report, and the main conclusions reached.

4. For each manuscript so submitted, a special committee of the Directors (including Directors Emeriti) shall be appointed by majority agreement of the President and Vice Presidents (or by the Executive Committee in case of inability to decide on the part of the President and Vice Presidents), consisting of three Directors selected as nearly as may be one from each general division of the Board. The names of the special manuscript committee shall be stated to each Director when notice of the proposed publication is submitted to him. It shall be the duty of each member of the special manuscript committee to read the manuscript. If each member of the manuscript committee signifies his approval within thirty days of the transmittal of the manuscript, the report may be published. If at the end of that period any member of the manuscript committee withholds his approval, the President shall then notify each member of the Board, requesting approval or disapproval of publication, and thirty days additional shall be granted for this purpose. The manuscript shall then not be published unless at least a majority of the entire Board who shall have voted on the proposal within the time fixed for the receipt of votes shall have approved.

5. No manuscript may be published, though approved by each member of the special manuscript committee, until forty-five days have elapsed from the transmittal of the report in manuscript form. The interval is allowed for the receipt of any memorandum of dissent or reservation, together with a brief statement of his reasons, that any member may wish to express; and such memorandum of dissent or reservation shall be published with the manuscript if he so desires. Publication does not, however, imply that each member of the Board has read the manuscript, or that either members of the Board in general or the special committee have passed on its validity in every detail.

6. Publications of the National Bureau issued for informational purposes concerning the work of the Bureau and its staff, or issued to inform the public of activities of Bureau staff, and volumes issued as a result of various conferences involving the National Bureau shall contain a specific disclaimer noting that such publication has not passed through the normal review procedures required in this resolution. The Executive Committee of the Board is charged with review of all such publications from time to time to ensure that they do not take on the character of formal research reports of the National Bureau, requiring formal Board approval.

7. Unless otherwise determined by the Board or exempted by the terms of paragraph 6, a copy of this resolution shall be printed in each National Bureau publication.

(Resolution adopted October 25, 1926, as revised through September 30, 1974)

To my parents,
Robert Aaron Gordon (1908–78)
and Margaret S. Gordon

Contents

Preface

This book has been in the works for many years. Its first draft was completed in June 1974, and was widely circulated for review and comment at that time. The long delay since that time has numerous causes, of which a principal culprit is the author's "other life" as a practicing macroeconomist. A large number of theoretical and empirical papers on macroeconomic issues emerged during 1974–88 while the durable goods project was fermenting in the back room.

But the delay has not been in vain. In recompense for the fourteen-year time lag since the first draft, the data coverage has been extended almost as much, by thirteen years from the initial termination year of 1970 to the new termination year of 1983. Much more important is the greatly expanded scope of the study. First, the study now has a coherent theoretical framework that extends earlier work on capital goods deflators. Because of the important changes in energy prices that have occurred since the 1974 version, it seemed appropriate to place major emphasis on improvement in the energy efficiency of capital goods. Extending the standard view that prices of different models of capital goods reflect their relative marginal products, the new theory shows that prices of different models of capital goods should reflect their relative contributions to net revenue, that is, to a firm's gross revenue minus variable operating cost. At the measurement level, this theoretical approach requires that price changes be adjusted for quality change, those adjustments taking the form not just of changes in performance but also of changes in energy use and in the frequency of repair. Quality adjustments for energy efficiency are undertaken here for commercial aircraft, electric utility generating equipment, household appliances, television sets, automobiles, and railroad equipment.

The 1974 version was heavily dependent for its price data on the Sears catalog. In this version, a bit less than half the weight in the final producers' durable equipment (PDE) deflator is carried by catalog data. Detailed studies of numerous major types of producer durables have been added, partly for their intrinsic interest, and partly to deal with the criticism that the 1974 results were too dependent on small items purchased from the Sears catalog by households, and that such results could not be extrapolated to the industrial sphere. New studies include chapter-length treatments of commercial aircraft, electric utility generating equipment, electronic computers, telephone transmission and switching equipment, and railroad equipment. Another important addition is a set of fifteen new product studies based on data and quality evaluations in *Consumer Reports*. Half these are used as the primary indexes for electric appliances, reflecting the judgment that they have broader brand-name coverage than the catalog indexes for the same products, and the other half are used to confirm and complement the catalog indexes for typewriters, outboard motors, and home power tools.

Thus, the delay in finishing the second version of the book has yielded as its benefit not just the increase in years covered, from twenty-four to thirty-seven, but also the theoretical contribution, the multidimensional treatment of quality change, and the greatly increased reliance on data sources other than the Sears catalog. The net result is a study that is significantly deeper, broader, and more convincing than the original draft.

Since this is a book about quality change and technological progress in durable goods, a word is in order about the change in the production technology of this book between the 1974 and 1988 versions. The draft of the first version was typed on a Smith-Corona portable typewriter and retyped in its entirety, often several times, by a secretary using an IBM selectric typewriter. Any change that I might have contemplated, particularly an extra paragraph early in a chapter, required extensive retyping by the secretary and a difficult cost-benefit calculation as to whether it was really worth it. Technology was a barrier to improvements in substance. In contrast, the new chapters written in 1988 were composed and printed at the level of professional typesetting inside my home by a 386 "clone" personal computer, a Hewlett-Packard laser printer, and WordPerfect 5.0. Revisions could be made instantly and chapters reprinted at the rate of eight pages per minute, all without any involvement of a secretary.

Despite recent technological advances that convert academic research and manuscript production into a cottage industry, no project of this scope and duration can be accomplished alone. I am grateful above all to the ongoing financial support of the National Science Foundation, and to the help of James Blackman and Dan Newlon through the years and more recently of Lynn Pollnow. For partial released time support during 1980–81 I thank the Guggenheim Foundation and during 1984–85 the Sloan Foundation, and particularly Al Rees, for an Officers Grant. Rees's original work on catalog price indexes in the Stigler committee report (National Bureau of Economic Research 1961) and in the context of his path-breaking (1961b) book on real wages during 1890–1914 continues to be an inspiration to me both for its substance and care in execution. The appendix notes to chapter 10, giving the detailed sources of the catalog price indexes, are explicitly modeled on an appendix in Rees's (1961b) book.

Most of the aforementioned financial support provided funds to support graduate student research assistants. A long line of students dating back to the early 1970s has carried out the tedious and demanding work of collecting the primary data developed in this study, including the data from thirty-seven years of Sears catalogs, census *Current Industrial Reports,* used auto and tractor manuals, prices of a multitude of electronic computer models from several sources, and plant-by-plant data on electric utility plant equipment costs and operating characteristics.

In this long list of students, at the very top as *primus inter pares* is Gabriel Sensenbrenner, without whose intense interest in and devotion to this project over the past three years little progress would have been made in translating this great body of data into a coherent set of results. Gabriel is unique in my experience in his curiosity and his ability to grasp broad ideas while making the smallest details come out right, not to mention his stamina to endure eighty-hour weeks. Gabriel also deserves special acknowledgment for his intense effort in the project on computer prices to convert recalcitrant data into coherent results.

Deserving to be singled out as well is James Wilcox, who worked on this project in the late 1970s and developed the new measures of automobile fuel economy that he published in 1984 and that are utilized in chapter 8 here. Peter Fisher did the final round of collection of catalog, automobile, and unit value data and, perhaps more important, transferred most of the catalog data from a pile of loose worksheets onto neat accounting pads suitable for inspection by curious outsiders.

Other students helping on the project, in rough chronological order, were Thomas Henrion, Gary Ericksen, Hans Genberg, and John Kienitz, all at the University of Chicago over the period 1969–73, and, at Northwestern since then, Dana Johnson, Ross Newman, George Kahn, Tim Stevens, and Janet Willer. In the final stages, George Williams did careful work in collecting and reentering for the full postwar period all the detailed product-by-product PPI data, and Dan Shiman was indispensable in converting previously written manuscript chapters from various obsolete technologies into WordPerfect 5.0, and again in reformatting the manuscript to meet the style requirements of the University of Chicago Press.

Projects like this need not only research assistant help but outside scrutiny, criticism, and encouragement. At the top of my list are Zvi Griliches and Robert Lipsey. Zvi's career has been an inspiration for me, and he has provided encouragement and chapter-by-chapter, version-by-version criticism since the beginning, culminating with his role as NBER staff reader of the final version. Robert Lipsey's gentle nagging was instrumental in my finishing the 1974 draft, and his detailed comments on that draft and inspection of the new data printouts at various stages since then led to many improvements. Useful suggestions also came in letters on the 1974 draft from Phil Cagan, Dale Jorgenson, John Kendrick, Sherwin Rosen, and Theodore Schultz. Helpful comments since then have come from George von Furstenberg, Martin Marimont, and F. Lee Moore. John Early of the Bureau of Labor Statistics (BLS) answered particular questions about the anomalous behavior of several specific PPIs. Important sets of detailed comments on specific chapters were received from Pete Dyvsand of the Boeing Company on aircraft, Franklin M. Fisher on computers, Brent Upson of General Motors on automobiles, and D. H. Clark and J. H. Seltzer of the Cummins Engine Company on diesel engine prices. Ken Flamm commented on the use made of his own work on computers and telecommunications equipment.

Reserved for last, but by no means least, is the contribution of Jack Triplett, at the BLS for most of the time span of this project and now chief economist at the Bureau of Economic Analysis. While an unfortunate adversarial tone entered into exchanges with Triplett early on, the substance of these exchanges has made an enormous difference to the scope, methodology, and detailed implementation of this project. Specific mention should be made of Triplett's criticism of earlier versions of my theoretical framework (chap. 2), my descriptions of what the BLS actually does (chap. 3), and the computer research (chap. 6). Perhaps most helpful of all were extremely long and detailed letters in the late 1970s on the automobile and Sears catalog research (chaps. 8 and 10). More than anything else, it was a desire to meet the challenge of Triplett's skepticism by expanding the scope of the project and fixing up the results at the level of detailed implementation that delayed the book for so long, and accordingly he deserves much of the credit for the improvement that has resulted.

Finally, a large bouquet to my wife Julie for listening endlessly over the years to my promises to finish what she cleverly called the "NVER" book "very soon," and for her patience and support in the summer of 1988, when the challenge of pulling all this together glued me to my computer for many long nights and weekends.

Robert J. Gordon
Evanston, Illinois
October 1989

I   Introduction and Methodology

1   Introduction and Summary of Findings

There is much to be said in favor of the recent impressive advances in quantitative techniques but to benefit from them there must be a real commitment to measurement. For want of commitment, we abide the lack of adequate data which greatly limits the usefulness of these new techniques. This sad state is a consequence of our dependency on data that have been collected for purposes other than economic analysis. Very few university economists are engaged in "making data" that will stand up under strong empirical analysis.

Theodore W. Schultz (1974, 1)

1.1   Introduction: Purpose of the Project and Statement of Main Result

This book describes the creation of a new set of price indexes for producer and consumer durable goods that differ fundamentally in methodology of measurement, sources of data, and empirical implications from the official U.S. government price deflators. In contrast to the official national income and product accounts' (NIPA) deflator for producers' durable equipment (PDE), the new index for exactly the same commodities increases at an annual percentage rate 2.9 percent slower over the full period 1947–83. When compounded over time, this implies that the ratio of the new PDE deflator to the existing deflator on a base 1983 = 100 has a 1947 value of 286. When compared with this major difference for producers' durables, the difference between the new deflator for consumer expenditures on durable goods and the official consumer durable deflator is a smaller but still noteworthy 1.5 percent per annum. When compounded over time, the ratio of the new consumer durable deflator to the existing deflator on a base 1983 = 100 has a 1947 value of 174. Since all data on the output of durable goods in the United States depend directly on the validity of durable goods price deflators, the new indexes substantially alter, for the entire postwar period, the official statistical picture of the behavior of investment, the capital stock, investment/output and capital/output ratios, the behavior of the prices of capital goods relative to consumer goods, and the growth rate of productivity in durable goods manufacturing as contrasted to other parts of the economy.

For instance, the annual rate of growth of real equipment investment during the period 1947–83, estimated to be 3.2 percent per annum in the official data, is a much higher 6.1 percent when the official deflator is replaced by the new index. The results overturn stylized facts that have reassured us about the relevance of standard economic growth models, particularly the rough constancy of the ratios of investment to GNP and the nonresidential capital stock to GNP. Even with no correction at all for possible errors in NIPA deflators for nonresidential structures, the new data indicate a continuous and rapid rise in the investment-GNP ratio over the entire postwar period. The ratio of equipment investment to GNP, as well as the ratio of equipment capital to GNP, almost triples in our new results. Another implication is a marked divergence of price changes for durable goods, as measured in this study, from price changes for nondurable goods and services.

1.1.1   Sources of Secular Drift of Alternative Relative to Official Price Indexes

The radical differences between this new PDE deflator and the official series reflect both theoretical and methodological innovations. I take seriously the old economic idea that capital goods are valued by their marginal products and extend it slightly to valuation by contribution to a firm's net revenue, that is, revenue less operating cost. Two capital goods are equivalent if they earn the same net revenue, in which case they will sell for the same age-adjusted price on the used asset market. This notion implies that an attempt must be made to value not just the change in performance of new models versus old models, but also changes in energy use and repair costs. Several of the product categories that exhibit the greatest differences between the alternative and the official deflators, particularly the new indexes for commercial aircraft and electric utility generating equipment, treat changes in operating characteristics explicitly. An important validation of the basic theoretical approach comes from the market for used aircraft; a price index that compares new and old models with quality relatives established by their subsequent value on the used aircraft market declines even more rapidly over the postwar period than an alternative index based on an explicit attempt to estimate net revenue, and the relative prices of individual models on the used aircraft market are highly correlated with our estimates of their ability to generate net revenue. Adjustments for energy use are applied as well for automobiles, railroad equipment, and almost all major consumer appliances. Adjustments for both energy use and repair frequency are made for television sets.

Most of the innovative empirical conclusions of this study stem, however, not from operating efficiency adjustments, but from a consistent implementation of current theoretical practice. The agency responsible for the NIPA data, the Bureau of Economic Analysis (BEA), already has introduced for the period extending back to 1969 a hedonic price index for computer systems; the BEA index is confirmed with new data and extended back fifteen years earlier. The widely accepted principles used by the BEA for computers are extended to communications equipment, the single most important category of PDE. The single largest body of data, however, comes from the Sears catalog and simply involves the application of the standard Bureau of Labor Statistics (BLS) specification technique, without explicit efficiency or reliability adjustments, carefully and consistently over a long period of time.

The results here go beyond current NIPA procedures, however, in order to repair the undesirable effects of the current official Paasche index number methodology for price deflators, in which the growth rate of an aggregate price index over a given time interval is highly sensitive to the choice of the base year, and in which products like computers with rapidly declining relative prices are severely underweighted in years prior to the base year and increasingly overweighted in years subsequent to the base year. Here, current NIPA practice is running well behind the widely accepted theoretical state of the art by failing to utilize the much superior Törnqvist (1936, 1937) index number formula, identified by Diewert (1976) as one of the class of what he calls "superlative" index numbers.[1] Throughout this study, the Törnqvist formula, in which nominal value share weights for aggregation are allowed to change each year, is used to aggregate price indexes across classes of products, for both producers durable equipment and consumer expenditures on durable goods. It should be emphasized that all statements contained in this chapter and in the rest of the book regarding "drift," that is, the growth rate of the ratio of the alternative index to the official price index for the same concept, always use identical weights for the numerator ("alternative index") and denominator ("official index") of any such ratio. Thus, the results on secular drift entirely reflect differences in the growth rates of the underlying price indexes and do not reflect differences in weighting schemes at all. Later in this chapter, results are exhibited on the drift of these new

1. What Diewert called "superlative" index numbers were those that provide a good approximation to a theoretical cost-of-living index for large classes of consumer demand and utility function specifications. In addition to the Törnqvist index, Diewert classified Irving Fisher's "Ideal" index as belonging to this class. Diewert's contribution is placed in the context of theoretical research on cost-of-living indexes by Triplett (1988) and is updated in Diewert (1989a).

indexes relative to the official indexes using three alternative weighting schemes, the Törnqvist formula, the NIPA method with 1982 weights, and the NIPA method with 1972 weights. The annual rate of drift of 2.86 percent for the PDE deflator refers to the Törnqvist version of the new index relative to a Törnqvist aggregation of the price indexes that underlie the NIPA deflator for PDE.

There is a need to stress not only what this study does demonstrate, but also what it does not. No claim is made that there is a consistent upward bias in the full range of government price indexes. In particular, there is no necessary conflict between these new results and the longstanding claim by Triplett (1975, 1988) that the overall bias in official price indexes is just as likely to be downward as upward. Triplett's claim has always been explicitly with reference to the CPI as a whole and does not conflict with the new results showing a major upward bias for durable goods in the PPI, and to the lesser extent for durable goods in the CPI. We cannot assess the direction of bias in the full CPI, and hence we cannot assess Triplett's claim, since we have no new data for the prices of consumer nondurables or services. This book makes no statement at all about the existence or direction of possible errors in price indexes for products other than durable goods. If the official price indexes for nondurable products are accurate, then these results imply major revisions in the relative prices and quantities of durables and nondurables, in the shares of durable goods in total output, and in the growth rate of capital input relative to total output. If, in contrast to the upward bias in the official price indexes for durable goods implied by these results, the official price indexes for products other than durable goods are biased downward—as has been suggested recently by Triplett (1988) for consumer nondurable goods and services—the suggested revisions in the relative prices and quantities of durables and nondurables would become even larger.[2] On the other hand, any finding in future research that the prices of consumer nondurables and services are on balance biased upward would reduce the

2. Triplett intends his assessment of downward bias to apply to the CPI as a whole and qualifies it to apply to the recent period: "However, because a number of large CPI components appear quite clearly downward biased, I suspect that the CPI has, if anything, understated inflation in the last several years" (1988, 67). Triplett's list of components claimed to be biased downward includes one type of consumer nondurables (clothing), two types of consumer services (housing and restaurant meals), and one type of durable good (new automobiles). He admits that there is upward bias in the CPI for used automobiles and states that evidence on other consumer services is inconclusive. His claim regarding new car prices does not necessarily conflict with my results since the major reason for his claim is that he disagrees with the BLS/NIPA treatment of safety and antipollution devices as quality improvements rather than price increases, whereas I accept the BLS/NIPA approach. Note in table 1.1 below that I find the PDE deflator for automobiles to be biased downward during 1973–83, owing to the erroneous CPI measure of the relative price of used to new cars, whereas that CPI error creates an upward bias in the consumer durable deflator. The opposite direction of these automobile biases results from the fact that on balance the business sector sells used cars to the household sector, resulting in a negative weight on used cars in PDE but a positive weight in consumer expenditures on durable goods.

magnitude of the suggested changes in the relative prices and quantities of durables and nondurables, but would correspondingly increase the magnitude of the estimated bias in absolute prices and quantities for GNP as a whole.

1.1.2   Sources of Data for the Alternative Deflators

Almost all the data on which the results are based have been newly collected for this study, and the final price indexes for producers' and consumer durables are weighted averages of 25,650 separate price quotations selected to satisfy the twin criteria of careful adjustment for quality change and measurement of transaction rather than list prices.[3] There is no overlap between the sources of the official deflators, based almost entirely on components of the consumer and producer price indexes, and the current project, which assembles and analyzes data from numerous sources.[4] Chief among these the following:

1. Mail-order catalog prices;
2. Price observations from *Consumer Reports* (*CR*) articles on household appliances, typewriters, outboard motors, and home power tools, as well as data on operating characteristics, repair records, and reliability for some products;
3. Unit value data from the census *Current Industrial Reports;*
4. Data from the Department of Transportation on prices paid by airlines for commercial aircraft, combined with data from the same source on the subsequent operating cost characteristics of specific aircraft models and from the Avmark Company on price quotations for used commercial aircraft;
5. Department of Energy data on equipment costs and operating characteristics of almost all the nonnuclear electric utility generating plants in the United States;
6. Data on prices and characteristics of mini- and mainframe computers from Phister (1979) and *Computerworld* magazine and also, for the last few years, from *PC* magazine on mail-order prices for personal computers and peripherals;
7. Data on the prices of new and used automobiles from the *Red Book* and the *NADA Official Used Car Guide;*

3. To use the technical terminology of chap. 12, this count includes only the data used in the sixteen "primary" categories of PDE. It is slightly overstated because it includes price observations for eleven Sears catalog indexes that are used twice, but it is also understated by excluding all the price observations collected for individual models in *Consumer Reports*. In addition, 8,000 additional observations were collected but were rejected for use in the final index. This total consists of about 4,500 unit values developed for an earlier unpublished study but not included in the analysis of chap. 11, and about 3,500 automobile list price quotations.

4. The one exception to the statement about overlap is that the CPI for new automobiles receives a weight of half in our automobile index. The new index for computer systems is entirely independent of data collected for the BEA computer deflator.

8. Data on the prices of new and used wheel and crawler tractors from the leading price guide for used tractors;
9. Data recently collected from AT&T sources by Kenneth Flamm (1989) on the prices of telephone transmission and switching equipment; and
10. Data collected from railroad industry magazines and other sources on the prices and quality characteristics of railroad locomotives and freight cars.

The primary focus of the study is on the detailed analysis of price data for individual products. This daunting task has in the end become a fascinating one, because the chapters of this book make up a detailed history of technological change and quality improvement for many types of durable goods. For each major product, in addition to incorporating adjustments for quality change to the maximum extent that the data allow, two additional exercises are central ingredients in establishing the credibility of the results. First, price comparisons are developed of "closely similar" models over long periods of time. If the new index says that there has been no price change over a particular interval for a specific product, while the PPI says that the price has doubled, it is reassuring to be able to provide a specific example of a model of roughly the same quality characteristics and size that has remained roughly unchanged in price. This technique is carried out mainly in chapter 10, where many such comparisons are developed for the catalog data. The methods of data collection used by the BLS to compile the PPI not only prevent outsiders like myself from carrying out any such comparisons of similar models on BLS data, but even prevent BLS specialists from accomplishing this task, particularly for the earlier part of the postwar period. Another important ingredient in the credibility of the results is the consistent attention throughout the book to unmeasured aspects of quality change. Below are summarized the numerous aspects of unmeasured quality change that, while difficult to quantify, imply that this study, however radical its results, still fails to capture the full range of quality improvements.

1.2 The Importance of Accurate Price Measures

Among the most important goals of aggregate economic policy are the achievement of full employment, price stability, and a high rate of economic growth. However, the evaluation of a nation's progress in achieving two of the goals, price stability and economic growth, depends on the accuracy with which prices are measured. Estimates of the overall rate of inflation and of changes in relative prices depend, of course, on accurate measurement of the prices of individual commodities. And estimates of the level and rate of growth of aggregate output and its components depend on the accurate deflation of current-dollar sales and production data. Because of their crucial role in output measurement, correct price quotations are also absolutely necessary for data on labor productivity (output per manhour) and the contribution of capital input and technical change to economic growth.

The scope of this book is limited to the prices of durable goods to the exclusion of nondurable goods and services, both to keep the scale of the research project at a manageable size and to concentrate on the segment of the economy where official price data are most vulnerable to inaccuracy, owing to the heterogeneity and changing specifications of durable goods. Why is a new set of price indexes necessary to replace the official government deflators for durable goods? The official indexes compiled by the BLS and other government agencies have been subjected to a steady barrage of criticism during the three decades that have passed since the publication of the "Stigler report" (NBER 1961). But, despite this fact, official deflators for durable goods today are based on essentially the same methodology as in the 1950s, with the new hedonic index for computers representing a rare exception to this statement.

One reason for the lack of progress is that most economic research on price measurement has been either too general or too specific to convince government officials that existing official deflators are very seriously in error. One research approach has been an exploration of the implications of casual empiricism, for example, the substitution by Jorgenson and Griliches (1967) of the CPI durable deflator for the producers durable equipment deflator (which has a faster rate of growth) on the grounds that, since "expenditures on the wholesale price index are less than those on the consumers' price index, adjustments for quality change are less frequent and less detailed (263).[5] This is obviously too general an approach to be convincing, since most types of producers' durables are not covered by the CPI, while the CPI itself has been subject to criticism regarding many of the same issues in the correction of quality change that raise problems for the PPI.

Most price research since the Stigler Committee report (NBER 1961), however, is at the opposite extreme, consisting of detailed regression studies of quality change in individual products (perhaps a dozen products in all), with relatively little attempt to evaluate the general implications of the studies for price, output, and input measurement. The concentration on one or two specific products is not surprising, since most tests have been conducted by professional econometricians more interested in refining their methodological techniques than in applying their conclusions to broader issues.[6] One indication that the authors of the first round of hedonic studies in the 1960s were mainly interested in econometric methodology rather than substantive implications is the way price research has essentially "died out"

5. The wholesale price index (WPI) was renamed the producers price index (PPI) in 1978. I have tried to purge the old WPI nomenclature from the book everywhere except in quoted material.

6. The most notable exception is the series of books and papers by Irving B. Kravis and Robert E. Lipsey on foreign trade prices, especially Kravis and Lipsey (1971).

since then. With the exception of research on computer prices, there have been remarkably few studies since 1971 requiring citation for the development of new product-level price indexes.

There are, of course, a few exceptions to this characterization. Since his earliest work on agriculture, Griliches has always been interested in extracting general implications from specific product studies of quality change using the hedonic and other methodologies. In addition to his work with Ohta on automobiles in the 1970s and 1980s, Griliches has written several follow-up pieces (including Griliches 1979) that supplement his well-known (1971) retrospective on hedonic research. Triplett is another leading figure who has written numerous surveys and evaluations of research on price measurement and quality change, most recently in his (1989) comprehensive survey of research on computer prices. Griliches and Triplett have generally taken opposing viewpoints about the importance and direction of price measurement bias due to problems in measuring quality change. In his first overall evaluation (1964) and again in his work with Jorgenson (1967, 1972), Griliches indicated the likelihood of a major upward bias in official measures of price change, while Triplett has consistently asserted that, "if individual components show both upward and downward errors, the overall error may go either way."[7] More recently, Triplett (1988) has argued that the reasons to believe that the CPI is downward biased outweigh those that work in the opposite direction.

The decisiveness of the results in this book stand in contrast to Triplett's (1971a, 1975) demonstration, on the basis of empirical studies predating the research reported here, that some hedonic regression studies indicate a downward rather than an upward bias in the CPI. As indicated above, these new results do not necessarily imply an upward bias in the official deflator for GNP as a whole, because I do not study prices of consumer nondurables and services. But most of the research reviewed by Triplett in the early 1970s, and indeed the great majority of price research carried out since the 1961 Stigler report, concerns durable goods. Within the limited sphere of durable goods, as measured in the PPI and in the household appliance and television components of the CPI, the results reported in this book decisively overturn the ambiguity of Triplett's appraisal. The bias in the durable components of both the CPI and the PPI is consistently in an upward direction. The annual percentage rate of "drift" of the ratio of my alternative price indexes to the official deflators is predominantly negative, with positive drift in only five of the sixty-six cells for subintervals in table 1.1 (which shows twenty-two PDE categories over the subintervals 1947–60, 1960–73, and 1973–83). This consistency in the direction of bias

---

7. The preceding sentence in the original is, "Notice that these studies do not point to a positive conclusion: we have not proved that price indexes are biased either upward or downward; rather, they establish only that the proposition that indexes are systematically upward biased is not conclusively confirmed by the available evidence" (Triplett 1971a, 31).

in the official PDE deflator is reassuring and shows that my results do not depend overwhelmingly on specific products or technologies. Very large rates of drift are identified for one or more of these subintervals for such diverse products as computers, telephone switching equipment, calculators, electric generating boilers and turbines, television sets, commercial aircraft, stationary air compressors, centrifugal pumps, and diesel engines.

1.2.1   Important Issues to Which Price Measurement is Related

While only a small minority of recent economic research has directly contributed to the improved measurement of prices, the conclusions of a much broader range of studies are affected by new estimates of durable goods prices.

1. Economic statisticians and historians have devoted much attention to accelerations or decelerations of output and productivity growth during various historical eras, for example, the acceleration in output growth after 1948 from the 1929–48 rate, or the productivity growth slowdown that started in the late 1960s and continues to this day. But few economists have attempted to determine the contribution of measurement error to these apparent historical events. If, for instance, the BLS made more detailed and widespread adjustments for quality change after 1947 than before (as seems to have been the case), much of the acceleration of productivity growth after World War II may have been caused by the improved statistical techniques of the BLS, rather than any event in the "real" economy outside Washington, D.C.[8] While the data in this book do not extend before 1947, and cannot answer questions about changes in growth rates that occurred on or about that date, the new measurement techniques have been applied consistently within the 1947–83 period and should thus eliminate spurious movements in durable goods output caused by intraperiod changes in the BLS deflation techniques. The only similar broad-scale effort to correct price data for a historical subperiod was Rees's (1961b) demonstration that the apparent cessation of real wage growth between 1890 and 1914 was an artifact of incorrect cost-of-living data and was eliminated by improved measurement techniques. Neither this study nor Rees's, of course, has anything to say about the true growth of prices and output before or after the historical subperiod under investigation. When we read that, in the forty years after 1865, the life of a rail increased from two years to ten, and the car weight it could bear from eight tons to seventy, we suspect that existing capital goods

---

8. Mills (1936) proves a perceptive early review of problems of price research that anticipates some of the themes of the Stigler report, written twenty-five years later. He cites (294–95) an engineering test showing that agricultural machinery in use in the United States in 1932 was 70 percent more efficient than that in use in 1910–14 and speculates that substantial improvements in the quality of "motor cars" had been missed in the WPI. However, Mills does not anticipate the potential contribution of the hedonic and other methods to improve the measurement of quality change and ends on a pessimistic note: "All commodities except a restricted number of staples are subject to quality changes that may not be reduced to quantitative form" (308).

deflators significantly overstate quality-corrected inflation in capital goods prices, and understate the increase in capital input, all the way back to the dawn of the industrial age.[9]

2. The growth rate of output minus the contributions of growth in labor and capital inputs is the growth rate in total factor productivity (TFP), often taken to represent the contribution of technical change or, more generally, advances in knowledge to economic growth (the latter contribution is sometimes called more neutrally the "residual" or "measure of our ignorance"). TFP growth is affected by errors in price measurement; in a steady state with constant growth rates of output and investment, the effect of price measurement errors on TFP growth is equal to the estimated bias in the deflator for investment goods times the difference between the share of capital in total income and the share of investment in total output. Assuming that the income share of capital exceeds the investment share of output, then the correction of any upward bias in price indexes for investment goods implies slower growth in TFP. However, this does not mean that advances in knowledge are less important. Slower growth of the "residual" is then more properly interpreted as the portion of labor productivity growth that is not contributed by technical change "embodied" in capital input. Solow's (1960) embodiment hypothesis held that productivity gains result, in large part, from the installation of capital goods that embody new technologies. Some studies, most recently Maddison (1987, 662–64), have interpreted this hypothesis to imply that explicit adjustments should be made to the BEA measures of the capital stock to account for embodied quality improvements.[10] However, it was shown long ago by Jorgenson (1966) and others that the Solow vintage argument could not contribute much to the explanation of economic growth, since the embodied quality improvements had the effect of raising both the growth rate of output (through faster investment growth) and the growth rate of capital input, leaving a minimum net effect on the growth rate of total factor productivity that depended on the small difference between the share of investment in output and the share of capital income in total income. The results in this book confirm Jorgenson's theoretical argument, in the sense that the very substantial revisions to the price deflators for PDE in the end "explain" only 13 percent of the 1.34 percent annual growth rate in conventionally measured total factor productivity over the postwar (1947–83) period. As in Jorgenson's model, the explanation of total factor productivity here is relatively small because the new deflators not only raise the growth rate of capital input, but also raise the growth rate of output.

3. Closely related to the previous paragraph are the behavior of the capital/output and investment/output ratios. The former exhibits puzzling

9. The source on rail quality is Rosenberg and Birdzell (1986, 247).
10. Some of this literature has been reviewed recently by Oliner (1988).

historical behavior, declining precipitously between 1929 and 1948, declining slowly from 1948 to 1966, and then reversing course to exhibit a slow increase from 1966 to 1983. The revised durable goods price data in this book suggest that the capital/output ratio rose dramatically rather than fell after 1948. These results naturally raise questions about the effect of possible measurement errors on its behavior in prior historical epochs.

4. A stimulus to several early hedonic regression studies of price and quality change was the need for accurate measures of relative prices for studies of the demand for durable goods. Indeed, the first such study of refrigerator prices (Burstein 1960) appeared in a book entitled *The Demand for Durable Goods*. The same need formed part of the motivation for Griliches's early work on automobile prices, including that in the Stigler report and that included in his well-known (1964) survey of measurement problems. Probably the best-known study in which the aim of the hedonic price research is the provision of a relative price measure for the purpose of demand analysis is Chow's (1967) paper on computer prices. Chow's work influenced me to urge (1971c) that the NIPA incorporate a hedonic price index for computer equipment, advice that was rejected at the time but then later accepted with a fifteen-year lag.[11]

5. Broader issues in macroeconomics that hinge on changes in the relative price of investment and consumption goods have been identified by R. A. Gordon (1961). Of more immediate interest may be the implications of this research for the terms of trade of different groups of nations. Assuming relatively accurate measurement of the prices of crude commodities exported by less-developed countries, the results reported here imply a substantial upward bias in the secular growth rate of the terms of trade of the developed world relative to the less-developed world, which imports much of its capital equipment.

6. Related to the previous topic is the dependence of measures of the user cost of capital on accurate indexes for the price of capital goods relative to output. The demand for a capital good depends on its user cost, which in the usual Hall-Jorgenson (1967) formula includes a term for the rate of change of the relative price of capital goods. The results in this study imply a substantial decline in the relative price of capital equipment, in contrast to the roughly constant relative price indicated in the NIPA over the period 1948–82. No new price indexes for structures are developed, and so the new results apply only to the equipment component of fixed investment (the nominal share of PDE in fixed nonresidential investment was 60 percent in 1948 and 70 percent in 1987).

11. One unfortunate side-effect of the fifteen-year lag is that the BEA would have discovered much earlier the pitfalls of its fixed-base-year Paasche index number formula. If a computer price index had been incorporated into the NIPA in the mid-1970s, the implicit GNP and PDE deflators would have been biased toward an increasingly severe understatement of inflation as a result of the fixed 1972 base year, used in the NIPA until the 1986 benchmark revision.

7. Studies of the payoff to research and development (R&D) are hamstrung by the misallocation of the fruits of research implied by the official price deflators for durable goods. Airlines do no research but "receive credit" for the R&D accomplished by the airframe and aircraft engine manufacturers. Electric utilities receive credit for the R&D performed by the makers of turbo-generator systems. The telephone communications industry receives credit for the achievements of the companies that manufacture telephone transmission and switching equipment. The approach here to the measurement of quality change creates a greater upward revision of the growth rate of output in industries where technical change has been rapid than in industries where it has been slow. This approach stresses the symmetric treatment of research on performance and operating attributes of capital goods. If R&D investment is shifted from making aircraft go faster to making them more fuel efficient, that R&D is still productive if it yields improvements in the ability of the new-model aircraft to earn profits for airlines. While the new theory calls for universal adjustments for improved energy efficiency that is not accompanied by proportional increases in the cost of durable goods, such adjustments are feasible only for a subset of products, and the improvements for other products that are not treated explicitly stand as an example of unmeasured quality change in this study.[12]

8. Accurate measures of the relation of transaction to list prices, that is, of discounts and premiums, are necessary to evaluate Stigler's contention that "it is not possible to make a direct test for price rigidity, in part, because the prices at which the products of oligopolists sell are not generally known. . . . Nominal price quotations may be stable although the prices at which sales are taking place fluctuate often and widely" (Stigler 1947). If discounting and premiums are important, vary procyclically, and are not adequately measured in present official statistics, existing national accounts may understate cyclical fluctuations in prices and overstate fluctuations in real output. To test this hypothesis, all price data collected for this book are either true transaction prices or close proxies, for example, prices of late-model used cars and tractors. This issue resurfaces in chapters 10 and 11.

1.3   The Scope of This Study

The original intention of the research project was simply to collect previous research and summarize its implications for the two major issues of "quality-adjustment" and "transaction-list" bias in the official producers' durable deflators. Primary attention to producers' durables was motivated by my longstanding interest in the measurement of capital input and in the

---

12. Additional research issues in the cross-industry allocation of the returns to R&D are considered by Griliches (1979, esp. 104–5).

sources of economic growth. After the initial results of the collection and summarization exercises were published (see Gordon 1971b), it became apparent that a new, larger-scale study was needed. Previous regression studies of the quality-adjustment problem were available for only short sample periods, in some cases were defective in methodology, and in almost all cases relied on list prices rather than transaction prices. Previous evidence on changes in unit values was unsuitable for application to the transaction-list problem, because inadequate attention had been paid to shifting product mix across size classes as an alternative source of fluctuations in unit values. The only solution was an effort to collect a large amount of new data for a long period of years and to perform an analysis that attempted to correct for quality change as thoroughly as possible, and to correct unit value data for shifts in product mix.

After the first draft of this project was completed in 1974, the scope of the study widened further. The stimulus for an explicit treatment of changes in energy efficiency came from the 1974 and 1979 oil shocks. Detailed case studies on aircraft and electric utility generating equipment (the latter treated only sketchily in the 1974 version) were added toward this end, and new evidence on changes in automobile fuel consumption was incorporated into that chapter. The criticism that the first-draft results were too dependent on mail-order catalogs led to the development of parallel evidence from *CR* for numerous appliances and other products, including typewriters, outboard motors, and home power tools, which results in a significant improvement in the robustness and credibility of my conclusions. Further, the scope of the study was broadened to include more "large" equipment that is sold directly to firms rather than to households. The improved evidence on electric utility generating equipment and the new evidence for the aircraft, computer, telephone, and railroad categories helps address this earlier criticism.

The following basic ground rules were set down to delimit the scope of this study.

1. The basic aim was to create a new index suitable for replacing the existing deflator for PDE in the NIPAs. Thus, the particular commodities eligible for data collection were those that are a component of the NIPA deflator for PDE.

2. Nineteen forty-seven was selected as the initial year of the sample period, since almost no capital goods were included before then in the PPI (on which the NIPA deflator is based). While an extension of the study back to 1929 or earlier would have been interesting and potentially important, the pre-1947 years carry the disadvantage for the present purpose that no estimates of official deflator bias are possible for individual commodities for those years. Any future study of the pre-1947 period will have to follow Rees (1961b) by developing price indexes from scratch, using available information on weights from the Census of Manufactures and other sources, since there is no product-by-product set of NIPA weights that can be used as

in this study. The terminal year of 1983 was chosen arbitrarily to bring the project to a halt, and work continued throughout the 1984–88 period to update to 1983 all the many data sources listed above.

3. Data were eligible only if they were obtained from sources independent of the PPI or CPI. The only exception is the inclusion of the CPI for new autos as part of the final auto index developed in chapter 8.

4. Data were eligible only if they could reasonably be interpreted either as transaction prices or as close proxies for transaction prices. This includes catalog prices, unit values, *CR* data, which after 1959 are based on market surveys of actual prices paid, buyers' prices for aircraft, electric generating equipment, telephone equipment, railroad equipment, and late-model used prices for automobiles and tractors.

Once the data were collected, they were adjusted for changes in quality by two basic methods. In the case of commodities where numerous observations were available in each year, hedonic regression studies were performed. Products for which hedonic regression estimates were obtained include electric generating equipment, computer processors, refrigerators, room air conditioners, washing machines, new and used automobiles, new and used wheel and crawler tractors, hot water heaters, and outboard motors. Given the fact that almost all the hedonic regression studies cover the full 1947–83 period and are thus based on a much longer span of time than the first generation of hedonic studies performed in the 1960s, it is likely that there are more "product years" covered in the hedonic regression studies of this book than in all previous hedonic research on durable goods combined.

The second basic method of quality adjustment was the conventional specification method, mainly used for the mail-order catalog items, where (with the exceptions of refrigerators, air conditioners, washing machines, hot water heaters, and outboard motors) only a few observations were available in each year for those products included in the study. Catalog specifications and illustrations were examined carefully to limit price comparisons to the subset of models that were absolutely identical in any given pair of years. An innovation in the discussion of both the hedonic regression results and the catalog indexes is the cross-checking of the hedonic price indexes by comparisons of "closely similar" models over long spans of time. This is done for automobiles with the aid of data on the value of specific options supplied by General Motors; in chapter 10 on the catalog data for almost thirty separate products; on diesel engines through correspondence with manufacturers; and on home appliances and several other products by developing parallel price indexes from *CR*.

The *CR* indexes are a relatively recent addition to the project and have proved to be so useful that they are the basis for all conclusions regarding home appliances. One of the most innovative and interesting aspects of the book is the set of explicit adjustments for energy efficiency and re-pair frequency of home appliances based on the *CR* data. Explicit energy adjustments are also carried out for individual pairs of aircraft models, electric generating equipment, automobiles, and railroad locomotives. Examples of products where improvements in fuel efficiency have occurred, but where no explicit adjustment is made, are tractors and diesel engines.

After all the individual product price indexes were developed, they were weighted together into deflators for the twenty-two categories of PDE and then for PDE as a whole. Weights within the twenty-two categories are identical to those used in the NIPA deflator for the same products, but across the twenty-two were calculated with the Törnqvist index number methodology discussed above rather than with the flawed implicit deflator method currently used in the NIPA. The only exception to this statement is that within the office machinery category computer and noncomputer equipment is aggregated with the Törnqvist formula. Chapters 6 and 12 show the substantial differences that emerge when the Törnqvist method is used in place of the implicit deflator method of aggregation.

A portion of the weight in the NIPA deflator for PDE is allocated to official price indexes for goods purchased not only by businessmen, but also by consumers. Chief among these are automobiles, large and small household appliances, radios, and television sets. The set of alternative price indexes developed for these products in this book can be used not just as a component in the alternative PDE deflator, but also as the basis for computation of an alternative deflator for consumer expenditures on durable goods. From the total of 105 unduplicated product indexes developed in this book for use in the alternative PDE deflator, a subset of eleven product indexes is used in the alternative deflator for consumer durables. Because nominal sales data can be easily obtained for these products, aggregation for consumer durables uses the Törnqvist formula throughout, in contrast to PDE, where NIPA weights are used within group categories and the Törnqvist formula is the basis for aggregating across those categories.

1.4 Summary of the Results

1.4.1 Methodological Innovations and Conclusions

In the deflation of durable goods, the proper criterion for quality adjustment is to consider as identical two different items if their ability to produce services for consumers, or their ability to generate net revenue for producers at a fixed set of output and variable input prices, is identical. Leaving aside changes in energy efficiency and repair frequency, there is no difference in principle between deflation based on equating goods in terms of their ability to generate net revenue and deflation based on equating goods in terms of their cost, as long as both concepts are measured for the same units, for example, the ability of a computer to perform calculations. Because firms may discover technological improvements that improve the net-revenue generating ability of a capital good by an amount greater than the effect of the improvement on the selling price of that capital good, the theory of quality adjustment must incorporate such changes, called ''nonproportional'' quality improvements in chapter 2.

A simple method for carrying out such an analysis is to calculate the ''real'' price change implied by the introduction of a new model as the percentage difference for the new and old models in the selling price and the ability to generate net revenue at a fixed set of output and variable input prices. If the introduction of a new model raises the selling price and ability to generate net revenue in exact proportion, then this ''proportional'' quality change implies no change in the ''real'' price caused by the new model introduction, and the nominal price change for this product can be measured by the behavior of nominal prices for models that remain unchanged in the two adjacent time periods affected by the new-model introduction. If, however, the introduction of a new model raises the selling price by less than the ability to generate net revenue, as occurred, for instance, with the introduction of the jet plane, a ''real'' price decline is recorded, and this negative change in the real price is added to the recorded nominal price change for models that remain identical in the time period affected by the introduction of the new model.

This technique amounts to ''crediting'' manufacturers for improvements in knowledge and techniques that achieve any such ''nonproportional'' improvements in quality. The approach is a straightforward extension of the treatment of computers already incorporated into the NIPA, which treats nonproportional changes in computer calculating power relative to computer prices as a price decrease, that is, which essentially measures changes in computer prices per unit of calculating power rather than per ''computer box.''

Problems in the implementation of the conceptual framework are the subject of chapter 3, which compares the advantages and disadvantages of the conventional ''specification'' technique used in the official deflators with those of the newer hedonic regression technique. The general conclusions of the chapter run counter to the view held in the 1960s that regarded the hedonic technique as a panacea that would make the conventional ''specification approach'' obsolete. While both methods are identical in principle, in practice their advantages are complementary. The conventional method is inferior to the hedonic approach in its inability to provide values or ''shadow prices'' for changes in overall dimensions or other physical characteristics, for example, length or horsepower. But the hedonic technique falls short when there is a change in the relation between quality characteristics that are, respectively, included in and excluded from the regression equation. Inclusion of all relevant variables in the regression is prevented in practice by multicollinearity, and by quality changes that occur on all models simultaneously and hence cannot be identified in a cross-sectional regression equation.

The emphasis in this book on improvements in energy efficiency leads to a further downgrading of the hedonic technique, since improvements in energy efficiency tend to be made on all models simultaneously (except in the interesting case of room air conditioners, where a variety of high-efficiency high-priced and low-efficiency low- priced units is for sale simultaneously). The hedonic technique is not well suited to measuring price for complex machines like tractors and automobiles, where handling, comfort, and other intangible characteristics are important attributes that are "missed" by the hedonic approach.[13] Instead, the hedonic approach is much more useful for simple products producing a homogeneous, easily measured output, represented in this book by the examples of electric utility generating equipment, hot water heaters, and outboard motors. Electronic computers fall somewhere in between the extremes of complex and simple, having two major quality attributes that can be measured relatively well, speed and memory, but also possessing other quality attributes that may cause shifts in the ratio of excluded to included variables in hedonic regressions, for example, multitasking ability and virtual memory.

Overall, a mix of measurement techniques is likely to be superior to the use of a single technique for all products. For products having a small number of characteristics that are valued by users and relatively easy to measure, and for which a substantial number of different models is available in each cross section for regression analysis, the hedonic technique may work well. In extreme cases where price variation is almost entirely explained by a single size or performance characteristic, for example, horsepower for diesel engines or number of circuits for telephone switching equipment, the price per unit of that quality characteristic, which amounts to a single-dimension hedonic function forced through the origin, may serve as an adequate price index.[14] For other products, and indeed for most of the Sears catalog data analyzed in this book, the standard BLS specification method may be superior to the hedonic method, since for many products the number of relevant quality characteristics seems to be too large relative to the number of available model observations in a single cross section to allow a regression to be run. The experience of developing Sears catalog indexes by the specification method for more than seventy products over thirty-seven

13. Triplett (1988, 57–58) also argues that "the automobile may be too complicated for hedonic studies." He concludes that "changes in the omitted characteristics can, without providing a clear signal to the investigator, swamp the effect of the included ones."

14. Mills (1936) speculates that a price index for automobiles based on price per pound or per horsepower might be a more adequate approximation to the unattainable true price index than the WPI methods used at the time he wrote. Triplett (1989) cites approvingly and uses as part of his final "best practice price index" an index of price per unit of computer calculating power developed by Flamm (1987).

years suggests that it is almost always possible to match models exactly along all listed quality characteristics without the need for linking or explicit cost adjustments. New models are usually introduced on a random basis in a particular year, replacing some models for a given product but leaving other models unchanged and available for price comparisons. This tacit endorsement of the specification method for some products is subject to the qualification that, even for low-tech products, there may be a tendency for quality improvements on new models to be "missed" in the linking procedure, just as matched-model (i.e., specification) indexes for computers show markedly slower rates of price decline than hedonic indexes.

Because the new price indexes often exhibit markedly different rates of growth than the PPI for the same product, I always ask a simple question of the indexes, one that seems rarely to have been asked in previous research. Does a comparison of the raw nominal price change at the beginning and end of the sample period for models of roughly similar quality "make sense"? Of course, quality does not remain unchanged over a span of two or three decades for most products. Nevertheless, for a surprising number of products in the Sears catalog study (chap. 10), it is possible to make such comparisons of "closely similar models" over periods of two decades or more. On average, the price change measured in such comparisons is smaller than that in the equivalent Sears catalog price index pieced together by cumulating year-to-year price changes for identical models. This implies that prices are more often reduced than increased relative to the quality change implicit in the new model introductions that are omitted from my matched-model Sears catalog indexes.

Whether the hedonic or the specification technique is used, however, it is often impossible to avoid a shift in the ratio of excluded to included quality attributes. This problem is inherent to the hedonic technique, as discussed above, but can also plague the conventional specification technique. The most important omitted quality changes in this study are improvements in fuel efficiency, repair frequency, and durability. With a full set of data from equipment users on the operating characteristics of new and old models, as in the studies of commercial aircraft and electric utility generating equipment, the value of such improvements can be calculated directly, although changes in durability may not be revealed until decades after the introduction of a new model. Analogous direct calculations can also be made for a few products, especially household appliances, where laboratory test data are available on energy efficiency, and where user questionnaires measure repair incidence. For other products, however, such supplementary data are not available, and the presumption must be that the new price indexes are on average biased upward by calculating fuel efficiency and repair adjustments for only a subset of the covered products.

Table 1.1   **Drift of the Ratio of Törnqvist Indexes, This Study and Corresponding PPIs, Over Selected Intervals**

	Annual Growth Rates			
NIPA Categories	Full Period of Data (1)	1947–60 (2)	1960–73 (3)	1973–83 (4)
Office, computing, and accounting machinery	−9.32	−3.94	−16.61	−6.83
Communication equipment	−5.84	−8.44	−2.89	−6.28
Instruments, photocopy and related equipment	−3.49	−3.18	−4.21	−2.97
Fabricated metal products	−1.80	−4.08	−1.28	0.49
Engines and turbines	−3.53	−7.16	−2.27	−0.44
Metalworking machinery	−1.15	−3.01	0.58	−0.96
Special industry machinery, n.e.c.	−2.48	−3.70	−1.01	−2.79
General industrial, including materials handling, equipment	−1.81	−2.87	−1.15	−1.29
Electrical transmission, distribution, and industrial apparatus	−2.11	−3.62	−1.89	−0.43
Trucks, buses, and truck trailers	−2.97	−5.74	−2.04	−0.59
Autos	−1.33	−5.02	−0.27	2.09
Aircraft	−8.29	−12.69	−7.48	−3.63
Ships and boats	−1.93	−3.17	−1.11	−1.39
Railroad equipment	−1.45	−1.24	−1.43	−1.76
Furniture and fixtures	−1.41	−2.72	−0.84	−0.46
Tractors	−1.35	−0.05	−1.28	−3.14
Agricultural machinery, except tractors	−0.70	−2.80	0.69	0.21
Construction machinery, except tractors	−1.63	−2.35	−1.63	−0.68
Mining and oilfield machinery	−1.63	−2.35	−1.63	−0.68
Service industry machinery	−3.15	−4.06	−1.91	−3.59
Electrical equipment, n.e.c.	−1.01	−2.56	−0.09	−0.20
Other	−1.99	−3.90	−0.30	−1.69
Total:				
Törnqvist	−2.96	−4.13	−2.44	−2.07
Implicit deflator, 1972 base	−2.90	−3.17	−1.88	−3.87
Implicit deflator, 1982 base	−1.97	−3.12	−1.20	−1.48

Sources: See the notes to table 12.2.

1.4.2   The Magnitude of Quality Bias in the Official Indexes

The overall results for PDE are summarized in table 1.1, which presents the difference in the annual rates of change of the new and official indexes for the twenty-two categories of PDE and for three different aggregations over the twenty-two categories. The overall "drift" in the ratio of the alternative to the official deflators, aggregated by the Törnqvist technique, occurs at the rate of 2.9 percent per year, which cumulates exponentially over thirty-six years to a ratio of the alternative to official price index in 1947 of 286 on a base of 1983 = 100. This Törnqvist-weighted average index for all PDE is compared to the official PDE deflator in figure 1.1. As shown at the bottom of table 1.1, an alternative PDE deflator aggregated over the twenty-two categories with the NIPA method and a fixed 1972 base

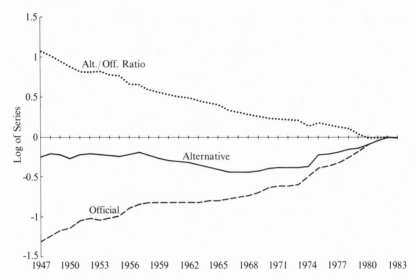

Fig. 1.1   Comparison of Törnqvist price indexes, this study and PPI, 22 categories, 1982 = 1.0

year yields a rate of drift for the full 1947–83 period that is almost exactly the same as the preferred Törnqvist index. But the flaws inherent in using a fixed base year lead the fixed 1972-base index to record too small a rate of drift before 1972 and too large a rate after 1972. In contrast, the fixed 1982-base index records too small a rate of drift throughout the 1947–83 interval.

The results displayed in table 1.1 indicate that the drift occurs at widely differing rates both across the twenty-two categories and across the three subintervals shown. Using either a fixed 1972 or fixed 1982 base year, the overall average rate of drift is smaller in 1960–73 then before or after. However, using the preferred Törnqvist method, the rate of drift is smaller in 1973–83 than in 1960–73. Several products stand out that have double-digit rates of drift for particular subintervals, for example, computers in 1960–73 and aircraft in 1947–60. Chapter 12 shows that there is a significant correlation between the growth rate of real investment already present in the NIPA data and the magnitude of the drift, lending credibility to the hypothesis that the measured drift is not a "fluke" but rather represents a systematic failure of the PPI to capture quality change adequately for those types of durable equipment having the most rapid rates of growth of nominal demand. This hypothesis is further supported by a regression analysis in chapter 10, which for the subset of indexes based on catalog data finds that the drift across sixty-eight products is significantly related to the technological complexity of the product and to the presence of electronic components,

Table 1.2   **Drift of the Ratio of Törnqvist Indexes, This Study and Corresponding NIPA
Implicit Deflators for Selected Consumer Durables, 1982 Base—Over Selected
Intervals**

	Annual Growth Rates			
NIPA Categories	Full Period of Data (1)	1947–60 (2)	1960–73 (3)	1973–83 (4)
1. Motor vehicles and parts	− 1.71	− 2.39	− 1.69	− 0.85
2. Furniture and household equipment:	− 1.79	− 2.52	− 1.26	− 1.55
2.1 Kitchen and other household appliances	− 3.22	− 4.39	− 2.37	− 2.83
2.2 Radios and TVs	− 5.94	− 9.07	− 3.77	− 4.69
3. Total consumer durables	− 1.54	− 2.21	− 1.24	− 1.05

Sources: See the notes to table 12.8.

but is not related at all to the closeness with which the individual Sears products are matched to individual components of the PPI.

Table 1.2 displays the estimated rates of drift for new consumer durable goods deflator relative to the official deflator. Since the new consumer durables index represents an alternative aggregation of a small subset of the individual price indexes originally collected for the purpose of deflating PDE, its coverage is substantially less complete. Fully half of consumer durable expenditures remain uncovered by the new indexes, and, at least for now, the existing NIPA deflators for these uncovered components are accepted as accurate. This limited coverage explains why the rate of drift for all consumer durables in row 3 of table 1.2 is smaller than the average of the rates of drift shown on rows 1 and 2, and also why the rate of drift on row 2 is less than the average of rows 2.1 and 2.2. As indicated above, the negative rate of drift for the consumer durable auto category is larger than for PDE, because the upward-biased official price index for used cars enters with a negative weight in the official PDE index but with a positive weight in the official consumer durable deflator. The rates of drift for the appliance and radio-television category may appear to be surprisingly high but are based on one of the most comprehensive and accurate parts of this study, the indexes developed from *CR,* which incorporate explicit energy efficiency adjustments for all major appliances, both energy efficiency and frequency of repair adjustments for television sets, and which since 1959 are based on market surveys of transaction prices.

1.4.3   Summary of Implications

This section briefly summarizes the main implications of the new PDE and consumer durable deflators developed here. Each of the implications is documented and discussed in more detail in chapter 12, which begins by treating issues involved in weighting together the new price indexes and in converting them into new measures of real investment, the capital stock, and total factor productivity.

One of the longstanding stylized facts about the U.S. economy is the stability of the investment/GNP ratio. The ratio of structures and equipment investment to real GNP in the current official NIPA was almost identical in 1947 and 1983, with ratios of 11.4 and 11.1 percent, respectively. One of the most important implications of this study is that this stylized fact has been far from the truth for the entire postwar era. In contrast to the NIPA ratio, which remains constant, the new ratio of real equipment investment to real GNP *triples*. Even though this study does not contain any new results on structures prices or real investment in structures, the ratio of real structures plus PDE investment to real GNP doubles when the new data on real PDE investment are substituted for the official data.

Because the new data on the investment/GNP ratios overturn standard impressions of the process of economic growth, they raise new issues that will need to be discussed. First among these is the most obvious from a longer historical perspective. If the investment/GNP ratio doubled between 1947–83, what happened in the 100 years prior to that? Is the large quality bias in official price indexes for capital goods a new problem or an age-old problem? More important for the near future, how long will investment continue to grow faster than GNP? Will the rapid growth rate of real equipment investment eventually lift the U.S. economy out of the productivity doldrums? Answers to these questions will require substantial further research, using the results of this book as a point of departure.

The alternative and official real investment series are then converted into capital stocks, using a simplified version of the perpetual inventory method used by the BEA. The equipment capital stock is calculated separately for the twenty-two categories of PDE, using an algorithm that extracts from the present official data the implicit service life for each category. The alternative and official NIPA capital stock growth rates for equipment, that is, PDE, differ by about 3 percent per annum, roughly the same amount as the difference between the annual growth rates of the alternative and official equipment investment series. For the subintervals, the differences in the growth rates of the equipment capital stock are, respectively, 3.06, 3.25, and 2.63 percent per annum. The growth rate of the equipment capital stock differs most, then, in the middle interval (1960–73), in contrast to the growth rate of equipment investment, which differs most in the first period (1947–60). This difference in timing reflects the fact that this study starts only in 1947 and has little effect on the growth of the capital stock in the first few years after 1947, when the majority of equipment capital consisted of items purchased before 1947.

Effects of the new price data on the growth of the capital stock of equipment and structures together are much smaller than for equipment alone, as would be expected in view of the facts that there are no new deflators for structures in this study, and that the stock of structures represents well over half the total capital stock. Despite the absence of new evidence on structures, however, this study has major implications for the behavior of the aggregate capital-output ratio. In the official data, the capital-output ratio is almost the same in 1947 and 1983, after displaying a substantial decline during 1947–67 and an increase during 1967–83. The capital-output ratio implied by this study is quite different. The increase in the capital-output ratio for equipment between 1947 and 1983 is 406 percent, compared to a much smaller 75 percent in the official data. For the aggregate of structures and equipment, the 1947–83 increase in the capital-output ratio is 44 percent, as contrasted to only 5 percent in the official data.

Just as the postwar price changes in producer and consumer durable goods have been much closer to each other with the new deflators than with the official deflators, the same conclusion applies to the shares of durable spending in GNP. A familiar fact in the existing NIPA is that the share of real consumer durable expenditures has increased substantially over the postwar period, by about two-thirds. Yet there has been virtually no increase in the NIPA share of real PDE in GNP. In contrast, the alternative deflators imply much greater 1947–83 increases in both investment shares, 178 percent for producer durables and 164 percent for consumer durables. As is true for the capital-output ratios discussed above, the denominator of these new investment/output ratios is not NIPA real GNP, but rather GNP recalculated with the alternative real PDE and consumer durable expenditure series in place of the official series for those two components.

The corollary of the rapid increase in the share of durable goods spending in the new data is, of course, a decline in the share of spending on categories of GNP other than durable goods. In contrast to the NIPA, in which the share of real nondurable consumption falls only by 0.7 percent from 1947 to 1983, in the new data that decline becomes 7.4 percent. The NIPAs already register a substantial 10.3 percent decline in the share of real GNP other than PDE and personal consumption expenditures, and this decline becomes 16.4 percent in the new data. In short, durable goods have been the most dynamic component of spending on GNP, and use of the new data to compute new industry productivity measures would indicate that the growth rate of productivity in durable manufacturing has been greatly understated, although by more before 1973 than since 1973.

An important question to ask of the new data is whether they contribute any explanation of the post-1973 productivity growth slowdown in the United States. It seems evident already from the results presented earlier in this chapter that there cannot be a major contribution, simply because the drift of the alternative relative to the official deflator extends over the whole postwar period. The 1947–73 annual rate of drift of the alternative relative to the official deflator (from table 1.1) is 3.3 percent, and a lower 2.1 percent for 1973–83. One would think that a finding of more rapid growth in

Table 1.3   **Effect of Alternative Durable Goods Deflators in Sources of Growth Calculation (annual growth rate over interval)**

	1947–60 (1)	1960–73 (2)	1947–73 (3)	1973–83 (4)	1947–83 (5)
Private GNP:					
Alternative	3.68	4.14	3.91	2.08	3.40
NIPA	3.35	4.02	3.68	1.82	3.17
Alternative—NIPA	0.33	0.12	0.23	0.26	0.23
Capital input:					
Alternative	4.60	5.73	5.17	4.97	5.11
NIPA	3.10	3.87	3.49	3.56	3.51
Alternative—NIPA	1.50	1.86	1.68	1.41	1.60
Capital contribution:[a]					
Alternative	1.15	1.43	1.29	1.24	1.28
NIPA	0.78	0.97	0.87	0.89	0.88
Alternative—NIPA	0.37	0.46	0.42	0.35	0.40
Private business labor hours	0.79	1.93	1.36	1.00	1.26
Labor Contribution:[b]	0.59	1.45	1.02	0.75	0.95
Multifactor productivity:[c]					
Alternative	1.94	1.26	1.60	0.09	1.17
NIPA	1.98	1.60	1.79	0.18	1.34
Alternative—NIPA	−0.04	−0.34	−0.19	−0.09	−0.17

Sources: See table 12.11.

[a]Equals capital input times 0.25.

[b]Equals labor input times 0.75.

[c]Equals growth in output minus capital contribution minus labor contribution.

capital input before 1973 would contribute to the productivity puzzle, since new data showing a greater slowdown in the growth rate of capital input would leave a smaller slowdown in total factor productivity ("Denison's residual").

This presumption, however, ignores the effect of the new deflators for producer and consumer durables on the growth rate of output; since the growth rate of output is increased more prior to 1973 than after, this implication of the new data deepens the productivity puzzle. The balance between the two effects, a greater speedup of the growth of both output and capital input before 1973 than after 1973, depends on the weight assigned to capital input as a source of growth. Unfortunately, existing estimates of capital's share differ widely. One can find weights for fixed capital input ranging from as low as 20 percent (Denison 1985, table G-2 for 1967) to 41 percent (Jorgenson and Griliches 1972, table 20 for 1962). Here, a compromise position sets the capital share at an arbitrary 25 percent. The results displayed in table 1.3, are set out in a format that allows them to be recalculated easily for any other assumed income share of capital.

Table 1.3 is arranged into five columns, corresponding to the three standard subintervals, the full 1947–83 period, and the extra 1947–73 subinterval that is of interest in discussions of the post-1973 productivity growth slowdown. Comparing columns 3 and 4, we can assess the effect of the new price indexes on the growth of GNP, capital input, the contribution of capital to output growth (using the arbitrary 0.25 weight), and multi-factor productivity (MFP), that is, the growth rate of output minus the contributions of capital and labor input. The row labeled "Alternative— NIPA" in the top section indicates that the effect of the new deflators on the growth rate of output is 0.23 percentage points in 1947–73 and 0.26 points in 1973–83, that is, almost exactly the same. The respective figures for capital's contribution to growth are 0.42 and 0.35 points. Using the same series on labor input to compute both alternative and NIPA versions of MFP growth, the new price deflators reduce the growth rate of MFP by 0.19 points before 1973 and 0.09 points after 1973. The MFP growth slowdown after 1973 is 1.61 points in the official data and 1.51 points in the new data. Thus, the new data contribute less than one-sixteenth (0.10/1.61) of the needed explanation of the post-1973 productivity growth slowdown. This conclusion is quite robust to variations in the arbitrary 0.25 capital share used in table 1.3; the explanation of the productivity slowdown is 0.08 points with a share of 0.15, 0.10 with a share of 0.25, and 0.13 with a share of 0.35.

1.5   What Is Wrong with the PPI?

The enormous difference between the alternative price indexes and the PPIs for the same products raises difficult questions for specialists at the BLS. Here, I can only speculate, for a fundamental limitation on anyone's ability to resolve this quandary is the confidentiality rule that prevents outsiders from inspecting individual price quotations. I corresponded in the late 1970s with BLS officials about the specific case of diesel engines, where the PPI shows prices more than doubling during 1947–72, while officials contacted at the leading firm producing the engines, which supplies data to the BLS, provided price schedules showing no change in price. Even in this specific case, BLS officials were unwilling or unable to provide a single example of a price change for a particular model number over that period and in their response offered only generalities about how in principle unit value data (the basis for my diesel engine index) could be flawed, without noting that my inquiry had been based not on unit value evidence but rather on explicit communications with one of their own price reporters.

As a second example, the BLS published an index for nonprinting electronic calculators over the period 1969–75 that fell only by about one-half, while Sears, *CR,* and everyone's personal recollections register a price decline by a factor of at least *ten* while at the same time a marked improvement in quality occurred over several dimensions, particularly the switch from LED to LCD displays, which eliminated the previous need for frequent battery recharging (the LED display soon became obsolete). What was the BLS pricing? How could it reach a conclusion so far from facts that are familiar to everyone, including BLS officials?

These examples suggest puzzles that this study identifies rather than resolves. However, even without any specific time series of BLS price quotations from individual reporters, several specific statements about the sources of bias in the PPI can be made.

1. The most obvious flaw in the PPI is that many price changes are compared without required quality adjustments being made at all. Mills (1936) was concerned about this long before the Stigler committee report, and most descriptions of BLS methods indicate that quality adjustments for products other than automobiles were spotty or nonexistent before 1960. For instance, an official with a diesel engine manufacturer (quoted in chap. 9 below) states explicitly that the BLS failed to make adjustments for the fact that his firm's engine was steadily upgraded in horsepower and fuel efficiency in the 1950s and 1960s even though it carried the same model number. Accordingly, it is not surprising that the negative drift of my alternative price indexes relative to PPIs for the same products is most rapid before 1960.

2. A weakness that has been discussed traditionally is that the PPI introduces new models too late and tracks obsolete models for too long. Until 1971, the BLS priced a steam-turbine generator in a size class that had been obsolete since the 1940s. Fluorescent lights were not introduced until 1961. An official with the firm that publishes the used tractor guides claims that the BLS perennially tracks tractor models that are "dogs" having a small market share. Triplett and McDonald (1977) found that "refrigerators in the sample were not a good reflection of the range of industry sales; the sample consisted, disproportionately, of 'bottom-end' or 'builder-model' refrigerators with a minimum of special features."[15] Finally, I have a personal anecdote regarding "obsolete models" with appalling implications if the practice is widespread. In my role as treasurer of the Econometric Society, I have been informed by our former printing firm that in 1988 *Econometrica* was still carried as part of the PPI for the printing industry, even though printing of that journal was shifted from the United States to the United Kingdom in 1984. When informed of this fact in 1984, the BLS commodity specialist told the U.S. printer to submit an imaginary price representing what the printing bill "would have been." We are now negotiating to return *Econometrica* to the same printer, but at a price much lower than the imaginary price, reflecting competitive bids on both sides of the Atlantic.

3. Another traditional criticism is that weights are out of date. In 1983 (the last year of my data coverage), the PPI was based on 1972 weights. As a

15. This interpretation of Triplett and McDonald is quoted from Triplett (1988, 73).

particularly stark example, the weight given in 1983 to electronic receiving tubes was greater than to integrated circuits of all types.[16]

4. For many traditional product lines, where the pace of technical advance is slow, the PPI is entirely adequate, as is confirmed by the low rate of drift in numerous product categories in the 1970s and 1980s. But when techno-logical change is rapid, the PPI is subject to a fatal weakness in its basic methodology of relying on reporters, that is, officials in manufacturing firms who have little concern with the purposes of their PPI price reports, to flag quality improvements and to introduce new models. The path of least resistance is to report the price for the same old model, even if its sales have almost disappeared. The PPI questionnaire, at least in its 1976 incarnation reproduced in the Ruggles report (U.S. Executive Office of the President 1977) fosters this fatal flaw by asking only for the value of quality changes on the current model, not for information on any new models that may have been introduced. An advantage of the catalog indexes is that the range of models covered for each product is *complete,* not a sample, and hence grows and shrinks automatically each year with the market, and no decision is necessary on when to change models (see the discussion of fig. 10.1 below).[17]

5. An obvious flaw in the PPI is that important products are not covered at all. There is no PPI for electronic computers, PCs, electric utility generating equipment, commercial aircraft, or telephone switching equipment, all of which are covered in this book.

6. Even if PPIs did exist for these products and others, the PPI specification method cannot cope with electronic products and those experiencing nonproportional changes in energy efficiency. In practice, if not in principle, the PPI is tied to the old-fashioned methodology that was implicitly rejected by the BEA's incorporation of a hedonic price index for computers into the NIPA. Technologically progressive products, like electronic computers and electronic telephone switching systems, are characterized by new model introductions in which performance is improved relative to price. The BLS questionnaire, at least its 1976 version, does not contain questions that would lead a manufacturer to report such changes in quality that are not accompanied by a change in cost. This problem is aggravated in the PPI by the linking in of new products like electronic calculators without any allowance for the price reduction implicit in the shift of users from the old model (in this example, rotary electric calculators).

How do these problems with the PPI help explain shifts in the alternative/official rates of drift over the three postwar time intervals? No

16. The 1983 relative importance of index 117801, receiving-type electron tubes, was 0.062 percent, and that of all types of integrated circuits was 0.051 percent (this is the sum of indexes 117841, 117842, 117845, and 117846).

17. Auto batteries represent the only product for which the Sears index is based on a sample of available models.

precise connection can be drawn, because some of the shifts over these intervals reflect the changing weight and pace of innovation in product categories for which there is no corresponding PPI, for example, computers and aircraft in the middle (1960–73) interval. Although shifts in the rate of drift reflect many factors, not just flaws in the PPI, I conjecture that the problems before 1960 and after 1973 were of a different nature. Prior to 1960, we know from many descriptions, which are referenced in chapter 3, that there was little systematic attempt to control for quality change in the PPI. The fact that many of the Sears catalog indexes for relatively simple products show significant drift through the early 1960s, but then little thereafter, supports this view. Another problem for the PPI is that it did not adequately capture the shift from premiums to discounts in the early postwar years, as is revealed by the behavior of the hedonic indexes for autos and tractors based on list prices of new models relative to similar indexes calculated from used-market prices of late models.

After 1973, the PPI has been undermined by electronics. Part of this comes out in the fact that a rapidly growing nominal expenditure weight in the Törnqvist indexes for aggregate PDE is allocated to the office machinery and communications categories, where electronic innovations are important yet where PPIs do not exist. Yet even in those few electronic products where there are explicit PPIs, for example, nonprinting calculators, ten-key adding machines, and electronic typewriters, the price increases registered by the PPI conflict starkly with everyday experience. The same phenomenon probably occurs in some other components of the PPI that are not covered in this study, for example, numerically controlled machine tools and electronic typesetting machines used by the printing industry.

Most of the electronic products priced by the PPI are not final goods but rather intermediate components used in the manufacture of other products, for example, electron tubes, capacitors, resistors, connectors, integrated circuits, and diodes. The ability of firms using electronic components to substitute transistors for tubes, and then integrated circuits for transistors, and then successively more powerful integrated circuits for less powerful circuits, is not taken into account at all. PPIs for integrated circuits were simply linked into the overall PPI in December 1974 as a totally new product, without any accounting for the implicit price reduction that their invention implied, just as electronic calculators were linked in as a new product in 1969 without any allowance for the price reduction when users switched from rotary electric calculators to electronic calculators. The late introduction of integrated circuits and the use of obsolete weights helps account for the remarkable fact that the PPI group index (1178) for "electronic components and accessories" displays a 1967–83 price increase of 83.6 percent, while the price of virtually every type of final electronic product covered in this study (computers, PCs, electronic calculators, electronic typewriters, VCRs) declines at a double-digit annual rate during the same interval.

This set of defects in the PPI leads to a simple explanation of the relatively low rate of drift observed in the middle period, 1960–73, for products other than electronic computers and aircraft. In these years, the early postwar readjustment was over, discounting had become established, the PPI had begun to make more systematic attempts to adjust for quality change on conventional products, and electronic products were still relatively unimportant. This is the period during which the PPI and CPI for automobiles are probably most accurate, for instance.

This study contains no explicit recommendations for reforms in organization or procedures at the BLS or BEA. As presently organized, the two agencies almost inevitably demote historical price index research to a low level of priority. The BLS has primary responsibility for price measurement but cannot revise its basic indexes, the CPI and PPI, because they are used to escalate legal wage and price contracts. Thus, the BLS is future oriented, interested in better procedures that may improve price indexes in the 1990s, but not in fixing up errors made in past time intervals.

The BEA is not bound by any limitation on historical revisions and indeed introduces major benchmark revisions every five years. But the BEA has many responsibilities, among which historical price research is low on the list. The development of a computer price index by the BEA and its introduction into the NIPA represents less a precursor of a major future commitment to historical price research than a recognition that the previous PDE deflator was seriously deficient in its assumption that computer prices were fixed. In this special case, the actual research on computer prices was carried out largely at IBM rather than at BEA. These limitations on historical price research at the BLS and BEA make it likely that primary responsibility for historical research on the accuracy of price indexes will continue to rest with the academic sector.

Nevertheless, there are several steps that the BLS and BEA might take in collaboration to use the results in the current book to improve the official indexes. Conversion of the entire set of NIPA deflators to the Törnqvist weighting methodology should occur formally at the next benchmark revision, and in the meantime the BEA should publish an article with alternative indexes of real GNP and its components based on this superior weighting method. At the level of individual prices, in the 1970s and 1980s the PPI is most prone to an upward bias in measuring the prices of electronic goods. This book shows that it is possible to create price indexes for electronic goods from catalog and *CR* data; the BLS could develop experimental indexes from those sources and others, for example, mail-order advertisements for personal computer processors and peripherals, and could obtain required specification data directly from manufacturers. The present procedure of collecting only price data from respondents, and leaving it to them to make corrections for quality change, is so clearly unsatisfactory for electronic goods that it will have to be abandoned. This book identifies a number of products where the PPI appears to have a consistent upward bias, indicating the need for the study of experimental indexes based on nontraditional sources in order to determine the source of the bias, while for many other products the evidence developed here suggests little or no difference between the alternative indexes and the PPI, particularly in the post-1973 period.

1.6   Qualifications to the Findings

1.6.1   Actual and Potential Criticisms

Several possible weaknesses should be considered in evaluating these results. First, no data have been collected for products representing a substantial fraction of investment in producers' durable equipment; roughly 77 percent of PDE by 1967 value is covered, and 23 percent remains uncovered. The treatment of the uncovered products involves the implicit assumption that, within any one of the twenty-two PDE categories, the observed drift for the covered products can be applied to uncovered products. Here, the crucial word is *within,* for the drift for the covered products is imputed to the uncovered products only inside each of the twenty-two PDE categories, not across them. Thus, the drift for covered metalworking machinery is imputed to uncovered types of metalworking machinery; the drift for office machinery or telephone equipment is not imputed to the uncovered types of metalworking machinery.

To take the opposite approach and do no imputation would amount to assuming that the PPIs are perfectly accurate for the uncovered products. This would doubtless be wrong, for it would overlook the systematic sources of bias in the PPI discussed in the previous sections. We cannot rule out the possibility that the uncovered products have a smaller "true" (and unobserved) drift than the covered products within the same category. But there are plenty of examples of uncovered products that have experienced radical decreases in price, from satellite television dishes to smoke detectors, or substantial increases in quality relative to price, including copying, photographic, and sports equipment, not to mention electronic medical testing equipment from CAT scanners to ultrasound testers.

An explicit criticism directed at the first (1974) version of this research by experts at the BLS was that several of the Sears catalog results involved the comparison of small items sold by Sears for home use with PPIs that priced much larger industrial varieties of the same product; the examples involved eight of the Sears-PPI comparisons, or about 10 percent of the products covered.[18] I have responded to this criticism in two ways. First, the

18. Memo from John Early to Jack Triplett, provided to me as an attachment to a letter from Jack Triplett, 16 December 1977.

catalog-to-PPI product matches were reviewed carefully and tightened. Some of the most convincing evidence of bias in the PPI comes from products where the specification of the PPI commodity index matches precisely what is priced here, for example, home utility quarter-inch electric power drills or stationary air compressors with PPI capacity levels exactly matched by the catalog products. In a statistical test in chapter 10, there is no correlation at all between the tightness of the catalog-PPI match and the drift in the catalog/PPI price ratios for particular products. Second, as discussed in the preface and earlier in this chapter, this criticism led me in the present version to broaden the study to include more ''large'' items such as aircraft and railroad locomotives.

While the study is no longer vulnerable to this criticism, it seems clear in retrospect that the earlier critique based on the ''small-large'' distinction rested on a false premise. It may be valid to complain that the use of Sears catalog prices involves a sample selection bias; I deal with this criticism at length in chapter 10 and argue that, if anything, the Sears catalog indexes are biased upward owing to a change in Sears's pricing policy after the mid-1970s. But it is not valid to argue that the comparison of small items with larger items creates a de facto presumption of downward bias in the alternative indexes. Internal evidence denying this claim is readily available in the PPI itself, where price changes can be tracked over long periods of time for detailed commodity indexes covering several sizes of the same product. These changes do *not* reveal any tendency for small items to increase in price less rapidly than large items. For instance, the PPI for home-model electric drills increased substantially more over 1967–83 than that for industrial-model electric drills.[19] For twelve product categories where a comparison could be made between PPIs for small and large sizes of the same machinery product, for example, centrifugal pumps with capacities of 90 and 1,000 gallons per minute, the 1967–83 price increase averaged over the twelve categories was 180.6 percent for the smallest variety listed and 178.5 for the largest variety, that is, about the same. This average disguises great differences in the price increases of small and large items for a given product category, but cases of lower price increases for small items are almost exactly balanced by cases of higher price increases for small items.[20]

Another qualification is the possible inaccuracy involved in the use of mail-order catalogs and used vehicle prices as close proxies for transaction

19. The 1967–83 increase was 128.6 percent for home utility drills (index 11320222) and 76.1 percent for industrial-line drills (index 11320301).

20. The twelve products are all those in PPI groups 11 and 12 (electrical and nonelectrical machinery) where eight-digit indexes are available for at least two size classes of the same product, where the product itself was introduced before 1980, and where the different size indexes, if introduced after the 1967 base year, were introduced at the same time. Of the twelve product groups, all but two were introduced in 1967 or before, one in 1972, and one in 1976.

prices. Improved or decreased relative operating efficiency or changed pricing strategies might have affected the price differential between catalog houses and walk-in retail stores. The relation between transaction prices of new cars and the prices of late-model used cars might have been affected by changes in tastes. But in the case of automobiles the new estimates of transaction prices correspond closely to scattered pieces of independent evidence on the magnitude of price premiums and discounts, as cited below in chapter 8. All the available evidence, both on the changes in Sears's pricing policy and on changes in the average level of Sears's prices compared to competitors, shows consistently that Sears's prices shifted from the low end of the spectrum to the middle over the postwar period, indicating that the dominant bias in our catalog indexes is likely to be upward, that is, that the negative drift of the alternative price indexes based on catalog data relative to the corresponding official indexes is understated. This verdict is supported by the *CR* indexes developed for appliances, which are based on market prices after 1959, which cover all major manufacturers, and which in almost every case exhibit an even greater drift relative to the PPI than the catalog indexes. The upward bias in the Sears catalog indexes relative to the *CR* indexes stems not from different methods of quality adjustment but from more rapid increases in Sears prices than prices of other manufacturers. Chapter 7 computes the ratio of the price of Sears models to the average of all models as listed in *CR* articles on refrigerators, air conditioners, and washing machines. This ratio increases from 80 percent in the earliest *CR* articles (published in 1949–59) to 102 percent in the most recent articles (published in 1974–84), indicating a systematic upward bias in price indexes based on Sears data and suggesting that the many results in this book based on Sears data may on average understate the upward bias in the PPI.[21]

In contrast to the many cross-checks of the results provided in this book, an outsider does not know what to make of the individual PPI commodity indexes when outside evidence reveals a major conflict. As in my example of the diesel engine index cited above, it is impossible for an outsider to obtain answers to the following basic questions. Which manufacturers submitted the BLS price quotations? Which models were included in each commodity index, and how often did they change? Precisely how were quality adjustments performed in each individual year?

In contrast to the evidence developed in this book on the basis of almost 100 separate product indexes that the PPI for machinery contains a

---

21. A needed qualification regarding refrigerators is that the achievement of greater energy efficiency, which is taken into account in the final indexes in this book, has come at the cost of the use of chlorofluorocarbons, or CFCs, which are members of a family of chemical that have been identified as major contributors to ozone depletion. A typical refrigerator now has 2.5 pounds of CFC 11 in its insulation and about eight ounces of CFC 12 in its cooling system. Because of concern about the ozone layer, use of these materials may be banned in the 1990s, leading to less efficient refrigerators. See Holusha (1989).

substantial upward bias, Triplett's recent (1988) review of the price measurement literature suggests only a single example of a downward bias in an official price index for a durable good.[22] This refers to the treatment in the auto component of both the CPI and the PPI of pollution and safety equipment as representing increases in quality rather than price. Triplett would prefer a treatment in which these items are treated as a "transportation tax" on consumers. In his preferred treatment, no quality adjustment would be made for these items, so that their introduction would be allowed to raise prices rather than quality. My analysis of automobiles accepts the present BLS approach, which treats pollution and safety devices as increasing quality rather than price. The only other place in this book where this issue arises is in the development of a price index for electric utility generating equipment, where I suggest a rough downward adjustment to the new price index in order to make the treatment of government-mandated scrubbers and other nonproductive components of generating equipment parallel to that of automobiles in the CPI and PPI.

Triplett's suggestion of downward bias in the official indexes for this reason involves a conceptual rather than a measurement issue. As discussed in chapter 2, legislated environmental and safety devices are the major reason why output and input price indexes need to be distinguished, since such devices drive a wedge between price indexes relevant for deflating the output of the industries producing capital goods and those relevant for deflating the capital input of the industries using those goods. Since productive inputs are used by capital goods manufacturing firms in producing environmental and safety devices, a study of output and productivity behavior in the producing industries should use price indexes that treat such devices as an increase in quality, whereas a study of productivity behavior in the capital-goods-using industries should employ price indexes that treat such devices as an increase in price, that is, as nonproductive. Whether such devices should also be treated as a price increase in the CPI and in the deflation of consumer expenditure depends on whether they yield any benefits in the form of reduced pollution and increased safety, and whether the CPI accurately measures the value of such benefits.

Because I accept the current official treatment of these devices, the new PDE deflators are suitable for the deflation of the output of industries producing producers' equipment, but are downward biased for the purpose

22. While Triplett had no access to the 1988 version of this book when writing his recent review (1988), he not only had access to the 1974 draft but also contributed copious comments on that draft, which have been incorporated into this version. In view of that access, it is astonishing to read the statement in his recent review (1988, 71) that "the PPI has a very large number of components and few of them have been examined in research," with no reference at all to the 1974 manuscript, which contained detailed annual comparisons over the 1947–70 period of alternative and PPI commodity indexes for more than 100 products.

of constructing indexes of capital input in the using industries and hence result in an overstatement of the growth of the productive capital stock in those industries. Since neither the CPI nor the consumer expenditures deflator in the NIPA contain any explicit adjustment for the benefits of mandated pollution and safety devices, the common treatment in the CPI and in this book of such devices as an increase in quality rather than price represents an arbitrary and unsupported judgment that the costs of such devices to consumers are exactly balanced by their benefits. If their costs exceed their benefits, then the alternative deflator for consumer durable goods contains a downward bias to this extent, and vice versa.

An implication of this qualification is that increased expenditures on mandated pollution and safety equipment cause the "true" growth of capital input to slow down more after 1973 than the growth rate of capital input displayed in table 1.3. While I have not developed an explicit measure of this source of bias, it does work in the direction of helping to explain part of the post-1973 productivity slowdown. For instance, if the growth rate of capital input were slowed by the adjustment for mandated equipment by 0.40 points, from 3.56 to 3.16 percent per year, the growth of multifactor productivity would be raised by one-quarter of this amount, from 0.09 to 0.19 percent per year. This would reduce the slowdown in multifactor productivity growth from 1.51 to 1.41 percent per year.

1.6.2   The Use of "Cross-Checks"

While the new results may appear startling in the magnitude of the drift that they reveal between the alternative and the official price indexes for particular products, the study has emphasized the collection of numerous "cross-checks" to make the recorded price changes "come to life" rather than lying inert on a computer printout. One source of cross-checks is contained in the popular literature on the history of particular products. These provide numerous examples of high prices in earlier years that might be compared to today's typical prices to dramatize the widespread occurrence of price declines for durable goods: $475 in 1947 for a 6,000 BTU Fedders room air conditioner that used much more energy than today's less expensive models; $425 in 1946 for a nine-inch black-and-white table-model television; $5,200 in 1948 for the first Ampex audio tape recorder; $1,000 in 1954 for a nineteen-inch console color television; $75,000 in 1956 for the first video tape recorder; $209 in 1958 for the first Smith-Corona portable electric typewriter with narrow carriage and manual return; $2,295 in 1975 for the first Betamax home videotape recorder without remote control or programming capability; and $1,000 in 1983 for a compact-disk player.[23]

---

23. All these examples are from Consumers' Union (1986), except for the 1958 Smith-Corona typewriter, which is the price quoted in the spring 1958 Sears catalog.

At a more formal level, developed as an integral part of the study of the mail-order catalog prices are many comparisons of "closely similar" models that provide specific examples of catalog models exhibiting price changes far below those implied by the PPI over periods of two or three decades. These comparisons undermine the credibility of many of the individual PPI commodity price indexes. In a case where the PPI doubles relative to the catalog index over two or three decades, it seems hard to believe that the PPI respondents would have any customers left except for the likelihood that the PPI price quotations are not corrected for quality change with the same exactness and consistency as are the Sears catalog price quotations. In fact, the long-term comparisons of similar models generally imply smaller price increases, and a greater drift away from the PPI, than is implied by the catalog price indexes themselves. This finding supports the view, so evident for computers, that new model introductions are often accompanied by an implicit price reduction that goes unmeasured in the conventional specification method.

Other sources of cross-checks should be stressed. The study includes both catalog and *CR* indexes for fourteen products. It includes the evidence of the market for used aircraft supporting the theory and practice of the new treatment of aircraft prices. It includes the thirty-year history of specific IBM mainframe computer models that supports the pace and timing of the new mainframe computer index. It includes written communications from the leading manufacturer of medium-sized diesel engines, itself a PPI respondent, explicitly supporting the conclusions of the case study of diesel engines, which yields one of the largest rates of drift from the PPI, and denying the validity of the PPI for diesel engines. Finally, it includes the correlations between technological complexity and the alternative/official drift that provide a rationale for the findings.

1.6.3   A Last Word on Unmeasured Quality Change

While there are substantial elements of plausibility and internal consistency in the results, there are two important reasons to suggest that the final results may actually understate the drift of the alternative indexes from the official indexes. First, as shown in table 12.1 below, 38 percent of the 1967 weight in the alternative PDE deflator is based on the Sears catalog indexes for products other than appliances. The comparisons of Sears and *CR* indexes for appliances, outboard motors, typewriters, and power hand tools reveal an upward bias in the Sears index in almost every case, on the presumption that the *CR* index is more accurate because of its greater coverage across manufacturers. Reflecting this presumption, the new price deflators for PDE and consumer durables are based on *CR* rather than Sears data for appliances. But this leaves open the possibility that the Sears indexes for products other than appliances, which are the basis for much of the final PDE index, on average contain an upward bias.

Probably more important as a source of upward bias in the final price indexes is a substantial margin of unmeasured quality change for several products. There is no better way to conclude this summary chapter than to list those elements of unmeasured quality change. In this book, no account is taken of the following dimensions of quality change, all of which are documented either in subsequent chapters, in sources cited in those chapters, or in footnotes here:

- Reduced vibration and noise of jet planes (recall that flight attendants were originally nurses on board to deal with air sickness), their ability to fly above thunderstorms, and their improved safety record relative to piston planes;
- The unmeasured value of time savings to travelers created by the transition to jet planes;
- Increased daily utilization rates of jet aircraft as compared to the piston aircraft that they replaced;
- Greatly increased realized service lifetimes of jet aircraft relative to the piston aircraft that they replaced;[24]
- A tripling of service lifetimes of automotive diesel engines between 1945 and 1975;
- Technical improvements in locomotives that reduce "wheel creep" and substantially improve hauling ability relative to horsepower, and improved fuel efficiency of locomotives made possible by lighter rail cars;
- Additional features on electronic typewriters and calculators that did not exist a decade ago;
- Reduced energy, space, and air conditioning requirements of electronic computers, photocopying machines, and other electronic products;
- Improved handling and riding capabilities of automobiles;
- Improved sound and reception quality and greater reliability of radio and audio/stereo equipment;
- Effective price reductions implied by the availability of personal computers to perform tasks formerly done on mini- and mainframe computers;

24. More than 100 of the original unstretched 727 aircraft are still in daily service with U.S. domestic trunk airlines, all having an age of twenty-four to twenty-six years in 1989. Their service lifetimes are likely to be extended well past thirty years, as a substantial number have been sold by United Airlines to Federal Express, for delivery during 1988–91. The Chairman of United Airlines recently declared that his airline's 29 DC–8–71 aircraft, built in 1968–69 and reengined in 1982–83, would last "indefinitely" and were being sold only because the price offered by the purchaser was irresistible (United Airlines quarterly financial report, second quarter, 1988). In 1988–89, there were several incidents of physical deterioration of older planes, most notably the 1988 Aloha Airlines incident, when corrosion caused part of the metal skin to fall off a twenty-year-old 737, resulting in the death of one flight attendant, and the 1989 United Airlines episode, in which a cargo door opened in flight on an eighteen-year-old 747, tearing off part of the metal skin and sucking nine passengers to their deaths. As this book went to press, however, these were isolated incidents, and there was no movement by the government or the airlines to ground old jet planes. In fact, the United plane was promptly repaired and put back into service in the fall of 1989.

- Greater ability of refrigerators to maintain a fixed low freezer temperature;
- A shift from metal to plastic parts on many products, which reduces weight and increases service lifetime by reducing corrosion (e.g., by eliminating the need to discard a dishwasher when the tub corrodes);[25]
- Double insulation and other safety devices on home power tools;
- Reduced weight of home power tools;
- Improved design of power lawn mowers, which has resulted in an order-of-magnitude reduction in injuries since the mid-1970s;
- Reduction in the variance of quality differences across brands, as implied by the great reduction in the frequency of "not acceptable" ratings by *CR;*
- Reduction of the frequency of service calls for refrigerators and washing machines (explicitly measured and taken into account only in the new index for television sets);
- Reduction of noise, weight, bulk, and installation cost of room air conditioners;
- Improved cleaning ability of automatic washing machines and dishwashers;
- Reduced size and improved safety of microwave ovens;
- Improved fuel economy of tractors, outboard motors, and diesel engines, and reduced electricity comsumption of condensers and compressors;
- And, finally, immeasurably better picture quality of color television sets.

25. Chapter 10 cites recent reports in *CR* on power tools that downgrade models containing metal rather than plastic cases.

2   Conceptual Issues in the Measurement of Price and Quality Changes

2.1   Introduction

The theory of price measurement is really the theory of output measurement in disguise, because every issue that arises in developing a conceptual basis for measuring price change ultimately hinges on the desired concept of output change.[1] This link between price and output measurement is seen most obviously in the identity that defines an index of real output (Q) as the ratio of an observed value aggregate (V) to a constructed price index (P): $Q \equiv V/P$. The primary purpose of many price indexes, called *deflators*, is to convert changes in observed value aggregates (dV) into changes in that aggregate expressed in the constant prices of some base year (dQ). Price changes themselves would appear to be of independent interest, since the rate of inflation is one of the primary arguments in the observed objective function of most macroeconomic policy authorities. Yet the most important cost of inflation, its effect in eroding the real value of fixed-interest securities (including money), "matters" ultimately because individuals hold these assets in order to purchase output in the future. Thus, the appropriate concept of price change to be used in discussions of the cost of inflation also depends on the desired concept of output change.

The measurement of prices would be straightforward if there were a single, generally accepted index of economic and social welfare that would tell us at a glance how much better or worse off we had become each year. Decisions made in the construction of an aggregate price index would be made entirely with a view to their effect on the aggregate welfare index; for instance, a quality adjustment would be made in the comparison of the prices of two products if one provided more final "welfare" than the other.

1. This chapter combines new material with elements of Gordon (1974, 1983). The notation in sec. 2.4 has been altered from that in the 1983 paper to improve the exposition.

As Denison (1971) and others have recognized, however, a single generally acceptable index of welfare cannot be constructed. There is no straightforward way to measure the welfare cost of increased crime, congestion, and pollution of the air and water, or the welfare benefit of improved medical care and of completely new products like the automobile, air conditioning, and home computers. And how are we to compare the present danger of nuclear war with past hazards, some of which are enumerated by Denison:

> Who would now think to consider the danger of attack by hostile Indians? Or the risk of being doused by slops thrown from windows as he walks the city streets? Even the very recent elimination of refrigerator doors that cannot be opened from within, and cost the lives of so many children, is almost forgotten. The annual series for "Persons Lynched" appears in the Census Bureau's *Historical Statistics* but not in its current *Statistical Abstract*. [1971, 5]

Fortunately, many of the issues that complicate the measurement of national welfare lie outside the sphere of the measurement of durable goods prices. We need not concern ourselves with changes in welfare that are unconnected with the development of new types of durable goods, including the changing incidence of crime, discrimination, and other social phenomena. Our task can be circumscribed by adopting four principles to guide our discussion of measurement concepts.

1. The valuation of changes in the characteristics of durable goods depends on the resulting change in the production of goods and services available to final consumers. Changes in well-being not directly attributable to changes in the types and characteristics of durable goods need not be considered.

2. Quality adjustments are to be carried out so as to "credit" manufacturers of durable goods for all changes in the quantity of final consumption goods and services that are caused by changes in the types and characteristics of "new vintage" durable goods. These include changes in the performance characteristics of consumer durables, changes in the quantity of consumer goods and services attributable to innovations in producer durables, changes in available resources attributable to changing fuel efficiency or maintenance requirements of new consumer and producer durables, and external economies and diseconomies, for example, the effect on air quality of smog control devices installed on new durable goods. In principle, then, we are interested in ex ante or "embodied" quality change, that which is designed into the good prior to installation.

3. Users of existing durable goods may also experience ex post changes in performance characteristics, energy efficiency, maintenance requirements, or external effects after the installation date. Possible causes may include changes in relative prices, changes in operating procedures, and environmen-

tal legislation applicable to existing machines. These ex post changes are not attributable to durable goods manufacturers and do not call for quality adjustments. A central measurement problem is to apply the ex ante criterion in practice, since part of the available data on operating performance comes from users rather than manufacturers.

4. It is recognized from the beginning that it is impossible in principle to measure every improvement in consumer welfare attributable to durable goods innovations, because the benefits of new types of activities made possible by totally new goods, for example, the automobile or air conditioning, cannot be quantified. Inevitably, decisions on the definition of product categories must be somewhat arbitrary, for example, whether to consider television a new product or a reduction in the transport cost of seeing baseball games and movies, or whether to compare the price of an electronic calculator at the time of its introduction to that of an old rotary electric calculator, or a slide rule, or neither. Similarly, the environmental and other external effects of changing durable goods characteristics are difficult and sometimes impossible to quantify adequately.

This chapter begins in sections 2.2–2.5 by providing formal definitions for aggregate input and output price indexes, and for the associated quality adjustments that are required when there are shifts in the cost function of producing performance characteristics. In these sections, my debt to Triplett (1983b) is great; the distinction between input and output price indexes and the expression of inputs and outputs in "characteristics space" both lean heavily on his paper. The main contributions of this part of the chapter are to introduce the idea of "nonproportional" quality change, to relate it to the cost function of the industry manufacturing the durable good, and to discuss practical measurement problems within the context of the input and output price index concepts.

Section 2.6 provides an analysis, using the concepts discussed in sections 2.2–2.5, of the debate in the earlier literature between the "resource cost" and "user value" concepts of quality change. This literature review seems necessary in light of previous statements by distinguished writers (e.g., Jaszi 1971, 203) that "most experts subscribe" to the principle that "quality improvements can be quantified only to the extent that they are accompanied by real cost increases." Prior arguments supporting this principle need to be considered carefully, since it appears to rule out the adjustments recommended here for nonproportional quality change.

The more novel part of the chapter, beginning in section 2.7, extends the discussion of changes in performance characteristics to changes in operating characteristics (fuel efficiency and maintenance requirements). A technique is proposed for adjusting capital goods prices for changes in operating efficiency, based on the criterion of improvement in net revenue relative to cost. The last substantive sections 2.9 and 2.10 consider the use of used asset prices as a cross-check on the methodology, and include interpretative comments on the proposed concepts. A summary section 2.11 concludes the chapter.

2.2 The Input Price Index

Durable goods are normally an input into the production of goods and services consumed by final users. Producer durables are an input, along with labor, structures, energy, and materials, in the production of consumer and producer goods. Consumer durables may also be considered an input, producing the services of durable goods. The cost-of-living index literature, including Pollak (1971), Fisher and Shell (1972), and Samuelson and Swamy (1974), treats the CPI as an input price index for consumption. The point of departure for the following analysis is Triplett's (1983b) treatment of the input price index, which is defined as a measure that answers the question, What is the cost change, between two periods, of collections of inputs sufficient to produce some specified output level?

I begin by assuming that the output of final product (y) is produced by a vector of market-purchased input characteristics (x):

$$(2.1) \qquad y = y(x), \quad y_x > 0, \, y_{xx} < 0,$$

where y_x represents the partial derivative of y with respect to x. An input characteristic is defined as any attribute of a market-purchased input that has a positive marginal product, including, in the case of durable goods, the horsepower and physical dimensions for a truck, or memory size and calculations per unit of time for a computer. In principle, the vector x also includes labor characteristics (education, experience, training), as well as effective inputs of energy and materials. In Triplett's more precise definition, a quantity is an input characteristic if it reduces the unexplained variation in output, given the explanation contributed by all the other arguments in the production function.

Consideration of energy and materials usage is postponed until section 2.7 of this chapter, and labor input is ignored entirely in order to concentrate on the measurement of the input and output of durable goods. Thus, (2.1) is interpreted as a production function that transforms a vector of a durable good's performance characteristics (x) into final output. By translating the term *quality* into changes in the quantity of performance characteristics, all quality changes are implicitly assumed to be quantifiable. For inventions of totally new consumer durables, this assumption may be overly optimistic.

The durable good is manufactured under competitive supply conditions, according to a cost function that exhibits constant returns in the quantity of goods produced, and diminishing returns in the number of units of the performance characteristic embodied in each physically separate durable good:[2]

$$(2.2) \qquad V(x) = Cc(x), \quad c_x > 0, \, c_{xx} > 0.$$

---

2. The assumption of costs that are constant in quantities, but increasing in quality characteristics, has been adopted by most previous papers in this literature, including Parks (1974) and Rosen (1974).

Adopting the convention that lower-case letters represent "real" variables and upper-case letters "nominal" variables (or, later, index numbers for real variables), c represents the real unit cost function, C represents a shift parameter in the cost of producing a given product due to changing profit margins and/or input prices, and V stands for the total value of each unit produced. Both (2.1) and (2.2) are on a "per unit" basis, dividing total output and cost by the number of physically separate durable goods used in the production process.

For any given level of technology, say that obtaining at time t, more inputs are required to produce more output. The input demand function depends on output and on the prices of inputs:

$$(2.3) \qquad\qquad x_t = x(y_t, C_t).$$

Here, equation (2.3) is a matrix showing the dependence of the demand for each input $(x_{1t}, \ldots, x_{nt})$ on the single output index and on the full set of input prices $(C_{1t}, \ldots, C_{nt})$. When the input demand function from (2.3) is substituted into the cost function of the supplying industry (2.2), we see that there is an indirect dependence of the cost of the good on the output produced by its user:

$$(2.4) \qquad\qquad V(x_t) = C_t c[x(y_t, C_t)].$$

The criterion of comparison on which the input price index (P_t^i) is based is that prices are compared holding constant output at a given level, say y^*. The optimal set of input characteristics (x^*) is defined by the demand functions for the characteristics at the given output level (y^*) and the differing input prices, C_t and C_0, respectively:

$$(2.5) \qquad\qquad x_t^* = x(y^*, C_t), \quad x_0^* = x(y^*, C_0).$$

The input price index can now be calculated as the ratio of the cost (V) of obtaining the optimum (minimum-cost) combinations of the vector of input characteristics sufficient to produce output level y^* in the reference and comparison-period input price regimes. Thus, the input price index is simply the ratio of (2.4) for the two price regimes, evaluated at the constant output level y^*:

$$(2.6) \qquad\qquad P_t^i = \frac{V(x_t^*)}{V(x_0^*)} = \frac{C_t c[x(y^*, C_t)]}{C_0 c[x(y^*, C_0)]}.$$

Because a change in input prices (C) between regimes can cause substitution in the quantities of the various input characteristics, the input price index allows for such substitution.

In this discussion, the inputs into the production function are the individual characteristics of goods, the vector x, so that a quality change involves a change in the quantity of one or more productive characteristics, which in turn must change the level of output. Since any such quality change would thus violate the criterion of constant output (y^*) on which the input price index is based, price measures must be adjusted "for changes in input characteristics that result in changed output (or reduced cost to the user), and the correct quality adjustment is exactly equal to the cost change or the value of the output change that they induce. In the literature, this is known as the user-value rule" (Triplett 1983b, 286).

2.3 Measuring the Input Price Index When Quality Change Is Nonproportional

Nonproportional technical innovations raise the performance of a good by increasing its built-in quantity of characteristics (x) relative to the resources used by the supplying industry. Thus, such innovations take the form of a downward shift in the real cost of producing a given quantity of characteristics, say computer calculations. The idea of nonproportional quality change can be brought into the measurement of the input price index by introducing a shift term λ_t into the cost function (2.4):

$$(2.7) \qquad V_t = C_t c[x(y_t, C_t), \lambda_t].$$

It is important to note that there is no shift in the using firm's production function (2.1), since a single calculation still produces the same amount of final output (y). Thus, the units of characteristics to be defined as x must be those that directly enter the using firm's production function, for example, a computer's "calculations per second" and not its dimensions. Also, the quality change, although "nonproportional," is not "costless." The reduction in cost must consume managerial and R&D resources, or else it would have occurred long ago. The R&D costs are not treated explicitly, nor is the capital stock in the machine-producing industry. Instead, the shift term λ represents the payoff achieved by the industry incurring those developmental costs. A virtue of our proposed accounting system is that it attributes the benefits of cost-reducing R&D expenditures to the industry that actually performs the R&D, unlike the present system, which often allocates improved productivity to the using rather than the producing industry, for example, to the airlines rather than to the aircraft engine manufacturers.

In this framework, the total change in input cost consists of four terms, obtained by taking the total derivative of (2.7):

$$(2.8) \qquad dV = dC[c + C_t c_x x_C] + C_t(c_x x_y dy + c_\lambda d\lambda).$$

These terms represent, respectively, the direct and indirect substitution effect of changing prices of the inputs to the supplying industry, the effect of changing input requirements due to changing input ($x_y dy$), and the effect of

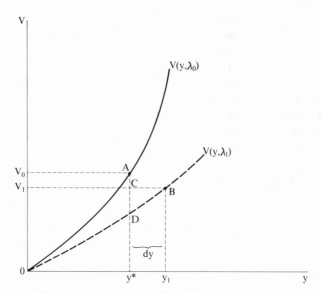

Fig. 2.1   Effect of a technological shift on the unit cost function

technical change in shifting the real cost function $(c_\lambda d\lambda)$. Since the input price index (P_t^i) as written in (2.6) holds the output level constant at y^*, the change in P_t^i can be written as the total change in cost from (2.8) minus the contribution to cost of the change in output:

$$(2.9) \quad \frac{dP^i}{P^i} = \frac{dV - C_t c_x x_y dy}{V(y^*, C_0, \lambda_0)} = \frac{dC[c + C_t c_x x_C] + C_t c_\lambda d\lambda}{V(y^*, C_0, \lambda_0)}.$$

Here, the middle expression indicates that the change in price is measured by adjusting the observed change in the cost of a new model for the change in its quantity of characteristics $(x_y dy)$ multiplied by the marginal cost of producing those characteristics $(C_t c_x)$. The right-hand expression shows that the price change can be caused either by changes in input prices or profit margins in the supplying industry (dC) or by a technical shift $(d\lambda)$. Because the middle expression is used in actual measurement, the technical shift itself $(d\lambda)$ does not have to be observed directly.

Figure 2.1 illustrates the measurement of changes in the input price index in the presence of nonproportional quality change. The two upward-sloping lines plot the unit cost function (2.7) for two different values of the technical shift parameter λ. Initially, output level y^* is produced at an input unit cost of V_0 at point A. The technological change represented by the shift from λ_0 to λ_1 improves quality by raising the quantity of input characteristics relative to their cost. This raises the demand for characteristics and the level of output, depicted by y_1 in the diagram. The unit cost of the durable good (V_1) could be either higher or lower than in the initial situation (V_0).

According to equation (2.9), the change in the input price index is equal to the change in unit cost (minus line segment AC) minus an adjustment factor equal to the change in output (CB) times the marginal cost (CD/CB) of building extra input characteristics capable of producing the extra output along a new supply schedule. Thus, the change in the input price index is $-AC - CD = -AD$, that is, the vertical downward shift in the supply schedule itself. Note that the change in the real input quantity is measured by the change in output times the marginal cost of producing extra output under the new supply conditions. The change in an index of the real quantity of input characteristics (dQ^i) can be written formally as the proportional change in the number of units of capital (du/u), plus the change in cost per unit (dV/V), minus the input price index:

$$(2.10) \qquad \frac{dQ^i}{Q^i} = \frac{du}{u} + \frac{dV}{V} - \frac{dP^i}{P^i} = \frac{du}{u} + \frac{C_t c_x x_y dy}{V(y^*, C_0, \lambda_0)}.$$

Because it is the marginal cost of producing characteristics that is used to make the actual quality adjustment in (2.9), the much-debated distinction between the "user-value" and "production-cost" criteria for the measurement of quality change is misleading, since both are used in (2.9) and in the corresponding figure 2.1. User value is the criterion used to define x, that is, the choice of calculations rather than dimensions as the characteristic desired by the user of a calculator. And production cost is the criterion used to make the actual quality adjustment. In essence, we have a hybrid criterion in which both the user-value and production-cost criteria are integral parts.

For the purpose of quality adjustment in practice, several alternative methods of estimating the marginal cost (c_x) are available. For instance, if an auto manufacturer were to make automatic transmission standard at no increase in price, and if the BLS had information either on the price of automatic transmission when it was an option or on a manufacturer's estimate of the cost of producing an automatic transmission, then the present BLS pricing methodology would be adequate to measure the marginal cost. Often, when quality change involves continuous rather than discrete change, for example, a change in automobile acceleration and dimensions or in computer performance, it is more convenient to use the hedonic regression technique to estimate the shadow price of a given characteristic, that is, its marginal cost. Clearly, the proper technique to use in each case is independent of whether the nature of the quality change is "cost-increasing" or "nonproportional."

2.4 The Output Price Index

Triplett (1983b) has made Fisher and Shell's (1972) distinction between input and output price indexes the centerpiece of his analysis of quality change. An output price index is used to calculate an aggregate output index by deflation. In the case of a machine that is both an input to a machine-using industry and the output of a machine-producing industry, the input price index should be used in calculating measures of real capital input in the using industry, while the output price index should be used in calculating output and productivity indexes for the machine-producing industry.

The distinction between input and output price indexes creates an obvious problem. The real net investment component of national product is defined as the change in the real capital stock. If the price change of a machine is measured differently by the input and output price indexes, then the resulting change in real capital input will not be compatible with the computed change in net investment. This section demonstrates that, fortunately, both cost-increasing and nonproportional quality changes are treated identically by input and output price index measures. The only justification for a distinction between the two index types arises when output and input change are not identical, as in the addition to a machine of a pollution-control device that does not actually produce output, and thus consumes resources in the machine-producing industry without raising input in the machine-using industry. This and other issues raised by external economies and diseconomies are discussed below.

In contrast to the input price index, the output price index uses a standard that compares prices by holding constant the economy's endowment of productive factors and its production technology. The new output symbol (q) represents a vector of output characteristics. Initially, nonproportional quality change is ignored. A vector of output characteristics (q) is produced in an amount that depends on the quantity of input characteristics (z) and the relative prices of output characteristics (P):

$$(2.11) \qquad q = q(z, P), \quad q_z > 0.$$

Triplett defines the output price index P_t^Q as the ratio of the revenue (R) obtained from the optimum (maximum-revenue) combination of output characteristics in the reference and comparison-period output price regimes, holding constant both input quantities (z^*) and production functions:

$$(2.12) \qquad P_t^Q = \frac{R(q_t^*, P_t)}{R(q_0^*, P_0)} = \frac{P_t q(z^*, P_t)}{P_0 q(z^*, P_0)}.$$

Here, P_t and P_0 represent, respectively, the vector of prices of output characteristics in, respectively, the reference and comparison periods. Note that I let z stand for input characteristics in the intermediate goods (i.e., computer-producing) industry, as distinguished from the x vector of inputs in the final goods (computer-using) industry. As we shall see below, output characteristics in the "intermediate" computer industry (the q vector) are the same as input characteristics in the final goods industry (the x vector).

The numerator and denominator of the output price ratio differ both in the price regime (P_t or P_0) and in the quantities of output characteristics (q_t^*) or q_0^*) that are optimal, given the fixed input quantities (z^*) and the fixed production functions that establish the various output combinations that can be produced from those inputs. A quality change now implies an increase in one or more output characteristics.[3] If we assume that the resources devoted to increasing quality are obtained by decreasing the output of some other good, in order to remain on the same production possibility frontier, the output price index must be adjusted for the resource cost of the added output characteristics. "The [quality] adjustment required is equal to the value of the resources required to move the set of output characteristics included in the index back to the same production possibility curve. This is precisely the resource cost quality measurement rule that has been argued in the literature" (Triplett 1983b, 299).

Do the input and output price index concepts give a consistent treatment to an identical technological innovation that was described in figure 2.1 as a cost-saving technological innovation? The nonproportional quality change can be introduced into the discussion of output price indexes by allowing the same shift term (λ) to enter the production function. A vector of output characteristics (q) is now produced in an amount that depends on the quantity of input characteristics (z), the prices of output characteristics (P), and the shift term (λ):

$$(2.13) \qquad q = q(z, P, \lambda), \quad q_z > 0, \ q_\lambda > 0.$$

Following Triplett's usage (1983b, 295), an output characteristic is defined as something that uses resources: "An output is not an output because someone wants it; being useful or desired is the definition of an input."

The output price index, as in (2.12), is now the ratio of revenue in two periods when output prices are allowed to change, holding constant the level of resources (inputs) and production technology:

$$(2.14) \qquad P_t^O = \frac{R(q_t^*, P_t)}{R(q_0^*, P_0)} = \frac{P_t q(z^*, P_t, \lambda^*)}{P_0 q(z^*, P_0, \lambda^*)}.$$

The total change in revenue between the reference and the comparison periods is the total derivative of the revenue function:

---

3. The vector of output characteristics (q) might be imagined to consist of $m - 1$ homogenous goods, plus an mth good that in turn consists of n separate characteristics: $y = (q_1, q_2, \ldots, q_{m-1}, q_{m1}, q_{m2}, \ldots q_{mn})$. Quality change involves an increase in one of the characteristics of the mth good. If resources and technology are fixed, this would in turn require a reduction in the output of one of the $m - 1$ other goods.

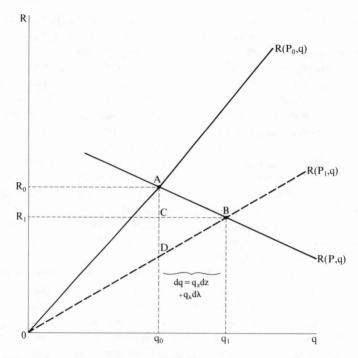

Fig. 2.2   Effect of a technological shift on the revenue function

$$(2.15) \qquad \frac{dR}{R} = \frac{dP(q + P_t q_P) + P_t(q_z dz + q_\lambda d\lambda)}{P_0 q(z^*, P_0, \lambda^*)},$$

where the terms represent, respectively, the direct and indirect substitution effects of changes in the output price, the effect on real output of increasing input usage, and the effect on real output of the technological shift itself.

The change in the output price index (2.14) consists of only two of the four terms in (2.15), since both input usage (z^*) and technology (λ^*) are being held constant:

$$(2.16) \qquad \frac{dP^O}{P^O} = \frac{dR - P_t(q_z dz + q_\lambda d\lambda)}{P_0 q(z^*, P_0, \lambda^*)} = \frac{dP(q + P_t q_p)}{P_0 q(z^*, P_0, \lambda^*)}.$$

The corresponding quantity index based on the output price index consists of the residual change in revenue:

$$(2.17) \qquad \frac{dQ^O}{Q^O} = \frac{P_t(q_z dz + q_\lambda d\lambda)}{P_0 q(z^*, P_0, \lambda^*)}.$$

What is the relation between changes in the output price index in (2.16) and in the input price index defined by (2.9)? Figure 2.2 illustrates the calculation of changes in the output price index and quantity index when there is a technological change represented by a shift from λ_0 to λ_1. The increase in the output that can be produced by the initial resource endowment raises output directly by the term $q_\lambda d\lambda$ in equation (2.17) and indirectly by raising the marginal product of inputs and hence the demand for inputs (the term $q_z dz$). If the higher level of output is to be sold, the output price (P) must drop, as indicated along the appropriate industry demand curve. The downward-sloping total revenue line in figure 2.2 is drawn on the assumption that demand is price inelastic. The upward-sloping lines indicate the revenue that would be obtained from varying levels of output if the price level were fixed. Starting from an initial equilibrium at point A, the innovation-induced increase in output leads to a new equilibrium at point B, where the price level has dropped from P_0 to P_1 and total revenue has declined from R_0 to R_1. According to equation (2.16), the change in the output price index is measured by the change in revenue (minus the line segment AC) minus the new price level (CD/CB) times the change in output (CB), or the distance $-AD$.

Now the connection between figures 2.1 and 2.2 becomes evident. When we consider the output of a capital good, for example, an electronic computer, a technological shift causes a decrease in price measured by the vertical distance AD in figure 2.2. Note that this vertical downward shift AD also appears in figure 2.1 as the change in input prices viewed by the user of the electronic computer. The input and output price index concepts are equivalent in this case and would include in both real GNP and in real capital input technological shifts that raise the output capacity of capital goods relative to their production cost.

The equivalence of the input and output price index concepts can be seen not just in the comparison of figures 2.1 and 2.2, but also in the comparison of equations (2.9) for the input price index and (2.16) for the output price index. First, because the output characteristics produced by the computer industry, the q vector, are identical to the input characteristics purchased by the final-goods industry, the x vector, we can write that in competitive equilibrium per-unit revenue $(R = Pq)$ equals per-unit cost $(V = Cc)$ in each time period:

$$(2.18) \qquad \begin{aligned} R_0 &= P_0 q_0 = V_0 = C_c c_0 \,, \\ R_t &= P_t q_t = V_t = C_t c_t \,. \end{aligned}$$

Further, in equilibrium, the price of an output characteristic produced by the computer industry (P) equals the marginal cost of producing a computer input characteristic for use in the final-goods industry:

$$(2.19) \qquad \begin{aligned} P_0 &= C_0 c_z \,, \\ P_t &= C_t c_z \,. \end{aligned}$$

Comparing (2.9) and (2.16) using the equilibrium conditions in (2.18), the denominator of the former, V_0, is identical to the denominator of the latter ($P_0 q_0$). The first terms in the numerator, respectively, dV and dR, are also identical. The terms subtracted in the middle expression of each equation, respectively, $C_t c_z dz$ and $P_t dq$, are also identical.

The model is applicable not just to "nonproportional" quality change, but also to "resource-using" or "cost-increasing" quality change. Imagine an upward shift in the demand for computers, without any change in technology. The previous equations are appropriate for measuring price and output change if we set the $d\lambda$ terms equal to zero. In figure 2.1, consider an initial equilibrium at point D, where the lower supply curve meets an initial demand curve (not drawn). Then let the demand curve shift upward sufficiently to move the new equilibrium position to point B. The change in unit cost (dV) is exactly offset by the increase in the marginal cost of the additional characteristics, leaving the input price index as measuring shifts in the price of producing a given output; in this case, there has been no such shift. The same conclusion applies to the output price index, which would be measured as unchanged, since the price of utilizing the initial level of resources has remained unchanged.

The previous comparison of equations (2.9) and (2.16) remains valid as well when quality change is resource using. In the case of each equation, the observed change in the value of a computer ($dR = dV$) is adjusted by the marginal cost ($C_t c_z dz$) of additional computer characteristics in the case of the input price index and the price ($P_t q_z dz$) of those characteristics in the case of the output price index.

2.5   The Equivalence of Input and Output Price Indexes

The conclusion of the previous section has been that both input price indexes and output price indexes treat quality change consistently, and that the user-value and resource-cost criteria lead to the same measures of prices of real output. This has always been recognized as true for "resource-using" quality change, where an increase in quality requires an increase in production cost. The novelty here is the demonstration that "nonproportional" quality change is also treated consistently by properly defined input and output indexes. Thus, a technological change that raises the user value of a durable good relative to its production cost will be treated in exactly the same way in input indexes that measure the changes in the real capital input of the using industry, and in output indexes that measure the real output of the producing industry.

This conclusion of equivalence between input and output indexes requires three assumptions for its validity.

1. The basic unit of observation in the theory is the characteristic. This may lead to measurement problems in practice, since we observe market prices in most cases only for physically discrete objects containing different bundles of characteristics.

2. The economy is competitive and in equilibrium, so that the price of characteristics is equal to their marginal cost. This equivalence of the "demand price" and "supply price" of a characteristic is familiar from the work of Rosen (1974).

3. Characteristics of durable goods must simultaneously make a difference for the output of the user (so that they can be counted as input characteristics for the using industry) and must require resources in their manufacture (so that they can be counted as output characteristics for the producing industry). This requirement may not be satisfied for some goods, for example, pollution-control devices.

If these three conditions are satisfied, the remaining theoretical ambiguity is limited to the usual Laspeyres/Paasche index number problem, for example, the different price indexes that result when base-period and current-period measures of marginal cost are used alternatively in (2.9) to adjust observed changes in the unit value of a durable good. Triplett (1983b) provides a full treatment of index number problems in the context of quality change adjustments and derives the direction of bias in the Laspeyres and Paasche indexes relative to the true input and output price indexes.

In practice, theoretical index number problems are likely to be of less importance than practical measurement issues. How is the marginal cost of an input characteristic, the key ingredient in the input price index formula (2.9), to be measured in practice? Similarly, how is the price of an output characteristic in (2.16) to be measured? Conventional, hedonic, and other measurement methods all involve developing proxies for these unobservables; their advantages and disadvantages are examined in chapter 3.

2.6 Comparison with Previous Approaches to the Quality Adjustment Issue

A complete survey of the large literature on quality change lies outside of the scope of this book. Instead, this section uses the preceding theoretical analysis to interpret the main arguments made by key participants in the debate between the "resource-cost" and "user-value" approaches to quality change, including Denison (1957, 1972), Gavett (1967), Gilbert (1961), Griliches (1964), and Jaszi (1964).

The analysis in the preceding section takes as its point of departure Triplett's insight that resource cost is the criterion used to define an output characteristic, and that user value is the criterion used to define an input characteristic. It goes beyond Triplett's analysis by making an explicit distinction between the quality-adjustment criterion and the estimator actually used to adjust price indexes for differences in characteristics across models.[4] For an input index, the preferred estimator is the marginal cost of producing an extra characteristic. For an output index, the preferred estimator is the demand price of an extra output characteristic. Both marginal cost and price information may be used to make quality adjustments in practice; the existing BLS quality adjustment procedures request manufacturers to estimate the cost of achieving a reported change in quality, whereas in the hedonic regression technique the dependent variable is the set of observed prices of models containing different quantities of characteristics. Thus, as Jaszi (1964) and some other early authors recognized, the issue of choosing the proper criterion is entirely independent of the practical issues involved in constructing the best possible estimator (e.g., the choice between the conventional and the hedonic methods).

Several authors, notably Denison and Jaszi, have opposed quality adjustments for the types of changes labeled here as *nonproportional,* that is, involving an increase in user value relative to resource cost. In Denison's original treatment of the subject, adjustments for nonproportional quality changes are opposed on grounds of infeasibility, not on the basis of a theoretical principle. Some other authors, however, have stated as a matter of principle that quality adjustments in price indexes are to be limited to cases where increased resources are required to produce an increase in quality.

The basic controversy revolves around the definition of the appropriate unit of measurement, which in this chapter is taken to be the *characteristic* (terminology used by Triplett and Lancaster), and which in some earlier work by myself (1970) and others was called the *quality attribute.* The proponents of the so-called resource cost position can often be described as choosing a more restrictive definition of the unit of measurement.

Another problem is the frequent confusion between movements along cost functions and shifts in those functions. In the computer example, any increase in multiplication speed or memory size raises costs and uses resources for any given technology (represented above by an initial value of the technological shift parameter, say λ_0). Thus, there should be no controversy about the desirability of making quality adjustments in price indexes for computers having different quantities of these resource-using characteristics. Disagreement arises, however, when a computer manufacturer introduces a new model containing twice as many characteristics as before with little or no increase in the computer's price. Here, the "resource cost" proponents argue against a quality adjustment, by stating in their terminology that a quality adjustment can be performed only when higher quality requires an increase in cost. Yet this terminology is appropriate only

4. Discussions with Triplett in 1979 and 1980 were instrumental in developing this distinction.

when cost functions remain fixed and fails to recognize the decline in the price of characteristics that occurs when there is a downward shift in the cost function, that is, a shift in technology from λ_0 to λ_1. The debate about the appropriate unit was best posed in the often-cited exchange between Griliches (1964) and Jaszi (1964). The question was stated concisely by Griliches (1964, 401–2):

> What should quality change be measured by—"cost" or "value"? The dosage of the new birth control pills (Enovid) has been recently cut in half, reducing thereby the price of this contraceptive method by half. This came about as the result of additional research which showed that half of the previously recommended dose is really enough to achieve the desired result. . . . How we should treat this change depends on our definition of "productivity." I would choose a measure that showed no decline in output, since in this way output would be defined in units comparable to the "market" for it, and such a definition would show a substantial increase in the productivity . . . of this industry. In fact, this is a rare actual example of the "pure-knowledge" no-increase-in-costs type of technological advance which crowds our textbooks.

Assume that before the technical advance two pills per day were required and afterward only one was necessary. Neither the cost of producing a pill nor a price index based on production cost has changed. Yet a price index based on the price of the "desired result," that is, on the ability of pills to produce birth control, has dropped by half. The apparent paradox disappears when we standardize the unit of transaction. While the cost per pill is unchanged, the cost per "desired result" has dropped by half, exactly the same proportion as the price index based on "value." The difference between the two approaches occurs only if the cost method is applied to "pill units" instead of "result units," and there is no conflict if the choice of unit, that is, the adjustment criterion, is based on the evaluation of users. If we observe on the marketplace that prices of pills are not identical but proportional to dosage, then we conclude that the consumer is buying dosage and does not care whether dosage comes in one-pill or two-pill bundles.

In his comment on Griliches's paper, Jaszi recognized that the definition of measurement units was crucial: the durability of automobile tires may be taken as the basic quantity dimension in some studies of transportation. It seems to me that this approach holds more promise than the two outlined before in some specific cases. Nevertheless, Jaszi took a relatively pessimistic attitude regarding the feasibility of measuring quality character-istics: "The difficulties involved in selecting the relevant quality character-istics, in finding good quantity indicators for them, and in assigning appropriate weights to these indicators tend to become unmanageable in most cases even of specific *ad hoc* analysis" (1964, 409).

Later, however, Jaszi shifted toward the view that the "real cost" criterion was desirable as an "underlying concept" rather than on grounds of practicality. Despite the precedent of Chow's (1967) hedonic study estimating the implicit prices of computer characteristics and showing a decline in characteristics prices of 25 percent per year, Jaszi defended his agency's practice of permanently setting the price deflator for computers equal to one by arguing that quality adjustments should not be made when an increase in computer performance relative to cost was made possible by a technological innovation:

> Recognition that we try to implement [the principle that quality changes must be reflected in real cost increases] is relevant in connection with R. J. Gordon's criticism of our assumptions about the prices of electronic computers. . . . The measurements presented in [Chow's] article do not seem to be based on the principle to which OBE [now BEA] and most experts subscribe, vis, that quality improvements can be quantified only to the extent that they are accompanied by real cost increases. [1971, 203]

Denison has contributed the basic theoretical paper (1957) that justifies the real cost criterion and that is cited in virtually every discussion, for example, that of Jaszi quoted in the preceding paragraph, written by those supporting that criterion. Denison distinguishes between a measure of real capital that equates units having the same real cost of production even if their quantity of input characteristics differ (K), a second measure that equates units having the same numbers of input characteristics (J), and a third that uses total output capacity as a proxy for capital input. I shall omit consideration of the latter here and agree with Denison that it is ''absurd'' because it would count increases in output due to a greater input of labor or land as attributable instead to capital. In Denison's discussion, units of capital goods that in my terminology have the same input characteristics are described as having the same marginal product.

Denison's attempt to distinguish between K and J rests on an arbitrary selection of the transaction unit. Any quality change that requires a higher price and cost of this transaction unit is taken into account in calculating K, but a quality change that leaves price and cost per transaction unit unchanged while reducing price and cost per quality characteristic should not be taken into account. It thus appears that Denison rejects J out of hand. Yet, according to my previous analysis, there should be no distinction between K and J if cost and price are defined in terms of the proper unit, the quality characteristic. Either K is identical to J, or it does not exist as a logically consistent concept.

Denison does not object to J on logical grounds. In fact, he calls it

> coherent and of extreme interest because all changes in real output could be traced to the responsible factor of production or to causes for which the factors were not responsible. Furthermore, it provides a measure of net capital formation which is theoretically meaningful. Zero net capital formation, or keeping capital intact, could be interpreted as that amount of

capital formation required to maintain the economy's output potential if the supply of all other productive factors were constant . . . and there were no changes in the institutional environment affecting productivity per unit of total input. [1957, 234]

Not only does Denison provide this degree of conceptual support for method 2 (J), but he presents two related arguments against the use of his own method 1 (K) as the only capital measure. First, he admits that "one aspect of method 1 at first sight appears curious. . . . Quality improvements in product not involving additional costs are usually considered as increases in output for industries producing consumers' goods but, by method 1, are not so considered in the case of durable capital goods." He defends this aspect of method 1 by claiming that capital goods are "instruments of production, not . . . products desired for their own own sake" (226–27). But, as Kuznets remarks in his comment on Denison's paper, this argument, if pushed to its logical conclusion, would cause investment to be excluded from national product altogether.

Second, Denison's own treatment of education in his studies of growth sources amounts to the "J approach" applied to people (see, e.g., his 1967 book). An index of quality change for labor is constructed with relative earnings of different education groups as weights on changes in the fraction of the labor force in each group. The weights are not based on the relative costs of educational inputs in each educational group. Thus, Denison's use of the J approach to measure labor input is inconsistent with his opposition to this approach for capital; in fact, the J approach should be used for both.

Then why does Denison oppose J as the appropriate concept? He claims that it simply cannot be measured and presents an example in which an improved variety of machines displaces labor in an industry and in which, he claims, the magnitude of J depends on the amount that the displaced labor can produce elsewhere. But the ratio of the quality of the new machines to that of the old depends only on the ratio of their input characteristics in the industries in which they are used and not on conditions in other industries to which displaced workers move. Denison rightly states that the macroeconomic data ordinarily employed by national income accounts will not reveal "the exact role of the change in the capital goods in isolation." But then he incorrectly rejects the use of macro data, for example, evidence on the relative prices of used assets, because the method "requires that buyers and sellers on the secondhand market have information which cannot be known to them . . . like the potential output of displaced workers" (234). The measurement of J requires micro data on relative prices, however, because relative prices measure relative marginal products, which are known to or can be estimated by the purchasers of the equipment. The effect of their purchases on conditions in other industries will not affect their price bids and are not relevant to the measurement of J.

Denison presents one last argument against J, which, even

> if there were no other difficulties, . . . would suffice to prevent [its]
> acceptance . . . as giving meaningful results. Very often production is
> increased simply because someone . . . has thought of a better way of
> organizing it. A more effective way to use a machine may be uncovered,
> either by change, through the initiative of its operator, as a result of time
> and motion study or other research project; or through an idea imported
> from abroad. The new way may involve no change at all in the machine.
> [233]

The introduction to this chapter, however, explicitly rules out price
adjustments for such ex post developments that could apply equally to new
or old machines. Events that change the marginal products of all machines
by the same proportion do not affect the price or quality change indices
defined in equations (2.9) and (2.16) because neither the quantity, nor the
implicit prices, nor the marginal costs, of characteristics would change.

Denison has subsequently supported his approach with an additional
argument that is conceptual rather than practical. The attempt to measure
quality change that raises the ratio of marginal product to cost

> would cause the capital stock in constant prices and hence capital input to
> rise more over time than the present procedure, and would transfer the
> gains provided by improved design of capital goods from advances in
> knowledge to capital. This would eliminate the possibility of a rise in the
> efficiency of capital and would destroy the possibility of analyzing
> advances of knowledge as a separate source of growth. [1972, 97]

But, as Rymes (1971) and I (1968) have previously pointed out, Denison's
argument goes only halfway if he wants to analyze advances of knowledge
as a separate source of growth. Technical advances in knowledge (''process
innovations'') that reduce the price of capital goods measured in transactions
units, relative to factor costs of inputs in those industries, cause ''the capital
stock in constant prices and hence capital input to rise more over time'' than
it would in the absence of advances in knowledge, and hence transfer the
gains provided by efficiency in the capital-goods-producing industry ''from
advances in knowledge to capital.'' Because the Denison (K) technique
already takes account of this source of growth, that is, productivity
improvements in the capital-goods-producing industries, but not the source
resulting from ''product innovations'' in those industries, it is a halfway
house that is not consistent with either of the two basic purposes of
investment statistics, the measurement of the output of real investment goods
or the identification of sources of growth. To identify the contribution of
advances in knowledge to growth, the proper distinction is to use the J
concept that attributes to capital goods manufacturers their own advances in
knowledge (both ''process innovations'' that raise productivity measured in
transactions units and ''product innovations'' that raise the quantity of
quality characteristics relative to the number of transactions units) but not
those ex post advances achieved by users of capital goods.

Recently Denison (1989, 24–32) has reentered the debate and gone beyond his previous advocacy of method 1 toward an endorsement of what he calls "method 4," the measurement of capital by consumption foregone. This has the effect of eliminating increases in the stock of capital made possible by process innovations, so that increases in GNP made possible by such innovations can be classified as due to advances in knowledge rather than as the result of capital investment. Allyn Young (1989b) provides a rebuttal to Denison's position in the context of defending the BEA's new computer deflators. The debate between Denison and Young does not change our previous conclusion that price deflators should be based on the J concept of capital.

Two more extreme positions may be cited. Gilbert presents the strongest statement defending the definition of price and cost in terms of the arbitrary units transacted on the market, rather than in terms of quality characteristics: "Our units of measurement are fixed transactions because they are the only measurable units" (1961, 21). But of course the conventional procedure already goes beyond transaction units, for example, a loaf of bread, and attempts to standardize for the units of a desired attribute, in this case weight per loaf. Once again, the disagreement revolves around an arbitrary and pessimistic presumption that all or most satisfaction-increasing quality changes are unmeasurable.

Gavett confronts an example that is exactly analogous to the case of nonproportional quality change, yet reaches the wrong conclusion:

> Suppose that an improved product can be produced without increasing the cost. If the price tag on the product remains the same, what should we conclude about the quality-adjusted price of this product? Cost considerations alone would suggest that the adjusted price is the same, if costs of the improvement are zero. This answer seems, at first blush, clearly wrong from the viewpoint of utility. After all, the product is better and the price tag the same. . . . Within the context of a pure price index, however, we must conclude that even utility consideration would lead to the conclusion that the quality-adjusted price is the same, not lower. [1967, 18]

The quotation states that the price is unchanged on the basis of both cost and utility considerations. This is wrong for costs, because the unit for measuring costs is wrongly chosen. While the cost of "this product" is indeed unchanged, the cost per unit of quality characteristic has declined. Thus, a properly defined cost measure yields a conclusion that price has declined. Gavett's second conclusion, that price is unchanged even on the utility criterion, is more surprising and equally incorrect. His justification is that the "increase in consumer surplus is not, however, attributable to a change in price but to a change in the quantity of the product purchased. That sort of gain in satisfaction is, however, excluded from a fixed weight index" (18). Yet the consumer's demand curve is exactly analogous to the situation in figure 2.2 above, which is defined with reference to the quality attributes that the consumer values. Thus, the quantity has increased because of the decline in price (and cost) per unit of quality attribute; the supply curve has shifted downward along an unchanged demand curve.

This section concludes, then, that there is no convincing case made in the previous literature that would warrant excluding quality adjustments to price indexes for quality changes that are "nonproportional." The basic Denison position, based on the infeasibility of measuring changes in quality characteristics, was written before Griliches's early work (1961) that demonstrated the feasibility of the hedonic regression technique. While choosing the appropriate unit of measurement may indeed be difficult when genuinely new products are invented, in many cases—like the invention of better-performing computer models—it will be possible to identify appropriate units in a cross section of different models. In these cases where objective evidence is available on the appropriate unit of measurement, there seems to be no articulate justification in the earlier literature for ignoring downward shifts in the cost function generated by reductions in the cost of producing these quality characteristics.

2.7   A Model Incorporating Operating Costs

The analysis to this point has followed the previous literature by analyzing concepts of quality adjustment for changes in performance characteristics, for example, changes in auto horsepower or computer memory. It now turns to a much less familiar topic, quality adjustments for changes in operating characteristics, for example, energy efficiency and maintenance requirements. While Griliches (1971) and others have recognized that fuel economy is a quality attribute that may help to explain some price differences across models, there is no previous theoretical treatment that explicitly integrates adjustments for operating efficiency into the index number literature.

Some research on the production technology of energy use (e.g., Hudson and Jorgenson 1974) assumes that energy (e) enters the production function symmetrically with labor hours (h) and capital input (x):

$$(2.20) \qquad y = y(h, x, e), \quad y_h > 0, \, y_x > 0, \, y_e > 0.$$

Thus, changing relative prices, in particular the rising relative price of energy observed during the 1970s, can cause substitution both between energy and capital and between energy and labor. Because the price of labor influences the amount of labor used per unit of capital, there is no presumption in this framework that changes in energy efficiency call for adjustments in the prices of capital goods.

Yet failure to do so would prevent the consistent treatment of performance-increasing and energy-saving technological change in the measurement of prices, output, and productivity. The previous sections show why a technological shift in the performance of a capital good per unit of resources used in capital-goods-producing firm A should be treated as an increase in real investment and real GNP. Now let us assume that another capital-goods-producing firm B achieves a technological improvement in one of its products, yielding energy savings having the same value to users as the performance improvement achieved by firm A. Should not the criteria for price measurement be designed to treat both types of technological change symmetrically?

In order to adjust the price of a capital good for changes in energy efficiency, it is necessary to assume that energy usage is "embodied" in capital goods, and that the production function (2.20) can be rewritten in the separable form:

$$(2.21) \qquad\qquad y = y[h, k(x, e)],$$

where $k(x, e)$ is a subfunction with two inputs, performance characteristics (x) and energy (e), that produces capital input (k). Berndt and Wood describe the subfunction as follows:

> For example, consider the production of industrial process steam of given specified physical characteristics. In such a context utilized capital services (k) refers to the quantity of steam produced per unit of time using capital . . . and fuel inputs. This assumption of a separable utilized capital subfunction implies that the optimal e/x ratios . . . depend solely on [the prices of x and e] and not on the other input prices or the level of gross output y. [1979, 344; my notation substituted for theirs]

Is this assumption of separability, which is essential to the discussion of price measurement in this paper, a reasonable one? Three arguments can be presented to support the procedures proposed here.

1. Berndt and Wood (1979) have reexamined previous econometric studies in an attempt to reconcile disparate findings regarding the degree of substitution or complementarity between capital and energy. In these reconciliations, "separability has played a prominent role" (350), and their own empirical evidence (1975) appears to support the separability assumption.

2. The study below makes the assumption not only that the production function is separable but that the technology is "putty clay," so that energy usage is "designed in" ex ante when the capital good is built. In some industries, the assumption that energy requirements are embodied in capital goods seems more reasonable than in others. The ability of a user ex post to improve the energy consumption of an automobile, commercial airplane, electricity generating plant, or appliance is relatively minor compared to the latitude available to the manufacturer. My study of the electric generating industry in chapter 5 below provides citations to previous literature, as well

as new evidence, supporting the proposition that energy efficiency is embodied ex ante, at least in that industry.

3. Although users can alter energy consumption even when technology is putty clay, for example, an automobile driver can save gasoline by careful avoidance of sudden starts, the techniques described below involve measuring an energy requirements function that holds constant the characteristics of users, for example, airline utilization or length of hop, and numerous characteristics of electricity generating plants. In addition, performance characteristics are held constant, yielding a function translating energy into performance that can fairly be said to be under the control of the capital-goods manufacturer.

2.8   Adapting the Input Price Index to Incorporate Nonproportional Changes in Net Revenue

The production of output (y) is now assumed not only to require the acquisition of durable goods having productive input characteristics (x), but also to involve a variable operating cost, the consumption of other inputs (e) times their price (S). In the present discussion, e may be taken to represent the yearly consumption of energy of a capital good having performance characteristics x. The energy requirements function is taken as given by the equipment user, reflecting my assumption of a separable putty clay technology:

$$(2.22) \qquad e = e(x, \sigma), \quad e_x > 0, e_\sigma < 0,$$

where the parameter σ represents a technological shift factor that can alter the energy consumption of a given set of input characteristics. A higher value of σ is assumed to be achieved by R&D expenditures by the equipment manufacturer and to allow a lower consumption of energy for a machine with a given set x of performance characteristics.

The net revenue (N) of the durable good user consists of gross revenue less variable operating cost. Gross revenue is the output price times the production function (eq. [2.1] above), and operating cost is the price of the operating input (S) times the consumption of operating inputs (e) from (2.22):

$$(2.23) \qquad N = Py(x) - Se(x, \sigma).$$

Here, to simplify the exposition, labor input is ignored and is implicitly assumed to be a fixed cost of operating capital with performance characteristics x. An expression for real net revenue (n) can be obtained by dividing (2.23) by the output price:

$$(2.24) \qquad n = y(x) - se(x, \sigma),$$

where s is the real price of the operating input ($s = S/P$).

Recall that the input price index was previously defined as the ratio for two time periods of the nominal cost of inputs that are capable of producing a given level of output (y^*). A natural extension of this concept in the presence of variable operating costs is to hold constant between the two periods the level of real net revenue (n^*). This criterion reflects the assumption that users of durable goods do not care about gross output but rather about the net revenue that durable goods provide. Thus, a user is assumed to be indifferent between ten units of real net revenue obtained in situation A with fifteen units of real output and five units of real operating cost, and an alternative situation B with sixteen units of real output and six units of real operating cost, holding constant his investment in capital goods (and the assumed fixed complement of labor required to operate the capital).

The introduction of variable operating costs makes the demand for input characteristics depend on real net revenue (n), the vector of prices of input characteristics (C), the real price of operating inputs (s), and the technological shift parameter (σ):

(2.25) $x_t = x(n_t, C_t, s_t, \sigma_t), \quad x_n > 0, x_s > 0, x_\sigma < 0.$

Comparing the arguments here to the previous input demand function in equation (2.3) above, note that real output has been replaced by real net revenue and that the two parameters of variable operating cost have been added (s and σ). The signs of the derivatives of (2.25) assume that the firm is operating in the region in which additional net revenue requires extra energy input and capital performance characteristics to produce more gross output. An increase in operating cost requires an increase in gross output (and hence capital input) to yield any fixed level of net revenue; hence, the derivative is positive with respect to the relative price s and negative with respect to the technological parameter σ.

When the new input demand function in (2.25) is substituted into the input characteristic cost function that allows for technical change (eq. [2.7] above), we obtain an expanded equation for the cost function:

(2.26) $V_t = C_t c[x(n_t, C_t, s_t, \sigma_t), \lambda_t].$

The input price index is defined as the ratio of the cost function in the comparison period to that in the reference period of producing a given real net revenue, holding constant the relative price of operating inputs:

(2.27) $$P_t^i = \frac{V(n^*, C_t, s_0, \sigma_t, \lambda_t)}{V(n^*, C_0, s_0, \sigma_0, \lambda_0)}.$$

The decision to hold constant the relative price of operating inputs (s) in the numerator and denominator reflects the desire to limit changes in the input price index to factors internal to the firm manufacturing the durable

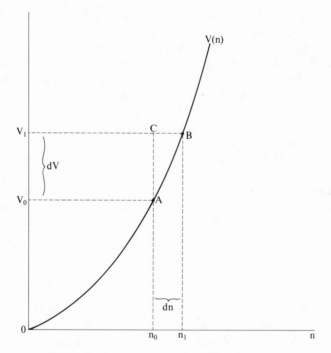

Fig. 2.3   The relation of unit cost for a capital good to its net revenue

good—its input prices and profit margin (C) and the level of technology built
into the good (σ, λ). In this way, changes in the relative price of an
operating input like energy are not treated as changes in the price of capital
input.

The change in the input price index can be written in two equivalent ways:

$$(2.28) \qquad \frac{dP^i}{P^i} = \frac{dV - C_t c_x(x_n dn + x_s ds)}{V(n^*, C_0, s_0, \sigma_0, \lambda_0)}$$
$$= \frac{dC(c + C_t c_x x_C) + C_t(c_x x_\sigma d\sigma + c_\lambda d\lambda)}{V(n^*, C_0, s_0, \sigma_0, \lambda_0)}.$$

The extended model incorporating operating costs can be illustrated in figure
2.3, which repeats the vertical axis of figure 2.1 and replaces y on the
horizontal axis by n. The upward-sloping schedule plots equation (2.26) and
shows the increasing unit cost of input characteristics required to generate
additional net revenue. The initial equilibrium position, where the quantity
of output is chosen to make marginal net revenue equal to marginal cost, is
shown at point A.

Consider first the proper treatment in price measurement of an improvement in quality that occurs when an equiproportionate increase in the prices
P and S relative to C leads users to demand higher-quality capital goods.

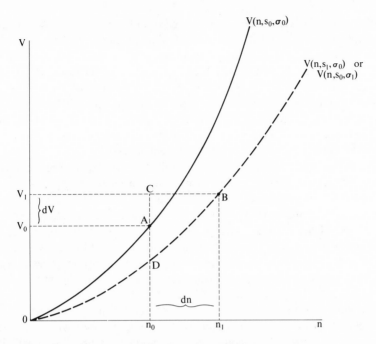

Fig. 2.4   Effect of a reduction in the real price of energy

Because the higher prices P and S shift the nominal marginal net revenue schedule upward, the equilibrium position shifts from A to B. If the manufacturer reports to the BLS that the entire addition to the price of the good from V_0 to V_1 is due to the higher cost (CA) of raising the specification of characteristics embodied in the good, the BLS would correctly conclude that there has been no price change. Note that the manufacturer's cost estimate does not represent simply the effect of higher performance holding constant operating cost, but rather the net extra cost of raising performance while allowing energy consumption to increase along the $e(x, \sigma)$ function. There is no danger that the substitution toward greater operating cost will be misinterpreted as a change in input price as long as the marginal cost (CA/CB) of the extra quantity of input characteristics is correctly measured.

Does the general formula (2.28) for the change in the input price index correctly conclude that there has been no price change? From the change in the cost of the durable good (CA) is to be subtracted the marginal cost (CA/CB) of the extra input characteristics required to raise real net revenue by the actual observed amount (CB). Thus, the observed change in input cost (CA) minus the correction factor (CA) equals zero.

A second case, a reduction in the relative price of energy, is illustrated in figure 2.4. A decrease in the price of energy from S_0 to S_1, while the product price is held constant at P_0, shifts the unit cost schedule rightward, since a smaller nominal operating cost must be deducted from gross revenue for any given quantity of the input characteristic, thus raising net revenue for any given value of V. The new equilibrium position is assumed to shift from point A to point B. The input price index subtracts from the observed change in price (CA) the marginal cost (CD/CB) of the extra input characteristics required to raise real net revenue by the observed amount (CB) adjusted for the effect on input cost $(+AD)$ of lower real energy prices (ds) when real net revenue is constant. Once again, the observed change in input cost (CA) minus the correction factor $(-CD + AD)$ equals zero.

As an example of this second case, note that lower relative gasoline prices in the 1950s and 1960s induced firms and consumers to shift to larger automobiles that consumed more fuel.[5] But if an automobile with given horsepower had maintained its previous fuel consumption along a fixed $e(x, \sigma)$ schedule, then no change would be imputed to the price of automobiles as a result of this substitution toward greater fuel consumption. The interesting research on automobiles by Wilcox (1984) describes energy efficiency as a function of performance characteristics and thus provides an estimate for that industry of the $e(x)$ function.

As a third example, let us consider a technological innovation that allows a given quantity of the input characteristic (x) to be used with a smaller consumption of fuel. To simplify the illustration in figure 2.4, it will be assumed that the shift takes the special form of reducing the marginal energy cost of a change in input quantity by the same amount as the decrease in the relative energy price examined in the previous two paragraphs:

$$(2.29) \qquad s_0 e(x, \sigma_1) = s_1 e(x, \sigma_0).$$

The lower schedule in figure 2.4 is relabeled to correspond to the new, more efficient energy consumption schedule in which σ_1 replaces σ_0.

In this third case, as in the first two cases, the equilibrium position moves from point A to point B. But now the input price index registers a decline in price instead of no change in price. From the change in the unit cost of the input characteristic $(dV = CA)$ is subtracted the marginal cost (CD/CB) of the extra input characteristics required to raise real net revenue by the actual observed amount (CB). Thus, the observed change in input cost (CA) minus the correction factor (CD) equals the change in the input price index $(-AD)$.

2.9   Implementation of Operating Cost Adjustments

In each of the cases considered in the previous section, the observed change in unit cost of a durable good was adjusted for changes in net

---

5. During the two-decade period 1953–72, the nominal price of gasoline in the CPI increased 34 percent, compared to 56 percent for the all-items CPI, representing a reduction in the relative price of 14.4 percent.

revenue caused by a shift in either an exogenous price or a technological parameter. In each case, the adjustment involved determining the marginal cost of whatever extra quantity of input characteristics would have been required to yield the observed increase in net revenue in the absence of the observed parameter shift. The foregoing discussion implies that, in practice, price changes across different models of a durable good can be measured as the change in unit value relative to the change, if any, in net revenue. The main obstacle to implementation of this idea, as we shall see, is nonlinearity in the function relating unit value to net revenue.

The discussion of measurement can usefully be set in the context of a competitive firm that uses capital goods to produce net revenue. Its user cost of capital multiplies the unit price of a durable good (V) times the interest rate r (representing some combination of borrowing costs and the opportunity cost of the firm's own funds), plus a geometric depreciation rate δ that measures the rate of decay with the asset's age of the stream of services that it provides. The capital market is assumed to set only a single interest rate that each firm takes as given, and the capital gains component of user cost is ignored.[6]

Firms using the durable good are price takers in both input and output markets. They have no influence on the price of the durable assets they purchase (V), on the price of the output they produce (P), or on the price of operating inputs (S) or cost of ownership ($r + \delta$) they must pay. In addition, I assume that the operating efficiency parameter (σ) is fixed by a technical constraint. Firms simply choose the level of output that maximizes yearly profit (π), the difference between nominal net revenue and the user cost of capital:

$$(2.30) \quad \pi = N - (r + \delta)V = Py(x) - Se(x, \sigma) - (r + \delta)V(x).$$

The only choice variable in the simplified structure of (2.30) is the quantity of input characteristics (x). If all producers and users of the durable asset are identical, then there will be a single model produced that embodies enough of the durable input characteristic to equate its real marginal cost of production to the present value of its real marginal net revenue:

$$(2.31) \qquad v_x(x) = \frac{y_x(x) - se_x(x, \sigma)}{r + \delta} = \frac{n_x(x, s, \sigma)}{r + \delta} \, ,$$

where $v_x(x) = V_x(x)/P$. The fact that the market usually provides numerous varieties containing different quantities of input characteristics has been

---

6. The depreciation rate should depend both on the built-in durability characteristics of the good and on the user-chosen intensity of repair and maintenance services. In the simple version of the model considered here, with only a single composite operating cost characteristic, the depreciation rate is assumed to be fixed.

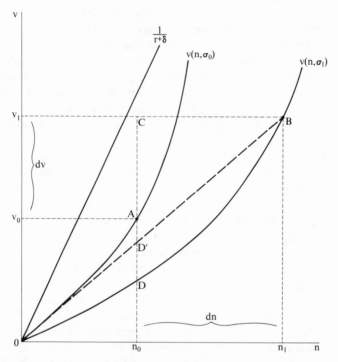

Fig. 2.5   Effect of improved operating efficiency on the real net unit cost function

explained by Rosen (1974) as resulting from the different tastes of consumers and technologies of producers.[7]

Figure 2.5 illustrates the equilibrium described in equation (2.30), with the real unit cost of durable goods on the vertical axis and real net revenue on the horizontal. As in figures 2.3 and 2.4, the purchase of additional input characteristics raises both unit cost (v) and net revenue (n), but the response of net revenue exhibits diminishing returns, both because of diminishing returns in the production function relating output to input characteristics, and because of the increasing marginal cost of producing input characteristics. When the technical level of operating efficiency is represented by σ_0, the initial equilibrium occurs at point A, where the $v(n, \sigma)$ function is tangent to a straight line having the slope $1/(r + \delta)$. The $v(\ )$ function also depends on C/P and x, but these parameters are held constant in the present discussion of adjusting capital input prices for changes in operating efficiency, $d\sigma$.

If the level of operating efficiency were to shift to the improved level represented by σ_1, the firm would move to a new equilibrium position at

7. For some qualifications, see Muellbauer (1974).

point *B*, where the new $v(n, \sigma)$ function again has the slope $1/(r + \delta)$.[8] The change in the input price index, as in figure 2.4, is the observed change in unit cost (dv = line segment *CA*) minus an adjustment factor equal to the observed change in net revenue (dn = *CB*) times the marginal cost of producing input characteristics capable of providing that amount of net revenue, the slope *CD/CB*. Although points *A* and *B* can be observed, and thus *dv* and *dn* can be measured, point *D* cannot be observed directly. How can the slope *CD/CB* be calculated in practice in order to compute the quality change adjustment factor *AD?*

As figure 2.5 illustrates, the problem of estimating point *D* arises because of the curvature of the $v(n, \sigma)$ function. If the function were a straight line, then the unobservable point *D* would coincide with point *D'*,which lies along a ray from the origin to point B having the slope v_1/n_1. But as long as there are either diminishing returns in producing net revenue in response to an increase in the quantity of input characteristics or an increasing marginal cost of producing input characteristics, then the curvature of the function will always make point *D'* lie above point *D*, and will make the segment *AD'* an underestimate of the required quality adjustment, segment *AD*.

Since the exact form of the function is unobservable, and because data are unlikely to be available to estimate it in many cases, the estimation of the quality adjustment factor must inevitably be based on some assumption about the function. Consider, for instance, the particularly simple relation

(2.32) $$v = \beta n^\alpha,$$

where the curvature of the function depends on the parameter α. Technological changes that alter the position of the function are represented by shifts in the β parameter.

To use this function in the estimation of changes in input price, first rewrite the basic formula (2.28) for a comparison in which the price of operating inputs (ds) is held constant:

(2.33) $$\frac{dp^i}{p^i} = \frac{dv - v_n dn}{v_0},$$

where the real unit cost (v) of the capital input replaces the nominal cost (V) appearing in (2.28), and the input price index is now expressed in real (p^i) rather than nominal (P^i) form, on the assumption that the output price can be held constant while comparing the new and old types of durable goods. Converting (2.33) from continuous to discrete changes, we obtain

8. Imagine that point *B* were to lie along an extension of the ray *OA*. Then the new level of net revenue per dollar of capital ($v_1 B/0 v_1$) would be the same as before ($v_0 A/0 v_0$). Since the percentage user cost per dollar of capital ($r + \delta$) is constant, the rate of return on capital would remain constant.

$$(2.34) \qquad \frac{\Delta p^i}{p^i} = \frac{\Delta v - [v(n_1, \sigma_1) - v(n_0, \sigma_1)]}{v(n_0, \sigma_0)}$$

$$= \frac{v(n_0, \sigma_1)}{v(n_0, \sigma_0)} - 1.$$

When the assumed functional form (2.32) is substituted into the general formula (2.34), the resulting expression depends only on observable variables and the ''curvature'' parameter:

$$(2.35) \qquad \frac{\Delta p^i}{p^i} = \frac{\beta_1 n_0^\alpha}{\beta_0 n_0^\alpha} - 1 = \left[\frac{v_1 n_0}{v_0 n_1}\right]\left[\frac{n_0}{n_1}\right]^{\alpha-1} - 1.$$

To make sense of the right-hand side of (2.34), imagine first that the $v(n, \sigma)$ function is linear, that is, that $\alpha = 1$, so that the second term in brackets becomes unity. Then the remaining expression states that the ''real'' price change will be zero if both unit cost and net revenue grow in proportion in the shift to the new model, $(v_1/v_0) = (n_1/n_0)$. This is the case of ''resource-using'' or ''cost-increasing'' quality change. A nonproportional quality change, as illustrated in figure 2.5, would raise net revenue relative to cost and would result in an estimated change in the ''real'' input price index that is less than the observed change in price of models that remain identical.

When the $v(n, \sigma)$ function is strictly convex, then $\alpha > 1$, and the second term in brackets in (2.35) becomes a fraction less than unity, corresponding in figure 2.5 to the fact that the unobservable point D lies below point D'. There seems to be no alternative in the estimation of equation (2.35) to making an arbitrary assumption about the value of the α parameter, or to presenting results for several alternative assumptions regarding the curvature of the $v(n, \sigma)$ function. To make the easy assumption that $\alpha = 1$ would be just as arbitrary as any other choice.

It is important to note that (2.35) is to be used to calculate a quality adjustment when comparing two different models, while holding constant output prices and the prices of operating inputs. Since this means in practice that the net revenue performance of two models must be compared in a particular year when both are in operation, equation (2.35) must be calculated in a way that holds constant any factors that change the cost of manufacturing a given model in the given year of comparison, that is, changes in profit margins and/or the prices of inputs into the manufacturing process. Thus, for practical measurement, equation (2.35), which computes the price change involved in the shift from one model to another, must be combined with an index of changes in the cost of producing identical models. Changes in the nominal input price index, then, are equal to changes in the real input price index plus changes in the cost of producing identical models:

$$(2.36) \qquad \frac{\Delta P^i}{P^i} = \frac{\Delta p^i}{p^i} + \frac{\Delta C[C_t c_x(x^*)]}{C_0 c(x^*)} \, .$$

Thus, if there is a 10 percent annual increase in the price of identical models, and if all quality change is resource using as in figure 2.3, the quality change adjustment in equation (2.35) will be zero, and the nominal input-cost index in (2.36) will be recorded to increase at a 10 percent annual rate. But if the real quality change adjustment were minus 5 percent, then the increase in the nominal input-cost index would be reduced to a 5 percent annual rate.

2.10   Used Asset Prices and the Accuracy of Quality Adjustments

The above analysis was based on the assumption that firms maximize profits and hence are indifferent between two machines with the same purchase cost and depreciation rate that yield the same net revenue. One of these might have low performance with low operating costs, and the other might have high performance with high operating costs. A corollary to this assumption is that the market for used assets must incorporate the effects of changes in operating costs due to changes either in technological design or in energy prices. Although data on used assets are available for only a relatively small number of durable goods, notably transportation equipment, tractors, and other equipment that is not "bolted down," the study of used asset price data may serve as a useful cross-check on the accuracy of quality adjustments carried out on data for new products.

Let us compare two used assets selling at time t at prices A_{0t} and A_{1t}. The firm is indifferent between the two if they each offer the opportunity to earn the same rate of return, say ρ_t^*. The implications for the relation of used asset prices and net revenue can be seen if we take (2.30), substitute the price of the used asset (A_{it}) for the price of the new asset (V), and divide through by A_{it}:

$$(2.37) \qquad \rho_t^* = \frac{\pi_{0t}}{A_{0t}} = \frac{N_{0t}}{A_{0t}} - (r + \delta),$$

$$\rho_t^* = \frac{\pi_{1t}}{A_{1t}} = \frac{N_{1t}}{A_{1t}} - (r + \delta).$$

Here, assume for convenience that the two assets are different models of the same product, and that the interest rate (r) and depreciation rate (δ) on the two alternative models are identical and constant. If so, then when the upper and lower lines in (2.37) are equated, we obtain:

$$(2.38) \qquad \frac{A_{1t}}{A_{0t}} = \frac{N_{1t}}{N_{0t}} \, .$$

Given the restrictive assumptions of the previous paragraph, used asset prices of different models for the same product observed at a given moment should be observed to be proportional to their respective ability to earn net revenue. Substituting the definition of nominal net revenue used in the right-hand expression of (2.30), we can relate the ratio of used asset prices to the determinants of net revenue:

$$(2.39) \quad \frac{A_{1t}}{A_{0t}} = \frac{P_t y(x_1) - S_t e(x_1, \sigma_1)}{P_t y(x_0) - S_t e(x_0, \sigma_0)} = \frac{y(x_1) - s_t e(x_1, \sigma_1)}{y(x_0) - s_t e(x_0, \sigma_0)}.$$

Here, it is assumed that the output price (P_t) and energy price (S_t) applicable to the two models are identical and are functions only of time, whereas the performance characteristics (x) and operating efficiency factor (σ) of each model are embodied ex ante and do not change over time.

The expression (2.39), together with the set of assumptions required to derive it, summarize both the benefits and the pitfalls of utilizing used asset price data as a cross-check on quality adjustments for new products. The benefit is that used asset prices should reflect differences in operating efficiency, so that actual observations on used asset prices can be compared with a theoretical calculation of net revenue for the two models based on their ability to generate gross revenue and on their operating costs. A close similarity of the used asset price ratio with the theoretical price ratio would tend to confirm the methodology developed above to perform quality adjustments, and major differences would introduce an important note of caution and qualification.

There are, however, a number of pitfalls.

1. The used asset price comparison cannot shed light on the proper treatment of nonlinearity, discussed above in the context of figure 2.5. If model 1 yields real net revenue n_1 and has a used asset price shown by the vertical distance at B, then a model 0 that yields net revenue n_0 has a used asset price shown by the point D' that lies along the ray OB. Used asset prices can give no information on the unobservable point D, since users care only about net revenue and not about curvature in the production function.

2. Expression (2.37) is overly simplified by assuming that users care about profits only at time t. More realistically, they want to maximize the present value of profits over the expected lifetime of the assets, and correspondingly they care about expected future real energy prices, not just current energy prices. This creates two problems in practice. First, it suggests that quality adjustments for operating efficiency improvements must be based on expected future energy costs, not current energy costs in the year of manufacture. Second, it complicates the task of comparing used asset prices with theoretical calculations of net revenue, since the expected lifetime relevant for expected future energy prices will cover a different interval and

be of a different length for the used asset comparison than for the quality adjustment applied to new equipment.

3. Expressions (2.38) and (2.39) are derived on the assumption that both the more efficient and the less efficient models have the same depreciation rate, and that the depreciation rate is constant. In fact, the depreciation rate on the two models may be different and may (as in the case of gas-guzzling automobiles and commercial aircraft after the 1974 oil price shock) depend on the level of energy prices. A related problem is that the more and less efficient models observed in the used asset market may be of different vintages and may have different expected lifetimes.

Despite all these caveats, comparisons between used asset price ratios and theoretically calculated ratios are of great value, because of their potential for providing verification of the basic approach suggested above, and of the specific assumptions made in quality adjustments for individual products. The qualifications do not seem serious enough to warrant discarding used asset data but rather indicate that their interpretation should be performed with care.[9]

2.11   Interpretation of the Proposed Conceptual Framework

The first part of this chapter explored the concept of nonproportional quality change in performance characteristics, and section 2.6 related this approach to important papers in the previous literature. Sections 2.7 and 2.9 have covered less familiar ground, nonproportional quality change taking the form of changes in operating efficiency. Because there is no significant earlier literature on this topic, it is worthwhile to pause here to consider possible caveats to the proposed treatment.

Triplett (1983a) objects to the proposal in the previous sections that an increase in fuel efficiency calls for a quality adjustment to the prices of fuel-using durable goods. His discussion is framed in terms of a theoretical total input cost index:

> If a fuel-efficiency improvement occurs in the second period, then the cost of the collection of inputs necessary to produce a given level will fall by the decrease in expenditure on fuel. . . . No additional adjustment to the price of aircraft is necessary. . . . the cost of saving from an improvement in fuel efficiency occurs precisely from an adjustment in quantity of fuel required for a fixed amount of output. Therefore, in the total input cost index, adjusting the price of airplanes for fuel savings would double-count

9. Diewert (1989b, chap. 5) presents a useful summary of the theory of used asset prices in the context of the measurement of the user cost of capital. His discussion, however, does not treat the problem addressed here: the use of used asset prices to assess quality differences between new and old models.

the effect of increased fuel efficiency, for that saving already shows up in decreased quantities of fuel purchased by airlines. [1983a, 260]

To consider the implications of Triplett's position, it is best to distinguish (as he does) between a fixed-weight Laspeyres index (L) and a theoretical or exact index number (I). We write L as

$$(2.40) \qquad L = \frac{P_t^F X_0^F + P_t^K X_0^K}{P_0^F X_0^F + P_0^K X_0^K}.$$

Here, the superscript F refers to fuel, and K to capital. P is the price of each input, and X is its quantity. In the airline fuel efficiency example, where we assume a constant price of fuel, the Laspeyres input cost index would take the cost of fuel to be unchanged ($P_t^F X_0^F = P_0^F X_0^F$). Thus, the actual decline of input cost would not be reflected unless the price index of capital input (P_t^K) were to decline, as would be accomplished by the procedures suggested above. Triplett does not object to the proposed adjustments in the fixed-weight index case but cautions that "the theory provides no guidance. The theory of index numbers is a theory of the exact or theoretical index" (1983a, 262).

However, it appears that there is no case for objecting to the proposed treatment even for the theoretical input cost index. No double counting is involved. In Triplett's notation, the theoretical index (I) is the ratio of the minimum cost of acquiring inputs sufficient to produce a given output in the reference period relative to the comparison period:[10]

$$(2.41) \qquad I = \frac{P_t^F X_t^F + P_t^K X_t^K}{P_0^F X_0^F + P_0^K X_0^K}.$$

The reduction of input cost comes in the reduced quantity of fuel, ($X_t^F < X_0^F$). However, the proposed adjustment to the price index of capital goods does not affect I in (2.41), simply because quantity is measured as nominal expenditure on capital divided by the proposed deflator. Adjustment of the capital goods deflator by any multiplicative constant, say $P_t^{K*} = \gamma P_t^K$, has no effect on the nominal magnitude entering (2.41). Since $X_t^K = P_t^K X_t^K / P_t^K$, it follows that

$$(2.42) \qquad P_t^K X_t^K = P_t^{K*} X_t^{K*} = P_t^K (P_t^K X_t^K / P_t^K).$$

Thus the case for including energy efficiency adjustments to capital goods price indexes cannot be opposed on the grounds of double counting, since the "γ adjustment" makes no difference for the total input cost index. Since

10. The formula for I comes from eq. (4) in Triplett (1983b), and the formula for L comes from eq. (5).

it makes no difference, Triplett is correct that it is redundant, insofar as the creation of a total input cost index is the sole objective of price measurement. The justification for such adjustments must hinge on other objectives of price measurement, particularly the creation of deflators required to compute time series on real investment, real capital stock, and productivity in particular industries manufacturing durable goods.

Triplett's second major criticism is that the separability assumption written above in equation (2.21), $y = y[h, k(x, e)]$, while plausible, "does not permit forming an index of capital goods prices, independent of energy. . . . the theoretically appropriate subindex is an index for airplanes combined with fuel" (1983a, 261). Triplett is correct that the technology specification in (2.21) does not allow the measurement of real capital input or a price index for capital goods that is independent of the relative price of energy. The connection with that relative price is explicit in the discussion above, particularly in equation (2.39). There it is recognized that quality adjustments must be based on expected future energy costs, and alternative adjustments would be implied by alternative assumptions about the expected energy price regime.

This criticism, while valid, introduces the familiar debate between measures that are "imprecisely right" and those that are "precisely wrong." In the airplane example, it would be incorrect to treat as a price increase rather than a quality increase that portion of the higher sales price of a Boeing 767 relative to a Boeing 727 that can be attributed to improved fuel economy. It is correct in principle to construct the aircraft price index on the basis of an estimate of the value of the fuel savings, and a necessary evil that a range of such adjustments can be calculated on the basis of alternative assumptions about expected fuel prices. This imprecision does not represent a quantum jump from the types of imprecision that have been accepted for years, for example, in the use of hedonic price regressions as the basis for the official residential construction deflator, despite the fact that alternative indexes emerge from the use of different econometric specifications and techniques.

In preference to my approach, which involves introducing quality adjustments for energy efficiency changes into the price indexes for durable goods, Triplett would rather measure the input service price of durable goods as the flow price per unit of time of the combined costs of capital, fuel, and maintenance ("the BLS would be pricing the cost per mile of a constant quality automotive service" [1983a, 262]). This approach would be sensible if the only function of official price measurement were to deflate consumer expenditures on a flow of services. But it would leave us bereft of sensible deflators for the output of producer and consumer durables, and industry output measures that properly allocate productivity gains across industries.

Quality adjustments in durable goods deflators for efficiency changes are necessary for these supplementary purposes of price indexes, while yielding the same results as Triplett's preferred measure. First, in the case of a "proportional" quality change taking the form of an improvement in energy efficiency, neither the service price nor my durable goods price index would register any change. Consider a situation in which a change in relative prices leads a refrigerator producer to add the quality characteristic "energy efficiency" up to the point where its marginal cost equals its value in energy saving to the consumer. There will be no change in the service price of the new-model refrigerator compared to that of an old model in the new energy price regime, since the reduction in the annual value of energy consumption will offset the increase in the annual depreciation and interest cost of the higher-quality refrigerator. In exactly the same way, my own procedure would find that there had been an increase in net revenue measured at constant fuel prices that was proportional to the higher unit price of the equipment, and consequently no quality adjustment would be called for.

Second, consider a "nonproportional" innovation that cut annual expenditures on energy by $20 while increasing the annual capital cost of a refrigerator by only $10. Triplett's service price of refrigerators would register a decline, as would my price index for refrigerators based on a finding that net revenue had increased by more than equipment cost. Either measure of price would be adequate for a study of the demand for refrigerators in a period of constant energy prices and would be far preferable to an index that failed to register any decline in price. In the case of commercial aircraft, a demand study would be highly misleading if it used the official BEA price index.

Consider the following division of annual operating revenue: (a) labor cost, (b) fuel cost, (c) capital cost (interest plus depreciation), and (d) profit. Triplett's service price includes b plus c. A nonproportional improvement in energy efficiency by definition reduces b more than it raises c, thus reducing the service price. Our "net revenue" is c plus d. A nonproportional improvement in energy efficiency by my definition raises net revenue (c plus d) by more than capital cost (c) when calculated at fixed prices of output, labor, and fuel. Thus, both criteria give the same answer; the reduction in service price parallels the decline in the equipment price index that results from the method proposed here.

There is an important conceptual distinction between the service price approach and the proposed quality adjustments in durable goods deflators. Measures of service prices will pick up any factors that alter operating efficiency, whether achieved by equipment manufacturers or users. In contrast, my approach requires explicit attention to the distinction between ex ante and ex post improvements. Ideally, quality adjustments using my method should be based on engineering data provided by manufacturers or, as a second best, operating data gathered from a variety of users soon after the introduction of the durable good. Subsequent improvements achieved by users should not be credited to manufacturers.

The discussion of changes in operating efficiency has focused on changes in fuel efficiency. Yet other changes that affect operating costs are equally relevant, including changes in maintenance requirements and in durability achieved by manufacturers. It is likely to be harder to maintain the ex ante versus ex post distinction for maintenance and durability changes, since these are unlikely to be observed until several years after installation.

2.12   Summary and Conclusion

The primary emphasis in this chapter has been on devising methods to make quality adjustments in the computation of price indexes so as to "credit" manufacturers of durable goods for all changes in the quantity of final consumption goods and services that are caused by changes in the types and characteristics of "new vintage" durable goods. The methodology is devised to allow a parallel treatment of technological developments that reduce the cost of purchasing a given quantity of performance characteristics and those that reduce costs of operation, for example, fuel and maintenance.

"Nonproportional" quality changes are those that increase the value of a durable good (specifically, its ability to generate net revenue) relative to its purchase price. These can take the form of higher quantities of performance characteristics provided relative to purchase price, the "price-performance" ratio so often discussed in the example of computers. They can also take the form of improvements in operating efficiency that yield a greater increase in net revenue than in purchase price. Although the literature on quality change adjustments has frequently debated the merits of the "user-value" and "production-cost" criteria for the measurement of quality change, *both* criteria are used in the proposed adjustment procedure. User value is the criterion used to choose the attributes or quality characteristics of each product, whereas production cost is the estimator used to make the actual adjustment. A literature survey finds that much of the past debate has involved disagreements over the choice of attributes.

It is shown that input and output price index concepts give a consistent treatment to a given technological innovation. The only reason to distinguish between the concepts is in cases where manufacturers use resources to produce output characteristics that are not valued by users, for example, antipollution equipment purchased by users of durable goods only as the result of government mandate. In such cases, input and output price indexes can diverge, and explicit accounting is required, as is accomplished by the present procedures that break out the fraction of the capital stock consisting of antipollution equipment.

The last half of the chapter is devoted to quality adjustments for changes in operating efficiency. The basic approach is to estimate the ability of old and new models to generate net revenue ex ante, that is, when calculated with manufacturers' specifications and a constant set of prices for output and fuel input. If the prices of the two models differ in proportion to their ability to generate net revenue, then no quality adjustment is called for. But if net revenue increases relative to the price of the newer model, then a quality adjustment would be performed.

In addition to requiring quality adjustments in price indexes for durable goods, efficiency improvements in new models should also be reflected in relative prices observed in markets for used assets. The main difficulties in achieving actual measures of the recommended quality adjustments include their sensitivity to alternative assumptions about future energy prices and depreciation rates, and problems created by curvature in the production function of durable goods manufacture. Data on used asset prices, while interesting, cannot really resolve the basic ambiguities inherent in this type of measurement.

The quality adjustment procedures proposed in this chapter seem necessary to capture the higher level of net investment and the higher level of aggregate productivity resulting from energy-saving innovations, as well as to allocate correctly the credit for the innovations to the industry achieving them. In the study of commercial aircraft in chapter 4, this involves allocating the credit for improved operating efficiency to the airframe and aircraft engine industries rather than to the airline industry. The importance of a correct allocation is obvious for those who are attempting to trace the current U.S. productivity slowdown to changes in capital and R&D input in particular industries (Griliches 1980).

3   The Methodology of Quality Adjustment

3.1   Introduction

A central theme of chapter 2 was the distinction between the criterion used in choosing quality characteristics for input cost indexes, and the estimator used to adjust durable goods price indexes for differences in characteristics across models. The theoretical discussion identified "user value" as the quality criterion and seller's marginal cost as the quality adjustment estimator. This chapter is concerned with the practical problems involved in computing quality adjustments. It concentrates on general measurement issues applicable to a variety of products; special problems particular to individual products are discussed in the subsequent product chapters.

The primary aim of this book is to use alternative data sources to produce new price deflators for selected types of durable goods. These are compared with existing deflators compiled by BEA, and the implications for BEA measures of output, productivity, and capital stock are then discussed. The great majority of BEA deflators for individual types of consumer durables are based on underlying commodity price components of the CPI, while deflators for individual types of producer durables are based on components of the PPI. Since the BEA is thus largely a "conduit" for the CPI and PPI price data collected by the BLS, this chapter refers mainly to the techniques of the latter agency.

The chapter begins with a description of present quality adjustment techniques used by the BLS. For exposition purposes, the BLS techniques are collectively called the *conventional method*. The advantages and disadvantages of these techniques are then compared with those of available alternatives, the best known of which is the hedonic regression approach. At the outset, it should be emphasized that the choice between estimation techniques does not correspond to the debate reviewed in chapter 2 regarding quality-adjustment criteria. Although some descriptions of government methods(e.g., Jaszi 1971) have ruled out adjustments for the types of quality change called *nonproportional* in chapter 2, in fact the use by the BLS of manufacturers' cost data for making quality adjustments corresponds closely to the general procedure advocated in chapter 2. In that conceptual discussion, the choice of quality characteristics is based on user value, and the estimator used for adjustment is the marginal cost of producing those quality characteristics along a fixed cost schedule. Correspondingly, "the criterion for measuring quality change in a BLS input price index is always user value. . . . The estimator, on the other hand, is sometimes manufacturing cost because that may be the only information available" (Triplett 1983b, 255). Thus, any criticism of BLS methodology, and any suggestion that alternative techniques should be substituted in some cases, involves not a theoretical dispute but rather concentrates on sins of omission and on detailed procedures. Each of the several available techniques has weaknesses, and it may be preferable in some cases to use techniques in combination (partly to serve as cross-checks on each other) rather than to adhere to the mechanical application of a single technique.

This chapter is not a comprehensive review of either the CPI or the PPI (formerly the WPI). For these, the reader is referred to the report of the NBER Price Statistics Review Committee (NBER 1961), or Stigler report, and to the more recent and comprehensive *Wholesale Price Index: Review and Evaluation* (U.S. Executive Office of the President 1977)), or the Ruggles report. These reports take up numerous issues that are not treated here, including sampling methodology, revision of weights, transaction versus list prices, and order versus shipment prices. As will soon become evident, the issues involved in quality adjustment are complex enough to warrant limiting our attention to that single issue.

3.2   Official Price Indexes: Coverage and Procedures

Primary emphasis in this section is on durable goods price information collected in the PPI, the basic source for the national income accounts deflators for PDE. Supplementary information on the CPI and the consumer durable deflator is contained at the end of the next section. The PDE deflator is based (with a few exceptions) on PPI eight-digit "item indexes," weighted by the estimated share of each commodity in gross domestic private investment. The BEA publishes twenty-two separate group deflators for major types of equipment, for example, office machinery and communications equipment. Current-dollar expenditures in the twenty-two groups are deflated separately to yield constant-dollar group expenditure, constant-dollar aggregate PDE expenditure, and the aggregate PDE deflator. Within the twenty-two groups, the individual PPI commodity indexes are combined with unpublished weights based on expenditures in about 150 detailed components of PDE (a list is provided in Appendix A).

Before 1947, motor vehicles, agricultural machinery, and office furniture were the only capital goods included in the PPI; data are available beginning in 1947 for a large number of different types of machinery, with the gradual introduction of new products and replacement of obsolete items throughout the postwar period. One measure of the extent of coverage is the percentage of a four-digit SIC industry's shipments represented by the value of individual seven-digit products that are priced directly. Based on the 1958 Census of Manufacturers, coverage in the PPI in the early 1960s was quite spotty in the machinery and transportation equipment industries (SIC 35, 36, and 37), with less than 10 percent of products priced directly in four-digit industries that contribute 42 percent of total value added, and with coverage of 50 percent or greater in industries contributing only 27 percent of value added. Among the important industries with very low or no coverage were construction machinery, special dies and tools, machine shop equipment, telephone and radio-television communication equipment, aircraft and aircraft engines, and ship building (Searle 1964, 358–59).

By the early 1970s, the situation had improved somewhat as coverage was broadened. Table 3.1 shows computations for six major two-digit durable goods industries based on the value of shipments recorded in the 1972 Census of Production. The first row indicates the number and value of shipments of all five-digit SIC product classes when classified into two-digit SIC major industries. Then row 2 shows the percentage of the five-digit SIC product classes in each two-digit major industry that were directly priced by the BLS by number and value of shipments. By this measure, the extent of coverage seems quite wide, ranging from 44 to 72 percent by value.

Another more meaningful criterion is the percentage of the seven-digit SIC product classes that were "directly priced" within each five-digit SIC product class. This is the criterion used by the BLS for publishing price indexes for the five-digit classes. Here, the extent of coverage is less impressive, as shown on row 3, with the percentages by value ranging from just eight in SIC 38 to fifty-five in SIC 25. In the machinery and transportation equipment industries (SIC 35, 36, and 37), the average percentage had risen from the 27 percent figure quoted above for 1958 to an average of 36 percent for 1972.[1] Thus, one justification for the exploration of alternative sources of price data, as in this book, is to fill in for coverage gaps in the PPI. Since coverage has improved over time, it is important to create alternative indexes over as long a historical time path as possible, in order to determine whether any bias in one direction or another has been created by changing coverage.

The last section of table 3.1 identifies manufacturers' reports as the major source of price information for the PPI. In all the durable goods industries shown, company reports account for between 97 and 100 percent of the total

---

1. The criterion changed from percentage of four-digit industries in the earlier comparison to percentage of five-digit industries in the later comparison.

Table 3.1   Data on PPI Coverage and Methods, Selected Two-Digit Industry Groups

	Two-Digit Industry and SIC Code					
	Furniture and Wood Products 25 (1)	Fabricated Metal Products 34 (2)	Nonelectrical Machinery 35 (3)	Electrical Equipment 36 (4)	Transportation Equipment 37 (5)	Instruments and Related 38 (6)
1. Total five-digit SIC product classes:[a]						
Number	43	127	190	117	71	48
Value ($billions)	11	51	64	54	103	16
2. Percent directly priced in PPI:[a]						
Percent by number	37	54	60	62	18	29
Percent by value	60	72	62	60	68	44
3. Percent published by BLS:[a]						
Percent by number	30	27	36	33	7	6
Percent by value	55	45	33	36	38	8
4. Sources of price reports:[b]						
Total number of reports	156	672	1771	992	191	140
Percent from trade sources	0	2	1	1	0	1
Percent from government agencies	2	1	1	3	0	0
Percent from companies	98	97	98	97	100	99
Value of shipments directly priced as percent of total	26	16	19	24	22	7

Source: U.S. Executive Office of the President (1977, tables I-2 and I-3).

[a]Computed from the *WPI Weight Diagram for 1972.*

[b]As of March 1975.

reports. Virtually none of the reports come from equipment purchasers, virtually all from equipment sellers. In a sample survey carried out in 1975, it appeared that about two-thirds of the durable goods reports were submitted by company headquarters, and the other one-third by individual establishments.

The essence of the "conventional method" used by the BLS is called *specification pricing*. If a product is specified by all quality characteristics (x) that influence user value, then none of the increase in sales revenue per unit due to increases in x is erroneously considered as a price change. The focus in the PPI has always been on obtaining prices for a given commodity from several producers. Thus, the specifications for the eight-digit item indexes must be detailed enough to eliminate the influence of important types of quality change, while at the same time broad enough to admit price reports from several manufacturers. The level of detail in specifications varies across commodities. For some relatively homogeneous commodities where manufacturers are basically producing identical items, it is possible to make the specification so detailed that it is quite unlikely that quality change slips through unnoticed. An example is the following specification for an eight-digit item index for wire rods:

10–13–01–11.02   Wire rods: 7/32'' diameter, coils, hot rolled carbon steel, CI 008 industrial or standard quality, base quantity 20 net tons and over; mill to user, f.o.b. mill, per 100 lbs.

For other commodities where technical innovation is frequent and features vary across manufacturers, commodity specifications are less detailed. Consider this specification for an eight-digit item index for color television sets:

12–52–01–56   Color television receiver, console model, 21'', 23'', or 25'' picture tube, veneer cabinet; manufacturer to dealer or distributor, f.o.b. factory, or warehouse, each.

Since the only specification of the quantity of x here is the size of the picture tube, many other features of color television sets could be ignored and some part of a change in price associated with a new or altered model might be treated as price change instead of quality change. Among the omitted features are remote control capability (and even this varies in the number of functions that can be controlled remotely), capability for cable television, headphone equipment, automatic tuning, type of built-in antenna, and so on.

The NBER review of the PPI carried out a test to determine whether the eight-digit PPI item indexes were defined for homogeneous products by computing the coefficient of variation of individual price reports relative to the average price within each PPI commodity. The coefficients of variation in percentages for the six durable goods categories were 41.3 (furniture), 16.1

(fabricated metal), 24.6 (nonelectrical machinery), 18.7 (electrical equipment), 16.0 (transportation equipment), and 21.6 (instruments). The review also pointed out that these differences persisted over a year between 1975 and 1976, suggesting substantial heterogeneity within eight-digit item groups (U.S. Executive Office of the President 1977, I-24, I-25). This intraitem heterogeneity does not necessarily cause a problem for the specification method, for if the manufacturer alters his product in any significant way, the change is supposed to be reported to the BLS. The BLS then decides whether the change warrants an explicit quantity adjustment or should be ignored. Its standards are sufficiently tight that broad specifications are not allowed to permit dimensional changes to be treated as price changes. For instance, Triplett (1971b, 184) reports that, despite a range in the refrigerator specification of 13.5–16.5 cubic feet, anything over a 0.4-cubic-foot change calls for an explicit quality adjustment. Thus, three different varieties of color television sets sold by three different manufacturers could be included in item index 12–52–01–56, with the top grade costing 50 percent more than the lowest grade, but there would be no problem for the index if the price reports from each of the three sellers were effectively adjusted for quality change.

3.3 Methodology of Quality Adjustment in the BLS Indexes

Since heterogeneity within PPI item indexes is common, the crucial issue becomes the adequacy of the quality adjustments carried out on the individual price reports within the eight-digit commodity classifications. To the extent that quality improvements occur within the eight-digit classes for which no quality adjustments are made, the overall PPI will rise faster than the "true" change in price. When informed by a manufacturer of an alteration on a model, the BLS commodity specialists make a choice among four alternative procedures.

This section first describes the mechanical method of adjustment under each of the four methods, using the formulas suggested by Early and Sinclair (1983, 110). It then turns to the frequency of use for each method, and some of the problems and potential biases that they might introduce.

If there is no model change brought to the attention of the BLS, then the price change between two successive months is simply P_t/P_{t-1}. In each of the four methods that the BLS uses when informed of a model change, we can express the calculated price change as P_t/L_{t-1}, where L_{t-1} is the "link price" of the new model. Each method calculates L_{t-1} by a different procedure. Under "direct comparison," the model change is ignored, so that $L_{t-1} = P_{t-1}$. Under "deletion," the price change between the two months for this particular product is omitted from the index calculation, which has the effect of setting $L_{t-1} = P_t/(P_t^*/P_{t-1}^*)$ where the term in parentheses is the average price change recorded for the other price reports in the eight-digit item index. Under the "link, no change" method, then, by definition there is no price change, and so $L_{t-1} = P_t$. Finally, with a producer cost adjustment amounting to Q_t (in dollars), $L_{t-1} = P_{t-1} + Q_t$.[2]

3.3.1   Direct Comparison.

The simplest procedure is simply to neglect the change. This occurs when the alteration is considered to be "small," for example, less than a 0.4-cubic-foot change in refrigerator capacity, or less than 2 inches of length variation for a rug. Within these limits, whatever price change is observed to accompany the model alteration will be treated as price change, not as quality change. As an example of the frequency of direct comparison, in the CPI in 1965, 23.1 percent of all price comparisons of appliances involved substitutions caused by nonidentical models, and 59.2 percent of these substitutions were handled by the method of direct comparison (Triplett 1971b, 187).[3]

The use of the direct comparison method does not necessarily impart a positive bias to the rate of price change recorded by the PPI. Some model alterations may represent a decline in performance quality or durability. Also, Triplett (1971b) has pointed out that a quality characteristic included in a BLS specification, for example, a frost-free freezer or a refrigerator, may "trickle down" over the years to models that have smaller quantities of other quality characteristics that are not included in the BLS specification. If this phenomenon were frequent, it could impart a negative bias to the PPI.

3.3.2   Deletion

In the example cited above for the 1965 CPI appliance indexes, 40.8 percent of the substitutions were not handled by direct comparisons. In most of this remaining group, the price quotation of the new model was simply deleted (39.4 percent), with a small remainder (1.4 percent) related to the previous observation by linking based on information for overlapping models. The choice between direct comparison and deletion depends on the size of the change in price between the old and the new quotations, with the deletion method chosen if the price change exceeds a predetermined but unpublished limit. Since quality improvements are frequently introduced on models with no change in price, the predetermined limit will not be exceeded in this case, and the new and the old models will be compared directly, causing the true decline in price to be missed and the index to be biased upward. When the limit is exceeded and the price quotation is deleted, the

2. Early and Sinclair point out that, since Q_t is valued in dollars as of time t rather than, as should occur, at time $t - 1$, the value of the adjustment is overstated during periods of inflation. The correct formula, apparently used now but not before 1978, is $L_{t-1} = (P_t P_{t-1})/(P_t - Q_t)$.

3. The data reported refer to all reported price quotations for nonfood items for two large cities.

index is based on one fewer observation, so that the average price change on the other included varieties is implicitly applied to the excluded variety.

If the most frequent cause of deletion is a sizable quality change, then the official price indexes consist disproportionately of commodities of constant quality. In some of the detailed product studies later in the book, we find that the quality adjusted price of new models is often below that of the models they replace. If so, the effect of deletion is to reduce the weight given in the index to the price declines relative to price increases and thus to bias the overall index upward. In principle, the opposite effect is also possible, if the typical introduction of a new model involves a mixture of quality improvement and "true" price change, since deletion will therefore reduce the weight given to true price change in the index. If the mixture tilted toward more true price change in periods of high inflation, then it is conceivable that the direction of bias might be inversely proportional to the inflation rate, with a positive bias in low inflation periods and a negative bias in high inflation periods.

3.3.3   Linking

When a model with a new quality characteristic is introduced, and price data are available for models with both quality characteristics at a given date, the new price is "linked" to the old one with a difference between the prices of new and old models on the transition date used to estimate the change in quality. This method is equivalent in principle to the hedonic regression method discussed below but is much less useful in practice, because old models often disappear completely. In the next month's price report, a replacement model often appears containing different quantities of one or more quality attributes, thus preventing the necessary simultaneous comparison of the prices of the two models. As recently as 1965, only 4.8 percent of all nonfood substitutions in the CPI were handled by linking, as compared to 61.4 percent by direct comparison and the remaining 33.8 percent by deletion (Triplett 1971b, 187).

3.3.4   Explicit Adjustment Based on Cost Estimate

The cost-adjustment method is saved for last. While it corresponds most closely to the conceptual framework suggested in chapter 2, it is carried out less frequently than the other methods. As described by Triplett (1983a, 254–55), the adjustment takes place in two steps. First, employing the user-value criterion, the BLS must decide whether the model alteration is to be considered as a quality change at all. Examples of changes not allowed as quality improvements by the BLS in the past include a change from a conventional to a digital clock face, and a redesigned speedometer that did not register extremely high speeds.

The second step is to estimate the value of the change. This is most straightforward when an item previously offered as optional equipment at a published price is made standard equipment. This gradual upgrading process was a common feature of quality change for automobiles in the 1950s and 1960s. However, the option price may exaggerate the cost of adding the item to all units in a standardized production run. When no such option price is available, the BLS must accept an estimate of added cost from the manufacturer. It is unclear how these estimates are monitored or audited. There may be an incentive for manufacturers to exaggerate the extra cost of added equipment; although neither sales nor profits are directly affected, manufacturers may want to understate the extent of price increases for public relations and labor relations purposes.

Because quality change is a pervasive feature of durable goods, and because the requisite overlapping models needed for linking are often not available, the extent to which the official price indexes (both CPI and PPI) adjust for quality improvements appears to depend crucially on cost estimates by manufacturers. Yet published descriptions of official methodology agree that, during most of the postwar period, the cost estimates have been made for only a few types of goods and for only a portion of the quality improvements that occurred in those goods. Before 1960, the method was applied in the CPI only to automobile accessories added to the standard model that were previously optional at a stated price: "For example in the case of automobiles our practice has been to substitute the new model car for the previous model, assuming no quality change except for those features which affect some easily observed difference in operational characteristics and for which a value can be determined. . . . In such a comparison we would make no allowances for such changes as greater length or more wrap in the windshield, because we have no objective standard by which to determine the relationship between quality and price for such features" (Jaffe 1959, 195). In 1961, "the most important items [in the CPI] for which this procedure is used regularly are automobiles, gas for heating and cooking, hospitalization insurance, and contract rents" (Hoover 1961, 1178). By implication, no cost-based explicit adjustments were performed then for any other important consumer durables, for example, washing machines, refrigerators, or radio-television equipment.

For automobiles, published reports describe a clear break in technique in 1959: "The guidelines followed in making adjustments for quality differences between the 1965 and 1966 models of automobiles are the same as those adopted by the Bureau in 1959 and were made possible by quality and cost data supplied by manufacturers. Prior to 1959, most adjustments for quality differences involved changes in optional equipment. . . . For the WPI, some additional adjustments for product changes had been taken into account in earlier years, but the extent of such adjustments was limited by the unavailability of the required information" (Stotz 1966, 178). Yet no explicit description or example is available that indicates precisely how changes in dimensions, for example, length or horsepower, have been handled since 1959. Furthermore, as late as 1965, prices of other consumer durables

Table 3.2   Classification of Quality Adjustments in Selected Major PPI
                   Commodity Groups

	Major Group and Two-Digit PPI Code			
	Metals and Metal Products 10 (1)	Machinery and Equipment 11 (2)	Furniture and Household Durables 12 (3)	Transportation Equipment 14 (4)
1. Tally as of July 1975:				
Number of items	373	799	94	104
Number of price quotations	1,225	2,893	431	242
2. 1976 quality adjustments as percent of all price quotations	0.4	0.5	1.3	2.4
3. 1976 percent share by quality adjustment method:				
Direct comparison	32.2	32.4	29.0	11.9
Link, no change	49.1	38.8	56.4	20.9
Cost estimate	18.7	28.8	14.5	67.1
	100.0	100.0	99.9	99.9

Sources by row: (**1**) *BLS Handbook of Methods,* Bulletin 1910 (U.S. Bureau of Labor Statistics, 1976). (**2, 3**) Early and Sinclair (1983, table 2.1).

were still not adjusted explicitly for quality change, and, in one published example for the year 1965, there was not one single explicit quality adjustment based on cost data in the entire nonfood component of the CPI (Triplett 1971b, table 6.2, row 4, p. 187). In another example, for all nonfood items in 1966, the division among the four methods was 59.1 percent by direct comparison, 36.2 percent by deletion, 1.9 percent by linking, and 2.6 percent by an explicit size or quality adjustment (Triplett 1971b, table 6.1, p. 186).

More recently, Early and Sinclair (1983) have summarized the classification of quality adjustments in the PPI for 1976, as shown in table 3.2. Row 2 shows all types of quality adjustments, excluding deletion, as a percentage of all price quotations. For the PPI as a whole, there were surprisingly few quality adjustments, 455 total cases out of 108,756 total price observations for the year. However, as shown in row 3, explicit cost estimates accounted for a much larger share of the quality adjustments than in the CPI examples for the mid-1960s cited above, and direct comparison for a much smaller share. This evidence that the BLS is investing more resources in making explicit quality adjustments with manufacturers' cost data would suggest, ceteris paribus, the possibility that any quality adjustment bias in the PPI might be less in the 1970s than in earlier decades. Nevertheless, the incidence of only 455 cases of adjustment for more than 100,000 price observations also would suggest that some cases of quality change may be missed, or that some types of rapidly changing products (particularly in the electronics area) are not included in the indexes at all. And the incidence of producers' cost estimates outside transportation equipment is still relatively low, ranging from 15 percent for furniture and household durables to 29 percent for machinery and equipment.

Because the greater frequency of explicit cost adjustments in transportation equipment, particularly autos and trucks, still occurs as it has since 1959, the differential rates of price change recorded by different components of the PPI may be partly due to differences in measurement techniques. Compare, for instance, the following recorded percentage changes by decade:

	1950–60	1960–70	1970–80
Agricultural machinery (PPI 11–1)	32.0	31.5	129.0
Motor vehicles (PPI 14–11)	31.2	8.6	84.2
Difference	0.8	22.9	44.8

If one assumes that agricultural machinery and motor vehicles use roughly comparable technology, then one might argue that the slower rate of price change of motor vehicles in the 1960s and 1970s is at least partly due to the greater resources devoted to explicit quality adjustments. This still leaves open the possibility that the quality adjustments for motor vehicles have been too large as a result of manufacturer's overvaluations of the true cost of quality changes.

3.4   The Hedonic Regression Technique: Basic Features

The hedonic regression approach, as developed by Court (1939) and Griliches (1961), can be viewed as an alternative method to manufacturers' cost estimates in making quality change adjustments. It assumes that the price of a product observed at a given time is a function of its quality characteristics (x), and it estimates the imputed prices of such characteristics by regressing the prices of different models of the product on their differing embodied quantities of characteristics. Papers by Muellbauer (1974) and Lucas (1975) relate the hedonic method to Lancaster's (1971) theory of consumer choice. In equilibrium, Rosen (1974) has shown that the hedonic price schedule traces out differences both in user value and in manufacturing cost across models. Thus, the hedonic price approach represents not a new concept in the measurement of quality change, but rather an alternative to cost estimates to be used when practical factors make it more suitable than the conventional method.

The empirical problem is the estimation of the implicit prices of characteristics (x_{ij}) in which the dependent variable is a vector of observations on prices on n different models at a given time, and each of the m independent variables is a vector of data for a quality attribute for the different models.[4] The regression is most often specified in semilog form:

$$(3.1) \qquad \log p_i = a_0 + \sum_{j=1}^{m} b_j x_{ij} + u_i, \quad i = 1, \ldots, n.$$

The regression coefficients (b_j) from (3.1) are combined with the data on changes in quality attributes (dx_{ij}) to yield the estimated change in quality, a calculation that implicitly assumes that all quality changes can be treated as variations in the quality of the x_{ij}, and any change in the quantity of particular product attribute can be converted into an equivalent amount of quantity in the product itself through multiplication by the estimated b_j weights. Then the change in a quality-adjusted price index for the product can be calculated by subtracting for each model the change in its quality index (i.e., the change in each quality characteristic multiplied by its estimated implicit price) from the change in its actual transaction price or unit value.

An alternative approach to the estimation of quality-adjusted price change is to estimate the coefficients on one or more time dummy variables (D_t) in cross-sectional regressions for two or more years:

$$(3.2) \qquad \log p_{it} = a_0 + \sum_{t=1}^{N} d_t D_t + \sum_{j=1}^{m} b_j x_{ijt} + u_{it},$$
$$i = 1, \ldots, n; t = 0, \ldots, N.$$

An aggregate index of price change then is obtained either from the series of d_t coefficients obtained in one regression like (3.2) run on data for a number of years, or from a string of d_t coefficients obtained from a series of "adjacent year" regressions on data for successive pairs of years. To the extent that the prices of quality characteristics are changing through time, the latter two-year technique allows the regression coefficients on the x_{ijt} to change frequently and is preferable.

There is no difference in principle between the two methods of estimating price change, deflation by a quality index and estimation of coefficients on time dummy variables. Results differ only to the extent that the time period for which the b_j implicit price weights are estimated in (3.1) differs from the time period in the adjacent year regression. For instance, Griliches's (1961) original hedonic study of automobiles contains three separate hedonic price indexes based on deflation by three quality indexes with b_j weights estimated in equation (3.1) for the initial year of the sample period alone, the final year

---

4. The partial regression coefficients of p_i and x_{ij} are precisely equal to Mp_i/Mx_{ij} only if a linear relation is postulated between the p_i and x_{ij}. If the variables are in semilog form, the coefficients stand for the percentage change in price with respect to a unit change in each quality attribute.

alone, and each year separately. The results differ in each case because of the standard index number problem that occurs when the estimated implicit prices of characteristics (b_j) shift from year to year. The results must be identical to the adjacent year technique if the b_j weights are estimated for the same pair of years.

Most studies have in practice chosen the time dummy variable approach, simply because it conveniently allows the "true" rate of price change to be read directly from the computer printout without any intermediate transformations. As Griliches (1967) has pointed out, however, changing samples of models in a regression like (3.2) for two adjacent years will cause some of the sample variation to be picked up in the time dummy coefficients, unless the sum ($\Sigma\ u_{it}$) of the "model effects" (the effect of left-out qualities) for both groups of models is identical. For instance, if we run a regression for two years, 1959 and 1960, and include only in the latter period models of compact cars that are more expensive per unit of size than full-sized cars, the regression will yield a positive coefficient on the 1960 time dummy, even in the absence of "pure" inflation, because the coefficients on the x_{ijt} variables are constrained to be equal in the next two years. This does not strike me as a major obstacle to the use of (3.2), however, because it is relatively easy, with only a small reduction in sample size (in most cases), to restrict the sample in years t and $t + 1$ to contain the same models and then include the new models in a regression on years $t + 1$ and $t + 2$. In his work with Ohta, Griliches explicitly endorses this view that the number of observations should be reduced where necessary to maintain constancy in the sample of models over time (Ohta and Griliches 1976).

Prices of used capital goods offer two advantages over new good prices for the study of quality change. First, they are by definition transaction prices rather than list prices. Second, the relative prices of two models of differing quality are determined by buyers' evaluations rather than by the decisions of sellers. But used good prices can usefully be studied only in conjunction with the hedonic technique, not by themselves. Any observation in a used asset market can be cross-classified along three dimensions, the time of the observation (t), the age of the asset (s), and its model designation (i). Differences in observed prices can be attributed to changes in "pure" price (P_t), differences in quality (X_{iv}) among models of different vintages ($v = t - s$), and the effect of depreciation on models of different ages (A_s). Maintaining the semilog approach,

$$(3.3) \qquad\qquad p_{its} = e^{P_t}e^{X_{iv}}e^{A_s}.$$

This parametization of price involves some strong but necessary assumptions, as pointed out by Hall (1971). Equation (3.3) can be converted into a semilog regression equation if the errors (u_{its}) are assumed to enter multiplicatively in (3.5):

(3.4) $\log p_{its} = P_t + X_{iv} + A_s + u_{its}$.

In this regression, the right-hand variables are dummy variables corresponding to the appropriate time periods, vintages, and ages, and their coefficients can be converted directly into index numbers. The major problem with (3.4) is that, without further assumptions, the rate of quality change cannot be identified, since observed prices that are consistent, say, with a given depreciation rate, low inflation, and rapid quality change, are also consistent with lower depreciation rates, more rapid inflation, and slower quality change.

Hall's major contribution is the suggestion that (3.4) can be combined with data on the quality characteristics of the different models and vintages in a single regression that generalizes the hedonic regression for new goods written in (3.5):

$$(3.5) \qquad \log p_{its} = a_0 + d_1 D_1 + \sum_{s=1}^{L} a_s A_s + \sum_{j=1}^{m} b_j x_{ijt} + u_{its} .$$

The constant term now refers to a new item in the first year of the adjacent year regression, d_1 is the coefficient on the dummy variable for observations recorded in the second year and represents pure price change, and the L separate age coefficients measure the relative prices of models of different ages that are otherwise identical, and their difference is the year-to-year rate of depreciation. In more refined versions, the rate of depreciation, which is assumed constant for all makes and quality dimensions in (3.5), can be allowed to vary along these dimensions.

3.5   The Hedonic Regression Technique: Pitfalls

The hedonic technique has been regarded in some quarters as a replacement for the conventional method and as a general solution to the problem of quality change measurement. The Stigler Committee report endorsed the technique as "potentially of wide applicability" (NBER 1961, 36). But whether the technique is applied to new or used goods, it raises as many problems as it solves; minor changes in specification yield hedonic indexes that differ substantially in both secular trend and year-to-year movements. Existing hedonic studies contain conclusions about price trends that are too divergent to be useful without close critical inspection to resolve differences. In Griliches's original study of automobiles, for instance, the estimated change in "true" price ranges from -18.4 to 14.1 percent over the 1950–60 period, depending on the particular time period used to estimate the b_j implicit price weights in the quality change index (Griliches 1961, 187, table 9). Similarly, more recent studies contain estimates of price change for 1960–65 that range from -0.8 to 6.4 percent (Ohta and

Griliches 1976). The reluctance of the BLS to use the hedonic technique regularly in the CPI and WPI may in part reflect the ambiguous results of past hedonic studies.

There are a number of econometric specification problems that contribute to the ambiguity inherent in the hedonic technique.

3.5.1   The General Excluded Variable Problem

Many of the specific specification difficulties encountered in applications of the hedonic technique are subclasses of the excluded variable problem. Assume that the correct structural model determining the price of two different models in two adjacent years can be completely described with no error:

$$(3.6) \qquad \log p_{it} = a_0 + d_1 D_1 + \sum_{j=1}^{m} b_j x_{ijt} + b_{m+1} x_{i,m+1,t} .$$

If a regression is run that erroneously includes only the first m quality attributes, and if the $m + 1$ variable is uncorrelated with the first variables, then the estimate of the rate of true price change (d_1) will be biased as follows whenever the quantity of the excluded quality attribute varies:

$$(3.7) \qquad \hat{d}_1 = d_1 + b_{m+1} \Delta x_{i,m+1} .$$

Sometimes a variable is excluded not because of negligence or lack of data, but because in one or more periods it has been observed to be perfectly collinear with one of the included characteristics, let us say the first:

$$(3.8) \qquad b_{m+1} x_{i,m+1,t} = \alpha x_{i1t}, \quad t = 1.$$

No problems arise if (3.6) is valid for both of the adjacent time periods, for the estimated value of b_1 will include the effect of the omitted variable, and the estimate of pure price change will be correct:

$$(3.9) \qquad \hat{b}_1 = b_1 + \alpha; \quad \hat{d}_1 = d_1 .$$

Trouble arises, however, if, in period 2, the additional quality characteristic yields a marginal product per unit of the first quality characteristic that increases by ϵ over its value in period 1, so that (3.8) is replaced by:

$$(3.10) \qquad b_{m+1} x_{i,m+1,t} = (\alpha + \epsilon) x_{i1t}, \quad t = 2.$$

The coefficient of b_1 estimated in a regression that excludes variable $m + 1$ understates the combined influence of characteristics 1 and $m + 1$ in period 2, and the extra "quality" of characteristic 2 is soaked up by the time dummy and is thus interpreted as pure price change:

$$(3.11) \qquad \hat{b}_1 = b_1 + \alpha; \quad \hat{d}_1 = d_1 + \epsilon.$$

The preceding simple example generalizes to the statement that the d_1 coefficient is biased whenever there is a shift between one year and the next in the relation between the omitted variables and the included variables.

3.5.2   Performance versus Physical Characteristics

Users of capital goods value quality attributes for their ability to produce output, not for their physical specifications alone. The value of a locomotive depends on the ton capacity of freight cars it can pull at a specific speed, not on the horsepower of its diesel engine. If pulling power is always a constant multiple of horsepower, the hedonic price index will be unaffected by the choice between them as independent variables in the hedonic regression. But if technical progress increases the efficiency of the driving mechanism that transmits locomotive power from engine to wheels, and if horsepower rather than pulling power is the independent variable in the hedonic regression, then the increasing ratio of pulling power to horsepower is an omitted variable that by (3.11) causes an upward bias in the estimated increase in "true" price.

Almost every previous hedonic study has employed data on physical rather than performance data because the former have been more readily available. Two recent exceptions are Ohta and Griliches (1976) and Hogarty (1972); both have experimented with performance variables in automobile regressions. The empirical chapters below report scattered pieces of evidence on performance characteristics and attempt where possible to correct hedonic price indexes in cases where a changing ratio of performance to physical characteristics seems to have occurred.

3.5.3   Make Effects

Most studies have combined price and quality attribute data for all manufacturers. Dhrymes (1971) was the first to test and reject the null hypothesis that pricing behavior by different manufacturers is identical. In a much more extensive exploration, Ohta and Griliches (1976) presented evidence to support make effects, defined as significant coefficients on make dummy variables (M_k) in regressions that identify each model (i) by its make designation:

$$(3.12) \qquad \log p_{itk} = \alpha_0 + d_1 D_1 + \sum_{k=1}^{r} m_k M_k + \sum_{j=1}^{m} b_j x_{ijt} .$$

In regressions for automobiles containing roughly four models per make, Ohta and Griliches find positive make effects for the three "luxury" makes (Cadillac, Imperial, and Lincoln) that imply prices roughly 25–35 percent higher than can be explained by the physical characteristics included in the regression. In previous studies, the high prices of these makes had been partly explained by high coefficients on the weight variable in regressions without make dummies, partly by upward biased coefficients on other variables, and had partly been reflected in positive residuals for these makes.[5]

Evidence on make effects has been subject to different interpretations. Dhrymes has argued that the make effect invalidates the basic hedonic assumption that the implicit prices of characteristics reflect consumer evaluations and instead implies that prices are marked up over cost by formulas that differ among manufacturers. Ohta and Griliches take the more sensible position that make effects stand as proxies for omitted characteristics, for example, the prestige associated with a luxury car, for which consumers are willing to pay a price. They test for the presence of the make effects in used car markets and discover that the "Cadillac prestige effect" persists permanently throughout the car's life, whereas that of Imperial and Lincoln is transient and evaporates quickly. Although Ohta and Griliches do not comment on the cause of the divergence between Cadillac and Imperial-Lincoln prices in the used car market, the result seems to be rather convincing evidence that the omitted quality variable for which the make effects stands as proxy represents primarily a subjective rather than an objective attribute. If the omitted variable were an objective feature, for example, fancy upholstery or electric windows, it would presumably be valued similarly in the used car market for the various luxury makes. It is possible, however, that the rapid depreciation of Lincoln and Imperial may at least partly reflect their relatively poor repair records.[6]

The make effects serve as a warning that comparisons of individual models of different makes across time must be performed carefully. In his original article on hedonic indexes, Court (1939) compared 1920 models of relatively expensive cars with 1939 models of relatively inexpensive cars that by then had grown to be almost identical in size. But at least part of the dramatic price reductions that he recorded may have been due to the positive make effect of the relatively expensive models in the early year.

3.5.4 New Products

The most intractable aspect of quality measurement has always been the introduction of a totally new characteristic that did not exist before, for example, the invention of television or of the automobile. The hedonic

5. See, e.g., Triplett (1969, 408–17). Triplett's truncated regressions contain estimates that the presence of automatic transmission, power steering, and power brakes raises the average car price by 30 percent, or about $900, although the value of these items as options was only about $350 at that time. The high value of this coefficient stands as a proxy for the "make effect" of the luxury cars. Although Triplett explicitly recognizes this (414), he fails to recalculate his regressions to include a dummy variable for make or price class and computes hedonic price indexes on the basis of his biased coefficients.

6. The frequency of repair record of Cadillac was distinctly superior to the other two luxury makes, as illustrated for the 1966–71 period that concerned Ohta and Griliches. See *Consumer Reports*, April 1972, 237–41.

approach can only evaluate quality improvements that either raise the quantity of characteristics that previously were included in a model or introduce characteristics that were formerly available only on higher-priced models and that "trickle down" to relatively lower-priced makes.

The most important single innovation in the capital goods industry during the postwar period has been the replacement of the clerk working with a calculating machine by the electronic computer. The hedonic technique has been used to evaluate quality improvements in computers, but not to evaluate the relative quality of computers and calculating machines. Similarly, no attention has been given to the saving in time made possible by the replacement of the rotary electric calculating machine by electronic calculators. Hedonic studies that ignore these aspects of technical change omit a variable and create an upward bias in price indexes. One can employ the "user-value" criterion to determine, at least subjectively, whether new products perform operations similar to the products they replace. If so, the relative performance of new and old products can be compared and changes in cost per equivalent operation can be calculated. The reduction in the cost of clerks made possible by the invention of electronic computers could in principle be estimated from time-and-motion studies of the calculations performed per clerk. The value of the invention of television might be estimated by the saving in time spent traveling to and from movie theaters.

3.5.5 Multicollinearity

Even if data were available on all relevant characteristics, multicollinearity usually precludes the estimation of separate implicit price coefficients for each. In comparison with a subcompact model, a full-sized Cadillac has greater weight *and* length *and* horsepower *and* includes as standard equipment automatic transmission, power options, and other accessories. Separate coefficients for each of these characteristics can be estimated only if the regression sample includes models that are short but heavy in weight, powerful but light in weight, and so on. Triplett (1969) showed that length and horsepower were so collinear with weight in his sample that the goodness of fit in automobile regressions was virtually unaffected when the length and horsepower variables were omitted. This poses a dilemma that weight is not desired for itself but only for the comfort that tends to be associated with it, and an innovation that reduces weight without reducing comfort (e.g., thin-wall casting of the engine) will be erroneously interpreted by the hedonic technique as a decline in quality (Triplett 1969, 416). In the absence of adequate data that directly measure performance variables like comfort, then, multicollinearity increases the likelihood that a bias will be caused by excluded variables.

3.5.6 The Treatment of Accessories

In most studies, multicollinearity has prevented the estimation of reliable and sensible implicit price coefficients on accessories like automatic trans-

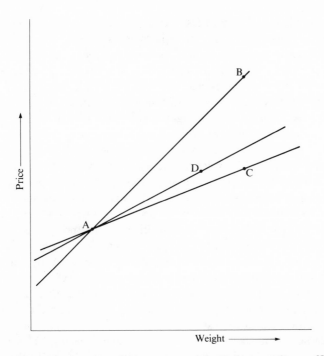

Fig. 3.1   Effect of accessory adjustments on estimated regression coefficients

mission or power steering for automobiles, or central air conditioning in hedonic studies of single-family houses. An alternative technique would be to adjust the price of each model for differences in standard equipment using the prices of accessories published in option lists. Similar adjustments could be made for the addition of accessories that were previously options or unavailable as standard equipment. No published hedonic study has made systematic adjustments of this type for accessories and optional equipment.

A problem is created, however, if a Cadillac is normally sold with air conditioning but its price in a hedonic regression is included net of this accessory. In this case, the weight variable is incorrect, because the published shipping weight includes the weight of the air conditioning equipment. In figure 3.1, point A represents the price and weight of a subcompact sold without air conditioning as standard equipment, and B represents the published price and weight of a Cadillac sold with this accessory standard. The slope of AB represents the coefficient of weight computed in a regression on published data. If the price per pound of the air conditioning unit is higher than the price per pound of the rest of the car, D is the Cadillac's price with both the price and the weight of air conditioning excluded, and AD is the "true" slope of weight for the car by itself. If the price of air conditioning is erroneously omitted without a weight adjustment, the weight coefficient is underestimated as AC.

Most previous studies have taken the approach of estimating the price of accessories without making an adjustment for weight and have thus estimated *AC* in figure 3.1 as the downward-biased weight coefficient. In their more recent investigation, Ohta and Griliches (1976) have argued that a high rate of purchase of power steering on large cars implies a market evaluation that this accessory is a necessary feature. If so, they argue, power steering is part of the price of weight, and the true weight coefficient is *AB*, not *AD*. While the argument may be valid for a single cross section, it is untenable in long historical studies. For instance, the 1948 Buick Road-master and the 1971 Chevrolet Impala are virtually identical in length and weight, but no units of the former and virtually all units of the latter model were equipped with power steering.[7] The market did not shift its tastes between 1948 and 1971, but simply responded to an invention that was unavailable in the earlier year. A comparison of true price change between the two years should be based on the prices of comparably equipped models. The 1971 price and weight of the power steering option (and anything else not included on the Buick) must be excluded from the Chevrolet's specifi-cations before a valid comparison can be made. If the price per pound of each accessory is identical to that of the rest of the car, these adjustments make no difference to the estimated coefficient on weight, but in fact the price per pound of an accessory like automatic transmission is relatively high, $2.74 versus $0.85 for the basic car in the case of the 1971 Chevrolet Impala V-8.[8] The Ohta-Griliches procedure leads to a coefficient on weight that is biased upward and a hedonic price index that is biased upward by registering as a price increase the introduction of power steering as standard equipment on a car of a given weight that previously offered power steering as an option.

3.5.7 Functional Form

Almost all studies of automobiles and most other commodities have continued Griliches's original practice of fitting regressions in semilog form. A unit change in a quality characteristic is thus assumed to be associated with a fixed percentage change in price, that is, an increase in weight by one pound raises the price of a 1971 Cadillac by three times as much as that of a 1971 subcompact. The popularity of the semilog form and its acceptance in formal tests by Dhrymes may simply reflect the nonlinear make effect of the luxury nameplates. Another standard assumption is that multiplica-tive interaction terms are absent; weight and horsepower influence price

7. The weight and length of the 1948 Buick were 4,160 pounds and 217.5 inches, respectively (*Consumer Reports,* May 1948, 209), while the same dimensions for the 1971 Chevrolet were 4,014 and 216.8 (*Automotive News 1971 Almanac Issue,* 46). In 1970 full-sized Chevrolets, 95.3 percent of all units were sold with power steering included (*Automotive News 1971 Almanac Issue,* 62).
8. Information obtained from the General Motors Corp. in letter dated 27 July 1972.

separately but not jointly, even though an increase in weight requires an increase in horsepower to maintain performance.

3.5.8   List Prices versus Transaction Prices

In most hedonic regression studies, the dependent variable is the manufacturer's list price. Discounting that causes variations in the ratio of transaction prices to list prices is not reflected in this dependent variable or, therefore, in the final hedonic price index. The best evidence that list prices are an unreliable guide to actual transactions prices refers to retail sales of automobiles. In his study of the auto industry, White (1982, 105) reports that, "although list prices get all the publicity in any discussion of auto prices, in fact they are only symbolic. Few sales actually get made at list prices." During the early postwar period, transaction prices were above list prices as a "gray market" in automobiles developed, whereas, during most of the period after the Korean War, discounting was common. For instance, a series of studies by Jung (1950, 1960) on the Chicago retail auto market reported an average discount off list price of 16 percent in 1959–60. A Federal Trade Commission survey for 1968 and 1969 reported that half the full-sized models in the survey sold for 15–20 percent below list prices, and that about 60 percent of the intermediates sold for 10–15 percent below list prices (quoted in *Consumer Reports,* April 1971, 203). Because the ratio of transaction to list prices was higher in the early postwar period than after 1953, the secular rate of change of any hedonic price index based on list prices for the entire postwar period is biased upward. And, to the extent that the size of discounts and rebates has varied procyclically, existing hedonic price indexes understate the true variability of auto prices over the business cycle.

In lieu of detailed data on transaction prices of new cars, one possible alternative would be to use prices for one-year-old used cars. The prices of these close substitutes for new cars may reflect to a substantial degree the variations of discounts on new cars. Unfortunately, previous studies have largely ignored the wealth of data available on used car prices. Ohta and Griliches have studied used car prices for the interval since 1961, but not for earlier years, when the main variations in discounts apparently occurred.

3.6   Relative Advantages of the Hedonic and Conventional Methods

The conventional specification method is similar in principle to the hedonic method. A hedonic study that has sufficient data to perform regressions of price on three characteristics, say length, horsepower, and weight, also provides sufficient data to compute a conventional price index for each of several length-horsepower-weight classes. In a period during which no pure price change occurs and any excluded quality characteristics are unaltered, an increase in unit value due to a shift in quality to a higher length-horsepower-weight class is treated as quality change rather than price change in the conventional method because there is no price change for any individual commodity class.

While the conventional method would be able to come close to the results of the hedonic method if more observations were collected, and if exactly the same quality characteristics were used, in practice there could never be enough continually occupied classifications to avert the need for special adjustments when a new higher-quality model is introduced but remains within the same length-horsepower-weight class as the old model. Even in this case, the methods would be identical if a simultaneous overlapping price observation on the new and the old model were available, since the same market price information used to estimate quality change in the hedonic regressions could be used for a special adjustment in the conventional method. But when no overlap is available, the conventional method has no systematic method of adjustment, whereas the hedonic method "creates" an overlap observation by estimating a regression line relating price to quality and calculating the implicit price of a model containing any given amount of the quality characteristics used in the regressions.

The most serious disadvantage of both methods is that neither can measure changes in the relation between excluded and included quality dimensions. A bias will result unless all excluded quality characteristics maintain a fixed relation with included characteristics. For instance, when we estimate the difference between the price of a 1948 Buick and that of a 1948 Chevrolet as depending on differences in length, weight, and horsepower, our coefficients are also picking up the influence of the Buick's carpeting, fancy doorknobs, and plush upholstery. If we discover that a 1970 Chevrolet has the same length, weight, and horsepower as a 1948 Buick, a quality index computed from the 1948 coefficients implies that both cars are identical in every other respect. In fact, the 1970 Chevrolet could be either higher or lower in quality in other respects than the 1948 Buick.

There is no escape from the excluded variable problem with either the hedonic or the conventional methods. An increase in the ratio of excluded to included characteristics creates an upward bias in the coefficient on the time dummy variable in hedonic regressions. Similarly, in the conventional method, an increase in the amount of "excluded quality" relative to the quality attributes included in a product's specifications shows up as an increase in the price index. Only if changes in quality attributes outside the written specification are explicitly adjusted by linking or a manufacturer's cost estimate does the conventional method treat the change as representing an increase in quality. The hedonic technique is superior in its ability to estimate the value of increases in dimensions like length, horsepower, and weight but is prevented by multicollinearity from estimating reasonable coefficients for the value of accessories.

No methodological rulebook states that one technique must be used exclusively. The best procedure for empirical price measurement is to combine the conventional and hedonic methods, taking advantage of the relative strengths of each. To the maximum extent possible, the conventional approach should be used to adjust the prices of different models for discrete options, accessories, and added features. Then the hedonic method should be employed to explain the remaining price difference as a function of basic dimensions or performance characteristics. Care must be taken that the two types of adjustments are consistent by adjusting not only price but also weight and performance characteristics for the effect of added accessories.

One possible procedure would be to proceed in steps as follows:

1. A preliminary hedonic regression should be run to determine the major price-determining quality characteristics. The effects of multicollinearity should be explored and characteristics with coefficients that are unstable, unreasonable, or of incorrect sign should be excluded.
2. Lists of option prices or manufacturers' cost estimates should be obtained to adjust the transaction price of each model for changes in discrete features and accessories.
3. Interactions between the variables in the hedonic regression and the adjustments in 2 should be investigated. If weight is variable in the regression, for instance, a correction should be made for the weight as well as the price of accessories, using weight data obtained from manufacturers or from mail-order catalogs.
4. Then a "final" hedonic regression can be estimated from the observations on adjusted price and adjusted physical or performance characteristics. A hedonic price index can be calculated from the time dummy variables in the final regression.

3.7 Implementation of Quality Adjustments for Changes in Operating Efficiency

A major theme of chapter 2 was the need to make quality adjustments for changes in the operating efficiency of durable goods. This section discusses practical problems in implementing such adjustments. While the analysis is framed in terms of changes in fuel economy, many of the same points could be made about changes in maintenance requirements.

Although little attention has been paid to changing fuel economy in past studies of quality change, it should be possible in principle to make appropriate quality adjustments using either the conventional or the hedonic method. In the conventional method, a manufacturer would report that a new model has improved fuel economy as compared to the model it replaces, owing, say, to electronic fuel ignition. The BLS can then ask for an estimate of the extra cost of the new ignition system and make an appropriate adjustment. Since, as we saw in chapter 2, in equilibrium the value to users of fuel efficiency improvements should be equal to their manufacturing cost, the conventional method should be adequate in this case. A problem is created for the conventional method, however, in another example where the electronic ignition replaces the previous mechanical ignition and yields improved fuel economy with no increase in manufacturing cost. This is what we have previously called a "nonproportional" quality improvement. Under present procedures, no adjustment would be made, even though the cost of producing the quality characteristic "fuel economy" has fallen. In terms of figure 2.5, what needs to be estimated is the marginal cost of producing the extra quantity of input characteristics that would have been required to yield the observed increase in net revenue or consumer value in the absence of the technical change. The hedonic method could in principle cope with the nonproportional improvement if the marketplace provides models with a broad mix of performance and fuel economy characteristics, thus allowing the imputed price of fuel economy to be estimated in the hedonic regression. However, in fact, a single cross section for a given year does not typically provide the required mix of automobiles. Because large cars have poor fuel economy, and small cars have good fuel economy, there is negative collinearity between dimensional variables and fuel usage. It is the absence of large cars with excellent fuel economy, or small cars with poor fuel economy, that prevents the reliable estimation of a coefficient for the imputed price of fuel economy. While the proliferation of foreign cars in recent years has provided a broader product mix, including relatively large cars with relatively good fuel economy, foreign and domestic cars differ in numerous other dimensions as well (frequency-of-repair record, extent of standard accessories).

Widespread interest in the effects of changing fuel prices after the two oil shocks (1973–74 and 1979–80) is reflected in two papers by Kahn (1981) and Ohta-Griliches (1986) that focus on the role of fuel efficiency in hedonic regressions. However, neither paper yields significant estimates of the value of fuel economy changes that could be used to produce suitable quality-adjusted price indexes. Further, their main focus is on the way in which changing fuel prices alter consumer evaluations of dimension and performance attributes in the used car market, not the imputed value of fuel economy in the new car market.

Because the conventional method cannot deal with nonproportional changes in fuel efficiency, and because the hedonic method is plagued by multicollinearity in this case, an alternative technique must be devised. The principle outlined in chapter 2 is to base a quality adjustment on a comparison of the price of old and new models with their respective ability to earn net revenue. In terms of the conventional method, the observed increase in the actual price of the new model is adjusted by the calculated increase in discounted future net revenue. The results of such calculations will always admit to a wide range of possible estimates, depending on the assumed real discount rate and future time path of the real price of fuel. It is possible that changing prices on the market for used cars and airplanes could be used to check the validity of the computed adjustments.

In the study of aircraft prices in chapter 4, the "net revenue" method is used by itself, not in combination with either the hedonic or the conventional methods. Changes in net revenue due to changes either in performance characteristics (plane size and speed) or in fuel usage are treated symmetrically in the calculation of net revenue, and then quality adjustments are computed from a comparison across pairs of old and new models of their ability to earn net revenue. This method cannot be used for automobiles used by consumers, since no net revenue is generated. Here it is preferable to compute quality adjustments by the conventional or hedonic method, and then to make an extra adjustment for the value of fuel savings. As Wilcox (1984) has shown, it is possible to compute an index of "pure" changes in fuel efficiency, by running a regression of fuel economy on other fuel-using characteristics like weight and engine displacement. Then changes in this fuel economy index can be converted into user value terms with suitable assumptions regarding the discount rate and future real fuel prices.

Consider a hypothetical example in which the price increase in a particular model car between 1956 and 1957 is observed to be $150. Let us assume that there are no changes in quality characteristics between the two years besides a modest increase in weight, and that there is no change in observed fuel economy. A hedonic regression across all models yields an imputed value for the increase in weight of, say, $40. Let us also assume that the Wilcox-type fuel economy regression indicates that the observed increase in weight should have reduced fuel economy by, say, two miles per gallon (mpg). The fact that observed mpg did not decrease signals a pure change in fuel economy that requires a quality adjustment. If the computed present value of the fuel economy improvement is, say, $50, then the final quality adjustment is $90 ($40 for weight and $50 for fuel economy), and the observed price of $150 is reduced by the quality adjustment to $60.

The need for a fuel economy adjustment in this example can be stated in another way. The hedonic regression of auto price on characteristics excluding mpg yields a downward-biased coefficient on weight due to a negative correlation between weight and the excluded mpg variable. The estimated coefficient understates the true user value of extra weight (which partly proxies for the other beneficial excluded variables that are positively correlated with weight), since it includes a negative component corresponding to the fuel cost imposed by extra weight. If there were never any technological shift in the Wilcox-type fuel economy regression, then the conventional application of the hedonic technique would properly adjust for the effects of added weight, combining both its positive and its negative aspects. But the shift in the fuel economy regression occurs because the new model does not require as much fuel, given its weight, as would have been expected given the correlation between fuel usage in weight across the old models and across the new models taken separately, and this shift amounts to a nonproportional quality change that must be taken into account.

A further complication occurs in the first half of the 1970s, when there was an adverse shift in fuel economy associated with antipollution regulations. This book accepts the official government treatment of antipollution devices, which is to treat their extra cost as a quality change rather than as a price change, on the grounds that society at large has received benefits that roughly balance the costs. Thus, if we can determine from industry commentaries that the fuel economy deterioration was due entirely to regulation, then we can ignore it and not apply a negative quality correction.

After 1975, fuel economy improved dramatically, but the price of automobiles soared. It is possible that this episode of improving fuel economy represented a proportional quality change, with the marginal cost of achieving higher mpg balancing the user value of the improvements. It will be interesting to determine in chapter 8, which calculates the explicit fuel economy adjustments, whether the BLS practice of ignoring shrinking dimensions in the process of automobile "downsizing" represents an adequate approximation to the "net" quality adjustment called for by the combination of smaller size and improving fuel economy.

To which price index should a fuel economy adjustment be applied? It has been suggested that a fuel efficiency adjustment is acceptable for an "input" price index, that is, one used to measure the purchase price of a capital good by a final user, but not for an "output" price index for use in deflating the production of machines. The skepticism for output price indexes concerns changes in fuel prices. Should the productivity of the machinery industry change when fuel prices change? The proposed method, as set out previously in section 2.9, is free from such objections, because it is based explicitly on a comparison in which the prices of variable inputs (labor, materials, and fuel) are held constant. Net revenue obtainable from new and old models is calculated with the same output price and variable input prices applying to both models.

Thus, a change in fuel prices by itself does nothing to alter the productivity of the machine-producing industry. If a change in fuel prices induces the introduction of a new model that moves up the cost function by introducing greater fuel efficiency at a higher capital goods price, the technique does not register a quality improvement (more precisely, there is no quality change when the capital goods price and net revenue rise in proportion). However, a technical change that allows an improvement in fuel economy with a less-than-proportional increase in the capital goods price *does* count as an improvement in quality. The only ambiguity involved in this technique is a standard index number problem: the value of a nonproportional improvement in fuel efficiency will differ in different fuel pricing regimes. To minimize the sensitivity of my adjustments to this problem, in the aircraft chapter differences in net-revenue generating ability between new and old models are evaluated at several different regimes of output and input prices and then averaged (see sec. 4.5).

3.8   Comparison of "Closely Similar" Models

To cross-check for secular bias in the conventional or hedonic methods, the secular change in price between two widely separated years can be compared. This approach was first used by Court (1939, p. 106) in his original paper on hedonic indexes to compare automobile models of roughly similar dimensions in 1920 and 1939. I used the same approach to compare 1959 and 1970 models in two early papers (1970, 1971b). A particular advantage of the method is that available resources can be invested in a more extensive effort to collect detailed information on specifications, on the presumption that forty specifications of two models manufactured twenty years apart will yield a more accurate index of secular quality change than information on two specifications for two models in each of the intervening years.

A major difficulty with the technique is the standard index number problem that prices of specifications or accessories in widely separated years may be quite different and yield differing estimates of quality change. Another drawback is the difficulty of estimating the implicit price of changed specifications when option or manufacturers' cost estimates are unavailable or unreliable. Finally, items twenty years apart will rarely be identical in size; if we find that a 1948 Buick is 100 pounds heavier and two inches shorter than a 1970 Chevrolet, what implicit prices should be applied to these differences? Presumably, the technique should be used to supplement and check the hedonic or conventional methods, and information from hedonic regressions or any other source can be used to estimate the implicit prices of a change in specifications. Finally, the comparison of a relatively high-priced model in an early year with a relatively low-priced model in a later year that has grown to the same overall size may err if prices are influenced by the "make effects" or "prestige effect" discussed above.

Most of the problems and ambiguities of the hedonic method discussed earlier in this chapter apply as well to the comparison of "closely similar" models. Performance variables should be used in place of physical characteristics where data are available. When we compare the prices of a 1946 DC-6 airplane with a 1971 DC-10, we are interested in the price per unit of seat-mile capacity (adjusted if possible for the saving of time made possible by jet speeds), not in relative length, weight, or horsepower. Comparisons of "closely similar" models also must take into account secular changes in fuel economy and decompose these into changes accounted for by altered quantities of performance characteristics and a residual "pure shift" effect.

3.9 Summary and Conclusion

This chapter examines the conventional and hedonic techniques of quality adjustment and suggests circumstances in which they should be used in combination rather than separately. Then it adds two additional techniques to be used where appropriate, adjustments for "pure shifts" in energy usage not connected with changes in the quantity of other quality characteristics, and comparisons of "closely similar" models.

In the conventional method, one of four explicit quality adjustment procedures comes into play when the BLS is notified by manufacturers that one or more characteristics of a new model are altered from those on the old model. The most satisfactory procedure is an explicit estimate of the cost of the quality change, provided by the manufacturer. While explicit cost adjustments have become more common in the past decade, the other three procedures have normally been used. Under "direct comparison," any change in price between the two models is assumed to be entirely a price change and not a quality change; under "linking," any change in price is assumed to be entirely due to a quality change and not to a price change. The fourth procedure, deletion, imputes to the new model a price increase equal to all the other price reports in the eight-digit commodity classification. One major problem with the conventional method is the possibility of a shift over time toward more accurate measurement as the fraction of explicit cost adjustments has increased. The prevalence in the first half of the postwar era of quality adjustments by the direct comparison procedure, which amounts to no adjustment at all, suggests that price, output, and productivity measures for durable goods indexes might contain a greater bias in the earlier years than more recently.

The hedonic method seems to be more naturally suited than the conventional method to quality adjustments that take the form of changes in dimensions or performance along a continuous dimension, for example, weight, horsepower, or acceleration. The conventional method seems more suited to discrete changes in characteristics than can be valued by manufacturer cost estimates or by option prices, for example, air conditioning and power brakes. Because multicollinearity limits the number of explanatory variables that can be included in a hedonic regression, the potential bias introduced by excluded variables, and the instability of coefficients on variables like air conditioning, is more serious than in the conventional method. An offsetting advantage is that the hedonic technique can be applied uniformly to a long time series of data, for example, 1947–80, as in this book, whereas the prevalence of quality adjustments in the official indexes has not been uniform over the years. The complementary advantages of the two techniques can be utilized in actual measurement by using both, so long as care is taken to avoid double counting.

The chapter suggests two different approaches to quality adjustments for nonproportional changes in energy efficiency. One method, probably well suited for automobiles and electric generating equipment, is to estimate a fuel economy function separately and to compute a quality adjustment for the present value of energy efficiency improvements as a supplement to the conventional and/or hedonic method. Another method, better suited for commercial aircraft where sample sizes are too small for adequate hedonic regressions, is to implement the comparison of selling price with net revenue, as suggested in chapter 2.

A final suggestion in the chapter is that the validity of all quality adjustments, whether by the conventional or the hedonic technique, and whether involving performance characteristics or fuel economy, can be cross-checked by comparisons of "closely similar" models over long time spans. Sometimes, there will be no such models, particularly in industries like computers with pervasive technical change. But in other cases, for example, automobiles and appliances, it is sometimes possible to find models sold ten or twenty years apart that share roughly the same dimensions and differ in other respects to which a value can be attributed. Such comparisons are provided in this book, not only to serve the cross-checking purpose, but also because comparisons of models widely separated in years help provide an interesting chronicle of types and forms of quality change.

II Studies of Individual Products

4   Commercial Aircraft

4.1   Introduction

Two factors motivate the choice of commercial aircraft as the first case study of the techniques proposed in chapter 2. First, throughout the postwar era, and particularly between 1958 and 1972, profound quality changes occurred in both performance characteristics and operating efficiency of commercial aircraft. Second, a wealth of data is available on all aspects of the airline industry, as a result of its history of federal government regulation. The U.S. Civil Aeronautics Board (CAB) continued to collect the same continuous data base both before and after the passage of the airline deregulation act in late 1978, at least through the "sunset" of the CAB at the end of 1984, allowing the study in this chapter to cover the years 1947–83.[1] Among the relevant CAB data are the prices paid by airlines for each individual aircraft, and numerous details on operating costs and revenue-generating ability for each aircraft type.

The commercial airframe and aircraft engine manufacturers provide a case study of what was called in chapter 2 *nonproportional quality change*. With only a few exceptions, most new aircraft models introduced since 1958 have, in comparison with the preceding model, provided a percentage increase in net revenue exceeding the percentage increase in price. During the heyday of the transition from piston to jet aircraft, from 1958 to 1972, the relatively small extra price charged by aircraft manufacturers for new models resulted in the transfer of benefits from performance and efficiency gains to airlines

---

1. Much of the data base relevant for this study has been maintained since the demise of the CAB in the aviation public reference room at the U.S. Department of Transportation. In particular, a complete record is maintained of purchase prices of aircraft and aircraft engines and operating costs by airline and aircraft type, allowing the study reported in this chapter to be updated by future investigators.

and ultimately to airline customers in the form of a declining real price of airline transportation.

There can be no doubt in the case of the aircraft industry that changes in operating efficiency are viewed, along with changes in performance characteristics, as relevant dimensions of quality change. In 1982, fuel expenses represented between 38 and 57 percent of total operating expense for the fourteen major aircraft types operated by the domestic trunk airline industry (U.S. CAB, *Aircraft Operating Cost and Performance Report,* July 1983). Aircraft purchase decisions have involved trade-offs, widely discussed in the trade press, among price, performance, and operating efficiency. Airlines have been observed to incur substantial capital costs in order to replace one type of plane by another having no greater speed or carrying capacity, just to gain an improvement in operating efficiency.

The study in this chapter and that of electric generating equipment in chapter 5 are intended to provide examples of practical methods for implementing the rather general and abstract measurement framework outlined in chapter 2. The basic formula for quality adjustment (eq. [2.35]) requires the comparison of the observed change in the price of a new model with the extra net revenue that the new model provides relative to the old model, holding constant the prices of output and operating inputs. Because data on changes in net revenue are required, the airline and utility industries are ideal testing grounds for the methodology, since the government requires the publication of detailed information on operating costs of specific units of capital equipment. Changes in operating efficiency have been important for some other products, for example, automobiles and consumer appliances. While data on operating costs are available, there is no direct measure of "net revenue," and a different approach to quality measurement must be adopted.

The quality corrections suggested in this chapter are large in magnitude and primarily reflect the effect of jet technology in raising the ability of commercial aircraft to generate net revenue. Turbine engines produce greater thrust and faster speeds and have resulted in a quantum decline in the "real" unit costs of crew salaries, fuel cost, and maintenance. Crew costs declined, because jet aircraft produce many more seat miles per crew hour, and maintenance expenses declined, because jet aircraft typically fly at least twice as long between overhauls as piston engines, and failures between overhauls have become much less frequent (Straszheim 1969, 84). Decreased maintenance requirements have increased feasible daily aircraft utilization, although the estimates in this chapter err on the conservative side in calculating quality adjustments by attributing to piston aircraft the daily utilization achieved by jet aircraft in the mid-1960s.

The new estimates understate the "true" extent of quality change in another much more important way, and this is the choice of an aircraft seat mile as a homogeneous output "characteristic" over the entire postwar period. This ignores the value of time savings to passengers due to the fact that the introduction of the jet aircraft cut travel times roughly in half on given routes and made possible longer stage lengths that reduced the necessity for making intermediate stops. Less tangible dimensions of quality improvement, for example, elimination of piston-engine vibration, the ability of jet aircraft to fly above thunderstorms and reduce the incidence of turbulence, and the improved safety record of jet aircraft, are also ignored. But these additional aspects of quality change can serve as a counterweight to those who may find the large size of the basic quality adjustments difficult to believe.

The approach outlined in chapter 2 calls for a price index for identical models to be multiplied by a quality adjustment factor based on changes in net revenue relative to changes in aircraft purchase prices. The first step is the development of a price index for identical aircraft. Next are provided estimates of gross revenue, operating costs, and net revenue for pairs of aircraft. These pairs are new models and the old models they typically replaced on routes of approximately the same stage length (long haul, medium haul, and short haul). The resulting "adjacent model" net revenue ratios are then compared with purchase price ratios. The last step in the analysis is an examination of cross-model ratios of used aircraft prices at different points in time, intended to provide a check on the quantitative magnitude of the estimated cross-model quality differentials. The resulting used aircraft price ratios can be converted into a price index, and this confirms the previous suggestion that the net revenue method yields quality adjustments that are too conservative.

4.2   Postwar Performance of the Airline Industry

As a preliminary to the subsequent investigation, table 4.1 displays data on the postwar performance of the airline industry, exhibited as annual average growth rates over five-year intervals. The first three rows identify a sharp break in the relation between employment cost and productivity before and after 1972. In the twenty-five years before 1972, the average annual increase in employee compensation was 6.3 percent and that of productivity was 7.9 percent, so that unit labor cost declined by 1.6 percent per year. After 1972, however, productivity growth virtually ceased, indicating that the airline industry made its own contribution to the post-1972 "puzzle" of a productivity growth slowdown for the U.S. economy as a whole. Without productivity growth, most of the rapid post-1972 growth in employee compensation flowed down to row 3 to become a relatively rapid rate of increase in unit labor cost.

Shown in row 4 is the soaring cost of aircraft fuel resulting from the two OPEC "shocks" of 1973–74 and 1979–80. This followed a much slower annual increase in fuel cost of only 1.7 percent per year during 1947–72.

Table 4.1   Airline Fares, Costs, and Productivity, Annual Growth Rates for Five-Year Intervals, 1947–82

	1947–52 (1)	1952–57 (2)	1957–62 (3)	1962–67 (4)	1967–72 (5)	1972–77 (6)	1977–82 (7)	1947–82 (8)
1. Compensation per FTE employee	7.95	4.41	5.09	4.66	9.54	8.97	8.31	6.99
2. Output per FTE employee	9.67	8.05	5.47	6.68	9.76	0.45	1.31	5.91
3. Unit labor cost	−1.72	−3.64	−0.38	−2.02	−0.22	8.52	7.00	1.09
4. Fuel cost per gallon	4.08	2.82	−1.59	−0.28	3.64	24.36	22.92	7.52
5. Average operating cost	−1.83	−1.44	1.02	−2.36	1.15	7.85	10.53	2.13
6. Average passenger yield	1.87	−1.07	3.88	−2.83	2.29	5.99	7.54	2.52
7. BEA index of equipment cost	5.82	4.26	1.97	1.92	3.80	8.76	10.24	5.25
8. GNP deflator	3.18	2.34	1.67	2.30	4.80	6.96	8.12	4.20
9. Real average cost	−5.01	−3.78	−0.65	−4.66	−3.65	0.89	2.41	−2.07
10. Real average yield	−1.31	−3.41	2.21	−5.13	−2.51	−0.97	−0.58	−1.68
11. Real equipment cost	2.64	1.92	0.30	−0.38	−1.00	1.80	2.12	1.05

Sources by row: **(1, 2)** Compensation, from NIPA, table 6.5A, row 43. Full-time equivalent employees (FTE), table 6.8A, row 43. Output is measured by available seat miles for the domestic industry (trunkline and local service), from Bailey, Graham, and Kaplan (1983, apps. A and B). **(3)** Row 1 minus row 2. **(4)** 1965–82: U.S.CAB, *Aircraft Operating Cost and Performance Report,* various issues, price paid for jet fuel for all carriers operating narrow-bodied four-engine jet aircraft. 1947–65: PPI for refined petroleum products (index 07-5). **(5, 6)** Bailey,Graham, and Kaplan (1983, app. A). **(7)** This chapter, table 4.3, col. 3. **(8)** NIPA, table 7.1 **(9)** Row 5 minus row 8. **(10)** Row 6 minus row 8. **(11)** Row 7 minus row 8.

Average operating cost per available seat mile in row 5 shows an acceleration corresponding to that in labor and fuel cost, from an average of −0.7 percent per year in 1947–72 to 9.2 percent per year in 1972–82. Average yield growth accelerated less than growth in average cost, from 0.8 to 6.8 percent per year, providing an explanation of the sharp drop in operating profit margins (which were −5.9 percent in 1947, 5.8 percent in 1972, and −4.5 percent in 1982; Bailey, Graham, and Kaplan 1985, app. A).[2]

Equipment cost also displayed a post-1972 acceleration, although this was less marked than for operating cost, from an average in row 7 of 3.6 percent per year in 1947–72 to 9.5 percent in 1972–82. This acceleration was slightly sharper than for the GNP deflator (2.9–7.5 percent). It is interesting to compare the increase in equipment cost in row 7 with compensation per employee in row 1, in an attempt to determine indirectly the behavior of productivity growth in the aircraft manufacturing industry. This comparison is meaningful only on the assumption that employee compensation in the

2. The 1982 figure is for the twelve months ending 30 June.

aircraft manufacturing industry increased at about the same rate as in the airline industry (there is no separate BEA index for average compensation or productivity in the aircraft manufacturing industry, which is lumped together with automobiles and other components of "transportation equipment"). If profit margins were roughly constant, then differences between the growth rates of employment cost and the prices of aircraft provide an indirect measure of productivity growth in aircraft manufacturing. This difference was 2.7 percent for 1947–72 and −0.9 percent for 1972–82, an indirect comparison that would seem to indicate that, after 1972, productivity growth in the aircraft manufacturing industry was somewhat less rapid than in U.S. manufacturing as a whole. This conclusion is consistent with the increase in the real cost of aircraft relative to the GNP deflator displayed in row 11.

The figures displayed in table 4.1 raise a question about the sources of the rapid productivity growth in the airline industry achieved prior to 1972, as displayed in row 2, and the reason for the sharp post-1972 productivity growth slowdown. This experience was much more severe than for the U.S. economy as a whole, since productivity grew much more rapidly in the airline industry than in the rest of the economy prior to 1972, but more slowly thereafter. One possible explanation of rapid productivity growth in a particular industry or sector of the economy might be a decline in the cost of capital equipment at a rate greater than for the economy as a whole, inducing through substitution a greater rate of increase in real capital input than in the rest of the economy. However, this explanation does not appear promising for the airline industry, in view of the increasing real cost of equipment during the period of rapid productivity growth between 1947 and 1962, as shown in row 11.

A working hypothesis to be investigated in this chapter is that the official price index for equipment cost is incorrect, and that the true price of equipment decreased rapidly before 1972 in real terms, motivating airlines to purchase equipment and substitute away from labor and fuel toward capital. If this decline in the real price of equipment ended around 1972, at least some part of the productivity growth slowdown might be explained as the result of a lower incentive to substitute capital for labor. One possible reason for the official price index to have been more accurate after 1972 than before could have been a decrease in the importance of *nonproportional* quality change.

4.3 Index of Sale Prices of Identical Models

The existing national income accounts deflator for the aircraft category of purchases of producers' durable equipment, shown on row 7 of table 4.1, has been compiled by the CAB's Financial and Cost Analysis Division for the years since 1957. Airlines report purchases and retirements regularly for each individual aircraft in their fleet, and since these aircraft are identified on

CAB's Form 41 (Schedule B-7) by their month of acquisition and type (e.g., Boeing 707-331B), the CAB has been able to construct an aircraft price index by measuring the year-to-year change in the unit price for each type of equipment delivered in *both of two adjacent years*. Because only identical pieces of equipment are compared in adjacent years, the index ignores any "true" price change involved in the transition from one aircraft type to another. As an example, the substantial price reduction involved in the switch by Douglas in 1958–59 from the manufacture of the DC-7 to that of the DC-8 is simply ignored, and the price index for the year of transition is based only on price changes for planes that were manufactured in both the adjacent years. The CAB index, shown in column 3 of table 4.4, begins in 1957 and increases from 1957 to 1983 by 270 percent, somewhat more than the 232 percent increase in the GNP deflator.[3]

Even viewed on its own terms as a price index for identical models, the CAB index has weaknesses. First, its criterion of identical quality is that any aircraft with the same model number retains the same quality, no matter how long it remains in production: "The fundamental assumption is that any significant change in specifications for new equipment results in a change in the type or model number of the equipment as reported on CAB Form 41" (U.S. CAB 1977, 1). However, as we shall see below, significant quality improvements were made over the production lifetime of some major types of jet aircraft, for example, the Boeing 727-200. The second problem is that the CAB index measures price changes between adjacent years for a given model, without any attention to which airlines were purchasing that model. As we shall see, different airlines pay quite different prices for a given model in the same year, so that the price change measured by the CAB combines true price change with mix effects, as the weight of airlines paying relatively high and low price changes. A third problem, the fact that the CAB index extends back only to 1957 and leaves the 1947–57 decade uncovered, is sufficient to warrant an effort to construct an alternative price index for identical aircraft. However, in the process of constructing the alternative index, sufficient information has been gathered to allow an assessment of the first two problems as well.

Our index is based on unit prices of commercial aircraft, obtained from the same source as the CAB index, that is, CAB Form 41. To save time in copying the data, there was no attempt to look up the initial report of each aircraft purchase on Schedule B-7, since an inspection of forty of these quarterly forms would have been required just to cover a single airline for a single decade. Instead, the source of the price data is schedule B-43, which lists the complete inventory of aircraft owned by each airline at the end of each year, and shows acquisition year, serial number, historical cost,

3. The CAB index is extrapolated before 1957 by weighting together several components of the PPI unrelated to aircraft manufacture, including diesel engines and fabricated metal parts.

and number of seats. Because aircraft engines are not listed separately for each airframe and are not dated by acquisition year, the index covers only airframes. This should not be a major handicap, since aircraft engines have rather continuously represented roughly one-quarter of the value of the associated airframe. The forms used were those for 1961 (covering 1947–61), 1967 (covering 1961–67), 1973 (covering 1967–73), 1978 (covering 1973–78), 1982 (covering 1978–82), and 1983 (covering 1982–83).

Like the CAB index, the new index excludes leased aircraft and used aircraft. Another similarity is that only the domestic trunklines are covered, and local service carriers are excluded.[4] Coverage is also similar, with the new index having slightly greater coverage in 1958–67, and the CAB index having greater coverage in 1968–76.[5]

| | Coverage as Percentage of Value of Aircraft Purchased by Domestic Trunk Carriers | |
	CAB Index	Table 4.2, Column 4
1958–67	47.9	51.6
1968–76	70.4	58.2

The criterion for coverage is to include the seven largest domestic trunk carriers, American, Delta, Eastern, Northwest, Pan American, TWA, and United.

A basic decision in constructing a price index from the available data is whether to treat as identical all aircraft bearing the same model number or only aircraft of a given model number purchased by a given airline. In what follows, two indexes are developed, respectively dubbed the "same model" (SM) index and the "same model same airline" (SMSA) index. The importance of this distinction becomes evident in an examination of the raw data, which show, for instance, that in 1952 Pan American paid $1.27 million each for twelve DC-6Bs, almost 50 percent more than United's purchase price of $0.86 million each for eleven aircraft. A more recent example is Delta's purchase of five 727-200 aircraft in 1981 at an average price of $12.0 million, one-third more than American's purchase of ten 727-200 aircraft in the same year at an average price of $8.9 million. These discrepancies in purchase price reflect some unknown combination of

4. The CAB index for 1957–76, which is described in U.S. CAB (1977), covers only the domestic trunkline industry. Since then, airlines have been reclassified as "major," "national," and "regional," and in recent years the CAB index has included the first two categories.

5. The source for coverage of the CAB index is U.S. CAB (1977, table 2). My coverage is calculated as half the value listed in table 4.2, col. 2, divided by the total of aircraft acquired as listed in the same CAB table.

differing features and options on the aircraft itself, and differing contract terms (in the 1979–81 period, Delta's purchase price for 727-200 aircraft increased each year, indicating an escalated contract, while American managed to escape escalation).

The distinction between the two types of indexes can be illustrated with a simple numerical example illustrating the evolution of aircraft prices over a four-year period:

	Year 1	Year 2	Year 3	Year 4
Model 1, airline 1	1 @ $1.00	10 @ $1.00	10 @ $1.00	1 @ $1.00
Model 2, airline 1	5 @ $1.00	. . .	8 @ $1.21	5 @ $1.32
Model 2, airline 2	. . .	7 @ $1.32	. . .	10 @ $1.58

Here, we have model 1, which is sold at the same price to airline 1 in each year. In the early years of jet aircraft, it was common for airlines to receive aircraft over a number of years on a single fixed-price contract, for example, purchases by Eastern, United, and American of Boeing 727-100 aircraft at a single price for each airline extending over the five-year period 1963–67. As for model 2, its price is assumed to increase at 10 percent per year. It is purchased by airline 2 only in years 2 and 4, while airline 1 does not purchase model 2 in year 2. Also, airline 2 for some reason pays 20 percent more for model 2 than does airline 1.

The CAB index is constructed for adjacent year pairs by using second-year quantity weights to construct a ratio of revenue in each year:

$$(4.1) \qquad R_t = \frac{\sum\limits_j P_{tj} Q_{tj}}{\sum\limits_j P_{t-1,j} Q_{tj}} .$$

The price index that links together the R_t ratios is

$$(4.2) \qquad I_t = 100 \prod_{k=1}^{t} R_k .$$

Just as the CAB index treats as a single homogeneous commodity any aircraft bearing a given model designation, regardless of which airline has done the purchasing, so we can construct an analogous SM index, and contrast it with an SMSA index. The alternative SM index differs from the CAB index only in the index number formula, which is based on the Törnqvist approach that applies value weights or logarithmic changes. The price change between two adjacent years is

$$(4.3) \qquad r_t = \frac{\sum_j (V_{t-1,j} + V_{tj})(\log P_{tj} - \log P_{t-1,j})}{\sum_j (V_{t-1,j} + V_{tj})},$$

where $V_{tj} = P_{tj}Q_{tj}$. The price index that links together these adjacent year changes is

$$(4.4) \qquad I_t = 100 \prod_{k=1}^{t} (1 + r_k).$$

The SMSA index is calculated with (4.3) and (4.4), differing only in that the index in (4.3) refers to a given model for a given airline, rather than a given model purchased by all airlines.

The difficulty in developing the SMSA index, which treats a given model purchased by different airlines as a different commodity, is evident in the numerical example. This more demanding criterion of quality homogeneity results in a drastic reduction in the sample of observations available, since no single airline purchased model 2 in adjacent year pairs 1 and 2 or 2 and 3. A straightforward calculation of the SMSA index would give a misleading result, since it would place no weight at all on model 2 in the first two year pairs. By placing all the weight on model 1, the resulting SMSA index would yield a zero rate of price change for the first three years, ignoring the increasing price of model 2.

A simple solution to this puzzle is to interpolate the observations for purchases of a given model by the same airline, "filling in" years with no purchases by interpolating between years when purchases were actually made. By interpolation, we can fill in the values of $1.10 for model 2 and airline 1 in year 2, and $1.45 for model 2 and airline 2 in year 3. The following table shows the results of applying these different index number methods to the example:

| Year | CAB Method (SM) | Törnqvist Index | | |
		SM	SMSA Raw Data	SMSA with Interpolation
1	100.0	100.0	100.0	100.0
2	122.4	110.8	100.0	103.4
3	107.6	106.3	100.0	109.6
4	123.8	120.1	104.9	116.0

The SM indexes, whether constructed by the CAB or by the Törnqvist methods, exhibit a common zigzag pattern, jumping in years 2 and 4 while declining in year 3. This is strictly a mix effect and reflects the fact that the high-price airline 2 purchased model 2 in years 2 and 4 but not in years 1 and 3. Another feature of the SM indexes is that the CAB method registers a higher rate of price change. This results from the formula (4.1), which exaggerates price change by using the prior year price in the denominator, instead of the average of the current and prior year price, which would give a closer approximation to the theoretically preferable Törnqvist index formula (4.3).

The three Törnqvist indexes also differ. The column labeled "SMSA Raw Data" registers no price change in years 1 through 3, since it gives a 100 percent weight to the unchanged price of model 1 and no weight at all to the rising price of model 2. This occurs because there is no available comparison for model 2 in adjacent year pairs 1 and 2 or 2 and 3, because no single airline purchases that model in both those adjacent years. The column labeled "SMSA with Interpolation" provides the closest approximation to "what is really happening," that is, a steady price for one model and a price increasing steadily at roughly 10 percent per year for the second model. The rate of change of the interpolated SMSA index is 3.4, 5.8, and 6.0 percent in the three adjacent year pairs, with the differences reflecting only the relatively smaller number of model 2 aircraft sold in year 1. The only apparent defect of the interpolated SMSA index is an exaggeration of price change, due to the inclusion of interpolated prices (using prior year's sales as weights), which attributes to any model for which interpolated observations are used a higher weight than is warranted by actual sales.

Table 4.2 displays rates of price change for the two Törnqvist indexes, equivalent to the SM and interpolated SMSA indexes in the above example. The SM index treats a single model as a homogeneous commodity, regardless of which airline makes the purchase, and registers a price change when there is a change in the mix of airlines paying relatively high and low prices for the same model. In table 4.2, column 1 shows the total value of purchases in each adjacent year pair, for example, $2,659 million in the 1982–83 pair (listed by the second year, 1983, in the table). Column 2 displays the ratio of the value in column 1 to the total value of aircraft purchases in the PDE component of the NIPA. Since coverage in the new SM index and the CAB index is similar, the fact that coverage in the new index is in the 15–25 percent range must reflect categories of aircraft that are excluded from both the SM and the CAB indexes, including aircraft leased by trunk carriers, aircraft purchased or leased by other airlines, and all general aviation aircraft, as well as the fact that the new data exclude the value of engines while the PDE component of the NIPA includes them. Like the PDE component of the NIPA, the new index excludes exports and, at least in principle, includes imports (the only imported aircraft included in the sample is the Airbus A-300 during the years 1978–82).

As in the above example, the interpolated SMSA index treats as a homogeneous commodity a given model purchased by a given airline. Interpolated

Table 4.2   **Weighted Price Changes for Identical Aircraft**

	Adjacent-Year Pairs					Weighted Percentage Change	
	Same Model (SM)		Same Model Same Airline (SMSA)				
Second Year of Pair	Value of Aircraft ($ million) (1)	Percent of NIPA Value (2)	Number of Aircraft (3)	Value of Aircraft ($ million) (4)	Percent Value Interpolated (5)	SM (6)	SMSA (7)
1983	2,659	22	80	2,659	. . .	2.4	2.8
1982	673	4	24	597	. . .	15.1	11.2
1981	1,235	7	52	954	. . .	6.1	9.9
1980	1,774	14	98	1,611	. . .	11.0	10.1
1979	1,572	19	128	1,608	6	7.2	6.2
1978	1,105	22	109	1,178	9	11.0	9.2
1977	638	13	54	545	27	8.0	11.3
1976	613	16	79	865	49	−3.7	7.9
1975	1,041	24	94	1,236	31	8.2	6.5
1974	1,274	25	73	753	14	3.0	5.1
1973	1,260	26	69	935	. . .	5.3	3.6
1972	1,015	31	45	511	18	2.2	1.2
1971	1,296	35	106	1,399	7	4.5	4.2
1970	1,010	20	41	341	12	5.8	3.2
1969	817	13	202	854	8	1.2	2.5
1968	1,346	22	258	1,337	4	4.5	3.1
1966	921	30	191	830	25	1.4	0.8
1965	533	25	181	842	48	0.0	1.8
1964	146	11	97	496	66	0.7	2.0
1963	28	2	65	320	70	9.4	3.9
1962	232	15	62	266	58	−13.9	0.6
1961	594	37	152	653	27	1.3	−1.3
1960	781	48	147	549	18	−3.4	2.7
1959	244	20	85	208	. . .	9.2	0.4
1958	150	17	86	130	. . .	−0.9	−0.3
1957	179	20	110	170	5	1.7	0.7
1956	135	25	83	125	26	−3.9	1.6
1955	81	22	49	70	38	10.8	3.0
1954	54	13	56	57	19	8.5	6.7
1952	88	31	107	75	10	7.5	7.3
1951	21	13	29	24	3	−4.5	−3.6
1950	8	4	20	14	47	18.6	11.3
1949	33	19	44	23	44	3.2	6.7
1948	59	31	82	54	5	6.2	0.1

Sources by column: (**1, 3–7**) U.S. CAB, Schedule B-43, 31 December 1961, 1967, 1973, 1978, 1982, and 1983. See explanation in text. (**2**) Column 4 divided by the sum for pairs of adjacent years of private purchases of aircraft, NIPA, table 5.6, row 21.

purchase prices are created when a given airline purchases a given aircraft model in two years separated by one or more years when no such aircraft were purchased. The price attributed to these purchases is based on a linear interpolation of the prices paid in years when actual purchases were made, and the weight attributed to these purchases was a value equal to the interpolated prices times the quantity sold in the earlier year. As an example,

Table 4.3   **Ratios to SMSA Value without Interpolation**

	SM Value (1)	SMSA Value with Interpolation (2)
1948–57	1.28	1.22
1958–67	1.30	1.45
1968–77	1.40	1.19
1978–83	1.07	1.02

Source: Calculated from table 4.2, cols. 1 and 4.

TWA purchased two model 727-200 aircraft in 1969 at $5.0 million each and five in 1971 at $5.88 million each. A 1970 observation is created as two 727-200 TWA aircraft purchased at $5.44 million each. After 1966, it was necessary to create interpolated observations only for gaps of a single year. But in the early 1960s there was a substantial period between the initial purchases by trunk carriers of first-generation jet aircraft in 1958–61 and a second wave of purchases of the same models in 1966–68. In this period, interpolated observations are created to fill a six-year gap for the American Airlines 707-100B between 1959 and 1966, and a four-year gap for the United Airlines DC8-50 between 1961 and 1966.

In table 4.2, columns 3 and 4 exhibit the number and value of aircraft included in the interpolated SMSA index, including the value attributed to the interpolated observations, and column 5 displays the percentage of the weight in each adjacent year pair attributed to interpolated observations. In some years, no interpolation is necessary, while in other years, particularly 1949–50, 1962–65, and 1975–76, a heavy weight is given to interpolated observations. The effects on sample size of interpolation and of the distinction between the SM and the SMSA criteria can be summarized by expressing the average ratio of the values displayed in column 1 for the SM index and in column 4 for the interpolated SMSA index to the equivalent value for the SMSA index without interpolation, shown in table 4.3.

With the exception of the post-1977 period, when the effects on sample size of both interpolation and the SM-SMSA distinction are minimal, the effect of interpolation is to increase sample size by between 20 and 45 percent, and the effect of using the SM instead of the SMSA criterion (without interpolation) is to increase the sample size by between 28 and 40 percent.

The two final columns of table 4.2 display the weighted percentage price change for each adjacent year pair for both the SM and the interpolated SMSA index. Several periods (1959–60, 1962–63, 1976–77) display zigzag movements for price change in the SM index that are not present in the interpolated SMSA index and are analogous to the zigzag movements in the SM index calculated for the above example. The two series for price change are converted into index numbers (1972 = 100) and compared with

Table 4.4   Price Indexes for Identical Aircraft (1972 = 100)

	SM (1)	SMSA (2)	BEA (3)
1983	201.8	223.4	253.3
1982	197.0	217.3	247.8
1981	171.1	195.4	224.1
1980	161.2	177.8	204.3
1979	145.2	161.5	182.2
1978	135.6	152.1	163.6
1977	122.1	139.3	152.2
1976	113.1	125.1	138.8
1975	117.3	116.0	123.4
1974	108.5	108.9	115.2
1973	105.3	103.6	104.1
1972	100.0	100.0	100.0
1971	97.8	98.8	98.1
1970	93.6	94.8	94.0
1969	88.5	91.9	88.7
1968	87.4	89.7	85.6
1967	83.6	87.0	83.0
1966	80.9	86.9	80.0
1965	79.6	86.2	78.7
1964	79.6	84.7	77.1
1963	79.1	83.0	78.7
1962	72.2	79.9	75.5
1961	82.3	79.4	73.2
1960	81.2	80.4	72.3
1959	84.0	78.3	72.1
1958	76.9	78.0	69.6
1957	77.6	78.2	68.5
1956	76.2	77.7	65.2
1955	79.2	76.4	59.8
1954	71.5	74.2	57.5
1953	65.9	69.6	56.8
1952	62.5	66.4	55.6
1951	58.2	61.9	55.9
1950	60.8	64.1	49.0
1949	51.3	56.6	46.5
1948	49.7	54.0	44.7
1947	46.8	53.9	41.9

Sources by column: (1–2) Table 4.2, cols. 6 and 7. (3) NIPA, table 7.20, row 21.

the BEA aircraft deflator in table 4.4. The latter consists of the CAB index for the period after 1957 spliced for 1947–57 to a proxy index developed by the BEA that includes various PPI series unrelated to aircraft, including "fabricated metal products" and "diesel engines."

The implications of the three indexes displayed in table 4.4 for the long-run rate of price change in the aircraft manufacturing industry can be summarized by calculating average annual rates of price change for each decade through 1977, and for the period since 1977, seen in table 4.5. As shown in the bottom row, the average rate of price change of the SM and the interpolated SMSA indexes is virtually identical and is roughly 1 percentage

Table 4.5   Average Annual Rates of Price Changes for Identical Aircraft

	SM	Interpolated SMSA	BEA
1947–57	5.19	3.79	5.04
1957–67	0.75	1.07	1.94
1967–77	3.86	4.82	6.25
1977–83	8.74	8.19	8.86
1947–83	4.14	4.03	5.13

Source: Calculated from table 4.3.

point less per annum than that of the BEA index. In each of the four subperiods, the interpolated SMSA index increases less rapidly than the BEA index by a roughly uniform amount, between 0.67 and 1.43 percentage points per annum. The differential between the SM and the BEA indexes is more erratic, and the SM index actually grew more rapidly than the BEA index in the first subinterval, 1947–57.

4.4   Price Changes and Quality Improvements for Particular Models

To assess the slower rate of price increase registered by both the SM and the interpolated SMSA indexes as compared to the BEA index within the last decade, we can examine price changes on aircraft that were purchased by a single airline year after year. In the last half of the 1970s, Delta was the only major airline that purchased the same aircraft in numerous successive years. The following is a comparison of 1974 and 1982, chosen because Delta purchased the L-1011 and 727-200 aircraft in both years:

	($ million) 1974	($ million) 1982	1982/1974
Delta L-1011	15.9	31.3	1.969
Delta 727-200	6.7	13.0	1.940
Interpolated SMSA index	108.9	217.3	1.995
CAB index	115.2	247.8	2.151

My interpolated SMSA index is substantially closer to an average of the price increases registered by the two Delta aircraft than the CAB index.

The price increase registered on the Delta 727-200 is a particularly important cross-check of the two indexes, since that aircraft model represented the great bulk of the airline purchases by major airlines during the 1973–80 period, when the two indexes diverge. Another check is to take the average price paid by all airlines for the 727-200 in the first round of purchases (1969) and the last year in which several of the large airlines purchased the same model (prices are listed, with numbers purchased in

Table 4.6   Average Price Paid by All Airlines for the 727-200

	1969	1980	1980/1969
American	5.4 (10)	8.9 (4)	
Delta	. . .	11.6 (9)	
TWA	5.0 (2)	. . .	
United	5.2 (6)	10.6 (4)	
Weighted average for 727-200	5.3	10.7	2.019
Interpolated SMSA	91.9	177.8	1.935
CAB index	88.7	204.3	2.303

parentheses), listed in table 4.6. Here, too, the new index is closer to the increases in prices paid for the 727-200.

There is an indirect piece of evidence that the interpolated SMSA index may overstate price increases rather than understate them. The ratio of this index for 1978 to its value in 1967 is 1.75. This ratio, when multiplied by the $3.1 million price paid for a DC9-30 model in 1967, implies that the same model would have sold for $5.4 million in 1978. However, in that year, a stretched version of the same aircraft, having 27 percent more seats, the DC9-50, was sold for only $5.6 million. I conclude that the CAB index is biased upward in the late 1970s, even by its own criterion of measuring price changes of identical aircraft.[6]

A common weakness of all the price indexes discussed thus far, including the interpolated SMSA index as well as the CAB index, is the assumption that a given model designation, for example, Boeing 727-200, indicates homogeneous quality. However, this does not prove to be a warranted assumption. The Boeing 727-200 was produced for seventeen years prior to termination of production in 1983, the Boeing 737-200 was produced for seventeen years, and the Boeing 747-200 was still being produced in 1988 after sixteen years. During these long production runs, substantial changes were made to these aircraft. In fact, in the used aircraft market, B727-200 aircraft produced after 1974–75 are classified separately as "B727-200 ADV," standing for *advanced*. For each aircraft model shown in table 4.7, standard specifications are listed for both 1983 and the first year of the production run. In all cases, the 1983 version of the same model designation incorporates substantial improvements. Chief among these are improvements in engine thrust and fuel economy that allow the addition of more fuel and more seats to increase range, payload, and airline profitability. For instance, the stretched 727 models purchased by United in the late 1960s could not fly nonstop from Chicago to San Francisco, whereas the models delivered in the

6. A qualification to the comparisons in the text is that they do not include all aircraft manufactured during this period. The B-727, L-1011, and DC-9 accounted for 53 percent of the number of commercial aircraft sold in 1976–80 (*Aerospace Facts and Figures*, 1981–82 ed., 37).

Table 4.7   Quality Changes on Boeing Aircraft Carrying Identical Model Numbers (prices include engines)

	737-200		727-200		747-200	
	1968 (1)	1983 (2)	1967 (3)	1983 (4)	1971 (5)	1983 (6)
1. Engine thrust (pounds)	14,000	15,500	14,000	16,000	48,570	54,750
2. Gross weight	95,000	115,500	170,000	197,000	775,000	833,000
3. Range (nautical miles)	1,300	1,850	1,700	2,250	5,160	6,130
4. Standard seats[a]	101	110	139	156	395	452
5. Fuel burn (pounds/mile)	15.6	15.4	27.6	25.0	51.6	46.1
6. Fuel burn (pounds/seat/mile)	.154	.140	.199	.160	.131	.102
7. Theoretical 1983 price of configuration ($ million)	14.0	15.9	19.5	21.8	71.6	85.0

Source: Boeing Commercial Airplane Co., internal records, 1984.

[a]Seating configuration adjusted from Boeing data to hold constant the number of rows devoted to the first-class cabin.

late 1970s could do so. Full-sized 747-200 aircraft produced in the 1970s could not fly nonstop from New York to Tokyo, but those produced in the 1980s could do so (prematurely making obsolete the shortened 747-SP designed explicitly for those long routes). Also included on the newer versions (and not shown in table 4.7) are improved avionics that provide better navigation and flight management systems to achieve a flight path that is closer to optimal.[7] Aircraft models developed in the 1980s, especially the Boeing 767 and 747-400 (as well as the Airbus, which is foreign made and thus not relevant for the U.S. GNP deflator), have completely computerized cockpits with sophisticated self-diagnostic capabilities. For instance, a mechanic can now plug a computer terminal into an engine on a 767 and watch the engine diagnose its own problems.

Two figures are shown on rows 5 and 6 for the improvement in fuel efficiency. Row 5, showing fuel burned in pounds per mile, understates the improvement in efficiency, because the newer aircraft are able to carry a higher payload for a given amount of fuel. The second figure in row 6 shows fuel burned in pounds per seat mile and obviously improves more over the years, by 9.5 percent for the 737-200, 21.8 percent for the 828-200, and 25.0 percent for the 747-200. The increase in number of seats per aircraft shown in row 4 holds constant the 1983 mix between first-class and coach seating and calculates a hypothetical number of seats for the earlier year (by taking the actual earlier seating configuration, which in each case included a larger share of first-class seating, and converting sufficient rows of first-class seats to coach to achieve the same number of first class seats as in 1983). The total number of coach seats in 1983 is greater than in the earlier years for each aircraft, reflecting a combination of thinner seats (allowing more seats to be added without sacrificing leg room), less leg room, and higher aircraft payload capacity. The earlier version of the aircraft may have been physically capable of holding more seats than were actually used, but only by sacrificing range (increasing the number of passengers always results in decreased range for a given plane with given engines operating at a given gross weight, since more weight devoted to passengers means less weight can be devoted to carrying fuel). So, leaving aside a minor decrease in passenger comfort, the evidence of improved fuel economy in row 6 of table 4.7 is more relevant than in row 5.

The final row of table 4.7 shows a calculation by Boeing of the marginal cost of production of the 1983 configuration as compared to the earlier configuration. The figure shown for the earlier year is the 1983 price adjusted for the cost of the increase in the capability of the airplanes through changes in gross weight, range, engines, fuel consumption, and avionics.

---

7. All data in table 4.7 and in this section of the text were provided by W. G. Loeken of the Boeing Commercial Airplane Co. in several letters sent to me in 1984.

The improvements on the 737-200 are estimated to have added 13.5 percent to its price, as compared with 11.8 percent for the 727-200 and 18.7 percent for the 747-200. If we take an unweighted average of these three figures, 14.7 percent, we can calculate the implications for the price index of identical models. Assume that similar improvements were made to aircraft produced by other manufacturers, for example, the Douglas DC-9 and DC-10 and the Lockheed L-1011.[8] The period 1972–82 is chosen for comparison, since aircraft sales in this decade were dominated by the three Boeing models and the three other models produced by Douglas and Lockheed:

	1982/1972
CAB index	2.478
Interpolated SMSA index	2.173
SMSA index adjusted for 14.6 percent quality change	1.896

Thus, the CAB index exaggerates the 1972–82 price increase of commercial aircraft by roughly 30 percent. No information is available to assess the importance of this problem in earlier decades, but similar quality improvements may have been introduced over the lifespan of planes that remained in production for a decade, for example, the DC-6B and the Boeing 707-100B and 707-300B. The substantial number of aircraft that remained in production only for a short interval of three to five years, however, including the DC-7, the Convair 880, the Boeing 720, and the

8. The three Boeing aircraft dominated deliveries by the U.S. commercial aircraft industry during the 1972–80 period. The following figures are from *Aerospace Facts and Figures*, various issues, and are not available to me from the same source for years since 1980. These figures cover all aircraft manufactured in the United States, including exports and leased aircraft, and thus cover a larger universe than the SMSA or the CAB indexes in tables 4.2 and 4.4:

Share of Deliveries, 1972–80, Total U.S. Industry (percentage of aircraft produced by number, not value)	
1. Boeing 737	18.5
2. Boeing 727	36.6
3. Boeing 747	14.1
Total, rows 1–3	69.2
4. Lockheed L-1011	8.6
5. Douglas DC-10	7.5
6. Douglas DC-9	8.3
7. Other	6.4
Total, rows 1–7	100.0

Boeing 727-100, suggest that the "hidden quality improvement phenomenon" was probably less important in the 1950s and 1960s than in the 1970s.

4.5 Quality Adjustments Based on Net Revenue Data

The technique of price measurement proposed in chapter 2 adjusts price differences between models of a given product for changes in net revenue yielded by new models, because firms purchase capital goods for their ability to produce "net revenue" (defined as gross revenue minus operating costs—thus, net revenue is the amount available to pay depreciation and interest charges). Holding constant the prices of unchanged models, if a 10 percent increase in the price of new model B compared to old model A is accompanied by a 10 percent increase in net revenue, no quality adjustment is required to an index of the prices of identical models, like those developed in table 4.4. However, an increase in the net revenue provided by model B relative to model A that is greater than the excess of the price of model B over model A would call for a quality adjustment to the table 4.4 price index. To repeat equation (2.35) from chapter 2, the change in the *real* input price index $(\Delta p^i / p^i)$ that holds constant the cost of producing identical models is

(4.5)
$$\frac{\Delta p^i}{p^i} = \left[\frac{v_1 n_0}{v_0 n_1}\right] \left[\frac{n_0}{n_1}\right]^{\alpha - 1} - 1.$$

Here, v designates the purchase price of models 1 and 0, and n designates their respective net revenue.

If $\alpha = 1$, then the second term in brackets becomes unity, and the remaining expression states that the "real" price change will be zero if both purchase price and net revenue change in proportion in the shift to the new model, $(v_1/v_0) = (n_1/n_0)$. If the cost schedule that allows a manufacturer to produce a higher-cost model exhibits diminishing returns in the extra net revenue produced, then $\alpha > 1$, and the second term in brackets becomes a fraction less than unity. Why is the second term in brackets, the "curvature adjustment," required? In the presence of diminishing returns, a movement along a fixed cost function should yield a less-than-proportionate increase in n for a given increase in v, and the first bracketed term would erroneously register a price increase when in fact the cost function had not shifted. Imagine a downward shift in the cost function sufficient in the presence of diminishing returns to yield an increase in n proportionate to that in v. Again, the first bracketed term would erroneously register no change in price when in fact the cost function has shifted downward. Thus, the curvature adjustment corrects for the fact that, in the presence of diminishing returns in the production of n in response to increased v, the first term in brackets always overstates the real price increase.

The nominal input price index $\Delta p^i / p^i$ is then obtained by adding the increase in the real input price from (4.5) to the change in the price index for identical models ($\Delta C / C$). Copying (2.36) for convenience, we have:

$$(4.6) \qquad \frac{\Delta P^i}{P^i} = \frac{\Delta p^i}{p^i} + \frac{\Delta C}{C} .$$

Thus, the purpose of this section is to develop measures of net revenue suitable for creating the year-to-year changes in the real input price index from equation (4.5). Subsequently, these changes will be added to the changes in the interpolated SMSA price index for identical models shown above in column 2 of table 4.4.

Any attempt to calculate changes in real input price using (4.5) will yield results that are sensitive to the assumptions made about expectations. In comparing a new and an old model at a particular time, the ratio of current-period prices (v_1 / v_0) can be observed in a straightforward manner, but the ratio of net revenue (n_1 / n_0) depends on expected output prices, expected output productivity, expected input prices, and expected input requirements, not to mention the expected lifetimes of the new and old models (the lifetime itself is an economic decision that depends on the unpredictable evolution of aircraft revenues and costs). A number of assumptions could be made about the revenue and cost calculations of users making aircraft purchasing decisions over the years, including static expectations, extrapolation of past trends, and expectations that are accurate *ex post*.

It would make no sense to proxy expectations as an extrapolation of past trends in the airline industry, since the introduction of the jet plane created a clean break with past operating conditions. Static expectations would also be a weak assumption, since labor expenses are a major component of airline operating costs, and wage rates have risen regularly every year (recall table 4.1 above).

The assumption that seems easiest to justify is accurate expectations *ex post*. In the analysis that follows, the sales price of a new model is compared with that of an old model (v_1 / v_0) in the year of introduction of the new model. However, when possible, the ratio of net revenue for the two models (n_1 / n_0) is calculated not only for that year, but also for several years in the future. The exact procedure is to calculate net revenue ratios for several years, starting with the year of introduction of the new model and continuing with years spaced five years apart (1967, 1972, 1977, etc.) until the date of retirement of the old model. Two factors prevent this procedure from being carried out for every model pair. First, the CAB operating cost data are not available in their present form before 1965, and, for comparisons involving the transition from late-model piston aircraft to early-model jet aircraft, only a single observation (in some cases taken from previous research monographs on the industry) is available. The second limitation occurs when only a short time interval is available between the introduction of a new model and the retirement of the corresponding old model. Since the Lockheed Electra (L188) was retired shortly after 1965, only one comparison is available between that aircraft and the Boeing 727-100 (the successor aircraft that typically replaced the Electra on medium-length routes). However, since the 727-100 has remained in service to this date, four comparisons of operating cost are available between the Boeing 727-100 and the ''stretched'' 727-200, in 1968, 1972, 1977, and 1982.[9] Whatever the limitations of this procedure, it seems to be the best available alternative and has the advantage that each pairwise comparison applies to a single year, thus holding constant output prices and the prices of operating inputs, particularly fuel and the wages of flight crews and maintenance labor.

The most important determinant of aircraft operating costs per seat mile at a given level of technology is ''stage length'' or ''length of hop.'' A very short flight mainly consists of expensive takeoff and landing operations, with a slow average speed, whereas a long flight amortizes the takeoff and landing over a multihour flight segment at cruising speed. This fact dictates that the pairs of new and old models in the net revenue comparisons must be chosen to have roughly similar stage lengths in actual operation. Basic operating characteristics and cost data for successive generations of aircraft are presented in the three parts of table 4.8, that is, part A for long-range aircraft, part B for medium range, and part C for short range. Fifteen comparisons appear in the three sections of the table, involving eighteen different aircraft models. In size, the aircraft range from the small, two-engine piston short-range Convair 340/440, with forty-four seats, to the large wide-bodied long-range turbofan Boeing 747-100, with over 400 seats and capable of providing roughly twenty-five times the annual capacity. In chronological time, the aircraft models span the entire postwar period, beginning with the staple of early postwar air travel, the Douglas DC-6B, and continuing through the newest generation of jet aircraft, the Boeing 767-200 and the McDonnell-Douglas DC9-80 (now called the MD-80). The major types of aircraft that are excluded (to limit the time devoted to the analysis) are planes that are virtual duplicates of those analyzed here (e.g., the Boeing 707-100B, which is similar to the Douglas DC8-50), and a few planes that had short production runs (e.g., the Convair 880/990). There is also no coverage of aircraft used by commuter airlines.

The three sections of table 4.8 are arranged to present for each pair of models all the data used to calculate net revenue. Annual net revenue in

---

9. The limitation to comparisons at five-year intervals, rather than shorter intervals, was chosen to control the time devoted to this phase of the research.

Table 4.8 Revenue and Operating Cost Data: Long, Medium, and Short Range

Plane Types	Year	Revenue Hours per Year (1)	Air Speed (mph) (2)	Seats (3)	Annual asm (millions) (4)	Stage Length (5)	Load Factor (6)	Gross Revenue per rpm (7)	Net Revenue per asm (8)	Operating Cost per asm (9)	(7)-(8) (10)	Annual Net Revenue ($million) (11)
A. Long range:												
1. B767-200	1982	2,478	462	196.7	265.6	1,026	.667	.1254	.0435	.0310	.0125	3.328
L1011-100		2,894	471	287.7	388.4	1,038	.537	.1254	.0435	.0325	.0110	4.272
2. A300-B2	1982	2,823	450	241.0	317.2	908	.562	.1274	.0400	.0311	.0089	2.823
L1011-100		2,894	471	287.7	378.7	1,038	.537	.1274	.0400	.0339	.0061	1.755
3. L1011-100	1982	2,894	471	287.7	351.4	1,038	.537	.1279	.0403	.0328	.0075	2.636
DC8-61		2,473	444	199.5	244.9	860	.559	.1279	.0403	.0378	.0025	0.612
	1977	2,750	475	250.5	324.4	969	.515	.0896	.0274	.0195	.0088	2.855
		2,832	453	193.5	250.6	858	.548	.0896	.0274	.0195	.0079	1.980
	1972	2,356	489	213.7	305.3	1,237	.483	.0648	.0179	.0114	.0065	1.984
		3,001	463	175.0	250.0	942	.477	.0648	.0179	.0093	.0083	2.150
4. DC10-10	1982	2,963	491	264.8	336.5	1,453	.617	.1231	.0416	.0321	.0095	3.196
DC8-61		2,473	444	199.5	253.5	860	.559	.1231	.0416	.0378	.0038	0.963
	1977	3,174	487	244.2	344.7	1,283	.583	.0861	.0294	.0163	.0131	4.510
		2,832	453	193.5	273.1	858	.605	.0861	.0294	.0195	.0099	2.704
	1972	2,834	483	224.6	318.8	1,067	.452	.0658	.0176	.0082	.0094	3.000
		3,001	463	175.0	248.4	942	.477	.0658	.0176	.0093	.0083	2.062
5. B747-100	1982	3,344	508	405.6	647.0	2,101	.682	.1157	.0423	.0296	.0127	8.210
B707-300B		. . .	446	154.5	246.4	793	.589	.1157	.0423	.0445	-.0022	-0.541
	1977	3,436	503	374.3	561.5	1,794	.620	.0808	.0283	.0162	.0121	6.794
		2,802	459	154.4	231.6	1,026	.597	.0808	.0283	.0224	.0059	1.367
	1972	3,147	507	317.1	519.1	1,962	.458	.0576	.0162	.0085	.0077	3.997
		3,454	485	143.0	234.1	1,429	.528	.0576	.0162	.0103	.0059	1.381

Model	Year											
6. DC8-61	1977	2,832	453	193.5	250.4	858	.548	.0895	.0289	.0195	.0094	2.063
DC8-50		· · ·	461	133.8	173.2	946	.574	.0895	.0289	.0270	.0019	0.288
	1972	3,398	463	175.0	256.4	867	.477	.0626	.0193	.0095	.0098	2.513
		2,937	462	128.9	188.8	847	.515	.0676	.0193	.0121	.0072	1.359
	1968	3,633	470	196.6	342.1	1,094	.450	.0582	.0160	.0068	.0092	3.147
		3,749	473	134.1	233.4	910	.510	.0582	.0160	.0096	.0064	1.494
7. DC8-50	1965	3,699	479	125.5	222.4[c]	841	.523	.0668	.0211	.0113[e]	.0098	2.180
DC-7		· · ·	286[a]	77.0	81.5[c]	750[d]	.585	.0668	.0211	.0198[e]	.0013	0.106
B. Medium range:												
8. DC9-80	1982	3,179	441	147.0	191.7	701	.530	.1345	.0426	.0252	.0174	3.336
B727-200		2,789	434	143.7	187.4	639	.575	.1345	.0426	.0368	.0058	1.087
9. B727-200	1982	2,789	434	143.7	157.8	639	.575	.1371	.0460	.0376	.0084	1.326
B727-100		2,248	438	109.0	119.7	666	.594	.1371	.0460	.0478	−.0018	−0.215
	1977	2,935	424	132.0	155.6	506	.565	.1047	.0353	.0221	.0132	2.054
		2,580	431	99.4	117.2	571	.608	.1047	.0353	.0296	.0057	0.068
	1972	2,613	427	123.3	136.0	550	.530	.0778	.0238	.0117	.0121	1.641
		2,519	433	96.2	106.1	542	.537	.0778	.0238	.0150	.0088	0.934
	1968	2,909	433	128.6	159.0	545	.474	.0702	.0212	.0076	.0136	2.162
		2,829	429	95.7	118.3	492	.579	.0702	.0212	.0129	.0083	0.982
10. B727-100	1965	2,518	389	94.1	92.8[c]	510	.612	.0775	.0266	.0123[e]	.0143	1.327
L-188		2,550	297	79.6	59.9[c]	500[d]	.589	.0775	.0266	.0143[e]	.0123	0.737
11. B-720B	1965	3,221	468	113.0	152.6[c]	698	.553	.0775	.0253	.0132[e]	.0123	1.846
L-188		2,550	297[a]	79.6	68.2[c]	500[d]	.589	.0775	.0253	.0143[e]	.0110	0.750
12. L-188	1965	2,550	297[a]	79.6	60.3[c]	500[d]	.589	.0775	.0253	.0143[e]	.0110	0.663
DC-6B		· · ·	225[a]	69.5	39.9[c]	500[d]	.513	.0775	.0253	.0203[e]	.0050	0.197

(*Continued*)

Table 4.8 (continued)

Plane Types	Year	Revenue Hours per Year (1)	Air Speed (mph) (2)	Seats (3)	Annual asm (millions) (4)	Stage Length (5)	Load Factor (6)	Gross Revenue per rpm (7)	Net Revenue per asm (8)	Operating Cost per asm (9)	(7)-(8) (10)	Annual Net Revenue ($million) (11)
C. Short range:												
13. DC9-50	1982	2,655	390	124.5	124.9	367	.558	.1704	.0550	.0314	.0169	2.948
DC9-30		2,516	386	100.5	100.8	371	.571	.1704	.0550	.0396	.0154	1.552
	1977	2,694	375	114.9	118.5	387	.560	.1187	.0398	.0139	.0259	3.069
		2,763	381	91.4	94.3	348	.611	.1187	.0398	.0219	.0179	1.688
14. DC9-30	1982	2,516	386	100.5	94.1	371	.571	.1747	.0575	.0396	.0179	1.684
DC9-10		2,375	380	83.5	78.2	297	.579	.1747	.0575	.0448	.0127	0.993
	1977	2,763	381	91.4	88.5	348	.611	.1161	.0415	.0219	.0196	1.735
		2,362	397	70.3	68.1	435	.640	.1161	.0415	.0291	.0124	0.844
	1972	2,927	382	89.4	92.0	331	.595	.0916	.0311	.0113	.0198	1.822
		2,449	384	66.7	68.7	312	.594	.0916	.0311	.0152	.0159	1.092
	1968	2,373	360	90.1	81.8	283	.605	.0832	.0281	.0098	.0183	1.497
		2,533	379	69.9	63.4	287	.575	.0832	.0281	.0118	.0163	1.035
15. DC9-10	1965	2,789	389	66.6	77.3[c]	299	.716	.0803	.0294	.0148	.0146	1.128
CV340-440		…	211[a]	43.6	21.3[c]	250[d]	.570	.0803	.0294	.0243	.0051	0.109

Sources by column: (In the following notes, AOCPR refers to U.S. CAB, *Aircraft Operating Cost and Performance Report*, issued annually, 1965–84.) (**1**) Revenue hours per year, from AOCPR for the year in question. Blanks indicate that no figures are shown for piston planes, which are allocated the same yearly utilization as the first plane listed in each comparison. Also, the extremely low utilization of the B707-300B in 1982 and DC8-50 in 1977 is ignored, and the utilization of the comparison aircraft is used instead in those years. (**2**) Air speed is from AOCPR, except for comparisons noted by [a], which are from Douglas and Miller (1974), where block speeds shown are converted to air speed using the air/block ratio for the first plane listed in each comparison. (**3**) Average available seats per aircraft mile from AOCPR. (**4**) Annual available seat miles equals col. 3 times the average for each pair of models of revenue hours from col. 1 times the average for the two models in each comparison of air speed from col. 2. For comparison marked with [c], involving comparisons of jets with turboprops or piston planes, the calculation of annual available seat miles uses air speeds in col. 2 for each separate aircraft, rather than the average of the two. (**5**) Stage length is taken from AOCPR, except for comparisons marked with [d], where operating cost comparisons for both planes in the pair are taken from Strazheim (1969, 74) for the stage length indicated. (**6**) Load factors are from AOCPR for the year shown. (**7**) Gross revenue per revenue passenger miles is taken from a yield curve for 1971 adjusted for discounts, as displayed in Douglas and Miller (1974, 90). Points on the curve not shown in the Douglas-Miller table are interpolated linearly. The resulting yield is converted from a 1971 basis to the yield for each comparison year by using a conversion factor equal to the ratio of average passenger yield in that year to average passenger yield for 1971, from Bailey, Graham, and Kaplan (1985, app. A). (**8**) Net revenue per available seat mile is obtained by multiplying gross revenue per revenue passenger mile in col. 7 by two ratios. The first is the average load factor for the two planes in each comparison, from col. 6. The second is the ratio of aircraft operating costs plus flight equipment maintenance plus depreciation plus interest to total gross revenue minus imputed profit, 57.2 percent for the twelve months ending 30 June 1981, from Bailey, Graham, and Kaplan (1985, table 3.3, p. 136). (**9**) Flying operations costs plus flight equipment maintenance per available seat mile are from AOCPR, and are calculated by dividing average cost per block hour by seating capacity times block speed. The average speed for the two aircraft in a pair is used to adjust for the tilt of the cost curve. Average cost figures denoted by [e] are taken from Strazheim (1969, 74, 86), which refers to 1965. Straszheim's average cost figures refer to the stage length denoted by [d] in col. 5 and are adjusted to deduct depreciation in order to make them comparable to the other entries in this column. (**10**) Equals col. 7 minus col. 8. (**11**) Equals col. 10 times col. 4.

millions of dollars is shown in the right-hand column 11, and the ingredients in arriving at that figure are shown in the other columns. The stages in the calculation are as follows.

1. Annual available seat miles, that is, total output per year, is calculated as the product of hours per year, times air speed, times the number of seats. For jet aircraft, hours per year is the actual time flown, but, for piston aircraft by the 1960s, hours per year were very low—far below the actual time flown in the prejet era, and so the annual hours for the comparison aircraft are used instead. Since piston aircraft, even in their heyday, had more frequent maintenance downtime, this procedure overstates the annual output of piston aircraft. This error is one of several, including the decision to ignore the value of time savings and greater comfort, that make the final index understate the quality improvement involved in the transition from piston to jet aircraft. Since jet aircraft generally fly at the same speed on a given route, annual capacity (col. 4) is calculated by taking the average speed of the two jet aircraft shown. For comparisons involving piston aircraft, speeds are taken from a source that displays speeds for different aircraft types at given stage lengths. As for seating capacity, this is taken as the actual figure in different years. Note that the seating capacity of jet aircraft has generally increased since the early 1970s, reflecting a marketing decision to reduce the space devoted to the first-class cabin, the development of thinner seats, the development of overhead baggage racks that allow passengers to occupy less space without a proportional loss of comfort, and new engines that have increased the range and passenger-carrying capacity of aircraft carrying an unchanged model number. Effects of changing seating configurations are examined in table 4.11 below.

2. Gross revenue per revenue passenger mile, or passenger "yield," is *not* based on published fares, which overstate the increase in fares over the years by neglecting discounts. Instead, the yield calculation begins with a yield curve adjusted for discounts from Douglas and Miller (1974). Then the yield for a particular stage length for years before and after 1971 is calculated by taking the point on that curve and multiplying it by the change in average passenger yield (this takes account both of discounts and of the changing mix between first class and coach) between 1971 and the year of the model comparison.

3. The definition of load factor (lf) is revenue passenger miles (rpm) divided by available seat miles (asm) (lf = rpm/asm). Since operating costs are collected on an asm basis, it is necessary to convert yield per rpm (col. 7) to yield per asm. Another adjustment is to subtract from gross revenue that fraction that must be set aside to cover airline operating costs other than direct costs of flying operations. Gross revenue is converted to a net basis by a multiplicative factor equal to the ratio of aircraft operating costs, including flight equipment maintenance plus depreciation and interest, to total gross revenue minus imputed profit, from the recent study by Bailey, Graham, and

Kaplan (1985). The resulting figure, expressed in column 8 on a basis per asm, is the amount available to cover costs of flying operations and maintenance shown in column 9. The difference, shown on an asm basis in column 10 and on a per-annum basis in column 11, is then available to cover depreciation and interest, with any residual contributing to operating profit.

The resulting estimates of net revenue display a fairly consistent pattern. In those comparisons, in which net revenue estimates are available for several successive five-year intervals, note that the relative advantage of the newer model in generating net revenue seems to increase as time goes on. For instance, the net revenue per asm of the 747-100 is only slightly above that of the 707-300 in 1972, but by 1982 the figure for the 747-100 has increased while that for the 707-300 has become negative. Similarly, the 1982 estimate for the 727-100 is negative. Thus, it is not surprising that by 1982 most U.S. airlines had grounded and/or retired their fleets of 707 aircraft and were operating 727-100 aircraft at relatively low utilization rates. Overall, it appears that the DC-9 series of short-haul aircraft produces the highest net revenue per asm, but total annual net revenue is highest for the Boeing 747-100, owing to its large annual capacity of asms.

Table 4.9 combines these net revenue estimates with data on the sales prices of various plane types. The prices are the same as those used in table 4.2 to compute the price indexes for identical models. In most cases, the "old" and "new" models being compared were not actually constructed simultaneously, requiring the adjustment of the price of the old model for changes in the price of identical models (using the interpolated SMSA index) between the year of its disappearance and the first sales year of the new model. In this way, the sales prices of the two planes in each comparison are computed for the same year, allowing the price of output and operating inputs to be held constant. For instance, in part A of table 4.9, there was no overlap in the construction dates of the L-1011 and DC8-61. The comparison for 1972 uses the average sales price for that year for the airlines purchasing the L-1011, from the data base used in developing tables 4.2 and 4.4 above. The price for the DC8-61 is the average 1968 price from the same data base, times the 1972/1968 ratio of the interpolated SMSA index in table 4.3. The 1977 and 1982 comparisons exhibit the implied prices when the 1972 price comparison is adjusted for the change in the interpolated SMSA index after 1972.

Each table is arranged with the comparisons of the most recent models at the top of each of the three sections (for long range, medium range, and short range), while at the bottom are displayed the comparisons for the transition between piston and jet aircraft. Column 4 shows the ratio of annual net revenue to the implied replacement price and indicates the enormous profitability of jet planes, compared to the piston planes they replaced. Because most airlines depreciated their piston planes over seven- or eight-year intervals, it is apparent that the DC-7 in part A of table 4.9 must have have

Table 4.9   Calculation of Price Change: Long, Medium, and Short Range

Plane Types	Year	Original Price (Year) (1)	Price in Comparison Year (2)	Net Revenue in Comparison Year (3)	n_t/v_t (4)	v_{1t}/v_{0t} (5)	n_{1t}/n_{0t} (6)	(5)/(6) −1 (7)	(7) With Curvature Adjustment (8)
A. Long range:									
1. B767-200	1982	33.9 (1983)	33.0	3.328	0.101	1.003	0.779	0.288	0.354
L1011-100	1982	33.8 (1983)	32.9	4.272	0.130				
2. A300-B2	1982	22.7 (1981)	25.2	2.823	0.112	0.778	1.609	−0.516	−0.560
L1011-100	1982	29.1 (1981)	32.4	1.755	0.054				
3. L1011-100	1982	15.4 (1972)	33.5	2.636	0.077				
DC8-61	1977	7.5 (1968)	18.2	0.612	0.033	1.840	4.307	−0.573	−0.681
			21.5	2.855	0.129				
			11.7	1.980	0.169	1.840	1.442	0.276	0.185
	1972		15.4	1.984	0.129				
			8.4	2.150	0.256	1.840	0.923	0.933	1.026
4. DC10-10	1982	15.3 (1972)	33.2	3.196	0.093				
DC8-61	1977	7.5 (1968)	18.2	0.963	0.053	1.820	3.319	−0.452	−0.569
			21.3	4.510	0.212				
			11.7	2.704	0.231	1.820	1.486	0.225	0.131
	1972		15.3	3.000	0.196				
			8.4	2.062	0.245	1.820	1.455	0.251	0.160
5. B747-100	1982	21.2 (1972)	46.1	8.210	0.130	2.986	⋮	⋮	⋮
B707-300B	1977	6.2 (1966)	15.5	−0.541	−0.026				
			29.5	6.794	0.223	2.986	4.970	−0.399	−0.564
			9.9	1.367	0.138				
	1972		21.2	3.997	0.189	2.986	2.894	0.032	−0.166
			7.1	1.381	0.175				

(continued)

Table 4.9 (continued)

Plane Types	Year	Original Price (Year) (1)	Price in Comparison Year (2)	Net Revenue in Comparison Year (3)	n_t/v_t (4)	v_{1t}/v_{0t} (5)	n_{1t}/n_{0t} (6)	(5)/(6) −1 (7)	(7) With Curvature Adjustment (8)
6. DC8-61	1977	7.5 (1968)	11.7	2.063	0.176	1.316	7.163	−0.816	−0.876
DC8-50		5.5 (1966)	8.8	0.288	0.033				
	1972		8.4	2.513	0.299	1.316	1.849	−0.288	−0.370
			6.3	1.359	0.216				
	1968		7.5	3.147	0.420	1.316	2.106	−0.375	−0.461
			5.7	1.494	0.262				
7. DC8-50	1965	4.4 (1959)	4.8	2.180	0.422	2.670	20.573	−0.873	−0.929
DC-7		1.6 (1958)	1.8	0.106	0.059				
B. Medium range:									
8. DC9-80	1982	22.4 (1983)	21.8	3.336	0.153	1.703	3.069	−0.445	−0.557
B727-200		9.5 (1979)	12.8	1.087	0.085				
9. B727-200	1982	5.3 (1969)	12.5	1.326	0.106	1.147	…	…	…
B727-100		4.6 (1969)	10.9	−0.215	−0.020				
	1977		8.6	2.054	0.257	1.147	3.075	−0.627	−0.702
			7.0	0.668	0.095				
	1972		5.8	1.646	0.283	1.147	1.762	−0.349	−0.418
			5.0	0.934	0.187				
	1968		5.2	2.162	0.416	1.147	2.202	−0.479	−0.555
			4.5	0.982	0.218				
10. B727-100	1965	3.9 (1963)	4.1	1.327	0.324	2.158	1.801	0.198	0.065
L-188		1.7 (1959)	1.9	0.737	0.388				
11. B-720B	1965	3.7 (1961)	4.0	1.846	0.462	2.105	2.461	−0.145	−0.286
L-188		1.7 (1959)	1.9	0.750	0.395				
12. L-188	1965	1.7 (1959)	1.9	0.663	0.326	1.727	3.374	−0.488	−0.599
DC-6B		1.0 (1958)	1.1	0.197	0.156				

C. Short range:

	Comparison year	(1) Price (year)	(2)	(3)	(4)	(5)	(6)	(7)	(8)
13. DC9-50	1982	5.6 (1978)	8.0	2.948	0.369	1.038	1.900	−0.453	−0.519
DC9-30		3.1 (1967)	7.7	1.552	0.202				
	1977		5.1	3.069	0.602	1.038	1.818	−0.429	−0.493
			5.0	1.688	0.338				
14. DC9-30	1982	3.1 (1967)	7.7	1.684	0.259	1.100	1.696	−0.352	−0.417
DC9-10		2.8 (1966)	7.0	0.993	0.070				
	1977		4.9	1.735	0.354	1.100	2.056	−0.464	−0.536
			4.5	0.844	0.188				
	1972		3.5	1.822	0.521	1.100	1.668	−0.340	−0.405
			3.2	1.092	0.341				
	1967		3.1	1.497	0.483	1.100	1.449	−0.241	−0.291
			2.8	1.033	0.369				
15. DC9-10	1965	2.8 (1966)	2.8	1.128	0.403	4.000	10.349	−0.613	−0.758
CV340/440		0.6 (1957)	0.7	0.109	0.156				

Sources by column: **(1)** All price data are for airframes, excluding engines, from CAB Form 41, Schedule B-43. Table 4.7 shows the average price paid by the following airlines, with the year of the schedule B-43 shown in parentheses for all comparisons but the first. *Long range:* (1) Schedule B-7, price paid by Delta for both the 767 and the L-1011 in the quarter ending 6-30-83; (2) A-300, Eastern, price paid in 1981 (12-31-82); L-1011, Delta, price paid in 1981 (12-31-82); (3) L-1011, average price paid by Eastern and TWA in 1972 (12-31-73); DC8-61, average price paid by Delta and United in 1968 (12-31-73); (4) DC10-10, average price paid by American and United in 1972 (12-31-73); (5) B747-100, average price paid by United in 1972 (12-31-73); DC8-50, same as comparison 3; DC8-61, same as comparison 3; DC8-50, average price paid by Delta and United in 1966 (12-31-67); (7) DC8-50, same as comparison 6; DC-7, average price paid by United in 1958 (12-31-61). *Medium range:* (1) DC9-80, average price paid by PSA in the quarter ending 6-30-83, from schedule B-7; B727-200, average price paid by American, TWA, and United in 1969 (12-31-73); (2) B727-200, average price paid by American, TWA, and United in 1969 (12-31-73); B727-100, average price paid by TWA in 1969 (12-31-73); (3) B727-200, average price paid by United in 1963 (12-31-67); L-188, average price paid by American in 1959 (12-31-73); B727-100, average price paid by TWA in 1969 (12-31-73); (4) B-720B, average price paid by American, Braniff, and United in 1961 (12-31-61); DC-6B, average price paid by United in 1958 (12-31-61); (5) L-188, same as comparison 3; DC-6B, same as comparison 4. *Short range:* (1) DC9-50, average price paid by Eastern in 1978 (12-31-78); DC9-10, same as comparison 2; CV-440, average price paid by Delta and Eastern in 1957 (12-31-61); (3) DC9-10, same as comparison 1; DC9-30, average price paid by TWA in 1966 (12-31-67); (3) DC9-30, average price paid by Eastern in 1966 (12-31-67). **(2)** Price in comparison year is the price shown in col. 1, multiplied by the ratio of the interpolated SMSA price index for identical models in the comparison year relative to the year shown in col. 1, from table 4.4, col. 11. **(3)** Table 4.4, col. 11. **(4)** Ratio of col. 3 to col. 2. **(5)** Ratio of col. 3 to col. 2 for first-listed model to second-listed model. **(6)** Ratio of col. 5 to col. 6, minus 1.0. **(7)** Ratio of col. 5 to col. 6, times col. 6 raised to the −0.2 power, minus 1.0. **(8)** Ratio of col. 5 to col. 6, times col. 6, minus 1.0.

been operated at a loss, with an n/v ratio of just 0.027, while the DC-6B and Convair 340/440 exhibit n/v ratios of 0.156 each, just sufficient to pay depreciation without leaving anything left over for profit. The most profitable aircraft appear to have been the DC8-61 in 1968, the 727-200 in 1968, and the DC9-50 in 1977, with respective n/v ratios of 0.420, 0.416, and 0.478. These ratios may seem unreasonably high, and one reason for this is that the aircraft prices shown in table 4.9 exclude engines, implying a total price about 25 percent higher than shown in column 1 and an n/v ratio about 20 percent lower than that shown in column 4. As long as there has been no significant drift over time in the ratio of engine prices to airframe prices, the omission of engine prices should not influence the remaining results discussed below.

Seven of the fifteen model comparisons in table 4.9 provide net revenue data that cover more than one year. This allows us to examine the pattern of change in the net revenue of new relative to old models as the new models "age" following their year of introduction. To the extent that new models are larger than old models and allow a reduction in labor cost and fuel cost per passenger, we should expect to find that the relative profitability of new models declines less rapidly than that of old models over time as fuel and labor costs rise. And we should expect a discontinuity after the two oil shocks of 1973–74 and 1979–80, since these were events that caused quantum jumps in the price of airline fuel and should have resulted in substantial declines in the profitability of older, less fuel-efficient models compared to new models.

The seven model comparisons in table 4.9 that cover more than one year are based on identical ratios of sales prices (v_1/v_0), but ratios of net revenue (n_1/n_0) that reflect the differing operating conditions of each year. Since the relative price changes displayed in column 7 depend only on these two ratios, they provide a concise summary of changes in profitability over time. The expected decline over time in the profitability of the old model relative to the new model should be reflected in relative price changes in column 7 that shift in a negative direction (either from positive to negative or from negative to more negative).This presumption of a negative shift in the price changes displayed in column 7 is confirmed by each of the seven multiyear model comparisons. Consider, for example, the four multiyear model comparisons displayed for long-range aircraft in part A of table 4.9. The first three of these (L-1011 vs. DC8-61; DC10-10 vs. DC8-61; and B747-100 vs. B707-300B) indicate a relative price *increase* in the year of introduction, but by 1982 a substantial relative price *decrease*. In the fourth comparison, a price decrease of 37.5 percent in 1968 becomes a decrease of 81.6 percent in 1977, as shown in column 7.

While increasing fuel and labor costs were mainly responsible for making older models uneconomical in the 1972–82 period, an additional factor was a change in marketing philosophy. Originally, the new larger aircraft, especially

Table 4.10   **Number of Seats, Seat Widths, and Pitch for United Airlines, for Various Models of Jet Aircraft**

	Total Number of Seats	Seat Width (inches)[a]	Pitch (inches)[a]
Boeing 747	429	17	34
Douglas DC-10	254	17	36
Boeing 767	197	18	34
Douglas DC8-71	191	17	36
Boeing 727-200	147	17	32
Boeing 727-100	108	17	34
Boeing 737-200	109	17	32

Sources: Seating capacity and dimensions from *Great Seats in the Friendly Skies,* brochure, United Airlines, July 1983.

[a]Seat widths and pitch are just for the economy cabin, but the first-class cabin generally contains 10 percent or less of the total seats

the wide-bodied 747, DC-10, and L-1011, were introduced with wider seats and greater "pitch" (i.e., distance between seats) than the narrow-bodied models that they replaced. It is impossible to place a quantitative value on the benefit that passengers received in the early years of the wide-bodied aircraft, since there was no fare differential to test the passengers' willingness to pay for comfort. However, as rising fuel prices created tough times for the airline industry, marketing executives recognized an opportunity to equalize the seating density of wide-bodied and narrow-bodied aircraft. Thus, note in part A of table 4.8 that average seats in the 747 increased between 1972 and 1982 from 317 to 406, in the DC-10 from 225 to 265, and in the L-1011 from 214 to 288.

The presumption is that this shift made the comfort of a wide-bodied aircraft equivalent to that of a narrow-bodied aircraft like the DC8-61 or B707-300, rather than inferior to that of a narrow-bodied aircraft. This is supported by evidence that the seating configurations that have been typical in recent years provide comparable seating width and pitch in older and newer models of jet aircraft. Corroborative figures are available for United Airlines, given in table 4.10. Since seat width is virtually the same, differences in passenger comfort could be attributed only to pitch. However, these figures for seat pitch do not suggest any substantial revision in the net revenue calculations in table 4.8 for 1982, and they *do* suggest that the net revenue of wide-bodied aircraft in their early years (e.g., 1972) was understated due to the temporary provision to the passenger of extra comfort.[10]

10. For instance, that 1982 ratio for the comparison of the DC10-10 with the DC8-61 indicates a seating ratio of 1.327. The ratio for the United configuration displayed in the text is 1.330, almost the same, and these two aircraft as flown by United offer passengers the same seating pitch (the airframe of the DC8-71 is identical to that of the DC8-61, since the two models differ only in the quieter, more fuel-efficient engines installed on the DC8-71). The tighter pitch of the 727-200 than the 727-100 in the United configuration might call for a

The final column in table 4.9 provides an estimate of the relative price change that takes account of the curvature of the function that links the relative price of new models to their relative capacity of earning net revenue. There appears to be no direct way of estimating this function by examining the cross section of planes built at any given time, because the planes built in the long-range, medium-range, and short-range categories are really separate products that defy comparisons. Further, at any given time, only the most advanced plane in each category is constructed. In lieu of any direct evidence on the curvature of the function by which aircraft manufacturers translate extra cost into extra ability to generate net revenue, the curvature parameter used in the calculations in column 8 of table 4.9 has been assigned a value of 1.2, implying diminishing returns, with an elasticity of net revenue to increases in manufacturing cost of $1/1.2 = 0.833$. If an increase in net revenue can be achieved with constant returns in manufacturing cost, then the relative price changes exhibited in column 7 are relevant, whereas a greater degree of diminishing returns would imply the need for a greater curvature adjustment than that shown in column 8.

As noted above, some of the relative price comparisons in table 4.9 are influenced by changes in seating configurations over time; wide-bodied aircraft introduced in the early 1970s initially offered passengers the comfort of wider seats than on narrow-bodied aircraft, but gradually these seats were replaced by the standard seats with which other jet aircraft were equipped. At least part of the relatively low profitability of wide-bodied aircraft in table 4.9 in 1972 can be explained by low seating capacities. To investigate the importance of this point, table 4.11 repeats the curvature-adjusted price changes from column 8 of table 4.9 and compares these with equivalent price changes recalculated to hold constant the seating capacity of aircraft (the base year is the most recent year shown in table 4.11, designated by an asterisk). For instance, the first pair of models shown, the L1011-100 and DC8-61, exhibit a relative price *increase* of 102.6 percent in the introductory year of 1972, but when net revenue for both aircraft is recalculated with 1982 seating capacities(which raises annual capacity and reduces operating cost per unit of capacity), the relative price increase is a much smaller 22.8 percent. The average relative price *decline* in the comparisons displayed in table 4.11 is 22.3 percent with actual seating capacities and 28.0 percent with standard base-year seating capacities.

The relative price changes with standardized seating configurations exhibit a consistent pattern in almost all the model comparisons. There is little

---

"comfort adjustment." But this would be minor: the seating capacity ratio in pt. B of table 4.8 for 1982 is 1.319, and the United ratio for 1983 with the differing comfort is 1.361. Assuming that a thirty-four-inch pitch for the coach cabin of the United 727-200 would reduce seating capacity from 147 to 139, for a seating capacity ratio for the 727-200 vs. the 727-100 of 1.287. This would reduce the annual net revenue figure for the 727-200 given in pt. B of table 4.8 by only 2.4 percent, not enough to create any appreciable change in the results.

Table 4.11   **Relative Price Changes Calculated with and without Standard 1982 Seating Configuration (includes curvature adjustment)**

Models in Pair	Year	Actual Configuration (1)	Standard Base-Year Configuration (2)
L1011-100	1982*	−0.681	−0.681
DC8-61	1977	0.185	−0.076
	1972	1.026	0.228
DC10-10	1982*	−0.569	−0.569
DC8-61	1977	0.131	−0.112
	1972	0.160	0.123
B747-100	1982*	. . .	. . .
B707-300B	1977	−0.564	−0.647
	1972	−0.166	−0.391
DC8-61	1977*	−0.876	−0.876
DC8-50	1972	−0.370	−0.436
	1968	−0.461	−0.447
B727-200	1982*	. . .	. . .
B727-100	1977	−0.702	−0.592
	1972	−0.555	−0.447
DC9-30	1982*	−0.417	−0.417
DC9-10	1977	−0.536	−0.338
	1972	−0.405	−0.213
	1967	−0.291	−0.180
Average for years Other than Base Year		−0.213	−0.280

Source: Tables 4.8 and 4.9; method explained in text.

*Base year.

difference in the relative price changes recorded for 1967–68 and 1972, but then the relative price change shifts in a negative direction between 1972 and 1977 and again between 1977 and 1982. The pattern reflects the influence of the 1973–74 and 1979–80 oil shocks, which had a greater impact in reducing the estimated net revenue of older models, and hence increasing the estimated relative price decline between the old and new models, due to the higher fuel consumption per seat mile of older models. (The two comparisons designated by ellipses points for 1982 are consistent with a greater advantage of newer models than in 1977, i.e., a greater relative price decline, but in these cases the net revenue of the older model has become negative, preventing the calculation of the extent of the relative price decline.)

4.6   Used Aircraft Prices and Pairwise Model Quality Comparisons

All the pairwise model relative price changes developed in the last section were based on constructed estimates of net revenue. However, the "true" value of one aircraft model compared to another is established in the marketplace for used assets. While many categories of capital goods are either "bolted down" or require high moving costs to be sold, commercial aircraft are among the most mobile of capital goods, and are bought and sold constantly on an active market for used aircraft. It has been estimated that the value of used aircraft transactions involving U.S. airlines has cumulated to $4.5 billion over the 1970–83 period (Avmark 1984). Since it is possible to obtain price quotes or estimates from the used aircraft market for most of the models involved in the comparisons of tables 4.8, 4.9, and 4.11, we can test the implication of the theoretical analysis in chapter 2. There was derived the condition that used asset prices of different models observed at a given moment should be observed to be proportional to their respective ability to earn net revenue. Repeating equation (2.38), we have:

$$(4.7) \qquad \frac{A_{1t}}{A_{0t}} = \frac{N_{1t}}{N_{0t}},$$

where A is the price of the used asset at a given time, and N is net revenue for the same model. In this light, we can view the investigation of used aircraft prices as a test of the validity of the estimates of net revenue (N) contained in the last section. An important reason why the valuation of two models in the marketplace may differ from the net revenue estimates is a different depreciation rate on model 1 and model 2, in contrast to the assumption of identical depreciation rates in the derivation of (4.7) and of the net revenue ratios in table 4.8. For instance, the marketplace knew in 1982 that the DC8-61 aircraft would become obsolete in 1985 under then-announced federal antinoise regulations, and this model is valued less by the used aircraft market than would be implied by our net revenue estimates.[11]

Table 4.12 displays used price quotations for the same years that were chosen above for the pairwise model net revenue comparisons (no quotations for 1967–68 are available). Every model that appears in the net revenue comparisons is also listed here, with the single exception of the recently introduced Boeing 767. Figures enclosed in parentheses indicate actual price quotations (asking prices for 1965, transaction prices for other years), while other figures are estimates made by the *Avmark Newsletter,* a trade publication that covers activity in the used aircraft market. It is evident from table 4.12 that there is a high correlation between price quotations and estimates when both are available for the same model and the same year, and that discrepancies are mainly in the direction of Avmark underestimating the value of newer models, for example, the advanced Boeing 727-200 and the DC9-50. The advantage of including the Avmark estimates is that they provide figures for 1977 and 1982 covering several planes for which no

11. The residual value of the DC8-61 in 1982 was for its conversion potential. It was economically feasible to attach new modern engines to this aircraft model, which was then rechristened the DC8-71. Such conversions were not economical for the nonstretched B-707 and nonstretched DC8-50 models, and so their prices by 1982 had fallen close to scrap value.

Table 4.12   **Prices of Used Commercial Aircraft, Various Years, by Model (in $million)**

	1965 (1)	1972 (2)	1977 (3)	1982 (4)
Long range:				
1. A300-B2	. . .	. . .	19.0	22.5
2. L1011-100	. . .	. . .	22.3	19.0
3. D10-10	. . .	. . .	21.5	18.0
4. B747-100	. . .	. . .	24.0	22.5
5. DC8-61	. . .	(6.7)	6.3 (6.0)	3.0
6. DC8-50	. . .	(2.3)	1.4 (1.7)	0.5
7. B707-300B	. . .	(3.3)	4.0 (3.8)	0.8 (1.3)
8. DC-7	(0.25)	. . .	. . .	. . .
Medium range:				
9. DC9-80	. . .	. . .	. . .	17.5
10. B727-200(ADV)[a]	. . .	. . .	. . .	6.8 (10.2)
11. B727-200	. . .	(5.0)	7.5	5.8 (5.3)
12. B727-100	. . .	(2.7)	2.9 (3.1)	2.0 (1.7)
13. B-720B	. . .	(1.5)	. . . (1.0)	. . .
14. L-188	(1.00)	. . .	. . . (0.4)	. . .
15. DC-6B	(0.35)	. . .	. . .	. . .
Short range:				
16. DC9-50	. . .	. . .	7.0 (9.2)[b]	9.5 (10.7)[c]
17. DC9-30	. . .	(3.8)	4.3 (4.2)	5.3 (5.3)
18. DC9-10	. . .	(2.2)	2.2 (2.8)	2.5 (1.9)
19. CV-340	(0.30)	. . .	. . .	. . .

Note: All numbers in parentheses are actual price quotes, i.e., the average price paid for all aircraft of a given type sold in a given year. Sources for price quotes by year are: 1965: *Aircraft Exchange and Services Newsletter,* no. 130, 8 January 1965 (prices shown are asking prices); 1972, 1977, 1982: prices actually paid are read off charts published in the *Avmark Newsletter,* various dates. The charts cover the period 1970–82 and indicate for each year (1970–77) and each quarter (1978–82) the number of aircraft of a given type sold and the average price received. The charts used and dates of publication are as follows: DC8-50, DC8-61: March 1982, 16; Boeing 720B, 707-120B, 707-320B: March 1983, 16; DC9-10, DC9-30, DC9-50, Boeing 737-200: September 1983, 18; B727-100, B727-200, B727-200 (ADV): October 1983, 20; All numbers not in parentheses are estimates of current market value published semiannually in the *Avmark Newsletter.* Price quotes shown are from the July issue of 1977 and 1982.

[a]ADV stands for the "advanced" B727-200 model.

[b]Price quote refers to 1978 rather than 1977.

[c]Price quote refers to 1981 rather than 1982.

direct price quotations are available, and this allows the study to include virtually the full range of models for which net revenue estimates have been compiled. The fact that Avmark tends to underestimate the value of newer models implies that the use of Avmark estimates tends correspondingly to understate the quality and/or efficiency advantage of new models and the associated relative price decline.

Equation (4.7) suggests that, at a given moment of time in comparing a new model with an old model, the ratio of their used asset price should be equal to the ratio of their net revenue. Table 4.13 displays pairwise model comparisons of net revenue and used price ratios. In the columns labeled u_0/u_1, the numbers in parentheses indicate used price comparisons in which both the numerator and denominator are price quotations as opposed to price

Table 4.13   Net Revenue and Used Price Ratios for "New" and "Old" Model Comparison Pairs

Comparison	1965		1972		1977		1982	
	n_1/n_0 (1)	u_1/u_0 (2)	n_1/n_0 (3)	u_1/u_0 (4)	n_1/n_0 (5)	u_1/u_0 (6)	n_1/n_0 (7)	u_1/u_0 (8)
1. A-300/L-1011	...	...	...	...	...	0.85	1.61	1.18
2. L-1011/DC8-61	...	...	0.92	...	1.44	3.54	4.31	6.33
3. DC-10/DC8-61	...	...	1.46	...	1.49	3.58	3.32	6.00
4. B-747/B-707	...	...	2.89	...	4.97	6.00	...	28.13
5. DC8-61/DC8-50	...	...	1.85	(2.91)	7.16	4.50 (3.53)	...	6.00
6. DC9-50/DC-7	20.57	19.20*	...	...	...	...	...	...
7. DC9-80/B727-200	...	...	...	...	...	...	3.07	3.01
8. B727-200/B727-100	...	...	1.76	1.85	3.08	2.59	...	2.90 (3.11)
9. B727-100/L-188	1.80	4.10*	...	...	...	... (7.75)	...	...
10. B-720B/L-188	2.46	4.00*	...	...	...	... (2.50)	...	...
11. L-188/DC-6B	3.37	2.86	...	...	...	...	...	...
12. DC9-50/DC9-30	...	...	...	...	1.82	1.62	1.90	1.79 (2.00)
13. DC9-30/DC9-10	...	...	1.67	(1.72)	2.06	1.95 (1.50)	1.70	2.12 (2.79)
14. DC9-10/CV-340	10.35	9.33*	...	...	...	...	...	...

Sources by column: (**1, 3, 5**) Table 4.9, col. 6. (**2, 4, 6**) Table 4.12.

Note: Parentheses indicate that both components of the ratio are actual price quotations. An asterisk indicates that the price quotation for the newer model is the1965 price of a new aircraft. See text.

estimates, and numbers without parentheses indicate that both numerator and denominator are Avmark price estimates.[12] A count of table 4.13 indicates twenty-one cases in which a pairwise net revenue ratio can be compared with a used asset price ratio (when both price quotations and Avmark estimates are available, only the ratio based on the former is counted). The unweighted average of the twenty-one used asset price ratios is 4.26, considerably higher than the 3.89 average for the twenty-one corresponding net revenue ratios. Excluding the extreme values for the comparison of the DC8-50 and DC-7, with a used asset price ratio of 19.2 and a net revenue ratio of 20.57, the respective averages are 3.52 and 3.06. A cross-sectional regression of the twenty net revenue ratios (n) on the twenty used price ratios (u) yields the following:

$$(4.8) \qquad n = 0.105 + 0.839u, \quad R^2 = 0.556, \; SEE = 1.49,$$
$$[0.15] \quad [4.98]$$

12. In comparisons for 1965 designated with an asterisk, no used price quotation is available for the newer model. In these cases, the price of the newer model is taken to be the price of that model sold new in 1965, from table 4.9. Recall that the data on new prices paid do not include engines, while the price quotations for used models do include engines. Assuming that engines contribute roughly 25 percent of the final total price of a new model, we implicitly treat the used price of a new model in 1965 as equal to $1.00/1.25 = 0.8$ of the price of the corresponding newly produced aircraft. This approach is supported by a comment that appears in the *Avmark Newsletter* (July 1982, 2): "These prices are for the earlier models, with newer models approaching new aircraft prices in value."

where *t*-ratios are in brackets. There is a strong positive association between *n* and *u*, but the standard error of estimate is quite high.

Several speculations may be offered to explain the largest discrepancies between the *n* and the *u* ratios in table 4.13. In the first comparison, that between the B-767 and the L-1011, the net revenue technique registers a relative price *increase* of 35 percent, while the used price comparison registers a relative price *decrease* of 49 percent. This comparison should not be given much weight, since there is no used price observation available for the brand-new 767 in 1982, and I use the price of the new aircraft instead (see n. 13 below). Most of the 767 aircraft sold in 1982 and 1983 were to airlines that had placed orders in 1978–79 when expected fuel prices for 1982 were much higher than actual prices turned out to be. The relative price increase indicated by the net revenue calculation in column 3 suggests that the operating efficiency of the 767 did not compensate for its high purchase price at the actual fuel prices of 1982. Airlines that might have wanted to back out of this transaction may have been prevented from canceling orders by stiff cancellation penalties. The makeshift device of comparing the price of the new 767 with the price of a used L-1011 may appear to be responsible for the problem, but the same technique leads to a close correspondence of the net revenue ratio and the new/used price ratio in the 1965 comparisons of the DC8-50 and DC-7 and of the DC9-10 with the Convair 340/440.

The net revenue technique appears to value the DC8-61 significantly more highly than does the used aircraft market. This probably occurs because the net revenue approach treats the expected lifetime of all aircraft as identical in a given year, whereas the used aircraft market "knew" that federal antinoise regulations would make the DC8-61 obsolete in 1985 without expensive engine "retrofitting" (see n. 12 above). The net revenue technique also appears to undervalue the B727-100 and B720B relative to the Lockheed Electra (L-188), since the net revenue calculation is based strictly on profit potential and assumes that both new-model and old-model aircraft operate at the same load factor. This neglects the additional passenger comfort and time savings made possible by the B727-100 and other early-generation jet aircraft that made the L-188 obsolete less than ten years after its introduction in 1958–59.

The treatment of used aircraft prices incorporates a feature that may appear to be peculiar, and this is that depreciation is assumed to be purely economic, with no depreciation attributed to physical wear and tear or to the passage of time. Thus, prices of used aircraft are compared in tables 4.12 and 4.13 without regard to their age. This would seem to create a bias when the used price ratios are interpreted as measuring the relative quality of new and old models of a given age, since part of the higher used price paid for the newer model must surely include an allowance for depreciation. While plausible, this qualification is not likely to be of major importance. First, physical depreciation is much less important for aircraft than for automobiles and trucks, both because of virtually continuous maintenance and because of the absence of direct contact with corrosive materials like road salt. Second, in table 4.13, we have successive observations on the used aircraft price ratios of new and old models of roughly the same age—B727-100 and early B727-200 aircraft manufactured in, respectively, 1964–67 and 1967–70, and DC9-10 and DC9-30 aircraft manufactured only a few years apart, in 1966–68 and 1968–70. While the newer model in these pairs was substantially younger in 1972, by 1982 the newer model was only marginally younger (e.g., fourteen vs. seventeen years). Thus, if physical depreciation had been important, we should have expected the price differential between the newer and the older model to narrow, but in fact the differential was substantially wider for both cases, supporting the hypothesis that economic depreciation dominates physical depreciation. Another persuasive example of the importance of economic depreciation is the case of the piston DC-7, since aircraft of this type that were newly manufactured in 1958 were declared to be worth only scrap value just a year later.[13] Some of the most dramatic implied relative price declines between old and new models were those involving the first-generation long-range jets, for example, the DC8-50 and the B707-100, and these aircraft replaced final-generation piston aircraft that in many cases were only two or three years older.

4.7   Price Indexes Adjusted for Changes in Operating Efficiency

Overall, it appears from the used price comparisons that the measures of relative price change between old and new models based on net revenue data may be too conservative. But, by not allowing at all for physical depreciation, the measures of relative price change based on comparisons of used aircraft prices may be too liberal, and this section develops real and nominal price indexes based on both data sources. Table 4.14 summarizes the ingredients in the calculation. The various pairwise model comparisons are listed as before by stage length and are allocated to chronological "generations." Several aircraft of a given stage length are allocated to the same generation if they were manufactured simultaneously for a substantial length of time, as in the case of the B-747, L-1011, and DC-10, but to different generations if the manufacture of the older model was terminated on the introduction of the newer model or soon thereafter. The newer model of each comparison is indicated in column 1, and column 2 lists other similar models that are treated as being essentially identical for the purpose of assigning weights. Relative price changes between old and new models

13. Thus, a study completed in February 1959 predicted that, by the end of 1959, a brand-new DC-7 would be worth only scrap value (see Sobotka 1959, table 6, p. 18). Other models predicted to reach scrap value by 1961 include the DC-3, DC-6, and all models of the Lockheed Constellation (L-049, L-749, etc.).

Table 4.14   **Relative Price Changes and Weights Used in Calculating Quality-Adjusted Relative Price Index**

Generation Number and New Model (1)	Other Models Included (2)	Relative Price Change (Tables 4.6–4.7) (3)	Ratio of Used Aircraft Prices (4)	Relative Price Change from (4) (5)	Years of Transition and Weight (6)	
Long range:						
1. DC8-50	B707-100B	− .929	19.20	− .923	1959–60	1.00
	B707-300B					
2. DC8-61	. . .	− .586	4.15	− .761	1967–68	0.35
3. L1011-100	. . .	− .126	4.94	− .729	1972–73	0.10
					1974–75	0.01
DC10-10	. . .	− .186	4.79	− .722	1971–72	0.22
					1974–75	0.02
B747-100	. . .	− .519	6.00[a]	− .652	1970–71	0.59
					1974–75	0.06
4. B767-200	B-757	.354	1.76	− .491	1982–83	0.50
A300-B2	. . .	− .560	1.01	− .236	1978–79	0.25
Medium range:						
1. L-188	. . .	− .599	2.86	− .511	1958–59	1.00
2. B727-100	CV880,990	.065	5.92	− .745	1964–65	0.70
B-720B	. . .	− .286	3.25	− .488	1961–62	0.30
3. B727-200	. . .	− .478	2.52	− .622	1967–68	1.00
4. DC9-80	. . .	− .557	3.01	− .546	1982–83	1.00
Short range:						
1. DC9-10	. . .	− .758	9.33	− .726	1966–67	1.00
2. DC9-30	B737-200	− .287	2.00	− .521	1968–69	1.00
3. DC9-50	. . .	− .506	1.81	− .491	1978–79	0.20

Sources by column: **(1)** Models shown are the ''new models'' chosen for the comparisons in tables 4.5 and 4.6. The ''old models'' in each comparison are those displayed in tables 4.5 and 4.6. **(2)** These models were treated as being essentially identical with the new models displayed in col. 1 for the purposes of establishing the weights for individual models shown in col. 6 and those for the long-range, medium-range, and short-range classifications shown in table 4.10. **(3)** These figures are from table 4.7, col. 2, for those comparisons where several years of alternative net revenue data are available. Figures for the other comparisons not shown in table 4.7 come from table 4.6, col. 8. **(4)** This is the ratio of the used aircraft price of the new model to the used aircraft price of the old model in the same comparison. In each case, the figure shown is the ratio of the price shown for each model in table 4.9, averaged over the years in that table where a price estimate or quotation for both models is available. For instance, table 4.9 shows that a price comparison for the A-300 with the L-1011 is available only for 1982, whereas a price ratio between the DC9-30 and DC9-10 can be established for three years, 1972, 1977, and 1982. In those cases where both a price estimate and a price quotation are available for both models in a given year, the quotation is always used in preference to the estimate. In several comparisons, the ''new model'' was so new that no price quote or estimate was available. In these cases, the used price was estimated as the new aircraft price for that year (from table 4.6). Since the new aircraft prices do not include engines, allowing 25 percent of the value of the airframe for engines would imply that these proxy prices are 80 percent of the price of the new aircraft. Used prices were estimated in this way for the following models and years: B-767 (1982), DC8-50 (1965), B727-100 (1965), B-720B (1965), and DC9-10 (1965). **(5)** This is calculated in the same way as table 4.6, col. 6, with the used aircraft price ratio in col. 4, u_1/u_0, substituted for the net revenue ratio n_1/n_0. **(6)** The years of transition are those used in table 4.11 to phase in the relative price changes shown in table 4.10. In each case, they are pairs of years, with the first chosen to be the initial year when significant deliveries were made to domestic trunk airlines. Weights were established for particular aircraft in a particular generation by taking its share of total sales in the relevant category. Source for numbers of aircraft sold by model is *Aerospace Facts and Figures,* issues dated 1961, 1969, 1974/75, and 1981/82. Source for average price of each model is the set of worksheets underlying table 4.2.

[a]The extreme value for 1982 is omitted.

implied by the net revenue ratios and used price ratios are indicated in columns 3 and 5, respectively.

The task of converting the relative price changes in columns 3 and 5 into Törnqvist price indexes is carried out in two steps, the first of which is to determine weighted average relative price changes within the three length-of-haul categories, and the second of which determines the weighted average of these three sets of price changes. The first step allocates the relative price changes between old and new models to pairs of "transition years,"chosen as the first two years of production of the new model. The choice of two transition years, rather than one, helps smooth the final price index and also takes account of the fact that production may continue on the last few aircraft in an older generation after production has started on the first aircraft in the new generation. Then a weight, based on the value of production, is determined for each model within its "generation" of long-haul, medium-haul, or short-haul aircraft. In several cases, this is straightforward, since there was only a single model in a given generation, and it can be allocated a weight of 100 percent. In other cases, there are several models within a given generation, as for the third generation of long-haul aircraft comprising the L-1011, DC-10, and B-747, and weights based on the value of production are determined by the share of each aircraft in the total production run of its generation (1970–77 for long-haul generation 3, and 1961–66 for medium-haul generation 2). When a previous generation remains in production, the weights on the next generation do not sum to 100 percent, as in the case of the short-range DC9-30 and B737-200, which were produced simultaneously along with the newer DC9-50, and the long-range B707-100 and B707-300, which remained in production along with the stretched DC8-61.

The weights shown in column 6 of table 4.14 then determine the relative price change within each length-of-haul category for each year. As an example, the "third generation" DC9-50 is allocated a weight of 20 percent in the short-haul category. The relative price change between the second and the third generations based on net revenue data from table 4.9 is indicated as -50.6 percent in column 3. Thus, the price change on the net revenue basis for the short-haul category in the two transition years 1978–79 is calculated as $(-.506)(.2)(.5)$, which equals -5.06 percent. On the used price basis, the relative price change in column 5 is indicated as -49.1 percent, implying a corresponding price change in the short-haul category for 1978–79 of -4.91 percent. In years between transition years for each category, the relative price change is set equal to zero. Thus, in the short-haul category, the relative price change on the net revenue basis is calculated as -37.9 percent for 1966–67, -14.35 percent for 1968–69, -5.06 percent for 1978–79, and zero for all other years between 1958 and 1983. Since no data are available to make model comparisons on either the net revenue or the used price basis before 1958, assume zero relative price change in all three categories for the period 1947–57.

Table 4.15   Two "Real" Price Indexes for Commercial Aircraft and Weights by Category, 1957–83

	Value Weights (Percent)			Real Price Indexes	
	Long Range (1)	Medium Range (2)	Short Range (3)	Net Revenue Basis (4)	Used Price Basis (5)
1983	51	32	17	0.78	0.65
1982	33	38	29	0.82	0.77
1981	45	36	18	0.88	0.90
1980	68	19	14	0.88	0.90
1979	63	24	13	0.88	0.90
1978	53	34	14	0.93	0.92
1977	55	30	15	0.97	0.94
1976	66	17	18	0.97	0.94
1975	60	22	19	0.97	0.94
1974	65	19	16	0.98	0.95
1973	75	19	6	1.00	0.97
1972	78	11	11	1.00	1.00
1971	78	8	14	1.02	1.10
1970	76	10	14	1.18	1.39
1969	37	22	41	1.35	1.63
1968	37	25	38	1.42	1.83
1967	40	26	34	1.69	2.36
1966	37	46	17	2.18	3.18
1965	46	52	2	2.33	3.39
1964	39	61	. . .	2.31	3.92
1963	53	47	. . .	2.28	4.66
1962	55	45	. . .	2.29	4.66
1961	35	65	. . .	2.32	4.82
1960	80	20	. . .	2.39	5.06
1959	67	32	1	3.91	8.02
1958	48	47	5	6.73	13.23
1957	. . .	. . .	. . .	7.83	15.11

Sources by column: **(1–3)** Same as table 4.10, col. 6. **(4)** Relative price changes from table 4.10, col. 3, phased in during the transition years shown in table 4.10,col. 6, using the weights shown in the same column. **(5)** Same as col. 4, using relative price changes from table 4.11, col. 5.

The second step is to convert these relative price changes within the three length-of-haul categories into two aggregate real price indexes, one on the net revenue basis and one on the used price basis. Weights based on the value of production for each of the three categories are exhibited in the first three columns of table 4.15.[14] These weights are used to combine the relative price changes for the three length-of-haul categories into the two Törnqvist indexes displayed in columns 4 and 5 of table 4.15. As we might expect, the most rapid decline in both real price indexes occurred in 1958–60, as a result of the replacement of the piston DC-6 and DC-7 series by the turboprop Lockheed Electra (L-188) and the pure jet Boeing 707 and

14. Sources for the value of production are the same as those listed in the notes to col. 6 of table 4.14.

720, and the Douglas DC-8. Both indexes also decline rapidly during the period of the introduction of the first short-haul jet airliner, the DC9-10, in 1966–67, and the introduction of the stretched DC8-61, B727-200, and DC9-30 in 1967–69. There is little further decline in the net revenue index, while there is a substantial further decline after 1970 in the index based on used aircraft price ratios. This discrepancy reflects the greater quality differential attributed by the used price method to the long-range DC-10 and L-1011. An even greater discrepancy occurs between 1963 and 1966, because the used price method rates the medium-range B727-100 as much higher in quality than the L-188 that it replaced, whereas the net revenue method places no value on passenger time or comfort and treats the two aircraft as comparable. The fact that the L-188 was retired from trunk airline service by the late 1960s, whereas several hundred B727-100 aircraft were still in trunk airline service in 1985, suggests that the net revenue method is too conservative in this example. A straightforward way to summarize the two different real price indexes is to display their annual percentage rates of growth before and after 1972:

	Net Revenue Basis	Used Price Basis
1957–72	− 12.8	− 16.6
1972–83	− 2.2	− 3.8

Table 4.16 (as well as Fig. 4.1) displays four nominal price indexes for commercial aircraft. The SMSA and BEA indexes are copied from table 4.3 and refer to identical models, with no attempt to measure the price change that occurs when one model is replaced by another. The two new indexes consist of the SMSA index for identical models multiplied by the two real price indexes from table 4.15, one on the net revenue basis and one on the used price basis, that measure the change in price between one model and its replacement. Overall, the two new indexes provide a radically different verdict on price changes in the commercial aircraft industry than do the SMSA and BEA indexes, which implicitly ignore nonproportional quality change between old and new models. The difference between the SMSA and the BEA indexes appears to be minor when compared to the enormous contrast with the two new indexes, and between the two new indexes themselves.

4.8 Conclusion

A review of the estimation procedures suggests little reason to doubt the overall implications of the index based on used aircraft price ratios, although

Table 4.16   **Nominal Price Indexes for Identical Models and After Adjustment for Quality Change (1972 = 100)**

	SMSA Index (1)	BEA Index (2)	Net Index Net Revenue Basis (3)	New Index Used Price Basis (4)
1983	223.4	253.3	174.3	158.6
1982	217.3	247.8	178.2	173.8
1981	195.4	224.1	172.0	173.9
1980	177.8	204.3	156.5	158.2
1979	161.5	182.2	142.1	143.7
1978	152.1	163.6	141.5	138.4
1977	139.3	152.2	135.1	129.6
1976	125.1	138.8	121.4	116.3
1975	116.0	123.4	112.5	107.9
1974	108.9	115.2	106.7	103.5
1973	103.6	104.1	103.6	100.5
1972	100.0	100.0	100.0	100.0
1971	98.8	98.1	100.8	108.7
1970	94.8	94.0	111.9	137.5
1969	91.9	88.7	124.1	162.7
1968	89.7	85.6	127.4	176.7
1967	87.0	83.0	147.0	219.2
1966	86.9	80.0	189.4	283.3
1965	86.2	78.7	200.9	297.4
1964	84.7	77.1	195.7	330.3
1963	83.0	78.7	189.2	374.3
1962	79.9	75.5	183.0	360.4
1961	79.4	73.2	184.2	369.2
1960	80.4	82.3	192.2	389.9
1959	78.3	72.1	306.2	592.7
1958	78.0	69.6	524.9	954.7
1957	78.2	68.5	612.3	1,087.8
1956	77.7	65.2	608.4	1,080.8
1955	77.4	59.8	598.2	1,062.7
1954	74.2	57.5	581.0	1,032.1
1953	69.6	56.8	545.0	968.1
1952	66.4	55.6	519.9	923.6
1951	61.9	55.9	484.7	861.0
1950	64.1	49.0	501.9	891.6
1949	56.6	46.5	443.2	787.3
1948	54.0	44.7	422.8	751.1
1947	53.9	41.9	422.0	749.8

Sources by column: **(1–2)** Table 4.3, cols. 2 and 3. **(3–4)** Table 4.3, col. 1, times table 4.11, cols. 4 and 5.

there is obviously a margin of error in the sense that different data sources and different choices of weights and transition years would influence the final price index. But it is hard to "argue with the market," especially with the basic fact that the used price ratio of new to old models is much higher than the ratio of their prices when new. And the fact that these ratios of used aircraft prices widened rather than narrowed over time, despite the narrowing

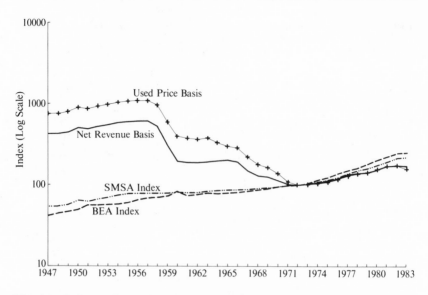

Fig. 4.1   Indexes of new aircraft prices, 1972 = 100

relative difference between the ages of the new and the old models, suggests that economic depreciation dominates any minor effect of physical depreciation in the used aircraft market.

As for the net revenue ratios, they are more likely to be too conservative, in the sense of attributing too little rather than too much net revenue advantage to the newer models and thus understating the rate of relative price decline. As several of the examples above suggested, the net revenue method understates the advantage of new models by placing no value on passenger time or comfort, and by assuming that the expected lifetime of all models is the same. Likewise, no value is placed on intangibles like reliability, in contrast to the market contrast in reliability of piston and jet aircraft suggested by the following quote: "In the piston era, experience showed a dual engine failure rate of one per 8 million operating hours, compared with a 'probability rate' of one per 1 billion hours for jet transports. There is so far no recorded instance of such a dual failure in 25 years of jet operations" (*Aviation Week and Space Technology,* 17 December 1984, 24).[15] Yet speed, comfort, and reliability can all be valued by the used aircraft market, and on average the ratios of used aircraft prices between new and old models are greater than the corresponding net revenue ratios.

15. Another achievement of modern jet technology has been witnessed as two-engine jet aircraft have been allowed to fly the North Atlantic. As reliability has been proven, the rules for the number of minutes these aircraft can remain away from the closest airport have been extended. As of mid-1989, there has been no single instance of an engine failure on a two-engine jet aircraft since such flying began in 1985.

Table 4.17   **Comparison of Growth Rates of Various Indexes of Prices and Employee
Compensations, in Annual Percentage Growth Rates**

	1947–72	1972–83
1. Compensation per FTE employee	6.3	8.6
2. BEA price index	3.5	8.8
3. New index net revenue basis (NRB)	−5.6	5.2
4. New index used price basis (UPB)	−7.7	4.3
5. Addenda: Comparison-BEA	2.8	−0.2
6. Addenda: Comparison-NRB	11.9	3.4
7. Addenda: Comparison-UPB	14.0	4.3

Sources: Rows 1–4 from table 4.16. Rows 5–7 from table 4.1.

One subtle source of error may create a further presumption that the net revenue technique understates the advantage of new models. Consider the amazingly high ratios of net revenue to aircraft price arrayed in table 4.8, column 4, ranging as high as 60 percent. This is far higher than the likely cost of capital and makes us wonder why the airline industry has not been more profitable. One possibility is that the approach used in tables 4.8 and 4.9 may systematically overstate revenue or understate costs, leading to exaggerated estimates of net revenue. If this tendency were corrected, all net revenue figures would be squeezed, and the older planes would be pushed closer to break-even status, thus increasing the relative net-revenue advantage of the newer models. Another important source of conservatism in the estimates is the decision to use the same utilization rates for new and old models. The actual utilization rates for piston aircraft were uniformly lower than for jets, allowing them to earn even less net revenue than indicated in my calculations. One hopeful note is that the net revenue earned on the older models declines over time and becomes negative at roughly the date when these aircraft were retired from U.S. trunkline service, for example, the estimated net revenue of the B707-300 becomes negative in 1982, about the same time that this model was phased out by the last airlines using it (American and TWA) in 1981–83.

This chapter began with the working hypothesis that the official BEA index for equipment cost overstates aircraft price increases more before 1972 than afterward, leading to a corresponding understatement of the growth rate of real equipment investment and the real capital stock of aircraft. The observed post-1972 slowdown in the growth of labor productivity in the airline industry thus might be partly explained by a slowdown in the growth rate of capital input that is greater than is implied by official equipment price indexes. The chapter supports the hypothesis and yields two new price indexes for aircraft that decline in nominal terms before 1972 and rise thereafter. An interesting contrast is provided by the juxtaposition of the growth rates of the various price indexes from table 4.16 with the growth rate of employee compensation from table 4.1, listed in table 4.17. Thus, according to either of the new indexes, the incentive to substitute capital for labor was much greater before 1972 than afterward, and the BEA index understates this post-1972 shift by a wide margin. It remains to be seen whether studies of other major capital goods indicate a similar tendency for a greater overstatement of price increases prior to 1972 than afterward.

To the extent that this study "explains" the slowdown in productivity growth in the airline industry by the mismeasurement of nonproportional quality change in the production of aircraft, it just shifts the puzzle of the productivity slowdown back one industry from airlines to aircraft manufacturing. At the beginning of this chapter, I suggested that, if profit margins were constant, then the difference in the growth rates of compensation per employee and in equipment cost could serve as a proxy for productivity growth in the aircraft manufacturing industry. As shown by table 4.17, the difference between compensation per employee and the two new equipment price indexes (NRB and UPB) is much greater than for the BEA equipment price index. This difference decelerated after 1972 by 8.5 points according to the NRB index and by 9.7 points according to the UPB index, as contrasted to a slowdown of 3.0 points according to the BEA index. The leading hypothesis to explain this slowdown in the rate of nonproportional quality improvements is Nordhaus's (1982) "depletion hypothesis." The aircraft airframe and engine industry had no "bag of tricks" to match the discovery of the jet engine and the swept-back wing, and many of the quality improvements made after 1960 took the form of making aircraft larger. But the limit was reached with the Boeing 747 and Douglas DC-10, and it is likely that we will be traveling in those aircraft (or slightly improved versions thereof) well into the twenty-first century.

5 Electric Utility Generating Equipment

5.1 Introduction

Electric utility generating equipment is the second case study of the methodology proposed in chapter 2. Like the commercial aircraft that were the subject of the previous chapter, data availability and the importance of energy as a factor input justify the choice of electric generating equipment for detailed scrutiny. As in the case of aircraft, government regulation of the industry using the equipment provides a wealth of data on the performance of equipment, as well as its operating characteristics. Another similarity to aircraft is the sequence of rapid technical improvements in the first part of the postwar era, followed by a sharp slowdown in the pace of improvements just as the oil shocks boosted the price of energy inputs. As for aircraft, most of the rapid improvements and the subsequent slowdown were achieved by the equipment manufacturer, yet the user industries (airlines and electric utilities) receive credit for the earlier productivity advances and the later slowdown in official productivity data. The main difference between the utility and the airline examples, as we shall see, is that there has been negative efficiency improvement along several dimensions in the electric utilities, while airline efficiency has continued to improve, albeit at a slower pace.

The electric utility industry has attracted a large number of studies by industrial organization economists interested in issues raised by regulation (e.g., Joskow and Schmalensee 1983), as well as by econometricians interested in using the extensive available data to test hypotheses about factor and product demand.[1] More closely related to this study of equipment prices are the studies that attempt to compile quality-adjusted price indexes for the

1. Examples of econometric studies include Bushe (1981), Christensen and Greene (1976), Nerlove (1963), and Wills (1978). A survey is provided by Cowing and Smith (1978).

equipment used in the production of electricity by Barzel (1964), Ohta (1975), and Wills (1978). While these studies cover only the earlier part of the 1947–82 sample period, their results are compared with mine for overlapping intervals in a later section of this chapter.

The basic data source for this chapter is a set of reports submitted by electric utilities to the Federal Energy Administration and its predecessor agencies on equipment costs, quantities and costs of variable factor inputs, and output for each electric generating plant. Coverage is limited to fossil-fueled steam-electric generating plants. Excluded are gas turbine and nuclear generation equipment, as well as equipment involved in the distribution and marketing of electricity. However, this limited coverage still includes the equipment that produces the majority of U.S. electricity, and the dominant role of fossil-fueled generating equipment in causing the slowdown of productivity growth in the electric utility industry is seen in the similarity of the path of postwar productivity growth for the plants covered in this chapter and for the electric utility industry as a whole (see tables 5.2 and 5.3 below).

Section 5.4, after a brief overview of data on changes in productivity and prices of output, inputs, and equipment for the electric utility industry as a whole, presents a display of data on the same variables for the sample of fossil-fuel steam generating plants. The task of creating quality-adjusted price indexes for equipment begins in section 5.5, where hedonic regression equations are run for a cross section of new plants that explain equipment prices in adjacent years ("vintages") by a set of variables that includes equipment characteristics and dummy variables for particular vintages. Then section 5.7 provides estimates of the net revenue provided by each vintage of equipment, so that indexes of quality-adjusted price changes can be constructed from ratios of net revenue to equipment cost, using the methodology of chapter 2.

The implementation of the quality-adjustment methodology in this chapter is more straightforward than in the chapter on commercial aircraft. One simplifying factor is that electricity is a homogeneous commodity, and we do not have to speculate about changes in its quality. More important, electric generating plants are all different, and there is no analogy here to the "model runs" of tens or hundreds of identical units of a particular aircraft model. Thus, in contrast to the involved analysis of the net revenue provided by individual aircraft models in chapter 4, in this chapter the estimates of net revenue are based on simple averages of performance for all units of a given vintage.

5.2   The Technology of Electricity Generation

Although electric utilities are monopolists in the local markets they serve, the aggregate number of these individual monopolies is substantial, in contrast to the very small number of major producers of generating equipment. The relatively large number of buyers in relation to sellers is even more evident when the existence of a substantial export market for equipment is taken into account.[2] Thus, utilities can accurately be described as price takers in the market for new equipment, and they are also "quality takers" in the sense that their choice set is constrained by whatever price-quality combinations are offered by equipment manufacturers on the market at any given time. The R&D expenditures that (at least in the past) have improved efficiency and productivity have taken place in the manufacturing sector, not in the utility industry.

The basic output of the utility industry can be expressed as a stock or a flow. The production process generates "electric power," an instantaneous concept, and the capacity of a generating unit is measured by the amount of electric power that it can produce at a moment in time, measured in kilowatts (KW) or megawatts (1,000 kilowatts, or MW). "Electricity," the flow measure, is the total energy that is produced by creating electric power for a duration of time and is measured in kilowatt hours (kWh). The production process involves the transformation of the internal energy in a fuel source into electrical energy. It takes place in a "power generation cycle" that can be divided into four stages: fuel combustion, steam generation, steam expansion, and power generation. A power generation "unit" operates independently of any other units at a given plant location and consists of a boiler to burn the fuel and to generate and expand the steam, and a turbo-generator that converts high-pressure steam into electric energy through the rotary motion of a turbine shaft. A condensor converts the steam into water to complete the cycle. The entire unit is called a "boiler-turbo-generator," or BTG unit. For the purposes of this chapter, the important aspect of the technology is the jointness of production by the BTG unit, making it impossible to develop price indexes for boilers and turbo-generators separately. Although individual units can be started and stopped independently, the plant is normally treated as the relevant economic entity for regulatory, accounting, and managerial purposes, and the data set, where the plant is the observation, contains no information on the characteristics of the individual units within the plant other than their number.

A central measure of the efficiency of the technical transformation process is the "heat rate" of the cycle, the ratio of input in British thermal units to one kWh of output. The higher the heat rate, the more fuel is being consumed in the production of a given amount of electricity, and the less efficient is the generation process. Although all the data on fuel efficiency in the industry appear to be expressed in terms of the heat rate, a concept that

2. Ohta (1975, 7) cites evidence that in 1957 about 80 percent of the total boiler supply was provided by two firms, Combustion Engineering and Babcock & Wilcock, and that in 1957–59 almost all the turbogenerators were produced by General Electric, Westinghouse, and Allis-Chalmers.

seems to be expressed in more natural units is "thermal efficiency," which represents the fraction of a unit's efficiency as related to a theoretical and unattainable standard of unity.[3] Thus, in assessing changes in the quality of BTG units, heat rate or thermal efficiency is as central a concept as is labor productivity in other applications.

Technical change in the design of BTG units has been aimed primarily at improving the thermal efficiency of the generating cycle by increasing the temperature to which the steam is heated, increasing the pressure of the steam entering the turbine, and reducing the heat that is transferred out of the cycle in the condenser. The technical design frontiers have been limited by the ability of boilers to withstand high temperatures and pressures, and the frontier has been pushed out by advances in metallurgy involving the development of high-temperature steel alloys. In 1948, three-quarters of all planned installations were designed for an operating pressure of under 1,200 psi (pounds per square inch) and over 80 percent for a temperature under 1,000° F. By 1977, over 80 percent were designed to operate at pressures of 2,400 psi and above, and virtually all had temperature ratings above 1,000° F (Bushe 1981, 44–46).

Another improvement was the addition of reheat cycles, which involve draining off steam at an intermediate stage and reheating it to raise the average temperature of the cycle and reduce the moisture content of the steam. As we shall see below, thermal efficiency and labor productivity improved through the mid-1960s and then deteriorated. This is related to the fact that the shift to higher temperatures and to reheat cycles was largely completed during the 1948–57 decade, with little further change thereafter, although the increase in pressure rating continued until the mid 1970s. Another technical development in the 1960s was the "supercritical" boiler (achieving a pressure above 3,200 psi). After reaching a 30 percent share in new installations in the late 1960s, the share of supercritical units fell to 13 percent in 1977, a phenomenon that has been variously attributed to an increase in the cost of capital, uncertainty about future demand growth, and (more important in assessing the quality of capital goods) an unexpected increase in the maintenance burden required by supercritical units.

Throughout the postwar period, the average scale of BTG units has increased, with 70 percent of new units rated below 50 MW in 1948, and 66 percent above 500 MW in 1977. Increased scale has also been a source of improved thermal efficiency, since many of the technical improvements required greater capital expenditures, the expense of which could be partially offset by increased scale. Engineers use a "six-tenths" rule for approximating the additional cost of a capacity increase; that is, a 1 percent increase in capacity increases capital cost by 0.6 percent, reflecting the geometric fact

3. Because the energy contained in one kWh is 3,415 BTU, thermal efficiency equals 3,415 divided by the heat rate, or $TE = 3,415/HR$.

that a 1 percent increase in the volume of a sphere increases its surface area by about 0.6 percent (Moore 1959). Cowing (1970) has dubbed this interaction between increasing scale and technical improvements "scale-augmenting technical change," but it is important to note that its benefits were exhausted in the first half of the postwar era. As Wills (1978, 500) demonstrates, there is little further improvement in thermal efficiency as unit sizes increase beyond 250 MW, and, indeed, after increasing from 21.7 percent in 1948 to 32.6 percent in 1963, thermal efficiency in new plants showed no increase at all from 1963 to 1985.[4]

While economies of scale with respect to thermal efficiency may have been exhausted in the 1950s, as the average size of new units advanced beyond the range of 150–250 MW, there is no evidence that there was a similar termination of improvements in labor productivity due to increased scale. Wills (1978, 501) plots the number of employees against plant capacity and finds increasing returns to scale at all plant sizes. However, in parallel research on labor productivity, I have found that the steady downward shift in labor requirements over new plant vintages continued only through 1968 and then reversed itself from 1968 to 1980 (Gordon 1985).

5.3 Postwar Performance of the Electric Utility Industry

The data used in this chapter cover only a segment of the capital equipment of the electric utility industry, the boilers and turbine generators that produce electricity with fossil fuel ("steam plants"). Excluded are not only nuclear and hydro plants, but also equipment used in transmission, distribution, and bill collection. As shown in table 5.1, steam plants account for roughly two-thirds of electric utility operating expenses (excluding purchased power and taxes), but for just one-third of the book value of the capital stock in place ("plant in service"). Of the $88.3 billion of steam plant in service, $65.3 billion consists of the boiler and turbogenerator equipment with which we are concerned in this chapter, and the remainder consists of land, structures, and auxiliary electrical equipment.

Corresponding to the fact that steam plants account for much less of capital than of operating expenses, the ratio of capital to operating expense is lower for steam plants than for the other major types of capital—nuclear plants and transmission/distribution equipment. Unfortunately, there is no known source of price data for transmission and distribution equipment by vintage, and so it is not possible to extend the coverage of this chapter to that large category of equipment used in the electric utility industry.

4. U.S. Department of Energy (1987, table 14) shows that heat rate did not move outside the rate 32.6–33.0 percent over the entire period between 1963 and 1985.

Table 5.1   **Distribution of Operating Expenses and Plant in Service, Electric Utility Industry, 1983**

	Operating Expenses		Plant in Service		Ratio of Capital to Operating Expense
	$Billion	(%)	$Billion	(%)	
Steam plants:	39.3	(66.8)	88.3	(35.6)	2.2
Fuel	34.0				
Other	5.9				
Land			0.6		
Structures			14.5		
Boiler equipment			48.0		
Turbogenerators			17.3		
Electric and other			8.0		
Nuclear plants	4.1	(6.9)	30.4	(12.2)	7.4
Hydro plants	0.3	(0.5)	6.1	(2.5)	20.3
Other plants (gas turbine, etc.)	0.9	(1.5)	4.5	(1.8)	5.0
Transmission	1.2	(2.0)	38.0	(15.3)	31.7
Distribution	4.0	(6.7)	73.3	(29.5)	18.3
Customer accounts and general administration	9.3	(15.6)	7.4	(3.0)	0.8
Total[a]	59.7	(100.0)	248.0	(99.9)	4.2

Source: U.S. Department of Energy (1983, tables 3 and 2).

[a]Excludes purchased power.

Table 5.2 displays the growth rates over five-year intervals of data on the performance of the utility industry as a whole. The data are obtained mainly from the NIPAs. Unfortunately, the NIPA data include not just electric utilities but also gas and "sanitary services" utilities.[5] In table 5.2 we observe that, while compensation per full-time equivalent (FTE) employee accelerates after 1967, output per FTE employee displays a steady deceleration throughout the postwar period. This pattern of a steady deceleration in productivity growth (with no apparent breaks) contrasts with the airline industry (table 4.1), where there is a sharp break before and after 1972.

The difference between per-employee compensation and output is unit labor cost, and in row 3 this exhibits a small negative growth rate through 1967, followed by a jump in each of the last three periods. The price of coal, represented by the PPI shown in row 4, exploded in the 1967–72 period, well before the first OPEC oil shock, and it seems remarkable that the rate of increase in the price of electricity during the 1967–72 period should have remained so far below the increase in the price of coal.[6] During 1972–77, the rate of increase in the price of electricity was in between that for unit

5. In 1983, there were 513,200 employees in investor-owned electric utilities (Edison Electric Institute 1984, table 90), as compared to 875,000 in the electric, gas, and sanitary category of the national accounts (NIPA, table 6.7B), or 59 percent.

6. In 1980, coal was the fuel used for 66 percent of the electricity generated by fossil-fuel steam plants. Gas (20 percent) and oil (14 percent) account for the remainder.

Table 5.2   **Utility Prices, Costs, and Productivity Annual Growth Rates for Five-Year Intervals, 1947–82**

	1947– 52 (1)	1952– 57 (2)	1957– 62 (3)	1962– 67 (4)	1967– 72 (5)	1972– 77 (6)	1977– 82 (7)	1947– 86 (8)
1. Compensation per FTE employee	7.25	5.46	4.93	5.63	7.57	9.36	9.67	6.95
2. Output per FTE employee	8.01	6.09	5.77	4.57	3.76	1.51	−1.11	4.05
3. Unit labor cost	−0.76	−0.63	−0.84	−0.04	3.81	7.85	10.78	2.90
4. Price of coal	4.31	2.74	−0.82	1.31	14.15	14.97	6.55	5.83
5. Price of electricity	0.76	0.76	0.85	−0.02	3.52	9.95	11.03	3.75
6. PPI used for PDE steam turbine generators	4.09	9.65	−1.79	2.35	4.64	10.15	8.37	5.35
7. GNP deflator	3.18	2.34	1.67	2.30	4.80	6.96	8.12	4.20
8. Real price of coal	1.13	0.40	−2.49	−0.99	9.35	8.01	−1.57	1.63
9. Real price of electricity	−2.42	−1.58	−0.82	−2.28	−1.28	2.99	2.91	−0.45
10. Real price of equipment	0.91	7.31	−3.46	0.05	−0.16	3.19	0.25	1.15

Sources by row: (**1, 2**) Compensation from NIPA, table 6.5A, row 49. Full-time equivalent (FTE) employees, table 6.8A, row 49. Output from table 6.2, row 15. (**3**) Row 1 minus row 2. (**4**) PPI index 05-1. (**5**) NIPA, table 7.12, row 50. (**6**) PPIs used by NIPA to deflate steam turbine generators: 1947–69: 11-73-01-27, "steam turbine generator set"; 1969–82: 11-73-02, "generators and generator sets." (**7**) NIPA, table 7.1, row 1. (**8**) Row 4 minus row 7. (**9**) Row 5 minus row 7. (**10**) Row 6 minus row 7.

Note: NIPA indexes referenced here refer to the numbering system prior to the 1986 benchmark revision.

labor cost and for coal, while after 1977 inflation in electricity prices exceed that in both unit labor cost and coal.

Row 8 computes a "real price of coal" as the difference between the growth rates of the nominal price of coal in row 4 and the GNP deflator in row 7. On average, the real price of coal increased over the postwar period, but this average behavior disguises marked shifts between the 1947–57 decade in which the real price of coal increased slightly, the 1957–67 decade in which a modest decline was observed, the 1967–77 decade in which the real price of coal increased sharply, and the final 1977–82 period in which the real price of coal, somewhat surprisingly, registered a decrease. There were fewer twists and turns for the real price of electricity, as shown in row 9. A continuous decrease occurred from 1947 through 1972, followed by a substantial increase during the 1972–82 decade.

The last piece of information contained in table 5.2 concerns the main topic of this chapter, the price of equipment used by the electric utility generating industry. Expenditures by the utility industry on equipment purchases are deflated in the NIPA by the PDE deflator for "engines and turbines." In recent years, roughly two-thirds of the weight for this PDE component deflator, presumably that accounted for by electric utility spending on new turbine generators, is attributed to the six-digit PPI commodity index for "generators and generator sets" (11-73-01). This, in turn, is based mainly on an eight-digit commodity index for "electric generating plant" (110-125 KW). The specification of this commodity index indicates that it is a gasoline or diesel water-cooled engine, not a steam turbine generator. In contrast, the PDE deflator for generators during the period 1947–69 is based on the 11-73-02-27 index for "steam turbine generator set," an index that was discontinued after 1969. The reason for discontinuance was doubtless the highly atypical small size of the unit priced for the index, since the specification refers to a generator of thirty to forty MW. In contrast, the average size of a new unit in my sample as long ago as 1953 was 118 MW, and by 1967 this average unit size had grown to 530 MW. Assuming that the PPI index for steam turbine generators was discontinued because the unit had become obsolete and was no longer manufactured, it is somewhat surprising that this index was not replaced with one for the typical large unit. Instead, since 1969 neither the PPI nor the PDE deflator have contained any information at all on the prices of steam turbine generators, nor has the PDE deflator been retrospectively revised to adjust for the obvious flaws in the pre-1970 PPI.[7]

The rate of change of the two linked PPI indexes that are used to deflate electric utility generating equipment in NIPA PDE is shown in nominal terms in row 6 of table 5.2 and in real terms in row 10. The most rapid real increase in the real price of equipment occurred in the 1952–57 interval, the period of the electrical equipment conspiracy. There was a modest real decline between 1957 and 1967, followed by a real increase in equipment prices thereafter, with a significant real increase occurring in the period 1972–77. On average, there was an increase in the real price of equipment over the full 1947–82 postwar period.

5.4   Characteristics of the Sample of Generating Plants

Numerous interesting features of the data set are summarized in table 5.3, where the top section shows plant means, the middle section exhibits selected ratios, and the bottom section provides comparisons with the aggregate industry indicators reviewed above in table 5.2. The selected years are chosen to correspond to the years in table 5.2, except for the initial (1948) and terminal (1983) dates, which are dictated by the span of the data. Each cell contains two numbers, the top number indicating the mean for all plants in the sample in a given year, and the bottom in parentheses indicating the mean for new plants built in that year and the two successive years. New plant means are shown for three years rather than one to smooth out erratic

---

7. Information on the history of PPI specifications within the 11-73-02 commodity group was provided in a letter dated 14 May 1979 to me from John Early, chief of the Division of Industrial Prices and Price Indexes of the BLS.

Table 5.3   Basic Characteristics of Plant Sample Means for All Plants (new plants in parentheses)

	1948	1952	1957	1962	1967	1972	1977	1980	1983
Number of plants in sample (new plants per year)	55 (39)	105 (29)	133 (23)	179 (19)	206 (15)	236 (28)	226 (26)	280	186 (11)[a]
Plant means:									
1. Capacity (MW)	148 (87)	167 (184)	244 (221)	348 (349)	460 (661)	630 (850)	835 (891)	847 (878)	1,131
2. Output (million kWh)	817 (478)	896 (991)	1,278 (1,218)	1,623 (1,788)	2,275 (2,979)	3,003 (3,139)	3,708 (3,186)	3,544 (2,463)	4,519
3. Employees (56)	161 (49)	135 (69)	126 (59)	112 (59)	110 (75)	120 (107)	139 (184)	171 (117)	215
4. Maintenance cost ($million)	0.41 (0.08)	0.37 (0.20)	0.47 (0.20)	0.57 (0.40)	0.85 (0.75)	1.74 (1.77)	4.3 (3.9)	6.7 (3.1)	10.4
5. Fuel cost ($million)	3.4 (1.4)	3.5 (2.6)	4.1 (3.3)	4.7 (4.2)	6.2 (6.7)	12.6 (14.3)	49.3 (37.3)	73.9 (45.2)	107.5
6. Equipment cost ($million)	10.4 (8.3)	15.7 (20.6)	24.0 (23.9)	36.7 (38.7)	46.2 (55.6)	66.9 (123.1)	122.1 (228.7)	139.4 (320.1)	217.1
Ratios:									
7. Utilization rate (percent)	66.1 (64.6)	64.2 (65.5)	57.8 (65.1)	50.5 (60.5)	56.0 (55.4)	56.0 (43.9)	50.1 (42.2)	45.0 (33.9)	44.6
8. Output/employee (million kWh/employee)	6.0 (8.2)	7.9 (14.2)	12.1 (22.5)	15.9 (28.9)	22.6 (39.7)	27.6 (31.2)	30.0 (19.0)	23.6 (25.3)	28.5
9. Maintenance cost/ouput ($/thousand kWh)	0.49 (0.25)	0.45 (0.23)	0.52 (0.21)	0.49 (0.23)	0.47 (0.24)	0.70 (0.60)	1.40 (1.55)	3.9 (1.63)	3.2
10. Fuel cost/output ($/thousand kWh)	4.3 (3.2)	3.5 (2.8)	3.6 (2.8)	3.2 (2.7)	3.0 (2.5)	4.6 (5.5)	14.9 (13.8)	27.3 (20.6)	28.9
11. Equipment cost/capacity($/kw)	78 (116)	99 (104)	104 (120)	108 (115)	104 (89)	109 (137)	140 (243)	161 (346)	187
Indexes (1972 = 100):									
12. Row 9/industry wage rate	(164)	(80)	(114)	(69)	(58)	(100)	(165)	(105)	
13. Row 10/price of coal	(134)	(121)	(116)	(102)	(87)	(100)	(124)	(127)	
14. Row 11/PPI for equipment	(219)	(160)	(114)	(120)	(83)	(100)	(107)	(100)	

Note: New plant means in parentheses refer to the average of the vintage indicated by the column label plus the two succeeding vintages, e.g., the means shown for new plants for 1948 actually include the three years 1948–50.

[a]The last three years have been grouped for the means of new plants.

fluctuations in the means attributable to the small number of plants built in each year, and the figures shown for all new plants refer to the first complete year of operation, that is, the year after the year of initial operation that establishes a plant's "vintage." Thus, the new plant means in the column labeled "1948" refer to plants of vintage 1948–50 as operated during the years 1949–51.

In 1980, the sample contained 280 plants, and this coverage represents 30 percent of all fossil steam plants in the United States, but 55 percent of the capacity. The relation between the total industry and the sample is as follows for 1980.[8] The ratio of capacity in the sample to capacity in the total industry has gradually increased over time, from roughly 20 percent in the late 1940s, to 30 percent in the early 1960s, to over 50 percent by the end of the 1970s.[9] The book value of equipment investment in the sample rose from $0.6 billion in 1948 to $40.1 billion in 1980.

Throughout its history, the electric generating industry has been characterized by increasing scale. For new plants, the mean size increased from 100 MW in 1948–50 to 878 MW in 1980–83.[10] Thus, one would expect that the mean size for new plants would always exceed the mean size for the stock of existing plants. This does not always occur in row 1 of table 5.3, because some of the older plants contain added units that were installed subsequently to initial operation. The fact that a plant can contain more than one unit, and that in some cases all units are not installed simultaneously, is the main defect of this data set, since the date of a plant's "vintage" does not uniquely identify the date of installation of all its units. This limitation does not, however, affect the results reported in this chapter, which are based entirely on new plants.

Just as plant capacity increases over time, so does plant output. However, an interesting pattern is evident in the behavior of plant utilization, calculated as output divided by capacity times 8,760 (the number of hours in a year). As shown in row 7, the utilization rate of all plants fell gradually throughout the postwar period. One important cause for this overall downtrend in utilization has nothing to do with the quality of generating plants, and this is the change in seasonal patterns associated with the development and spread of air conditioning (the difference in the average summer and winter peak load is greater now than in the late 1940s, when the winter peak load was somewhat higher owing to the need for more lighting

---

8. Figures for the total U.S. industry are from U.S. Department of Energy (1983, 3).

9. The data set for 1948–71 was obtained from Thomas Cowing and was developed by an unknown method of sampling the available data on steam plants. This is the data set used in the regression study by Wills (1978). Data for 1972–83 were added by my research assistants as new annual versions of the source volume were published by the Department of Energy. Starting in 1972, *all* new plants of vintage 1972 or later were included, as were current operating data for each year for pre-1972 plants already in the sample.

10. The discrepancy between these average plant sizes and the average unit sizes cited earlier is accounted for by the fact that the average number of units in a new plant has ranged from 1.5 to 2.0 over the postwar years (with no noticeable trend).

Table 5.4   **Comparison of Output per Employee for Utility Industry and for Sample, 1948–82**

	Output per Employee (annual percentage growth rate)	
	Utility Industry	Sample
1948–52	8.6	6.9
1952–57	6.1	8.5
1957–62	5.8	5.5
1962–67	4.6	7.0
1967–72	3.8	4.0
1972–77	1.5	1.7
1977–82	−1.1	−1.0
Average growth rate	4.2	4.7

on short winter days). New plants had higher utilization rates than all plants during the 1952–62 interval but had substantially lower utilization rates from 1967 on. This phenomenon of relatively low utilization on new plants constructed in the late 1960s and 1970s may be indicative of unanticipated maintenance problems already alluded to above in connection with the rise and fall of supercritical units; it also may reflect the influence of environmental legislation, which makes some new plants more expensive to operate than their older brethren.

Row 3 exhibits the average number of employees per plant, and row 8 indicates the level of labor productivity, that is, output per employee. The universe of all plants shows rapid productivity growth through 1972, then a leveling off through 1983. An interesting comparison is provided by the growth in output per employee for the entire utility industry (including electric, gas, and sanitary) from row 2 of table 5.2, with the growth in output per employee for our sample of fossil-fuel steam generating plants, given in table 5.4.

The basic pattern of rapid growth followed by a leveling off and decline is observed for both series, but with differences. The deceleration of productivity growth for the entire industry is more gradual and for my sample of plants is more precipitous, with fairly steady and rapid growth through 1967, followed by a rapid slowdown and negative growth rate in the final half-decade interval at about the same rate as for the industry as a whole.

Rows 9 and 10 of table 5.3 display maintenance and fuel cost per unit of output. These both decline in nominal terms through 1967 and rapidly increase thereafter, reflecting both inflation and declining efficiency. Equivalent series are calculated in real terms in rows 12 and 13, where per-unit maintenance cost is deflated by the industry wage rate, and per-unit fuel cost is deflated by the price of coal.[11] This allows us to see more clearly

11. The industry wage rate and the price of coal are taken from table 5.2.

the "U-shaped" pattern of both real unit cost series, with the figures for all plants indicating a trough for real per-unit maintenance cost in 1967 and for real per-unit fuel cost in 1972. For new plants, the pre-1967 decline in real per-unit maintenance cost is less sharp, and the trough for real fuel cost is reached in 1967 rather than 1972.

Finally, row 11 exhibits equipment cost per unit of capacity. After increasing substantially between 1948 and 1952, this remains relatively constant for all plants until 1972, when a rapid increase begins. For new plants, the increase begins after 1967. When expressed as a ratio to the linked PPIs used by BEA in the PDE deflator, there is very rapid decline through 1967, followed by a modest increase.

The methodology developed in chapter 2 calls for the price change from an old model to a new model to be compared with their relative ability to generate net revenue at a fixed set of input and output prices. Since each electric plant is different, the concept of a "model" is not relevant, and I shall treat average figures for each successive "vintage" as if they represented successive models. The figures shown in rows 12 and 13 indicate an improvement in the efficiency of new plants in the usage of maintenance inputs and fuel until 1967 or 1972, and a deterioration after that. The methodology applied below translates this into a greater quality-adjusted decline in equipment prices before 1967 relative to the nominal equipment cost measure in row 11, but a greater increase after 1967.

5.5   Hedonic Price Regressions for Equipment Cost

The first step in the empirical analysis is to estimate hedonic price regression equations for the sample of new plants in which the dependent variable is the ratio of equipment price to capacity. All observations on new plants, as in table 5.3, refer to the year after the "vintage" (i.e., opening year) of the plant. Since the latest year of observation is 1983, the sample of new plants covers the vintages 1947–82. Because of relatively small sample sizes for each vintage, in which the mean values of equipment cost and quality attributes jump around substantially from vintage to vintage, the initial regression results reported in table 5.5 are based on a single equation estimated for the full sample period. The implicit prices (β_j) of j quality attributes (x_{ijt}) are constrained to remain the same over time, and price change is estimated by a string of time dummy variables (D_t):

$$(5.1) \qquad \log p_{it} = \beta_0 + \sum_{t=1}^{N} d_t D_t + \sum_{j=1}^{m} \beta_j x_{ijt} + u_{it} .$$

To test whether the β_j coefficients remained stable over the full set of vintages (1947–79), equation (5.1) is also estimated over shorter sample periods and is tested for structural change.

Table 5.5   **Hedonic Regression Equations Explaining the Log of Equipment Cost per Unit of Capacity All New Plants in Sample, Installation Years 1947–83**

	1947–79	1947–66		1966–79	
	(1)	(2)	(3)	(4)	(5)
1. Log capacity	−0.01	−0.15**	−0.20**	0.05	0.05
2. Log heat rate	0.61*	0.42	. . .	−0.01	. . .
3. Log number of units	−0.07	0.12*	0.16**	−0.15	−0.12
4. Fuel use:					
a. Coal only	0.17*	0.19**	0.16**	0.04	0.03
b. Oil only	−0.00	0.05	0.02	−0.24	−0.25
c. Gas only	−0.07	−0.13	−0.15*	−0.04	−0.05
5. Construction type					
a. Conventional	−0.05	−0.01	−0.02	−0.12	−0.11
b. Semioutdoor	−0.10	−0.04	−0.05	−0.25	−0.24
6. Vintage					
1949–50	0.02	0.04	0.04	. . .	. . .
1951–52	0.01	0.11	0.09	. . .	. . .
1953–54	0.16*	0.29**	0.27**	. . .	. . .
1955–56	0.10	0.31**	0.28**	. . .	. . .
1957–58	0.18	0.36**	0.33**	. . .	. . .
1959–60	0.29*	0.54**	0.51**	. . .	. . .
1961–62	0.26*	0.46**	0.42**	. . .	. . .
1963–64	0.08	0.35**	0.34**	. . .	. . .
1965–66	−0.08	0.24**	0.24*	. . .	. . .
1967–68	−0.04	. . .	. . .	−0.06	−0.06
1969–70	0.20	. . .	. . .	0.23*	0.22*
1971–72	0.33**	. . .	. . .	0.35**	0.36**
1973–74	0.54**	. . .	. . .	0.62**	0.62**
1975–76	0.76**	. . .	. . .	0.86**	0.85**
1977–78	0.73**	. . .	. . .	0.79**	0.79**
1979–80	1.47**	. . .	. . .	1.64**	1.65**
1981–82	1.61**	. . .	. . .	1.79**	1.79**
$\bar{R}^2$	.702	.625	.617	.736	.753
S.E.E.	.229	.153	.154	.270	.259
Observations	231	134	136	101	124

Note: All equations also include a constant and five location dummies, and two additional construction dummies.

*Indicates significance at the 5 percent level.

**Indicates significance at the 1 percent level.

Before turning to the results, a major limitation of the results should be recognized. This is a defect in common with previous hedonic regression studies of this industry and is not unique to this effort. With reference to section 3.4 of chapter 3, we have the "general excluded variable problem." The most important excluded variables are detailed specifications of the units composing each new plant, for example, pressure, temperature, type of coal used (high or low sulphur), and type of air and water pollution control equipment installed. The last omission is potentially serious and may lead us to interpret as price increases the substantial cost increases of generation equipment due to government-mandated pollution control equipment. To treat price indexes for this industry consistently with existing BLS price indexes for automobiles, which treat the cost of mandated pollution control and safety equipment as a quality change rather than a price change, the value of this equipment should be used to adjust the price changes implied by the hedonic coefficients.[12] The absence of variables in the data set for these types of equipment specifications will require us below to introduce rough ad hoc adjustments for this problem.

Fortunately, however, many of the other methodological problems with the hedonic methodology are not present here. For instance, the shifting relation between measured physical and unmeasured performance characteristics, which may have occurred for automobiles, is no problem for electric utilities, where the basic variables in the regression refer to performance, that is, the ability to generate a homogeneous unit of electricity. There is no problem of a shifting relation between list and transaction prices, since the data on the installed cost of equipment are obtained from buyers rather than sellers. Make effects are unlikely to be an important issue, since just two or three manufacturers dominate the industry, and in any case equipment makes are not identified in the data set. There is no "new product" problem, since we are measuring price change for the same product, which converts the same inputs into a homogeneous output, over the full postwar sample period. The only qualification is that factor inputs have not been homogeneous, due to the government-mandated replacement of high-sulphur by low-sulphur coal for some utilities, but this is another aspect of the more general "unobserved pollution control equipment" issue discussed above.

An issue that is of unique importance in the measurement of equipment prices for electric generation is the treatment of economies of scale. That is, if equipment price per unit of capacity declines with increasing average capacity per plant, should this be treated as a decline in the price index for equipment? This issue can be addressed if we write a simplified version of (5.1) in which there are only two vintages being observed, just one dummy variable, and a single quality characteristic, capacity (k_{it}):

$$(5.2) \quad \log(p_{it}/k_{it}) = \beta_0 + \delta_1 D_1 + \beta_1 \log k_{it} + u_{it}, \quad t = 0, 1.$$

If the coefficient on capacity is significantly negative, then economies of scale are present and must be allocated between the manufacturer of equipment and increased market size. If there is an increase in the average capacity of each vintage, then measuring the price change between vintage 0 and vintage 1 as the coefficient on the vintage dummy (δ_1) amounts to attributing all the effect of economies of scale to increased market size. The alternative approach is to measure the change in the equipment price index

12. I defer to the conceptual chapters of the book the more general issue as to whether the BLS treatment of safety and antipollution devices as quality rather than price change is a desirable approach.

(P_t) as the coefficient on the dummy plus the effect of economies of scale in reducing equipment price per unit of capacity, thus crediting the full effect of economies of scale to the manufacturer:

(5.3) $$\log P_1 - \log P_0 = \delta_1 + \beta_1(\log k_1 - \log k_0),$$

where β_1 is the coefficient on capacity in the regression equation (5.2), and k indicates the mean capacity of a given plant.

Since the role of scale economies has a substantial effect on the final price index that emerges from our calculations, some consideration of the proper treatment is appropriate. Reviewing the summary statistics in table 5.3, note that the issue is more important in the first half of the sample period, for the average capacity of new plants increased eight-fold in the interval between 1948 and 1967, but only by about 30 percent from 1967 to 1972, and virtually not at all after that. In the first published study of this industry based on the hedonic regression technique, Barzel (1964) attributed the full effect of economies of scale to the manufacturer, but without any substantive discussion. Ohta (1975) ignores the proper attribution of scale economies and thus implicitly assumes that equipment users consider a 100 percent increase in the capacity of a unit to represent less than a 100 percent increase in its quality. Wills (1978) also presents a price index based entirely on dummy variables for particular years without crediting the manufacturer for any of the effect of higher capacity in reducing equipment cost per unit of capacity.

One way to approach the issue is to ask why generator units were so small in the early part of the postwar period. Either manufacturers did not have the technical competence to produce larger units at reasonable cost, or markets were too small to support the purchase of larger units. If the first explanation is closer to the truth, the increase in scale over time was due to technological progress in the equipment producing industry, which reduced the cost of large units relative to small, and Barzel was right to adjust his price index for the scale effect. If market size rather than technical capability was the operative constraint, the approach taken by Ohta and Wills is correct.

One indirect piece of evidence that supports Barzel is that the average number of units installed per newly constructed plant during the early 1947–50 period was 2.0 rather than 1.0, and six plants in the data set were built with three or four units during that four-year interval. If larger pieces of equipment had been available at a lower cost per unit of capacity, they would have been purchased in place of two or more of the smaller units. This is even more true of boilers than generators, since early practice had been to install more than one boiler per generator.[13] It is universal in technical

---

13. Among the "major advances in the art" of steam-electric power generation in the early postwar years was "almost universal adoption of unit type construction—that is, a single boiler

descriptions of the industry's progress for the increased scale of units (and of plants, since the number of units per new plant did not change) to be attributed to technical progress. For instance, Cowing (1970, 39–40) writes that "the most important design advances contributing to this increased factor productivity have been significant increases in the feasible size of the turbine-generator units and the associated boiler, and in steam conditions. . . . This significant rate of technical change in steam-electric generation has been the result of significant advances in high-temperature metallurgy and in boiler and turbine design concepts." Similarly, Komiya (1962, 166), in his early path-breaking study, attributes increasing scale to the manufacturer: "The fact that it has become possible to build larger and larger generating units realizing the benefit of increasing returns is to be considered as the major achievement of technological progress in this industry." Indirect support of the view that size was constrained by technology comes from an engineering study (Kirchmayer et al. 1955, 613) carried out on units in the range of 50–100 KW: "we have every confidence that continued progress in metallurgy and design skill will make units larger than those now in operation economically feasible." One of their conference discussants stressed that "size must not run ahead of our proved progress in metallurgy. From recent evidence it seems that size has now outrun progress" (609).

The basic regression results are exhibited in table 5.5, where the functional form is assumed to be logarithmic (i.e., all variables other than dummy variables are entered as natural logs). The dependent variable is equipment cost per unit of capacity, and the explanatory variables are capacity, heat rate, and the number of units per plant. In addition, dummy variables are included for type of fuel used, type of construction, location in one of six regions of the country, and, corresponding to the D_t variables in (5.1) and (5.2), plant vintage. Because vintage dummies estimated for individual vintages tend to jump around owing to the small sample size, vintage dummies are included for pairs of years (e.g., 1949–50).

A notable feature of the results, as shown in column 1 of table 5.5, is an absence of price increase over the first two decades of the postwar period, as indicated by the coefficients on the vintage dummies, with a 29 percent increase from 1947–48 to 1959–60 more than offset by a 37 percent decline from 1959–60 to 1965–66. But then price increases began to be substantial, with an increase of 169 percent from 1965–66 to 1981–82 (these percentage changes are calculated as 100 times the change in the log). These price changes compare with increases in the linked PPIs used in the PDE deflator of 72 percent from 1947 to 1967 and 116 percent from 1967 to 1982.

The coefficients on the other variables contain some surprises. In contrast to an economies of scale parameter (β_1) of -0.185 found by Barzel (1964)

---

for each turbine-generator—[which] has helped to reduce plant investment costs as well as annual operating costs" (U.S. Federal Power Commission 1969, ix).

for his early 1947–58 sample period, the scale parameter in column 1 is zero
(−0.01). However, this single parameter disguises a shift in structure over
the postwar years. Columns 2 and 4 display separate equations for the first
and second parts of the postwar period, with the heat rate variable included,
while columns 3 and 5 display separate equations with the heat rate variable
excluded. When equations (with heat rate included) are estimated for the
separate 1947–64 and 1965–82 subperiods, the $F(13,198)$ ratio for a change
in structure in comparison with the full-period equation in column 1 is 2.40,
which is significant at better than the 1 percent level.

Interestingly, this evidence of a change in structure occurs only when the
regional location dummies are included. Without these variables, the F-ratio
for the column 1 specification versus a break at 1965 falls well below the
borderline for 5 percent significance. Yet the regional equipment cost
differences are highly significant and widen substantially after 1965, perhaps
indicating that environmental standards differed widely across regions. For
instance, the regional location dummies indicate that, holding constant other
attributes, equipment cost in the South was 28 percent less than in the
Northeast before 1965, widening to 40 percent less after 1965. Even more
radical was the difference between the Southwest (Texas, Oklahoma, etc.)
and the Northeast, widening from 24 percent before 1965 to 69 percent after
1965.[14] These regional differences seem enormous, especially in light of the
following table, which exhibits regional mean equipment cost per unit of
capacity (in dollars per kilowatt), as well as the number of observations in
each mean, for four subperiods:

Vintage	Northeast	North Central	South	Southwest
1947–55	123 (13)	131 (22)	100 (20)	96 (8)
1956–64	139 (17)	122 (10)	99 (13)	94 (4)
1965–71	111 (8)	122 (14)	89 (14)	77 (4)
1972–79	228 (8)	248 (20)	197 (14)	165 (12)

Between the first and last subperiod, there was no widening of the mean
among the first three regions, while the mean increased in the Southwest by
only 8 percent less (in logs) than in the Northeast. The discrepancy between
the widening gap in the regional dummies, as contrasted with the absence of
such widening in the regional means, may be explained by the shift in the
fuel use dummies, which show a narrowing in the extra cost of coal
compared to gas from 32 percent in 1947–64 to 7 percent in 1965–82.
Thus, in the first period, the fuel dummies play more of a role in explaining
the higher cost of equipment in the North, while, in the second period, the
regional dummies provide more of the explanation.

14. All percentage changes in the text, as in table 5.5 to be discussed below, are calculated as
changes in coefficients on dummy variables, i.e., changes in natural logs, multiplied by 100.

Previous investigators, especially Wills (1978), have devoted considerable attention to the distinction between ex ante and ex post substitution possibilities in the electric generating industry. While factor substitution is difficult and limited after a plant is built, it should be possible to substitute at the design stage, for example, to build a plant with a higher capital cost that uses less fuel. Thus, Joskow and Schmalensee (1983, 47) in their description of generation technology state that "designers of steam-electric plants can increase fuel efficiency at the expense of capital cost." Evidence of this type of ex ante substitution would be found in a negative coefficient on the "heat rate" variable, indicating that a plant with a lower heat rate (i.e., lower fuel use per unit of output) has a higher equipment cost.

Thus, another surprising feature of the results in table 5.5 is the positive coefficient on the heat rate, and this coefficient is significant in the first column. Wills (1978, 503) reports the same finding of perverse coefficients on fuel efficiency and interprets this as the result of omitted attributes. Plants with expensive extra equipment (that is part of the dependent price variable but is not revealed by any of the independent variables) may use extra fuel, thus accounting for the positive coefficient on the heat rate variable in columns 1 and 2 of table 5.5. Because of this finding, Wills rejects all the "many" substitution models that he investigated and concludes that (ex ante) "substitution possibilities are poor" (503). While the heat rate variable is omitted by Wills in his final equipment price regression, table 5.5 exhibits equations for the two subperiods with and without this variable.

Wills's skepticism about the scope for ex ante substitution is also based on results in which labor input (employees per unit of capacity) is entered as an additional explanatory variable in the equipment cost regression. If firms can choose from a menu in which higher capital cost "buys" lower labor input, then one would expect a negative coefficient on the labor input variable. Wills finds, and my research confirms, that the coefficient on labor input is positive. When the log of the employment/capacity ratio is added to the equations in columns 2 and 4 of table 5.5, the respective coefficients (elasticities) are 0.09 and 0.14, respectively, both significant at the 10 percent (but not the 5 percent) level. It seems most plausible to regard the positive coefficients on both the heat rate and labor input as proxying for omitted quality attributes.

5.6 Price Indexes Implied by Hedonic Regression Equations

The price indexes implied by the regression coefficients of table 5.5 are summarized in table 5.6 and are compared there to the linked PPI series used in the PDE deflator and to indexes developed in other studies. All figures in the table are percentage changes (calculated as 100 times the log difference) over selected intervals, and the right-hand column shows the percentage change over the full period between the 1947–48 and the 1981–82 vintages. The linked PPI series is listed in row 1, with a full-period change of 186.8

Table 5.6   Percentage Changes over Selected Intervals in Alternative Price Indexes for Steam-Electric Generating Equipment

	1947–48 to 1957–58	1957–58 to 1965–66	1965–66 to 1971–72	1971–72 to 1981–82	1947–48 to 1981–82
1. NIPA engines and turbines	70.6	−7.9	30.0	94.1	186.8
2. Table 5.5 without capacity adjustment:					
a. Column 1	18.1	−26.4	40.6	128.4	160.7
b. Columns 2 and 4	35.7	−11.4	35.8	143.7	203.8
c. Columns 3 and 5 with heat rate omitted	32.6	−8.9	36.4	142.5	202.6
3. Table 5.5 with capacity adjustment:					
a. Column 1	16.7	−27.6	40.2	127.8	157.1
b. Columns 2 and 4	14.2	−28.8	37.6	146.8	169.8
c. Columns 3 and 5 with heat rate omitted	3.9	−32.1	38.2	145.6	155.6
4. Addendum: change in capacity (table 5.7)	143.4	115.8	36.9	61.5	358.7
5. Barzel	2.8	. . .	. . .	. . .	. . .
6. Wills	−7.5	−24.6	. . .	. . .	. . .

Sources by row: (**1**) See table 5.2 above, notes to row 6. (**2, 3, 4**) Regression coefficients underlying tables 5.5 and 5.7. (**5**) Barzel (1964, table 6, col. 1). (**6**) Wills (1978, fig. 4, p. 507). Wills used dummies for the average of three years. Figures reported in the 1947–48 column are his 1947–49, in the 1957–58 column are his 1956–58, and in the 1965–66 column are his 1965–67.

Note: All percentages are changes in logs multiplied by 100.

percent, as compared with the three indexes in row 2 calculated from the vintage dummy variable coefficients of table 5.5, with full-period changes ranging from 161 to 204 percent. The linked PPI series rose considerably faster than the hedonic indexes during the 1947–48 to 1965–66 subperiod and rose much more slowly between 1971–72 and 1981–82.

The next section of the table calculates changes in price indexes that adjust for the effect of changing capacity, as in equation (5.3). Rather than taking the arithmetic mean of capacity for these calculations, changes in capacity are taken from a regression equation for capacity, as shown in the first column of table 5.7. This "explains" the log of capacity by vintage and by the various dummy variables on fuel use, construction type, and region. Changes in capacity over successive vintages are shown by the vintage dummy variables in table 5.7 and are summarized in row 4 of table 5.6. Thus, the change in the price index shown in row 3 of table 5.6 is simply the change in the corresponding row and column of section 2 plus the change in capacity from row 4 times the coefficient on capacity from table 5.5.

There is no impact of the capacity adjustment with the specification of table 5.5, column 1, which holds constant the coefficient on capacity over the whole period and yields a zero coefficient. Larger adjustments occur in the other two specifications. The first of these, taken from columns 2 and 4 of table 5.5, estimates separate equations for the first and last part of the

Table 5.7   Equations Explaining Fuel and Labor Input, All New Plants in Sample, Installation Years 1947–79

	Log Capacity (1)	Log Heat Rate (BTU/kWh) (2)	Log Employees/ Capacity (3)
1. Log capacity	. . .	−0.08**	−0.73**
2. Log output	. . .	. . .	0.26**
3. Log number of units	1.18**	0.05**	−0.01
4. Fuel use:			
a. Coal only	0.37*	−0.03	0.27**
b. Oil only	−0.11	−0.05**	−0.08
c. Gas only	−0.00	−0.01	−0.09
5. Construction type:			
a. Conventional	−0.04	−0.01	0.05
b. Semioutdoor	−0.26	−0.01	−0.18*
6. Vintage:			
1949–50	0.24	−0.03	0.07
1951–52	1.04**	−0.06**	0.08
1953–54	1.24**	−0.09**	−0.21
1955–56	1.90**	−0.13**	−0.41*
1957–58	1.43**	−0.12**	−0.43**
1959–60	1.89**	−0.13**	−0.57**
1961–62	1.83**	−0.17**	−0.59**
1963–64	2.07**	−0.10**	−0.64**
1965–66	2.57**	−0.09**	−0.74**
1967–68	2.80**	−0.08*	−0.71**
1969–70	2.71**	−0.03	−0.67**
1971–72	2.98**	−0.03	−0.60**
1973–74	2.92**	0.00	−0.40*
1975–76	2.79**	0.01	−0.50*
1977–78	3.09**	0.04	−0.06
1979–80	2.91**	0.01	−0.48*
1981–82	3.59**	0.07	−0.53
$\bar{R}^2$	.756	.698	.808
S.E.E.	.592	.068	.371
Observations	268	229	268

Note: All equations also include a constant and five location dummies.

*Indicates significance at the 5 percent level.

**Indicates significance at the 1 percent level.

sample period (with an overlap in 1965–66). The second is identical but omits the heat rate variable, as in columns 3 and 5 of table 5.5. Because the shift in structure after 1965–66 involves a turnaround in the capacity coefficient from negative to positive, which is disguised by the zero coefficient in the full-period equation, the split equations yield larger estimated scale effects (−0.15 and −0.20, respectively) for the 1947–66 period when most of the capacity increase took place. During the 1947–66 interval, the three specifications summarized in row 3 of table 5.6 yield adjusted price declines of 10.9, 14.6, and 28.2 percent, respectively, a relatively narrow range, especially when compared with the NIPA increase of 62.7 percent. During the 1965–79 interval, the three specifications imply adjusted price increases of 169.0, 179.5, and 168.9 percent, all much greater than the NIPA increase of 124.1 percent.

Why is the lowest cumulative price increase over 1947–66 registered when the heat rate variable is excluded, as in row 3c? This occurs because the omission of the heat rate variable raises the scale effect in this period from -0.15 to -0.20, thus increasing the capacity adjustment made in the transition from row 2c to row 3c. Essentially, the specification that includes the heat rate, which appears with a positive coefficient, explains some of the decline in equipment price per unit of capacity before 1966 as stemming from the decline in the heat rate (i.e., improvement in fuel efficiency). When the heat rate variable is omitted, more of the explanation is "picked up" by the negative coefficient on capacity.

Previous research on price indexes for electric generating equipment has been carried out over shorter sample periods, precluding a full comparison with these results. A table in Barzel's (1964) paper allows a direct comparison with his results over the first decade of the postwar period, indicating that his scale-adjusted price change of just 2.8 percent is extremely close to the 3.9 percent in row 3c, which, like his approach, omits the heat rate variable. This similarity of results, despite several differences in the details of execution (including Barzel's omission of location dummies and technique of smoothing year-to-year equipment price changes by using the GNP deflator as an interpolator), reflects in part an extremely close estimate of the scale effect (-0.185 for Barzel and -0.20 in table 5.5, col. 3). In Wills's (1978) results, summarized in row 6 of table 5.6, the estimated price decline is greater than in any of my results for the first decade, but less than my scale-adjusted results in the second decade. Differences are due to Wills's use of a linear rather than a logarithmic specification and of an instrumental variable technique, as well as his omission of location dummies.[15]

5.7   Adjusting for Changes in Operating Cost

The technique of price measurement proposed in chapter 2 centers around the concept of "net revenue," defined as gross revenue minus operating costs, that is, the amount available for depreciation, interest, and before-tax profits. As applied in the analysis of chapter 4 on commercial aircraft, price differences between old and new models of a given product are adjusted for changes in net revenue yielded by new models. Holding constant the price of a model that remains unchanged, a quality adjustment is made if the ratio of net revenue generated by the new model relative to the old model does not

---

15. Wills (1978, table 2, p. 506) presents an alternative set of results with random coefficients estimation that exhibits virtually no price decline between 1947–49 and 1965–67.

equal their ratio of sales prices. To repeat equation (2.35) from chapter 2, the change in the real input price index (dp/p) that holds constant the cost of producing identical models is

(5.4) $$dp/p = [v_1 n_0]/[v_0 n_1] - 1,$$

where v designates the purchase price of models 1 and 0, and n designates their respective net revenue.[16] For the purpose of the calculations in this chapter, it is convenient to express (5.4) in logs:

(5.5) $$d \log p = d \log v - d \log n.$$

Expressions (5.4) and (5.5) both state that the "real" price change will be zero if both purchase price (v) and net revenue (n) change in proportion between model 0 and model 1. The nominal price index P is then obtained by adding the change in the real input price from (5.4) to the change in the price index for identical models (C). Copying (2.36) and converting to logs, we have:

(5.6) $$d \log P = d \log p + d \log C.$$

The task of this section is to compute a time series on net revenue for my sample of generating plants to be inserted into (5.5) and (5.6). In contrast to my study of commercial aircraft, where data on discrete "models" are available, the data set on electric generating plants contains no such model identification, and in fact each boiler-generator unit is unique. An obvious alternative is to treat each "vintage" of electric generating plants as a "model" for the purpose of computing the components of (5.5) and (5.6). Because the size and average equipment cost of plants tend to jump erratically from year to year, we compute the net revenue and equipment cost ratios needed in (5.4) for *pairs* of vintages (e.g., 1947–48, 1949–50, etc.). This is the same procedure already followed in the hedonic regression equations presented in table 5.5 above.

In the aircraft study, the change in the price of identical models (C) could be measured directly. For electric generating equipment, where there is no "model" concept, I choose instead to identify the price of a constant-quality model with the coefficients on the vintage dummies in the hedonic regression equations of table 5.5. Then the comparison of net revenue and sales price ratios, required in (5.4) for the computation of the change in the "real" price index, is based on changes in net revenue per unit of capacity and in equipment cost per unit of capacity between one vintage pair (say 1947–48) and the next vintage pair (say 1949–50), holding constant input and output prices at the values of 1947–48.

---

16. The "curvature adjustment" included in the analysis of chap. 2 is omitted here to simplify the discussion.

The change in the real equipment price ($d \log v$) is taken from the hedonic regression equations of table 5.5. Since the price changes captured by the vintage dummies are already included in the constant-quality price index ($d \log C$), the remaining "real" price change per unit of capacity is computed as the coefficient on capacity (β) times the change in capacity ($d \log k$):

$$(5.7) \qquad d \log v = \beta \, d \log k.$$

For this calculation, the β coefficients are taken from the split regression that excludes the heat rate variable, that is, columns 3 and 5 of table 5.5, and the sum of the two change components ($d \log C$ and $d \log v$) corresponds exactly to the change summarized in table 5.6, row 3c.

Since an electric utility earns revenue from the joint activities of generation, transmission, distribution, and bill collection, no figure is recorded for the gross or net revenue of a generating plant. However, as in the case of commercial aircraft, it is possible to prorate revenue among the different cost categories if we assume that the same operating margin is earned in each category. In 1983, for instance, the electric utility industry earned net revenue equal to 40.7 percent of operating cost, calculated as follows (all figures are billions of dollars):[17]

Gross revenue	$ 117.3
Less taxes included in operating expense	− 17.4
Equals available revenue	99.9
Less operating expense	71.0
Equals net revenue (depreciation, amortization, and net operating income)	28.9

Thus, net revenue/operating expense = $28.9/71.0 = .407$.

Letting z stand for the ratio of net revenue to operating expense, and assuming that the industry ratio (e.g., .407) also applies to each generating plant, the net revenue of a plant can be computed from its operating expense (x):

$$(5.8) \qquad n = (1 + z)(x) - x = zx.$$

We want to measure the change in net revenue that occurs when, holding gross revenue constant, a change in fuel or labor requirements creates a change in operating cost. This is simply[18]

17. The source is U.S. Department of Energy (1984, table 3, p. 11).
18. Again denoting an initial and subsequent situation with subsequent subscripts 0 and 1, we have the change in net revenue, caused by a change in input requirements when gross revenue is held constant, as:

$$\frac{n_1 - n_0}{n_0} = \frac{-dx}{n_0} = \frac{-dx}{zx_0}.$$

(5.9) $d \log n = -(1/z)d \log x.$

The last step is to define operating cost (x) as the sum of fuel and labor maintenance cost. Fuel cost in turn is equal to the price of fuel (p^f) plus fuel requirements measured in BTU per kWh (f). Labor maintenance cost is equal to the price of maintenance labor per employee (p^e) plus labor requirements measured in employees per kWh (e):

(5.10) $x = p^f f + p^e e,$

and the change in operating cost at fixed input prices is

(5.11) $d \log x = \alpha d \log f + (1 - \alpha)d \log e,$

where α is the share of nominal fuel expense in total operating expense. Combining (5.9) and (5.11), the change in net revenue is

(5.12) $d \log n = -(1/z)[\alpha d \log f + (1 - \alpha)d \log e].$

Finally, the change in the real price index is, from (5.5) and (5.7) above, is

(5.13) $d \log p = \beta d \log k + (1/z)[\alpha d \log f + (1 - \alpha)d \log e].$

This equation identifies three sources of a reduction in the real price index (p), the reduction in price per unit of capacity associated with an increase in capacity, the benefit of which is credited to the manufacturer, to a reduction in fuel requirements per unit of output, and to a reduction in labor requirements per unit of output. All three of these factors were important sources of reductions in the real price index prior to the late 1960s, but not since then.

To calculate the change in net revenue in (5.12), we need only the share of fuel expense in total operating expense (α) and changes in fuel and labor input requirements per unit of output. The α weights are taken from the means for new plants in the data set of nominal fuel and maintenance labor expense for each vintage pair. The latter $(d \log f$ and $d \log e)$ are taken from the regression equations of table 5.7, where heat rate and the employee/capacity ratio are explained by the same set of variables that appear in my hedonic regression equations for equipment cost. The negative coefficients on capacity indicate substantial scale effects for fuel use and especially for labor. An improvement in fuel efficiency occurred between the 1947–48 and the 1961–62 vintage pairs, followed by a steady deterioration through the end of the sample period. Labor efficiency improved through 1969–70 and deteriorated thereafter. Holding capacity constant, fuel efficiency was slightly worse in 1981–82 than in 1947–48, while labor efficiency was 53 percent better.

Just as we attribute the scale effects in the price equation to the manufacturer, those in the fuel and labor efficiency equations are also treated in the same way. Thus, the change in efficiency between two vintage pairs is

Table 5.8 **Components of Operating Cost Adjustment**

Year Pair	$d \log v$ $= \beta \, d \log k$ (1)	α (2)	$d \log f$ (3)	$d \log e$ (4)	$d \log n$ (5)	$d \log p^i$ (6)
1947–48		94.0				
1949–50	−4.8	94.4	−4.9	−10.5	−12.8	−17.6
1951–52	−16.0	94.7	−9.4	−57.4	−29.3	−45.3
1953–54	−4.0	93.1	−4.6	43.6	−3.1	−7.2
1955–56	−13.2	94.4	−9.3	−68.2	−31.0	−44.2
1957–58	9.4	94.1	4.8	32.3	15.8	25.2
1959–60	−9.2	90.7	−5.5	−47.6	−23.1	−32.1
1961–62	1.2	93.0	−3.5	2.4	−7.6	−6.4
1963–64	−4.8	91.4	4.9	−22.5	6.2	1.4
1965–66	−10.0	92.9	−3.0	−46.5	−15.0	−25.0
1967–68	1.2	89.0	−0.8	−13.8	−5.5	−4.3
1969–70	−0.5	89.0	5.7	10.6	15.3	14.8
1971–72	1.4	88.4	−2.2	−12.7	−8.4	−7.0
1973–74	−0.3	91.5	3.5	24.4	13.0	12.7
1975–76	−0.7	92.7	2.4	−0.5	5.4	4.7
1977–78	1.5	90.2	0.6	−20.9	−3.7	−2.2
1979–80	−0.9	88.5	−1.6	14.1	0.5	−0.4
1981–82	3.4	91.7	0.6	−54.6	−9.8	−6.4
Sum of log change	−46.3		−22.3	−227.8	−93.1	−139.4

Sources by column: (**1**) Change in time coefficients in capacity equation from table 5.7, col. 1, times coefficient on capacity in table 5.5, col. 3, until 1965–66, and col. 5 thereafter. (**2**) Share of fuel cost in sum of fuel and maintenance cost, from sample means for new plants. (**3**) Change in time coefficients in heat rate equation from table 5.7, col. 2, plus change in time coefficients in capacity equation from table 5.7, col. 1, times coefficient on capacity in table 5.7, col. 2. (**4**) Change in time coefficients in employment equation from table 5.7, col. 3, plus change in time coefficients in capacity equation from table 5.7, col. 1, times coefficient on capacity in table 5.7, col. 3. (**5**) The fraction $1/z$, where $z = .407$, times the weighted average of cols. 3 and 4, using col. 2 as weights. (**6**) Column 1 plus col. 5.

the coefficient on the vintage dummy in the fuel and labor requirement equations of table 5.7, plus the coefficient on capacity times the change in capacity (where the change in capacity in each vintage pair is taken from the regression coefficients in the first column of table 5.7). Because I have no data on the effect of environmental regulations on operating efficiency or on equipment cost, my approach lumps together the effects of technological improvements achieved by the manufacturer with retrogression caused by environmental regulations; I deal separately with this problem below.

The calculations are carried out in table 5.8. The first column lists the price change associated with the direct effect of changing capacity on price ($\beta d \log k$); this is identical to the capacity effect taken into account in the middle of table 5.6. Column 2 lists the weight of fuel cost in total operating cost; this remains over time in a relatively narrow range of 88–95 percent and is lower on average in the last half of the sample period. The changes in fuel and labor requirements are reported in columns 3 and 4, where the numbers shown combine the direct changes measured by the time dummy coefficients listed in table 5.7 with the scale adjustment. A negative entry indicates improved efficiency, and a positive number indicates deteriorating

Table 5.9   **Alternate Price Indexes for Electric Generating Equipment, 1947–82 (1971–72 = 100)**

	Linked PPIs used to Deflate PDE (1)	Hedonic with Capacity Adjustments (2)	Hedonic with Capacity and Operating Expense Adjustments (3)	Same as (3) with 1973–78 Adjustment for Environmental Regulation (4)
1947–48	40.7	117.7	315.2	315.2
1949–50	42.2	114.5	269.7	269.7
1951–52	47.4	104.6	183.9	183.9
1953–54	52.0	107.8	183.7	183.7
1955–56	60.0	89.0	111.2	111.2
1957–58	80.4	105.9	155.0	155.0
1959–60	82.1	107.8	125.2	125.2
1961–62	72.7	105.9	114.0	114.0
1963–64	72.6	84.3	96.6	96.6
1965–66	74.3	65.0	64.1	64.1
1967–68	81.6	68.5	63.9	63.9
1969–70	93.2	86.6	94.2	94.2
1971–72	100.0	100.0	100.0	100.0
1973–74	109.6	123.0	140.1	133.4
1975–76	152.7	152.2	182.9	166.2
1977–78	177.7	149.9	173.7	150.1
1979–80	209.1	281.8	328.1	266.7
1981–82	248.7	335.3	354.0	274.3

Sources: Column 1 from table 5.2, row 6. Column 2 calculated from table 5.5, cols. 3 and 5. Column 3 calculated from tables 5.5 and 5.8. Column 4 adjustment as described in text.

efficiency. Negative entries predominate until 1967–68, and positive entries thereafter. Finally, the two right-hand columns exhibit the change in net revenue (n) calculated with equation (5.12) and the change in the real price index (p) calculated with (5.13). The cumulative improvement in fuel efficiency is 31.3 percent through 1967–68, followed by a 9.0 percent decline thereafter. For labor, the improvement through 1967–68 is 188.2 percent, followed by a further but smaller improvement of 39.6 percent. For the real price index shown in the final column, the cumulative real price change through 1967–68 is 155.6 percent, followed by an increase of 16.2 percent from then until 1981–82.

The end result of these computations is displayed in columns 2 and 3 of table 5.9. The table begins in column 1 with the linked PPIs used in the NIPA to deflate PDE in steam turbine generators. In the second column is the index, corresponding to table 5.6, row 3c, based on the hedonic price equations with an adjustment for the capacity scale effect, but with no treatment of changes in operating efficiency. The third column contains the nominal price index with the full set of operating efficiency adjustments. The change between vintage pairs of this index is computed from equation (5.6), where the change in the price of a constant-quality unit, $d \log C$ (taken as the change in the vintage dummy coefficients in cols. 3 and 5 of table 5.5), is added to the change in the "real" price index ($d \log p$) from the right-hand column in table 5.8.

5.8   The Impact of Environmental Legislation

The price indexes in table 5.9 show a consistent pattern. Both of the new indexes decline relative to the NIPA index before 1971–72 and exhibit a relative rise thereafter. Because both fuel and labor efficiency per unit of capacity improved prior to the late 1960s and deteriorated thereafter, the final index that incorporates the operating efficiency adjustments declines relative to the other two indexes before the late 1960s and increases thereafter. Using either of the two new indexes as a deflator for investment spending in the national accounts would lead to the conclusion that the growth rate of real investment in the NIPA is drastically understated before the late 1960s and overstated thereafter.

However, we have not yet taken into account the effects of environmental legislation, which probably has a greater impact on the electric utility industry than on any other, with the possible exception of automobiles and steel. Since World War II, most coal has been burned in pulverized form in furnaces at sufficiently high temperatures to produce not only the steam that drives the turbines, but also nitrogen and sulfur oxides, both linked to acid rain. The 1970 Clean Air Act contained amendments that divided responsibility for control of emissions from electric utility generating stations. States were given responsibility for designing standards for plants built before August 1971, while new plants built (or old plants substantially modified) after that date were subject to explicit quantitative emissions controls (measured in pounds of sulfur dioxide per million BTUs of fuel input). Under 1977 amendments, new plants are required to install an emissions desulfurization system, usually called "scrubbers."[19]

In the national accounts, price changes due to environmental legislation are omitted in the calculation of real investment in consumer and producers' durables. That is, a catalytic converter added to an automobile is treated as an improvement in the quality of the automobile, even if the consumer would not purchase the device freely, on the assumption that society as a whole receives benefits from such devices in an amount roughly equal to their cost. To treat electric utility equipment symmetrically with automobiles, those price increases in generating equipment attributable to environmental legislation must be omitted from the price indexes developed here.

The impact of environmental legislation on quality-adjusted price indexes for electric utility generating equipment takes two main forms. First, there is

19. Details of environmental legislation and regulations can be found in Gollop and Roberts (1983).

the direct expense incurred in purchasing pollution control equipment, which primarily consists of scrubbers. If possible, we should subtract from the price increases in table 5.9 those attributable to the added cost of scrubbers and similar equipment. Second, environmental legislation can impair both fuel and labor efficiency, by requiring the use of nonpolluting types of fuel that require more BTUs to generate a unit of electricity and by requiring additional maintenance labor to service the scrubbers and other pollution-control equipment and to remove the wet sludge that collects in the scrubbers as part of the mechanical process by which they remove pollutants. To correct for this effect, we should adjust changes in fuel and labor requirements previously used to develop fuel and energy efficiency adjustments for the estimated impact of environmental legislation. A third effect of environmental legislation, the addition of high cooling towers to reduce pollution, has the same economic effects as scrubbers but is included in the cost of the plant structure, not in the separate total for plant equipment, which concerns us in this chapter.

There is substantial evidence and even more hearsay regarding the direct increase in the price of equipment attributable to scrubbers and other mandated equipment. The best academic evidence is that of Joskow and Rose (1985), who provide econometric estimates explaining total plant construction cost, using a data set that contains specific technical variables not available in my data. Their estimates of the coefficient on a scrubber dummy variable average out to 0.15, that is, scrubbers have added an estimated 15 percent to the construction cost of coal-fired plants. Joskow and Rose stress that this estimate does not include the capital costs of all environmental control equipment, for which they cite (1985, 20) an industry source as indicating a 20–30 percent addition to the cost of a typical unit. In a totally different ballpark is an estimate that refers to all government-mandated equipment; a 1979 study by Ebasco Services estimated that fully 62 percent of the cost of a new coal-burning plant in that year was attributable to the cost increase "from statutory and regulatory changes" (quoted in Faltermayer 1979, 118). Bain (1986) cites a figure of one-third of the cost of building a power plant. Prewitt (1988) estimates a cost of 14–20 percent.[20]

On maintenance requirements, one source estimates that scrubbers require as much maintenance as the rest of the plant taken together.[21] In earlier research (Gordon 1985), I conducted telephone interviews with plant managers to investigate sources of the productivity slowdown in the electric generating industry and the existence of "left-out variables" that could

20. The cost of add-on scrubbers is stated to be $200–$300 per kilowatt of capacity as compared with a total estimated plant cost of $1,500 "required to build a new coal-burning plant from scratch" (Prewitt 1988, 180).

21. The source is Weaver (1975), who cites the Cholla plant in Arizona, the first to have a "working" scrubber, as requiring a 50 percent increase in its maintenance labor force.

affect the results of econometric equations explaining employment (like that presented in table 5.7, col. 3). I found that no plant manager cited work force additions connected with pollution control equipment exceeding 25 percent. The conflict between this finding and the other evidence cited above is that my survey was conducted over a sample of existing plants, not necessarily newly constructed. Recall that the environmental regulations call for scrubbers on new plants after 1977, but not necessarily on earlier plants. Only one of the plants in my survey was equipped with a scrubber, and its manager stated that fully 25 percent of the plant work force was required for the operation and maintenance of the scrubber; other plants in the survey were equipped with electrostatic precipitators, which appear to have much less onerous maintenance requirements.

Overall, it would appear that 20 percent would be a conservative estimate for the early 1980s of the fraction of equipment cost in new plants consisting of environmentally mandated devices, including not only scrubbers but all other equipment designed to reduce both air and water pollution. If we assume that plant scale has not been affected by legislation, then we can simply subtract 20 percent from the estimated time dummy coefficients in the equipment cost regression of table 5.5 in the most recent year covered, 1981–82, and interpolate that adjustment linearly back to 1971–72, the time when the legislation first went into effect. As for maintenance labor, 20 percent is subtracted from the 1981–82 labor requirement used in the calculation of net revenue in table 5.8. In the absence of any specific quantitative evidence, no adjustment is made for any effect of environmental regulations on fuel efficiency, which, in view of the widespread shift to less efficient fuel, makes it likely that the overall adjustment is too conservative.

The "environmentally adjusted index" is shown in column 4 of table 5.9. The adjustment begins in the 1973–74 year pair and becomes larger until, in 1981–82, the resulting adjusted index number is 77.4 percent of the unadjusted index number. Almost all the adjustment is due to the direct vintage coefficient in the price equation of table 5.5, that is, the cost of the equipment itself, and relatively little to the additional adjustment for changes in labor efficiency. Before adjustment, the 1972–82 annual growth rate of the new index, 12.6 percent, greatly exceeded the 9.1 rate registered by the PPI, but, after adjustment, the rate of 10.1 percent is substantially closer to that of the PPI. Since there are few examples in this book of new price indexes that rise substantially faster than the PPI over any period, the more moderate inflation registered by the adjusted new index has a certain plausibility.

5.9 Conclusion and Topics for Further Research

There are a number of questions that could be addressed in future extensions of this research. First, the statement of net revenue per unit of

Table 5.10   Equation Explaining Log Utilization Rate, All Plants in Sample, Years of Operation 1948–80

1. Log capacity		0.01
2. Log heat rate		−1.24**
3. Log number of units		−0.06**
4. Fuel use:		
a. Coal only		0.18**
b. Oil only		−0.08**
c. Gas only		−0.03
5. Construction type:		
a. Conventional		−0.03*
b. Semioutdoor		0.05*

6. Vintage and time:	Vintage	Time
1949–50	0.08**	−0.20**
1951–52	0.10**	−0.20**
1953–54	0.10**	−0.29**
1955–56	0.10**	−0.42**
1957–58	0.19**	−0.54**
1959–60	0.12**	−0.68**
1961–62	0.16**	−0.72**
1963–64	0.19**	−0.67**
1965–66	0.15**	−0.62**
1967–68	0.16**	−0.62**
1969–70	0.06	−0.61**
1971–72	0.06	−0.59**
1973–74	−0.01	−0.60**
1975–76	−0.04	−0.85**
1977–78	0.06	−0.79**
1979–80	−0.02	−0.86**
1981–82 (1983)	−1.35**,[a]	−0.89**
$\bar{R}^2$		0.344
S.E.E.		0.458
Observations	6,479	

*Indicates significance at the 5 percent level.

**Indicates significance at the 1 percent level.

[a]No new plants in sample for 1983.

capacity in (5.12) assumes no change in utilization, since fuel expense per unit of capacity is defined as heat rate times fuel cost per BTU times output per unit of capacity. However, over the postwar period, there have been significant changes in the utilization rates of different vintages, observed over their lifetimes. A regression equation (shown in table 5.10) for all plants in the sample, that is, each vintage is observed from the year after its installation to 1983, shows an improvement in average utilization, holding year of operation constant, over vintages from 1947–48 to 1965–66, followed by a marked deterioration. If this change in utilization by vintage is attributed to the manufacturer, because technical change can make a new vintage more efficient and therefore more attractive for base-load capacity, then the adjustment for fuel efficiency in (5.7) would be calculated as the existing heat rate change, plus the effect of capacity on heat rate, plus the vintage and capacity effects on utilization. Any such additional adjustment would simply accentuate the differences evident in table 5.9, with a greater decline in the index shown in the third column through the mid-1960s, and a greater relative increase thereafter. However, this conclusion would be premature, pending an investigation of the effects of seasonality and other market demand factors on utilization. For instance, reduced utilization may be primarily due to an increased dispersion of summer and winter peak loads as the use of air conditioning has spread.

Second, the net revenue adjustments are based on the experience of operating a new plant only in the first year after its installation. Firms might, however, make a calculation that takes into account different expectations about the future time path of fuel and labor prices. For instance, if wage rates were expected to increase relative to fuel prices during the first two decades of the postwar period, then the present value of future maintenance expense would be a greater share of the present value of total future operating expenses than indicated by the share of maintenance in the first year of operation. Since the labor efficiency adjustments in table 5.8 are greater in percentage terms than the fuel efficiency adjustments, placing a greater weight on labor cost would add to the overall size of the adjustments and further accentuate the differences of the final operating-cost-adjusted price index in comparison with the other indexes before and after 1970.

While there is much to be done, one conclusion emerges clearly in this chapter. Over the first half of the postwar era, few, if any, products exhibit a greater difference between the fully adjusted alternative price index (table 5.9, col. 4) and the equivalent PPI. The drift over 1947–48 through 1967–68 amounts to a staggering −11.5 percent per year. In the official BLS breakdown of productivity growth, the electric utility industry exhibits rapid growth in the early postwar years, followed by a steady slowdown, to virtual stagnation since 1973. This chapter demonstrates that this history cannot be blamed on any aspect of behavior by employees or managers within the utility industry itself. Instead, credit for the early achievements and blame for the subsequent failures should be directed toward the manufacturing sector, both the companies making generators and boilers, and those in other companies and industries responsible for the advances in metallurgy that ultimately made possible much of the increase in scale of equipment and the accompanying decline in price per unit of capacity.

6 Computer Processors and Peripherals

Economics is a one or two digit science.[1]

If the auto industry had done what the computer industry has done in the last 30 years, a Rolls-Royce would cost $2.50 and get 2,000,000 miles to the gallon.[2]

6.1 Introduction

It is now thirty-nine years since the first delivery of the UNIVAC I electronic computer, and thirty-six years since the introduction of IBM's first electronic computer model. It is well known that the price of mainframe computers per unit of performance has fallen radically since those early days, by a factor of hundreds or even thousands, and that a modern personal computer costing a few thousand dollars has more memory and a faster speed than mainframes costing a million dollars or more as recently as the mid-1970s. Yet to this day, the BLS in its PPI includes no price index for computers (either mainframe or personal), despite its inclusion of many hundreds of commodity indexes for less important types of mechanical and electrical machinery. And only in its December 1985 benchmark revision did the BEA introduce a deflator for the computer component of PDE dating back to 1969, after more than two decades of publishing NIPAs based on the assumption that the prices of electronic computers remained fixed year after year.[3] The NIPAs still assume that computer prices remained fixed before 1969.

---

1. This was a remark of Norbert Weiner's, apparently quoted with approval by Oskar Morgenstern in his work on the accuracy of economic statistics (Phister 1979, 4).
2. *Forbes,* 22 December 1980, 24, attributed to *Computerworld* magazine.
3. The BEA's deflation procedures are described by Cartwright (1986) and are based on hedonic price indexes for computer processors and peripherals developed in Cole et al. (1986).

This chapter attempts to construct a single price deflator for electronic computers for the full period 1951–84, based on an application of the hedonic regression technique to two different data sets. The source of one of these data sets (Phister 1979) also forms the basis of a recent study by Flamm (1987), although this chapter is the first to estimate hedonic regression equations for the Phister data, which cover the period 1951–79.[4] The other data source, *Computerworld* magazine, covers 1977–84 and is studied here for the first time.[5] While the "final" price index developed in the chapter is based entirely on the Phister and *Computerworld* data sets, the equations are also reestimated for the new-model portion of two other data sets used previously by Chow (1967) and Dulberger (1989). This allows us to explore the sensitivity of the implied hedonic price indexes to alternative data sources, while holding constant other aspects of the methodology.

The coverage of the study includes mainframe computer processors for the full 1951–84 period, minis from 1965 to 1984, and personal computers for 1982–87. This is the first study of computers to cover such a long sample period and to provide separate treatment of mini and micro computers.[6] The final price index for mainframe and mini computer processors exhibits a 1951 index number, on a base 1984 = 100, of 133,666, implying an annual rate of change over the thirty-three years of −21.8 percent.[7]

The desire for complete time coverage of the postwar period is partly dictated by the need to maintain consistency with the time coverage adopted for the other chapters. But the inclusion of the full period is also important for substantive reasons, since one objective of this line of research is to understand the relation (if any) between the measurement of durable goods prices and the mysterious decline in productivity growth that began about 1970. If computers have been so productive, why has the cyclically adjusted rate of productivity growth in the U.S. economy outside manufacturing slowed in the 1980s to a rate close to zero? Any contribution of the possible mismeasurement of PDE deflators to the productivity slowdown puzzle requires not simply the identification of a price measurement bias, but rather depends on identifying either a *change* in the bias or a change in the weight attributed to the product exhibiting the bias. The share of computers in PDE expenditure was obviously much higher after 1970 than before, but it

4. Also, Flamm's index is based on the price-performance ratio of the installed stock of computers, not on the flow of newly produced models, as in this study.
5. The BEA also uses *Computerworld* data to update its computer price index for years after 1984.
6. The only other hedonic price index that covers both the 1950s and the late 1970s is the Knight (1983) index, as quoted by Alexander and Mitchell (1984, table 9, p. 48). Triplett's (1989) survey paper summarizes results of other studies over our period but does not present new research results.
7. Some might prefer to omit the 1951–54 interval, which is based on a single 1951 observation. The 1954 index number on a 1984 base is 33,293, for an annual rate of change over thirty years of −19.4 percent. These indexes are presented in table 6.7 below.

remains to be seen whether the net impact of changing weights and the absence of a BEA price index for computers before 1969 implies a significant change in the extent of mismeasurement of the PDE deflator.

The chapter begins with three sections providing background material. Section 6.2 provides a brief overview of the postwar development of the computer industry and exhibits data on value and numbers of computers sold by major type (the same data are subsequently used to supply weights for the separate mainframe and minicomputer price indexes). Section 6.3 examines aspects of the hedonic regression methodology that are relevant to this study, including data availability and definitions, specification, functional forms, structural stability, and make effects.

Section 6.4 provides an introduction to the data sets, while section 6.5 discusses the hedonic regression estimates and section 6.6 the issues involved in choosing one equation in preference to another, including equations covering the same time interval yielded by alternative data sets. Section 6.7 discusses two weighting issues involved in converting a price index for computer processors into an index for computer systems, where a system is defined as the processor and its associated peripherals. Using the computer system index, the chapter then computes an index for the overall "office, computing, and accounting machinery" (OCAM) category of PDE. Traditional index number problems that are of only minor importance in most aspects of deflation assume major importance in combining computer price indexes into deflators for aggregates like OCAM. Two main problems are discussed. First, results are sensitive to the choice of base year for any price index (whether an implicit deflator or fixed-weight index) in which calculations require the source of a single base year. In the case of the implicit deflator method, the use by the BEA of the base year 1982, when computers were relatively cheap, tends to yield a low weight on computers in earlier years and understate the importance of price decreases that occurred prior to the mid-1970s. Correspondingly, the contribution of computers to real investment is understated before 1982 and overstated after 1982.

The second problem is that with the implicit deflator method, regardless of the base year chosen, the weight of computers is zero for any year prior to the introduction of computers, assumed to be 1958 in the NIPAs. Thus, in a comparison between 1957 (or any earlier year) and the base year, in this case 1982, the rapid price decline of computers has no effect at all on the growth rate of real investment or real GNP. This result, which may seem surprising, in fact reflects well-known properties of the Paasche implicit deflator methodology rather than any mistake made by the BEA. This chapter deals with both weighting problems by using the Törnqvist approximation to an ideal index number, in which the weights on computers shift every year to reflect their share of nominal expenditures within OCAM.

There are a number of studies that have created price indexes that may be compared to this one, including Knight (1983), Chow (1967) as extended by Miller (1980), Archibald and Reece (1979), Cole et al. (1986), and Dulberger (1989). Other hedonic regression studies of computer prices have not attempted to develop price indexes, but rather have been within the industrial organization literature concerned with whether IBM overprices or underprices its computers over relatively short time periods (Kelejian and Nicoletti 1974; Ratchford and Ford 1976; Stoneman 1978; Brock 1979; Michaels 1979; Fisher, McGowan, and Greenwood 1983). Other studies of technological change (Alexander and Mitchell 1984; Bresnahan 1986) and of functional form (Horsley and Swann 1983) have used the previous hedonic studies by Chow and/or Knight rather than producing their own. To limit its scope, this chapter provides only new research results and does not present any comparison of its results with the previous literature. Such comparisons are amply provided in the recent survey paper by Jack Triplett (1989).

6.2 The Postwar Development of the Computer Industry

This study develops price indexes for computer processors displaying enormous changes over time; a price index that shrinks from 100,000 to 100 over a span of thirty-three years is probably unprecedented in economic history (although changes in the opposite direction, from 100 to 100,000, over shorter periods have occurred in hyperinflations). A bit of intuition to support these startling numbers is provided by a few details on the first electronic computer, the ENIAC, which was developed during World War II. The ENIAC had a trifling computational capacity in comparison with today's PCs, yet was gigantic in size, measuring 100 feet long, ten feet high, and three feet wide, and containing about 18,000 vacuum tubes. This machine was programmed by setting thousands of switches, all of which had to be reset by hand in order to run a different program. It is reported to have broken down "only" about once per day.[8]

The first major successor to the ENIAC was the UNIVAC I, originally built on contract with the U.S. government for use in the 1950 census. All the UNIVACs built through 1953 were purchased by the government, and an initial commercial purchase occurred in 1954. Unlike the ENIAC, the UNIVAC operated with stored programs rather than hand-set switches, and is the first machine in my hedonic regression sample from the Phister (1979) data source.[9]

8. This section is based on Cole et al. (1986), the conference draft of Dulberger (1989), Einstein and Franklin (1986), and Fisher, McKie, and Mancke (1983).

9. The vintages associated with each observation in the Phister sample are those listed in the source. Thus, the UNIVAC I is attributed to the 1951 vintage, the year that the first unit was delivered to the Census Bureau. Those that may be interested in extending my price index

The development of computer technology is often described with a terminology of technical "generations." Early first-generation machines through the late 1950s operated with vacuum tubes, followed by the second-generation machines based on transistors, starting with the IBM 7000 series introduced in 1959. The first IBM third-generation machines with integrated circuits were the series 360 models, first installed in 1965. Since the introduction of semiconductor chips, continuous improvements have been achieved by packaging increased numbers of circuits closer together, both lowering the marginal cost of additional memory and reducing instruction execution time.

The evolution of the computer industry is quantified in table 6.1, which displays domestic purchases (i.e., including imports and excluding exports) for mainframes, mini computers, and micros (mainly PCs in the 1980s). Both numbers of units and the value of shipments are exhibited for each group.[10] Unit values are not shown to save space but can be calculated. These range for mainframes from $420,000 in 1955 to $968,000 in 1984; for minis from $110,000 in 1965 to $58,000 in 1984; and for micros from $15,000 in 1975 to $3,690 in 1984. Prior to 1965, virtually all computers were mainframes, and unit sales grew at a 50 percent annual rate, while the value of shipments grew at a 44 percent rate (1955–64). In subsequent decades, the annual growth rate of mainframe units tapered off to 4 percent (1964–74) and 2 percent (1974–84), while the value of shipments grew at annual rates of 14 and 5 percent in these two decades, respectively. For these two decades, growth rates were much faster for minis (48 and 23 percent for units versus 40 and 22 percent for values for 1965–74 and 1974–84, respectively). The annual growth rate for micro units during 1975–84 was 95 percent and for value was 67 percent.

In assessing the data in table 6.1, note the shift from mainframes to minis and micros; the value share of mainframes declined from 97 percent in 1969 to 46 percent in 1984. Since this is the period covered by the new BEA deflator for computers, which excludes both minis and micros, that deflator becomes less representative of the total computer industry as the years go on.

---

further back in time should note that the price/performance ratio of the ENIAC to UNIVAC I is 10.9, according to Knight's commercial index (1966, 45). This would imply a 1946 price index on a 1984 base of roughly 1.5 million.

10. The source for table 6.1 defines the breakpoint between micros and minis at $20,000 per units and between minis and mainframes at $250,000. The $250,000 figure corresponds precisely with Phister (1979, fig. 1.21.5, p. 13), which shows that $250,000 remains a consistent borderline between mainframes and mini computers over the 1955–74 period. Correspondingly, all machines in the Phister data set with prices below $250,000 are classified as "minis." When the minimum, mean, and maximum memory configurations of a model straddle the $250,000 boundary, the classification is decided by whether the mean configuration lies below or above $250,000.

Table 6.1   **U.S. Domestic Purchases of Electronic Computers, 1955–84 (value in millions of dollars)**

Year	Mainframes Units	Mainframes Value	Minis Units	Minis Value	Micros Units	Micros Value	Total Units	Total Value
1955	150	63	. . .	. . .	. . .	. . .	150	63
1956	500	152	. . .	. . .	. . .	. . .	500	152
1957	660	235	. . .	. . .	. . .	. . .	660	235
1958	970	381	. . .	. . .	. . .	. . .	970	381
1959	1,150	475	. . .	. . .	. . .	. . .	1,150	475
1960	1,790	590	. . .	. . .	. . .	. . .	1,790	590
1961	2,700	880	. . .	. . .	. . .	. . .	2,700	880
1962	3,470	1,090	. . .	. . .	. . .	. . .	3,470	1,090
1963	4,200	1,300	. . .	. . .	. . .	. . .	4,200	1,300
1964	5,600	1,670	. . .	. . .	. . .	. . .	5,600	1,670
1965	5,350	1,770	250	29	. . .	. . .	5,610	1,799
1966	7,250	2,640	385	40	. . .	. . .	7,635	2,680
1967	11,200	3,900	720	69	. . .	. . .	11,920	3,968
1968	9,100	4,800	1,080	100	. . .	. . .	10,180	4,900
1969	6,000	4,150	1,770	152	. . .	. . .	7,770	4,302
1970	5,700	3,600	2,620	210	. . .	. . .	8,320	3,810
1971	7,600	3,900	2,800	218	. . .	. . .	10,400	4,118
1972	10,700	5,000	3,610	271	. . .	. . .	14,310	5,271
1973	14,000	5,400	5,270	369	. . .	. . .	19,270	5,769
1974	8,600	6,200	8,880	577	. . .	. . .	17,480	6,777
1975	6,700	5,410	11,670	642	5,100	77	23,470	6,128
1976	6,750	5,580	17,000	816	25,800	374	49,550	6,770
1977	8,900	6,600	24,550	1,203	58,500	761	91,950	8,563
1978	7,500	7,590	29,550	1,596	115,600	1,098	152,650	10,284
1979	7,200	7,330	35,130	2,038	160,000	1,488	202,330	10,856
1980	9,900	8,840	41,450	2,487	250,500	2,104	301,850	13,431
1981	10,700	9,540	44,100	2,699	385,100	2,503	439,900	14,842
1982	10,600	10,300	47,820	2,821	735,000	4,190	793,420	17,311
1983	9,985	10,480	45,420	3,330	1,260,000	5,300	1,315,405	19,110
1984	10,700	10,360	72,130	4,185	2,100,000	7,750	2,182,005	22,295

Source: 1960–84: Einstein and Franklin (1986, table 1); 1955–59: Phister (1979, table II.1.21).

6.3   Implementation of the Hedonic Regression Methodology

6.3.1   "Matched Model" versus Hedonic Regression Indexes

Triplett (1986) has provided a concise introduction to the interpretation of hedonic price indexes. These indexes can be distinguished from the "conventional method" used by the BLS to construct the CPI and the PPI. In the recent literature on computer price indexes, the conventional method has been called the "matched model" method, since it involves comparing prices only for models that are identical in quality from one year to the next.

The most important potential defect in a matched model index is the omission of price changes implicit in the introduction of new or "unmatched" models. A matched model index assumes that the price change implicit in the introduction of new models is identical to the price change of the matched models over the same time interval. While this might be a valid assumption for some products, it is clearly invalid for electronic computers, as has been demonstrated recently by Cole et al. (1986) in their comparison of matched model and hedonic price indexes for the same sample of computers. The effect of the introduction of new technology that reduces the price of quality characteristics (e.g., computer speed and memory) is to cause the price of old models to be bid down. The prices of old models included in the matched model price indexes may fail to duplicate the price reductions on new models either because firms may sell old models at a discounted price but report list prices to the compiler of the price index or because firms may fail to reduce the transaction price of old models, thus causing their sales to disappear at a speed that depends on lags in information, lags in consumer reaction (due perhaps to employee training costs for switching to new models), and supply bottlenecks or backlogs on new models.

6.3.2   The Hedonic and Imputation Methods

The hedonic regression approach can be viewed as one of several methods to estimate the slope of the function relating the cost of a product to its quantity of characteristics. A common approach to the estimation of quality-adjusted price change is to include time dummy variables (D_t) in cross-sectional regressions explaining price (p_{it}) for two or more years:

$$(6.1) \qquad \log p_{it} = \beta_0 + \sum_{t=1}^{N} \delta_t D_t + \sum_{j=1}^{m} \beta_j \log y_{ijt} + u_{it},$$
$$i = 1, \ldots, n; t = 0, \ldots, N.$$

Here y is the quality characteristic. Equation (6.1) uses a log-linear (or "double log") specification, following the majority of hedonic regression studies of computers. An alternative would be a semilog specification, with the log of price of the left and the unlogged values of the y variables on the right. Whatever the functional form, as long as the log of price is related to linear time dummy variables like the D_t in (6.1), a hedonic price index with a base of unit y in year $t = 0$ can be calculated from the antilogs of the δ_t coefficients. This has been the most common procedure in hedonic regression studies and is what Triplett (1989) calls the dummy variable method.

The leading alternative is the imputation method, in which an imputed base-year price for each model is calculated as the fitted value of (6.1), with the time coefficient for year t (δ_t) replaced by the time coefficient for the base year ($\delta_0 = 0$). If, for instance, the regression equation covers 1954–65 and 1954 is the base year, the imputed 1954 price of a 1965 model can be calculated as the fitted value with the time coefficient set to zero. Since computer prices fell rapidly from 1954 to 1965, the imputed 1954 price of a 1965 model will be much higher than the actual price charged in 1965. Triplett (1989) compares the dummy variable and imputation methods and on balance prefers the latter. In this chapter, I compute price indexes using both methods. To his list of advantages of the imputation technique we can add the extremely useful role of imputed prices in providing a straightforward measure of base-year quality that can be used to edit a data set. If the ratio of the actual to the imputed price for a given model is much higher than the average of all models for a given year, that model is "overpriced," that is, its actual price in year t is much higher relative to base-year quality than the average model. Below, I adopt this criterion to omit selected models from the Phister data set, following the precedent set by Knight (1966).[11]

Returning to equation (6.1), there remains the problem of determining the optimal sample period for the regression. At one extreme, we can obtain an aggregate index of price change from the series of δ_t coefficients obtained in a single regression for an entire data set, and at the other extreme an index can be calculated by linking together a string of δ_t coefficients obtained from a series of "adjacent year" regressions on data for successive pairs of years. To the extent that the prices of quality characteristics are changing through time, the adjacent-year technique allows the regression coefficients on the y_{ijt} to change every year. The disadvantage of the adjacent-year technique is that sample sizes are sometimes too small to yield efficient estimates, and estimated coefficients on the quality characteristics jump erratically from year to year and may even change sign.

Clearly, there is no reason to choose either the extreme of running a single regression or N separate adjacent-year regressions. Instead, we can begin with numerous equations estimated for overlapping short periods and successively pool the data into longer periods, checking for structural change with the conventional "Chow test" for aggregation. This chapter tests for aggregation not only over time but also across different types of computer models.

6.3.3   Interpreting Residuals in Hedonic Regression Equations

No hedonic regression equation will fit the data perfectly. The estimated residuals (u_{it}) represent the effects of excluded attributes, incorrect specification of functional form, marketing practices unrelated to production costs, demand discontinuities, and time lags due to the fact that a new model

---

11. This discussion omits the third type of price index described by Triplett (1989), the "characteristics price index," since this technique is not used here.

may have a lower price than an older model containing the same quantity of characteristics. Some variables are omitted because they are highly correlated with other variables that are included. The coefficients on an included variable thus represent not just its own effect on price, but also that of the omitted variables. Thus, the estimated coefficients cannot necessarily be interpreted as representing the value that users place on a particular attribute.

Omitted attributes afflict all hedonic regression studies but may be particularly important in research on computer prices, since no study, including this one, has been able to quantify software maintenance, engineering support, or manufacturer's reputation. If these omitted variables differ systematically across manufacturers, then their effect on prices can be captured by manufacturer dummy variables or "make effects." Since my major emphasis is on changes in computer price indexes over time, my investigation of make effects is limited to the inclusion of IBM make-effect dummy variables in all those regression equations that include IBM models.

Related to make effects is the question of commodity boundaries. In a sense, this study does not extend back far enough in time, since the first electronic computer may have represented a decline in the price-performance ratio of the previous "computer," some mixture of a punched card sorting machine and a clerk with a calculator.[12] The same issue arises in a cross section, since one can ask whether mainframe, mini, and micro computers are all the same product. Below, we find that pooling tests reject the aggregation of minis and mainframes into a single equation.

6.4 The Data

The results in this study are based on two overlapping data sources. For the years 1951–79, we have the compilation of Phister (1979), which provides for roughly 100 mainframe models a long list of quality characteristics, as well as a variety of sales prices and rental rates. For many but not all of the models, the Phister tables list ninety-five separate quality characteristics, including a wide variety of different performance measures (e.g., included memory, several dimensions of speed, and the Knight commercial and scientific indexes) as well as a number of attributes of more dubious importance (e.g., floor space, weight, and price per pound of both central processor and memory), and twenty lines of information on prices and rental rates.

For the period 1977–84, the data source is *Computerworld* magazine, published by the International Data Corporation (IDC), which also publishes the bimonthly *EDP Industry Report*, the source of data in several earlier

12. Fisher, McKie, and Mancke (1983, 3) report that the first electronic computer, the ENIAC, carried out calculations between 100 and 500 times faster than punched card machines with electromagnetic relays.

studies. The *Computerworld* annual hardware issue makes available all the required information in a single place for each year of the sample period. Unfortunately, the annual hardware issue began only in 1981, making an issue-by-issue search necessary for earlier years. It was possible to search back only to 1977 within the span of time available for this study.

Two other data sources are used to check the sensitivity of these results to data sources. Gregory Chow provided the data used in his original 1967 article, and the BEA provided the data used by Ellen Dulberger (1989) and Cole et al. (1986) for computer processors. In the following sections, the Phister and *Computerworld* data are described in some detail, since these are used here for the first time, and the Chow and Dulberger data in less detail, since these are described by those authors.

6.4.1 The Phister Data

Phister's data on speed and memory mainly come from *Auerbach Computer Technology Reports,* a comprehensive guide published since the early 1960s by Auerbach Information, Inc. His sources for system prices include General Service Administration catalogs, price lists published by various manufacturers, and Auerbach. Phister dates his prices as pertaining to roughly two years after a model was introduced, where the introduction dates come from IDC.[13]

The Phister data include, for most computer models, two types of prices. First, there is a system price accompanied by information on the amount of memory included in that price. Second, there is information on the price of incremental memory. A pitfall in working with the Phister data is that the prices of several machines are listed with zero memory included. For most but not all machines, information is given on the incremental price of memory, and for each such machine three observations were created, corresponding to the price and characteristics of models configured with minimum, maximum, and mean memory sizes. This procedure is identical to that carried out by Dulberger in creating her sample, except that she creates two observations corresponding to minimum and maximum memory. In short, in the Phister data set, each model is entered three times if data on the price of incremental memory are provided, but only once if only a single price at a fixed memory configuration is provided without any supplemental information on the price of incremental memory.[14]

Seven indexes of speed are provided by Phister, including memory cycle time and several different measures of addition and multiplication speed.

---

13. This two-year-lag criterion is not consistently applied, however, since Phister presents prices for the IBM 4331 and 4341 models, which were introduced in 1979, the same year as his book was published.

14. Eighty-nine models are entered as triplets and eight as single observations, for a total of 287 total observations. Dulberger's data set includes sixty-six new models (twenty-seven IBM and thirty-nine plug-compatible), for a total of 132 observations on new models.

Initially, I included memory cycle time and multiplication speed, as did Chow (1967), but soon found that they are highly collinear in the Phister sample. Multiplication speed is omitted from the results presented in section 6.5 of this chapter, which include only memory and memory cycle time for the regressions estimated for the Phister data.

Also available from Phister are the Knight commercial and scientific performance indexes, which use a formula to weight together memory, processor time, and input-output time factors, and these are calculated from more basic specifications of each computer. Because the Knight indexes are composite blends of memory and speed based on ''the opinions of 43 senior computer engineers and programmers'' (Phister 1979, 358) in the early 1960s, the weighting factors may be obsolete, and so the weights on memory and speed are freely estimated and do not include the Knight indexes as explanatory variables. In the last part of the chapter, the Knight indexes are used as part of a comparison of the quality of particular IBM models over time. It is interesting that, as an example of the extent of reduction in the price-performance ratio in the industry, the Knight commercial index increases from 119 for the 1954 IBM model 650 to 564,000 for the 1979 IBM model 4331, yet the nominal price of the 4331 was less than half that of the 650.[15]

6.4.2   The Computerworld Data

The *Computerworld* data set for 1977–84 includes several quality attributes not available from Phister, including minimum and maximum number of input-output channels, cache buffer size, and, most important, millions of instructions per second (MIPS) beginning in 1981. Additional input-output channels allow a computer to use its central processor and memory more efficiently by loading instructions and data from several devices at the same time, and a cache buffer memory allows a powerful processor to use a low-cost, relatively slow integrated circuit memory (Phister 1979, 524). Triplett (1989) discusses the advantages of MIPS over machine cycle time as a quality attribute, and for the 1981–84 period equations are estimated that contain both MIPS and cycle time. Because these additional variables are available in the *Computerworld* sample but not in the Phister sample, separate equations are estimated for each sample and are not pooled.

6.4.3   Other Data Sources

The new data from Phister and *Computerworld* are supplemented by two other data sets, the original Chow (1967) data set covering 1954–65, and the

---

15. This implies an annual rate of change of the performance/price ratio of 36.9 percent, when we use the price of the 4331 with the mean memory configuration. Price and performance data come from Phister (1979, 339, 359, 631).

Dulberger (1989) data set covering IBM and compatible machines for 1972–84. The Chow data set is considerably larger than the Phister sample for the years of overlap but yields similar results. The main defect of the Chow data set, as discussed in section 6.6, is its underrepresentation of IBM mainframes and overrepresentation of mini computers. The Dulberger data set includes information on the technological class of computers not available in either the Phister or the *Computerworld* samples.[16] The main limitation of the Dulberger data set is its relatively small size, particularly when it is limited to new models only. During 1972–79, the Dulberger data set includes just nineteen new models (all IBM except for four plug-compatibles), as contrasted to forty-one new models in the Phister data set. In the 1981–84 period, the Dulberger data set includes forty-two new models (eleven IBM and thirty-one plug compatible), in contrast to the 266 new models in the *Computerworld* data set (thirty-four IBM and 232 others, including sixty-eight minis and superminis).[17]

There are several differences among these data sets that we need to keep in mind. Chow (with a few exceptions) and Phister include only computers in their first year of production (new models), while Dulberger and *Computerworld* cover all models in production. Dulberger's data cover a narrower range of manufacturers (IBM and three plug-compatible manufacturers) but are the most carefully developed for the consistency of price and quality characteristics. I deal with the first aspect of noncomparability by editing the Chow, Dulberger, and *Computerworld* data sets to include only new models. The importance of the data consistency issue is assessed by comparing the estimate of performance improvements on specific IBM models implied by the estimated coefficients from the Phister, Dulberger, and *Computerworld* data sets.

6.4.4 Data Issues

New Models versus All Models

Numerous pitfalls in applying the hedonic regression technique have surfaced in the literature, but one seems to apply with particular force in the computer industry. The Rosen (1974) equilibrium interpretation of a hedonic surface may not apply in the computer case, because the computer market has ''never been close to long-run equilibrium in its entire existence'' (Fisher, McGowan, and Greenwood 1983, 149). Old inferior models do not just

16. The Dulberger data set includes a technological class variable for each mainframe processor (those produced by IBM and three other ''plug-compatible'' manufacturers), including two classes of ''bipolar'' semiconductors and five classes of field effect transistor (FET) semiconductors, which gradually increased from one to sixty-four kilobits per chip.

17. Each of these comparisons refers to separately numbered models. In the Dulberger data set, each model appears twice, priced at minimum and maximum memory. In the Phister data set, most but not all models appear three times, priced at minimum, mean, and maximum memory. The *Computerworld* data set is unduplicated.

disappear when a new superior model is introduced, nor are they repriced at a lower price/performance ratio equal to that of the new model. This suggests that new and old models may lie on different hedonic surfaces.

When new models are introduced, they tend to offer a lower ratio of price to performance than existing models. Instead of falling until price/performance ratios are equalized across machines, older models that remain in production tend to be overpriced. This phenomenon suggests two possible arguments for excluding old models in hedonic regressions. First, mixing old and new models having different price-to-performance ratios together in the same hedonic regression equation may lead to biased estimates of the rate of price change. Second, the rate of price change will be sensitive to the changing fraction of the same, consisting of old models in a given year. For these reasons, Fisher, McGowan, and Greenwood (1983) argue forcefully that a hedonic regression study should include only new models.

By including only new models, the hedonic price index traces out the technological "frontier" as successively more powerful new models are introduced. The main limitation of such a price index is that the total production of computers includes both new and old models, and so for deflation of current-dollar computer sales the price index should take into account existing models as well as new models. Thus, a case can be made for producing two hedonic price indexes, both including and excluding old models. To be consistent over time, a hedonic price index should be of one form or another, rather than mixing forms. If a data source included both old and new models, there would be no problem, since separate indexes could be developed based on all and only new models. Unfortunately, the Phister data source used in this chapter contains only new models, and thus to be consistent the resulting Phister-data price index should be compared to price indexes for the other data sets based on only new models. To maintain consistency, the basic results for the *Computerworld* data set include new models only. The results for both the Chow and the Dulberger data sets estimate hedonic indexes only for the subset of new models in those data sources; hence the hedonic price indexes for the Chow and Dulberger data do not constitute a replication of those authors' results and would not be expected to be identical to the results published by those authors.[18]

Weighting by Market Shares

Ideally it would be desirable to weight each observation by market share in each year. However, the requisite market share data are not available from the data sources. Phister presents an inventory of the installed number of computers for some but not all models, and *Computerworld* does not provide numbers produced or installed. The regression equations weight each

18. Readers can find price indexes based on the full Chow and Dulberger samples in the original papers by those authors and in Triplett (1989).

observation equally, which results in an underweighting of IBM machines, which had a share ranging from 60 to 75 percent in the total revenue of the data-processing industry, but represent only about half the observations in the Phister sample and only about 18 percent of the observations in the *Computerworld* sample. To deal with the weighting issue, separate price indexes for mainframe and mini computer processors are estimated over 1965–79, and the separate rates of price change are weighted by market shares in each year. Yearly market share weights are also applied to separate indexes over 1979–84 and IBM and plug-compatible mainframes, other mainframes, and minis and superminis. I also present a linked imputed price index over the entire sample period for major IBM mainframe models, in order to assess the plausibility of the final price index for those models that had the dominant market share.

Rental Rates versus Purchase Prices

The dependent variable in all the regressions is the log of purchase price. How different would the results be if the log of the rental rate were instead taken as the dependent variable? Phister provides data for all models on the rental rate, purchase price, and price/rental ratios. A scan of this ratio of purchase price to monthly rental indicates that it falls within the range of forty to sixty for almost all models in the Phister sample, with no evident time trend. The variance of this ratio over time is trivial compared to the variance of the price/performance ratio over time, suggesting that alternative regressions using the rental rate would yield similar results to those exhibited in section 6.5. Further evidence that this distinction is not important comes from the similarity of the price indexes yielded by the Phister and Chow data sets over 1954–65 (see table 6.3 below), where the Phister results are based on prices and the Chow results are based on rental rates.

Peripherals

While price/performance ratios for peripheral equipment (tape and disc drives, printers, etc.) fell over time by substantial amounts, the available evidence, especially that presented by Cole et al. (1986) and Flamm (1987), suggests that the rate of price decline was less than that for mainframe processing systems. Below, the Flamm series for peripherals is linked to that of Cole et al., so that the final price index properly weights together the price experience of computer processors and peripherals.

Software

The regressions cover only hardware prices, not the full operating cost of performing "computations," which would also include costs of software, maintenance, electricity, and rent on floorspace. However, the hardware prices include the basic system software that a manufacturer supplies with each machine. This has increased manyfold in quality and quantity, along with the increase in system performance. For instance, in 1954, IBM supplied only about 6,000 lines of code as programming support for the model 650 computer. The company provided an assembler and a few basic utility routines, but that was all. But as new models were introduced, the software provided grew exponentially. By the late 1960s, the operating system for the IBM 360 series, designed to improve system performance and to provide a wide variety of useful operating features, included over 5 million lines of code. From 1965 to 1975, software was a constant share (roughly 35 percent) of the total developmental cost of computer manufacturers (Phister 1979, 26–27).

Then, in 1969, IBM announced its "unbundling" decision, that separate charges would be made for systems engineering services and education and for new program products, "as distinct from system control programming." IBM also reduced its prices by 3 percent, an amount that represented its estimate of the value of the excluded services. No adjustment is made in this study for unbundling, partly on the ground that 3 percent is a small number, and partly because software developments had led to increasingly sophisticated operating systems that have relieved customer programmers of various complex tasks and made them more self-sufficient of the manufacturers' systems engineering personnel (Fisher, McKie, and Mancke 1983, 173–79). This would lead us to overstate the rate of decline of computer processor prices, particularly because unbundling progressed further during the 1970s, with IBM separately pricing more and more operational software until, by the end of the 1970s, all software was separately priced. Set against this bias are other omissions that work in the opposite direction, including the reduced energy and space requirements of computer processors.

6.5   Regression Results

6.5.1   Phister Data: General Procedures

All regressions estimated for the Phister data include two basic quality characteristics, memory and speed ("memory cycle time"). In addition, two types of dummy variables were included. First, an intercept dummy, equal to unity for an IBM machine and zero for a non-IBM machine, was included to test for an "IBM effect." Second, the data source listed the type of memory, allowing tests for the effect of memory types other than the standard core or integrated circuit types.

Perhaps the most important difference in memory type occurred in the early years of the sample period, when "drum" memory was supplanted by "core" memory. Although it would have been preferable to include a dummy for drum memory, this was precluded by the unfortunate fact that all the 1954 observations but *none* of the 1955 observations have drum memory.

Hence, the drum memory coefficient is collinear with the 1954–55 price change and prevents the estimation of plausible price coefficients in 1954–55. However, in the 1969–72 period, several isolated machines with unusual memory types ("wire" memory and "rod" memory) were identified. Because only a few machines had these memory types, inclusion of a memory-type dummy in this period did not preclude estimating the time coefficients. The form of the memory-type dummy was left to the computer, which selected an interactive memory type and memory slope dummy in preference to a shift in the intercept or in the speed coefficient.[19]

Lacking a priori evidence whether coefficients on quality characteristics could be assumed to remain constant over long periods, our estimation procedure began with short periods. Equations were first estimated for overlapping "triplets" of years, extending from 1951, 1954, and 1955 through 1977, 1978, and 1979.[20] Subsequently, groups of triplets were joined together and subjected to aggregation (or "pooling") tests to determine whether coefficients were stable across three-year periods. In the tables below, the triplet results are not presented, and the estimates shown are for the longer sample periods that accept aggregation over time.

For each of these longer sample periods, the ratio of the actual price to imputed base-year price was then inspected for "overpriced" models (see the discussion of the imputation method above following eq. [6.1]. Models selected for exclusion were those that had a log ratio of actual price to imputed price greater than 1.5 times the standard error of the estimated regression equation (in most equations, this criterion translates into the statement that the excluded models had an actual price double or greater the imputed price). Then the equations were reestimated with the overpriced models excluded. A precedent for excluding observations is Knight (1966, 49), who excluded overpriced models lying more than half a standard error above an initially fitted regression line.[21] It should be noted that less than 10 percent of the observations in this study are excluded by this procedure,

19. Thus, the "other memory" dummy is equal to the value of memory for those machines with wire or rod memory and zero otherwise. The estimated coefficient on this dummy in table 6.4 below is positive, indicating that extra memory raises price more for these other memory types than for standard memory types. I also tested for a difference between integrated circuit and core memory, but did not obtain any significant coefficients.

20. In some previous versions of this chapter, regressions for pairs of adjacent years were presented. Since sample sizes in some of those regressions were so small, in this version the first estimates were for triplets of years.

21. This sentence translates Knight's actual procedure into the language of this paper. As shown by Triplett (1989, eqq. [9] and [10]), Knight's procedure amounts to a regression of performance on price, rather than the usual regression of price on performance, and a price index can be calculated from the antilogs of the negatives of the estimated time dummy coefficients. Hence, when Knight states that he eliminates observations lying more than half a standard deviation below the regression line, he means that he eliminated overpriced observations, i.e., those that had a low ratio of performance to price. I was guided to this precedent for omitting observations by Triplett (1989, sec. II.B.3).

Table 6.2   **Hedonic Regressions, Phister Sample, 1951–69**

	1951–60 (1)	1960–69 (2)	1951–69 (3)
Memory	0.64**	0.65**	0.70**
Memory cycle time	−0.17**	−0.55**	−0.22**
IBM dummy	−0.25	0.11	0.08
Other memory[a]	. . .	0.16*	0.20**
1951	1.32*	. . .	1.46**
1954	base	. . .	base
1955	−0.01	. . .	−0.45
1956	no data	. . .	no data
1957	excluded	. . .	excluded
1958	−0.29	. . .	−0.42
1959	−0.62	. . .	−0.88*
1960	−0.72	base	−1.02**
1961	. . .	−0.40**	−1.30**
1962	. . .	−0.49**	−1.33**
1963	. . .	−0.54**	−1.26**
1964	. . .	−1.04**	−1.67**
1965	. . .	−1.81**	−2.33**
1966	. . .	−2.06**	−2.64**
1967	. . .	−2.28**	−2.58**
1968	. . .	excluded	excluded
1969	. . .	−3.07**	−3.52**
$\bar{R}^2$	0.808	0.894	0.872
S.E.E.	0.427	0.431	0.451
Observations	39	110	133

[a]"Other memory" is a dummy that allows for a shift in the coefficient on memory for models having wire or rod memory.

*Indicates significance at the 5 percent level.

**Indicates significance at the 1 percent level.

in contrast to Knight, who appears to have discarded about half his observations.[22]

6.5.2   The Phister Sample: Regression Results

The regression results are presented beginning in table 6.2 for the 1951–69 period. The specification is double log, as in equation (6.1) above, with asterisks used to designate the significance levels of the coefficients so as to avoid an excessive clutter of numbers in the tables. The base year for each equation is indicated by the word *base*. The implied price index in each other year can be calculated by taking the antilog of the coefficient shown opposite each year.

22. This procedure led to the exclusion of nine of the ninety-seven models in the Phister data set (twenty-one observations of 287). The list of overpriced models and their ratios of actual to imputed prices is presented in the Appendix. Knight (1966) does not report how many observations were omitted, but the number must have been substantial, since he began with 225 observations (45–46) but reports that "over 120 observations were used [in the final regressions]" (49).

Successive aggregation tests suggested that pooling was accepted over the entire decade 1960–69, but not beyond. There is a decisive break in 1969 revealed by the failure of 1960–69 to pool with 1969–72, 1969–75, and 1969–79. The break in 1960 is less decisive. One can test for such a break in two ways, by asking (1) whether the addition of, say, 1951–59 to 1960–69 passes an aggregation test, but also (2) whether the addition of 1960–69 to 1951–59 passes an aggregation test. These are two separate questions, and there is no statistical reason why the answer to them should be the same. Aggregation test 1 is accepted at the 5 percent level, but 2 is rejected at the 1 percent level. In light of this mixed finding, the final price index for 1951–65 is based on the average of the price changes shown in columns 1 and 2 and those shown in column 3. For the years after 1965, there are sufficient data to split the sample into two separate segments for minis and mainframes, as shown below in table 6.5.

In table 6.2, the coefficients on memory and speed ("memory cycle time") are highly significant. That on memory is stable across the 1960 break, as shown in a comparison of columns 1 and 2, while that on speed increases in absolute value after 1960. The "other memory" dummy variable is significant in both columns 2 and 3; the IBM dummy is not significant but is included to remain consistent with results displayed below that extend after 1969. The other point of interest in table 6.2 is that the time coefficients imply a relatively smooth rate of price decline. There are no price increases registered in any year in columns 1 and 2, while in column 3 there are small increases of 7 and 6 percent, respectively, in 1963 and 1967.

Data source effects are explored in table 6.3, which compares results for the Phister and Chow data sources. The sample period ends in 1965, which is the last year in the Chow data set. The "other memory" dummy is excluded, since it is not defined over 1951–65, and the IBM dummy is excluded in light of its insignificance in table 6.2. The only difference in the specification of the Chow equations is in the differing speed variables included in the data, "access time" and "multiplication time," as contrasted with the single Phister speed variable, "memory cycle time."

The Chow data used in table 6.3 refer only to new models, not to both new and old models, as in the original Chow (1967) article. Editing the Chow data in this way is necessary to achieve consistency with the Phister data set. While the overall rate of price decline over 1954–65 is not affected by excluding old models, one aspect of Chow's original research is altered. When all models are included, an aggregation test to add 1954–59 to 1960–65 is rejected at the 5 percent level, but this is not true for new models only. The new-only data set easily passes an aggregation test over 1954–65 by either method 1 or 2 listed above.

Thus, the basic Chow result is that presented in column 6. Because of the ambiguous results in aggregating the Phister data over 1954–65, we can compare the Chow estimates in column 6 with either columns 1 plus 2, or 3

Table 6.3   Comparison of Hedonic Regressions, Phister versus Chow (new models only), 1951–65

	Phister			Chow (new models only)		
	1951–60	1960–65	1951–65	1954–60	1960–65	1954–65
	(1)	(2)	(3)	(4)	(5)	(6)
Memory	0.67**	0.66**	0.71**	0.38**	0.58**	0.54**
Memory cycle time	−0.21**	−0.57**	−0.21**	. . .	. . .	. . .
Access time	. . .	. . .	. . .	−0.16**	−0.14**	−0.15**
Multiplication time	. . .	. . .	. . .	−0.13**	−0.06**	−0.07**
1951	1.59**	. . .	1.43**	. . .	. . .	. . .
1954	base	. . .	base	base	. . .	base
1955	0.03	. . .	−0.42	−0.02	. . .	−0.03
1956	no data	. . .	no data	−0.17	. . .	−0.33
1957	excluded	. . .	excluded	−0.18	. . .	−0.22
1958	−0.11	. . .	−0.45	−0.60**	. . .	−0.56**
1959	−0.40	. . .	−0.92*	−0.63**	. . .	−0.74**
1960	−0.54	base	−1.01*	−1.20**	base	−1.14**
1961	. . .	−0.42**	−1.31**	. . .	0.13	−1.24**
1962	. . .	−0.56**	−1.37**	. . .	−0.47**	−1.62**
1963	. . .	−0.56**	−1.24**	. . .	−0.58**	−1.72**
1964	. . .	−1.15**	−1.73**	. . .	−0.91**	−2.03**
1965	. . .	1.86**	−2.33**	. . .	−1.15**	−2.29**
$\bar{R}^2$	0.801	0.887	0.856	0.932	0.896	0.902
S.E.E.	0.435	0.433	0.456	0.340	0.387	0.380
Observations	39	86	109	43	81	115

*Indicates significance at the 5 percent level.

**Indicates significance at the 1 percent level.

alone. The most interesting similarity is in the overall rate of price decline: on a base 1965 = 100, the implied Chow index number for 1954 is 987, while the implied Phister index number for 1954 in column 3 is 1,028 (cols. 1 and 2 together imply 1,102). A further similarity between columns 3 and 6 is the roughly similar rate of price decline over the 1954–60 and 1960–65 subperiods; columns 1 and 2 differ in this regard in exhibiting a much slower price decline over 1954–60 and a much faster price decline over 1960–65. The other notable differences in table 6.3 are in the pattern of coefficients: both sets of results indicate a shift in coefficients after 1960, but for the Phister data in columns 1 and 2 this takes the form of a jump in the absolute value of the speed coefficient, whereas for the Chow data in columns 4 and 5 the jump is in the coefficient on memory.

Table 6.4 displays the Phister results covering the remainder of the sample period through 1979. The sample periods shown are 1960–69, 1969–79, and 1960–79. These periods emerged as the outcome of a set of aggregation tests. The period 1960–65 could be extended to 1960–69 but not beyond 1969, and 1969–72 could be pooled with 1973–79. But pooling any period

Table 6.4 Hedonic Regressions, Phister Sample, 1960–79

	1960–69 (1)	1969–79 (2)	1960–79 (3)
Memory	0.65**	0.73**	0.71**
Memory cycle time	−0.55**	−0.43**	−0.51**
IBM dummy	0.11	1.25**	0.70**
Other memory[a]	0.16*	0.20	0.19
1960	base	. . .	base
1961	−0.40**	. . .	−0.34
1962	−0.49*	. . .	−0.23
1963	−0.54**	. . .	−0.57
1964	−1.04**	. . .	−0.70*
1965	−1.81**	. . .	−1.82**
1966	−2.06**	. . .	−2.05**
1967	−2.28**	. . .	−1.83**
1968	excluded	excluded	excluded
1969	−3.07**	base	−2.84**
1970	. . .	−0.19	−3.07**
1974	. . .	−0.60	excluded
1972	. . .	−0.81	−3.43**
1973	. . .	−0.80	−3.41**
1974	. . .	−1.37**	−3.96**
1975	. . .	−1.28**	−3.95**
1976	. . .	−2.12**	−4.54**
1977	. . .	−1.52**	−4.05**
1978	. . .	−2.04**	−4.44**
1979	. . .	−3.04**	−5.32**
$\bar{R}^2$	0.894	0.896	0.885
S.E.E.	0.431	0.626	0.604
Observations	110	139	243

[a] "Other memory" is a dummy that allows for a shift in the coefficient on memory for models having wire or rod memory.

*Indicates significance at the 5 percent level.

**Indicates significance at the 1 percent level.

before 1969 with any period after 1969 is rejected, usually at the 1 percent level.

It is evident from a comparison of columns 1 and 2 in table 6.4 that the large coefficient shifts are not in memory and speed, but in the dummy variables for IBM. The IBM dummy has an enormous coefficient of 1.25 during 1969–79, which implies that IBM charged more than triple the price per unit of quality during this interval as other manufacturers. It seems puzzling that IBM would pursue such an extreme price policy during the decade of the famous antitrust case. However, as we shall see in the next table, this finding results from an aggregation error, the inclusion of mini and mainframe computers in the same equation.

We have already examined the coefficients on the time dummies for the 1960–69 equation in table 6.2. The time dummies for 1969–79 in column 2 of table 6.4 exhibit more of a tendency to zigzag around a declining trend. We should view these results as more useful for indicating the magnitude of price changes for periods of several years than for annual changes between successive pairs of years.

It is important to note that this tendency to zigzag can occur in any data set consisting of new models. Note in table 6.3 that the Chow data display a price increase of 10 percent in 1957. Columns 3 and 4 in table 6.5 indicate that the Dulberger data for new-only models display price increases of 10 percent in 1973, 21 percent in 1974, and 23 percent in 1976 (this occurs when her technological class variables are omitted; price increases still remain in 1974 and 1976 when those variables are included).

Aggregation tests were also carried out for minis and mainframes. This test is carried out for 1965–79, since this is the first year when we have substantial data on minis, and for various subperiods. In each period, the test rejects the aggregation of minis and mainframes at a 1 percent significance level or better, confirming a similar result reported below for the *Computerworld* data. However, a combined test of time and type aggregation indicates that both mini and mainframe equations accept aggregation over the full 1965–79 period.

These results are shown in the first two columns of table 6.5. Note that minis tend to have a higher coefficient on memory and that mainframes have a higher speed coefficient. This suggests one source of the aggregation problem. The pooled equation for 1969–79 (table 6.4, col. 2) has a coefficient of 0.73 on memory, higher than for either minis or mainframes separately in table 6.5. This implies that the marginal price of memory is greater when a purchaser shifts from a mini to a mainframe than when a purchaser shifts to a larger machine within each category. A sensible interpretation is that minis and mainframes are different products, and mainframes provide extra services, for example, more channels and input-output ports, that justify their high relative prices.

Another interesting result is that the IBM dummy, which was implausibly high in the 1969–79 regression in table 6.4, declines substantially in table 6.5. The mainframe IBM coefficient of 0.30 seems consistent with the range of 0.24–0.34 in the results for IBM and plug-compatible mainframes for 1977–84 in the *Computerworld* data set (table 6.6). The coefficient of 0.75 for minis still seems high; an inspection of imputed prices traces this mainly to two particular 1970 models (S3/6 and S3/10).

Time dummy coefficients are missing for some years where we are missing an observation on minis, mainframes, or both. Hence, price indexes cannot be constructed for every year. Also, partly because of smaller sample sizes, the separate mini and mainframe time coefficients display more of a tendency to "jump" than the pooled results in table 6.4. For minis, there are three periods when the overall price decline is interrupted, 1966–67 and by lesser amounts in 1973 and 1977. These jumps clearly result from the small

Table 6.5   **Hedonic Regressions for Mini and Mainframe Models, Phister Sample, 1965–79, and for New-Only Portion of Dulberger Sample, 1972–84**

	Phister Data		Dulberger Data, Technology Variables	
	Minis (1)	Mainframes (2)	Excluded (3)	Included (4)
Memory	0.59**	0.47**	0.19**	0.24**
Memory cycle time	−0.31**	−0.45**	. . .	. . .
IBM dummy	0.75**	0.30**	−0.01	0.02
Other memory[a]	. . .	0.06	. . .	. . .
MIPS	. . .	. . .	0.84**	0.80**
Core 72	. . .	. . .	. . .	−0.60**
FET1K77	. . .	. . .	. . .	0.33
FET4K77	. . .	. . .	. . .	0.59**
FET24K80	. . .	. . .	. . .	0.40**
FET2K81	. . .	. . .	. . .	0.33
F16K81	. . .	. . .	. . .	0.36**
F16K82	. . .	. . .	. . .	0.40*
1965	1.17**	0.95**	. . .	. . .
1966	1.48**	−0.13	. . .	. . .
1967	1.44**	0.77*	. . .	. . .
1968	excluded	no data	. . .	. . .
1969	no data	−0.07	. . .	. . .
1970	0.37	no data	. . .	. . .
1971	no data	no data	. . .	. . .
1972	base	base	base	base
1973	0.07	−0.52	0.11	0.29
1974	−0.16	no data	0.41	−0.01
1975	−0.40	−0.05	−0.49	−0.84**
1976	−1.13**	−0.52	−0.23	−0.65**
1977	−1.01**	−0.48	−0.57	−1.07**
1978	no data	−0.83*	−1.03**	−1.44**
1979	−1.41**	−2.08**	−1.66**	−2.36**
1980	. . .	. . .	−1.65**	−2.33**
1981	. . .	. . .	−1.65**	−2.28**
1982	. . .	. . .	−1.94**	−2.40**
1983	. . .	. . .	−2.12**	−2.52**
1984	. . .	. . .	−2.35**	−2.76**
$\bar{R}^2$	0.599	0.953	0.951	0.965
S.E.E.	0.637	0.220	0.256	0.217
Observations	111	68	133	133

Note: Because only new models are excluded, there are too few observations to permit the following technology variables from the original Dulberger specification to be entered: BP1K73, BP1K74, FET2K75, FET2K76, FET2K77, FET1K78, FET1K79, FET2K79.

[a]"Other memory" is a dummy that allows for a shift in the coefficient on memory for models having wire or rod memory.

*Indicates significance at the 5 percent level.

**Indicates significance at the 1 percent level.

Table 6.6 Hedonic Regressions by Type of Machines, *Computerworld* Sample, 1977–84 and 1981–84

	IBM and Plug-Compatible Machines			Other Mainframes			Minis (including superminis)		
	(1)	(2)	(3)	(4)	(5)	(6)	(7)	(8)	(9)
Memory	0.43**	0.43**	0.31**	0.21**	0.20*	0.18**	0.44**	0.43**	0.44**
Machine cycle time	−0.23**	−0.16	−0.08	−0.93**	−0.93**	−0.20*	−0.31	−0.05	−0.09
MIPS	⋯	⋯	0.43**	⋯	⋯	0.79**	⋯	⋯	−0.06
Minimum number of channels	0.58**	0.28*	0.20*	0.36*	0.36*	0.10	⋯	−0.04	−0.02
Maximum number of channels	0.16**	0.50**	0.27**	0.16	0.17	−0.05	⋯	0.27**	0.26*
Cache buffer size[a]	0.003**	0.003**	0.001	0.002	0.002	0.000	⋯	0.005	0.005*
IBM dummy	0.24**	0.34**	0.28**	⋯	⋯	⋯	⋯	⋯	⋯
1977	1.43**	⋯		⋯	⋯		⋯	⋯	
1978	1.30**	⋯		⋯	⋯		⋯	⋯	
1979	1.06**	⋯		1.94**	⋯		1.33**	⋯	
1980	0.84**	⋯	⋯	no data	⋯	⋯	0.84**	⋯	⋯
1981	0.50**	0.55**	0.67**	0.53	0.52	0.99**	0.62**	0.81**	0.83**
1982	0.32**	0.44**	0.43**	0.43	0.43	0.54**	0.42	−0.05	−0.09
1983	0.17	0.26	0.34**	0.75**	0.74**	0.85**	0.06	0.17	0.15
1984	base	base	base	base	base	base	base	base	base
$\bar{R}^2$	0.866	0.890	0.928	0.776	0.780	0.920	0.398	0.508	0.502
S.E.E.	0.472	0.470	0.380	0.759	0.761	0.457	0.660	0.664	0.669
Observations	191	110	112	94	92	92	111	68	68

[a]This variable is not in log levels because it often takes a zero value.

*Indicates significance at the 5 percent level.

**Indicates significance at the 1 percent level.

sample size, just two mini models in 1966, two in 1967, one in 1973, and one in 1977. For mainframes, there are substantial jumps in 1967 (one model) and 1975 (two models). Below, in constructing the final price index, the estimated time dummy coefficients for mainframes are smoothed over the 1966–76 period, but this does not prove to be necessary for minis.

Columns 3 and 4 of table 6.5 display equations for the new model component of the Dulberger data set (which includes only mainframes, not minis) over the 1972–84 period. These results do not correspond to the equations estimated in Dulberger (1989), which covers both new and old models (132 new models and 164 old models). Column 3 omits Dulberger's technology-type variables for purposes of comparison with the Phister results, and column 4 reestimates the equation with the technology variables included. While the standard errors are not comparable, since the sample periods are different, they are of the same order of magnitude in the mainframe results (col. 2) and the two Dulberger equations. On a base 1972 = 100, the implied price index for 1979 in columns 2–4 is 12.6, 19.0, and 10.6, respectively.

6.5.3   The *Computerworld* Sample: Regression Results

The *Computerworld* sample is very large in comparison to the other data sets studied in this chapter. The number of new model observations is fifty per year, as contrasted with 9.6 for Chow, 5.1 for Dulberger, and 3.8 for Phister (all these calculations refer to individual models, not observations created by doubling and tripling, as in the Dulberger and Phister data sets). Compared to the Dulberger data set that overlaps its 1977–84 time period, it not only covers minis, superminis, and mainframes of noncompatible manufacturers, which are excluded from Dulberger's data set, but also it provides a much greater coverage of IBM and plug-compatible mainframes (191 new models over 1977–84 as contrasted with fifty-five for Dulberger), hereafter abbreviated I/PC. It also makes available additional variables (minimum and maximum channels and cache buffer size). Its main limitation, in addition to lacking the Dulberger technology variables, is that coverage of non-I/PC mainframes begins only in 1981 (plus two 1979 models), mini and supermini coverage begins only in 1979, and the MIPS measure of quality is available beginning only in 1981.

In table 6.6, the results are presented in three groups: I/PC mainframes, other mainframes, and minis. A pooled regression equation is not presented for the entire *Computerworld* data set, since aggregation tests indicate that these three subsets cannot be merged. Because the MIPS variable is not available before 1981, for each group results are displayed for an equation that omits MIPS from 1977–84, then one that omits MIPS for 1981–84, and finally an equation that includes MIPS from 1981–84. In every case, the third equation that includes MIPS indicates a more rapid rate of price decline between 1981 and 1984 than either equation omitting MIPS. The third equation also indicates a faster 1981–84 rate of price decline for other mainframes and minis for I/PC mainframes. The other main difference in the three groups is that the price decline for I/PC mainframes is smooth, while the other mainframes have a price jump in 1983. Columns 8 and 9 also display a smaller and statistically insignificant price jump for minis in 1983.

There are several interesting features of the estimated coefficients for the various quality characteristics. For I/PC mainframes, almost all the estimated coefficients are significant. The inclusion of MIPS in column 3 greatly improves the fit and reduces the coefficient on memory but still leaves room for a significant contribution of the minimum and maximum channels variables. Cache buffer size is significant when MIPS is omitted but insignificant in conjunction with MIPS. The IBM dummy is quite stable in the range of 0.24–0.34 and highly significant. The elasticity on MIPS is considerably lower than in the Dulberger data set results (table 6.5, cols. 3 and 4), probably because those results do not include any variables for the number of channels.

For other mainframes, the results including MIPS (col. 6) yield memory and MIPS coefficients very similar to the Dulberger data set results, and it is interesting that the inclusion of MIPS still leaves a significant role for cycle time. Interestingly, MIPS is not significant for minis. In light of the high standard error in this equation, it would appear that mini prices are largely explained by variables omitted from the data set.

6.6   The New Processor Price Index and Its Interpretation

6.6.1   Linking the Component Indexes

With the hedonic regression equations now estimated, there are only a few decisions required to develop a final index of computer processors. This section presents the basic results for indexes constructed from tables 6.2, 6.5, and 6.6 using the dummy variable technique. Indexes for the same equations are also developed using the imputation technique. Because the year-to-year changes are extremely similar when the two different methods are used, only the dummy variable indexes are presented in annual detail, while subsequently growth rates over multiyear intervals are presented for the imputation indexes.

The final processor price index and its ingredients are displayed in table 6.7. The first eight columns of table 6.7 exhibit the components. Because the aggregation test yielded an ambiguous conclusion regarding the feasibility of pooling the 1951–60 and 1960–69 regressions on the Phister data set, both the separate 1951–60 and 1960–69 results are included in columns 1–2 with the pooled 1951–69 results in column 3. Since aggregation tests reject the pooling of minis and mainframes in the post-1965 period, separate indexes are shown for these two components over 1965–79. This

Table 6.7   **The Final Price Index for Computer Processors, 1951–84 (1984 = 100; all indexes shown are based on the dummy variable method)**

	Phister Data Set (1965 = 100)					Computerworld (1984 = 100)			Final Price Index
	All Models			1965–79					
	1951–60	1960–69	1951–69	Minis	Mainframes	I/PC Mainframes	Other Mainframes	Minis (including supermini)	
	(1)	(2)	(3)	(4)	(5)	(6)	(7)	(8)	(9)
1951	4,699	⋯	4,426	⋯	⋯	⋯	⋯	⋯	133,666
1954	1,255	⋯	1,028	⋯	⋯	⋯	⋯	⋯	33,293
1955	1,243	⋯	655	⋯	⋯	⋯	⋯	⋯	26,452
1956	no data	⋯	no data	⋯	⋯	⋯	⋯	⋯	25,373
1957	excluded	⋯	excluded	⋯	⋯	⋯	⋯	⋯	24,337
1958	939	⋯	675	⋯	⋯	⋯	⋯	⋯	23,344
1959	675	⋯	426	⋯	⋯	⋯	⋯	⋯	15,726
1960	611	611	371	⋯	⋯	⋯	⋯	⋯	13,948
1961	⋯	410	280	⋯	⋯	⋯	⋯	⋯	9,928
1962	⋯	374	272	⋯	⋯	⋯	⋯	⋯	9,349
1963	⋯	356	292	⋯	⋯	⋯	⋯	⋯	9,444
1964	⋯	246	193	⋯	⋯	⋯	⋯	⋯	5,992
1965	⋯	100	100	100	100	⋯	⋯	⋯	2,931
1966	⋯	57	73	136	34	⋯	⋯	⋯	1,583
1967	⋯	90	78	131	84	⋯	⋯	⋯	1,582
1968	⋯	excluded	excluded	excluded	no data	⋯	⋯	⋯	1,296
1969	⋯	28	30	no data	36	⋯	⋯	⋯	1,058
1970	⋯	⋯	⋯	45	no data	⋯	⋯	⋯	1,065

(*continued*)

Table 6.7 (continued)

| | Phister Data Set (1965 = 100) | | | | | Computerworld (1984 = 100) | | | |
| | All Models | | | 1965–79 | | | | | Final Price |
	1951–60 (1)	1960–69 (2)	1951–69 (3)	Minis (4)	Mainframes (5)	I/PC Mainframes (6)	Other Mainframes (7)	Minis (including supermini) (8)	Index (9)
1971	⋯	⋯	⋯	excluded	no data	⋯	⋯	⋯	1,084
1972	⋯	⋯	⋯	31	39	⋯	⋯	⋯	1,099
1973	⋯	⋯	⋯	33	23	⋯	⋯	⋯	846
1974	⋯	⋯	⋯	26	no data	⋯	⋯	⋯	831
1975	⋯	⋯	⋯	21	37	⋯	⋯	⋯	813
1976	⋯	⋯	⋯	10	23	⋯	⋯	⋯	606
1977	⋯	⋯	⋯	11	24	495	⋯	⋯	638
1978	⋯	⋯	⋯	no data	17	435	⋯	⋯	554
1979	⋯	⋯	⋯	7.6	4.8	342	1,102	466	439
1980	⋯	⋯	⋯	⋯	⋯	275	no data	286	307
1981	⋯	⋯	⋯	⋯	⋯	195	269	229	211
1982	⋯	⋯	⋯	⋯	⋯	154	58	91	138
1983	⋯	⋯	⋯	⋯	⋯	140	234	116	145

Sources by column: **(1–3)** Table 6.2, cols. 1–3. **(4–5)** Table 6.5., cols. 1–2. **(6–8)** Table 6.6, cols. 1, 4, and 7, linked in 1981 to cols. 3, 6, and 9. **(9)** 1977–84: Törnqvist index of cols. 6–8. 1965–77: Törnqvist index of cols. 4–5, with the mainframe index smoothed by taking an average of 1966–67 as the value for both years; an average of 1972–73 as the value for both years; and by omitting 1975. 1951–65: A geometric average of Törnqvist indexes of col. 1 linked to col. 2, and of col. 3.

Geometric interpolation is used to span any year where an index value is missing because of no data or excluded observations.

Source of weights for value share of mainframes and minis, table 6.1. Source of weights for value share of I/PC mainframes and other mainframes, *Computerworld*, various issues.

aggregation test result leads me to make no use at all of the equation estimated for the full Phister data set over 1969–79, as displayed in table 6.4. Columns 6–8 exhibit the *Computerworld* results. In each case, the indexes displayed for 1981–84 use the results with the significant MIPS variable included, and these are linked at 1981 to the 1977–84 equations that omit the MIPS variable.

The separate components are aggregated using the Törnqvist approximation to an ideal index number. This simply weights the logarithmic changes between year t and $t + 1$ of each component index by the average in t and $t + 1$ of the value shares of the components being combined. Then the string of weighted changes is cumulated starting with zero in the base year and converted into a price index by taking antilogs. In table 6.7 the final processor price index is presented with a base of 1984 = 100. For instance, with hypothetical 1983 index values for components A and B of ninety-eight and 150, and a value share for A in 1983 of .40 and in 1984 of .48, the weighted change would be

$$(0.44)[\log(100/98)] + (0.56)(\log[100/150)] = -0.218,$$

and the resulting 1983 index value would be $100[\exp(0.218)] = 124.4$.

Working backward from 1984, for 1979–84 the index combines the *Computerworld* indexes from columns 6–8 with value shares for I/PC mainframes, other mainframes, and minis (see source notes to table 6.7). For 1977–79, only the *Computerworld* I/PC mainframe index (col. 6) is used. An alternative would have been to weight this index with the Phister index for minis (col. 4), interpolated through the missing year 1978. By coincidence, the 1977/1979 ratio for these two indexes is identical (1.45), indicating that the alternative would have made no difference. More important is the fact that the choice of the *Computerworld* indexes after 1977 implies that no use is made of the Phister mainframe index for 1977–79, which has a drastically different 1977/1979 ratio of 5.0. This large discrepancy implies that the decision to omit the 1977–79 decline in the Phister mainframe index has an important effect on the final results. A close examination of actual and imputed prices for individual models has convinced me that the *Computerworld* results are more reliable because of their larger sample size and lesser dependence on particular unusual models. The excessive reliance of both the Phister and the Dulberger samples on a particular atypical model in 1979 causes both resulting indexes to overstate the rate of price decline during 1977–79 and to understate it during 1979–84.

The aggregation test results suggest that the separate Phister mini and mainframe indexes should be used as far back as possible, that is, from 1977 back to 1965. Note that the choice of the component indexes makes no use of the 1960–69 or 1951–69 results for all Phister models during the years

1966–69. Over the period 1951–65, the ambiguity of the aggregation test results suggests the use of an unweighted geometric average of separate Törnqvist indexes of the 1951–60 linked to the 1960–69 equation (cols. 1 and 2) and the pooled 1951–69 equation (col. 3).

6.6.2   The Price and Performance History of IBM Mainframes

The next section exhibits the annual percentage growth rates of the final processor price index over several basic multiyear intervals (e.g., 1954–60, 1960–65, etc.). While the overall growth rate of the final processor price index is in the same general range as other research, – 19.4 percent per year, the pace of its decline is irregular, with rates of – 22.1 percent in 1954–65, – 12.7 percent in 1965–77, and – 26.5 percent in 1977–84. The relatively slow rate of price decline observed between 1965 and 1977 conflicts with some other research, including some of that surveyed by Triplett (1989).

What would seem a hopeless task of reconciling conflicting results becomes a bit more feasible when one considers the dominant market share of IBM.[23] By comparing major IBM models of succeeding computer "generations," we can determine whether the evolution of the price-performance history of IBM models is consistent with the behavior of the final processor price index. This history is displayed in table 6.8. For each of thirty-seven different IBM models, plus the early ENIAC and UNIVAC I machines, data are shown on the memory, speed, the Knight "commercial index" of computation power, MIPS (since 1972), the actual system price with the memory configuration shown, and the imputed system price in the 1965 base year. The latter is calculated separately for each of the regression equations that serves as a component of the final index, and, if 1965 is not part of the sample period of that equation, the resulting imputed price is linked to 1965 at some common overlap period (see notes to table 6.8). The ratio of the actual to the imputed 1965 price is shown in column 8 as an index number (1965 = 100) and again in column 9 on the basis 1984 = 100.

6.6.3   Using the IBM History to Evaluate Index Discrepancies

We need to examine table 6.8 in conjunction with table 6.9, which converts all the relevant price indexes discussed thus far into annual percentage growth rates over key intervals divided in 1960, 1965, 1972, 1977, 1979, and 1981. The year 1960 was a dividing point within Chow's study; 1965 marks the end of Chow's study; 1972 the beginning of Dulberger's data; 1977 the beginning of the *Computerworld* data; and 1981 the year when the MIPS variable becomes available in the *Computerworld*

---

23. IBM's 360 line accounted for about 70 percent of mainframe revenue in the last half of the 1960s; IBM's overall share of world mainframe revenues in 1987 was 76 percent. See *Business Week*, 30 November 1987, 121.

Table 6.8   The History of Price and Performance for Selected IBM Computer Processors

Year	IBM Model (1)	Memory (kbytes) (2)	Memory Cycle Time (milliseconds) (3)	Knight Commercial Index (4)	MIPS (5)	Actual System Price ($000) (6)	Imputed 1965 Price ($000) (7)	Actual/Imputed (1965 = 100) (8)	Actual/Imputed (1984 = 100) (9)	Regression (10)
1946	[ENIAC]	...	...	0.04	...	...	...	47,753	1,095,252	A
1951	[UNIVAC I]	8	220	0.29	...	750	17	4,406	101,055	B,D
1954	650	10	2,400	0.27	...	174	19	998	22,890	B,D
1955	704	108	12	3.79	...	1,054	153	588	13,486	B,D
	705	30	17	2.09	...	608	62	864	19,817	B,D
1958	709	108	12	10.23	...	1,108	149	642	14,725	B,D
1959	7090	197	2.2	45.47	...	1,652	282	465	10,615	B,D
1960	7070	37	6.0	5.14	...	488	81	506	11,606	B,D
1961	1410	45	4.5	4.7	...	424	91	380	8,716	C,D
	7074	88	4.0	31.7	...	1,012	196	473	10,849	C,D
	7080	100	2.2	30.9	...	1,366	244	508	11,651	C,D
1962	7094	197	2.0	95.9	...	1,274	435	278	6,376	C,D
1963	7010	70	2.4	11.5	...	578	201	272	6,238	C,D
	7044	122	2.0	23.4	...	963	318	290	6,651	C,D
1965	360–20	10	3.6	4.5	...	41	49	81	1,858	E,D
	360–30	36	1.5	17.1	...	132	138	90	2,064	E,D
	360–40	136	2.5	50.1	...	340	500	82	1,881	F,D
	360–50	288	2.0	149	...	721	784	103	2,362	F,D
	360–65	1,088	0.75	810	...	2,458	2,255	115	2,638	F,D
1966	360–44	144	1.0	858	...	252	813	33	757	F
1972	370–135	304	0.94	172	0.16	472	1,123	42	963	F
	370–145	1,184	0.61	446	0.30	798	2,574	31	711	F
	370–155	1,152	0.12	1,203	0.55	1,553	5,355	29	665	F
	370–165	1,792	0.08	3,515	1.90	2,647	7,785	34	780	F

(continued)

Table 6.8 (continued)

Year	IBM Model (1)	Memory (kbytes) (2)	Memory Cycle Time (milliseconds) (3)	Knight Commercial Index (4)	MIPS (5)	Actual System Price ($000) (6)	Imputed 1965 Price ($000) (7)	Actual/Imputed (1965 = 100) (8)	Actual/Imputed (1984 = 100) (9)	Regression (10)
1973	370–125	176	0.48	70	0.08	266	1,209	22	505	F
1974	370–115	165	0.48	39	0.05	147	474	31	711	E
1975	370–158–3	3,328	0.12	2,423	0.83	2,593	8,643	30	688	F
1976	370–138	768	0.94	496	0.21	395	1,717	23	528	F
1977	370–148	1,000	0.23	1,014	0.42	687	3,440	20	459	G
1978	3031	2,000	0.12	2,317	1.05	831	6,812	12	280	G
	3032	2,000	0.08	6,921	2.50	1,905	13,004	15	336	G
	3033	6,000	0.06	19,019	5.90	3,613	15,757	23	526	G
1979	4341	2,000	0.12	1,863	0.72	247	3,555	6.9	160	G
1980	3081	16,000	0.03	…	10.40	3,723	56,927	6.5	150	G
1981	8140	1,000	0.80	…	0.36	81	780	9.2	211	G
	3033-M	16,000	0.06	…	9.10	2,678	2,880	4.1	93	G
1982	4321	1,000	0.90	…	0.19	85	1,284	6.7	153	G
1984	4361–5	2,000	0.10	…	1.14	201	4,518	4.4	102	G
	4381–2	4,000	0.07	…	2.70	499	11,560	4.4	99	G

Sources by column: (2, 3, 6) Phister data set 1951–76, Computerworld data set 1977–84. Cycle time linked by dividing Computerworld machine cycle time by 1,000; by this method, cycle times coincide exactly on five models that overlap the Phister and Computerworld data sets in 1977–79. (4) Phister data set. (5) Dulberger data set 1972–80, Computerworld data set 1981–84. (7) Obtained from predicted value of regression indicated in col. 10. Regressions C, D, and E all have 1965 base year. B is linked at 1960, F by the average of the five overlapping observations in 1977–79. (8) 100 times col. 6 divided by col. 7, except for 1954–65, for which is reported the average of imputed indexes from the regressions indicated in col. 10. (9) Col. 8 divided by 0.0436, which is the 1984 index number of a 1965 base implied by the average of the five overlapping observations in regressions E and F. (10) A: ENIAC linked to UNIVAC I with Knight's performance/price ratio (1966, table 6.1, col. 4 divided by col. 5). B: Phister 1951–60, table 6.2, col. 1. C: Phister 1960–69, table 6.2, col. 1. D: Phister 1951–69, table 6.2, col. 3. E: Phister minis 1965–79, table 6.5, col. 1. F: Phister mainframes 1965–79, table 6.5, col. 2. G: Computerworld IBM and plug compatibles, 1977–84, table 6.6, col. 1.

Table 6.9   Comparison of Alternative Indexes for Computer Processors, Annual Percentage Growth Rates, Various Intervals, 1954–84

	1954–60 (1)	1960–65 (2)	1965–72 (3)	1972–77 (4)	1977–79 (5)	1979–81 (6)	1981–84 (7)	1954–65 (8)	1972–84 (9)	1977–84 (10)	1954–84 (11)
Mainframes:											
1. Phister (51–60) (imputed)	−12.0	...	...	...	...	...	...	...	...	...	...
	−7.2										
2. Phister (60–69) (imputed)	...	−36.2	...	...	...	...	...	...	...	...	...
		−32.6									
3. Phister (51–69) (imputed)	−17.0	−26.2	...	...	...	...	...	−21.2	...	...	...
	−15.1	−26.8						−20.4			
4. Chow new-only (54–65) (imputed)	−19.0	−23.0	...	...	...	...	...	−20.8	...	...	...
	−18.8	−22.7						−20.6			
5. Phister mainframe (imputed)	...	...	−13.6	−9.2	−80.5	...	...	...	...	...	...
			−13.5	−9.7	−81.1						
6. Dulberger N-O (A) (imputed)	...	...	...	−11.4	−54.5	+0.5	−23.3	...	−19.6	−25.4	...
				−12.7	−54.2	+0.4	−23.1		−20.0	−25.3	
7. Dulberger N-O (B) (imputed)	...	...	...	−21.4	−64.5	+4.0	−16.0	...	−24.1	−23.0	...
				−22.1	−64.7	+4.9	−15.5		−23.7	−23.1	
8. *Computerworld* I/PC (imputed)	...	...	...	...	−18.5	−28.0	−22.3	...	...	−22.9	...
					−12.9	−27.1	−22.8			−20.3	
9. Linked mainframe (imputed)	...	−31.2	−13.6	−9.2	−18.5	−28.0	−22.3	−22.1	−17.2	−22.9	−18.2
		−29.7	−13.5	−9.7	−12.9	−27.1	−22.8	−19.6	−15.9	−20.3	−16.7
10. IBM imputed mainframe	...	−33.6	−13.8	−10.6	−53.2	−2.6	−14.0	−21.4	−17.2	−21.9	−17.9
Minis:											
11. Combined Phister and *Computerworld*	...	...	−16.7	−20.2	−20.0	−35.5	−27.6	...	−24.5	−27.7	...
Mainframes and minis:											
12. Final price index	−14.5	−31.2	−14.0	−10.9	−18.7	−36.6	−24.9	−22.1	−20.0	−26.5	−19.4

Sources by row: **(1–3)** Table 6.2, cols. 1–3. **(4)** Table 6.3, col. 6. **(5)** Table 6.5, col. 2. **(6–7)** Table 6.5, cols. 3–4. **(8)** Table 6.7, col. 6. **(9)** 1954–77 this table rows 1–3 and 5. 1977–84 this table row 8. **(10)** Table 6.8. **(11)** Table 6.5, col. 1, and table 6.7, col. 8. **(12)** Table 6.7, col. 9.

data. Also included is 1979, since this is the introduction date of the IBM 4300 series, which plays such an important role in explaining the divergent behavior of alternative indexes in the 1977–81 period.

The IBM price index in column 8 or 9 can be interpreted as an imputation index for a subset of the available data. In order to isolate the effects of the selection of particular IBM models as opposed to the effect of using the imputation technique itself, most of the indexes in table 6.9 are displayed as pairs; the index constructed by the dummy variable technique is shown as the top member of the pair, with the corresponding imputation index directly below. Comparing the growth rates of the IBM index in row 10 of table 6.9 with the mainframe component of the final processor price index in row 9 and with the results for the Chow and Dulberger new-only (''N-O'') samples in rows 4, 6, and 7, we can isolate four main discrepancies that warrant discussion. These are the differing growth rates for the Chow and Phister samples within the 1954–65 period; the slow price decline of the final index during 1965–72, which differs from some of the results surveyed by Triplett; the slow price decline of the final index during 1972–77; and the differing time path of the price decline of the final index from the Dulberger results during 1977–84.

1954–65: Chow versus Phister

All the indexes for 1954–65 summarized in column 8 agree on a rate of price decline in the range of 20–22 percent per annum. Particularly remarkable is the close agreement over 1954–65 of the pooled Phister equation with the new-only component of the Chow sample (rows 3 and 4). A greater discrepancy occurs in the timing of price changes before and after 1960. The Phister sample registers a smaller price decrease before 1960 and a faster price decrease between 1960 and 1965. This is particularly pro-nounced in 1963–65, and more so for the separate regressions split at 1960 (rows 1 and 2) than the pooled regression (row 3).

The IBM history provides a clue as to the source of this phenomenon; for the IBM subset, the imputed price index shows a tendency to decline slowly during 1954–60 and more rapidly during 1960–65. Some intuition about this is provided by the Knight commercial index, which is not used in the regressions. Taking pairs of machines with roughly equivalent Knight indexes, we get an annual rate of decline of the price/performance ratio from 1955 (model 704) to 1961 (model 1410) of 19 percent, from 1959 (model 7090) to 1965 (model 360–40) of 28 percent, and from 1961 (model 1410) to 1965 (model 360–20) of 57 percent. The differing pattern for the Phister and Chow samples is largely due to the greater IBM share of the observations in the Phister sample (49 percent) than in the Chow sample (21 percent). Another indication that the Chow sample is less representative comes from its higher proportion of mini computers, which, as is evident in table 6.1, had negligible sales before 1965.[24] Particularly worth noting is the much higher representation in the Phister sample of the third-generation IBM 360 series in 1965 (fifteen of twenty-four observations) than in the Chow sample (five of sixteen observations, of which twelve are minis). This helps explain why the Phister indexes drop so fast between 1963 and 1965. Although the agreement between the two samples over 1954–65 is reassuring, an index weighted by market shares would show more similarity to the slow-fast pattern over the 1954–60 and 1960–65 subperiods evident in the Phister data than the more evenly paced tempo of Chow's price decline.

1965–72: Comparing the 360 and 370 Series

Timing of new-model introductions is uniform across data sets: the same five 360-series IBM models are introduced in the Chow and Phister data in 1965, and the same four 370-series models in the Dulberger and Phister data in 1972. Given the dominant market share of IBM and the miniscule value share of minis during this period, the price history of 1965–72 boils down to a single question. How much did the quality-corrected price of 370s decline relative to 360s? The imputed base-year prices (1965 = 100) for the 1972 370s in table 6.8 indicate an average 1972 price index of 34 percent. This is a far more modest price decline than in the evidence for 1965–72 surveyed by Triplett, which leads him to a 1972 index number of 15 (1989, table 6-A).

It seems inconceivable that anyone could compare the 1972 370 models and the 1965 360 models and conclude that a quality-corrected price index had declined from 100 to fifteen. In fact, it is hard to justify an index of thirty-four. Note, for instance, that the average Knight performance index for the 370–145 and 370–155 is 825, close to the 360–65 value of 810. Yet the ratio of the average 1972 price of the two 370 models to the 360–65 price in 1965 is 0.48. To use the information contained in the Knight index more systematically, an additional regression equation is estimated only for the thirty-six Phister model 360 and model 370 observations over 1965–74 with the speed variable replaced by the Knight index.[25] Because we are comparing like with like, the standard error is just 0.139, far lower than in any other equation estimated in this chapter. Both the memory and the

---

24. Chow's data provides monthly rentals and Phister's provides both monthly rental and purchase prices. As noted above, price tends to equal forty to sixty times monthly rental. Corresponding to the $250,000 dividing line between minis and mainframes would be about a $10,000 monthly rental. Fifty-seven percent of Chow's new-only observations are minis by this definition, vs. 36 percent of the Phister sample.

25. This use of the Knight index in preference to speed is an afterthought. If I were beginning this research again, I would have tested each equation to learn if the Knight index was superior to speed as an explanatory variable, or whether it and speed should enter together along with memory.

Knight index variables are highly significant, with respective coefficients of 0.44 and 0.40, and the price indexes (1965 = 100) are as follows:

	1966	1972	1973	1974
Dummy variable method	23	52	60	47
Imputation method	23	48	61	44

Thus, the use of the Knight index yields an even slower rate of price decline over 1965–72 than the basic Phister index for mainframes. The underpricing of the single 1966 model (360–44) stands out as well.[26] These results suggest that, far from understating the rate of price decline over 1965–72, the indexes in column 3 of table 6.9 may have overstated it.

1972–77: The Second-Generation 370s

The next discrepancy in table 6.9 occurs during 1972–77. The Phister mainframe index in row 5 agrees fairly well with price index (A) from the Dulberger new-only sample, registering a 9.2 percent annual rate of decline, compared to 11.4. But both indexes decline far more slowly than the 21.4 percent rate registered for price index (B), which is based on the same sample but adds the Dulberger technology variables. On the basis 1972 = 100, in 1977 the Phister price index is at sixty-one, the Dulberger (A) at fifty-seven, and the Dulberger (B) at thirty-four. Which rate of change is more plausible? Once again, turning to the IBM data in table 6.8, we note that the only new 1977 model is the model 370–148. This is the only new IBM model introduced in 1977 in either the Dulberger or the Phister sample.

To assess the rate of price change over 1972–77, we can compare the price-performance characteristics of the 370–148 with the similar-sized 370–155 in 1972. The Phister 1977/1972 ratio of actual prices for these two models is 0.48; the equivalent Dulberger ratio is an identical 0.48. The imputed quality ratio is 0.58 for Phister, 0.69 for Dulberger (A), and 2.56 for Dulberger (B).[27] The implied imputed price index, expressed as the actual ratio over the imputed quality ratio, is eighty-three for Phister, seventy for Dulberger (A), and nineteen for Dulberger (B). The Dulberger (B) result seems implausible. By every measure of quality listed in table 6.8, the 1977

26. Further support for the view that the IBM 360-44 was underpriced, and should not be given undue weight in the final processor price index, is provided in a letter from Franklin M. Fisher. According to Fisher, "the 360/44 was deliberately stripped-down to be a 'lean' machine. . . . Any study that didn't show the 360/44 as underpriced wouldn't be doing its job. Perhaps more important for your purposes, since we know that this was done off the pricing surface, it may be a mistake to use 360/44 observations in your sample. This is particularly true because the machine didn't sell very well."

27. Using the substitute equation that employs the Knight commercial index instead of speed, the Phister quality ratio is 0.87.

vintage 370–148 is inferior to the 1972 vintage 370–155: it has 87 percent of the memory, operates at half the speed, has 84 percent of the Knight performance index, and has 76 percent of the MIPS performance measure. The only reason the B result attributes such high quality to the 370–148 is the contribution of the technology variables—these alone imply that the 370–148 has 255 percent of the quality of the 370–155 simply because of the different materials used in the memories of the two machines (magnetic core vs. semiconductor). However useful the technology variables may be in explaining price differences of particular machines within a given year, they seem misleading in evaluating quality across a span of years.[28] Viewed from the standpoint of the user, who neither knows nor cares about chip technology but values quality characteristics like memory, cycle time, and MIPS, it seems implausible to argue that the 370–148 had a higher quality than the 370–155, much less 2.5 times the quality. Fully two-thirds of the contribution of the Dulberger technology variables to the implausible imputation of the 1972–77 price increase comes from the 1972 coefficient, which rates the 370–165 as having seven times the quality of the 370–135, as contrasted to twelve times the quality when the technology variable is omitted. Rather than concluding that the 370–165 and 370–155 were of low "quality" relative to their content of memory and MIPS, I prefer the alternative conclusion that the price-to-MIPS gradient was unusually flat in 1972, and that the Dulberger variable is standing as a proxy for an equally plausible MIPS-slope dummy in that year.[29] As is evident from the growth rates displayed in table 6.9, the implausible discrepancy between the A and the B results for the Dulberger sample applies only to 1972–77, and for 1977–84 both the A and the B indexes decline at about the same rate as the *Computerworld* index for mainframes.

1977–84: The Influence of the IBM 4341

Recall that the final processor price index is based on the *Computerworld* results from 1977 to 1984 and ignores the rapid rate of price decline exhibited by the Phister mainframe results in the overlapping years 1977–79. Overall, from 1977 to 1984, there is no conflict between the rate of change of the *Computerworld* and Dulberger price indexes, both A and B. The big difference is in timing within that interval: the Dulberger indexes fall at a fifty-five to sixty-five annual rate in 1977–79 and then rise in 1979–81

28. On this discussion, Franklin M. Fisher cautions that the 370/148 was a virtual memory machine, while the 370/155 was not.

29. The same evaluation applies to Dulberger's own results (1989), which differ from those here by including both old and new models. However, the Dulberger (1989) sample consists entirely of new models in 1972, and her estimate of the 1972 technology dummy of −0.55 is close to the estimate of −0.66 shown in table 6.5 above. It should be noted that the Dulberger sample for 1972, in addition to the four 370 models shown in table 6.8, also includes a model 2022. However, as a minicomputer priced at just $46,000 with maximum memory, the Phister results suggest that it should not be pooled with the much larger mainframes in her sample.

before resuming their decline. In complete contrast, the *Computerworld* mainframe index declines at a relatively constant rate over 1977–84, with if anything an acceleration after 1979.

This discrepancy is explained entirely by the small sample size of the Dulberger data set for new models, which contains only two new models in 1979. One of these is the IBM 4341, which is famous in the history of the computer industry for its low price in relation to performance, which suggested at the time to observers that IBM was adopting a newly aggressive marketing strategy.[30] The other model is a plug-compatible; both it and the IBM 4341 have an actual-to-imputed price ratio on a 1984 = 100 base of about 150, quite similar to the imputed ratio for the IBM 4341 in the *Computerworld* regression of 160. Quite simply, these two models introduced the price level of 1982–83 about three years early. But an index based only on these two models is misleading if other new models sold in 1979 were not similarly underpriced. The *Computerworld* sample contains not two but forty-two observations on new IBM and plug-compatible models introduced in 1979, having actual-to-imputed ratios on a 1984 base ranging from 111 to 644. The IBM models alone range from 160 to 474. Since the model 4341 was a relatively small mainframe, it is likely that other larger new machines with much less favorable prices had a substantial market share in 1979, suggesting that the *Computerworld* index is more reliable than the Dulberger A and B indexes. Gradually in the years after 1979, lower-priced machines are introduced into the *Computerworld* sample, so that over the entire period 1977–84 its rate of price decline is roughly the same as in the Dulberger sample. The heavy reliance of the Dulberger sample on the two unusual 1979 models explains the starkly different timing of price decline evident in table 6.9.

6.7 Peripherals and Weighting Issues

Table 6.7 has shown how the different indexes developed in this study are integrated to form the final index for computer processors displayed in its column 8. A computer processor is a "box" containing the central processor and its internal memory. The index of table 6.7 needs to be augmented by price indexes for the various peripherals that are essential to make a computer processor accessible to its users. Such a price index for computer systems would then be comparable to the index published by the BEA. Further, this index for computer systems could then be weighted together with the BEA price deflator for other products in the OCAM category of PDE. Thus, we construct a new deflator for OCAM machinery comparable in coverage to the one published in the NIPA. As in developing the index for processors, the method of weighting together the successive layers of indexes, from the computer box to OCAM, is the Törnqvist index formula.

30. See "IBM's New Models Jolt the Industry," *Business Week,* 12 February 1979, 42.

As suggested in the introduction to this chapter, differences among the alternative price indexes for computer processors that might be used in such an exercise are trivial compared to the major impact of alternative methods of weighting. A Törnqvist index has the triple advantage of maintaining year-to-year comparability, of being immune to distortions in weighting due to the choice of the base year, and of reflecting the continual shift in the importance of its components by using moving weights.

This chapter does not create new price indexes for peripherals similar to the one constructed for computer processors. To maintain consistency with the hedonic index for computer processors, I rely on the hedonic regression coefficients of the study by Cole et al. (1986, table 7). Their hedonic price indexes are available for three types of computer peripherals—disk drives, printers, and displays—but only over the 1972–84 interval. The source for the earlier years is the study by Flamm (1987, table A-3, p. 218), which covers four types of computer peripherals—moving-head disk files, line printers, card readers and punchers, and magnetic tape units. Flamm also displays weights for these four types of peripherals and for processors covering the period 1955–78. These weights are used throughout, with the 1955 weights extrapolated prior to 1955 and the 1978 weights after that year. Flamm's four series are linked to Cole's three series in 1972; to ascribe Flamm's four sets of weights to these three products priced by Cole, card readers and punchers were matched with displays, line printers with printers, and the weights of magnetic tape units and moving-head disk files were merged and applied to disk drives. Also, in order to match the time coverage of the peripherals index with the processor index, a price index for peripherals is created over the 1951–57 interval by backcasting, using the annual average growth rate of this index over 1957–65. The effect of this arbitrary choice on the final results is minimal, since Flamm's weight on peripherals in 1957 is only 11 percent (see table 6.10).

Results are displayed in table 6.10 and figure 6.1. The following summarizes the quantitative evidence of table 6.10 over selected intervals:

	Annual Percentage Rate of Change		
Alternative Deflators	1957–65	1965–72	1972–84
Computer processors	−26.5	−14.0	−20.0
Peripherals	−23.4	−17.5	−16.5
Difference: processor-peripherals	−3.1	3.5	−3.5
Computer systems	−24.3	−14.9	−18.5

Since the index for peripherals does not decelerate as much over 1965–72 as the processor index, inclusion of peripherals makes the final index for systems decline at a slightly slower rate than for processors over 1957–65 and 1972–84, but at a slightly faster rate over 1965–72.

Table 6.10   Components of and Final Index for Computer Systems, 1982 = 100

Year	Weight of Computers (1)	Index for Computers (2)	Weight of Peripherals (3)	Index for Peripherals (4)	Final Index for Computer Systems (5)
1951	89.11	96,859.42	10.89	21,863.93	56,208.97
1952	89.11	60,942.35	10.89	17,299.33	36,259.53
1953	89.11	38,343.92	10.89	13,687.69	23,390.46
1954	89.11	24,125.36	10.89	10,830.07	15,088.82
1955	84.08	19,168.12	15.92	8,569.04	11,982.96
1956	75.50	18,386.23	24.50	6,780.05	11,147.21
1957	69.00	17,635.51	31.00	5,364.56	10,199.54
1958	63.68	16,915.94	36.32	4,323.94	9,269.68
1959	58.71	11,395.65	41.29	3,649.38	6,777.39
1960	56.00	10,107.25	44.00	3,013.42	5,836.24
1961	56.44	7,194.20	43.56	2,152.32	4,160.46
1962	56.16	6,774.64	43.84	1,308.30	3,237.64
1963	52.50	6,843.48	47.50	961.47	2,844.75
1964	48.74	4,342.03	51.26	891.32	2,161.14
1965	45.23	2,123.91	54.77	824.03	1,464.99
1966	45.73	1,147.10	54.27	779.62	1,075.62
1967	50.75	1,146.38	49.25	694.86	1,010.20
1968	53.96	939.13	46.04	570.46	828.44
1969	55.94	766.67	44.06	482.57	687.48
1970	55.94	771.74	44.06	412.11	643.67
1971	54.23	785.51	45.77	313.32	576.12
1972	51.74	796.38	48.26	242.70	516.40
1973	51.24	613.04	48.76	243.52	451.75
1974	54.00	602.17	46.00	219.75	425.76
1975	58.00	589.13	42.00	194.99	398.25
1976	61.50	439.13	38.50	178.81	323.84
1977	64.00	462.32	36.00	135.63	300.51
1978	65.00	401.45	35.00	137.57	275.96
1979	65.00	318.12	35.00	108.56	218.35
1980	65.00	222.46	35.00	100.05	168.19
1981	65.00	152.90	35.00	98.07	130.89
1982	65.00	100.00	35.00	100.00	100.00
1983	65.00	105.07	35.00	41.52	75.92
1984	65.00	72.46	35.00	33.69	55.43

Sources by column: (1) Flamm (1987, p. 220), assumed to be constant after 1978. (2) Table 6.7, col. 9. (3) 1.0 minus col. 1. (4) 1951–72 Flamm (1987, table A-3, p. 218) linked to 1972–84 Cole et al. (1986, table 7). (5) Törnqvist index of cols. 1–4.

Figure 6.2 compares the new index for computer processors with Triplett's "best practice index" (1989, tables 13-A and 14). Except after 1976, there is a broad agreement in their time paths. As discussed earlier, Triplett's index behaves differently at this point partly because of two "outlier" models that were underpriced in 1979. Figure 6.3 compares the new index for computer systems with the BEA and Triplett indexes. The BEA index is based on actual information only in 1969 and assumes computer prices to be constant before that date; thus, comparisons are meaningful only beginning in 1969. Note that all three indexes exhibit

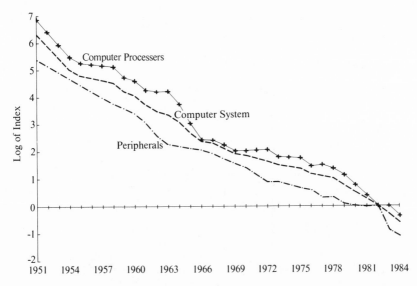

Fig. 6.1   Components of index for computer systems, 1982 = 100

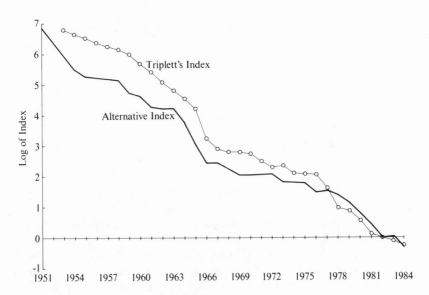

Fig. 6.2   Comparison of indexes for boxes

roughly the same rate of price decline during 1969–82, with the BEA and Triplett indexes sharing the feature of relatively more rapid decline until 1979 and the new index a relatively more rapid decline after 1979.

As shown above, the inclusion of peripherals makes the price index for systems decline somewhat more slowly than the price index for processors.

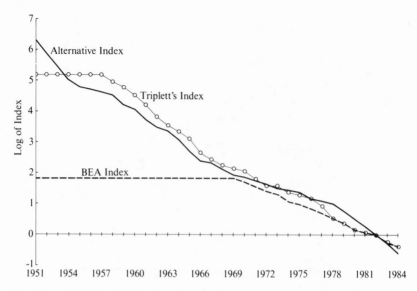

Fig. 6.3   Comparison of indexes for systems

But there are numerous dimensions of quality improvement that have been omitted and have the effect of making both the processor and the systems indexes understate the true rate of price decline (some of these factors may apply to peripherals as well). First, no allowance at all is made for the value of reduced repair, energy, and maintenance costs on computers. Chapter 7 finds for television sets that an allowance for the value of such cost savings increases the rate of price decline over the 1947–84 period from −4.4 to −6.9 percent per annum. I would be surprised if savings of a similar magnitude, say 2 percentage points per year, were not achieved on computer equipment. Any casual or anecdotal comparison of the energy, space, and maintenance requirements of the vacuum-tube processors of the 1950s with today's desktop PCs would reinforce this point.

Second, to the extent that price reductions were more rapid on mini and micro (i.e., PC-type) computers than on mainframes, a "true" price index for computer processors would decline more rapidly than the processor index developed here, which has no coverage of micro computers at all or of mini computers before 1977. As shown in section 6.8 below, a price index for personal computer (i.e., micro) processors has declined more rapidly over the 1981–87 period than the 1972–84 rate of decline of the IBM mainframe processor price index obtained by imputation in table 6.9.

Third, note from Table 6.1 above that the combined value of mini and micro sales had exceeded the value of mainframe sales by 1984. After 1966, the growth in the number of mainframe units purchased was very slow relative to the growth in the number of mini and micro units purchased.

Clearly, many computer users have found that the growing power of minis and micros allowed them to perform certain tasks at a lower cost than by continuing to rely on mainframes (any economist who in the past five years has shifted from mainframes to PCs will share this reaction). The price reduction implicit in this shift in mix is not taken into account in any of the indexes for computer processors developed in this chapter or in other studies.[31] A simple example dramatizes the importance of this point. In October 1987, one could buy for $5,718 a Compaq Deskpro 386 (20 MHz model) with a processing speed of 4.6 MIPS, a 1 MB memory, and a 130 MB disk drive.[32] This machine can be compared with the 1972 mean of Dulberger's sample: 0.59 MIPS, 0.79 MB memory, no disk drive, and a price of $1,143,640. The Compaq is superior in speed, memory, and disk drive, but lacks the multiple input-output channels and some of the multi-tasking capability that are the main distinguishing features of mainframe computers. If we call it a draw, we can calculate the annual rate of change of the price between the 1972 Dulberger mean and the 1987 Compaq price, −36.7 percent, as an indication of the enormous understatement of the decline in computer prices inherent in any index that ignores the shift from mainframes to minis, and from minis to micros.

The above three factors all were concerned with computer hardware. The presumption that processor price indexes understate the true rate of price decline is offset to some degree (although only over the 1969–79 decade) by the "unbundling" of computer operating software, discussed above. However, even if the cost of "free" operating software before 1969 amounted to 10 percent of the value of the typical processor, which seems improbable, the unbundling issue could only create an overstatement of the rate of price decline of 1 percent per annum over the decade of the 1970s. The magnitude of the three sources of bias in the opposite direction is doubtless much greater than that.

6.7.1 Aggregating the Computer Index into a Deflator for OCAM

Table 6.11, column 5, displays the implicit BEA deflator for OCAM, calculated with the following formula:

(6.2) $$P_t^{BEA} = (V_t^C + V_t^O)/(W_t^C + W_t^O),$$

where

$$W_t^C = V_t^C/P_t^C, \; W_t^O = V_t^O/P_t^O \,,$$

---

31. Up to this point, this chapter contains results identical to those reported in Gordon (1989). From this point on, the rest of the chapter is new.

32. Price quote for Compaq 386–20 from ad for Computer Discount Software, *PC* magazine, 27 June 1989. MIPS for Compaq 386–20 taken from ad for Everex Computer Systems, *PC* magazine, 27 June 1989.

Table 6.11   Calculation of BEA Deflator for OCAM, 1982 = 100

Year	Weight of Computers (1)	Deflator for Computers (2)	Weight of Other OCAM (3)	Deflator for Other OCAM (4)	Implicit Deflator for OCAM (5)	Fixed Weight Deflator for OCAM (6)
1947	0.00	617.30	100.00	59.55	59.55	. . .
1948	0.00	617.30	100.00	54.14	54.14	. . .
1949	0.00	617.30	100.00	66.17	66.17	. . .
1950	0.00	617.30	100.00	59.55	59.55	. . .
1951	0.00	617.30	100.00	63.16	63.16	. . .
1952	0.00	617.30	100.00	63.16	63.16	. . .
1953	0.00	617.30	100.00	66.17	66.17	. . .
1954	0.00	617.30	100.00	66.17	66.17	. . .
1955	0.00	617.30	100.00	68.71	68.71	. . .
1956	0.00	617.30	100.00	72.78	72.78	. . .
1957	0.00	617.30	100.00	73.13	73.13	. . .
1958	0.06	617.30	99.94	72.81	73.13	. . .
1959	0.17	617.30	99.83	70.73	71.68	627.90
1960	1.74	617.30	98.26	73.23	82.71	627.90
1961	2.88	617.30	97.12	77.07	92.63	627.90
1962	3.93	617.30	96.07	70.70	92.16	627.80
1963	7.45	617.30	92.55	70.94	111.66	628.00
1964	9.47	617.30	90.53	72.49	124.06	628.00
1965	10.82	617.30	89.18	69.13	128.44	628.10
1966	11.94	617.30	88.06	68.21	133.77	628.20
1967	13.61	617.30	86.39	69.85	144.36	628.60
1968	14.22	617.30	85.78	65.97	144.36	628.70
1969	15.87	617.30	84.13	72.30	158.80	628.70
1970	21.50	552.10	78.50	74.50	177.20	552.90
1971	27.61	473.80	72.39	79.29	188.20	487.50
1972	32.51	408.10	67.49	77.98	185.30	430.40
1973	27.00	369.30	73.00	78.19	156.80	431.30
1974	28.26	291.10	71.74	80.34	139.90	382.30
1975	32.40	265.10	67.60	86.85	144.60	347.70
1976	36.50	231.10	63.50	86.37	139.20	323.30
1977	39.68	199.70	60.32	88.30	132.50	247.30
1978	48.88	169.30	51.12	90.66	129.10	159.80
1979	57.09	146.20	42.91	92.37	123.10	140.30
1980	64.34	117.50	35.66	94.79	109.40	115.80
1981	71.24	107.40	28.76	95.93	104.10	105.10
1982	72.20	100.00	27.80	100.00	100.00	100.00
1983	78.05	77.10	21.95	103.98	83.00	88.80
1984	80.70	68.50	19.30	98.03	74.20	78.60

Sources by column: (**1**) Provided by David Cartwright of BEA. (**2**) Cartwright (1986, table 1, col. 1). (**3**) 1.0 minus col. 1. (**4**) Solved out as residual, given values in cols. 1–3 and 5. (**5**) NIPA, row 4 in table 5.6 divided by row 4 in table 5.7. (**6**) NIPA, table 7.13, row 4.

and where each variable refers to the current time period (t), and the price indexes P are expressed with 1982 as base year. In (6.2), W is the real value of shipments in 1982 prices, V is the value of shipments in current dollars, the superscript BEA stands for the BEA's OCAM deflator, the superscript C stands for computers, and the superscript O stands for other products within OCAM. Implicit in this formula are "weights" of the form

$W_t^C/(W_t^C + W_t^O)$. These are the implicit weights of an implicit deflator calculation.

The components of this calculation are shown in table 6.11. The first column displays the implicit weights for computers. The fact that they are computed in 1982 prices means that the current value shipments of computers, V, are divided by larger and larger P^c prices as one proceeds back into the 1970s and 1960s. The BEA's own current-value weight for computer systems within OCAM is 26.3 percent for 1962, but the implicit weight is a mere 4 percent for that year, as reported in table 6.11. This illustrates the distortion in weighting that the implicit deflator conveys.

Another problem of any implicit deflator is that its methodology precludes making year-to-year price comparisons, since measures of price change are valid only between each year separately and the base year, but not between one year and another nonbase year. The implicit deflator in column 5 represents the level of the OCAM deflator, which is in fact calculated relative to 1982 separately for each year. This implies that, since the computer weight is zero for 1957, the change of the OCAM deflator from 1957 to 1982 is identical to that for other OCAM products, for example, typewriters. This is evident by comparing columns 4 and 5. Consequently, the price decline of computers between 1957 and 1982 has absolutely no impact on the recorded change of the OCAM deflator over that interval. For a year like 1968, when computers have a 14 percent implicit weight, the computer deflator of 617 is averaged together with the "other" deflator of sixty-six, to yield an OCAM deflator of 144. One hundred forty-four is two times higher than the deflator for 1957, although the index for "other" declines over the 1957–68 period, while the index for computers remains constant. Figure 6.4 displays this phenomenon vividly and illustrates how the implicit deflator is pulled up by the level of the computer processor index as the weight of processors increases in systems. The implicit deflator distorts the information contained in its subcomponents, because it fails to cumulate them in a meaningful way, by cumulating the levels instead of the growth rates.

Because the implicit deflator methodology treats separately each year relative to 1982, year-to-year changes of the OCAM implicit deflator have no interpretation. This characteristic of the implicit deflator methodology is allegedly well known, and yet the only data for real OCAM investment produced by the BEA are based on the same OCAM implicit deflator, in the sense that the ratio of nominal OCAM expenditures to real OCAM expenditures equals by definition the OCAM implicit deflator.[33] It should be

---

33. The "well known" claim comes in correspondence with Jack Triplett. In my younger days, the implicit deflator was the only GNP concept of inflation, and we were aware that its quarter-to-quarter rate of change could be distorted by mix effects, but according to Triplett neither the BEA nor the press should ever have published quarter-to-quarter changes of the implicit deflator. Yet, to this day, the quarterly GNP report published in the *New York Times* contains the most recent quarterly change in both the fixed-weight and implicit deflators.

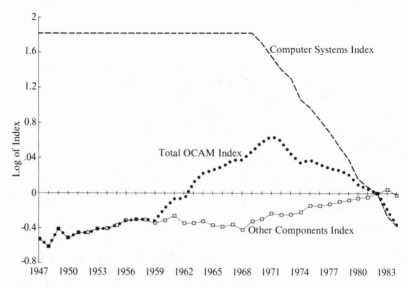

Fig. 6.4   BEA components for OCAM index

emphasized that the implicit deflator is only one of two price indexes for OCAM published by the BEA. Table 7.13 of the NIPA publishes a fixed-weight index for OCAM that, as shown in the right-hand column of table 6.11, and again in figure 6.5, displays a monotonic decline between 1969 and 1984, in contrast to the hump-shaped pattern of the implicit deflator. I emphasize the pitfalls of the implicit deflator methodology in this section for two reasons. First, the implicit deflator for OCAM was the only deflator displayed by Cartwright (1986, table 1, col. 2, p. 8) and is referred to by him as "the" BEA deflator. Second, and more important, the implicit deflator by definition is used to convert nominal investment expenditures into real investment expenditures. The BEA produces no alternative series of real OCAM investment based on a fixed-weight or moving-weight (e.g., Törnqvist) deflator.[34]

The results of the alternative Törnqvist method of weighting are illustrated in table 6.12, column 5.[35] The formula, using the same notation as in equation (6.2) but expressing logarithmic growth rates with lower-case letters, is

---

34. The BEA has calculated PDE and other major components of GNP for the period 1982–88 in 1987 prices as an alternative to 1982 prices (see Young 1989a). However, 1987-base measures of real GNP are even less accurate for the period before 1982 than 1982-base measures.

35. The name *Törnqvist* for a moving-weight average of percentage growth rates is suggested by Ruist (1968). The spelling is suggested by his reference to the original article by Törnqvist (1937). Diewert (1976) shows that the Törnqvist index is a so-called superlative index number.

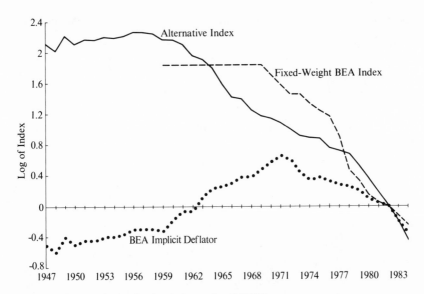

Fig. 6.5   Comparison of price indexes for OCAM

$$(6.3) \qquad\qquad P_t^T = P_{t-1}^T \exp(p_t),$$

where

$$(6.4) \qquad p_t = \sum_i [(V_t^i + V_{t-1}^i)/2] (\ln P_t^i - \ln P_{t-1}^i).$$

In words, this states that the Törnqvist index is a cumulative exponential index of growth rates, each of which aggregates the underlying subcomponent growth rates by a weighted average of the expenditure (or value of shipment) shares (V^i) in the two periods used to compute the growth rate between t and $t - 1$.

The value of shipments used to compute the V^i weights is the same as used by the BEA in equation (6.2) back to 1965 but differs before that date.[36] The resulting OCAM index falls relative to the BEA index, as shown in the comparison of the implicit BEA deflator in table 6.11 with the right-hand column of table 6.12. Two graphs are provided to summarize these results. Figure 6.4 displays the BEA indexes. It extracts from table 6.11 the BEA computer systems deflator (including peripherals), the BEA "other OCAM" deflator, and the BEA OCAM deflator that results using the implicit deflator weighting methodology as in equation (6.2). Note that the implicit OCAM

36. The BEA current-value weights are used from 1966 to 1984 (shown in their Törnqvist form in table 21). For 1951–65, I have created my own weights by taking the ratio of the value of U.S. computer shipments from Phister (1979) to total current-dollar OCAM, and linking that ratio to the BEA weight in 1966. This procedure results in a higher current-value weight on computers in the 1950s and early 1960s. For instance, my current-dollar weight for computers in OCAM in 1958 is 15 percent, as compared to the BEA's implausibly small value of 0.5 percent.

Table 6.12   New OCAM Index Combining Computer System Index from This Study with BEA Deflator for Other OCAM Weighted by Törnqvist Method, 1982 = 100

Year	Weight of Computers (1)	Index for Computers (2)	Weight of Other OCAM (3)	Deflator for Other OCAM (4)	Deflator for Total OCAM (5)
1947	0.00	56,208.97	100.00	59.55	827.88
1948	0.00	56,208.97	100.00	54.14	752.67
1949	0.00	56,208.97	100.00	66.17	919.92
1950	0.57	56,208.97	99.44	59.55	827.88
1951	1.41	56,208.97	98.59	63.16	877.78
1952	2.11	36,259.53	97.89	63.16	872.37
1953	2.95	23,390.46	97.05	66.17	904.64
1954	3.78	15,088.82	96.23	66.17	893.02
1955	5.80	11,982.96	94.20	68.71	917.96
1956	8.35	11,147.21	91.65	72.78	965.04
1957	12.07	10,199.54	87.94	73.13	962.13
1958	17.84	9,269.68	82.16	72.81	947.43
1959	21.32	6,777.39	78.69	70.73	874.88
1960	27.61	5,836.24	72.39	73.23	870.92
1961	39.21	4,160.46	60.79	77.07	823.12
1962	42.00	3,237.64	58.01	70.70	707.92
1963	42.46	2,844.75	57.54	70.94	671.81
1964	47.80	2,161.14	52.20	72.49	605.29
1965	52.38	1,464.99	47.62	69.13	490.34
1966	56.65	1,075.62	43.35	68.21	414.44
1967	59.50	1,010.20	40.50	69.85	404.10
1968	61.25	828.44	38.75	65.97	350.90
1969	64.35	687.48	35.65	72.30	324.33
1970	68.25	643.67	31.75	74.50	314.21
1971	70.55	576.12	29.45	79.29	297.14
1972	67.60	516.40	32.40	77.98	273.71
1973	61.20	451.75	38.80	78.19	250.27
1974	59.10	425.76	40.90	80.34	243.91
1975	60.00	398.25	40.00	86.85	242.06
1976	60.20	323.84	39.80	86.37	213.34
1977	61.95	300.51	38.05	88.30	205.75
1978	65.95	275.96	34.05	90.66	197.13
1979	68.45	218.35	31.55	92.37	170.01
1980	71.30	168.19	28.70	94.79	143.36
1981	72.85	130.89	27.15	95.93	120.30
1982	72.35	100.00	27.65	100.00	100.00
1983	73.50	75.92	26.50	103.98	82.82
1984	73.50	55.43	26.50	98.03	64.70

Sources by column: (1) BEA weights are used for 1966–84. For 1951–65, weights are calculated by taking the ratio of the value of U.S. computer shipments from Phister (1979) to current-dollar OCAM, and linking that ratio to the BEA weight in 1966. (2) Table 6.10, col. 5. (3) 1.0 minus col. 1. (4) Table 6.11, col. 4. (5) Törnqvist index of cols. 1–4.

deflator rises relative to either of its components between 1958 and 1968. Figure 6.5 contrasts this implicit deflator from table 6.11 and figure 6.4 with the alternative Törnqvist index from table 6.10. Figure 6.5 also reports the NIPA fixed-weight index for OCAM. The following is a summary of the growth rates of the two alternative OCAM deflators over selected intervals:

| | Annual Percentage Rate of Change | | |
Alternative Deflators	1947–57	1957–72	1972–84
BEA OCAM implicit (table 6.11)	2.08	6.39	−7.34
BEA OCAM fixed weight (table 6.11)	. . .	−2.49	−13.20
This study OCAM (table 6.10)	1.50	−8.38	−12.02
Difference: This study OCAM minus BEA implicit OCAM	−0.58	−14.77	−4.68

Thus, the difference between the new index for OCAM and the corresponding BEA index is negligible before 1957, and is much larger between 1957 and 1972 than after 1972. While it may be illegitimate to compare changes in the BEA implicit deflators for OCAM for intervals like 1957–72 that do not include the 1982 base year, there is no denying the fact that the features of the table listed above carry over to the only published NIPA measures of real investment in OCAM. For instance, shifting from the BEA implicit deflator to the Törnqvist deflator raises the annual growth rate of OCAM investment for 1957–72 from the BEA figure of 2.3 percent to the new figure of 16.8 percent; for 1972–84 the BEA figure of 24.2 percent is raised to 28.1 percent. Figure 6.6 compares the time patterns of these two series. Much of the discrepancy between the two paths occurs before 1971. The divergence is particularly striking and reflects less the choice of the index used for deflating nominal investment than the method used to construct this index. Figure 6.6 is therefore just an echo of figure 6.5.

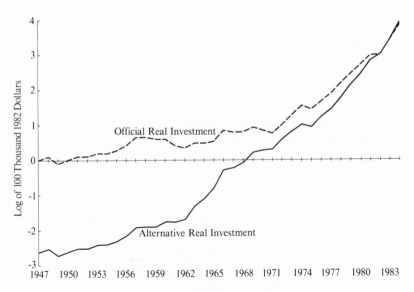

Fig. 6.6   Comparison of OCAM real PDE

6.8   Price Indexes for Personal Computers: A Pilot Study

There are few people in the academic profession who have not observed the rapid descent in the prices of personal computers and peripherals in the 1980s. It would be very difficult to compile the data required for a hedonic price index of PC processors and peripherals, because the number of relevant quality characteristics is very large, and so a large sample would be necessary to obtain sensible coefficient estimates. However, a matched model index can be created from a much smaller sample of observations, and the results of such a "pilot study" are shown in table 6.13.

For 1981–84, the only information shown in the table is the price decline for an IBM PC equipped with a standard and fixed configuration. For price changes covering 1984–85, 1985–86, and 1986–87, I have access to issues of *PC* magazine for the fall period in each of the three years. As explained in the notes to table 6.13, price changes for 1984–87 were calculated from advertisements of mail-order firms for several of the most popular models of IBM and IBM-compatible processors and peripherals. Each change that is labeled "matched model" (MM) compares identical models and configurations. The "matched characteristics" (MC) comparisons allow the purchaser to switch from brand-name equipment to "clones" in the first year that such a choice is available. Obviously, the MC comparisons make no allowance for possible quality differences in brand names and clones in warranties, quality of instruction manuals, or other dimensions, and presumably the "true" price decrease as perceived by a purchaser lies somewhere in between the MM and MC indexes.

For processors, the resulting price decreases appear to be substantially more rapid than my computer processor index in table 6.7, with annual rates of price change between 1981 and 1987 of − 26.4 percent for the MM index and − 30.0 percent for the MC index, as compared with − 21.3 percent for the table 6.7 processor index over the 1972–84 interval. An unweighted average of the MM indexes for printers (including the MC hard drive index) exhibits an annual rate of price change for 1984–87 of − 26.1 percent, and this increases to − 34.9 percent when the MC index for other peripherals is substituted for the MM index. In light of the issues discussed above about the conversion of processor indexes into indexes for processors plus peripherals, it is interesting to note the result that the rate of price decline for peripherals is of roughly the same order of magnitude as for processors. The next research task should be an attempt to collect analogous MM and MC measures of price change for years before 1984–85. For the period 1982–87, an alternative price index for IBM PCs developed at the BEA declines at an annual rate of 19.6 percent, somewhat slower than our evidence in table 6.13 (see Cartwright and Smith 1988, table 1).

Table 6.13   **Price Changes for Personal Computers and Peripherals, 1982–87 (numbers of models indicated in parentheses)**

	1982 (1)	1983 (2)	1984 (3)	1985 (4)	1986 (5)	1987 (6)
Processors:						
1. Matched model	−22.8(1)	−26.3(1)	−25.8(1)	−32.6(2)	−26.4 (6)	−24.4 (7)
2. Matched characteristics	. . .	. . .	. . .	. . .	−36.0 (6)	−36.7 (7)
Peripherals:						
3. Printers—matched model	. . .	. . .	. . .	−26.2(7)	−21.0(19)	−13.0 (16)
4. Hard drives—matched characteristics	. . .	. . .	. . .	−78.7(2)	−21.6 (6)	−30.6 (11)
5. Other—matched model	. . .	. . .	. . .	−11.0(5)	−12.3 (7)	−20.4 (7)
6. Other—matched characteristics	. . .	. . .	. . .	−45.1(5)	−23.2 (7)	−54.6 (6)

Sources by row: ("1985" refers to comparison of 1984 with 1985, etc. *Code: PC Magazine,* 1 September 1984, 26 November 1985, 28 October 1986, and 10 November 1987; ACP: ads for Arlington Computer Products; PCN: ads for PC Network; PCL: ads for PC's Limited; LS: ads for Logic Soft, all from the same issues.) (**1**) *1981–84: Business Week,* 25 March 1985, 29. Refers to IBM PC with 256K, 1 floppy drive, DOS, and monochrome monitor. *1985:* PCN: IBM basic unit with 256K and 2 floppy drives but no monitor, IBM-XT with 256K and no monitor. *1986:* PCN: IBM basic, IBM-XT, Compaq portable 20MB, Compaq Deskpro 20MB hard drive, IBM AT basic unit; ACP: IBM AT (512K, 20MB, monochrome). *1987:* PCL: Turbo with 20MB hard drive, 286–8 with 20MB hard drive, 268-12 with 40MB hard drive, all equipped with standard B&W monitor and graphics card; PCN: Compaq Deskpro 640K with 20MB hard drive; ACP: IBM AT with 30MB hard drive and monochrome with 1986 price comparison for same unit from LS, Compaq basic portable with 20MB hard drive, and Compaq 286 portable with 640K and 20MB hard drive. (**2**) *1986:* Replaces IBM basic and IBM-XT with PC Network Turbo, without and with 10MB hard drive. *1987:* Replaces Compaq Deskpro with PCL Turbo, and IBM AT with PCL 286–8. (**3**) *1985:* PCN: Epson FX-80 (FX-85 in 1985), LQ-1500, NEC 3530, 3550, Qume Spring, Texas Instruments 855, Toshiba P1351 (P351 in 1985). *1986:* PCN: Citizen MSP-10, MSP-15, MSP-25, NEC 2050, 3550, 8850, and Toshiba P351; LS: Citizen MSP-10, MSP-15, MSP-20, MSP-25, Juki 6100, 6300, Epson LQ-1500 (LQ-1000 in 1986), Okidata 182P, 192P, 193P, 2410P, and Toshiba P351. *1987:* ACP: Epson LQ-800, LQ-1000, IBM Proprinter, Proprinter XL; LS: HP Laserjet (500 + in 1986, 500 + series 2 in 1987), Epson LQ-800, LQ-1000, Okidata 182P, 2410P, Toshiba P351, Citizen MSP-10, MSP-15, Premier 35; PCN: Epson LQ-1000, Citizen MSP-10, Premier 35. (**4**) *1985:* PCN: Teac half height drive (pair), Cogito 10MB internal hard drive ("THE" clone in 1986). *1986:* PCN: Iomega Bournoulli Box, Clone 10MB internal, 20MB internal, 10MB tape, Maynard 20MB drive with 20MB tape (clone 20 + 20 in 1986), clone half height drive. *1987:* PCN: Clone 20MB internal and 20MB card; LS: Mountain 20MB and 30MB cards, Plus 20MB card, Seagate 20MB half and full height, 30MB half and full height, 40MB and 80MB full height. (**5**) *1985:* PCN: Hayes Smartmodem 1200B, AST 6 Pak, Hercules monochrome card, Amdek 310A monitor, and 10 DSDD diskettes. *1986:* PCN: Same as 1985 with addition of Hayes 2400 modem and Prometheus Promodem. *1987:* LS: Hayes Smartmodem 1200B and 2400B, each with Smartcom, AST 6 Pak Plus and 6 Pak Premium, Hercules monochrome card, Amdek 310A B&W monitor, 722 Color monitor. (**6**) *1985:* PCN: Replaces AST 6 Pak and Hercules monochrome card with clones. *1986:* PCN: Replaces Hayes Smartmodem 1200B with clone, continues with clones for AST 6 Pak and Hercules monochrome card. *1987:* LS: Replaces Hayes Smartmodem 2400B with clone and two Amdek monitors with clones, continues with clones for Hayes Smartmodem 1200B, AST 6 Pak, and Hercules monochrome card.

6.9 Conclusion

This chapter has developed a single price index for mainframe and mini computer processors over the entire history of the computer industry, extending from 1951 to 1984. The chapter shares with others the conclusion that computer processor prices have declined rapidly, at roughly a 20 percent annual rate. The unique contribution of this chapter is its consistency: the price index is based only on new models in their year of introduction. In contrast, other studies are based on a mixture of only new models (Knight 1966), mainly new models (Chow 1967), or a mixture with old models in the majority (Dulberger 1989). One would expect ex ante that the behavior of new-only and all-model indexes would be different: a new-only price index can exhibit a sharp decline when new technology is introduced, as in my index during 1963–66. An all-model index will introduce the effect of new technology more gradually, reflecting the influence of old models that remain in production. Both types of indexes are useful, a new-only index for indicating changes in the pace of technological change, and an all-model index for the purpose of deflating the nominal value of current computer production. But it is clear that the two types of indexes measure two different concepts, and they should not be compared or mixed across historical eras. This can easily lead to double counting a technological improvement if, for instance, an index for new-only models that incorporates a new generation of computers in year t is linked to an all-model index that incorporates the effect of the growing share of new-generation models in year $t + 1$.

The resulting "final" processor price index for new-only models in this chapter has the additional advantage that it is based on only two data sources, and the overlap between the two in 1977–79 has been handled to avoid double counting the technological improvement that occurred at that time. The plausibility of the final index has been checked against the price-performance history of major IBM mainframe models. Given the dominant market share of IBM in mainframe sales, this cross-check is extremely important to avoid placing undue weight on models having a low market share. The final index tracks an imputation index for IBM mainframes very closely except in the final interval, 1981–84, when the growing share of minis and the rapidly falling prices of minis lead to a somewhat faster decline for the final index than for IBM mainframe prices.

Section 6.6.3 above considered at length several discrepancies between the final results and the results implied by estimating similar equations on the new-only subset of the observations compiled by Chow for 1954–65 and Dulberger for 1972–84. For 1954–65 the final results and Chow's are similar for the period as a whole but differ in the timing of price decline before and after 1960, and the timing of the new index corresponds more closely to the evolution of IBM mainframe models reflecting the greater share of IBM mainframes and smaller share of minicomputers in the present sample than in Chow's. For 1972–77, the final results accord with Dulberger's new-only subsample as long as her technology variables are omitted; the technology variables yield an implausible relation between the quality of the major 1972 and 1977 IBM models and should be excluded in the calculation of price and quality indexes. For 1977–84, the final results are similar to those for the Dulberger new-only subsample but differ radically as to the pace within the period, a discrepancy attributed to the overweighting of two underpriced machines in the Dulberger sample in 1979. Finally, for the "mystery period" 1965–72 that spans the gap between the Chow and the Dulberger studies, the final index produces a result of relatively slow price decline that is confirmed by a detailed quality comparison of IBM 360 and 370 series models.

Proceeding from the price index for computer processors to the price index for systems, the index for computer peripherals is based on the hedonic results of Cole et al., and the nonhedonic results of Flamm for the pre-1972 period. Peripherals and processors are weighted together with a Törnqvist scheme. The annual rate of price change over the 1957–84 period for the "final" index of systems is −19.3 percent per year (col. 5 of table 6.10), which compares to the −20.4 percent for the price decline of processors. Over the same interval, this is slightly slower than the −20.6 percent rate of price change for Triplett's "best practice" index for systems, as developed in his survey based on the same data for peripherals (his tables 13-A and 14).

Several arguments developed in the text suggest that the rate of price decline developed in this study is in fact too slow. These include the failure in this or any study to allow for reductions in energy and maintenance costs; the possibility that mini and micro prices may have declined faster than mainframe prices before 1981; and, by far the most important, the fact that minis and micros provide "computation services" far more cheaply than mainframes. One suggestive example for the 1972–87 period indicates that the rate of price decline for users able to switch from a typical 1972 mainframe to a 1987 PC using a 386 chip would have enjoyed an annual rate of price decline of more than 35 percent, not the 20 or 21 percent that emerges from this study and Triplett's.

The final section of the chapter was concerned with aggregating the new price index for computer systems into a deflator for the OCAM component of PDE, using the Törnqvist index methodology that allows value-of-shipments weights to change each year. Possibly the most dramatic result in this study is not the rate of price decline in the price index for computer processors, which is of the same order of magnitude as in several other studies covering parts of the postwar period, but the finding that the BEA understates the growth rate of real OCAM investment at an annual rate of 14.8 percent during the period 1957–72. Primarily weighting issues also account for a 3.9 percentage point understatement in the growth rate of real OCAM investment in the more recent 1972–84 period.

When these alternative OCAM deflators are aggregated into deflators for all PDE, the differences are much more modest, amounting to about 0.75 percent for the period since 1957. When the Törnqvist index for OCAM is used in the calculation of total PDE, the 1957–72 BEA growth rate of real investment is raised from 4.45 to 5.20 percent; for 1972–84 the BEA figure of 4.33 percent is raised to 4.94 percent. There is little difference in the contribution of the new indexes to the PDE deflator for 1957–72 and 1972–84, since the growing weight of OCAM offsets the shrinking size of the difference between my OCAM deflator and that of the BEA. The fact that my implied PDE deflator registers about the same difference from the BEA deflator for PDE in 1957–72 as in 1972–84 suggests that the results of this chapter have few if any implications for the post-1972 slowdown in U.S. productivity growth, even though electronic computing machines are, among all the products studied in this book, the product with the most dramatic revisions of its price index.

Appendix

Data Sources

Phister 1979, table 2.11, pp. 338–57, continued p. 630 et seq.

Computerworld: 1977: 10 and 17 October, and two other issues.
1978: 16 January, 5 June, and one other issue.
1979: 8 January, 5 and 12 February, 16 July, and 5 November.
1980: 21 January, 17 March, 12 May, 28 July, 22 September, 20 October, 17 and 24 November, and one other issue.
1981: 13 July.
1982: 2 August.
1983: 8 August.
1984: 20 and 27 August, 3 September.

Omitted Observations in Phister Data Set

The following observations were omitted after the discovery that on the first round of the research they yielded actual to imputed prices more than 1.5 times the standard error of the relevant regression equation. Note that only a single IBM model is excluded. Numbers in parentheses are the ratios of actual to imputed prices for the mean memory configuration from the regressions listed in table 6.8, column 10.

1957: IBM 305 (2.11), Univac II (2.43).
1968: Burroughs 500 (2.66).
1969: Univac 1106 (1.93).
1971: NCR 50 (7.69).
1973: Cyber 76 (3.23), Univac 1110 (3.35).
1978: DEC VAX 780 (3.74).

7   Electrical Appliances

7.1 Introduction

Next to automobiles and electronic computers, household appliances have been the most popular product for study with the hedonic regression technique. In addition to the pioneering studies by Burstein (1960, 1961), both Dhrymes (1971) and Triplett and McDonald (1977) have published hedonic regression studies of appliance prices, with a heavy emphasis on refrigerators. In addition to the presence of a previous literature, appliances are an appealing subject for inclusion in this book, with its emphasis on quality changes taking the form of changes in operating efficiency. Energy cost is a large fraction of total operating cost for several types of appliances, particularly refrigerator-freezers, room air conditioners, and clothes dryers, and the effect of adjustments for the value of changes in energy efficiency will be a central focus of the chapter. As an example, it has been estimated that electrical power accounts for 58 percent of the lifetime cost of owning a refrigerator, purchase cost 36 percent, and servicing costs the remaining 6 percent (*Consumer Appliances*, n.d., 6).

The price indexes for major appliances developed in this chapter are based on two separate sources of information. Hedonic regression equations for refrigerators, room air conditioners, and washing machines (both wringer and automatic) are estimated from the earliest feasible postwar date to 1983, using data on prices and quality characteristics transcribed from successive Sears, Roebuck catalogs. A separate source of data on prices and characteristics is provided by successive *Consumer Reports (CR)* evaluations of appliances. In this chapter, the *CR* data are not used to estimate hedonic regression equations, but are employed to develop a separate set of price indexes based on the technique of comparing "closely similar models" discussed in chapter 3. *CR* data on energy usage allow the estimation of the value of changes in

energy efficiency, and these energy adjustment factors are then applied to the
CR specification indexes of price change. This chapter develops *CR* indexes
for eight products (refrigerators, room air conditioners, washing machines,
clothes dryers, TV sets, under-counter dishwashers, microwave ovens, and
VCRs). Additional *CR* indexes are developed that incorporate energy efficiency adjustments for four of these products (refrigerators, room air conditioners, clothes dryers, and TV sets), and an additional adjustment for
reductions in the cost of repairs is developed for TV sets.

In total, this chapter develops seventeen new price indexes from thousands
of price observations (both from the Sears catalog and from *CR*) that are
independent of the prices collected by the BLS for the CPI and PPI. Because
the *CR* indexes are developed from price quotations for all major brands and
for the most popular models of each product, they are in most cases based on
more information than the PPI for a given product at a given moment of time.
The PPI is computed at a monthly frequency and so may be based on more
total information for these products, but the informational advantage of the
PPI lies in its ability to track intrayear and year-to-year price movements.
When comparing price changes over periods of two or more years, the *CR*
indexes probably have an informational advantage.

Of the eight products covered in this chapter, the first five (in the order
listed above) are compared to both of the indexes compiled by the BLS, the
CPI and PPI, for the same product. The new indexes for dishwashers and
microwave ovens are compared just with the PPI, and the new index for VCRs
stands alone, since there is no CPI or PPI for that product. For some products,
and in some time intervals, the rate of price change in the CPI and PPI differ
substantially, and some products are introduced into the two government
indexes at different dates (e.g., air conditioners entered the PPI in 1952 and
the CPI in 1964). The PPI is of more concern than the CPI, since a central
focus of this book is the development of alternative deflators for PDE to be
compared to the BEA deflators for PDE that rely entirely on the PPI and never
use the CPI.[1] But the CPI is also relevant for a broader evaluation of the

---

1. The following PPI indexes for household appliances are used within the "service industry
machinery" subcomponent of PDE. The following are the PPI indexes used and their percentage
weights within the service industry machinery component in 1967 and 1981 (the source of the
table is unpublished BEA worksheets):

	Weights	
	1967	1981
Household laundry equipment (124102)	8.30	5.40
Household refrigeration equipment (124103)	17.94	10.28
Household room air conditioners (12410338)	11.17	6.31
Household under-counter dishwashers (12410441)	6.00	8.42
Household canister-type vacuum cleaners (12430111)	1.17	2.97

Table 7.1   **Home Appliances and Electronic Goods, 1949 and 1983, Manufacturers**
                          Shipments in Units and Retail Value

	Units (thousands)		Value ($million)		Mean Value ($/unit)	
	1949	1983	1949	1983	1949	1983
Air conditioners	89	2,696	31	1,054	352.37	390.95
Kitchen appliances	7,362	23,274	1,847	10,105	251.01	434.18
Refrigerators	4,450	5,255	1,134	3,607	255.00	686.39
Microwave ovens	. . .	6,006	. . .	2,586	. . .	430.57
Ranges	2,112	4,521	486	2,060	230.00	455.65
Dishwashers	160	3,054	44	1,205	275.00	394.56
Freezers	485	1,166	162	568	335.00	487.14
Other	155	3,666	21	441	135.00	120.29
Home laundry	3,866	7,426	640	3,034	165.52	408.56
Compact appliances	25	1,259	. . .	334	. . .	265.29
Video	3,000	34,190	970	10,881	323.33	318.25
Audio/hi-fi	7,805	81,274	329	4,620	42.21	56.84
Personal electronics (excluding PCs)	1,350	126,724	9	4,545	5.75	35.87
Small electrical appliances	18,942	84,330	303	3,877	16.00	45.97
Floor care	2,900	10,152	222	1,271	76.49	125.20
Personal care	1,725	60,217	37	1,273	21.50	21.14
Other	1,040	181,349	95	3,173	91.73	17.50
Total	55,441	612,891	6,330	44,167	114.18	72.06
Of which, major appliances	11,342	34,655	2,518	14,527	222.01	419.19

Sources: 1949: *Electrical Merchandising Week,* January 1959. 1983: Statistical Abstract of the United States, 1985, table 1394, p. 777, with some categories reorganized and combined.

adequacy of quality adjustments by the BLS. There are sharp differences between the CPI and the PPI for refrigerators (discussed in this chapter) and between the CPI for new cars and for used cars (discussed in the next chapter). These differences are too great to be accounted for by wholesale-to-retail markups (for refrigerators) or depreciation rates (for used cars), and may suggest the need for some internal procedure to invest extra resources in the reconciliation of such differences when they exceed some minimum value.

7.2   The Postwar Development of the Appliance Industry

A comprehensive view of the postwar development of the appliance industry is provided in table 7.1. Included are both "white goods," that is, kitchen appliances, home laundry appliances, and room air conditioners, and "brown goods," that is, video and audio/hi-fi, as well as small appliances and electronic devices.[2] The table indicates that the list of consumer appliances is a long one, and it helps provide perspective on the coverage of this chapter. Leaving aside TV sets, which are not included in the totals for major appliances at the bottom of table 7.1, the four appliances receiving the most

2. The classification of room air conditioners, which are usually brown and never white, is an anomaly, confirmed by the classification in Hunt (1975).

attention here (refrigerators, air conditioners, washers, and dryers) made up 72 percent of the value of major appliances in 1949 and 53 percent in 1983. Refrigerators alone constituted 45 percent of the value of major appliances in 1949, but only 25 percent in 1983. In the major appliance category, the only important product not covered in this chapter is the kitchen range. In turn, major appliances accounted for 39.8 percent of all products listed in 1949 and for 32.9 percent in 1983, with the decline largely due to the growing importance of "brown goods," particularly TV sets and VCRs, both of which are covered here.

The very rapidly declining price indexes for electronic computers developed in the last chapter and by other investigators suggest that quality changes may have been more pervasive in consumer electronic goods than in major appliances. This fact, and the growing importance of electronic goods evident in table 7.1, from 20.6 percent of the total in 1949 to 45.4 percent in 1983, suggests that some attention must be paid to electronic products in this chapter. This task is inherently difficult, however, since many of the dimensions over which quality has improved, for example, picture quality, are difficult to quantify within the context of the hedonic regression technique. Although most of the space in this chapter is devoted to appliances, considerable attention is devoted to the development of a *CR* index for TV sets, and a briefer treatment of VCRs is included as well.[3]

The right-hand two columns in table 7.1 exhibit unit values for each major product category in 1949 and 1983. Changes in these unit values can be compared with changes in the PPI for the same products over the same period. If both the unit value and the PPI doubled, this would imply that quality per unit remained unchanged, while if the unit value doubled and the PPI remained fixed, the quality per unit implied by the PPI would have doubled. The following are the (logarithmic) annual rates of change of unit values, the PPI for each product, and the implied PPI quality per unit over the 1949–83 interval:

	Unit Value	PPI	Quality per Unit
Refrigerators	2.95	1.36	1.59
Air conditioners (PPI used 1953–63)	0.31	0.35	−0.05
Home laundry (used PPI for washing machines)	2.69	1.73	0.96
Video (used CPI for TV sets, 1950–83)	−0.05	−1.40	1.35

These implied growth rates of quality per unit raise intriguing questions. Could video equipment really have increased in quality at a slower rate than

---

3. Another reason for devoting less attention to electronic goods is that they are primarily manufactured abroad, and thus, while entering the deflators for consumer and producers durable expenditures, are netted out of the GNP deflator. Thus, any bias in official price indexes for consumer electronic goods would have little effect on aggregate measures of the growth rates of output and productivity.

refrigerators? Is it reasonable to conclude that the average quality per unit of air conditioners did not improve at all, since part of the technology of air conditioners is similar to that of refrigerators?

7.3 Data Sources: The Sears Catalog and *CR*

Ideally, the data source for each product studied in this volume would be comprehensive collection of price quotations (preferably transaction prices) and quality characteristics collected for all available manufacturers and models on a consistent basis over the entire postwar period. Some studies (e.g., Triplett and McDonald 1977) come close to this ideal, but only for a particular product and for a particular subset of years (1960–72 in that study represents only thirteen years of the thirty-six-year span of this book covering 1947–83). The paucity of hedonic studies and their limited product and time coverage forces us to carry out new investigations of major products over an extended sample period. To maintain the overall research within a feasible scope, compromises must be made in the collection of data. In particular, the results in this chapter are based entirely on Sears catalogs and *CR* product evaluations.

The Sears data set has the advantage that prices have a specific meaning, that is, freight on board (f.o.b.) the Sears warehouse net of shipping expense, and these prices are not subject to discounting. Thus, we need not speculate as to the possibility that discounts from list price varied over time. Further, quality characteristics (specifications) are relatively complete and are reported in full each year, whether or not a model is changed from its counterpart in the preceding catalog.[4] This allows the Sears data base to be used for the compilation of a price index either by the specification technique, which for adjacent years compares models that are absolutely identical in their printed specifications (a technique used for clothes dryers and TV sets in this chapter and for numerous Sears products in chapter 10), or by the hedonic technique (as in this chapter for refrigerators, room air conditioners, and washing machines).

There are several obvious disadvantages of the Sears data base that apply both to the specification indexes in chapter 10 and to the hedonic indexes in this chapter, and specific disadvantages applicable to the hedonic regressions developed here. The most important disadvantage is that the Sears catalog reports prices for only a single brand name. In contrast, Triplett and McDonald (1977, table 3) estimate coefficients of "make effect" dummy variables for eleven makes, and *CR* product evaluations usually cover as many as fifteen to twenty models, most of which represent different manufacturers.[5]

---

4. Actually, the Sears catalog is issued twice a year. Data for this study were collected only from the spring catalog.

5. Most *CR* product reports for refrigerators cover thirteen to fifteen models, even in the late 1940s and early 1950s. Product evaluations for washing machines cover as many as twenty-four models. Numbers of models are listed explicitly for most of the *CR* price comparisons in this chapter.

Further, the range of prices across models included in the typical *CR* evaluation is quite wide, and the Sears price may not be equal to or even close to the mean price across all models.[6]

Fortunately, the Sears model is included in the *CR* evaluation often enough to allow a statement about the likely direction of bias involved in basing the hedonic regression equations only on Sears catalog price quotations. It appears that the Sears price quotation listed by *CR* was consistently at the bottom of the price spectrum in the late 1940s and 1950s, but by the 1970s and 1980s was much closer to the mean. The following are ratios (in percentages) of the Sears price to the mean price in the first two and last two *CR* evaluations covered later in the chapter:[7]

	First Two (years)	Last Two (years)
Refrigerators	76.4 (1949, 1952)	105.5 (1974, 1983)
Air conditioners	80.3 (1953, 1959)	101.4 (1976, 1982)
Washing machines	84.2 (1950, 1954)	98.2 (1982, 1984)

This consistent pattern implies that the hedonic regression indexes based solely on data from the Sears catalog are probably biased in the direction of indicating a faster price increase or a slower price decline than the appropriate universe of all models. This conclusion would be qualified to the extent that Sears models had consistently improved in quality relative to the average, or to the extent that the *CR* price quotations are misleading by shifting in the 1960s from catalog to retail store prices.[8]

Because of their more complete coverage of different manufacturers, the *CR* product evaluations would seem to be unambiguously superior to the Sears catalog quotations. Indeed, considerable emphasis is placed below on "closely similar" model comparisons based on the *CR* data. Except for automobiles, no category of consumer expenditures has received more consistent or detailed coverage by *CR* over the postwar period than major consumer appliances. Successive *CR* product evaluations not only provide information on changes in prices and quality characteristics over the entire postwar period, but also constitute our sole source of data on changes in energy usage of major appliances.

6. That is, if a Sears model is included, which does not always occur.

7. Sears prices are catalog prices until the early 1960s, when they are means of retail prices in a survey of *CR* shoppers. Catalog prices in this comparison (but not in the hedonic regressions below) include an extra $10 for shipping, an add-on factor suggested in the June 1949 *CR* evaluation of refrigerators.

8. Fortunately, sufficient data are available to rule out this last possibility. In scattered cases, *CR* lists both the catalog and the mean shopper retail price quotation for the same model, and the two are almost always within 3 percent of each other after adding an arbitrary $10 shipping cost factor to the listed catalog quotation.

However, the *CR* data have limitations of coverage that inhibit their use in a formal hedonic regression study. First, *CR* does not print a report on each product every year. Instead, an irregular span of years separates reports on a given product. For instance, refrigerator reports appeared roughly every three years between 1949 and 1970, but there was then a gap between 1970 and 1974, and again between 1974 and 1983.

A further problem is that a *CR* evaluation for a given year typically includes only a single model of each manufacturer, in contrast to the Sears catalog, which typically lists eight to ten models of each major appliance. For instance, between 1964 and 1983, *CR* reported on refrigerators without automatic freezer defrost only once, in 1974, thus precluding a hedonic estimate of the "freezer defrost" characteristic for the intervening years. Estimates of the value of other characteristics are similarly inhibited when *CR* lists only a single model of each brand, and especially when the models of each brand are selected to be as close as possible to each other in the set of included characteristics.

This aspect of the *CR* sample that makes it unsuitable for the estimation of hedonic regression equations actually facilitates the alternative technique of "comparison of closely similar models." For instance, the *CR* sample allows us to compare models with bottom-located freezers having automatic defrost in 1959, 1960, 1964, and 1968; top-located freezers having automatic defrost in 1968, 1970, 1974, and 1983; and top-located freezers without automatic defrost in 1954, 1957, 1959, 1962, 1964, and 1974. While the technique of comparing "closely similar" models is appropriate for some of these comparisons, it suffers from the defect that, in other comparisons, the size of the refrigerator compartment and/or the freezer compartment changes significantly. In these cases, a straightforward comparison cannot be made, and adjustments for changing size are made, employing hedonic coefficients from the Triplett-McDonald study and from the hedonic regression estimates for the Sears catalog sample. In other cases (e.g., dishwashers), insufficient evidence on changing size is provided, and no adjustments are made beyond direct price comparisons between models having roughly comparable features; in these cases, informal evidence on increasing size or other changes is provided to support the view that the new price indexes make insufficient allowance for quality change.

7.4 Common Features of the Hedonic Regression Equations

The data source for the hedonic regression equations estimated in this chapter is the spring Sears Roebuck catalog for every year from 1948 to 1983. When a particular product (e.g., room air conditioners) was not available in 1947, the starting date of the regression equation coincides with the first appearance of the product in the catalog (e.g., 1952 for room air conditioners). For refrigerators and washing machines, the Sears indexes begin in 1948, while the CPI and PPI are available for 1947. The Sears data for room air conditioners begin in 1952, one year before the 1953 appearance of the PPI index for this product, and twelve years before the 1964 appearance of the CPI index.

In addition to price quotations (always net of shipping costs), data were copied from the Sears catalog on all listed quality characteristics. In the case of refrigerators, these took the form of numerical magnitudes for the total cubic foot capacity and the capacity of the freezer, and dummy variables for the presence of other characteristics (e.g., refrigerator automatic defrost, freezer automatic defrost, presence of crisper, porcelain-on-steel interior, powermiser, shelves in door, etc.). Freezer capacity was sometimes listed in pounds and sometimes in cubic feet, and these were placed on a consistent basis of pounds, using the *CR* conversion factor of thirty-five pounds per cubic foot. The quantitative and dummy variables for other products are discussed below in the appropriate sections.

More variables were available than the coefficients that could be estimated, owing to the limited size of the sample, and this limitation is especially binding in the first half of the postwar period. For instance, in the case of refrigerators, sample sizes in adjacent-year regressions (i.e., the number of observations available for two successive years) ranged from six to thirteen from 1948 to 1952, from sixteen to twenty-three from 1952 to 1969, with a jump then to from thirty to forty-eight between 1969 and 1983. The criterion for inclusion of variables was to give first priority to the size and defrost dummy variables, and then to include additional dummy variables on the criterion of goodness of fit. When the list of additional dummy variables had to be shortened and two alternative lists yielded about the same goodness of fit, variables were chosen that seemed to be given more emphasis in *CR* product evaluations.[9]

All regression equations were specified in the double-log functional form, that is, with the log of price as dependent variable, and the log of quantitative variables as explanatory variables, in addition to the dummy variables. Thus, all coefficients can be interpreted as elasticities, for example, the percentage increase in price associated with a 1 percent increase in capacity, with the presence of automatic freezer defrost and other characteristics held constant. Some other studies (e.g., Triplett and McDonald 1977) use the semilog form, with the log of price regressed on the arithmetic values of quantitative variables. This has the disadvantage for expositional purposes that one cannot extract the elasticities from the tables of coefficients without knowing the means of the variables. For the portion of the refrigerator sample that overlaps Triplett-McDonald (1960–72), I estimated a semilog version of my pooled regressions, and the standard error of estimate was almost the same as with the double-log version. I did not experiment with semilog versions for products other than refrigerators.[10]

Two types of hedonic regression equations were estimated from the Sears catalog data, which I call *pooled* and *adjacent-year* equations. For refrigerators, adjacent-year regressions were estimated for each year pair from 1948–49 to 1982–83, and pooled regressions were estimated for periods of five to nine years (1948–57, 1957–62, 1962–69, 1969–76, and 1976–83). Break points in the pooled regressions were generally chosen to be years when particular characteristics first appeared. Each pooled regression includes a string of dummy variables for each year except for the first year, and each adjacent-year equation includes a single time dummy variable for the second year of the pair. In each case, the price change from the beginning to the end of the sample period in the pooled regression equation is compared with the cumulative sum of the time coefficients in the adjacent-year equations covering the same period. The price indexes calculated from the time coefficients of the pooled and adjacent-year regressions are compared with *CR* indexes (with and without energy adjustments) and with both the CPI and the PPI.

7.5   Household Refrigerators and Refrigerator-Freezers

The presentation of results begins with refrigerators and refrigerator-freezers for three reasons. This product has been the subject of substantial previous research, while relatively little has been done on other products; refrigerators account for the largest share of sales of major appliances (i.e., "white goods" excluding audio and video) in table 7.1 in both 1949 and 1983; and the product itself is more complex than air conditioners, washing machines, and the other products examined in this chapter. Also, refrigerators were introduced earlier than air conditioners or washing machines.

The first home refrigerator units went on sale in 1918, but they were of distinctly lower quality than even early postwar units: "Food kept for any length of time in them tended to dry out. Ice accumulated relentlessly around the freezing elements, demanding frequent defrosting" (Consumers' Union 1986, 150). Refrigerators began to sell in substantial numbers in the 1930s, and *CR* began rating refrigerators in its first year, 1936. In June 1938, it compared the energy efficiency of electric and gas refrigeration with the traditional icebox, and reported that an electric refrigerator could cool at one-third the cost of an icebox. This is an example of a quality improvement that is not taken into account in this book but would be relevant if this study were extended to the interwar period.

---

10. The Dulberger (1989) study of computers cited in chap. 6 finds the double-log functional form distinctly superior to the semilog form.

This section on refrigerators begins with the hedonic regression study of Sears catalog data and then proceeds to the comparison of "closely similar" models with *CR* data, both with and without explicit adjustments for changes in energy efficiency. The resulting indexes are then compared with the CPI and PPI. The section concludes with a discussion of omitted dimensions of quality that have improved over the postwar years and impart to the quality adjustments a downward ("conservative") bias and to the new price indexes a corresponding upward bias.

7.5.1 Hedonic Regression Results

The results of estimating hedonic regression equations from Sears catalog data are presented in a uniform format for refrigerators, room air conditioners, and washing machines. Each table is broken into parts (A, B, etc.) corresponding to the coverage of each pooled regression. The adjacent-year regressions covering the same period as the pooled regression are shown alongside. Thus, part A of table 7.2 exhibits results from estimating a pooled equation for 1948–57 and also nine adjacent-year regression equations for the year pairs 1948–49 to 1956–57. To save space, the significance of the time dummy variables is indicated by asterisks (one for significance at the 5 percent level and two at the 1 percent level).

The pooled equation contains all the available variables that are significant in the pooled regression whether or not they are significant in the adjacent-year regressions (smaller sample sizes imply that *t*-ratios would be lower in the adjacent-year results). When a variable does not appear in the adjacent-year regressions (e.g., refrigerator defrost from 1948–49 to 1951–52), either the feature was not offered on any model in the Sears catalog or the coefficient on that feature cannot be estimated owing to multicollinearity. Automatic refrigerator defrost was first offered in the Sears catalog in 1952; the first *CR* evaluation of models having that feature also appeared in 1952.

The coefficients in table 7.2, part A, do not all have the correct positive sign because of multicollinearity. Coefficients that are negative also are insignificant. Otherwise, the magnitudes seem plausible; the coefficient of 0.04 on crisper is reasonable, even though a crisper may act as a proxy for additional attributes included on "deluxe" models (e.g., shelves in door, deluxe trim). The coefficient of 0.20 on refrigerator defrost can be compared with an estimate of 0.16 that can be extracted from *CR* for 1952.[11] The standard error of estimate for the pooled regression of 0.081 improves on the standard error of 0.112 in the Triplett-McDonald 1963–65 equation, which has a much larger sample size of 303, as compared with sixty-nine in table 7.2, part A. The price decline of 44 percent between 1948 and 1957 implied

---

11. The January 1952 *CR* evaluation estimates that the presence of refrigerator defrost added $50 in that year. This is 16 percent of the mean price of $306.91 for the models not equipped with automatic refrigerator defrost evaluated in the October 1951 issue.

Table 7.2 Pooled and Adjacent-Year Double-Log Regression Equations for Refrigerators, Sears Catalog Data, 1948–57, 1957–62, 1962–69, 1969–76, 1976–83 (t-ratios in parentheses)

A. 1948–57

	Pooled 1948–57	1948–49	1949–50	1950–51	1951–52	1952–53	1953–54	1954–55	1955–56	1956–57
Total capacity	0.24	0.23	0.35	0.51	0.44	−0.19	−0.39	0.04	0.27	0.33
	(2.30)	(1.05)	(4.38)	(2.30)	(0.54)	(−0.26)	(−1.38)	(0.14)	(1.06)	(1.43)
Freezer capacity	0.33	0.44	0.38	0.27	0.24	0.60	0.74	0.40	0.28	0.30
	(7.04)	(2.13)	(2.60)	(2.57)	(0.50)	(1.17)	(4.98)	(3.85)	(3.03)	(3.02)
Refrigerator defrost	0.20	...	...	...	...	0.22	0.18	0.21	0.20	0.17
	(6.85)					(2.61)	(3.66)	(4.09)	(3.85)	(2.92)
Crisper	0.04	0.08	0.07	0.05	0.05	−0.06	−0.12	0.01	0.07	0.06
	(1.42)	(0.90)	(1.72)	(0.75)	(0.16)	(−0.21)	(−1.59)	(0.24)	(0.95)	(0.73)
Constant	3.33	2.97	2.54	2.16	2.53	4.22	4.69	3.90	2.94	2.60
	(9.12)	(3.64)	(4.82)	(2.61)	(0.96)	(2.24)	(5.15)	(4.38)	(3.38)	(3.41)
1949	−0.10	−0.06								
1950	−0.13*		−0.05							
1951	−0.23**			−0.08						
1952	−0.18**				0.05					
1953	−0.20**					−0.02				
1954	−0.13*						0.04			
1955	−0.41**							−0.28**		
1956	−0.42**								0.01	
1957	−0.44**									−0.02
$\bar{R}^2$	0.907	0.839	0.917	0.904	0.703	0.802	0.896	0.890	0.885	0.934
S.E.E.	0.081	0.070	0.046	0.061	0.118	0.117	0.083	0.090	0.092	0.079
Observations	69	6	9	9	7	13	18	22	23	19

(continued)

Table 7.2 (continued)

	B. 1957–62					
	Pooled 1957–62	1957–58	1958–59	1959–60	1960–61	1961–62
Total capacity	0.22	0.11	0.28	0.27	0.36	0.70
	(1.41)	(0.77)	(1.11)	(0.97)	(0.98)	(3.13)
Freezer capacity	0.36	0.30	0.34	0.40	0.32	0.27
	(5.00)	(3.78)	(2.82)	(2.70)	(1.94)	(2.42)
Refrigerator defrost	0.14	0.21	0.12	0.21	0.27	0.25
	(3.48)	(3.97)	(1.84)	(3.45)	(2.91)	(3.32)
Freezer defrost	0.19	−0.01	0.09	0.19	0.12	0.22
	(5.58)	(−0.16)	(1.68)	(3.01)	(1.74)	(5.60)
Door	0.10	0.07	0.18	0.12	0.04	−0.08
	(2.60)	(1.46)	(2.03)	(1.45)	(0.45)	(−1.20)
Color	0.10	0.06	0.01	0.04	0.18	0.15
	(2.68)	(1.17)	(0.17)	(0.73)	(2.63)	(3.14)
Constant	3.41	3.87	3.30	2.91	2.92	2.33
	(15.0)	(16.9)	(8.56)	(6.27)	(4.26)	(5.86)
1958	−0.04	0.01				
1959	−0.11**		−0.08			
1960	−0.21**			−0.11*		
1961	−0.28**				−0.03	
1962	−0.27**					−0.01
$\bar{R}^2$	0.938	0.970	0.932	0.960	0.954	0.968
S.E.E.	0.084	0.054	0.093	0.075	0.078	0.059
Observations	56	20	20	17	16	19

C. 1962–69

	Pooled 1962–69	1962–63	1963–64	1964–65	1965–66	1966–67	1967–68	1968–69
Total capacity	1.02	0.48	0.62	1.81	1.36	1.64	1.73	0.74
	(7.68)	(4.78)	(2.84)	(5.83)	(3.90)	(3.73)	(2.60)	(2.17)
Freezer capacity	0.23	0.38	0.48	0.12	0.35	0.04	-0.01	0.38
	(3.46)	(4.06)	(2.22)	(1.01)	(1.71)	(0.19)	(-0.04)	(2.39)
Door	-0.11	-0.12	-0.09	-0.02	-0.45	...	-0.16	-0.29
	(-1.41)	(-1.69)	(-0.58)	(-0.16)	(-1.28)		(-0.86)	(-1.67)
Refrigerator defrost	0.04	0.17	-0.16	-0.07	0.42	0.19	0.25	0.12
	(0.45)	(2.03)	(-0.76)	(-0.37)	(1.58)	(1.10)	(1.71)	(0.91)
Freezer defrost	0.20	0.29	0.27	...	...	...	...	...
	(3.15)	(8.84)	(2.66)					
Constant	1.88	2.43	1.75	0.32	0.46	0.93	0.99	1.92
	(-8.68)	(6.79)	(2.70)	(0.48)	(0.86)	(1.83)	(4.56)	(5.66)
1963	-0.06	-0.10**						
1964	-0.22**		-0.14					
1965	-0.08			0.11				
1966	-0.15*				-0.05			
1967	-0.18**					-0.06		
1968	-0.27**						-0.10	
1969	-0.25**							0.03
$\bar{R}^2$	0.851	0.959	0.788	0.802	0.879	0.908	0.897	0.892
S.E.E.	0.132	0.061	0.134	0.130	0.114	0.121	0.119	0.123
Observations	84	20	19	19	17	15	16	30

(continued)

Table 7.2 (continued)

	D. 1969–76							
	Pooled 1969–76	1969–70	1970–71	1971–72	1972–73	1973–74	1974–75	1975–76
Total capacity	0.68	0.65	0.66	0.54	0.51	0.69	0.65	0.45
	(9.00)	(4.96)	(5.45)	(3.00)	(2.95)	(4.08)	(4.59)	(3.04)
Freezer capacity	0.15	0.15	0.02	0.09	0.18	0.15	0.23	0.34
	(4.44)	(2.64)	(0.30)	(1.57)	(2.71)	(1.95)	(3.67)	(4.33)
Freezer defrost	0.05	0.10	0.19	0.11	0.07	0.11	0.03	−0.04
	(1.55)	(1.89)	(3.61)	(1.73)	(1.04)	(1.53)	(0.55)	(−0.72)
Icemaker	0.17	0.23	0.27	0.13	0.06	0.11	0.12	0.13
	(7.75)	(5.48)	(7.60)	(2.75)	(1.24)	(2.62)	(3.45)	(3.77)
Powermiser	0.18	0.18	0.20	0.23	...	...	...	0.13
	(7.51)	(4.21)	(5.46)	(4.87)				(3.73)
Cold water dispenser	0.14	...	0.11	0.23	0.22	0.14	0.13	0.15
	(4.83)		(1.60)	(3.82)	(3.59)	(2.62)	(2.89)	(3.64)
Constant	3.01	3.02	3.56	3.58	3.33	2.99	2.71	2.98
	(25.6)	(15.2)	(17.3)	(14.7)	(12.8)	(11.8)	(11.5)	(12.7)
1970	−0.01	−0.00						
1971	−0.00		0.00					
1972	0.04			0.05				
1973	0.03				−0.00			
1974	0.02					−0.02		
1975	0.22**						0.20**	
1976	0.10**							−0.10**
$\bar{R}^2$	0.949	0.954	0.954	0.932	0.937	0.953	0.966	0.957
S.E.E.	0.086	0.085	0.082	0.092	0.087	0.072	0.062	0.066
Observations	156	47	48	42	34	27	30	40

E. 1976–83

	Pooled 1976–83	1976–77	1977–78	1978–79	1979–80	1980–81	1981–82	1982–83
Total capacity	0.56	−0.19	−0.05	0.30	0.78	0.97	0.88	0.82
	(5.28)	(−0.98)	(−0.26)	(1.38)	(3.84)	(7.11)	(5.98)	(3.47)
Freezer capacity	0.32	0.64	0.52	0.42	0.28	0.19	0.17	0.18
	(6.65)	(7.30)	(6.03)	(4.33)	(2.85)	(2.92)	(2.64)	(1.89)
Icemaker	0.17	0.13	0.21	0.21	0.14	0.08	0.10	0.17
	(5.79)	(2.59)	(4.46)	(4.29)	(2.73)	(1.95)	(1.71)	(1.88)
Coldwater dispenser	0.10	0.09	0.07	0.07	0.10	0.14	0.16	0.18
	(2.78)	(1.73)	(1.11)	(1.03)	(1.69)	(3.01)	(2.59)	(1.63)
Adjustable shelves	0.15	0.18	0.23	0.21	0.20	0.26	0.26	−0.00
	(6.47)	(4.96)	(6.67)	(5.37)	(4.47)	(6.21)	(3.25)	(−0.04)
Constant	2.63	3.18	3.29	2.85	2.29	2.26	2.73	3.27
	(17.6)	(12.7)	(10.9)	(8.86)	(7.89)	(11.4)	(13.5)	(9.42)
1977	−0.03							
1978	0.03	−0.06						
1979	0.11**		0.05					
1980	0.17**			0.08				
1981	0.34**				0.05			
1982	0.47**					0.15**		
1983	0.53**						0.13**	−0.01
$\bar{R}^2$	0.945	0.933	0.924	0.918	0.928	0.974	0.971	0.927
S.E.E.	0.099	0.084	0.086	0.092	0.090	0.068	0.075	0.116
Observations	131	40	37	37	35	31	26	23

*Indicates significance at the 5 percent level.

**Indicates significance at the 1 percent level.

by the coefficients on the time dummy variables in the pooled regression equation compares with a cumulative 41 percent implied by successive time dummy coefficients in the adjacent-year equations.

The next period, 1957–62, is covered in part B of table 7.2. Dummy variables for freezer defrost, "door" (i.e., two doors), and "color" (available in colors other than white) are added, while the crisper variable disappears. The coefficients in the pooled equation are all positive, significant, and reasonable in size; the coefficient on total capacity shrinks slightly and that on freezer capacity rises slightly as compared with part A of table 7.2. A few of the coefficients in the adjacent-year equations have a negative (albeit insignificant coefficient). The standard error of 0.084 in the pooled equation is almost identical to that for the 1948–57 period, and the 1957–62 price reduction of 27 percent in the pooled equation compares with the smaller cumulative reduction of 22 percent in the adjacent-year equations.

The next period, 1962–69, overlaps the Triplett-McDonald sample period. The composition of the Sears sample prevents coefficients on freezer defrost from being estimated in most of the adjacent-year regressions. The coefficients in the pooled equation are less satisfactory than before, in that the elasticity on total capacity jumps from 0.22 in part B of table 7.2 to 1.02 in part C of table 7.2, the coefficient on door is negative, and no variables are included for numerous deluxe features that one might have expected to be important. For instance, variables included by Triplett-McDonald for their 1963–65 pooled regression, but excluded here, are "meat pan," "bottom freezer location," and "side freezer location."

It is likely that the omission of these variables accounts both for the large coefficient on total capacity and for the larger standard error of estimate than in the previous tables (0.132 vs. 0.084 and 0.081). Although the Triplett-McDonald equation is estimated in a semilog form, their coefficients applied to the means of the *CR* sample for 1964 imply elasticities of 0.39 for refrigerator capacity and 0.24 for freezer capacity. Reflecting the difference in the coefficients, the 1962–69 price decline in the pooled equation of 25 percent and in the adjacent-year equations of 33 percent are not very close to the 19.7 percent decline registered by Triplett-McDonald's central index "C" (1977, table 5, p. 148).

For the 1969–76 period, the average sample size is larger than in previous tables, and the standard errors of estimate are lower. Dummy variables for three luxury features, "icemaker," "powermiser," and "cold water dispenser," are included and are significant in the pooled and in almost all the adjacent-year equations. The coefficients on total capacity, freezer capacity, and the presence of freezer defrost differ again from the previous table, and the omission of several variables may account for this instability. In their pooled regression for 1970–72, Triplett-McDonald include the following dummy variables that are excluded here: meat pan, bottom or side freezer location, cantilever shelves, reversible doors, and rollers. The 1969–76 price increase in the pooled equation of 10 percent compares with a cumulative 13 percent in the adjacent-year equations.

The final table of results covers the 1976–83 interval. Once again, the sample sizes are larger than in the early years, all the estimated coefficients are highly significant in the pooled equation, and many are significant in the adjacent-year equations. The coefficients in the pooled equation for 1976–83 are quite similar to those in the 1969–76 pooled equation in the previous table. The price increase of 53 percent in the pooled equation compares with a cumulative increase of just 40 percent in the adjacent-year equations. I will turn to a comparison of these price changes with those registered by the CPI and PPI after developing the alternative price indexes based on *CR* data.

7.5.2   Comparisons from *CR* Product Evaluations

As noted above, *CR* has published detailed product evaluations of major appliances throughout the postwar years. The *CR* data base is complementary to the Sears catalog data. The catalog provides a wide variety of models under one brand name, while *CR* evaluates a single model type for a wide variety of brand names. By linking together *CR* price and quality data for "closely similar" models, a price index can be developed that is similar in principle to the specification method used to compile the CPI and PPI.

The price indexes developed in this section are based on thirteen reports on refrigerators and refrigerator-freezers that appeared between 1949 and 1983.[12] Because several reports included two model types rather than a single model type, the *CR* price indexes link together sixteen averages of *CR* price quotations, as shown in table 7.3. For each model type, simple averages of the listed price, refrigerator capacity, and freezer capacity are calculated, as well as the average monthly energy cost. The price per kilowatt hour used in computing the energy cost was also recorded, as well as any significant comments about other dimensions of quality change.

Two changes in the criteria of measurement occurred over the postwar period. Starting in 1960, *CR* shifted from reporting the manufacturer's list price to an average price reported by *CR*'s own shopping survey. Fortunately, in the overlap report (September 1960), both list prices and average shopper prices are reported, and the latter are only 2.8 percent below the former ($559 vs. $575 for type E, as identified in the notes to table 7.3). While this may seem surprising, it appears from the wide range of prices in the shopping survey that in 1960 many outlets sold refrigerators at a price *above* manufacturer's list price. Because the difference in the mean list and the shoppers' prices was so small, the effect of this shift in pricing criteria is ignored in the price comparisons. A further change in criteria in the late 1950s was a shift from manufacturers' capacity measurements to *CR*'s own

---

12. After completing the calculations, I discovered that I had missed evaluations published in 1966, 1971, and 1979.

Table 7.3   Comparisons of "Closely Similar" Models of Refrigerator-Freezers from *Consumer Reports*, 1949–83 (all changes are in percentages)

Dates	Type (1)	Size (cubic feet) Refrigerator (2)	Freezer (3)	Price Change (dP/P) (4)	Adjustments to Price Change Size $(-adC/C)$ (5)	Energy[a] $(dE/[P + dE])$ (6)	Annual Rate of Price Change Without Energy Adjustment (7)	With Energy Adjustment (8)
1. 1949–51	A	8.0/ 7.1	0.42/0.68	−7.2	−6.9	−1.1[b]	−7.3	−11.7
2. 1949–51	B	7.3/ 7.5	1.50/1.21	−21.4	3.2	−8.1[c]	−9.6	−12.3
3. 1951–54	B	7.5/ 8.1	1.21/1.00	−10.4	0.6	−24.4[d]	−3.4	−12.8
4. 1951–54	D	8.5/ 9.5	1.66/1.90	1.5	−7.9	−18.1[e]	−2.2	−12.2
5. 1954–57	D	9.5/10.1	1.90/2.37	−11.1[f]	−8.0	12.2[g]	−6.8	−5.2
6. 1954–59	C	9.5/ 9.5	1.90/2.00	−22.3	−1.2	2.6[i]	−5.2	−4.9
7. 1957–59	D	7.2/ 7.2[h]	2.15/2.65[h]	−7.9	−5.1	13.1[j]	−3.3	−2.5
8. 1959–60	E	7.0/ 7.2	3.00/3.18	−20.1	−2.5	5.3[k]	−22.6	−19.8
9. 1959–62	C	7.5/ 7.0[h]	1.53/1.61[h]	−15.9	1.5	4.0[l]	−5.1	−3.1
10. 1959–62	D	7.2/ 7.5	2.65/2.73	−29.3	−2.8	−2.0[m]	−12.1	−14.2
11. 1962–64	D	7.5/ 7.6	2.73/2.73	−3.0	−0.5	−3.7[n]	−1.8	−3.9
12. 1960–64	E	7.2/ 7.3	3.18/3.24	−23.7	−1.0	6.8[o]	−6.8	−5.1
13. 1964–68	E	7.3/ 8.0	3.24/3.45	−20.7	−5.3	−7.1[p]	−7.3	−11.4
14. 1968–70	F	8.1/ 9.4	3.05/3.63	22.3	−10.6	14.3[q]	5.7	7.4
15. 1970–74	F	9.4/ 8.8	3.63/3.48	12.9	3.5	0.0[r]	3.9	3.9
16. 1974–83	F	8.8/10.3	3.48/4.65	81.3	−14.2	−4.3[s]	5.9	4.5

Note: Type A: U-type, no refrigerator or freezer defrost. Type B: Cross-top freezer, single zone, no refrigerator or freezer defrost. Type C: Same as B, but with refrigerator defrost. Type D: Same as C, but dual zone. Type E: Bottom freezer, dual zone, refrigerator and freezer defrost. Type F: Same as E, but cross-top freezer.

[a]All energy costs in the calculations in these notes are converted to a per-month basis at $.03 per kilowatt hour, except for 1949–51 ($.04 per kilowatt hour) and 1974–83 ($.0675 per kilowatt hour).

[b]From $1.81 to $1.79 per month; present value of saving = $2.75.

[c]From $2.42 to $2.17; present value of saving = $34.30.

[d]From $1.63 to $0.91; present value of saving = $98.77.

[e]From $2.36 to $1.64; present value of saving = $98.77.

[f]Deducted $35 from 1957 price to take account of additional features not present in 1954.

[g]From $1.64 to $2.00; present value of extra cost = $49.38.

[h]Starting with the 1957–59 comparison, dimensions shift from manufacturers' claims to *CR* remeasurement basis.

[i]From $1.05 to $1.11; present value of extra cost = $8.22.

[j]From $2.00 to $2.37; present value of extra cost = $50.75.

[k]From $3.42 to $3.67; present value of extra cost = $34.99.

[l]From $1.11 to $1.18; present value of extra cost = $9.60.

[m]From $2.37 to $2.31; present value of saving = $8.23.

[n]From $2.31 to $2.23; present value of saving = $10.98.

[o]From $3.67 to $3.93; present value of extra cost = $35.67.

[p]From $3.93 to $3.69; present value of saving = $3.92.

[q]From $3.07 to $3.32; present value of extra cost = $34.29.

[r]No data available for 1974; 1974–83 comparison refers to 1970–83.

[s]Change from $7.47 in 1970 to $7.29 in 1984 (at $06.75 per kwh); present value of saving = $16.07.

measurements. Since both sets of measurements are given in the 1957 and 1959 product evaluations, it is straightforward to "link out" the effect of this change. Because *CR*'s measurements in 1957 are about 25 percent smaller than manufacturer's measurements for refrigerator capacity and about 10 percent smaller for freezer capacity, columns 2 and 3 understate the overall postwar increase in capacity between 1949 and 1983.

Each of the sixteen comparisons in table 7.3 is exhibited in a uniform format. First are listed the dates of the product evaluations where the data appeared for the comparison, then the model type (identified at the bottom of the table), and then the average refrigerator and freezer capacity in the first and second years of the comparison. Column 4 lists the percentage change in price between the first and the second year, without any quality adjustments at all, except in comparison 5 for 1954–57, discussed below.

Two types of adjustments are made for changing quality. In column 5, the size changes from columns 2 and 3 are converted into value changes, using the estimated coefficients on size from the Triplett-McDonald study. Their coefficients are used in preference to mine in table 7.2 because they are based on a full range of brand names and a larger sample. Further, their implied size elasticities are smaller than mine in table 7.2 for most of the sample period, reflecting their longer list of additional characteristics included in the regression equations. As they comment in discussing their results (1977, 143), price per incremental unit of capacity fell over their 1963–72 sample period, and this is true of the implied elasticities as well. This suggests that their elasticities may be too low when extrapolated for my pre-1963 adjustments, and therefore that my size adjustments could be on the conservative side before 1963 and on the liberal side after 1972.

As an example of the calculation of the size adjustment, the implied Triplett-McDonald elasticity for refrigerator capacity is 0.397 and for freezer capacity is 0.223.[13] Thus, in the fifth comparison, where refrigerator size increased by 6.3 percent and freezer size increased by 24.7 percent, we have:

$$(6.3)(.397) + (24.7)(.223) = 8.0.$$

This increase in value is equivalent to a 8.0 percent decline in quality-adjusted price and is listed in column 5, row 5.

Thus far, this method has controlled for six quality characteristics that appear to be important determinants of cross-sectional price differences in the Triplett-McDonald study and in my Sears catalog hedonic regressions. The first two, refrigerator capacity and freezer capacity, are subject to the explicit

13. To simplify the calculations, a single elasticity was used for the entire period and was calculated as follows. The Triplett-McDonald semilog coefficients for refrigerator capacity (from table 2, p. 142) were .054 in 1963–65 and .041 in 1969–72, for a mean of .0475. Refrigerator capacity in table 7.3 for model E in 1964 of 7.3 and model F in 1970 of 9.4 average out to 8.35, implying an elasticity of 0.397 (= 8.35 × .0475). The same calculation for freezer capacity yields an elasticity of 0.223.

adjustments described in the preceding paragraph. The other four are part of the specifications of the "model types" (A, B, etc.) identified at the bottom of table 7.3, that is, refrigerator defrost, freezer defrost, freezer location, and the "dual zone" feature (which involves separate cooling coils for refrigerator and freezer).

There remains the question of adjustment for the many other features that appeared on refrigerators gradually over the postwar period, including shelves in the door, egg compartment, heated butter compartment, vegetable crispers, meat compartment, adjustable shelves, reversible doors, door stops, rollers, and heaters to prevent condensation. The addition of these features over time interacts with the shift between model types. If type A (U-type, no refrigerator or freezer defrost) lacks all the extra features, while types E and F (dual-zone, top or bottom freezer, refrigerator and freezer defrost) are equipped with all these features in all years, then the procedure of linking in a new model type would automatically incorporate the value of the extra features. However, in both my hedonic regression study and the Triplett-McDonald study, separate coefficients are estimated for features beyond the basic characteristics that define the model types. Further, note that type D (dual-zone, top freezer, refrigerator defrost, no freezer defrost) spans numerous evaluations during the main period when refrigerator prices were declining (this model appears in the 1952, 1954, 1957, 1959, 1962, and 1964 reports), yet appears to add features.

For instance, of the seven type D refrigerators in the 1952 evaluation, only four had adjustable-temperature butter compartments, only three had door shelves, and only two are listed as having "full cold-wall construction" (i.e., the dual-zone feature). By 1957, we learn that all but one of seventeen top-freezer models tested were dual zone, all models had shelves in the door, all models but one had one or more "slide-out" shelves, four models had arrangements for altering the height of some shelves, and some had freezer doors with dispenser racks and/or shelves. How can a value be established for these extra features? The 1957 report includes both a deluxe and a standard version of one brand, the Kelvinator, which differed in price by $70, and half that amount, $35, is taken as a one-time adjustment for extra features (see n. f in col. 4). I suspect that this is a substantial underestimate of the cumulative value of extra features over the full postwar period.

7.5.3 Adjustments for Improvements in Energy Efficiency

Thus far, neither the Sears hedonic regression study nor the *CR* comparisons have taken into account reductions over time in the energy consumption of refrigerators. Fortunately, in all product evaluations but one (1974), *CR* lists the monthly energy cost and the price per kilowatt hour assumed in making the calculation. The notes to column 6 of table 7.3 list the mean monthly energy cost in the first and second years of each comparison and the present discounted value of the change, calculated at a 3 percent discount rate and a fourteen-year lifetime. A 3 percent discount rate is a common choice for such comparisons, and the fourteen-year lifetime is suggested by *Consumer Appliances* (n.d.).[14] The present discounted value of the change in energy cost (dE) is then divided by the sum of that change plus the average refrigerator price in the first year of each comparison period to establish the percentage adjustment factors listed in column 6. Thus, the adjustment factor is calculated as $dE/(P_0 - dE)$. This approach treats the value of an improvement in energy efficiency as part of the price of the unit in the first year of the comparison but not in the second year of the comparison. The method also assumes static expectations regarding the future evolution of energy prices.

A difficult problem in implementing the energy adjustment is the treatment of the correlation between energy cost and other quality characteristics. Increasing refrigerator capacity adds to energy requirements, as does the addition of extra features like refrigerator and freezer defrost. By using the six separate model types A–F, I control for the extra energy consumption required by refrigerator and freezer defrost and the dual-zone feature.[15] There remains the necessity of adjusting energy consumption for refrigerator and freezer capacity. The method can be set out by decomposing the change in the energy-adjusted price index (dI^E/I^E) into four components:

$$(7.1) \qquad dI^E/I^E = dP/P - adC/C + dE/(P - dE) - gdC/C.$$

The first component is the change in the average price itself (dP/P), without any adjustment for changing size or energy consumption, and appears in column 4 of table 7.3. The next component is the change in capacity (dC/C) times the hedonic coefficient (a) that translates the change in capacity into a change in value, and this component appears in column 5. The third component ($dE/[P + dE]$) is the change in the present value of energy consumption evaluated at a constant price of electricity, appearing in column 6. The final component is the effect of changing capacity on energy consumption, represented by the unknown elasticity g. The last term is included so that an increase in energy consumption solely due to larger capacity is not treated as a price increase.

---

14. "Based on industry information, the MIT study team established that the color TV has a life of about 10 years, the refrigerator a life of about 14" (*Consumer Appliances,* n.d., 11). *CR* in most product evaluations calculates the monthly cost of electricity use and does not indicate a lifetime, except in 1968, when it calculates the lifetime electricity cost on the assumption of a fifteen-year life (September 1968, 476, 479). The 3 percent discount rate, although appropriate for producers' purchases of appliances, may be too low for consumers. For a discussion of the evidence that consumers may "overdiscount" in making purchases of durable goods, see Hausman and Joskow (1981, 9).

15. For instance, in the *CR* report of August 1964, the average monthly energy cost of units with freezer defrost was 1.76 times that of the cost of units without freezer defrost. This compares with the comment by *CR* that freezer defrost raises energy consumption by a factor of "two-thirds," i.e., would imply a ratio of 1.67 times. The difference between 1.76 and 1.67 may be accounted for by extra features and by the fact that the 1964 freezer-defrost models had on average a 19 percent larger effective freezer capacity than the no-freezer-defrost models.

An argument could be made that the effect of larger capacity on energy consumption (g) is larger than the effect of larger capacity on manufacturing cost (a), since the former should depend on cubic area while the latter should depend on the surface area of the refrigerator "box." Applying this reasoning, the g elasticity to increased capacity should be unity and the a elasticity should be two-thirds. In contrast, the values of a used in column 5 of table 7.3, that is, the Triplett-McDonald price elasticities for refrigerator size (0.40) and freezer size (0.22), sum to a bit less than two-thirds, probably because manufacturing cost contains fixed elements as well as depending just on the surface area of the box. While a case could be made that the g elasticity should be unity, I take the more conservative approach here of assuming that $g = a$, so that year-to-year changes in my energy-adjusted price index are calculated as

$$(7.2) \qquad dI^E/I^E = dP/P - 2adC/C + dE/(P - dE)$$

and the change in the price index without an energy adjustment (dI^N/I^N) is calculated as

$$(7.3) \qquad dI^N/I^N = dP/P - adC/C.$$

Note that $dI^E/I^E = dI^N/I^N$ only if $dE/(P - dE) = adC/C$, that is, in the case when higher energy consumption is neither more nor less than is explained by the extra energy requirements of a larger capacity. Scanning down column 5 of table 7.3, which shows $-adC/C$, and column 6, which exhibits $dE/(P - dE)$, we note numerous comparisons (rows 5, 7, 8, 9, and 12) in which $dE/(P - dE)$ is positive and is substantially greater than $-adC/C$. This could indicate that the choice of g (as equal to a instead of equal to some higher elasticity) is too small, and/or that added features on a given model-type (C, D, etc.) raised energy consumption without increasing capacity. Either alternative would make the energy adjustments too conservative, and understate the secular rate of decline of the energy-cost-adjusted price index (I^E).

The final two columns of table 7.3 convert the price change over the multiyear comparison intervals into geometric annual rates of change. These rates of change for the non-energy-adjusted index (I^N) from (7.3) are shown in column 7, and for the energy-adjusted index (I^E) from (7.2) in column 8. The implications of the two *CR* indexes in comparison with the CPI, PPI, and Sears hedonic regression indexes are examined in the next section.

7.5.4   Alternative Price Indexes for Refrigerator-Freezers

The outcome of the investigation of refrigerator prices is presented in table 7.4. Here are contrasted the CPI and PPI with five other indexes, including the Triplett-McDonald "C" index, the two Sears catalog hedonic indexes, and the two *CR* indexes. In converting the annual rates of change of the *CR* price

Table 7.4   Alternative Price Indexes for Refrigerator-Freezers, 1947–83 (1967 = 100)

	CPI (1)	PPI (12-41-03-35) (2)	Triplett-McDonald Index C (3)	Sears Hedonic Pooled (4)	Sears Hedonic Adjacent Year (5)	Consumer Reports Without Energy Adjustment (6)	Consumer Reports With Energy Adjustment (7)
1947	174.5	121.5	. . .	. . .	. . .	. . .	. . .
1948	192.7	130.2	. . .	243.5	238.7	. . .	. . .
1949	186.8	126.7	. . .	220.3	224.8	302.8	468.9
1950	182.7	129.1	. . .	213.8	213.8	278.4	415.9
1951	192.4	132.4	. . .	193.5	197.4	256.0	368.8
1952	185.1	131.8	. . .	203.4	207.5	251.4	325.5
1953	178.1	133.1	. . .	199.4	203.4	246.9	287.3
1954	166.0	134.1	. . .	213.8	211.6	240.1	253.5
1955	156.0	128.0	. . .	161.6	161.1	226.1	241.0
1956	134.6	123.7	. . .	160.0	161.6	213.0	229.3
1957	123.8	116.6	. . .	156.8	158.4	200.6	217.9
1958	119.6	114.3	. . .	150.7	160.0	192.1	209.9
1959	119.2	114.0	. . .	140.5	147.7	184.0	202.3
1960	116.8	108.7	137.0	127.1	132.3	161.1	178.8
1961	115.2	105.2	133.1	118.5	128.4	147.8	166.0
1962	112.5	102.0	127.4	119.7	127.1	135.7	154.0
1963	109.6	98.7	115.4	112.7	115.0	130.0	147.2
1964	107.4	98.2	107.7	96.1	100.0	124.5	140.8
1965	104.2	96.6	103.8	110.5	111.6	115.7	125.6
1966	100.2	97.6	100.4	103.0	106.2	107.6	112.1
1967	100.0	100.0	100.0	100.0	100.0	100.0	100.0
1968	101.3	104.3	103.2	91.3	90.5	93.0	89.2
1969	103.1	105.3	102.3	93.2	93.2	98.4	96.1
1970	105.8	106.1	105.1	92.3	93.2	104.2	103.5
1971	108.1	108.1	109.4	93.2	93.2	108.3	107.6
1972	108.1	105.3	106.0	97.0	98.0	112.6	111.9
1973	108.3	105.1	. . .	96.1	98.0	117.1	116.3
1974	114.6	113.4	. . .	95.1	96.1	121.8	120.9
1975	128.7	131.6	. . .	116.2	117.4	129.2	126.5
1976	134.8	140.6	. . .	103.0	106.2	137.0	132.3
1977	139.7	147.6	. . .	100.0	100.0	145.4	138.4
1978	146.2	154.8	. . .	106.1	105.1	154.2	144.8
1979	153.2	160.2	. . .	115.0	113.8	163.6	151.4
1980	162.4	170.3	. . .	122.1	119.7	173.5	158.4
1981	173.5	184.4	. . .	144.7	139.1	184.0	165.7
1982	187.3	194.5	. . .	164.8	158.4	195.2	173.3
1983	193.3	200.8	. . .	175.0	156.8	207.1	181.3

changes from table 7.3 to price indexes in table 7.4, equal weights were applied to each comparison when more than one price change is available for a particular year. This procedure is symmetric with the hedonic regression studies, which give each observation an equal weight regardless of its sales.

The behavior of the various price indexes differs over alternative subperiods of the 1949–83 period. Table 7.5 summarizes for three intervals. The first is 1949–72, starting with the first year when both the Sears hedonic and the *CR*

Table 7.5   **Annual Percent Growth Rates of Alternative Price Indexes for Refrigerators, 1949–83 and Subintervals**

	1949–72	1960–72	1972–83	1949–83
CPI	−2.35	−0.64	5.42	0.10
PPI	−0.80	−0.26	6.04	1.49
Triplett-McDonald	. . .	−2.12	. . .	. . .
Sears pooled	−3.59	−2.21	5.51	−0.68
Sears adjacent year	−3.55	−2.47	4.36	−1.05
CR without energy	−4.21	−2.94	5.70	−1.11
CR with energy	−6.04	−3.83	4.55	−2.76

indexes are available. The second is 1960–72, chosen for comparability with the Triplett-McDonald hedonic regression study. The third is 1972–83. The geometric annual growth rates of the seven alternative indexes over the three intervals and the full period are presented in table 7.5.

The annual growth rates shown in table 7.5 embody striking similarities and differences among the alternative indexes. The two main similarities are the relatively narrow range of growth rates for the most recent 1972–83 period and the close similarity of the hedonic regression results for the Triplett-McDonald and Sears pooled indexes for the overlap period of 1960–72. The fact that the Sears adjacent-year price index is based on a relatively small sample in each regression and that this index deviates more than the pooled index from Triplett-McDonald in 1960–72 and from the other indexes in 1972–83 suggests that we should disregard the behavior of the adjacent-year index in the subsequent discussion.

Despite these similarities, however, the differences in the annual growth rates are remarkably large for 1949–72, ranging from −0.80 for the PPI to −6.04 for the CR index including the energy cost adjustment. In evaluating these differences, three main issues arise. First, why does the CR index without an energy adjustment decline more rapidly than the Sears pooled hedonic index from 1949 to 1972? Second, why does the CR index without an energy adjustment decline more rapidly than the Triplett-McDonald hedonic index from 1960 to 1972? Third, is there any explanation for the difference in timing of the time path of the CPI and of the CR specification index that is not adjusted for energy prices, since both are based on the specification method and cover a wide variety of brand names?

The first contrast between the Sears pooled hedonic and the CR no-energy indexes is largely resolved by the upward shift of the Sears Kenmore brand in the price structure. As noted above in section 7.3, the average Sears price for refrigerators (adjusted for shipping costs) was 76.4 percent of the CR mean for the same model type in the first two CR product evaluations (1949 and 1952) and 105.5 percent in the last two CR evaluations (1974 and 1983). Assuming that all this shift occurred before 1972, the shift in price structure would have occurred at an annual rate of 1.41 percent during

1949–72, which is greater than the 1.08 percent difference in the growth rates of the Sears pooled hedonic and *CR* no-energy indexes. While this upward shift in the relative price of the Sears brand may have been accompanied by an improvement in relative quality, this quality shift must have occurred in characteristics that are not taken into account in the hedonic or *CR* specification comparisons.[16]

The second contrast is between the Triplett-McDonald hedonic index and the *CR* no-energy index for the period of their overlap, 1960–72, with a more rapid decline in the *CR* index at an annual rate of 0.8 percent. Both indexes have in common a comprehensive coverage of all the major brand names, with between thirteen and fifteen brand names rated by *CR* in each product evaluation between 1960 and 1974. The issue of discounting is not a problem for the *CR* index during this period, since the quotation of mean shoppers' prices began in 1960; on this ground, the Triplett-McDonald PPI price quotations obtained from manufacturers may not represent true transaction prices at the retail (or even wholesale) level. Since most of the price decline in the *CR* index is accounted for by the behavior of model type E (bottom freezer, full defrost) in 1960–68, it is interesting to compare the average 1960 price of $559 to the average 1968 price of $339, for a price decline of 39 percent in comparison to the 42 percent decline in the *CR* index. This raw unadjusted price change does not take account of an 11 percent increase in refrigerator capacity between 1960 and 1968, a 8 percent increase in freezer capacity, and numerous other quality improvements.[17] Further, there is an additional aspect to the decline in price, in that full-defrost models were originally introduced in 1958–59 only in the bottom-freezer configuration, and *CR* in 1959, 1960, and 1964 tested only the bottom-freezer models. By the mid-1960s, however, top-freezer full-defrost models were available, and in 1968 *CR* stated that they outsold bottom-freezer units by a margin of five to one.[18] If one compares the 1968 top-freezer unit with the 1960 bottom-freezer unit on the ground that the

16. There is a tendency for the Sears Kenmore model to be among the lowest priced and lowest rated in the early years of the *CR* product evaluations. By the September 1968 *CR* evaluation, however, we find that the top-freezer model (type F) is second rated out of fourteen models and priced 4 percent above the mean, while the bottom-freezer model (type E) is third rated out of nine models and priced 2 percent above the mean.

17. One of the most obvious quality improvements is impossible to quantify: in 1960 only five of fourteen models were rated "acceptable-good" and the other nine models were downgraded as "good-to-fair" and "fair" because of "performance deficiencies," particularly inability to hold a zero temperature in the freezer and/or uneven temperatures. In 1968, however, there was only one "acceptable" category for all nine models rated, and the only deficiencies discussed were in the category of convenience rather than performance.

18. By 1974, *CR* called bottom-freezer units a "vanishing breed" and stated that their frequency-of-repair record is of "mainly antiquarian interest" (811). In 1983, *CR* mentions that top-freezer units had accounted for three-quarters of sales in recent years, with the remainder being side-by-side units.

top-freezer unit is preferable but was unavailable in 1960, the raw unadjusted price decline becomes 51 percent.[19]

The third and last contrast is between the CPI and the *CR* index without the energy cost adjustment. The contrast between the two indexes is highlighted by choosing 1957 and 1967 as break points for calculating annual growth rates:

	1949–57	1957–67	1967–77
CPI	− 5.01	− 2.11	4.21
CR (no energy adjustment)	− 5.02	− 6.73	4.65

The 1957 and 1967 break points highlight the similarity of the two indexes before 1957 and after 1967, and their enormous difference between 1957 and 1967. There may be two explanations for this discrepancy. First, the CPI may have placed too much weight on obsolete models. While I have been unable to locate a time series of changes in specifications, I have found the CPI specification for refrigerators in 1956, which specifically instructs field agents to exclude models with two doors and automatic defrost, yet by then automatic (refrigerator) defrost had become so dominant in the marketplace that *CR* did no further testing on no-defrost models after 1954. Second, the CPI may not have accounted adequately for discounting. Particularly striking is the contrast for the year 1960, when the CPI registers a price decline of just 2.1 percent, while the *CR* index drops by a much greater 12.4 percent. The CPI in this case seems inconsistent with the *CR* description of market conditions in 1960:

> CU's shoppers made their price survey during the last two weeks in June. Since that time retail prices for refrigerators have dropped even further; the price toboggan, which began this Spring, has been so severe this Summer that trade and financial papers like *The Journal of Commerce* and *Home Furnishings Daily* have carried headlines about how "High Stocks [Are] Causing Refrigerator Cuts." As CU goes to press, there is every indication that this downward trend in prices will reach even lower levels. [September 1960, 461]

As a final comment on the official price indexes, the PPI seems totally at variance with the new price indexes for the period before 1967 and even with the CPI for the period before 1957. Yet it is the PPI, not the CPI, that is used by the BEA for deflation of PDE.

---

19. This does not make any allowance for a 13 percent increase in refrigerator capacity of a 4 percent decrease in freezer capacity, nor does it include a 18 percent decline in energy consumption, having a present value of $82.30 (15 percent of the average price of the 1960 models).

7.5.5   Unmeasured Dimensions of Quality Improvement

All the quality adjustments for refrigerators discussed thus far have been quantitative in nature. In addition, there have been quality improvements in refrigerators that cannot be quantified, but that indicate that my indexes understate the total magnitude of quality improvement over the postwar period. In addition to providing the quantitative data assessed above, the successive product evaluations in *CR* include numerous comments that suggest additional dimensions of quality improvement, at least through the late 1960s.

Temperature Criteria

A primary criterion for the *CR* performance evaluation of refrigerators has always been the ability to hold a desired level of temperature in the refrigerator and freezer under normal and adverse conditions. After the early 1960s, the standard requirement was for the refrigerator compartment to be able to hold a temperature of thirty-seven degrees and the freezer compartment zero degrees. By the 1964 report, all models apparently had gained the ability to perform at this standard, and there was rarely any mention after that date of temperature-holding ability, except that the January 1983 report (23) explicitly stated that all models met the thirty-seven- and zero-degree criteria at a room temperature of seventy degrees and that only two failed at ninety degrees. But in 1949 the situation was far different. The criterion was more lenient, forty-three degrees for the refrigerator. More important, only two models were able to maintain zero degrees in the freezer, and the others ranged from five to twenty-two degrees. In 1951, *CR* continued to complain about warm spots in the freezer, with only three models out of thirteen capable of holding the freezer temperature at ten degrees, much less zero. By 1954, the refrigerator criterion (at a ninety-degree room temperature) had been tightened from forty-three to thirty-nine degrees, and by 1957 to the present thirty-seven degrees. Also by 1957, freezer performance had improved, so that all models could hold five to ten degrees. By 1964, all models had reached the zero- to five-degree range in the freezer.

Overall Quality

The tone of the *CR* product evaluations has changed over the postwar years. In the beginning, the main emphasis was on the overall range of quality, and one can link together comments into a time-series commentary on improvements in quality. The earliest postwar refrigerators seemed to be a great advance over their prewar ancestors:

> It is likely that present refrigerators will last longer without trouble than their predecessors of a decade ago. CU's consultants report that a very high percentage of service calls on prewar refrigerators were for repair of

slipping belts, poor piping and shaft seals, trouble with expansion valves, and thermostat trouble. This year's refrigerators, with sealed motor-compressor units and capillary tubes instead of expansion valves, appear to have eliminated the first three problems almost entirely, and the likelihood of thermostat trouble appears to have been reduced. [June 1949, 248]

But early postwar refrigerators were no paragons. CU tests "revealed a very wide range of quality," with two models listed as not acceptable (October 1949, 445). By 1957, matters had improved, but "major shortcomings of performance were found among models high in 'showroom appeal.' A number of defects in design and construction showed up. . . . But from the total of the tests several good refrigerators emerged" (August 1957, 360). But by 1959, "all of these models tested by CU . . . performed considerably better than their predecessors tested two years ago, and on the average were more compact. These units are more-or-less deluxe models, so widely pictured in the ads, usually available in various colors, and boasting a variety of convenience features." Nevertheless, "although refrigerator-freezers seem to have come of age, and the conventional refrigerators can be generally trusted to perform adequately, CU encountered a number of models with some design bloopers which could irritate and infuriate the user" (September 1959, 457–58).[20] By 1964, we read, "The generally high level of performance demonstrated by the tested models is as it should be, CU believes, in an appliance on the market as long as refrigerators have been" (August 1964, 368). In 1971, a further improvement is recorded: "When we totaled our scores for all the units, we found that overall quality differences between models were generally smaller than they had been. And a notable uptrend in quality had emerged" (September 1971, 562). After 1971, there were no further comments on overall quality.

Quality Control

Manufacturing defects provoked major complaints by *CR* during the period 1960–64, in contrast to the pre-1960 period, when uneven performance was the main problem, and to the post-1964 period, when there were virtually no complaints at all. The 1960 evaluation lamented "nearly half of these high-priced 'no-frost' models were defective as received. . . . In the majority of these cases, the defects required service calls. . . . many of [these defects] could have resulted only from slipshod assembly and inadequate quality control, neither of which, in CU's view, should be present in so expensive an appliance" (September 1960, 457). The 1964 report complains of "annoying flaws" and a "deplorable lack of quality control" (August 1964, 368). The 1968 and subsequent evaluations, in contrast, make no mention of quality control problems of any kind.

20. These comments refer to the models classified as type D in table 7.3.

Frequency of Service Calls

There are no comments in *CR* to indicate any change in the frequency of service calls for refrigerators. However, the MIT report (*Consumer Appliances*, n.d., 23) reports that the incidence rate for first-year service calls for refrigerators fell steadily from 68 percent in 1958 to 32 percent in 1972. While most first-year service calls may be free, covered by warranties, they still "matter" to households who may in some cases face the possible deterioration or loss of frozen foods. No data are provided for service calls after the initial year, but one might assume that service reliability in subsequent years would improve in tandem with the first-year record. This is clearly the case for TV sets, as documented in section 7.9 below. I make no separate adjustment for this aspect of quality change, but note that it provides another reason to suspect that my indexes understate the extent of quality improvement (explicit repair cost adjustments are provided for TV sets in sec. 7.9 below).

7.6 Room Air Conditioners

In contrast to household refrigerators, which were sold widely in the 1930s, room air conditioner sales began later. The first electrical air conditioning system appeared in Grauman's Metropolitan Theater in Los Angeles in 1923, and by the mid-1930s air conditioning had been installed in the U.S. Capitol building, the White House, the Supreme Court, the Kremlin, and about 10,000 U.S. homes (Consumers' Union 1986). But as a commonly purchased major appliance, room air conditioners are a postwar phenomenon. From a modest 48,000 units in 1946, sales rose to over 450,000 in 1952 and 750,000 in 1953. The first models appeared in the Sears catalog in 1953, and the first *CR* product evaluation also appeared in 1953. Room air conditioners entered the PPI in 1953 as well, but did not enter the CPI until 1964. By 1957, when sales of room air conditioners approached 2 million units, *CR* was ready to call air conditioning a "wonderful thing," and more recently has enthused, "Without air conditioning, we wouldn't have Las Vegas. Or Miami, or Houston, or Los Angeles. At least, not in their modern metropolitan forms that, collectively, make up the Sunbelt, the fastest growing area of the United States. Nor would we have jet air travel, manned spaceflight, submarines, or computers" (Consumers' Union 1986, 2).

7.6.1 Hedonic Regression Results

The study of room air conditioner prices is considerably simpler than that of refrigerators, since air conditioners produce a much more homogenous product. Whereas refrigerators have separate capacity measurements for refrigerator and freezer, frost free or not in both compartments, alternative locations of the freezer, and a host of convenience features, room air conditioners basically provide a single "service," cooling, and have few fancy features.

The results of the hedonic regression study of Sears catalog data begins in part A of table 7.6, where the format is the same as table 7.2. A pooled regression is displayed for a particular interval, and adjacent-year regression equations alongside. The first interval, 1954–58, is chosen to reflect the shift in the catalog from quoting the overall capacity measurement as horsepower in the early years and as BTU beginning in 1958. In part A of table 7.6, the pooled equation indicates an elasticity of price to capacity of 0.53 and an insignificant coefficient on volts, which nevertheless is included to maintain uniformity with the other intervals. It is plausible that the elasticity of price to capacity should be less than unity; the estimate here of 0.53 compares to the Triplett-McDonald elasticity for refrigerator capacity of 0.40 discussed in the previous section. The standard error of estimate of 14 percent is somewhat higher than those in the hedonic regression study of refrigerator prices. The price decline of 41 percent between 1954 and 1958 implied by the coefficients on the time dummy variables compares with a cumulative 42 percent implied by the successive time dummy coefficients in the adjacent-year equations. The next interval, 1958–67, is covered in part B of table 7.6. Now the basic capacity measure is BTU rather than horsepower, and the elasticity rises from 0.59 in the earlier period to 0.74 in the pooled equation. Six of the nine capacity elasticities in the adjacent-year equations fall into the range of 0.52–0.86. Unlike the previous table, the coefficient on volts is significantly negative and indicates in the pooled equation that a doubling of volts from 115 to 230 reduces price by 15 percent. The 1958–67 price decline implied by the time dummy coefficients in the pooled equation is 9 percent, as compared to 12 percent in the adjacent-year equations.

Part C of table 7.6 continues with the period 1967–74. The explanatory variables continue to be BTU and volts, and the respective estimated elasticities of 0.70 and −0.17 are similar to those for 1958–67. The coefficients on both variables are more stable in the adjacent-year equations, and for BTU range only from 0.63 to 0.76. The standard error in this period is just 6 percent for the pooled equation and is as low as 3.6 percent for the 1971–72 equation, and the estimated 1967–74 price increase of 8 percent for the pooled equation compares to an almost identical 7 percent cumulatively for the adjacent-year equations.

The interval 1974–77 in part D of table 7.6 is presented separately, since the variable "watts" becomes available and supplants "volts." The watts variable is highly significant in each equation. The coefficients on the time dummy variables imply a price increase between 1974 and 1977 of 13 percent in the pooled equation and 12 percent in the adjacent-year equation. Since the energy efficiency ratio (EER) is BTU/watts, the inclusion of watts amounts to an energy-efficiency adjustment for this period.

Results for the final interval, 1977–83, are shown in part E of table 7.6. Now two additional explanatory variables are available, "fan speed" and "high efficiency," with highly significant coefficients for all equations.

Table 7.6   Pooled and Adjacent-Year Double-Log Regression Equations for Air Conditioners, Sears Catalog Data, 1954–58, 1958–67, 1967–74, 1974–77, 1977–83 (t-ratios in parentheses)

A. 1954–58

	Pooled 1954–58	1954–55	1955–56	1956–57	1957–58
Horsepower	0.53 (5.77)	0.75 (3.54)	0.63 (3.25)	0.26 (1.37)	0.37 (1.54)
Volts	−0.01 (−0.12)	−0.17 (−0.72)	−0.13 (−0.86)	0.11 (0.81)	0.13 (0.82)
Constant	5.77 (67.34)	5.85 (55.5)	5.73 (64.3)	5.53 (101.)	5.43 (89.7)
1955	−0.08	−0.08			
1956	−0.22*		−0.15*		
1957	−0.29**			−0.07	
1958	−0.41**				−0.12
R^2	0.584	0.655	0.619	0.546	0.603
S.E.E.	0.143	0.149	0.135	0.132	0.141
Observations	40	9	17	24	19

B. 1958–67

	Pooled 1958–67	1958–59	1959–60	1960–61	1961–62	1962–63	1963–64	1964–65	1965–66	1966–67
BTU	0.74 (10.4)	1.17 (14.0)	0.52 (3.57)	0.55 (4.74)	0.57 (5.59)	0.57 (7.27)	0.86 (5.26)	0.42 (5.63)	0.69 (10.4)	0.37 (3.94)
Volts	−0.15	−0.10 (−2.62)	−0.12 (1.92)	−0.10 (−1.77)	−0.06 (−1.16)	−0.07 (−1.50)	−0.29 (−2.49)	−0.33 (−2.74)	−0.15 (3.21)	−0.15 (· · ·)
Constant	3.83 (23.6)	2.74 (14.7)	4.43 (12.9)	4.25 (16.7)	4.17 (18.2)	4.19 (24.4)	3.58 (9.71)	3.32 (9.07)	3.84 (25.9)	4.57 (18.3)
1959	0.07	0.04								
1960	0.01		−0.08							
1961	−0.01			−0.01						
1962	−0.01				−0.00					
1963	−0.04					−0.02				
1964	−0.17**						−0.13			
1965	−0.11							0.05		
1966	−0.16*								−0.04	

1967	−0.09			0.07
R^2	0.674	0.662	0.935	0.749
S.E.E.	0.123	0.182	0.051	0.085
Observations	70	17	12	6

C. 1967–74

	Pooled 1967–74	1967–68	1968–69	1969–70	1970–71	1971–72	1972–73	1973–74
BTU	0.70	0.67	0.70	0.65	0.63	0.76	0.72	0.73
	(32.8)	(10.1)	(18.4)	(15.5)	(11.6)	(26.1)	(23.7)	(18.3)
Volt	−0.17	−0.15	−0.16	−0.11	−0.11	−0.24	−0.19	−0.21
	(−6.84)	(−2.12)	(−3.70)	(−1.97)	(−1.54)	(−6.65)	(−5.39)	(−4.76)
Constant	3.85	3.92	3.82	3.87	4.01	3.69	3.80	3.81
	(60.8)	(24.9)	(47.1)	(41.2)	(34.5)	(61.5)	(59.7)	(43.1)
1968	−0.03	−0.03						
1969	−0.06		−0.04					
1970	0.02			0.07*				
1971	−0.02				−0.04			
1972	−0.01					0.01		
1973	0.02						0.03	
1974	0.08							0.07*
R^2	0.970	0.942	0.966	0.966	0.962	0.991	0.988	0.965
S.E.E.	0.060	0.079	0.066	0.066	0.069	0.036	0.039	0.062
Observations	79	14	23	16	15	19	21	30

D. 1974–77

	Pooled 1974–77	1974–75	1975–76	1976–77
BTU	1.15	1.05	1.12	1.27
	(17.0)	(12.3)	(12.3)	(11.8)
Watts	−0.59	−0.50	−0.60	−0.69
	(−6.69)	(−4.34)	(−5.01)	(−5.20)
Volts	0.04	0.06	0.07	−0.00
	(0.09)	(0.82)	(0.94)	(−0.11)
Constant	7.09	6.70	7.36	7.68
	(14.4)	(10.2)	(10.9)	(10.24)

(continued)

Table 7.6 (continued)

D. 1974–77

	Pooled 1974–77	1974–75	1975–76	1976–77
1975	0.15**	0.14**		
1976	0.12**		−0.02	
1977	0.13**			−0.00
R^2	0.944	0.953	0.936	0.937
S.E.E.	0.088	0.079	0.093	0.096
Observations	69	39	44	30

E. 1977–83

	Pooled 1977–83	1977–78	1978–79	1979–80	1980–81	1981–82	1982–83
BTU	0.95	0.87	0.50	0.57	0.72	0.93	1.02
	(15.8)	(4.93)	(2.19)	(2.65)	(7.29)	(11.7)	(13.5)
Watts	−0.41	−0.31	0.26	0.08	−0.18	−0.40	−0.49
	(−6.28)	(−1.42)	(0.99)	(0.32)	(−1.69)	(−4.75)	(−6.00)
Fan speed	0.23	0.29	0.32	0.28	0.24	0.20	0.20
	(11.0)	(6.74)	(6.33)	(6.55)	(8.84)	(5.92)	(4.44)
High efficiency	0.03	0.09	0.23	0.17	0.12	0.04	−0.01
	(1.31)	(1.41)	(2.88)	(2.25)	(3.66)	(7.39)	(−0.44)
Volts	−0.05	...	...	−0.00	−0.09	−0.02	0.01
	(−1.56)			(−2.61)	(−2.43)	(−0.59)	(0.15)
Constant	6.21	5.64	2.39	3.62	5.18	6.54	7.10
	(17.6)	(4.63)	(1.66)	(2.86)	(9.15)	(14.8)	(16.0)
1978	0.08*	0.07**					
1979	0.14**		0.05				
1980	0.18**			0.04			
1981	0.30**				0.12**		
1982	0.38**					0.09**	
1983	0.44**						0.06**
R^2	0.977	0.966	0.917	0.941	0.984	0.976	0.976
S.E.E.	0.070	0.055	0.083	0.079	0.052	0.064	0.064
Observations	121	21	25	29	39	49	47

Note: Volts is defined as 0 for 110, 1 for 220. High efficiency is 1 for high efficiency, 0 otherwise.

Perhaps because of the data on the additional variables, the elasticity on capacity drops from 1.18 in the previous table to 0.95 here. For all years, the standard errors of estimate in all the equations are well below 10 percent. The price change for 1977–83 of 44 percent in the pooled equation is identical to the 43 percent cumulative change implied by the time dummy coefficients in the adjacent-year equations.

By and large, these hedonic regression results are straightforward and do not indicate any obvious problems. It is worth noting that the sample size in the adjacent-year equations increases markedly from the first three equations for 1954–57 containing an average of seventeen observations, to the last three equations for 1980–83 containing an average of forty-five observations. The large number of models sold under a single brand name in a single year reinforces the reality of product heterogeneity even for so simple a product as a room air conditioner.

7.6.2   Comparisons from *CR* Product Evaluations

Although the room air conditioner was introduced later than the refrigerator, nevertheless it is possible to develop even more comparisons of "closely similar" models (eighteen for room air conditioners vs. sixteen for refrigerators) owing to the greater frequency of product evaluations of air conditioners after 1970. All seventeen *CR* product evaluations of room air conditioners that appeared between 1953 and 1986 were consulted in the preparation of this section. In contrast to the refrigerator analysis, which used six classifications of "model types," this section uses the straightforward criterion of comparing machines of similar size. Thus, for instance, in rows 14–16, we have three overlapping comparisons of air conditioners of, respectively, 6,000, 8,000, and 5,000 BTU. The interval for each comparison depends on the appearance of models of a particular size class in the *CR* evaluations, since (as in the case of refrigerators) each evaluation tends to cover just one size class.

The criterion of capacity measurement in the *CR* evaluations changed from horsepower to BTU in 1959, about the same time that the same change occurred in the Sears catalog.[21] Fortunately, data are provided by *CR* to translate horsepower to BTU in both 1953 and 1959, and these translation factors are consistent with those given in the Sears catalog in 1958. Another minor complication that can be handled in a straightforward way results from a technological change that altered the relation of both BTU and energy consumption to horsepower, and details on the shift in this relation are provided by *CR* in the 1957 evaluation (see table 7.7, nn. c and e). The format of the comparisons in table 7.7 is the same as for refrigerators in table 7.3. Column 1 lists capacity in BTU in the first and second year of each comparison, and column 2 lists the percentage change in the average price of all models rated by *CR*.

21. This transition is described by *CR*, June 1959, 283.

Three adjustments are made to the raw price change calculated from the average unadjusted price for the models listed in each *CR* evaluation. First, as indicated by equation (7.3) above, the change in value attributable to changing size is calculated using an estimated elasticity of price on capacity. The coefficient *a* in (7.3) is set at 0.74, which is the coefficient on BTU in the pooled Sears catalog equation for 1958–67 in part B of table 7.6 and not far from the 0.72 coefficient for 1967–74 in part C. Two other adjustments are made that do not relate directly to energy efficiency. The second involves the transition from 230 to 115 volts in 1957, and this is taken into account using the coefficient of −0.15 on volts in part B of table 7.6. Third, an adjustment is made for the convenience value of reduced installation cost. Initially, room air conditioners were extremely heavy, with an average weight in 1957 for 6,400 BTU units of 180 pounds (May 1957, 302), and were bulky, with an average projection inside the room of ten to twenty inches (July 1953, 286). As a result, an extra installation expense was required, estimated at $35 by *CR* in 1953 (July, 280) and $25–$35, excluding the possible need for house rewiring, in 1959 (June, 286). Gradually, weight declined, reaching seventy pounds in 1970 for 6,000 BTU units, and brackets for self-installation were provided with each unit, making possible installation by the purchaser. Further, the bulk of the units also declined, with a projection into the room of three inches or less for eleven of seventeen models tested in 1970. To allow for this improvement in the price-change calculations of column 2, I include $30 in the price for installation cost before 1961, $15 in 1961, and nothing thereafter. While it could be argued that self-installation at zero pecuniary cost is not actually costless in time or effort, there is the offsetting fact that lower weight allows purchasers to remove the unit each fall and reinstall each spring, as recommended by *CR* in cold climates (e.g., July 1986, 444), thus providing savings in heating expense and an improvement in comfort and aesthetics during the winter that are not taken into account.[22] Implicitly, this approach assumes that there is an exact offset between the inconvenience of self-installation and the benefits of lower weight that makes possible winter removal. Of the adjustments discussed in the preceding paragraph, the first two are combined and listed in column 3 of table 7.7. The third (the installation cost adjustment) is taken into account in the basic calculation of

22. In the transition year of 1961 (June, 336), *CR* contains an explicit discussion of the installation issue: "In the past, all window installations were of the 'permanent' type, often done by a skilled serviceman, at a cost which could range from $10 on up. . . . once the installation is completed, the conditioner remains in place the year-round, and is an obstruction to light and air. . . . In contrast, some of the recently introduced, simplified 'do-it-yourself' mountings (see Ratings) are relatively simple to install, even for a layman. . . . The flexibility of such an arrangement is obvious. You can remove the conditioner for storage during the winter months, and then have full use of the window. You can readily move the unit to another location . . . should you later decide to do so. The disadvantage of this type of installation lies principally in the fact that the unit is not likely to be so securely mounted as it should be, and may not be well sealed against outside air."

price change in column 2. There are other aspects of quality change for which I do not adjust, and these are discussed below.

7.6.3   Adjustments for Improvements in Energy Efficiency

The adjustments for changes in energy efficiency are based on similar information as that for refrigerators, with the minor inconvenience that data on energy consumption are not provided in the evaluations between 1957 and 1965. As for refrigerators, the listed monthly energy cost data are averaged across all models of a given size in a given year, and the average monthly energy cost is standardized to an electricity price of $0.03 until 1974 and $0.0675 after 1974. Then the present discounted value of the change in energy cost from one product evaluation to the next was calculated, using the same discount rate as for refrigerators (0.03) and a shorter ten-year average lifetime. Monthly cost was converted to annual cost assuming 4.2 months of use per year (taken from *CR*'s own 1973 translation of $3.55 per month to $15.00 per year).[23]

Over the postwar period, energy cost savings in the operation of room air conditioners have been very significant, as indicated by the large negative adjustment factors in column 4 of table 7.7. Also, in contrast to refrigerators, where the energy savings were concentrated at the beginning and end of the 1949–83 postwar period, energy efficiency improvements for air conditioners were virtually continuous. I discuss the plausibility of these large adjustments in the next section, where alternative price indexes for air conditioners are compared.

7.6.4   Alternative Price Indexes for Room Air Conditioners

The alternative price indexes for room air conditioners are listed in table 7.8. The CPI and PPI are contrasted with four new indexes, including the pooled and adjacent-year indexes using Sears catalog data, and the *CR* indexes without and with an energy efficiency adjustment.[24] As for refrigerators, equal weights were applied when more than one *CR* price comparison in table 7.7 applied to a particular year. For instance, the price change between 1975 and 1976 for the *CR* price index without the energy adjustment (table 7.8, col. 5) is the average of the annual rates in rows 13, 14, and 15 of table 7.7 (12.7, 9.4, and 5.2 percent).

Since the behavior of the various price indexes differs over alternative subperiods of the 1953–83 interval, the differences are displayed for three subintervals. The first is 1953–72, starting with the earliest possible date. The second is

23. The monthly cost of a particular GE model is given in July 1973, 450, and the yearly cost of the same model at the same assumed electricity price, BTU capacity, and EER rating is given in July 1974, 520.

24. While the Sears hedonic regression equations in table 7.6 begin in 1954, we have two Sears observations for 1953 that allow the index to be extended back one year. Both these two models were also sold in identical form in 1954 at an average price 8.2 percent lower than in 1953.

Table 7.7   Comparisons of "Closely Similar" Models of Room Air Conditioners from *Consumer Reports*, 1953–86

			Adjustments to Price Change		Annual Rate of Price Change	
Dates	Capacity (BTU) (1)	Price Change (%) (2)	Capacity and Volts (3)	Energy[a] (4)	Without Energy Adjustment (5)	With Energy Adjustment (6)
1. 1953–57	7,500/6,375[c]	−13.4[b]	1.0[c,f]	−13.8[c]	−3.3	−7.0
2. 1953–57	7,500/8,625[c]	−5.2[b,d]	−21.8[e,f]	0.0[e]	−7.6	−11.4
3. 1957–61	6,375/6,875	−35.0[b]	−5.8	−3.2[h]	−12.3	−15.8
4. 1957–59	8,625/8,575	−39.3[b]	0.6	−10.0[i]	−21.7	−28.0
5. 1957–60	8,626/10,246	−26.1[b]	−4.0[f]	0.0[i]	−11.3	−13.0
6. 1959–71	8,575/8,000	−2.6[b]	6.8	−43.6[j]	0.3	−3.2
7. 1961–65	6,875/5,117	−36.0[b]	18.9	−8.5[h]	−4.6	−1.7
8. 1965–67	5,117/6,320	14.9	−17.4	−9.7[k]	−1.3	−16.1
9. 1967–70	6,320/6,000	−1.7	3.7	−0.4[l]	0.7	2.0
10. 1970–72	6,000/6,000	2.8	0.0	−5.8[m]	1.4	−1.5
11. 1971–75	8,000/7,916	26.0	0.8	−11.3[n]	6.1	3.8
12. 1972–74	6,000/6,000	7.6	0.0	−13.3[o]	3.7	−2.9
13. 1973–76	5,000/5,150	45.4	−2.2	−22.7[p]	12.7	5.8
14. 1974–79	6,000/6,120	57.9	−1.5	−18.8[q]	9.4	6.4
15. 1975–79	7,916/8,130	24.5	−2.0	7.1[r]	5.2	6.3
16. 1976–80	5,150/5,070	23.6	1.1	−8.9[s]	5.7	4.0
17. 1979–82	8,130/8,085	18.9	0.4	0.3[t]	6.1	6.3
18. 1980–86	5,070/5,565	28.0	−7.2	−2.2[u]	3.2	1.8

[a]All energy calculations prior to 1974 use $0.03 per kilowatt hour. After 1974, $0.0675 is used. Notes below give monthly figures. These are converted to present values assuming 4.2 months of use and a real interest rate of 0.03 percent.

[b]Prices before 1961 include $30 for installation, 1961 models include $15 for installation, while nothing is included for installation after 1961.

[c]1957 *CR* states (212) that three-quarter-horsepower models produce 0.85 times as much cooling for 0.60 as much energy as "their predecessors." Energy cost in 1957 of $5.00 per month at $.02 per kWh ($7.50 at $0.03 per kWh) implies 1953 energy cost of $12.50 per month. However, this contradicts the explicit listing of energy costs in 1953 that average out to $9.34. By choosing the latter figure for 1953, I take the lower of the two energy cost adjustments that could be made for this comparison. The decline from $9.34 to $7.50 yields a present value of energy saving of $66.69.

[d]Comparison of price of the three-quarter-horsepower model in 1953 with the one-horsepower model in 1957, both including $30 for installation.

[e]1957 *CR* states (212) that one-horsepower models produce 1.15 times as much cooling for the same energy as previous three-quarter-horsepower models. Energy cost in 1957 listed as $8.00 per month at $0.02 per kWh, or $12.00 per month at $0.03 per kWh.

[f]Adjustment includes allowance for charge in volts, using hedonic coefficient of −0.15.

[g]Using equation (7.2), but applying the capacity adjustment ($-gdC/C$) only to the charge in BTU, not the charge in volts. The geometric annual rate of energy adjustments in col. 6 are computed by calculating the annual rate of charge of the monthly energy cost converting that to a present value for the first year of the comparison, including the price in the first year of the comparison, and then combining that annual rate with the annual rates of charge in cols. 2 and 3 as in eq. (7.2).

[h]No energy consumption data are given for 1959 and 1961. Energy cost was linearly interpolated between the three-quarter-horsepower figure for 1957 (see n. c) and the 1965 average figure of $6.25 per month. This implies the following first- and second-year per-month cost and implied present value of saving: 1957–59: $7.50, $7.17, $11.96; 1959–61: $7.17, $6.85, $11.18; 1961–65: $6.85, $6.25, $21.75.

[i]No information given for 1960; no energy adjustment attempted in view of change in size and volts.

Table 7.7 (continued)

[j]The annual rate of change of the monthly energy cost between 1957 and 1971 is -5.2 percent per annum. This implies a present value of savings for 1957–59 of $4.08 and for 1959–71 of $184.94.

[k]From $6.25 to $5.81; present value of saving $= $15.95. Temporary change in size from 1961 to 1965 and then back again in 1967 is ignored.

[l]From $5.81 to $5.79 (midpoint of range of p. 351); present value of saving $= $0.72.

[m]From $5.79 to $5.50 (single figure given, p. 433); present value of saving $= $10.51.

[n]Shifted from monthly cost to EER. EER conversion as follows. July 1973 states special GE model used 625 watts of power (p. 443), for monthly cost of $3.55 (p. 450) at $0.03 per kWh. This implies a conversion factor for other units of:

$$\text{Monthly cost} = (\text{BTU/EER}) \times (\$3.55/625).$$

For models rated in 1975, this comes out at $4.88. Saving from 1971 figure of $5.70 has a present value of saving $= $29.72.

[o]From $5.50 to $4.77, calculated from EER $= $7.15 as in n. n; present value of saving $= $26.46.

[p]From $5.20 to $3.99, calculated from EER $= $8.33 as in n. n; present value of saving $= $43.86.

[q]Now using $0.0675 per kWh, from $10.73 to $9.54, calculated from EER $= $8.20; present value of saving $= $43.13.

[r]From $10.98 to $11.52, calculated from EER $= $9.02; present value of extra cost $= $19.53.

[s]From $8.98 to $8.39, calculated from EER $= $7.72, present value of saving $= $21.38.

[t]From $11.52 to $11.53, calculated from EER $= $8.96; present value of extra cost $= $0.36.

[u]From $8.39 to $8.23, calculated from EER $= $8.64; present value of saving $= $5.80.

1964–72, reflecting the earliest date when a comparison can include the CPI. The third is 1972–83. The geometric annual growth rates of the six alternative indexes over the three intervals and the full period are given in table 7.9.

The relation among the indexes in table 7.9 differs in the three subperiods and the full 1953–83 interval. In the first period, the two Sears indexes agree almost exactly with the non-energy-adjusted *CR* index, but all three indicate a rate of price decline at double the rate of the PPI, or an absolute difference of 1.69 percentage points below the PPI and the *CR* no-energy. For the 1953–64 segment of the first subinterval, the absolute difference is an even larger 2.74 points, with a rate of decline for the PPI of 3.39 percent compared with an average for the other three of 6.13 percent. In the second subinterval, there is a close correspondence among the indexes that are not explicitly adjusted for energy efficiency; the CPI, PPI, Sears adjacent-year, and *CR* indexes grow at almost exactly the same rate, and the Sears pooled index grows at a slightly faster rate. In the final subinterval, the two Sears indexes and the non-energy-adjusted *CR* index increase much more rapidly than do the CPI and PPI, and the latter two indexes even increased at a slightly slower rate than the energy-adjusted *CR* index.

Overall, the results seem consistent with the view that the CPI and PPI have gradually improved their corrections for quality change, and the divergences for 1972–83 imply that both the CPI and the PPI must have taken considerable care to treat improvements in energy efficiency as a quality improvement. There remains the question as to whether the greater rate of price decline in the new indexes before 1972 is credible. Starting with the

Table 7.8   Alternative Price Indexes for Room Air Conditioners, 1953–83 (1967 = 100)

			Sears Hedonic		Consumer Reports	
					Without	With
		PPI		Adjacent	Energy	Energy
Year	CPI	(12-41-03-38)	Pooled	Year	Adjustment	Adjustment
	(1)	(2)	(3)	(4)	(5)	(6)
1953		153.6	178.7	185.6	207.8	345.3
1954		153.5	165.2	171.6	196.7	315.0
1955		144.6	152.1	158.4	186.3	287.3
1956		137.7	132.4	136.3	176.4	262.0
1957		132.7	123.6	127.1	167.1	239.0
1958		127.8	109.4	112.7	145.4	197.8
1959		119.2	117.4	115.0	126.6	163.6
1960		115.5	110.5	108.3	117.1	147.1
1961		109.0	108.3	107.3	110.2	133.8
1962		107.8	108.3	107.3	107.9	130.5
1963		106.4	105.1	104.1	105.5	127.4
1964	105.5	105.1	89.6	92.4	103.3	124.3
1965	97.8	99.7	98.0	97.0	101.0	121.3
1966	98.0	98.7	93.2	93.2	100.5	110.1
1967	100.0	100.0	100.0	100.0	100.0	100.0
1968	102.3	101.6	97.0	97.0	100.5	99.4
1969	105.0	101.3	94.2	93.2	101.0	98.8
1970	107.1	104.2	102.0	100.0	101.5	98.2
1971	110.2	108.4	98.0	96.1	102.4	95.9
1972	110.7	109.4	99.0	97.0	106.3	97.0
1973	110.1	107.7	102.0	101.0	111.6	97.5
1974	113.4	114.8	108.3	108.4	120.3	99.7
1975	123.8	126.5	125.9	124.7	132.1	105.1
1976	129.5	125.3	122.1	122.2	144.8	111.8
1977	135.1	126.2	123.4	122.2	154.9	118.2
1978	138.3	131.3	133.6	131.1	165.7	124.9
1979	147.4	138.3	141.9	137.8	177.3	132.1
1980	154.0	150.1	147.7	143.4	188.1	137.5
1981	160.1	158.0	166.5	161.7	197.1	143.2
1982	167.7	164.2	180.4	176.9	206.4	145.7
1983	170.7	174.5	191.6	187.9	213.1	148.4

non-energy-adjusted *CR* index, which in 1972 has an index value equal to 0.512 times its 1953 value, we find confirming evidence in comparing the average 1972 price of a 6,000 BTU unit of $173.75 with the $415.63 price of a 7,500 BTU unit in 1953.[25] Raising the price of the 1972 unit by 18 percent (25 percent greater capacity times the hedonic coefficient of 0.74), we have a 1972 price of $205.03, which is 0.493 of the 1953 price. The same exercise with the average price of a 8,000 BTU unit in 1971 yields a price ratio of 0.535. Both are quite close to the ratio for the *CR* index and differ markedly from the implied 1972/1953 PPI price ratio of 0.712.

The non-energy-adjusted *CR* index implies that the price ratio between the beginning and end of the entire period, 1982/1953, was 0.993. We can take the

25. The 1953 price includes $30 for installation, as discussed above.

Table 7.9   **Annual Percent Growth Rates of Alternative Price Indexes for Room Air Conditioners, 1953–83 and Subintervals**

	1953–72	1964–72	1972–83	1953–83
CPI	. . .	0.60	4.02	. . .
PPI	−1.77	0.50	4.34	0.43
Sears pooled	−3.06	1.26	6.18	0.23
Sears adjacent year	−3.36	0.61	6.19	0.04
CR without energy	−3.46	0.40	6.53	0.08
CR with energy	−6.46	−3.05	4.43	−2.61

average price for 8,000 BTU units in 1982 of $435.31, and adjust this down to $408.78 to compare with the 7,500 BTU capacity of 1953 units; this yields a 1982/1953 price ratio of 0.984, which corresponds almost exactly to the CR index ratio of 0.993.

There remains the question of the extremely rapid rate of decline of the energy-adjusted CR index. Using the explicit cost per month figures in CR for 1957, we can develop a comparison with 1971. The $12.00 monthly cost in 1957 for the average unit of 8,625 BTU compares with the average $5.71 cost in 1971 for 8,000 BTU. Using the same method as in table 7.7, the present value of the difference between $12 and $5.71 per month is $227.99, or 58 percent of the price (including installation) of the 1957 model. If one takes the ratio of the actual 1971 price adjusted to 8,625 BTU ($246.66) to the price of the 1957 model plus the present value of the extra energy consumption ($622.14), one has a ratio for 1971/1957 of 0.396, compared to a ratio of 0.401 for the index in column 6 of table 7.8, indicating a very close correspondence.

As for the more recent period of 1973–86, the average EER rating of models in the 5,000 BTU range improved from 6.0 to 8.64, for a saving having a present value at the post-1974 electricity price of $125.77, or 84 percent of the average 1973 price for 5,000 BTU units. Adding this to the 1973 price, one obtains a price ratio for 1986/1973 of 1.248, considerably less than the 1983/1973 ratio for the energy-adjusted CR index of 1.511. A similar exercise for 8,000 BTU units between 1971 and 1982 yields a ratio of only 1.166 for the 1982 price ($435.31) to the 1971 price ($233.18) plus the present value of energy saving on the 1982 model compared to the 1971 model ($140.09). Both these comparisons suggest that the CR index may overstate the increase in prices in the post-1972 subinterval.

7.6.5 Unmeasured Dimensions of Quality Improvement

In the previous study of quality changes for refrigerators, we found aspects of quality improvement that could not be taken into account in price indexes, either by the hedonic or by the specification method. These included a tightening of the CR criteria for temperatures in the refrigerator and freezer, a greatly improved ability of the average unit to hold the required temperatures, improvements in design to eliminate previous inconvenience, improvements in quality control, and a reduced frequency of service calls. In the case of air conditioners, dimensions of unmeasured quality improvement are fewer, partly because the air conditioner is a simpler product to begin with. In particular, there seems to have been no improvement at all in the ability of a unit to maintain a fixed temperature, unlike refrigerators in which temperature control ability improved markedly.

Nevertheless, there are a few aspects of quality improvement that deserve note. I have already remarked on the weight and bulk of the early units, and the impossibility of taking them in for the winter or of moving them from room to room. A rough adjustment for this change is made by including installation cost in the price of models before 1961. In that adjustment, I made no allowance for the requirement that air conditioners of the 1950s required their own fifteen-ampere electric circuit, requiring extra wiring in homes without extra circuits, but by the 1960s and 1970s drew as little as 7.5 amps, allowing an existing circuit to be shared with lighting or other electrical requirements. A second issue is that the 1953 models were not equipped with some features that became common later. Of the sixteen models rated in 1953, nine lacked thermostats, although all could be equipped with thermostats for an average extra cost of $14.61, and allowance for this would add another 2 percent to the average 1953 price. Also, eleven of the sixteen models had only one fan speed. By 1967, all models had at least two fan speeds and most had three. Another difference is noise. *CR* commented in 1953 that "all are noisy," but by 1965 that the "top-rated models are very quiet" (June, 276). Overall, however, these improvements seem minor, and there is little reason to suspect that the new indexes miss major dimensions of quality change.

7.7   Washing Machines

The first electric washing machine was introduced in 1911, when Maytag added electricity to a wringer model known as the "Hired Girl." The first automatic model was introduced by Bendix in 1940, but sales of automatic washers did not pass those of wringer-style models until 1952.[26] In the subsequent decade, automatic washing machines added a host of features, including wash-and-wear cycles, and multiple temperature and water-level choices. The main issue in developing price indexes for washing machines is to make adequate corrections for the steady increase in features and options. As in the two previous sections, I begin with the results of estimating hedonic regression equations from Sears catalog data on prices and specifications and then turn to a comparison of "closely similar" models from successive *CR* product evaluations.

---

26. Historical details are from Consumers Union (1986, 232).

7.7.1   Hedonic Regression Results

The regression results for 1948–54 are presented in part A of table 7.10 and cover wringer models until 1952 and automatic models for 1952–54.[27] The equations for wringer models include as explanatory variables capacity and dummy variables for the presence of automatic drains and timers. The coefficients on capacity are relatively large, ranging from 0.87 to 1.47, and are highly significant, as are most of the coefficients on the dummy variables. The 1952–53 equation for automatic models includes only a capacity variable, because the small number of observations for that equation precludes adding additional variables. A greater range of models is available in 1953–54, and so variables are entered for the number of machine cycles and the number of speed settings. The cumulative price change between 1948 and 1954 implied by the six adjacent-year equations is − 17 percent.

The next table (7.10, pt. B) covers the full decade from 1954 to 1964, with the pooled regression equation displayed in the first column, followed by the ten adjacent-year equations. The capacity variable is joined by the number of cycles and the level 1 variable, which is a dummy variable indicating the presence of more than one water-level setting.[28] The large semielasticity on the level variable, 19 percent in the pooled equation, suggests that this variable may partly be standing as a proxy for other "deluxe" features. The standard error on the pooled equation is about 10 percent, similar in magnitude to the equations for refrigerators and air conditioners estimated in previous sections. The standard errors in the adjacent-year equations are less after 1961, and it is interesting to note that the elasticity of price to capacity fell sharply after 1961 as well. The cumulative price change of − 44 percent in the pooled equation compares with − 33 percent in the adjacent-year equations.

Part C of table 7.10 for 1964–71 contains the same variables as the previous table. The elasticity of price to capacity is markedly lower than in the period before 1961. In the pooled regression for 1964–71, the coefficient on the cycles variable is somewhat higher than for 1954–64, and the coefficient on level 1 is considerably lower. The standard error in the pooled equation is also lower than in the previous table. The cumulative price change in the pooled equation of 8 percent is identical to that implied by the adjacent-year equations.

Part D of table 7.10, covering the 1971–76 period, introduces a new definition of the level variable (indicating the presence of a continuous level

27. Part A of table 7.10 is arranged in a slightly different format than the other tables presenting hedonic regression results in this chapter, since these results are taken from the 1974 draft of this book.

28. The "cycle" variable is the number of cycles, entered linearly. The coefficient of 0.03 in the pooled regression indicates that the addition of one more cycle adds 3 percent to price. Since the average number of cycles on the machines in my sample for 1960 was almost six, the coefficient on the cycles variable implies that a machine with an average number of cycles would have a price 15 percent higher than a machine with a single cycle.

Table 7.10   Pooled and Adjacent-Year Double-Log Regression Equation for Washers, Sears Catalog Data, 1948–54, 1954–64, 1964–71, 1971–76, 1976–80, 1980–83 (t-ratios in parentheses)

A. 1948–54

	1948–49	1949–50	1950–51	1951–52	1952–53	1953–54
Type	Wringer	Wringer	Wringer	Wringer	Auto	Auto
Capacity	0.87	1.085	1.28	1.47	2.03	1.34
	(10.4)	(21.2)	(19.3)	(8.7)	(6.48)	(1.99)
Automatic drain	0.06	0.08	0.07	0.05	...	...
	(2.32)	(5.10)	(4.29)	(1.11)		
Automatic timer	...	...	...	...	...	...
Cycles	...	0.21	0.16	0.12	...	0.13
		(8.78)	(9.73)	(3.09)		(1.10)
Temperatures	...	...	...	...	...	0.13
						(2.00)
1949	−0.16**					
1950		0.02				
1951			0.07			
1952				0.01		
1953					0.02	
1954						−0.13
$\bar{R}^2$	0.974	0.997	0.998	0.993	0.978	0.955
S.E.	0.039	0.019	0.017	0.034	0.030	0.061
Observations	8	8	8	7	4	8

B. 1954–64

	Pooled 1954–64	1954–55	1955–56	1956–57	1957–58	1958–59	1959–60	1960–61	1961–62	1962–63	1963–64
Capacity	0.62	2.33	2.07	1.11	0.86	0.68	1.09	1.02	0.37	0.34	0.36
	(4.33)	(3.73)	(2.94)	(2.70)	(2.70)	(1.53)	(2.69)	(2.41)	(1.46)	(3.18)	(3.88)
Cycles	0.03	0.04	−0.04	...	0.09	0.17	0.03	0.03	0.04	0.04	0.03
	(4.20)	(0.64)	(−0.28)		(0.63)	(2.05)	(2.69)	(2.96)	(7.68)	(8.25)	(5.84)
Level 1	0.19	−0.01	0.17	0.28	0.20	0.00	−0.02	0.05	0.18	0.19	0.20
	(5.22)	(−0.08)	(0.80)	(3.87)	(0.80)	(0.00)	(−0.13)	(0.45)	(4.01)	(5.64)	(6.48)
Constant	3.95	2.58	0.79	3.71	3.06	3.47	2.72	2.85	4.15	4.18	4.13
	(12.7)	(3.07)	(0.53)	(3.10)	(3.40)	(3.58)	(3.18)	(3.07)	(7.48)	(17.9)	(19.3)

	(1)	(2)	(3)	(4)	(5)	(6)	(7)	(8)	(9)	(10)	(11)
1955	−0.11										
1956	−0.20**	−0.10									
1957	−0.28**		−0.06								
1958	−0.20**			−0.09							
1959	−0.28**				0.06						
1960	−0.26**					−0.08					
1961	−0.33**						−0.04				
1962	−0.37**							0.03			
1963	−0.44**								−0.01		
1964	−0.44**									−0.00	
$\bar{R}^2$	0.782	0.808	0.709	0.773	0.673	0.687	0.808	0.826	0.969	0.967	0.958
S.E.E.	0.099	0.082	0.098	0.107	0.146	0.121	0.097	0.094	0.034	0.039	0.042
Observations	63	9	10	12	12	13	13	12	10	12	14

C. 1964–71

	Pooled 1964–71	1964–65	1965–66	1966–67	1967–68	1968–69	1969–70	1970–71
Capacity	0.25	0.39	0.36	0.34	0.21	0.19	0.17	0.06
	(4.20)	(4.77)	(8.08)	(10.2)	(3.12)	(2.55)	(1.52)	(10.5)
Cycles	0.05	0.04	0.04	0.04	0.05	0.06	0.06	0.42
	(14.3)	(6.92)	(13.0)	(14.6)	(8.62)	(9.68)	(9.86)	(3.32)
Level 1	0.08	0.16	0.14	0.20	0.14	0.08	0.09	−0.17
	(2.70)	(5.10)	(7.64)	(14.1)	(3.97)	(1.82)	(1.23)	(−2.26)
Constant	4.39	4.06	4.07	4.11	4.47	4.47	4.50	4.50
	(31.6)	(21.3)	(38.5)	(57.9)	(27.0)	(25.4)	(18.7)	(19.2)
1965	−0.05	−0.04						
1966	−0.05		−0.00					
1967	−0.04			0.01				
1968	−0.03				0.00			
1969	−0.04					−0.01		
1970	−0.03						0.01	
1971	0.08*							0.11*
$\bar{R}^2$	0.908	0.969	0.991	0.995	0.964	0.944	0.923	0.888
S.E.E.	0.067	0.038	0.021	0.015	0.041	0.047	0.057	0.075
Observations	60	13	12	12	15	17	17	18

(continued)

Table 7.10 (continued)

D. 1971–76[a]

	Pooled 1971–76	1971–72	1972–73	1973–74	1974–75	1975–76
Capacity	0.06	0.17	0.22	−0.04	−0.00	0.02
	(1.80)	(2.44)	(3.54)	(−0.51)	(−0.03)	(0.64)
Cycles	0.02	0.04	0.04	−0.00	0.00	0.04
	(3.11)	(3.06)	(4.28)	(−0.12)	(0.08)	(4.70)
Level 2	0.14	0.10	0.12	0.23	0.19	0.04
	(3.35)	(1.42)	(2.41)	(3.08)	(2.42)	(4.70)
Filter	0.16	0.08	0.14	0.22	0.17	0.15
	(4.19)	(1.23)	(3.26)	(2.96)	(2.33)	(3.80)
Constant	5.13	5.10	5.04	5.15	5.19	5.22
	(126.)	(107.)	(126.)	(75.0)	(72.1)	(135.)
1972	0.00	0.00				
1973	−0.04		−0.03			
1974	−0.04**			0.02		
1975	0.10**				0.15**	
1976	0.10**					−0.02
R^2	0.776	0.838	0.938	0.755	0.679	0.865
S.E.E.	0.095	0.082	0.054	0.108	0.115	0.062
Observations	51	17	16	16	16	18

E. 1976–80

	Pooled 1976–80	1976–77	1977–78	1978–79	1979–80
Capacity	0.07	0.09	0.12	0.08	0.04
	(3.57)	(3.36)	(2.76)	(2.14)	(1.75)
Cycles	0.03	0.02	0.03	0.03	0.04
	(6.90)	(2.67)	(4.02)	(4.30)	(1.27)
Filter	0.08	0.08	0.09	0.07	0.08
	(2.95)	(1.83)	(1.68)	(1.24)	(2.29)
Saver	0.10	· · ·	0.02	0.10	0.12
	(4.28)		(0.54)	(2.79)	(5.33)

Speed	0.10	0.14	0.14	0.08	0.02
	(3.64)	(3.20)	(2.65)	(1.37)	(5.20)
Constant	5.10	5.05	5.08	5.19	5.26
	(125.)	(103.)	(76.9)	(78.2)	(116.)
1977	0.06	0.05**			
1978	0.08**		0.04		
1979	0.19**			0.10	
1980	0.20**				0.04
$\bar{R}^2$	0.899	0.910	0.904	0.814	0.904
S.E.E.	0.070	0.078	0.070	0.070	0.057
Observations	70	19	25	25	35

F. 1980–83

	Pooled 1980–83	1980–81	1981–82	1982–83
Capacity	0.06	0.05	0.05	0.14
	(2.04)	(1.74)	(1.23)	(1.72)
Cycle	0.03	0.03	0.03	0.03
	(7.60)	(6.66)	(5.34)	(4.39)
Speed	0.18	0.17	0.21	0.24
	(4.67)	(4.25)	(4.50)	(2.77)
Constant	5.22	5.26	5.29	5.20
	(76.1)	(7.89)	(67.8)	(29.8)
1981	0.09**	0.09**		
1982	0.18**		0.09**	
1983	0.26**			0.08*
$\bar{R}^2$	0.817	0.832	0.804	0.669
S.E.E.	0.090	0.077	0.082	0.105
Observations	61	34	30	27

[a]From 1971 on, "capacity" becomes a dummy variable (0, 1), where 1 represents "large capacity."

adjustment) and a new variable indicating the presence of a lint filter. Another change is that the capacity variable is now a dummy variable rather than an actual measurement. Reflecting the fact that now all the variables in the equation are dummy variables, the title of the table indicates that the equations should be interpreted as having a semilog specification. The coefficient on capacity is smaller than before, while the coefficients on the cycles and level variables are similar to those in the previous table. The coefficient on filter seems implausibly large, suggesting that this variable has now taken on the role of acting as a proxy for other deluxe features. The cumulative price change indicated by the pooled equation is 10 percent, somewhat less than the 12 percent implied by the successive coefficients on the time dummy variables in the adjacent-year equations. There are problems with the signs and significance of the adjacent-year coefficients of capacity.

The next period, 1976–80, is covered in part E of table 7.10. Here, a linear variable for the number of speed settings replaces the dummy variable for water level. A new variable for the presence of a water-saving feature (which reduces the amount of hot water needed, thus saving energy) is added. All the explanatory variables are significant in the pooled equation and most in the adjacent-year equations. The standard error in the pooled equation is lower than before, and the number of observations per year is much higher. The 1976–80 price increase of 20 percent in the pooled equation compares with a larger 23 percent increase in the adjacent-year equations.

The final table (7.10, pt. F) covers the 1980–83 period. The number of explanatory variables is smaller than before, and the standard error of the pooled equation is also higher. The price increase in the pooled equation is 26 percent, and the indicated price increases for 1980–81, 1981–82, and 1982–83 are identical in the pooled and adjacent-year equations.

7.7.2   Comparisons from *CR* Product Evaluations

The *CR* price index developed in this section is based on nineteen reports on automatic washing machines that appeared in *CR* between 1948 and 1983.[29] The procedure for converting the *CR* price listings into a price index is simpler than for refrigerators and room air conditioners, because no adjustment is made for changes in energy efficiency. Washing machines have very small direct energy requirements in comparison with the indirect energy used in heating the water that they use. Thus, the main way in which manufacturers could have accomplished a reduction in the total energy cost involved in washing a load of dirty clothes would have been to devise methods of saving hot water. Consumption of hot water averaged eighteen gallons in 1950 and twenty-three gallons in 1980, but the capacity of washers increased by about 50 percent in the meantime, probably more than accounting for this

---

29. The report that I use for 1983 prices was actually published in January 1984.

Table 7.11   Comparisons of "Closely Similar" Models of Automatic Washing Machines from *Consumer Reports*, 1948–83

Dates	Price Range (1)	Price Change[a] (2)	Quality Adjustment (3)	Annual Rate of Price Change with Quality Adjustment (4)
1. 1948–50	Low	−4.3[b]	0.0	−2.2
2. 1950–54	Low	−0.5[b]	−13.0[c]	−3.6
3. 1954–60	Low	−22.5	0.0	−4.2
4. 1959–60	Top	−5.7	0.0	−5.7
5. 1960–62	Middle	−21.8[d]	0.0	−11.6
6. 1962–64	Middle	−3.4	−2.0[e]	−2.7
7. 1964–66	Middle	2.7	−2.0[e]	0.3
8. 1966–69	Middle	−1.4	−2.0[e]	−1.1
9. 1969–70	Middle	3.7	−1.0[e]	2.7
10. 1970–71	Middle	2.6	−1.0[e]	1.6
11. 1971–73	Middle	1.7	−2.0[e]	−0.2
12. 1973–74	Middle	−3.3	−1.0[e]	−4.3
13. 1974–75	Middle	22.5	−1.0[e]	21.5
14. 1975–78	Middle	18.5	−3.0[e]	4.9
15. 1978–79	Middle	5.8	−1.0[e]	4.8
16. 1979–80	Middle	9.5	−1.0[e]	8.5
17. 1980–81	Middle	7.8	−1.0[e]	6.8
18. 1981–82	Middle	3.7	−1.0[e]	2.7
19. 1982–83	Middle	1.7	0.0	1.7

[a]Unless otherwise noted, price change is between the unweighted average of *CR* price listings in each year excluding Tumbler-type models. Also excluded are deluxe models when two models are included for the same brand name.

[b]Excludes bolt-down models in 1948 and 1950.

[c]Adjusts for increase from one to two temperatures, using 1953–54 hedonic coefficient of 0.13.

[d]Comparison of top-range 1960 models with mid-range 1962 models assumes that mid-range models in 1960 would have been priced midway between average price of top-range and economy models.

[e]One percent per annum quality improvement applied from 1962 to 1982. See text.

difference.[30] The most important energy-saving innovation in the postwar period was the development of cold-water detergents, allowing some types of loads to be washed with no hot water at all, but any credit for this development should go to the soap industry rather than the appliance industry.

The year-by-year price comparisons for the *CR* price index are listed in table 7.11. Only a few decisions need to be made in compiling the index. The first is the linking of models in different price classes. In the 1950s, *CR* was not consistent in its choice of models to be tested. The 1948, 1950, and 1954 evaluations are based on very simple machines by present standards. In contrast, "top-of-the-line" super deluxe models were tested in 1959 and

30. The 1950 figures are a simple average of the hot water consumption figures given in the detailed ratings. The 1980 figure is an in-text remark (November, 680) that does not specify the size of the load used in the test.

1960. Beginning in 1962, *CR* consistently rated only mid-range models that had certain minimum features but not all the bells and whistles of the super deluxe models. The difficulties caused by this shift in the model-selection criterion are greatly eased by the fact that *CR* rated both deluxe and economy models in 1960. The inclusion of simple models for 1960 establishes a price link between 1954 and 1960 (row 2), and the presence of both top- and bottom-grade models in 1960 allows us to estimate a midpoint for comparison with the mid-range models tested in 1962 and thereafter.

The second issue is the adjustment for improvements in quality over the years. The first adjustment is made in row 1 for the 1950–54 comparison. The 1950 models had no optional settings at all for speed, temperature, or water level. But 1954 machines could be set to wash with either hot or warm (but not cold) water. The value of the extra temperature setting is taken from the coefficient on temperature settings in the Sears hedonic regression equation for 1953–54. Another improvement, for which no explicit adjustment is made, is that three of the ten non-bolt-down machines in 1950 required that the water first be turned on manually and that the user wait until the machine was full before switching on the wash cycle (for two of these three models, "the water may flood over onto the floor if you aren't there to turn it off" [November 1950, 503]). Also, five of the ten models lacked an automatic cut-off in the case of excessive vibration.

The other quality adjustment made is to take account of the gradual improvement in capacity and other features on the mid-range models between 1962 and 1982. Unfortunately, *CR* does not provide explicit and consistent measures of capacity in each report, yet enough information is provided to allow a guess that capacity must have increased by at least 50 percent after 1962. In the 1962 report (380), four models claimed twelve-pound capacities, "while six others are rated at 9 to 10 pounds."[31] And *CR* found that even these claims were exaggerated: "Most of the machines tested simply did not have the physical capacity to take a 12-pound mixed load, and many could not handle 10 pounds without the obvious signs of overloading—clothes becoming tightly packed, items of clothing escaping into the outer tub, or the machine stopping frequently. In general, even where machines could handle large loads, washing ability and uniformity fell off as the load increased" (August 1962, 380). In contrast, in 1981 (October, 558), *CR* wrote that "Nearly half of the machines sold last year were identified as 'large' models. (Some manufacturers define 'large' as an 18- to 20-pound capacity; others don't define it.) The 12 machines we tested are in that class." Further, there are no comments in the 1981 report disputing the capacity claims of manufacturers. I surmise that this increase in capacity must have occurred

31. "Most of the remaining models do not, to CU's knowledge, claim specific load weights" (August 1962, 380).

gradually, because comments on capacity in 1971 indicate an in-between status. Some but not all models claimed eighteen-pound capacities, and these were described by *CR* as "very large" and "capacious." But other tubs were described as "medium" and "small." Further, in contrast to the quote from 1962, "all the machines with medium or larger tubs accepted our 11-pound load easily; we had to cram the smaller tubs."

Overall, these quotes suggest an increase in average capacity from ten pounds in 1962 to eighteen pounds in 1981. To be conservative, I estimate the increase as 50 percent and multiply it by the Sears hedonic coefficient for 1964–71 (0.25) to arrive at an upward quality adjustment of 12.5 percent for capacity over the 1962–82 period. Further adjustments must be made, however, for the numerous features on 1982 models that were not present in 1962. The selection criterion in 1962 was "the least expensive model in each line that offered two agitator and spin speeds." There was no criterion for number of water levels, temperature combinations, or number of automatic cycles. The detailed model-by-model ratings indicate that some models could be preset to three alternative water levels, while in other cases "user must be present to push button when water has reached desired level." Most machines offered three wash temperatures and two rinse temperatures, but there is no mention for any of the brands of multiple cycles. Further, no dispensers were included for liquid bleach or fabric softener.[32]

By 1971, quality had improved. All machines offered at least one cycle in addition to the regular cycle, and all offered bleach dispensers. And, by 1984, further improvements had been introduced. In a detailed chart listing features of machines rated by *CR* and other models of the same brands, we learn that all rated machines provided three cycles, two separate automatic dispensers (for bleach and softener), and continuous rather than discrete control of water level (which *CR* considered preferable). To adjust for these improvements, I raise the estimate of 1962–82 quality improvement from the 12.5 percent warranted by the capacity increase to 20 percent. Since the hedonic regression equations estimate that two extra cycles raise price by 6–10 percent, depending on the sample period, this adjustment would seem to be conservative in that it makes no explicit allowance for the improved control of water level and the addition of automatic dispensers. As shown in column 3, the estimated 20 percent quality improvement is introduced at the rate of 1.0 percent per year over the twenty years from 1962 to 1982.

7.7.3   Alternative Price Indexes for Automatic Washing Machines

The alternative price indexes for automatic washing machines are compared in table 7.12. The CPI and PPI are compared with the pooled and

32. The exception is the Blackstone, which is listed in 1966 (431) as a top-of-the-line model. To maintain consistency, all Blackstone models are excluded in calculating the price comparisons of table 7.11.

Table 7.12   **Alternative Price Indexes for Automatic Washing Machines, 1947–83
(1967 = 100)**

Year	CPI (1)	PPI (12-41-02-01) (2)	Sears Hedonic Pooled (3)	Sears Hedonic Adjacent Year (4)	Consumer Reports (5)
1947	112.7	111.5	. . .	. . .	. . .
1948	121.2	117.7	191.5	169.0	208.3
1949	119.6	113.6	163.2	144.8	203.7
1950	118.1	112.9	166.5	147.7	199.3
1951	126.2	122.9	178.6	158.4	192.2
1952	126.7	122.4	180.4	160.0	185.4
1953	124.8	122.0	184.0	163.2	178.8
1954	121.8	121.8	161.6	143.3	172.5
1955	118.5	118.5	144.8	129.6	165.4
1956	115.7	115.7	132.3	122.1	158.6
1957	117.1	117.1	122.1	111.6	152.1
1958	115.8	115.8	132.3	118.5	145.8
1959	113.6	113.6	122.1	109.4	139.9
1960	110.7	110.7	124.6	105.1	133.7
1961	107.4	107.4	116.2	101.0	119.1
1962	104.5	104.5	111.6	104.1	106.1
1963	103.0	103.0	104.1	103.0	103.3
1964	101.6	101.6	104.1	103.0	100.5
1965	100.2	100.2	99.0	99.0	100.8
1966	99.7	99.7	99.0	99.0	101.1
1967	100.0	100.0	100.0	100.0	100.0
1968	102.5	102.5	101.0	100.0	98.9
1969	104.6	103.8	100.0	99.0	97.8
1970	107.3	105.9	101.0	100.0	100.5
1971	109.4	105.7	112.8	111.6	102.1
1972	110.5	106.9	112.8	111.6	101.9
1973	111.0	107.2	108.4	108.3	101.7
1974	117.1	117.7	108.4	110.5	97.4
1975	131.9	132.5	124.6	128.4	120.8
1976	141.0	143.9	124.6	125.9	126.9
1977	145.5	148.9	132.4	132.3	133.2
1978	154.0	155.0	135.0	137.7	139.9
1979	164.1	162.9	150.7	152.2	146.8
1980	177.1	173.0	152.2	158.4	159.8
1981	189.8	184.8	166.5	173.3	171.1
1982	203.6	196.8	182.2	189.6	175.7
1983	212.7	203.5	197.4	205.4	178.8

adjacent-year Sears hedonic indexes and with the *CR* index.[33] The geometric
annual growth rates of the five alternative indexes over three intervals and the
full period are given in table 7.13. The first interval is 1950–60, starting with
the first year when both the Sears hedonic and the *CR* indexes are available.

33. I extrapolate the pooled Sears hedonic index prior to 1954 with the Sears adjacent-year
index and replace the implausible 1980–81 price change in the adjacent-year index with that in
the pooled index.

Table 7.13   Annual Percent Growth Rates of Alternative Price Indexes for Automatic
                  Washing Machines, 1950–83 and Subintervals

	1950–60	1960–72	1972–83	1950–83
CPI	−0.66	−0.02	6.13	1.80
PPI	−0.20	−0.29	6.03	1.80
Sears pooled	−2.86	−0.83	5.22	0.52
Sears adjacent year	−3.35	0.50	5.70	1.01
CR	−3.91	−2.24	5.24	−0.33

The second is 1960–72, chosen for comparability with the presentation of results in the refrigerator section. The third is 1972–83.

These annual growth rates indicate a relatively close correspondence between the CPI and PPI and the Sears hedonic indexes after 1960, but with an average absolute difference of 2.7 percentage points in the first decade between 1950 and 1960. The growth rate of the *CR* index is lower than that of the CPI and PPI in every period, with the difference narrowing from an average 3.48 points for 1950–60, to 2.09 points for 1960–72, to a mere 0.84 points in 1972–83. The discrepancy between the *CR* and the Sears hedonic indexes can be partly explained by the fact (introduced above in sec. 7.3) that Sears models were at the low end of the price spectrum in the 1950s but close to the mean price in the 1980s. For washing machines, the Sears price rose from 84.2 percent of the mean in the 1950 and 1954 reports to 98.2 percent of the mean in the 1982 and 1984 evaluations. The growth rate of this ratio is 0.5 percent per year, accounting for most of the 0.85-point difference between the growth rates of the Sears pooled and *CR* indexes.

7.7.4   Unmeasured Dimensions of Quality Change

A contrast between the 1950 and the 1982 product evaluations reveals relatively few unmeasured aspects of quality improvement. In 1982, *CR* comments explicitly on how much automatic washers had changed since their introduction in 1937, but "the most conspicuous difference is that the 1982 machines are very versatile—they can give you a great deal of control over the way the laundry is handled." These convenience features, including continuous water level control, temperature control, and automatic cycles, are taken into account explicitly in my quality adjustments.

However, one does note several remarks in the 1950 evaluation that suggest improvements. One 1950 machine was rated "not acceptable" because "it tangled clothes so badly and so consistently." In contrast, the only other strongly negative evaluations were for two models rated "not acceptable" in 1962 and three rated "conditionally acceptable" in 1966. We note in 1960 that, with three exceptions, "most of the remaining washers were unable to get rid of large quantities of sand, or tended occasionally to reposit some of the sand they removed onto subsequent loads" (August, 414), whereas in

1982 "most machines do a fairly good job of getting rid of any sand that's collected in beach towels and clothing" (October, 509). Further, lint was a problem even on the deluxe models tested in 1960: "Many housewives complain that their washers deposit too much lint on clothes. . . . The problem of deposition is something else again; CU can offer no complete solution. The fact is that all of the machines tested . . . left some lint on the items washed" (August, 414). In contrast, we read in 1982 that "all the machines are designed to prevent lint from resetting on clothing during the wash."

As for quality control, the only comment is in 1964: "Now, as in the past, the odds are unfortunately in favor of your having some trouble with a new washer" (September, 419). In contrast, a 1979 chart (November, 684) lists the percentage of washers needing repair as ranging from 11 percent on one-year-old models to 28 percent on ten-year-old models. Unfortunately, there is no quantitative information in *CR* to allow a comparison over time of frequency of repair records.

7.8   Clothes Dryers

The indoor clothes dryer is a comparative latecomer in the world of household appliances. It was apparently invented in 1930 by J. Ross Moore of North Dakota, who "deplored the fact that his mother had to hang out wash in 40-below temperatures. . . . [he] designed a series of proper drying machines that could be brought into the house, although one prototype weighed 700 pounds. They didn't sell" (Consumers' Union 1986, 234). Although clothes dryers began to sell in quantity in the early 1950s, and warranted a report by *CR* in 1951, they did not appear in the PPI until 1954 or in the CPI until 1963.

This section provides a briefer evaluation than the previous sections, mainly because there are too few models in the Sears catalog to warrant estimating hedonic regression equations. The main information consists of a comparison of "closely similar" models from successive *CR* product evaluations. The end of this section compares the resulting *CR* price index with an index of matched models from the Sears catalog.

7.8.1   Comparisons from *CR* Product Evaluations

The comparisons of gas and electric dryers are presented in table 7.14, which is arranged like the previous *CR* comparisons of refrigerators, room air conditioners, and automatic washing machines. Since product evaluations appeared less frequently for clothes dryers than the other products, the resulting price index extends over longer spans of years and thus may miss some year-to-year price variations. But this should not alter the accuracy of the trend rate of price change over long periods, which is the main orientation of this study.

Table 7.14   **Comparisons of "Closely Similar" Models of Clothes Dryers from *Consumer Reports*, 1951–84**

Years	Price Range (1)	Number of Models (2)	Price Change		Annual Rate of Price Change	
			Gas (3)	Electric (4)	Gas (5)	Electric (6)
1. 1951–54	Low	6/6	1.6[a]	0.0[b]	0.5	0.0
2. 1954–57	Low	8/8	0.0[a]	−1.4[c]	0.0	−0.5
3. 1957–61	Low	8/8	−20.1[d]	−19.2[d]	−5.5	−5.2
4. 1961–66	High	27/20	−18.7[e]	−27.5[e]	−4.1	−6.2
5. 1961–72	Low	9/20	−20.1[f]	−20.5	−2.0	−2.1
6. 1966–74	High	20/21	−5.8[f]	−4.8	−0.7	−0.6
7. 1974–75	High	21/23	20.9[g]	15.4[g]	20.9	15.4
8. 1975–82	Medium	23/11	46.4[h]	46.2[h]	5.6	5.6
9. 1982–84	High	11/11	6.8[i]	5.2[i]	3.3	2.6

[a]1951–54 and 1954–57 price changes calculated for two matched models of the same brand both having automatic ignition, timer control, and temperature control.

[b]1951–54 price change calculated for four matched models of the same brand all having timer control and temperature control, but not having a "dryness" control.

[c]1954–57 price change calculated for six matched models of the same brand, all having timer control and temperature control, but not having high speed, automatic control, or other special features.

[d]Excludes models having automatic dryness control. No comparison for gas models is possible; gas price is estimated as $32.50 above the electric model price, based on two otherwise identical models.

[e]Excludes Easy brand, which does not have automatic dryness control.

[f]Excludes models not having automatic ignition.

[g]1975 prices are for mid-range models lacking automatic dryness control. $30 added to 1975 price to incorporate automatic dryness control, using the figure in *CR* (November 1975, 686).

[h]Medium-range models chosen rather than high-priced models since the latter contain permanent press (cool-down) cycles, "added tumble," electronic touch switches, and other features not available in 1975.

[i]1982–84 comparison based on models matched by model number (seven electric and four gas).

Like washing machines, the evolution of clothes dryers mainly involved the addition of more and more complex controls. In the first *CR* product evaluation (1951), most dryers had a simple timer or a simple temperature control, and in a few cases both. Some gas dryers had automatic ignition, but some had a pilot light that required lighting by hand each time the dryer was used. By the last report in 1984, controls had become much more complex. The top-of-the-line models rated in 1984 had not only automatic sensors that turned off the dryer when clothes were dry, but permanent press cycles and in some cases electronic switches.

Particularly in the 1950s and 1980s, the rated dryers were sufficiently heterogeneous that it was necessary to match them model by model to allow a legitimate price comparison. For instance, the 1951, 1954, and 1957 comparisons include matched models having both time and temperature controls (not "either-or") and lacking automatic dryness control, "high-speed drying," and other features. The 1951–54 and 1954–57 comparisons link prices of identical brand names. An invaluable aid was the presentation by *CR* of prices and ratings of both deluxe and economy models in 1961. This allowed the linking of the economy-model prices with the simple models of earlier years, as well as with a single further rating of economy models in 1972, and the linking of the deluxe-model prices with the more complex models of later years.

By the 1980s, the models that incorporated the same features as the deluxe models of the 1960s and 1970s had slipped to the mid-range of the price spectrum, and new features had been added to the most expensive models that had not been previously available, including permanent-press and delicate-fabric cycles, and "added tumble time" (an extended period of cool tumbling to keep clothes from wrinkling until the user has time to empty the machine). Thus, 1975 mid-range models, with their prices adjusted to incorporate automatic dryness control, are compared with 1982 mid-range models. The 1982–84 comparison is for deluxe models matched by brand and model number to have similar features.

7.8.2   Adjustments for Improvements in Energy Efficiency

CR does not present detailed model-by-model data on energy usage, but the text of each product evaluation report contains a statement regarding the energy consumption or energy cost of a load of a specified weight. The remarks are mainly included as an attempt to advise readers on the length of time needed for the lower energy usage of gas dryers than electric dryers to compensate for their higher purchase price. But the listed monthly energy cost can be used to calculate an energy-efficiency adjustment. Until 1974, the monthly electricity cost of electric dryers does not show any clear trend, as it is reported to be $3.29 in 1954, $2.93 in 1954, $2.73 in 1961, $3.61 in 1966, and $2.73 in 1974.[34] The 1966 figure seems to be inconsistent with a trend that otherwise would be slightly downward; however, there can be no misreading the text of the evaluation, which states clearly in 1966 that "it would cost you $3.38 to dry 26 loads a month with the least power-hungry dryer tested" (September, 443).

However, there is no ambiguity about the improvement in energy efficiency after 1974. Using *CR*'s own figure of $0.0775 per kWh, and noting that it had increased the dry weight of its test load from 8 to 10.5 pounds, we have monthly electricity costs of $8.65 in 1974, $8.86 in 1975, $5.17 in 1982, and $5.53 in 1984. The 1984 figure is 63.9 percent of the 1974 figure. Another consistent way of calculating the energy saving is to note (October 1984, 583) that 1984 electric dryers drew 5.4 kilowatts and required thirty minutes to dry a 10.5 pound load, for a consumption of 2.7 kWh. This implies a

---

34. Sometimes *CR* provides the cost per load, sometimes the cost per month, and sometimes both, using a translation factor of twenty-six loads per month. In 1957 and 1961, the electricity consumption in kWh is given per load. All figures given in the text are on an equivalent energy price basis of $0.03 per kWh.

consumption of 2.18 kWh for a load of eight pounds, or just 58 percent of the 3.75 kWh requirement explicitly stated in *CR* for 1957 (July, 308).[35]

Similar calculations for gas dryers produce a consumption in cubic feet of 13.5 in 1957, 13.0 in 1961, and 11.8 in 1974 for an eight-pound load, and 15.8 in 1974, 14.6 in 1975, 7.9 in 1982, and 7.8 in 1984 for an eleven-pound load. The 1984/1974 ratio is just 49.4 percent, an even greater proportional saving than for electric dryers.[36] To convert these figures into a quality adjustment for the improvement in energy efficiency, I make one calculation for 1954–74 using pre-1974 energy prices and an eight-pound load, and a second calculation for 1974–82 using post-1974 energy prices and a 10.5 pound load. For electricity, the present value of the saving from the 1954 monthly electricity cost of $3.29 to the 1974 monthly cost of $2.73, assuming a ten-year lifetime, comes to $58.05. Using the same method as for refrigerators and air conditioners (adding the energy saving to the base-year price), we have an adjustment factor of − 1.07 percent per year for 1954–74. The present value of the saving from the monthly electricity cost of $8.65 to the 1982 electricity cost of $5.35 is $342.12, implying an adjustment factor of − 12.93 percent per year from 1974 to 1982.[37] The present value of the saving from the 1954 monthly gas cost of $0.33 to the 1974 monthly gas cost of $0.29 is $4.31, implying an adjustment factor of a minuscule −0.08 percent per year in the twenty years before 1974. But there was a more sizable drop from the monthly gas cost of $2.42 in 1974 (calculated at post-1974 gas prices and a larger 10.5 pound load) to $1.21 in 1982, implying a present value of energy saving of $125.45 and a yearly adjustment factor of − 5.73 percent.[38]

7.8.3   Alternative Price Indexes for Clothes Dryers

As with the other products, the behavior of the various price indexes displayed in table 7.15 differs over alternative subperiods of the 1951–84 period. Table 7.16 summarizes over three subintervals the CPI, PPI, Sears matched model index, and four *CR* indexes for gas and electric dryers, without and with an energy adjustment. The Sears index is calculated by the

35. In 1974, *CR* states that the cost of drying a load of eleven pounds is 1.289 times the cost of drying a load of eight pounds, for an elasticity of cost to weight of 0.77.

36. None of these figures are reported directly in *CR*. But the text of the evaluations provides enough information to make the necessary calculations. For instance, in 1975 we read that with gas at $0.25 per 100,000 BTU and electricity at $0.09 per kWh, 300 eleven-pound loads would cost $11.58 for gas and another $6.75 for electricity to run the dryer's motor. At 1,055 BTU per cubic foot, the price becomes $0.2637 per 100 cubic feet. A cost of $11.58 per 300 loads implies a cost per load of $0.0386, or 14.64 cubic feet of gas (and 0.25 kWh of electricity) per load.

37. I choose the period 1974–82 rather than 1974–84, since the transition to lower energy usage had already occurred by 1982. To make the adjustment slightly more conservative, I take the average of the 1982 and 1984 monthly electricity cost figures rather than the lower 1982 figure.

38. I use the gas price in the 1984 *CR* evaluation of $0.617 per therm, which is less than the 1982 price of $0.7 per therm.

Table 7.15   **Alternative Price Indexes for Clothes Dryers, 1951–83 (1967 = 100)**

				Consumer Reports			
				Without Energy Adjustment		With Energy Adjustment	
Year	CPI	PPI (12-41-02-32)	Sears Matched Models	Gas	Electric	Gas	Electric
	(1)	(2)	(3)	(4)	(5)	(6)	(7)
1951	. . .	. . .	. . .	144.8	155.1	146.1	179.2
1952	. . .	. . .	. . .	145.5	155.1	146.8	179.2
1953	. . .	. . .	. . .	146.4	155.1	147.6	179.2
1954	. . .	103.4	144.6	147.1	155.1	148.4	179.2
1955	. . .	100.5	118.0	147.1	154.3	148.3	176.3
1956	. . .	102.5	113.3	147.1	153.6	148.3	173.6
1957	. . .	106.5	108.4	147.1	152.8	148.2	170.9
1958	. . .	106.5	108.4	139.2	145.1	140.2	160.5
1959	. . .	108.7	116.9	131.8	137.7	132.6	150.8
1960	. . .	105.2	116.9	124.7	130.7	125.4	141.6
1961	. . .	103.5	100.6	118.0	124.1	118.6	133.0
1962	. . .	102.3	110.8	114.5	119.2	115.0	126.3
1963	105.8	102.3	112.0	110.1	114.5	110.4	119.8
1964	105.5	101.0	112.0	107.7	109.9	108.0	113.7
1965	103.0	97.8	108.4	104.5	105.5	104.7	107.9
1966	100.0	98.1	93.9	101.4	101.4	101.4	102.4
1967	100.0	100.0	100.0	100.0	100.0	100.0	100.0
1968	103.1	102.6	100.0	98.6	98.6	98.5	97.6
1969	105.2	104.9	104.8	97.3	97.3	97.2	95.3
1970	108.4	108.4	113.3	96.0	96.0	95.8	93.0
1971	112.4	110.1	120.5	94.7	94.7	94.4	90.8
1972	114.2	108.8	120.5	93.4	93.5	93.1	88.6
1973	114.4	110.8	120.5	92.8	92.9	92.4	87.2
1974	121.4	120.7	130.1	92.2	92.3	91.7	85.7
1975	136.7	134.8	156.6	113.6	107.8	106.7	87.8
1976	148.6	148.8	169.8	120.1	113.9	106.6	81.6
1977	155.1	154.0	175.9	127.1	120.5	106.4	75.9
1978	163.7	161.2	162.6	134.4	127.4	106.3	70.5
1979	174.5	172.3	206.0	142.1	134.8	106.1	65.5
1980	188.3	191.4	215.7	150.3	142.5	106.0	60.9
1981	201.8	207.0	236.1	158.9	150.8	105.8	56.6
1982	216.5	223.6	260.2	168.1	159.4	105.7	52.6
1983	226.2	232.5	283.1	173.8	163.6	109.3	54.0
1984	231.8	238.7	. . .	179.6	168.0	112.9	55.4

methods described in detail in chapter 10. The subintervals are 1954–63, 1963–74, and 1974–83, and the full 1954–83 period (1954 is the first year of the PPI; the 1963 break point corresponds to the first year of the CPI; and the 1974 break point corresponds to the year that divides the two subintervals of our energy adjustment).

These annual growth rates indicate a relatively close correspondence of the Sears and *CR* no-energy indexes in the first subinterval, and between the PPI and the Sears indexes in the second subinterval. The CPI, PPI, and *CR* no-energy indexes are also quite close together in the final subinterval. The greater rate of price decline in the *CR* no-energy indexes than in the Sears

Table 7.16   **Annual Percent Growth Rates of Alternative Price Indexes for Clothes Dryers, 1954–83 and Subintervals**

	1954–63	1963–74	1974–83	1954–83
CPI	. . .	1.26	7.16	. . .
PPI	−0.11	0.73	7.55	2.83
Sears matched model	−2.80	0.67	9.02	2.34
CR gas no energy	−3.17	−1.60	7.30	0.57
CR electric no energy	−3.31	−1.94	6.57	0.18
CR gas with energy	−3.23	−1.67	1.97	−1.05
CR electric with energy	−4.38	−3.00	−5.00	−4.05

index between 1963 and 1974 may be the counterpart of the gradual shift in Sears's location in the price structure from well below average to average. The rapid rate of increase in the Sears index after 1974 is something of a puzzle that should be resolved.[39] As for the *CR* indexes incorporating the energy adjustments, these are dependent on the validity of the same assumptions used to calculate the energy adjustments for refrigerators and room air conditioners, namely the use of a 3 percent discount rate and the evaluation of post-1974 energy savings at the energy prices of the early 1980s.

7.8.4   Unmeasured Dimensions of Quality Improvement

Like washers, dryers have mainly improved over the years through the addition of extra controls and convenience features. Because models with comparable features are linked in table 7.14, there are few additional dimensions of quality change to discuss. By far the most important is the remarkable improvement in energy efficiency achieved in an appliance that (at least for electric dryers, which account for about two-thirds of sales) over its lifetime consumes electricity worth more than double its purchase price (125 percent more at 1972 prices and 100 percent more at 1982 prices).

The only evidence of quality improvement along other dimensions appears in 1957, when *CR* (July, 308) wrote that "you can buy a better dryer today than you could three years ago," and cited two major improvements (lower temperatures and faster drying speed) and several minor additions that are not taken into account in the explicit quality adjustments (shut-off switch when door is opened, foot-pedal door openers, and magnetic door closers). Another area of improvement may have been larger capacity, although no explicit comments are made on this issue. The chief hint that capacity increased is that *CR*'s "standard load" for testing and the calculation of energy costs was eight pounds until 1974, both eight and eleven pounds in 1974 and 1975, and 10.5 pounds thereafter. In 1966, but not before, *CR* mentions testing dryers with a twelve-pound load on which "they still performed quite well." Since it seems

39. As of this writing, I have not had the opportunity to attempt to match Sears models in the catalog to those rated by *CR*.

clear from the previous section that the capacity of automatic washing machines increased significantly, it makes sense to infer that dryer capacities must have increased as well. However, I have no basis on which to make a quantitative adjustment for increased capacity, and so I leave this as one dimension of improvement that suggests that my *CR* index may not adjust sufficiently for quality change.

7.9   TV Sets

No consumer product has improved more over the postwar era taken as a whole than TV sets. It is startling to look back and discover that, in September 1946, RCA introduced the first black-and-white (B&W) table model with a 10-inch diagonal screen for a selling price of $375, plus $50 for installation and the first year's service.[40] A Rip Van Winkle who had gone to sleep in 1946 and woken up in 1986 would have been dazzled by the incredibly sharp and bright picture on a 19-inch color TV set that sold for just $168.[41] In contrast to this history, the price decline registered by the CPI price index for TV sets from its inception in 1950 to 1984 is just 40 percent. It seems likely that a careful attempt to link the prices of "closely similar" models over the postwar period would yield a price index that declines by substantially more than this.

The first half of the postwar era was dominated by B&W receivers. Although TV was invented before World War II and demonstrated at the New York World's Fair of 1939, mass production of TV sets did not become feasible until 1946–47, when the first stations went on the air on a full-time basis. Even as large a city as San Francisco did not have a single TV station until 1948. Yet by 1949 the production and sales of TV sets had taken off, with 3 million sets sold in that year (see table 7.1 above). Quality changes for B&W sets over the postwar period have included increases in picture size, improvements in picture quality, reductions in weight that made possible portable sets, and a decreased incidence of service calls.

The current broadcast system for color TV was adopted in 1953, but the first color sets produced to meet this standard were unsuccessful in the marketplace. RCA managed to sell only thirty of its $1,000 set in its first month on the market in 1955. Only in the 1965–66 season did all three networks begin to broadcast most of their evening programs in color, after years when RCA's NBC division had run scattered programming in a feeble

40. "The RCA TS630, c. 1946, had a 10-inch picture tube and weighed 85 pounds. . . . The first mass-produced model, the TS630 made television ownership practical and possible for many, opening the way for the age of television" (*CR*, January 1954).

41. This was a 19-inch set with remote control advertised by a chain store in the *Chicago Tribune* on 23 October 1986. It is an extreme example, but there were many different chains advertising 19-inch sets with quartz tuning, automatic fine tuning, and remote control in the price range of $279–$298 during the same week.

attempt to sell color sets. Not until 1973 were half of U.S. homes equipped with color sets. Color sets did not outsell black and white sets in numbers until 1972, but in value they became dominant several years earlier. And the improvement in quality of color sets from the 1960s to the 1980s has been phenomenal: "Those venturesome consumers who bought color sets in the 1960s were plagued by the difficulty of tuning them and by inordinately frequent, lengthy, and expensive repairs. 'Of all types of products, only autos generate more complaints,' *CR* wrote in its May 1968 issue" (Consumers' Union 1986, 34).

The goal of this section is to quantify improvements in quality along as many dimensions as possible, while admitting in advance that some dimensions, particularly picture quality and portability, are inherently unquantifiable. The year-by-year comparisons are set out in table 7.17, which exhibits thirty-nine different pairwise comparisons of particular types of TV sets. In some years, *CR* published as many as two or three evaluations of TV sets of different sizes and types. Only two or three of these comparisons are excluded, and so table 7.17 summarizes essentially *all* the information of prices of TV sets in *CR* over the four decades between 1947 and 1986.[42] A total of 384 models is included in the comparisons, a figure taken as the sum of the number of models listed for the first year of each comparison in column 2 of table 7.17.

Just as refrigerators are separated into separate categories by type of defrost and location of freezer for the comparisons of "closely similar models," here TV sets are subdivided by B&W or color, size of screen, and type of cabinet (console, table model, or portable). As the string of zeros in column 4 demonstrates, it is possible to make most pairwise comparisons of a given type of TV set without any explicit adjustment for quality change. This section describes the major adjustments that were made. The comparison in row 12 includes an allowance for the introduction of a bonded picture tube, using a *CR* statement about the difference in cost, and an arbitrary $10 allowance for increased ease of servicing from the introduction of pull-out chassis units. The 1965–67 comparison in row 19 involves an allowance for the introduction of UHF tuners, using the price difference between VHF-only and VHF-UHF tuners listed in 1965.

Several other adjustments are made, sometimes involving arbitrary but plausible estimation of the value of particular features, including $20 for a cart when included for a portable set, $20 for the addition of quick warmup and automatic or one-button fine tuning, and $5 for a cable connection.

42. The exceptions are a 1957 evaluation of 14-inch B&W sets, which could not be directly compared with the same size of set for either earlier or later years; a 1960 evaluation of "minor-brand" B&W consoles, which I felt might not be fully comparable to the major brand sets; and a 1981 evaluation of 19-inch color sets loaded with all conceivable "bells and whistles" and sold at very high prices, with no information provided on less-complex models that would be comparable to the 19-inch sets included for earlier years.

Table 7.17   Comparisons of "Closely Similar" Models of Television Sets from *Consumer Reports*, 1947–84

Years	Type (1)	Number of Models (2)	Price Change (3)	Quality Adjustment (4)	Annual Rate of Price Change (5)
1. 1947–48	10'' table B&W	1/1	−13.3[a]	0.0	−13.3
2. 1948–49	10'' table B&W	4/10	−21.9	0.0	−21.9
3. 1949–50	12'' table B&W	5/8	−38.1	0.0	−38.1
4. 1949–51	16'' table B&W	1/7	−33.2[b]	0.0	−18.3
5. 1951–52	17'' table B&W	7/7	−21.9	0.0	−21.9
6. 1952–53	21'' table B&W	9/10	−12.9[c]	0.0	−12.9
7. 1953–55	21'' table B&W	10/10	−21.9	0.0	−11.6
8. 1955–57	21'' table B&W	10/7	12.8	0.0	6.2
9. 1957–58	21'' table B&W	7/10	−1.9	0.0	−1.9
10. 1958–59	17'' portable B&W	7/17	−0.6	0.0	−0.6
11. 1959–61	17/19'' portable B&W	17/13	13.0	−16.6[d]	−1.8
12. 1961–62	19'' portable B&W	13/14	−5.2	0.0	−5.2
13. 1961–62	23'' console B&W	14/14	−2.7	0.0	−2.7
14. 1962–63	19'' portable B&W	14/15	−17.9	0.0	−17.9
15. 1962–64	23'' console B&W	14/15	−3.5	0.0	−1.8
16. 1963–65	19'' portable B&W	15/14	−2.1	0.0	−1.1
17. 1964–66	23'' console color	1/2	−18.8	0.0	−9.9
18. 1965–66	25'' console color	1/3	−4.7	0.0	−4.7
19. 1965–67	19''/18'' portable B&W	14/15	−5.0	−6.0[e]	−5.7
20. 1966–68	23'' console color	2/9	4.7	0.0	4.7
21. 1967–68	18'' portable B&W	15/5	4.2	0.0	4.2
22. 1967–68	23'' console color	10/9	−10.3	0.0	−10.3
23. 1966–73	12'' portable B&W	11/12	−1.7[f]	0.0	−0.2
24. 1968–70	23'' console color	9/7	7.5[g]	0.0	3.7
25. 1968–73	19'' portable B&W	5/8	15.4	−7.1[h]	1.6
26. 1969–71	19'' table color	15/17	4.5	−4.5[i]	0.0
27. 1970–72	23'' console color	7/6	−17.2	0.0	−9.0
28. 1973–74	12'' portable B&W	12/12	6.3[f]	0.0	6.3
29. 1972–74	25'' console color	7/11	7.7	−4.2[k]	1.7
30. 1971–73	19'' table color	17/15	8.2	5.0[j]	1.6
31. 1973–75	19'' table color	15/15	9.9	0.0	4.8
32. 1973–76	19'' portable B&W	8/11	0.5	0.0	0.2
33. 1974–77	12'' portable B&W	12/10	3.6	0.0	1.2
34. 1974–77	25'' console color	11/12	12.1	0.0	3.9
35. 1975–78	19'' table color	15/15	3.9	0.0	1.3
36. 1977–80	12'' portable B&W	10/14	−5.7	0.0	−1.9
37. 1977–80	25'' console color	12/11	6.4[l]	0.0	2.1
38. 1979–85	13'' portable color	16/21	−13.5	−1.4[m]	−2.7
39. 1980–82	12'' portable B&W	14/16	3.6	0.0	1.8
40. 1980–86	25'' console color	11/14	−28.9	0.0	−5.5

[a]Based on price history for RCA given in *CR* (July 1950, 297). 1947 price is that listed for September 1946, and 1948 price is that listed for September 1947, which corresponds also to the price listed in the January 1948 report.

[b]Sixteen inch in 1949, seventeen inch in 1951.

[c]Prices in the January 1953 *CR* were used for 1952, November 1953 used for 1953.

[d]*CR* states that the new nineteen-inch screen was 5.5 percent larger than the old seventeen-inch screen; 5.5 percent was added to the 1959 price to make the quality adjustment, based on an approximate unitary elasticity of price to screen size implied by picture tube (for *CR* $10 figure, see January 1961, 9) and $10 for improved serviceability (10). A 1957 comment states that a seventeen-inch set was priced 20 percent higher than an otherwise comparable fourteen-inch set.

Table 7.17 (continued)

ᵉ1965 models listed both with and without UHF tuners. 1967 UHF models compared with 1965 UHF-equipped models. No adjustment made for picture size, since *CR* states that the new-style eighteen-inch is equivalent to the old-style nineteen inch.

ᶠExcludes Sony in 1973 and 1974 (not sold in 1966).

ᵍIncludes only models without remote control.

ʰHalf include a cart in 1973. Allowing $20 as the value of the cart, $10 is deducted from the 1973 price. Also, all models have automatic VHF tuning.

ⁱIn 1969, all lack automatic fine tuning; in 1971, all have this feature. To adjust for this improvement, the quality change is arbitrarily set equal to the price change.

ʲ$25.00 arbitrary adjustment for addition of quick warm-up, cable connection, and one-button tuning.

ᵏ$20.00 arbitrary adjustment for addition of quick warm-up and one-button tuning.

ˡAverage prices exclude Sony and models with quartz tuning.

ᵐ1985 price adjusted downward $5.00 to allow for incorporation of cable connection.

ⁿRated models in 1986 include stereo, multiple audio and video jacks, remote control, and ability to handle twenty-three or more cable channels. However, prices are given for models excluding all these features that are comparable to models sold in 1980 and prior years.

Balancing any possible overestimate of the value of these improvements is the failure to allow for other additional features (e.g., lighted channel numbers and automatic color control). Also, the degree of similarity across models in particular comparisons is improved by excluding sets that had an attribute not available in an earlier year, including remote control, quartz tuning, stereo speakers, multiple audio and video jacks, and tuners able to handle more than the original eighty-two VHF-UHF channels.[43]

7.9.1 Improved Service Reliability and Reduced Energy Consumption

One estimate (*Consumer Appliances,* n.d., 13) divided up the lifetime cost of owning a color TV set into 53 percent for the purchase price, 35 percent for servicing costs, and 12 percent for electrical power costs. While costs other than the purchase price were not as large a share of the lifetime cost of TV sets as of refrigerators, nevertheless reductions in servicing costs and energy costs over time have been a major component of quality change. The details of the adjustments are laid out in table 7.18, where the top half refers to color TV sets and the bottom half to B&W sets. Using information from the MIT report and from *CR* product evaluations, it is possible to piece together the history of improvements in the incidence of repairs and of reductions in energy use. The sources tell a straightforward and relatively consistent story of a reduction

43. Some idea of the wide variety of new features on top-of-the-line TV sets in the 1980s can be gleaned from *CR* (January 1986, 16–17). Some, most, or all of these sets included quartz frequency-synthesized tuners with channels preprogrammed at the factory and allowing the change from one channel to any other while skipping any in between, stereo decoder and speakers, infrared wireless remote control, a self-censor feature to block children from watching particular channels, cable-readiness for up to 125 cable channels, a comb filter to increase resolution by about 20 percent (not available until "a few years ago"), direct video and audio inputs for using a VCR or computer, room-light sensor, one-button control to lock picture adjustments into a preset range, sleep timers, last-channel recall, and screen shield.

Table 7.18   Repair and Energy Costs of Television Sets, Various Years and Intervals

Year	Estimated Lifetime Repair Incidence (1)	Cost per Repair (2)	Lifetime Repair Cost (3)	Energy Use (watts) (4)	Adjustments (percent) Repairs (5)	Energy (6)
Color:						
1964	11.0[a]	$20[b]	$220	350[j]	. . .	. . .
1972	5.5[c]	30[b]	165	200[j]	− 11.8	− 7.5
1978	2.2[d]	45[e]	99	150[k]	− 12.7	− 6.2
1981	1.5[f]	65[f]	98	116[l]	− 5.2	− 3.9
1986	0.8[g]	80[h]	64	. . .	− 7.3	. . .
B&W:						
1948	10.0[i]	10[i]	100	230[m]	. . .	. . .
1964	4.4[i]	10	44	200[n]	− 18.2	− 4.1
1972	2.2[i]	15	33	110[o]	− 10.8	− 17.8
1978	0.9	23	21	73[o]	− 8.5	− 19.9
1981	0.6	36	22	60[p]	− 3.5	− 6.4
1986	0.3	40	12	. . .	− 5.5	. . .

[a]Two repairs in the first year, from *Consumer Appliances* (n.d., 25) and one repair per year thereafter (*CR*, May 1969, 258).

[b]*Consumer Appliances* (n.d., 24).

[c]One repair in the first year from *Consumer Appliances* (n.d., 25) and one repair every two years thereafter (*CR*, January 1972, 15).

[d]Interpolated between 1972 and 1981.

[e]*CR*, January 1978, 14.

[f]Average set required .125 repairs in a given year (*CR*, January 1981, 36). Repair cost of $65 for average set from the same source.

[g]*CR* (January 1986, 16) states that 40 percent of sets bought in 1980 have needed at least one repair, and 10 percent of sets bought in 1984.

[h]Estimated on basis of growth in an economy-wide wage index.

[i]1974 and 1972 incidence for B&W sets is half that for color sets, from *Consumer Appliances* (n.d., 25). Forty percent figure used for other years, and 1950 figure is estimated. B&W cost per repair for 1981 from *CR* (January 1981, 36) estimated to be half color cost in other years. Cost for 1948 is based on a *CR* statement that RCA offered a service contract for an unspecified flat fee plus $5.95 per visit, implying that the cost per visit paid for without a contract must have exceeded $5.95. Also, note that all makes reviewed in January 1948 (10) offered installation plus a one-year parts and labor warranty for $55 above the listed price of the set, which apparently did not include any warranty. *CR* (July 1949, 302) estimates the yearly cost of repairs and service at $50.

[j]*Consumer Appliances* (n.d., 9) states that power consumption had been reduced from 300–400 watts on earlier all-tube sets to "as few as 140 watts in some of today's solid-state sets." On this basis, 1964 was set at 350 watts and 1972 at 200, on the grounds that not all sets sold in 1972 were solid state.

[k]Interpolated between 1972 and 1981.

[l]Average of actual reported figures in ratings of twenty-five-inch consoles from *CR* (January 1980).

[m]Power consumption range of 210–250 watts given in *CR* (January 1948), and 150–300 watts in *CR* (July 1949, 302).

[n]*CR* (January 1967) states that a B&W set was 200 watts, in comparison to 350 watts for a typical color set.

[o]Interpolated from 1964 to 1981.

[p]Nineteen-inch color sets had a power consumption ranging from 61 to 115 watts, with a mean of 88 watts (*CR*, January 1981). Power use of B&W sets, which are mainly sold in smaller sizes, is set at 60 watts, the lower end of the range for nineteen-inch color sets.

in servicing requirements by a factor of more than ten for color TV sets between 1964 and 1986, and by combining the same sources with plausible guesses, we arrive at an improvement in the repair incidence of B&W TV sets by a factor of thirty between 1950 and 1986.[44] The basic source of evidence on the improvement in repair incidence, the *CR* frequency of repair surveys, is particularly good, since it is based on hundreds of thousands of questionnaire responses.

The data on energy usage in table 7.18 are also pieced together from both the MIT report and *CR* product evaluations. Fortunately, both sources provide a consistent figure of 350 watts of power consumption for the color TV sets of the mid-1960s, and *CR* has a model-by-model listing of power consumption (averaging 116 watts) in 1980. I take no account of any added power requirements of the many extra features present on 1980 sets compared to 1964 sets. For B&W sets, we also have two consistent figures for power consumption in the late 1940s and one little-changed consumption figure for the mid-1960s. The real saving in energy use came in the 1970s with the transition to all solid-state sets, and in the column 4 of table 7.18 this is phased in gradually between 1964 and 1981.

In valuing the saving in repair costs and electricity consumption, I use the same 3 percent discount rate as in the previous calculations for refrigerators, room air conditioners, and clothes dryers. The assumed lifetime is ten years, taken from the MIT report (11). If anything, these estimates may be on the conservative side, since, even without applying a discount factor, the $165 lifetime repair cost for 1972 (table 7.18, col. 3) plus the implied $87.60 power cost is well under the price of a typical color TV set ($650 for a 25-inch color console and about $430 for a 19-inch table model), whereas the MIT report states that for 1972 the lifetime cost of repair and energy consumption is 47/53 of the purchase price. Also, the 1948 figure for repair costs on the early B&W sets implies a yearly cost of just $10, in contrast to the explicit statement in *CR* (July 1949, 302) that purchasers should plan on a $50 annual repair and servicing cost over the lifetime of a TV set, and that power and servicing made up 63 percent of the lifetime cost of owning a TV set, even when a seven-year lifetime was assumed. Thus, there is a good case for believing that the price indexes adjusted for the reduced cost of service and energy, as presented in the next section, may significantly understate the true reduction in price achieved by continuous technical advances by the firms manufacturing TV sets.

44. The only inconsistency is that the MIT report (*Consumer Appliances,* n.d.) states that color TV sets in 1965 required an average of two service calls per year and in 1972 one service call per year (23). However, the results of the *CR* frequency-of-repair questionnaire cited in nn. a and c to table 7.18 yielded an estimate of once per year in 1969 for sets manufactured between 1964 and 1968, and once every two years in 1972 for sets manufactured through 1972. I combine the lower *CR* figures with the MIT figures for the incidence of repair in the first year of ownership.

Table 7.19   Alternative Prices for Television Sets, 1947–84 (1967 = 100)

				Consumer Reports	
				Unadjusted	Adjusted
		PPI	Sears Matched	for Repairs	for Repairs
Years	CPI	(12-52)	Models	and Energy	and Energy
1947	. . .	. . .	. . .	505.1	723.9
1948	. . .	. . .	. . .	442.2	623.7
1949	. . .	. . .	. . .	355.2	493.1
1950	159.7	. . .	. . .	267.9	366.0
1951	156.3	. . .	. . .	223.1	300.0
1952	137.9	124.1	220.9	179.2	237.1
1953	132.6	124.1	199.1	157.5	205.1
1954	123.9	118.5	159.4	140.3	179.8
1955	116.8	115.1	142.5	124.9	157.5
1956	117.3	116.0	139.6	132.9	165.0
1957	122.4	117.4	145.2	141.4	172.7
1958	124.6	117.7	145.2	138.7	166.8
1959	126.2	116.3	149.1	137.9	163.2
1960	127.1	114.9	140.6	135.5	160.2
1961	123.8	113.8	122.6	133.0	157.4
1962	117.7	110.3	122.6	127.9	148.9
1963	114.7	108.1	122.6	115.9	132.8
1964	112.1	106.4	112.3	114.2	126.5
1965	107.3	103.6	108.5	108.2	115.7
1966	102.1	101.8	100.0	100.5	104.0
1967	100.0	100.0	100.0	100.0	100.0
1968	99.8	97.5	100.0	102.9	99.5
1969	99.6	92.6	100.0	104.7	97.8
1970	99.8	91.9	96.2	106.1	95.8
1971	100.1	92.8	98.1	104.1	90.8
1972	99.5	90.7	94.3	102.5	86.5
1973	98.0	88.4	94.3	103.7	83.7
1974	98.9	88.9	103.8	107.1	82.8
1975	101.6	92.2	103.8	109.9	81.3
1976	102.9	91.8	109.4	111.7	79.0
1977	101.7	85.6	109.4	114.1	77.3
1978	101.6	84.4	113.2	114.7	74.3
1979	103.0	85.8	113.2	114.8	72.0
1980	104.4	89.0	107.5	113.9	69.1
1981	105.3	88.3	107.5	111.5	65.5
1982	103.9	86.1	109.4	109.1	63.3
1983	100.3	83.2	109.4	104.7	60.0
1984	95.3	80.0	. . .	100.5	56.8

7.9.2   Alternative Price Indexes for TV Sets

The alternative price indexes for TV sets are presented in table 7.19. Table 7.20 contrasts the CPI and PPI with three other indexes, a matched model index from the Sears catalog (compiled by the same method as for clothes dryers, as described in chap. 10), and two *CR* indexes for "closely similar models", both without and with adjustments for reductions in the costs of repairs and power consumption. The break years are 1950 (the first year of the

Table 7.20   **Annual Percent Growth Rates of Alternative Price Indexes for Television Sets, 1950–83 and Subintervals**

	1950–72	1952–72	1972–83	1952–83
CPI	−2.13	−1.62	0.07	−1.02
PPI	. . .	−1.56	−0.78	−1.28
Sears matched model	. . .	−4.17	1.36	−2.24
CR unadjusted	−4.27	−2.67	0.19	−1.72
CR adjusted for repairs and energy	−6.35	−4.92	−3.27	−4.34

CPI), 1952 (the first year of the PPI and the Sears index), and 1972. The final year is 1983.

Ignoring the CR index that is adjusted for the decline in repair and power costs, the main disagreement among the indexes in table 7.20 occurs before 1972, when both the Sears and the CR indexes indicate more rapid rates of price decline than the CPI or PPI. Particularly interesting are the almost identical annual growth rates of the CPI and unadjusted CR indexes after 1972. TV sets represent the only product category for which the pre-1972 Sears index declines at an appreciably faster rate than the unadjusted CR index. Such a discrepancy might occur because the CR index links together the model types that appear in the product evaluations, whereas the Sears index represents a broader range of model types in the year-to-year price comparisons. In particular, the decline in the Sears index relative to the unadjusted CR index occurs in the 1950s, when the CR index is based mainly on a single model type for each pair of years. Possibly new types of models registering greater price declines were introduced more rapidly into the Sears catalog than into the CR testing program. A further discrepancy is in the more rapid rate of increase of the Sears index than the unadjusted CR index after 1972; this also occurs for clothes dryers and may reflect a shift in marketing strategy that resulted in an upward adjustment of Sears's rank in the price-quality ranking.

7.9.3   Unmeasured Dimensions of Quality Improvement

While the CR price indexes developed above incorporate quantitative adjustments for the addition of particular features to TV sets, and while a second index includes adjustments for reduced repair and energy costs, there remain other dimensions of improvement for which no adjustments have been made. The most important of these are the improved provision of warranties and a continuous improvement in picture quality.

No adjustment is made for warranties, because it is difficult to put together a consistent time series, and because the valuation of warranties is complex, in light of changes in repair incidence that have occurred. But there seems little doubt that consumers receive better warranty protection now than they did in the late 1940s. The prices of TV sets in the CR index for 1948 do not include the extra $55 that was charged for installation and first-year service; of this, in-text comments by *CR* indicate that about $15 was for installation and the rest was for service. The introduction of the one-year warranty apparently dates to the 1960s:

> Since the advent of the consumer advocacy movement in the early 1960s, the television industry has seen the one-year labor and parts warranty become an industry standard, primarily due to consumer and competitive pressures that caused manufacturers to assume greater responsibility for early failures of their products. This is a vast change from prior warranty practices which had manufacturers typically assuming responsibility only for parts failures during the first 90 days of ownership, putting much heavier service-cost burden on the consumer. [*Consumer Appliance*, n.d., 15]

The *CR* ratings of January 1974 confirm the MIT statement; all sets are listed as including not just a two-year warranty on the picture tube, but also a one-year warranty on parts and labor, while one set offered a two-year warranty on parts and labor and another a four-year warranty on parts and the picture tube. By 1986, matters had become more complex. The two-year warranty on the picture tube was still almost universal for the eighteen sets listed, with the only exceptions being one case of thirty months and one of forty-eight months. Parts warranties were thirteen cases of one year, three of two years, one of thirty months, and one of forty-eight months. Labor warranties included seven of three months, eight of twelve months, and one each of twenty-four, thirty, and forty-eight months. It is difficult to place a value on improved warranty coverage, although the MIT report (15) places a value of $3.00 per set on the ninety-day parts-only warranty common before the mid-1960s, and a value of $25 per set for the period 1969–72. This difference would reduce the *CR* price index by another 5 percent over the period when the extended warranty was introduced, presumably the mid-1960s.

The record on improved picture quality consists of a series of quotes from *CR* over the years. In 1950, five of fourteen rated sets were labeled "poor" or "unacceptable" in regard to their picture quality. By 1953, we read that all nine receivers tested were acceptable, and that "the performance of most of the sets was appreciably better than the TV sets of the same brands which CU tested in 1952" (January, 15). There was a brief period of quality deterioration noted in 1962; most of the sets suffered from "pincushion distortion" and "horizontal nonlinearity," apparently as the consequence of a shift to shorter picture tubes that allowed "slim sets." But by 1967 there was no mention of these problems, and "the top-ranked sets showed clearer, crisper pictures than any we have seen for a number of years" (March, 135).

As for color sets, *CR* branded their picture quality universally poor in 1964. In 1968, the complaint was the difficulty of tuning: "Troublesome as color adjustment is, most users would probably accept the bother cheerfully if they could get it over with at the start of each viewing session'' (January, 17). But matters improved rapidly. By 1972, large consoles as well as 19-inch table sets were equipped with automatic fine tuning and automatic gain control, and ''the picture quality of the three check-rated models was just about the best we've ever seen'' (January 1972, 8). In January 1978 (13), we find that ''the technology needed to produce a fine color television picture has apparently reached the point where every TV manufacturer can turn the trick. All fifteen of the 19-inch sets CU tested for this report delivered pictures of very high quality.'' By 1980, we read that, ''as a group, all the tested sets proved admirably sharp'' and that the new quartz tuners were ''very impressive'' (January, 13). Finally, in January 1981 (34), ''CU's tests suggest that good picture quality can almost be taken for granted in today's color-TV sets. A majority of the sets delivered a picture that was nearly as good as the picture on the 'state-of-the-art' receiver/monitor in our laboratory.''

There is other confirming evidence on improved quality. Comparing 1974 TV sets with their 1967 counterparts, Kleinfield (1974) wrote: ''Today's color set differs from its 1967 counterpart in that it is all solid-state, its parts last longer and are easier to service, it consumes less electricity, it is two to four times brighter, it has better contrast and it has automatic tuning.'' In a more recent evaluation, Fantel (1984) wrote that, on the latest models, ''The first thing you notice is that the picture is sharper, brighter, and more ''contrasty'' in broad daylight. . . . The main reason the picture is sharper than in the past is that many of the better sets use a so-called comb filter, which separates the color signal from the black-and-white signal. Up to now this fancy circuit was too bulky and expensive to use in TV sets. . . . But in recent years new electronic chips have been developed to perform these filter functions.'' Fantel (1986) quantifies the improvement further: ''In the specifications of a television set or video monitor, resolution . . . is indicated mainly by the horizontal line count. . . . Over the years, video designers have been working hard, and with considerable success, to increase the count. Only a short time ago, horizontal line counts as low as 230 were not uncommon. Today, some of the best sets go as high as 500.'' Other dimensions of quality improvement in TV sets, cited by Fantel (1984), include the addition of terminals for connecting VCRs, reduction of optical distortion in better-shaped picture tubes made possible by better glass-molding methods, the use of a ''black matrix'' to improve contrast and reduce reflections, and reduction in picture shrinkage and ''overscan,'' allowing the full transmitted picture to be routinely displayed.

7.10   Other Products

While the evaluation of appliance prices in this chapter has treated some of the most important consumer durable goods, others have been omitted. Taking the figures for 1983 in table 7.1, the most important omissions by value of

Table 7.21   Comparisons of "Closely Similar" Models of Three Products from Consumer Reports

	Type[a]	Number of Models	Price Change
Under-counter dishwashers:			
1. 1952–65	A	4/4	−34.3
2. 1965–71	A	4/3	0.7
3. 1965–71	B	9/6	−4.5
4. 1971–74	A	3/1	−18.9
5. 1971–74	B	6/8	−11.2
6. 1971–74	C	7/6	−12.4
7. 1974–80	B	8/2	26.3
8. 1974–80	C	6/10	41.8
9. 1980–83	B	2/1	6.1
10. 1980–83	C	10/8	22.2
Microwave ovens:			
1. 1968–73	A	1/12	−24.8
2. 1973–76	A	12/5	−22.3
3. 1976–81	B	11/7	−6.0
4. 1981–85	C	10/5	−47.3
Videocassette recorders:			
1. 1980–82	A	3/4	−38.7
2. 1982–85	B	4/8	−65.0

[a]*Dishwashers:* type A: one cycle only; type B: basic cycle and rinse-hold cycle; includes dispenser and rinse conditioner; type C: at least three cycles, including heavy duty, scour, or pots and pans. *Microwave ovens:* type A: only one heat setting, mechanical controls; type B: basic setting and at least one reduced setting; type C: temperature probe, variable heat settings, touch panel controls with facility for more than one programmable setting. *Videocassette recorders:* (VHS only): type A: two heads, wire remote with pause control only, no search; type B: multifunction infrared remote, two heads, fourteen-day multiprogram capability, cable ready.

shipments are kitchen ranges, dishwashers, microwave ovens, and VCRs. I do not compute a price index for gas or electric kitchen ranges, because *CR* product evaluations have appeared only infrequently, making it difficult to control for the numerous relevant quality characteristics of this complex product. However, it is feasible to develop *CR* price indexes of "closely similar" models for the other three products. In order to limit the scope of this chapter, each of the three indexes is described more briefly in this section than the other five products treated previously.

7.10.1   Under-Counter Dishwashers

The automatic electric dishwasher is a postwar product, introduced at about the same time in the late 1940s as the clothes dryer, and accounting for about the same value of shipments (as shown by the weights in the notes to table 7.23 below). Although not introduced into the PPI until December 1966, *CR* rated under-counter dishwashers as early as 1952. Measures of price change displayed in the top section of table 7.21 are based on six *CR* evaluations between 1952 and 1983.[45] The only quality adjustment made prior to

45. There was also a report in 1959, but this could not be included here as the *CR* volume was missing from the Northwestern library at the time this chapter was written.

calculating the price change between pairs of years was to sort the rated models into three type classes differing by the number of automatic cycles.

Because 1952 models had only one basic cycle, just this simple type (A) could be compared between 1952 and 1966. However, for the other pairs of years, at least two model types could be compared, and three for 1971–74. Both types B and C have more than one cycle; type B machines have a basic cycle and a rinse-hold cycle, while type C machines add a heavy-duty wash cycle (called variously "extended wash," "scour," "pots-and-pans," or other such names). Machines became still more complex in the 1980s, and to maintain homogeneity I omitted complex models having such features as heater turnoff, choice of 120- or 140-degree water temperature, or all push-button control.

As shown in table 7.22, the resulting *CR* price index declines during the 1952–65 period, when there was no PPI, and increases at only about half the rate of the PPI after 1966. Nevertheless, there are at least four reasons to suspect that the *CR* index may understate the extent of quality improvements and thus overstate the rate of price increase. First, dishwashers appear to have increased in capacity (as did automatic washing machines and clothes dryers). In 1952, larger models were reported to accommodate eight place settings, while the rest held six settings. However, by 1980, *CR*'s standard test load was ten place settings, and several models held eleven. Second, performance improved. *CR* wrote in 1965 that "all do wash better than most of the models tested in 1959" (November, 527). Third, there may have been some improvement within the model-type classes. For instance, *CR* complained in 1952 that with some of the models (all of which had just one basic cycle) there was no ability to vary the cycle at all by interrupting or speeding it up. Fourth, there appears to have been an energy-saving reduction in the use of hot water in relation to capacity, but insufficient data are provided to allow a formal adjustment for energy efficiency. Overall, the *CR* dishwasher index seems to understate the extent of the 1952–83 price decline, in light of the observed facts that the average price in 1952 was $328 for simple models with a single cycle, whereas in 1980 and 1983 models with two automatic cycles were available for an average of $290 and $310, respectively.[46]

7.10.2 Microwave Ovens

The two "hot" household appliances of the 1980s are microwave ovens and VCRs. As shown in the notes to table 7.23, microwave ovens by 1983 outsold any of the products covered in this chapter, with the exceptions of refrigerators and color TV sets. Microwave sales were stimulated by a dramatic decline in prices, by improved quality, and by eased concerns about safety, but, strangely enough, the PPI for microwave ovens, introduced only in 1978, shows only an 8 percent price decline between 1978 and 1985. Five

---

46. These are the type B models shown in the 1980–83 comparison in table 7.21.

Table 7.22   Alternative Indexes for Three Products, 1952–85 (1982 = 100)

| Year | Under-counter Dishwashers | | Microwave Ovens | | Videocassette Recorders |
	PPI (1)	CR (2)	PPI (3)	CR (4)	CR (5)
1952		121.0			
1953		117.3			
1954		113.6			
1955		110.0			
1956		106.6			
1957		103.2			
1958		100.0			
1959		96.9			
1960		93.4			
1961		90.9			
1962		88.1			
1963		85.3			
1964		82.7			
1965		80.1			
1966		79.8			
1967	53.9	79.6			
1968	53.6	79.3		207.1	
1969	54.5	79.0		196.0	
1970	52.3	78.7		185.5	
1971	56.1	78.5		175.4	
1972	55.4	74.7		166.0	
1973	54.6	71.1		157.1	
1974	55.7	67.6		144.9	
1975	58.8	71.1		133.7	
1976	66.5	74.8		123.3	
1977	69.0	78.6		121.8	
1978	72.5	82.6	100.4	120.3	
1979	80.0	86.9	98.9	118.8	
1980	87.0	91.3	108.4	117.4	154.3
1981	93.1	95.6	103.8	115.9	124.2
1982	100.0	100.0	100.0	100.0	100.0
1983	103.1	104.6	99.4	86.3	74.4
1984			98.9	74.4	55.4
1985			92.7	64.2	41.2

CR product evaluations of microwave ovens were published between 1968 and 1985, and the pairwise price comparisons are shown in the middle section of table 7.21.

As for dishwashers, the only quality adjustments are the identification of model types. Type A has mechanical controls, a timer dial, and a single power setting. Type B offers at least one reduced power setting but still has mechanical controls and a timer dial. Type C is much improved, having a temperature probe, many variable power settings, and touch-panel controls with at least two automatic programmable settings. One reason for the growing popularity of microwave ovens in the 1980s was their increased availability in compact sizes; I control for size, using *CR*'s measurements, and include only those 1985 models with capacities of 1.0 cubic foot or more. This explains why only five models are included in 1985. To provide examples of prices, in 1981 type B models were available at an average of $393 and type C at an average of $556. By 1985, the type C price of large 1.0-cubic-foot models had fallen to $293, while thirteen additional models with capacities of 0.6–0.7 cubic foot were available for an average of $272. By November 1986, the eight type C models of 0.6-cubic-foot capacity had fallen further in price to $191. These prices contrast with type A, sold in 1968 for $495.

The *CR* price index for microwave ovens is compared with the PPI in table 7.22. The overall geometric annual rate of change of the *CR* index between 1968 and 1985 is − 6.7 percent, and the rapid decline in the *CR* index between 1980 and 1984 differs from the PPI by more than 10 percent per year.

As with other products, there are additional dimensions of quality improvement. The most important is safety. As *CR* wrote in 1985, "In the early 1970s, we found that some microwave ovens leaked radiation in troubling amounts when we subjected them to deliberate abuse. Since then—and partly as a result of CU's efforts—the design of microwave ovens has improved. . . . As in our last two reports on microwave ovens, we found radiation leakage to be quite low in all models" (November, 647). The other main improvement is size, since for a microwave oven compactness is a virtue rather than a defect, at least within limits. As *CR* stated in 1985, "Smaller sizes have solved one of the biggest problems consumers have had with microwave ovens—too much oven in too little kitchen" (November, 644). Despite the virtues of small sizes, the price comparisons in table 7.21 compare models of identical capacities. Nevertheless, it seems clear from the smaller sizes of models tested by *CR* in 1986 than in 1985, and in 1985 than in 1981, that consumers prefer small sizes. In addition to the space-saving aspects, smaller ovens consume less energy to achieve routine chores like defrosting frozen food, although there is not enough information to attempt an energy-efficiency adjustment, and I doubt that it would amount to much, given the limited number of hours per year that a microwave oven would typically be used (especially in contrast to refrigerators, color TV sets, and clothes dryers).

7.10.3   VCRs

The VCR was introduced in the mid-1970s and was first rated by *CR* in 1978. Yet its popularity was so great that by 1983 the value of shipments of VCRs was equal to that of washing machines and was greater than the value of shipments of room air conditioners and clothes dryers combined (see the notes to table 7.23). Only three *CR* evaluations are used in developing the price comparisons of table 7.21 (1980, 1982, and 1985), since the 1978 report included models that were so simple (no remote control, no programming capability) that they could not be compared to the standard models of 1980.

Just two model types are identified. Type A has a wired remote control only able to make the tape action pause but having no other feature, and this type also lacks search and cue capability. Type B, which was a super deluxe model in 1982 but standard in 1985, has a "full-featured" infrared remote control and fourteen-day programming capability, but just two recording heads. By 1985, VCRs with three and four recording heads had begun to appear, but these are not included. Despite the plummeting price of type B from the $1,500 to the $600 range between 1982 to 1985, the best was yet to come. Such models were widely available for $275 in late 1986, and higher-priced models included still more features not available in type B machines, including slow motion and stereo sound.

Table 7.23   **Divisia Price Indexes for Eight Appliances, 1947–84[a]**

	Annual Growth Rates			Price Indexes (1967 = 100)		
	Unadjusted CR (1)	Adjusted CR (2)	PPI (3)	Unadjusted CR (4)	Adjusted CR (5)	PPI (6)
1947	. . .	. . .	. . .	307.1	441.0	117.5
1948	−0.2	−0.8	6.4	306.4	437.6	125.4
1949	−12.2	−12.7	−3.0	271.3	385.4	121.7
1950	−13.8	−16.0	1.1	236.3	328.4	123.0
1951	−10.7	−12.9	4.4	212.2	288.7	128.6
1952	−8.9	−14.2	−0.4	194.2	250.5	128.0
1953	−5.8	−11.1	0.4	183.2	224.3	128.5
1954	−5.8	−10.6	−1.2	172.9	201.8	126.9
1955	−7.4	−7.5	−3.7	160.6	187.1	122.3
1956	−1.5	−1.7	−1.8	158.2	184.1	120.2
1957	−1.5	−1.7	−2.0	155.8	180.9	117.8
1958	−3.9	−5.0	−0.8	149.8	172.0	116.9
1959	−3.2	−4.4	−1.4	145.1	164.7	115.3
1960	−5.2	−5.3	−2.4	137.7	156.1	112.5
1961	−5.1	−5.1	−2.2	130.9	148.3	110.1
1962	−5.7	−6.4	−2.8	123.6	139.1	107.1
1963	−6.6	−7.5	−2.1	115.7	129.1	104.9
1964	−2.5	−4.3	−1.3	112.9	123.7	103.6
1965	−4.6	−7.3	−2.5	107.6	115.0	101.0
1966	−5.4	−8.6	−0.8	102.0	105.5	100.2
1967	−2.0	−5.3	−0.2	100.0	100.0	100.0
1968	−0.3	−2.9	0.2	99.8	97.1	100.2
1969	1.6	0.2	−1.8	101.3	97.3	98.4
1970	1.9	0.5	0.2	103.3	97.8	98.5
1971	−0.0	−2.0	1.7	103.3	95.9	100.3
1972	−0.1	−2.0	−1.5	103.1	94.0	98.8
1973	1.3	−1.3	−1.3	104.4	92.9	97.5
1974	1.9	−0.6	4.1	106.4	92.3	101.6
1975	6.9	3.4	8.0	114.0	95.5	110.1

Table 7.23 (continued)

	Annual Growth Rates			Price Indexes (1967 = 100)		
	Unadjusted CR (1)	Adjusted CR (2)	PPI (3)	Unadjusted CR (4)	Adjusted CR (5)	PPI (6)
1976	3.9	0.4	3.5	118.5	95.9	113.9
1977	3.2	0.7	−1.0	122.5	96.5	112.0
1978	2.6	0.0	1.9	125.5	96.5	114.9
1979	2.4	0.3	2.9	128.6	96.8	118.3
1980	2.4	0.2	6.0	131.8	97.0	125.7
1981	−1.6	−3.5	2.6	129.7	93.7	124.0
1982	−3.5	−4.8	1.4	125.3	89.3	130.8
1983	−5.5	−6.3	0.3	118.6	83.9	131.2
1984[b]	−5.7	−6.4	0.1	112.0	78.7	131.4

[a]The percentage weights applied to the appliances are as follows:

	1948–57	1958–68	1969–76	1977–84
Refrigerators	43.5	21.2	19.1	18.2
Room air conditioners	1.0	8.5	8.8	4.6
Washing machines	20.1	13.8	11.7	8.9
Clothes dryers	1.3	5.0	6.6	4.4
TV sets	32.5	51.4	45.5	33.1
Dishwashers	1.5	3.8	6.5	5.3
Microwave ovens	0.0	0.0	1.3	11.3
VCRs	0.0	0.0	0.0	14.3

Sources for weights: 1948–57 are based on 1949 and 1977–84 based on 1984 from table 7.1. 1958–68 are based on 1965 and 1969–76 based on 1972, both from *Statistical Abstract.* The weight for video equipment in table 7.1 is divided between TV sets and VCRs from details in the 1985 *Statistical Abstract* (777).

Note: Weights are set equal to zero in years when no index change is available, and remaining products are reweighted so that weights sum to 100 percent.

[b]Change in PPI used for 1984 for these three products.

There is no PPI with which the *CR* index can be compared, for the simple reason that no VCRs are produced in the United States. Any difference between official price indexes and the alternative price indexes introduced by the inclusion of the VCR price index is relevant for the deflation of U.S. consumption, investment, capital stock, and imports, but not for the deflation of GNP. The same is true for the imported component of all the other products discussed in this chapter, a qualification of more importance for microwave ovens and TV sets than for the others.

7.11 Overall Price Indexes and Conclusion

This chapter has created seventeen new price indexes for eight major household appliances: refrigerators, room air conditioners, automatic washing machines, clothes dryers, TV sets, under-counter dishwashers, microwave ovens, and VCRs. These represent all the "white goods" produced by the appliance industry (as listed in table 7.1) except for electric and gas ranges. Included are the most important types of "brown goods," but excluded are radios and other audio equipment. The new price indexes can be classified as follows:

1. eight *CR* price indexes lacking any adjustment for energy efficiency or repair costs;
2. four additional *CR* price indexes incorporating such adjustments (refrigerators, room air conditioners, clothes dryers, and TV sets);
3. three hedonic regression indexes based on Sears catalog data and available in two versions for each product, one with six to nine years pooled together, and the second with adjacent years only (the three products are refrigerators, room air conditioners, and washing machines); and
4. two matched model indexes based on Sears catalog data (clothes dryers and TV sets).

These new "alternative" price indexes are compared to the official PPI in two tables. First, table 7.23 reports weighted averages of the two types of *CR* indexes and of the corresponding PPI indexes (the behavior of the Sears indexes are summarized subsequently). The columns labeled "adjusted *CR*" are based on the energy- and repair-adjusted *CR* indexes for the four products listed above and the unadjusted *CR* indexes for the other four products. These are Divisia indexes, in which current value weights are applied to annual percentage price changes of the individual commodity price indexes. A zero weight is applied in years when no price change can be computed because a component index is unavailable, and the remaining indexes are reweighted to sum to 100 percent. Because the PPI is introduced later than the *CR* index for some products, the greater rate of decline (or smaller rate of increase) of the *CR* indexes combines two sources of difference—different index behavior in overlapping years together with the impact of rapid price declines in the early years of a product cycle before the PPI is introduced (these two different sources are disentangled in table 7.24 below). To maximize the period of comparability for the two products where the PPI starts prior to the *CR* index (two years earlier for refrigerators and one year earlier for washing machines), the change in the *CR* index is set equal to the change in the Sears index or the PPI in those years.[47]

The first three columns in table 7.23 show percentage changes at annual rates for the three indexes, and the next three columns convert these to price indexes on a base of 1967 = 100. The value weights and their sources are listed in the notes to the table. For the period 1948–57, the weights are dominated by three products, refrigerators, washing machines, and TV sets, accounting for 96.2 percent of the value of shipments. By 1977–84, the three

47. Thus, the percentage change in the *CR* index for refrigerators is set equal to that of the Sears index for 1948–49 and the PPI for 1947–48; the change in the *CR* index for washing machines is set equal to that of the PPI in 1947–48.

Table 7.24   Average Annual Rates of Change, by Type of Price Index, Selected Intervals 1947–84

	1947 or Earliest Date to 1957	1957–67	1967–77	1977–83/84	1947 or Earliest Date to 1983–84
Full period, eight products:					
1. PPI	0.03	−1.63	1.21	2.20	0.30
2. *CR* unadjusted	−6.56	−4.34	2.03	−1.25	−2.69
3. *CR* adjusted	−8.53	−5.76	−0.36	−2.02	−4.55
4. *CR* unadjusted—PPI	−6.59	−2.71	0.82	−3.45	−2.99
5. Energy-repair effect	−1.97	−1.42	−2.39	−0.77	−1.86
Comparable periods, five products, earliest date to 1983					
6. PPI	−0.86	−1.63	1.22	2.40	0.24
7. Sears	−5.09	−3.39	1.45	3.97	−0.79
8. *CR* unadjusted	−4.07	−4.38	2.29	2.71	−0.89
9. *CR* unadjusted—PPI	−3.21	−2.75	1.07	0.31	−1.13
10. Sears—*CR* unadjusted	−1.02	0.99	−0.84	1.26	0.10
11. *CR* vs. PPI	−8.56	−4.13	−1.57	−4.22	−4.85
a. Mix effect	−3.38	0.04	−0.25	−3.76	−1.72
b. Price index effect	−3.21	−2.75	1.07	0.31	−1.13
c. Energy-repair effect	−1.97	−1.42	−2.39	−0.77	−1.86

Sources for row 11: Row 11a: row 3 minus row 1 minus row 11b minus row 11c. Row 11b: row 9. Row 11c: row 5.

top products are refrigerators, TV sets, the VCRs, but these account for just 65.5 percent of the weight. In contrast to the PPI listed in column 6, which is at 111.8 percent of its 1947 value in 1984, the unadjusted *CR* index declines in 1984 to 36.5 percent on a 1947 base, and the adjusted *CR* index declines in 1984 to 17.8 percent.

The differences between the *CR* and the PPI indexes are quite radical in size and implications, especially in contrast to the much smaller differences found by Triplett and McDonald (1977) between the PPI for refrigerator-freezers and their quality-adjusted PPI based on hedonic regression coefficients. Part of the greater rate of decline of the *CR* indexes occurs because they generally commence earlier than the PPI and for some products display rapid rates of price decline in the years when the PPI for that product does not exist (an extreme case is the VCR, which has no PPI at all). To address this issue, table 7.24 summarizes the annual growth rates of alternative price indexes for appliances. The top section of the table simply reports the average growth rates of the three indexes in table 7.23 over selected intervals. The bottom part of the table summarizes growth rates of the five products where we also have Sears indexes (pooled rather than adjacent-year hedonic indexes are used for three products and matched model indexes for two products). The five-product comparisons differ in that the growth rates are computed only for those years when *CR*, Sears, and the PPI are all available, and thus none of the differences displayed in rows 9 and 10 can be attributed to differences in the time span of coverage.

The implications of the alternative indexes and methods of calculation are shown in rows 4, 5, and 9–11. For the full period when the *CR* indexes are available, the unadjusted *CR* index changes at an annual rate of −2.99 percent relative to the PPI (row 4), and this difference ranges from −6.59 percent in 1947–57 to 0.82 in 1967–77. In addition, the adjustment of the *CR* indexes for energy and repair costs (row 5) introduces an additional average annual change of −1.86 percent, and this ranges between −2.39 percent in 1967–77 to −0.77 percent in 1977–84.

The average annual difference between the *CR* index and the PPI shown in row 9 for five products and comparable time periods is much smaller than for eight products and the full time period in row 5. This difference is called the *mix effect*, is reported separately in row 11a, and is very large in 1947–57 and in 1977–84, but is quite small during the middle two decades (1957–77). In the early period, this difference reflects primarily the extremely rapid rate of decline of the *CR* price index for television sets from 1947 to the introduction of the PPI for TV sets in 1952. Yet this typical "new product learning-curve effect" was not limited to a product with a tiny initial sales volume. Instead, the value of TV set shipments was already very significant by 1949, with a one-third share of the six products covered in this chapter (see the notes to table 7.23). In the final interval of 1977–84, the "mix effect" in line 11a reflects the influence of both microwave ovens and VCRs, with the *CR* index for microwaves having a much more rapid rate of decline than that of the PPI, and with the very fast decline in VCR prices missing from the PPI. Recall that the change in the *CR* index for VCRs applies only to the limited time period 1980–84.

The unadjusted *CR* index is compared to the Sears indexes for five products in row 10. As in rows 6–9, indexes for a given product are compared only for the time span for which all three indexes (PPI, Sears, and *CR*) are available. In row 10, we see that, on average from the earliest comparable date to 1983, the weighted average change in the Sears index was just 0.10 percent per annum greater than that of the unadjusted *CR* index. Differences were greater in individual subintervals, ranging from −1.02 percent from the earliest date through 1957, to 1.26 percent for the final subinterval (1977–83).

The final results of the chapter are summarized in row 11, which reports the difference between the adjusted *CR* index and the PPI, and decomposes this difference into a mix effect, the "price index effect" (i.e., different measures of price change for the same product over the same period), and the energy-repair cost effect. The mix effect is a slight misnomer, since it combines a different mix of products for the years when the PPI is unavailable with the different rates of price change for two of the products (dishwashers and microwave ovens) included in the group of eight but not the group of five. The energy-repair cost effect is simply the difference between the two *CR* indexes and is copied from row 5 into row 11c. The price index effect applies to the five common products and is copied from row 9 into row 11b. The mix effect is a residual, calculated as row 11 (which in turn equals row 3 minus row 1) minus row 11b minus 11c.

We can see that the three sources of difference between the adjusted *CR* index and the PPI vary in importance over the different subintervals. The mix effect and price index effect are of roughly equal importance before 1957. The mix effect is close to zero from 1957 to 1967, when the price index effect is of greatest importance. The differences between the unadjusted *CR* index and the PPI during this period occur by a similar order of magnitude for four out of the five common products, with virtually no difference for TV sets. After 1967, the pure price index effect reverses sign, since the PPI increases less rapidly than the unadjusted *CR*. This finding is supportive of the hypothesis that the BLS has adjusted for quality improvements (excluding energy and repair costs) more completely and accurately in the last half of the postwar period than in the first half. After 1967, the continued decline of the *CR* adjusted index relative to the PPI is mainly attributable to the energy-repair adjustment in 1967–77 (this was the period of the greatest improvements in the repair and energy costs of TV sets), and to the mix effect (mainly microwave ovens and VCRs after 1977).

This chapter concludes that the PPI radically understates the enormous decline in the prices of electric appliances that has occurred over the postwar years. The conclusion for the CPI is the same, since the CPI and PPI exhibit similar behavior, except that the greater decline in the CPI than in the PPI for refrigerators and TV sets from 1947 to 1957 would add about 1.3 percent to the weighted average annual rate of price decline exhibited by the PPI for that interval in table 7.24.[48] This difference between the new indexes and the PPI is attributed to three main factors. First is the conceptual difference that no explicit allowance is made by the PPI for changes in energy and repair costs attributable to the manufacturer (i.e., changes from one model to the next computed at constant energy and repair prices). Second is the fact that the PPI is often introduced several years after the introduction of new products that typically exhibit their greatest rates of price decline in the first part of their product cycle. Late introductions in the PPI are most important for TV sets and dishwashers. The CPI is even worse, with indexes for room air conditioners and clothes dryers introduced more than a decade after the comparable PPIs. The third factor is the traditional concern of the literature on quality change—an upward bias in the PPI due to the failure to adjust adequately for quality improvements (other than energy and repairs) for comparable products over comparable time intervals. This bias was significant before 1967, at a rate of about 3 percent per year, but disappeared after 1967.

The extent of the pure quality-change effect is based on the behavior of the unadjusted *CR* indexes, which, unlike the Sears catalog indexes, compare the prices of all the best-selling models, with as many as fifteen or twenty brands included in the majority of the price comparisons. The PPI has greater coverage across time, since monthly price changes are compiled, but this

---

48. As in the rest of the book, I stress the behavior of the PPI here, since it is the source of the NIPA deflators for producers durable equipment.

advantage is unimportant for the study of price changes over multiyear intervals. Outweighing the greater temporal time coverage of the PPI is the greater brand-name coverage of the *CR* indexes, and the fact that *CR* reflects market trends by concentrating on the model types that account for the greatest share of sales of a given product.[49] Thus, in the sense relevant for multiyear price comparisons, the *CR* indexes are probably based on more brands and more observations than the PPI. This is particularly true after 1959, when the *CR* published prices for most products are themselves averages of shopper surveys that collect numerous price quotations for each specific model included in the ratings. Thus, the *CR* indexes after 1959 can be interpreted as quality-adjusted indexes of true "transactions prices."

There is little reason to believe that the PPI is any more accurate for products omitted from this chapter than from those included. The most important omission, by value of shipments in 1983, is audio equipment. There can be no doubt that solid-state technology, quartz tuning, and other improvements have resulted in dramatic reductions in the price of audio equipment relative to performance. Prices of compact-disk players have been dropping as rapidly as those of VCRs. Yet the 1985 PPI for "other home electronic equipment" was 100.5 on a 1967 base. And electronics are also becoming more common in "white goods" (i.e., major appliances), allowing very rapid reductions in the price of including advanced electronic control features.[50]

As radical as the *CR* price indexes may seem, with a weighted average rate of price *decline* for appliances (including the energy-repair adjustment) of 4.55 percent a year compared to the 0.30 percent annual *increase* registered by the PPI, for each of the eight product categories this chapter has provided information on dimensions of quality improvement that are not taken into account in the quantitative measures of price change taken from *CR*. Thus, surprising as it may seem, a good case can be made not only that the PPI (and to a lesser extent the CPI) understates the rate of price decline by a large amount, but that even the new *CR* indexes contain at least a modest further understatement as the result of additional unmeasured quality improvements.

49. Triplett and McDonald (1977, 140) comment that "the number of refrigerator-freezer prices collected for the WPI is far too small to estimate reliable hedonic functions."

50. General Electric has introduced refrigerators that have an array of diagnostic options and a sensor that notes when the door is left open, and dishwashers that have a programmable timer and washer load options and that also shut off and alert the user if the spray arm is blocked. The electronics on the first "digital dishwasher" cost $200, but by 1984 had fallen to $50 and were projected to decline to $25 in subsequent years ("Look Ma, No Dials," *Business Week*, 12 November 1984, 97).

8　New and Used Automobiles

8.1　Introduction

Along with computers, new and used automobiles have received more attention in studies of price and quality change than any other product. In fact, it has been suggested that there is no need for yet another study of automobile prices, since it is possible to piece together a hedonic price index for automobiles, at least through 1971, from the various papers written by Zvi Griliches, both by himself (1961, 1964) and in collaboration with Makoto Ohta (1976).[1] My justification for including this chapter on automobiles is twofold. First, the most interesting issues and puzzles in the measurement of auto prices emerge in the period after the sample period of the Griliches and Ohta-Griliches regression equations (which spans 1947–71).[2] In particular, there is a much greater discrepancy between a hedonic regression index and the CPI for new cars after 1971 than over the 1947–71 period, which has been studied before. Second, the most important changes in automobile quality characteristics in the period after 1971, particularly safety and pollution equipment and changing fuel economy, are not particularly suited to the hedonic method. A full treatment of quality and price changes since 1971 requires that the hedonic technique be combined with the specification method and with a comparison of "closely similar" models over time. Thus, the main focus of this chapter is on the questions that cannot be answered by running "one more hedonic regression." This section introduces the main puzzles,

---

1. This point was made forcefully by Jack Triplett in his comments on the 1974 draft of this chapter.
2. In the original Griliches (1961) paper, the sample period includes 1937, 1950, and 1954–60. Griliches (1964) covers 1947–61. The Ohta and Griliches (1976) paper presents hedonic price indexes for new cars covering each year over the interval 1955–71 and for used cars over 1961–71. Ohta and Griliches (1986) estimate regression equations for the 1970s but do not include time dummy variables or calculate a hedonic price index from the estimated coefficients.

and the rest of the chapter is primarily devoted to combining old and new evidence in a way that helps solve them.

1. In contrast to the 1940s and 1950s, the time period covered in Griliches's first hedonic regression study, when a hedonic price index for new autos rises at a slower rate than the BLS indexes (CPI and PPI), the relation was completely reversed in the 1970s and 1980s. The hedonic price index for new cars developed here rises much faster than the BLS indexes after 1970, with an annual rate of increase for 1970–83 of 8.0 percent compared to an annual rate of increase for the CPI of just 5.0 percent. Can a case be made that the BLS indexes are biased downward, that the hedonic indexes are biased upward, or that the "truth" lies somewhere in between? To what extent can adjustments for safety and pollution devices in the BLS indexes explain this discrepancy, given that the hedonic technique cannot cope with changes in quality that take place on all models at the same time?[3]

2. A new issue that arises after 1970 is the divergent behavior of the CPI indexes for new and used cars. The annual rates of increase for 1970–84 are, respectively, 4.8 and 9.6 percent. If the average price of a one-year-old car was 22 percent less than the price of a new car in 1970, then the average price of a one-year-old car in 1984 would have been 45 percent more than that of a new car![4] Since this remarkable implication is at odds with the basic facts of the auto market in the 1980s, something must have gone wrong at the BLS to account for the inconsistent time-series behavior of the CPI indexes for new and used cars. I address this question by attempting to provide new quality adjustments for used cars that are consistent with the CPI quality adjustments for new cars.

3. The inconsistent behavior of the BLS price indexes for new and used cars is not just a harmless quirk, but has profound consequences for the PDE deflator, the main focus of this book. PDE for automobiles is calculated by adding purchases of new cars and then subtracting sales of used cars from the business sector to the household sector.[5] Because the price index for new cars (a component of the PPI that behaves similarly to the CPI for new cars) increases much more slowly than the CPI used car index used to deflate used car sales in the PDE, the resulting implicit deflator for auto PDE displays a time series path that can only be described as bizarre. As shown below in table 8.8 in columns 1 and 3, after increasing at an annual rate of 6.4 percent per year between 1970 and 1980 (not too far above the CPI rate of 5.2 percent), the PDE deflator for cars decreases at a rate of 7.1 percent per year from 1980 to 1984. This absolute decrease of over 25 percent in three years occurs at a time when the CPI index for new cars rises by 16 percent.

---

3. This limitation of the hedonic technique is discussed by Triplett (1969, 416–17).

4. In 1970, the nine Buick models in the data set sold as one-year-old cars for 78 percent of the price of the same models when new in 1969, according to the *NADA Used Car Guide*. The calculation in the text implicitly assumes that the CPI index for used cars, which applies to all ages of used cars, can be used to compute the price increase of one-year-old cars.

5. My understanding is that automobiles are the only category of PDE for which used purchases are subtracted from new purchases.

4. In keeping with the emphasis in this book on quality adjustments to take account of changes in energy efficiency, this chapter assesses the implications of previous studies of changes in automobile gas mileage by Crandall et al. (1986) and Wilcox (1984). Fuel economy changes are an important type of quality change with which the hedonic regression technique cannot cope, and previous investigators have found that fuel economy enters regression equations either insignificantly or with the wrong sign, partly because it is collinear with weight.[6] Changes in fuel economy call for explicit quality adjustments, like those introduced in the previous chapter on appliances. One might expect the neglect of improvements in fuel economy to impart an upward bias to an automobile price index. However, some of the improvement in fuel economy may already be implicit in the BLS indexes, which did not treat the "downsizing" of cars in the late 1970s as a quality deterioration, at least partially on the ground that smaller size was balanced by improved fuel economy.

A large number of technical topics in the construction of hedonic price indexes for automobiles is treated in the Ohta and Griliches (1976) paper (hereafter O-G), and I do not retrace the same ground here. The construction of hedonic price indexes is straightforward, and the presentation of results is brief, for the new work goes beyond previous hedonic studies mainly by extending the time coverage over the entire 1947–83 interval. Thus there are thirty-six adjacent-year regression equations for both new and used cars, compared to fourteen postwar new car equations in Griliches (1964), sixteen for new cars in O-G, and ten for used cars in O-G.[7]

After examining the hedonic regression results, I then turn to further adjustments needed to reconcile the behavior of the hedonic indexes and the CPI, and to explain the behavior of the used car indexes (both CPI and hedonic) relative to the corresponding new car indexes. Among the data sources used for these adjustments are the studies of safety and environmental equipment by Crandall et al. (1976), and of fuel economy by the Crandall team and by Wilcox (1984). Also examined is the time series of BLS quality adjustments made to the CPI over the 1968–84 period, based on BLS press releases, and a related unpublished list of year-to-year quality changes compiled by General Motors over the full postwar period.

8.2 Issues That Arise in Estimating Hedonic Regressions for Automobiles

8.2.1 The Distinction between Performance and Physical Characteristics

The hedonic analysis assumes a two-stage process in which the utility of the automobile user (for autos used as consumer goods) and the ability of autos

---

6. Hogarty (1972, 9) reports this negative finding and states that similar results were reported by Cowling and Cubbin (1972).

7. Other sources are Kravis and Lipsey (1971), which presents a hedonic price index for automobiles for the years 1953, 1957, and 1961–64, and Triplett (1969), which presents a hedonic index for 1960–66.

to produce capital services (for autos used as PDE) are functions of a vector of performance characteristics (z), which is in turn "produced" by a vector of physical characteristics (x):

(8.1) $U = U(z_1, \ldots, z_N) = U(z),$

(8.2) $z = h(x_1, \ldots, x_N; t) = h(x; t),$

where t enters (8.2) on the assumption that the production function converting physical into performance characteristics can change over time.

The principal performance characteristics (z) of an automobile are interior dimensions, opulence of upholstery and trim, quality of ride, trunk space, handling, braking, acceleration, fuel economy, frequency and cost of repair, and depreciation. Ideally, these characteristics could be used to explain the prices of automobiles in hedonic regression equations. However, owing to data limitations, most hedonic regression studies have been based on physical characteristics (x), typically weight, length, horsepower, and dummy variables for accessories (automatic transmission, power steering, power brakes, air conditioning, etc.). If relative input prices remain steady, and if technological change can be ignored (i.e., if the h function does not vary over time), then physical characteristics may be acceptable proxies for performance characteristics in hedonic regression equations. Indeed, O-G demonstrate (367–78) that performance and physical characteristics are able to explain automobile prices with an approximately equal fit for the short period 1963–66.[8] This would tend to indicate that the h function is stable, allowing the investigator to choose variables based on the accessibility of data.

But the use of either physical or available performance data entails problems. The existing performance data are imperfect and could introduce measurement error that might have a significant secular bias. While dimensions, fuel economy, and acceleration are amenable to precise measurement, quality of ride, handling, and quality of trim are not. Such descriptions as we have of these characteristics are qualitative. CR, which is the major source of performance data used in previous studies, explicitly warns readers that qualitative descriptions of ride or handling as "good" or "excellent" are valid only for comparisons of cars in a given year and do not have the same meaning in other years. For instance, CR intoned in 1957 (April, 160) that "a car reported as having a good ride in 1940 would by today's standards be intolerably poor."[9] While there are more precise engineering measures of ride

---

8. This simply indicates that the z and x variables were highly correlated over their particular time period and does not rule out secular shifts in the h function over longer periods. Hogarty (1972) also estimates hedonic regression equations with performance attributes over the longer period 1958–71 and finds only a minimal difference in the resulting price indexes compared to similar equations using physical characteristics.

9. The problem of comparability over time of qualitative remarks about performance is recognized by O-G, but then ignored in practice.

Table 8.1   **Physical Characteristics of the 1976 and 1977 General Motors Full-sized Cars**

	1976	1977	Change (%)
1. Exterior:			
Length (inches)	226.0	213.8	−5.4
Width (inches)	78.9	75.4	−4.4
Wheel base (inches)	123.4	115.9	−6.1
Weight (pounds)	4423	3685	−16.7
2. Interior:			
Front head room (inches)	38.3	38.8	1.3
Rear head room (inches)	37.2	38.0	2.2
Rear leg room (inches)	38.5	39.5	2.6
Rear knee clearance (inches)	3.6	3.7	2.8
Trunk capacity (cubic feet)	18.8	20.3	8.0
3. Other:			
Horsepower	145	145	0.0
EPA fuel rating (city/highway)	13/18	16/21	23/17
List price	$5,013	$5,357	6.9

Source: Sections 1 and 2 are from Callahan (1976) and refer to the Pontiac Catalina. Other figures refer to the Chevrolet Caprice.

("spring rate") and handling ("skid pad tests"), these are only imperfect proxies for what the consumer thinks of as "ride" and "handling," and they are difficult to compile for a statistical study.[10]

While the physical characteristics used in this and other studies are quantitative, the h function linking them to performance may shift over time. In fact, one could view a basic function of engineers as working to achieve shifts in that function by finding ways of improving performance relative to "physical inputs." A dramatic example of such a shift is provided by the downsizing of General Motors "full-sized" cars in 1977. In the course of a single model changeover, there were decreases in quantities of the physical characteristics that enter hedonic regression equations as explanatory variables, while simultaneously there were increases in many of the measures of performance characteristics.[11] As shown in table 8.1, weight declined by 738 pounds, or 16.7 percent, overall length dropped by over a foot, and exterior width was reduced by three inches. At the same time, each of the five interior dimensions rose. Further, there was no decrease in other aspects of performance. *CR* (February 1977, 81) praised the downsized Chevrolet Caprice (a twin of the Pontiac Catalina): "General Motors has already shrunk its 'full-sized' [models]. And, judging by our tests of the Chevrolet Caprice, GM has in the process improved gas mileage while losing nothing in the comfort and interior roominess one expects of a large car. . . . So General Motors,

10. These examples of engineering proxies were suggested by Jack Triplett.

11. For an illuminating earlier discussion of the shifting relation between the weight characteristic and "true quality," see Triplett (1969, 414–17). He points out that weight is actually an undesirable characteristic, and that this problem was also recognized by Griliches (1961) and Court (1939).

Table 8.2 Factory Installed Equipment on U.S.-Made Cars, Selected Years, 1953–83 (all figures are percentages of total cars manufactured)

	1948	1953	1958	1963	1968	1973	1978	1983
1. Automatic transmission	33.3	49.4	76.8	76.3	89.0	93.4	93.1	86.6
2. Four-speed transmission	N.A.	0.0	0.0	3.8	3.8	4.1	6.4	6.1
3. Air conditioning	0.0	0.0	4.6	14.1	44.3	72.6	80.8	83.5
a. Manual control						65.3	70.3	71.0
b. Automatic control						7.3	10.5	12.5
4. Disc brakes	0.0	0.0	0.0	0.0	12.7	85.7	100.0	95.2
5. Power steering	0.0	11.7	42.8	50.1	80.0	87.7	92.7	90.5
6. Power brakes	0.0	8.2	29.8	27.2	44.9	75.5	86.0	95.2
7. Radial tires	0.0	0.0	0.0	0.0	0.0	13.3	84.8	99.9
8. Radio	0.0	0.0	0.0	61.6	87.9	94.0	80.2	86.8
a. AM only						64.0	31.0	14.6
b. AM-FM only						9.3	12.6	3.7
c. Stereo radio						15.4	21.1	42.4
d. Stereo tape				0.0	2.4	5.3	15.5	26.1
9. Power door locks						13.8	26.1	39.0
10. Power seats, four or six way			9.0	7.3	9.3	14.3	19.5	30.3
11. Power windows		6.6	6.3	12.2	17.6	25.7	28.4	37.9
12. Vinyl roofs						48.9	35.5	26.5
13. Tinted glass		31.6	27.7	51.7	69.5	78.9	86.9	89.0
14. Wheel covers						72.0	70.8	N.A.
15. Clock						42.0	51.3	59.2
16. Adjustable steering column				2.5	9.5	18.6	38.7	56.2
17. Rear window defogger						16.4	39.1	59.0
18. Remote control side mirror						58.6	77.4	85.5
19. Cruise control				0.0	4.1	10.6	35.7	N.A.

Sources: Wards Automotive Yearbook and *Automotive Facts and Figures,* various issues.

long the champion of big cars, has proved that with good design a car doesn't need all that 'road-hugging weight' to handle well and ride comfortably."[12]

8.2.2 The Treatment of Extra Equipment, Both Standard and Optional

A problem with either physical or performance characteristics is the probable existence of omitted characteristics. Automobiles have been including more and more types of additional equipment that go beyond the traditional physical characteristics of weight, length, and horsepower. Table 8.2 brings together for selected years the available evidence on factory-installed equipment in domestic U.S. automobiles. For almost every type of equipment, the percentages indicate increased coverage over time, and only a few of these, particularly automatic transmission (AT), air conditioning (AC), power steering (PS), and power brakes (PB), have been explicitly taken into account in previous hedonic studies. A serious problem of interpretation of the

12. For further praise of this model, voted *Motor Trend*'s 1977 "Car of the Year," see *Motor Trend,* February 1977, 26–32.

data in table 8.2 arises, however, because, except for a few major items, we do not know what fraction of factory-installed equipment is standard equipment and what fraction is purchased as optional equipment. Since the dependent variable in a regression for new cars is the price including standard equipment but excluding options, while the price in a used-car regression includes both standard equipment and options, a growing share of optional equipment might create an inconsistency between new car and used car price indexes and might possibly help account for the greater relative rise over time of used car than of new car indexes.

Two approaches to the "extra equipment" issue have been taken in the past. A direct approach is to include dummy variables for the presence of each item. Multicollinearity may lead to unstable or wrongly signed coefficients on some of these variables, and, rather than estimating the price of a piece of equipment, the coefficients may pick up luxury models or classes of cars that come "highly equipped." A more direct approach, which is feasible only for some of the major pieces of equipment, is to "strip" the price of the item from the price of cars on which it is included as standard equipment. Two types of prices are defined in the data below, "loaded" with all items included as standard, and on a standardized "stripped basis" that includes only a heater and AM radio but is adjusted to exclude AT, AC, and other major types of equipment included as standard. For a car that includes a heater and AM radio as standard equipment, but that is equipped with AT and AC purchased as optional equipment, the loaded and stripped price would be the same.

O-G also standardize their price data to eliminate the need to include dummy variables for extra items of equipment. Instead of stripping, they standardize their observations to include the price of a heater, AT, and PS, and to exclude AC.[13] If the price of AT and PS increase at a slower rate than the "basic car," then the standardized O-G price would increase more slowly than the "stripped" price computed for this study.

Tables 8.3 and 8.4 list means of prices and the major physical characteristics separately for new cars and used cars, respectively. Both the loaded and the stripped price are shown for each year between 1947 and 1983, and table 8.5 shows the ratio of the stripped to the loaded price for both new and used cars. For new cars, the ratio of the stripped to the loaded price declined from 100 percent in the late 1940s to 87–89 percent after 1973. For used cars, the stripped price fell from 101 percent in the late 1940s to 88 percent since 1975.

A problem that O-G ignore, and I handle only partially, was initially raised in chapter 3. This concerns the inconsistency of the price and weight data. The data on shipping weight used as an explanatory variable refer to the car

---

13. A second variant treats power steering as a "cost of weight and size" and includes the price of power steering only for those cars where it is standard equipment. However, a comparison of tables 8.2 and 8.3 indicates that power steering seems to be desired for itself, not as a byproduct of weight and size, since the average weight of new cars in the early 1980s plummeted well below the levels of the late 1940s and early 1950s, yet power steering was included on 91 percent of 1983 models, as compared to just 12 percent in 1953.

Table 8.3   Mean Values of New Car Sample, 1947–83

	Price Loaded	Price Stripped	Weight	Length	Brake Horsepower
1947	1,554	1,554	3,503	206.7	106
1948	1,737	1,735	3,482	207.0	105
1949	1,974	1,964	3,422	202.5	109
1950	2,023	1,997	3,525	204.8	111
1951	2,192	2,150	3,545	205.2	113
1952	2,390	2,343	3,600	206.3	124
1953	2,381	2,365	3,571	205.5	129
1954	2,326	2,313	3,557	207.0	140
1955	2,276	2,261	3,481	205.7	167
1956	2,347	2,290	3,514	206.0	192
1957	2,660	2,561	3,642	208.4	214
1958	2,858	2,747	3,743	213.0	229
1959	2,848	2,725	3,746	214.1	230
1960	2,753	2,640	3,658	211.0	208
1961	2,615	2,517	3,419	206.5	186
1962	2,593	2,495	3,164	201.6	167
1963	2,566	2,468	3,176	202.9	173
1964	2,580	2,481	3,253	205.7	184
1965	2,540	2,388	3,192	203.7	184
1966	2,578	2,426	3,261	204.1	187
1967	2,637	2,470	3,280	206.3	190
1968	2,796	2,624	3,356	207.0	197
1969	2,912	2,651	3,434	208.9	209
1970	3,059	2,768	3,549	211.4	216
1971	3,287	2,958	3,566	210.8	205
1972	3,333	2,984	3,591	210.4	200
1973	3,304	2,941	3,697	212.6	195
1974	3,783	3,348	3,847	213.6	212
1975	4,234	3,726	3,731	211.8	186
1976	4,484	3,924	3,763	211.1	192
1977	4,626	4,030	3,559	208.7	181
1978	5,111	4,461	3,402	205.8	178
1979	5,119	4,484	3,161	200.5	164
1980	5,677	4,996	3,077	200.4	152
1981	7,092	6,262	2,892	194.2	144
1982	7,588	6,822	2,879	191.1	138
1983	7,857	6,984	2,766	187.4	141

equipped with whatever equipment is provided as "standard" (i.e., as part of the price). While I attempt to strip out the weight of AT and PS, as discussed below in section 8.3, this has not been possible for other accessories for which the price is adjusted (e.g., air conditioning in the more recent years). If the price-to-weight ratio of AC is higher than that of the rest of the car, then the process of stripping price but not weight will slightly reduce the coefficient on weight. Similarly, when O-G add the price of AT to a car that is not so equipped, they are raising price without adjusting weight, leading to an upward bias on their coefficient on weight.

The possible inconsistency of the weight and price data raise two more general problems with the hedonic regression equations. First, weight is

Table 8.4   Mean Values of Used Car Sample, 1947–83

	Price Loaded	Price Stripped	Weight	Length	Brake Horsepower
1947	1,862	1,887	3,509	207.0	106
1948	2,017	2,032	3,477	206.4	105
1949	1,558	1,596	3,493	207.6	105
1950	1,545	1,571	3,462	207.2	108
1951	1,719	1,734	3,539	204.9	110
1952	1,860	1,873	3,577	206.0	114
1953	1,810	1,837	3,605	206.6	121
1954	1,624	1,660	3,561	205.9	126
1955	1,711	1,742	3,662	208.7	141
1956	1,684	1,661	3,649	208.8	163
1957	1,843	1,766	3,614	207.9	189
1958	1,800	1,712	3,675	208.9	208
1959	1,939	1,840	3,756	211.4	230
1960	1,896	1,773	3,857	214.4	245
1961	1,857	1,765	3,786	213.5	238
1962	1,760	1,676	3,549	209.1	204
1963	1,804	1,740	3,296	203.4	179
1964	1,790	1,723	3,228	202.7	176
1965	1,817	1,707	3,257	199.0	186
1966	1,693	1,577	3,249	204.5	191
1967	1,757	1,630	3,245	203.8	191
1968	1,910	1,777	3,331	205.6	198
1969	1,837	1,637	3,396	208.5	204
1970	2,100	1,867	3,465	209.9	213
1971	2,138	1,899	3,501	210.7	215
1972	2,321	2,058	3,548	210.5	212
1973	2,310	2,047	3,600	211.6	206
1974	2,479	2,194	3,674	212.5	200
1975	2,977	2,632	3,760	215.7	194
1976	3,452	3,048	3,776	209.4	197
1977	3,393	2,987	3,730	211.0	186
1978	3,763	3,311	3,564	208.1	182
1979	3,750	3,300	3,420	205.7	179
1980	4,142	3,644	3,283	203.5	170
1981	5,080	4,470	3,149	201.6	159
1982	5,574	4,905	3,051	200.0	149
1983	6,037	5,316	2,922	193.4	142

highly unsatisfactory as a proxy for desired performance characteristics, particularly "quality of ride." Even prior to the post-1973 era of high fuel prices, engineers strived to eliminate unnecessary weight, and cars of equivalent quality have become lighter. The downsizing of the full-sized GM models detailed in table 8.1 is the best example of this phenomenon, and the earlier examples of the "thin-wall" casting process and the utilization of aluminum, plastics, and light alloys were suggested by Triplett (1969, 416). Particularly in the post-1973 era of higher fuel prices, the inclusion of weight in a hedonic regression equation seems increasingly an anachronism. Weight acts as an unsatisfactory proxy both for size and for luxuriousness of equipment. An improved approach would be to replace the standard weight

Table 8.5   Ratios from Tables 8.3 and 8.4

	Stripped Used Price/New Price	Stripped Used/New 1.5 Years Back	New Cars Stripped/Loaded	Used Cars Stripped/Loaded
1947	1.21		1.00	1.01
1948	1.17		1.00	1.01
1949	0.81	0.97	0.99	1.02
1950	0.79	0.85	0.99	1.02
1951	0.81	0.88	0.98	1.01
1952	0.80	0.90	0.98	1.01
1953	0.78	0.82	0.99	1.01
1954	0.72	0.71	0.99	1.02
1955	0.77	0.74	0.99	1.02
1956	0.73	0.73	0.98	0.99
1957	0.69	0.78	0.96	0.96
1958	0.62	0.71	0.96	0.95
1959	0.68	0.69	0.96	0.95
1960	0.67	0.65	0.96	0.94
1961	0.70	0.66	0.96	0.95
1962	0.67	0.65	0.96	0.95
1963	0.71	0.69	0.96	0.96
1964	0.69	0.69	0.96	0.96
1965	0.71	0.69	0.94	0.94
1966	0.65	0.65	0.94	0.93
1967	0.66	0.68	0.94	0.93
1968	0.68	0.73	0.94	0.93
1969	0.62	0.64	0.91	0.89
1970	0.67	0.71	0.90	0.89
1971	0.64	0.70	0.90	0.89
1972	0.69	0.72	0.90	0.89
1973	0.70	0.69	0.89	0.89
1974	0.66	0.74	0.89	0.89
1975	0.71	0.84	0.88	0.88
1976	0.78	0.86	0.88	0.88
1977	0.74	0.78	0.87	0.88
1978	0.74	0.83	0.87	0.88
1979	0.74	0.78	0.88	0.88
1980	0.73	0.81	0.88	0.88
1981	0.71	0.94	0.88	0.88
1982	0.72	0.87	0.90	0.88
1983	0.76	0.81	0.89	0.88

Sources by column: (**1**) Table 8.4 col. 2 divided by table 8.3 col. 2. (**2**) Table 8.4 col. 2 divided by average of table 8.3, col. 2, dated one and two years earlier. (**3**) Table 8.3 col. 2 divided by table 8.3 col. 1. (**4**) Table 8.4 col. 2 divided by table 8.4 col. 1.

and length variables with interior dimensions and trunk capacity, and then to handle discrete items of equipment on a one-for-one basis. This procedure is not attempted here, simply because the basic data source, the used car guides, list the standard physical variables for each model but not the required interior dimensions and trunk space. While these are available from *CR,* the effort to match these with the corresponding new car and used car prices was beyond the feasible scope of the study.

The second problem applies to the suggestion in the previous paragraph that discrete items of equipment might be handled on a one-for-one basis, as in the CPI. The application of such adjustments to a hedonic index raises the possibility of double counting, due to the likelihood in principle that any left-out performance characteristic may be correlated with one or more of the variables included in the hedonic regression. For instance, environmental control or safety equipment (e.g., crash-resistant bumpers) may affect weight and/or horsepower, and an adjustment to subtract out the value of such equipment from a hedonic regression index that already incorporates the effect of weight and horsepower would involve double counting. I return to this issue below when examining differences in the secular behavior of the CPI and the hedonic regression index in the period since 1967, during which a substantial amount of environmental and safety equipment has been added to U.S. automobiles.

In addition to the major accessories (AT, PS, PB, and AC), numerous smaller items have been added to the standard equipment of automobiles over time (e.g., directional signals, seat belts, two-speed windshield wipers, and many others). If a complete list of the price and weight of these items were available for every model, the process of stripping could be applied to them as well. An improved hedonic index would result, subject to the limitation imposed by the second qualification above, that in principle there could be a correlation between one or more of these items and some variables besides weight that is included in the hedonic regression equation. Unfortunately, a complete list detailing all items added or subtracted from every model in every year is not available, preventing the technique of stripping from being applied.

In this study, government-mandated safety and antipollution devices are treated as improvements in quality rather than increases in price. This approach is followed to conform to BLS practice in the PPI and CPI, facilitating comparisons of those indexes with these results. There is a debate as to whether the BLS approach is appropriate. Some approve the BLS procedure of treating government-mandated devices as a quality improvement rather than a price increase, on the assumption that the democratic process that mandates these devices reflects "the will of the people" and that, implicitly, benefits from increased safety and cleaner air balance the costs. Others claim that the regulations have gone too far and have been inefficiently administered, leading to costs that have outweighed benefits (see, in particular, Crandall et al. 1976, 155–61). Probably the best approach is to keep track of quality adjustments for these government-mandated items separately, since it may be appropriate to include them as quality rather than price increases for some purposes (e.g., measuring productivity changes in the automobile-producing industry), while treating them as price rather than quality increases for other purposes (e.g., measuring the effective capital input of automobiles in industries using automobiles as a producer durable good).

8.2.3   Used Car Prices and the Transaction Prices of New Cars

The ideal price index for automobiles, as for any product, would be based on changes in transaction prices fully adjusted for changes in quality. Previous hedonic indexes for new cars have been based on manufacturers advertised list prices, which may differ from true transactions prices in the presence of discounts or premiums. Since about 1960, the CPI has kept track of discounts and thus is probably closer to a transaction price measure than a hedonic index based on list prices. However, the validity of allowance in the CPI for discounts and premiums before 1960 is open to question.

The last section of this chapter examines the effects of taking an index of late-model used car prices, adjusted for changes in the depreciation rate, as a proxy for the transaction prices of new cars. This makes a substantial difference in the late 1940s and early 1950s, due to premiums charged on new cars at that time.[14] By far the greatest difference between the CPI and my "final" index occurs in the early years of the postwar period, and I interpret this shift as a result of a change from premiums to discounts in the relation of transactions prices of new cars to list prices. Large differences also arise between hedonic indexes for new cars and the new car CPI, but these differences are probably the result of inadequate quality corrections in the hedonic indexes.

8.3   Data Used in the Hedonic Regression Study

The basic data for the hedonic regression equations in this chapter come from two sources. For the period 1947–69, the source is the 1 July edition of National Market Reports' *Red Book: National Used Car Market Report* (hereafter NMR), which was published every six weeks during that time period.[15] For the period 1969–83, the source was the October edition of the *NADA Official Used Car Guide,* which is published monthly.[16] Both guides contain data on physical characteristics, new car list prices, and estimates of retail used car transaction prices for all automobile models produced in the United States (and, recently, all major imports).

New car list prices in the guides are supplied by manufacturers. These include the cost of all standard equipment but no optional equipment. They also exclude state and local taxes, shipping charges, and dealer preparation charges. Where do the guides obtain their estimates of used car prices? There

14. In January 1949, *CR* calculates the percentage of the new list price that must be paid for used 1948 models as follows: Chevrolet 168 percent, Ford 153 percent, Buick 151 percent, Pontiac 165 percent, and Plymouth 148 percent. In contrast, in April 1970 (198), *CR* quotes an FTC study documenting the prevalence of discounts of from 15 to 20 percent of the sticker price.

15. I am grateful to Fred Heffinger, president of National Market Reports, for allowing me to monopolize his xerox machine for almost two days to copy the data.

16. Both sources apply to the central United States ("region A" for NMR, "Midwest region" for NADA). We have both sources for the overlap year 1969.

are two main sources.[17] First, sales reports are submitted from dealers. The number of transactions is claimed to be "large," and prices are presumably free from influence by any single dealer or group of dealers.[18] The second major source of information is the wholesale auto auction report. There are over 100 auto auctions located throughout the United States. Auctions may be better indications of value than dealer reports on wholesale prices, since the latter involve problems of interpreting inflated trade-in values. The major limitation of auctions is their thinness, but variations of prices so caused would presumably be dampened by the process of averaging over 100 auction reports. The NADA *Guide* is based roughly one-third on retail dealer used car reports, one-third on wholesale dealer used car reports, and one-third on auto auction reports.[19]

8.3.1   Characteristics of the Sample

The sample includes observations on every four-door sedan manufactured by Chrysler, Ford, and General Motors (the "Big Three") and by American Motors since 1977, except for the three luxury makes (Imperial, Lincoln or Continental, and Cadillac). The luxury makes are excluded to avoid biasing coefficients. Previous research has shown that these luxury makes are substantially overpriced in relation to their "quality" as measured by the standard hedonic physical characteristic variables.[20] Cars made by firms other than the Big Three are also excluded; this reduced the clerical time in collecting the data set while excluding only a small portion of sales. Imported cars are also excluded, so that the resulting hedonic price index (like the PPI) applies to domestic U.S. production, not domestic U.S. purchases.

In comparison to the O-G paper, the regression equations in this chapter include more observations in each year for new cars and fewer for used cars. This reflects a difference in emphasis. O-G included six vintages of used cars in each year of their sample period (1961–71) and made an extensive study of depreciation patterns and their interaction with make effects. There is no reason to duplicate this aspect of the O-G study, and instead only a single depreciation rate from one-year-old to two-year-old status is estimated. Other differences are that O-G include both four-door sedans and four-door hardtops, while I include only sedans; I include all trim variations and engine

17. The following description is paraphrased from the introduction of the *NADA Official Used Car Guide,* July 1973, E-1–E-8.

18. Fred Heffinger of NMR in a discussion with me estimated that, at the time (1970), roughly 10,000 dealer reports and other pieces of information are digested for each issue, and that each report refers to multiple transactions.

19. The NADA explanation also states that the raw data received by the publishers are edited to reduce measurement error. High and low limits from a norm are established to weed out clerical errors and "junker" sales.

20. Although most hedonic regression studies have included dummy variables for luxury cars ("prestige effects"), the original Griliches (1961) study did not. O-G report an average new car "make effect" for Cadillac, Continental, and Imperial beginning in 1960 of 31.4 percent relative to Chevrolet.

types (at least through 1976) while they include only a subset; and I treat accessories differently. As we shall see, these differences appear to make little difference in the results, as the new index for new cars is a virtual mirror image of the O-G index during the overlap period (1955–71), and the used car index is almost as close (for 1961–71). Because of this overlap, the discussion below concentrates on the periods where the new coverage is unique (1972–83 for new cars and both 1947–60 and 1972–83 for used cars).[21]

All the regression equations include make dummies, but these are not reported in tables 8.6 and 8.7 to save space. The make dummies control for systematic variations in price by make, and thus they minimize errors due to the changing number of observations of each make in adjacent years. An additional control is provided by excluding compact cars from any regression in which they would appear for only a single year, on the grounds that since compact cars tend to be overpriced in relation to quality, including such a car in only the second year of an adjacent-year equation might bias upward the coefficient on the time dummy.

Despite these exclusions, the sample is unnecessarily large. Models with identical weight, length, and engine characteristics are entered into the regressions between two and four times, reflecting differences in trim. Originally, this duplicative procedure was chosen to avoid possible errors that might have been introduced by the arbitrary choice of a single trim type, but the similarity of the new results to those of O-G suggest that it was not worth the trouble. Another related point is that the size of the sample may be misleadingly large because of the overlap in quality characteristics among different brand names of the same manufacturer (e.g., Ford and Mercury), further cutting the "true" degrees of freedom in this study. To some extent, the instability of some of the coefficients on the physical characteristic variables may reflect an inadequacy of sufficient independent variation over these dimensions.

8.3.2   The Process of "Stripping"

The general principle was to make each observation comparable by excluding all accessories except for a radio and heater. The practical procedures for carrying out the adjustments were as follows.

1. Beginning with medium-priced models in the 1950s, and extending to most large models in the 1960s, prices in the guides sometimes included AT and, later, PS. In the 1970s and 1980s, prices for many large cars also included AC. In most cases, the guides provided the required information on the list price (for new cars) or the amount to deduct (for used cars) that

---

21. Ohta and Griliches (1986) estimate cross-sectional regressions for used cars for April and October in each year from 1970 to 1981, but they do not include time dummies, nor do they calculate a hedonic price index.

allowed the price to be adjusted for the presence of this equipment. The adjustments were double-checked with the annual automobile issue of *CR*, which notes the list price of each test car and the options with which it is equipped.[22]

2. The used car price was calculated in the same way by adjusting the listed "retail price" in the guide. In the first decade, radios and heaters were not included in the basic price, but a separate table in the front of the book listed option prices of radios and heaters by vintage. After about 1956, the value of radios and heaters was included in all used car "retail price" estimates. Accessory lists are provided immediately adjacent to the prices of each model, indicating by how much to reduce the price if a car was lacking a particular item (AT, PS, etc.), and these lists were the source of the "stripping" adjustments.

3. The weight data published in the guides were adjusted for those models with AT and/or power steering included as standard equipment, using an estimation of the contribution of each item to the weight of a 1974 Chevrolet Impala.[23] This adjustment was performed on only a small number of models over most of the years of the study, since AT and PS did not become standard equipment on the full-sized Chevrolet until 1971, and later (or never) on smaller cars.

8.4 Regression Estimates for New Cars

The estimated hedonic regression equations are presented for the full period 1947–83 in table 8.6 for new cars and table 8.7 for used cars. Each table has the same format as for the hedonic regression studies of Sears catalog appliance data in chapter 7. In the left-hand column is a pooled regression for a set of years, and in the rest of the table are separate regressions for pairs of adjacent years. All these regression equations are based on a standardized approach.

1. A semilog specification is used to facilitate comparison with other studies. Each physical characteristic is entered as its arithmetic value (weight in thousands of pounds, brake horsepower in hundreds, and overall length in hundreds of inches). Dummies are entered for trim level (from 4 for cheapest to 1 for most expensive), type of engine (4, 6, straight 8, or V-8), and time.

2. While both pooled and adjacent-year equations are estimated, to maintain a consistent format with the appliance chapter, they yield similar results, and I compute hedonic indexes only for the adjacent-year equations.

22. When no information was given to allow a deduction for, say, AT, the price adjustment was taken from the next lower priced model of the same brand name, e.g., the Chevelle price for AT was used if the Impala price was missing. The radio adjustments for the last half of the 1960s were made by extrapolating the last available radio price listing on the assumption of a constant price. Radio prices appear to have been roughly constant for several decades, as shown in App. table B.2B.

23. Obtained from Robert T. Welch of the General Motors Corp.

Table 8.6   Semilog Hedonic Regressions for New Cars and Four-Door Sedans, 1947–55, 1955–62, 1962–69, 1969–76, 1976–83

A. 1947–55

	1947–55	1947–48	1948–49	1949–50	1950–51	1951–52	1952–53	1953–54	1954–55
Weight	0.26 (8.07)	0.87 (10.9)	0.27 (4.07)	0.06 (1.94)	0.07 (1.58)	0.01 (0.12)	0.38 (8.14)	0.41 (7.64)	0.64 (6.04)
Length	0.76 (6.80)	−0.72 (−3.11)	0.26 (1.23)	1.40 (9.91)	1.37 (8.03)	1.34 (4.28)	0.46 (2.94)	0.66 (3.37)	−0.23 (−0.67)
Brake horsepower	0.14 (4.43)	−0.26 (−2.23)	0.47 (4.11)	0.49 (7.16)	0.20 (3.09)	0.24 (2.86)	0.17 (4.96)	0.13 (3.27)	0.03 (0.40)
6 cylinder	0.02 (1.62)	⋯	⋯	0.04 (2.08)	−0.01 (−0.55)	−0.04 (−1.33)	0.02 (1.40)	0.03 (1.80)	0.06 (1.72)
Straight 8	0.03 (2.03)	−0.06 (−2.80)	−0.07 (−2.93)	⋯	⋯	−0.06 (−1.40)	0.01 (0.45)	0.03 (1.45)	0.11 (0.01)
Trim	−0.03 (−6.01)	−0.04 (−3.90)	−0.03 (−4.43)	−0.02 (−4.66)	−0.02 (−3.64)	−0.04 (−3.42)	−0.04 (−5.68)	−0.04 (−4.88)	−0.04 (−3.45)
Intercept	4.68 (28.7)	6.05 (19.9)	5.42 (15.6)	3.92 (17.6)	4.31 (16.8)	4.68 (12.0)	5.21 (25.9)	4.75 (17.2)	5.88 (12.6)
1948	0.12**	0.14**							
1949	0.30**		0.16**						
1950	0.27**			−0.04**					
1951	0.35**				0.08**				
1952	0.37**					0.02			
1953	0.37**						0.00		
1954	0.34**							0.03**	
1955	0.35**								0.05*
R^2	0.941	0.961	0.936	0.970	0.955	0.951	0.990	0.978	0.903
S.E.E.	0.060	0.039	0.048	0.033	0.041	0.047	0.025	0.036	0.066
Observations	344	73	79	84	80	69	69	76	83

B. 1955–62

	Pooled 1955–62	1955–56	1956–57	1957–58	1958–59	1959–60	1960–61	1961–62
Weight	0.21 (7.48)	0.59 (4.69)	0.45 (5.74)	0.58 (6.90)	0.50 (4.27)	0.20 (2.59)	0.13 (2.20)	0.03 (0.80)
Length	0.12 (0.98)	0.57 (1.35)	1.08 (4.17)	0.48 (1.49)	1.70 (3.16)	−0.14 (−0.47)	0.17 (0.65)	0.68 (4.24)
Brake horsepower	0.05 (3.04)	0.07 (1.00)	0.03 (0.74)	0.00 (0.11)	0.08 (2.96)	0.12 (3.59)	0.07 (2.73)	0.09 (3.92)
Trim	−0.05 (−9.1)	−0.04 (−4.77)	−0.05 (−7.06)	−0.06 (−6.42)	−0.05 (−7.88)	−0.04 (−3.65)	−0.04 (−4.77)	−0.05 (−7.14)
Intercept	6.70 (37.7)	4.58 (7.35)	4.09 (10.9)	4.93 (10.3)	2.43 (2.83)	7.32 (17.7)	6.94 (19.3)	6.25 (27.7)
1956	0.00	−0.02	⋯	⋯	⋯	⋯	⋯	⋯

1957	0.06**		0.01**					
1958	0.08*			−0.01				
1959	0.10**				0.02			
1960	0.09**					−0.01		
1961	0.02**						0.01	
1962	0.17**							0.04**
$\bar{R}^2$	0.857	0.909	0.966	0.944	0.971	0.845	0.856	0.903
S.E.E.	0.074	0.057	0.038	0.050	0.027	0.067	0.064	0.052
Observations	368	83	83	83	79	86	101	116

C. 1962–69

	Pooled 1962–69	1962–63	1963–64	1964–65	1965–66	1966–67	1967–68	1968–69
Weight	0.16 (15.1)	0.06 (1.59)	0.23 (6.97)	0.13 (7.79)	0.07 (3.10)	0.19 (12.5)	0.19 (13.9)	0.19 (7.10)
Length	0.11 (3.10)	0.58 (3.86)	−0.02 (−0.21)	0.16 (2.54)	0.35 (4.52)	0.03 (0.82)	0.05 (1.46)	0.06 (0.66)
Brake horsepower	0.08 (11.6)	0.08 (3.40)	0.01 (0.43)	0.10 (6.83)	0.11 (7.26)	0.04 (3.38)	0.05 (4.84)	0.10 (8.65)
6 Cylinder	0.02 (3.35)	0.01 (0.34)	⋯	0.04 (3.78)	0.04 (3.29)	0.01 (0.72)	⋯	0.05 (4.49)
Trim	−0.04 (−16.5)	−0.05 (−6.29)	−0.05 (−7.54)	−0.05 (−11.6)	−0.04 (−11.5)	−0.04 (−12.4)	−0.04 (−13.1)	−0.04 (−9.82)
Intercept	7.02 (148.9)	6.44 (30.0)	7.22 (45.7)	6.97 (78.9)	6.73 (65.6)	7.12 (139.)	7.09 (153.)	6.97 (63.6)
1963	−0.00	−0.02						
1964	0.00		−0.01					
1965	−0.04*			−0.02				
1966	−0.03				0.01*			
1967	−0.02					0.01**		
1968	0.02**						0.04**	
1969	0.02**							−0.02*
$\bar{R}^2$	0.903	0.886	0.895	0.939	0.931	0.941	0.954	0.923
S.E.E.	0.047	0.057	0.049	0.033	0.033	0.030	0.027	0.039
Observations	701	125	134	155	174	177	170	245

(*continued*)

Table 8.6 (continued)

| | D. 1969–76 | | | | | | | |
	1969–76	1969–70	1970–71	1971–72	1972–73	1973–74	1974–75	1975–76
Weight	0.30 (22.8)	0.17 (7.87)	0.22 (11.1)	0.31 (12.3)	0.31 (7.87)	0.37 (8.88)	0.30 (11.4)	0.19 (6.25)
Length	0.01 (0.15)	0.17 (2.14)	0.39 (5.46)	0.27 (2.82)	0.21 (1.50)	−0.10 (−0.68)	−0.11 (−1.60)	−0.10 (−1.48)
Brake horsepower	0.06 (6.80)	0.12 (10.8)	0.08 (6.23)	0.04 (2.71)	0.15 (3.90)	0.08 (1.74)	0.08 (1.88)	0.14 (3.26)
4 Cylinder	0.05 (1.53)	0.09 (3.42)	0.10 (3.24)	0.13 (3.17)	⋯	⋯	⋯	⋯
6 Cylinder	0.02 (3.05)	0.06 (5.73)	0.04 (3.61)	0.01 (1.22)	⋯	⋯	⋯	⋯
Trim	−0.03 (−10.1)	−0.04 (−9.99)	−0.03 (−7.72)	−0.03 (−6.11)	−0.04 (−5.12)	−0.04 (−5.71)	−0.04 (−4.95)	−0.07 (−7.58)
Intercept	6.80 (110.1)	6.79 (62.2)	6.26 (65.1)	6.36 (53.0)	6.37 (36.8)	6.86 (37.0)	7.22 (68.1)	7.83 (65.4)
1970	0.02**	0.03*						
1971	0.08**	⋯	0.07**					
1972	0.05**	⋯	⋯	−0.04				
1973	0.02**	⋯	⋯	⋯	−0.02			
1974	0.10**	⋯	⋯	⋯	⋯	0.07**		
1975	0.25**	⋯	⋯	⋯	⋯	⋯	0.16**	
1976	0.30**	⋯	⋯	⋯	⋯	⋯	⋯	0.05**
R^2	0.932	0.930	0.955	0.970	0.955	0.931	0.881	0.884
S.E.	0.059	0.041	0.038	0.035	0.045	0.054	0.065	0.065
Observations	612	246	170	127	114	142	113	97

E. 1976–83

	1976–83	1976–77	1977–78	1978–79	1979–80	1980–81	1981–82	1982–83
Weight	0.01 (1.00)	−0.01 (−0.25)	−0.06 (−0.99)	0.09 (1.46)	0.06 (0.84)	0.05 (0.82)	0.01 (0.90)	0.01 (0.59)
Length	0.44 (8.53)	0.74 (3.79)	0.81 (4.75)	0.11 (0.59)	−0.01 (−0.08)	0.00 (−0.02)	0.35 (4.33)	0.70 (8.29)
Brake horsepower	0.12 (5.80)	0.17 (3.24)	0.00 (1.14)	0.06 (0.67)	0.09 (1.05)	0.16 (2.55)	0.08 (2.29)	0.23 (3.62)
4 Cylinder	0.03 (1.67)	⋯ ⋯	−0.10 (−1.54)	⋯ ⋯	0.09 (2.06)	0.07 (1.89)	0.00 (−0.14)	⋯ ⋯
6 Cylinder	0.01 (0.90)	⋯ ⋯	−0.02 (−0.07)	⋯ ⋯	0.03 (1.14)	0.04 (1.69)	⋯ ⋯	−0.02 (−0.88)
Trim	−0.08 (−8.11)	−0.07 (−5.53)	−0.05 (−2.91)	⋯ ⋯	⋯ ⋯	⋯ ⋯	⋯ ⋯	⋯ ⋯
Intercept	7.41 (73.4)	6.47 (29.2)	6.98 (35.9)	7.90 (39.0)	8.25 (45.4)	8.29 (57.5)	8.04 (54.3)	7.32 (50.3)
1977	0.03*	0.03						
1978	0.18**		0.14**					
1979	0.23**			0.04*				
1980	0.34**				0.11**			
1981	0.59**					0.23**		
1982	0.68**						0.08**	
1983	0.71**							0.04**
$\bar{R}^2$	0.862	0.720	0.707	0.485	0.532	0.834	0.643	0.822
S.E.	0.092	0.091	0.081	0.078	0.066	0.056	0.072	0.075
Observations	424	120	122	106	102	98	89	100

*Indicates significance at the 5 percent level.

**Indicates significance at the 1 percent level.

Table 8.7 Semilog Hedonic Regressions for Used Cars and Four-Door Sedans, 1947–55, 1955–62, 1962–69, 1969–76, 1976–83

A. 1947–55

	1947–55	1947–48	1948–49	1949–50	1950–51	1951–52	1952–53	1953–54	1954–55
Weight	0.11 (5.73)	0.05 (1.30)	0.08 (2.36)	0.06 (2.25)	0.07 (3.36)	0.32 (6.57)	0.22 (4.91)	0.04 (1.40)	0.11 (2.50)
Length	0.58 (8.47)	0.74 (4.22)	0.28 (2.51)	0.04 (0.41)	0.05 (0.59)	−0.37 (−2.24)	0.25 (1.63)	1.11 (10.5)	1.16 (6.95)
Brake horsepower	0.22 (8.68)	−0.08 (−0.08)	0.02 (0.21)	0.26 (3.73)	0.33 (4.77)	0.11 (2.54)	0.10 (2.72)	0.12 (3.81)	0.09 (2.09)
Age	−0.20 (−36.9)	−0.16 (−13.4)	−0.15 (−21.1)	−0.20 (−24.5)	−0.21 (−27.2)	−0.17 (−28.2)	−0.20 (−28.9)	−0.22 (−31.1)	−0.24 (−20.9)
6 cylinder	−0.02 (−2.47)	−0.03 (−1.63)	−0.03 (−2.02)	⋮	⋮	⋮	−0.01 (−0.72)	⋮	⋮
V 8	0.01 (0.89)	0.01 (0.30)	0.02 (0.92)	0.06 (2.25)	0.05 (2.21)	0.03 (1.74)	0.03 (2.27)	0.06 (3.67)	0.04 (1.55)
Trim	−0.02 (−5.12)	−0.04 (−4.34)	−0.03 (−4.27)	−0.02 (−3.66)	−0.03 (−5.30)	−0.02 (−4.60)	−0.02 (−3.84)	−0.05 (−7.67)	−0.04 (−3.27)
Intercept	5.93 (57.40)	6.07 (21.7)	6.98 (38.2)	7.07 (42.0)	6.91 (44.4)	7.20 (33.4)	6.40 (32.3)	5.22 (33.9)	4.86 (19.3)
1948	0.18**	0.17**							
1949	−0.09**		−0.27**						
1950	−0.08**			0.00					
1951	0.01				0.08**				
1952	0.08**					0.08**			
1953	0.01						−0.06**		
1954	−0.09**							−0.10**	
1955	−0.12**								−0.04**
R^2	0.904	0.886	0.955	0.902	0.927	0.954	0.960	0.971	0.941
S.E.E.	0.062	0.047	0.040	0.051	0.048	0.038	0.039	0.039	0.056
Observations	608	95	136	155	167	169	157	143	144

B. 1955–62

	1955–62	1955–56	1956–57	1957–58	1958–59	1959–60	1960–61	1961–62
Weight	0.25 (7.99)	0.44 (6.88)	0.29 (3.58)	0.43 (3.89)	0.12 (2.09)	0.14 (3.00)	0.14 (2.51)	0.07 (1.41)
Length	−0.03 (−0.22)	0.53 (2.38)	0.66 (2.41)	0.06 (0.16)	1.03 (3.96)	0.96 (4.01)	−0.13 (−0.59)	0.01 (0.04)
Brake horsepower	−0.01 (−0.36)	0.00 (0.06)	0.05 (1.02)	−0.03 (−0.39)	0.14 (3.25)	0.03 (1.30)	0.05 (2.34)	0.08 (4.07)
Age	−0.29 (−33.3)	−0.28 (−20.9)	−0.29 (−17.4)	−0.28 (−13.3)	−0.23 (−14.0)	−0.25 (−19.3)	−0.29 (−25.1)	−0.29 (−27.4)
6 cylinder	−0.10 (−6.01)	−0.04 (−1.61)	⋮	⋮	⋮	⋮	⋮	−0.09 (−1.77)
Straight 8	−0.09 (−2.04)	−0.03 (−0.93)	⋮	⋮	⋮	⋮	⋮	
Trim	−0.03 (−0.67)	0.03 (1.19)	⋮	⋮	⋮	⋮	−0.06 (−0.95)	−0.05 (−0.86)
Intercept	7.09 (34.4)	5.20 (16.2)	5.34 (1.40)	6.26 (9.92)	5.10 (10.9)	5.31 (12.3)	7.63 (24.6)	7.60 (29.2)
1956	−0.03**	0.02	⋮	⋮	⋮	⋮	⋮	⋮

1957	0.01**	⋮	⋮	⋮	⋮	⋮	⋮
1958	0.04**	⋯	0.04**	⋯	⋯	⋯	⋯
1959	0.02**			−0.07**			
1960	0.01**					−0.06**	
1961	0.03*				0.01		−0.01
1962	0.01**						0.01
R^2	0.862	0.949	0.943	0.899	0.916	0.936	0.924	0.937
S.E.E.	0.083	0.051	0.055	0.070	0.062	0.055	0.057	0.054
Observations	660	155	160	161	164	164	169	178

C. 1962–69

	1962–69	1962–63	1963–64	1964–65	1965–66	1966–67	1967–68	1968–69
Weight	0.13 (8.48)	0.09 (1.98)	0.06 (1.49)	0.19 (8.81)	0.20 (8.61)	0.05 (1.10)	0.05 (0.89)	0.23 (5.46)
Length	0.02 (0.68)	−0.05 (−0.23)	0.13 (0.71)	−0.03 (−1.27)	−0.02 (−0.76)	0.34 (1.89)	0.27 (1.27)	−0.34 (−2.38)
Brake horsepower	0.10 (7.31)	0.07 (3.28)	0.08 (3.14)	−0.01 (−0.22)	0.06 (2.30)	0.16 (4.67)	0.16 (4.46)	0.12 (6.38)
4 cylinder	−0.10 (−3.74)	−0.21 (−5.49)	−0.20 (−6.27)	−0.21 (−6.45)	−0.13 (−3.88)	−0.06 (−0.99)	0.02 (−0.28)	−0.06 (−1.48)
6 cylinder	−0.02 (−1.60)	−0.04 (−2.05)	−0.06 (−2.82)	−0.08 (−3.74)	⋯	0.04 (1.22)	0.04 (1.24)	0.04 (2.54)
Age	−0.26 (−36.8)	−0.29 (−26.3)	−0.27 (−25.7)	−0.25 (−23.1)	−0.27 (−23.9)	−0.29 (−18.9)	−0.25 (−16.1)	−0.24 (−30.1)
Trim	−0.07 (−7.17)	⋯	⋯	−0.06 (−0.88)	−0.06 (−0.84)	−0.07 (−0.67)	−0.07 (−0.70)	−0.07 (−10.1)
Intercept	7.26 (125.0)	7.58 (27.4)	7.34 (28.8)	7.41 (78.2)	7.21 (72.6)	6.70 (25.1)	6.84 (22.5)	7.61 (43.1)
1963	0.04*	0.08**						
1964	0.04*		0.00					
1965	0.03**			−0.02				
1966	−0.07**				−0.10**			
1967	−0.02*					0.06**		
1968	0.04**						0.07**	
1969	0.01**							−0.03
R^2	0.842	0.932	0.939	0.935	0.927	0.853	0.814	0.918
S.E.E.	0.092	0.059	0.059	0.061	0.067	0.097	0.098	0.062
Observations	1117	201	213	253	283	318	329	327

(continued)

Table 8.7 (continued)

D. 1969–76

	1969–76	1969–70	1970–71	1971–72	1972–73	1973–74	1974–75	1975–76
Weight	0.11 (7.59)	0.23 (5.07)	0.21 (4.76)	0.17 (4.76)	0.28 (8.55)	0.18 (4.69)	−0.01 (−0.68)	0.03 (1.14)
Length	−0.11 (−2.48)	−0.45 (−2.86)	−0.69 (−4.21)	−0.34 (−2.78)	−0.38 (−3.26)	−0.50 (−3.41)	−0.06 (−1.00)	0.02 (0.41)
Brake horsepower	0.16 (18.2)	0.15 (7.90)	0.23 (12.1)	0.18 (9.42)	0.04 (2.52)	0.12 (5.57)	0.17 (4.81)	0.13 (3.63)
4 cylinder	0.02 (0.64)	−0.04 (−1.29)	0.16 (3.79)	0.09 (1.82)	−0.05 (−0.81)	−0.19 (−2.00)	... ...	... ...
6 cylinder	0.04 (4.34)	... ...	0.12 (6.90)	0.07 (−4.10)	−0.02 (−1.36)	0.02 (1.44)	... ...	... ...
Age	−0.26 (−44.1)	−0.25 (−23.6)	−0.26 (−23.6)	−0.23 (−23.2)	−0.22 (−16.2)	−0.28 (21.4)	−0.27 (−26.5)	−0.25 (−22.3)
Trim	−0.05 (−16.1)	−0.06 (−10.8)	−0.05 (−8.23)	−0.03 (−4.70)	−0.05 (−7.37)	−0.05 (−7.39)	−0.06 (−8.84)	−0.06 (−7.50)
Intercept	7.49 (115.5)	7.84 (38.7)	8.14 (39.1)	7.73 (48.4)	7.81 (51.9)	8.40 (45.0)	8.23 (96.4)	8.21 (87.9)
1970	−0.02	−0.01						
1971	0.13**	...	0.16**					
1972	0.18**	...	...	0.06**				
1973	0.22**	...	...	...	−0.01**	...		
1974	0.27**	...	...	...	...	0.03**		
1975	0.46**	...	...	...	...	...	0.20**	
1976	0.57**	...	...	...	...	...	...	0.11**
R^2	0.903	0.912	0.890	0.877	0.887	0.818	0.863	0.892
S.E.E.	0.085	0.067	0.067	0.076	0.075	0.086	0.071	0.066
Observations	1007	326	243	263	254	302	208	157

E. 1976–83

	1976–83	1976–77	1977–78	1978–79	1979–80	1980–81	1981–82	1982–83
Weight	0.04 (4.03)	0.10 (3.03)	0.19 (3.26)	0.00 (−0.05)	−0.12 (−1.35)	−0.10 (−2.31)	0.09 (1.55)	0.07 (4.40)
Length	0.10 (2.04)	−0.10 (−0.97)	−0.45 (−2.32)	−0.02 (−0.06)	0.08 (0.34)	0.24 (2.08)	0.14 (1.03)	0.39 (5.80)
Brake horsepower	0.03 (1.34)	0.14 (3.13)	0.13 (2.43)	0.08 (0.78)	0.16 (1.44)	0.02 (0.37)	0.08 (1.33)	0.20 (2.91)
4 cylinder	−0.03 (1.57)	...	−0.02 (−0.22)	0.02 (0.27)	0.02 (0.41)	−0.01 (−0.35)	0.07 (1.90)	...
6 cylinder	−0.01 (−0.80)	...	−0.01 (−0.26)	...	...	0.00 (−0.23)	0.02 (1.10)	−0.03 (−1.18)
Age	−0.22 (−16.0)	−0.23 (−17.0)	−0.24 (−18.3)	−0.21 (−8.82)	−0.19 (−8.23)	−0.23 (−20.1)	−0.23 (−20.1)	−0.23 (−17.4)
Trim	−0.06 (−5.77)	−0.05 (−5.70)	−0.03 (−1.94)	...	...	...	...	...
Intercept	8.14 (90.6)	8.20 (60.0)	8.54 (38.0)	8.49 (26.2)	8.54 (30.5)	8.47 (65.1)	8.21 (60.6)	7.78 (73.5)
1977	−0.01	−0.01	...					
1978	0.14**		0.15**	...				
1979	0.14**			−0.02	...			
1980	0.27**				0.11**	...		
1981	0.48**					0.20**	...	
1982	0.58**						0.09**	...
1983	0.67**							0.11**
R^2	0.787	0.713	0.725	0.377	0.389	0.824	0.775	0.816
S.E.E.	0.129	0.098	0.098	0.167	0.161	0.074	0.078	0.086
Observations	897	226	237	218	224	218	204	192

*Indicates significance at the 5 percent level.

**Indicates significance at the 1 percent level.

Turning now to table 8.6, which presents five pooled equations and thirty-six adjacent-year equations, the included variables appear to provide a good explanation of automobile prices, with an average standard error in the adjacent-year equations of about 5 percent, less in some years, and more in others, particularly after 1976. The values and significance levels of the coefficients on the three physical characteristic variables are erratic due to multicollinearity, and twelve out of the 108 coefficients on these variables in the adjacent-year equations have the wrong (negative) sign. All the coefficients on these variables in the pooled equations, however, have the correct sign.

The significance of the weight variable exhibits cycles, with high significance in adjacent-year regressions beginning in 1947, 1948, 1952–60, and 1964–76. Interestingly, the weight variable becomes very insignificant after 1976, reflecting in part the down-sizing of some cars without a corresponding reduction in their price. The significance of the length variable exhibits shorter cycles, with relatively high significance in 1949–54, 1961–66, 1970–72, 1976–78, and 1981–83.

The coefficients on the time dummies for the adjacent-year equations are converted into a hedonic price index for new cars in table 8.8 and compared there with the CPI and with hedonic indexes developed by Griliches (1964) and Ohta and Griliches (1976). Despite differences in methodology, the new index agrees very closely with O-G over the full 1955–71 interval, including both the secular rate of increase and the year-to-year fluctuations. The correspondence with the Griliches (1964) index is much less close. While the year-to-year pattern is quite different, the overall rate of increase between 1951 and 1961 is not too far apart, with total increases of 4.1 percent for the new index and 1.3 percent for the Griliches index. There is also less than a perfect correspondence between the Griliches (1964) index and those (not shown) presented in his first paper (1961), which covers only 1937, 1950, and 1954–60. The two Griliches indexes for 1950–54 show growth rates of 2.8 and 11.2 percent, respectively. But the story is radically different from 1947 to 1951, with an increase in the new index of 40.5 and in the Griliches (1964) index of 8.2 percent. The Griliches index seems implausible, in view of the sample means in table 8.3 that show a 41.1 percent increase in price from 1947 to 1951, with hardly any change in weight, length, or horsepower. Griliches does not exhibit his sample means, but for the low-priced three subset of his sample, the mean price increases by 49.1 percent (even more than the 41.1 percent in my sample, as shown in table 8.3), yet there is only a small increase in the three main physical characteristics.[24]

---

24. Griliches (1964, table 6, p. 395). Between 1947 and 1951, weight increased only from 3,166 to 3,303, length increased from 197.4 to 199.3, and horsepower increased from 92 to 103. The G_A quality index increased only by 6.7 percent.

Table 8.8   **Alternative Price Indexes for New and Used Cars (1967 = 100)**

	New Cars						Used Cars		
	CPI (1)	PPI (2)	PDE Deflator (3)	Griliches (4)	O-G (5)	This Study Hedonic (6)	CPI (7)	O-G (8)	This Study Hedonic (9)
1947	69.2	69.8	57.4	91.1		67.7			124.6
1948	75.6	77.2	65.3	96.4		77.9			147.7
1949	82.8	87.9	69.8	101.7		91.4			112.7
1950	83.4	88.2	70.6	99.5		87.8			112.7
1951	87.4	88.7	84.8	98.6		95.1			122.1
1952	94.9	96.0	95.6	104.8		97.0			132.3
1953	95.8	95.6	77.0	104.7		97.0	89.2		124.6
1954	94.8	96.8	86.1	102.3		94.2	75.9		112.7
1955	90.9	88.1	80.3	98.3	98.1	99.0	71.8		108.3
1956	93.5	93.5	113.8	99.1	100.2	97.0	69.1		106.2
1957	98.4	98.2	106.3	100.3	100.5	98.0	77.4		110.5
1958	101.5	102.0	116.1	101.4	98.7	97.0	80.2		103.0
1959	105.9	107.1	101.6	101.7	97.5	99.0	89.5		104.1
1960	104.5	105.8	99.1	101.6	98.3	98.0	83.6		98.0
1961	104.5	105.0	103.3	99.9	99.9	99.0	86.9	91.9	97.0
1962	104.1	105.0	98.9		102.5	103.0	94.8	92.2	98.0
1963	103.5	105.0	100.9		101.3	101.0	96.0	104.2	106.2
1964	103.2	103.0	98.1		100.0	100.0	100.1	103.9	106.2
1965	100.9	101.6	93.9		94.1	98.0	99.4	103.5	104.1
1966	99.1	100.0	97.5		98.5	99.0	97.0	98.2	94.2
1967	100.0	100.0	100.0		100.0	100.0	100.0	100.0	100.0
1968	102.8	103.6	98.9		103.1	104.1	104.0	103.4	107.3
1969	104.4	104.6	101.6		104.1	102.0	108.1	106.2	104.1
1970	107.6	108.5	118.0		106.5	105.1	104.3	104.3	103.0
1971	112.0	111.9	110.6		113.3	112.7	110.2	117.8	120.9
1972	111.0	111.9	108.3			108.3	110.5		128.4
1973	111.1	111.1	105.6			106.2	117.6		127.1
1974	117.5	118.5	106.1			113.9	122.6		131.0
1975	127.6	128.8	127.9			133.6	146.4		160.0
1976	135.7	136.7	124.9			140.5	167.9		178.6
1977	142.9	143.1	124.6			144.8	182.9		176.8
1978	153.8	154.8	139.3			166.5	186.5		205.3
1979	166.0	166.3	156.5			173.3	201.0		201.4
1980	179.3	180.2	189.8			193.5	208.1		224.8
1981	190.2	191.3	166.7			243.5	256.9		274.6
1982	197.6	198.4	156.5			263.8	296.4		300.4
1983	202.6	203.6	151.2			274.6	329.7		335.4
1984	208.5	209.5	141.5				375.7		

Sources by column: (**1, 2**) *Business Statistics* (U.S. Department of Commerce), 1975 and 1984 editions. (**3**) NIPA May 1986 tape, deflator for new cars from gross auto output table, table 1.17 divided by table 1.18. (**4**) Griliches (1964, D coefficients in table 4, p. 393). (**5**) Ohta and Griliches (1976, table 26, col. 1, p. 384). (**6**) This study, table 8.6, computed from adjacent-year coefficients. (**7**) Same as col. 1. (**8**) Ohta and Griliches (1976, table 24, col. 1, p. 381). (**9**) This study, table 8.7, computed from adjacent-year coefficients.

Returning now to the comparison of new car indexes in table 8.8, it seems ironic that there is a very small difference in the total price increase registered by the CPI and by the new hedonic index over the full period between 1947 and 1974, 69.8 and 68.2 percent, respectively. The lack of a major difference with the CPI seems surprising in light of the widespread impression that the extent of quality adjustments in the CPI was less extensive before 1960 than afterward. Even between the CPI and the linked Griliches indexes, the difference is relatively minor over the 1951–71 period, with increases of 28.1 and 12.9 percent, respectively, a difference that amounts to an annual growth rate over the period of just 0.6 percent, not much to get excited about, and very small compared to the differences between the new "alternative" indexes and the PPI in other parts of this book. The closeness of the new index to that of O-G after 1955 supports their conclusion (and that of Triplett) that the CPI may have understated the rate of price increase during the period 1960–66, although such a conclusion hinges on the validity of the hedonic price technique using these physical "proxy" variables, which are subject to the criticism (reviewed above) that it makes a virtue of increased weight over periods when engineers may have been working to reduce weight. I return to this question below in a comparison of several "closely similar" models that span the 1960s.

After 1974, however, there is a substantial difference between the CPI and the hedonic index for new cars. From 1974 to 1983, the CPI increases by 77.4 percent, much less than the 141.8 percent increase in my hedonic price index for new cars. At annual rates, the hedonic index increases at 10.3 percent, a rate 3.7 percent faster than the 6.6 percent annual rate of increase of the CPI over this period. As we shall see below, *all* this discrepancy can be explained by the allowance in the CPI for quality improvements taking the form of government-mandated safety and antipollution devices, in contrast to the hedonic index that makes no such allowances.

8.5   Hedonic Regression Estimates for Used Cars

We enter into more virgin territory in the treatment of used car prices. Although he estimated cross-sectional regressions for used cars in several papers (Griliches 1961; Ohta and Griliches 1986), Griliches has published a hedonic price index for used cars covering only the limited period 1961–71 (Ohta and Griliches, 1976). Because my used and new car samples are comparable, in the sense that the one-year-old and two-year-old used cars in the sample are exactly the same makes and models as are the new cars (except in introductory years), the ratio of the mean stripped price of used cars relative to new cars is a meaningful indicator of the postwar history of the relative price of used cars. This ratio, shown in the first column of table 8.5, remained in the range of 64–71 percent through the period 1957–74. In the first decade, from 1947 to 1957, the used/new price ratio fell dramatically, reflecting the transition from premiums to discounts on new cars. In the final decade, the ratio increased from an average of 67.1 percent in 1964–73 to 72.9 percent in 1974–83. This transition may have reflected, at least in part, reduced discounts on new cars resulting from reduced margins allowed to dealers by manufacturers and hence less "bargaining room."

The regression estimates for 1947–83 are presented in table 8.7; all details of implementation are identical to those in the new car regressions. The average standard error is somewhat higher than the average for new cars, perhaps because of measurement error in the used car price estimates, a greater importance of "left-out" variables, or the extra variance introduced by including two vintages for each year.[25] The coefficients on the major quality characteristics are somewhat more erratic than in the new car equations, with horsepower and the V-8 dummy relatively more significant in many years, and length relatively less important. The rate of depreciation between ages 1 and 2 appears to have been relatively slow in the first few years of the postwar period, with an average rate of 18 percent in the four equations spanning 1947–53, as compared to an average rate of 27 percent for 1953–63, 25 percent for 1963–73, and 23 percent for 1973–83.

Returning now to table 8.8, we can compare the hedonic price index for used cars with the O-G index covering 1961–71 and the CPI used car index covering the full period since 1953. The correspondence between my index and that of O-G is almost as close as for new cars, except for their much greater price increase in 1962–63. For 1963–71, the increases in my index and theirs are a very close 13.8 and 13.9 percent, respectively.

Several interesting ratios are provided in table 8.9 to summarize the results for used cars. The first column lists the average stripped price of used cars relative to new cars, set on a base of 1967 = 1.0, from tables 8.3 and 8.4. This shows, as we saw previously in table 8.5, that the index of raw (quality unadjusted) used car prices stayed in a relatively constant relation to a similar index of new car prices from 1957 to 1974. Prior to 1957, used car prices declined relative to new car prices, as did the used hedonic index relative to the new hedonic index in column 2. After 1974, used car prices averaged 112 percent of new car prices on a base of 1967 = 100; this increase may have reflected some combination of a reduction in the magnitude of dealer discounts and a reduction in the depreciation rate, as occurs in the coefficients on age in the hedonic regression equations for used cars.

The next column (2) in table 8.9 shows that the ratio of the used hedonic price index from table 8.8 rises relative to the new hedonic index, particularly in the 1970–72 period. It is interesting to recall that this was a period of price controls on new cars, so that the jump in used car prices might reflect an

---

25. For the adjacent-year equations spanning 1961–71, my standard error is 0.069, compared to 0.098 for Ohta and Griliches. However, the samples are not comparable, since I include several trim classes for each model, and they include six vintages instead of my two.

Table 8.9   **Key Ratios for Automobiles, 1947–83 (1967 = 1.0 or 100)**

	Used/New Means (1)	Used/New Hedonic (2)	Used Mean/ Used Hedonic (3)	(1)/(2) (4)	Used Hedonic/ Used CPI (5)	Transaction Price Adjustment (6)
1947	1.84	1.84	0.93	1.00		164.4
1948	1.77	1.90	0.84	0.94		161.9
1949	1.23	1.23	0.87	1.00		115.6
1950	1.19	1.28	0.85	0.93		117.4
1951	1.22	1.28	0.87	0.95		113.2
1952	1.21	1.36	0.87	0.89		120.5
1953	1.18	1.28	0.90	0.92	1.40	118.2
1954	1.09	1.20	0.90	0.91	1.49	112.6
1955	1.17	1.09	0.99	1.07	1.51	117.7
1956	1.10	1.09	0.96	1.00	1.54	115.9
1957	1.04	1.13	0.98	0.93	1.43	113.1
1958	0.94	1.06	1.02	0.89	1.28	97.6
1959	1.02	1.05	1.08	0.97	1.16	103.7
1960	1.02	1.00	1.11	1.02	1.17	106.6
1961	1.06	0.98	1.12	1.08	1.12	107.8
1962	1.02	0.95	1.05	1.07	1.03	104.0
1963	1.07	1.05	1.01	1.02	1.11	108.9
1964	1.05	1.06	1.00	0.99	1.06	105.7
1965	1.08	1.06	1.01	1.02	1.05	110.2
1966	0.98	0.95	1.03	1.04	0.97	102.3
1967	1.00	1.00	1.00	1.00	1.00	100.0
1968	1.03	1.03	1.02	1.00	1.03	101.5
1969	0.94	1.02	0.96	0.92	0.96	97.7
1970	1.02	0.98	1.11	1.04	0.99	101.4
1971	0.97	1.07	0.96	0.91	1.10	99.5
1972	1.04	1.19	0.98	0.88	1.16	107.0
1973	1.05	1.20	0.99	0.88	1.08	117.0
1974	0.99	1.15	1.03	0.86	1.07	109.8
1975	1.07	1.20	1.01	0.89	1.09	113.2
1976	1.18	1.27	1.05	0.93	1.06	119.1
1977	1.12	1.22	1.04	0.92	0.97	115.6
1978	1.12	1.23	0.99	0.91	1.10	111.8
1979	1.12	1.16	1.01	0.96	1.00	105.4
1980	1.11	1.16	0.99	0.95	1.08	110.4
1981	1.08	1.13	1.00	0.96	1.07	107.6
1982	1.09	1.14	1.00	0.96	1.01	108.5
1983	1.15	1.22	0.97	0.94	1.02	115.6

Sources by column: (1) Table 8.4, col. 2, divided by table 8.3, col. 2, expressed as an index number, 1967 = 1.0. (2) Table 8.8, col. 9, divided by col. 6. (3) Table 8.4, col. 2, rebased to 1967, and divided by table 8.8, col. 9. (4) Table 8.9, col. 1, divided by col. 2. (5) Table 8.8, col. 9, divided by col. 7. (6) Exponential index created from the logs of two indexes, (1) the average of the ratio of the used/new means and the ratio of the used/new hedonic (cols. 1 and 2), and (2) an index of $1/(1 - d_1)$, where d_1 is the absolute value of the "age" coefficients for each year from the adjacent-year used-car regressions in table 8.7.

excess demand for cars, as one might expect during a period of controls. The partial reversal of this phenomenon in 1973–74 reinforces the view that an effect of controls may have been involved. Nevertheless, there does seem to have been an increase in quality-adjusted used car prices in the past decade. One good measure of this is the ratio in column 2 for the postcontrols period (1976–83) of 119 percent, as compared to the 1962–71 decade, when the same ratio was 102 percent. This increase in the relative price of used cars seems implausibly large to be accounted for solely by a shrinkage in discounts; another source may be an inconsistency in the number of options included in the new car and used car observations in the hedonic regression equations. I return to this issue below in section 8.8.

An interesting index of the quality of used cars, as evaluated on the used car market, is provided in column 3, which displays the ratio of an index of the mean price of used cars to the used hedonic index. When this ratio increases, it indicates an increase in the quality of used cars. For instance, if the actual price of used cars increased by 15 percent while the hedonic index remained constant, this set of facts could be interpreted as implying a 15 percent improvement in quality. As shown in column 3 of table 8.9, there was a marked improvement in quality from 1947 to 1958, with a "quality peak" reached in 1961 at a level 20 percent higher than 1947, but then a decline in quality set in, until in the last decade the implicit quality index in table 8.9 reached an average level of 101, the same level as 1958, and only a modest improvement from 1947.

The next column in table 8.9, column 4, shows the ratio of the used/new mean ratio in column 1 to that for the used and new hedonic indexes in column 2. This column can be interpreted as providing a relative quality evaluation index, since high numbers indicate that quality is valued more highly in the used car market, while low numbers indicate that quality is valued more highly in the new car market. While the numbers jump around, reflecting in part the lag in the adjustment of the used car market to the new car market, there is no trend over the full period, and the 1982–83 figures are not far from the 1947 and 1967 values of one.

Finally, column 5 exhibits the ratio of the used hedonic price index to the used auto price component of the CPI. There was a major downtrend of the hedonic index that lasted from the inception of the used car CPI in 1953 through the mid-1960s. After that, there was little trend, as indicated by the ratio of 1.02 in 1983 on a 1967 = 1.00 base. The discrepancy between my index and the CPI for used cars before 1965 is large but not unexpected. Only Chevrolets, Fords, and Plymouths were priced by the CPI before 1962, no allowance was made for optional equipment before 1966, and there has been no other allowance for changes in quality.[26] More interesting is the lack of

---

26. These statements are based on "Seasonal Demand and Used Car Prices," *Monthly Labor Review* (March 1967): 12–16.

difference in the growth rate of the hedonic used car index after 1965 and the CPI for used cars. If the latter incorporates few if any quality adjustments, then we might infer either that on balance there was no net quality improvement, or alternatively that the hedonic index for used cars misses some types of quality change.

8.6 Changes in Quality Mandated by Safety and Environmental Regulations

The three major types of government regulation affecting the automobile are safety standards, air pollution standards, and the regulation of fuel economy. This section treats the value of equipment added to automobiles to comply with safety and pollution regulations, and the next section reviews evidence on changes in fuel economy. The safety and environmental adjustments cover only the period after 1967, since the major legislation has taken effect only since that date, particularly the National Traffic and Motor Vehicle Safety Act of 1966, the Motor Vehicle Information and Cost Savings Act of 1972, the Clean Air Act Amendments of 1970 and 1977, and the Energy Policy and Conservation Act of 1975. In the next section, the measures of changing fuel economy extend over the whole postwar period, since changes in fuel economy are desirable in themselves and have occurred continuously, although their pace was accelerated after the early 1970s not only by fuel economy legislation but by the 1973–74 and 1979–80 increases in the relative price of gasoline.

Details on the legislation are provided by Crandall et al. (1986) and White (1982). The 1970 Clean Air Act set the ambitious target of reducing the level of auto emissions by 90 or 95 percent of the average 1968 level, although this standard was relaxed to about 80 percent by the 1977 Clean Air Act Amendments. Safety standards are set by the National Highway Traffic Safety Administration (rather than by Congress, as in the case of emissions regulations) and include more than fifty separate standards for passenger vehicles. The 1966 act that began the process of safety regulation occurred before the major environmental legislation, and thus major changes in automobile equipment in the late 1960s involved safety items (e.g., seat belts).

The most controversial issues involving safety and environmental regulations involve measuring their benefits, rather than their costs. Beginning with the 1967 model year, the BLS has issued an annual release providing a breakdown of the value of its quality adjustments for automobiles into three categories, safety equipment, emissions control equipment, and other changes. In some years, the safety equipment is further subdivided into two categories, items formally mandated and those added voluntarily or in anticipation of future regulations. The CPI adjustments are displayed in table 8.10 and are subsequently incorporated into the final price index for new cars.

Table 8.10   **Components of CPI Price and Quality Adjustment and of Hedonic Price and Quality Change, Index Numbers, 1967 = 100**

| | Components of CPI Price and Quality Change | | | | | | Hedonic | | |
| | | | Components of Quality Adjustment | | | | | | |
	Unadjusted Price Change (1)	Total Quality Adjustment (2)	Safety (3)	Environ-mental (4)	Other (5)	Net Price Change (6)	Sample Mean Price Change (7)	Quality Adjust-ment (8)	Price Index (9)
1967	100.0	100.0	100.0	100.0	100.0	100.0	100.0	100.0	100.0
1968	103.9	101.8	101.3	100.5	100.0	102.0	106.2	102.1	104.1
1969	105.7	101.8	101.9	100.5	99.4	103.8	107.3	105.2	102.0
1970	110.3	103.7	103.0	100.7	100.0	106.4	112.1	106.6	105.1
1971	117.2	103.9	103.5	100.7	99.8	112.9	119.8	106.2	112.7
1972	118.1	104.6	103.6	100.9	100.2	112.9	120.8	111.6	108.3
1973	123.6	109.4	106.8	101.9	100.6	113.0	119.1	112.1	106.2
1974	136.5	114.0	110.8	102.0	100.9	119.7	135.5	119.0	113.9
1975	155.0	118.8	111.2	106.0	100.9	130.5	150.9	112.9	133.6
1976	164.5	119.2	111.6	106.2	100.7	138.0	158.9	113.1	140.5
1977	182.0	121.2	111.9	106.6	101.7	150.2	163.2	112.7	144.8
1978	201.6	122.6	111.9	106.8	102.7	164.4	180.6	108.5	166.5
1979	215.3	123.9	112.0	107.1	103.4	173.8	181.5	104.8	173.3
1980	232.1	130.2	112.3	109.7	105.8	178.2	202.3	104.5	193.5
1981	257.0	144.1	112.4	120.0	106.9	178.4	253.5	104.1	243.5
1982	282.9	147.3	112.4	121.8	107.7	192.1	276.2	104.7	263.8
1983	296.2	150.5	112.4	123.1	108.9	196.8	282.8	103.0	274.6
1984	306.2	153.1	112.2	124.2	110.0	200.0			
1985	318.4	156.5	112.2	124.6	112.1	203.4			

Sources by column: **(1–6)** The source was a complete set of annual BLS press releases covering the 1967–85 model years. Each press release gives the dollar change in total price and the dollar change in quality, subdivided into three categories, safety, environmental legislation, and "other." The net price change, when not given specifically, is computed as the dollar change in the unadjusted price minus the dollar quality adjustment. Adjustments were given in both dollars and percentage of retail price in 1967 and 1968, allowing the computation of the unadjusted price each year. Percentage changes are computed from the dollar changes divided by the unadjusted price, updated each year. Index numbers are developed from the cumulative percentage changes, using the formula $100 \times \exp[\ln(X_{t-1}) + x_t]$, where X_{t-1} is last year's value (starting from 1967 = 100), and x_t is the change in the item from last year to this year. **(7)** Table 8.3, col. 2. **(8)** Index created exponentially from col. 7 divided by col. 9. **(9)** Table 8.8, col. 6.

Previous authors have presented time series of the dollar cost of safety regulation (Crandall et al. 1986, 35–37; White 1982, 60–65). In some cases, the cumulative dollar costs are actually exhibited without any correction for inflation, which seems inappropriate in light of the tripling of the average selling price of new cars (table 8.3) over the 1967–83 period. Fortunately, the BLS releases on safety and emission control equipment provide enough information to convert the value of the changes in each year to a percentage figure, expressed as a percent of the average selling price of cars in that particular year. This is feasible because, in 1967 and 1968, the BLS lists each change both in dollar terms and as a percentage of the average retail selling price. Each successive release provides the information only in dollars, but these can be converted into percentages by cumulating the 1968 selling price by the total dollar price change in each year. Both the dollar price changes and the 1968 selling price are expressed as retail rather than wholesale values, so that the percentage changes are computed on a consistent basis. The index of the average unadjusted price is shown in column 1 of table 8.10, where it can be compared with the mean unadjusted price in the new car hedonic sample. Over the full 1967–83 period, the unadjusted CPI price grows at an annual rate of 7.0 percent, close to the 6.7 percent growth rate of the hedonic sample mean. Over shorter periods, the growth rates of the two average price figures differ by more than this, with the CPI figure growing more rapidly from 1974 to 1980, while the hedonic sample mean grows much more rapidly from 1980 to 1981.

Column 2 displays the total CPI quality adjustment as an index number, computed from the dollar quality adjustments expressed as a percentage of the previous year's average selling price. The total quality adjustment is then broken down into its three components—safety, emission control, and other—in columns 3–5. The safety adjustments came in the first decade after 1967 and were minimal after 1975. The emission control adjustments were made in two stages, 1973–75 and 1979–81. The "other" adjustments were surprisingly small from 1967 to 1976, and then proceeded at a rate of about 1 percent per year thereafter. One puzzle involving the small "other" adjustments between 1967 and 1976 is that data from General Motors (discussed below) indicate that important options, especially AT and PS, became standard equipment on full-sized Chevrolets in 1971, and presumably around that time on other popular makes.

Overall, the quality adjustments reduce the annual 1967–83 increase in the CPI from an unadjusted 7.0 percent to an adjusted 4.3 percent.[27] In contrast, columns 8–9 show that, on balance, there was virtually no quality improvement implicit in the hedonic regression estimates, in that the increase in the hedonic regression price index in column 9 was almost as rapid as in the raw unadjusted mean price in the hedonic sample displayed in column 7. The hedonic quality index in column 8 simply picks up the fact, already obvious in the means of table 8.3, that cars became larger and heavier through the mid-1970s and then became smaller. An interesting artifact of the shifting coefficients in the adjacent-year regressions is that, although the average values of all three physical characteristics were significantly lower in 1983 than in 1967, the implicit quality index in column 8 is 3 percent higher. This is possible in principle if the coefficients in the 1967–75 period placed a higher value on the increase in physical characteristics than the coefficients of

27. The index values in col. 6 of table 8.10 may not correspond exactly to the published CPI in col. 1 of table 8.8, since the former are based on price changes between introductory months one year apart, usually September or October, while the published CPI is an annual average of monthly figures. However, the difference in the annual growth rates is small, 4.3 percent for table 8.10 vs. 4.5 percent for the published CPI.

the 1976–83 period placed on the decline in those characteristics. In particular, recall that the coefficient on weight drops to a low or even negative value in the new car hedonic regression equations of table 8.6 beginning in 1975–76 and in the used car regression equations of table 8.7 beginning in 1974–75.

8.7 Fuel Economy

Fuel economy has long been recognized as an important performance attribute of automobiles, and Crandall et al. (1976, 133) quote a government estimate that the ratio of the present value of gasoline costs to that of capital costs for a car held for four years was 31 percent for 1972 model automobiles and 42 percent for 1981 model cars. Recently Ohta and Griliches (1986) have carried out an extensive study of hedonic regression equations including fuel economy variables (but without time dummies—hence the omission of this study from table 8.8). In the past, the main problem precluding quality adjustments for changes in fuel economy was the very high negative correlation of fuel economy and weight, precluding independent estimates of coefficients for the fuel economy and weight variables. However, recent research on fuel economy, particularly that of Wilcox (1984), has circumvented this problem by estimating constant-quality fuel economy indexes based on hedonic-like regression equations in which fuel economy is the dependent variable and various physical characteristics are explanatory variables.[28]

Wilcox's basic index is displayed as column 1 of table 8.11. It displays a slow increase through 1968, a small decline through 1971, and then a rapid increase to 1980. For the overlap period 1971–80, we also have a regression-based fuel economy index developed by Crandall et al. (1976), and this increases much less during the overlap period than the Wilcox index. There are three reasons to prefer the Wilcox estimates. First, he estimates adjacent-year equations rather than a single pooled equation, thus allowing coefficients to shift. Second, and probably more important, he includes many explanatory variables that are missing from the Crandall study, yet are known to affect fuel economy.[29] Third, the gas mileage concept explained by the Wilcox regressions is constant speed gas mileage, whereas Crandall uses the more ambiguous figures for "city driving" and "highway driving." As Wilcox

28. As an historical note, Wilcox was a research assistant working on this book in the mid-1970s and carried out his research on fuel economy as an independent project (later updated through 1980), using my complete file of postwar *CR* articles on automobiles.

29. Both studies include weight and front-wheel drive. Crandall includes displacement as an indicator of engine size, whereas Wilcox chooses acceleration as a measurement of engine performance. Variables included by Wilcox but omitted by Crandall are dummy variables for PS, PB, AT, AC, overdrive, extra forward transmission gears, and diesel engines. Crandall also includes three "corporate" dummies that are all insignificant.

Table 8.11   **Alternative Fuel Economy Indexes**

	Wilcox Fuel Economy Index (1)	Crandall Fuel Economy Index (2)	White Emissions Control Penalty (3)	Linked Emission-adjusted Index (4)
1947				82.5
1948				82.5
1949	82.5			82.5
1950	85.0			85.0
1951	85.0			85.0
1952	86.8			86.8
1953	86.4			86.4
1954	84.5			84.5
1955	84.3			84.3
1956	84.5			84.5
1957	84.2			84.2
1958	84.3			84.3
1959	88.6			88.6
1960	95.3			95.3
1961	92.4			92.4
1962	91.6			91.6
1963	92.8			92.8
1964	92.0			92.0
1965	95.0			95.0
1966	99.8			99.8
1967	100.0			100.0
1968	101.3			101.3
1969	98.9			98.9
1970	97.7			97.7
1971	96.0	98.0	100.0	96.0
1972	101.2	98.0	100.0	101.2
1973	107.4	99.0	108.0	115.9
1974	119.2	99.0	108.0	128.8
1975	113.4	102.0	101.0	114.6
1976	114.7	112.7	101.0	115.8
1977	120.9	112.7	103.0	124.6
1978	132.6	112.7	103.0	136.6
1979	139.2	113.9	103.0	143.4
1980	143.2	113.9	106.0	151.8
1981		118.5	107.0	159.5
1982		119.7	107.0	161.1
1983		131.0	107.0	176.2
1984		123.4	107.0	166.0

Sources by column: (1) Wilcox (1984), index computed by taking exponents of successive changes recorded in table 1, pp. 378–79. (2) Crandall et al. (1976), index computed by taking exponents of successive changes recorded in table 6–4, col. 4, p. 129. (3) Same source as col. 2, table 6–5, col. 2, p. 130. (4) *1947–48:* linked to col. 1 in 1949. *1949–70:* same as col. 1. *1970–80:* exponential index created from col. 1 times col. 3. *1981–83:* column 2 linked to col. 4 in 1980, adjusted by col. 3.

(1984, 382) shows for 1953–66, regression indexes based on these vague standards are biased downward, since they fail to hold speed and acceleration constant and because *CR* has gradually changed the tests to make them "tougher."

The Crandall discussion points out an additional issue that Wilcox neglects, and this is the fact that regression-based gas mileage indexes do not take into account the penalty imposed by pollution control equipment. If the latter is classified as part of the cost of environmental legislation, then "true" gas mileage should be adjusted upward to take out the negative effect of emissions control equipment. The Crandall study uses the estimates by White (1982), shown in column 3 of table 8.11. My linked gas mileage index combines the Wilcox figures through 1980 and the linked Crandall index for 1980–84 and adjusts both for the emissions control penalty. The Wilcox index is extended back from 1949 to 1947, assuming no change in those two years.

8.8   Discounting, Premia, and the "Transaction Price Proxy"

8.8.1   Perfect Substitutability and the Estimation of First-Year Depreciation

An important defect of all hedonic regression studies of new car prices, including mine, is the use of manufacturers' list prices. However, the price quotations in the used car regressions (coming from dealer reports and auctions) are much closer to the desired transaction price concept. A useful working assumption is that late-model used cars are perfect substitutes for new cars, except for age. Since the depreciation rate from the true transaction price at age 0 to the transaction price at age 1 is not observable, perfect substitutability can be interpreted as imposing the assumption that depreciation is geometric from the initial date of sale, that is, that the unobserved depreciation rate from age 0 to age 1 is the same as the observed rate from age 1 to age 2 (or, more generally, to the average observed depreciation rate over all ages after the first year). This implies that price fluctuations in quality-adjusted used car prices relative to the quality-adjusted list prices of new cars reflect changing discounts or premiums of new car transaction prices from new car list prices.

This section first describes the procedures followed to implement the assumption that age-adjusted prices of used cars can be used as a proxy for the transaction prices of new cars, and then it considers possible objections and qualifications to the assumption. To supply the missing proxy for the depreciation from the "true" new price to the observed age 1 price, it seems reasonable to assume a zero-to-one depreciation rate (d_0) equal to the one-to-two year depreciation rate (d_1) estimated in the hedonic regression equations of table 8.7. This rate rises from an average of 17 percent for

1947–51 to the range of 27–29 percent during most of the postwar period, with a slight decline to around 23 percent toward the end of the 1970s. Since by definition the observed price at age 1 (P_1) equals the true new price (P_0) adjusted for the true depreciation rate,

(8.3) $$P_1 = (1 - d_0)P_0 ,$$

by assuming $d_0 = d_1$, we can calculate the "transaction price proxy" (*TPP*, or P^*_0) as

(8.4) $$P^*_0 = P_1/(1 - d_1).$$

By allowing the geometric depreciation rate to vary each year, this procedure does not impute to new car prices changes in used car prices due solely to changes in depreciation rates observable on used cars.

8.8.2   Calculation of the Transaction Price Proxy

In order to carry out the calculation of the TPP, we need some measure of quality-adjusted used car prices relative to quality-adjusted new car prices. We cannot use the CPI, since quality adjustments are not carried out consistently in the CPI new and used car indexes. The obvious choice would seem to be the ratio of the used to the new hedonic index. This has the advantage that the same physical characteristics enter the quality-adjustment procedure for new cars and used cars. The main disadvantages are two: both the new and used hedonic indexes are prone to implausible jumps up and down, due to erratic movements in the estimated coefficients on the time dummy variables, and the coefficients in the used car regressions differ from those in the new car regressions and may not reflect buyer tastes in the new car market.

An alternative would be to use the ratio of the raw unadjusted mean price in the used car sample to the new car sample. This has the advantage that these are unadulterated raw numbers, not prone to jumps imposed by the regression procedure, but with the disadvantage that quality improvements that are accompanied by price increases are introduced into the new car mean 1.5 years prior to their introduction in the used car mean, causing a drop in the ratio when new car quality improves, and vice versa. The used/new ratio of mean prices appears in table 8.9, column 1, and can be compared to the used/new hedonic index ratio in column 2 of the same table. The overall secular behavior of both ratios is similar, although year-to-year movements are quite different. Because the case for either index is not overwhelming, the calculations of table 8.11 are based on an average of the used/new mean price ratio and the used/new hedonic index ratio.

The TPP adjustment displayed in column 6 of table 8.9 is simply this average ratio from columns 1 and 2, times an index of $1/(1 - d_1)$ from the used car regressions in table 8.7, restated as an index number with

1967 = 100. After the very large adjustments of 1947–48 reflecting premia over list prices (discussed below), the discount adjustment (expressed as an index number on a 1967 base) averages 116 for 1949–57, 103.5 for 1958–72, and 112.2 for 1973–83. How should these movements be interpreted? First, to take a year when the index is at a low level, and using data in table 8.12 for the full-sized Chevrolet as an example, the used price of a one-year-old V-8 Impala model in 1969 was $1,970 and the estimated transaction price of a new 1969 model (using the estimated 25 percent depreciation rate) is $2,627, indicating a discount of 12.4 percent from the 1969 list price of $2,999.[30] In 1977, the same calculation (using a depreciation rate of 21 percent) indicates a discount of 7.2 percent. In contrast, the used price of a one-year-old model in 1948 was $2,045 and the estimated transaction price of a new 1948 model was $2,400, indicating a premium of 71 percent over the 1948 list price of $1,345.

Are these values plausible? *CR* in 1970 (April, 198) reported the results of an FTC study indicating that half the full-sized models "went at prices from 15 to 20 percent less than the sticker price," which is regrettably vague but at least not inconsistent with my implied discount of 12.4 percent. The 1977 value also seems plausible in light of the calculation by Bresnahan and Reiss (1985, 267) that the average new car retailed at 95 percent of list in 1977, and we would expect the discount of a large Chevrolet to be higher than average since the markup of list price over dealer cost is greater for larger models.[31]

As for 1948, the problem is more complicated. Why would purchasers pay so much more for a used car than a new model? The first reason is that the list prices were fictitious, as illustrated in the invoice for a 1948 Hudson displayed in *Consumer Reports* (May 1948, 205). Although the list price was $1,870, the price actually paid net of sales tax was $2,315, or about 24 percent above the list price. It is probably no coincidence that the price of a used 1948 Hudson in the 1 July 1948 *Red Book* (equipped with heater) was 29 percent higher than the stripped list price. Of the 24 percent premium, 14 percent represents extra amounts needed to obtain the basic stripped model, and the other 10 percent reflects the costs of accessories.

But this example cannot explain a 71 percent premium in price as calculated above for the Chevrolet. Part may be due to the greater popularity of the Chevrolet than the Hudson in 1948, since the ratio of used to new Chevrolet prices (69 percent) was higher than for any other make displayed by *CR* (January 1949, 10). Much of the rest may be explained by the fact that, in a period of shortages and waiting lists, purchasers were willing to pay a premium for a used unit to the extent that the waiting period for a new model

30. In this and the following example, the prices refer to the most expensive Chevrolet four-door sedan equipped with radio and heater but not AT, PS, or PB.
31. The Bresnahan-Reiss study refers only to 1977 and does not provide data for any other year.

Table 8.12   New and Used Prices for Top-of-Line Chevrolet, 1947–83

	New Car List Price (1)	Used Price			Depreciation		
		Age 0 (2)	Age 1 (3)	Age 2 (4)	List to Age 0 (5)	List to Age 1 (6)	Age 1 to Age 2 (7)
1947	1,256		1,620			1.29	
1948	1,407		2,045	1,695		1.45	0.83
1949	1,601		1,485	1,350		0.93	0.91
1950	1,591		1,545	1,200		0.97	0.78
1951	1,862		1,530	1,335		0.82	0.87
1952	1,811		1,710	1,455		0.94	0.85
1953	1,936		1,560	1,280		0.81	0.82
1954	1,946		1,575	1,130		0.81	0.72
1955	1,994		1,550	1,275		0.78	0.82
1956	2,126		1,530	1,150		0.72	0.75
1957	2,452		1,825	1,320		0.74	0.72
1958	2,609		1,815	1,440		0.70	0.79
1959	2,772		1,925	1,625		0.69	0.84
1960	2,759		1,980	1,445		0.72	0.73
1961	2,759		1,975	1,565		0.72	0.79
1962	2,769		1,990	1,555		0.72	0.78
1963	2,769		2,030	1,635		0.73	0.81
1964	2,779		2,025	1,625		0.73	0.80
1965	2,779		1,975	1,630		0.71	0.83
1966	2,783		1,875	1,475		0.67	0.79
1967	2,828		1,930	1,515		0.68	0.78
1968	2,951		2,150			0.73	
1969	2,999		1,970	1,555		0.66	0.79
1970	3,132		1,770	1,375		0.57	0.78
1971	3,742		2,500	1,925		0.67	0.77
1972	4,009		2,475	1,950		0.62	0.79
1973	4,176		2,875	2,100		0.69	0.73
1974	4,877	4,200	3,300	2,650	0.86	0.68	0.80
1975	5,290		3,600	2,725		0.68	0.76
1976	5,465		4,050	3,100		0.74	0.77
1977	5,864	5,450	4,300	3,400	0.93	0.73	0.79
1978	6,408	6,000	5,050	3,725	0.94	0.79	0.74
1979	7,229	5,675	4,525	3,775	0.79	0.63	0.83
1980	7,824	6,150	5,075	4,025	0.79	0.65	0.79
1981	8,419	7,950	6,400	5,125	0.94	0.76	0.80
1982	9,152	8,750	7,100	5,925	0.96	0.78	0.83
1983	9,898	9,650	8,150	6,800	0.97	0.82	0.83

Sources by column: (**1–4**) Sources for prices are the same as for the new car and used car hedonic regression equations. Prices are standardized for both new and used cars as follows: all years include radio and heater; 1971–73 observations include automatic transmission and power steering; 1974–83 observations include automatic transmission, power steering, and air conditioning. Engine is six-cylinder 1947–56 and V-8 for the interval 1957–83. (**5**) Column 2 divided by col. 1. (**6**) Column 3 divided by col. 1. (**7**) Column 4 divided by col. 3.

Table 8.13   **New and Used Price Ratios for Top-of-Line Chevrolet, Selected Intervals, 1947–83**

| | Depreciation | | |
	List to Year 1	Year 1 to Year 2	Implied Discount
1949–53	0.89	0.85	1.05
1954–58	0.75	0.76	0.99
1959–63	0.72	0.79	0.91
1964–68	0.69	0.80	0.86
1969–73	0.64	0.77	0.83
1974–78	0.72	0.77	0.94
1979–83	0.73	0.82	0.89
1982–83	0.80	0.83	0.96

Source: Table 8.12.

imposed a nonpecuniary cost on them. In an attempt to explain the high used car prices during this period, *CR* (January 1949, 10) cited ''dealer acceptance of tips or bonuses, juggling of waiting lists, loading of cars with accessories, and 'stealing' of used cars traded in by allowing only a fraction of their worth.''

While the decline in used car prices relative to the list prices of new cars in the first postwar decade can plausibly be attributed to the transition from premiums to discounts, the increase in the relative value of used cars in the post-1970 period requires further discussion. To facilitate this, table 8.12 presents the price data from the hedonic regression data base for one particular model, the most expensive full-sized Chevrolet four-door sedan listed in each year. Original sources have been checked again to maintain a consistent treatment of accessories on each model observed in a given year. Engine types and included equipment are upgraded in 1957, 1971, and 1974 (see notes to table 8.12), implying that no comparisons can be made of the raw prices over time, but only between new and used models in a given year.

The information in table 8.12 is summarized in table 8.13 by taking five-year averages. Here, the final column labeled ''Implied Discount'' is stated as the implied ratio of the new car transaction price to the new car list price. This ratio shows a sharp jump (i.e., discounts dropped) between the 1969–73 and the 1974–78 periods. The apparent reversal of this change in 1979–83 is due to the temporary decline in the prices of used large ''gas guzzlers'' in the years of peak gasoline prices, 1979–80. By 1982–83, the ratio was above 95 percent, indicating that discounting had almost disappeared.

8.8.3   Possible Objections to the Transactions Price Proxy

The assumption that quality- and age-adjusted used car prices can be taken as a proxy for the unobservable transactions prices of new cars may ignore factors that can cause short-run deviations between true new car prices and observed new car prices. A used-car price quotation represents the price of a stock and can fluctuate in response to demand shifts over a wider range than the price of a new car. When there is a sharp drop in the demand for a particular model car, as in the case of large cars in the aftermath of the 1974 and 1979 oil price shocks, the price of the used car may fall below the transaction price of the new car. A dealer may limit the new-car discount that is offered, choosing to retain unsold cars as inventory (in the hope that demand will revive) rather than selling them at a loss. When there is a sharp rise in the demand for a particular model car, the price of the used car may rise above the transaction price of the new car, although there is no limit in the premium that dealers can charge (and dealers are known to have charged substantial premiums in 1983–85 on Japanese cars in short supply because of import quotas).

While correct in principle, this objection to the transaction price proxy methodology seems to have more force for individual models than for the U.S. car market as a whole. Episodes of shortage and surplus, while common for individual models, have been relatively rare and short lived for the aggregate car market. The major exception is the early postwar period, when high used car prices may reflect a combination of premiums above list price and the imputed value of waiting time for new cars in scarce supply. For this period, the transaction price proxy amounts to a shadow price of new cars as viewed by the consumer.

A second problem with my approach is that the used car price quotations do not refer to a uniform month of the year. Quotations are for July during 1947–69, October during 1977–83, and a mixture of months (April, July, and October) during 1970–76. The use of October rather than July in recent years tends to impart a slight downward bias to the increase in the hedonic used car price index (and to the used car price averages) in table 8.9. Another difficulty is that model years run from September to September, beginning in the year before the designation of the model's year, so that the average age of a "one-year-old" 1982 car observed in October 1983 is actually 1.5 years. Assuming that depreciation begins with the date of delivery, the use of the depreciation rate for year 1–2 to proxy the unobserved depreciation rate for year 0–1 may understate the depreciation that actually occurs over the 1.5 years before the "age 1" price quotation, and hence overstate the discount.

Further information on the behavior of prices during that initial 1.5-year period is provided in table 8.12 for full-sized Chevrolet models. For the years based on October observations, 1974 and 1977–83, I show in column 2 the price of an "age 0" car, that is, a 1983 model sold as used in October 1983. Although just 86 percent of the new list price in 1974, the "age 0 used price" rose to a remarkable 97 percent in 1983. Even if there were no discount at all on a new model, it seems implausible that people would have been willing to pay almost as much for a used 1983 model having an average age of six months as for a brand new model.[32] I am not aware that full-sized Chevrolets were being sold at a premium in 1982–83.

This leads to the third objection, that more optional equipment may be included in the used-car quotations than in the new-car list price, causing an upward bias in the transaction price proxy for new cars. The list prices of new cars and the retail values of used cars are adjusted to provide a consistent treatment of automatic transmission, power steering, and air conditioning. But, as shown in table 8.2, there has been a marked increase in the fraction of automobiles equipped with particular types of factory-installed equipment. And, within categories, there has also been a shift to higher quality, for example, from AM radios to stereo tape decks, and from manual to automatic control air conditioning. To the extent that my prices of used cars fail to "strip out" the value of these additional items that are not included as standard in the list price of the new car, there will be a spurious increase in the ratio of the used price to the new list price and a spurious finding of a reduction in discounting.

Fortunately, the used car guides that serve as data sources for this study make a fairly careful attempt to list the retail value of optional equipment separately from the value of the car equipped with standard items. For instance, the price for a one-year-old full-sized 1982 Chevrolet in the 1983 *NADA Official Used Car Guide* explicitly lists separate retail values for the following items, thus excluding them from the used one-year-old price quotation: vinyl roof, AM/FM/stereo with or without tape, power seats, power windows, power door locks, rear window defroster, wire wheel covers, tilt steering wheel, cruise control, luggage rack, and custom paint. Air conditioning is included, although not standard equipment, but I have stripped the value of air conditioning, automatic transmission, and power steering, from both the new list and the used price quotations. Of the items in table 8.2 that might be optional equipment but are not listed separately in the *Used Car Guide,* this leaves deluxe (automatic control) air conditioning, tinted glass, adjustable steering column, and remote control side mirror. Other items that are not listed in table 8.2 but that might be included as optional equipment are

---

32. An interesting comparison can be made between year 0–1 and year 1–2 depreciation rates for 1974 and 1977–83. From table 8.12, we have:

	1974	1977	1978	1979	1980	1981	1982	1983
0–1	21	21	16	19	17	19	19	16
1–2	20	21	26	17	21	20	17	17

For 1974–77 and 1981–83, the depreciation rates are quite close. The zigzags in 1979–80 may have been related to the oil price shocks. As for 1978, it is interesting to speculate that the used-car market treated the 1977 downsized Chevrolet as substantially more valuable than the previous larger-size 1976 model.

deluxe interior and exterior trim packages, bumper guards, and other items. It seems plausible to guess that the typical one-year-old full-sized Chevrolet in 1983 might have been equipped with $200–$300 in optional equipment that was not included in the list price of the new 1983 model. This would imply that the transaction price proxy overstates the 1983 price by 2–3 percent. Since this degree of possible overstatement seems relatively minor in comparison with other possible sources of error, it is neglected in the final calculations in the next section.

8.9   The "Final Alternative" Index

Tables 8.14 and 8.15 exhibit the steps taken to create the "final alternative" price index. Shown in the first three columns of table 8.14 are the CPI, the CPI before adjustment for quality change (available only after 1966), and the new car hedonic index from table 8.8. The ratio of the hedonic index to the CPI through 1966 and to the unadjusted CPI after 1966 is shown in column 4. This ratio shows remarkably little trend, remaining flat between 1947 and 1967, declining to 0.83 in 1980, and then jumping back to 0.90 in 1983. The 1967–80 decline indicates an improvement in quality as evaluated by the hedonic index, relative to the quality implicit in the unadjusted CPI. Another reason for the lesser rise in the hedonic index during the 1972–80 period and 1980–83 turnaround is that it excludes the prices of imported cars, which are included in the CPI. The depreciating dollar during 1972–80 boosted the relative prices of imported cars, while the appreciating dollar during 1980–83 reduced the relative prices of imported cars.

Because the CPI (unadjusted after 1966) and hedonic index have different strengths and weaknesses, I take their average as the "base price" for further quality adjustments. The feature they share in common is that neither index adjusts for the value of safety and pollution devices or changes in fuel economy. The unadjusted CPI has the advantage that (at least in theory) it takes into account changing discounts and warranty provisions, while the hedonic index has the advantage that it provides at least a crude adjustment for major changes in weight, length, and horsepower. The average of these two indexes is displayed in column 5 of table 8.14 and in column 6 is compared with the adjusted CPI.

Turning now to table 8.15, the "base" price index is copied into column 1. But the base index does not take account of safety and emission-control equipment. To achieve a correction for the value of this equipment, I take the component of the CPI quality adjustment due to safety and emissions-control equipment from table 8.10, columns 3 and 4, and display an index of the combined CPI adjustment in table 8.15, column 2. This is stated as an inverse of the quality index, in order to indicate the amount by which the price index needs to be reduced to account for the addition of safety and emission-control equipment.

Table 8.14   Calculation of "Base" Price Index for New Cars, 1947–83 (1967 = 100)

	CPI (1)	Unadjusted CPI (2)	New Car Hedonic Index (3)	Ratio of (3) to (1) or (2) (4)	Average of (3) and (1) or (2) (5)	Ratio of (4) to CPI (6)
1947	69.2		67.7	0.98	68.5	0.99
1948	75.6		77.9	1.03	76.7	1.02
1949	82.8		91.4	1.10	87.1	1.05
1950	83.4		87.8	1.05	85.6	1.03
1951	87.4		95.1	1.09	91.3	1.04
1952	94.9		97.0	1.02	96.0	1.01
1953	95.8		97.0	1.01	96.4	1.01
1954	94.8		94.2	0.99	94.5	1.00
1955	90.9		99.0	1.09	95.0	1.04
1956	93.5		97.0	1.04	95.3	1.02
1957	98.4		98.0	1.00	98.2	1.00
1958	101.5		97.0	0.96	99.3	0.98
1959	105.9		99.0	0.93	102.5	0.97
1960	104.5		98.0	0.94	101.3	0.97
1961	104.5		99.0	0.95	101.8	0.97
1962	104.1		103.0	0.99	103.6	0.99
1963	103.5		101.0	0.98	102.3	0.99
1964	103.2		100.0	0.97	101.6	0.98
1965	100.9		98.0	0.97	99.5	0.99
1966	99.1		99.0	1.00	99.1	1.00
1967	100.0	100.0	100.0	1.00	100.0	1.00
1968	102.8	104.7	104.1	0.99	104.4	1.02
1969	104.4	106.3	102.0	0.96	104.2	1.00
1970	107.6	111.5	105.1	0.94	108.3	1.01
1971	112.0	116.3	112.7	0.97	114.5	1.02
1972	111.0	116.1	108.3	0.93	112.2	1.01
1973	111.1	121.6	106.2	0.87	113.9	1.03
1974	117.5	133.9	113.9	0.85	123.9	1.05
1975	127.6	151.5	133.6	0.88	142.6	1.12
1976	135.7	161.8	140.5	0.87	151.2	1.11
1977	142.9	173.1	144.8	0.84	159.0	1.11
1978	153.8	188.6	166.5	0.88	177.6	1.15
1979	166.0	205.6	173.3	0.84	189.5	1.14
1980	179.3	233.5	193.5	0.83	213.5	1.19
1981	190.2	274.0	243.5	0.89	258.7	1.36
1982	197.6	291.0	263.8	0.91	277.4	1.40
1983	202.6	305.0	274.6	0.90	289.8	1.43

Sources by column: (1) Table 8.8, col. 1. (2) Table 8.10, col. 1, multiplied by ratio of CPI in col. 1 to adjusted CPI in table 8.10, col. 6. (3) Table 8.8, col. 6. (4) Column 3 divided by col. 1 through 1966 and by col. 2 after 1966. (5) Average of cols. 3 and 1 through 1966 and of cols. 3 and 2 after 1966. (6) Ratio of col. 4 to col. 1.

The adjustment for premiums and discounts displayed in column 3 is taken to be half the transaction price adjustment from table 8.9, column 6. I choose to include only half this adjustment, for two reasons. First, the base index is based on both the CPI and the hedonic index, but the CPI (at least since about 1960) is in principle already adjusted for changing discounts, and thus the transaction price adjustment should be applied only to the hedonic part of the base price index. Second, I suggested above that part of the large transaction price adjustment for 1947–48 represents the imputed value of consumer

Table 8.15   Calculation of Alternative Price Index for New Cars, 1947–83 (1967 = 100)

	"Base" Price Index (1)	CPI Safety and Environmental Quality Adjustment (2)	Adjustment for Discounts (3)	Adjustment for Value of Fuel Economy (4)	Final Alternative Index (5)	Ratio of (5) to New Car CPI (6)
1947	68.5		128.2	106.1	93.1	134.6
1948	76.7		127.2	106.1	103.6	137.1
1949	87.1		107.5	106.1	99.4	120.0
1950	85.6		108.4	105.2	97.6	117.0
1951	91.3		106.4	105.2	102.1	116.8
1952	96.0		109.8	104.5	110.1	116.0
1953	96.4		108.7	104.6	109.7	114.5
1954	94.5		106.1	105.3	105.6	111.4
1955	95.0		108.5	105.4	108.6	119.5
1956	95.3		107.6	105.3	108.0	115.5
1957	98.2		106.3	105.5	110.2	111.9
1958	99.3		98.8	105.4	103.4	101.9
1959	102.5		101.8	103.8	108.3	102.3
1960	101.3		103.2	101.5	106.1	101.5
1961	101.8		103.8	102.5	108.3	103.6
1962	103.6		102.0	102.8	108.5	104.2
1963	102.3		104.3	102.4	109.2	105.5
1964	101.6		102.8	102.6	107.2	103.9
1965	99.5		105.0	101.6	106.1	105.1
1966	99.1		101.1	100.1	100.2	101.1
1967	100.0	100.0	100.0	100.0	100.0	100.0
1968	104.4	98.2	100.7	99.6	102.8	100.0
1969	104.2	97.6	98.8	100.3	100.9	96.6
1970	108.3	96.4	100.7	100.7	105.9	98.4
1971	114.5	96.0	99.7	101.3	111.1	99.2
1972	112.2	95.7	103.5	99.6	110.7	99.7
1973	113.9	91.9	108.2	95.5	108.1	97.3
1974	123.9	88.4	104.8	92.5	106.2	90.3
1975	142.6	84.9	106.4	95.9	123.4	96.7
1976	151.2	84.4	109.1	95.5	133.0	98.0
1977	159.0	83.9	107.5	93.4	133.9	93.7
1978	177.6	83.7	105.7	90.8	142.7	92.8
1979	189.5	83.4	102.7	89.4	145.0	87.3
1980	213.5	81.1	105.1	87.9	159.9	89.2
1981	258.7	74.2	103.7	86.5	172.2	90.5
1982	277.4	73.1	104.2	86.3	182.1	92.1
1983	289.8	72.3	107.5	83.9	188.9	93.2

Sources by column: (1) Table 8.14, col. 5. (2) Exponential index created from minus the logs of the indexes exhibited in table 8.10, cols. 3 and 4. (3) Exponential index created from 0.5 of the log of the transaction price adjustment displayed in table 8.9, col. 6. (4) Exponential index created by taking -0.31 times the log of the fuel economy index in table 8.11, col. 4. (5) Exponential index created from the sums of the logs of the indexes in this table, cols. 1–4. Column 2 excluded from 1947 to 1966. (6) Column 5 divided by table 8.14 col. 1.

waiting time, rather than a pecuniary premium paid to automobile dealers, and the inclusion of this imputed value of waiting time would be inappropriate for an automobile price index intended for the deflation of expenditures on producer durable equipment.

The adjustment for fuel economy needs to place a value on the linked fuel economy index from table 8.11, column 4. I join Crandall et al. (1976, 133) in using a Department of Transportation estimate of 31 percent for the present value of gasoline costs to that of capital costs for 1972 (the other figure given is 42 percent for 1981, but I ignore this larger figure in order to arrive at a relatively conservative adjustment). To convert the index of improved fuel economy into an index of saving in capital cost, -0.31 is multiplied by the log of the fuel economy index and converted to an index in column 4 of table 8.15.

This procedure is subject to several qualifications. The use of the new hedonic index as half the base index is subject to all the criticisms of hedonic indexes and in particular the possibility that the hedonic index may exaggerate the decline in quality associated with downsizing since 1976. The CPI "other" quality adjustments indicate a 10 percent improvement in quality between 1967 and 1983, beyond the effect of safety and emission-control equipment. By excluding any adjustment for these "other" quality improvements, I lean toward an overstatement of price increases. However, an offsetting understatement of price increases may occur if there is double counting of the value of fuel economy. Unfortunately, the BLS press releases are inconsistent, mainly including changes involving fuel economy in the "other" category (which I exclude), but sometimes including those changes in the emission-control category, with no information on the portion attributable to fuel economy. Without further information on their relative sizes, the size of these offsetting biases cannot be estimated.

The final alternative price index in column 5 of table 8.15 combines the base price index with the three adjustment factors in columns 2, 3, and 4. The ratio of the alternative index to the CPI for new cars is shown in column 6. There are up-and-down movements but essentially no drift in this ratio from 1958 to 1976, and a decline in the ratio to an average for 1977–83 of 91.2 percent. Considering the large differences between the new car hedonic index and the new car CPI, or between the used car and new car CPI, the differences between the final index and the CPI over the 1957–83 period seem relatively minor. In the first decade of 1947–57, however, the differences are more substantial. These differences are mainly due to the discounting and fuel economy adjustments, since there is very little difference in the growth rates of the new car hedonic index and the CPI between 1947 and 1958.

8.10   Comparisons of "Closely Similar" Models

In a previous paper (Gordon 1971b), and in an earlier version of this book, substantial attention was paid to comparisons over a decade or more of models having roughly the same physical and performance attributes. Because such comparisons have been rightly criticized as subjective and anecdotal, I do not place much emphasis on them here. Nevertheless, such comparisons are interesting in providing another view of at least the order of magnitude of price changes over substantial periods. Both comparisons involve full-sized Chevrolet four-door sedans and cover, respectively, the intervals 1960–71 and 1962–77. Numerous details on specifications are provided in the exhibits prepared by General Motors (tables 8A.1 and 8A.2). This section compares the price changes over the intervals calculated by General Motors, after adjustment for changes in standard equipment, as well as safety and pollution equipment, with the CPI and a version of the "final alternative index" for new cars that incorporates the CPI safety and emissions-control adjustments but excludes the fuel economy and discounting adjustments, since the General Motors data are for list prices and make no adjustment for fuel economy.[33]

Change In:	1960–71	1962–77
General Motors adjusted price	6.6	35.3
CPI	7.6	37.3
New hedonic index with safety and emissions control adjustments	10.8	17.4

In both comparisons, the change in the CPI is closer to the General Motors adjusted price change than is the adjusted new hedonic index. This is not surprising, since General Motors is one of the main sources of the CPI data, and the General Motors adjustments for safety, emission-control, and optional equipment made standard are among the main sources of the CPI quality adjustments. The adjusted hedonic index is fairly close to the General Motors adjusted price change for 1960–71 but registers less than half the increase for 1962–77, with the discrepancy presumably occurring between 1971 and 1977.

A hint as to the problem with the new hedonic index is that the mean unadjusted price in the hedonic sample rises by just 36 percent between 1971 and 1977, compared to 55 percent for the unadjusted CPI price mean (in contrast to the full 1967–83 period in table 8.10, when the respective increases are 183 and 196 percent). This suggests that there may be a timing problem in using the hedonic index over short intervals, since the unadjusted price means agree fairly closely over longer intervals. A related fact is that the ratio of the used hedonic to the new hedonic index rises by 15 percent between 1971 and 1977 (table 8.9, col. 2), which could reflect in part shrinking discounts on new cars, but also a decline in quality as measured by the used car regression coefficients as contrasted with the new car coefficients.

8.11 Conclusion

This chapter has presented a wide variety of new evidence on new and used automobile prices, including hedonic regression indexes estimated from data on both new cars and used cars over the full 1947–83 period, and has

___

33. Also excluded is the dealer preparation fee for the 1971 car, since it was not included in 1960.

developed adjustments from the BLS statements on the value of safety and emissions-control equipment, and adjustments from previous investigators on the value and extent of improved fuel economy. The result is a price index that increases at roughly the same rate as the CPI between 1958 and 1983 (annual growth rates of 2.4 percent for the new index and 2.8 percent for the CPI). Before 1958, the new index declines substantially relative to the CPI, reflecting primarily the effects of a shift from premiums to substantial discounts from list price in new car transaction prices.

There are greater differences between the new index and the CPI over shorter intervals. These timing differences could reflect any number of factors, including shifts in the mix of the hedonic sample, erratic changes in hedonic coefficients, and the fact that the hedonic prices and characteristics are copied from a used car guide for a single month each year, in contrast to the CPI, which is an annual average. However, there is a clear substantive reason that explains in part why the final index falls relative to the CPI in the late 1970s and recovers in the early 1980s. Since the CPI includes imported cars, but the final index does not, one would expect the CPI to rise more rapidly when the foreign exchange rate of the dollar is depreciating, as in 1976–80, and to rise more slowly when the exchange rate of the dollar is appreciating. The timing in column 6 of table 8.12 is just right for this interpretation, since the ratio of the final index to the CPI dips from 98.0 percent in 1976 to 89.2 percent in 1980, and then recovers to 93.2 percent in 1983. Another period when the final index rises relative to the CPI is 1959–65. This is consistent with the previous work of Ohta and Griliches and of Triplett, in that both studies concluded that the CPI may have registered too low a rate of price change in the first half of the 1960s.

Despite these differences, the general agreement between the new index and the CPI after 1957 is reassuring, and the differences are relatively small as compared to the enormous differences since 1970 in the used car CPI contrasted with the new car CPI, and between an unadjusted hedonic price index for new cars and the new car CPI. It is clear that a hedonic index cannot be used by itself and must be adjusted for changes in quality taking the form of safety and emission-control equipment, and for changes in fuel economy. As for the CPI used car index, it suffers from exactly the same flaw as the unadjusted hedonic price index for new cars. As shown in column 5 of table 8.9, there is virtually no secular drift in the ratio of the used car hedonic index and the CPI for used cars from 1964 to 1983. Since there is no drift in the same period between the used hedonic index and the unadjusted mean price of used cars in the sample, we can deduce that there is essentially no adjustment for quality change in either the used car hedonic index or in the CPI for used cars.

Thus, the CPI indexes for new cars and used cars are simply inconsistent, and the latter index should be discarded. As long as the BLS continues to publish its misleading used car index, users of the statistics will be tempted to compare the CPI used car and new car indexes and reach erroneous conclusions. The most obvious example of this is the use of both indexes by the BEA in its PDE deflator for automobiles. Since business purchasers of new cars are deflated by the new car CPI (or equivalent new car PPI), while business sales to households are deflated with the inconsistent and non-quality-adjusted used car CPI, the BEA is mixing apples and oranges and as a result publishes a nonsensical PDE deflator for automobiles that actually declines by 25 percent from 1980 to 1984 (see table 8.8). It would be far better for the BEA to construct its own used car index, by introducing the published quality adjustment factors from the new car CPI (as recorded in table 8.10, cols. 3–5), assuming that the CPI ''other'' quality adjustment (excluded from the final index) at least partially takes into account improvements in fuel economy.

Appendix

Table 8A.1   **General Motors Comparison of Price and Quality Characteristics of 1960 and 1971 Chevrolet Impala**

	1960 Impala Four-Door Sedan	1971 Impala Four-Door Sedan
V-8 engine:		
Gross horsepower	250	245
Cubic-inch displacement	348	350
Gross torque at 2,800 rpm	355	350
Curb weight (pounds) with powerglide and power steering	4,025	4,093[a]
Exterior dimensions (inches):		
Wheelbase	119.0	121.5
Overall length	210.8	216.8
Overall width	80.8	79.5
Overall height—Loaded	56.0	54.1
Tread width		
Front	60.3	64.1
Rear	59.3	64.0
Interior dimensions (inches):		
Head room		
Front	39.5	38.9
Rear	38.2	38.0
Leg room		
Front	44.5	42.5
Rear	42.5	39.2
Hip room		
Front	65.3	62.0
Rear	65.4	61.9
Shoulder room		
Front	60.5	64.3
Rear	59.0	63.5
Entrance height		
Front	29.4	30.9
Rear	28.0	31.0

Table 8A.1 (continued)

	1960 Impala Four-Door Sedan with V-8 Engine, List ($)	1971 Impala Four-Door Sedan with V-8 Engine, List ($)
Base car price	2,462.00	3,542.00
Options offered in 1960 made standard:		
Heater and defroster	69.00	Standard
Luggage compartment lamp	2.25	Standard
Permanent coolant	5.00	Standard
Instrument panel pad	17.00	Standard
Outside rearview mirror	4.25	Standard
Two-speed wipers and washers	15.00	Standard
Nonglare inside rearview mirror	4.00	Standard
Increased tire size	14.00	Standard
Increased engine size	75.00	Standard
	205.50	
Subtotal	2,667.50	3,542.00
Options offered after 1960 made standard:		
Padded sun visors	6.00	Standard
Two rear seat belts	12.00	Standard
Two front seat belts	17.50	Standard
Front seat belt retractors	4.00	Standard
Hazard warning flasher	11.00	Standard
Exhaust emission control (including PCV valve)	47.50	Standard
Shoulder belts	22.00	Standard
Front and rear center seat belts	12.00	Standard
Depressed park windshield wipers	18.00	Standard
Head restraints	16.00	Standard
Variable ratio power steering	110.00	Standard
High-level ventilation system	15.00	Standard
Bias belt tires	30.00	Standard
Turbo-hydra-matic transmission	205.00	Standard
Evaporative emission control	35.00	Standard
Power disc brakes	61.00	Standard
Increased wheel size	8.00	Standard
	630.00	
Total base car adjusted to 1971 standard equipment	3,297.50	3,542.00[b]
Optional equipment:		
AM pushbutton radio	65.00	63.00
Whitewall tires	34.00	29.00
Electric clock	Standard	16.00
	99.00	108.00
Total car and options	3,396.00	3,650.00

Note: Standard equipment in 1971 is not identical to the optional items shown in prior years: the optional items most nearly comparable were selected.

[a]Shown for comparability purposes; effective 1 May 1971, the turbo-hydra-matic transmission became standard, increasing the weight by seventy-three pounds.

[b]Includes $31 dealer preparation charge that may be claimed by dealer on completion of new car preparation.

Table 8A.2   **General Motors Comparison of Price and Quality Characteristics of 1962 and 1977 Chevrolet Impala (from General Motors News Release #8210, July 1977)**

DETROIT—Today's American automobile is worth more than its 1962 ancestor, from the standpoint of both adjusted price and technological improvement.

Commenting on a recent study of vehicle design over a 15-year period, Robert D. Lund, Chevrolet general manager and General Motors vice president, believes the automobile has not only maintained, but increased its value compared with its 1962 predecessor. The results of the study seem to dispell the myth that "they don't build 'em the way they used to."

"We think the 1977 full-size Chevrolet, for example, has far greater value than its 1962 counterpart from virtually any standard of comparison including economy, performance, maintenance, ride, handling, durability, quietness, comfort and interior roominess," Lund said.

"To prove this contention, we took the base prices of a 1962 and 1977 Chevrolet Impala sedan and adjusted them according to the standard U.S. Bureau of Labor cost of living scale.

"Adjusting the list price of the 1962 Impala for increases in the Consumer Price Index (all items average) as published by the U.S. Department of Labor, and including adjustments for equipment, safety and emission items, the price level today would approximate $6,000," said Lund.

"This simply means that the Manufacturer's Suggested Retail Price of our 1977 Impala at $4,900.65 is nearly $1,100 *less* than the adjusted price of the 1962 Impala, a definite bargain when considering increases in the cost of living scale since 1962."

Lund noted the recent study showed a price breakdown of the two vehicles as follows:

	List Price
1962 Impala 4-Door Sedan	$2,529
1977 Impala 4-Door Sedan	4,887
Net Increase	$2,358
Detail of Net Increase:	
Safety and Emissions	$ 537
Added Value-Equipment	546
Economics and Other	1,275
Total	$2,358

The 1977 Chevrolet Caprice and Impala are the first of a new wave of more cost effective vehicles and Lund believes these cars will become increasingly popular "because of dramatically changing social, economic and environmental conditions in the world today."

Besides having an overall roominess index superior to the 1962 Impala, the '77 model shows dimensional advantages in rear head room, front and rear leg and shoulder room. The '77 also has greater total glass area, more usable luggage space, and a lower curb weight.

Lund said the EPA city/highway fuel economy rating for the '77 is 16 and 21 mpg respectively, while figures simulated by GM for the 1962 Impala are 14.6 and 15.9 mpg. Acceleration at zero-to-sixty mph favors the 1977 Impala with 12.3 seconds to 14.2 seconds for the 1962.

Seven complete emission control systems are offered on the '77 Impala: fuel evaporation control, positive closed crankcase ventilation, controlled combustion system, carburetor hot air, early fuel evaporation, exhaust gas recirculation and underfloor catalytic converter. The 1962 Impala offered only the positive crankcase ventilation system.

The study also shows that 1962 recommended service intervals called for vehicle maintenance every 1,000 miles, or 50 times in 50,000 miles. Current vehicle service intervals require visits for maintenance only six or seven times in 50,000 miles.

Lund commented on the marked improvement of automobile engineering and design technology, particularly with the debut of the 1977 Chevrolet Caprice, recipient of the MOTOR TREND "Car-of-the-Year" award.

Table 8A.2 (continued)

"The 1977 Caprice and Impala use the most advanced automobile technologies available including computer finite element modeling, plastic model stress analysis, ride simulation and aerodynamic wind-tunnel testing.

"As a result, the '77 Caprice and Impala provide greater fuel economy, more interior and trunk space, and significant overall reduction in vehicle mass.

"We feel that the significant improvement in value to our customers over the past 15-year period is typical of the kind of progress our industry has made since 1962," Lund said.

#   #   #

CHEVROLET VALUE COMPARISON

	1977 Caprice Sedan	1962 Impala Sedan	
	DIMENSIONS AND WEIGHTS		1977 over (+) under (−) 1962
Wheelbase	116.0	119.0	−3
O.A. length	212.1	209.6	+2.5
Overhang—front	40.0	32.7	+7.3
—rear	56.1	57.9	−1.8
Tread —front	61.8	60.3	+1.5
—rear	60.8	59.3	+1.5
O.A. height	56.0	56.1	−.1
O.A. width	76.0	79.0	−3
Front—head (effective)	39.0	39.0	0
—leg (effective)	42.2	41.8	+.4
—hip	55.0*	63.5	−8.5
—shoulder	60.8*	58.7	+2.1
Rear—head (effective)	38.2	38.0	+.2
—leg (effective)	39.5	38.2	+1.3
—hip	55.3*	63.4	−8.1
—shoulder	60.8*	57.8	+3
Glass area	4363.2 Sq.In.	4195.6 Sq.In.	+167.6
Luggage (usable)	20.2 Cu.Ft.	19.0 Cu.Ft.	+1.2
Curb weight—lbs.	3716	3775	−59

*Not directly comparable to 1962 model because of industry changes to measuring methods enacted in 1975.

GENERAL

Computer assisted design program for body and chassis —finite element models —plastic ⅜ scale models —electronic analyzer —wind tunnel tests	Conventional engineering design and laboratory test methods of that time.
Comprehensive 27-step design level corrosion protection program—extensive use of zincrometal and galvanized metal.	Conventional production and assembly applications of that time.

BODY

Halo roof construction	Conventional
Very extensive acoustical insulation	Adequate insulation
Flow through ventilation	None

(continued)

Table 8A.2 (continued)

1977 Caprice Sedan	1962 Impala Sedan
Thin shell seat design for increased interior space	Conventional frame construction
Full molded foam seat cushions and backrests	Foam pads over conventional spring construction
Folding front seat center armrest	None
1-piece floor carpet extends fully under front seat	Separate front & rear carpets—minimal coverage under front seat
Simplified dash—improved sealing & noise reduction	Conventional construction
Ash tray lamp	Not available
Column mounted headlamp dimmer switch	Conventional floor mounted switch
Luggage compartment lamp	Extra cost
Wiring harness with bulkhead connectors	Conventional harness design with multiple individual connectors
1-piece formed headliner with polyfoam sound insulation	Vinyl headlining on lacing wires

EMISSION CONTROL SYSTEMS

FEC (Fuel Evaporation Control System)	Not available
PCV (Positive Closed Crankcase Ventilation)	Positive Crankcase Ventilation
CCS (Controlled Combustion System)	Not available
CHA (Carburetor Hot Air)	Not available
EFE (Early Fuel Evaporation)	Not available
EGR (Exhaust Gas Recirculation)	Not available
UFC (Underfloor Catalytic Converter)	Not available

SAFETY

Seat belts with pushbutton buckles for all six passenger positions. Two front combination seat and inertia reel shoulder belts for driver (with reminder light and buzzer) and right front passenger.	Seat belts available at extra cost. No shoulder belts available.
Adjustable front seat head restraints	Not available
Energy absorbing padded instrument panel	Extra cost
Safety steering wheel	Not available
Thick laminate windshield	Not available
Safety armrests	Not available
Contoured windshield header	Not available
Energy absorbing steering column	Not available
Passenger guard door locks	Not available
Safety door latches and hinges	Not available
Inertia seat back lock (coupes only)	Not available
Side marker lamps and reflectors	Not available
Parking lamps that light with headlamps	Not available
Four way hazard flasher	Extra cost
Lane change feature in turn signal control	Not available
Two speed windshield wipers with washers	Extra cost (single speed wipers without washers standard)
Day-night inside mirror (vinyl edged, shatter resistant glass, deflecting support)	Day-night mirror extra cost, safety features not available
Dual master cylinder brake system with warning light	Single circuit, no warning light
Starter safety switch	
Outside rear view mirror	Extra cost

Table 8A.2 (continued)

1977 Caprice Sedan	1962 Impala Sedan

CHASSIS

1977 Caprice Sedan	1962 Impala Sedan
Radial ply tires—fiberglass belted—FR78 × 15	Bias ply tires—fabric plies—7.50 × 14
Power steering	Extra cost
Front disc brakes, finned drum rear. Power standard	Drum brakes—front & rear. Power extra cost
Audible front brake wear sensors	Not available
Front ball joint wear indicators	Not available
15 × 6 wheels	14 × 5 wheels

Table 8A.3   **List of Changes and Added Features on Four-Door Chevrolet Sedans, 1948–85**

	List Price of Former Option Made Standard ($)

1948 Six-cylinder Fleetmaster:
  Thermal circuit breakers replace fuses.
  Three-position ignition switch.
  Precision replaceable main bearings.
  Increase in crankcase rigidity.
  Pressure cooling system.
1949 Six-cylinder De Luxe 2100 Fleetline:
  Pushbutton door handles.
  Pushbutton starting motor control.
  Curved windshield—30 percent larger and two piece.
  Concealed fuel tank filler and vent pipe added.
  Deck lid—counterbalanced and keyless lock feature.
  Integral rear fenders part of quarter panel.
  Automatic dome light switches—two.
  Dash panel vents—ducts to front of car.
  Direct double-acting shock absorbers, front and rear.
  Center point steering linkage.
  Bonded brake lining—life approximately doubled.
  New 6.70 × 15 low-pressure tires and wide base rims.   ?
  New mechanical gear shift.
  Improved front suspension.
  Dual rear license lights.
  Foam rubber seat cushions.
  Integral exhaust pipe and muffler.
  Improved transmission.
  Rear window 70 percent larger.
  Larger radiator core.
  Wrap-around front bumpers.
  New windshield wiper assemblies.
  Ventipanes added to rear doors.
  Larger spark plugs—stronger shells.
1950 Six-cylinder De Luxe 2100 Fleetline:
  External hood release.
  Larger exhaust valves.
  Box section roof rails—formerly channel design.

(continued)

Table 8A.3 (continued)

	List Price of Former Option Made Standard ($)

Improved fuel filler pipe.
New front door seal.
New carburetor—concentric float bowl design.
Frame side rails strengthened.
1951 Six-cylinder De Luxe 2100 Fleetline:
Self-energizing brakes—duo serve.
1952 Six-cylinder De Luxe 2100:
Improved shock absorbers.
Four-point engine mounts.
New carburetor and automatic choke.
1953 Six-cylinder 210:
Built-in provision for backup lights.
Improved body structure.
Needle bearings replace bushings—Pitman arm.
One-piece curved windshield.
More rigid crankshaft.
Strengthened engine structure.
Key-turn starter control.
Aluminum pistons.
Cable drive windshield wipers.
Swing-out front door hinges.
Bypass added to cooling system.
Wrap-around rear window area 41 percent greater.
Direction signals.   ?
45-ampere generator replaces 37 ampere.
1954 Six-cylinder 210:
Strap drive clutch—increased torque capacity.
Rear door locks—"free-wheeling" type.
Nylon inserts in rear springs.
Muffler—30 inch replaces 16 inch; back pressure reduced;
   improved silencing.
Engine—compression ratio increased to 7.5:1 from 7.1:1; horsepower
   increased to 115 from 108.
Full pressure lubrication.
Aluminum pistons offset pinned.
New clutch—improved pressure plate.
Improved transmission—use of needle bearings on countershaft; gears shot peened.
1955 Six-cylinder 2100:
New 265 cubic inch V-8 engine—first availability (an option).
Twelve-volt electrical system.
Panoramic wrap-around windshield.
Cowl plenum chamber—vent system.
Hotchkiss drive replaces torque drive.
Spherical joint front suspension.
Brake redesigned for better accessibility; passenger comfort; reduced weight.
Tubeless tires—standard.
Transmission—greater torque transmitting capacity; increased durability.
Rear window visibility increased 21 percent.
Frame—integrated front suspension; cross member lighter; more rigid frame.
Torsion rod deck lid hinges.
Suspended brake and clutch pedals.

Table 8A.3 (continued)

	List Price of Former Option Made Standard ($)
Telltale lights replace ammeter oil gauge.	
Recirculating ball-nut steering gear.	
Automatic transmission indicator mounted on instrument panel.	
Concentric gearshift control.	
New hood lock—improved hinges and catch.	
New rear axle housing assembly—stronger; extra torque capacity; more durability.	
New rotary-type door lock.	
1956 Six-cylinder 2100:	
Full flow oil filter provisions.	
Electric temperature gauge and sending unit.	
Ribbed insulator spark plugs.	
Provision for precision head lamp aiming.	
Improved sealed beam head lamps.	
Bumpers—heavier and wider.	
Frame—stronger.	
Self-cancelling directional signals—standard.	13.08
Improved parking lamps.	
Battery—capacity from 50 to 53 amps per hour; increased durability; guarantee increased from 21 to 36 months.	
Engine—provisions for full-flow oil filter; high lift camshaft; improved carburetor deicing.	
New clutch drive disc.	
Improved tail lamp.	
1957 Six-cylinder 2100:	
Improved rear suspension.	
Rear wheel bearings larger—higher capacity.	
Wheels—14 × 5; larger bead seat; improved cornering.	
Tires—7.50 × 14 replace 6.70 × 15; wider; lower pressure.	?
Bumpers stronger.	
New starter—fully enclosed; greater efficiency; current requirement reduced 36 percent.	
Improved ventilation—substantial increase in air flow.	
More rigid chassis frame.	
Brakes—improved lining and shoe mechanism.	
Windshield visibility increased 69 square inches.	
Head lamps redesigned with provision for air scoop.	
Improved clutch assembly—semicentrifugal.	
New gas filler vent—lessens spill; faster filling rate.	
Improved wiring harness and connectors.	
Improved seat cushions.	
1958 Eight-cylinder Biscayne:	
"X" frame—30 percent greater torsional rigidity; permits lower center gravity.	
Four-link rear suspension with coil springs.	
Two-speed electric windshield wiper.	?
Improved three-speed transmission.	
Improved clutch—new centrifugal feature.	
Foot-operated parking brake.	
283 cubic inch V-8 engine now standard.	
Redesigned front suspension and steering.	
New dual head lamp assembly—formerly single.	

(continued)

Table 8A.3 (continued)

	List Price of Former Option Made Standard ($)
Windshield visibility—4 percent increase.	
Hood panel—inner panel added.	
Fan shroud added.	
New radiator—more effective cooling; "tube-on-center."	
Wrap-around bumpers.	
Propeller shaft—new two-piece with bearing.	
Rocker panels strengthened—inner and outer.	
1959 Eight-cylinder Bel Air:[a]	
Acrylic lacquer—better luster retention; greater stain resistance.	
Dry-type air cleaner more efficient—replaces oil bath cleaner.	
Tyrex tires—longer wearing; improved rayon; 7 percent greater tread life.	
Windshield area increased 53 percent.	
Rear window area increased 15 percent.	
Brakes—improved cooling; 17 percent increase effective lining.	
Frame design change—improved rigidity.	
Improved rear suspension—tie rod added.	
Wheels—short spoke disc wheels replace full spoke disc wheels; improves brake cooling.	
Improved steering mechanism.	
1960 Eight-cylinder Impala:	
Double stroke parking brake.	
Tires—improved Tyrex cord; 12 percent greater tread life; better traction; less squeal.	
Economy Turbo-Fire 283 cubic inch V-8 engine.	
Corrosion-resistant muffler.	
Full-flow oil filter.	?
Improved front seat back.	
Improved braking—less pedal pressure; proportioning of pressure between front and rear.	
Frame—redesigned at "X" member to decrease tunnel; added rear suspension cross member.	
1961 Eight-cylinder Impala:	
Parallel-acting windshield wipers.	
Concentric fuel filler neck.	
Removable instrument console.	
Five-position ignition switch.	
Luggage space increased 15 percent.	
More durable front wheel bearing—tapered roller.	
Straight element windshield glass replaces compound curved glass.	
1962 Eight-cylinder Impala:	
Front fender skirt—corrosion prevention.	
Two-ply tires standard.	
Heater and defroster standard.	69.00
Luggage compartment lamp.	2.25
Heavier bumpers and reinforcements.	
Stronger seat belt attachment.	
1963 Eight-cylinder Impala:	
Washed-dried body rocker panels.	
Self-adjusting brakes—new.	
Delcotron replaces conventional generator.	
Amber directional signals.	
Permanent coolant—antifreeze.	5.00

Table 8A.3 (continued)

	List Price of Former Option Made Standard ($)
Positive crankcase ventilation standard.	5.00
Battery—44 amp replaces 53 amp.	
Horn blowing ring replaces buttons at outer spokes.	
Muffler aluminized.	
1964 Eight-cylinder Impala:	
Two front seat belts standard.	17.50
Front fender reinforcement—new.	
Plastic cowl kickpads replace pressboard.	
Seat belt anchors improved.	
1965 Eight-cylinder Impala:	
New body, trim, glass, and hardware.	
7.35 × 14 nylon tires replace 7.00 × 14.	
Improved front suspension.	
New Salisbury-type rear axle housing.	
New double-walled exhaust pipe.	
New molded hood insulator.	
New frame—perimeter type; all welded with torque box construction.	
Rear bumper—center face bar of heavier gauge steel.	
New relay-type steering linkage and gear.	
New link-type rear suspension.	
New propeller shaft—one-piece shaft replaces two-piece shaft.	
1966 Eight-cylinder Impala:	
Two rear seat belts.	12.00
Instrument panel pad.	17.00
Outside rearview mirrors.	4.25
Two-speed wiper and washer.	15.00
Padded sun visors.	6.00
Ignition switch—push-turn accessory position.	
Windshield strengthened—double thickness laminate.	
Brake lines—super terne-coated; increased thickness.	
Wrap-around taillight provides side visibility.	
7.75 × 14 tires replace 7.35 × 14.	14.00
Addition of no. 6 body mounts—right and left.	
Aluminum distributor housing replaces iron.	
Improved water pump.	
Door rubber seal added.	
1967 Eight-cylinder Impala:	
Nonglare inside rearview mirror—day/night.	4.00
Increased tire size—8.25 × 14 replaces 7.75 × 14.	14.00
Front seat belt retractors.	4.00
Hazard warning flasher.	11.00
Energy absorbing steering wheel.	
Energy absorbing steering column.	
Fusible link wiring harness.	
Stamped steel door hinges—replace malleable iron.	
Dual master cylinder brake system & warning light.	
Larger fuel tank—improved retention; new metering unit.	
Carburetor linkage—anti-hangup feature.	
Air cleaner—reduced height; smaller diameter.	

(continued)

Table 8A.3 (continued)

	List Price of Former Option Made Standard ($)
Window regulator knobs—soft vinyl.	
Front and rear seat belts—new pushbutton belt buckles replace lever releases (less retractors).	6.00
Steering linkage improved—less effort.	
Exhaust pipe and crossover improved.	
New "energizer" storage battery.	
Head lamp housings eliminated.	
Breakaway rearview mirror support.	
Seat belt anchorages improved.	
Instrument cluster—printed circuit replaces wiring.	
Fiber optics—light ignition key hole.	
Seat back and latch—improved seat construction.	
1968 Eight-cylinder Impala:	
Exhaust emission control including PCV valve.	47.50[b]
Shoulder belts.	22.00
Front and rear center seat belts.	12.00
Depressed park windshield wipers.	18.00
Electric clock deleted.	(16.00)
Nonglare finish—horn button and spokes; windshield garnish molding.	
Dome light replaces two side roof rail lights.	
Bumper guards—front.	15.00
Instrument panel cover size increased.	
Rotary action glove box door lock.	
Hood insulator deleted.	
Protective vinyl insert—side moldings.	
Side marker lights—front and rear.	
Ignition buzzer alarm.	
Energy absorbing seat back.	
Larger V-8 engine—307 cubic inch replaces 283 cubic inch.	
Heavier radiator.	
1969 Eight-cylinder Impala:	
Windshield skid header.	
Cowl panel upper strengthened.	
Luggage compartment forward barrier.	
Side impact barrier added.	
Front door locking knobs moved forward.	
Head restraints standard (1/1/69).	16.00
Improved fuel tank security.	
New steering column—ignition lock on column; new ball-type energy absorbing provision.	
Upper level ventilation system.	15.00
Brake pipes—spiral wire protection.	
Engine—235 horsepower 327 cubic inch replaces 200 horsepower 307 cubic inch.	75.00
Variable ratio power steering.	
New double-cushioned chassis sheet metal mounts—two added; metal vibration noise reduction.	
Odometer—antireversing provision.	
Radiator and shroud mounting change provides improved air flow.	
1970 Eight-cylinder Impala:	
New bias-ply, glass-belted tires—G78 × 15 replace 8.25 × 14.	30.00

Table 8A.3 (continued)

	List Price of Former Option Made Standard ($)
Increased wheel size—14 to 15 inches.	8.00
Lights—front parking from class B to A; class A reflexes added to side markers; rear lights from class B to A.	
Improved window regulators—vertical tube guide.	
Exhaust emission control—TCS added in conjunction with CCS.	
Yielding windshield pillar molding.	
Improved body sound insulation.	
New 350 cubic inch engine replaces 327 cubic inch.	
New interlock front engine mounts.	
Improved exhaust system—welded connections and brackets.	
Hood stop pins added.	
New ignition lock—detent accessory position.	
1971 Eight-cylinder Impala:	
Turbo-Hydra-Matic transmission.	205.00
Evaporative emission control.	35.00
Power disc brakes.	61.00
Increased wheel size—15 × 5 to 15 × 6.	
Improved rear lamp reflectors.	
Wheel opening moldings—deleted.	
Single horn replaces dual horns.	
New side terminal battery.	
Improved body mounts—front impact.	
Improved frame—longer; "C" section side rails replace box section; gauge increased.	
Remote hood latch release.	
Bumpers strengthened—gauge increased; rear brackets heavier.	
Emission control—engine adopted for low lead and other emission control improvements.	
Double shell roof construction.	
Thinner windshield glass—visibility increased 11.6 percent.	
New underbody—larger panels; less welding; improved sealing.	
Improved windshield wiper—longer blades and arms; new drive and linkage.	
Improved body ventilation.	
Rear window visibility increased 43 percent.	
New door glass weather seal.	
New molded full-foam—front seat and back; rear seat cushion only.	
Improved body wiring harness.	
Improved front suspension.	
Improved rear axle assembly.	
Steering linkage new—incorporates forward steering.	
1972 Eight-cylinder Impala:	
Three-point seat belt and warning system.	
Front and rear bumper reinforcement—GM 2.5 mph barrier.	
Floor pan construction simplification.	
Emission control—TCS reinstated replacing CEC; new idle stop solenoid.	
Alternator—integral diode set.	
Shoulder belt mounting provisions—rear passengers.	
Body ventilation system—improvements and simplification.	
Exhaust pipes and crossover—gauge increase.	

(continued)

Table 8A.3 (continued)

	List Price of Former Option Made Standard ($)
1973 Eight-cylinder Impala:	
Doors—right and left side impact improvement.	
Frame transmission crossover—heavier gauge.	
Interior trim—flammability.	
Bumpers—front 5 mph impact; rear 2.5 mph impact; enersorbers added to front; rear reinforced.	
Addition of brake proportioning valve.	
Exhaust emission control—addition of AIR and EGR; TCS deleted.	
Simplified evaporation emission control.	
Enclosed bushing engine mounts.	
Alternator—addition of integrated voltage regulator.	
1974 Eight-cylinder Impala:	
Ignition interlock front seat—three-point belt restraint system.	
Front and rear bumpers—5 mph barrier impact; 3 mph corner impacts; enersorbers added rear.	
Roof crush resistance.	
Accelerator control—secondary linkage return.	
Emission control—addition of TVS to EGR.	
Serviceable CV universal joint.	
1975 Eight-cylinder Impala:	
Underfloor catalytic converter system.	
Tandem-type power brakes.	
New brake hoses.	
Speedometer numerals changed.	
Threaded fuel filler cap.	
Improved corrosion resistance.	
Moldings—changed to bimetal sandwich.	
Stationary vent window.	
Frame—gauge increase.	
Front suspension lower control arm front bushing.	
Steel-belted radial tires HR78 × 15—standard.	157.10
1976 Eight-cylinder Impala:	
Hydraulic brake system.	
Exterior protection—new front bar, changed bumpers.	
Check valve at fuel inlet filter.	
1977 Eight-cylinder Impala:[c]	
Exhaust recirculation valve, distributor spark advance curve and carburetor recalibrated.	
Fuel tank—reinforcement and attachment revised.	
Front seat restraint system redesigned.	
Corrosion resistance improved.	
Engine electrical diagnostic connector.	
Acoustics improved.	
Air conditioner compressor changed to cycling clutch orifice tube.	
Four cylinder air conditioning compressor.	
1978 Eight-cylinder Impala:	
Fuel evaporation control.	
Restraint system—front seat portion revised.	
Brake system—active carbon filter added; brake pressure switch from nylon.	
Improved corrosion resistance.	
Bright metal roof drip moldings—standard.	17.00

Table 8A.3 (continued)

	List Price of Former Option Made Standard ($)

1979 Eight-cylinder Impala:
Improved antitheft ignition lock.
Thermac engine temperature sensor in air cleaner.
Improved EGR system.
New single stage two-barrel carburetor.
Cold trapped ignition sparks.
Corrosion resistance improved.

1980 Eight-cylinder Impala:
Air injection reactor.
Electric choke.
Two aluminum steel heat shields.
Low dispersion acrylic lacquer paint.
Reinforcement of each rear end frame.
Solid bumper guard impact stripes.
Improved door locking mechanism.
4.4 liter—267 CID, two-barrel, V-8 engine (optional, part of reported car).
Engine inlet manifold changed to aluminum.
Automatic transmission with torque converter clutch.
High-pressure compact spare and tire.
Lightweight plastic tape drive window regulators.
Two gas spring assists in rear compartment deck lid.
Power steering pump rotor redesigned.
Thickness of rear window reduced.
Reduced weight front rubber floor mats.
Smaller, lighter weight floor mats.
Door impact bar design changed.
Transmission support diameter reduced.
Intermediate exhaust pipe diameter reduced.
Smaller, high efficiency radiator.
Steel-belted radial tire (P205/75 R-15) replaces the FR 78-15/B.
Chassis changes due to tire change.
Improved corrosion resistance.
Removal of air conditioning system diagnostic connector.
Side-lift frame jack.
Removable body rear end finishing panel.
Deluxe seat and shoulder belts—standard.   24.00

1981 Eight-cylinder Impala:
Computer command control emission and fuel control system.
Dual-lead oxidizing reducing converter.
Computer-controlled exhaust gas recirculation valve solenoid replaces thermal
     vacuum switch.
Additional oil separator baffles.
Carburetor vacuum break—tamper proof.
Electronic spark timing.
Heater in-line water shut-off valve.
Activated carbon element added to air cleaner assembly.
Heat activated thermo vacuum switch.
Improved carburetor sealing.
ISO identifying pictures on controls.
Vehicle Identification Number plate.
Electronically controlled converter clutch.
Rear wheelhouse deadener material changed.

(continued)

Table 8A.3 (continued)

	List Price of Former Option Made Standard ($)
Engine inlet manifold changed back to cast iron.	
Reduced front brake drag.	
"Freedom II" battery (F-15) replaces "Freedom I."	
Improved corrosion resistance.	
"Resume speed" memory feature added to cruise control.	
Powertrain protection extended to 24 months or 24,000 miles.	
1982 Eight-cylinder Impala:	
Refinements of the emission control system.	
Changes in fuel evaporation control system.	
Improvement in corrosion resistance.	
New fluidic windshield washer system.	
1983 Eight-cylinder Impala:	
Two flexible plastic tabs sewn to rear seat covers.	
New engine design encloses alternator cooling fan.	
"Dish" reservoir added to fuel tank.	
Improved corrosion resistance.	
Instrument panel radio speakers upgraded.	
Engine electrical diagnostic connector removed.	
1984 Eight-cylinder Impala:	
Altitude sensing switch assembly/barometric pressure sensor.	
Exhaust gas recirculation valve recalibrated and vacuum reducer added.	
Housing pressure altitude advance solenoid added.	
Improved corrosion resistance.	
Improved fuel filter system.	
Refinements to engine compression and oil rings.	
Wheel trim covers—standard.	52.00
1985 Eight-cylinder Impala:	
Computer controlled exhaust gas recirculation system.	
Component parts of THM-2000 automatic transmission modified.	
New antenna.	
"All Seasons" tires size P205/75 R15.	

Note: This table is not explicitly discussed in the text of chap. 8, since the value of most of these changes are difficult to quantify. However, since this material has not been published anywhere else and provides a unique time series on the nature of quality changes throughout the postwar period, it is included here as an appendix.

[a]From 1959 to date, changes in a four-door Impala are noted. For comparability purposes prior to the introduction of the four-door Impala in 1959, four-door, middle-of-the-line vehicles were followed. The eight-cylinder engine did not become available until 1955, and only then as an option. The first V-8 model was introduced in 1958.

[b]Deduct $5.00 for PCV valve reported in 1963.

[c]In view of the significant change in the 1977 model Impala compared with the 1976 model, the BLS ruled that it would be impractical to determine the quality changes on the traditional basis. An acceptable alternative was to report only those quality changes that were clearly identifiable and unrelated to the weight and size reduction of the vehicle.

9   Other Products

9.1   Introduction

This chapter contains shorter studies of three product categories within PDE that do not fit into the other chapters. The three studies have in common only that their exposition does not require the length of a full chapter. By far the most radical results, and among the most important in this book, are obtained for communications equipment, which has emerged in the 1980s as the single most important industry group within PDE. Also included here is railroad equipment; while my results are based on fragmentary data, they represent, I believe, the only academic study that has ever been carried out on price trends for this type of equipment. The third product group is tractors, both the wheel and the crawler types, which are used within agriculture and construction. The studies of railroad equipment and tractors are based on primary data newly collected for this study, while the results for communication equipment are based entirely on a pathbreaking recent study by Kenneth Flamm (1989), who in turn assembled a variety of price data from industry sources. Because the analysis of tractor prices is based on the hedonic regression technique and is similar in many respects to the examination of auto prices in the last chapter, the tractor results are presented as an "appetizer" for the more exciting findings on communication equipment as the chapter's "main course," leaving railroad equipment for dessert. Those readers who are most interested in those product categories where the new results differ radically from the official government price indexes may want to turn first to the study of communication equipment in section 9.3 below.

9.2   Tractors

The new evidence on tractors consists of hedonic regression equations estimated for new and used wheel and crawler tractors. The time periods

383

covered by the hedonic regressions are 1947–76 for new and used wheel tractors, 1950–70 for new crawler tractors, and 1950–74 for used crawler tractors. As will be evident from the description in this section, the need to adjust prices for changes in equipment attachments makes a hedonic regression study of tractor prices a time-consuming enterprise. In order to obtain a tractor price index for the full 1947–83 period covered in this book within the available time constraint, the indexes are extended after the end of the regression sample by constructing matched model indexes for identical new and used wheel tractor models in pairs of adjacent years. For crawler tractors, a paucity of available data dictated a shift from the hedonic to the matched model method for new crawler tractors in 1971 and for used crawler tractors in 1974.

9.2.1 Hedonic Methodology in This and Previous Studies

One of the earliest hedonic regression studies was performed by Lyle Fettig (1963a, 1963b) for farm tractors on data for the periods 1950 and 1953–62. His results indicated only a modest disagreement with the PPI; the overall price increase between 1950 and 1962 was 23.4 percent for his hedonic index and 28.9 percent for the PPI.[1] A new study of tractors seemed warranted not only to extend the sample period beyond Fettig's eleven years to the much longer time interval covered in this book, but also to examine the relation between used and new tractor prices, both as a means of providing a comparison with my study of new and used auto prices in the last chapter, and as a means of determining whether deviations between transaction and list prices have been important in the market for tractors.

A second major regression study was performed by John Muellbauer (1971a) for the period 1958–69 on a very large sample of used tractor prices. Taken together, the Fettig and Muellbauer indexes when spliced together cover about half the thirty-seven year 1947–83 sample period, that is, 1950 and 1953–69. However, this spliced index cannot be used to study either cyclical variations in prices or shifts in the secular growth rate of prices between the decade of the 1950s and the decade of the 1960s, because the two studies differ in their methodology in two major respects. First, Fettig's dependent variable is the list price of the model when new, whereas Muellbauer's is the price of a used model observed at a particular age. This allows Muellbauer to estimate coefficients not only for the various quality characteristics and for the passage of time, but also for depreciation that occurs with age (one to ten years in his data). Second, Fettig adjusts the list prices for changes in the value of attachments and accessories included as standard equipment, whereas Muellbauer does not.

---

1. The increase cited in the text is for the average of the linear and semilog indexes from (Fettig 1963b, 50), as compared with PPI index 11-11-01 for "wheel-type tractors."

The methodology of the hedonic study follows the guidelines set down in chapter 3 above and followed in chapter 8 on automobiles. The dependent variable is the price of late-model used items, which should be a good proxy for the true transaction prices of new items, if late model used tractors are close substitutes for new models. In a period of weak demand, one would expect to observe a decline relative to the list price of new models both in the actual transaction price of new models, as a result of discounting, and in the price of used models. Regression equations are estimated below both for the list prices of new models and for used one-year-old and two-year-old models, and the behavior over time of the used/new ratio is interpreted as evidence of cyclical fluctuations in tractor demand.[2]

While this study follows Muellbauer in its use of prices for used items, it follows Fettig in its adjustments for the value of attachments and accessories. A hedonic regression equation with engine power as its only right-hand quality variable will tend to exaggerate the increase in tractor prices, since the price of a 1976-vintage tractor with a given horsepower engine includes as standard equipment a substantial number of attachments that were absent from a 1947-vintage model of the same horsepower. While the value of these attachments may in principle be estimated by separate dummy variables in the hedonic regression equation, in practice multicollinearity results in erratic and insignificant coefficients. The discussion in chapter 3 above recommends the direct adjustment of the dependent price variable for the value of attachments, and this approach has been carried out for auto accessories in chapter 8. Fortunately, the used tractor guides contain lists of prices suitable for adjusting the dependent price variable in the hedonic regressions. The attachment prices are listed for new tractors. The total value of the attachments on a given model is summed and then subtracted from the list price of the tractor in the same year to yield a "stripped" list price. Then the ratio of the stripped to the actual list price is multiplied by the price of used versions of that model to obtain the "stripped" price of the used model.

Although most readers have personal experiences with the automobile accessories that have been gradually converted from options to standard equipment—heater, outside mirror, multispeed window washers, sun visors, tinted glass, seat belts, head restraints, automatic transmission, power steering, and power brakes—the tractor attachments may be less familiar. Whereas a 1947 tractor was equipped simply with starter, lights, and "power takeoff" (i.e., a drive shaft to connect attachments to the tractor's engine), with even basic equipment like tires priced on some models as an optional

---

2. *The Official Tractor and Equipment Guide* is issued twice each year. Since the vast majority of tractor sales are made in the spring, all prices were copied from the spring edition. I am grateful to F. Wakefield for his hospitality during my visit to the St. Louis headquarters of the National Farm and Power Equipment Dealers Association, where these data were copied in February 1973. Data for the years 1971–83 were obtained by mail from the same source.

extra, by the 1960s the list of standard equipment had grown to include hydraulic systems equipped with sensors to detect changes in terrain and soil conditions, allowing a tractor operator to preset and maintain the draft of ground-working tools. Transmissions also became more complex, with more speeds and the introduction of both semiautomatic and automatic types. Other developments included independent power takeoff, which continues to drive an attachment even when the tractor clutch is disengaged, and the addition of fenders, deluxe seats, and, more recently, enclosed and air-conditioned cabs, as well as electronic monitors that measure and regulate the rate of chemical and seed application. The standard equipment on a 1975 forty-five horsepower International Harvester model 464 gas tractor included, according to the *Official Tractor and Equipment Guide*, ''adjustable front axle; fenders; hydrostatic power steering; starter and lights; independent PTO; 8-speed transmission; 3-point hitch with hydraulic draft control and rockshaft; swinging drawbar.'' Fully 26.4 percent of the price of the average 1970 wheel tractor in my sample was accounted for by equipment that was not included on the average 1947 model.

The procedure of stripping tractors of attachments was performed separately for each model, since the price of a given attachment often varies with the overall size of the tractor. Since the calculation was performed only once when the model was introduced, the price of attachments in years after the model introduction is implicitly assumed to have behaved in the same manner as the price of the stripped tractor. Clearly, this technique requires the willingness to accept the maintained hypothesis that depreciation of used attachments proceeds at the same rate as for the used basic tractor itself. In some cases, when the prices of attachments are not listed separately in the *Guide,* it was necessary to estimate prices for them by finding the current price of an attachment of similar description on a comparable size tractor of the given manufacturer, and if this was not available, of another manufacturer.

9.2.2   Results: Wheel Tractors

Considering that the prices of some attachments had to be estimated in both this study and Fettig's, that the worksheets for Fettig's detailed calculations are unavailable, and that the sample in this study is smaller, the two studies arrive at remarkably similar adjustments for the time interval that both have in common, as illustrated in table 9.1. The ratio of the actual price to the stripped price in this study rises by 19.9 percent from the average 1950 model to the average 1962 model, whereas in Fettig's study the same ratio rises by 19.7 percent. The year-to-year behavior of the ratios in table 9.1 is also reasonably similar, with little change during 1950–57, a very rapid increase during 1957–60 for this study and 1957–59 for Fettig, and then approximate constancy until 1962. Overall, the 1947–70 increase in the ratio in this study

Table 9.1		Ratio of Actual List Price of Wheel Tractors to Price "Stripped" of Attachments, Average over All Models in Sample in Each Year, 1947–70	

Year	This Study (1)	Fettig (2)	Ratio, This Study/Fettig (3)
1947	0.923	. . .	. . .
1948	0.931	. . .	. . .
1949	1.012	. . .	. . .
1950	1.012	1.012	1.000
1951	1.021	. . .	. . .
1952	1.032	. . .	. . .
1953	1.013	1.064	0.952
1954	1.013	1.091	0.928
1955	1.023	1.076	0.950
1956	1.050	1.068	0.983
1957	1.042	1.073	0.972
1958	1.126	1.141	0.986
1959	1.178	1.218	0.967
1960	1.214	1.205	1.007
1961	1.211	1.206	1.004
1962	1.214	1.211	1.002
1963	1.251	. . .	. . .
1964	1.297	. . .	. . .
1965	1.239	. . .	. . .
1966	1.239	. . .	. . .
1967	1.237	. . .	. . .
1968	1.290	. . .	. . .
1969	1.268	. . .	. . .
1970	1.244	. . .	. . .

Sources: This study (see text), and Fettig (1963b, table 10, p. 40). The level of the index is arbitrary, depending on what equipment is included on the "stripped" model, and is set equal to Fettig's index in 1950.

is 35.8 percent, that is, hedonic regressions estimated from data on unadjusted prices and engine characteristics would exaggerate inflation in tractor prices by 35.8 percent relative to regressions based on adjusted prices.[3]

The treatment of attachments changed after 1970, simply because many items previously listed as attachments became standard, and attachment prices were no longer available. As stated above, for the period after 1970 the new results are based on hedonic regressions for wheel tractors over 1970–76 and matched model indexes over 1976–83. For crawler tractors, all results are for matched models, except for hedonic regressions estimated over 1970–74. All results after 1970 have in common that the only models included in pairs of adjacent years are absolutely identical in model numbers and in the details of standard equipment listed in the used tractor manuals. This feature of the study may make control for quality change better after 1970 than before, for

3. The ratio for this study falls below unity in 1947 and 1948, because models in those years had smaller tires than in 1950; the level of the index is set to equal Fettig's in 1950.

no attempt is made to limit comparisons to observations with identical model numbers before 1970.

While the methodology of this study combines the better features of the previous work by Fettig and Muellbauer, a possible handicap is a much smaller sample size. To minimize the burden of data collection, given the large number of products included in the coverage of this book, tractor price data were collected for only one large manufacturer—International Harvester—and for only two ages of used equipment, one and two years old. Fortunately, Muellbauer's results indicate that the change in tractor prices is virtually identical across manufacturers, and so it would appear that little is lost by the decision to economize on data collection.[4] Similarly, the closely parallel ratios of unadjusted to adjusted prices in table 9.1 indicate that attachments were added to International Harvester tractors to the same extent and at about the same time as for the eight manufacturers included in Fettig's study.[5]

As pointed out in chapter 3, adjustments for attachments must be applied not only to price, but also to any quality characteristics that interact with the attachments. When weight is a quality characteristic included in a hedonic regression, for instance, both price and weight must be "stripped" of the value and weight of attachments. If only the price is adjusted, the coefficient on weight will be biased downward. Fortunately, this problem does not arise in the case of tractors, since the only quality characteristics included in the regressions are horsepower and a dummy variable for diesel engines, and weight is not included.[6] It would be desirable to make an adjustment for improvements in fuel economy, as was so important in the case studies of commercial aircraft and steam-turbine generators earlier in the book, because quality-adjusted fuel economy appears to have improved during the postwar period, but a lack of data precludes explicit fuel economy adjustments.[7]

---

4. Muellbauer (1971, 26) states, "This latest piece of information shows that brand effects do not simultaneously dominate price and depreciation behavior. This suggests that features that might be associated with market imperfections, such as strong brand advertising and brand loyalty more generally, are probably not very powerful."

5. The sample contains all International Harvester wheel-type gas and diesel tractors listed in the *Guide* except for "duplicate models," i.e., models in a given series having differences from included models only with respect to front-end design, high clearance features, special equipment for canefield or orchard operations, or steel wheels in place of rubber tires.

6. Experiments with other variables were conducted by Fettig, who supported the decision to eliminate variables other than belt horsepower and engine-type dummy variables "for either or a combination of two reasons. The first of these is non-significance of the estimated coefficient for the variable and the second is very high correlation with belt horsepower, so that the variable adds to additional explanation of price variance" (Fettig 1963b, 36).

7. Fettig (1963b, 37–38). Barger et al. (1963, 437) explain this phenomenon as follows: "It would appear, superficially, that the efficiency of tractor engines has not increased since 1940. Actually the engine efficiency has increased, but so has the number of power-absorbing accessories and equipment such as hydraulic systems, generators, and more complex transmissions. The result of the addition of accessories to tractors since 1940 has been to offset the increase in engine efficiency since that time." This implies that constant-quality fuel economy

Table 9.2   Adjacent-Year Logarithmic Regressions for Used Gas and Diesel Wheel Tractors, Prices Adjusted for Attachments, 1947–76

Year Pair	Horse power (1)	Dummy = 1 if Diesel (2)	Dummy = 1 if Two Years Old (3)	Time Dummy for Second Year (4)	$\bar{R}^2$ (5)	S.E.E. (6)	Number of Observations (7)
1947–48	0.87**	0.27**	−0.08*	0.19**	0.954	0.092	35
1948–49	0.84**	0.25**	−0.08*	0.19**	0.952	0.081	31
1949–50	0.92**	0.25**	−0.11**	−0.12**	0.951	0.086	31
1950–51	0.91**	0.33**	−0.11**	0.22**	0.974	0.068	35
1951–52	0.85**	0.33**	−0.10**	0.02	0.979	0.057	36
1952–53	0.88**	0.33**	−0.10**	−0.06**	0.976	0.063	37
1953–54	0.93**	0.31**	−0.07**	−0.04	0.965	0.077	34
1954–55	0.89**	0.27**	−0.06	−0.17**	0.947	0.092	23
1955–56	0.49**	0.37**	−0.11**	0.06**	0.981	0.046	18
1956–57	0.60**	0.33**	−0.12**	0.03	0.985	0.057	16
1957–58	0.78**	0.28**	−0.10**	0.10**	0.988	0.042	16
1958–59	0.87**	0.26**	−0.09**	0.09**	0.980	0.064	23
1959–60	0.85**	0.22**	−0.07	−0.07	0.890	0.140	31
1960–61	0.82**	0.19**	−0.10	0.01	0.900	0.131	34
1961–62	0.85**	0.18**	−0.10**	0.06**	0.978	0.064	34
1962–63	0.85**	0.13**	−0.08**	−0.03	0.977	0.063	34
1963–64	0.88**	0.11**	−0.05**	0.04*	0.981	0.053	35
1964–65	0.90**	0.13**	−0.05*	−0.04*	0.972	0.060	37
1965–66	0.88**	0.11**	−0.06**	0.00	0.967	0.068	34
1966–67	0.83**	0.10**	−0.10**	0.05*	0.976	0.062	36
1967–68	0.84**	0.09**	−0.08**	0.05*	0.954	0.085	42
1968–69	0.93**	0.11**	−0.09*	0.03	0.931	0.116	41
1969–70	0.92**	0.12**	−0.10*	0.05	0.914	0.129	36
1970–71	0.79**	0.05*	−0.09**	−0.01	0.960	0.082	44
1971–72	0.81**	0.07*	−0.09**	0.04	0.958	0.091	50
1972–73	0.83**	0.08**	−0.09**	−0.00	0.950	0.100	52
1973–74	0.85**	0.08*	−0.08*	0.05	0.958	0.097	40
1974–75	0.95**	0.05	−0.10**	0.48**	0.977	0.100	51
1975–76	0.98**	0.10**	−0.10**	0.05*	0.979	0.081	60

*Indicates significance at the 5 percent level.

**Indicates significance at the 1 percent level.

The detailed regression results for twenty-eight pairs of adjacent years are listed in table 9.2. As in previous studies in this book (e.g., electric generating equipment, appliances, and electronic computers), all regressions are fitted in double-log form. The tractor equations fit reasonably well, with an average standard error for 1953–62 of 0.0781, as compared to 0.0986 for Fettig's semilog-adjacent-year equations for the same time interval. Compared to the previous equations for appliances in chapter 7, the coefficients on quality characteristics in the tractor regressions are more stable, which may at least partly be a consequence of the larger sample size (which ranges between sixteen and sixty). With the exception

improved, but to take this into account it would be necessary to carry out a study like that of Wilcox (1984) for automobiles, running a regression of fuel economy on a host of quality characteristics. Unfortunately, my data do not permit this additional step.

of the three years when the sample size falls below twenty, the coefficient on horsepower lies in the relatively narrow range of 0.8 to 1.0, with no discernible trend over the postwar period.[8] The coefficient on the diesel dummy declines fairly steadily from an average of 0.29 in the earliest five equations to 0.07 in the last five. The depreciation coefficient (i.e., the dummy variable for two-year-old models) fluctuates between -0.05 and -0.12 but has an average value that agrees closely with Muellbauer's estimate.[9]

Table 9.3 compares the hedonic price index for used tractors derived from the coefficients on the time dummy variables in table 9.2 with three indexes for new tractors—a parallel set of regression equations for new list prices from this study, Fettig's results, and the PPI index for new wheel tractors. Recall that a time constraint led us to extend the hedonic indexes after 1976 with an index of matched models for both new and used tractors. These should be quite reliable, as they are based on a large number of models for both new and used tractors (again, used tractor prices are recorded only for ages of one and two years). Another change made after 1976 is to recognize the supplanting of International Harvester by John Deere as the market leader; all prices for wheel tractors over the period 1977–83 are for John Deere models ranging from the smallest to the largest. The post-1976 matched model index for new wheel tractors is based on as many as seventeen models in a single adjacent-year price comparison, and as many as fifteen for used tractors (i.e., thirty comparisons including both ages, one and two years).

As is shown by the ratios displayed in columns 5–7, the overall rate of secular price change measured by the two hedonic indexes is similar to that of the PPI and, for his limited sample period, to Fettig's index. In contrast to many of the price indexes developed elsewhere in this book for other products, the drift of the three ratios shown in columns 5–7 proceeds at a trivial rate over time. Given the substantial difference in sample size and detailed implementation of the hedonic technique, it is reassuring to find that the ratio of the new list price hedonic index to that of Fettig (col. 6) remains within the narrow range of 0.95–1.04 during the common 1950–62 sample period. We would expect a hedonic price index to exhibit greater fluctuations in price change than the PPI, and indeed such fluctuations are evident in the new/PPI ratio displayed in column 7.

Fluctuations in the ratio of the used hedonic index to the new hedonic index, displayed in column 5, are caused both by variations in the ratio of used prices to the true transactions prices of new tractors, and by variations in transaction relative to list prices. We observe in column 5 greater fluctuations

8. The coefficient averages 0.878 in the first five equations displayed in table 9.2 and 0.884 in the last five equations.

9. For 1958–69, Muellbauer (1971, 26) estimates an average rate of depreciation between one- and two-year-old models of International Harvester wheel tractors of 0.074, with the coefficient constrained to be fixed over the entire time period. The average of my depreciation coefficients for his sample period is 0.078.

Table 9.3   **Alternative Price Indexes for New and Used Wheel Tractors, and Selected Ratios among Indexes, 1947–83**

	This Study, New List Price[a] (1)	Fettig, New[b] (2)	This Study, Used Price[a] (3)	PPI (4)	Ratio, Used/New (5)	Ratio, New/Fettig (6)	Ratio, New/PPI (7)
1947	43.5		51.4	46.9	1.181		0.928
1948	47.8		61.9	52.2	1.294		0.916
1949	54.3		74.7	55.0	1.377		0.987
1950	54.7	57.7	66.1	55.8	1.208	0.948	0.980
1951	68.4		82.3	59.2	1.203		1.156
1952	69.2		83.9	60.0	1.213		1.153
1953	67.6	65.2	78.7	60.3	1.164	1.038	1.121
1954	63.3	63.3	75.4	59.2	1.192	1.000	1.068
1955	60.8	61.3	63.9	58.3	1.050	0.993	1.043
1956	64.7	64.0	67.6	59.7	1.045	1.012	1.084
1957	69.1	66.3	69.9	62.8	1.012	1.041	1.100
1958	70.0	73.8	77.5	65.8	1.107	0.949	1.064
1959	70.2	72.2	84.4	68.3	1.203	0.972	1.028
1960	68.2	72.0	78.7	69.2	1.154	0.947	0.986
1961	73.9	74.5	79.4	70.6	1.074	0.992	1.047
1962	74.9	74.9	84.3	72.5	1.125	1.000	1.034
1963	73.5		81.8	73.3	1.114		1.002
1964	69.9		85.3	74.7	1.220		0.936
1965	75.3		81.8	76.1	1.086		0.990
1966	76.2		81.6	78.6	1.071		0.969
1967	79.1		85.4	81.1	1.079		0.976
1968	85.0		90.0	84.4	1.059		1.007
1969	91.2		93.1	88.3	1.021		1.033
1970	96.5		92.3	92.8	0.957		1.040
1971	100.0		96.1	95.3	0.961		1.049
1972	100.0		100.0	100.0	1.000		1.000
1973	108.5		99.9	101.9	0.921		1.065
1974	120.4		104.8	117.2	0.871		1.027
1975	163.6		169.3	138.6	1.035		1.180
1976	182.9		177.5	150.6	0.971		1.214
1977	200.1		197.3	164.3	0.986		1.218
1978	200.1		215.4	176.8	1.076		1.132
1979	214.4		243.6	194.9	1.136		1.100
1980	233.6		257.8	224.2	1.104		1.042
1981	265.2		294.2	253.3	1.109		1.047
1982	308.2		299.6	277.9	0.972		1.109
1983	322.5		293.4	294.1	0.910		1.097

Sources: Column 3 is constructed by cumulating and taking antilogs of time dummy regression coefficients shown in table 9.2. Column 1 is index calculated in the same way from coefficients in an analogous regression equation for new list prices, not shown separately. Column 4 is PPI index 11-11-01, from App. table B.11.

[a]Indexes for this study in cols. 1 and 3 are matched model rather than hedonic regression indexes for 1976–83.

[b]Fettig index is the average of linear and semilog indexes in Fettig (1963b, 50) and is linked to my new list price hedonic index in 1962.

Table 9.4   Adjacent-Year Logarithmic Regressions for Used Gas and Diesel Crawler
Tractors, Prices Adjusted for Attachments, 1950–74

Year Pair	Horse-power (1)	Dummy = 1 if Diesel (2)	Dummy = 1 if Two Years Old (3)	Time Dummy for Second Year (4)	$\bar{R}^2$ (5)	S.E.E. (6)	Number of Observations (7)
1950–51	1.35**	0.15**	−0.11**	0.20**	0.945	0.052	16
1951–52	1.13**	0.09*	−0.09*	−0.02	0.929	0.068	17
1952–53	1.15**	0.08	−0.10**	−0.01	0.952	0.073	19
1953–54	1.21**	0.08**	−0.12**	0.08**	0.976	0.057	20
1954–55	1.22**	0.09**	−0.10**	−0.07**	0.981	0.051	20
1955–56	1.20**	0.12**	−0.11**	0.04	0.979	0.053	20
1956–57	1.05**	0.12*	−0.11*	−0.09	0.908	0.099	16
1957–58	0.59**	0.20**	−0.11**	0.17**	0.968	0.047	12
1958–59	0.82**	0.17**	−0.10**	0.06**	0.999	0.005	12
1959–60	0.81**	0.19**	−0.10**	0.05**	0.999	0.003	12
1960–61	0.79**	0.18**	−0.09**	0.08**	0.998	0.012	12
1961–62	1.25**	0.10	−0.09*	−0.00	0.949	0.095	18
1962–63	1.40**	0.08	−0.10**	−0.05	0.956	0.088	23
1963–64	1.53**	0.07	−0.11**	0.02	0.953	0.080	21
1964–65	1.74**	0.06*	−0.10**	0.02	0.966	0.063	20
1965–66	1.82**	0.03	−0.10**	0.00	0.967	0.059	19
1966–67	2.42**	−0.04	−0.08	0.04	0.956	0.077	15
1967–68	3.30**	−0.11**	−0.10**	−0.01	0.999	0.086	12
1968–69	1.42**	0.11	−0.13	0.07	0.852	0.168	16
1969–70	1.33**	0.08	−0.12	0.05**	0.998	0.13	18
1970–71	0.74**	. . .	−0.09	−0.02	0.665	0.19	12
1971–72	0.74**	. . .	−0.09	0.02	0.663	0.19	12
1972–73	0.69**	. . .	−0.13	0.04	0.689	0.184	11
1973–74	0.50*	. . .	−0.14	0.05	0.708	0.166	8

*Indicates significance at the 5 percent level.
**Indicates significance at the 1 percent level.

in the ratio of the two hedonic indexes than in the ratio of the new hedonic
index to the PPI: the used/new ratio in column 5 displays a substantial bulge
at the beginning of the sample period and then a gradual downdrift. This ratio
averages 1.252 in the first five years and 1.046 in the last five years of the
sample period. The overall pattern of the used/new ratio for wheel tractors
mirrors many of the features of the used/new hedonic ratio for automobiles
discussed in the previous chapter (see table 8.9), except that the immediate
postwar bulge in the used/new ratio is greater for automobiles, and the
used/new ratio for automobiles increases in 1971–72 to a level about 10
percent higher than that observed in the 1960s, whereas a similar jump for
tractors occurs somewhat later, over the 1978–81 interval.

9.2.3   Results: Crawler Tractors

Separate regression equations were estimated for crawler tractors and are
exhibited in table 9.4. All methodological details, including the adjustments
for attachments, are identical to those for wheel tractors, and the average
standard error is similar for the period 1950–70 (0.0681 compared to 0.0781

for wheel tractors), after which the standard error for crawler tractors is larger, probably due to a much smaller sample size. The smaller average sample size may also explain the less stable coefficients on horsepower and the diesel dummy. Most of the instability occurs in the period 1964–70, when the range of horsepower covered in the sample is quite narrow, only 27–40 hp. In most earlier and later years, larger models are included and help stabilize the coefficient on horsepower. As compared to the wheel tractor regressions, the depreciation coefficients for crawlers are more stable and fluctuate in the relatively narrow range − .09 to − .14.

The hedonic index implied by the regression coefficients of table 9.4 is displayed in column 2 of table 9.5 and is compared there to an analogous hedonic price index based on new list prices (col. 1) and the PPI for crawler tractors (col. 3). Recall that small sample sizes force a switch to the matched model (specification) method for new crawler tractors in 1970 and for used crawler tractors in 1974. Only International Harvester models are included until 1976 but all manufacturers after 1976. The matched model pairs for adjacent years during 1976–83 cover a total of six manufacturers, and those for used crawlers cover three firms (this occurs because the tractor books give new list prices but no used prices for several small firms, probably indicating a small used market for these brands). Until the final decade (1973–83), there is no net drift in the ratio of the hedonic index for new list prices to the PPI, as shown in column 5. This ratio is almost identical in 1947 and 1972, rises above unity during 1951–56, and falls below unity during the period 1957–71.

The sharp decline in the ratio of the new-list-price crawler index to the PPI during 1972–78 is startling. In contrast to the 76 percent increase in the PPI over this six-year period, my index increases only 17 percent. For most of the period, this index is based on two large models (International Harvester TD-15-C and TD-20-C), which exhibited list price increases over 1973–77 of just 11 and 17 percent, respectively. To check on the plausibility of this new list price index, we can examine the price history of these models in the used tractor market, for, if they were underpriced in later years, any price differential compared to similar models should have been eliminated by arbitrage in the used market. Yet we find an increase over 1974–79 of just 31 percent for a one-year-old TD-20-C and just 32 percent for a two-year-old version of the same model, in contrast to an increase of 75 percent in the PPI over the same interval.

The ratio of the used hedonic to new hedonic index (col. 4) displays a substantial downdrift over time, like the used/new ratio for wheel tractors discussed above in table 9.3, but the timing is different. The used/new ratio for wheel tractors exhibits most of its decline during 1949–55, while that for crawler tractors declines mainly between 1967 and 1975, with another decrease during 1979–83 after a temporary increase in between. The final two columns in table 9.5 exhibit the ratio of the crawler to the wheel tractor

Table 9.5   Alternative Price Indexes for New and Used Crawler Tractors, and Selected Ratios among Indexes, 1950–83

	This Study, New List Price[a] (1)	This Study, Used Price[a] (2)	PPI (3)	Ratio, Used/New Crawler (4)	Ratio, New Crawler/ PPI (5)	Ratio, New Crawler/ New Wheel (6)	Ratio, Used Crawler/ Used Wheel (7)
1950	38.5	54.4	37.4	1.411	1.030	0.705	0.823
1951	45.6	66.2	41.1	1.453	1.108	0.666	0.804
1952	47.6	64.7	42.6	1.358	1.119	0.688	0.771
1953	49.1	64.0	45.4	1.303	1.082	0.727	0.813
1954	51.4	69.1	46.9	1.345	1.096	0.812	0.916
1955	53.0	64.8	48.6	1.223	1.091	0.871	1.014
1956	58.1	67.2	54.0	1.157	1.075	0.898	0.994
1957	51.4	61.4	58.6	1.195	0.877	0.744	0.878
1958	56.6	72.8	61.4	1.287	0.921	0.808	0.939
1959	56.7	76.9	63.7	1.357	0.889	0.807	0.911
1960	62.7	80.5	65.7	1.284	0.954	0.920	1.023
1961	66.6	86.7	66.9	1.301	0.996	0.902	1.092
1962	62.2	86.6	67.4	1.391	0.923	0.831	1.027
1963	63.7	82.2	68.9	1.291	0.925	0.866	1.005
1964	64.4	83.9	71.4	1.303	0.902	0.921	0.984
1965	63.9	85.1	73.1	1.331	0.874	0.849	1.040
1966	68.9	85.5	74.9	1.241	0.920	0.904	1.048
1967	69.3	89.1	78.3	1.285	0.886	0.877	1.043
1968	71.4	88.2	84.3	1.235	0.847	0.840	0.980
1969	84.4	94.8	88.6	1.123	0.953	0.926	1.018
1970	84.4	99.8	92.3	1.182	0.915	0.875	1.081
1971	84.4	98.1	96.6	1.162	0.874	0.844	1.021
1972	100.0	100.0	100.0	1.000	1.000	1.000	1.000
1973	105.8	104.5	104.0	0.988	1.017	0.975	1.046
1974	108.7	109.4	122.9	1.006	0.885	0.903	1.044
1975	116.5	116.3	149.7	0.998	0.778	0.712	0.687
1976	116.5	121.5	160.6	1.044	0.725	0.637	0.685
1977	116.5	149.4	176.2	1.283	0.661	0.582	0.757
1978	116.5	152.8	194.3	1.312	0.600	0.582	0.710
1979	116.5	148.0	214.9	1.270	0.542	0.543	0.569
1980	116.5	146.6	239.0	1.259	0.487	0.499	0.569
1981	147.2	151.9	260.7	1.032	0.565	0.555	0.516
1982	159.3	161.2	286.2	1.012	0.557	0.517	0.538
1983	165.1	155.2	295.8	0.941	0.558	0.512	0.529

Sources: Column 2 is constructed by cumulating and taking antilogs of time dummy regressions coefficients shown in table 9.4. Column 1 is index calculated in the same way from coefficients in an analogous regression equation for new list prices, not shown separately. Column 3 is PPI index 11-28-02, from app. table B.11. Column 4 is the ratio of col. 2 to col. 1; col. 5 is the ratio of col. 1 to col. 3; col. 6 is the ratio of col. 1 to col. 1 of table 9.3; col. 7 is the ratio of col. 2 to col. 3 of table 9.3.

[a]Indexes for this study in cols. 1 and 2 are matched model rather than hedonic regression indexes for 1974–83.

hedonic indexes, both new and used. Here we find substantial changes in relative prices that are mimicked in the new and used index ratios, with a substantial increase in the relative price of crawler tractors over the period 1950–60, followed by a sharp decline after 1973.

As in Chapter 8's study of used and new automobile prices, changes in the ratio of the used to new hedonic price index are interpreted as an indicator of shifts in transaction prices for new models relative to list prices. Anecdotal evidence suggests that new tractors have sold for substantial discounts off list price in some periods, and it is plausible that they may have sold for premiums over list price during the farm export boom after World War II, as did automobiles.[10] For this reason, the alternative price index for the tractor component of PDE developed in chapter 12 utilizes the hedonic price indexes for used wheel and crawler tractors displayed in tables 9.3 and 9.5. Any tendency of the used tractor index to overstate the downdrift of true transaction prices relative to list prices should be more than offset by the incomplete adjustment for quality change in the hedonic regression equations. First, no adjustment at all is made for improved "constant-quality" fuel economy or, second, for the types of improvements in riding and handling quality that have occurred in the auto industry.[11]

9.3   Telephone Transmission and Switching Apparatus

In recent years, communications equipment has been the largest single industry group within PDE and accounted for 12.7 percent of nonresidential PDE in 1986, more than either the office and computing (OCAM) or the trucks and busses categories. Within communications equipment, almost all the weight in the PDE deflator is applied to equipment installed by telephone companies for the purpose of transmitting and switching local and long-distance telephone calls.[12] The communications equipment category is of central interest in any study of durable goods prices, not only because of the importance of the category within PDE, but also because of the unusually high rate of R&D spending by manufacturers of telephone equipment and the resulting rapid rate of technological change. Western Electric (hereafter abbreviated WE), the AT&T-owned manufacturing subsidiary, spent 5.8

10. There is no evidence that used late-model tractors sold for more than the list price of new tractors, as was true for autos in 1947–48. However, regarding discounting, a dealer is quoted in 1977 as stating, "Our biggest seller is the 135-hp tractor, which lists for $26,000 . . . but many dealers are selling it for $22,000, just to move tractors off the lot and make enough cash to keep the doors open." This amounts to a discount of 15.4 percent (see "Farm Equipment Sales Go Slow," *Business Week,* 25 July, 1977, 49).

11. In a story about relatively inexpensive imported Russian tractors, a reporter for *Forbes* magazine took a ride both on the 70 hp Russian Belarus and a 65 hp Deere model: "The Deere is quiet, smooth-shifting, with a short turning radius, a steering wheel that responds to one finger and push-button four-wheel drive. The Belarus, by contrast, is loud, smoky and cantankerous; Richards had to play with the gearshift for almost a minute to get it into neutral" (Zweig 1988, 108). I take this to be indirect evidence that the handling characteristics of the 1988 American model are superior to a 1947 American model on the logic that, however far behind the Russians may be, surely the 1988 Russian model is superior to the typical 1947 American one.

12. The weight in App. table A.1 for 1967 is 95 percent (this is the sum of the weights applied to the AT&T index used for annual deflation; the other indexes designated by n. b in that table are used for quarterly interpolation). For 1986, the BEA list of price indexes used in the PDE deflator indicates a weight of 74 percent applied to the PPI for switchgear and the Engineering-News-Record wage index for skilled construction labor.

percent of net sales on R&D during the 1961–70 decade, substantially more than the chemical (3.8 percent), electrical equipment (3.6 percent), or total manufacturing (2.0 percent) industries (Billingsley 1973, 19). Partly as a result of the R&D spending, many types of equipment used in telephone transmission and switching have been subject to order-of-magnitude improvements in performance. For instance, the capacity of coaxial cable systems increased from 600 simultaneous conversations in 1941 to 132,000 in the late 1970s.[13] The introduction of electronic switching systems in the mid-1970s increased speed by an order of magnitude, provided more flexibility in routing calls, and reduced requirements for electricity, maintenance labor, and space.[14] Because of the sharp increases in the carrying capacity of transmission lines and the introduction of electronic switching equipment, it is quite likely that a "true" price index for telephone equipment would exhibit a decline in price over the postwar period, although probably at a rate considerably slower than the 20 percent annual rate of price decline experienced by electronic computers (see chap. 6 above). However, the existing PDE deflator for telephone equipment registers a substantial postwar increase in price rather than a decline and may fail to capture much of the technological change that has occurred.

9.3.1   Existing Price Indexes for Telephone Equipment

Over the postwar interval through 1983, the PDE deflator for telephone equipment is set equal to a component of the AT&T telephone plant and equipment price indexes (TPI) called "inside plant." Since 1983 the AT&T index has been unavailable, and the BEA has switched to a crude approximation, deflating the entire telephone equipment category by the PPI for "Switchgear" (with a two-thirds weight) and an index of skilled construction labor (with a one-third weight), making no adjustment at all for productivity change. This assumption of no productivity increase in telephone equipment is ironic, in view of the fact that the communications industry itself (as distinguished from the portion of manufacturing that makes communications equipment) exhibits the fastest postwar increase in productivity of any major industry group. As one example of a significant rate of productivity improvement within Western Electric, the main manufacturer of telephone equipment, a Bell publication (Billingsley 1973, 22) shows that, in the manufacture of rotary telephone sets over 1955–71, an increase in wage rates at an annual rate of 5.2 percent was largely offset by a reduction in labor

---

13. Bell Lab/Western Electric advertisement, *Commentary* magazine, July 1977, 2. Ellinghaus (1970) cites figures of 480 simultaneous messages for coaxial cables in 1941, 5,580 in 1953, and 32,400 in 1970.

14. Heralding the introduction of the no. 4 Electronic Switching System, McElheny (1976) compared it to its electromechanical predecessor 4-A Crossbar system: "The No. 4 E.S.S., costing far less per unit of capacity than its predecessor, using only 60 percent as much electricity, and requiring small maintenance and operating crews, also occupies so much less space . . . that virtually all the No. 4's can go into existing telephone buildings" (37).

Table 9.6   Annual Growth Rates for Telephone Equipment, 1947–80

	Annual Growth Rates
1. BEA PDE deflator for communications equipment	2.09
2. AT&T TPI for inside plant	2.57
3. WE index for all manufactures	1.13
4. WE index for apparatus and equipment (excludes cable and wire)	0.65
5. PPI for Switchgear, 11-75-04 (used by BEA after 1982)	4.54
6. BEA compensation per hour in construction industry (1948–80; analogous to construction wage index used by BEA after 1982)	5.91
7. AT&T average embedded cost per circuit mile	−5.35

Sources by row: **(1)** Table 9.7, col 1. **(2)** Table 9.7, col. 4. **(3)** Table 9.7, col. 2. **(4)** The Western Electric embedded cost index is available only through 1980. **(5)** PPI for Switchgear is from the PPI file described in chap. 12. **(6)** BEA compensation per hour is from NIPA table 6.4A divided by table 6.11. **(7)** AT&T embedded cost is from Flamm (1989, fig. 5, p. 28), available only through 1980.

content per set at an annual rate of 3.6 percent, resulting in an annual increase in labor cost per set of 1.6 percent rather than the 5.2, percent that would be implied by the BEA's post-1982 method.

To demonstrate the sharp divergence among alternative indicators that have been or might be used as deflators for telephone equipment, annual growth rates are contrasted over the 1947–80 interval in table 9.6. Annual data for the indexes shown in the first three rows are displayed in table 9.7, columns 1, 2, and 4. These growth rates raise several questions. I have no explanation for the small discrepancy between the BEA PDE deflator and the AT&T TPI, since the former is supposed to be composed of the latter with a weight of 95 percent prior to 1983.[15] The substantially slower rate of price increase recorded by the WE index reflects the fact that the AT&T TPI includes an installation labor component, while the WE index refers to manufactured products only. The much faster rates of increase shown by the Switchgear PPI and construction wage index suggest that the BEA deflator may be biased upward after 1982, even if the AT&T TPI is correct. Finally, the rapid decline in the AT&T embedded cost index suggests the possibility that technological progress may have reduced effective capital cost in ways that are not captured by either the AT&T TPI or the WE indexes. Any such finding would be important not only for our primary focus, the secular rate of change of the PDE deflator, but also for microeconomists interested in the production process within the telephone industry and who have in the past used the AT&T TPI to measure capital costs (see, e.g., Nadiri and Schankerman 1981).

For perspective on the new evidence discussed below, a review of the available data can begin with the methodology of the AT&T TPI and WE equipment indexes. The TPI includes separate components for transmission

15. The 95 percent weight comes from app. table A-1 (see also n. 12 above). The information that the particular AT&T TPI chosen by the BEA is the "inside plant" category comes from Flamm (1989, 30).

systems (circuit and radio equipment in central offices, cable and wire, pole lines, and underground conduits) and switches (manual, panel, step by step, crossbar, and electronic) and is based on the standard BLS specification methodology. No allowance is made for changes in price per unit of the desired quality characteristic, that is, per circuit mile for transmission equipment or line capacity for a switching system. In effect, only price changes following the initial introduction of a new model have any effect on the aggregate TPI. We learned in studying computer prices that much of the rapid rate of price decline measured by hedonic price indexes occurs with the introduction of new models, and the evidence of Cole et al. (1986) was cited showing that a matched model index for computer processors declined during 1972–84 at a much slower rate than a hedonic regression index. It would be surprising if price declines in telephone equipment did not also occur with the introduction of new models.

The WE index, compiled annually from 1920 to 1980, is a ''chain index'' compiled by specification methodology and thus differs from the PPI in its use of current sales weights, which change annually, as compared to the fixed weights and infrequent weight changes in the PPI.[16] It measures changes in the level of prices charged to Bell System customers for products sold to them by WE and differs from the AT&T TPI indexes by excluding any costs incurred by the Bell customers in the installation of the equipment. All significant items in each division (''sales class'') of WE are included, and ''the sum total of the item individually priced for the indexes is in the order of 90–95 percent of the total sales in most cases.'' Thus, the WE index introduces new products faster than is typical in the PPI and also has unusually complete coverage. However, the WE index suffers from the same basic defect as the TPI, and this is the failure to measure price change at the time that new models are introduced. The description of the index states explicitly that, ''frequently, redesigned or new products have to be introduced into the indexes. When this is necessary the redesigned or new product is 'linked' into the index in a manner which does not change the level of the index at the time of introduction.[17]

9.3.2 Technological Innovation: A Brief Historical Review

The pace and timing of new model introductions that might incorporate unmeasured price declines have differed between transmission and switching equipment. Improvements in transmission technology have included a

---

16. I am grateful to S. Dale Jones, manager, Corporate Analysis, Western Electric Co., for providing me in 1973 with the Western Electric price indexes and background on their methodology. Updates through 1980 were provided by T. F. Clifford, manager, Corporate Analysis, Western Electric.

17. Details on the WE index included in this paragraph come from a mimeographed document obtained in 1973 from WE entitled ''Basic Characteristics of the W. E. Selling Price Indexes.''

hundred-fold increase in the carrying capacity of coaxial cables, the introduction of microwave transmitters and satellite transmission, and, more recently, optical fiber cable. Evidence examined below suggests that a substantial decline in the cost of transmission capacity occurred in two stages, the first between the early 1950s and the mid-1960s, and the second beginning in the late 1970s and extending into the mid-1980s. Indirect evidence is provided of further rapid price declines before 1950.

The technology of switching equipment was purely electromechanical until 1965, and the transition to electronic switches did not begin in earnest until the mid-1970s. The three main types of electromechanical switches were step by step, panel, and crossbar, serving, respectively, 47.5, 5.6, and 49.1 million telephones in 1970 (Brand 1973, 5). These were progressively more sophisticated in their programming ability: the first could send a call only through a fixed path and returned a busy signal if that was unavailable; the second and third allowed a limited ability to reprogram the calling path from a central location independently of the sequence dialed by the customer. The first full-scale central office electronic switching system was introduced in 1965, followed by the first fully digital electronic system in 1976. The transition to electronics also included the upgrading of old crossbar equipment to include limited electronic programming capability.[18]

9.3.3 New Evidence on Secular Price Movements

The new evidence presented in this section is all based on Flamm's (1989) pathbreaking study, which assembles evidence on costs and prices from a variety of sources, including internal Bell System records.[19] My contribution is to distill this evidence into a single price index for telephone transmission and switching equipment that can be used to replace the inadequate TPI on which the official PDE deflator is now based. Flamm's evidence is of three basic types. All have in common that they are measures of capital cost divided by some measure of the productive capacity of a capital good (e.g., circuit miles or lines handled by a switching system). Thus, these measures are analogous to the indexes for computer processors developed in chapter 6, where the unit of capital is taken to be the "quality characteristic" (e.g., memory, speed) of the computer rather than the number of computer boxes. In the same way, here I take the unit of measurement to be a circuit mile or telephone line rather than a "wire mile" (independent of handling capacity) or "switching system box."

---

18. Details in this paragraph come from Flamm (1989, 19–27), who emphasizes the much slower diffusion of electronic technology in the telephone industry than in the electronic computer industry.

19. Some of my source notes also refer to Flamm (1988), the working paper version of Flamm (1989), which contains several data series in appendix tables that were not reprinted in the published 1989 version.

Flamm's first measure is the AT&T embedded capital cost per circuit mile, which is a measure of the book value of installed capital in the AT&T Long Lines Department (i.e., excluding local service) divided by the number of circuit miles in the system at the same time. Because this concept measures the unit capital cost embedded in the current capital stock over all past vintages still on the books, its timing is inappropriate to represent the price of currently produced investment goods. Only if price change proceeded at an absolutely unchanged geometric rate would an embedded stock measure yield the same rate of price change as a price index based on current production. A further problem is that the depreciable lifetime of capital for accounting purposes may well be different from the actual lifetime over which the capital is counted in the cumulation of "circuit miles," the denominator of the AT&T ratio. Because of its disadvantages, this measure is used only to extrapolate the new index from 1952 back to 1947, a period for which no other adequate information is available.[20] A precedent for adopting a measure of the unit capital cost embedded in the current capital stock as part of a price index is provided by Jack Triplett, who as part of his "best practice" price index for computer processors attached a sizable weight to Flamm's (1987) price index of the installed capital stock of computers (in the case of computers measured at market prices rather than historical cost).

The second type of evidence taken from Flamm is a measure of incremental capital cost for new transmission and switching capacity. For transmission equipment, capital cost is the annual change in the net book value of central office circuit and radio equipment, as well as in that of toll and exchange lines, and the change in capacity is measured in circuit miles. For switching equipment, capital is measured by the annual change in the net book value of central office switching equipment, and switching activity is assumed to be proportional to total local calls plus ten times long distance messages. The resulting ratios of incremental capital cost to incremental capacity have a zigzag appearance and are exhibited in table 9.7, columns 5 and 6, as three-year moving averages. The rapid decline in transmission cost between 1952 and 1968 is striking, as is the reversal between 1969 and 1978. Incremental switching cost declined much more slowly than transmission cost until the mid-1960s and increased less from then until the mid-1970s.

Flamm suggests three defects of the incremental capital cost measures. First, there is a time lag between an investment and the completion data of the resulting increase in capacity. Second, the denominator in the switching measure is actual traffic, rather than capacity, and thus incremental cost for switching moves inversely to capacity utilization, and vice versa. Third,

20. In discussing Flamm's evidence, I omit his measure, taken from Phister (1979), of the cost of data communication per bit transferred, following his own verdict that this mainly reflects improvements in interface technology (i.e., cheaper modems) rather than lower line costs. To the extent that modems are treated as a computer peripheral in PDE within the OCAM category, lower modem costs are already taken into account in the PDE deflator.

Table 9.7   Alternative Price Indexes for Telephone Transmission and Switching Equipment, 1947–84

	NIPA Deflator for Communications Equipment (1)	Western Electric All Manufactures (2)	AT&T TPI General Equipment (3)	AT&T TPI Inside Plant (4)	AT&T Marginal Capital Cost Transmission (5)	AT&T Marginal Capital Cost Switching (6)	Bellcore 6 Switching Equipment Types (7)	AT&T Bellcore Transmission and Switching Equipment (8)
1947	68.4	97.7	47.8	63.3				273.9
1948	68.4	96.4	52.2	63.9				256.7
1949	66.4	96.3	54.2	63.3				240.6
1950	68.4	93.0	56.0	64.8				225.5
1951	78.7	104.9	60.8	67.9				211.6
1952	73.1	94.6	62.2	65.9	265.8	100.0		198.6
1953	68.7	87.2	62.7	60.9	178.1	101.9		164.1
1954	66.4	87.3	63.4	64.4	190.4	83.5		153.5
1955	71.2	87.9	65.6	64.6	233.3	61.2		145.5
1956	68.4	89.6	70.0	66.3	253.5	65.0		156.4
1957	74.3	88.6	72.8	69.1	207.9	77.7		141.6
1958	75.5	91.4	76.3	70.7	163.2	69.9		119.0
1959	76.7	92.1	77.9	71.2	129.8	58.3		96.9
1960	76.4	90.3	78.2	71.0	128.1	68.0		104.0
1961	74.8	88.7	78.2	70.9	115.8	71.8		101.7
1962	72.2	85.7	77.9	71.0	118.4	79.6		108.2
1963	75.3	85.0	76.7	72.0	107.0	68.0		95.1
1964	74.4	84.0	78.3	73.5	106.1	68.9		95.4
1965	75.5	81.7	78.7	73.8	82.5	60.2	74.8	78.5
1966	75.5	81.9	79.4	75.4	82.5	65.0	78.0	80.2
1967	77.5	83.2	81.5	78.2	72.8	68.9	81.3	76.9
1968	81.3	88.1	84.5	81.7	71.1	68.0	84.7	77.6
1969	85.3	90.5	86.9	86.1	71.1	72.8	88.3	79.2
1970	87.6	94.4	90.7	90.0	78.1	88.3	92.0	84.8
1971	94.1	96.2	94.8	94.9	92.1	101.0	95.9	94.0
1972	100.0	100.0	100.0	100.0	100.0	100.0	100.0	100.0
1973	102.6	100.8	99.9	104.0	100.0	96.1	99.4	99.7
1974	104.1	110.9	111.1	113.9	113.2	116.5	105.8	109.4
1975	117.6	120.0	125.1	124.7	131.6	115.5	92.5	110.3
1976	126.3	128.0	130.3	132.3	149.1	109.7	76.6	106.9
1977	130.0	130.7	132.3	137.4	152.6	76.7	72.7	105.3
1978	130.1	130.9	132.3	137.9	159.6	75.7	69.0	104.9
1979	132.9	134.7	138.4	141.5	137.7	82.5	66.4	95.6
1980	136.1	141.6	147.0	147.8	105.3	106.8	65.2	82.9
1981	149.5		163.0	160.4			67.4	85.6
1982	166.1		176.9	176.0			70.0	88.9
1983	176.6		183.9	185.4			59.8	76.0
1984	183.7						51.2	65.0

Sources by column: (**1**) NIPA implicit deflator, table 5.6, row 5, divided by table 5.7, row 5, rebased to 1972. (**2**) From Western Electric prior to divestiture (see text). (**3, 4**) From Flamm (1988, app. A). (**5, 6**) Three-year moving averages of Flamm (1988, app. B, cols. 3 and 4). (**7**) Constructed by cumulating and taking antilogs of annual log changes displayed in table 9.8, applying equal weights to each piece of equipment. (**8**) Törnqvist index of cols. 5 and 6 for 1952–65 and cols. 5 and 7 for 1965–82, extended to 1984 by col. 7, and extended before 1952 by Flamm (1989, fig. 5, p. 28), reading off the graph annual growth rates of −6.47 percent for 1947–50 and −6.37 percent for 1950–55.

Table 9.8   Annual Growth Rates of Prices for Six Types of Telephone Switching
                   Equipment, 1965–84

	Small (1)	Medium (2)	Large (3)
	2,500 lines	5,000–20,000 Lines	80,000 Lines and Over
Local office switches:			
1972–73	4.14	−25.92	5.56
1973–75	4.14	18.05	2.31
1975–76	−8.87	1.81	−0.87
1976–78	−8.87	0.30	−0.87
1978–79	1.78	−1.79	−0.66
1979–80	11.37	−4.94	4.77
1980–81	11.37	13.26	4.77
1981–82	6.45	13.26	13.58
1982–84	−22.20	−10.20	−14.65
	15,000 Trunks	30,000 Trunks	60,000 Trunks
Toll and tandem switches:			
1965–72	4.15	4.15	4.15
1972–74	4.26	4.26	4.26
1974–76	−25.26	−36.53	−43.25
1976–80	−6.11	−7.46	−8.47
1980–82	−4.81	−3.31	−2.08

Source: Calculated from Flamm (1989, app. B, pp. 404–5).

capital cost per mile is inversely proportional to route length, so a reduction in average route length would spuriously raise the transmission incremental cost measure, and vice versa. However, the first two factors will mainly contribute year-to-year fluctuations in the incremental cost measures rather than creating a secular bias; the bias caused by changing route length is unknown. The Flamm incremental cost measures are greatly superior to the WE and TPI indexes, which omit all price changes associated with the introduction of new models and new products.

Flamm's third set of evidence, and doubtless the best, consists of estimates by Bell Communications Research (''Bellcore'') specialists of the cost of representative central office switches per line served in offices of varying sizes. These estimates are also available for toll and tandem switches. Displayed in table 9.8 are the annual rates of price change over the intervals spanning the estimated prices. The price changes are erratic, with substantial price declines concentrated in particular years. Trunk line switches plummet in 1974–76, reflecting an assumed shift from the No. 4 crossbar system to the No. 4 Electronic Switching System (ESS). To the extent that the transition of overall Western Electric production from crossbar to ESS switches did not occur instantaneously, the indicated rates of price change may exaggerate the price decline in 1974–76 and overstate it in other periods.

Because the Bellcore estimates are closer in principle to true prices than are the incremental capital cost measures, the final price index (displayed in table 9.7, col. 8) is based on the Bellcore switch estimates for their period of availability, 1965–84. The six Bellcore size classes are combined into logarithmic chain indexes (i.e., Törnqvist indexes), using equal weights, and then are combined again with the incremental capital cost measure for transmission equipment (available only through 1980), again with equal weights. Since Flamm provides data on cost per circuit mile, number of circuit miles, switching cost per line, and number of lines, it is possible to aggregate the implicit transmission and switching capital stock, and this calculation yields 1973 shares of transmission and switching equipment in the capital stock of 49.3 and 50.7 percent, respectively, thus validating the choice of equal weights for the two components of telephone equipment.[21] From 1952 to 1965, the final index is an unweighted Törnqvist index of incremental capital cost for transmission and switching, and prior to 1952 is based on Flamm's embedded capital cost per circuit mile measure. The annual growth rate of the final index over 1947–52 is − 6.4 percent, over 1952–65 is − 7.1 percent, and over 1965–84 is a mere − 1.0 percent.

As was true for many of the indexes developed in other chapters, there are numerous unmeasured aspects of quality change that are not taken into account in the final index, thus supporting the verdict that it understates the "true" rate of price decline. First, reduced maintenance cost and energy use in electronic switching systems creates value for the user beyond the sheer carrying capacity of the switches. We found in chapter 7 that saving in maintenance cost and energy use was important for several types of appliances and were able there to develop rough adjustments for the value of these improvements, but here we do not have quantitative evidence and must rely on qualitative descriptions.[22] In addition to these savings, electronic switching equipment has made possible radical reductions in equipment space occupied per line served, thus allowing many telephone companies to eliminate whole multistory buildings that would have been required with the previous technology to accommodate today's calling volumes.[23] Second, for switching equipment, the basic measurement unit is taken to be the "line,"

---

21. The calculation for 1973 is 550 million circuit miles times $18 average cost, or $9.9 billion, and 62 million lines at about $165 switching cost per line, or $10.2 billion. These figures are taken from Flamm (1989, figs. 4 and 5); and Flamm (1988, app. C).

22. See, e.g., the McElheny (1976) quote in n. 14 above.

23. In addition to McElheny (1976), an additional citation on space-saving is Urquhart (1985), who states that, as a result of space-saving equipment, Bell Canada was able to eliminate plans to build a third office building in Toronto, and was able to sell a regional headquarters building with 660,000 square feet of office space: "The company has also realized that the introduction of compact digital switching equipment that requires one-quarter as much space as old electro-mechanical equipment,is freeing up all sorts of existing space for other uses. As the old equipment was replaced, Bell said, 'Holy smoke, look at all that valuable real estate' " (29).

but a telephone line is not the same as it was twenty or forty years ago. Today's switches allow calls to be completed much faster than before, saving time for customers, and the programming capabilities of modern switches allow the equipment to search for alternative routings, thus reducing the incidence of "circuit busy" signals. Third, today's digital switches (by converting analog voice signals into digits) reduce distortion and provide a clearer line. Finally, modern switches allow the provision of additional services, including the routine provision of itemized bills for subscribers, as well as paging and electronic call transfer services.[24]

Regarding transmission equipment, there are fewer dimensions of unmeasured quality change, but no doubt that transmission quality has improved over the postwar period. People calling their relatives across the continent who in earlier decades may have sounded "far away" now sound as if they were "next door," and the difference in sound quality between local and transcontinental calls, and even for some types of international calls, is rapidly disappearing. A further indication that the final index may understate the rate of decline in telephone equipment prices occurs after 1980, when the index is entirely based on switching equipment, with no contribution from transmission equipment. If anything, the transition to fiber optic cable must have created a decline in the effective cost of transmission equipment during this period even more rapid than that of switching equipment. As one specific piece of evidence, Flamm (1988) exhibits a chart indicating a rate of price decline for fiber optic cable of 45 percent *per year* from 1980 to 1985. This piece of evidence is not included in the final price index, however, because it refers to the cable itself, not the complete transmission system, which contains an unknown mix of other equipment besides cable.

9.4 Other Types of Communication Equipment

This book develops alternative price indexes for components of PDE and, in chapter 12, combines the alternative and current official price indexes with an identical set of weights, that used by the BEA at present in combining its own set of detailed official price indexes (mainly PPIs) into deflators for the separate industry groups within PDE. There seems to be some indication that the 95 percent weight applied (before 1973) by the BEA to the AT&T TPI index of telephone transmission and switching equipment is excessive, simply because the remaining 5 percent (about $1.6 billion in 1984) seems to leave too little room for other types of communication equipment.

Contrasting evidence is given by *Current Industrial Reports,* which lists 1984 shipments of telephone switching and switchboard equipment ($5.5

---

24. On the last two points, see "Princes and Pumpkins at the Digital Switching Hour," *Economist,* 29 August 1987, 74–75.

billion), other telephone equipment ($8.1 billion), nontelephone nonbroadcast communications systems and equipment ($8.5 billion), and broadcast and studio equipment ($1.4 billion). Thus, there is clearly a substantial production of communications equipment other than telephone equipment, and the broadcast/studio category alone amounts to almost as much ($1.4 billion) as the entire amount ($1.6 billion) that the BEA allocates to communications equipment other than telephone.

This section provides some qualitative and anecdotal evidence on several of the other types of products involved. Previously, in chapter 6 on computers, in the section of chapter 7 on home television sets, and in the previous section on telephone equipment, quantitative evidence has been provided to show that prices of electronic equipment have uniformly fallen over the postwar period. And, as we found for telephone switches and as we shall find again for typewriters in chapter 10, the transition from electromechanical to electronic components for a given product can easily involve a discrete decline in price to one-third or less of the previous price, not counting the additional dimensions of quality (spellcheckers on typewriters, call forwarding by telephone equipment) that were previously unavailable. In discussing these additional types of equipment, this section implicitly assesses the validity of the PPIs to which the BEA applies the remaining 5 percent weight in the PDE deflator for communications equipment; these are the PPIs for magnetic tape, home tape recorders, home television sets, and phonographs.

One product that experienced a shift to electronic technology beginning in the mid-1970s was the office telephone and internal office switching equipment (PBX, for "private branch exchange"). Until 1968, AT&T had a monopoly and owned the entire installed base of PBX equipment, but the historic Carterfone decision in that year allowed non-Bell equipment to be connected to Bell System lines. Because AT&T had no incentive to introduce modern technology, PBX equipment designs seldom changed, and one telephone company was offering in 1971 a model first introduced in 1937. Competing firms took time to get established in the face of delaying tactics applied by Bell companies to "foreign attachments," but by 1975 these firms were applying intense competitive pressure through the introduction of modern electronic PBX systems.

In the old technology, physical rewiring was required to change the telephone configuration in a customer's office. Electronic PBX devices allowed the addition of numerous features that today are taken for granted, including call forwarding, automatic call back, call waiting, automatic setting up of conference calls, automatic routing of long-distance calls, and restrictions on toll use by some branch extensions. By 1976, prices of full electronic systems had fallen to roughly the level charged by old-fashioned electromechanical PBX equipment lacking all these advanced features. In one case, a new system in a large 1,000-line office saved 26 percent on long-distance charges, and 75 percent on operator costs.[25] It should be noted also that deregulation and divestiture opened the market to new suppliers that undercut Bell system prices, so that an internal Bell price index for PBX equipment, even if one existed, would understate the rate of price decline during the 1970s. More recently, in the 1980s, a study has estimated that PBX prices fell at an annual rate of 10 percent per annum over 1981–84, while smaller PBXs called "key systems" fell at an annual rate of 16 percent over the same period; the same study quotes a decline in central office switching equipment costs over 1980–84 at an annual rate of 7–10 percent, which is somewhat faster than the 6 percent rate of decline used in the final telephone equipment index in the previous section.[26]

In the 1980s, the most dramatic new product innovations have been the cellular telephone and the fax machine. In each of these cases, drastic cost reductions have stimulated exponential increases in use. One estimate is that the price of the least-expensive model cellular phone declined at an annual rate of 23 percent between 1983 and 1987, comparable to the rate of price decline of personal computer equipment over the same period.[27] Until 1985, fax machines were large, cumbersome machines, usually found in the corporate mailroom, which were difficult to operate, often unreliable, and took as long as six minutes to transmit one page of a document. The new generation of fax machines are small, easy to use, transmit a page in fifteen seconds, and are fast becoming ubiquitous in corporate offices and even in universities. According to one estimate, the prices of fax machines have fallen at about 15 percent per year during the 1985–88 period, with signs of an acceleration at the end of the period as small personal units were introduced in the $1,000–$1,500 range having many of the features previously available on more expensive office units.[28]

Broadcast and studio equipment has, of course, been of electronic design throughout the history of the industry, but has benefited from the same transition from vacuum tubes to transistors to integrated circuits that yielded for home television sets a −6.6 percent rate of price change over the 1952–83 period. Much broadcast equipment consists of transmission equipment, the price of which should behave roughly like that of telephone transmission equipment, and of television sets and monitors, which should mimic the prices of home television sets. In the area of transmission equipment, the most dramatic price change has been in satellite earth

25. Details about PBX equipment come from "Technology Changes the Office Telephone," *Business Week,* 19 January 1976, 42–44.

26. These growth rates are from a study by an industry group and are quoted in "Telecommunications Survey," *Economist,* 23 November 1985, 12.

27. *Business Week,* 21 September 1987, 90. On personal computer equipment, see chap. 6.

28. "Faxually Speaking," *Forbes,* 13 June 1988, 114–16.

terminals, which in one three-year period (1975–78) fell in price at an annual rate of 54 percent per year (Cooper 1978, 34). The study of home appliances in chapter 7 above found that the most dramatic rate of price decline, −26 percent per annum over the 1980–85 period, occurred for VCRs. So we should expect that dramatic price declines have occurred for types of broadcast equipment that involve videotape recording technology.

In the early years of television, video cameras weighed hundreds of pounds. They were mobile only in the sense that they were mounted on dollies and rolled into position on the studio floor. As for the equipment that recorded picture and sound, it weighed tons and could not be moved at all. Until the introduction of instant video replay technology in 1957, those of us who lived on the West Coast saw all prime-time television programs not in the original fidelity enjoyed in the rest of the country but through the grainy screen of off-the-screen sixteen-millimeter film reproduction used to achieve the required three-hour time delay. In the 1950s, any outside gathering of television news was accomplished by film cameras, not video cameras, and transmission required the physical transport of the film back to the studio and a time delay required for film developing. Live remote broadcasts, such as sporting events or political conventions, required that portable video cameras be connected by cable to a truck containing the 1.5 tons of equipment required to record on two-inch videotape.

By 1975, the weight and size of portable camera and recording units had been reduced to eighty-five pounds and could be carried by two men; tape width had fallen to one inch. Only a few years later, a broadcast-quality unit had been reduced in weight to fifteen pounds, and one person could operate a single unit housing a camera, complete recording system (on one-quarter-inch tape), and battery.[29] By the mid-1980s, "camcorders" in several tape formats had fallen enough in price to make the transition into the home market, making home movie equipment obsolete. The reduction in television news equipment prices had proceeded far enough by 1988 that hundreds of local television stations sent live transmissions from the floor of the two political conventions.

Overall, the experience of home television sets, with their postwar annual rate of price decline of 6.6 percent per year, may be an acceptable proxy through the mid-1970s, but since then the rate of price decline for nontelephone communications equipment seems to have accelerated. Scattered examples in this section over selected three to five-year intervals since 1975 reported annual rates of price decline for particular products in the rate of 10–50 percent. Even if these examples are atypical, reporting price declines in the particular intervals when technical innovations were concentrated, the

29. Details on size and weight of equipment from an advertisement of Robert Bosch GmbH in the *Wall Street Journal*, 5 April 1982, 12.

implied rate of price decline for all these products could easily have been in the range of 5–10 percent per annum.

9.5 Railroad Equipment

A great deal of information is available on prices of railroad equipment, but time limitations permitted only the assembly of scattered bits and pieces. These, however, cover freight locomotives and several of the most important types of freight cars, which together account for the great majority of PDE in railroad equipment. To capture secular price trends, data collection is limited to the beginning, middle, and end of the 1947–83 coverage period. The aim is to develop estimates of the secular rate of price change for locomotives and freight cars over the intervals 1947–70, 1970–79, and 1979–83.[30]

Just as the new price measures for telephone equipment are developed for a single quality unit, circuit miles for transmission equipment and lines for switching equipment, here the new price measures are based on price per horsepower for locomotives and price per ton of carrying capacity for railroad freight cars. This procedure introduces the implicit assumption that the cross-sectional relation of price to horsepower or price to ton is unit elastic, that is, the plot of price against horsepower at a moment of time is a ray extending through the origin. The unit elasticity assumption has been used in some previous studies, including Flamm's (1987) work on computers, discussed in chapter 6, and telephone equipment, discussed in section 9.3 above. Dulberger's (1989) and this study's hedonic regression equations for computers in chapter 6 tend also to exhibit a unit elasticity of price to the two most important quality characteristics, memory and speed.

The new evidence on railroad equipment prices is based on three different data sources. For 1947 and 1970, tables are listed in the monthly periodicals *Railway Mechanical Engineer* and its successor, *Railway Locomotives and Cars*. These tables, published every month, list almost all orders for new locomotives and freight cars, including for all orders the number of units ordered and the horsepower or ton capacity. For a very small subset of the orders the aggregate price is included, allowing calculation of a per-unit and per-horsepower or per-ton price. For instance, of the roughly 150 order transactions for locomotives and a like number of freight car transactions in calendar 1948, suitable price information was provided for just twelve locomotive transactions and six freight car transactions. Some price information could not be used, because the price provided was the aggregate value of

---

30. For annual interpolation, the only available source is the single PPI used in the POE deflator for this category. This is PPI index 14-4, which began in 1961. The notes to the BEA list of PPIs have the following ambiguous explanation of the pre-1961 source: "Extrapolated back prior to 1961-I using previously published quarterly series."

an order containing several sizes of locomotives or types of freight cars. Unfortunately, these periodicals eventually suspended publication, and similar information has not been published since the early 1970s. In assessing this new evidence, it is important to note that the prices are *not* sampled; the results are based on literally every shred of usable information published in the sources for the two years 1948 and 1970.

The twelve priced transactions for locomotives in 1948 are particularly valuable information, because the wide range of sizes ordered provides clear evidence of a unit elasticity of price to horsepower. Despite a range of sizes from 1,000 to 6,000 hp, the price per horsepower was in the extremely narrow range of $91.70–$106.10, and most of the locomotives were priced at precisely $100 per horsepower, that is, a price of $100,000 each for an order of thirteen 1,000 hp locomotives and $600,000 each for an order of six 6,000 hp locomotives. Exactly the same information was available in the same format in 1970, although the range of price per horsepower was much wider ($92.50–$150). However, there is no evidence in the 1970 sample to conflict with the assumed unit elasticity of price to horsepower; both the orders at $150 per horsepower were of the mid-range 2,000 hp size, and other order transactions occurred for the 1,000, 2,000, and 3,000 sizes in the narrow range of $92.50–$100 per horsepower. If a larger number of transactions containing price information had been available, one might well have concluded that there was no increase at all in price per horsepower between 1948 and 1970; however, when one averages the price-per-horsepower quotations with equal weights across each order, one concludes that the average price increased 14 percent (see table 9.9, rows 1 and 2).[31]

For freight cars, exactly the same sources are used in the same way. As shown in rows 5 and 6 of table 9.9, prices are collected separately for open and covered hopper cars. (Additional price information was available on gondola and box cars in 1970, but not in 1948.) The prices listed indicate that freight car prices almost doubled over this interval, in contrast to virtually no increase in locomotive prices. This difference in price behavior is consistent with evidence provided from the Sears Roebuck catalog in chapter 10 that simple products fabricated from metal with few moving parts exhibited faster price increases, and benefited less from technological change, than more complex devices, for example, a 1948–70 price increase of 87 percent for steel safes and 131 percent for cast-iron radiators versus an increase of 14 percent for stationary air compressors and 7 percent for centrifugal pumps.

---

31. If I had weighted by the dollar value of each order, my conclusion would have been that price did not change at all, since one order of $28.3 million, with an average price per horsepower of just $97.50, dwarfs all other orders combined (adding to $12.0 million).

Table 9.9   **Summary of Information Collected on Railroad Locomotives and Freight Cars, 1948–83**

	1948	1970	1979	1983
Locomotives, price per horsepower:				
1. Twelve transactions, 103 locomotives, range 1,000–6,000 hp, range $/hp $91.7–$106.1.	102.42			
2. Eight transactions, 173 locomotives, range 1,000–3,000 hp, range $/hp $92.5–$150		116.88		
3. Electro-Motive new unit, 3,000 hp model SD-40-2			216.67	
4. Electro-Motive new unit, 3,500 hp model SD-50				342.90
Freight cars, price per ton:				
5. Six transactions, 3,800 hopper cars:				
Open	67.40			
Covered	107.14			
6. Four transactions, 3,500 hopper cars:				
Open		132.50		
Covered		180.56		
7. Average cost per car (size not specified):				
Gondola		14,203	31,760	37,655
Open Hopper		12,726	34,585	39,687
Covered Hopper		16,221	36,858	37,334
Price indexes, 1970 = 100:				
8. BEA implicit deflator for PDE, railroad equipment	52.8	100.0	231.3	293.3
9. Alternative, locomotives	87.6	100.0	176.5	244.6
10. Alternative, freight cars	54.9	100.0	208.8	218.5
11. Törnqvist-weighted alternative, railroad equipment	69.4	100.0	192.0	231.2

Sources by row: **(1, 5)** *Railway Mechanical Engineer,* various monthly issues during calendar year 1948, feature titled "Orders and Inquiries for New Equipment Placed Since the Closing of the [last month] Issue" **(2, 6)** *Railway Locomotives and Cars,* various monthly issues during calendar 1970, feature having same title as in 1948. **(3)** Young (1979, 1). **(4)** "Electro-Motive Gets Big Conrail Order," *Chicago Tribune,* 17 November 1983, sec. 2, 14. **(7)** *Railroad Facts, 1985 Edition* (Washington, D.C.: Association of American Railroads, August), 49. **(8)** NIPA, table 5.6, row 20, divided by table 5.7, row 20, rebased in 1970. **(9)** 1948–70, directly from rows 1 and 2. 1970–79 and 1979–83, adjusted for 5 and 14.2 percent estimated present value of fuel saving (see text). **(10)** 1948–70, directly from rows 5 and 6. 1970–79 and 1979–83, annual percentage change in "Cost of New Freight Cars" (row 7 source, p. 49) is reduced by annual percentage change in "Average Freight Car Capacity" (in tons, from row 7 source, p. 48). **(11)** Törnqvist unweighted average index computed from rows 9 and 10.

Independent evidence to support these results on locomotive prices was obtained directly from the Electro-Motive division of General Motors, which for most of the postwar period had a market share of about 75 percent (thus making its price experience as relevant for a locomotive price index as IBM's experience is for a computer price index).[32] In addition to manufacturing

32. In the early 1980s, Electro-Motive lost ground to General Electric, which in 1983 had gained a market share of 45 percent. See "GM Locomotive Production Lines May Shut," *Chicago Tribune,* 15 July 1982, sec. 4, 1.

locomotive diesel engines for use in its own locomotives, Electro-Motive sells the same engine for a variety of uses, including inland marine use (e.g., tow boats on the Ohio River), for standby emergency power generation, and in oil well drilling. Its standard locomotive engine was gradually upgraded from 1,605 to 3,300 hp between 1950 and 1970 and increased in price per horsepower by 14 percent over that two-decade interval, by coincidence the same percentage increase as is shown in table 9.9 for locomotives between 1948 and 1970.[33]

To update the study for the period after 1970, when the order transaction data are unavailable, I rely on separate sources for locomotives and freight cars. The locomotive data are for the dominant Electro-Motive model sold in 1979 and 1983, as reported in newspaper accounts (see the notes to table 9.9). The freight car observations are the average purchase price, without any adjustment for size, available annually from the Association of American Railroads. The reported annual rate of change in freight car prices is adjusted for the annual rate of change in average freight car size, from the same source, so that the resulting price index calculated in row 10 is on the same per-ton basis as the computed 1948–70 price change. For locomotives, an adjustment is made for improved fuel economy. Railroads achieved a 36 percent increase in fuel economy per ton mile carried between 1971 and 1983; of this, a 20 percent increase is allocated to locomotives, and the rest to some combination of lighter freight cars and improved operating procedures.[34] The present discounted value of the fuel saving is then used to adjust the observed change in locomotive price per horsepower, using the same procedure as in chapter 7, in which the dollar fuel saving is added to the price in the first year and the price change then recalculated. Data on locomotive lifetimes and fuel prices are averages for the railroad industry as a whole. Fuel prices are those at the beginning of each interval (1970 for 1970–79 and 1979 for 1979–83), thus assuming static expectations and greatly underestimating the true fuel savings that were made ex post.[35] The resulting adjustments are 5 percent of the 1970 price over 1970–79 and 14 percent of the 1979 price over 1979–83.

33. The price per horsepower increased from $20.40 to $23.33. Price quotations were obtained by phone in 1973 from H. L. Smith, chief engineer of Electro-Motive, McCook, Ill., and are listed in detail in chap. 11.

34. Of the 20 percent increase in fuel economy, 10 percent is allocated to 1970–79 and the remaining 10 percent to 1979–83. Electro-Motive achieved a substantial improvement in fuel economy in shifting from the model SD-40, introduced in 1965, to the SD-40-2, introduced in the mid-1970s. This was "designed to save fuel by idling at lower horsepower, equipped with a better cooling system, and capable of being shut down completely in cold weather when the locomotive is not needed. [One of the biggest headaches faced by railroads is the cost of idling locomotives around the clock in cold weather because of the difficulty in restarting a diesel engine.] 'It's the most reliable unit we own,' said Deane H. Ellsworth, manager of motive power planning and development for Amtrak, of that agency's 71 SDP40-Fs"(Young 1979, 3).

35. The necessary data are obtained from the source listed in table 9.9, row 7, p. 44 for fuel consumed per revenue-ton mile, p. 45 for the average age of locomotives in 1984, and p. 60 for average price paid annually by railroads for diesel fuel.

The resulting price indexes for locomotives and freight cars are shown separately in rows 9 and 10 of table 9.9 and are aggregated into a single unweighted Törnqvist index for railroad equipment in row 11. The application of equal weights to locomotives and freight cars is supported by the PPI, which reports the "relative importance" of its locomotive index (14–41) as 0.146 and of its railroad car index (14–42) as 0.151.[36] Despite the adjustment for improved locomotive fuel efficiency, there is no doubt that the final index for railroad equipment overstates the true quality-adjusted price increase. Two specific pieces of evidence can be cited. First, technical improvements in locomotives have been made that improve hauling ability relative to horsepower. There was little change in average horsepower per locomotive between 1971 and 1984 but an increase in revenue ton miles per locomotive of 38 percent.[37] In the specific case of Electro-Motive, the new model SD-50, introduced in 1979–80, had a 16 percent increase in horsepower (from 3,000 to 3,500) but could haul 33 percent more tonnage, which was accomplished through a newly designed system for controlling "wheel creep," improving the adhesion between wheel and rail by between 18 and 24 percent (Young 1979, 3). I make no adjustment at all for the improved fuel efficiency made possible by lighter freight cars, yet part of the increased cost per ton, counted here as a price increase, actually represents a quality increase. For instance, flat cars redesigned in the 1980s to use lighter-weight materials produced fuel savings equal to fully one-third of their capital cost, evaluated at 1983 fuel prices.[38]

9.6   Conclusion

This chapter has provided new evidence on secular price trends for four different classes of products, tractors, telephone equipment, nontelephone communications equipment, and railroad equipment. The overall secular drift of the new alternative indexes relative to official price indexes covers a wide range, suggesting that there is no alternative to the nitty-gritty business of examining as many products as possible, and that overall conclusions may be sensitive to alternative weighting schemes.

The secular annual rate of price change over the full intervals of available data for the new price indexes developed here are listed in table 9.10. The secular drift exhibited for crawler tractors and railroad equipment is in the range found for many other products in this book, as summarized below in

36. See *PPI Supplement: Data for 1983*, October 1984, table 13, p. 239.
37. See the source to table 9.9, row 7, p. 44.
38. Specifically, Santa Fe railroad designed a new "Ten Packer" train of piggyback-carrying flat cars that saved 6,000 gallons of fuel per trip, or $600,000 per year, for a capital cost of $2 million. "The principal savings on fuel come because the cars are lighter and are designed to reduce aerodynamic drag on trains." (Young 1983, 2).

Table 9.10   **Annual Rate of Price Change for New and Official Price Indexes**

	Interval	Alternative	Official	Alternative/Official
Wheel tractors	1947–83	4.84	5.10	−0.26
Crawler tractors	1950–83	3.18	6.27	−3.09
Telephone equipment	1947–84	−3.89	2.67	−6.56
Railroad equipment	1948–83	3.44	4.89	−1.45

Sources: Alternative/official calculated from alternative and official growth rates. Wheel tractors data from table 9.3, cols. 3 and 4. Crawler tractors data from table 9.5, cols. 2 and 3. Telephone equipment data from table 9.7, cols. 8 and 1. Railroad equipment data from Table 9.9, rows 11 and 8.

chapter 12. Wheel tractors, like automobiles, exhibit virtually no drift, suggesting perhaps that the BLS has devoted unusual attention to purging observed price observations of quality change. Telephone equipment, with its transition to electronics, is an unusual case, exhibiting a rate of secular drift much less than that of electronic computers, but similar to that of noncomputer office machinery.

III Sources for the Pricing of Numerous Products

10   Specification Price Indexes from Sears Catalog Data

10.1   Introduction

Chapters 4–9 developed new price indexes for a number of products. In most cases, these chapters included a detailed treatment of measured and unmeasured quality change, as well as a comparison of alternative indexes or data sources. Among these comparisons were those of the Chow, Phister, Dulberger, and *Computerworld* data sets for computers in chapter 6, the Sears catalog and *Consumer Reports (CR)* price indexes for appliances in chapter 7, and the new hedonic, used hedonic, and BLS indexes for automobiles in chapter 8. However careful these chapters may have been, they were limited to a small number of products. Yet the official NIPA deflator for PDE is based on about 150 group or product components of the PPI.

As contrasted with the "narrow but deep" coverage of the previous chapters, this chapter and the next are "broad but shallow," developing new price indexes for a large number of products from data in the Sears catalog and, in chapter 11, from unit value data. The coverage is "shallow" in the sense that there is not the detailed comparison of quality attributes and unmeasured quality change that characterized, for instance, the study of appliances in chapter 7. Nevertheless, for seven products (two types of typewriters, two sizes of outboard motors, and three power hand tools) it is possible to compare the catalog results with indexes of roughly matched models from *CR*. Subsequently, in chapter 12, the indexes developed in this chapter and the next are joined together with indexes from chapters 4–9 to compute new "alternative" price indexes from all the information in chapters 4–11 for many of the individual commodity classes included in the NIPA deflator for PDE.

The main focus of this chapter is on comparisons of mail-order catalog price indexes with PPI commodity price indexes for the same or similar

417

products.[1] Reassured by Rees's (1961a) finding that his results were similar for prices obtained from the Sears and Wards catalog, I have limited data collection to Sears, which in the postwar period has had substantially greater catalog sales than Wards.[2] Sixty-eight unduplicated Sears catalog price indexes have been compiled for study in this chapter, excluding the five Sears indexes for appliances developed and discussed in chapter 7. A total of 7,242 individual price observations make up the sixty-eight Sears catalog indexes over the thirty-seven-year period 1947–83. Taking account of product categories that are not available for the full thirty-seven-year interval, we have an average of 59.4 product categories per year, 235 observations per year, and 3.3 model observations per product category per year. Just as the NIPA deflator for PDE contains duplication, with eleven PPI indexes used twice, my alternative PDE index developed in chapter 12 also uses eleven of the Sears indexes twice, for a total of seventy-nine Sears catalog indexes excluding appliances.

The focus in this chapter is on the "drift" of the Sears indexes relative to the corresponding PPIs, where drift is defined as the growth rate over specified periods of the log ratio of the Sears index to the corresponding PPI. The methodological section of the chapter discusses alternative interpretations of this drift, including the possibility that the drift represents an estimate of quality change unmeasured by the PPI. The major methodological issues that receive attention are possible sources of secular drift in the prices charged by catalog outlets selling to households relative to manufacturers' prices reported to the PPI, and the possibility that the individual pairings of Sears catalog indexes with PPI commodity indexes may be inappropriate.

The conclusion of the chapter discusses the substantial difference between the average growth rate of the Sears catalog price indexes and that of the corresponding PPIs. This difference is calculated with two weighting schemes. With equal weights for all sixty-eight indexes, the average annual percentage "drift" of the Sears/PPI ratio is − 1.30 percent per year, that is, the average growth rate of the Sears catalog price indexes is 1.3 percent per year slower than the corresponding PPIs. When the Sears products are weighted in proportion to their importance in the PDE deflator by the weighting scheme described in chapter 12, the annual rate of drift becomes − 1.56 percent per year, implying that the more important products have higher rates of drift than the less important products. Also examined are summary data on the drift over specified subintervals of the full 1947–83 coverage period, and the frequency distribution of the drift for the sixty-eight

---

1. I acknowledge my debt to Jack Triplett for his close scrutiny of the earlier (1974) version of my work on catalog pricing; the extended discussion of advantages and disadvantages in sec. 10.3 owes much to his earlier critique, as do numerous comments and qualifications in the subsequent sections discussing the detailed product indexes.

2. In the late 1970s, Sears's catalogue sales were at a level of about $3 billion per year, compared to just under $1 billion for Wards. See Hendrickson (1979, 250).

unduplicated Sears/PPI ratios over these subintervals. In attempting to determine whether the resulting drift might be related to the adequacy of adjustments for quality change, the drift is related to the technological complexity of each product and to the extent of model coverage in the catalog. Finally, the chapter, in section 10.16.3, examines implications of the year-to-year behavior of the Sears/PPI ratios for the behavior of transaction prices relative to list prices, and for the efficacy of the Nixon-era price controls.

The new information in this chapter is based on the Sears, Roebuck catalog. Mail-order catalog price indexes have the dual advantages that they are true transaction prices, and that detailed specifications facilitate control for quality change. For a few of the Sears catalog products, there are sufficient observations to estimate hedonic regression indexes. Sears hedonic indexes for refrigerator-freezers, room air conditioners, and washing machines were presented in chapter 7, and outboard motors and gas hot water heaters are discussed in this chapter. For most of the Sears products, however, insufficient numbers of price observations for differing models are published in a given catalog to allow estimation of hedonic regressions. This dictates the use of the conventional "specification" method for the great majority of the Sears-PPI comparisons. As we shall see, an important advantage of the catalog data is that it is possible to implement the specification method in its "pure" form, in the sense that price comparisons for each pair of years refer to models that are identical in all quality characteristics listed in the catalog.

10.2   The Colorful History of the Sears Catalog

While the history of the Sears catalog is interesting in itself, it is of importance for this chapter because of its implications for the relative price of Sears catalog products as compared to the average price of similar products sold by noncatalog suppliers. A central theme of the history is that Sears (and Wards) catalogs became popular as a source of supply for rural residents, because they undercut the high prices charged by the typical rural merchant of the late nineteenth century. By the late 1970s, however, there is direct evidence that the pricing position of the catalog had shifted from below average to average or even above average. Subsequent sections return to the implications of this history for comparisons of catalog prices with PPI commodity price indexes.

While this study concentrates on mail-order catalog listings of durable goods, the variety of products sold is far broader. Catalogs have sold apparel, shoes, and processed foods from the beginning, and from 1909 to 1937 Sears sold cumulatively more than 100,000 complete kits for its "Honorbilt" residential houses. Some of the products were more unusual, as suggested by this letter:

Dear Montgomery Ward: Do you still sell embalming fluid? I saw it in your old catalog but not the new one. If you do, please send me enough for my husband, who is five foot eleven inches tall and weighs 165 pounds when in good health.

Another time a Montana rancher ordered a wife from Sears. She was supplied when an order clerk quit her job and went West to marry him.[3]

Benjamin Franklin has been called "the father of the mail-order catalog," because he issued in 1744 a list of 600 books he would sell by mail. But the catalog business as we know it today was founded by Charles Thompson in 1866, and the expression "mail-order" is first recorded in the language in 1867. Aaron Montgomery Ward founded his famous firm in 1872 after working as a traveling salesman in rural areas for Chicago dry goods stores and finding that farmers complained bitterly about the prices they were forced to pay for goods at traditional country stores, as well as limited selections and dishonest merchants.[4] Ward's was an idea whose time had come, for the spread of railroads throughout the United States made it possible for Ward and other early catalog operations to bypass the high-markup middlemen and retailers who were responsible for high retail prices.

Much of the early impetus to catalog sales came from established retail merchants like John Wanamaker and R. H. Macy, who established their mail-order departments in 1872 and 1874, respectively. Wanamaker was a leading advocate of improved mail service to facilitate mail-order shipments to rural residents and lobbied to achieve rural free delivery (1896) and the parcel post system (1913). Parcel post raised the previous four-pound limit on mail parcels; no longer would mail-order companies have to cut an overcoat into halves and send it in separate parcels along with needle and thread, as did Wards in the 1870s.

The threat of low-priced mail-order goods was not ignored by local retail merchants. The first mass book burners in American history were the anti-mail-order fanatics of the 1890s. Local merchants tried to persuade local residents to toss their catalogs into a bonfire in the public square every Saturday night. The mail-order merchants struck back with editorials in their catalogs urging sympathy for the local merchants who were honest but just inefficient, since they paid too much for their goods and could not obtain the volume discounts available to the giant mail-order houses.

Richard Sears began with a mail-order watch business in 1887, the success of which was facilitated by the skill of Alvah Curtis Roebuck, a former watch repairer, in organizing an assembly line to assemble inexpensive watches. The full-scale "Sears, Roebuck, and Company" catalog operation began in 1893, fully two decades after Wards, but by 1895 the Sears catalog already

---

3. Hendrickson (1979, 205–6). This book is the source for many of the details in this section.
4. A storekeeper is said to have enjoined his clerk to "come to the prayers after you have sanded the sugar and watered the molasses."

numbered 507 pages, and its cover proclaimed itself "The Cheapest Supply House on Earth."[5] By 1900, sales reached $11 million (about $150 million at 1982 prices), and Sears passed Wards in sales, a lead it was never to relinquish. Sears overtook the early lead of the older company because of the inspired combination of Richard Sears's promotional genius (which often descended into the sleazy, particularly in his advertisements for patent medicines and "electric belts") and the administrative skill of his new partner Julius Rosenwald, who organized the Sears shipping operation so well that Henry Ford studied it before setting up his first automobile assembly line.[6]

Much of Sears's early success in the late 1890s and early 1900s was due to its drastic price cutting on sewing machines and bicycles. When most other firms were selling sewing machines for $35–$55, Sears began in the $14–$16 range, and soon reduced the price of its most popular model to $12.50. Bicycles sold by local merchants for $75 were undercut by Sears models selling for $14 and $20 (Emmet and Jeuck 1950, 66–71). Sears prices in the postwar era have never been so low relative to the average retail price of other makes.

The rapid growth of the Sears catalog operation witnessed catalog circulation grow from 318,000 in 1897 to 3.6 million in the fall of 1908 and sales grow from $1.4 million in 1896 to $50 million in 1907 (Emmet and Jeuck 1950, table 11, p. 172). This early period culminated with the construction in 1906 of its westside Chicago headquarters and distribution center, a building of awesome proportions even by current standards. The 3-million-square-foot complex was proudly described as "the largest business building in the world,"and boasted a two-block-long railroad yard rolling through its center that connected Sears to every major trunk line emanating from Chicago.[7] More than 7,000 workers operated the miles-long system of conveyor belts and bin sorters that wound through the nine-story facility. The building even including a printing department for printing the millions of catalogs distributed annually, complete with railroad tracks to carry paper straight to the printing presses. The building's water tower, built to a height of sixteen stories in neo-Venetian style, set the design standard for subsequent Sears distribution plants and retail stores, all of which had real or fake towers in the same style until about 1940.[8]

5. The catalog reached 1,200 pp. in 1906, roughly its present size (it peaked at roughly 1,500 pp. in the early 1970s).

6. In 1895, Roebuck insisted on being bought out of his partnership by Sears for the princely sum of $25,000.

7. The quotation is from Worthy (1984, 29), who also records this description from the 1905 Sears, Roebuck catalog: "Miles of railroad tracks run through, in and around this building for the receiving, moving and forwarding of merchandise; elevators, mechanical conveyors, endless chains, moving sidewalks, gravity chutes, apparatus and conveyors, pneumatic tubes and every known mechanical appliance for reducing labor, for the working out of economy and dispatch is to be utilized here in our great Works."

8. Details about the distribution center come from *Crain's Chicago Business*, 21 September 1987, 3, in an article written on the occasion of its closing after eighty-one years in operation.

Sears grew rapidly with the agricultural prosperity that followed the outbreak of World War I, and, by the end of the war, Rosenwald found himself one of the world's wealthiest men. During this period, Rosenwald established a testing laboratory to check on the quality of merchandise being bought by his buyers and introduced review procedures to assess the validity of claims made in the catalog about particular goods. The company came close to bankruptcy during the 1920–21 postwar deflation-depression and was saved when Rosenwald pledged $20 million from his personal fortune as a guarantee to Sears' creditors.[9]

For almost a century, the Sears catalog has been an American institution, reflecting the styles and fashions of each era. Space in the catalog has always been allocated by sales, which allows individual products to appear and disappear faster in a catalog-based price index than in the official BLS price indexes. Using the catalog, for example, one can establish that bosom boards were widely used by women during the 1890s, that pyjamas were introduced about 1908 and twin beds about 1921, and that the last covered wagon was sold in 1924.

By the 1920s, however, the golden age of the catalog was already in decline.[10] Catalog sales depended heavily on farmers and other residents of rural areas and were bound to decline in relative importance as the United States became urbanized and, later, suburbanized. The prescient General Robert Wood, who assumed the management of Sears in 1922, foresaw these trends and decided to use the regional mail-order plants Rosenwald had built as supply bases for a sprawling network of stores. By the end of 1929, there were 324 retail stores, and in 1932 and every succeeding year the volume of retail store sales exceeded that of catalog sales.

As of the late 1970s, 315 million copies of Sears catalogs were printed each year, generating sales of $3 billion per year from 28 million customers.[11] Sears's catalog sales were larger than its next four rivals combined—Wards, Penney, Spiegel, and Alden. Nevertheless, the relative competitive position of the Sears catalog eroded in the 1970s; the number of catalog customers actually declined in 1979 for the first time in twenty-five years. Internally, Sears executives realized that problems with catalog sales were due in part to the rise of new competitors selling more stylish goods at lower prices, and that Sears had deliberately moved its prices from low to upper middle in the

9. The most detailed description of this fascinating episode is contained in Emmet and Jeuck (1950, 211–15). A shorter version is in Weil (1977, 56–58). The net effect of Rosenwald's "gift" was to make him and his heirs even richer, since his contribution was in the form of company stock with an option to repurchase later at a favorable price, and through the purchase of Sears buildings and real estate, which were later repurchased by the company.

10. The main source of the remainder of this section is Katz (1987).

11. Hendrickson (1979, 250). Katz (1987, 198) gives the figure of 350 million catalogs sent to 25 million households during 1979. These figures obviously include a multitude of small specialty catalogs. Distribution in 1988 of the two semiannual general merchandise catalogs was 15 million each, or 60 million copies in total (Barmash 1988).

preceding decade.[12] A Sears executive is quoted as stating in 1979, "The catalog was once the jewel of Sears, but now it's full of last year's goods at next year's prices." So dramatic was Sears's attempt to "trade up" to higher-quality goods, higher prices, and higher markups, that Sears has been called a "traitor to its class" (Weil 1977, 256).

Things went from bad to worse in the 1980s. Catalog sales as a percentage of total Sears retail sales declined from 100 percent in 1924, to 50 percent in 1932, to 22 percent in 1979, to 18.1 percent in 1984, to 15.5 percent in 1987.[13] The absolute level of nominal catalog sales was flat from 1981 to 1987, implying a decline of 20 percent in real catalog sales (deflating by the NIPA implicit consumption deflator). This occurred despite the demise of several important Sears rivals; Montgomery Ward closed its 113-year-old catalog operation in 1985, as did Aldens in 1982. Sears was undermined not just by its own pricing policy, but by an explosion of specialty catalog operations (our household buys from Williams Sonoma and Lands' End but never, ironically, from Sears). Some observers predict that the general catalog, the bible on which this chapter is based, may disappear in the 1990s. A preview may have occurred in 1986, when the "big book" was split into two parts, an annual durable goods catalog and a semiannual "soft goods" catalog.

To a large extent, the difficulties of the catalog mirrored the broader competitive weakness of Sears's retail merchandising operations in competing against an increasing variety of specialty stores that stocked a much deeper selection of goods in a narrow category. Sears has been described as a "sluggish behemoth clashing with smaller, more agile adversaries," and it can no longer boast, as it could fifty years ago, that only Sears extended credit to middle America or backed its merchandise with its own store guarantee.[14] In a broad sense, the struggle of Sears is an inevitable effect of the sovereignty of consumer choice in an affluent society. For the narrower purpose of price measurement carried out in the rest of this chapter, we should note that Sears is not as competitive as it once was. To the extent that the price-quality relation of Sears merchandise has deteriorated relative to that for durable goods retailing as a whole, the Sears catalog indexes will overstate the rate of price increase and understate the downdrift of the ratio of "true" quality-adjusted prices to the PPI.

12. "Awesome in size . . . Sears began trading up its price lines between 1967 and 1973. It raised its markups by selling higher-priced goods and gave up its lowest price lines" (Barmash 1977).

13. The 1924 figure is for the year before the opening of the first retail store; the 1932 figure is for the year given by Hendrickson (1979) that retail stores passed the catalog in sales; 1979 is from *Business Week,* 8 January 1979, 83; 1984 and 1987 are from Snyder and Waldstein (1988, 28).

14. This pessimistic verdict on the future of Sears and the Sears catalog is extracted from Snyder and Waldstein (1988), which is the best available study of the competitive and marketing difficulties of Sears (in contrast to Katz) [1987], which concentrates on the clash of personalities).

10.3   Catalog Price Indexes: Advantages and Disadvantages

This is not, of course, the first study to be attracted by the price and quality information available in mail-order catalogs. W. I. King was the first to use catalog data, constructing a Sears catalog cost-of-living index for 1909–28 that was published in bulletins of the National Bureau of Economic Research.[15] Albert Rees (1961a) published what is probably the best-known comparison of catalog price quotations with official price indexes, in his case the CPI. There is no overlap between the information collected by Rees and by this study, since Rees's concern was with price indexes for selected nondurable goods. One of Rees's main conclusions was that, when "there has been considerable stability in the physical characteristics of commodities over time," the catalog indexes "turn out to be surprisingly good approximations" of BLS indexes "based on much larger samples of outlets and areas" (1961a, 168–69). The presumption in this study is that, if the catalog indexes can come close to the BLS for simple items experiencing quality change, they may do better than the BLS for complex items undergoing continuous quality change, both because the catalogs adjust the model mix faster to reflect market tastes, and because the detailed catalog specifications make it easier to hold constant quality changes.

A closer analogue to this study is the catalog price index for thirty-six clothing items and nineteen home furnishing items developed by Rees (1961b) for the period 1890–1914. As does this study, Rees found a substantial amount of secular drift between his catalog indexes and the BLS WPI, with an average rate of change of the catalog/WPI ratio of -1.40 per year for clothing and -2.14 per year for home furnishings. Rees's study differs from the approach taken in this chapter, in that he did not attempt to match catalog price indexes with WPI indexes on an item-for-item basis, but rather used catalog prices and expenditure survey weights to construct a completely new index that might be compared with the overall WPI for clothing and home furnishings. Because Rees made no attempt to compare identical items, his index might differ from the PPI due to a different selection of items and the earlier introduction of new items. In contrast, the drift in the catalog/PPI ratios recorded in this chapter relates to identical items, within the limits of feasibility in matching catalog products with detailed eight-digit PPI commodity classifications.

10.3.1   Advantages

The purpose of this book is to investigate the behavior of price indexes for durable goods compiled from data sources that are different than those used in compiling the official government price indexes for durable goods. Mail-order catalogs seem ideally suited for this purpose. The following discussion compares catalog price indexes with both of the official BLS price

15. This fact is reported by Rees (1961b, 80).

indexes, the CPI and PPI, although the quantitative results of this chapter are entirely based on comparisons of catalog indexes with corresponding PPI commodity indexes (CPI indexes for selected appliances were compared with catalog indexes for appliances in chap. 7).

Among the advantages of catalog price indexes are the following.

1. Most important, specifications and illustrations published in catalogs allow closer control for changes in quality than in the official price indexes. The continuity of item codes from one catalog to the next is often helpful in following a particular item, and there is usually a long list of specifications that can be checked to ensure that the models being compared are absolutely identical. In contrast, compilers of the PPI must trust the manufacturers who submit mail questionnaires to hold quality constant, and the relatively low frequency of product substitutions in the PPI suggests that specification changes may frequently go unreported (see below).[16] This advantage of catalog indexes needs to be qualified, of course, if the catalogs do not disclose a true change in quality of an item described as identical in two successive catalogs.

2. Leaving aside the small number of hedonic indexes developed from the catalog data, the specification methodology used to compare catalog items over time (discussed in more detail below) ensures that price comparisons are included only for items that are absolutely identical in every dimension reported in the catalog specification. In contrast, most BLS specifications are not as detailed as the printed catalog specifications, and, in contrast to the catalog indexes, both the CPI and the PPI make direct comparisons between nonidentical goods if both fall within the same specification.[17]

3. Related to the first two advantages is the fact that catalog price indexes can in principle be replicated by anyone with access to a library containing historical catalog volumes. In contrast, the submissions by manufacturers to the PPI are confidential, and there is no way that PPI commodity price indexes can be replicated by anyone except BLS employees. For historical periods twenty-five or thirty years ago, even BLS employees may not have access to the original manufacturers' submissions.[18]

16. An exception is the automobile, to which the BLS gives special attention. BLS representatives travel to Detroit to discuss quality changes with manufacturers and see not just illustrations, but the actual models of the cars involved.

17. This statement about the CPI comes from Rees (1961a, 141), who states, "The BLS makes direct comparisons between nonidentical goods if both fall within the same specification." Triplett (1971b, 186, table 6.1) quotes a study showing that, for nonfood items in the CPI in April 1966, more than half of all product substitutions were handled by direct comparison of prices of the old and new model, and well under 1 percent were handled by an "explicit size or quality adjustment." For the PPI, Early and Sinclair (1983, 111) state, that of the 455 cases for 1976 in which nonidentical items were compared in the PPI, 142 of the cases (31 percent) were handled by "direct comparisons," i.e., all the recorded price change was treated as a price change and none as a quality change. See pp. 84–89 above.

18. Nor would a BLS employee have any incentive to study the original manufacturers' submissions, since the PPI and CPI are never revised retrospectively. With the exception of an occasional research study using historical data (e.g., Triplett and McDonald 1977; and Early and

4. The selection of products and individual models sold in catalogs responds automatically to the needs of the marketplace. This has always been true, as in the comment, "space to items always having been allotted on the basis of sales" (Hendrickson 1979, 249). This gives catalog price indexes two inherent advantages over the CPI and PPI, at least prior to the introduction of improved methodology in the CPI in 1978 and in the PPI beginning in 1982. First, for products sold in a large number of models or varieties, "it seems reasonable to assume that the number of different detailed varieties in the catalog will be greatest where the volume of sales is greatest, so that we probably weight the major varieties of an item in rough proportion to their importance" (Rees 1961a, 141). There is no such assurance that product indexes are sales weighted across models within a product category in the pre-1978 CPI, which was based on an expenditure survey taken many years previously that did not reflect the current range of models on the market. This advantage of catalogs is even more true in contrast to the PPI, which prior to 1982 gave equal weight to each price reporter within individual commodity categories.

Second, products tend to be introduced into the catalogs soon after they become marketable, in contrast to the CPI and PPI, which often introduce new products many years after they become commercially important. In fact, given the expense of distributing catalogs, it is likely that the catalog firms wait longer to "take a chance" on new items than do normal retail shops.[19] In this sense, neither the catalog nor the BLS indexes are ideal, and both may be late in the introduction of new products, although in most cases the catalogs move faster than the BLS. This timing factor is one reason for preferring the *CR* indexes for appliances in chapter 7 to either the catalog or the BLS indexes; the first report in *CR* appeared before the earliest appearance in the Sears catalog in most cases, and well before the BLS indexes in every case where there was a difference *(CR* and the Sears catalog beat the CPI for room air conditioners by eleven years, although not the PPI; *CR* beat the PPI by fifteen years on under-counter dishwashers and by ten years on microwave ovens—these last two products are not included in my Sears sample).

Sinclair 1983, all the research effort at the BLS is oriented toward improving the construction of the indexes in the future rather than toward evaluating the behavior of the indexes in the past. This orientation helps explain why it was the BEA rather than the BLS that took the lead in developing the price indexes for computers discussed in chap. 6 above.

19. The fact that Sears, Roebuck followed the market even in its first twenty years is described in this interesting passage from Emmet and Jeuck (1950, 108–9): "The first appearance of any new item in a Sears catalogue had seldom marked the date when that item first became popular. It had simply marked the date when the item had established beyond peradventure that it was here to stay and the date when Sears, Roebuck was able to make satisfactory arrangements with sources for mass delivery of the item. . . . Yet, with due allowance for this time lag, the catalogue offerings of the company have remained one of the best yardsticks in most respects of the needs and wants of the people of this country during the period of Sears, Roebuck's existence. No item could long be in great demand without cropping up in the big book; and, by the same token, few items could hang on in the catalogue for any length of time after the public ceased to fancy them. As that public fancy expanded in scope, as America came of age, . . . the Sears catalogue kept pace, albeit a cautious pace indeed."

Further, for a given product, the selection of models available in catalogs is adjusted with each newly issued catalog to respond to changes in demand, automatically allowing weights on different model types to change (e.g., for refrigerator-freezers from "U-type" to "dual-zone" to cross top to side-by-side arrangements). In contrast, both the PPI and the CPI adhere to fixed specifications over a long period of time, which may lead to disproportionate weight for obsolete items. In discussing the wording on the PPI questionnaire below, I note that manufacturers are instructed to report changes in existing models but not the introduction of additional models. Thus, if an existing model, say an old U-type refrigerator, remains in production without changes, and a new cross-the-top model is introduced, the change is not reported spontaneously by the manufacturer but must be discovered by the BLS commodity specialist. As a result, the old model may be priced after sales have shifted to a new model.

The adherence by the BLS indexes to fixed specifications may also lead to a systematic choice of items that are lower in quality than the typical item actually being sold on the market, and may severely limit the coverage of the BLS indexes to a fraction of the different model types actually being sold on the market.[20] While the new methodology used in the CPI since 1978 and that phased in for the PPI in the early 1980s allow those indexes to respond more rapidly to changes in the marketplace, there have been no retrospective revisions, and, for this reason, these improvements have no bearing on comparisons of catalog indexes with either the CPI or the PPI before 1978 and 1982, respectively.

5. Prices printed in the catalogs are actual transaction prices. If retail and wholesale outlets that compete with catalog firms price items at varying discounts, catalog houses must adjust their published prices to remain competitive. Their prices should therefore be reasonably good proxies for those of their major competitors.

6. Since postage and shipping costs, credit charges, and taxes (except for federal excise taxes) are not included in the published catalog prices, the services provided with each item are held constant. This does not represent any advantage over the PPI, which measures prices at the manufacturers' (not wholesale) level. However, the CPI may reflect a changing mix of services. Although prices in different stores are not directly compared in the CPI, services in the same store may change over time (e.g., Marshall Field's, a full-service department store, eliminated free delivery service in the 1970s

20. As reported by Rees (1961a, 141–42), "It seems probable to us that the selection of specified-in-detail items for the CPI is often at too low a quality level for the index population, probably because the index population moved up to better qualities after the item was specified. In a number of cases we were unable to find any variety of an item in the catalogs of either house whose quality was as low as that specified by the BLS." Rees further reports (142) that rigid adherence to BLS specifications would require excluding a large fraction of the observations that can be collected from the catalog, in one case reducing the sample by a factor of ten.

under pressure from discount-store competition). Also, otherwise identical catalog and CPI indexes can differ, since the CPI includes state and local sales taxes.

Although there are numerous advantages to using mail-order catalogs as a source of data for price indexes, these should not be overstated. For instance, there is no presumption that the catalog price index for a given product in this study is based on more individual models than the PPI. A proliferation of different models and types was a characteristic of Rees's (1961a) study, which made breadth of model coverage a criterion for choosing products to be studied. Here, in contrast, the main criterion is to find as many catalog products as possible that can be compared to the specific PPI commodity indexes used to deflate PDE in the NIPA, and this leads me to develop product indexes with a wide range of model coverage, from one model to more than ten models per product category per year. Subsequently, I shall compare my model coverage with the number of PPI price observations per commodity index.

10.3.2   Disadvantages

The case against reliance on catalog price indexes takes two forms. First, there are clear disadvantages of relying on catalogs. Second, criticisms can be offered of the advantages listed above.

The most serious problem in the use of catalog prices is the possibility of a systematic difference in the secular growth rates of the same product sold by catalog and noncatalog outlets, due, for instance, to differential growth in the efficiency of catalog operations or changes in pricing policies. Regarding efficiency, there are different issues involved in comparing catalog prices with retail prices as recorded in the CPI and with producer prices as recorded in the PPI. For a comparison with the CPI, catalog prices include payment for warehouse and distribution services and would have a slower secular rate of increase than prices of retail competitors if the growth of efficiency in the provision of these services by catalog houses had been relatively rapid. It is hard to believe such a bias could be major, since innovations in warehouse technology are likely to have been adopted by noncatalog competitors. In fact, the bias appears to operate in the opposite direction. The secular rate of decline of prices for three major appliances in the Sears catalog appears to have been slower than for an average of all makes reported in *CR*, as documented above in chapter 7 for washing machines, refrigerators, and room air conditioners. In this chapter, seven new *CR* indexes are developed, and five of these seven also show the same pattern of a slower secular price increase than the equivalent catalog index (leaving aside outboard motors for 1971–75; see sec. 10.8 below). Further, the model-by-model prices recorded by *CR* indicate that Sears and Wards models for major appliances tended to be at the lower end of the price range in the early postwar period but drifted toward the middle of the price range over time. Such behavior is consistent with the quotes in the historical section (10.2) above, indicating a shift in pricing strategy by Sears in the late 1960s and early 1970s. This evidence suggests the possibility that the downward drift of most Sears catalog indexes relative to comparable CPIs may understate the downward drift of a more representative range of "true" prices relative to the CPI.

These remarks on comparing catalog prices with components of the CPI are relevant for the study of appliances in chapter 7. However, in this chapter, all the comparisons are with the PPI. Here, note that warehouse and distribution services are included in the catalog price quotations but not in the PPI, which for the durable goods categories studied here collects virtually all its price quotations directly from manufacturers. There are numerous reasons why the implicit value-added deflator of the wholesaling and distribution component of the catalog price might rise at a different rate than the manufacturers' price of a given product, including differential improvements in efficiency, a differential component of automation and computerization, a differential share of purchased materials, and so on. All these factors caution us against treating the catalog price indexes themselves as necessarily representing a best estimate of the required "true" price index, and remind us that drift of the catalog indexes relative to the PPI can occur for numerous reasons, not just as the result of different procedures for controlling quality change.

The inclusion of wholesaling and distribution operations in the catalog prices may be an advantage rather than a disadvantage from the perspective of the PDE deflator in the NIPA. Many types of durable goods go through warehouse and distribution channels en route from manufacturer to the business firms that purchase durable goods. While large durable goods built to order (e.g., Boeing 747s) are delivered directly from the manufacturer to the final user, the smaller mass-produced durable goods studied in this chapter may often be sold by wholesalers or other distributive middlemen.

Another inherent problem in using catalog information is the need to match the dates on the catalog price quotations with the corresponding PPIs. Should the prices published in the spring-summer catalog be compared with the PPI for a single month in the spring, for an average of months in the spring and summer, or for some earlier period on the ground that decisions on prices in the spring-summer catalog are made in the preceding autumn? Below, I discuss my selection criterion and compare it to that of Rees (1961a). But, whatever month is selected for the PPI, this issue makes little or no difference for secular comparisons over decades or longer periods.

Some of the advantages of catalog price indexes discussed in the previous section have been called into question. First, the availability of explicit specifications, model numbers, and illustrations in catalogs does not necessarily constitute a unique advantage. Model numbers and illustrated brochures are available for some types of producer durables, and these may be used by BLS commodity specialists. Further, as recognized above, printed specifications and illustrations cannot reveal unreported changes in the quality of catalog items. In fact, an extreme view might hold that a catalog price index has "no advantage at all" over the PPI in this regard.[21]

To evaluate this skeptical view, it is worth reviewing the source of price data for durable goods in the PPI, discussed previously in section 3.2 and 3.3. Close to 100 percent of price quotations for machinery and transportation equipment are based on reports submitted from producers by mail on a uniform questionnaire form.[22] Identification of quality changes and evaluation of their "value" are left entirely up to the initiative of the producers submitting the price reports, and there is no request on the printed questionnaire that producers routinely submit documentary evidence on the nature or value of changes, whether in the form of brochures, specification lists, or anything else.[23] There is simply a blank space with the instruction, "Commodity description (Please indicate all changes)," and, under the heading "changes," the label "date, nature and value of change."

While there is no documentation of the frequency with which BLS commodity specialists physically examine submitted printed evidence on specification changes, one suspects that such careful scrutiny was relatively rare for products other than automobiles, at least until recently. Section 3.2 cited evidence that virtually no explicit quality corrections were made for durable goods other than automobiles before 1965 and, even in that year, showed that the majority of changes in product specifications were handled by "direct comparison" of new and old models (i.e. by ignoring the quality change), and that virtually none of such changes were handled by explicit adjustments based on cost estimates. Further, as pointed out above, the wording of the questionnaire asks respondents to report changes in existing models but not the introduction of additional models. For this reason, the PPI may continue to price an old unchanged model after sales have shifted to a newly introduced model. Perhaps the best response to the extreme view that BLS commodity specialists regularly review printed specifications and illustrations comes from the BLS itself: "Firms are trusted to make accurate estimates of quality change. The BLS does not normally question their estimates.[24]

A sharp contrast can be drawn between the mail-order catalog price indexes, where all price comparisons are based on an examination of printed specifications and pictures, and the BLS procedures, which depend on the diligence of individual commodity specialists, and which have doubtless

21. "Thus, not only is the picture-specification 'advantage' over WPI prices no advantage at all, but the method of controlling for quality change that it implies is just as inadequate in your data as it is in the WPI" (letter to the author from Jack E. Triplett, 30 November 1977).

22. The "Ruggles report" is cited in the references under its official author, U.S. Executive Office of the President (1977). Data on price reports by type are provided in table I-4 and a sample of the BLS questionnaire, form BLS 47JA, dated January 1976, is included as exhibit I-1.

23. Again, autos are an exception. See n. 8 above.

24. Telephone conversation with Alvin Roark, a machinery specialist in the then WPI (now PPI), 12 July 1973.

varied over time. The Ruggles report noted the dependence of the BLS procedures on possibly dissimilar criteria of the individual specialists, in the context of the choice of individual commodities and particular reporters:

> The determination of both the commodity selection and the price reporter thus in large measure depends on the diligence of the commodity specialist, and the personal contacts which he can build up. Just as in most libraries the collection of books in various areas of specialization is a direct reflection of the scholars working in those areas, so also are the prices collected by the Bureau of Labor Statistics a reflection of the commodity specialists in different areas. [U.S. Executive Office of the President 1977, III-1]

Even as recently as 1976, out of 108,756 price observations, Early and Sinclair (1983) report that only 455 created the need to make a comparison between dissimilar items. As Griliches observed in his comment on their paper (144), "Either many true comparability problems are not reported or the PPI by design excludes most of the rapidly changing commodity areas from its purview. I assume that both are true." The low frequency of product substitutions reported by Early and Sinclair suggests that some specification changes may slip through without being reported on the questionnaires, possibly for the simple reason that reporters do not want to take the time to estimate the value of the changes, as requested. Below, we shall see that the frequency of model changes in the catalog data base is substantially more frequent than is implicit in the PPI.[25]

Another criticism of the preceding section on the advantages of catalog price indexes concerns reproducability, where we need to distinguish two issues. An unambiguous advantage of a catalog price index is that in principle it can be reproduced by anyone with access to the same catalogs. However, there is no guarantee that any such reproduction would inevitably yield an identical index, because subjective decisions must inevitably be made in situations where models change without an overlap model, or when only a subset of available information is used in order to economize on research resources. The methods used to develop the catalog indexes were, however, designed to minimize subjective decisions, since the actual data collection was carried out by a succession of research assistants. Subsequently, the price and quality of individual models are examined over long time intervals to see if the resulting catalog indexes "make sense," particularly when they record

---

25. The implied frequency of product substitutions for machinery cannot be extracted from the Early-Sinclair paper, which does not report the total number of price observations by industry. However, table IV-1 of the Ruggles report lists 409 "linked series" in 1974 for machinery (SIC 35 and 36) out of 31,441 monthly observations, which translates to 2,620 annual observations. Thus, just 15.6 percent of the 1974 machinery reports involved a product substitution, for an implied frequency of about one every 6.5 years. This figure rises to 22.2 percent when the replacement of discontinued series by new series is included, for an implied frequency of one product substitution per observation every 4.5 years.

a significantly different rate of price change from the closest comparable PPI commodity index.

10.3.3   A Balanced Assessment

Catalog price indexes are clearly no panacea to the age-old dilemma of adjusting durable goods deflators for quality change. Even if catalog prices are fully corrected for quality change, they may not accurately reflect the unobserved "true" quality-corrected price index for all suppliers, because of differences between catalog firms and all firms in the growth of efficiency or in the evolution of pricing policies. The comparison of catalog prices with individual PPI commodity indexes rests in part on a belief in the efficacy of economic competition in keeping catalog prices for a given narrowly defined product roughly in line with what is charged by other suppliers. Even so, the perfect functioning of competition would not prevent drift between the catalog and the PPI commodity indexes in a case where there is a major difference in the secular price trend of the warehousing and distribution services provided by catalog houses and the underlying prices of manufactured goods collected by the PPI, or where the selection of models or types of products sold through catalogs is different from that sold by other outlets, for example, if catalogs typically sell more items that are small or lightweight in order to minimize shipping costs. This difference could make catalog indexes behave differently than the PPI, although there is no presumption for the direction of the drift.

Further, catalog prices may not adequately control for all types of quality change. As noted above, some changes may be introduced without being explicitly acknowledged in the printed catalog descriptions. Further, catalog indexes based on the specification method are subject to all the criticisms directed toward the specification method as used in the PPI. Both types of specification index delete price change when new models are introduced and rely only on unchanged overlapping models; this could impart a downward bias if the timing of price increases typically coincides with the introduction of new models or an upward bias if improvements in performance-price ratios coincide with the introduction of new models, as clearly is the case for electronic computers (chap. 6) and appliances (chap. 7).

Consequently, there can be no blanket claim that the catalog indexes developed here are superior to the individual PPI commodity indexes with which they are compared. This chapter attempts to determine which types of commodities exhibit the greatest drift, and to examine possible generalizations that might explain such drift. For instance, a consistent tendency for technologically complex products to exhibit more of a downward drift of the catalog indexes relative to the PPI than simple products with constant quality characteristics might indicate that the catalog indexes do a better job of correcting for quality change. Also, a tendency for the drift to become smaller or disappear might support the view that quality-change procedures at the BLS have improved over the postwar years. A final question is whether the drift is greater for products where the catalog indexes are based on a relatively large number of models.

10.4   Catalog Price Index Methodology

10.4.1   Criteria for Selection of Catalog Price Quotations

For any given investment of research resources, there is a trade-off between the number of different catalogs consulted for a given product and the number of separate products that can be included. Since Rees did not comment on any significant discrepancy between prices for a given item in the Sears, Roebuck and Montgomery Ward catalogs, an initial decision was made to limit this study only to Sears (the largest catalog house) and thus to allow time to copy data for additional products and models. This procedure is consistent with Rees's conclusion that too many outlets and insufficient varieties are priced in the official indexes.[26] Sears's catalog sales in the 1970s were triple Wards's and equal in fact to Wards's and the next three competitors combined. To allow time to copy prices for more products, prices were copied only from one catalog per year (spring-summer), even though two catalogs are published annually.[27] This decision has the disadvantage, of course, that the resulting indexes may understate the extent of flexibility in the catalog prices.[28]

Since the primary purpose of this study is a comparison of the catalog prices with PPI indexes for the same products and time periods, a decision was required on the choice of time periods for that comparison. The catalog data in this study were collected from the Chicago-area edition of the Sears, Roebuck spring-summer general catalog.[29] According to a Sears official, however, prices are set long in advance of catalog distribution. Since the catalogs go to press in October of the previous year, and final price decisions are made in October, the most closely comparable PPI indexes would be those for October of the year previous to the date printed on the Sears catalog.[30]

26. "This suggests that too large an amount of resources may be devoted to maintaining large outlet and area samples for some commodities, and that an improvement of the official indexes could be obtained within a fixed budget by reducing the size of outlet samples and increasing the size of samples of items or varieties. . . . if it is cheaper to sample several varieties in one outlet rather than one variety in several outlets (and we suspect that it sometimes is) this again suggests a possible gain from the reallocation of resources devoted to the price statistics programs" (Rees 1961a, 169).

27. The decision to limit indexes to annual observations was also made in order to maintain comparability with the new price indexes developed in other chapters of this book for which only annual observations are available. Few of my data sources allow measurement of intrayear price movements, except for the used car guides.

28. Sears also issues periodic special "sale" catalogs for a subset of items, again indicating that the catalog indexes compiled here understate the true extent of price flexibility.

29. In a very few instances, particular items were not listed in the spring-summer catalog, and prices were substituted from the previous fall-winter edition.

30. These dates for the pricing decision and printing of the catalogs were obtained from a 1973 conversation with J. Karp, an official of the Sears credit department at Chicago headquarters.

However, another interpretation is that the correct PPI is that of the following spring, contemporaneous with the period when the catalog prices are in effect, because of aspects of Sears's pricing strategy that are forward looking. For instance, in some past periods, Sears purchased futures in cotton and rubber to cover their anticipated sales of tires in the following six months. They also owned part of corporations supplying them with products, including appliances, particularly Whirlpool, and arranged to buy forward at a price established for conditions of the following six months.[31] While in some earlier stages of this research PPI prices in year $t - 1$ were compared with prices in the spring-summer Sears catalog for year t, in the end both were compared in year t. It might have been preferable to use monthly PPI indexes for, say, September or October of the previous year, but monthly data for eight-digit PPI commodity indexes were not as complete as for annual data. This choice to adopt contemporaneous pricing is made partly because it is probably more accurate, and also to simplify the presentation of the results in light of the many indexes in this book developed from sources other than the Sears catalog. While there may be a case for comparing the catalog indexes with a month prior to the beginning of the year when the catalog is in use, there is no such case in the many comparisons involving sources other than Sears discussed in other chapters (e.g., *CR*, unit values, used auto prices, and computer prices). Thus, all PPI series listed in the tables in this chapter and in Appendix B are reported for the same year as published by the BLS.

The selection of products and models is straightforward, except for the fact that products were selected in two stages. Of the sixty-eight unduplicated catalog products, fifty-eight were included in the original 1974 first draft of this study, and were originally collected for the period 1947–70. The point of departure was the list of PPI commodity indexes included in the NIPA index for PDE (listed in App. table A.1). Each such product was included if it was carried in the Sears catalog for most of the 1947–70 period. In cases where the PDE deflator is based on a four-digit or six-digit group index rather than an eight-digit commodity index, an attempt was made to locate Sears products that matched eight-digit commodity indexes within the relevant four-digit or six-digit group. Thus, some eight-digit PPI commodity indexes are used for comparison that are not included in the PDE deflator.

Catalog prices for the original fifty-eight products were gradually updated throughout the late 1970s and early 1980s, and then in the final data collection in 1984–85 an additional ten catalog products were added. The steps taken to develop the additional products were, first, to make a list of new producer

Another report states that "most price decisions must be made eight months before the general books expire," and implies that the expiration date of the spring-summer catalog is normally 1 July, soon after the fall-winter books are mailed. This would date the price decision for the spring-summer catalog at 1 November of the previous year. See "Catalog Sales Thrive on Inflation," *Business Week,* 20 July 1974, 27.

31. On Sears's pricing policy, the use of futures contracts and forward thinking was stressed in a letter to me from Theodore W. Schultz, dated 17 December 1973.

durable products in the PPI since 1970, and then to check that the product was
carried in the Sears catalog from 1970 to 1983 with a sufficient number of
year-to-year model matches.

In general, all models listed in the catalog for a given product are included.
An exception is made in the case of several products (e.g., auto batteries)
where a very large number of closely similar models was listed in the catalog,
and to save copying time only a subset was included in this study. Other
exceptions were as follows:

1. PVC piping: all sizes of straight lengths of PVC piping were included;
2. Prefabricated metal buildings: the largest size of each building type was
   included;
3. Chain link fence: a combination of gates, posts, and fabric for various
   sizes of industrial fence was used;
4. Drill bits: only standard drill bits were included.

10.4.2   Implementation of the Specification Technique

For those products priced by the specification method, price comparisons
for each pair of years are facilitated by Sears's policy of carrying several
models in each product category. Changes in specifications usually affect only
a subset of models in any one year, so for almost every product at least a few
identical models are available for a price comparison between a pair of years.
Because model changes occur at irregular intervals, the number of price
comparisons of identical models for a given product may be on the order of,
let us say, ten for a series of years and then collapse to two or three in a year
of substantial model changes.

The detailed application of the specification methodology from the catalog
price indexes in this study differs from that used by the BLS in the
construction of PPI product indexes. For most products, the BLS specifications remain identical over a long period of years, and a "product substitution" is flagged only when the respondent's questionnaire indicates a change
in some characteristic. As discussed above, only about one-fifth of the PPI
price observations for machinery in 1974 required any substitution at all, and
this fraction was even lower in the 1950s and 1960s. In contrast, each pair of
years is treated separately in this study, and (with the exceptions noted above)
the list of included models is allowed to change annually. Table 10.1 is a
schematic representation of the methodology for a hypothetical product, with
the models included in this study for each pair of years indicated by boxes.

The asterisks indicate models whose prices might be included in a
hypothetical PPI index. Model D represents the type of model that remains in
the PPI year after year, as implied by the low percentage of PPI product
substitutions that appear to occur each year. The replacement of model A by
model F indicates another characteristic of the PPI, that in between major
revisions new models are linked into the index only when a respondent flags
the disappearance of an old model. The Ruggles report (table IV-1) states, for

Table 10.1   Models Listed in Sears Catalog for a Hypothetical Product by Year

	Years					
	1	2	3	4	5	6
	A*	A*	A*			
	B	B				
	C	C	C			
	D*	D*	D*	D*	D*	D*
		E	E	E	E	
		F	F	F*	F*	F*
				G	G	G
				H	H	H
				I	I	I
						J
Total number of model comparisons included in this study		4	5	3	6	5
Total number of model comparisons included in hypothetical PPI		2	2	1	2	2

Note: Asterisks indicate models whose prices are included in hypothetical PPI index: boxes indicate models whose prices are included in hypothetical catalog index.

instance, that the number of new machinery series in 1974 was 175, almost exactly the same as the number of discontinued machinery series (176).

The advantages of the approach used in this study are the inclusion of extra models that appear and disappear between major PPI revisions (e.g., model E in table 10.1), and the more rapid inclusion of new models. Ideally, this approach should lead to the inclusion of more total models per product, as was true in Rees's (1961a) study. However, several products are included where only one or two models are available, in order to include in the study as many as possible of the PPI products used in the NIPA PDE deflator. Thus, there is no general presumption that the catalog index is based on more models per product category than the PPI. A question for subsequent study is whether the drift of the catalog indexes relative to the comparable PPI indexes is related to the number of catalog model observations per product. Once it was decided to include a catalog product, the procedure was to compare all identical models in every pair of adjacent years. For two models to be considered identical, and thus for their prices to be compared directly, it was necessary that all the following quality characteristics must match exactly: weight, accessories, capabilities, electrical use, dimensions, efficiency ratings, and all other listed characteristics. Identical catalog numbers do not ensure that two products are identical, and so the determining criterion for direct comparison is the exact match of characteristics, not an exact match of model numbers.

Nevertheless, the model numbers are very useful in quickly spotting changes in characteristics in the set of models available in two adjacent years.

Since no information is available on the relative volume of sales for the models of each product, an equal weight is applied to the price change of each model within a product category. Formally, the method used to calculate the price change (p_t) for each of the sixty-eight product categories was

$$(10.1) \qquad p_t = (1/n)\sum_{i=1}^{n}(\log P_{it} - \log P_{i,t-1}),$$

where the index i refers to the n individual models within each product category. The price change for each pair of adjacent years (p_t) as calculated in (10.1) was cumulated into a price index in logs by simple addition, and then converted into a conventional price index by taking antilogs. While the use of equal weights for each model may introduce an element of misrepresentation into the indexes, the mix of models that Sears carries for a given product responds to changes in the relative volume of sales. Examples of this response are the shifts from manual to electric adding machines, galvanized to glass-lined water heaters, seven- or 8-inch to 9- or 10-inch power saws, manual-prime to self-priming centrifugal pumps, and so on.

The indexes created from this study have the advantage that they are open to public inspection and can be reproduced by anyone with access to a library that holds back issues of the Sears catalog. To facilitate any such attempt to reproduce our indexes, the Appendix to chapter 10 provides exact model numbers and page numbers in the Sears catalog for each product in the final year covered by the index. The same table lists the average number of models priced per year, the total number of models priced, and the number of quality attributes held constant. In addition, for many products, the text of this chapter describes the characteristics and prices of models available at the beginning and end of the sample period as a cross-check that the secular rates of price change of the new catalog indexes are reasonable.

As stated above, the catalog indexes are subject to the same problem as any specification index, including those compiled by the BLS. Any price change that occurs on the introduction of a new model is deleted, as in the changeover in table 10.1 in year 4 from old models A and C to the new models G, H, and I. If manufacturers typically postpone price increases during the life of a model for the occasion of a new model introduction, then deletion causes the exclusion of major price changes and leads to a downward secular bias in price indexes. If, on the other hand, quality improvements in new models tend to be introduced with no change in price, the deletion technique causes the exclusion of reductions in "true price" and leads to an upward secular bias.

The hedonic technique provides a solution, where sufficient data are available, since all available models can be included, and the hedonic regression coefficients can be used to establish a value for changes in quality between old and new models of the same product. In this study, hedonic regressions are performed for those products with relatively frequent quality changes. In the extreme case of refrigerators, models tend to be changed completely every year, with virtually no overlap of identical models. No hedonic regressions were performed for those products where insufficient models were listed to provide a sample of at least ten for each pair of years (i.e., at least five in any single year) or for some products with many listed models where quality appeared to remain identical over a long series of years (e.g., the cases of automobile batteries and electric motors). The individual catalog product regressions (for gas hot water heaters, outboard motors, automatic washing machines, refrigerators, and room air conditioners) are described in chapter 7 for appliances and later in this chapter for the other two products.

10.4.3   Weighting Issues and Presentation of Results

The primary discussion of weighting issues in this book is contained in chapter 12, which treats all the issues involved in converting the evidence developed in chapters 4–11 into an alternative version of the PDE deflator, as well as the deflator for consumer expenditures on durable goods. In this chapter, the primary emphasis is on the development of individual catalog/PPI price ratios for as many products as possible, and the discussion is primarily devoted to an examination of the ratios on an individual basis. The overall conclusions of the chapter are summarized by presenting an aggregate of the catalog and PPI indexes, as well as the catalog/PPI ratio, based on both an unweighted and a weighted average, where the latter uses the PDE weights from chapter 12.

The following text sections describe the individual product indexes within each industry group and vary considerably in length and amount of detail, depending on the complexity of the products within each group and the availability, in a few cases, of additional evidence from *CR*. To avoid a multiplicity of tables for the various industry groups and to allow a compact tabular presentation, the supporting tables each cover all catalog products and are grouped together at the end of the chapter for easy reference. Each text section begins by describing the selection of PPI commodity indexes used by the BEA to deflate PDE and indicates the subset of these indexes for which corresponding Sears products are available. The list of the PPIs used in the PDE deflator was obtained from the BEA in 1977 and refers to the PPI commodity indexes available and in use at that time.[32] This complete list, together with the 1967 weight applied to each PPI index, is presented in

32. There is an equivalent list of PPIs in the PDE deflator in 1986, after the late 1985 benchmark revision. There are a few minor additions and subtractions, but the overall list is basically the same. The 1986 list provided by the BEA is much less useful than the one obtained

Appendix A at the end of the book. Table 10.8 below lists each catalog product and the PPI commodity index and (and PPI code number) with which it is compared. At this stage, each section comments on any problems in "matching" the specifications of the catalog and PPI products, as might occur, for instance, if a smaller variety sold by the catalog for home use were compared with a larger-sized PPI product intended for industrial use.

Then each section proceeds to discuss the individual catalog products, with reference to tables at the end of the chapter. The Appendix to this chapter contains details about each Sears product: years covered, average models per year, total models priced, and number of quality attributes held constant. For the final year covered, it also lists the price range of models included, model numbers, and the page number in the relevant catalog. The drift of the catalog/PPI ratios for each product is listed for the full period and three subintervals in table 10.9 below by product category and in table 10.10 below by the size of the drift. For almost all products where the secular downward drift in the ratio of the catalog price index to the comparable PPI index is relatively large, it has been possible to carry out a comparison of "closely similar" models in order to assess the evolution of quality-adjusted prices over long periods of time. Usually the criterion for carrying out such a comparison is that the downdrift averages out to −2.0 percent or more over the postwar period as a whole. This growth rate is sufficient to imply a 1947 Sears/PPI index ratio of 206 on a base of 1983 = 100.

For further reference, additional tables relevant for the book as a whole, not just this chapter, are contained in appendixes in the back of the book. A complete listing of PPIs used in the PDE deflator is presented as Appendix A. The detailed annual values of all the catalog and PPI commodity indexes covered in this chapter, together with the indexes developed in other chapters, are presented in Appendix tables B.1–B.16.

10.5   Office, Computing, and Accounting Machinery

In its 1986 benchmark revision of the NIPA, the BEA reorganized the listing of the industry subgroups of PDE and promoted the office, computing, and accounting machinery (OCAM) component to the first-listed category, thus reflecting its rapidly growing importance. By far the most important product within OCAM is the electronic computer and its associated peripherals, and these were subjected to a full-scale study in chapter 6. The other PPI commodity indexes used in the PDE deflator for noncomputer OCAM are two eight-digit commodity indexes for electric and manual typewriters, and

---

in 1977, because the 1986 list lacks the PPI code numbers of the specific PPI indexes used and contains no information on what was done to deal with the historical disappearance of specific PPI indexes and the initiation of new indexes.

two six-digit group indexes for calculating and accounting machines. Four related products were sold in the Sears catalog over most or all of the postwar period—ten-key adding machines, cash registers, manual typewriters (both standard and portable), and electric portable typewriters—and a fifth product, the electronic calculator, that was carried in the catalog beginning in 1970.

There are several comparability problems in matching the catalog indexes for these products to individual PPIs. These are evident in table 10.8, which lists the precise PPI commodity indexes matched with each Sears catalog product. For ten-key adding machines, there is an exact match only for 1961–75. Before that date, the PPI did not price ten-key machines, and it was necessary to substitute the PPI for full-keyboard adding machines (which are much inferior because they do not allow for touch adding and have long been obsolete). After 1975, the eight-digit PPI index for ten-key machines was discontinued, requiring a switch to the six-digit PPI index for "computing and related machines." The PPI for cash registers begins only in 1961, and before that date the same six-digit group PPI was substituted. The Sears indexes for manual and electric typewriters are matched with PPI eight-digit indexes for manual and electric typewriters, with the PPI for manual portable typewriters used throughout and with a switch from the PPI for "electric typewriters" to that for "portable electric typewriters" when the latter index commences in 1969. For this product, then, we have a very close match, since Sears sold primarily portable manuals (some standards before 1965) and only portable electrics. Finally, the Sears and PPI indexes for electronic calculators are matched only through 1980, after which the PPI was not published, and the six-digit group index was substituted.

10.5.1   Case Study: Ten-Key Adding Machines

Of the first four products, the most rapid downward drift of the catalog/PPI price ratio is for the ten-key adding machine, and a brief case study for this product demonstrates a few of the details of the method. As shown in table 10.8, the annual rate of drift for ten-key adding machines during 1947–60 is −5.3 percent and for 1960–73 is −2.5 percent. The drift is a similar −2.8 percent per annum for 1973–83. The PPI rises slightly from 104 in 1948 to 109 in 1970, while the catalog index declines from 353 in 1954 to 100 in 1970 (on a base 1972 = 100). One possible source of the drift is the oft-cited lag in the introduction of new products in the PPI. There was no separate index for ten-key adding machines in the PPI before January 1960, and prior to that date the PPI (and NIPA) represents all electric adding machines by an index for the obsolete full-keyboard models, which accounted for only 24 percent of sales in 1960, compared to 76 percent for the ten-key models.[33] The catalog index

33. The equivalent sales ratio in 1953 was fifty-four to forty-six in favor of full-keyboard models. The source for these figures on the value of production is *Current Industrial Reports*, the basic source of the unit value data discussed in chap. 11.

is available over the full 1947–83 period. Among the quality characteristics held constant are the ability to multiply and subtract directly, number of columns listed, whether electric or manual, presence of clear key, repeat key, nonadd key, and metal casing. Although no single model can be traced through the entire thirty-seven years, it is possible to find identical models in each pair of adjacent years and to construct a chain index.

The decline in the catalog index by a factor of four is supported by a comparison of nearly identical models. A ten-key electric adding machine with seven digits of display was listed for $285.69 in 1953 and $64.44 in 1970. The only appreciable difference between the two machines was the replacement of metal by plastic casing, which the 1959–60 comparison indicates accounted for no more than $29 of the total $221 drop in price. Although the failure of the PPI to register a price decline before 1960 can be attributed to the pricing of an obsolete model, the behavior of the PPI between 1960 and 1970 is more puzzling. The PPI fell from 1960 to 1970 by just 20 percent, while the catalog index fell by 58 percent. Yet we can find an identical Sears model sold in the two years that registers a decline of 46 percent.[34] Supporting the view that the catalog index is closer than the PPI to the true price of noncatalog suppliers, a unit-value index for ten-key adding machines has a 1960 index value of 189 on a base 1970 = 100.[35]

Over the longer period 1947–83, the linked PPI used here for ten-key adding machines declines only from 104 to 81 on a 1972 base. Perhaps for no other comparison in this chapter is the evidence against the PPI and in favor of the catalog index as compelling. Opening the 1947 catalog, we find listed a ten-key *manual* adding machine listing nine columns for $108.65.[36] Yet for only $67.99 a 1983 customer could purchase a full-fledged printing electronic calculator, offering not just addition but subtraction, multiplication, division, a four-function memory, percentage and square-root keys, a gross margin key, and four decimal settings. In between, in 1970, a ten-key electronic adding machine with automatic multiplication, but no division and no memory, sold for $177.95.

For the years when the PPI for cash registers is available, 1961–76, there is a negative drift in the catalog/PPI ratio of −4.1 percent per year. The drift may reflect in part the relatively late shift (1974) of the PPI from the obsolete electromechanical cash register to the more modern electronic variety. The catalog-PPI comparison for this product is an example of an inexact match due to the difference in varieties sold in the catalog and priced by the PPI. The most expensive Sears cash register sold for only $260 in 1970, much less than

34. The 1960 model sold for $119.95 and the 1970 model for $64.44.

35. This unit-value index was created as part of an earlier unpublished study. The methodology is discussed in chap. 11 of this volume, which reports an updated subset of indexes from that earlier study and plots the unit-value index for ten-key adding machines as fig. 11.5.

36. See spring 1947, 565. The only other notable listed feature is "auto ribbon reverse." There is no mention of the facility to list a debit balance or the availability of a two-color ribbon.

the $4,000 that was a typical price for the typical large electromechanical variety of that era. Below, I discuss some of the common technical improvements shared by cash registers and typewriters in recent years.

10.5.2 Case Study: Typewriters as Viewed through Forty Years of *CR*

For manual typewriters, the catalog/PPI ratio (summarized in table 10.9 and App. table B.1) drifts downward at an annual rate of -2.1 percent between 1948 and 1973 but is flat thereafter. The downdrift of the ratio of electric typewriters is at an annual rate of -4.4 percent between 1958 and 1973 and -1.1 percent thereafter. Thus, the catalog index, like the other indexes in this industry group for calculators and cash registers, yields a downdrift relative to the PPI.

We have already in chapter 7 made extensive use of *CR* as a source for the development of price indexes for appliances, and there we concluded that *CR* is superior to the Sears catalog as a source because of both its wide range of brands covered and its provision of qualitative evaluations of quality change. All the price indexes based on *CR* data in chapter 7 uniformly exhibit a downdrift relative not just to the CPI and PPI, but also to the equivalent Sears catalog index. This section develops a *CR* index for electric typewriters that agrees closely with the Sears index prior to 1979 but declines much faster than the Sears index after 1979. In contrast, the *CR* index for manual typewriters declines more slowly than the catalog index between 1957 and 1972.

The *CR* matched model index is computed by linking the reported prices in successive *CR* articles on portable typewriters. The method is exactly that followed in chapter 7 on appliances: for each chronological pair of *CR* articles, the models listed are reduced to a subset that has roughly the same quality characteristics. For the next pair of *CR* articles, different models may be compared to hold quality constant, since for typewriters, as for many products, quality is steadily upgraded. For instance, the 1968-vintage electric typewriters compared with the earliest 1957 model have manual return, but those compared with the 1977 models are limited to those with power return.

The distinction between "rough matching" and "exact matching" of models is helpful in gaining insight into the differences that emerge between the catalog and the *CR* indexes. It is impossible to prevent a gradual improvement in quality across vintages in the *CR* indexes, since the reports are published with a gap of several years, over which one model is typically replaced by another with an upgraded mix of features. Because the catalog indexes are developed year by year, in contrast, it is possible to obtain exact matches. Specific examples are provided below to illustrate how this process works in the case of typewriters, and how the radical innovations introduced with electronic typewriters have reversed the relation between the catalog and the *CR* indexes.

The right-hand column of table 10.2 lists the quality dimensions where improvements occur in *CR* across models whose prices are compared directly.

Table 10.2   **Comparisons of "Closely Similar" Model Typewriters from *Consumer Reports*, 1948–87**

	Years (1)	Number of Models (2)	Average Price (3)	Price Change (4)	Description of Models Compared (5)
Manual portables:					
1.	1948 –1957	4 10	91.33 123.95	30.5	"Convenient" margin-setting device, flexible tabulator, adjustable paper guide, "heavyweight" (16–23 pounds), 9½-inch platen, no horizontal half spacing. 1957 models same as 1948, except that most 1957 models have touch control, 2-color and stencil selection.
2.	1957 –1960	10 13	123.95 113.61	−8.7	Same as above, except most 1960 models have "convenient line adjustment," erasure plate, paper support, and most permit horizontal and vertical half spacing.
3.	1960 –1966	13 9	113.61 111.53	−1.8	Same as above, except some 1966 models have two removable keys. One has 19 type styles.
4.	1966 –1972	9 9	111.53 105.90	−5.0	Same as above. 1972 average price excludes Canadian models. Most models have typing pressure control. Every model can use two-color ribbon.
5.	1972 –1979	9 3	105.90 133.33	25.9	Excludes models with page-end indicator, jammed-type key, ribbon cartridge, repeat-space feature.
Electric portables (typebar):					
6.	1957 –1968	1 5	209.50 143.57	−31.5	Manual carriage return, manual backspace, no horizontal or vertical half spacing, 9½-inch platen (three 1968 models have one changeable type key, one has vertical half space).
7.	1968 –1977	1 4	209.50 248.33	18.5	Power carriage return and backspace, horizontal half space, 11.7–12.8-inch platen. Excludes models with automatic vertical spacing or index key, extra repeat keys, page-end indicator.
8.	1977 –1982	1 1	255.00 295.00	15.7	Only models with spool ribbon, adjustable tab, no half spacing, no page-end indicator. 1982 model has built-in cover-up ribbon.
9.	1982 –1984	7 2	337.29 267.00	−20.8	All models have adjustable tabs and self-correction but lack automatic repeat return or index key. Excludes machines weighing more than 30 pounds.
Electronic portables:					
10.	1982 –1984	4 7	600.00 491.28	−18.1	All models have daisy-wheel element and are self-correcting. All 1984 models have a memory of between 10 and 20 characters, while *CR* makes no mention of any memory on 1982 models.

Table 10.2 (continued)

Years (1)	Number of Models (2)	Average Price (3)	Price Change (4)	Description of Models Compared (5)
11. 1984 –1987	4 3	572.50 214.00	– 62.3	All models are of "medium" size and have daisy-wheel element and full-line memory capability for correction but no further text memory. All models lack visual display and spell checker. Some 1987 models have the following features not mentioned in 1984: variable pitch, word correct, line-by-line mode. Three 1987 models lack automatic underlining.

Source: Consumer Reports, November issues of the following years: 1948, 1957, 1960, 1966, 1968, 1972, 1977, 1979, 1984, 1987.

The most difficult comparison is for electric typewriters between 1978 and 1982, since no models in the earlier year but all models in the later year have some form of self-correction. To make any comparison at all over this period, it is necessary to narrow the many models listed in each report down to a single model in each year that represented the closest possible comparison of quality, and yet the otherwise identical 1982 model offered a built-in correction ribbon, while the 1978 model did not.

One emerges from these comparisons with the impression of a great acceleration in the pace of quality change in the 1970s and particularly in the 1980s. Between the late 1940s and the 1970s, quality improvements in manual typewriters were relatively minor, whereas in the case of electric typewriters many new convenience features became available, but at a substantial cost, so that the average price of machines listed increased much more than the matched model index. These quality changes pale beside the dramatic improvements in electronic machines, which exhibit a price decline over 1982–87 at an annual rate of 24 percent, comparable to the price decline for computer processors over this period. Electronic typewriters were first featured by *CR* in 1982 and were rated as greatly superior to, albeit much more expensive than, the electric "typebar" models that then dominated sales. These early electronic models were relatively crude by later standards, lacking memory capability or visual display, much less such advanced computer-like features as spell checkers. By 1987, each leading brand name sold a product "line," with numerous models available in a whole hierarchy of quality characteristics; the bottom-of-the-line models selling in 1987 for about $225 had numerous features that were unavailable on the 1982 models selling for $600. Fortunately, this gap is bridged by a 1984 report that allows the comparison of almost identical models.

The *CR* pairwise comparisons are linked together into a price index in table 10.3. In addition to showing a much faster decline than the PPI over 1982–87

Table 10.3   **Alternative Price Indexes for Portable Typewriters, Selected Years, 1972 = 100**

	Manual			Electric/Electronic			Average		
	Sears (1)	CR (2)	PPI (3)	Sears (4)	CR (5)	PPI (6)	Sears (7)	CR (8)	PPI (9)
1948	121	86	69	. . .	. . .	63	117	93	66
1957	147	117	101	. . .	136	85	142	127	93
1960	139	107	116	129	125	89	134	116	103
1966	116	105	107	99	106	96	108	106	102
1968	110	103	106	96	93	99	103	98	103
1972	100	100	100	100	100	100	100	100	100
1977	125	118	126	122	110	123	124	114	125
1979	135	126	133	123	120	140	129	123	137
1982	150	. . .	154	145	130	142	148	133	148
1984	. . .	. . .	. . .	146	106	131	149	108	137
1987	. . .	. . .	. . .	74	57	132	76	58	138

Sources: Sears and PPI, 1947–83, see App. table B.1. No PPI for electric portables or even for typewriters is published after 1984. PPI is extended for 1984–87 using 11-93-02, "typewriters, word processors, and parts." CR index from table 10.2. Index for average in cols. 7–9 is computed by applying equal weights to the manual and electric indexes.

(with annual rates of -24.3 percent vs. -1.5 percent), the *CR* index exhibits a substantial drift over 1957–68 (showing an annual decline of -2.4 percent vs. an increase of 1.1 percent for the PPI). The major disagreements between *CR* and Sears are for portable typewriters during the period 1960–72 and for electric and electronic typewriters after 1979.

Regarding the first period, the Sears index exhibits a decline of 28 percent during 1960–72, while the *CR* index declines by only 6 percent. To choose between the indexes, we can examine the characteristics of individual models. In 1957, Sears sold a 9.5-inch platen model with a full tabulator for $86.50, whereas in 1972 for 20 percent less ($68.99) a model of the same size and weight was available with several extra features, including buttons to set the tabs on the keyboard instead of reaching behind the machine, and both horizontal and vertical half spacing. For $88.99 in 1972, one could buy from Sears a heavier machine with a 12.6-inch platen offering horizontal and vertical half spacing, platen release, and a key to clear jams, all of which were unavailable on the 1957 machine. The slower decline of the *CR* index is mainly due to the failure to control for all the extra features that were added over time, but also may be partly due to shifts in the mix of relatively high-priced and low-priced models.

In the 1980s, the electronic revolution led to a drastic decline in the prices of constant-quality machines. Sears sold its first electronic model in 1983 and its last nonelectronic electric model in 1986. By early 1986, electronic typewriters accounted for virtually all business typewriter sales and more than half the 2.6 million typewriters sold annually in the United States. One of the major factors accounting for the decline in price of electronic models was an order-of-magnitude reduction in the number of moving parts, from 4,000 to

700.[37] In dropping conventional models, Sears reflected the verdict of the marketplace as succinctly summed up by *CR* (November 1987, 683): "The manual typewriter and the old-fashioned electric typewriter—the kind that's basically a manual typewriter with a power assist—are moribund products, with a slimmer and slimmer slice of the market each year. In their place: the electronic typewriter."

The reason for the much slower decline in the Sears index than in the *CR* index is clear: in the Sears catalog, the turnover of electronic models was so rapid between 1983 and 1986 that the adjacent-year Sears comparisons are largely based on obsolete electric models that then subsequently disappear from the catalog in the following year. Because of rapid model turnover, there are few adjacent-year comparisons of electronic models available, at least if we adhere to the rigid criterion that catalog models must be absolutely identical in all listed characteristics. However, if we apply to the catalog the same criterion as to *CR*, that models be "roughly" similar, we can compare models that are excluded from the catalog index. For instance, a 1983 electronic model selling for $544.99 can be compared to a 1987 model selling for $197.99.[38] A catalog index for electric and electronic typewriters that includes nine additional "roughly similar" model comparisons over the 1977–87 decade has a 1987 index number (1972 = 100) of fifty-seven, which is identical to the 1987 *CR* index number and can be contrasted with seventy-four for the basic catalog index displayed in table 10.3.

10.5.3   Electronic Calculators and Conclusions Regarding Office Machinery

Of all the products in this category, that which shows the largest rate of drift is the electronic calculator. The PPI for an electronic calculator was available only between December 1969 and April 1981 and, over that time interval, declined in price only from 115 to 41 (1972 = 100).[39] In contrast, the catalog index for an electronic calculator declined from 329 in 1970 to 24 in 1983. Once again, though, it is possible to find evidence in *CR* that the Sears index declines too slowly. Over the period 1973–82, the Sears index declines from 100 to 24 (1972 = 100), for an annual rate of change of − 15.9. *CR* published reports on hand-held electronic calculators in 1973, 1975, and 1983 that yield an annual rate of price change of − 27.1 percent, and even this takes no

37. Facts in these two sentences come from "Smith-Corona Is Typing in Black Ink Again," *Business Week,* 9 June 1986, 70.

38. Both have full-line memory, a vertical index key, and automatic centering. The 1987 machine lacks automatic underscoring available on the 1983 machine, but the 1987 machine has an extra feature called "Word Correct." *CR* (November 1987, 689) reports paying just $165 for the 1987 model 53002, recorded in my catalog index at its list price of $198 (both prices plus shipping).

39. All Sears observations are for nonprinting electronic calculators. Unfortunately, the PPI for nonprinting calculators, introduced in December 1969, was discontinued in 1976, requiring the substitution of the PPI for printing electronic calculators after that date. The latter index was subsequently discontinued, requiring the substitution of the six-digit group index for calculating and accounting machinery after 1980.

account of the improvement in quality that occurred when the replacement of LED by LCD displays eliminated the need for frequent battery recharging.[40]

Furthermore, even these dramatic changes understate the decline in price that occurred when the rotary electric calculator was replaced by the earliest electronic calculators in 1968–70. Instead of treating the initial price change from roughly $1,000 for the rotary electric model to roughly $250 for the earliest electronic models as a price decline, the PPI staff linked the two indexes, that is, the price change in the transition between the old and the new types of calculators was ignored. Leaving aside entirely the ability of modern electronic calculators to do scientific calculations, to use one or more electronic memories, and to perform calculations instantly (in contrast to the need to wait for the "clunk-clunk" calculations of the rotary electric models), and to be completely portable, the price of bare-bones nonprinting machine capable of performing multiplication and division has fallen since 1968 by roughly a factor of 100, from $1,000 to $10. Because Sears did not sell four-function calculators before 1970, much of this drastic decline in price is excluded from the aggregate PDE index developed in chapter 12.

Overall, a sample selection bias causes the catalog indexes for the noncomputer component of the OCAM category greatly to understate the error in the PPI. The improvement in performance made possible since 1970 by electronics is not adequately captured by the catalog indexes, because Sears did not sell full-sized electronic cash registers or typewriters, and hence these are not included here. In 1986, one could purchase a modern IBM office electric with automatic correction for about $600 or for $1,000 one with multipage memory and a host of automatic features. An equivalent IBM memory typewriter in 1978 cost $5,500, was much larger, heavier, more difficult to use, and lacked many features available on the 1986 machine.[41] A key aspect of unmeasured quality improvement in this section concerns reliability: the electronic revolution reduced the number of moving parts on an IBM Selectric by a factor of ten and increased reliability by a factor of ten. An IBM executive recently stated that "with these new approaches, based on our statistics, we have achieved near lifetime performance. That is a significant quality jump."[42] Similarly, there has been a ten-fold improvement in the frequency-of-repair record of Xerox photocopying machines.[43] Overall, this detailed study of the industry groups provides evidence that the specification

40. In the 1973 report, the average price of nine models is $108.67. All have eight digits, a decimal point, a constant K function, and no memory. In the 1975 report, the average price of three models is $46.66. All have eight-digit red LED displays. Only models lacking independent memories are included; all included models have "totalizing memory," absent in 1973. In the 1982 report, the average price of the two models with no or limited memory was $9.46.

41. Prices quoted are both IBM machines purchased by the business office of the Econometric Society at Northwestern University.

42. "For Better Products, Use Fewer Parts," *New York Times,* 26 June 1988, Sunday Financial sec., 2.

43. Photocopying machines are a separate category of PDE and are not covered directly by alternative price information in this book. However, App. C uses the average of the alternative price information for noncomputer office machines as a proxy for the missing alternative price of

method, by pricing only identical models, may miss quality improvements that are introduced on new models that provide additional features at the same or a reduced price.

10.6   Communication Equipment

Fully 96 percent of the weight attributed to the communication equipment category of PDE is allocated to telephone transmission and switching equipment. Several alternative indexes for such equipment were examined in chapter 9. The small remaining weight is allocated to home electronic equipment. I have developed two catalog indexes for comparison with the PPI, a matched model index of television sets already discussed above in section 7.9, and a similar matched model index for radio sets introduced here.

The catalog index for radio sets is based on an average of 3.3 models per year for the full period 1947–83. The eight-digit PPI commodity index for table radios is published only during 1953–72 and is supplemented before 1953 and after 1972 with appropriate PPI group indexes for radio receivers. Both the catalog and the PPI indexes for radios decline on average over the postwar period; the annual rate of price change is −1.9 percent for the catalog index and −1.4 percent for the PPI. The rate of drift of the catalog/PPI price ratio is a relatively small 0.2 percent per annum 1947–60, −0.7 percent per annum 1960–73, and −1.1 percent per annum 1973–83.

It is not surprising to discover that no comparison of closely similar models in 1947 and 1983 is possible for radio receivers, since quality characteristics changed so much between those dates. However, there is substantial evidence to support the catalog index, which falls by 49 percent over that time interval, implying that a radio priced at $30 in 1983 would have cost $60 in 1947. First, consider this comparison of 1947 and 1983 radio sets. In the 1947 catalog, we find for $25.50 an AM-only table radio with a plastic case, a four-inch speaker, and slide-rule tuning. In 1983, one could purchase for $29.95 a clock radio with not just AM but also FM, a three-inch speaker, solid-state chassis, slide-rule tuning, tone control, AFC, and a wood-grained vinyl overlay on the plastic case.

For the first half of the postwar period, it is possible to gain further insight on radio prices from *CR*. The price of a five-tube radio with a four-inch speaker declined from an average of $18.20 for thirty-one models in 1949 to $12.98 for fourteen models in 1966, or a decline of 33.8 percent as compared to a decline of 32 percent for the Sears catalog index. However, the *CR* comparison significantly understates the "true" decline in price for several reasons:

1. List prices are published in both years, but the 1966 report states that "discounts are generally available," whereas the 1949 report makes no mention of discounts (this is not a defect of the catalog index).

---

photocopying equipment, and for this reason the improving repair record is relevant. For anecdotal evidence on improving repair records, see chap. 12, n. 8.

2. Ten of the thirty-one models in 1949 were rated "not acceptable" because of "poor speech reproduction," and four more were so rated because of "short circuit hazard." In 1966, only one model out of fourteen was rated not acceptable, in that case because of a shock hazard.
3. Of the seventeen acceptable 1949 models, eight were rated "poor" or "poor-to-fair" in music reproduction, whereas only one 1966 model was rated "poor-to-fair."
4. Eleven of the seventeen acceptable models in 1949 were rated "poor" in interference rejection, and two more were rated "very poor." In 1966, no model rated below "fair" in this characteristic.
5. Unfortunately, the ratings do not directly compare models of different vintages. However, the qualitative descriptions of quality have a distinctly different tone in the 1949 and 1966 reports. In the earlier year, the ratings include the following comments: "music somewhat distorted," "objectionable hum," "an almost total lack of sibilants in speech reproduction."[44] The 1966 report states, "Our test results showed that an inexpensive AM radio can be of reasonably good quality. In fact, it is our opinion that many of the relatively low-priced sets are good enough to satisfy most listeners."

Unfortunately, these differences in quality cannot be quantified, because there were no models available in 1949, even at the high end of the price range, that provided all the advantages of inexpensive 1966 models. This comparison stands as evidence that the Sears indexes may understate the secular upward drift in the PPI. A similar tendency is exhibited by *CR* ratings of AM-only portable radios. At first glance, the decline in portable radio prices appears smaller than that of the Sears table radio index, with respective 1950–64 declines of 5 and 13 percent. But during this period, a revolution in operating efficiency occurred. The average battery cost per hour declined from $0.0764 to $0.01, which at a listening rate of one hour per day for three years would yield a saving of $72.70. This, when added to the 1950 price, implies an "adjusted" 1950–64 price decline of 67 percent. This too is an understatement of quality improvement, since fully half the 1950 models were rated "not acceptable" because of shock hazards or "very weak sound even when tuned to nearby stations."[45]

10.7 Fabricated Metal Products

The NIPA PDE deflator for the "fabricated metal products" category is based on fourteen different PPI indexes for barrels, steam and hot water

44. This comparison is based on *CR* (November 1949, 515–16; July 1966, 351). All models with special features are excluded, e.g., those with wood cabinets, short-wave tuners, clocks, and three-gang tuners in 1949, and all transistorized models in 1966.
45. These comparisons are based on *CR* (November 1950, 481–84; November 1964, 550–53). Since the 1964 reports are confined to medium-sized models, those identified as "small" in the 1950 report are excluded from the price comparison.

equipment, storage tanks, valves, and office safes. Sears catalog data have been gathered for hot water heaters, water storage tanks, brass gate valves, steel safes, and several additional products that seem to fall naturally in this category: warm air furnaces, prefabricated metal buildings, chain link fencing, and PVC (plastic) plumbing pipe. While the last listed is not, of course, made of metal, its inclusion allows us to make a modest allowance for the possibility of substituting plastic for metal that has occurred during the postwar period. All these catalog indexes are compiled by the specification technique, with the single exception of gas hot water heaters, where the hedonic technique is used. There are only minor comparability problems in associating each catalog index with a PPI eight-digit commodity index. The brass gate valve prices are generally for half- or three-quarter-inch models, while the PPI specification is for one inch. The PPI for PVC piping begins four years later than my catalog index, and I have substituted a PPI index for copper pipe to cover this interval. Otherwise, the only noncomparability problems may be those of size. Sears probably sells a smaller size of some of these products than is priced by the PPI, particularly in the case of water storage tanks.

Overall, the drift of the indexes in this industry group is smaller than in the case of office machinery. As shown in table 10.9, only one of the ten catalog indexes exhibit an annual rate of drift of −2.0 percent or greater, and five exhibit a positive drift. One of the three products exhibiting relatively rapid negative drift is the gas hot water heater, the subject of a hedonic regression study described below. The other two are brass gate valves and steel safes. For valves, the Sears index yields a 1983 index value of 219, compared to 57 in 1947; the figures for the PPI are, respectively, 212 and 33. Did the price of such valves increase by a factor of 3.8 or 6.4? In the 1947 catalog, we find a price of $1.59 for three-quarter-inch brass gate valves; the price of a similar three-quarter-inch valve in 1983 was $7.99, or 5.0 times as much. This ratio is roughly halfway between that for the Sears and PPI indexes. Why does this discrepancy occur? In 1970, the Sears price ratio to 1947 is 1.7, which is approximately reflected in a price increase of an identical valve from $1.59 to $2.39. The discrepancy occurs in 1973–74, when there is a complete switchover of models and a direct comparison of prices is made. This is an example showing that the specification method can yield a downward-biased index, for here the model substitution was accompanied by a price increase for a product that was "roughly similar." This is exactly the reverse of the case of electronic typewriters discussed above.[46]

46. This is an example where a long-departed research assistant made a decision that is different than the one I would have made. It was not feasible to rework the catalog indexes for every such case. Instead, I stress the virtue of the thirty-six-year comparisons of closely similar models as a cross-check on the overall plausibility of the results. I can also offer as an offsetting bias for the gate valve index the availability in the 1983 Sears catalog of a plastic gate valve, which

For steel cabinet safes, the 1947 and 1983 Sears models cannot be compared directly. The Sears index exhibits a 1983/1947 ratio of 3.5 and the PPI of 5.7. One can find roughly similar models in 1947 ($72.50) and 1983 ($259.99), yielding a price ratio of 3.6, much closer to the Sears index than to the PPI.[47]

The hedonic regressions for gas hot water heaters are carried out for all thirty-five pairs of adjacent years between 1947 and 1983 (the thirty-five individual sets of regression coefficients are not displayed here in order to save space).[48] The dependent variable is the log of the Sears catalog price, and the independent variables are the logarithms of each listed specification that differs among models. For instance, only some models were glass lined before 1957, and so this characteristic is a variable in the regressions only before that date, but after that date all models were glass lined, and this variable is then collinear with the constant term and cannot be included. The specifications listed in the catalog shifted over the postwar period; at first, heating power was measured by gallons per hour, which could be raised 60 degrees in temperature, then those that could be raised 100 degrees, and after 1961 by BTU. Other explanatory variables include tank size, presence of two stages, three stages, power miser, liquid propane fuel capability, and the time dummy that measures price change between adjacent years. While the coefficients on some of the independent variables are not statistically significant, the significant variables are of the expected sign and reasonable magnitude. The number of observations grows over time, starting at two in 1947–48 and reaching twenty-nine in 1982–83. In the 1970s and 1980s, the R^2 is in the range of 97–99 percent, and almost all variables are significant in almost every pair of years.

The coefficients on the time dummy variables can be cumulated into the Sears hedonic index summarized in table 10.9 and listed annually in Appendix table B.3. The 1987/1947 price ratio is 1.31 for the catalog index and 2.31 for the PPI. A comparison of closely similar models in 1947 and 1983 suggests that even the catalog index overstates the rate of price change: a glass-lined thirty-gallon model with a twenty-eight gallon per hour recovery rate and no relief valve sold for $87.50 in 1947 and $89.99 in 1983. The 1970/1947 ratio is 0.67 for the hedonic index, 1.01 for the PPI, and 0.68 for an identical model. For this product category, then, it appears that the difference between the hedonic index and the PPI is greatest after 1973.

---

could perform the same service (in conjunction with plastic pipe) for $2.89 instead of $7.99 for the brass model. Allowing for this substitution would bring the 1983/1947 ratio down to 1.8.

47. One should note that the 1983 model is somewhat smaller, having 3,360 interior cubic feet vs. 4,410 for the 1947 model. The problem seems to involve substitutions before 1970, since the 1983/1947 Sears index ratio of 1.9 is roughly validated by a 1970 model with 3,744 interior cubic inches selling for $129.95 (yielding a 1983/1970 ratio for the models cited of 2.0).

48. The twenty-three regressions for 1947–70 were presented in the 1974 first draft of this book, and a copy of that table is available to anyone who is interested.

A similar comparison suggests that the specification index constructed for gas warm air furnaces may overstate the rate of price change. The Sears specification index exhibits a 1976/1951 ratio of 1.39. However, it is possible to find virtually identical models selling for $229.50 in 1950 and $209.95 in 1976, for a ratio of 0.91.[49] Overall, these model comparisons lead to the conclusion that the catalog index probably does not substantially overstate or understate the rate of price increase in this category. There is modest evidence of overstatement for brass gate valves and steel safes, and modest evidence of understatement for hot water heaters and warm air furnaces.

10.8 Engines and Turbines

By far the most important products in this category are turbines and boilers used in electricity generation, the subject of chapter 5. Gasoline and diesel engines are treated in chapter 11. The only Sears catalog index for this industry group is a hedonic regression index for outboard motors.

The format of the regression equations is the same as for gas hot water heaters. Again, there are thirty-five regression equations for all pairs of adjacent years between 1947 and 1970. The dependent variable is the logarithm of price, and the explanatory variables are the logs of horsepower, fuel capacity, and fuel use (starting in 1973), as well as dummy variables for one or two gears shifted forward and one gear shifted in reverse, electric starting, and the time dummy that measures price change between adjacent years. For each pair of adjacent years, several equations were estimated with different subsets of the explanatory variables, since multicollinearity prevented inclusion of all variables. The particular equation selected was that with the highest R^2, unless one or more variables had coefficients that were insignificant or had the wrong sign, and in these cases the equation with the next lowest R^2 was chosen. Once again, the detailed regression results are not presented here to save space.[50]

In most years, the coefficient on horsepower is the most significant statistically and is relatively stable in size, ranging from 0.40 to 0.60. Coefficients on the other variables vary in their level of significance and fall within the range of 0.10–0.30 when significant. In most years, a price index controlling for horsepower alone would not have adjusted adequately for quality change, since the presence of gear shifting, electric starting, and a larger fuel tank each add from 10 to 30 percent to price.

The 1983/1948 ratio for the Sears hedonic price index is 3.65 and that of the PPI is 5.11. Much of this difference occurs in the first decade of the period, during which the respective increases in the hedonic and PPI indexes

---

49. The 1950 model has 80,000 BTU output, a five-inch flue, and a ⅙ hp motor; the 1976 model has 80,000 BTU output, a four-inch flue, and a ⅙ hp motor.
50. See n. 42 above.

are 3 and 43 percent. The catalog models listed in 1948 and 1958 are not identical, so that no straightforward comparison is possible. A 5.5-horsepower model sold in 1948 for $129.95 and 1958 for $199.50, but the 1948 model had no gear shift, and a 6.5-pint fuel capacity that allowed cruising for only 1.25 hours at full speed, whereas the 1958 model was equipped with both forward and reverse shift, and had a thirty-six-pint fuel capacity that allowed cruising for four hours at full speed. Since the average estimated coefficient on fuel capacity in the 1950s is about 0.20, the 5.5 times increase in fuel capacity on this model alone would account for a doubling of price, not to mention the contribution of the gear shift. Thus, if anything, the hedonic index appears to overstate the increase in "true" price in this period.

Other comparisons over longer periods can also be made. A 7.5-horsepower model with forward shift but no reverse or electric start was priced at $149.50 in 1950 and $199.50 in 1970, for a 33 percent increase in price, compared to the 60 percent increase registered by the hedonic index and 75 percent for the PPI. Unfortunately, no comparisons are possible between 1970 and 1983. In the latter year, all engines larger than 3.0 horsepower had electric start, and all smaller engines had at least one forward gear, while, in the former year, no engines had electric start, and all small engines lacked gears. The closest available comparison is between 1968 and 1983 for 7.5 horsepower engines, which yields a 1983/1968 price ratio of 1.87, compared to the Sears hedonic index of 2.60 and the PPI ratio of 3.10.[51]

As in the case of typewriters, it is possible to link together successive *CR* articles on outboard motors into a price index for "roughly matched" models. The details of the comparisons made are listed in table 10.4. The main obstacle is the extreme irregularity of the *CR* publication schedule: there were yearly articles between 1953 and 1956, then every other year, then nothing between 1960 and 1968, then frequent articles, and then nothing at all after 1975.[52] Because of frequent publication, the comparisons in the mid-1950s are of exactly identical models, down to the brand name and model name. However, subsequently, the models are only "roughly similar," owing to *CR*'s practice of reporting only on newly introduced models, and owing to the long gap between articles on models of a given size after 1958. Since prices of models sold through catalogs (not only Sears and Wards but also Western Auto) were considerably lower than the list prices of "brand names" like Evinrude and Mercury during the 1950s and 1960s, the prices of catalog models were not compared with those of noncatalog models.

51. The 1968 model had a price of $289, 7.5 hp, two forward gears, and no electric start. The 1983 model had a price of $540, 7.5 hp, one forward gear, and was equipped with electric start. A scan of the Sears data for this size class reveals a premium for electric start in 1968 of 40.1 percent and for a second forward gear of 26.5 percent in 1972.

52. In addition to the years listed in the notes to table 10.4, additional articles were published in 1952 and 1959, but these issues were missing from our library when this study was carried out. A careful search of the annual indexes in the November issues for each year between 1976 and 1987 uncovered no article on outboard motors over that long interval.

Table 10.4   **Comparisons of "Closely Similar" Model Outboard Motors from** *Consumer Reports*, **1953–75**

	Years (1)	Number of Models (2)	Average Price (3)	Price Change (4)	Description of Models Compared (5)
Small motors (5–16 hp):					
1.	1953	2	238.75	−0.1	Two models newly introduced in 1953,
	−1954	2	238.50		identical in 1954, one 3.0 hp and one 10.0 hp.
2.	1954	8	217.18	4.1	All selected models have identical brand
	−1955	8	226.14		names, model names, and hp in both years. Hp of models included: 3.0, 5.5, 7.5, 10, 12, 15. All models but 3 hp have one forward gear, neutral, and reverse; 3 hp models have pivot.
3.	1955	3	245.58	1.6	As above, with three identical models of 3.0,
	−1956	3	249.52		7.5, and 15 hp, all equipped with manual start.
4.	1956	2	269.50	0.2	As above, with two identical models of 5.5
	−1958	2	270.00		and 10 hp, all equipped with manual start.
5.	1958	1	230.00	2.2	No models rated in 1960 larger than 7.5 hp.
	−1960	1	235.00		Identical 5.5 hp model, same brand name, model name. Ratings indicate a 5.0 hp ("Gale") model with the same brand name in each year changed a defective fuel tank configuration that was criticized in 1958.
6.	1960	3	162.16	−10.0	Few models can be compared, because most
	−1971	3	146.00		have auxiliary fuel tanks in 1971 but not in 1961. Compared are 5.0 hp and 3.5 hp noncatalog models, and a 3.0 hp catalog model.
7.	1971	5	331.00	37.5	Models compared are one of 7.5 hp, three of
	−1975	5	455.00		6.0 hp, and one of 4.0 hp. All models compared have same brand name and hp, have manual start and same gear-shift equipment and fuel tank size.
Medium-size motors:					
8.	1954	2	506.50	5.6	Identical brand names, model names, both
	−1955	2	535.00		25 hp, one-speed forward and reverse, and equipped with electric start.
9.	1955	2	535.00	−2.8	All 25 hp with electric start, 1956 models
	−1956	2	520.00		are all newly introduced with different brand names than 1955 models, but to maintain comparability no catalog models are included.
10.	1956	0	. . .		No models listed in both years with the
	−1958	0			same hp.

(*continued*)

Table 10.4 (continued)

	Years (1)	Number of Models (2)	Average Price (3)	Price Change (4)	Description of Models Compared (5)
11.	1956	2	645.26	6.9	Two models, one 33 hp and one 40 hp
	−1968	2	690.00		in each year, both with electric start
					and without remote controls.
12.	1968	4	809.30	33.9	Four models, one 50 hp, one 45 hp,
	−1973	4	1083.50		and two 40 hp in each year, all
					including electric start and optional
					battery-charging system (if not
					standard) and one-lever remote
					control.

Sources: Consumer Reports, June 1953, July 1954, June 1955, 1956, 1958, May 1960, June 1968, 1971, 1973, July 1972, 1975.

Table 10.5   **Alternative Price Indexes for Outboard Motors, Selected Years, 1972 = 100**

	Sears (1)	CR (1971 = 100) (2)	PPI (3)
1953	71	81	60
1954	75	81	63
1955	70	85	63
1956	75	85	65
1958	75	85	73
1960	77	87	71
1968	101	84	84
1971	98	100	99
1973	109	127	101
1975	122	179	139

Sources: Sears and PPI indexes from app. table B.3. *CR* indexes from table 10.4, with changes between successive *CR* articles converted into annual percentage rates and then averaged for the small and medium models with equal weights.

As shown in table 10.4, this exercise is carried out separately for "small" and "medium" outboard motors. Over time, the average size of outboard motors purchased increased, from 3.6 horsepower in 1941, to 12.9 hp in 1955, to 30 hp in 1967.[53] This suggests that the weights should gradually shift toward larger models, but, unfortunately, we do not have sufficiently detailed and continuous market share information to carry out this refinement. Instead, the annual percentage change over each interval in the small and medium categories is averaged with equal weights and cumulated into the index that is displayed in table 10.5. There, the comparison with the Sears catalog index and the PPI yields very different results before and after 1971. In the earlier

53. The figures for 1941 and 1955 are from *CR* (June 1956, 276), and for 1967 from *CR* (June 1968, 292).

period, the CR index increases less (23 percent for 1953–71) than the PPI (65 percent), with the Sears index (38 percent) somewhat closer to the CR index. This is the "typical" pattern that we found in chapter 7 for appliances. Yet, after 1971, the CR index shows an explosive price increase relative to either the Sears index or the PPI.

Why does the Sears index increase so slowly from 1968 to 1975? The CR index for this period is based on articles for medium-sized models in 1968 and 1973, and for small models in 1971 and 1975. Unfortunately, no Sears (or other catalog) models were included in the 1973 report, so we are limited for a comparison to the 1971 and 1975 articles. Here, we find two Sears models listed in 1971 (3.0 and 5.5 hp) and six in 1975 (5.0, 5.5, 7.0, 7.5, 9.9, and 15 hp). There is overlap only for the single size category of 5.5 hp, and here we find a modest price increase of 29 percent, as compared to 24 percent for the catalog index.[54] Looking at the hedonic data, we find virtually identical models of 3.0, 5.0, and 7.0 hp in 1971 and 1975, with an average price increase of 26 percent. Perhaps the main reason for the discrepancy is simply a lag in Sears's pricing decisions. Note in Appendix table B.4C that the catalog index lagged behind the PPI by about a year, finally catching up in 1982.

A central quality characteristic that is not held constant in the index for electric motors is fuel consumption. Since fuel consumption is listed in the Sears catalog beginning only in the early 1970s, it is not possible to create a time series of this characteristic for the whole postwar period. A spot check of several models indicates that, at least on the limited selection of small models offered by Sears in 1983, fuel consumption was the same as on similarly sized models in 1976.

CR articles on outboard motors substantiate a significant improvement in fuel economy for the medium-size motors that dominated the value of sales at that time. Over the period 1968–73, it is possible to match exactly by horsepower and brand name one model of 50 hp and two of 40 hp. These register an improvement in fuel economy of 42 and 23 percent, respectively. The increases in list price are, respectively, 24 and 12 percent, as compared to 20 percent for the PPI and −3.5 percent for the Sears hedonic index. But if we were to add the value of the 1968–73 fuel saving to the price of the 1968 CR models, the price change would be converted into −20 percent for the 50 hp model and −19 percent for the 40 hp model.[55] For the light motors tested in 1975, we find no improvement in fuel economy over 1971.[56] For earlier periods, the first report to list fuel

54. From $170 to $219. Other than the gearshift difference noted in the text, both models have 0.7-gallon integral fuel tanks.
55. For the Mercury 50 hp models, the 1968 and 1973 prices are $870 and $1,080, and the miles per gallon figures "top speed, normal load" are 3.6 and 5.1. For two 40 hp models in 1968 and three 40 hp models in the same years (Johnson and Evinrude) the figures are $695, $778, 4.3, and 5.3. I assume 100 hours of operation per year for ten years at an average speed of 15 mph and a fuel price of $0.40, leading to an undiscounted fuel saving for the 50 hp models of $490 and for the 40 hp models of $263.

economy was published in 1958. Comparing three models in 1958 and 1968 of 35 hp motors and one of 40 hp, we find almost identical fuel economy, indicating that the improvement between 1968 and 1973 may have been a special one-time event.[57]

Overall, rough matches of individual Sears models over long periods of time support the verdict of the Sears hedonic index that the PPI substantially exaggerates the rate of price increase for outboard motors. While raw price comparisons from *CR* are closer to the PPI than the Sears hedonic index during the 1968–75 period, these do not take account of major improvements in fuel economy and other important dimensions of quality change, particularly reliability.[58] Further, even in the 1954–68 period, when the *CR* index increases more slowly than the PPI, there were numerous quality improvements that received explicit mention in *CR* articles, including self-winding starters, reductions in noise and vibration, and greater convenience in operation.[59]

10.9 Metalworking Machinery

The PDE for the "metalworking machinery" industry group includes seven PPIs for various groups of machines (two three-digit, one four-digit, and four

56. To control for different loads on the *CR* tests, I measure mpg at constant speed, 7.0 mph for four models of 6.0 hp and 6.5 mph for five models of 4.0 hp. The mpg figures for the 6 hp engines improved from 7.5 to 8.0 but for the 4 hp engines declined from 12.0 to 11.3.

57. The loads defined as "light" and "heavy" in the *CR* tests are not held constant over time. To assess the meaning of the loads, I inspected the maximum speeds of motors of a given horsepower and concluded that a "medium" load in 1958 was equivalent to a "light" load in 1968 for a 35 hp motor. The mpg figures compared are thus those reported for the light load in 1968 and the average of the light and heavy load for 1958 (when mpg for medium load was not reported). The resulting average mpg figures for the four models are 5.57 in 1958 and 5.40 in 1968.

58. Comments relevant to unmeasured quality improvement in *CR* (November 1972, 408–9) are as follows: "Since [1968] outboard motor manufacturers have been busy eliminating overboard unburned fuel drains—long a wasteful characteristic of two-stroke cycle outboard engines. We can only conclude that the manufacturers' efforts have not only improved fuel economy but have helped to reduce water pollution. . . . The electronic ignition systems of the 2-stroke motors, together with their 50:1 gas-to-oil ratio seem to have pretty well eliminated chronic spark-plug fouling and—if our experience can be considered typical—increased the overall reliability of the outboard." In the June 1973, report, we read on 384 that "spark-plug servicing is not the frequent nag that it used to be." The July 1975, report (430) comments that "no motor was observed puddling unburned fuel overboard by way of the exhaust— a common sight some years back."

59. Comments on the evolution of quality over time are as follows: "Subtle improvements made over the years within the engines make for smoother operation and generally greater reliability. Other improvements are more obvious—for example, self-winding starters, now standard equipment on almost all motors" (July 1954, 305). "Today's outboards are generally more convenient to operate; starter cords and knobs are of better quality, controls are generally simpler. . . . considerable improvement has also been made in hood design" (June 1955, 261). "In the opinion of CU's consultants, vibration is no longer a serious problem in outboard motors, because so much has been done toward isolating the engine from the boat by means of shock-absorbing mountings" (June 1956, 280). "That oil requirement is notably lower than it was for the outboards we reported on in 1959" (June 1968, 292).

six-digit indexes), but no index at the detailed eight-digit product level. Comparability problems are aggravated by the failure of the PPI to publish any six-digit or eight-digit indexes for metal-cutting machine tools (drill presses, lathes, etc.) until 1972. Given Sears's prominence as the dominant seller of power tools for home use, we have an embarrassment of riches in this category, and this study treats fourteen different Sears products, the most of any industry group.[60] For eleven of the fourteen products, it is possible to locate comparable eight-digit PPI product indexes that allow a close match (e.g., "light-duty ¼ inch drill," "home-utility ½ inch drill," "power saw, light duty"). No PPIs are available before 1972 for drill presses, lathes, and free-standing power saws, requiring the use of the overall average index for metalworking machinery. While this lack of a close match between the catalog index and the PPI for these three products may seem to create a problem, actually we find that the secular drift of the Sears/PPI ratio is less than for some products with very closely matched PPIs (e.g., quarter-inch home-utility light-duty hand power drills).

As shown in table 10.9, the tendency for the Sears indexes to exhibit a slower secular price increase than the PPI is quite pervasive across the fourteen product groups, with ten increasing more slowly, two slightly more rapidly, and two about the same. Six of the fourteen Sears indexes exhibit a downward drift relative to the PPI of more than 2 percent per annum over the entire postwar period. These are the free-standing power saw, the two indexes for power drills, the acetylene cutting tool and single-stage welding outfit, and the power saw blade.

A comparison of closely similar models at or near the beginning and end of the sample period can be made for some of the products where the Sears and PPI indexes diverge substantially, although in some cases a better match is possible between an early year and a middle year like 1968 or 1970. An identical free-standing power saw increased in price between 1948 and 1969 by 28 percent, as compared to 32 percent for the Sears index of all power saws, and 120 percent for the PPI used in the NIPA to deflate power saws.[61] After 1969, the catalog index and PPI agree fairly closely. An identical hand power drill declined in price between 1949 and 1967 by 15.4 percent, as compared to an increase in the catalog index of 1 percent and an increase in the PPI of 36 percent.[62] We can also compute a price decrease of 32 percent between 1947 and 1970 for nearly identical models (the PPI increased 38 percent between these years).[63]

60. In a poll taken in 1988, an amazing 52 percent of those surveyed nationwide selected Sears as "the best place to buy home improvement goods" (see Snyder and Waldstein 1988, 18).

61. The models compared both have a ten-inch blade, a 1 hp motor, no speed adjustment, no blade guard, and a twenty-by-twenty-seven-inch work space. The maximum cutting depths were 3.38 and 3.25 inches in 1968 and 1947, respectively.

62. Both models are half-inch hand power drills, with a no-load speed of 450 rpm, and appear from catalog illustrations and specifications to be identical in all other respects.

63. The 1947 model was an unadorned quarter-inch model selling at $21.50; single-speed quarter-inch models were offered in the 1970 catalog at $8.33 for "light duty" and $14.69 for

The other products with a relatively rapid downward drift of the catalog index relative to the PPI are acetylene welding outfits and power saw blades. For an acetylene cutting tool, the catalog index registers an increase of 56 percent between 1947 and 1970, in contrast to that of 77 percent for the PPI; we find an identical tool in the 1970 catalog at 56 percent more than in 1947, except that the 1970 model was equipped with a tip, and the 1947 model was not. There is also a discrepancy over the period 1976–83, when the increase in the catalog index of 35 percent contrasts with the 70 percent increase for the PPI. In the catalog, we find the same model exhibiting an increase of 33 percent over this interval.[64] For the welding outfit, the 1947–69 increases in the Sears index and PPI are 68 and 158 percent, respectively, and the Sears index is based on a single identical model throughout. In the early 1970s, there are many substitutions in the Sears index, but the identical model increased in price between 1976 and 1983 by 45 percent, as compared to 42 percent and 66 percent for the catalog and PPI indexes, respectively. For circular saw blades of the 1947–67 period, the increases in the catalog and PPI indexes are −44 and 1 percent, respectively, as compared to an increase for an identical Sears model of −11 percent.[65] Frequent model substitutions prevent a comparison for closely similar models after 1975.[66]

Portable electric power tools constitute one of the few categories where it is possible to compare the Sears catalog indexes with prices for a wider variety of models from *CR* over a substantial portion of the postwar period. The details of the comparison of ''roughly similar'' models from *CR* are displayed in table 10.6 for three products, power drills, finishing sanders, and saber saws. The technique is exactly the same as for typewriters, discussed above in section 10.6. In each pair of years when a *CR* report was published, the list and quality ratings of all models were compared until a subset could be located that had roughly the same quality characteristics. In the case of power drills, the major criterion of comparison was output under load, while for sanders and saws it was speed of operation. In the later years, when variable-speed models began to replace single-speed models of drills and saws, these were treated as separate products. Likewise, three-eighths-inch drills were treated separately from quarter-inch drills (the latter disappeared in the early 1970s). Over time, *CR* changed its method of listing these quality

---

''medium duty.'' For only a bit more than the 1947 price, \$24.69 would buy a variable-speed three-eighths-inch model.

64. This is model 54407 (changed to 54408 in 1982, with no change in listed specifications), which sold for \$39.95 in 1976 and \$52.99 in 1983.

65. A cross-cut eighteen-gauge six-inch diameter circular saw blade cost \$2.35 in 1947 and \$2.09 in 1967.

66. For instance, the only listed ten-inch circular saw blade in the 1983 catalog sold for \$24.99, 3.5 times the 1947 price, as compared to an increase in the Sears index of just 1.8 times. Yet the 1983 blade is listed as ''diamond ground with carbon tips,'' two characteristics absent in both 1947 and 1970. Note that the 1983/1947 ratio for these two blades is still well below the PPI ratio of 5.5 times.

Table 10.6   **Comparisons of "Closely Similar" Model Power Tools from** *Consumer Reports*, **1954–87**

	Years (1)	Number of Models (2)	Average Price (3)	Price Change (4)	Description of Models Compared (5)
Small power drills:					
1.	1954 –1958	3 7	26.65 25.10	–6.0	Single-speed ¼ inch, produced 100–120 watts under load.
2.	1954 –1958	2 13	34.98 37.50	7.0	Single-speed ¼ inch, produced 150–175 watts under load.
3.	1958 –1966	7 2	25.10 17.41	–36.6	Single-speed ¼ inch, produced 100–120 watts output under load, defined as "adequate" in the 1966 rating system.
4.	1958 –1966	1 3	37.50 31.94	–16.0	Single-speed ¼ inch, produced 150–175 watts output under load, defined as "high" in the 1966 rating system.
5.	1966 –1971	4 2	28.07 11.50	–89.2	Single-speed ¼ inch, rated "fairly high" for output under load in both years.
6.	1966 –1971	2 2	32.73 27.50	–17.4	Variable-speed ⅜ inch, rated "high" for output under load in both years.
7.	1971 –1975	6 4	14.67 18.25	21.8	Single-speed ⅜ inch, rated "fairly low" for output under load in both years.
8.	1971 –1975	2 5	27.50 40.60	38.4	Variable-speed ⅜ inch, rated "high" for output under load in both years.
9.	1975 –1979	4 4	18.25 16.25	–11.6	Single-speed ⅜ inch, rated "fairly low" for output under load in 1975 and "fair" in 1979; rpm under load limited to range 600–750.
10.	1979 –1982	1 5	45.00 58.25	25.8	Variable-speed ⅜ inch, rated "very good" for output under load; rpm under load limited to range greater than 800.
Finishing sanders:					
11.	1959 –1965	5 5	42.77 22.75	–63.1	For 1959 included models rated as sanding 14–17 grams per 10 minutes, described as three times as fast as by hand. For 1965 included models described as "fairly slow," which is shown in a table to be defined as three times as fast as by hand.
12.	1965 –1971	5 4	38.62 25.75	–40.5	Includes models rated as sanding "fast" in both years.
13.	1971 –1978	4 4	25.75 31.00	18.6	Orbiter models only; includes models rated sanding "fast" in 1971 and as "very good" in 1978.
Saber saws:					
14.	1964 –1967	9 6	42.76 43.13	0.9	Single speed; includes only models check-rated in both years.
15.	1967 –1972	6 1	43.13 50.00	14.8	Single speed; includes models check-rated in 1967 and rated in top category in 1972.

Table 10.6 (continued)

	Years (1)	Number of Models (2)	Average Price (3)	Price Change (4)	Description of Models Compared (5)
16.	1972 –1976	1 3	50.00 15.33	–118.2	Single speed; rated in top category in both years.
17.	1972 –1976	2 4	45.00 22.00	–71.6	Two speeds; took only non-Canadian model in top category in 1972 and top half of listed models in 1976.
18.	1972 –1976	3 4	40.33 46.75	14.8	Variable speed; took those listed in top rating category in 1972 and those rated as having "fast" speed in 1976 (the highest listed category).
19.	1976 –1984	3 1	15.33 21.00	31.5	Single speed; top-rated category in both years; excluded two models described as "commercial" in 1984 (both had prices over $100).
20.	1976 –1984	4 3	22.00 40.33	60.6	Two speeds; top-rated category in both years.
21.	1976 –1984	4 6	46.75 80.33	54.1	Variable speed, included all models rated as having "very good" speed in both years.

Source: Consumer Reports, selected issues from the years listed.

attributes, usually beginning with specific quantitative measures ("17 grams of wood sanded in 10 minutes") and later shifting to relative ratings ("fast" and later "very good"). Fortunately, there were in-text remarks, and for drills an explicit table, allowing the translation of the quantitative measures into the qualitative categories, as, for instance, when in 1966 a table lists "fast" as describing drills with 150–175 watts of output under load.

Unfortunately, it was not possible to control for several important quality attributes. By 1971, all power drills were double insulated, a safety feature to which *CR* attached considerable importance in its 1966 article but that was not mentioned in the 1954 or 1958 articles. In 1975, all variable-speed power drills were reversible, whereas in the 1971 article none were reversible. By 1975, some power drills began to offer a second handle. Similarly, all power saws were double insulated by 1972, and in 1984 seven of those listed had a scrolling feature. Other extra features listed for some models in the 1984 report were trigger switches that could be locked at any speed and antisplinter slots.

An important quality improvement that can be quantified in the first half of the period is a reduction in weight. *CR* states in several articles that weight is a disadvantage for power hand tools (holding performance constant), and it explicitly lists the presence of metal rather than plastic cases as a disadvantage of particular models in its 1982 report on drills. From the listed weights, we can calculate a decline in weight of one-third from 4.3 to 2.8 pounds between 1954 and 1971 for quarter-inch drills with the same output under load and a

Table 10.7   Alternative Price Indexes for Power Tools, Selected Years, 1972 = 100

	Power Hand Drills			Finishing Sanders			Saber Saws		
	Sears (1)	CR^a (2)	PPI (3)	Sears (4)	CR^a (5)	PPI (6)	Sears (7)	CR (8)	PPI (9)
1954	105	219	99	. . .	. . .	. . .	. . .	. . .	. . .
1958	116	220	102	. . .	. . .	. . .	. . .	. . .	. . .
1959	. . .	. . .	. . .	106	282	109	. . .	. . .	. . .
1964	. . .	. . .	. . .	. . .	. . .	. . .	88	86	117
1965	. . .	. . .	. . .	93	150	110	. . .	. . .	. . .
1966	82	171	95	. . .	. . .	. . .	. . .	. . .	. . .
1967	. . .	. . .	. . .	. . .	. . .	. . .	88	86	110
1971	92	100	109	100	100	101	. . .	. . .	. . .
1972	. . .	. . .	. . .	. . .	. . .	. . .	96	100	101
1975	94	136	129	. . .	. . .	. . .	. . .	. . .	. . .
1976	. . .	. . .	. . .	. . .	. . .	. . .	119	56	120
1978	. . .	. . .	. . .	84	120	136	. . .	. . .	. . .
1979	86	136	169	. . .	. . .	. . .	. . .	. . .	. . .
1982	. . .	176	222	. . .	. . .	. . .	. . .	. . .	. . .
1984	. . .	. . .	. . .	. . .	. . .	. . .	210^b	91	183

Sources: Sears and PPI, 1947–83 (see App. table B.5). *CR* indexes from table 10.6.

[a]Base year for *CR* drill and sander indexes is 1971 rather than 1972.

[b]Sears index shown is for 1983.

further decrease from 4.0 to 3.2 pounds between 1971 and 1982 for variable-speed three-eighths-inch models having a similar performance rating.

The *CR* comparisons are converted into index numbers in table 10.7. When price comparisons of several varieties are available for the same pair of years, the logarithmic change in price of each variety is given the same weight, and the average change is converted into an index by taking antilogs. The growth rates between the earliest and latest *CR* article are as follows:

	Sears	CR	PPI
Power drills (1954–79)	0.1	−1.9	2.2
Finishing sanders (1959–78)	−0.8	−4.5	1.2
Saber saws (1964–84)	4.9	0.3	2.3

For drills and sanders, the results display the same pattern as we found in chapter 7 for appliances, and in section 10.6 for electric/electronic typewriters, and that is a slower rate of price increase (or faster decline) in the *CR* index than in the catalog index, which in turn grows slower than the PPI. In the case of saws, the Sears index increases faster than the PPI over the particular years shown, even though over the full postwar period it displays a downdrift relative to the PPI. This occurs because the Sears index is at its minimum relative to the PPI in the year that the *CR* index begins, 1964. Also, the Sears index is for circular power saws, not for saber saws, which might explain some of the difference.

An obvious qualification to this section is that many products sold by the metalworking machinery industry are industrial-use metal-cutting and metal-forming tools that are much larger than anything sold in the Sears catalog or rated by CR. The mere difference in size does not necessarily indicate that the PPI is more accurate for large industrial machines than for small machines intended for home use. We have found in this section a fairly consistent downward drift in the Sears and CR indexes relative to the PPI, even when the latter is very precisely and narrowly defined to cover the same exact product as is sold by Sears or covered by CR (e.g., ''home-utility light-duty power hand drills'').

In fact, there is every reason to think that the PPI is severely biased upward in the late 1970s and throughout the 1980s for large machine tools, simply because of the revolution created by numerically controlled machine tools. First-generation machine tools developed in the 1960s began to be replaced by second-generation tools that combined traditional machines with minicomputers in the late 1970s.[67] Since machine tools are now part traditional machine and part computer, we would expect their ''true'' price to behave as a weighted average of the rising prices of machines and the rapidly declining prices of computers. Indeed, there are scattered remarks to this effect in the press. A 1978 article commented that the declining prices of computers had allowed the price of electronic equipment to decline to 15 percent of the cost of a computerized machine tool, compared with 50 percent in the late 1960s (Salpukas 1978, F-12). Any attempt to measure price changes for large-scale machine tools would be very difficult. Just as for some products it is necessary to take account of improved energy efficiency, for machine tools account needs to be taken not only of improved reliability but of the lower level of skills needed by operators.[68]

10.10 General Industrial Equipment

Sears catalog products are available in PPI categories representing about 45 percent of the 1967 weight in the PDE deflator applied to general industrial equipment. Excluded are industrial-process furnaces and ovens and industrial material handling equipment. There is no obvious reason to consider the included products as more or less technically complex than the excluded products, and no way to appraise the bias introduced by partial coverage. Sears coverage is particularly good in the categories of air compressors and centrifugal pumps, with year-to-year comparisons based on as many as eleven models of the former and thirteen of the latter.

67. ''Machine Tools Keep Humming,'' *Business Week,* 29 May 1978, 84.
68. See the source cited in n. 67.

The match between the Sears products and the PPI is very close in this group. There is no problem with a larger size being priced by the PPI, since PPI eight-digit indexes are defined by size and are available for relatively small sizes, for example, 5 hp stationary air compressor and ninety-gallon-per-minute centrifugal pump.[69] Despite this close match, the downdrift of the catalog indexes relative to the PPI for air compressors, pumps, and fans is one of the most rapid recorded in this chapter. For each product, the downdrift is more rapid before 1960 than afterward, but is still significant after 1973.

A comparison of closely similar models can be provided to lend credence to the catalog index. Stationary air compressors show a dramatic contrast between the catalog index and PPI over 1947–70, with respective price increases of 17 versus an incredible 272 percent. Over this period, one can compare models registering a 29 percent price increase in a larger size category and a price decline of 26 percent in a smaller category, and in the second case the smaller model is significantly improved in quality in 1970 relative to 1947. Over 1970–83, the respective increases of the catalog index and PPI are 122 and 171 percent. Individual models in the larger size category increased in price by 30 and 84 percent, respectively.[70]

In the case of centrifugal pumps, the 1947–70 increase in the PPI was 122 percent, in contrast to a 3 percent decline registered by the catalog index. An identical model fell in price over the same period by 19 percent. For the more recent period, the catalog index increases by 116 percent from 1970 to 1983 and the PPI by 154 percent, yet it is possible to find a model with significantly improved quality selling for 111 percent more.[71]

Propeller fans exhibit a postwar downdrift of the catalog index relative to the PPI throughout all subintervals of the postwar period. Between 1948 and 1970, the Sears index increased by 22 percent and the PPI by 134 percent. A thirty-inch one-speed Sears attic fan increased in price over the same interval by 27 percent but delivered 20 percent more air per minute. Between 1970 and 1981, the respective figure for the Sears index and PPI are 121 and 194 percent. A similar thirty-inch fan increased in price over the same interval by 100 percent.[72]

69. These particular indexes are available since 1972 and 1974, respectively.

70. The larger category refers to a stationary model of 1.5 hp and 5.3 cfm (cubic feet per minute) air delivery in 1947 for $310.00, 1.5 hp and 5.0 cfm in 1970 at $399.95, and 6.6 cfm for $519.99 in 1983. The smaller category refers to a portable model of 0.5 hp and 1.2 cfm for $169.50 in 1947, 0.75 hp and 2.2 cfm for $124.95 in 1970, and 0.5 hp and 2.5 cfm for $229.99 in 1983.

71. A 5 hp model providing an output of 100 gallons per minute is listed at $235.95 in 1947 and $189.95 in 1970. A 5 hp model providing an output of 132 gallons per minute is listed at $399.95 in 1983 and ninety-one gallons per minute for $279.95.

72. All are thirty-inch one-speed models, delivering 6,500 cfm in 1947 for $54.95, 7,800 cfm in 1970 for $69.95, and 7,800 cfm in 1981 for $129.99. Interestingly, the weight of the unit fell from 100 to 49 pounds between 1947 and 1983.

10.11   Electrical Transmission, Distribution, and
Industrial Equipment

The PDE deflator for electrical equipment is based on fourteen PPI six-digit and eight-digit indexes for welding machines, electrical direct measuring instruments, electric motors, transformers and power regulators, and switchgear equipment. Welding machines are included in the metalworking machinery category discussed above. This leaves ten unduplicated Sears catalog products to be compared with the closest available PPIs, covering direct measuring instruments, electric motors, and a variety of electric switches and panelboards.

There are several comparability problems in developing ratios of the catalog products to the closest available PPI. There are no published PPI eight-digit indexes for specific direct measurement instruments, requiring that each of the three catalog instrument indexes be compared to the PPI six-digit group index for "direct measurement electric instruments." For the other seven catalog products, there are specific eight-digit PPI product indexes available that make a relatively good match. The comparison is particularly close for electric motors, panelboards, and indoor safety switches.

Of the ten ratios that can be computed from the catalog and comparable PPIs, one exhibits a positive drift of 1.6 percent per annum, two exhibit a small rate of positive drift of 0.5 percent per annum, while the remaining seven exhibit negative drift, and this is at a rate greater than -2.0 percent per year for three products. In order of decreasing drift, the top five products are tachometers, electronic auto testers, circuit breakers, panel-style ammeters, and indoor safety switches. These range from relatively simple products that have changed little over time—circuit breakers and safety switches—to the auto testers where the electronic revolution had completely changed the nature of the product.

For tachometers, the 1947–83 increases in the catalog index and PPI are, respectively, 22 percent and an incredible 442 percent. While the items priced in the catalog changed substantially over time, it is possible to compare items having a 1976 price just 38 percent higher than the 1951 price, in contrast to the 171 percent increase registered by the PPI over this period.[73] Electronic auto testing outfits, with a catalog index rising 33 percent between 1947 and 1983, are compared with the same PPI group index, which rises by 442 percent. Here we find no contest between the clumsy seven-gauge 1947 tester and the 1983 professional electronic analyzer capable of performing thirty different tests for a price 46 percent lower.[74] Another comparison is between

73. The 1951 model ($39.95) has a four-inch dial and a range from 0 to 5,000 rpm. The 1976 model ($49.99) is solid state, has a 3.5-inch dial and a range from 0 to 8,000 rpm.

74. The seven-gauge output in 1947 was priced at $186. The "professional" thirty-test analyzer in 1983 was listed at $99.99 and the plain seventeen-test "analyzer" at $69.99. The eight-test 1983 meter was priced at $39.99.

a 1947 generator tester with dual meters that displayed only the generator's amps and volts with, for a 1983 price only 16 percent higher, an eight-test meter capable of testing rpm, dwell, alternator/generator, voltage regulator, point resistance, and battery voltage. There seems little doubt that the matched-model Sears index overstates the true increase in price for this product. Model substitutions are too frequent to allow a comparison of panel-type ammeters for the full postwar period, but for the shorter period 1947–67 Sears sold exactly the same model with a twenty-year price increase of just 10 percent (over which period the comparable PPI rose by 105 percent).

Comparisons are easier for simple indoor electric safety switches. Over 1947–83, the catalog index rises 314 percent and the detailed PPI eight-digit index for exactly the same product 644 percent, more than twice as much. Identical Sears thirty-amp two-fuse switches increased in price over the same period by 336 percent (the catalog index increases less than this switch because of the presence for part of the postwar period of other models that exhibited a smaller price increase). For circuit breakers, the Sears and PPI indexes increase between 1947 and 1967 by 155 and 550 percent, respectively. It is actually possible to find a single-pole fifteen-amp circuit breaker in the 1983 catalog for only 5 percent more than the same product in 1947.[75] The Sears index increases more than this, because it is based on larger 60 and 100 amp multibranch breakers.

While the catalog index covers only relatively small items sold directly to consumers, we should recall that evidence was provided in early hedonic research of a marked bias in the PPI for large electrical transformers and other apparatus. I have linked together a hedonic regression index created by Irving Kravis and Robert Lipsey (1971) for power transformers over the period 1957–64 with a regression index for 1954–57 developed by Charles Dean and Horace DePodwin (1961) using a similar methodology.[76] Both the Kravis-Lipsey and Dean-DePodwin studies were notable for their use of prices paid by buyers instead of list prices charged by sellers. Their linked regression index declines by 57 percent over a decade in which the PPI index increases by 6 percent; the annual rate of drift of their index relative to the PPI is very high, −9.2 percent per annum, which is higher than for any other product studied in this chapter, with the single exception of electronic calculators. Unfortunately, evidence on large electrical apparatus is not available for the years since 1964, and even the Kravis-Lipsey evidence has the disadvantage that it is based on export prices, not domestic prices, and could be expected to differ from the PPI for that reason alone. I doubt that the export-domestic distinction could come close to explaining the drift of the Kravis-Lipsey index

75. The price in 1947 was $4.75 and in 1983 was $4.99.
76. The Kravis-Lipsey index is reported in (1971, table 13.28, p. 418, eq. 12).

relative to the PPI, since there is no apparent reason why such a divergence should have happened in this period, which is entirely one of fixed exchange rates when there were no changes in exchange rates between the United States and its major trading partners.

10.12   Furniture and Fixtures

The NIPA PDE deflator for the "furniture and fixtures" industry group combines four PPI three-digit and four-digit group indexes for household and commercial furniture, general millwork, and metal doors. Since most of the NIPA weight in this group is allocated to a PPI group index that includes just a few types of basic metal commercial furniture, matched model catalog indexes were developed for these items, while wood commercial and household furniture was excluded. Catalog indexes were developed for six products. Four of these—steel desk, swivel office chair, fluorescent lighting fixtures, and filing cabinets—exactly match eight-digit PPI commodity indexes (which are not used directly in the PDE). Two other products—typewriter tables and card files—are included as well.

The comparability of the catalog indexes and the eight-digit PPIs for the first four of these products is quite close, although we must recognize that furniture comes in many sizes and styles, so that the catalog indexes must be constructed with more than the usual attention to careful matching of models in pairs of adjacent years. For the other two products, the match is less close. Typewriter tables are compared to the four-digit group index for metal commercial furniture, and card files to the PPI for filing cabinets.

All six catalog indexes rise more slowly than the comparable PPIs. The annual rate of drift ranges from −0.1 percent for steel desks to −2.0 percent per year for office swivel chairs. The rate of drift for typewriter tables is quite rapid through 1967 (see App. table B.8), and in fact the Sears index registers only a small increase of 11 percent between 1947 and 1967, as contrasted to an increase of 77 percent in the PPI. We find exactly the same model sold in the 1948 and 1966 catalogs for $5.29 and $4.89, respectively.[77] The story is similar for card files, with all the downdrift concentrated in 1947–70, over which period the catalog index increased by just 33 percent, in contrast to 125 percent for the PPI. Two models of card files were priced and were identical throughout the 1947–70 period, so that a comparison of similar models yields the same increase as the matched-model index.[78] For fluorescent lighting fixtures, the 1947–83 increase is 111 percent for the catalog index and 294 percent for the PPI, yet the 1983 catalog contains a chain fluorescent

77. The model is 26.5 inches in height, 14 × 35 with shelves up, 14 × 18 with shelves down, has no drawer and no brakes.
78. A recheck of the 1947 and 1970 catalogs indicates that four rather than two identical models can be compared, with an overall price increase of 33 percent.

worklight, with two forty-watt bulbs and "rapid start" selling for only 19 percent more than the same fixture in 1947 without rapid start.[79]

Steel metal desks are the product exhibiting the closest price increase of the catalog index and the PPI over the 1950–83 interval, 324 and 345 percent, respectively. Yet an inspection of the 1950 and 1983 catalogs shows that similar steel desks could be purchased at a price increase in the latter year of just 132 percent.[80] For filing cabinets, the respective increases of the catalog index and PPI over the interval 1950–83 are 206 and 415 percent. One can find essentially identical models in 1950 and 1983 exhibiting a price increase of just 120 percent.[81] This result is particularly interesting, since filing cabinets are a familiar product that has remained essentially untouched by technological change for many decades. Finally, the respective catalog and PPI increases over 1950–83 for swivel office chairs are 129 and 342 percent. One can find a 1982 model of roughly the same size and weight of a 1952 model at a price that is 80 percent higher (for this interval, the increases of the catalog index and PPI are 93 and 255 percent).

10.13 Agricultural Machinery (Including Garden Tractors and Excluding Farm Tractors)

The PDE deflator for agricultural machinery (excluding tractors) is based on eleven six-digit PPI group indexes for the different major types of agricultural machinery. We have nine catalog products, four of which are tractor-drawn apparatus, with good representation in most of the PPI categories but none at all in the most important, combines and other harvesting machinery. This section also discusses a tenth Sears product, garden tractors (the hedonic price index for full-scale farm tractors was developed in chapter 9).

The match between the Sears and PPI indexes is quite close, since eight-digit PPI product indexes are available for comparison with all but one of the Sears products. Overall, except for garden tractors, the ratio of the Sears index to the PPI exhibits less of a tendency to drift downward than in any of the other industry groups covered in this chapter. The annual rate of change of the ratio ranges from 1.6 to −1.7 percent, with moderate positive drift for five products, no drift for one, and moderate negative drift for five.

---

79. The respective prices are $15.95 and $18.99. The only difference evident is that the 1947 model is fifty inches long, versus forty-eight inches in 1983. Bulbs are included in both cases.

80. Both the 1947 and 1983 are 30 × 60 inch steel desks with a file drawer and lock. The top of the 1947 model is linoleum and that of the 1983 model is walnut-grain plastic. The prices are $94.50 and $219.99.

81. Both are two-drawer metal file cabinets with a lock and built-in card holders on the front of each drawer. The 1983 model is superior both because it is eighteen inches deep as contrasted to sixteen inches for the 1947 model, but also because the listing describes "large rollers," in contrast to no mention of rollers in 1947.

This leaves garden tractors, where the downdrift of the Sears/PPI ratio is relatively rapid. The 1949–83 increase in the Sears index is only 43 percent, as contrasted with 276 percent for the PPI. No direct comparison is possible, since the sole 1949 model was a 1.6 hp "walk-behind" recoil-start model sold without tires (!) for $182.50, while in 1983 the smallest model was a 16 hp riding tractor with tires, electric start, and a variable three-speed transmission for $1,999.99. However, in between there is a comparison that dramatizes the slow rate of price increase for this product. The first riding model introduced by Sears at $615.00 in 1954 had 6 hp and recoil start; in 1977 for $789.00 one could purchase an 8 hp model with electric start, four-speed transmission, and "auto-type differential." This increase of 28 percent over 1952–77 for what is clearly a superior model contrasts with the respective increases of the catalog index and PPI of 27 and 114 percent, respectively.

10.14 Construction Machinery (Except Tractors)

The NIPA PDE deflator is based on nine PPI indexes; five of these are four-digit group indexes, one is a six-digit group index, and three are eight-digit commodity indexes for "tractors other than farm." This category is probably the one covered in this chapter for which the coverage is most inadequate. We face the same problem as for agricultural machinery, but in a more aggravated way: the largest and most complex items included in the NIPA deflator are not listed in the Sears catalog. We have two products, a post-hole digger and a roto-spader, for which the PPIs are in a four-digit category allocated 18 percent of the 1967 weight in the PDE deflator. Also included is a portable concrete mixer, and three products previously described in section 10.11 on general industrial equipment, stationary air compressors, centrifugal pumps, and chain hoists.

The comparability of the catalog indexes and PPIs is mixed at best. Both the post-hole digger and roto-spader are compared to the closest available PPI eight-digit index, that called "trencher." The portable concrete mixer is compared to a PPI eight-digit index, which presumably prices much larger units. On the other hand, the catalog indexes described above for air compressors, pumps, and chain hoists are matched quite closely.

The ratio of the catalog index to the PPI for all three of the new products introduced in this section exhibits a downdrift over the postwar period. The annual rate of drift is a relatively rapid − 3.3 percent for the post-hole digger (1956–83) and − 3.0 percent for the roto-spader (1948–81) but a negligible − 0.8 percent for the portable concrete mixer. The catalog index and PPI for post-hole diggers increase by very different percentages, 128 and 461, over the 1956–83 interval. One can find almost identical models listed in 1956 and 1976 exhibiting a price increase of 39 percent over that interval, as compared to 30 percent for the catalog index and 149 percent for the PPI.[82] For roto-spaders over the interval 1948–80, the catalog indexes and PPI increase by 123 and 422 percent. For this product, the catalog index seems to overstate the price increase implied by a comparison of similar models. Between 1948 and 1970, the catalog index is almost constant when the PPI nearly doubles, yet one can compare a 1948 model of only 2 hp having a cut width ranging from fourteen to twenty-one inches and priced at $137.95 with a 1970 model of 3.5 hp having a cut width of from eleven to twenty-two inches and priced at $117.88. The same 1970 model was available in 1976 for $194.95, a price increase of 41 percent over the inferior 1948 model, in contrast to 1948–76 price increases of 77 and 196 percent for the catalog index and PPI. This kind of difference suggests that the price per unit of quality must have fallen substantially when new models of this product were introduced, since the Sears index is based only on the prices of identical models.

Mention should be made here of the Early and Sinclair (1983) hedonic regression study of power cranes (hydraulic, truck, and crawler). Their results yield a hedonic price index for all three types of cranes for the period 1971–77 that is essentially indistinguishable from the PPI for the same product. This small tidbit of evidence supporting the PPI does not detract from the large number of indexes developed here that differ from the PPI. Of the products discussed in this book, that closest to power cranes is tractors, for which hedonic price indexes were developed in chapter 9. We find less than a 2 percent difference in the 1971–77 increase of the PPI tractor index and the new tractor index (see App. table B.12), suggesting that the PPI could well be right for some products in this period but misleading for other products and over longer periods.

10.15 Service-Industry Machinery and Electrical Equipment, n.e.c.

The industry-by-industry examination concludes with the two final industry categories, service-industry machinery and electrical equipment "not elsewhere classified." This section is short, simply because most of the Sears catalog indexes used in these two categories have already been discussed. Fully 64 percent of the 1967 weight in the service-industry machinery category of PDE is allocated to PPI product indexes that we have already examined. About 43 percent of the weight is allocated to five major household appliances that we studied in chapter 7 (washers, dryers, refrigerators, room air conditioners, and under-counter dishwashers). Another 18 percent is allocated to products examined previously in this chapter (power sanders, pumps and compressors, and domestic water heaters). Most of the remaining

---

82. A 3 hp, one-man digger, two-cycle engine, at $114.95 in 1956 and $159.95 in 1976. There was a model change in 1970, but the models overlapped and sold for within 2 percent of the same price in that year.

weight is allocated to a four-digit group code for "food products machinery" and a six-digit group for coin-operated vending machines.

This section develops only two new indexes for minor appliances, commercial vacuum cleaners and automatic coffee makers, that had new eight-digit PPI product indexes introduced in the early 1970s, thus allowing a close comparison with Sears catalog prices. The match between the catalog and the PPI product definitions is exact for coffee makers but not for vacuum cleaners, since unfortunately the PPI for vacuum cleaners was published in some but not all years over the 1972–83 interval. The resulting Sears/PPI ratios show a negligible downdrift for vacuum cleaners but a significant downdrift for automatic coffee makers at a rate of -7.0 percent per annum over 1972–83. The Sears index registers a 14 percent decline, while the PPI more than doubles. An examination of the catalog suggests a partial explanation, as this product category appears to be one in which old-fashioned electric perk coffee makers increased in price, while the more modern automatic drip models introduced in the early 1970s have fallen in price. For instance, a 1975 four- to eight-cup electric perk model can be matched exactly with the same model in 1983 at a price 48 percent higher. Yet over the same interval it is possible to find automatic drip models that declined in price 22 percent while improving in quality.[83]

In the electrical equipment n.e.c. category, 25 percent of the 1967 weight in the PDE deflator is allocated to PPIs for which we have already developed alternative indexes, including water heaters, lighting fixtures, major appliances, vacuum cleaner, and small electric appliances. The only new product introduced in this section is storage batteries, which receive a 1967 weight of 17 percent. The Sears catalog index for automobile replacement batteries is matched with the PPI for precisely the same product. The 1948–83 drift of the Sears/PPI ratio is a positive 0.8 percent per annum, and this occurs entirely in the last two years (1981–83), when the PPI falls while the Sears index increases rapidly. Perhaps it is fitting that we end with this product, which shows that the Sears/PPI drift can go in either direction.

10.16 Behavior of the Average Sears/PPI Ratio

10.16.1 Alternative Average Indexes

The study of Sears catalog price quotations summarized in this chapter has compiled sixty-eight unduplicated product price indexes based on 7,242 unduplicated price observations for adjacent-year price changes of individual models. This works out at 196 observations per year, and 3.3 models per

---

83. In 1975, a ten-cup automatic drip model with no water-level indicator or on-off switch was priced at $29.49, while a ten-cup automatic drip model with 1983 with water-level indicator, signal light, and off-on switch sold for $22.99.

Table 10.8   **Sears Products and Corresponding PPIs by Component of NIPA PDE Deflator**

Sears Products (1)	PPI Code by Year (2)	PPI Description (3)
Office, computing, and accounting machinery:		
1. 10-key adding machine	1947–60: 11-53-02	10-key adding machine
	1961–76: 11-93-01-07	Adding machine, electric, 10 key
	1977–83: 11-93-01	Calculating and accounting machines
2. Cash register	1953–59: 11-93-01	Calculating and accounting machines
	1960–76: 11-93-01-06	Cash register, electro-mechanical
	1977–78: 11-93-01-11	POS cash register, electric
	1979–83: 11-93-01	Calculator and accounting machines
3. Manual typewriter	1948–83: 11-93-03-13	Typewriter, manual portable
4. Electric typewriter	1958–68: 11-93-03-12	Typewriter, electric
	1969–83: 11-93-03-14	Typewriter, portable electric
5. Calculator	1970–76: 11-93-01-03	Calculator, electronic, nonprinting
	1979–80: 11-93-01-05	Calculator, electronic, printing
	1981–83: 11-93-01	Calculating and accounting machines
Communication equipment:		
6. Radio receiver	1947–52: 12-5	Home electronic equipment
	1953–72: 12-51-01-02	Radio, table
	1973–83: 12-51	Radio receivers
Fabricated metal products:		
7. Gas warm air furnace	1951–83: 10-62-01-42	Warm air furnace, steel, forced air, gas
8.*Gas hot water heater	1948–67: 10-66	Water heater, domestic
	1968–83: 10-66-01-13	Water heater, domestic, gas
	1948–80: 10-72-01-01	Pressure tank, above ground
9. Water storage tank	1981–83: 10-72	Metal Tanks
10. Brass gate valve	1947–82: 11-49-01-02	Gate valve, brass or bronze, one inch
	1983: 11-49-02-01	Gates, globes, angles, and checks
11. Steel safe	1947–83: 11-93-05-21	Safe, cabinet-type
12. PVC piping	1967–69: 10-25-02-52	Copper water tubing, straight lengths
	1970–78: 07-21-01-02	Rigid PVC pressure pipes
	1979–83: 07-21	Plastic construction products
13. Electric furnace	1972–82: 10-62-01-59	Electric furnace, forced-air, ten kilowat
14. Electric hot water heater	1968–83: 10-66-01-01	Water heater, domestic
15. Prefabricated metal building	1961–81: 10-74-01-45	Metal building, steel, rigid frame
	1982–83: 10-79	Prefabricated metal buildings
16. Chain link fence	1955–83: 10-88-06-13	Chain link fencing
Engines and turbines:		
17.*Outboard motor	1948–83: 11-94-02-11	Outboard motor, 5–15 hp.
Metalworking machinery:		
18. Drill press	1947–72: 11-3	Metalwork, machinery and equipment
	1973–83: 11-37-12	Drilling machines
19. Metal lathe equipment	1947–71: 11-3	Metalwork, machinery and equipment
	1972–83: 11-37-14	Lathes
	1977–83: 11-3	Metalwork, machinery and equipment
20. Free-standing power saw	1947–83: 11-3	Metalwork, machinery and equipment
21. ¼ inch hand power drill	1947–79: 11-32-02-21	Drill quarter inch
	1980–83: 11-32-02	Home utility line, electrical
22. ½ inch hand power drill	1947–79: 11-32-03-02	Drill half inch
	1980–83: 11-32-03	Industrial line, electrical
23. Hand power saw	1947–82: 11-32-02-23	Circular saws
	1983: 11-32-02	Home utility line, electrical
24. Hand electric sander	1947–83: 11-32-02-24	Sanders, orbital
25. Transformer arc welder	1947–83: 11-33-01-01	Arc welder, transformer type
26. Acetylene welding torch	1947–82: 11-33-04-52	Welding torch, blow type
	1983: 11-33-04	Gas welding, machine and equipment

Table 10.8 (continued)

Sears Products (1)	PPI Code by Year (2)	PPI Description (3)
27. Acetylene cutting tool	1947–83: 11-33-04-53	Cutting tool, blow type
28. Acetylene single-stage welding outfit	1947–83: 11-33-04-54	Flame cutting machine
29. Drill bit	1947–83: 11-35-01-03	Twist drill
30. Power saw blades	1947–82: 11-35-01-29	Power saw blades, hack
	1983: 11-35-03	Metal working power saw
31. Micrometer caliper	1947–83: 11-35-02-42	Micrometer caliper
General industrial, including materials handling, equipment:		
32. Stationary air compressor	1947–70: 11-41-03-03	Stationary air compressor, 75–125 hp
	1971–83: 11-41-03-01	Stationary air compressor, 5 hp
33. Centrifugal pump equipment	1947–70: 11-41-02-08	Centrifugal pump, 3,000 gpm
	1971–72: 11-41-02-21	Centrifugal pump
	1973–83: 11-41-02-04	Centrifical pumps, 90 gpm
34. Differential chain hoist	1948–77: 11-44-94-01	Hand chain hoist, spur gear
35. Propeller fan	1948–83: 11-47-01-11	Propellor fan
36. Fire extinguisher	1947–83: 15-99	Fire extinguisher
Electrical transmission, distribution, and industrial apparatus:		
37. Tachometer	1947–83: 11-72-01	Electrical (direct measurement) instrument
38. Electronic auto tester	1947–83: 11-72-01	Electrical (direct measurement) instrument
39. Panel-type ammeter	1947–83: 11-72-01	Electrical (direct measurement) instrument
40. Fractional HSP electric motor	1947–82: Average of 11-73-01-05, 11-73-01-06	A-C fractional electric motor
	1983: 11-73-03	Fractional HP motors and generators
41. Voltage regulator	1947–80: 11-74-01-21	Feeder voltage regulators
	1981–83: 11-74	Transformers and power regulators
42. Fusible-type panelboard	1950–83: 11-75-01-01	Panelboard, distribution, fusible
43. Circuit breaker-type	1954–83: 11-75-01-02	Panelboards, lighting, circuitbreaker
44. Indoor safety switch	1947–83: 11-75-02-12	Safety switch, a-c, 3 pole, 60 A
45. Circuit breaker	1947–83: 11-73-03-21	Air circuit breaker, a-c
46. Outdoor power switch	1947–64: 11-75-02-12	Safety switch, a-c, 3 pole, 60 A
	1965–74: 11-75-04-51	Disconnect switch, 600 A
	1975–82: 11-75-04-53	
Furnitures and fixtures:		
47. Typewriter table	1947–83: 12-22	Metal commercial furniture
48. Card file	1947–78: 12-22-01-21	Metal filing cabinets
49. Fluorescent lighting	1947–60: 12-22	Metal commercial furniture
	1961–80: 10-83-01-31	Commercial fluorescent, non–air handling lighting fixtures
	1981–83: 10-83-03-23	Commercial fluorescent fixtures, recessed non-air
50. Steel desk	1947–67: 12-22	Metal commercial furniture
	1968–76: 12-22-01-01	Clerical and secretarial desks
	1977–79: 12-22	Metal commercial furniture
	1980–83: 12-22-03-21	Desks and extensions
51. Filing cabinet	1950–79: 12-22-01-21	Metal filing cabinet
	1980–83: 12-02-02-01	Vertical filing cabinets
52. Office swivel chair	1947–83: 12-22-01-11	Office swivel chair
Tractors:		
53. Garden tractor	1949–83: 11-11-05-22	Garden tractor, riding type

(continued)

Table 10.8 (continued)

Sears Products (1)	PPI Code by Year (2)	PPI Description (3)
Agricultural machinery, except tractors:		
54. Tractor-drawn plow	1948–83: 11-12-01	Plow
55. Tractor-drawn harrow	1948–82: 11-12-02-13	Harrow, disc drawn
	1983: 11-12-03	Planting, seeding, and fertilizing machinery
56. Seeder	1947–83: 11-12-03-22	Drawn corn planter
57. Manure spreader	1950–83: 11-12-03-25	Manure spreader, PTO driven
58. Tractor-drawn cultivator	1949–72: 11-12-04	Cultivators
	1973–82: 11-12-04-36	Cultivators, rear mounted, 4 row
	1983: 11-12-04	Cultivators
59. Sprayer	1947–61: 11-12-05	Sprayers and dusters
	1962–82: 11-12-05-44	Field sprayer, tractor mounted
	1983: 11-12-05	Sprayers and dusters
60. Tractor-mounted mower	1949–83: 11-12-07-62	Mower, mounted
61. Portable farm elevator	1947–67: 11-12	Agricultural machinery, except tractors
	1968–75: 11-12-09	Farm elevators and blowers
	1976–83: 11-12-09-81	Farm elevator, portable, double chain
62. Poultry brooder	1947–77: 11-13-01-03	Gas poultry brooders
	1978–83: 11-13-01	Poultry equipment
Construction machinery, except tractors:		
63. Post-hole digger	1956–83: 11-23-01-01	Trencher
64. Roto spader	1948–81: 11-23-01-01	Trencher
65. Portable concrete mixer	1947–83: 11-27-01-11	Portable mixers, 3.5 cubic feet and over
[32] Stationary air compressor	1947–70: 11-41-03-03	Stationary air compressors, 75–125 hp
	1971–83: 11-41-03-01	Stationary air compressors, 5 hp
[33] Centrifugal pump	1947–70: 11-41-02-08	Centrifugal pump, 3,000 gpm
	1971–72: 11-41-02-21	Centrifugal pump
	1973–83: 11-41-02-04	Centrifugal pump, 300 gpm
[34] Differential chain hoist	1948–83: 11-44-94-01	Hand chain hoist, spur gear
Service industry machinery:		
[7] Gas warm air furnace	1951–83: 11-62-01-42	Warm air furnace, steel, forced air, gas, 72–88 thousand BTU
[8] Gas hot water heater	1948–66: 10-66	Water heaters domestic
	1967–83: 10-66-01-13	Gas water heaters, domestic
[24] Hand electric sander	1947–83: 11-32-02-24	Orbital sanders
66. Commercial vacuum cleaner	1972–81: 12-43-01-11	Canister, tank, and other general purpose vacuum cleaners
	1982–83: 11-68-01-11	Commercial and industrial vacuum cleaners and parts
67. Automatic coffee maker	1972–83: 12-44-01-13	Automatic coffee maker
Electrical equipment, n.e.c.:		
68. Replacement auto battery	1948–83: 11-79-01-01	Storage battery, automotive, 12-volt, replacement
[37] Tachometer	1947–83: 11-72-01	Electrical (direct measurement) instrument
[38] Electronic auto tester	1947–83: 11-72-01	Electrical (direct measurement) instrument
[39] Panel-type ammeter	1948–83: 11-72-01	Electrical (direct measurement) instrument

Table 10.8 (continued)

Sears Products (1)	PPI Code by Year (2)	PPI Description (3)
[49] Fluorescent lighting fixtures	1947–60: 12-22	Steel furniture and store fixtures
	1961–80: 10-83-01-31	Commercial fluorescent non-air handling lighting fixtures
	1981–83: 10-83-03-23	Commercial fluorescent fixtures, non-air
[66] Commercial vacuum cleaner	1972–81: 12-43-01-11	Canister, tank, and all general purpose vacuum cleaners
	1982–83: 11-68-01-11	Commercial and industrial vacuum cleaners

Note: Brackets indicate a product appearing for the second time. The number inside the bracket is the chronological number of its first appearance. No product appears more than twice.

*Indicates hedonic.

Table 10.9   **Growth Rates of Ratio of Sears Indexes to Corresponding PPIs, 1947–83 and Subintervals, by NIPA PDE Order**

	Annual Growth Rates			
Sears Products[a]	Full Period of Data (1)	1947–60 (2)	1960–73 (3)	1973–83 (4)
Office, computing, and accounting machinery:				
1. 10-key adding machines	−3.6 (1947–83)	−5.3	−2.5	−2.8
2. Cash registers	−2.3 (1953–78)	1.2	−4.1	−2.5
3. Manual standard typewriters	−1.3 (1948–83)	−2.5	−1.7	0.8
4. Standard electric typewriters	−2.2 (1958–83)	−15.1	−2.7	1.1
5. Electronic calculators	−12.7 (1970–83)	b	−34.0	−6.3
Communication equipment:				
6. Radio receivers	−0.5 (1947–83)	0.2	−0.7	−1.1
Fabricated metal products:				
7. Gas warm air furnaces	0.2 (1951–83)	1.1	−0.7	0.7
8.*Gas hot water heaters	−1.6 (1947–83)	−1.2	−1.9	−1.7
9. Water storage tanks	0.2 (1948–83)	0.7	0.7	−1.0
10. Brass gate valves	−1.4 (1947–83)	−4.7	0.3	0.5
11. Steel safes	−2.2 (1947–83)	−3.3	−2.6	−0.4
12. PVC piping	0.8 (1967–83)	b	−3.1	3.1
13. Electric furnaces	−1.3 (1972–82)	b	−0.7	−1.3
14. Electric hot water heaters	1.4 (1968–83)	b	3.2	0.5
15. Prefabricated metal buildings	0.6 (1961–83)	b	−0.1	1.5
16. Chain link fences	−0.2 (1955–83)	−1.1	−0.3	0.3
Engines and turbines:				
17.*Outboard motors	−0.9 (1948–83)	−2.1	−0.1	−0.7
Metalworking machinery:				
18. Drill presses	−1.0 (1947–83)	−2.6	0.4	−0.8
19. Metal lathes	−0.2 (1947–83)	1.2	−0.1	−2.1
20. Free-standing power saws	−2.3 (1947–83)	−4.5	−2.0	−0.1
21. ¼ inch hand power drills	−2.0 (1947–83)	−1.2	0.1	−5.8
22. ½ inch hand power drills	−2.3 (1949–82)	−1.0	−2.5	−3.5

(continued)

Table 10.9 (continued)

	Annual Growth Rates			
Sears Products[a]	Full Period of Data (1)	1947–60 (2)	1960–73 (3)	1973–83 (4)
23. Hand power saws	−0.4 (1947–83)	−2.8	0.4	1.9
24. Hand electric sanders	−1.3 (1947–83)	0.1	0.0	−4.9
25. Transformer arc welders	0.0 (1947–83)	3.9	−0.5	−4.4
26. Acetylene welding torches	−1.4 (1947–83)	−3.6	1.0	−1.6
27. Acetylene cutting tools	−1.5 (1947–83)	−2.0	0.5	−3.6
28. Acetylene single-stage welding outfits	−2.0 (1947–83)	−4.0	0.0	−2.2
29. Drill bits	0.4 (1947–83)	−4.0	3.7	1.6
30. Power saw blades	−2.5 (1947–83)	−6.9	2.0	−2.7
31. Micrometer calipers	0.7 (1947–83)	−0.3	1.3	1.3
General industrial, including materials handling, equipment:				
32. Stationary air compressors	−3.8 (1947–83)	−4.5	−4.9	−1.4
33. Centrifugal pumps	−2.8 (1947–83)	−6.9	0.0	−1.1
34. Differential chain hoists	−0.5 (1948–83)	−0.8	−0.6	0.0
35. Propellor fans	−2.7 (1948–83)	−3.2	−2.9	−2.0
36. Fire extinguishers	−0.9 (1947–83)	0.2	0.1	−3.6
Electrical transmission, distribution, and industrial equipment:				
37. Tachometers	−4.1 (1947–83)	−5.6	−4.1	−2.2
38. Electronic auto testers	−3.9 (1947–83)	−3.9	−3.5	−4.3
39. Panel-type ammeters	−1.8 (1948–83)	−2.7	−1.8	−0.8
40. Fractional HSP electric motors	0.5 (1947–83)	1.5	0.9	−1.4
41. Voltage regulators	0.5 (1947–79)	−3.7	1.6	7.0
42. Fusible-type panelboards	1.6 (1950–83)	4.2	1.2	−0.5
43. Circuit breaker-type panelboards	−0.7 (1954–83)	−2.3	−0.6	−0.2
44. Indoor safety switches	−1.6 (1947–83)	−4.4	0.5	−0.8
45. Circuit breakers	−2.5 (1947–83)	−1.7	−3.6	−2.2
46. Outdoor power switches	−0.2 (1948–82)	−1.3	3.1	−3.3
Furnitures and fixtures:				
47. Typewriter tables	−1.0 (1947–83)	−3.3	−1.5	2.6
48. Card files	−1.0 (1947–78)	−3.7	−0.9	5.7
49. Fluorescent lighting fixtures	−1.5 (1947–83)	−3.9	0.9	−1.6
50. Steel desks	−0.1 (1950–83)	1.6	−0.5	−1.3
51. Filing cabinets	−1.6 (1950–83)	−1.8	−2.6	0.0
52. Office swivel chairs	−2.0 (1949–83)	−4.3	−0.5	−1.4
Tractors:				
53. Garden tractors	−2.8 (1949–83)	−4.7	−1.0	−3.1
Agricultural machinery, except tractors:				
54. Tractor-drawn plows	0.7 (1948–83)	−4.5	5.7	0.5
55. Tractor-drawn harrows	0.9 (1948–83)	1.0	0.8	0.9
56. Seeders	−1.2 (1947–83)	−1.8	−1.2	−0.3
57. Manure spreaders	0.1 (1950–83)	−0.5	−0.6	1.5
58. Tractor-drawn cultivators	−0.9 (1949–83)	−1.0	0.2	−2.1
59. Sprayers	1.6 (1947–83)	0.7	1.7	2.6
60. Tractor-mounted mowers	−1.7 (1949–83)	−2.6	−0.3	−2.5
61. Portable farm elevators	0.5 (1948–83)	−2.6	0.3	4.5
62. Poultry brooders	−0.2 (1947–83)	−3.1	−0.3	−3.5

Table 10.9 (continued)

	Annual Growth Rates			
Sears Products[a]	Full Period of Data (1)	1947–60 (2)	1960–73 (3)	1973–83 (4)
Construction machinery, except tractors:				
63. Post-hole diggers	−3.3 (1956–83)	−3.2	−2.6	−4.4
64. Roto spaders	−3.0 (1948–81)	−3.7	−2.3	−2.9
65. Portable concrete mixers	0.8 (1947–83)	−0.1	−0.2	3.4
[32] Stationary air compressors	−3.8 (1947–83)	−4.5	−4.9	−1.4
[33] Centrifugal pumps	−2.8 (1947–83)	−6.9	−0.0	−1.1
[34] Differential chain hoists	−0.5 (1948–83)	−0.8	−0.6	0.0
Service industry machinery:				
66. Commercial vacuum cleaners	0.4 (1972–83)	b	2.7	0.2
67. Automatic coffee makers	−7.0 (1972–83)	b	−0.8	−7.6
[7] Gas warm air furnaces	0.2 (1951–83)	1.1	−0.7	0.7
[8]* Gas hot water heaters	−1.6 (1947–83)	−1.2	−1.9	−1.7
[24] Hand electric sanders	−1.3 (1947–83)	0.1	0.0	−4.9
Electrical equipment, n.e.c.:				
68. Replacement auto batteries	0.8 (1948–83)	−0.4	0.6	2.5
[37] Tachometers	−4.1 (1947–83)	−5.6	−4.1	−2.2
[38] Electronic auto testers	−3.9 (1947–83)	−3.9	−3.5	−4.3
[39] Panel-type ammeters	−1.8 (1948–83)	−2.7	−1.8	−0.8
[49] Fluorescent lighting fixtures	−1.5 (1947–83)	−3.9	0.9	−1.6
[66] Commercial vacuum cleaners	0.4 (1972–83)	b	2.7	0.2

[a]Entry number from table 10.8.

[b]No data for this subinterval.

*Indicates hedonic.

Table 10.10   **Growth Rates of Ratio of Sears Indexes to Corresponding PPIs, 1947–83 and Subintervals, in Ascending Order**

	Annual Growth Rates			
Sears Products	Full Period of Data (1)	1947–60 (2)	1960–73 (3)	1973–83 (4)
5. Electronic calculators	−12.7 (1970–83)	b	−34.0	−6.3
67. Automatic coffee makers	−7.0 (1972–83)	b	−0.8	−7.6
37. Tachometers	−4.1 (1947–83)	−5.6	−4.1	−2.2
38. Electronic auto testers	−3.9 (1947–83)	−3.9	−3.5	−4.3
32. Stationary air compressors	−3.8 (1947–83)	−4.5	−4.9	−1.4
1. 10-key adding machines	−3.6 (1947–83)	−5.3	−2.5	−2.8
63. Post-hole diggers	−3.3 (1956–83)	−3.2	−2.6	−4.4
64. Roto spaders	−3.0 (1948–81)	−3.7	−2.3	−2.9
33. Centrifugal pumps	−2.8 (1947–83)	−6.9	0.0	−1.1
53. Garden tractors	−2.8 (1949–83)	−4.7	−1.0	−3.1
35. Propellor fans	−2.7 (1948–83)	−3.2	−2.9	−2.0

(continued)

Table 10.10 (continued)

Sears Products	Full Period of Data (1)	1947–60 (2)	1960–73 (3)	1973–83 (4)
		Annual Growth Rates		
30. Power saw blades	−2.5 (1947–83)	−6.9	2.0	−2.7
45. Circuit breakers	−2.5 (1947–83)	−1.7	−3.6	−2.2
2. Cash registers	−2.3 (1953–78)	1.2	−4.1	−2.5
20. Free-standing power saws	−2.3 (1947–83)	−4.5	−2.0	−0.1
22. ½ inch hand power drills	−2.3 (1949–82)	−1.0	−2.5	−3.5
4. Standard electric typewriters	−2.2 (1958–83)	−15.1	−2.7	1.1
11. Steel safes	−2.2 (1947–83)	−3.3	−2.6	−0.4
21. ¼ inch hand power drills	−2.0 (1947–83)	−1.2	0.1	−5.8
28. Acetylene single-stage welding outfits	−2.0 (1947–83)	−4.0	0.0	−2.2
52. Office swivel chairs	−2.0 (1949–83)	−4.3	−0.5	−1.4
39. Panel-type ammeters	−1.8 (1948–83)	−2.7	−1.8	−0.8
60. Tractor-mounted mowers	−1.7 (1949–83)	−2.6	−0.3	−2.5
8.*Gas hot water heaters	−1.6 (1947–83)	−1.2	−1.9	−1.7
44. Indoor safety switches	−1.6 (1947–83)	−4.4	0.5	−0.8
51. Filing cabinets	−1.6 (1950–83)	−1.8	−2.6	0.0
27. Acetylene cutting tools	−1.5 (1947–83)	−2.0	0.5	−3.6
49. Fluorescent lighting fixtures	−1.5 (1947–83)	−3.9	0.9	−1.6
10. Brass gate valves	−1.4 (1947–83)	−4.7	0.3	0.5
26. Acetylene welding torches	−1.4 (1947–83)	−3.6	1.0	−1.6
3. Manual standard typewriters	−1.3 (1948–83)	−2.5	−1.7	0.8
13. Electric furnaces	−1.3 (1972–82)	b	−0.7	−1.3
24. Hand electric sanders	−1.3 (1947–83)	0.1	0.0	−4.9
56. Seeders	−1.2 (1947–83)	−1.8	−1.2	−0.3
18. Drill presses	−1.0 (1947–83)	−2.6	0.4	−0.8
47. Typewriter tables	−1.0 (1947–83)	−3.3	−1.5	2.6
48. Card files	−1.0 (1947–78)	−3.7	−0.9	5.7
17.*Outboard motors	−0.9 (1948–83)	−2.1	−0.1	−0.7
36. Fire extinguishers	−0.9 (1947–83)	0.2	0.1	−3.6
58. Tractor-drawn cultivators	−0.9 (1949–83)	−1.0	0.2	−2.1
43. Circuit breaker-type panelboards	−0.7 (1954–83)	−2.3	−0.6	−0.2
34. Differential chain hoists	−0.5 (1948–83)	−0.8	−0.6	0.0
6. Radio receivers	−0.5 (1947–83)	0.2	−0.7	−1.1
23. Hand power saws	−0.4 (1947–83)	−2.8	0.4	1.9
16. Chain link fences	−0.2 (1955–83)	−1.1	−0.3	0.3
19. Metal lathes	−0.2 (1947–83)	1.2	−0.1	−2.1
46. Outdoor power switches	−0.2 (1948–82)	−1.3	3.1	−3.3
62. Poultry brooders	−0.2 (1947–83)	−3.1	−0.3	−3.5
50. Steel desks	−0.1 (1950–83)	1.6	−0.5	−1.3
25. Transformer arc welders	0.0 (1947–83)	3.9	−0.5	−4.4
57. Manure spreaders	0.1 (1950–83)	−0.5	−0.6	1.5
7. Gas warm air furnaces	0.2 (1951–83)	1.1	−0.7	0.7
9. Water storage tanks	0.2 (1948–83)	0.7	0.7	−1.0
29. Drill bits	0.4 (1947–83)	−4.0	3.7	1.6
66. Commercial vacuum cleaners	0.4 (1972–83)	b	2.7	0.2
40. Fractional HSP electric motors	0.5 (1947–83)	1.5	0.9	−1.4
41. Voltage regulators	0.5 (1947–79)	−3.7	1.6	7.0
61. Portable farm elevators	0.5 (1948–83)	−2.6	0.3	4.5
15. Prefabricated metal buildings	0.6 (1961–83)	b	−0.1	1.5
31. Micrometer calipers	0.7 (1947–83)	−0.3	1.3	1.3
54. Tractor-drawn plows	0.7 (1948–83)	−4.5	5.7	0.5

Table 10.10 (continued)

	Annual Growth Rates			
Sears Products	Full Period of Data (1)	1947–60 (2)	1960–73 (3)	1973–83 (4)
12. PVC piping	0.8 (1967–83)	b	−3.1	3.1
65. Portable concrete mixers	0.8 (1947–83)	−0.1	−0.2	3.4
68. Replacement auto batteries	0.8 (1948–83)	−0.4	0.6	2.5
55. Tractor-drawn harrows	0.9 (1948–83)	1.0	0.8	0.9
14. Electric hot water heaters	1.4 (1968–83)	b	3.2	0.5
42. Fusible-type panelboards	1.6 (1950–83)	4.2	1.2	−0.5
59. Sprayers	1.6 (1947–83)	0.7	1.7	2.6

[a]Entry number from table 10.8.

[b]No data for this subinterval.

*Indicates hedonic.

product. In this section, I discuss the average growth rates of the Sears indexes and the counterpart PPIs, which are, for the most part, closely matched to cover the same products. Two weighting schemes are used. The first simply averages the yearly growth rates of the sixty-eight Sears product indexes and cumulates them into the "unweighted" Sears catalog index. The same is done for the sixty-eight corresponding PPIs, and the unweighted Sears/PPI ratio is calculated. The second is a Törnqvist index of the sixty-eight Sears and PPI growth rates, applying the weighting scheme developed below in chapter 12. There the annual Sears and PPI price index growth rates within each major PDE category (i.e., metalworking machinery) are weighted with the current share of nominal PDE in that category to total nominal PDE in the thirteen categories for which we have Sears catalog data. As in any Törnqvist index, nominal value shares for the average of the current year and most recent year are averaged and applied to the current year's growth rate. Within each of the thirteen PDE categories, the Sears and PPI indexes are weighted with the weight allocated to each particular covered product within the PDE deflator. Weights allocated to uncovered products are omitted. Thus, imagine that, in the PDE deflator within category 1 (say, metalworking machinery), a weight of 0.2 is allocated to product A, 0.1 to product B, 0.4 to product C, and 0.3 to product D. Imagine also that we have a Sears price index for products A and B, a price index from some other chapter of the book for product C, and no new information on product D. Then the Törnqvist index developed for this chapter will average together price changes for products A and B only within category 1, allocating weights of 0.1/0.3 and 0.2/0.3, with the remaining 0.7 weight unallocated.

The result of these two alternative weighting schemes is shown in table 10.11, where all figures shown are average annual logarithmic rates of growth, converted into percentages. The overall annual rate of drift of the

Table 10.11   Annual Growth Rates of Sears Catalog and PPI Indexes, Alternative Weighting Schemes and Selected Intervals, 1947–83

	1947–60	1960–73	1973–83	1947–83
Unweighted averages:				
68 Sears indexes	1.18	1.27	6.49	2.69
68 Matched PPIs	3.49	1.90	7.32	3.98
Difference, Sears/PPI	−2.30	−0.63	−0.83	−1.29
Törnqvist indexes:				
68 Sears indexes	0.76	−0.16	4.08	1.35
68 Matched PPIs	3.01	1.01	5.24	2.91
Difference, Sears/PPI	−2.25	−1.17	−1.16	−1.56

Sears/PPI ratio is -1.29 percent for the unweighted indexes and -1.56 percent per year for the Törnqvist indexes. As is evident in the behavior of the Sears and PPI indexes themselves, the Törnqvist method allocates more weight to those products that have less inflation in *both* the catalog indexes and the PPIs, in addition to yielding a greater average annual rate of drift. This occurs because there is a relatively large number of products (twenty-three out of the sixty-eight total) in two relatively small industries that have relatively rapid inflation and small drifts—the agricultural machinery industry (average Törnqvist PPI inflation $= 5.49$ percent per annum over 1947–83; drift $= 0.70$ percent per annum) and metalworking machinery industry (average Törnqvist PPI inflation $= 4.58$ percent; drift $= -1.15$ percent).

10.16.2   Determinants of the Drift

Could the drift between the catalog indexes and the corresponding PPIs be related to the technological complexity of products? If the problem with the PPI is a failure to control adequately for quality change, then this should be a more important problem for complex than for simple products. Another hypothesis, suggested by critics of earlier versions of this work on catalog price indexes, is that the drift results from mismatch between the catalog indexes and the PPIs. The PPI, it could be claimed, often prices items that are larger and of a heavier, industrial grade than the items intended for home and farm use that are sold by Sears.

To test these two hypotheses, I estimate a cross-sectional regression for the sixty-eight products, giving equal weight to each observation. The variable to be explained is the annual percentage rate of drift of the Sears/PPI ratio for each product over its full period of availability (recall that some Sears indexes begin after 1947 or end before 1983). Three explanatory variables are defined for each product. First is an index of technological complexity (TC), which assigns a "grade" to each of the sixty-eight products. Products with few or no moving parts (e.g., drill bit or chain-link fence) are assigned 1. More complex products lacking engines, motors, or heating devices are graded 2 (e.g., typewriter table, card file, and fire extinguisher). Products primarily involving a heating device are graded 3 (e.g., hot water heater, furnace, and arc welder). Products primarily involving an engine or motor are graded 4 (e.g., power drill, power saw, and centrifugal pump). Products receiving the top grade of 5 involve both a motor or an engine and additional complexity in the form of moving parts and additional functions (e.g., garden tractor, drill press, metal lathe, and electric typewriter). To provide an additional dimension of complexity, a second variable (ED) was defined as a dummy for electronic components during part or all of the period. Products rated 1 rather than 0 for the ED variable were ten-key adding machine, cash register, electric typewriter, electronic calculator, and electronic auto tester. Then to test the hypothesis that the drift results from poor matching of Sears products with the corresponding PPIs, an index of the closeness of the Sears-PPI match (M) is developed. This starts at a grade of 1 for poor matches, where a Sears product is compared with a four-digit PPI group index rather than a specific six-digit or eight-digit product index. Examples are drill presses, metal lathes, and auto testing equipment. Grades of 2 or 3 are given where there is a presumption that the PPI typically prices larger items than are sold by Sears (e.g., water storage tanks). Grades of 4 or 5 are given for very close matches, where the Sears index corresponds exactly to a six-digit or eight-digit PPI that is specified to be in the same price range sold by Sears. Examples of products receiving grades of 5 include radio receivers, chain link fence, outboard motors, quarter-inch hand power drills (the PPI is explicitly for "home utility use"), differential chain hoist, fire extinguisher, indoor safety switch, filing cabinet, garden tractor, and replacement auto battery.

The estimated regression equation explaining the drift in the Sears/PPI ratio (S_i/I_t) is

$$(10.2) \quad 100 * d \log(S_i/I_i) = 0.21 - 0.44TC_i - 2.77ED_i - 0.03M_i ;$$
$$[0.21][-2.28] \quad [-3.36] \quad [-0.15]$$
$$R^2 = 0.25, \; S.E.E. = 1.87,$$

where t-ratios are shown in parentheses. Evidently, technological complexity and electronic components both contribute to a downdrift of the Sears indexes relative to the corresponding PPIs. It is also interesting that there is absolutely no relation between the closeness of the Sears-PPI match and the drift of the Sears/PPI ratio. The coefficients imply that the average annual percentage rate of drift for the simplest nonelectronic product is predicted to be -0.23, for the most complex nonelectronic product -1.99, for an average electronic product -3.88, and for the most complex electronic product -4.76.

10.16.3 Time Series Properties of the Sears Indexes

Several questions might be asked about the time series relation between the Sears index and the PPI. Is the average Sears index more or less volatile over the business cycle than the PPI? Does the adjustment of the typical Sears index typically lag behind changes in the PPI? Figures 10.1 and 10.2 present

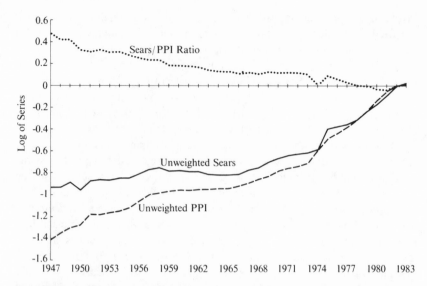

Fig. 10.1   Comparison of price indexes, unweighted, 68 products, Sears and corresponding PPI, 1982 = 1.0

time series plots of the unweighted and Törnqvist indexes, including the Sears catalog and corresponding PPI, and the Sears/PPI ratio, all in log form on a base of 1982 equals unity. The main features evident in the figures are, first, the downdrift of the Sears/PPI ratio, which is fastest in the early period 1947–62, then slackens off, and then speeds up again, particularly for the Törnqvist version in figure 10.2. The two most interesting aspects of the Sears indexes that leap out from the page are their absolute drop in 1950, perhaps responding to the 1949 recession, and their decline relative to the PPI in 1974. This latter episode is probably an artifact of the price control period, since the controls were lifted in May 1974, too late to affect the prices in the spring-summer catalog used for the index. Thus, the great leap of the Sears price indexes in 1975 combines into one year the inflation of both 1974 and 1975.

Is there a systematic cyclical response of the Sears indexes relative to the corresponding PPIs? This question is addressed by regression equations in which both versions of the average Sears index, unweighted and Törnqvist, are explained by current and lagged values of the PPI, by time trends, and by the same cyclical indicator used in chapter 11 to analyze the time series properties of the unit value indexes, that is, the detrended ratio of unfilled orders to capacity in the nonelectrical machinery industry.

Since the issue of cyclical volatility is a minor side issue in connection with the Sears indexes, the reader is referred to chapter 11 for a discussion of the background of the debate over spurious cyclical rigidity in the PPI, and for details of the definition of the cyclical variable. Table 10.12 presents the

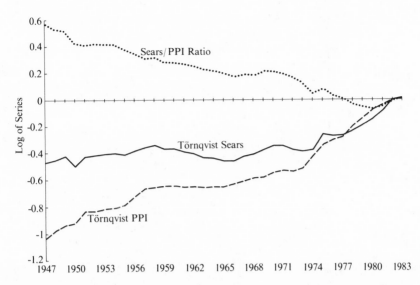

Fig. 10.2   Comparison of Törnqvist price indexes, Sears and corresponding PPI, 1982 = 1.0

regression results. The explanatory variables are listed in columns 1–9. First comes a constant, then the current and two lagged values of the corresponding PPI (unweighted or Törnqvist), then a time trend broken at 1969, then both the level and the first difference of the detrended ratio of unfilled orders to capacity in the nonelectrical machinery industry, and finally a dummy variable to capture the effect of the end of price controls in 1974. The dummy variable is defined as minus one in 1974 and one in 1975, so that no long-run effect is allowed on the Sears/PPI ratio, but only an additional lagged adjustment for Sears beyond that present in normal years.

Two versions of the equations for each index are exhibited in table 10.12. The first version is unrestricted. The second restricts the sum of coefficients on the current and lagged PPI variables to unity. The PPI coefficients on the unrestricted version sum to about 0.7, indicating a systematic tendency for the Sears index to respond less to basic inflationary forces than the PPI. This result misinterprets the downdrift of the Sears/PPI ratio by a mixture of a below-unity elasticity of the PPI response and low coefficients on the trend terms. The restricted versions are preferable, since they force the long-run response of the Sears index to the PPI to have a unitary elasticity and correspondingly allocate more of the downdrift of the Sears/PPI ratio to the time trend terms. The 1974–75 dummy terms are quite strong statistically for the unweighted series, but weak for the Törnqvist series.

Finally, the cyclical effects are very weak. If anything, there is slight evidence in the unrestricted versions of a negative cyclical effect for the change in the demand variable. This implies that the Sears index responds less

Table 10.12   Regression Equations Explaining Time Series Behavior of Sears Catalog Indexes, 1949–83

| | Constant (1) | PPI at Lag | | | Time Trend | | Unfilled Orders Capacity | | Dummy 1974–75 (9) | $\bar{R}^2$ | S.E.E. | Durbin-Watson |
		Current (2)	One (3)	Two (4)	1949–68 (5)	1969–83 (6)	Level (7)	Change (8)				
Unweighted series:												
Unrestricted	27.16**	0.16	0.73**	−0.21	−0.43**	1.23*	0.85	−0.03*	4.64**	0.997	1.96	1.00
	[5.36]	[1.04]	[2.71]	[−1.12]	[−4.76]	[2.61]	[0.41]	[−2.41]	[2.87]			
Restricted	−1.50	0.61**	0.33	0.06	−0.81**	−1.37**	3.20	−0.03	5.42*	0.992	2.98	0.39
	[−0.56]	[2.94]	[0.83]	[0.22]	[−8.03]	[−4.68]	[1.01]	[−1.65]	[2.21]			
Törnqvist series:												
Unrestricted	30.90**	0.14	0.30	0.26	−0.85**	−0.38	−0.18	−0.04*	3.35	0.957	3.02	0.58
	[2.85]	[0.51]	[0.75]	[0.93]	[−5.54]	[−0.62]	[−0.05]	[−2.15]	[1.43]			
Restricted	1.59	0.46	0.19	0.35	−1.17**	−2.02**	1.50	−0.04	3.26	0.945	3.38	0.39
	[0.50]	[1.69]	[0.43]	[1.15]	[−9.77]	[−8.00]	[0.40]	[−1.87]	[1.24]			

Note: Construction of detrended unfilled orders–capacity variable discussed in chap. 11 in connection with table 11.1, which presents similar regressions explaining the ratios of unit value indexes to the corresponding PPIs. 1974–75 dummy defined as minus one in 1974, one in 1975, and zero otherwise. *t*-ratios are in parentheses.

*Indicates significance at the 5 percent level.

**Indicates significance at the 1 percent level.

to cyclical ups and downs of demand than does the PPI. The advantage that the Sears price quotations represent true transaction prices may be offset by the time delays in printing the catalogs and the fact that the printed price lists are "locked in" for six months. This reduces the incentive to catalog firms to respond promptly to temporary shifts in demand that may have disappeared by the time the catalog is printed and distributed.

10.17 Conclusion

This chapter has developed sixty-eight new price indexes from Sears catalog price quotations covering the postwar interval from 1947 to 1983. The indexes are based on an average of about three models per product index per year, and the number of models per product varies from as few as a single model to as many as ten or more. Each Sears product is chosen so that it may be compared to a detailed PPI commodity price index that is used in the construction of the NIPA deflator for PDE, and the overall conclusions of the chapter relate to the behavior of the individual Sears/PPI ratios for the sixty-eight products, and to two averages for the sixty-eight products.

Of the sixty-eight product groups, forty-nine exhibit a secular downdrift in the Sears/PPI ratio, one exhibits no net change, and the remaining eighteen exhibit a secular updrift in the ratio. The sixty-eight products are listed in order of the drift in table 10.10, from that with the largest negative drift through that with the largest positive drift. Not only do far more products exhibit a negative drift, but the negative drift tends to be larger. Only three products have a positive drift greater than 1.0 percent per annum, but thirty-four products have a negative drift of more than 1.0 percent and eighteen more than 2.0 percent. Two averages are computed of the sixty-eight Sears indexes and corresponding PPIs. The first applies equal weights to each product. The second is a Törnqvist index based on the weighting scheme described in chapter 12 based on the weight allocated to each product's PPI in the construction of the official PDE deflator. The annual rate of change of the unweighted Sears/PPI ratio is -1.29 percent and for the Törnqvist index is -1.56 percent.

The Sears indexes tend to increase at a slower rate than the PPIs because the PPI makes inadequate allowance for quality change. A cross-sectional regression for the sixty-eight products shows that the Sears/PPI drift tends to be greater for products of greater technological complexity, and products that incorporate electronic components. An alternative hypothesis, that the Sears/PPI drift occurs mainly or entirely in products where the Sears product specifications are poorly matched to the PPI specifications, receives no support at all in the regression analysis.

A central feature of this chapter, which both contributes to its length and contributes valuable insights on the history of technological change and product improvements, is the set of "comparisons of closely similar models" that serve as a cross-check on the Sears indexes. Each comparison is documented in footnotes with details of price and quality. Looking back through the text, we can find twenty-nine such comparisons for twenty-three of the sixty-eight products over one or more long intervals ranging from a decade to the full thirty-seven-year span of the study. Of the twenty-nine comparisons, fully sixteen indicate a long-term decline in price of the quality-matched model relative to the catalog index of more than 10 percent, whereas only four indicate a long-term increase in price of more than 10 percent. For these twenty-nine comparisons, the unweighted price increases are 215 percent for the PPI, 84 percent for the catalog index, and 65 percent for the matched model comparisons. Taking out the two products where the matched model comparisons seemed to indicate a downward bias in the Sears indexes, we have average increases of 194 percent for the PPI, 71 percent for the catalog index, and just 42 percent for the matched model comparisons. The conclusion implied by these comparisons is that the catalog index is biased upward by missing price decreases that occur with the introduction of new models.

Equally important as a check on the catalog indexes, and an indication that they are biased upward, is the development of seven new *CR* indexes for typewriters, outboard motors, and small power tools. With the exception of outboard motors in the 1971–75 period, the new *CR* indexes generally increase less or decrease more than the corresponding catalog indexes, strengthening the overall conclusion that the significant downward drift of the catalog indexes relative to the PPI documented in this chapter actually understates the secular upward bias in the PPI.

Appendix

(Table 10A.1 follows on pp. 487–89.)

Table 10A.1   Details on Sears Products Observations by Order of Appearance on NIPA PDE List

Sears Products (1)	Years Covered[a] (2)	Average Models per Year (3)	Total Models Priced (4)	Number of Attributes Held Constant (5)	Price Range (6)	Final Year Covered	
						Model Range[b] (total models) (8)	Page(s) of Catalog (9)
Office, computing, and accounting machinery:							
1. 10-key adding machines		2.1	22	5	118	5807 (1)	675
2. Cash registers	1953–78	1.3	7	7	240	5964 (1)	1029
3. Manual typewriters	1948–83	2.7	35	9	77–147	5210–50 (2)	673
4. Electric typewriters	1958–83	3.8	39	10	200–295	5390–62 (4)	672
5. Electronic calculators	1970–83	6.3	25	6	18	58087 (1)	675
Communication equipment:							
6. Radio receivers	1951–83	3.5	47	12	20–70	24041–2411 (5)	703
Fabricated metal products:							
7. Gas warm air furnaces		3.1	34	5	580–730	76262–124 (4)	1014
8. *Gas hot water heaters	1948–83	10.4	79	6	130–340	33214–664 (29)	959
9. Water storage tanks		3.1	16	9	90–195	2950N–52N (4)	964
10. Brass gate valves		1.8	4	4	8	1775 (1)	958
11. Steel safes		1.8	22	5	260–360	6558–60 (2)	661
12. PVC piping	1967–83	6.6	8	3	1.6–13	59001–23111 (8)	970
13. Electric furnaces	1972–82	5.4	6	8	300–420	58751–58756 (5)	1089
14. Electric hot water heaters	1968–83	7.3	53	8	130–360	31194–156 (16)	957
15. Prefabricated metal buildings	1961–83	7.5	83	5	130–1,180	60815–60849 (7)	897
16. Chain link fencing	1955–83	8.1	12	3	2.2–21	9852–17537 (8)	967
Engines and turbines:							
17. *Outboard motors	1948–83	6.6	48	6	230–1,050	58513L–635N (7)	630
Metalworking machinery:							
18. Drill presses		1.9	11	5	100–280	1197–21381 (3)	831
19. Metal lathes	1947–76	2.9	10	5	320	2142 (1)	659
20. Free-standing power saws		4.2	34	7	95	10916C (1)	824
21. ¼ inch hand power drills	1947–83	1.8	14	8	45–60	1024–1051 (2)	830
22. ½ inch hand power drills	1949–83	2.3	15	8	90–150	1149–2711 (2)	831
23. Hand power saws		2.9	33	6	55	1091 (1)	824
24. Hand electric sanders		3.2	26	7	85	2264 (1)	828

(continued)

Table 10A.1 (continued)

Sears Products (1)	Years Covered[a] (2)	Average Models per Year (3)	Total Models Priced (4)	Number of Attributes Held Constant (5)	Price Range (6)	Final Year Covered	
						Model Range[b] (total models) (8)	Page(s) of Catalog (9)
25. Transformer arc welders		3.5	26	6	100–200	20143–20137 (2)	837
26. Acetylene welding torches		1.2	6	1	240	5441 (1)	837
27. Acetylene cutting tools		1.1	5	1	53	54408 (1)	837
28. Acetylene single-stage welding outfits		1.1	6	1	240	5446 (1)	837
29. Drill bits		3.1	12	2	18–23	6830–09 (2)	830
30. Power saw blades		2.4	19	3	17–38	32489–3257 (4)	824
31. Micrometer calipers		2.6	14	4	80–160	40185–40186 (3)	820
General industrial, including materials handling, equipment:							
32. Stationary air compressors		5.5	44	6	1,680–2,150	17515–317 (3)	854
33. Centrifugal pumps		6.5	31	6	145–280	2600–10 (4)	966
34. Differential chain hoists	1948–77	2.1	7	4	140–250	78703–05 (3)	703
35. Propellor fans		1.9	16	5	230–250	64066–77 (2)	1003
36. Fire extinguishers		8.5	56	11	10–85	58033–5808 (5)	817
Electrical transmission, distribution, and industrial apparatus:							
37. Tachometers		1.7	27	6	22–40	2177–2195 (2)	571
38. Electronic auto testers		2.0	30	5	40–100	2161–21040 (3)	616–17
39. Panel-type ammeters	1948–83	1.0	9	2	10	2176 (1)	819
40. Fractional horsepower electric motors		4.3	37	3	80–130	1216–1215C (5)	836
41. Voltage regulators	1947–78	1.3	8	3	10–12.3	1492–1487 (2)	686
42. Fusible-type panelboards	1950–83	2.8	6	2	16	51281 (1)	819
43. Circuit breaker-type panelboards	1954–83	3.7	5	4	5–12.5	5330–53321 (3)	818
44. Indoor safety switches		2.1	3	2	13	5230 (1)	818
45. Circuit breakers		3.7	15	3	60–130	5470–5202 (4)	818
46. Outdoor power switches	1948–82	2.0	5	2	30	5109–5131 (2)	819
Furnitures and fixtures:							
47. Typewriter tables		1.6	15	6	38–60	5401C–5405C (3)	670
48. Card files	1947–78	2.1	5	4	16–24	63052–6 (3)	1024
49. Fluorescent lighting fixtures		2.6	18	4	16–35	89013C–8903C (3)	1022
50. Steel desks	1950–83	1.5	11	8	110–220	77051N–77054N (3)	663
51. Filing cabinets	1950–83	6.1	25	5	50–150	60141N–60702N (8)	660
52. Office swivel chairs	1949–83	1.2	13	4	120	7720N (1)	663

Tractors:

53. Garden tractors	1949–83	2.0	32	7	2,000	25372N (1)	882
Agricultural machinery, except tractors:							
54. Tractor-drawn plows	1948–83	2.5	16	3	330	26291N (1)	882
55. Tractor-drawn harrows	1948–83	2.3	16	7	220–870	26294–80853 (4)	882–83
56. Seeders		2.5	19	5	180–600	78266–78303 (8)	884
57. Manure spreaders	1950–83	3.4	25	2	180–600	78266–78303 (8)	884
58. Tractor-drawn cultivators	1949–83	2.2	20	4	70–200	29085–26293 (3)	879–83
59. Sprayers		3.8	37	2	80–970	1512–46134 (9)	884
60. Tractor-mounted mowers	1949–83	2.2	25	4	490–1,150	25364–26511 (3)	882
61. Portable farm elevators	1948–83	1.9	9	2	400	78911 (1)	834
62. Poultry brooders		3.4	20	2	15–280	88028–88031 (6)	921
Construction machinery, except tractors:							
63. Post-hole diggers	1956–83	2.0	12	2	22–450	72005–72026 (3)	921
64. Roto spaders	1948–76	3.5	35	7	295–680	29944–25237 (2)	770–71
65. Portable concrete mixers		2.3	16	5	450–540	7575–7595 (2)	953
[32] Stationary air compressors		5.5	44	6	1,680–2,150	17515–317 (3)	854
[33] Centrifugal pumps		6.5	31	6	145–280	2600–10 (4)	966
[34] Differential chain hoists	1948–77	2.1	7	4	140–250	78703–05 (3)	703
Service industry machinery:							
66. Commercial vacuum cleaners	1972–83	2.8	31	5	265–390	22961L–23991L (4)	724
67. Automatic coffee makers	1972–83	1.7	19	4	17–50	67129–67952 (4)	806–7
[7] Gas warm air furnaces	1951–83	3.1	34	5	580–730	76262–124 (4)	1014
[8]* Gas hot water heaters		10.4	79	6	130–340	33214–664 (29)	959
[24] Hand electric sanders		3.2	26	3	85	2264 (1)	828
Electrical equipment, n.e.c.:							
68. Replacement auto batteries	1948–83	5.7	24	4	38–71	4334N–4362N (4)	609
[37] Tachometers		1.7	27	6	22–40	2177–2195 (2)	571
[38] Electronic auto testers		2.0	30	5	40–100	2161–21040 (3)	616–17
[39] Panel-type ammeters	1948–83	1.0	9	2	10	2176 (1)	819
[49] Fluorescent lighting fixtures	1948–83	2.6	18	4	16–35	8903C–89013C (3)	1022
[66] Commercial vacuum cleaners	1972–83	2.8	31	5	265–390	22961L–23991L (4)	724

Note: Brackets indicate a product appearing for the second time. The number inside the bracket is the chronological number of its first appearance. No product appears more than twice.

aWhen no entry in this cell, the period spans 1947–83.

bModel numbers indicate the first-listed and last-listed model in the final year covered. Numbers listed out of sequence indicate that models are listed out of sequence in the catalog.

*Indicates hedonic.

11   Using Unit Value Indexes to Measure Transaction Prices and Quality Change

11.1   Introduction

Up to this point, this book has been entirely concerned with the development of new price indexes for durable goods that are corrected to the maximum extent possible for changes in quality. In addition to quality change, a second issue that has received considerable attention in the price measurement literature is the cyclical sensitivity of transaction prices relative to list prices. Macroeconomists have long been interested in the incredible rigidity of the price indexes for many individual commodities. One of the advantages claimed in earlier chapters for the use of mail-order catalog prices, as well as prices of late-model used automobiles and tractors, is that catalog prices represent actual transaction prices, and that late-model used asset prices should be close proxies for the true transaction prices of new models. An even better source of information on transaction prices comes from the collection of prices directly from buyers, as contrasted to the PPI procedure of collecting from sellers. The well-known book by Stigler and Kindahl (1970) reported the results of a data-collection project in which buyers of industrial equipment were directly approached for price quotes. Another source of information on transaction prices can come from a hedonic regression index if it is based on prices collected from buyers on mail-order catalogs, or on the actual sales prices of late-model used items.

A separate data source, unit values in the Census of Manufacturers, has severe limitations for the study of both secular quality change and changes in the relation of transaction to list prices. Nevertheless, on the basis of an extensive earlier research project, I believe that unit value indexes for several basic and simple industrial goods can provide a useful complement for the other data sources utilized in this book.[1] The two basic weaknesses of unit

---

1. The earlier research, which was widely distributed in mimeographed form in 1972–73, was included in the first draft of this book in 1974. This chapter extends to 1983 the unit value indexes

value data are that they allow correction for at most one dimension of quality change (e.g., horsepower for diesel engines), and they are subject to spurious movements that reflect changes in product mix rather than true changes in price. The products chosen for analysis in this chapter are one-dimensional in quality, primarily engines, compressors, and condensing units, and have data available in sufficient detail to allow control for changes in product mix along that single quality dimension.

11.2   Background of the Transaction Price Issue

Soon after the inception of the WPI, observers took notice of the incredible rigidity of the price indexes for many individual commodities.[2] Price quotations remained unchanged month after month through prosperity and depression. Accepting the validity of the WPI price quotations, Means (1935) and others cited their rigidity relative to "classically competitive market prices" as support for the proposition that industrial prices are "administered" by firms rather than determined by the interaction of market supply and demand. The implication was not merely that administered pricing was responsible for the relatively large adjustment of real output and small adjustment of prices during business contractions, but also that the entire structure of classical economics had been called into question: "Until economic theory can explain and take into account the implications of the neoclassical behavior of administered prices, it provides a poor basis for public policy. The challenge which administered prices make to classical economics is as fundamental as that made by the quantum to classical physics" (Means 1972, 304).

An alternative explanation for the relative rigidity of some industrial prices is that WPI price quotations are sellers' list prices, which do not reflect actual market conditions. One of the first to suggest this possibility was Stigler in his critique of the kinked demand curve: "It is not possible to make a direct test for price rigidity, in part, because the prices at which the products of oligopolists sell are not generally known. For the purpose of such a test we need transaction prices; instead we have quoted prices on a temporal basis, and they are deficient in two respects. The first deficiency is notorious: Nominal price quotations may be stable although the prices at which sales are taking place fluctuate often and widely" (Stigler 1947). Flueck (1961, 422) offers several reasons why actual market prices might differ from list prices, of which the most important is discounting: "Apparently the most popular and widely used method is to offer discounts of varying degrees (depending on the market supply and demand situation) from the list price which is quoted in

---

for a subset of eight of the fifty-two products that were studied in the earlier report, copies of which are still available on request.

2. For references to the literature, see Stigler and Kindahl (1970, 11–20).

trade journals, newspapers, by trade associations, and unfortunately for many commodities, the WPI. For discounting appears to be very common in normal markets, rampant in weak (buyers') markets, and zero or negative in strong (sellers') markets.''

Evidence on transaction prices would be useful in providing an indication of the accuracy of the conventional PPI commodity indexes. If discounting and premiums are important and vary procyclically, the existing national accounts may understate cyclical fluctuations in prices and overstate fluctuations in real output. New insights may be gained about particular historical episodes, for example, were price controls in World War II and during the Korean War as effective as the official indexes imply, or did the actual transaction prices include premiums? If discounts are important for those commodities with relatively inflexible "administered" PPI quotations, and if PPI quotations in competitive markets are relatively accurate, then improved measures of transaction prices may reduce or even eliminate the contrast between administered and competitive price behavior.

If discounting were equally prevalent in sales of producer and consumer goods, the official U.S. price deflators would be more accurate for the latter, since the CPI is based on field reports of actual retail transaction prices, whereas the primary source of producer good prices, the PPI, relies primarily on reports of list prices mailed in by manufacturers.[3] Several studies, most notably that by Stigler and Kindahl (1970), have attempted to remedy this inadequacy of the PPI by collecting data on actual prices paid by buyers and comparing these "true" quotations with the PPI list prices. Unfortunately, with a few exceptions, these studies have been limited to relatively homogeneous crude and intermediate goods (e.g., steel). Virtually no information is available on transaction prices of finished capital goods.

This chapter reports on an exploratory attempt to analyze evidence on transaction prices of capital goods. The U.S. Census of Manufacturers regularly publishes data on the value and quantity of products shipped, and in some cases these are collected for very narrowly defined commodity classifications. The ratio to quantity shipped, the "unit value," is a transaction price (f.o.b. plant, after discounts and allowances, excluding freight charges

---

3. In March 1975, according to the Ruggles report (U.S. Executive Office of the President 1977, table I-5), 98 percent of PPI commodity indexes in SIC industries 34–38 were based on company reports, and of these 95 percent were based on "list prices minus discounts" rather than on "list prices" or on "average realized unit selling price." This still leaves open whether the companies report transaction prices or list prices. Clorety (1970, 34) writes, e.g., that "the WPI for motor vehicles reflects . . . actual transaction prices." And, in general, when "the trade press or other publications report discounting," it is typical "for the appropriate commodity analyst to check the reports immediately with reporting companies and other sources of information. Like quality adjustment, the pursuit of actual transaction prices is virtually a daily problem in calculating the PPI." But my impression, based on the time I spent copying monthly PPI commodity quotations, is that these efforts are sporadic rather than general. Most PPI commodity quotations for machinery remain absolutely fixed for long periods of time, often twelve months or more, suggesting continued heavy reliance on list price reports.

and excise taxes) that can be compared to PPI price quotations for the same products to determine the prevalence of price discounts on capital goods not taken into account in the PPI. Annual unit value data are a potentially valuable yet almost untapped source of information, and as many as twenty-four annual observations are available for some products.[4] The basic hypothesis to be tested is that the ratio of census unit value to PPI price for a given commodity fluctuates procyclically, indicating an increase in the prevalence of discounting in weak (buyers') markets.

The unit value indexes developed in this chapter can do "double duty," both serving as an indication of cyclical fluctuations in the ratio of transaction to list prices, and providing alternative quality-adjusted price indexes to add to those developed in the previous chapters of the book. A basic flaw of unit value data is that changes in unit values may indicate either changes in prices or changes in the size/quality mix. Unit value data for some products (e.g., "standard nonelectric typewriter") are collected with absolutely no information available to estimate the importance of shifts in quality mix. Others are collected in "cells" differentiated by a major quality characteristics (e.g., horsepower for diesel engines). If the single quality dimension along which the cells are differentiated also happens to be the dominant quality characteristic of the product, then use of unit value indexes as a proxy for quality-adjusted price indexes may be possible. If, however, there are multiple dimensions of quality, then unit value indexes will not be up to the task. For this reason, coverage in this chapter is limited to only eight products that perform fairly simple tasks and for which the assumption of a single dimension of quality should be valid. These are cast iron radiators, gasoline and diesel engines, and several types of compressors and condensing units. In an earlier version of this study, many more products were included, but previous chapters have now developed evidence for many of these (e.g., tractors) that corrects for multiple dimensions of quality change.

11.3 Conceptual Problems in the Use of Census Unit Values

11.3.1 Previous Critiques

The U.S. Census Bureau collects data on the value of shipments and the number of units shipped for numerous manufacturing commodities, and the

---

4. Previous studies of unit value data include the following. McAllister (1961) calculated two annual unit value indexes for machinery: standard typewriters (1948–59) and a ½ hp "Jet Type Deep Well Water System" (1952–56). Two other studies are exclusively concerned with the "secular drift" in several unit value/WPI ratios and do not discuss annual changes (Jorgenson and Griliches 1972; and Searle 1970). The Searle report contains two appendices: "A Study of Differences between Census and Price Index Deflators," by Cornelia Motheral and Alexander Yeats (app. A); and "A Study of Census Unit Value Relatives and Comparable Wholesale Price Indexes for Selected Manufactured Products, 1958–1963," by Edward D. Gruen and Mary E. Lawrence (app. B).

unit values (i.e., value shipped divided by number of units shipped) can be compared with PPI quotations. In considering unit value data for narrowly defined individual commodities as potential replacements for PPI quotations, this chapter evaluates the feasibility of a recommendation of the 1961 Stigler report: "Where buyers' prices are not available, we recommend extensive use of unit values, at least as benchmarks to which the monthly prices are adjusted. Unit values are inferior to specification *transaction* prices, but when unit values are calculated for fairly homogenous commodities, they are more realistic than quoted prices in a large number of industrial markets" (NBER 1961, 71).

The Stigler recommendation was later challenged, and the use of unit value data as price quotations has been seriously questioned, by an unpublished report chaired by Allan D. Searle of the Bureau of Labor Statistics, henceforth the "Searle report" (Searle 1970). The report is based on two staff studies that tip the scale against unit values, rejecting the Stigler call for unit values calculated for "fairly homogenous commodities" as unattainable, since even at the census seven-digit product level changes in unit values are dominated by shifts in product mix:

> This [first] study suggested that any gains in precision which may arise because unit values reflect a comprehensive universe representing actual transaction prices are offset by problems of product and transaction mix. This arises because a 7-digit Census product may include a relatively wide range of specifications and transaction types. This mix may change markedly from Census year to Census year. The other study, in depth, of 25 items, at the 7-digit product level, showed a "persistent tendency of unit values between 1958 and 1963 to reflect shifts in product mix, usually to the lower end of the quality—or price line." [Searle 1970, 4]

More recently, Lichtenberg and Griliches (1989) have carried out a wide-ranging comparison of unit value indexes with PPI indexes at the seven-digit product level. Their study was limited to price changes over a single interval, 1972–77. Their major conclusion regarding unit value indexes is that these have a much lower signal-to-noise ratio than the PPIs, 0.53 as compared to 2.72 by their estimate. They estimate that the PPI captures about two-thirds of actual quality change over their period of study. The Lichtenberg-Griliches study confirms Searle's previous verdict that unit value indexes cannot be used as a universal replacement for PPIs, because of the problem of changes in product and transaction mix. However, because their study contains no criterion for selecting the "best" unit values and makes no attempt to correct for shifts in product mix, its negative verdict on a universal, unselected, and unadjusted unit values has no relevance to this study, with its narrower focus on carefully selected and adjusted unit value indexes.

This chapter attempts to minimize the quantitative importance of shifts in product mix by limiting the analysis to commodities that the census subdivides into explicit size cells or classes (e.g., gasoline engines of thirty-six to forty horsepower). Yet, even within commodity groups that are defined as narrowly as this, shifts in product mix may occur. One of the twenty-five commodities included in the second staff study of the Searle report, gasoline engines, is included in the evidence evaluated in the present chapter. The report explains an increase in the ratio of unit values to PPI indexes for large gasoline engines as being due to changes in product mix both across and within size cells.

11.3.2   Adjustments for Changes in Product Mix

I deal with the Searle report criticism in two ways. First, the change from one year to the next in the unit value is calculated separately in each size cell, so that the unit value index is not influenced by changes in product mix across cells. Second, changes in product mix within cells are controlled by using information on changes in product mix in adjacent cells. While there is no X-ray to see what is happening inside individual product classes, a plausible assumption is that class lines are arbitrary, and that any significant changes in product mix within classes are revealed by similar changes in mix between adjacent classes.[5] If we are considering adjacent product cells A, B, and C, for instance, a shift in product mix from items in small-size class A to items in medium-size class B, and from items in class B to class C, should indicate that the average size of items within class B is increasing as well. In another situation, when sales of both border commodity groups (A and C) are increasing relative to the subject commodity group (B), the negative adjustment contributed by the lower border class will roughly balance the positive component of the upper class. A simple product mix adjustment is developed to deal with these cases.[6]

The product mix adjustment will be least accurate in the bottom and top size cells, since only half as much information is available on mix movements in adjacent cells. The inaccuracy may be particularly acute when the quantities sold in the smallest or largest class constitute an important share of the product group, for example, the less than 7 hp gasoline engines that, as the second Searle staff study noted, accounted for a large share of quantities and values in the 1963 census statistics. In a class as important as this, the product

5. Another alternative assumption is that class limits are set so as to place the bulk of production at the center of each class. In that case, the average size within a class might well remain constant, even though there is a shift of production up the size scale. The primary reason for rejecting this possibility is that most shifts in class definitions retain arbitrarily, usually even-numbered boundaries, and combine or subdivide these arbitrary classes when production shifts. For instance, class boundaries may shift from 10-20-30-50 to 10-30-40-45-50 as average size increases.

6. The formulas are involved, since they take account of the relative width of each size cell, and are omitted here to simplify the presentation. Intuitively, any changes in the share of total units contributed by units in the two adjacent classes are weighted by the mean relative unit value of each adjacent class and by the width of the cell.

mix index may be virtually useless, because its key assumption of a linear relation between price and quantity changes may be invalid. To deal with the problem posed by the bottom and top cells, an initial test calculates alternative unit value indexes that exclude the bottom and top classes. Where these indexes differ from the indexes that include all classes, the bottom or top class is eliminated. This test leads to the exclusion of all data for gasoline engines from size classes below 11 hp, thus eliminating the main problem to which the Searle report called attention for this product (the only product for which there is any overlap between that report and this chapter). For other products, it was not deemed necessary to eliminate the bottom or top classes, either because they were unimportant, or because the product mix was relatively stable. For instance, in the case of diesel engines, subject of a case study later in the chapter, the value of sales in the smallest size class in the 1970s was only 3 or 4 percent, and so changes in unit value in that size class can have only a trivial effect on the final results.

11.4   Characteristics of the Data and Calculation of Indexes

Current Industrial Reports, which publishes annual and in some cases monthly data on the value of shipments and quantity shipped for individual seven-digit census commodities, is a relatively little-known adjunct to the Census of Manufacturers.[7] The *Reports* covers the industry as completely as the census and is not based on a sample survey, as is the Annual Survey of Manufacturers. Standard report forms are submitted by all known producers of the products listed in each *Report*. The incompleteness of the *Reports* compared to the census lies not in the extent of coverage but in the scope of information provided, which includes only the value of shipments and number of units shipped, while omitting the usual census questions on payrolls, value added, geographic origin, and so on.

Although the *Reports* data represent transaction prices and have the advantage of completeness, the method of their compilation and presentation has posed numerous problems for this study. In order to minimize the heterogeneity of products and implement the procedure for product mix adjustments as outlined above, I require that quantities and values for product groups be subdivided into product classes defined by an explicit size dimension, but the criteria for selecting products to be subdivided by size in the census and *Reports* are capricious at best. Although several types of construction and agricultural machinery and virtually all types of refrigeration and air conditioning equipment are subdivided into explicit size classes, not a single product is included within many important categories of PDE. Many of the products that are subdivided (e.g., moldboard plows) are much less

7. Before 1960, the *Current Industrial Reports* was called *Facts for Industry*. The starting date varies among products; the earliest *Facts* for a few products was issued during World War II.

important than those excluded (e.g., lathes). Even within a product group (e.g., electric motors), the selection criteria have no apparent basis. Some seven-digit product classes consist of the entire production of an item in all its various forms and sizes (e.g., product 3621101, "automobile accessory electric motors"). Yet others are arrayed in many separate size categories, as in the extreme example of nonautomotive fractional horsepower electric motors, for which data are available in forty-one separate classes (e.g., product 3621152, "fractional horsepower motors, alternating current, conventional type shaded pole motors, 3¾ inches in diameter and over but less than 4½ inches in diameter, ¹⁄₂₀ hp and over but less than ¹⁄₁₀ hp").

Just eight product groups are selected for this study, a small subset of the forty-two types of PDE for which data are collected in subclasses with explicit size dimensions. An early version of this study covered all forty-two types, plus an additional ten for which no size classes were available, for a total of fifty-two. Here, however, the scope of the investigation is limited by excluding all those products for which some other source of information is available, or for which quality change occurs on a multidimensional basis. For instance, both criteria lead to the exclusion of tractors. The availability of alternative information from the Sears catalog leads to the exclusion of many others, including electric motors, stationary air compressors, and centrifugal pumps. The multidimensional quality issue dictates the exclusion of complex agricultural equipment (e.g., combines and mechanized corn pickers). The product groups selected for this study, then, are as follows, listed here with their average number of size classes over the period 1947–70 indicated in parentheses:

1. cast iron radiators and convectors, measured in square feet (1);
2. gasoline and other carburetor engines, except automotive, aircraft, and outboard (15.9);
3. diesel and semidiesel engines, except automotive (22.0);
4. compressors, all refrigerants except ammonia, open-type, over 10 hp (9.0);
5. compressors and compressor units, ammonia refrigerants (10.8);
6. condensing units, air cooled, hermetic type (7.7);
7. condensing units, water cooled, open type (15.9); and
8. condensing units, water cooled, hermetic type (8.5).

The unit value indexes are the antilogs of log indexes cumulated from the log changes for each of the eight product groups in each pair of adjacent years between 1947 and 1983, exactly the same procedure used to convert the year-to-year log change in the Sears catalog prices in chapter 10 into price indexes.[8] However, the procedure to aggregate the unit value changes in the

8. Data for water-cooled hermetic condensing units begin in 1952; data on gasoline and diesel engines are not available for 1948 and 1949, so that the first year pair is 1947–50.

individual size cells is superior to that used to aggregate price changes for individual Sears models. In the catalog index, no market share information is available for individual models, and equal weights are applied to aggregate the separate model-by-model price changes into a single price change for that product in an adjacent-year pair. Here, for unit values, we can construct a true Törnqvist index, weighting each log change in unit value in each size cell by the average value share of that size cell in each year of the adjacent-year pair.

The number of separate size cells often changes between adjacent-year pairs as class boundaries shift and alter the number of comparisons that can be made between identically defined classes. Assume, for instance, that the available size classes for a product group in three successive years are as follows:

1963	1964	1965
0.0–7.0	0.0–7.0	0.0–9.0
7.0–10.9	7.0–13.9	9.0–13.9
11.0–15.0	14.0–15.0	14.0–15.0

The 1963–64 growth rate would be calculated for the two classes 0.0–7.0 and 7.0–15.0, while the 1964–65 growth rate would be calculated for the two classes 0.0–13.9 and 14.0–15.0. In each pair of years, the maximum number of homogeneous comparisons is two. Shifting boundaries account for the changing number of class comparisons in each pair of years.

In what sense are the size classes for each product group "wide" or "narrow"? If the largest items of a product were only moderately more expensive than the smallest, even two size classes might be sufficient to control for shifts in product mix, but if a large item in a group is 100 times more expensive than a small item, even twenty size classes will each be quite "wide." We can calculate a measure of width as the ratio of the unit value in one class to that in the next smallest class, averaged with quantity weights over all classes. In the original study, class widths ranged from 1.07 for room air conditioners (a product for which I now have information from both the Sears catalog and *Consumer Reports*) to 16.5 for portable air compressors. Leaving aside cast iron radiators, for which no size classes are available, the average size widths for 1947–70 for the remaining seven products are, in the respective order listed above, 1.25, 1.39, 1.29, 1.24, 1.27, 1.28, and 1.29. Thus, the class boundaries are relatively narrow and are quite uniform across these seven product categories. These seven product classes constitute fully half of all the available products for which class boundaries are of an average width of 1.4 or narrower.

The original study constructed four separate unit value indexes for each of the original fifty-two product groups in order to study the effect of disaggregation. The indexes are as follows, moving from the most to the least disaggregated.

1. The fully disaggregated index P_1 uses all available size class information, and, in addition, adjusts for estimated shifts in product mix within each class, using information on mix shifts across adjacent classes as described above.
2. Index P_2 uses all available size classes, as does index P_1, but excludes the adjustment for changes in product mix within individual classes.
3. Index P_3 is calculated for half the available size classes; half the class boundaries are "thrown away," and the unit values for the remaining classes are set equal to the sum of values in two adjacent classes divided by the sum of units sold.
4. Index P_4 uses no size class information at all. Unit value is defined simply as the ratio of the total value of shipments in the product group as a whole to the total number of units shipped.

A cross-sectional study of the difference between the growth rates of the indexes revealed that the less disaggregated indexes were more error prone in proportion to the average growth rate of size over time and as a positive function of average cell width. For the products that concern us, with relatively narrow cell widths, there were only minor differences between indexes P_1 and P_2. The results discussed in the rest of the chapter are based on the most disaggregated index P_1 for the period of the initial study, 1947–70. For the update of the study over the period 1971–83, the index P_2 was used in light of the minor difference between P_1 and P_2 in the earlier period.[9]

11.4.1 The Selection of PPI Indexes for Comparison with the Unit Value Indexes

While the unit value indexes for product groups are interesting in themselves, the purpose of this chapter is to compare the behavior of machinery prices as measured by unit value indexes with the NIPA deflator for PDE. Since the NIPA deflators are weighted averages of individual PPI six-digit or eight-digit commodity indexes, the unit values for each of the eight product groups are compared here with the appropriate PPI indexes for the same product groups. Previous studies (e.g., the Searle report) were based on unit values for a few isolated size classes (e.g., gas engines of 81–100 hp) chosen for close correspondence with a particular PPI index for, for example, gas engines of 86–104 hp.[10] Yet this procedure has four flaws.

1. Most important, the census size boundaries do not remain constant, so that the unit values are composed of different sized items in different years.

9. While I would have preferred to calculate a P_1 index for the full 1947–83 interval of the study, the original vintage-1972 computer program designed to calculate the intracell mix adjustment needed for P_1 has been lost in the sands of time and was not judged to be worth the time to reconstruct.

10. This is the size boundary for the largest gas engine priced by the PPI during most of the postwar period, index 11-94-01-04.

2. In some year-to-year comparisons, the 81–100 class is subdivided into 81–90 and 91–100. The use of a combined 81–100 class "throws away" valuable information available to improve the control of product mix shift in some years, if not in all years.
3. The use of unit values only for isolated size classes chosen to correspond with PPI definitions (e.g., 7–10.9 hp, 21–30 hp, and 81–100 hp) discards valuable information on the omitted size classes. Prohibitive compilation cost prevents the PPI from maintaining a separate index for every size class, and the value weights for the omitted classes are imputed to the relatively small number of PPI indexes that are collected, but there is no parallel justification to exclude unit value classes, since the marginal cost of including all published size classes is virtually zero.
4. The use of unit values only for isolated size classes prevents the calculation of the intraclass product mix estimate that adjusts unit value index P_1.

Since each product group unit value index in this study contains all available size classes, the most appropriate comparison is the PPI index used in the NIPA PDE deflator to deflate the value of production for that product group as a whole. In some cases, appropriate four-digit or six-digit PPI group indexes are readily available that correspond perfectly to the unit value product groups (gasoline and diesel engines). In the important "service-industry equipment" industry (refrigeration equipment), unfortunately, there are no PPI indexes collected at all for most of the product groups, and the unit values are compared with the proxies selected in the national accounts.[11] A detailed list of the specific PPI commodities chosen for comparison is contained in Appendix table B.17.

11.5   Tests of Cyclical Behavior

11.5.1   Review of Previous Techniques

The previous literature contains a few attempts to test the cyclical relation between transaction and list prices. In most cases, very small sample sizes have precluded formal statistical analysis and have required other expedients.

1. McAllister compared the year-to-year change in the unit value/PPI ratio for steel with the simultaneous change in the steel industry rate of capacity utilization. He found the expected positive correlation on average for 25 steel products in "5.2 out of a possible 10 times" and concluded "clearly, the data as analyzed in the above fashion do not substantiate the hypothesis that the unit values are more flexible on an annual basis than the PPI prices" (1961, 400).

---

11. Proxy indexes used in the national accounts are listed in App. table A.1.

2. A staff study in the Searle report (1970, 15–24) included cross-sectional regressions within each two-digit manufacturing industry, with the 1963 difference between unit value and PPI commodity indexes (1958 = 1.00) as dependent variable and the change in output between 1958 and 1963 as an explanatory variable. The relation was significant in only seven of eighteen industry groups, and in almost all cases the sign of the estimated coefficient was negative rather than positive.

3. In their study of prices paid by buyers, Stigler and Kindahl compare the average rate of change of their buyers' price index with that of the corresponding PPI series over NBER reference cycles, both before and after correction for trend. On balance, they concluded that the behavior of the PPI and buyers' indexes "uncorrected for trend are essentially identical in their behavior," and "on balance we found slightly better conformity of prices and business changes in contractions than in expansions prior to trend corrections" (1970, 63).

11.5.2 Regression Specification

Because it can allow automatically for the differing length and strength of cycles, because lagged variables can be easily introduced, and because the statistical significance of results can be easily evaluated, time series regressions are preferable to the cycle-average technique. The small sample sizes that have inhibited time series regression studies carried out in the 1960s are no longer an impediment. The model to be tested is that the unit value index P_1 of a product group differs from the PPI index for that group (I) both in its secular trend and in its response to variations in the excess demand for commodities (E) over the business cycle:

$$(11.1) \qquad \log(P_{1t}/I_t) = \alpha_0 + \alpha_1 t + \alpha_2 \log(E_t) + \epsilon_t \,,$$

where ϵ_t is the error term, and the basic cyclical hypothesis is that the coefficient α_2 is significantly greater than zero. The sign of the time trend parameter α_1 cannot be specified a priori, since either the unit value index or the PPI could do a better job of controlling for secular quality change. Equation (11.1) closely resembles a model of price behavior frequently employed in time series studies of aggregate economy-wide price data, in which the aggregate price index (in level or difference form) is regressed on "standard" unit labor cost and a measure of excess demand like E above. In (11.1), the PPI variable (I_t) already incorporates the influence of cost and at least a portion of the effect of excess demand, and so the cyclical hypothesis to be tested is that there is an additional effect of excess demand present in P_{1t} over and above that present in I_t .

The most difficult step in the implementation of (11.1) is the choice of a specific variable to stand as a proxy for excess demand. In my own work on aggregate price equations in the early 1970s (1971a, 1975), I found significant demand effects for the ratio of unfilled orders to capacity in durable manufacturing as an excess demand proxy, based on the idea that excess demand spills into both price increases and increases in unfilled orders, and that unfilled orders in a recession should be compared not with the relatively low shipments that are actually being produced but with the potential shipments that could be produced if capacity were fully utilized.[12] This variable is calculated as the ratio of unfilled orders to shipments multiplied by the capacity utilization rate. An exact analog of this aggregate variable is not available for the disaggregated product groups, so I use the ratio of unfilled orders to capacity (F_t) in the nonelectrical machinery industry, SIC 35, estimated as the ratio of unfilled orders to shipments for that industry multiplied by the capacity utilization ratio for all durable manufacturing.[13]

In estimating the regression model (11.1) over the sample period 1950–83, the excess demand and time trend coefficients were allowed to shift after 1968. Also, the excess demand term was initially entered in the form of lags 0, 1, and 2, and only the significant terms were retained for the estimates presented in table 11.1. Equations were estimated for an unweighted average of all eight products, and for three "industry groups", radiators (one product), engines (two products), and compressors/condensing units (five products).

The results, shown in table 11.1, are presented only for the variant that displayed the strongest evidence of a procyclical movement of the P_{1t}/I_t ratio. Significantly positive coefficients on F_t were obtained for at least half the postwar period, either the early period 1950–68 or the later period 1969–83, or both in the case of engines. However, the results are not as strong as they appear, because the low Durbin-Watson statistics for the aggregate and compressor equations indicate positive serial correlation, and inclusion of the lagged dependent variable in these equations reduces the significance of the F_t terms to zero. However, the radiator equation survives a transformation to first difference form, with the lagged dependent variable entered here to correct for negative serial correlation. The engine equation provides the clearest evidence of a procyclical effect, with reasonable elasticities of 0.2 that are highly significant at better than the 1 percent level and stable across the two subperiods. This elasticity estimate implies that in a typical business expansion, when F_t rises by about 50 percent, the unit value index for engines rises about 10 percent relative to the PPI.

---

12. This ratio was first developed in deMénil (1969).

13. Unfilled orders and shipments data are taken from the 1975 and 1986 editions of *Business Statistics*. These data are not available prior to 1953; the same variables for durable manufacturing were substituted, from the same source. Capacity utilization in durable manufacturing is taken from *Economic Report of the President*, February 1988, table B-51. This variable was not available prior to 1967; the same variable for total manufacturing was substituted, from the same source.

Table 11.1   Regression Equations Explaining Ratio of Unit Value Index to PPI, 1950–83

Form (1)	Lagged Dependent Variable (2)	Time, 1950–68 (3)	Time, 1969–83 (4)	F_t, 1950–68 (5)	F_t, 1969–83 (6)	$\bar{R}^2$	S.E.E.	Durbin-Watson
Aggregate Level	···	-4.42** [13.79]	0.00 [0.14]	0.09 [1.39]	0.17** [3.28]	0.949	5.88	0.67
Radiators First Difference	-0.58** [-3.94]	-1.43 [-1.18]	3.45 [1.85]	0.00 [0.13]	0.50** [4.46]	0.501	5.16	2.14
Engines Level	···	-4.45** [16.47]	-1.32** [-4.48]	0.21**a [3.25]	0.18**a [3.12]	0.973	5.46	1.65
Compressors/condensing units Level	···	-5.27** [-11.03]	0.00 [0.65]	0.11 [1.20]	0.26** [3.25]	0.910	8.77	0.47

Note: Initially, the F_t variable was entered in the form of lags 0,1, and 2 in levels or 0 and 1 in first differences. Each coefficient on F_t shown here is on the current (0) variable only, except for those designated by [a], where the figures shown are the sums of coefficients on lags 1 and 2, with lag 0 omitted. *t*-ratios are in brackets.

**Indicates significance at the 1 percent level.

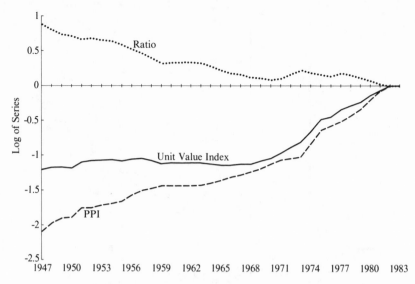

Fig. 11.1   Comparison of price indexes, this study and PPI, 1982 = 1.0

11.6   Secular Drift in the Unit Value Ratios

Another interesting feature of the regression estimates is an extremely large and significant negative coefficient on the time trend variable in the pre-1969 period. The strong downward drift of the aggregate unit value index relative to the PPI (both calculated as an unweighted Törnqvist index of the eight product indexes) is evident also in figure 11.1. As shown by that figure, and evident when growth rates are calculated over three periods (1947–60, 1960–73, and 1973–83), there was a hiatus in the downward drift in the middle period, followed by a resumption of the downward drift in the third period at a much slower rate than in the initial period.

The tendency of the unit value indexes to drift down relative to the PPI, particularly in the 1947–60 interval, applies to all the products except for radiators. While the rates of drift for several products in the compressor and condensing unit group are rapid, the most interesting evidence is for diesel engines. The diesel engine unit value index may indicate convincing evidence of secular bias in the PPI, both because it is so precisely matched to the PPI group index for nonautomotive diesel engines, and because the unit value index for diesel engines is based on so many different size cells (twenty-two, the most for any product in this study or in my broader initial study). Because of the importance of the product and the high quality of the comparison, the unit value and PPI indexes for diesel engines are compared in figure 11.2.

11.6.1   Unit Values as a "Signal" of Unmeasured Quality Change

In addition to their usefulness as indicators of cyclical fluctuations in transaction prices, unit value indexes can also perform a secondary function

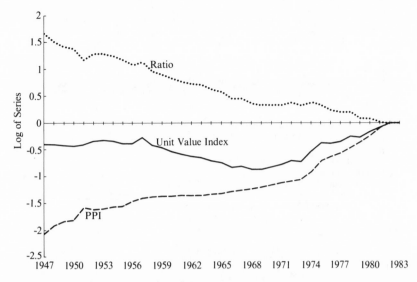

Fig. 11.2   Comparison of price indexes, this study and PPI, for diesel engines, 1982 = 1.0

as a "signal" when they deviate to a very great degree from comparable PPI indexes. A discrepancy might be due to flaws in either the unit value or the PPI and can signal an area in which a search of a third independent outside source of information may yield a high research payoff. The marked discrepancies between unit values and national income accounts deflators for diesel engines, compressors, and condensing units are evident in the regression study above and suggest an inappropriate choice of deflators in the national accounts. Unit values would be particularly good substitutes for the PPI for these products, because census size classes are defined very narrowly in most cases, and the products are simple utilitarian items free from complications of unmeasured quality attributes (with the possible exception of improvements in energy efficiency, which presumably cause the unit value indexes developed here to overstate the true rate of price increase).

This section examines outside evidence for two product groups that display large discrepancies between unit value and PPI indexes. The first is for diesel engines, where the quality of the unit value index is relatively good. The second is for ten-key adding machines, based on a unit value index developed in the earlier study but not used in the alternative price index developed in chapter 12, since we already have the Sears catalog index for ten-key adding machines from chapter 10.

11.6.2   A Case Study: Diesel Engines

The difference between the behavior of the unit value and PPI indexes for diesel engines can only be described as enormous, as shown in figure 11.2. Between 1947 and 1972, the PPI increases by 150 percent, while the unit

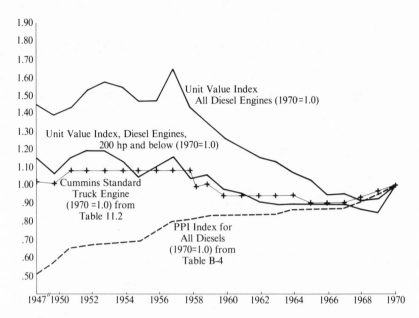

Fig. 11.3   Alternative price indexes for all diesel engines and for medium-sized diesel engines, 1970 = 1.0

value index declines by 25 percent. The unit value index, in addition, exhibits considerably more year-to-year variation than the PPI, and the unit value/PPI ratio in the regression study has a statistically significant correlation with the ratio of unfilled orders to capacity in nonelectrical machinery. Unfortunately, mail-order catalog houses do not sell new diesel engines, and there is no easily accessible alternative source of data on engine prices.[14] In this section, scattered pieces of information are examined that provide most if not all of the needed explanation of the puzzling behavior of the unit value/PPI ratio.

The unit value data for diesel engines are especially useful because so many different size classes are defined in the census, and these allow us to examine disaggregated information to pin down the source of the unit value/PPI puzzle. First, separate unit value indexes are calculated for "small" and "large" engines, with a dividing line selected so that half the size classes fall in each group. The dividing line falls fairly consistently at 200 horsepower, and the index for engines below 200 horsepower is displayed in figure 11.3 as the lower of the two solid lines. Unit values of small engines dropped only 14 percent between 1947 and 1970, as compared to 55 percent for large engines. The impression conveyed by the PPI subindexes is diametrically opposite. The respective rates of price increase between 1947 and 1970 were 76, 109,

---

14. Warshawsky, a Chicago mail-order automotive catalogue firm, sells a few models of *used* diesel engines, but their condition and mileage differ from one sample to another.

Table 11.2   Manufacturers' Price Data for Diesel Engines, 1945–75

	Cummins VT12			Cummins "Standard" Truck Engine			Electromotive "Standard" Locomotive Engine		
	Price (1)	Hp (2)	Price/Hp (3)	Price (4)	Hp (5)	Price/Hp (6)	Price (7)	Hp (8)	Price/Hp (9)
1945				2,690	200	13.4			
1950							33,600	1,650	20.4
1951				2,867	200	14.3			
1955	9,255	600	15.4				39,250	1,925	20.4
1958	9,000	600	15.0	3,160	220	14.4			
1959				2,975	220	13.5			
1960				2,800	220	12.7	37,800	2,650	21.8
1965				2,899	230	13.8	64,200	2,750	23.4
				3,050	250	12.2			
				3,410	275	12.4			
				3,685	335	11.0			
1967				2,750	230	11.9			
1970	9,757	635	15.4	3,051	230	13.2	77,000	3,300	23.4
				3,400	250	13.6			
				3,900	280	13.9			
				4,125	330	12.5			
				4,375	350	12.5			
				4,875	370	13.2			
1975				4,325	230	18.8			
				4,850	250	19.4			
				4,860	280	17.4			
				5,915	350	16.9			
				6,600	400	16.5			

Sources: Obtained by telephone from internal company data. Cummins data verified and extended for the period 1965–75 by letter from company officials, 10 April 1975 (see text). Columns 4–6 refer, respectively, to the NH-220 line in 1965, the NHC-250 line in 1970, and the NTC-290 line in 1975. These were chosen by company officials as "most representative."

Note: Blank space indicates data unavailable.

and 72 percent for the three "small engine" indexes included in the PPI, and an incredible 207 percent increase in the one index for a "large" engine.[15] To simplify the discussion, let us deal with small and large engines separately.

Three leading manufacturers of diesel engines were contacted to obtain further information on price movements. To minimize the burden on the respondent, and because the major puzzle regards secular rather than cyclical movements, prices were obtained only for scattered years and not in the form of an annual series. Prices of three engines are displayed in table 11.2. The first engine listed, upgraded from 600 to 635 horsepower, is used primarily in "off-highway" vehicles (e.g., front-end loaders and other construction and mining machinery). The second is for Cummins's truck engines. Prices are for

15. The horsepower specifications of the three "small" indexes in 1957 were 56–75, 120–190, and 147–200 hp. By 1970, the specifications had shifted to 50–99, 101–200, 200–399, and "over 600" hp.

models chosen by company officials as "most representative," and for 1965, 1970, and 1975 it was possible to obtain price quotes for the entire horsepower range of these model designations.[16] The third is the standard locomotive engine sold by the Electro-Motive Division of General Motors, which until the early 1980s was the dominant manufacturer of diesel electric locomotives. This engine, which was gradually upgraded from 1,605 to 3,300 hp between 1950 and 1970, is also widely used in inland marine use (e.g., tow boats on the Ohio River), for standby emergency power generation, and in oil well drilling.

The first of the three indexes, for the 200–300 hp Cummins truck engine, is exhibited in figure 11.3 and appears to be in extremely close agreement with the unit value index for engines below 200 hp. Both series show virtually no change between 1947 and 1970; the price per horsepower of the truck engine was $13.40 in 1947 and $13.20 in 1970 (after reaching a low point of $11.90 between 1965 and 1967). Unfortunately, only three prices were obtained for the 600–635 hp engine, but there also appears to have been no secular change in price per horsepower ($15.40 in both 1955 and 1970). The locomotive engine increased in price per horsepower by 14 percent between 1950 and 1970, far below the 207 percent increase in the PPI for large engines.

Thus, the first answer to our puzzle is that the PPI is simply inconsistent with historical data provided by manufacturers. The secular rate of change of the unit value index for engines below 200 hp is much more consistent with the manufacturer's information than is the PPI, which is based on questionnaires submitted by manufacturers! It seems unlikely that the price behavior of the particular models selected for the PPI questionnaire could be sufficiently different from the particular models in my unofficial survey to account for the discrepancy. The only plausible explanation is that the PPI must price the same model year after year without taking account of the gradual upgrading of horsepower that typically occurs. For example, the Electro-Motive standard locomotive engine, model 567, retained the same basic appearance and model number as it rose in horsepower from 1,650 in 1950 to 2,750 in 1965 (the 1970 quotation is for the new model 645).[17]

16. The Cummins price and horsepower data were originally obtained by telephone in 1972. Company officials reviewed the draft of the 1974 version of this case study, verified the data, and added supplementary data for 1965–75, as shown in table 11.2. This is contained in a letter with attachments from D. L. Clark and J. H. Seltzer of Cummins, 10 April 1975. This is referenced subsequently as the "1975 Cummins letter." The Detroit Diesel Division of General Motors was also contacted but did not provide a specific price series. They did confirm that the Cummins series was consistent with their experience. Robert Lipsey also provided me with the prices of eleven diesel engines in the 90–263 horsepower range for various years within the 1953–64 period. The average 1953–64 price change for the two models available over that span was −4.4 percent, as compared to −14.7 percent for the Cummins price/horsepower ratio for 1951–65 (table 11.2), where the 1965 figure is calculated as the average for all models shown.

17. The exact horsepower figures were obtained in a telephone conversation with H. L. Smith, chief engineer of Electro-Motive, McCook, Ill. Further evidence on price changes for locomotives is provided in chap. 9.

Table 11.3   Dimensions of Quality Improvement in Automotive Diesel Engines, 1931–75

General dimensions of improvement:

1. Since 1945, product line has been through a complete evolution. We are selling completely different products today.

2. While this product evolution occurred, it allowed the trucking industry to upgrade from approximately 150 hp in 1945 to 250 hp in the late 1960s and on to over 300 hp in 1974.

3. With the introduction of turbochargers and improved fuel systems on our products, they now have both higher output and better fuel consumption characteristics.

4. The durability (or life to overhaul) of our products has been increased by nearly a factor of three since 1945. That is, engine life which was below 100,000 miles is now around 300,000 miles.

Examples of specific product evolutions:

1931	"H" series engine (672 cubic inches) introduced. 150 hp at 1,800 rpm.
1944	"HR" series engine (743 cubic inches) introduced. Added fully counterweighted crank and vibration dampers, allowing 2,100 rpm. 180 hp at 2,100 rpm.
1945	"NH" series engine (743 cubic inches) introduced with 4 valve heads versus 2 valve previously. 200–220 hp at 2,100 rpm.
1954	Turbocharged versions introduced allowing increased horsepower. 335 hp at 2,100 rpm.
1954	The "NH" series had its displacement increased to 855 cubic inches. Power range extended to 370 hp at 2,300 rpm.
	New PT fuel system added to product line in the mid-1950s.
1960s	Continuous product evolution extending the life and reliability of products. Includes improved gaskets; cylinder liner designs and materials upgraded; piston designs and materials upgraded; improved piston rings; fillet-hardened crankshafts and improved bearings; alloyed cylinder blocks; improvements in fuel pump and injectors.

Source: Company letter, 10 April 1975 (see text).

Direct evidence that the PPI obtains price quotations for obsolete items and fails to correct for quality change is provided by a manufacturer that is a major source of PPI data in this category. As of 1975, the model priced in the PPI was not the most representative model, but rather the previous line, which was still in production but with diminished market share. The manufacturer concludes that the PPI "does not reflect the dramatic technical improvements in diesel engines" and provides the information contained in table 11.3 as "the primary factors which it [WPI] doesn't account for." In contrast to the 150 percent increase in the PPI registered between 1947 and 1972 for diesel engines, the manufacturing official concludes, "while these improvements [listed in table 11.3] added cost to our product and resulted in dramatic improvement in product performance, cost reductions in other areas and productivity allowed us to hold prices nearly stable."[18] While, strictly speaking, the unit value and the PPI data are for nonautomotive (i.e., nontruck) diesel engines, while the data in table 11.3 are for automotive diesel engines, the manufacturer states explicitly that the same improvements have been applied to nonautomotive diesel engines.

18. All quotes in this paragraph come from the 1975 Cummins letter.

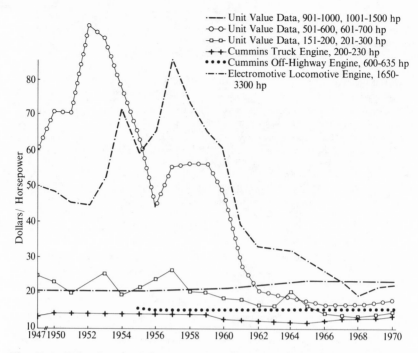

Fig. 11.4   Price data for large diesel engines

However, there is still the remaining puzzle that even if the secular trend of manufacturers' prices corresponds closely to the unit value index for small engines, this leaves unresolved the large discrepancy between the stable manufacturers' prices and the very rapid decline of unit values for large engines. Figure 11.4 illustrates the dramatic narrowing of unit value per horsepower for large and small engines through 1970. Unit values per horsepower are all in the $14–$24 range in the late 1960s but ranged as widely as $22–$100 in 1952. In the late 1960s, the unit values per horsepower of large engines are quite close to the prices per horsepower quoted by manufacturers, but in the early period are several orders of magnitude higher. My hypothesis is that the decline in unit value per horsepower for large engines was due to a shift in product mix at a given horsepower level from large, heavy, slow-speed engines to lighter high-speed engines with a much lower price per horsepower. This could not be treated as a price decline if there was also a shift in the composition of users from those who are limited to low-speed engines (e.g., because of less vibration) to those who can take advantage of high-speed engines. But, on the contrary, I conjecture that the composition of users remained stable, while engineering improvements in the durability and vibration characteristics of high-speed engines made them available to users who formerly had no choice but to buy low-speed engines.

While there are no detailed data on the end-use composition of diesel purchasers, this conjecture is supported in conversations with industry experts. One official, for instance, reports that "the market for tugboat and barge engines was formerly dominated by the large very slow-speed high price-per-horsepower engines of Waukashaw, Sterling, Alco, and others. Then large firms like Cummins came along and adapted their lighter, higher speed engines for these uses and took away the market.[19] Commenting on this quote, a Cummins official responds that his company had made "measurable inroads into this market previously dominated by slow speed engines, but . . . slow-speed diesels still account for approximately 40 percent of this market." Further support is offered by another expert, who reports that locomotive diesel engines are now used in a substantial number of Ohio River barge tow boats.[20]

The hypothesis is also consistent with the history of the technical development of the diesel engine, which has been marked by a steady and continuous reduction in engine weight per horsepower of output, from 250 lb/hp in the early 1930s, to 45 lb/hp in the late 1940s, to 28 lb/hp in 1960 (Rice 1946, 3; Taylor 1962, 14, fig. 3). In the early period, high-speed engines were plagued by vibration, low durability, and high maintenance cost, but these problems were gradually solved: "Prior to 1936 . . . a large part of diesel development was accomplished at the level of the slow-speed or medium-speed diesel. Not until the 1940s did the high-speed diesel receive a full measure of attention" (Rice 1946, 7).

Nor is the hypothesis inconsistent with Kravis and Lipsey's (1971, 16) cross-sectional regressions, which yield a significant positive coefficient on weight when horsepower is held constant. Further verification comes from the fact that Caterpillar price per horsepower ratios for their 1,300 rpm engines are 1.5–2.0 times those for their 2,200 rpm engines at nearly identical horsepower ratings.[21] Clearly, large, heavy engines have always cost more per household than lighter models, and undesirable characteristics of the lighter models have yielded users sufficient utility to lead them to buy the heavier types. But technical advances have steadily reduced these undesirable characteristics and have allowed more and more users to shift from the heavier to the lighter types. As far as these users are concerned, "best-practice" price per horsepower declines dramatically when they are able to make the switch.

A final factor adds plausibility to the declining relative price of large engines and argues against acceptance of the PPI indication that the relative price of large engines has increased. This is the simple fact that the average size of diesel engines more than doubled from 98 hp in 1947 to 205 hp in

19. Telephone conversation with Raymond Prussing of the Pricing Office, Detroit Diesel Division of General Motors, 13 July 1972.

20. Telephone conversation with H. L. Smith, chief engineer of the Electro-Motive Division of General Motors, 8 August 1972.

21. Letter to the author from D. L. Clark and J. H. Seltzer of Cummins, 10 April 1975.

1970.[22] The misleading impression conveyed by the single PPI index for large engines is a particularly dramatic example of the often-cited "new model" problem. The PPI has continued to price as its only large engine a low-speed model, which my hypothesis suggests has become less and less typical of the average large engine sold. As the relative price of low-speed engines has increased, users have shifted from the item priced by the PPI to lower-priced items that are not in the PPI sample.[23]

Many of the product studies in other chapters have concluded by listing dimensions of quality change that could not or have not been taken into account. Here the most important by far is the tripling of durability cited in table 11.3. If we were to redefine the basic unit of quality of automotive diesel engines as the "horsepower mile" instead of plain horsepower, we would conclude that price per unit of quality fell by two-thirds between 1947 and 1970. This seems the clear implication of the evidence gathered in this section, but in the absence of more detailed model-by-model information on durability, I omit any correction for this improvement. Instead, the durability issue is added to numerous other unmeasured dimensions of quality change recorded in previous chapters that stand as evidence that these new durable goods price indexes, no matter how radical they may seem, understate the required extent of correction for quality improvement.

11.6.3   Case Study: Ten-Key Adding Machines

The earlier and more complete version of the study of unit value indexes developed the unit value index for ten-key adding machines displayed in figure 11.5. I have not included this unit value index in the final price index developed in chapter 12, because there is a satisfactory Sears catalog index that can be used in its place. But here the main focus is on unit value indexes. A comparison of the Sears catalog index previously developed in chapter 10 with the unit value index displayed here helps to demonstrate the usefulness of unit value indexes in signaling problems with the PPI.

How can we account for the incredible 6.4 percent annual rate of decline of the unit value index relative to the PPI for ten-key adding machines? One possible problem is the often-cited lag in the introduction of new products in the PPI. There was no separate index for ten-key machines in the PPI until January 1960, and before that date the PPI (and the national accounts) represent all-electric adding machines by an index for the obsolete full-keyboard models, which accounted for only 24 percent of sales in 1960,

22. This fact comes from the size averages implied by the unit value data. The 1975 Cummins letter contains an exhibit showing an increase in average horsepower of diesel engines sold by Cummins from 215 hp in 1962 to 310 hp in 1974.

23. Concluding its review, the 1975 Cummins letter states that, "although working from limited data and understanding of the diesel engine industry, Professor Gordon has drawn fundamentally valid conclusions concerning the 'unit value' trends over the long term."

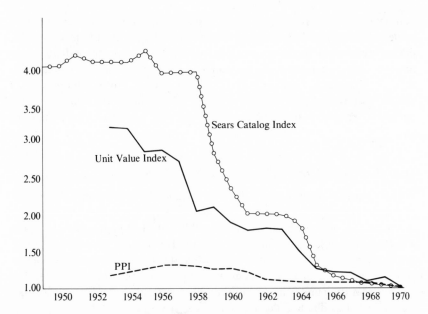

Fig. 11.5   Alternative price indexes for ten-key adding machines, 1970 = 1.0

compared to 76 percent for the ten-key models.[24] Yet this cannot explain the discrepancy, since the unit value/PPI ratio declines by 47.5 percent in the 1966–70 interval when the PPI ten-key index is available, as compared to a 41.5 percent decline in the 1953–60 period.

Chapter 10 demonstrated the usefulness of mail-order catalog price indexes. There we noted that a ten-key electric adding machine with seven digits of display was listed for $285.69 in 1953 and $64.44 in 1970. The only appreciable difference between the two machines was the replacement of metal by plastic casing, which the 1959–60 comparison indicates accounted for no more than $29 of the total $221 drop in price. The catalog index for ten-key adding machines from chapter 10 is displayed in figure 11.5 alongside the unit value and PPI indexes for the same product. The unit value index is strongly confirmed, both in its secular rate of decline and in the timing of the price reductions as concentrated in two episodes, 1957–61 and 1963–65. The major difference is the greater secular rate of decline in the catalog index, perhaps indicating a narrowing of Sears's markup relative to manufacturers' prices, and in the exact timing of the price decline in the 1957–59 interval. Another possibility is that the Sears index accurately measures the true

24. The equivalent sales ratio in 1953 was 54 to 46 in favor of full-keyboard models. The source for these market share data is my file of value-of-shipments data collected for the full unit value study.

transaction price of machines sold by other manufacturers, but that the unit value index declines less in response to an upgrading of the product mix. On the assumption that Sears's prices maintain a rough competitive relation with prices in other retail and wholesale outlets, we can conclude only that the PPI is grossly incorrect as a description of price movements for this product. The unanswered puzzle is the basis of the PPI's information. Perhaps price quotations have been based on the obsolete model with a shrinking share of sales.

11.7   Concluding Evaluation of Unit Value Indexes

The controversy over the use of unit values as a replacement for PPI quotations has developed in two stages. First, the 1961 Stigler report recommended their widespread use and published study papers that contained a few comparisons of unit values and the PPI. The tide was turned by the 1970 Searle report, which recommended against unit values on the grounds that the product mix problem is insurmountable. Previous conclusions of a secular downward drift in unit values relative to PPI quotations in the 1958–63 period were rejected as due to a decline in average size.

The results of this study imply that neither side is correct. Indeed, unit values can be seriously misleading unless explicit size-class information is available for fairly narrow classes. But if this size-class information is available, unit values can serve two useful functions. First, their historical behavior provides valuable information on the importance of deviations between transaction and list prices. Of the eight unit value indexes developed here for products with relatively narrow size cells, convincing evidence of procyclical movements in the ratio of unit values to the corresponding PPI was found only for gasoline and diesel engines. For the other products, the relation did not stand up to detailed scrutiny and testing. This negative finding may be helpful in suggesting that the PPI does *not* understate the cyclical variability of prices, at least for the products studied here. This negative finding would tend to reaffirm previous tests of macroeconomic price rigidity based on official government price indexes.

Second, and more important for this book, marked deviations between the secular rate of growth of unit values and the PPI indexes serve as a "signal" that further research is necessary. In some cases, the PPI may be more accurate and may be confirmed by outside data, and in some cases the unit values may be confirmed. In the two case studies of this chapter, for diesel engines and ten-key adding machines, we have found convincing outside evidence that strongly confirms the behavior of the unit value index and contradicts the behavior of the PPI. It took the outside data to lend credibility to the unit value index; the important function served by unit value data is to pinpoint such areas where further research is likely to have a high benefit-cost ratio.

Remaining unanswered in this chapter is the source of the puzzling behavior of the PPI. The diesel engine case study collected information for the period 1945–75 directly from the dominant manufacturers, which are also the main source of data for the PPI. Their reports deny the validity of the PPI diesel engine index. However, because of confidentiality regulations, there is no way that an outsider can determine the source of the PPI's error. I did make such an attempt in the case of diesel engines, since the evidence reviewed in the case study seems so convincing, and because diesel engines are such an important and basic industrial product. It would have been desirable to examine, for instance, the Cummins questionnaires submitted to the BLS over the period 1947–58, when the PPI states that diesel engine prices doubled, whereas Cummins says they did not change. My request was flatly denied. Further, when I raised the puzzle of the behavior of the PPI for diesel engines with BLS officials, the only information I was able to obtain was the following:

A review of specification changes for diesel engines reported between 1947 and 1970 shows that there were between 12 and 16 major changes for each of the four non-automotive diesel engines priced for the PPI and two for the truck diesel between 1967 and 1970. Most of these changes resulted from changes in model, speed, horsepower, or other physical product changes which required adjustments to the reported price. We have not made an in-depth analysis of the impact of these changes.[25]

25. Letter to the author from W. John Layng, assistant commissioner, Prices and Living Conditions, BLS, 29 November 1977.

IV Weighting Issues and Final Results

12 Weighting the Alternative Data Sources into New Price and Output Measures for Producer and Consumer Durable Equipment

12.1 Introduction

The preceding chapters of this book have developed a large body of new data on the prices of durable goods. On the basis of more than 25,000 new price observations, unduplicated price indexes were constructed for 105 different product categories of producer durable equipment, seventy-five from the Sears catalog (sixty-eight in chap. 10, and the remaining seven in chap. 7), fourteen from *Consumer Reports* (*CR*), eight from unit value data, and eight from other diverse sources. This chapter asks the most important question of all. What does it mean? What is the time series behavior of the deflator for aggregate PDE and for consumer expenditures on durable goods implied by these new data? What are the implications for the growth rate of real investment and the real capital stock in the postwar period? While this chapter describes many of the details involved in aggregating the data, the basic principle is simple. I attempt to use existing NIPA weights for the product categories within PDE, so that differences between the new PDE deflator and the NIPA deflator for PDE will reflect the new data sources but not differences in weighting methods. For individual products within the twenty-two categories of PDE, I adhere tightly to the NIPA weighting scheme (except for the weighting of computers within the office equipment category, as already discussed above in chap. 6). However, to aggregate PDE across the twenty-two categories, the final deflator is based on the Törnqvist method rather than the BEA's implicit deflator method, in light of the undesirable features of the latter also discussed previously in chapter 6. An alternative aggregation of this new information using the implicit deflator method with 1972 and 1982 used as alternative base years is displayed for contrast.

The relatively small share of PDE investment in total GNP immediately enters an important qualification for the discussion of this chapter. No matter how radical the new deflators for producer durable goods may seem, they refer to only a small part of GNP. Even though durable goods prices have increased much less and real investment much more than in the NIPA, this does not imply that the economy-wide inflation rate or real growth rate are significantly biased. Such a conclusion would require a much broader study. A substantial component of consumer spending, the dominant component of GNP, would seem to be immune from the quality adjustment problems that have been the main focus of the book. Price indexes for lettuce, canned fruit, many types of apparel, gasoline, and many other consumer goods are probably quite accurate over the postwar period, if not before. The main questions about consumer spending, other than durables, concern services where there may have been an unmeasured improvement or deterioration. The task of examining consumer services deflators is explored in a separate research project (Baily and Gordon 1988). Pending further evidence, then, I emphasize here that the conclusions of this book should not be taken to apply to any other component of GNP besides durable goods themselves.

Also at this point I should stress the self-imposed limits on the questions asked in this, the final chapter of the book. The aim is to convert the individual product price series into new durable goods deflators. By dividing these new deflators into the existing nominal spending series, a new real investment series is obtained in a straightforward fashion. The resulting real investment series implies new measures of the real capital stock of PDE. In order to expedite publication of these results, I have chosen not to engage in an extensive investigation that uses the new data to redo past studies of the sources of economic growth. As we shall see, the growth rate of the new deflators differs substantially from the NIPA deflators throughout the postwar period, and the implications of these results for the behavior of the investment/output and capital/output ratio are more important than explaining changes in productivity growth from one segment of the postwar era to another.

12.2 Coverage of the Study

12.2.1 Sources of the Official PDE Deflator

The primary focus of this chapter is on the task of weighting together the new product indexes to create a new deflator for PDE. The study has been organized around the twenty-two group categories of PDE, as listed in table 12.1. The basic document from which the study begins is the list, reproduced in Appendix A, of PPIs for individual commodities and groups of commodities used by the BEA in the deflation of PDE. The research agenda was simply to assemble alternative sources of price data for as many of these specific PPIs as possible. When I began the study, the entire PDE deflator in the NIPA was based on components of the PPI, except for three indexes from

Table 12.1 Shares of Covered Products in PDE by Data Source, 1967 Weights

	Shares in Nominal PDE			Weight of Alternative Source by Category					
	1947 (1)	1967 (2)	1983 (3)	Sears Catalog (4)	Consumer Reports (5)	Unit Value (6)	Energy Adjusted (8)	Not Energy Adjusted (8)	Uncovered (9)
Office, computing	4.0	5.9	10.2	31.5	0.0	0.0	0.0	58.2	10.3
Communications	4.6	7.7	11.0	1.7	3.3	0.0	0.0	95.0	0.0
Instruments*	2.6	4.8	7.3	50.7	2.8	0.7	0.0	0.0	55.0
Fabricated metal	3.3	2.6	3.3	60.8	0.0	5.7	24.7	0.0	8.9
Engines, turbines	0.7	1.5	0.6	15.2	0.0	43.6	25.1	0.0	16.1
Metalworking	5.3	8.7	4.3	77.1	0.0	0.0	0.0	0.0	22.9
Special industry*	7.9	6.5	7.3	61.6	15.7	3.0	0.0	0.0	19.7
General industrial	6.6	6.1	5.0	80.1	0.0	0.0	0.0	0.0	19.9
Electric	5.3	5.9	4.0	70.1	0.0	0.0	0.0	0.0	29.9
Trucks, busses*	11.3	9.0	7.3	0.0	0.0	50.0	50.0	0.0	0.0
Automobiles	11.9	8.5	6.7	0.0	0.0	0.0	100.0	0.0	0.0
Aircraft	0.7	4.6	3.7	0.0	0.0	0.0	100.0	0.0	0.0
Ships*	4.0	1.1	7.7	41.6	0.0	26.9	0.0	0.0	31.5
Railroad	4.0	3.3	0.4	0.0	0.0	0.0	100.0	0.0	0.0
Furniture, fixtures	4.6	4.2	4.4	61.2	0.0	0.0	0.0	0.0	38.8
Tractors	3.3	3.1	2.1	8.1	0.0	0.0	0.0	76.5	15.4
Agricultural	4.6	4.1	2.6	54.9	0.0	0.0	0.0	0.0	45.1
Construction	3.3	3.5	2.6	52.3	0.0	0.0	0.0	0.0	47.7
Mining*	1.3	1.1	1.5	52.3	0.0	0.0	0.0	0.0	47.7
Service industry	6.6	3.9	2.5	25.9	51.9	10.0	0.0	0.0	12.2
Electric n.e.c.	1.3	0.9	2.3	26.7	14.3	0.0	0.0	0.0	59.0
Other*	2.7	3.0	3.2	58.1	0.0	0.0	8.8	0.0	33.2
Total	100.0	100.0	100.0	37.6	4.0	6.3	18.5	10.4	23.2

Source: App. B tables.

Note: Categories denoted with an asterisk are not part of the sixteen categories covered by the detailed tables of App. B. Alternative deflators were used in these categories when they matched the PPIs used for the PDE deflator in these categories, or under other special circumstances. See text and app. to chap. 12.

outside sources (the Civil Aeronautics Board—now Department of Transportation—index of aircraft prices, the Maritime Administration index of ship prices, and the AT&T telephone plant index). Other than these three, the PDE deflator is based on a large number of PPIs, 147 on the list in Appendix A, which covers most of the postwar period.[1] This number exaggerates somewhat the variety of independent PPIs included in the PDE deflator, for fifteen of the 147 are PPI group indexes that are averages of individual product indexes that are entered separately, and eleven of the 147 represent an index that appears twice or, in one case, three times in the count. The correct count of independent PPIs in the Appendix A list is 121. When the study was almost completed, I received a more recent exhibit of PPIs used in 1986; the number displayed had fallen from 147 to 121, including duplications and group indexes.[2] The new list also incorporates two additional sources of information beyond the PPIs, the BEA's price index for computer systems discussed in chapter 6 above, and the CPIs for new and used automobiles examined in chapter 8.

Compared to the 121 unduplicated PPIs in Appendix A, this study has compiled 105 independent product indexes. Of these, the fourteen *CR* indexes overlap fourteen Sears catalog indexes for the same product, and I choose only one or the other for use in the final averages, not both, reducing the number of products covered to ninety-one. Nevertheless, the number of products covered is of the same general order of magnitude as in the PDE deflator. To fix terminology for expositional purposes, in the detailed tables of Appendix B and in the description that follows, I call the new indexes the "alternative" series and those presently making up the PDE deflator the "official series"; in this usage, the word *official* refer not only to the individual PPIs but also the small number of additional data sources used in the PDE deflator, including the BEA computer index. The "official" deflator for a category of PDE (say, metalworking machinery) does not necessarily correspond to the PDE deflator for the same category, since both the alternative and the official deflators are averaged only over the subset of products for which we have new data, in contrast to the PDE deflator, which is averaged over all available PPI commodity indexes. The major contribution of the study is the estimated "drift" in the individual alternative/official price index ratios for each product, for each of the twenty-two groups of PDE, and

1. The App. A list exhibits 1967 weights for each PPI. I also have the same list from the BEA, dated 15 August 1977, with the same typed categories and 1967 weights, but with additional weights for 1958, 1963, and 1975 added in handwriting. I infer that this list of PPIs accurately reflects the sources of the PPI deflator for the period 1958–75, if not before. The list in App. A contains 161 indexes. The total of 147 cited in the text excludes the two for steel scrap and the twelve that are used only for quarterly interpolation of the three products for which outside information is available on an annual basis—aircraft, ships, and telephone equipment.

2. This new list, dated 22 February 1988, provides weights for 1986. No use of this new list is made in the present study, both because of its late arrival, and because it does not provide numerical codes for the PPIs.

for PDE as a whole. After discussing these ratios for PDE, I shall compute and discuss alternative/official price index ratios for consumer expenditures on durable goods.

If the number of products covered in this study and in the official PDE deflator is similar, what statement can be made about the number of individual price observations per product in each source? The PPI for machinery, transportation equipment, and instruments included in 1975 a total of 630 commodity indexes at the most disaggregated level, which in turn were based on a total of 1,999 price reports, for an average of 3.2 reports per index (U.S. Executive Office of the President 1977, table II-3). Some subset of these indexes is used in the PDE deflator, but it is difficult to count the size of this subset, since the PPIs included in the PDE deflator are a mixture of six-digit and eight-digit indexes at the detailed commodity level and three- or four-digit indexes that comprise groups of the detailed indexes. Roughly sixty of the indexes in the Appendix A list are at the three- or four-digit level, and the remaining eighty-seven are at the six- and eight-digit level; a rough guess is that the PDE deflator combines information from between half and two-thirds of the underlying detailed indexes in these groups, for, let us say, 1,000–1,300 price reports in 1975. In comparison, my index is based on 769 unduplicated price observations in the same year, for an average of 8.4 observations per unduplicated product index.[3] Earlier in the postwar period, coverage is smaller in both the PPI and the alternative index. There is no ready source of data on PPI coverage for machinery before 1961, although it must be based on many fewer indexes than in 1975 in view of the large number of new PPI categories introduced in 1961 and later years. In a year like 1953, my index is based on 451 unduplicated price observations, for 5.6 observations per product index. The fact that my index is based on substantially more observations per product index than the PPI is somewhat misleading, for the average number of observations per product index is inflated by the large number of yearly observations I have in just a few product categories, particularly in the hedonic price studies of automobiles and appliances. A more representative comparison is between the 3.2 reports per PPI commodity index in 1975 and the 3.3 models per product in our Sears catalog data over the full 1947–83 period.

12.2.2   Coverage by Category of PDE

Table 12.1 provides an overview of the product coverage in the twenty-two NIPA categories of PDE expenditures (these are the categories listed in NIPA

---

3. These figures do not include the fourteen extra products for which *CR* data have been gathered to supplement the Sears catalog indexes. The figures on observations listed in App. B refer to the number of models in the Sears catalog only. In addition are several hundred observations from *CR*. For appliances, the final results are based on the *CR* indexes, and for typewriters, outboard motors, and electric power tools on the catalog indexes. The Sears indexes for appliances and *CR* for the other products serve as a cross-check on the results.

tables 5.6 and 5.7 for nominal and real spending). Columns 1–3 list nominal expenditure shares for each of the twenty-two categories in 1947, 1967, and 1983. Here note the dramatic rise in the importance of office, computing, and accounting machinery (OCAM) on the first line and communications equipment on the second line. The most dramatic declines in shares have been experienced by transportation equipment, including trucks, buses, automobiles, and railroad equipment. Substantial declines are also observed in the shares of tractors and of agricultural, construction, and service-industry equipment. This shift in shares is of considerable importance in assessing the likely bias that might occur in the PDE deflator in years after 1983, the terminal year of this study. The categories with the greatest bias in the PDE deflator, OCAM and communications equipment, have rising nominal expenditure weights, while several categories having small errors, especially autos, tractors, and agricultural equipment, have declining nominal expenditure weights. The presumption that the rate of price increase registered by the PDE deflator after 1983 might be too low applies only with a properly constructed set of Divisia or Törnqvist weights. Any tendency for the PDE deflator to be biased upward after 1983 may be offset by the BEA's use of the implicit deflator method of calculation, which causes price increases to be understated in years after the base year for products with rapidly falling prices, like computers. Below, I shall demonstrate the extreme implications of the implicit deflator weighting system when 1972 instead of 1982 is used as a base year.

In this study, the twenty-two categories fall into two groups. The sixteen primary categories, listed without an asterisk, are those for which at least one new unduplicated source of data has been developed. The execution of the project began with the list of PPI commodity indexes for each of these sixteen categories to determine those products for which an alternative data source could be located, whether in the Sears catalog or somewhere else. Initially, the study relied heavily on unit value indexes, and then made a transition to greater reliance on Sears catalog data. The use of *CR* prices to serve as a cross-check on the Sears catalog results and as a richer source of information on quality change came relatively late in the project. Of the single-product studies for major durable goods, first came the hedonic price studies of autos, tractors, and electric generating equipment, and these were later supplemented by the new primary data and analyses of prices for aircraft, computer systems, telephone transmission and switching equipment, and railroad equipment. Listed across columns 4–9 of table 12.1 are the sources of data divided into five categories, Sears, *CR,* unit value, major product studies with explicit adjustments for energy efficiency, and major product studies without energy efficiency adjustments. The final column (9) shows the share of the weight in each category applied in the PDE deflator to PPIs for which we have no counterpart source of new information.

After all available data had been collected within the feasible time frame of the research for the sixteen primary categories, there remained the problem of what to do about the six remaining secondary categories (marked with an asterisk in table 12.1). One alternative would be to assume that the PDE deflator in those six categories is correct, another would be to apply to those six categories the average annual drift of the alternative deflators for the sixteen primary categories. In the end, the problem answered itself, because a close examination of the PPIs used by the BEA to deflate the six remaining categories revealed the use of numerous duplicate PPIs for which we have corresponding alternative product indexes. For instance, the PDE deflator for the "instruments" category is based in large part on individual PPI commodity indexes for power-driven hand tools, pumps, compressors, electrical direct measurement instruments, and metal commercial furniture, all of which are covered by the alternative data.[4] Similarly, the PDE deflator for the "other" category is based in part on individual PPI commodity indexes for lighting fixtures, metal commercial furniture, motor vehicles, and fire extinguishers. In categories where such duplicate PPIs are not used and where we have no direct evidence, plausible substitutions are made. For trucks and buses, the indexes for autos and for diesel engines are combined with equal weights (recall from chap. 11 that the main evidence supporting the unit value index for diesel engines and conflicting with the PPI came from the leading manufacturer of diesel engines for trucks). For ships and boats, I use the new indexes for products that the BEA employs for the intrayear quarterly interpolation of this category: steam and hot water equipment, pumps, compressors, electrical equipment, and nonautomotive diesel engines. This brings us to two final categories where we have no information and no obvious procedure for making substitutions: special industry machinery and mining-oilfield machinery, comprising together 7.6 percent of nominal PDE in 1967. For the former, I combine the average indexes for metalworking and service-industry machinery, and for the latter I use the index for construction machinery.

For each of the twenty-two categories, columns 4–9 show how the existing 1967 weights are allocated to the different data sources, and to products that are not covered in this study. The bottom line of the table lists the average shares of PDE allocated to the various data sources. The share of PDE that remains uncovered is 23 percent. Of the 77 percent covered share, about half is accounted for by Sears catalog indexes, and for the rest in descending order by major product energy adjusted, major product non-energy adjusted, unit

4. In the Musgrave (1986) capital stock data, the photocopy and instruments categories are combined into one category called "instruments." The NIPA publish separate data on photocopy equipment and instruments. For the photocopy category, the alternative indexes for office machinery other than electronic computers are taken and combined, using Törnqvist weights, with the instruments deflators listed in the text.

value, and *CR* indexes. The industries relying heavily on Sears catalog information are, in order of the shares listed in column 4, general industrial (e.g., pumps and compressors), metalworking, electrical, special industry, and furniture and fixtures. The *CR* indexes used here are mainly for appliances, the dominant product type in the service-industry category, and show up also in the special industry and electric n.e.c. categories. Unit value indexes provide a direct source of data for the engines and turbines and service industry categories (compressors and condensing units), and also for diesel engines in the proxy indexes for trucks, buses, and ships. Finally, the major product data sources dominate the alternative information sources for specific industries. In the energy-adjusted group (col. 7), the new index for electric utility generating equipment is used for both boilers (in the fabricated metal products category) and turbine generators (in the engines and turbines category). The auto index provides all the information for the auto category and half for trucks and buses, while the new indexes for aircraft and railroad equipment are the only source of information for those types of transportation equipment. In the non-energy-adjusted group, by far the most important are the new indexes for computer systems and for telephone transmission and switching equipment. Of much lesser importance are the alternative indexes for tractors.

12.3   The Overall Drift of the Alternative/Official Price Ratios

12.3.1   The Weighting Scheme

Thus far the alternative data have been placed into slots of the matrix displayed in table 12.1. The next step is to weight them together within each of the twenty-two categories, and then across the twenty-two categories. As stated in the introduction to this chapter, the weights should adhere to the present NIPA weights as closely as possible, so differences between the final alternative deflator and the current NIPA PDE deflator primarily reflect the new sources of data, rather than differences in weighting methods.

Within each of the twenty-two categories, the NIPA weights are followed as precisely as possible. The 1967 weights attached to each PPI ingredient of the PDE deflator are displayed in Appendix A, and the BEA has also provided the weights for the same list of PPI ingredients in 1958, 1963, 1975, and 1981. Weights for other years are interpolated linearly between these five years, and are assumed constant before 1958 and after 1981. The weights allocated by the BEA to PPIs for which we do not have alternative data series are set to zero. Details on the choice of weights from the Appendix A list are provided in the notes to the sixteen sets of tables of Appendix B, which list for each product in this study the alternative and official (usually PPI) indexes, the weight assigned for each year to each product within the PDE category, and the number of observations each year on which each "alternative" product index is based. The seventeen sets of tables in Appendix B correspond to the sixteen primary categories of PDE (those listed in table 12.1 without an asterisk) plus the "unit value industry," the aggregate of the unit value indexes developed in chapter 11. Details on the indexes and weights used for the six secondary categories are provided in Appendix C.

The alternative and official product price indexes are combined into deflators for the twenty-two categories by the Törnqvist formula, which applies the average of the current and last year's value weights to the growth rate of each price index between last year and this year. This procedure is repeated for all thirty-six sets of adjacent years, and the resulting weighted average log growth rate of the alternative and official deflators is cumulated into price indexes for each of the twenty-two categories. The resulting alternative and official indexes, as well as the alternative/official ratio, are plotted for the sixteen primary PDE categories in figures 12.1–12.16 in this chapter, and the annual data for these categories are listed as the last table in each numbered section of Appendix B. The indexes for the six secondary categories are not plotted separately, since they are based entirely on the duplication of data series already used in the sixteen primary categories. The annual time series for each of the six secondary categories is listed in the six tables of Appendix C.

12.3.2 Drift in the Alternative/Official Ratios

Table 12.2 provides a summary listing of the annual rate of drift of the alternative/official ratio for all twenty-two categories. Listed in the first

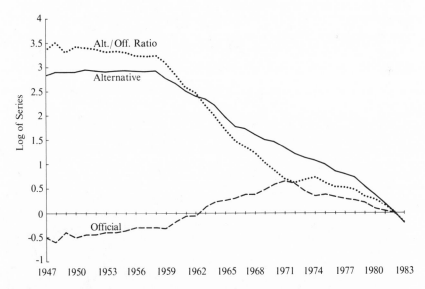

Fig. 12.1 Comparison of Törnqvist price indexes, this study and PPI, office, computing and accounting machinery, 1982 = 1.0

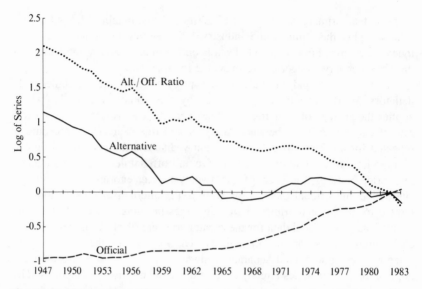

Fig. 12.2   Comparison of Törnqvist price indexes, this study and PPI, communication equipment, 1982 = 1.0

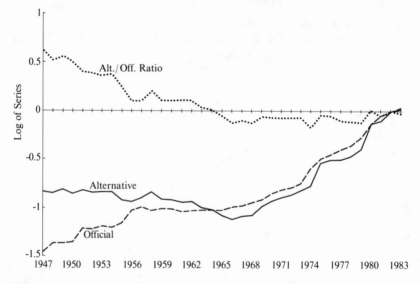

Fig. 12.3   Comparison of Törnqvist price indexes, this study and PPI, fabricated metal products, 1982 = 1.0

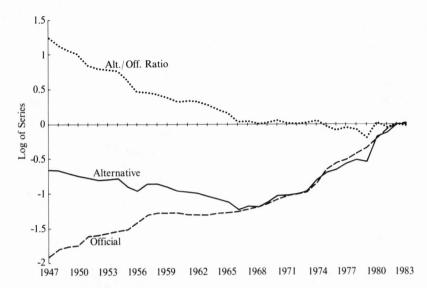

Fig. 12.4   Comparison of Törnqvist price indexes, this study and PPI, engines and turbines, 1982 = 1.0

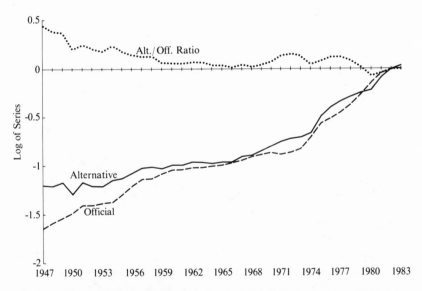

Fig. 12.5   Comparison of Törnqvist price indexes, this study and PPI, metal-working machinery, 1982 = 1.0

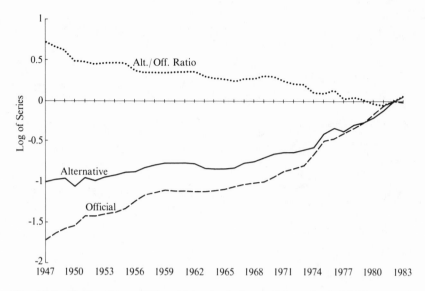

Fig. 12.6   Comparison of Törnqvist price indexes, this study and PPI, general industrial equipment, 1982 = 1.0

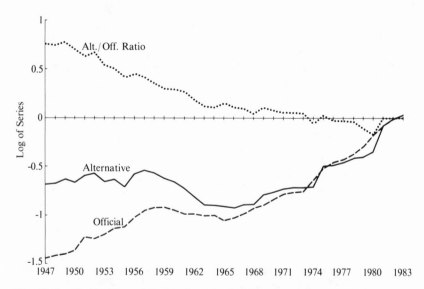

Fig. 12.7   Comparison of Törnqvist price indexes, this study and PPI, electrical transmission, distribution, and industrial apparatus, 1982 = 1.0

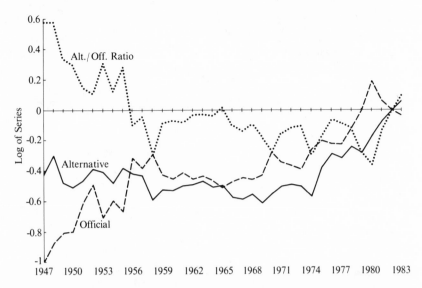

Fig. 12.8   Comparison of Törnqvist price indexes, this study and PPI, autos, 1982 = 1.0

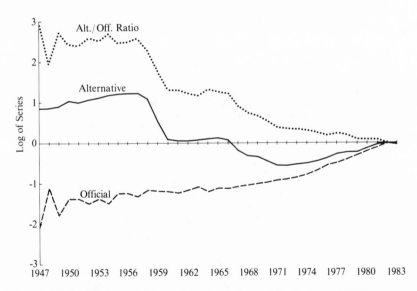

Fig. 12.9   Comparison of Törnqvist price indexes, this study and PPI, aircraft, 1982 = 1.0

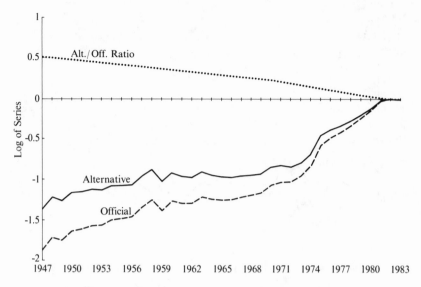

Fig. 12.10   Comparison of Törnqvist price indexes, this study and PPI, railroad equipment, 1982 = 1.0

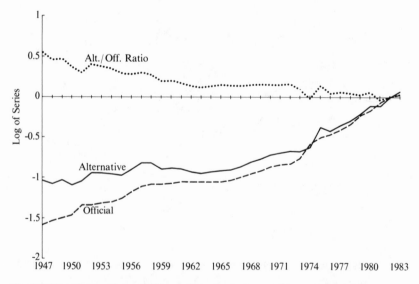

Fig. 12.11   Comparison of Törnqvist price indexes, this study and PPI, furniture and fixtures, 1982 = 1.0

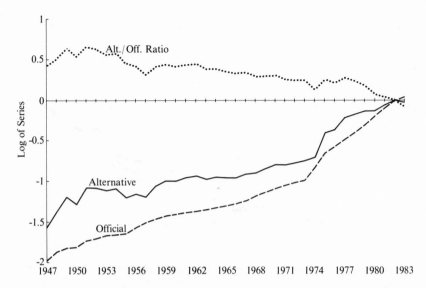

Fig. 12.12   Comparison of Törnqvist price indexes, this study and PPI, tractors, 1982 = 1.0

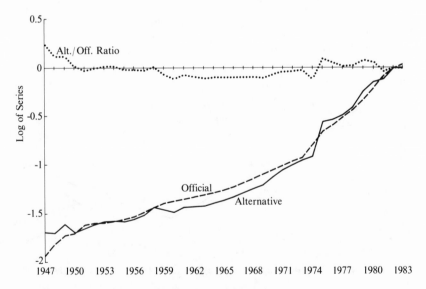

Fig. 12.13   Comparison of Törnqvist price indexes, this study and PPI, agricultural machinery, except tractors, 1982 = 1.0

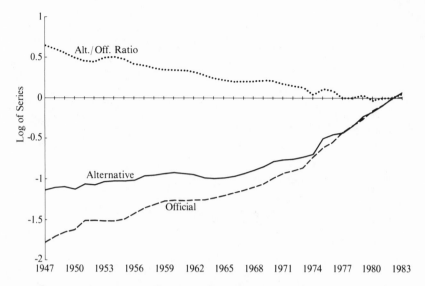

Fig. 12.14   Comparison of Törnqvist price indexes, this study and PPI, construction machinery, except tractors, 1982 = 1.0

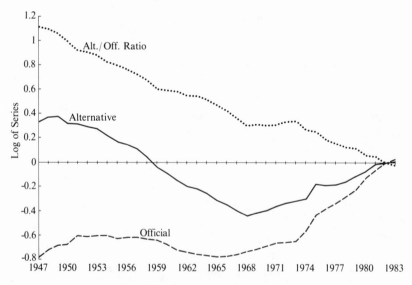

Fig. 12.15   Comparison of Törnqvist price indexes, this study and PPI, service industry machinery, 1982 = 1.0

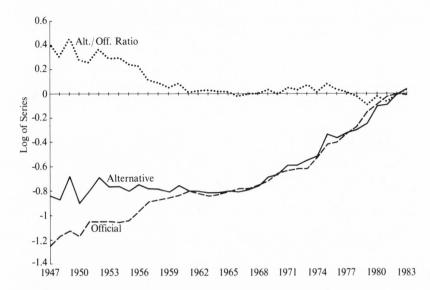

Fig. 12.16   Comparison of Törnqvist price indexes, this study and PPI, electrical equipment, N.E.C., 1982 = 1.0

column is the annual percentage rate of drift for each category over the entire period of data, usually 1947–83, and in the other columns over the three subperiods 1947–60, 1960–73, and 1973–83. At the bottom of table 12.2 is the weighted average drift, calculated by applying the Törnqvist formula to the indexes for each of the twenty-two categories, using annual NIPA nominal investment in each category as weights.

The line in the bottom section of table 12.2 labeled "Törnqvist" is really the bottom line of the whole study. For the full time period 1947–83, the Törnqvist-weighted average of the alternative price series increases at an annual rate fully 3 percent slower than the corresponding official series combined with identical weights. To appreciate the size of this number when compounded over thirty-six years, the 1947 alternative/official ratio calculated with a base year of 1983 = 1.0 is 2.94. Stated another way, the implied alternative price index in 1947 is an index number on a 1983 base almost *triple* the 1947 price index that is calculated for the official data sources with exactly the same weights (but combined with a different weighting formula, the Törnqvist). Across the postwar period, the annual rate of drift is 4.1 percent in the first subperiod, falls to 2.4 percent in the second subperiod, and then falls further to 2.1 percent in the last subperiod.

These results are based on the Törnqvist index number formula to aggregate the PDE deflator over the twenty-two categories of PDE, using NIPA weights to aggregate both the alternative and the official components of the deflator within each of the twenty-two categories. How would the results differ if we

Table 12.2   Drift of the Ratio of Törnqvist Indexes, This Study and Corresponding PPIs, Over Selected Intervals

| | Annual Growth Rates | | | |
NIPA Categories	Full Period of Data (1)	1947–60 (2)	1960–73 (3)	1973–83 (4)
Office, computing, and accounting machinery	−9.32	−3.94	−16.61	−6.83
Communication equipment	−5.84	−8.44	−2.89	−6.28
Instruments, photocopy and related equipment	−3.49	−3.18	−4.21	−2.97
Fabricated metal products	−1.80	−4.08	−1.28	0.49
Engines and turbines	−3.53	−7.16	−2.27	−0.44
Metalworking machinery	−1.15	−3.01	0.58	−0.96
Special industry machinery, n.e.c.	−2.48	−3.70	−1.01	−2.79
General industrial, including materials handling, equipment	−1.81	−2.87	−1.15	−1.29
Electrical transmission, distribution, and industrial apparatus	−2.11	−3.62	−1.89	−0.43
Trucks, buses, and truck trailers	−2.97	−5.74	−2.04	−0.59
Autos	−1.33	−5.02	−0.27	2.09
Aircraft	−8.29	−12.69	−7.48	−3.63
Ships and boats	−1.93	−3.17	−1.11	−1.39
Railroad equipment	−1.45	−1.24	−1.43	−1.76
Furniture and fixtures	−1.41	−2.72	−0.84	−0.46
Tractors	−1.35	−0.05	−1.28	−3.14
Agricultural machinery, except tractors	−0.70	−2.80	0.69	0.21
Construction machinery, except tractors	−1.63	−2.35	−1.63	−0.68
Mining and oilfield machinery	−1.63	−2.35	−1.63	−0.68
Service industry machinery	−3.15	−4.06	−1.91	−3.59
Electrical equipment, n.e.c.	−1.01	−2.56	−0.09	−0.20
Other	−1.99	−3.90	−0.30	−1.69
Total:				
Törnqvist	−2.96	−4.13	−2.44	−2.07
Implicit deflator, 1972 base	−2.90	−3.17	−1.88	−3.87
Implicit deflator, 1982 base	−1.97	−3.12	−1.20	−1.48

Sources: Drifts for the covered categories, App. B "group average" tables at the end of each category. For the uncovered categories, App. C. The total Törnqvist index is computed using NIPA table 5.6. The implicit deflators are computed using NIPA table 5.7.

used the NIPA weighting methodology completely, not just within the twenty-two categories, but also across categories in place of the Törnqvist formula? This would require that we calculate constant-dollar real investment in each of the twenty-two categories in 1982 prices, add up the twenty-two real investment series to form total real investment, and then calculate the implicit deflator on a 1982 base by dividing nominal PDE by this twenty-two-category real investment aggregate in 1982 dollars. To preview results that are discussed further below, the last two rows of table 12.2 display the rates of drift that are implied by the present NIPA weighting methodology, using 1972 and 1982 as alternative base years. The use of a single fixed base year, like 1972 or 1982, tends to underweight industries with declining relative prices (like computers) in years prior to the base year, and to overweight those industries in years after the base year, relative to a weighting formula like the Törnqvist that changes weights each year. This relation comes out clearly in the bottom three rows of table 2.2. While the overall 1947–83 rate of drift is similar using the Törnqvist formula or fixed 1972 weights, the latter method understates the rate of drift before 1973 and overstates it after 1973. Use of a fixed 1982 base year, as in the current NIPA, causes the rate of drift to be understated in all three periods. A subsequent graph displays the alternative and official PDE deflators that are implied by these three different sets of weights.

Having discussed differing methods of aggregation, let us now turn to the fascinating pattern of rates of drift for the twenty-two individual categories of PDE. These display a high variance both across categories and over time. Top ranked for drift is, perhaps not surprisingly, the OCAM category, where three major factors contribute to an enormous annual difference of almost 10 percent between the alternative and the official indexes. First, the BEA has no deflator for computer systems before 1969, so that the full impact of the rapid price decline for computer systems feeds straight through to the drift for OCAM during 1954–69. The rate of drift shown for OCAM in 1947–60 is much less than in 1960–73, simply because computers had a much higher weight within the OCAM category in the more recent period. Second, we have found that the PPI greatly overstates the price increase (or understates the decline) for noncomputer OCAM, particularly for adding machines, calculators, and, more recently, typewriters. Third, the BEA underweights the price change for computers before 1982 (and overweights it after 1982) by applying the implicit deflator methodology within OCAM. This practice, which was severely criticized in chapter 6, leads us to take as the "official" price index in the OCAM category not the Törnqvist-weighted average of the component price indexes but rather the actual BEA implicit deflator for OCAM (this is the only category for which the weights within the category differ from those of the BEA). While the BEA publishes a fixed-weight deflator for OCAM back to 1959, this has no bearing on the measurement of real investment in OCAM or PDE, which relies entirely on the implicit deflator.

The other two categories with extremely rapid rates of drift are communication equipment and aircraft. We saw in chapter 9 that the BEA price index for telephone transmission and switching equipment takes no account at all of the electronic revolution in telephone equipment since the early 1970s, or of the earlier advances in transmission technology. This category mirrors the rate of drift for OCAM, but at a slower rate (except during 1947–60, when computers were much less important than telephone equipment). The aircraft indexes have their greatest drift during 1947–60, mainly reflecting the enormous impact of the transition from production of piston to jet aircraft in 1958–59. The rate of drift is much lower after 1973, but still above the average Törnqvist rate of drift for all PDE.

Many other industries have much slower rates of drift. As we learned in chapter 10, the drift for the ratio of the Sears catalog indexes to the corresponding PPIs tends to be in the range of -1 to -2 percent, and fully thirteen of the twenty-two categories of table 12.2 fall into this range. When categories are ranked by the full-period rate of drift, agricultural equipment takes bottom place, reflecting the flat profile of the catalog/PPI ratio identified in chapter 10. When we count over all sixty-six cells of table 12.2 covering the twenty-two categories for the three subperiods, we find only five positive numbers, implying a more rapid price increase for the alternative than for the official deflator. The largest and doubtless the most interesting is that for automobiles during 1973–83, reflecting the spurious decline in the NIPA automobile deflator during 1980–83 that results from taking a reasonable price index for new cars to deflate new car purchases by business, but then deflating sales of used cars from the business to the household sector with a totally inconsistent deflator for used cars that greatly overstates the rate of price change. Because this used car index enters with a negative weight, it causes the PDE auto deflator to exhibit a spurious decline during 1980–83. Without this error, the rate of drift for autos during 1973–83 would be essentially zero, and the large negative drift for total PDE would be even larger.

While it is not possible to comment on every one of the cells in table 12.2, several other large negative rates of drift can be related to issues that were raised earlier in the book. The rapid annual drift of -7.16 percent for engines and turbines during 1947–60 combines the radical improvements in the efficiency of electric utility generating stations with the mysterious mismeasurement by the PPI of the price of diesel engines discussed in the detailed case study of chapter 11. By the final subperiod, the rate of drift in this category had fallen close to zero. The alternative index for service-industry machinery consists in large part of the *CR* indexes for home appliances, and the rapid rate of drift here after 1973 reflects not just the influence of improved electronics on television sets and microwave ovens, but also the explicit adjustments for improvements in energy efficiency and reliability for several types of appliances. With the exceptions of OCAM, communications equipment, and service-industry equipment, there is a fairly consistent tendency for the rate of drift in the other categories to be largest in the first subperiod, 1947–60. This would be consistent with the straightforward hypothesis that the PPI does a better job of correcting for quality change now than was true thirty-five or forty years ago.

12.3.3 Real PDE Investment by Category

The new set of alternative deflators have startling implications for real PDE investment. The bottom row of table 12.3 shows that the use of the new (''alternative'') set of deflators boosts the annual growth rate of real PDE

Table 12.3   **Average Annual Growth Rates of Real Investment, 1947–83, Applying This
                      Study Alternative and Official Deflators NIPA Investment Series**

NIPA Categories	This Study Real Investment (1)	NIPA Real Investment (2)	Difference (3)
Office, computing, and accounting machinery	18.97	9.65	−9.32
Communication equipment	13.51	7.67	−5.84
Instruments, photocopy and related equipment	11.13	7.63	−3.50
Fabricated metal products	4.95	3.15	−1.80
Engines and turbines	4.46	0.93	−3.53
Metalworking machinery	2.83	1.69	−1.15
Special industry machinery, n.e.c.	2.94	0.46	−2.48
General industrial, including materials handling, equipment	3.50	1.69	−1.81
Electrical transmission, distribution, and industrial apparatus	5.39	3.28	−2.11
Trucks, buses, and truck trailers	5.39	2.42	−2.97
Autos	4.93	3.60	−1.33
Aircraft	15.11	6.81	−8.29
Ships and boats	0.54	−1.39	−1.93
Railroad equipment	−2.07	−3.52	−1.45
Furniture and fixtures	5.00	3.58	−1.41
Tractors	2.74	1.38	−1.35
Agricultural machinery, except tractors	1.98	1.28	−0.70
Construction machinery, except tractors	3.23	1.61	−1.63
Mining and oilfield machinery	3.29	1.66	−1.63
Service industry machinery	5.57	2.41	−3.15
Electrical equipment, n.e.c.	6.28	5.27	−1.01
Other	6.93	4.94	−1.99
Total Törnqvist Constructed PDE	6.15	3.19	2.96

Sources: Column 1: col. 2 minus col. 1 of table 12.2. Column 2: NIPA table 5.7; total PDE includes scrap.
Total Törnqvist constructed PDE uses weights from NIPA table 5.6.

investment by 93 percent, from 3.19 to 6.15 percent per annum. An even
more dramatic contrast occurs when we apply the magic of compound interest
to these annual growth rates. The percentage increase in real PDE investment
between 1947 and 1983 was 815 percent, almost four times the 215 percent
registered by the NIPA.

The growth rates of investment by category display an interesting pattern.
The four highest growth rates in the NIPA data in column 2 are for OCAM,
communication equipment, instruments, and aircraft. These four rank in the
top five in terms of the percentage rate of drift registered in column 3, which
is precisely the rate of drift in column 1 of the previous table, 12.2, with the
sign reversed. In the new data, all four of these categories register double-
digit growth rates of real investment over the entire postwar period through
1983. Leaving aside railroad equipment, with negative growth in real
investment in both the NIPA and the alternative series, the slowest growth rate
of real NIPA investment is for agricultural equipment, and indeed this

category has the smallest drift of the alternative/official price ratio. The appearance of a strong correlation between columns 2 and 3 is confirmed by the following simple regression equation:

$$(12.1) \quad DR_i = 1.10 + 0.48GINIPA_i + \epsilon_i; \quad \bar{R}^2 = 0.38, \text{ S.E.E.} = 1.79,$$
$$[1.88] \quad [3.71]$$

where DR is the set of category drift rates in column 3, GINIPA is the set of NIPA investment growth rates from column 2, ϵ_i is the error term, and t-ratios are in brackets. A reasonable interpretation of this correlation is that official measurement methods make the greatest errors in measuring quality change of producer durable goods in those categories that are already the most dynamic in the official data. For stagnant products like tractor-drawn plows, there is very little quality change to be missed.

12.4   Time Series for the New PDE Deflator and Associated Real PDE Investment

To convert the alternative deflator series into a new deflator for PDE, we must take into account the fact that we leave uncovered about one-quarter of the total weight in the PDE deflator. This uncovered category represents those products where PPIs are used in the PDE deflator for which we have no new source of information. The final PDE deflator is based on the assumption that the drift for the uncovered products is the same as the average drift for the covered products within each of the twenty-two PDE categories. Thus, the drift in communications equipment is not applied to metal-forming equipment, for which we have no information. Instead, I assume that the drift for metal-forming equipment is equal to the average drift for the numerous covered products in the metalworking machinery category. As shown in column 9 of table 12.1, there are no uncovered products and thus no imputations in five of the twenty-two categories: communications equipment, trucks, buses, autos, aircraft, and railroad equipment.

The difference made by coverage is shown in the difference between columns 3 and 4 of table 12.4, where the former column displays the Törnqvist-weighted average of the official price indexes for the covered products, and the latter displays the NIPA PDE deflator in the same twenty-two categories. The 1947–83 growth rate in column 3 is 3.62 percent, somewhat slower than the 4.37 percent growth rate in column 4, indicating that on average the official price indexes for the covered products register lower price increases than for the uncovered products.

The rest of table 12.4 shows the calculation of the new PDE deflator and series on real PDE investment. Nominal NIPA PDE investment in column 1 is the starting point for all the real investment series. The next three columns contrast the alternative deflator for the covered products, the official deflator for the covered products, and the NIPA PDE deflator. The ratio of the

Table 12.4 **Alternative Annual Series for the PDE Deflator and Real PDE Investment, 1947–83 (Törnqvist method, 1982 base)**

		Deflators					Real PDE (1982$)	
	NIPA Nominal PDE (billions) (1)	Alternative Törnqvist (2)	Official Törnqvist (3)	NIPA Implicit Deflator (1982 = 100) (4)	Ratio (2)/(3) (5)	This Study Implied New PDE Deflator (4)*(5) (6)	This Study (1)/(6) (Billions) (7)	NIPA (Billions) (8)
1947	15.3	78.1	27.0	20.6	2.89	59.6	25.7	74.2
1948	17.3	81.1	29.5	22.5	2.75	62.0	27.9	76.9
1949	15.7	79.7	30.9	24.0	2.58	61.9	25.4	65.5
1950	17.8	75.6	31.6	25.0	2.40	59.9	29.7	71.2
1951	19.9	79.5	35.4	26.5	2.25	59.4	33.5	75.2
1952	19.7	80.5	36.1	26.9	2.23	59.9	32.9	73.3
1953	21.5	79.3	35.3	27.7	2.25	62.2	34.6	77.7
1954	20.8	78.4	36.4	28.6	2.15	61.6	33.8	72.7
1955	23.9	78.1	36.7	29.3	2.13	62.3	38.4	81.7
1956	26.3	79.3	41.4	31.0	1.91	59.3	44.4	84.9
1957	28.6	81.2	42.8	33.3	1.90	63.2	45.2	85.9
1958	24.9	78.8	44.2	34.0	1.78	60.6	41.1	73.3
1959	28.3	75.6	43.6	34.6	1.73	60.1	47.1	81.7
1960	29.7	73.9	43.9	35.7	1.69	60.1	49.4	83.3
1961	28.9	72.6	44.2	35.9	1.64	59.0	49.0	80.5
1962	32.1	71.4	43.9	36.1	1.63	58.8	54.6	88.9
1963	34.4	69.6	44.5	36.2	1.56	56.6	60.8	95.1
1964	38.7	68.1	44.8	36.2	1.52	55.0	70.3	107.0
1965	45.8	66.2	44.7	36.4	1.48	54.0	84.9	125.8
1966	53.0	63.9	45.8	37.2	1.40	51.9	102.0	142.4
1967	53.7	64.0	47.2	38.5	1.36	52.2	102.9	139.6
1968	58.5	63.8	48.4	39.9	1.32	52.7	111.1	146.5
1969	65.2	64.6	49.9	41.6	1.29	53.8	121.1	156.8
1970	66.1	66.8	53.0	43.2	1.26	54.5	121.3	152.9
1971	68.7	67.9	54.2	45.5	1.25	57.0	120.5	151.0
1972	78.5	67.6	54.5	46.9	1.24	58.2	134.9	167.5
1973	94.5	67.9	55.0	47.3	1.23	58.4	161.7	199.6
1974	103.6	69.5	60.7	51.1	1.14	58.5	177.1	202.7
1975	106.6	80.2	67.7	59.8	1.19	70.8	150.5	178.4
1976	119.9	81.5	70.1	64.4	1.16	74.9	160.1	186.2
1977	147.4	82.5	72.8	68.3	1.13	77.5	190.1	215.7
1978	178.0	86.1	77.6	73.3	1.11	81.3	218.9	242.8
1979	203.3	86.8	83.6	78.6	1.04	81.6	249.1	258.8
1980	208.9	90.6	91.3	86.0	0.99	85.3	244.8	243.0
1981	230.7	95.7	96.3	93.6	0.99	93.0	248.0	246.4
1982	223.4	100.0	100.0	100.0	1.00	100.0	223.4	223.4
1983	232.8	99.1	99.4	99.5	1.00	99.1	234.8	233.9

Sources: NIPA nominal and real PDE include scrap. Column 1: NIPA table 5.6. Columns 2 and 3: this study. Column 4: NIPA tables 5.6 and 5.7. Column 8: NIPA table 5.7.

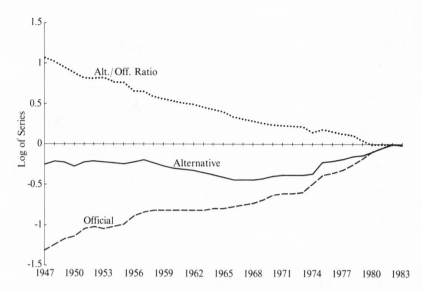

Fig. 12.17   Comparison of Törnqvist price indexes, this study and PPI, 22 categories, 1982 = 1.0

alternative and official deflators in columns 2 and 3 is displayed in column 5, and this ratio with its components is plotted in figure 12.17. There we see the smooth downward movement of the alternative series between 1957 and 1966, followed by a plateau and then inflation during 1975–82. The alternative/official ratio has the zigzag in 1974–75 that we have already identified as the delayed reaction of the Sears catalog prices to the end of price controls, and the ratio also has a sharp plunge in 1956 that is not evident in the Sears catalog index developed in chapter 10.

Returning to table 12.4, the final step is to calculate a new PDE deflator by applying the alternative/official ratio in each of the twenty-two categories to the NIPA PDE deflator in that category, thus imputing to the uncovered items the drift in the covered items within the same category. The resulting new PDE deflator in column 6 rises faster than the alternative deflator in column 2 as the result of the faster inflation already measured by the NIPA for the uncovered items. Finally, the two right-hand columns of table 12.4 list the implied real PDE investment series. That based on the new deflator developed in this study (col. 7) increases at 6.15 percent per annum over 1947–83, as contrasted with 3.19 percent in the official NIPA real PDE investment series. These growth rates are precisely the same as those appearing in the bottom row of table 12.3.

12.4.1   The Folly of the Implicit Deflator Method

Section 6.7.1 discussed the translation of computer prices into a deflator for the OCAM category and noted the defects for this purpose of the implicit deflator methodology, currently used throughout the NIPA to calculate real investment. There are four central flaws of the implicit deflator method. First, by applying the structure of relative prices in the base year to all other years, the method understates the importance of real spending in categories with rapidly falling prices in every year prior to the base year and overstates their importance after the base year. The reverse is true for components with rapidly rising prices. Second, the method relates the prices of each year separately to the base year, so that price changes calculated between adjacent nonbase years are invalid. A bizarre example occurs in the implicit OCAM deflator in the current NIPA, which rises rapidly from 1957 to 1972 even though both its computer and its noncomputer components are declining over this period. Third, the effect of relatively recent products is ignored in long historical comparisons, as in the case of computers; the change in the OCAM deflator between 1957 and 1982 is identical to that of noncomputer products, as if computers had never existed during that interval. Finally, an implication of the first flaw is the fourth, that the growth rate of prices and the resulting real investment series is totally dependent on which year is chosen as the base year. To reflect this sensitivity to the choice of base year, the bottom section of table 12.2 displays the difference in the rates of drift of the alternative and official price indexes made when the implicit deflator methodology is applied with 1972 and 1982 as alternative base years.

Since economists studying long-run growth issues have been using Törnqvist and the related Divisia-type indexes for several decades, at least since the work of Solow (1957) and Jorgenson and Griliches (1967), it is surprising that the U.S. national accounts should be based on such a deficient method of aggregation. The reason that the implicit deflator method has lasted so long is doubtless that, prior to the introduction of a price index for computers, the anomalies introduced by the implicit deflator method were not very important in practice. However, in this study, which yields such widely divergent deflator growth rates for the individual categories of PDE, the use of the Törnqvist approximation to the ideal index number is essential. In this section, I pause briefly to demonstrate the misleading results that would have been obtained if the new numbers had been combined with the implicit deflator method.

Recall that the implicit deflator overstates the importance of components with declining prices in every year after the base year. This phenomenon can be dramatized by choosing 1972 as a base year and recalculating the alternative and official price indexes for the twenty-two categories without the coverage adjustment. The time series for the alternative and official PDE deflators are displayed in figure 12.17 for the Törnqvist method, figure 12.18 for the implicit deflator method with 1972 weights, and figure 12.19 for the implicit deflator method with 1982 weights. In figure 12.18, we see that the alternative deflator would actually have declined from 1972 to 1983 with the implicit deflator method using a 1972 base year, despite the fact that prices in

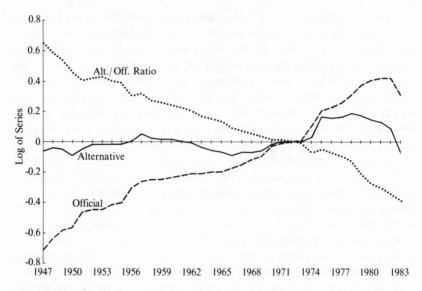

Fig. 12.18   Comparison of implicit price indexes, this study and PPI, 22 categories, 1972 = 1.0

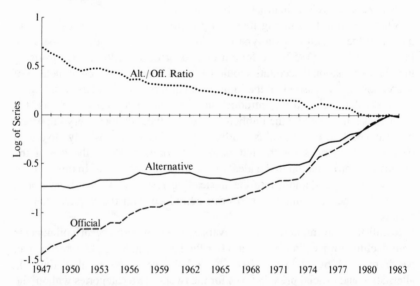

Fig. 12.19   Comparison of implicit price indexes, this study and PPI, 22 categories, 1982 = 1.0

twenty of the twenty-two categories increased over this period, most of them more than doubling. The 1972–83 increase in the implicit deflator would have been only 37 percent even with official price data. Figure 12.19 repeats the same calculation in precisely the same way but switches the base year from 1972 to 1982. With the alternative data, the implicit deflator grows from 1972 to 1983 by 63 percent instead of declining by 7 percent. With the official data, the implicit deflator grows by 94 percent instead of by 37 percent.

Clearly, any implications of this study that the PDE deflator overstates the rate of price increase become increasingly inappropriate the further the present method is extended after the current 1982 base year. Using the 1982 base year, the new PDE deflator shows much less inflation than the official series, whether the Törnqvist or implicit deflator method is used through the end of the study in 1983. For years after 1983, there is no implication that the growth in the PDE deflator is biased upward, and in fact it may be biased downward by an increasingly large amount the further time extends beyond 1982.

12.5 Investment/GNP and Capital Stock/GNP Ratios

One of the longstanding stylized facts about the U.S. economy is the stability of the investment/GNP ratio. As shown in table 12.5, column 4, the NIPA ratio of structures and equipment investment to real GNP was almost identical in 1947 and 1983, with ratios of 11.4 and 11.1 percent, respectively. One of the most important implications of this study is that this stylized fact has been far from the truth for the entire postwar era. The first two columns in table 12.5 contrast the official and the new ratios of PDE investment to GNP. The NIPA ratio remains constant, while the new ratio *triples*. Even though this study does not contain any new results on structures prices or real investment, the ratio of structures plus PDE investment to real GNP doubles when the new data are substituted for the official data.

Even with the Törnqvist method of aggregation, the absolute level of the investment/GNP ratio is sensitive to the choice of base year. With 1982 as a base, as in table 12.5, the investment/GNP ratio is very small in 1947. With 1929 as a base year, the investment/GNP ratio in 1983 would be huge. There is no escape from this inevitable arithmetic as long as we replace the stylized fact of equal growth rates of investment and GNP by the new fact that investment has been growing much faster than GNP. On any arbitrary base year, the investment/GNP ratio will be huge in a distant future year and tiny in a far distant past year.

Because the new data on the investment/GNP ratios overturn standard impressions of the process of economic growth, they raise new issues that will need to be discussed. First among these is the most obvious from a longer historical perspective. If the investment/GNP ratio doubled between 1947–83, what happened in the 100 years prior to that? Is the large quality bias in official price indexes for capital goods a new problem or an age-old problem?

Table 12.5   **Real Investment as a Percentage of GNP, NIPA, and This Study, in Constant 1982 Prices**

| | Equipment | | Structures, NIPA | Total | |
	NIPA (1)	This Study (2)	(3)	NIPA (4)	This Study (5)
1947	6.96	2.58	4.45	11.41	6.22
1948	6.94	2.70	4.55	11.49	6.45
1949	5.91	2.44	4.45	10.35	5.97
1950	5.92	2.62	4.39	10.30	6.22
1951	5.66	2.66	4.25	9.92	6.19
1952	5.31	2.51	4.15	9.46	5.91
1953	5.41	2.53	4.34	9.75	6.05
1954	5.13	2.50	4.58	9.72	6.13
1955	5.47	2.70	4.64	10.11	6.46
1956	5.56	3.05	4.95	10.51	7.12
1957	5.54	3.05	4.85	10.39	7.05
1958	4.76	2.77	4.59	9.35	6.50
1959	5.02	3.00	4.41	9.43	6.70
1960	5.00	3.07	4.57	9.57	6.89
1961	4.71	2.96	4.55	9.26	6.71
1962	4.94	3.13	4.52	9.46	6.93
1963	5.08	3.35	4.36	9.43	7.11
1964	5.42	3.67	4.45	9.88	7.60
1965	6.03	4.19	4.88	10.90	8.55
1966	6.45	4.75	4.89	11.34	9.24
1967	6.15	4.64	4.64	10.79	8.93
1968	6.19	4.80	4.57	10.76	9.07
1969	6.47	5.10	4.66	11.13	9.49
1970	6.33	5.12	4.60	10.93	9.47
1971	6.08	4.94	4.32	10.40	9.04
1972	6.42	5.28	4.20	10.62	9.33
1973	7.27	6.02	4.29	11.56	10.24
1974	7.43	6.60	4.22	11.65	10.78
1975	6.62	5.69	3.81	10.43	9.45
1976	6.59	5.76	3.69	10.28	9.41
1977	7.29	6.51	3.66	10.95	10.20
1978	7.79	7.11	3.83	11.62	10.99
1979	8.11	7.83	4.09	12.20	11.95
1980	7.62	7.69	4.27	11.90	11.96
1981	7.58	7.64	4.58	12.16	12.22
1982	7.06	7.06	4.53	11.58	11.58
1983	7.14	7.16	3.96	11.09	11.12

Sources: GNP for cols. 1, 3, and 4 is NIPA. GNP for cols. 2 and 5 is NIPA with the new PDE and new consumer durables substituted in by straight addition, not by Törnqvist. The numerator of col. 4 is NIPA table 5.7, row 2. The numerator of col. 5 is a Törnqvist of cols. 2 and 3.

More important for the near future, how long will investment continue to grow faster than GNP? Will the rapid growth rate of real equipment investment eventually lift the U.S. economy out of the productivity doldrums? Answers to these questions will require substantial further research, using the results of this book as a point of departure.

12.5.1 Constructing a New Times Series on the Capital Stock

The official BEA data on the fixed reproducible capital stock are constructed by a complex methodology involving the application of Winfrey decay distributions to each disaggregated category of investment. In this study, a shortcut method is used to calculate a new capital stock of PDE for the period 1947–83. Because we have no evidence covering the period before 1947, the new real investment series for 1947–83 must be linked to Musgrave's (1986) official series on flows of real equipment investment prior to 1947. Lacking the detailed Winfrey distributions for each PDE category, I assume a one-hoss shay distribution and estimate the service lifetime implicit in the Musgrave capital stock data. This involves searching through iteration for the implicit service lifetime for a particular category of PDE, which in a particular year is the number of years that investment must remain in the capital stock in order to obtain Musgrave's capital stock for that category of PDE. This approach allows us to calculate the implications of replacing NIPA investment for each category with the alternative series, holding constant the implicit service lifetime of capital in that category for each capital stock series, both that which we construct from the official deflators and the alternative capital stock series which we construct from the new alternative deflators.

The BEA and alternative capital stocks for equipment are shown in columns 1 and 2 of table 12.6 and are combined with the existing BEA series on the capital stock of nonresidential structures in columns 4 and 5. The stocks of equipment and structures are aggregated by the Törnqvist formula, using as weights the nominal gross flow of services, as explained in the notes to table 12.6. Table 12.7 summarizes the annual growth rates of the capital stock over key intervals for equipment using the official and alternative deflators, for the official structures series, and for the aggregate of equipment and structures.

The alternative and official NIPA capital stock growth rates for equipment, that is, PDE, differ by about 3 percent per annum in table 12.7, about the same amount as the difference between the annual growth rates of the alternative and official equipment investment series displayed above in tables 12.3 and 12.4. For the subintervals, the differences in the growth rates of the equipment capital stock are, respectively, 3.06, 3.25, and 2.63 percent per annum. The growth rate of the equipment capital stock differs most, then, in the middle interval (1960–73), in contrast to the growth rate of equipment investment, which differs most in the first period (1947–60). This difference in timing reflects the fact that this study starts only in 1947 and has little effect on the growth rate of the capital stock in the first few years after 1947, when the majority of equipment capital consisted of items purchased before 1947.

Table 12.6   Real Capital Stocks, BEA Wealth Data Base and This Study, Billions 1982 Dollars, and Real Capital Input Index, 1982 = 100

| | Equipment | | | Capital Input Index | |
	This Study (1)	BEA (2)	Structures, BEA (3)	This Study (4)	BEA (5)
1947	190.	548.	1,292.	16.5	29.0
1948	210.	593.	1,302.	17.2	30.0
1949	227.	628.	1,311.	17.9	30.9
1950	250.	669.	1,324.	18.7	31.9
1951	276.	713.	1,340.	19.7	33.1
1952	301.	755.	1,357.	20.6	34.2
1953	327.	799.	1,378.	21.7	35.4
1954	352.	836.	1,401.	22.7	36.5
1955	381.	877.	1,429.	23.8	37.8
1956	413.	919.	1,463.	25.1	39.2
1957	446.	959.	1,496.	26.4	40.5
1958	471.	982.	1,524.	27.4	41.3
1959	503.	1,011.	1,554.	28.7	42.4
1960	536.	1,039.	1,589.	30.0	43.4
1961	568.	1,063.	1,626.	31.3	44.4
1962	605.	1,093.	1,664.	32.8	45.6
1963	647.	1,128.	1,704.	34.4	46.9
1964	695.	1,173.	1,750.	36.2	48.5
1965	756.	1,234.	1,808.	38.6	50.6
1966	833.	1,308.	1,869.	41.4	53.1
1967	908.	1,379.	1,928.	44.1	55.5
1968	992.	1,456.	1,989.	47.0	58.0
1969	1,085.	1,541.	2,055.	50.2	60.8
1970	1,175.	1,620.	2,118.	53.3	63.4
1971	1,263.	1,693.	2,178.	56.2	65.8
1972	1,365.	1,779.	2,237.	59.4	68.5
1973	1,490.	1,892.	2,305.	63.2	71.8
1974	1,625.	2,005.	2,373.	67.2	75.1
1975	1,725.	2,084.	2,429.	70.1	77.5
1976	1,832.	2,166.	2,483.	73.1	79.9
1977	1,968.	2,273.	2,541.	76.8	82.9
1978	2,131.	2,400.	2,609.	81.1	86.4
1979	2,325.	2,539.	2,686.	86.1	90.2
1980	2,510.	2,652.	2,769.	91.0	93.7
1981	2,693.	2,759.	2,865.	96.0	97.2
1982	2,834.	2,834.	2,951.	100.0	100.0
1983	2,986.	2,913.	3,017.	103.9	102.5

Sources: BEA wealth data base, Musgrave (1986). See text for the calculation of col. 1.

The capital input index (col. 4) is obtained by a Törnqvist algorithm weighting the new equipment stock growth rate with the BEA structures stock growth rate. The weights are the respective shares in the gross nominal flow of services, as follows:

$$w_E = [0.15 \times \text{(gross nominal equipment stock)}]/[0.15 \times \text{(gross nominal equipment stock)} + 0.08 \times \text{(gross nominal structures stock)}], \ w_s = 1 - w_E .$$

The same algorithm is applied to obtain col. 5. 0.15 is the sum of the rate of return, 0.05, and the depreciation rate for equipment, 0.10. 0.08 is the sum of the rate of return, 0.05, and the depreciation rate for structures, 0.03.

Table 12.7   Average Annual Growth Rates of Alternative and Official Series for Real Investment, Selected Intervals, 1947–83

Capital Stock Concept	1947–83	1947–60	1960–73	1973–83
NIPA PDE	4.64	4.92	4.61	4.32
Alternative PDE	7.65	7.98	7.86	6.95
NIPA structures	2.36	1.59	2.86	2.69
NIPA total	3.25	2.74	3.60	3.45
Alternative total	4.31	3.66	4.96	4.31

Effects of the new price data on the growth of the capital stock of equipment and structures together are much smaller than for equipment alone, as would be expected in view of the facts that no alternative deflators for structures have been created in this study, and that structures represent well over half the total capital stock. Despite the absence of new evidence on structures, however, this study does have major implications for the behavior of the aggregate capital-output ratio. Table 12.8 exhibits ratios of capital to real GNP in 1982 prices for equipment, structures, and the total of equipment plus structures, using both the alternative equipment deflator and the official NIPA equipment deflators.[5] All columns of table 12.8 define the denominator of the capital/output ratio to be real GNP using the appropriate set of deflators for consumer and producer durables; that is, the real GNP is based on the alternative deflators for durables when compared with the capital stock based on the alternative deflators, whereas the official real GNP measure is compared with the capital stock based on the official deflators for expenditures on durables goods.

In the official data, the capital/output ratio is almost the same in 1947 and 1983, after displaying a substantial decline during 1947–67 and an increase during 1967–83. The capital-output ratio implied by this study is quite different. The increase in the capital-output ratio for equipment between 1947 and 1983 is 406 percent, compared to a much smaller 75 percent in the official data. For the aggregate of structures and equipment, the 1947–83 increase in the capital-output ratio is 44 percent, as contrasted to only 5 percent in the official data.

12.6 Alternative Deflators for Expenditures on Consumer Durable Goods

Although the primary emphasis of this study has been on price indexes for PDE, several of the price indexes can be used in compiling an alternative deflator for consumer durables. No new data have been collected for the

---

5. The official data in tables 12.6 and 12.7 are labeled "BEA" rather than "NIPA," because they are not part of the national income accounts, but rather are created as part of the ongoing BEA capital stock study.

Table 12.8   Real Gross Capital Stocks/Real GNP Ratios, BEA and This Study, in
                  Constant 1982 Prices

	Equipment		Structures, BEA	Total	
	BEA (1)	This Study (2)	(3)	BEA (4)	This Study (5)
1947	0.51	0.19	1.21	1.72	1.27
1948	0.54	0.20	1.17	1.71	1.27
1949	0.57	0.22	1.18	1.75	1.29
1950	0.56	0.22	1.10	1.66	1.23
1951	0.54	0.22	1.01	1.55	1.15
1952	0.55	0.23	0.98	1.53	1.14
1953	0.56	0.24	0.96	1.52	1.14
1954	0.59	0.26	0.99	1.58	1.20
1955	0.59	0.27	0.96	1.54	1.18
1956	0.60	0.28	0.96	1.56	1.21
1957	0.62	0.30	0.96	1.58	1.24
1958	0.64	0.32	0.99	1.63	1.28
1959	0.62	0.32	0.95	1.57	1.25
1960	0.62	0.33	0.95	1.58	1.27
1961	0.62	0.34	0.95	1.57	1.28
1962	0.61	0.35	0.92	1.53	1.26
1963	0.60	0.36	0.91	1.51	1.26
1964	0.59	0.36	0.89	1.48	1.25
1965	0.59	0.37	0.87	1.46	1.25
1966	0.59	0.39	0.85	1.44	1.25
1967	0.61	0.41	0.85	1.46	1.29
1968	0.62	0.43	0.84	1.46	1.30
1969	0.64	0.46	0.85	1.48	1.34
1970	0.67	0.50	0.88	1.55	1.42
1971	0.68	0.52	0.88	1.56	1.44
1972	0.68	0.53	0.86	1.54	1.44
1973	0.69	0.56	0.84	1.53	1.45
1974	0.73	0.61	0.87	1.60	1.53
1975	0.77	0.65	0.90	1.67	1.61
1976	0.77	0.66	0.88	1.64	1.58
1977	0.77	0.67	0.86	1.63	1.57
1978	0.77	0.69	0.84	1.61	1.56
1979	0.80	0.73	0.84	1.64	1.59
1980	0.83	0.79	0.87	1.70	1.67
1981	0.85	0.83	0.88	1.73	1.72
1982	0.90	0.90	0.93	1.83	1.83
1983	0.89	0.91	0.92	1.81	1.83

Sources: See the notes to table 12.5 for the GNP concept used in each column. The numerator of col. 2 is constructed, first by accumulation at the level of each category of the real investments of the BEA wealth data base (Musgrave 1986), using implicit service lives as described in the text, then by aggregation using a Törnqvist with weights being the gross nominal capital stocks. The numerators of cols. 4 and 5 are Törnqvist of equipment stock and structures stock, respectively, BEA and this study. The weights are calculated from the gross nominal capital stocks.

explicit purpose of developing a consumer durables deflator, although copious price data are available in the Sears catalog and in *CR* that could be used in a future study to provide more complete coverage of consumer durables. Here, the findings for consumer durables are based solely on the subset of the PDE price data that already refer to consumer durables, and that were

Table 12.9   **Relative Importance of Covered and Uncovered Categories of Consumer Durables in 1982**

	$ Billions in 1982	Percent
Covered categories:	130.7	51.8
New autos	53.3	21.1
Net purchases of used autos	19.6	7.8
Other motor vehicles	15.6	6.2
Kitchen and other household appliances	17.7	7.0
Radio and television receivers	24.5	9.7
Noncovered categories:	121.8	48.1
Tires, tubes, accessories, and other parts	20.2	8.0
Furniture, including mattresses and bedsprings	21.6	8.5
China, glassware, tableware, and utensils	10.4	4.1
Other durable house furnishings	21.5	8.5
Other	48.1	19.0
Total consumer durables	252.7	99.9

collected to match those components of the official PDE deflator that in fact refer to durable goods purchased by consumers as well as by business firms, including those for automobiles, kitchen and other household appliances, radios, and television sets. Existing official deflators for all other categories of consumer durables are assumed to be correct. Table 12.9 indicates the extent of the covered and noncovered categories of consumer durable expenditures in 1982. As shown in table 12.9, the fraction of 1982 consumer durable expenditures representing goods with new price indexes developed in this study stands at a bit more than half. Because the official NIPA deflators for the other half are assumed to be correct, at least for the purposes of the present computation, it is not surprising to find that the overall annual rate of drift of the alternative deflator relative to the official deflator is much smaller than for PDE.

The alternative price indexes are taken from the detailed product tables in Appendix B. Unlike the alternative PDE deflator discussed earlier in this chapter, which is compiled from NIPA weights within the twenty-two categories of PDE and then aggregated using the Törnqvist formula across the twenty-two categories, here for consumer durables all the component price indexes are aggregated using the Törnqvist method. The required nominal value weights are the retail value of sales of each product, including automobiles, each type of appliance, radio, and television. Details are given in the notes to table 12.10, and the body of that table displays the results. The bottom row exhibits the overall rate of drift for the consumer durables deflator, -1.54 percent per annum over the full 1947–83 period, and respective rates of -2.21, -1.24, and -1.05 percent per year over the three subintervals. In all three of the major subcategories for which we have new information, motor vehicles, appliances, and radio-television, the rate of drift

Table 12.10   Drift of the Ratio of Törnqvist Indexes, This Study and Corresponding NIPA Implicit Deflators for Selected Consumer Durables, 1982 Base—Over Selected Intervals

NIPA Categories	Annual Growth Rates			
	Full Period of Data (1)	1947–60 (2)	1960–73 (3)	1973–83 (4)
1. Motor vehicles and parts	−1.71	−2.39	−1.69	−0.85
2. Furniture and household equipment	−1.79	−2.52	−1.26	−1.55
2.1 Kitchen and other household appliances	−3.22	−4.39	−2.37	−2.83
2.2 Radios and TVs	−5.94	−9.07	−3.77	−4.69
3. Total consumer durables	−1.54	−2.21	−1.24	−1.05

Sources by row: (1) The official index is the implicit deflator for the combined categories of new autos, net purchases of used autos, and other motor vehicles, listed in rows 4, 5, and 6 in table 2.5 of the NIPA. The corresponding alternative index is taken from App. B.8, autos. The alternative and official indexes for the category of tires, tubes, accessories, and other parts are taken to be the implicit deflator for this category. The indexes for the overall category of motor vehicles and parts are Törnqvist indexes of the above two, respectively for the alternative and the official, using weights provided by the corresponding nominal series of NIPA table 2.4. (2) Furniture and household equipment results from a Törnqvist of 2.1, 2.2, and the implicit deflator of the categories listed as rows 9, 11, and 13 of NIPA table 2.5. The weights are from NIPA table 2.4. (2.1) The official index is the implicit deflator from the NIPA for this category. The alternative is a Törnqvist of price indexes for automatic washing machines, clothes dryers, refrigerators, microwave ovens, vacuum cleaners, automatic coffee makers, room air conditioners, and propeller fans as they appear in App. B. The weights are from retail value tables of the *Statistical Abstract of the United States,* various issues, in the listing for home appliances. I used data for 1950, 1955, 1960, 1965, 1970, 1975, 1979, 1981, and 1983, and interpolated to construct complete series of weights. (2.2) The official index is the NIPA implicit deflator for radios, TVs, records, and musical instruments. The alternative is a Törnqvist of the alternative indexes for radios and for TVs listed in App. B, table B.2. Weights are from the *Statistical Abstract of the United States.* (3) Row 3 is a Törnqvist of rows 1, 2, and the implicit deflator for the category other, row 14 of NIPA table 2.5.

Note: NIPA implicit deflators at the level of disaggregation considered include additional items not covered by the alternative indexes of this study. For instance, the alternative index for kitchen and other household appliances does not cover cooking ranges.

is more rapid before 1960 than afterward. For motor vehicles, the rate of drift decelerates further after 1973, while for appliances and radio-television, the rate of drift accelerates in the 1973–83 subinterval as compared to the middle 1960–73 interval. The rate of drift for consumer durables as a whole is quite close to the rate of drift for motor vehicles. The much faster rates of drift for appliances and, particularly, for radio-television are canceled out by the fact that the existing NIPA deflators for fully half of consumer durable expenditures are assumed to be correct.[6]

Table 12.11 converts the alternative deflator for consumer durable spending into a new series for real expenditures on consumer durables. The table is laid

6. The reader will note that there is a negative drift for motor vehicles in table 12.8 for consumer durables in the last subinterval, 1973–83, in contrast to the positive drift of 2.09 percent per annum shown for the PDE auto category in table 12.2 above. This discrepancy reflects entirely the role of the CPI index for used cars, which rises at a spuriously rapid rate due to the absence of quality adjustments, together with the fact that expenditures on used cars enter PDE with a negative weight but consumer durable expenditures with a positive weight.

Table 12.11   **Annual Series for the Consumer Durables Deflator and Real Consumer Durables Expenditures, This Study and NIPA, 1947–83 (Törnqvist method)**

	NIPA Nominal Consumer Durables (billions) (1)	Indexes			Ratio (2)/(3) (5)	Implied Deflator (5)*(4) (6)	Real Consumer Durables (1982 $)	
		Alternative Törnqvist (2)	Official Törnqvist (3)	NIPA Deflator (4)			This Study (1)/(6) (billions) (7)	NIPA (billions) (8)
1947	20.4	66.6	38.3	36.1	1.74	62.7	32.5	56.5
1948	22.9	67.9	39.0	37.1	1.74	64.6	35.4	61.7
1949	25.0	64.5	39.7	36.9	1.63	59.9	41.7	67.8
1950	30.8	63.2	40.4	38.2	1.56	59.7	51.6	80.7
1951	29.9	64.3	41.6	40.0	1.54	61.8	48.4	74.7
1952	29.3	65.1	41.6	40.1	1.56	62.7	46.7	73.0
1953	32.7	63.5	42.4	40.8	1.50	61.1	53.5	80.2
1954	32.1	61.2	40.8	39.4	1.50	59.1	54.3	81.5
1955	38.9	61.5	42.1	40.1	1.46	58.7	66.3	96.9
1956	38.2	61.8	42.5	41.2	1.46	59.9	63.7	92.8
1957	39.7	63.9	44.2	43.0	1.44	62.0	64.0	92.4
1958	37.2	60.8	43.6	42.8	1.39	59.6	62.4	86.9
1959	42.8	60.8	45.5	44.2	1.34	59.0	72.6	96.9
1960	43.5	59.7	45.7	44.4	1.31	58.0	75.0	98.0
1961	41.9	59.8	46.1	44.8	1.30	58.1	72.1	93.6
1962	47.0	59.1	47.0	45.6	1.26	57.4	81.9	103.0
1963	51.8	59.2	47.8	46.3	1.24	57.4	90.2	111.8
1964	56.8	57.9	48.2	47.0	1.20	56.5	100.6	120.8
1965	63.5	57.4	48.4	47.2	1.19	55.9	113.5	134.6
1966	68.5	55.1	48.0	47.4	1.15	54.4	125.9	144.4
1967	70.6	55.5	48.5	48.3	1.14	55.2	127.9	146.2
1968	81.0	56.3	50.5	50.1	1.11	55.9	145.0	161.6
1969	86.2	56.7	51.6	51.4	1.10	56.5	152.7	167.8
1970	85.7	58.8	52.8	52.7	1.11	58.7	145.9	162.5
1971	97.6	60.7	55.0	54.7	1.10	60.4	161.6	178.3
1972	111.2	62.7	55.8	55.5	1.12	62.3	178.6	200.4
1973	124.7	63.1	56.8	56.6	1.11	62.9	198.2	220.3
1974	123.8	66.8	60.2	60.4	1.11	67.0	184.7	204.9
1975	135.4	73.3	65.7	65.9	1.12	73.5	184.2	205.6
1976	161.5	75.8	69.6	69.5	1.09	75.7	213.4	232.3
1977	184.5	77.4	72.8	72.7	1.06	77.2	238.9	253.9
1978	205.6	81.6	77.2	76.9	1.06	81.3	252.9	267.4
1979	219.0	83.0	82.3	82.2	1.01	82.8	264.4	266.5
1980	219.3	90.2	88.8	89.2	1.02	90.6	242.1	245.9
1981	239.9	96.1	95.3	95.7	1.01	96.5	248.7	250.8
1982	252.7	100.0	100.0	100.0	1.00	100.0	252.7	252.7
1983	289.6	102.9	102.8	102.1	1.00	102.3	283.1	283.6

Sources: Column 1: NIPA table 1.1, row 3. Columns 2 and 3: table 12.8 (see sources). Column 4: NIPA tables 1.1 and 1.2, row 3. Column 8: NIPA table 1.2, row 3.

Note: The difference between cols. 3 and 4 is due entirely to the Törnqvist method of aggregation vs. the implicit deflator method.

Table 12.12   Average Annual Growth Rates of Alternative Deflators for Producer and
Consumer Durable Expenditures, Selected Intervals, 1947–83

Interval	Producer Durable Expenditure Deflator	Consumer Durable Expenditure Deflator
1947–83	1.41	1.36
1947–60	0.06	−0.60
1960–73	−0.22	0.62
1973–83	5.29	4.86

out just like table 12.4, which converted the new PDE deflator into a new series on real investment in producer durables. The result is an annual growth rate of real consumer durable expenditures of 6.01 percent with the alternative deflators, in contrast to a growth rate of 4.48 percent for the official NIPA series on real consumer durable expenditures. A particularly interesting conclusion in table 12.11 is the consumer durable deflator implied by the new data, displayed in column 6. As seen in table 12.12, the growth rate of this deflator over the postwar period is remarkably similar to the new PDE deflator from column 6 of table 12.4, despite the fact that the former is based on new price indexes for only eleven products, whereas the latter is based on new price indexes for ninety-one unduplicated products.

In short, the results imply that the average prices of both producer and consumer durable goods were essentially constant from 1947 to 1973 and rose roughly 5 percent per year from 1973 to 1983. In contrast, the official deflators imply that the prices of producer durables rose 50 percent faster than those of consumer durables over the full period (4.37 vs. 2.88 percent per year), that PDE prices more than doubled from 1947 to 1973, and that consumer durable prices increased by 57 percent between 1947 and 1973.

12.7   Implications for Shares of GNP and Sources of Growth

Just as we have found that postwar price changes in producer and consumer durable goods have been much more similar with the alternative deflators than with the official deflators, the same conclusion applies to the shares of durable spending in GNP. A familiar fact in the existing NIPA is that the share of consumer durable expenditures has increased substantially over the postwar period, 63 percent as shown in column 4 of table 12.13. Yet there has been virtually no increase in the NIPA share of PDE in GNP, with an increase in column 2 of only 3 percent. In contrast, the alternative deflators imply much greater 1947–83 increases in both investment shares, 178 percent for producer durables and 164 percent for consumer durables. As was true for the capital/output ratios in table 12.8, the denominator of these investment/output ratios is not NIPA real GNP, but rather that official concept of GNP with the addition of the difference between the alternative and the official real PDE and consumer durable expenditure series.

Table 12.13   Selected GNP Components as a Percentage of Real GNP Adjusted for the
Results of This Study, 1982 Base

	PDE		Consumer Durables		Other Consumption		Other GNP	
	This Study (1)	NIPA (2)	This Study (3)	NIPA (4)	This Study (5)	NIPA (6)	This Study (7)	NIPA (8)
1947	2.58	6.96	3.27	5.30	61.35	57.19	32.78	30.55
1948	2.70	6.94	3.43	5.57	60.00	55.93	33.87	31.57
1949	2.44	5.91	4.00	6.11	60.18	56.59	33.38	31.39
1950	2.62	5.92	4.55	6.70	57.59	54.22	35.24	33.17
1951	2.66	5.66	3.84	5.62	53.48	50.75	40.02	37.97
1952	2.51	5.31	3.56	5.29	53.19	50.62	40.76	38.79
1953	2.53	5.41	3.92	5.59	52.90	50.32	40.65	38.67
1954	2.50	5.13	4.02	5.75	54.90	52.34	38.58	36.77
1955	2.70	5.47	4.67	6.48	54.67	51.96	37.96	36.08
1956	3.05	5.56	4.38	6.08	55.42	52.89	37.15	35.46
1957	3.05	5.54	4.32	5.96	55.82	53.34	36.81	35.17
1958	2.77	4.76	4.21	5.65	57.06	54.96	35.96	34.63
1959	3.00	5.02	4.62	5.95	56.20	54.17	36.17	34.87
1960	3.07	5.00	4.66	5.89	56.41	54.48	35.86	34.64
1961	2.96	4.71	4.36	5.48	56.26	54.52	36.42	35.29
1962	3.13	4.94	4.69	5.72	55.39	53.68	36.78	35.65
1963	3.35	5.08	4.97	5.97	54.84	53.20	36.85	35.76
1964	3.67	5.42	5.25	6.12	54.78	53.20	36.30	35.26
1965	4.19	6.03	5.60	6.45	54.39	52.77	35.81	34.75
1966	4.75	6.45	5.86	6.54	53.72	52.28	35.69	34.74
1967	4.64	6.15	5.77	6.44	53.76	52.46	35.83	34.96
1968	4.80	6.19	6.27	6.83	53.78	52.60	35.15	34.38
1969	5.10	6.47	6.44	6.92	54.33	53.19	34.13	33.42
1970	5.12	6.33	6.16	6.73	56.14	55.02	32.57	31.92
1971	4.94	6.08	6.63	7.18	55.81	54.75	32.61	31.99
1972	5.28	6.42	6.99	7.68	55.66	54.49	32.07	31.40
1973	6.02	7.27	7.38	8.03	54.74	53.55	31.85	31.15
1974	6.60	7.43	6.88	7.51	54.75	53.83	31.77	31.24
1975	5.69	6.62	6.96	7.63	56.93	55.89	30.42	29.86
1976	5.76	6.59	7.67	8.22	56.50	55.60	30.07	29.60
1977	6.51	7.29	8.19	8.58	55.85	55.09	29.44	29.04
1978	7.11	7.79	8.22	8.58	55.04	54.36	29.62	29.26
1979	7.83	8.11	8.31	8.35	54.64	54.44	29.21	29.10
1980	7.69	7.62	7.60	7.72	55.08	55.05	29.63	29.61
1981	7.64	7.58	7.66	7.72	54.60	54.59	30.11	30.11
1982	7.06	7.06	7.98	7.98	56.79	56.79	28.17	28.17
1983	7.16	7.14	8.64	8.65	56.80	56.81	27.39	27.39

Sources: GNP for cols. 2, 4, 6, and 8 is NIPA. GNP for cols. 1, 3, 5, and 7 is adjusted for the new PDE and consumer durables. Columns 1 and 2: table 12.4. Columns 3 and 4: table 12.9. Columns 6 and 8: NIPA table 1.2.

The corollary of the rapid increase in the share of durable goods spending in the new data is, of course, a decline in the share of spending on categories of GNP other than durable goods. This is shown in the right half of Table 12.13. In contrast to the NIPA, in which the share of nondurable consumption falls only by 0.7 percent from 1947 to 1983, in the new data that decline becomes 7.4 percent. The NIPAs already register a substantial 10.3 percent decline in the share of GNP other than PDE and personal consumption expenditures, and this decline becomes 16.4 percent in the new data. In short, durable goods have been the most dynamic component of spending on GNP, and use of the new data to compute new industry productivity measures would indicate that the growth rate of productivity in durable manufacturing has been greatly understated, although by more before 1973 than since 1973.

An important question to ask of the new data is whether they contribute any explanation of the post-1973 productivity growth slowdown in the United States. It seems evident already from the results presented earlier in this chapter that there cannot be a major contribution, simply because the drift of the alternative relative to the official deflators extends over the whole postwar period. The 1947–73 annual rate of drift of the alternative relative to the official deflator (from table 2.1) is 3.3 percent, and a lower 2.1 percent for 1973–83. One would think that a finding of more rapid growth in capital input before 1973 would contribute to the productivity puzzle, since new data showing a greater slowdown in the growth rate of capital input would leave a smaller slowdown in total factor productivity ("Denison's residual").

This presumption, however, ignores the effect of the new deflators for producer and consumer durables on the growth rate of output; since the growth rate of output is increased more prior to 1973 than after, this implication of the new data deepens the productivity puzzle. The balance between the two effects, a greater speedup of the growth of both output and capital input before 1973 than after 1973, depends on the weight assigned to capital input as a source of growth. Unfortunately, existing estimates of capital's share differ widely. One can find weights for fixed capital input ranging from as low as 20 percent (Denison 1985, table G-2 for 1967) to 41 percent (Jorgenson and Griliches 1972, table 20 for 1962). Here, I take a compromise position and exhibit the effect of this study on the sources of growth when an arbitrary capital share of 25 percent is used. The results, displayed in table 12.14, are set out in a format that allows the results to be recalculated easily for any other assumed income share of capital.

Table 12.14 is arranged into five columns, corresponding to the three standard subintervals, the full 1947–83 period, and the extra 1947–73 subinterval that is of interest in discussions of the post-1973 productivity growth slowdown. Comparing columns 3 and 4, we can assess the effect of the new price indexes on the growth of GNP, capital input, the contribution of capital to output growth (using the arbitrary 0.25 weight), and multifactor productivity (MFP), that is, the growth rate of output minus the contributions of capital and labor input. The line labeled "Alternative-NIPA" in the top section indicates that the effect of the new deflators on the growth rate of output is 0.23 percentage points in 1947–73 and 0.26 points in 1973–83, that is, almost exactly the same. The respective figures for capital's contribution to growth are 0.42 and 0.35 points. Using the same series on labor input to compute both alternative and NIPA versions of MFP growth, the new price

Table 12.14   **Effect of Alternative Durable Goods Deflators in Sources of Growth Calculation (annual growth rate over interval)**

	1947–60 (1)	1960–73 (2)	1947–73 (3)	1973–83 (4)	1947–83 (5)
Private GNP:					
Alternative	3.68	4.14	3.91	2.08	3.40
NIPA	3.35	4.02	3.68	1.82	3.17
Alternative—NIPA	0.33	0.12	0.23	0.26	0.23
Capital input:					
Alternative	4.60	5.73	5.17	4.97	5.11
NIPA	3.10	3.87	3.49	3.56	3.51
Alternative—NIPA	1.50	1.86	1.68	1.41	1.60
Capital contribution:[a]					
Alternative	1.15	1.43	1.29	1.24	1.28
NIPA	0.78	0.97	0.87	0.89	0.88
Alternative—NIPA	0.37	0.46	0.42	0.35	0.40
Private business labor hours	0.79	1.93	1.36	1.00	1.26
Labor contribution[b]	0.59	1.45	1.02	0.75	0.95
Multifactor productivity[c]					
Alternative	1.94	1.26	1.60	0.09	1.17
NIPA	1.98	1.60	1.79	0.18	1.34
Alternative—NIPA	−0.04	−0.34	−0.19	−0.09	−0.17

Sources: The difference between alternative and NIPA real GNP is equal to the difference between alternative and NIPA real PDE from table 12.4 and real consumer durable expenditures from table 12.11. Growth rates of alternative and BEA capital stock are from table 12.6. Private business labor hours are from NIPA table 6.11, extrapolated back from 1948 to 1947 by use of full-time equivalent employment from NIPA table 6.7, part A.

[a]Equals capital input times 0.25.

[b]Equals labor input times 0.75.

[c]Equals growth in output minus capital contribution minus labor contribution.

deflators reduce the growth rate of MFP by 0.19 points before 1973 and 0.09 points after 1973. The MFP growth slowdown after 1973 is 1.61 points in the official data and 1.51 points in the new data. Thus, the new data contribute less than one-sixteenth (0.10/1.61) of the needed explanation of the post-1973 productivity growth slowdown.

12.8 Conclusion

This chapter has described the process by which new price series for almost 100 types of PDE have been converted into alternative versions of the PDE deflator, real PDE investment, the consumer durable expenditures deflator, and real expenditures on consumer durable goods. The aggregation process for PDE can be summarized as involving four steps. First, within each of twenty-two PDE categories, the existing weights applied to particular product price indexes (mainly components of the PPI) in the NIPA PDE deflator were used to aggregate both the new product price indexes and the official price indexes with which those new indexes are compared. The NIPA weights applied to uncovered products (i.e., those for which new data is not available) are set to zero at this step.[7] Second, the Törnqvist method rather than the conventional implicit deflator method is used to aggregate alternative and existing official price indexes across the twenty-two categories, using NIPA nominal investment shares in each category as weights. Third, a new deflator for total PDE is calculated by multiplying the alternative/official price ratio for each of the twenty-two categories by the existing PDE deflator. This has the effect of assuming that the ratio of the unobserved alternative price to the official price in the uncovered sector of each category is equal to that ratio for the average of the covered products in the same category. It should be stressed that information on the drift in the alternative/official price ratios is not applied from one category to the uncovered sector of another category. Finally, real investment is calculated by taking the existing NIPA nominal PDE aggregate and dividing by the new PDE deflator.

The final results have radical implications for the price deflator and quantity of PDE. The new PDE deflator rises almost 3 percentage points per annum less than the NIPA PDE deflator, and the annual growth rate of real investment is increased by 93 percent, from 3.2 to 6.2 percent per annum over the thirty-six-year period between 1947 and 1983. The most startling implication of these results is for the ratio of equipment investment to GNP, which almost triples during the postwar period, as compared to rough constancy in the NIPA data. A subset of the new price indexes applies equally well to consumer durable expenditures and is used to replace the official consumer durable deflator for products making up about half of consumer durable spending in 1982. The result is a smaller but still significant reduction in the growth rate of the consumer durable deflator of about 1.5 percent per year, and a corresponding increase in the growth rate of real consumer durable expenditures by the same amount. The study eliminates the differences between the behavior of inflation in producer and consumer durables that is present in the NIPA versions. Over 1947–83 both types of durable expenditures exhibit almost exactly the same rate of price increase in the new data, whereas in the NIPA data the inflation rate for producer durables is about 50 percent faster than for consumer durables. A similar revision is made to NIPA data on shares of durable spending in GNP. In contrast to the official data showing no increase in the share of PDE and a two-thirds increase in the share of consumer durable expenditures, the data imply that the share of both types of durable goods almost triples. Despite the radical nature of these conclusions, they have only minor implications for the puzzling decline in productivity growth since 1973. The 1.61 percentage point deceleration in the annual growth rate of MFP that occurs in the official data is reduced only to 1.51 percent in the new data.

---

7. The distinction between the sixteen primary categories listed in App. B and the six secondary categories for which duplicate indexes were used, as listed in App. C, is not made in this summary. See sec. 12.2 above.

The main questions remaining at the conclusion of this large research project regard the reliability of the findings regarding the PDE deflator. To avoid duplication, the main discussion of possible biases in either direction is contained in chapter 1. The radical difference between the new PDE deflator and the official series reflects both theoretical and methodological innovations. Capital goods are valued by their contribution to a firm's net revenue, that is, gross revenue less operating cost. Two capital goods are equivalent if they earn the same net revenue, in which case they will sell for the same age-adjusted price on the used asset market. This notion implies that an attempt must be made to value not just the change in performance of new models versus old models, but also any changes in energy use and repair costs. Several of the product categories that exhibit the most radical differences between the alternative and the official deflators treat explicitly changes in operating characteristics, particularly the new indexes for electric utility generating equipment and commercial aircraft. An important validation of the basic theoretical approach comes from the market for used aircraft; a price index that compares new and old models with quality relatives established by their subsequent value on the used aircraft market declines even more radically over the postwar period than an alternative index based on an explicit attempt to estimate net revenue. Adjustments for energy use and repair frequency also are applied for most major consumer appliances.

Most of the innovative conclusions of this study stem, however, not from operating efficiency adjustments but from a consistent implementation of current theoretical practice. The BEA already has a price index for computer systems extending back to 1969; this is confirmed with new data and extended back fifteen years earlier. The undesirable effects of the implicit deflator methodology are repaired by aggregating computers with other products using the much superior Törnqvist method, in which weights for aggregation respond each year to changes in value shares, and in which there is no effect of the choice of the base year. The widely accepted principles used by the BEA for computers are extended to communications equipment, the single most important category of PDE. The single largest body of data, however, comes from the Sears catalog and simply involves the application of the standard BLS specification technique, without explicit efficiency or reliability adjustments, carefully and consistently over a long period of time.

The most likely source of downward bias in the resulting durable goods deflator may occur in the process of aggregation. It is, of course, possible, that the PPI makes errors only in measuring the goods covered in this study, and measures all uncovered goods with perfect accuracy. This hypothesis seems implausible on its face when we consider the similarity between many covered goods and those that remain uncovered. An important uncovered area, for instance, consists of large numerically controlled machine tools that incorporate computerized controls and programming. There are probably very large errors in the PPI for these products, which essentially are combinations of computers with traditional machine tools, and yet I impute to omitted machine tools only the relatively small drift between the new index for covered machine tools and the PPI indexes for the same products. Similarly, large-scale agricultural harvesting and construction equipment is uncovered, and I impute only the very small drift in the new indexes for agricultural and construction machinery, with no impact at all allowed to creep into these categories from the PDE categories that exhibit major differences (e.g., computers and aircraft).

Many of the biases that contaminate the new indexes actually work in the direction of causing them to understate the difference with the existing official indexes. Almost every study in this book has ended with a discussion of unmeasured quality change. Lacking data for the prices of photocopying machines, I use the average of the new price indexes for noncomputer office machine products, which fail to take account of the radical improvement in the reliability of photocopying machines over the past several decades.[8] More important, no account is taken of reduced vibration and noise of jet planes, of improved fuel economy of tractors and outboard motors, of longer lifetimes of diesel engines, of additional features on typewriters and calculators that did not exist a decade ago, of improved handling capabilities of automobiles, of better sound quality for radios, and of better picture quality of television sets. While some of these unmeasured quality improvements influence the value of products for consumers, others make producers' equipment more valuable in ways that would raise their value on the market for used assets.

The value of many of these unmeasured quality improvements is difficult to estimate, but at least we know that they all work in the direction of causing the new PDE deflator to understate the extent of quality change. The opposite bias due to coverage gaps and mismatch between the alternative indexes and particular PPI components is speculative, and even its direction is unknown. With the large number of new price series that are introduced here, there is no doubt that experts at the BLS and elsewhere will be able to raise questions about individual products over individual time intervals. But there is no less doubt that the overall impact of unmeasured quality change is substantial and provides a protective "cushion" that lends credibility and value to the final results.

8. A Xerox repairman told me in mid-1988 that, whereas a repair interval of once each 5,000 copies was common "a few years ago," the average interval on the machine in our economics department was once each 40,000 copies, and even newer machines were averaging once each 80,000–100,000 copies.

Appendixes

Appendix A

PPIs and Weights Used for Deflating PDE in the NIPA, 1967 and Earlier Years

Table A.1

PDE Category	PPI Code	PPI Title	1967 Weights (percent)	Proxy Indexes Used for Earlier Years: PPI Code (prior to)
Furniture and fixtures: Household furniture				
	121	Household furniture	100.0	
Other furniture			100.0	
	0821	General millwork	17.3	082 (January 1964)
	1071	Metal doors sash and trim	21.5	
	122	Commercial furniture	61.2	
Fabricated metal products			100.0	
	10320111	Barrels, drums and pails, steel, barrels, 55 gallons	.9	
	1061	Steam and hot water equipment	22.6	
	10720101	Metal tanks, pressure tanks, above ground	6.9	
	10720103	Metal tanks, pressure vessel, 30,000 gallons	24.7	10720101 (January 1962)
	10720112	Metal tanks, bulk storage tanks, 6,000 gallons	2.2	
	10720113	Metal tanks, bulk storage, tanks, 10,000 gallons	1.5	
	10720116	Metal tanks, truck tank	1.4	

(continued)

561

Table A.1 (continued)

PDE Category	PPI Code	PPI Title	1967 Weights (percent)	Proxy Indexes Used for Earlier Years: PPI Code (prior to)
	10720121	Metal tanks, gas cylinder L.P.G.	5.0	
	1073	Sheet metal products	3.3	107 (January 1961)
	10730159	Sheet metal products, grain bin, farm	3.6	107 (January 1962)
	11350127	Cutting tools and accessories, power saw blade, hand	0.7	
	114901	Miscellaneous general purpose equipment, valves and fittings	20.2	
	1163	Woodworking machinery and equipment	1.1	113 (December 1960)
	1190521	Office and store machines and equipment, safes, cabinet type	6.3	
Engines and turbines: Steam engines			100.0	
	117302	Motor generators and generator sets	62.7[a]	117302 (June 1971)
	11703226	Motor generators water wheel driven	37.4	
Internal combustion engines			100.0	
	119401	Internal combustion engines, gasoline engines	33.7	
	119402	Internal combustion engines, outboard motors	25.4	1194 (December 1959)
	119403	Internal combustion engines, diesel engines, other than automotive	39.0	
	11940545	Internal combustion engines, natural gas engines	2.0	1194 (January 1967)
Tractors: Farm			100.0	
	111101	Farm, lawn and garden tractors, wheel type farm	83.8	
	111105	Farm, lawn and garden tractors and equipment	16.2	
Construction			100.0	
	11280104	Tractors, other than farm, off highway diesel, 250–350 hp	30.8	112802 (January 1967)
	11280211	Tractors, other than farm, crawler type diesel, 60–85 net engine hp	9.5	
	11280213	Tractors, other than farm, crawler type, diesel, 90–149 net engine hp	15.8	

Table A.1 (continued)

PDE Category	PPI Code	PPI Title	1967 Weights (percent)	Proxy Indexes Used for Earlier Years: PPI Code (prior to)
	11280215	Tractors, other than farm, crawler type, diesel, 150–199 net engine hp	16.6	
	11280217	Tractors, other than farm crawler type, diesel, 200 and over net engine hp	27.4	
Agricultural machinery (except tractors)			100.0	
	111201	Agricultural machinery excluding tractors, plows	5.6	
	111202	Agricultural machinery excluding tractors, harrows and rotary cutters	10.8	1112 (January 1967)
	111203	Agricultural machinery excluding tractors, planting and fertilizing machines	11.5	
	111204	Agricultural machinery excluding tractors,cultivators	4.6	
	111205	Agricultural machinery excluding tractors, sprayers	2.6	
	111206	Agricultural machinery excluding tractors, harvesting machinery	39.4	
	111207	Agricultural machinery excluding tractors, haying machinery	8.9	
	111208	Agricultural machinery excluding tractors, crop preparation machinery	5.2	1112 (January 1967)
	111209	Agricultural machinery excluding tractors, elevators	2.5	1112 (January1967)
	111301	Agricultural equipment, poultry equipment	3.2	
	111302	Agricultural equipment, barn equipment	5.8	
Construction machinery (except tractors)			100.0	
	1121	Power cranes excavators, and equipment	25.0	
	1122	Construction machinery for mounting	11.0	
	1123	Specialized construction machinery	18.4	

(continued)

Table A.1 (continued)

PDE Category	PPI Code	PPI Title	1967 Weights (percent)	Proxy Indexes Used for Earlier Years: PPI Code (prior to)
	1125	Scrapers and graders	14.9	
	1127	Mixers, pavers, spreaders, etc.	8.2	
	112801	Tractors other than farm, wheel type	8.0	11280213 (December 1963)
	11280218	Tractors other than farm, shovel loader 45–89 hp	2.7	112802 (January 1968)
	11280219	Tractors other than farm, shovel loader 90–129 hp	4.7	112802 (December 1963)
	11280601	Tractors other than farm, tractor loader 1.25 and under 2 cubic yards	7.2	
Mining and oilfield machinery			100.0	
	1191	Oilfield machinery and tools	57.4	
	119201	Mining machinery and equipment, underground	18.8	
	119202	Mining machinery and equipment, crushing, pulverizing and screening	14.5	
	119203	Other mining machinery and equipment	9.3	
Metalworking machinery			100.0	
	113	Metalworking machinery and equipment	45.9	113 (December 1966)
	113201	Power driven hand tools, production line	9.9	
	113202	Power driven hand tools, home utility line	1.9	
	113304	Welding machines and equipment, gas welding	1.6	
	113501	Cutting tools and accessories, small cutting tools	17.9	
	1138	Metal forming machine tools	21.6	113 (January 1967)
	116	Special industry machines and equipment	1.3	113 (January 1961)
Special industry machinery, n.e.c.			100.0	
	1161	Food products machinery	17.7[b]	
	1162	Textile machinery and equipment	15.7[b]	
	1163	Woodworking machinery and equipment	6.4[b]	
	1165	Printing trades machinery and equipment	15.8[b]	
	1166	Other special industry machinery	44.4[b]	

Table A.1 (continued)

PDE Category	PPI Code	PPI Title	1967 Weights (percent)	Proxy Indexes Used for Earlier Years: PPI Code (prior to)
General industrial, including materials handling, equipment			100.0	
	1124	Portable air conditioners	2.6	
	1134	Industrial process furnaces and ovens	12.6	
	114	General purpose machinery and equipment	20.6	
	1141	Pumps, compressors and equipment	17.0	
	1144	Industrial material handling equipment	36.1	
	1147	Fans and blowers, except portable	6.4	
	1161	Food products machinery	4.8	114 (December 1960)
Office, computing, and accounting machinery			100.0	
		Electrical computers	64.5[c]	
	1146	General purpose machines, scales and balances	2.6	
	119301	Office and store machines and equipment, calculating and accounting machines	15.5	
	11930312	Typewriters, electric	8.2	
	11930313	Typewriters, portable, manual	0.5	
	119307	Other office and store machines	8.8	
Service industry machinery			100.0	
	1066	Water heaters, domestic	3.1	
	11320111	Power driven hand tool, sander	4.6	
	1141	Pumps, compressors and equipment	10.0	
	1161	Food products machinery	25.5	average of 124101 (wt. 0.2914) and 124103 (wt. 0.7086) (December 1960)
	119306	Office and store machines, coin operated vending machines	12.2	
	124102	Household appliances, laundry equipment	8.3	
	124103	Household appliances, refrigeration equipment	17.9	

(*continued*)

Table A.1 (continued)

PDE Category	PPI Code	PPI Title	1967 Weights (percent)	Proxy Indexes Used for Earlier Years: PPI Code (prior to)
	12410338	Household appliances, room air conditioners	11.2	
	12410441	Household appliances, dishwasher, undercounter	6.0	124102 (January 1967)
	12430111	Household appliances, vacuum cleaner, canister type	1.2	
Electrical transmission, distribution, and industrial apparatus			100.0	
	113301	Welding machines and equipment, arc welding machines and supplies	4.8	
	113302	Welding machines and equipment, resistance welding machines	2.6	113 (December 1959)
	117201	Electrical (direct measuring) instruments	23.6	
	11730106	Electric motors, fractional hp, A.C., ½ hp	.6	
	1173011	Electric motors, integral hp, 3 hp	1.0	
	11730112	Electric motors, integral hp, 10 hp	1.3	
	11730113	Electric motors, integral hp, A.C., 250 hp	1.6	
	11730119	Electric motors, integral hp, A.C., 50 hp	1.2	1173 (January 1967)
	117302	Generator, and generator sets	5.4	
	1174	Transformers and power regulators	34.4	
	117501	Switchgear, switchboard, etc. equipment, panelboards	5.5	
	117503	Switchgear, switchboard, etc. equipment, circuit breakers	2.9	
	117504	Switchgear, switchboard, etc. equipment, switch gear	10.4	
	117507	Switchgear, switchboard, etc. equipment, industrial controls	4.6	
Communication equipment			100.0	
	10260151	Wire and cable, telephone cable, polyethylene	0.9	1026 (January 1967)
	1171	Electrical machinery and equipment, wiring devices	7.2[d]	

Table A.1 (continued)

PDE Category	PPI Code	PPI Title	1967 Weights (percent)	Proxy Indexes Used for Earlier Years: PPI Code (prior to)
	117210	Integrating and measuring instruments, electrical (device measuring) instruments	7.2[d]	
	1174	Switchgear, switchboard, etc. equipment	50.2[d]	
	117825	Electronic components and accessories, magnetic tape	0.5	117 (January 1969)
	11930633	Office and store machines and equipment, phonograph	1.2	
	125	Home electrical equipment	0.9	
	1252	Home electrical equipment, television receivers	1.0	
	12530102	Home electrical equipment, portable tape recorder	0.2	
		Index of hourly wage of skilled construction labor (ENR)	23.8[d]	
Electric equipment, n.e.c.			100.0	
	1066	Heating equipment, water heaters, domestic	1.1	
	1083	Lighting fixtures	3.2	12450111 (January 1961)
	10830123	Lighting fixtures, commercial or residential incandescent, square recessed	4.2	12450111 (January 1961)
	11710105	Electric machinery, lighting arrester, 9–10 KV	3.3	117 (January 1967)
	117901	Miscellaneous electrical machinery and equipment, storage batteries	16.9	
	11790533	Miscellaneous electrical machinery and equipment, medical X-ray unit	37.3	1179 (January 1968) 117 (December 1960)
	1241	Household appliances, major appliances	8.4	
	12420131	Sewing machines, portable type, with imported head	13.7	
	1243011	Vacuum cleaner, canister type	2.4	
	1244	Household appliance, small electrical appliances	5.9	
	1245	Household appliance, electric lamps	3.7	

(*continued*)

Table A.1 (continued)

PDE Category	PPI Code	PPI Title	1967 Weights (percent)	Proxy Indexes Used for Earlier Years: PPI Code (prior to)
Trucks, buses, and truck trailers			100.0	
	141102	Transportation equipment, motor trucks	99.2	
	141103	Transportation equipment, motor coaches	0.8	
Aircraft			100.0	
	107	Fabricated structural metal products	30.0[e]	
	113	Metalworking machinery and equipment	25.0[e]	
	117	Electrical machinery and equipment	25.0[e]	
	119403	Internal combustion engines, diesel engines, other than automotive	20.0[e]	
Ships and boats			100.0	
	0812	Lumber, hardwood	2.6	
	082	Lumber, millwork	5.3	
	0832	Plywood, hardwood	2.6	
	1061	Heating equipment, steam and hot water equipment	15.8[f]	
	1071	Fabricated structural metal products, metal doors, sash and trim	5.3	
	1072	Fabricated structural metal products, metal doors, sash and trim	15.8	
	1141	General purpose machinery and equipment, pumps, compressors and equipment	15.8[f]	
	117	Electrical machinery and equipment	15.8[f]	
	1194	Internal combustion engines	5.3	
	119403	Internal combustion engines, diesel engines, other than automotive	15.8[f]	
Railroad equipment			100.0	
	144	Railroad equipment	100.0[g]	
Instruments			100.0	
	11320221	Power driven hand tools, single or variable speed	2.5	
	113502	Cutting tools and accessories, precision measuring tools	15.6	

Table A.1 (continued)

PDE Category	PPI Code	PPI Title	1967 Weights (percent)	Proxy Indexes Used for Earlier Years: PPI Code (prior to)
	1141	Pumps, compressors, and equipment	2.3	
	1172	Integrating and measuring instruments	43.5	117201 (January 1967)
	117201	Integrating and measuring instruments, electrical (direct measuring) instruments	6.7	
	1222	Metal commercial furniture	24.2	
	1244	Small electric appliances	5.1	
Photographic equipment			100.0	
	1541	Photographic equipment	100.0	
Miscellaneous equipment			100.0	
	1083	Lighting fixtures	19.7	12450111 (December 1960)
	111211	Agricultural machinery excluding tractors, farm wagons	7.7	1112 (December 1961)
	1222	Metal commercial furniture	4.3	
	1231	Soft surface floor coverings	9.4	
	1266	Lawnmowers	32.2	
	141	Motor vehicles and equipment	9.7	
	1512	Sporting and athletic goods	6.4	
	1593	Musical instruments	10.0	
	1599	Fire extinguishers	1.0	
Scrap			100.0	
	1012	Iron and steel scrap	70.7	
	1023	Nonferrous scrap	29.3	

[a]Used to extrapolate forward from date indicated.

[b]Extrapolated back from December 1960 using previously published PDE deflators for this category (special industry machinery).

[c]Not a PPI; 100.0 for all periods (1986 benchmark revision uses BEA computer index 1969 to date).

[d]For annual deflation, these indexes are replaced by AT&T index.

[e]For annual deflation, these indexes are replaced by Civil Aeronautics Board index.

[f]For annual deflation, these indexes are replaced by Maritime Administration index.

[g]Extrapolated back prior to 1961 using previously published quarterly series.

Appendix B

Detailed Product-by-Product Annual Listing of Alternative and Official Price Indexes (1972 = 1.00)

List of Tables

Table B.1   Comparison of Alternative Price Indexes for PDE with Official Indexes from NIPA, Table 5.6, Row 4, Office, Computing, and Accounting Machinery

A. 10-Key Adding Machines

Year	Sears	PPI	Sears/PPI	Weight	Models
1947	3.28	1.04	3.15	.97	1
1948	3.53	1.12	3.16	.94	1
1949	3.48	1.12	3.12	.94	1
1950	3.48	1.16	3.01	.93	2
1951	3.64	1.27	2.85	.92	2
1952	3.56	1.27	2.79	.70	5
1953	3.53	1.26	2.79	.47	7
1954	3.53	1.32	2.67	.47	5
1955	3.66	1.36	2.68	.46	2
1956	3.40	1.41	2.41	.44	3
1957	3.40	1.44	2.37	.37	6
1958	3.40	1.41	2.41	.29	4
1959	2.57	1.36	1.89	.28	1
1960	2.17	1.37	1.58	.25	1
1961	1.86	1.33	1.40	.21	2
1962	1.86	1.20	1.54	.20	2
1963	1.86	1.20	1.55	.19	2

Table B.1A (continued)

Year	Sears	PPI	Sears/PPI	Weight	Models
1964	1.77	1.18	1.50	.17	2
1965	1.31	1.16	1.13	.14	1
1966	1.16	1.16	1.00	.12	2
1967	1.10	1.16	.95	.11	2
1968	1.05	1.16	.90	.11	3
1969	1.05	1.14	.92	.09	2
1970	1.00	1.09	.92	.07	1
1971	1.00	1.01	.99	.07	2
1972	1.00	1.00	1.00	.07	1
1973	1.09	.96	1.13	.09	2
1974	1.05	.95	1.10	.09	1
1975	1.05	.99	1.06	.09	2
1976	1.04	.94	1.11	.09	2
1977	.95	.91	1.05	.10	1
1978	.88	.91	.96	.10	1
1979	.74	.89	.83	.09	1
1980	.72	.86	.85	.08	1
1981	.70	.85	.82	.08	1
1982	.70	.83	.85	.08	1
1983	.70	.81	.86	.08	1

B. Cash Registers

Year	Sears	PPI	Sears/PPI	Weight	Models
1953	.95	.66	1.44	.47	1
1954	1.01	.67	1.51	.47	1
1955	1.01	.68	1.49	.46	1
1956	1.06	.71	1.51	.44	2
1957	1.06	.73	1.45	.37	2
1958	1.13	.74	1.53	.29	1
1959	1.13	.74	1.52	.28	2
1960	1.16	.74	1.57	.25	1
1961	1.19	.75	1.60	.21	2
1962	1.12	.75	1.49	.20	2
1963	1.10	.76	1.46	.19	1
1964	1.10	.77	1.44	.17	1
1965	1.12	.77	1.46	.14	1
1966	1.05	.78	1.35	.12	1
1967	1.04	.80	1.31	.11	2
1968	1.10	.80	1.37	.11	2
1969	1.09	.82	1.32	.09	1
1970	1.09	.88	1.23	.07	1
1971	1.00	.95	1.06	.07	1
1972	1.00	1.00	1.00	.07	1
1973	1.00	1.08	.92	.09	1
1974	1.00	1.16	.86	.09	1
1975	1.00	1.30	.77	.09	2
1976	1.02	1.19	.86	.09	1
1977	1.04	1.25	.84	.05	1
1978	1.04	1.28	.82	.00	1

(*continued*)

Table B.1 (continued)

C. Manual Typewriters

Year	Sears	PPI	Sears/PPI	Weight	Models
1948	1.19	.73	1.62	.06	2
1949	1.25	.73	1.70	.06	2
1950	1.27	.75	1.69	.06	2
1951	1.32	.77	1.71	.06	3
1952	1.31	.78	1.66	.05	3
1953	1.31	.87	1.51	.03	3
1954	1.37	.92	1.48	.03	3
1955	1.44	.96	1.50	.03	3
1956	1.48	.99	1.50	.03	4
1957	1.45	1.07	1.35	.03	2
1958	1.54	1.12	1.38	.02	5
1959	1.50	1.14	1.32	.02	5
1960	1.38	1.14	1.21	.02	1
1961	1.31	1.07	1.22	.01	2
1962	1.33	1.06	1.25	.01	2
1963	1.31	1.07	1.23	.01	1
1964	1.31	1.06	1.24	.01	3
1965	1.20	1.05	1.14	.01	4
1966	1.16	1.04	1.12	.01	5
1967	1.10	1.04	1.06	.01	2
1968	1.10	1.03	1.07	.01	5
1969	1.08	1.00	1.08	.01	3
1970	1.05	1.00	1.05	.01	3
1971	1.00	.99	1.02	.01	2
1972	1.00	1.00	1.00	.01	2
1973	1.00	1.03	.97	.01	1
1974	1.00	1.11	.90	.01	1
1975	1.20	1.20	1.00	.01	1
1976	1.25	1.25	1.00	.01	3
1977	1.27	1.26	1.00	.01	3
1978	1.30	1.31	.99	.01	3
1979	1.37	1.41	.97	.01	2
1980	1.37	1.46	.94	.01	1
1981	1.37	1.52	.90	.01	2
1982	1.53	1.49	1.03	.01	2
1983	1.52	1.46	1.05	.01	2

D. Electric Typewriters

Year	Sears	PPI	Sears/PPI	Weight	Models
1958	1.63	.85	1.91	.22	0
1959	1.44	.89	1.61	.21	1
1960	1.27	.90	1.41	.20	1
1961	1.11	.90	1.23	.17	1
1962	1.11	.91	1.21	.17	1
1963	1.09	.93	1.16	.17	2
1964	1.07	.94	1.13	.17	2
1965	1.06	.97	1.09	.18	2
1966	.99	.97	1.02	.18	2
1967	1.00	.99	1.01	.17	2
1968	.96	1.00	.96	.16	3

Table B.1D (continued)

Year	Sears	PPI	Sears/PPI	Weight	Models
1969	.99	1.02	.97	.13	3
1970	1.00	1.04	.96	.10	2
1971	1.00	.99	1.01	.09	2
1972	1.00	1.00	1.00	.10	2
1973	1.03	1.04	.99	.12	2
1974	1.05	1.12	.94	.12	2
1975	1.12	1.20	.93	.12	3
1976	1.14	1.22	.94	.12	5
1977	1.23	1.26	.97	.13	4
1978	1.24	1.39	.89	.13	6
1979	1.24	1.48	.84	.13	3
1980	1.37	1.44	.95	.12	2
1981	1.37	1.41	.98	.11	3
1982	1.47	1.40	1.05	.11	5
1983	1.46	1.32	1.11	.11	5

E. Electronic Computing Machines, BEA Deflator for Computer Systems

Year	Hedonic	NIPA	Hedonic/NIPA	Weight	Models
1951	108.85	1.51	71.96	.01	1
1952	70.22	1.51	46.42	.02	1
1953	45.30	1.51	29.95	.03	1
1954	29.22	1.51	19.32	.04	4
1955	23.21	1.51	15.34	.06	6
1956	21.59	1.51	14.27	.08	1
1957	19.75	1.51	13.06	.12	2
1958	17.95	1.51	11.87	.18	9
1959	13.12	1.51	8.68	.21	4
1960	11.30	1.51	7.47	.28	16
1961	8.06	1.51	5.33	.39	20
1962	6.27	1.51	4.14	.42	7
1963	5.51	1.51	3.64	.42	13
1964	4.19	1.51	2.77	.48	9
1965	2.84	1.51	1.88	.52	24
1966	2.08	1.51	1.38	.57	9
1967	1.96	1.51	1.29	.59	9
1968	1.60	1.51	1.06	.61	3
1969	1.33	1.51	.88	.64	9
1970	1.25	1.35	.92	.68	12
1971	1.12	1.16	.96	.71	3
1972	1.00	1.00	1.00	.68	36
1973	.87	.90	.97	.61	6
1974	.82	.71	1.16	.59	12
1975	.77	.65	1.19	.60	21
1976	.63	.57	1.11	.60	16
1977	.58	.49	1.19	.62	34
1978	.53	.41	1.29	.66	86
1979	.42	.36	1.18	.68	71
1980	.33	.29	1.13	.71	66
1981	.25	.26	.96	.73	92
1982	.19	.25	.79	.72	96
1983	.15	.19	.78	.72	107

(continued)

Table B.1 (continued)

F. Electronic Calculators

Year	Sears	PPI	Sears/PPI	Weight	Models
1970	3.29	1.18	2.80	.07	1
1971	2.11	1.20	1.76	.07	2
1972	1.00	1.00	1.00	.07	2
1973	1.00	.99	1.01	.09	6
1974	.84	.85	.99	.09	8
1975	.49	.68	.72	.09	9
1976	.40	.54	.73	.09	11
1977	.34	.48	.70	.10	19
1978	.31	.49	.64	.10	5
1979	.27	.48	.55	.09	6
1980	.26	.48	.55	.08	4
1981	.26	.48	.55	.08	6
1982	.26	.46	.57	.08	7
1983	.24	.45	.54	.08	2

G. Group Average

Year	Alternative	Official	Alternative/Official	Weight	Models
1947	5.14	.98	5.25	1.00	1
1948	5.52	1.05	5.26	1.00	3
1949	5.46	1.05	5.21	1.00	3
1950	5.47	1.09	5.03	1.00	4
1951	5.71	1.19	4.80	1.00	6
1952	5.56	1.19	4.66	1.00	9
1953	5.47	1.19	4.59	1.00	12
1954	5.57	1.23	4.53	1.00	13
1955	5.63	1.26	4.46	1.00	12
1956	5.55	1.30	4.26	1.00	10
1957	5.50	1.34	4.11	1.00	12
1958	5.57	1.33	4.18	1.00	19
1959	4.72	1.33	3.55	1.00	13
1960	4.28	1.34	3.20	1.00	20
1961	3.66	1.33	2.76	1.00	27
1962	3.28	1.31	2.51	1.00	14
1963	3.09	1.31	2.36	1.00	19
1964	2.71	1.31	2.07	1.00	17
1965	2.14	1.31	1.63	1.00	32
1966	1.75	1.32	1.33	1.00	19
1967	1.68	1.33	1.27	1.00	17
1968	1.48	1.33	1.12	1.00	16
1969	1.33	1.34	1.00	1.00	18
1970	1.27	1.25	1.02	1.00	20
1971	1.13	1.12	1.01	1.00	12
1972	1.00	1.00	1.00	1.00	44
1973	.92	.94	.98	1.00	18
1974	.87	.81	1.07	1.00	25
1975	.81	.77	1.04	1.00	38
1976	.70	.69	1.02	1.00	38
1977	.66	.63	1.06	1.00	62
1978	.62	.58	1.08	1.00	102
1979	.51	.53	.98	1.00	83

Table B.1G (continued)

Year	Alternative	Official	Alternative/Official	Weight	Models
1980	.43	.45	.97	1.00	74
1981	.36	.42	.86	1.00	104
1982	.30	.40	.76	1.00	111
1983	.24	.33	.75	1.00	117

Table B.2   **Comparison of Alternative Price Indexes for PDE with Official Indexes from NIPA, Table 5.6, Row 5, Communication Equipment**

A. Telephone Transmission and Switching Equipment

Year	Flamm	BEA	Alternative/BEA	Weight	Models
1947	2.74	.63	4.32	.95	1
1948	2.57	.64	4.02	.95	1
1949	2.41	.63	3.80	.95	1
1950	2.23	.65	3.43	.95	1
1951	2.12	.68	3.12	.95	1
1952	1.99	.66	3.01	.95	2
1953	1.64	.64	2.58	.95	2
1954	1.53	.64	2.38	.95	2
1955	1.45	.65	2.25	.95	2
1956	1.56	.66	2.36	.95	2
1957	1.42	.69	2.05	.95	2
1958	1.19	.71	1.68	.95	2
1959	.97	.71	1.36	.95	2
1960	1.04	.71	1.46	.95	2
1961	1.02	.71	1.43	.95	2
1962	1.08	.71	1.52	.95	2
1963	.95	.72	1.32	.95	2
1964	.95	.73	1.30	.95	4
1965	.79	.74	1.06	.95	4
1966	.80	.75	1.06	.95	4
1967	.77	.78	.98	.95	4
1968	.78	.82	.95	.95	4
1969	.79	.86	.92	.95	4
1970	.85	.90	.94	.95	4
1971	.94	.95	.99	.95	4
1972	1.00	1.00	1.00	.95	7
1973	1.00	1.04	.96	.95	7
1974	1.09	1.14	.96	.95	7
1975	1.10	1.25	.88	.95	7
1976	1.07	1.32	.81	.95	7
1977	1.05	1.37	.77	.95	7
1978	1.05	1.38	.76	.95	7
1979	.96	1.41	.68	.95	7
1980	.83	1.48	.56	.95	7
1981	.86	1.60	.53	.95	7
1982	.89	1.76	.51	.95	7
1983	.76	1.87	.41	.95	4

B. Radio Receivers

Year	Sears	PPI	Sears/PPI	Weight	Models
1947	1.38	1.58	.87	.02	2
1948	1.43	1.64	.87	.02	2
1949	1.28	1.70	.75	.02	4
1950	1.22	1.59	.77	.02	5
1951	1.25	1.53	.82	.02	3
1952	1.25	1.52	.82	.02	5
1953	1.32	1.53	.87	.02	4
1954	1.22	1.45	.84	.02	2
1955	1.29	1.42	.91	.02	2
1956	1.29	1.45	.89	.02	5

Table B.2B (continued)

Year	Sears	PPI	Sears/PPI	Weight	Models
1957	1.29	1.55	.83	.02	4
1958	1.30	1.56	.84	.02	3
1959	1.30	1.46	.89	.02	4
1960	1.29	1.44	.89	.02	3
1961	1.16	1.41	.83	.02	3
1962	1.13	1.40	.81	.02	6
1963	1.07	1.37	.78	.02	4
1964	1.06	1.35	.79	.02	4
1965	.95	1.32	.72	.02	4
1966	.89	1.31	.68	.02	4
1967	.91	1.30	.70	.02	4
1968	.94	1.26	.74	.02	4
1969	.94	1.15	.82	.02	2
1970	.94	1.12	.84	.02	1
1971	.94	1.06	.89	.02	11
1972	1.00	1.00	1.00	.02	15
1973	.83	1.01	.82	.02	6
1974	.83	1.05	.79	.02	2
1975	.73	1.02	.72	.02	4
1976	.66	1.11	.59	.02	2
1977	.64	1.01	.63	.02	5
1978	.64	1.19	.54	.02	3
1979	.61	1.16	.53	.02	3
1980	.65	1.10	.59	.02	4
1981	.66	.99	.67	.02	6
1982	.71	.97	.73	.02	5
1983	.71	.96	.74	.02	2

C. Table Television Sets

Year	*CR*	PPI	*CR*/PPI	Weight	Models
1947	8.37	1.42	5.90	.03	3
1948	7.21	1.48	4.89	.03	3
1949	5.70	1.53	3.73	.03	3
1950	4.23	1.43	2.97	.03	3
1951	3.47	1.37	2.53	.03	3
1952	2.74	1.37	2.00	.03	3
1953	2.37	1.37	1.73	.03	3
1954	2.07	1.31	1.58	.03	2
1955	1.82	1.27	1.43	.03	4
1956	1.91	1.28	1.49	.03	4
1957	2.00	1.29	1.54	.03	6
1958	1.93	1.30	1.49	.03	2
1959	1.89	1.28	1.47	.03	4
1960	1.85	1.27	1.46	.03	4
1961	1.82	1.25	1.45	.03	2
1962	1.72	1.22	1.42	.03	4
1963	1.54	1.19	1.29	.03	4
1964	1.46	1.17	1.25	.03	5
1965	1.34	1.14	1.17	.03	3
1966	1.20	1.12	1.07	.03	3
1967	1.16	1.10	1.05	.03	4
1968	1.15	1.07	1.07	.03	2
1969	1.13	1.02	1.11	.03	2

(continued)

Table B.2C (continued)

Year	CR	PPI	CR/PPI	Weight	Models
1970	1.11	1.01	1.09	.03	3
1971	1.05	1.02	1.03	.03	3
1972	1.00	1.00	1.00	.03	3
1973	.97	.97	.99	.03	3
1974	.96	.98	.98	.03	4
1975	.94	1.02	.92	.03	8
1976	.91	1.01	.91	.03	7
1977	.89	.94	.95	.03	4
1978	.86	.93	.92	.03	2
1979	.83	.95	.88	.03	1
1980	.80	.98	.81	.03	2
1981	.76	.97	.78	.03	4
1982	.73	.95	.77	.03	6
1983	.69	.92	.76	.03	3

D. Group Average

Year	Alternative	Official	Alternative/Official	Weight	Models
1947	2.81	.66	4.25	1.00	6
1948	2.63	.67	3.94	1.00	6
1949	2.45	.66	3.70	1.00	8
1950	2.25	.68	3.33	1.00	9
1951	2.13	.70	3.03	1.00	7
1952	1.99	.69	2.91	1.00	10
1953	1.66	.66	2.50	1.00	9
1954	1.54	.67	2.31	1.00	6
1955	1.46	.67	2.19	1.00	8
1956	1.57	.69	2.28	1.00	11
1957	1.43	.72	2.00	1.00	12
1958	1.21	.73	1.66	1.00	7
1959	1.00	.73	1.36	1.00	10
1960	1.06	.73	1.45	1.00	9
1961	1.04	.73	1.42	1.00	7
1962	1.10	.73	1.50	1.00	12
1963	.97	.74	1.31	1.00	10
1964	.97	.75	1.29	1.00	13
1965	.80	.76	1.06	1.00	11
1966	.81	.77	1.06	1.00	11
1967	.78	.80	.98	1.00	12
1968	.79	.83	.95	1.00	10
1969	.80	.87	.92	1.00	8
1970	.86	.91	.95	1.00	8
1971	.94	.95	.99	1.00	18
1972	1.00	1.00	1.00	1.00	25
1973	.99	1.04	.96	1.00	16
1974	1.08	1.13	.96	1.00	13
1975	1.09	1.23	.88	1.00	19
1976	1.05	1.31	.81	1.00	16
1977	1.04	1.35	.77	1.00	16
1978	1.03	1.36	.76	1.00	12
1979	.94	1.39	.68	1.00	11
1980	.82	1.45	.57	1.00	13
1981	.85	1.57	.54	1.00	17
1982	.88	1.71	.52	1.00	18
1983	.76	1.80	.42	1.00	9

Table B.3   **Comparison of Alternative Price Indexes for PDE with Official Indexes from NIPA, Table 5.6, Row 9, Fabricated Metal Products**

A. Gas Warm Air Furnaces

Year	Sears	PPI	Sears/PPI	Weight	Models
1951	1.06	1.09	.97	.08	2
1952	1.08	1.06	1.02	.08	1
1953	1.12	1.07	1.04	.08	2
1954	1.12	1.05	1.07	.08	3
1955	1.05	1.04	1.01	.07	2
1956	1.14	1.08	1.06	.07	2
1957	1.14	1.08	1.05	.07	2
1958	1.14	1.05	1.09	.07	2
1959	1.07	1.05	1.03	.07	3
1960	1.08	1.01	1.07	.06	3
1961	1.04	.92	1.14	.06	6
1962	.95	.88	1.08	.05	5
1963	.95	.86	1.11	.05	5
1964	.90	.85	1.05	.06	4
1965	.80	.84	.96	.06	4
1966	.81	.85	.96	.06	4
1967	.81	.85	.95	.06	2
1968	.78	.89	.87	.06	2
1969	.82	.91	.91	.06	2
1970	.83	.97	.86	.06	2
1971	.93	.99	.94	.06	2
1972	1.00	1.00	1.00	.06	2
1973	.98	1.01	.97	.06	2
1974	1.01	1.09	.92	.06	2
1975	1.43	1.21	1.18	.06	4
1976	1.47	1.28	1.15	.06	4
1977	1.47	1.35	1.09	.06	4
1978	1.57	1.43	1.09	.05	4
1979	1.75	1.58	1.11	.05	4
1980	1.80	1.78	1.01	.04	4
1981	2.12	1.99	1.07	.05	4
1982	2.05	2.15	.96	.05	4
1983	2.29	2.21	1.04	.05	4

B. Gas Hot Water Heaters

Year	Sears Hedonic	PPI	Hedonic/PPI	Weight	Models
1947	1.34	.90	1.48	.12	2
1948	1.42	.97	1.46	.09	5
1949	1.45	1.04	1.40	.09	5
1950	1.36	1.03	1.33	.08	5
1951	1.54	1.12	1.38	.08	3
1952	1.64	1.10	1.49	.08	3
1953	1.68	1.08	1.56	.08	4
1954	1.44	1.05	1.37	.08	4
1955	1.38	1.06	1.31	.07	7
1956	1.33	1.05	1.27	.07	7
1957	1.34	1.04	1.29	.07	9
1958	1.25	.99	1.26	.07	6
1959	1.15	.97	1.19	.07	8

(continued)

Table B.3B (continued)

Year	Sears Hedonic	PPI	Hedonic/PPI	Weight	Models
1960	1.13	.89	1.28	.06	8
1961	1.05	.81	1.29	.06	8
1962	.96	.80	1.19	.05	6
1963	.96	.82	1.16	.05	6
1964	.94	.80	1.18	.06	6
1965	.87	.80	1.08	.06	4
1966	.89	.82	1.09	.06	6
1967	.87	.80	1.08	.06	6
1968	.82	.81	1.02	.06	10
1969	.89	.84	1.06	.06	11
1970	.90	.91	.99	.06	11
1971	1.00	.95	1.05	.06	12
1972	1.00	1.00	1.00	.06	12
1973	1.01	1.02	.99	.06	11
1974	1.00	1.06	.95	.06	11
1975	1.24	1.22	1.02	.06	13
1976	1.35	1.40	.96	.06	14
1977	1.49	1.43	1.04	.06	20
1978	1.55	1.49	1.04	.05	25
1979	1.71	1.61	1.06	.05	20
1980	1.72	1.76	.98	.04	24
1981	1.72	1.86	.92	.05	19
1982	1.72	1.99	.86	.05	28
1983	1.75	2.08	.84	.05	29

C. Water Storage Tanks

Year	Sears	PPI	Sears/PPI	Weight	Models
1948	.61	.79	.77	.16	1
1949	.71	.74	.95	.16	2
1950	.67	.73	.92	.15	2
1951	.85	.80	1.06	.14	2
1952	.81	.80	1.01	.14	1
1953	.77	.81	.95	.14	2
1954	.74	.76	.97	.14	2
1955	.71	.80	.88	.14	2
1956	.71	.95	.74	.14	2
1957	.71	.99	.71	.14	2
1958	.74	.93	.80	.14	2
1959	.73	.95	.76	.15	3
1960	.79	.94	.84	.15	3
1961	.77	.92	.84	.16	4
1962	.83	.91	.90	.17	2
1963	.83	.90	.91	.17	2
1964	.87	.90	.97	.16	2
1965	.87	.89	.98	.16	4
1966	.89	.89	1.00	.14	4
1967	.90	.89	1.01	.13	4
1968	.97	.89	1.09	.13	4
1969	1.03	.89	1.16	.13	4
1970	1.00	.92	1.09	.13	5
1971	1.00	.95	1.06	.13	5
1972	1.00	1.00	1.00	.13	4

Table B.3C (continued)

Year	Sears	PPI	Sears/PPI	Weight	Models
1973	1.00	1.08	.93	.13	3
1974	1.05	1.36	.77	.14	3
1975	1.31	1.62	.81	.14	4
1976	1.39	1.62	.86	.13	4
1977	1.36	1.72	.79	.13	4
1978	1.45	1.84	.79	.12	4
1979	1.51	1.96	.77	.11	4
1980	1.76	2.42	.73	.10	3
1981	2.00	2.71	.74	.12	3
1982	2.25	2.78	.81	.14	4
1983	2.28	2.72	.84	.14	4

D. Steam Boilers for Electricity Generation

Year	Hedonic	PPI	Hedonic/PPI	Weight	Models
1948	3.15	.68	4.66	.30	14
1949	2.92	.64	4.59	.30	6
1950	2.70	.62	4.33	.29	9
1951	2.22	.68	3.25	.28	12
1952	1.84	.68	2.69	.28	5
1953	1.84	.69	2.67	.28	12
1954	1.84	.65	2.82	.27	10
1955	1.43	.69	2.08	.26	4
1956	1.11	.81	1.37	.26	5
1957	1.31	.85	1.55	.26	10
1958	1.55	.79	1.96	.27	7
1959	1.39	.81	1.71	.27	6
1960	1.25	.80	1.56	.27	7
1961	1.19	.78	1.53	.27	2
1962	1.14	.78	1.46	.27	8
1963	1.05	.79	1.33	.28	8
1964	.97	.79	1.22	.31	6
1965	.79	.80	.98	.33	8
1966	.64	.81	.79	.32	3
1967	.64	.82	.78	.30	7
1968	.64	.83	.77	.28	5
1969	.78	.86	.90	.27	3
1970	.94	.92	1.02	.26	11
1971	.97	.98	.99	.24	10
1972	1.00	1.00	1.00	.22	5
1973	1.18	1.08	1.10	.21	6
1974	1.40	1.19	1.18	.20	12
1975	1.60	1.31	1.22	.21	6
1976	1.83	1.45	1.26	.22	6
1977	1.78	1.59	1.12	.23	1
1978	1.74	1.62	1.07	.23	7
1979	1.39	1.72	.80	.24	7
1980	3.28	2.15	1.53	.24	10
1981	3.41	2.59	1.32	.12	5
1982	3.54	2.76	1.28	.00	6

(*continued*)

Table B.3 (continued)

E. Brass Gate Valves

Year	Sears	PPI	Sears/PPI	Weight	Models
1947	.57	.33	1.73	.30	2
1948	.52	.34	1.54	.21	2
1949	.52	.35	1.48	.21	2
1950	.50	.38	1.34	.20	2
1951	.57	.47	1.22	.19	2
1952	.62	.47	1.34	.19	2
1953	.64	.49	1.31	.19	2
1954	.69	.50	1.38	.19	2
1955	.69	.56	1.24	.19	2
1956	.81	.68	1.20	.19	2
1957	.75	.70	1.07	.19	2
1958	.75	.65	1.15	.19	2
1959	.64	.66	.98	.18	2
1960	.63	.67	.94	.18	2
1961	.63	.64	.99	.18	2
1962	.77	.67	1.15	.18	2
1963	.63	.68	.93	.17	2
1964	.63	.70	.91	.16	2
1965	.70	.71	.98	.16	2
1966	.77	.82	.94	.14	2
1967	.93	.84	1.11	.12	2
1968	.88	.86	1.02	.12	2
1969	.94	.82	1.14	.12	2
1970	.96	.88	1.09	.12	2
1971	.96	.96	1.00	.11	2
1972	1.00	1.00	1.00	.11	2
1973	1.04	1.06	.98	.11	2
1974	1.04	1.39	.75	.11	2
1975	1.31	1.56	.84	.11	2
1976	1.31	1.58	.83	.12	1
1977	1.31	1.59	.83	.12	1
1978	1.37	1.67	.82	.12	1
1979	1.64	1.88	.88	.12	1
1980	1.64	2.12	.77	.12	1
1981	1.92	2.16	.89	.15	1
1982	1.92	2.18	.88	.18	1
1983	2.19	2.12	1.03	.18	1

F. Steel Safes

Year	Sears	PPI	Sears/PPI	Weight	Models
1947	.54	.29	1.88	.23	1
1948	.49	.33	1.48	.16	1
1949	.59	.34	1.71	.16	1
1950	.59	.36	1.61	.16	1
1951	.62	.46	1.35	.15	1
1952	.64	.44	1.46	.15	1
1953	.64	.48	1.34	.15	1
1954	.64	.50	1.29	.15	1
1955	.65	.52	1.25	.15	1
1956	.70	.58	1.21	.15	1
1957	.75	.62	1.21	.15	1

Table B.3F (continued)

Year	Sears	PPI	Sears/PPI	Weight	Models
1958	.82	.64	1.27	.15	1
1959	.79	.66	1.19	.15	1
1960	.85	.69	1.23	.15	1
1961	.85	.70	1.22	.15	1
1962	.77	.73	1.07	.15	1
1963	.77	.73	1.05	.15	1
1964	.77	.74	1.05	.13	1
1965	.77	.74	1.05	.12	1
1966	.80	.74	1.08	.10	1
1967	.80	.78	1.03	.09	1
1968	.85	.86	.99	.09	1
1969	.90	.93	.97	.09	1
1970	.92	.93	.99	.09	1
1971	.95	.96	.98	.09	1
1972	1.00	1.00	1.00	.09	1
1973	.91	1.03	.88	.09	1
1974	.87	1.09	.80	.10	1
1975	1.19	1.16	1.02	.11	6
1976	1.19	1.23	.97	.13	6
1977	1.30	1.30	1.00	.14	6
1978	1.43	1.38	1.04	.16	5
1979	1.60	1.52	1.06	.18	5
1980	1.65	1.70	.97	.19	2
1981	1.65	1.87	.88	.24	2
1982	1.81	2.04	.89	.28	6
1983	1.88	2.23	.85	.28	2

G. Cast Iron Radiators and Convectors

Year	Unit Value	PPI	UnitValue/PPI	Weight	Models
1947	.35	.30	1.18	.12	1
1948	.42	.37	1.14	.09	1
1949	.45	.40	1.13	.09	1
1950	.45	.40	1.13	.08	1
1951	.51	.44	1.15	.08	1
1952	.54	.45	1.20	.08	1
1953	.56	.48	1.15	.08	1
1954	.59	.50	1.19	.08	1
1955	.57	.51	1.12	.07	1
1956	.60	.53	1.14	.07	1
1957	.59	.56	1.05	.07	1
1958	.61	.57	1.07	.07	1
1959	.60	.59	1.03	.07	1
1960	.60	.59	1.03	.06	1
1961	.63	.59	1.08	.06	1
1962	.66	.60	1.09	.05	1
1963	.64	.62	1.04	.05	1
1964	.66	.64	1.03	.06	1
1965	.65	.64	1.01	.06	1
1966	.66	.67	.97	.06	1
1967	.65	.69	.95	.06	1
1968	.71	.74	.95	.06	1
1969	.86	.78	1.09	.06	6

(continued)

Table B.3G (continued)

Year	Unit Value	PPI	UnitValue/PPI	Weight	Models
1970	.81	.94	.86	.06	6
1971	.93	1.00	.93	.06	6
1972	1.00	1.00	1.00	.06	6
1973	1.14	1.01	1.12	.06	6
1974	1.43	1.35	1.06	.06	6
1975	1.84	1.65	1.12	.03	6
1976	1.89	1.76	1.08	.00	6

H. PVC Piping

Year	Sears	PPI	Sears/PPI	Weight	Models
1967	1.02	.86	1.18	.12	5
1968	1.02	.91	1.13	.12	5
1969	1.02	1.00	1.02	.12	5
1970	1.00	1.08	.93	.12	5
1971	1.00	1.02	.98	.11	5
1972	1.00	1.00	1.00	.11	5
1973	1.00	1.02	.98	.11	5
1974	.87	1.28	.68	.11	5
1975	1.15	1.19	.97	.11	5
1976	1.05	1.07	.98	.12	5
1977	.96	1.14	.85	.12	8
1978	1.05	1.18	.89	.12	8
1979	1.64	1.27	1.29	.12	8
1980	2.01	1.33	1.51	.12	8
1981	1.68	1.34	1.26	.15	8
1982	2.21	1.28	1.72	.18	8
1983	1.89	1.41	1.34	.18	8

I. Electric Furnaces

Year	Sears	PPI	Sears/PPI	Weight	Models
1972	1.00	1.00	1.00	.06	5
1973	1.00	1.01	.99	.06	5
1974	1.00	1.09	.91	.06	5
1975	1.22	1.21	1.01	.06	5
1976	1.22	1.25	.98	.06	5
1977	1.22	1.30	.94	.06	5
1978	1.26	1.41	.90	.05	6
1979	1.35	1.48	.91	.05	6
1980	1.47	1.62	.91	.04	6
1981	1.54	1.81	.85	.02	6
1982	1.54	1.75	.88	.00	5

Table B.3 (continued)

J. Electric Hot Water Heaters

Year	Sears	PPI	Sears/PPI	Weight	Models
1968	.84	.91	.92	.06	8
1969	.89	.92	.97	.06	9
1970	.96	.95	1.01	.06	9
1971	.98	.97	1.02	.06	8
1972	1.00	1.00	1.00	.06	9
1973	1.09	1.01	1.08	.06	6
1974	1.08	1.05	1.03	.06	7
1975	1.38	1.20	1.14	.06	5
1976	1.48	1.39	1.07	.06	8
1977	1.55	1.40	1.11	.06	7
1978	1.57	1.43	1.10	.05	8
1979	1.73	1.51	1.15	.05	16
1980	1.90	1.67	1.14	.04	20
1981	1.95	1.74	1.12	.05	15
1982	2.15	1.86	1.16	.05	18
1983	2.18	1.94	1.13	.05	16

K. Prefabricated Metal Buildings

Year	Sears	PPI	Sears/PPI	Weight	Models
1961	.84	.83	1.01	.04	3
1962	.78	.83	.94	.04	1
1963	.73	.83	.88	.04	2
1964	.63	.84	.75	.03	9
1965	.63	.84	.75	.03	8
1966	.63	.85	.74	.02	7
1967	.75	.85	.89	.02	2
1968	.75	.85	.88	.02	11
1969	.79	.89	.89	.02	12
1970	.82	.93	.88	.02	11
1971	.94	.96	.98	.02	9
1972	1.00	1.00	1.00	.02	12
1973	.99	1.01	.99	.02	9
1974	1.38	1.29	1.07	.02	7
1975	1.87	1.46	1.28	.02	9
1976	1.93	1.51	1.27	.02	6
1977	1.93	1.63	1.18	.02	7
1978	1.96	1.75	1.12	.02	12
1979	2.22	1.94	1.14	.02	6
1980	2.28	2.05	1.11	.02	8
1981	2.27	2.19	1.04	.03	8
1982	2.51	2.30	1.09	.03	7
1983	2.59	2.24	1.15	.03	7

(*continued*)

Table B.3 (continued)

L. Chain Link Fences

Year	Sears	PPI	Sears/PPI	Weight	Models
1955	.75	.75	.99	.04	8
1956	.78	.80	.98	.04	8
1957	.84	.87	.96	.04	8
1958	.86	.91	.94	.04	8
1959	.86	.91	.94	.04	8
1960	.86	.91	.94	.04	8
1961	.80	.91	.88	.04	8
1962	.80	.91	.88	.04	8
1963	.75	.91	.82	.04	8
1964	.75	.85	.89	.03	8
1965	.74	.78	.95	.03	8
1966	.78	.79	.99	.02	8
1967	.86	.79	1.09	.02	8
1968	.88	.79	1.11	.02	8
1969	.88	.84	1.05	.02	8
1970	.92	.90	1.02	.02	8
1971	.92	.96	.96	.02	8
1972	1.00	1.00	1.00	.02	8
1973	1.02	1.12	.90	.02	8
1974	1.21	1.47	.82	.02	8
1975	1.60	1.52	1.05	.02	8
1976	1.34	1.56	.86	.02	8
1977	1.57	1.61	.98	.02	10
1978	1.42	1.75	.81	.02	10
1979	1.76	1.95	.90	.02	10
1980	1.80	2.08	.87	.02	10
1981	1.93	2.21	.87	.03	10
1982	2.15	2.35	.92	.03	10
1983	2.16	2.32	.94	.03	8

M. Group Average

Year	Alternative	Official	Alternative/Official	Weight	Models
1947	1.04	.52	2.01	1.00	6
1948	1.02	.56	1.80	1.00	24
1949	1.06	.56	1.87	1.00	17
1950	1.01	.57	1.77	1.00	20
1951	1.04	.65	1.60	1.00	23
1952	1.02	.65	1.57	1.00	14
1953	1.02	.67	1.53	1.00	24
1954	1.02	.66	1.56	1.00	23
1955	.94	.69	1.36	1.00	27
1956	.93	.79	1.18	1.00	28
1957	.97	.82	1.18	1.00	35
1958	1.03	.79	1.30	1.00	29
1959	.95	.80	1.19	1.00	32
1960	.95	.80	1.18	1.00	33
1961	.92	.78	1.19	1.00	35
1962	.93	.79	1.19	1.00	34
1963	.87	.79	1.10	1.00	35
1964	.85	.79	1.08	1.00	39

Table B.3M (continued)

Year	Alternative	Official	Alternative/Official	Weight	Models
1965	.80	.79	1.02	1.00	40
1966	.77	.82	.94	1.00	36
1967	.80	.83	.96	1.00	38
1968	.80	.85	.94	1.00	57
1969	.89	.88	1.01	1.00	63
1970	.94	.94	1.00	1.00	71
1971	.97	.98	.99	1.00	68
1972	1.00	1.00	1.00	1.00	71
1973	1.05	1.04	1.00	1.00	64
1974	1.10	1.22	.90	1.00	69
1975	1.38	1.34	1.03	1.00	73
1976	1.43	1.40	1.02	1.00	73
1977	1.44	1.48	.97	1.00	73
1978	1.49	1.55	.96	1.00	90
1979	1.61	1.68	.96	1.00	87
1980	2.09	1.93	1.09	1.00	96
1981	2.16	2.12	1.02	1.00	81
1982	2.37	2.20	1.08	1.00	97
1983	2.41	2.29	1.05	1.00	79

Table B.4   **Comparison of Alternative Price Indexes for PDE with Official Indexes from NIPA, Table 5.6, Row 10, Engines and Turbines**

A. Steam Turbine Generators

Year	Hedonic	PPI	Hedonic/PPI	Weight	Models
1948	3.15	.41	7.72	.34	14
1949	2.92	.41	7.14	.34	6
1950	2.70	.42	6.48	.34	9
1951	2.22	.45	4.94	.34	12
1952	1.84	.48	3.87	.34	5
1953	1.84	.50	3.64	.34	12
1954	1.84	.52	3.53	.34	10
1955	1.43	.54	2.65	.34	4
1956	1.11	.65	1.72	.34	5
1957	1.31	.77	1.70	.34	10
1958	1.55	.81	1.92	.34	7
1959	1.39	.82	1.71	.33	6
1960	1.25	.82	1.53	.33	7
1961	1.19	.73	1.63	.32	2
1962	1.14	.70	1.62	.32	8
1963	1.05	.71	1.48	.31	8
1964	.97	.72	1.34	.31	6
1965	.79	.73	1.08	.30	8
1966	.64	.75	.86	.30	3
1967	.64	.79	.81	.30	7
1968	.64	.81	.79	.30	5
1969	.78	.85	.91	.30	3
1970	.94	.93	1.02	.30	11
1971	.97	.97	1.00	.30	10
1972	1.00	1.00	1.00	.30	5
1973	1.18	1.03	1.15	.30	6
1974	1.40	1.14	1.23	.30	12
1975	1.60	1.43	1.12	.30	6
1976	1.83	1.60	1.14	.30	6
1977	1.78	1.66	1.07	.30	1
1978	1.74	1.80	.97	.30	7
1979	1.39	1.86	.74	.30	7
1980	3.28	2.20	1.49	.30	10
1981	3.41	2.53	1.35	.15	5
1982	3.54	2.60	1.36	.00	6

B. Gasoline Engines, 11 hp and Over

Year	Unit Value	PPI	UnitValue/PPI	Weight	Models
1947	.69	.47	1.48	.25	11
1948	.69	.53	1.30	.15	1
1949	.68	.56	1.23	.15	1
1950	.68	.56	1.21	.15	11
1951	.82	.62	1.33	.15	11
1952	.86	.63	1.35	.15	11
1953	.85	.64	1.33	.15	11
1954	.86	.64	1.36	.15	11
1955	.84	.65	1.30	.15	14
1956	.91	.69	1.32	.15	15
1957	.99	.72	1.37	.15	13

Table B.4B (continued)

Year	Unit Value	PPI	Unit Value/PPI	Weight	Models
1958	.90	.73	1.22	.15	12
1959	.85	.73	1.16	.15	10
1960	.88	.74	1.19	.15	8
1961	.91	.75	1.21	.15	10
1962	.93	.77	1.21	.15	11
1963	.89	.77	1.17	.16	13
1964	.90	.77	1.17	.19	13
1965	.99	.77	1.28	.21	12
1966	.88	.77	1.14	.23	9
1967	.98	.77	1.27	.24	9
1968	1.00	.80	1.24	.23	10
1969	1.01	.86	1.18	.22	11
1970	1.11	.91	1.22	.21	10
1971	1.09	.96	1.13	.20	10
1972	1.00	1.00	1.00	.19	10
1973	.91	1.01	.90	.18	11
1974	1.08	1.18	.91	.17	12
1975	1.19	1.38	.86	.16	10
1976	1.06	1.50	.71	.16	8
1977	1.73	1.60	1.08	.15	5
1978	2.02	1.80	1.12	.15	6
1979	2.20	1.99	1.11	.14	4
1980	2.61	2.26	1.16	.13	7
1981	2.87	2.54	1.13	.16	6
1982	2.91	2.75	1.06	.19	6
1983	3.03	2.85	1.06	.19	6

C. Outboard Motors

Year	Sears Hedonic	PPI	Hedonic/PPI	Weight	Models
1948	.72	.51	1.40	.23	4
1949	.69	.53	1.29	.23	4
1950	.65	.53	1.23	.23	5
1951	.67	.59	1.14	.23	5
1952	.68	.59	1.15	.23	1
1953	.70	.60	1.18	.23	4
1954	.75	.63	1.19	.23	4
1955	.70	.63	1.11	.23	5
1956	.74	.65	1.14	.23	5
1957	.74	.71	1.05	.23	6
1958	.74	.73	1.02	.23	7
1959	.79	.72	1.10	.22	11
1960	.77	.71	1.08	.21	10
1961	.80	.71	1.12	.21	4
1962	.82	.73	1.14	.20	8
1963	.80	.73	1.10	.20	8
1964	.81	.75	1.09	.19	7
1965	.87	.77	1.13	.19	6
1966	.89	.77	1.16	.18	7
1967	.98	.81	1.21	.18	9
1968	1.01	.84	1.20	.19	10
1969	1.03	.87	1.18	.19	7
1970	1.04	.93	1.11	.19	5

(continued)

Table B.4C (continued)

Year	Sears Hedonic	PPI	Hedonic/PPI	Weight	Models
1971	.98	.99	.99	.20	5
1972	1.00	1.00	1.00	.20	4
1973	1.09	1.01	1.08	.20	7
1974	1.16	1.15	1.02	.21	6
1975	1.23	1.39	.89	.21	5
1976	1.36	1.53	.89	.22	7
1977	1.40	1.57	.89	.22	6
1978	1.45	1.67	.87	.23	7
1979	1.67	1.86	.90	.23	6
1980	1.98	2.13	.93	.24	7
1981	2.10	2.36	.89	.30	15
1982	2.75	2.52	1.09	.35	15
1983	2.63	2.61	1.01	.35	14

D. Diesel Engines, Except Automotive

Year	Unit Value	PPI	Unit Value/PPI	Weight	Models
1947	1.34	.37	3.61	.47	20
1948	1.33	.43	3.10	.28	20
1949	1.31	.47	2.81	.28	20
1950	1.29	.48	2.71	.28	20
1951	1.32	.60	2.22	.28	20
1952	1.42	.58	2.44	.28	20
1953	1.45	.59	2.45	.28	19
1954	1.43	.61	2.35	.28	17
1955	1.36	.62	2.19	.28	18
1956	1.36	.68	2.01	.28	19
1957	1.52	.72	2.10	.28	16
1958	1.32	.74	1.79	.29	16
1959	1.26	.75	1.68	.30	18
1960	1.17	.75	1.56	.31	18
1961	1.11	.76	1.47	.32	17
1962	1.07	.76	1.41	.33	17
1963	1.05	.76	1.38	.33	16
1964	.99	.78	1.27	.31	15
1965	.96	.79	1.21	.30	11
1966	.88	.82	1.08	.29	10
1967	.90	.84	1.06	.28	12
1968	.85	.86	.98	.29	12
1969	.85	.89	.96	.29	36
1970	.89	.93	.96	.30	22
1971	.93	.97	.96	.31	22
1972	1.00	1.00	1.00	.31	28
1973	.98	1.03	.96	.32	24
1974	1.19	1.18	1.01	.33	16
1975	1.39	1.45	.96	.33	11
1976	1.38	1.58	.87	.33	12
1977	1.43	1.69	.85	.33	10
1978	1.58	1.87	.84	.33	10
1979	1.55	2.08	.75	.33	8
1980	1.73	2.34	.74	.33	14
1981	1.89	2.71	.70	.39	12
1982	2.01	2.94	.68	.46	13
1983	2.05	2.99	.69	.46	13

Table B.4 (continued)

E. Group Average

Year	Alternative	Official	Alternative/Official	Weight	Models
1947	1.42	.41	3.49	1.00	31
1948	1.41	.45	3.11	1.00	39
1949	1.35	.47	2.87	1.00	31
1950	1.30	.48	2.71	1.00	45
1951	1.27	.54	2.33	1.00	48
1952	1.22	.55	2.21	1.00	37
1953	1.24	.57	2.17	1.00	46
1954	1.25	.59	2.14	1.00	42
1955	1.11	.60	1.86	1.00	41
1956	1.05	.66	1.58	1.00	44
1957	1.16	.74	1.57	1.00	45
1958	1.16	.76	1.53	1.00	42
1959	1.11	.76	1.46	1.00	45
1960	1.05	.76	1.38	1.00	43
1961	1.03	.74	1.39	1.00	33
1962	1.01	.74	1.37	1.00	44
1963	.97	.74	1.31	1.00	45
1964	.93	.76	1.23	1.00	41
1965	.89	.76	1.17	1.00	37
1966	.80	.78	1.03	1.00	29
1967	.84	.80	1.04	1.00	37
1968	.83	.83	1.00	1.00	37
1969	.89	.87	1.03	1.00	57
1970	.98	.93	1.06	1.00	48
1971	.98	.97	1.01	1.00	47
1972	1.00	1.00	1.00	1.00	47
1973	1.05	1.02	1.02	1.00	48
1974	1.22	1.16	1.05	1.00	46
1975	1.37	1.42	.97	1.00	32
1976	1.43	1.56	.92	1.00	33
1977	1.56	1.64	.95	1.00	22
1978	1.65	1.79	.92	1.00	30
1979	1.61	1.95	.82	1.00	25
1980	2.29	2.24	1.02	1.00	38
1981	2.45	2.55	.96	1.00	38
1982	2.74	2.73	1.00	1.00	40
1983	2.75	2.80	.98	1.00	33

Table B.5   **Comparison of Alternative Price Indexes for PDE with Official Indexes from NIPA, Table 5.6, Row 11, Metalworking Machinery**

A. Drill Presses

Year	Sears	PPI	Sears/PPI	Weight	Models
1947	.49	.38	1.29	.14	3
1948	.46	.41	1.11	.14	3
1949	.51	.43	1.18	.14	3
1950	.47	.46	1.02	.14	2
1951	.51	.51	1.00	.14	3
1952	.50	.52	.97	.14	3
1953	.52	.53	.98	.14	2
1954	.55	.54	1.02	.14	2
1955	.60	.56	1.06	.14	2
1956	.60	.62	.97	.14	2
1957	.63	.66	.96	.14	2
1958	.67	.67	1.00	.14	2
1959	.67	.69	.97	.13	2
1960	.65	.71	.92	.13	2
1961	.68	.71	.95	.13	1
1962	.70	.73	.96	.13	1
1963	.69	.73	.95	.13	1
1964	.66	.74	.89	.14	1
1965	.66	.76	.86	.14	1
1966	.67	.80	.83	.15	1
1967	.75	.83	.90	.15	1
1968	.75	.87	.86	.15	1
1969	.77	.90	.86	.15	1
1970	.87	.95	.92	.15	2
1971	.94	.98	.97	.14	3
1972	1.00	1.00	1.00	.14	2
1973	1.03	1.06	.97	.14	2
1974	1.10	1.26	.87	.14	1
1975	1.56	1.49	1.04	.14	2
1976	1.56	1.68	.93	.13	2
1977	1.72	1.81	.95	.13	1
1978	1.78	1.95	.91	.13	1
1979	1.85	2.14	.86	.13	1
1980	1.83	2.35	.78	.12	1
1981	2.17	2.61	.83	.12	3
1982	2.26	2.61	.87	.12	3
1983	2.39	2.69	.89	.12	3

B. Metal Lathes

Year	Sears	PPI	Sears/PPI	Weight	Models
1947	.32	.38	.83	.14	1
1948	.37	.41	.90	.14	1
1949	.37	.43	.86	.14	1
1950	.31	.46	.68	.14	4
1951	.40	.51	.78	.14	4
1952	.39	.52	.76	.14	4
1953	.40	.53	.75	.14	4
1954	.46	.54	.85	.14	4
1955	.50	.56	.89	.14	4
1956	.51	.62	.83	.14	4

Table B.5B (continued)

Year	Sears	PPI	Sears/PPI	Weight	Models
1957	.59	.66	.89	.14	4
1958	.61	.67	.90	.14	4
1959	.57	.69	.83	.13	4
1960	.69	.71	.97	.13	2
1961	.69	.71	.97	.13	3
1962	.70	.73	.97	.13	3
1963	.77	.73	1.06	.13	3
1964	.77	.74	1.03	.14	3
1965	.77	.76	1.01	.14	3
1966	.77	.80	.97	.15	3
1967	.81	.83	.98	.15	3
1968	.82	.87	.94	.15	3
1969	.86	.90	.96	.15	3
1970	.89	.95	.94	.15	3
1971	.98	.98	1.00	.14	3
1972	1.00	1.00	1.00	.14	3
1973	1.04	1.08	.96	.14	2
1974	1.07	1.32	.81	.14	1
1975	1.34	1.51	.89	.14	1
1976	1.64	1.62	1.01	.13	1
1977	1.80	1.73	1.04	.13	3
1978	1.92	1.93	1.00	.13	2
1979	1.95	2.19	.89	.13	3
1980	2.19	2.57	.85	.12	2
1981	1.75	2.78	.63	.12	3
1982	1.89	2.88	.66	.12	1
1983	2.25	2.89	.78	.12	1

C. Free-Standing Power Saws

Year	Sears	PPI	Sears/PPI	Weight	Models
1947	.85	.38	2.23	.14	2
1948	.71	.41	1.72	.14	2
1949	.74	.43	1.71	.14	2
1950	.67	.46	1.45	.14	2
1951	.73	.51	1.42	.14	3
1952	.74	.52	1.42	.14	5
1953	.76	.53	1.44	.14	4
1954	.79	.54	1.47	.14	4
1955	.84	.56	1.48	.14	6
1956	.85	.62	1.38	.14	7
1957	.88	.66	1.34	.14	7
1958	.89	.67	1.33	.14	5
1959	.83	.69	1.20	.13	6
1960	.89	.71	1.25	.13	6
1961	.88	.71	1.23	.13	6
1962	.91	.73	1.25	.13	6
1963	.90	.73	1.24	.13	5
1964	.84	.74	1.13	.14	7
1965	.82	.76	1.08	.14	6
1966	.82	.80	1.02	.15	5
1967	.86	.83	1.03	.15	5
1968	.91	.87	1.05	.15	7
1969	.94	.90	1.05	.15	7

(*continued*)

Table B.5C (continued)

Year	Sears	PPI	Sears/PPI	Weight	Models
1970	.94	.95	.99	.15	4
1971	.96	.98	.98	.14	5
1972	1.00	1.00	1.00	.14	6
1973	1.01	1.04	.97	.14	6
1974	1.01	1.22	.83	.14	4
1975	1.11	1.43	.78	.14	4
1976	1.64	1.51	1.09	.13	2
1977	1.84	1.65	1.11	.13	1
1978	1.90	1.81	1.05	.13	1
1979	2.03	2.01	1.01	.13	1
1980	2.15	2.28	.94	.12	1
1981	2.47	2.51	.99	.12	2
1982	2.53	2.67	.95	.12	3
1983	2.61	2.72	.96	.12	1

D. Quarter-Inch Hand Power Drills

Year	Sears	PPI	Sears/PPI	Weight	Models
1947	.81	.78	1.04	.01	1
1948	.81	.81	1.00	.01	1
1949	.85	.81	1.05	.01	2
1950	.82	.83	.99	.01	2
1951	.91	.91	1.01	.01	2
1952	.87	.91	.96	.01	2
1953	.89	.94	.94	.01	2
1954	.96	.99	.97	.01	2
1955	.96	1.03	.93	.01	2
1956	1.01	1.03	.97	.01	2
1957	1.07	1.08	.99	.01	2
1958	1.07	1.02	1.05	.01	2
1959	.79	1.03	.76	.02	2
1960	.91	1.03	.89	.02	2
1961	.91	1.04	.88	.03	2
1962	.91	1.06	.86	.03	2
1963	.90	1.04	.86	.03	2
1964	.85	1.00	.85	.03	2
1965	.85	.95	.90	.03	2
1966	.81	.95	.85	.03	2
1967	.87	.95	.92	.03	2
1968	.92	.98	.94	.03	2
1969	.96	.98	.98	.03	4
1970	.90	1.08	.83	.03	2
1971	.91	1.09	.84	.03	2
1972	1.00	1.00	1.00	.03	2
1973	.89	.99	.89	.03	2
1974	.89	1.12	.79	.03	1
1975	.95	1.29	.73	.03	1
1976	.95	1.39	.68	.03	1
1977	1.01	1.50	.67	.03	1
1978	.88	1.63	.54	.02	2
1979	.98	1.69	.58	.02	2
1980	.96	1.86	.51	.02	4
1981	1.15	2.19	.52	.02	4
1982	1.15	2.22	.52	.02	3
1983	1.10	2.21	.50	.02	2

Table B.5 (continued)

E. Half-Inch Hand Power Drills

Year	Sears	PPI	Sears/PPI	Weight	Models
1949	.87	.58	1.49	.01	2
1950	.84	.59	1.43	.01	1
1951	.99	.62	1.60	.01	1
1952	.99	.61	1.63	.01	2
1953	.97	.61	1.58	.01	2
1954	.99	.62	1.58	.01	2
1955	.99	.65	1.52	.01	2
1956	1.04	.67	1.55	.01	3
1957	1.05	.70	1.50	.01	3
1958	.99	.70	1.43	.01	3
1959	.93	.71	1.30	.02	2
1960	.96	.72	1.34	.02	2
1961	.90	.74	1.21	.03	2
1962	.96	.76	1.26	.03	1
1963	.94	.77	1.22	.03	3
1964	.95	.77	1.24	.03	3
1965	.93	.77	1.21	.03	3
1966	.93	.78	1.18	.02	3
1967	.88	.79	1.10	.02	2
1968	.89	.81	1.10	.03	4
1969	.92	.83	1.11	.03	4
1970	.94	.92	1.02	.03	3
1971	.95	.97	.98	.03	3
1972	1.00	1.00	1.00	.03	4
1973	.98	1.02	.97	.03	4
1974	.99	1.13	.88	.03	1
1975	1.18	1.27	.93	.03	2
1976	1.18	1.43	.83	.03	2
1977	1.18	1.61	.73	.03	1
1978	1.36	1.68	.81	.02	1
1979	1.36	1.77	.77	.02	2
1980	1.33	2.02	.66	.02	1
1981	1.41	2.09	.68	.01	2
1982	1.51	2.14	.70	.00	0

F. Hand Power Saws

Year	Sears	PPI	Sears/PPI	Weight	Models
1947	1.57	1.11	1.41	.01	1
1948	1.61	1.11	1.45	.01	1
1949	1.65	1.10	1.50	.01	1
1950	1.53	1.06	1.45	.01	1
1951	1.55	1.07	1.45	.01	1
1952	1.42	1.07	1.33	.01	3
1953	1.44	1.10	1.32	.01	3
1954	1.38	1.11	1.25	.01	3
1955	1.15	1.15	1.00	.01	1
1956	1.22	1.18	1.03	.01	2
1957	1.24	1.23	1.01	.01	2
1958	1.24	1.23	1.01	.01	3
1959	1.16	1.19	.97	.02	2

(continued)

Table B.5F (continued)

Year	Sears	PPI	Sears/PPI	Weight	Models
1960	1.16	1.18	.98	.02	4
1961	1.15	1.22	.94	.03	4
1962	1.15	1.26	.91	.03	5
1963	.93	1.19	.79	.03	3
1964	.88	1.17	.75	.03	2
1965	.88	1.08	.81	.03	4
1966	.87	1.08	.81	.02	4
1967	.88	1.10	.80	.02	4
1968	.89	1.14	.79	.03	4
1969	.95	1.14	.84	.03	4
1970	.95	1.10	.87	.03	4
1971	.96	1.01	.95	.03	4
1972	1.00	1.00	1.00	.03	5
1973	1.00	.97	1.03	.03	4
1974	1.07	1.06	1.02	.03	5
1975	1.32	1.17	1.13	.03	6
1976	1.22	1.20	1.02	.03	3
1977	1.22	1.34	.91	.03	3
1978	1.42	1.42	1.00	.02	2
1979	1.58	1.54	1.03	.02	3
1980	1.97	1.67	1.18	.02	1
1981	2.09	1.80	1.16	.02	2
1982	2.09	1.81	1.15	.02	2
1983	2.25	1.81	1.24	.02	1

G. Hand Electric Sanders

Year	Sears	PPI	Sears/PPI	Weight	Models
1947	.79	.81	.98	.01	1
1948	.94	.81	1.16	.01	1
1949	1.02	.81	1.25	.01	1
1950	.96	.84	1.15	.01	1
1951	1.02	.91	1.11	.01	1
1952	1.00	.91	1.09	.01	2
1953	1.03	.93	1.11	.01	2
1954	1.04	.96	1.09	.01	2
1955	1.04	1.00	1.05	.01	3
1956	1.08	1.04	1.04	.01	3
1957	1.10	1.04	1.06	.01	3
1958	1.10	1.05	1.05	.01	3
1959	1.04	1.09	.95	.02	3
1960	1.07	1.08	.99	.02	4
1961	1.07	1.02	1.04	.03	4
1962	1.06	1.13	.94	.03	3
1963	.92	1.13	.82	.03	3
1964	.84	1.13	.75	.03	3
1965	.93	1.10	.85	.03	4
1966	.96	1.07	.90	.02	4
1967	.96	1.13	.85	.02	3
1968	.99	1.16	.85	.03	4
1969	1.00	1.14	.88	.03	4
1970	1.00	1.05	.96	.03	3
1971	1.00	1.01	.99	.03	3
1972	1.00	1.00	1.00	.03	6

Table B.5G (continued)

Year	Sears	PPI	Sears/PPI	Weight	Models
1973	.99	1.00	.99	.03	5
1974	.95	1.04	.91	.03	6
1975	1.03	1.16	.88	.03	6
1976	.79	1.19	.67	.03	4
1977	.76	1.24	.61	.03	4
1978	.89	1.36	.65	.02	4
1979	.95	1.43	.67	.02	4
1980	.95	1.54	.62	.02	5
1981	1.10	1.64	.67	.02	2
1982	1.10	1.77	.62	.02	3
1983	1.10	1.81	.61	.02	1

H. Transformer Arc Welders

Year	Sears	PPI	Sears/PPI	Weight	Models
1947	.75	1.19	.63	.01	2
1948	.72	1.19	.60	.01	2
1949	.76	1.16	.66	.01	2
1950	.74	1.10	.68	.01	3
1951	.87	1.08	.80	.01	4
1952	.87	1.07	.81	.01	1
1953	.91	1.07	.85	.01	1
1954	.98	1.07	.91	.01	4
1955	1.16	1.07	1.09	.01	1
1956	1.16	1.12	1.04	.01	3
1957	1.21	1.21	1.00	.01	5
1958	1.20	1.25	.96	.01	5
1959	1.20	1.16	1.03	.02	5
1960	1.18	1.12	1.05	.02	5
1961	1.19	1.02	1.17	.03	6
1962	1.11	.97	1.14	.03	4
1963	1.10	.95	1.16	.03	5
1964	.99	.92	1.07	.03	5
1965	.91	.87	1.04	.03	5
1966	.91	.88	1.03	.02	4
1967	.95	.89	1.07	.02	4
1968	.94	.89	1.07	.03	5
1969	.98	.90	1.08	.03	5
1970	.94	.96	.98	.03	4
1971	.97	.97	1.00	.03	3
1972	1.00	1.00	1.00	.03	3
1973	.99	1.00	.99	.03	4
1974	1.01	1.14	.89	.03	4
1975	1.21	1.25	.97	.03	2
1976	1.41	1.30	1.08	.03	4
1977	1.36	1.46	.94	.03	1
1978	1.36	1.59	.86	.02	4
1979	1.32	1.72	.77	.02	3
1980	1.23	1.89	.65	.02	3
1981	1.22	2.10	.58	.02	3
1982	1.37	2.26	.61	.02	2
1983	1.48	2.31	.64	.02	2

(*continued*)

Table B.5 (continued)

I. Acetylene Welding Torches

Year	Sears	PPI	Sears/PPI	Weight	Models
1947	.64	.47	1.37	.01	1
1948	.60	.49	1.22	.01	1
1949	.59	.51	1.15	.01	1
1950	.55	.53	1.04	.01	1
1951	.59	.56	1.06	.01	1
1952	.60	.56	1.06	.01	1
1953	.60	.58	1.03	.01	1
1954	.61	.59	1.04	.01	1
1955	.57	.60	.94	.01	1
1956	.57	.66	.87	.01	1
1957	.57	.67	.85	.01	1
1958	.57	.66	.87	.01	1
1959	.57	.69	.82	.01	1
1960	.61	.71	.86	.01	1
1961	.65	.72	.90	.01	1
1962	.69	.72	.96	.01	1
1963	.69	.73	.95	.01	1
1964	.69	.75	.93	.01	1
1965	.71	.75	.95	.01	1
1966	.72	.78	.93	.01	1
1967	.73	.81	.90	.01	1
1968	.79	.85	.94	.01	1
1969	.80	.86	.93	.01	1
1970	.98	.95	1.03	.01	1
1971	1.00	.96	1.04	.01	1
1972	1.00	1.00	1.00	.01	1
1973	1.00	1.02	.98	.01	2
1974	1.00	1.11	.90	.01	1
1975	1.03	1.14	.91	.01	1
1976	1.20	1.12	1.07	.01	2
1977	1.19	1.31	.91	.01	1
1978	1.19	1.36	.88	.01	1
1979	1.19	1.45	.82	.01	2
1980	1.21	1.60	.76	.01	2
1981	1.33	1.75	.76	.01	3
1982	1.47	1.86	.79	.01	1
1983	1.60	1.92	.83	.01	1

J. Acetylene Cutting Tools

Year	Sears	PPI	Sears/PPI	Weight	Models
1947	.63	.53	1.18	.01	1
1948	.63	.57	1.10	.01	1
1949	.58	.58	.99	.01	1
1950	.52	.58	.90	.01	1
1951	.57	.60	.95	.01	1
1952	.57	.60	.95	.01	1
1953	.57	.62	.93	.01	1
1954	.61	.64	.95	.01	1
1955	.57	.67	.85	.01	1
1956	.57	.71	.80	.01	1
1957	.66	.74	.90	.01	1

Table B.5J (continued)

Year	Sears	PPI	Sears/PPI	Weight	Models
1958	.66	.71	.93	.01	1
1959	.66	.72	.92	.01	1
1960	.66	.73	.91	.01	1
1961	.66	.73	.91	.01	1
1962	.71	.74	.96	.01	1
1963	.72	.75	.97	.01	1
1964	.73	.78	.94	.01	1
1965	.76	.79	.96	.01	1
1966	.78	.82	.96	.01	1
1967	.78	.84	.92	.01	1
1968	.84	.87	.97	.01	1
1969	.86	.87	.99	.01	1
1970	.98	.94	1.03	.01	1
1971	1.00	.98	1.02	.01	1
1972	1.00	1.00	1.00	.01	1
1973	1.00	1.02	.98	.01	2
1974	1.00	1.13	.88	.01	1
1975	1.03	1.15	.89	.01	1
1976	1.03	1.19	.86	.01	2
1977	1.10	1.29	.85	.01	1
1978	1.10	1.37	.80	.01	1
1979	1.10	1.47	.74	.01	2
1980	1.13	1.67	.68	.01	2
1981	1.25	1.89	.66	.01	2
1982	1.31	2.01	.65	.01	1
1983	1.39	2.02	.68	.01	1

K. Acetylene Single-Stage Welding Outfits

Year	Sears	PPI	Sears/PPI	Weight	Models
1947	.60	.36	1.67	.01	1
1948	.60	.38	1.59	.01	1
1949	.56	.59	.94	.01	1
1950	.54	.61	.89	.01	1
1951	.60	.63	.96	.01	1
1952	.59	.63	.94	.01	1
1953	.59	.66	.89	.01	1
1954	.62	.68	.92	.01	1
1955	.65	.68	.96	.01	1
1956	.65	.70	.94	.01	1
1957	.75	.70	1.07	.01	1
1958	.79	.75	1.05	.01	1
1959	.79	.77	1.02	.01	1
1960	.79	.80	.99	.01	1
1961	.83	.80	1.04	.01	1
1962	.86	.84	1.02	.01	1
1963	.86	.85	1.01	.01	1
1964	.86	.86	1.01	.01	1
1965	.90	.87	1.04	.01	1
1966	.88	.89	.99	.01	1
1967	.91	.90	1.01	.01	1
1968	.99	.92	1.07	.01	1
1969	1.01	.93	1.08	.01	1

(continued)

Table B.5K (continued)

Year	Sears	PPI	Sears/PPI	Weight	Models
1970	1.01	.95	1.07	.01	1
1971	.94	.99	.96	.01	1
1972	1.00	1.00	1.00	.01	1
1973	1.00	1.00	1.00	.01	1
1974	1.05	1.07	.98	.01	1
1975	1.07	1.12	.96	.01	1
1976	1.09	1.19	.92	.01	2
1977	1.09	1.36	.80	.01	1
1978	1.13	1.47	.77	.01	1
1979	1.16	1.57	.74	.01	2
1980	1.21	1.76	.69	.01	2
1981	1.31	1.94	.68	.01	2
1982	1.44	1.95	.74	.01	1
1983	1.58	1.96	.80	.01	1

L. Drill Bits

Year	Sears	PPI	Sears/PPI	Weight	Models
1947	.62	.62	1.01	.19	3
1948	.62	.64	.98	.19	3
1949	.64	.68	.95	.19	3
1950	.65	.73	.90	.19	3
1951	.73	.80	.91	.19	2
1952	.65	.77	.85	.19	3
1953	.65	.76	.85	.19	3
1954	.72	.76	.95	.19	3
1955	.66	.85	.77	.19	3
1956	.73	.93	.79	.19	2
1957	.73	.99	.74	.19	3
1958	.72	.95	.76	.19	3
1959	.70	1.04	.68	.18	3
1960	.70	1.17	.60	.17	3
1961	.69	1.16	.60	.17	3
1962	.71	1.17	.61	.16	3
1963	.69	1.17	.60	.15	3
1964	.69	1.18	.59	.14	3
1965	.69	1.21	.58	.13	3
1966	.73	1.25	.58	.13	3
1967	.73	1.25	.58	.12	3
1968	.74	1.39	.53	.12	3
1969	.86	1.42	.61	.12	3
1970	.93	1.27	.74	.12	3
1971	.95	1.00	.95	.12	3
1972	1.00	1.00	1.00	.13	3
1973	1.00	1.03	.97	.13	3
1974	1.06	1.12	.95	.13	3
1975	1.40	1.30	1.07	.13	3
1976	1.55	1.35	1.15	.15	7
1977	1.66	1.46	1.14	.16	3
1978	1.69	1.56	1.08	.17	8
1979	1.72	1.67	1.03	.18	3
1980	1.72	1.89	.91	.19	2
1981	2.04	2.11	.97	.20	2
1982	2.41	2.14	1.12	.20	4
1983	2.41	2.10	1.15	.20	2

Table B.5 (continued)

M. Power Saw Blades

Year	Sears	PPI	Sears/PPI	Weight	Models
1947	.80	.43	1.85	.19	2
1948	.79	.45	1.76	.19	2
1949	.79	.47	1.65	.19	2
1950	.55	.49	1.13	.19	2
1951	.63	.50	1.26	.19	2
1952	.59	.50	1.19	.19	2
1953	.56	.53	1.05	.19	2
1954	.56	.55	1.01	.19	2
1955	.56	.62	.90	.19	1
1956	.63	.71	.89	.19	2
1957	.66	.80	.83	.19	2
1958	.65	.80	.81	.19	2
1959	.67	.87	.77	.18	2
1960	.67	.88	.76	.17	2
1961	.67	.88	.75	.17	2
1962	.64	.90	.71	.16	2
1963	.64	.90	.71	.15	2
1964	.70	.90	.78	.14	2
1965	.70	.90	.78	.13	2
1966	.69	.89	.78	.13	2
1967	.71	.93	.76	.12	2
1968	.74	.94	.79	.12	2
1969	.93	.94	.99	.12	2
1970	.98	.96	1.02	.12	2
1971	.98	.96	1.02	.12	2
1972	1.00	1.00	1.00	.13	2
1973	1.02	1.04	.98	.13	2
1974	1.11	1.12	1.00	.13	2
1975	1.30	1.25	1.04	.13	4
1976	1.21	1.28	.95	.15	2
1977	1.23	1.27	.97	.16	2
1978	1.23	1.40	.88	.17	2
1979	1.31	1.73	.75	.18	2
1980	1.31	1.97	.66	.19	1
1981	1.76	2.22	.79	.20	8
1982	1.76	2.34	.75	.20	8
1983	1.76	2.36	.74	.20	4

N. Micrometer Calipers

Year	Sears	PPI	Sears/PPI	Weight	Models
1947	.45	.50	.90	.14	2
1948	.49	.56	.88	.14	2
1949	.53	.56	.95	.14	2
1950	.53	.58	.91	.14	2
1951	.56	.62	.91	.14	2
1952	.55	.62	.88	.14	2
1953	.55	.64	.85	.14	2
1954	.59	.62	.95	.14	2
1955	.62	.65	.95	.14	2
1956	.62	.69	.90	.14	2

(*continued*)

Table B.5N (continued)

Year	Sears	PPI	Sears/PPI	Weight	Models
1957	.66	.74	.89	.14	2
1958	.67	.76	.88	.14	2
1959	.69	.80	.87	.13	2
1960	.70	.81	.86	.13	2
1961	.70	.83	.84	.13	2
1962	.84	.87	.97	.13	2
1963	.84	.87	.97	.13	4
1964	.84	.92	.91	.14	3
1965	.94	.95	.98	.14	3
1966	.92	.96	.96	.15	2
1967	1.05	.97	1.09	.15	2
1968	.99	.97	1.03	.15	2
1969	.85	.97	.87	.15	2
1970	.91	.98	.93	.15	2
1971	1.00	.98	1.02	.14	2
1972	1.00	1.00	1.00	.14	2
1973	1.05	1.02	1.03	.14	2
1974	1.07	1.09	.98	.14	2
1975	1.11	1.30	.86	.14	2
1976	1.26	1.38	.91	.13	3
1977	1.36	1.43	.95	.13	3
1978	1.58	1.54	1.03	.13	5
1979	1.69	1.67	1.01	.13	5
1980	1.75	1.81	.97	.12	4
1981	2.08	1.95	1.07	.12	4
1982	2.47	2.08	1.18	.12	7
1983	2.47	2.12	1.17	.12	3

O. Group Average

Year	Alternative	Official	Alternative/Official	Weight	Models
1947	.62	.46	1.34	1.00	21
1948	.61	.49	1.26	1.00	21
1949	.64	.51	1.24	1.00	24
1950	.56	.54	1.05	1.00	26
1951	.64	.58	1.09	1.00	28
1952	.61	.58	1.05	1.00	32
1953	.61	.60	1.03	1.00	30
1954	.65	.60	1.08	1.00	33
1955	.66	.65	1.03	1.00	30
1956	.70	.71	.99	1.00	35
1957	.74	.76	.97	1.00	38
1958	.75	.77	.97	1.00	37
1959	.73	.80	.91	1.00	36
1960	.76	.84	.91	1.00	37
1961	.76	.84	.90	1.00	38
1962	.78	.86	.92	1.00	35
1963	.78	.85	.91	1.00	37
1964	.77	.87	.89	1.00	37
1965	.78	.88	.89	1.00	39
1966	.78	.90	.87	1.00	36
1967	.83	.93	.90	1.00	34
1968	.84	.96	.88	1.00	40

Table B.50 (continued)

Year	Alternative	Official	Alternative/Official	Weight	Models
1969	.88	.98	.90	1.00	42
1970	.92	1.00	.92	1.00	35
1971	.97	.98	.99	1.00	36
1972	1.00	1.00	1.00	1.00	41
1973	1.02	1.04	.98	1.00	41
1974	1.06	1.17	.90	1.00	33
1975	1.26	1.35	.93	1.00	36
1976	1.39	1.43	.97	1.00	37
1977	1.48	1.52	.97	1.00	26
1978	1.55	1.65	.94	1.00	35
1979	1.61	1.84	.88	1.00	35
1980	1.66	2.07	.80	1.00	31
1981	1.90	2.29	.83	1.00	42
1982	2.05	2.38	.86	1.00	39
1983	2.13	2.39	.89	1.00	23

Table B.6   **Comparison of Alternative Price Indexes for PDE with Official Indexes from NIPA, Table 5.6, Row 13, General Industrial Equipment**

A. Stationary Air Compressors

Year	Sears	PPI	Sears/PPI	Weight	Models
1947	.81	.25	3.29	.26	3
1948	.84	.27	3.08	.20	3
1949	.73	.29	2.53	.20	6
1950	.68	.30	2.29	.20	5
1951	.82	.34	2.41	.20	6
1952	.70	.34	2.05	.20	6
1953	.81	.36	2.28	.20	7
1954	.82	.37	2.24	.20	7
1955	.87	.40	2.16	.20	6
1956	.87	.46	1.89	.20	3
1957	.93	.49	1.91	.20	6
1958	.97	.53	1.85	.19	6
1959	1.05	.57	1.83	.19	6
1960	1.05	.58	1.82	.18	3
1961	1.05	.58	1.83	.18	6
1962	.98	.58	1.70	.17	3
1963	.78	.58	1.33	.16	3
1964	.78	.62	1.27	.15	7
1965	.81	.69	1.19	.13	3
1966	.88	.76	1.17	.11	10
1967	.88	.79	1.11	.11	7
1968	.87	.83	1.05	.11	8
1969	.89	.89	.99	.11	10
1970	.95	.93	1.02	.11	8
1971	1.00	.97	1.03	.11	8
1972	1.00	1.00	1.00	.12	8
1973	1.00	1.04	.97	.12	8
1974	1.02	1.21	.84	.12	11
1975	1.14	1.48	.77	.12	3
1976	1.16	1.52	.77	.13	4
1977	1.21	1.68	.72	.13	3
1978	1.28	1.92	.67	.13	3
1979	1.37	2.13	.64	.13	3
1980	1.41	2.36	.60	.14	3
1981	1.78	2.46	.72	.14	3
1982	1.95	2.53	.77	.14	6
1983	2.11	2.51	.84	.14	3

B. Centrifugal Pumps

Year	Sears	PPI	Sears/PPI	Weight	Models
1947	.98	.41	2.40	.26	2
1948	.89	.45	1.98	.20	2
1949	.88	.49	1.77	.20	1
1950	.82	.52	1.59	.20	2
1951	.88	.60	1.47	.20	2
1952	.89	.60	1.50	.20	2
1953	.89	.61	1.46	.20	2
1954	.94	.61	1.54	.20	2
1955	.94	.62	1.52	.20	6

Table B.6B (continued)

Year	Sears	PPI	Sears/PPI	Weight	Models
1956	.86	.70	1.22	.20	8
1957	.87	.76	1.14	.20	8
1958	.84	.79	1.06	.19	10
1959	.82	.82	.99	.19	12
1960	.78	.80	.98	.18	12
1961	.78	.79	.99	.18	11
1962	.79	.79	1.00	.17	13
1963	.79	.76	1.04	.16	13
1964	.78	.76	1.03	.15	12
1965	.77	.77	1.01	.13	7
1966	.77	.79	.97	.11	8
1967	.80	.81	.98	.11	8
1968	.80	.82	.97	.11	3
1969	.85	.84	1.01	.11	8
1970	.95	.91	1.05	.11	7
1971	1.00	.97	1.03	.11	5
1972	1.00	1.00	1.00	.12	5
1973	1.00	1.01	.99	.12	5
1974	1.04	1.23	.85	.12	5
1975	1.25	1.42	.88	.12	9
1976	1.35	1.51	.89	.13	9
1977	1.35	1.63	.83	.13	6
1978	1.45	1.77	.82	.13	6
1979	1.65	1.93	.85	.13	6
1980	1.79	2.13	.84	.14	6
1981	1.96	2.30	.85	.14	6
1982	1.96	2.32	.85	.14	7
1983	2.05	2.31	.89	.14	4

C. Differential Chain Hoists

Year	Sears	PPI	Sears/PPI	Weight	Models
1948	.47	.42	1.12	.34	2
1949	.50	.44	1.13	.34	2
1950	.46	.46	1.00	.34	2
1951	.54	.52	1.03	.34	2
1952	.52	.52	.99	.34	2
1953	.54	.55	.99	.34	2
1954	.55	.56	.99	.34	2
1955	.56	.58	.97	.34	2
1956	.56	.62	.91	.34	2
1957	.63	.68	.92	.34	2
1958	.69	.71	.97	.34	2
1959	.75	.75	.99	.35	2
1960	.77	.76	1.02	.36	2
1961	.77	.76	1.02	.36	2
1962	.79	.76	1.05	.37	2
1963	.76	.76	1.01	.39	2
1964	.76	.76	1.01	.40	2
1965	.76	.76	1.01	.42	2
1966	.76	.78	.97	.44	2
1967	.85	.80	1.06	.45	2
1968	.89	.82	1.08	.44	2
1969	.95	.83	1.15	.43	2

(*continued*)

Table B.6C (continued)

Year	Sears	PPI	Sears/PPI	Weight	Models
1970	1.00	.89	1.12	.42	2
1971	1.00	.97	1.03	.42	2
1972	1.00	1.00	1.00	.41	2
1973	1.00	1.05	.95	.40	2
1974	1.03	1.18	.88	.39	2
1975	1.29	1.37	.94	.40	2
1976	1.34	1.40	.96	.40	2
1977	1.34	1.50	.89	.41	2
1978	1.56	1.57	1.00	.42	3
1979	1.59	1.67	.96	.42	3
1980	1.69	1.86	.91	.43	3
1981	1.69	2.10	.81	.44	3
1982	1.91	2.22	.86	.44	3
1983	2.10	2.23	.94	.44	3

D. Propellor Fans

Year	Sears	PPI	Sears/PPI	Weight	Models
1948	.76	.38	1.99	.07	2
1949	.76	.43	1.75	.07	2
1950	.70	.45	1.54	.07	2
1951	.81	.53	1.52	.07	2
1952	.86	.53	1.63	.07	2
1953	.86	.54	1.59	.07	1
1954	.90	.56	1.60	.07	1
1955	.88	.58	1.52	.07	2
1956	.96	.64	1.50	.07	2
1957	.96	.65	1.46	.07	1
1958	.96	.65	1.48	.06	1
1959	.89	.65	1.37	.06	1
1960	.87	.64	1.35	.06	1
1961	.87	.63	1.37	.06	1
1962	.84	.65	1.30	.06	1
1963	.84	.65	1.29	.06	1
1964	.77	.65	1.18	.06	1
1965	.77	.68	1.14	.07	1
1966	.77	.71	1.08	.08	1
1967	.84	.76	1.11	.08	1
1968	.84	.79	1.07	.09	1
1969	.91	.83	1.10	.10	1
1970	.93	.89	1.04	.11	1
1971	1.00	.95	1.06	.11	1
1972	1.00	1.00	1.00	.12	1
1973	1.00	1.08	.93	.13	1
1974	1.07	1.32	.81	.14	1
1975	1.38	1.56	.89	.13	6
1976	1.36	1.66	.82	.12	6
1977	1.48	1.82	.81	.10	4
1978	1.51	1.95	.77	.09	4
1979	1.74	2.13	.82	.07	4
1980	1.88	2.38	.79	.05	2
1981	2.06	2.62	.79	.05	4
1982	2.15	2.77	.78	.05	4
1983	2.15	2.81	.76	.05	2

Table B.6 (continued)

E. Fire Extinguishers

Year	Sears	PPI	Sears/PPI	Weight	Models
1947	.86	.78	1.09	.27	7
1948	1.00	.82	1.23	.20	7
1949	1.10	.81	1.37	.20	5
1950	.90	.83	1.09	.20	5
1951	.88	.85	1.04	.20	11
1952	.89	.85	1.05	.20	11
1953	.88	.83	1.05	.20	15
1954	.88	.84	1.04	.20	13
1955	.98	.89	1.10	.20	11
1956	1.07	.97	1.11	.20	9
1957	1.06	1.03	1.04	.20	11
1958	1.06	1.00	1.06	.21	15
1959	1.01	.92	1.11	.21	15
1960	1.00	.89	1.12	.22	14
1961	1.01	.90	1.11	.22	11
1962	.98	.88	1.11	.23	12
1963	.99	.89	1.11	.23	10
1964	.97	.90	1.08	.24	11
1965	.97	.89	1.09	.25	11
1966	.97	.89	1.09	.25	4
1967	.97	.91	1.07	.26	4
1968	.98	.90	1.09	.25	5
1969	.98	.89	1.11	.25	6
1970	.98	.90	1.09	.24	6
1971	.99	.97	1.02	.24	7
1972	1.00	1.00	1.00	.24	7
1973	1.14	1.00	1.14	.23	6
1974	1.16	1.12	1.04	.23	8
1975	1.19	1.36	.87	.23	11
1976	1.46	1.38	1.06	.23	9
1977	1.15	1.41	.81	.23	4
1978	1.15	1.46	.79	.23	6
1979	1.11	1.56	.71	.24	6
1980	1.19	1.75	.68	.24	5
1981	1.42	1.99	.71	.24	5
1982	1.67	2.17	.77	.24	5
1983	1.67	2.09	.80	.24	5

F. Group Average

Year	Alternative	Official	Alternative/Official	Weight	Models
1947	.70	.42	1.68	1.00	12
1948	.71	.45	1.58	1.00	16
1949	.72	.48	1.51	1.00	16
1950	.65	.50	1.32	1.00	16
1951	.73	.56	1.31	1.00	23
1952	.70	.55	1.27	1.00	23
1953	.73	.57	1.29	1.00	27
1954	.75	.58	1.29	1.00	25
1955	.78	.61	1.28	1.00	27
1956	.78	.67	1.17	1.00	24

(continued)

Table B.6F (continued)

Year	Alternative	Official	Alternative/Official	Weight	Models
1957	.83	.72	1.14	1.00	28
1958	.85	.74	1.15	1.00	34
1959	.87	.76	1.14	1.00	36
1960	.87	.76	1.15	1.00	32
1961	.87	.76	1.15	1.00	31
1962	.86	.75	1.15	1.00	31
1963	.82	.75	1.09	1.00	29
1964	.81	.76	1.07	1.00	33
1965	.81	.77	1.06	1.00	24
1966	.82	.80	1.03	1.00	25
1967	.87	.82	1.06	1.00	22
1968	.89	.84	1.07	1.00	19
1969	.93	.85	1.10	1.00	27
1970	.98	.90	1.08	1.00	24
1971	1.00	.97	1.03	1.00	23
1972	1.00	1.00	1.00	1.00	23
1973	1.03	1.04	.99	1.00	22
1974	1.06	1.19	.89	1.00	27
1975	1.26	1.41	.89	1.00	31
1976	1.35	1.45	.93	1.00	30
1977	1.29	1.55	.83	1.00	19
1978	1.40	1.65	.85	1.00	22
1979	1.46	1.77	.82	1.00	22
1980	1.55	1.98	.79	1.00	19
1981	1.70	2.20	.78	1.00	21
1982	1.89	2.32	.82	1.00	25
1983	2.01	2.30	.87	1.00	17

Table B.7   Comparison of Alternative Price Indexes for PDE with Official Indexes from
NIPA, Table 5.6, Row 14, Electrical Transmission, Distribution, and
Industrial Apparatus

A. Tachometers

Year	Sears	PPI	Sears/PPI	Weight	Models
1947	1.41	.38	3.66	.15	2
1948	1.40	.40	3.47	.13	2
1949	1.40	.41	3.44	.13	2
1950	1.36	.42	3.21	.13	1
1951	1.36	.48	2.82	.13	1
1952	1.36	.47	2.88	.13	1
1953	1.24	.49	2.53	.10	1
1954	1.26	.51	2.45	.08	2
1955	1.18	.52	2.28	.08	2
1956	1.18	.54	2.17	.08	1
1957	1.18	.59	1.98	.08	1
1958	1.19	.63	1.89	.08	2
1959	1.19	.65	1.82	.08	1
1960	1.19	.68	1.76	.08	1
1961	1.31	.69	1.91	.08	2
1962	1.31	.70	1.89	.08	2
1963	1.11	.69	1.60	.08	1
1964	1.11	.70	1.60	.10	1
1965	1.00	.70	1.44	.12	1
1966	1.00	.74	1.35	.12	1
1967	.98	.78	1.26	.12	2
1968	.99	.83	1.19	.12	1
1969	.99	.87	1.14	.13	2
1970	.99	.92	1.08	.13	2
1971	1.00	.98	1.02	.13	2
1972	1.00	1.00	1.00	.13	2
1973	1.05	1.01	1.04	.13	2
1974	1.11	1.10	1.01	.13	2
1975	1.26	1.22	1.03	.13	4
1976	1.30	1.30	1.00	.13	2
1977	1.35	1.35	1.00	.14	2
1978	1.35	1.41	.95	.15	3
1979	1.25	1.49	.84	.17	2
1980	1.37	1.59	.86	.18	2
1981	1.56	1.78	.88	.18	1
1982	1.72	1.96	.88	.19	2
1983	1.72	2.06	.83	.19	2

(continued)

Table B.7 (continued)

B. Electronic Auto Testers

Year	Sears	PPI	Sears/PPI	Weight	Models
1947	.99	.38	2.58	.15	1
1948	.98	.40	2.43	.13	1
1949	.98	.41	2.40	.13	1
1950	.98	.42	2.32	.13	2
1951	.98	.48	2.04	.13	3
1952	.97	.47	2.06	.13	3
1953	.96	.49	1.96	.10	2
1954	.96	.51	1.87	.08	3
1955	.96	.52	1.85	.08	1
1956	1.13	.54	2.09	.08	3
1957	1.13	.59	1.91	.08	3
1958	1.13	.63	1.80	.08	2
1959	1.05	.65	1.60	.08	2
1960	1.05	.68	1.55	.08	1
1961	1.05	.69	1.53	.08	1
1962	1.05	.70	1.51	.08	1
1963	1.05	.69	1.51	.08	2
1964	.99	.70	1.42	.10	4
1965	.97	.70	1.39	.12	2
1966	.97	.74	1.31	.12	1
1967	.97	.78	1.24	.12	1
1968	.97	.83	1.17	.12	1
1969	.97	.87	1.12	.13	2
1970	.97	.92	1.06	.13	2
1971	1.00	.98	1.02	.13	2
1972	1.00	1.00	1.00	.13	2
1973	1.00	1.01	.99	.13	2
1974	.95	1.10	.86	.13	1
1975	1.23	1.22	1.00	.13	4
1976	1.07	1.30	.83	.13	3
1977	1.21	1.35	.90	.14	1
1978	1.30	1.41	.92	.15	3
1979	1.20	1.49	.81	.17	2
1980	1.01	1.59	.64	.18	1
1981	1.19	1.78	.67	.18	1
1982	1.20	1.96	.62	.19	4
1983	1.32	2.06	.64	.19	3

C. Panel-Type Ammeters

Year	Sears	PPI	Sears/PPI	Weight	Models
1948	.69	.37	1.88	.13	1
1949	.69	.37	1.86	.13	1
1950	.69	.38	1.80	.13	2
1951	.77	.44	1.76	.13	2
1952	.74	.43	1.73	.13	2
1953	.73	.44	1.65	.10	2
1954	.73	.47	1.58	.08	1
1955	.79	.47	1.69	.08	1
1956	.79	.49	1.61	.08	1
1957	.79	.54	1.47	.08	1
1958	.79	.57	1.38	.08	1

Table B.7C (continued)

Year	Sears	PPI	Sears/PPI	Weight	Models
1959	.80	.59	1.35	.08	1
1960	.84	.61	1.37	.08	1
1961	.87	.62	1.40	.08	1
1962	.91	.63	1.44	.08	1
1963	.95	.63	1.51	.08	1
1964	.99	.63	1.57	.10	1
1965	.98	.63	1.55	.12	1
1966	.87	.67	1.30	.12	2
1967	.87	.71	1.22	.12	1
1968	.87	.83	1.05	.12	2
1969	1.00	.89	1.13	.13	1
1970	1.00	.91	1.10	.13	1
1971	1.00	.92	1.09	.13	1
1972	1.00	1.00	1.00	.13	1
1973	1.00	.92	1.09	.13	1
1974	1.04	1.00	1.04	.13	1
1975	1.15	1.11	1.03	.13	1
1976	.94	1.18	.80	.13	1
1977	.94	1.22	.77	.14	1
1978	.94	1.29	.73	.15	1
1979	.94	1.35	.69	.17	1
1980	.94	1.45	.65	.18	1
1981	1.31	1.62	.81	.18	2
1982	1.69	1.78	.95	.19	2
1983	1.88	1.88	1.00	.19	1

D. Fractional Horsepower Electric Motors

Year	Sears	PPI	Sears/PPI	Weight	Models
1947	.52	.77	.68	.14	1
1948	.62	.74	.84	.13	1
1949	.62	.73	.84	.12	2
1950	.57	.75	.76	.12	5
1951	.65	.87	.74	.12	4
1952	.65	.86	.76	.12	5
1953	.64	.86	.75	.10	5
1954	.69	.83	.83	.08	5
1955	.63	.81	.78	.08	5
1956	.72	.82	.88	.08	4
1957	.71	.86	.83	.08	4
1958	.73	.84	.87	.07	5
1959	.69	.82	.84	.07	5
1960	.69	.84	.82	.07	4
1961	.75	.83	.90	.07	1
1962	.74	.81	.91	.06	2
1963	.61	.81	.75	.06	2
1964	.64	.79	.81	.08	5
1965	.67	.78	.85	.09	4
1966	.66	.80	.82	.09	4
1967	.74	.82	.90	.09	5
1968	.76	.85	.89	.09	4
1969	.83	.88	.93	.09	3
1970	.84	.95	.89	.09	3

(*continued*)

Table B.7D (continued)

Year	Sears	PPI	Sears/PPI	Weight	Models
1971	.89	.98	.91	.09	3
1972	1.00	1.00	1.00	.09	3
1973	.96	1.03	.93	.09	1
1974	1.01	1.23	.82	.09	3
1975	1.17	1.35	.87	.09	14
1976	1.17	1.47	.80	.08	14
1977	1.25	1.57	.79	.06	5
1978	1.34	1.70	.79	.06	5
1979	1.45	1.86	.78	.05	5
1980	1.55	2.04	.76	.04	3
1981	1.74	2.26	.77	.03	5
1982	1.78	2.32	.77	.03	6
1983	1.90	2.37	.80	.03	5

E. Power Transformers

Year	Kravis-Lipsey	PPI	Kravis-Lipsey/PPI	Weight	Models
1954	2.35	1.00	2.36	.35	30
1955	1.93	1.01	1.90	.35	30
1956	2.46	1.17	2.10	.35	30
1957	2.73	1.24	2.19	.35	30
1958	2.43	1.28	1.90	.35	1
1959	2.13	1.27	1.68	.35	1
1960	1.84	1.13	1.62	.35	1
1961	1.54	1.07	1.44	.35	30
1962	1.19	1.04	1.14	.35	30
1963	1.02	1.01	1.01	.35	30
1964	1.00	1.06	.94	.35	30

F. Voltage Regulators

Year	Sears	PPI	Sears/PPI	Weight	Models
1947	.82	.65	1.27	.28	1
1948	.87	.66	1.31	.25	1
1949	.96	.67	1.43	.24	1
1950	.96	.69	1.39	.24	1
1951	.96	.78	1.24	.24	1
1952	1.08	.78	1.39	.24	1
1953	.91	.85	1.07	.19	1
1954	.95	.90	1.06	.15	1
1955	.87	.91	.96	.15	1
1956	.91	1.05	.87	.15	1
1957	.83	1.15	.73	.15	1
1958	.84	1.17	.72	.15	1
1959	.85	1.17	.73	.15	1
1960	.91	1.17	.78	.15	1
1961	.82	1.02	.81	.15	1
1962	.82	1.04	.79	.15	1
1963	.82	.97	.85	.15	1
1964	.81	.89	.91	.20	1
1965	.80	.79	1.02	.25	1
1966	.77	.80	.96	.26	1

Table B.7F (continued)

Year	Sears	PPI	Sears/PPI	Weight	Models
1967	.82	.84	.98	.26	2
1968	.82	.87	.95	.25	2
1969	.93	.85	1.09	.25	2
1970	.98	.91	1.08	.24	2
1971	.97	1.00	.97	.24	2
1972	1.00	1.00	1.00	.23	2
1973	1.00	1.04	.96	.22	2
1974	1.00	1.15	.87	.22	1
1975	1.48	1.35	1.10	.22	2
1976	1.53	1.35	1.13	.21	2
1977	1.61	1.36	1.19	.21	2
1978	1.94	1.39	1.39	.10	1
1979	2.04	1.39	1.46	.00	1

G. Fusible-Type Panelboards

Year	Sears	PPI	Sears/PPI	Weight	Models
1950	.37	.65	.57	.04	4
1951	.45	.79	.58	.04	4
1952	.47	.69	.69	.04	4
1953	.43	.65	.65	.03	4
1954	.44	.66	.66	.03	4
1955	.48	.68	.70	.03	5
1956	.54	.70	.77	.03	4
1957	.59	.76	.78	.03	4
1958	.65	.76	.85	.03	5
1959	.65	.76	.85	.03	5
1960	.65	.75	.86	.03	4
1961	.64	.72	.89	.03	4
1962	.65	.73	.90	.03	4
1963	.64	.79	.82	.03	4
1964	.64	.76	.84	.04	4
1965	.64	.72	.89	.05	4
1966	.68	.72	.94	.04	4
1967	.71	.73	.97	.04	4
1968	.74	.80	.92	.04	4
1969	.86	.89	.97	.04	1
1970	.91	.97	.94	.04	1
1971	1.00	1.00	1.00	.05	1
1972	1.00	1.00	1.00	.05	1
1973	1.00	1.00	1.00	.05	1
1974	1.00	1.14	.88	.05	1
1975	1.18	1.36	.86	.05	1
1976	1.46	1.52	.96	.05	1
1977	1.35	1.62	.83	.06	1
1978	1.36	1.79	.76	.07	1
1979	1.53	1.96	.78	.09	1
1980	1.75	2.32	.76	.09	1
1981	2.60	2.51	1.03	.10	1
1982	2.60	2.69	.97	.10	1
1983	2.60	2.74	.95	.10	1

(*continued*)

Table B.7 (continued)

H. Circuit Breaker-Type Panelboards

Year	Sears	PPI	Sears/PPI	Weight	Models
1954	.88	.69	1.28	.03	2
1955	.93	.71	1.32	.03	3
1956	1.03	.73	1.41	.03	2
1957	1.11	.77	1.45	.03	2
1958	.89	.78	1.15	.03	2
1959	.87	.78	1.12	.03	4
1960	.87	.79	1.11	.03	4
1961	.81	.78	1.04	.03	4
1962	.82	.79	1.04	.03	4
1963	.82	.78	1.04	.03	4
1964	.82	.79	1.04	.04	3
1965	.82	.78	1.05	.05	4
1966	.82	.78	1.05	.04	5
1967	.85	.80	1.07	.04	3
1968	.83	.84	.99	.04	3
1969	.90	.88	1.02	.04	2
1970	.94	.95	1.00	.04	2
1971	1.00	.99	1.01	.05	2
1972	1.00	1.00	1.00	.05	2
1973	1.03	1.00	1.03	.05	2
1974	1.03	1.13	.91	.05	2
1975	1.27	1.27	1.00	.05	4
1976	1.33	1.43	.93	.05	4
1977	1.31	1.46	.90	.06	4
1978	1.27	1.65	.77	.07	4
1979	1.31	1.82	.72	.09	4
1980	1.42	2.18	.65	.09	4
1981	2.19	2.18	1.01	.10	3
1982	2.21	2.15	1.03	.10	3
1983	2.28	2.16	1.05	.10	3

I. Indoor Safety Switches

Year	Sears	PPI	Sears/PPI	Weight	Models
1947	.63	.38	1.65	.09	2
1948	.46	.40	1.16	.08	2
1949	.43	.43	1.01	.07	2
1950	.44	.45	.96	.07	2
1951	.50	.54	.93	.07	2
1952	.52	.53	.97	.07	3
1953	.45	.55	.83	.06	3
1954	.48	.57	.85	.05	3
1955	.52	.59	.88	.05	4
1956	.59	.66	.89	.05	3
1957	.64	.70	.92	.05	3
1958	.69	.74	.93	.05	3
1959	.69	.74	.93	.05	3
1960	.69	.74	.93	.05	3
1961	.68	.74	.92	.04	3
1962	.69	.74	.92	.04	2
1963	.68	.74	.92	.05	2

Table B.7I (continued)

Year	Sears	PPI	Sears/PPI	Weight	Models
1964	.68	.74	.92	.06	2
1965	.68	.73	.93	.08	2
1966	.71	.73	.98	.08	2
1967	.75	.75	1.00	.08	3
1968	.78	.82	.94	.08	3
1969	.88	.89	.99	.08	2
1970	.92	.96	.96	.08	2
1971	1.00	1.00	1.00	.08	2
1972	1.00	1.00	1.00	.08	2
1973	1.00	1.00	1.00	.08	1
1974	1.00	1.13	.88	.08	1
1975	1.14	1.30	.88	.08	1
1976	1.44	1.48	.97	.08	1
1977	1.44	1.54	.93	.08	1
1978	1.38	1.66	.83	.09	1
1979	1.50	1.83	.82	.10	1
1980	1.97	2.15	.91	.09	1
1981	2.61	2.40	1.09	.10	1
1982	2.61	2.64	.99	.10	1
1983	2.61	2.83	.92	.10	1

J. Circuit Breakers

Year	Sears	PPI	Sears/PPI	Weight	Models
1947	.71	.40	1.79	.09	4
1948	.70	.41	1.70	.08	4
1949	.82	.42	1.98	.08	4
1950	.78	.44	1.78	.08	4
1951	.81	.50	1.63	.08	4
1952	.83	.50	1.64	.08	4
1953	.69	.53	1.30	.06	4
1954	.66	.55	1.19	.05	4
1955	.68	.56	1.22	.05	4
1956	.75	.60	1.25	.05	4
1957	.81	.66	1.24	.05	4
1958	.88	.66	1.35	.05	4
1959	.90	.65	1.40	.05	4
1960	.91	.63	1.45	.05	4
1961	.85	.64	1.34	.05	4
1962	.86	.66	1.29	.05	4
1963	.82	.68	1.21	.05	4
1964	.82	.74	1.11	.05	4
1965	.82	.74	1.11	.05	4
1966	.84	.75	1.12	.05	4
1967	.82	.81	1.01	.04	4
1968	.81	.85	.95	.04	4
1969	.92	.88	1.04	.04	3
1970	.92	.93	.99	.04	3
1971	1.01	.99	1.02	.04	3
1972	1.00	1.00	1.00	.04	3
1973	.94	1.04	.91	.05	3
1974	.94	1.15	.82	.05	3
1975	1.27	1.38	.92	.05	3

(continued)

Table B.7J (continued)

Year	Sears	PPI	Sears/PPI	Weight	Models
1976	1.26	1.52	.83	.05	3
1977	1.19	1.29	.92	.05	3
1978	1.19	1.33	.89	.06	3
1979	1.26	1.84	.68	.06	3
1980	1.37	2.26	.61	.07	3
1981	1.74	2.47	.70	.07	4
1982	1.89	2.52	.75	.07	4
1983	1.89	2.60	.73	.07	4

K. Outdoor Power Switches

Year	Sears	PPI	Sears/PPI	Weight	Models
1948	.42	.56	.75	.08	1
1949	.50	.59	.84	.07	1
1950	.39	.63	.62	.07	1
1951	.52	.75	.69	.07	2
1952	.47	.74	.64	.07	2
1953	.46	.76	.61	.06	2
1954	.49	.78	.63	.05	2
1955	.52	.82	.64	.05	2
1956	.55	.91	.61	.05	2
1957	.60	.97	.63	.05	1
1958	.66	1.03	.64	.05	1
1959	.66	1.03	.64	.05	1
1960	.66	1.03	.64	.05	1
1961	.66	1.03	.64	.04	1
1962	.66	1.03	.64	.04	2
1963	.66	1.03	.64	.05	2
1964	.65	1.03	.64	.06	2
1965	.65	1.01	.65	.08	2
1966	.71	1.01	.71	.08	2
1967	.73	1.03	.71	.08	2
1968	.74	1.01	.73	.08	2
1969	.89	.99	.90	.08	2
1970	.91	1.02	.89	.08	2
1971	1.01	1.02	.99	.08	2
1972	1.00	1.00	1.00	.08	2
1973	1.00	1.04	.96	.08	2
1974	1.00	1.35	.74	.08	2
1975	1.09	1.53	.71	.08	3
1976	1.32	1.58	.83	.08	3
1977	1.30	1.70	.76	.08	3
1978	1.28	1.85	.69	.09	3
1979	1.36	2.13	.64	.10	3
1980	1.59	2.56	.62	.09	3
1981	2.21	2.87	.77	.05	3
1982	2.21	3.09	.71	.00	2

Table B.7 (continued)

L. Group Average

Year	Alternative	Official	Alternative/Official	Weight	Models
1947	1.03	.51	2.03	1.00	11
1948	1.04	.52	2.00	1.00	13
1949	1.09	.53	2.06	1.00	14
1950	1.05	.55	1.91	1.00	22
1951	1.13	.63	1.79	1.00	23
1952	1.15	.62	1.86	1.00	25
1953	1.06	.65	1.63	1.00	24
1954	1.08	.69	1.57	1.00	57
1955	1.00	.70	1.43	1.00	58
1956	1.15	.77	1.48	1.00	55
1957	1.19	.83	1.43	1.00	54
1958	1.16	.86	1.35	1.00	27
1959	1.10	.86	1.28	1.00	28
1960	1.06	.83	1.27	1.00	25
1961	.99	.80	1.23	1.00	52
1962	.91	.80	1.13	1.00	53
1963	.84	.78	1.07	1.00	53
1964	.83	.79	1.05	1.00	57
1965	.82	.75	1.10	1.00	25
1966	.81	.77	1.05	1.00	26
1967	.84	.80	1.04	1.00	27
1968	.84	.85	.99	1.00	26
1969	.93	.88	1.05	1.00	20
1970	.95	.93	1.02	1.00	20
1971	.98	.98	1.00	1.00	20
1972	1.00	1.00	1.00	1.00	20
1973	1.00	1.01	.99	1.00	17
1974	1.01	1.13	.89	1.00	17
1975	1.25	1.29	.97	1.00	37
1976	1.26	1.37	.92	1.00	34
1977	1.30	1.41	.92	1.00	23
1978	1.36	1.49	.92	1.00	25
1979	1.38	1.61	.85	1.00	23
1980	1.46	1.81	.80	1.00	19
1981	1.89	2.00	.95	1.00	21
1982	2.04	2.15	.95	1.00	25
1983	2.13	2.24	.95	1.00	20

Table B.8   Comparison of Alternative Price Indexes for PDE with Official Indexes from
             NIPA, Table 5.6, Row 17, Autos

A. Autos

Year	Chapter 8	NIPA	Car Ratio	Weight	Models
1947	1.07	.53	2.01	1.00	48
1948	1.21	.60	2.01	1.00	48
1949	1.01	.65	1.57	1.00	68
1950	.98	.65	1.51	1.00	78
1951	1.03	.78	1.31	1.00	83
1952	1.11	.88	1.25	1.00	85
1953	1.09	.71	1.53	1.00	78
1954	1.01	.80	1.27	1.00	71
1955	1.11	.74	1.50	1.00	72
1956	1.07	1.05	1.02	1.00	78
1957	1.06	.98	1.08	1.00	80
1958	.90	1.07	.84	1.00	81
1959	.96	.94	1.03	1.00	82
1960	.96	.92	1.05	1.00	82
1961	.99	.95	1.04	1.00	85
1962	1.00	.91	1.09	1.00	89
1963	1.02	.93	1.09	1.00	100
1964	.98	.91	1.08	1.00	115
1965	.99	.87	1.14	1.00	127
1966	.92	.90	1.02	1.00	141
1967	.90	.92	.98	1.00	159
1968	.93	.91	1.02	1.00	165
1969	.88	.94	.94	1.00	162
1970	.94	1.09	.86	1.00	164
1971	.99	1.02	.96	1.00	158
1972	1.00	1.00	1.00	1.00	178
1973	.99	.98	1.01	1.00	149
1974	.92	1.11	.83	1.00	155
1975	1.11	1.18	.94	1.00	175
1976	1.22	1.15	1.06	1.00	178
1977	1.19	1.15	1.03	1.00	167
1978	1.28	1.29	.99	1.00	155
1979	1.23	1.45	.85	1.00	151
1980	1.38	1.75	.79	1.00	149
1981	1.52	1.54	.99	1.00	155
1982	1.63	1.45	1.13	1.00	124
1983	1.74	1.40	1.25	1.00	144

Table B.8 (continued)

B. Group Average

Year	Chapter 8	NIPA	Ratio	Weight	Models
1947	1.07	.53	2.01	1.00	48
1948	1.21	.60	2.01	1.00	48
1949	1.01	.65	1.57	1.00	68
1950	.98	.65	1.51	1.00	78
1951	1.03	.78	1.31	1.00	83
1952	1.11	.88	1.25	1.00	85
1953	1.09	.71	1.53	1.00	78
1954	1.01	.80	1.27	1.00	71
1955	1.11	.74	1.50	1.00	72
1956	1.07	1.05	1.02	1.00	78
1957	1.06	.98	1.08	1.00	80
1958	.90	1.07	.84	1.00	81
1959	.96	.94	1.03	1.00	82
1960	.96	.92	1.05	1.00	82
1961	.99	.95	1.04	1.00	85
1962	1.00	.91	1.09	1.00	89
1963	1.02	.93	1.09	1.00	100
1964	.98	.91	1.08	1.00 [c]	115
1965	.99	.87	1.14	1.00	127
1966	.92	.90	1.02	1.00	141
1967	.90	.92	.98	1.00	159
1968	.93	.91	1.02	1.00	165
1969	.88	.94	.94	1.00	162
1970	.94	1.09	.86	1.00	164
1971	.99	1.02	.96	1.00	158
1972	1.00	1.00	1.00	1.00	178
1973	.99	.98	1.01	1.00	149
1974	.92	1.11	.83	1.00	155
1975	1.11	1.18	.94	1.00	175
1976	1.22	1.15	1.06	1.00	178
1977	1.19	1.15	1.03	1.00	167
1978	1.28	1.29	.99	1.00	155
1979	1.23	1.45	.85	1.00	151
1980	1.38	1.75	.79	1.00	149
1981	1.52	1.54	.99	1.00	155
1982	1.63	1.45	1.13	1.00	124
1983	1.74	1.40	1.25	1.00	144

Table B.9   Comparison of Alternative Price Indexes for PDE with Official Indexes from NIPA, Table 5.6, Row 18, Aircraft

A. Aircraft

Year	Chapter 4	NIPA	Air Ratio	Weight	Models
1947	4.22	.31	13.65	1.00	41
1948	4.23	.82	5.13	1.00	63
1949	4.43	.41	10.75	1.00	32
1950	5.02	.62	8.12	1.00	32
1951	4.85	.62	7.84	1.00	20
1952	5.20	.55	9.46	1.00	58
1953	5.45	.62	8.81	1.00	53
1954	5.81	.55	10.57	1.00	56
1955	5.98	.71	8.47	1.00	53
1956	6.08	.71	8.61	1.00	67
1957	6.12	.65	9.41	1.00	96
1958	5.25	.76	6.90	1.00	98
1959	3.06	.74	4.13	1.00	86
1960	1.92	.73	2.62	1.00	117
1961	1.84	.71	2.61	1.00	150
1962	1.83	.76	2.40	1.00	107
1963	1.89	.82	2.30	1.00	64
1964	1.96	.73	2.67	1.00	80
1965	2.01	.80	2.50	1.00	139
1966	1.89	.79	2.38	1.00	185
1967	1.47	.84	1.76	1.00	96
1968	1.27	.86	1.48	1.00	129
1969	1.24	.90	1.38	1.00	230
1970	1.12	.93	1.21	1.00	122
1971	1.01	.97	1.03	1.00	73
1972	1.00	1.00	1.00	1.00	95
1973	1.04	1.05	.99	1.00	57
1974	1.07	1.12	.95	1.00	71
1975	1.13	1.24	.91	1.00	83
1976	1.21	1.41	.86	1.00	86
1977	1.35	1.50	.90	1.00	66
1978	1.41	1.65	.86	1.00	81
1979	1.42	1.82	.78	1.00	118
1980	1.56	2.03	.77	1.00	115
1981	1.72	2.23	.77	1.00	75
1982	1.78	2.47	.72	1.00	38
1983	1.74	2.53	.69	1.00	52

Table B.9 (continued)

B. Group Average

Year	Chapter 4	NIPA	Air Ratio	Weight	Models
1947	4.22	.31	13.65	1.00	41
1948	4.23	.82	5.13	1.00	63
1949	4.43	.41	10.75	1.00	32
1950	5.02	.62	8.12	1.00	32
1951	4.85	.62	7.84	1.00	20
1952	5.20	.55	9.46	1.00	58
1953	5.45	.62	8.81	1.00	53
1954	5.81	.55	10.57	1.00	56
1955	5.98	.71	8.47	1.00	53
1956	6.08	.71	8.61	1.00	67
1957	6.12	.65	9.41	1.00	96
1958	5.25	.76	6.90	1.00	98
1959	3.06	.74	4.13	1.00	86
1960	1.92	.73	2.62	1.00	117
1961	1.84	.71	2.61	1.00	150
1962	1.83	.76	2.40	1.00	107
1963	1.89	.82	2.30	1.00	64
1964	1.96	.73	2.67	1.00	80
1965	2.01	.80	2.50	1.00	139
1966	1.89	.79	2.38	1.00	185
1967	1.47	.84	1.76	1.00	96
1968	1.27	.86	1.48	1.00	129
1969	1.24	.90	1.38	1.00	230
1970	1.12	.93	1.21	1.00	122
1971	1.01	.97	1.03	1.00	73
1972	1.00	1.00	1.00	1.00	95
1973	1.04	1.05	.99	1.00	57
1974	1.07	1.12	.95	1.00	71
1975	1.13	1.24	.91	1.00	83
1976	1.21	1.41	.86	1.00	86
1977	1.35	1.50	.90	1.00	66
1978	1.41	1.65	.86	1.00	81
1979	1.42	1.82	.78	1.00	118
1980	1.56	2.03	.77	1.00	115
1981	1.72	2.23	.77	1.00	75
1982	1.78	2.47	.72	1.00	38
1983	1.74	2.53	.69	1.00	52

Table B.10   **Comparison of Alternative Price Indexes for PDE with Official Indexes from NIPA, Table 5.6, Row 20, Railroad Equipment**

A. Railroad Locomotives and Freight Cars

Year	Chapter 9	NIPA	Rail Ratio	Weight	Models
1947	.60	.43	1.38	1.00	10
1948	.69	.50	1.37	1.00	10
1949	.66	.49	1.35	1.00	10
1950	.73	.55	1.33	1.00	10
1951	.74	.56	1.32	1.00	10
1952	.76	.58	1.30	1.00	10
1953	.75	.58	1.29	1.00	10
1954	.79	.62	1.27	1.00	10
1955	.79	.63	1.25	1.00	10
1956	.80	.65	1.24	1.00	10
1957	.89	.73	1.22	1.00	10
1958	.97	.80	1.21	1.00	10
1959	.84	.70	1.19	1.00	10
1960	.93	.79	1.18	1.00	10
1961	.89	.76	1.16	1.00	10
1962	.88	.76	1.15	1.00	10
1963	.94	.82	1.14	1.00	10
1964	.90	.80	1.12	1.00	10
1965	.88	.79	1.11	1.00	10
1966	.88	.80	1.09	1.00	10
1967	.89	.83	1.08	1.00	10
1968	.90	.85	1.07	1.00	10
1969	.92	.87	1.06	1.00	10
1970	.99	.95	1.04	1.00	10
1971	1.02	1.00	1.02	1.00	10
1972	1.00	1.00	1.00	1.00	10
1973	1.05	1.07	.98	1.00	10
1974	1.17	1.22	.96	1.00	10
1975	1.47	1.57	.94	1.00	10
1976	1.59	1.72	.92	1.00	10
1977	1.66	1.85	.90	1.00	10
1978	1.77	2.01	.88	1.00	10
1979	1.91	2.21	.86	1.00	10
1980	2.08	2.43	.85	1.00	10
1981	2.29	2.72	.84	1.00	10
1982	2.33	2.80	.83	1.00	10
1983	2.30	2.80	.82	1.00	10

Table B.10 (continued)

B. Group Average

Year	Chapter 9	NIPA	Rail Ratio	Weight	Models
1947	.60	.43	1.38	1.00	10
1948	.69	.50	1.37	1.00	10
1949	.66	.49	1.35	1.00	10
1950	.73	.55	1.33	1.00	10
1951	.74	.56	1.32	1.00	10
1952	.76	.58	1.30	1.00	10
1953	.75	.58	1.29	1.00	10
1954	.79	.62	1.27	1.00	10
1955	.79	.63	1.25	1.00	10
1956	.80	.65	1.24	1.00	10
1957	.89	.73	1.22	1.00	10
1958	.97	.80	1.21	1.00	10
1959	.84	.70	1.19	1.00	10
1960	.93	.79	1.18	1.00	10
1961	.89	.76	1.16	1.00	10
1962	.88	.76	1.15	1.00	10
1963	.94	.82	1.14	1.00	10
1964	.90	.80	1.12	1.00	10
1965	.88	.79	1.11	1.00	10
1966	.88	.80	1.09	1.00	10
1967	.89	.83	1.08	1.00	10
1968	.90	.85	1.07	1.00	10
1969	.92	.87	1.06	1.00	10
1970	.99	.95	1.04	1.00	10
1971	1.02	1.00	1.02	1.00	10
1972	1.00	1.00	1.00	1.00	10
1973	1.05	1.07	.98	1.00	10
1974	1.17	1.22	.96	1.00	10
1975	1.47	1.57	.94	1.00	10
1976	1.59	1.72	.92	1.00	10
1977	1.66	1.85	.90	1.00	10
1978	1.77	2.01	.88	1.00	10
1979	1.91	2.21	.86	1.00	10
1980	2.08	2.43	.85	1.00	10
1981	2.29	2.72	.84	1.00	10
1982	2.33	2.80	.83	1.00	10
1983	2.30	2.80	.82	1.00	10

Table B.11   **Comparison of Alternative Price Indexes for PDE with Official Indexes from NIPA, Table 5.6, Row 22, Furniture and Fixtures**

A. Typewriter Tables

Year	Sears	PPI	Sears/PPI	Weight	Models
1947	.81	.47	1.74	.21	1
1948	.80	.49	1.63	.17	1
1949	.95	.51	1.86	.10	1
1950	.75	.53	1.42	.07	1
1951	.86	.60	1.44	.07	1
1952	.84	.60	1.40	.07	1
1953	.86	.61	1.40	.07	1
1954	.88	.62	1.41	.07	1
1955	.90	.65	1.37	.07	1
1956	.98	.71	1.38	.07	1
1957	1.05	.76	1.38	.07	1
1958	1.05	.79	1.33	.07	1
1959	.95	.79	1.20	.07	1
1960	.90	.79	1.14	.07	1
1961	.89	.78	1.14	.07	1
1962	.89	.79	1.13	.07	1
1963	.89	.79	1.13	.07	1
1964	.89	.79	1.12	.07	1
1965	.88	.79	1.10	.07	1
1966	.74	.80	.93	.07	1
1967	.90	.83	1.08	.07	1
1968	.93	.86	1.08	.07	1
1969	.97	.89	1.09	.07	1
1970	.97	.95	1.02	.07	1
1971	.97	.99	.98	.07	1
1972	1.00	1.00	1.00	.07	1
1973	1.02	1.10	.93	.07	1
1974	1.05	1.31	.80	.07	1
1975	1.34	1.43	.94	.07	4
1976	1.45	1.51	.96	.07	4
1977	1.54	1.59	.97	.07	4
1978	1.95	1.72	1.14	.08	4
1979	2.17	1.88	1.15	.08	3
1980	2.17	1.97	1.10	.08	2
1981	2.26	2.16	1.05	.08	3
1982	2.61	2.32	1.13	.08	3
1983	2.91	2.41	1.21	.08	3

B. Card Files

Year	Sears	PPI	Sears/PPI	Weight	Models
1947	.70	.45	1.58	.24	2
1948	.69	.47	1.48	.20	2
1949	.66	.49	1.35	.12	2
1950	.63	.51	1.22	.08	2
1951	.66	.58	1.13	.08	2
1952	.75	.58	1.29	.08	2
1953	.74	.59	1.25	.08	2
1954	.72	.60	1.20	.08	2
1955	.72	.63	1.15	.08	2

Table B.11B (continued)

Year	Sears	PPI	Sears/PPI	Weight	Models
1956	.72	.69	1.04	.08	2
1957	.75	.74	1.01	.08	2
1958	.71	.76	.93	.08	2
1959	.71	.77	.92	.08	2
1960	.75	.77	.98	.08	2
1961	.70	.77	.90	.08	2
1962	.70	.78	.89	.08	2
1963	.70	.79	.88	.08	2
1964	.68	.79	.86	.08	2
1965	.66	.79	.83	.08	2
1966	.68	.80	.84	.08	2
1967	.77	.84	.92	.08	2
1968	.77	.87	.89	.08	2
1969	.89	.90	.98	.08	2
1970	.93	.95	.98	.08	2
1971	.97	.98	.99	.08	2
1972	1.00	1.00	1.00	.08	1
1973	.95	1.09	.87	.08	1
1974	1.13	1.34	.84	.08	2
1975	1.86	1.55	1.21	.08	1
1976	1.86	1.61	1.16	.08	3
1977	2.01	1.71	1.17	.04	3
1978	2.16	1.86	1.16	.00	3

C. Fluorescent Lighting Fixtures

Year	Sears	PPI	Sears/PPI	Weight	Models
1947	.72	.49	1.45	.55	2
1948	.67	.52	1.29	.45	2
1949	.72	.54	1.32	.27	2
1950	.63	.57	1.11	.19	2
1951	.66	.63	1.04	.19	1
1952	.72	.64	1.13	.19	2
1953	.72	.65	1.11	.19	2
1954	.69	.66	1.05	.19	2
1955	.68	.70	.97	.19	2
1956	.72	.76	.96	.19	2
1957	.73	.81	.90	.19	2
1958	.73	.84	.87	.19	2
1959	.73	.84	.87	.19	2
1960	.73	.84	.87	.19	2
1961	.73	.93	.79	.19	2
1962	.74	.88	.84	.19	2
1963	.74	.86	.86	.19	2
1964	.74	.86	.86	.19	2
1965	.74	.85	.88	.19	2
1966	.74	.87	.86	.19	2
1967	.75	.88	.85	.19	2
1968	.81	.91	.89	.19	2
1969	.89	.95	.93	.19	2
1970	.95	.99	.96	.19	2
1971	1.00	1.00	1.00	.19	2

(*continued*)

Table B.11C (continued)

Year	Sears	PPI	Sears/PPI	Weight	Models
1972	1.00	1.00	1.00	.19	6
1973	.99	1.01	.98	.19	5
1974	.95	1.13	.83	.19	2
1975	1.14	1.18	.96	.19	6
1976	1.14	1.19	.96	.19	6
1977	1.14	1.20	.95	.19	3
1978	1.14	1.26	.91	.20	3
1979	1.21	1.44	.84	.20	3
1980	1.38	1.59	.87	.20	3
1981	1.55	1.81	.85	.20	3
1982	1.62	1.94	.83	.20	3
1983	1.62	1.93	.84	.20	3

D. Steel Desks

Year	Sears	PPI	Sears/PPI	Weight	Models
1950	.45	.53	.84	.23	1
1951	.48	.60	.81	.23	1
1952	.57	.60	.94	.23	1
1953	.55	.61	.90	.23	1
1954	.55	.62	.89	.23	1
1955	.57	.66	.86	.23	1
1956	.64	.71	.89	.23	1
1957	.74	.76	.98	.23	1
1958	.74	.79	.94	.23	1
1959	.74	.79	.94	.23	1
1960	.78	.79	.98	.23	1
1961	.78	.78	.99	.23	1
1962	.81	.79	1.03	.23	1
1963	.74	.79	.94	.23	1
1964	.81	.79	1.02	.23	1
1965	.88	.79	1.11	.23	1
1966	.88	.80	1.10	.23	1
1967	.88	.83	1.06	.23	1
1968	.88	.88	1.00	.23	1
1969	.92	.91	1.02	.23	1
1970	.93	.96	.97	.23	1
1971	.97	.99	.98	.23	1
1972	1.00	1.00	1.00	.23	1
1973	1.03	1.11	.92	.23	1
1974	1.08	1.30	.83	.23	1
1975	1.16	1.36	.85	.23	3
1976	1.06	1.43	.75	.23	4
1977	1.16	1.52	.76	.24	3
1978	1.29	1.65	.78	.25	3
1979	1.46	1.80	.81	.25	3
1980	1.65	1.89	.87	.25	2
1981	1.59	2.06	.77	.25	2
1982	1.76	2.23	.79	.25	3
1983	1.91	2.36	.81	.25	3

Table B.11 (continued)

E. Filing Cabinets

Year	Sears	PPI	Sears/PPI	Weight	Models
1950	.79	.51	1.55	.25	2
1951	.81	.58	1.40	.25	2
1952	.97	.58	1.67	.25	2
1953	.97	.59	1.64	.25	2
1954	.98	.60	1.64	.25	2
1955	.92	.63	1.47	.25	2
1956	1.01	.69	1.47	.25	2
1957	1.11	.74	1.50	.25	2
1958	1.12	.76	1.47	.25	2
1959	.95	.77	1.24	.25	2
1960	.99	.77	1.29	.25	4
1961	.96	.77	1.25	.25	6
1962	.79	.78	1.01	.25	4
1963	.79	.79	1.01	.25	8
1964	.80	.79	1.02	.25	8
1965	.81	.79	1.03	.25	8
1966	.83	.80	1.04	.25	8
1967	.85	.84	1.01	.25	8
1968	.91	.87	1.04	.25	8
1969	.90	.90	1.00	.25	8
1970	.97	.95	1.02	.25	8
1971	.97	.98	.99	.25	8
1972	1.00	1.00	1.00	.25	8
1973	1.01	1.09	.92	.25	8
1974	1.11	1.34	.83	.25	8
1975	1.55	1.55	1.00	.25	8
1976	1.45	1.61	.90	.25	8
1977	1.58	1.71	.92	.26	8
1978	1.74	1.86	.93	.27	8
1979	1.82	2.07	.88	.27	8
1980	1.98	2.17	.91	.27	8
1981	2.00	2.38	.84	.27	8
1982	2.20	2.54	.87	.27	8
1983	2.42	2.63	.92	.27	8

F. Office Swivel Chairs

Year	Sears	PPI	Sears/PPI	Weight	Models
1949	.85	.54	1.58	.27	1
1950	.85	.55	1.55	.19	3
1951	.87	.61	1.41	.19	3
1952	.84	.61	1.36	.19	2
1953	.84	.63	1.33	.19	1
1954	.81	.64	1.25	.19	1
1955	.79	.65	1.22	.19	1
1956	.81	.68	1.19	.19	1
1957	.87	.71	1.23	.19	1
1958	.87	.72	1.21	.19	1
1959	.76	.72	1.06	.19	1
1960	.73	.74	.98	.19	1

(continued)

Table B.11F (continued)

Year	Sears	PPI	Sears/PPI	Weight	Models
1961	.73	.75	.97	.19	1
1962	.73	.75	.97	.19	1
1963	.73	.76	.96	.19	1
1964	.73	.77	.95	.19	1
1965	.73	.77	.95	.19	1
1966	.78	.81	.96	.19	1
1967	.81	.86	.94	.19	1
1968	.92	.89	1.04	.19	1
1969	.92	.93	1.00	.19	1
1970	.97	.96	1.01	.19	1
1971	.97	.99	.99	.19	1
1972	1.00	1.00	1.00	.19	1
1973	.97	1.05	.92	.19	1
1974	1.05	1.24	.84	.19	1
1975	1.41	1.36	1.04	.19	1
1976	1.28	1.46	.88	.19	1
1977	1.44	1.56	.92	.19	1
1978	1.35	1.68	.80	.20	1
1979	1.50	1.85	.81	.20	1
1980	1.65	1.98	.83	.20	1
1981	1.50	2.19	.69	.20	1
1982	1.80	2.33	.78	.20	1
1983	1.95	2.43	.80	.20	1

G. Group Average

Year	Alternative	Official	Alternative/Official	Weight	Models
1947	.70	.47	1.48	1.00	5
1948	.67	.50	1.35	1.00	5
1949	.70	.52	1.36	1.00	6
1950	.66	.54	1.23	1.00	11
1951	.69	.60	1.15	1.00	10
1952	.77	.60	1.27	1.00	10
1953	.76	.62	1.24	1.00	9
1954	.75	.63	1.20	1.00	9
1955	.74	.65	1.13	1.00	9
1956	.80	.71	1.13	1.00	9
1957	.86	.75	1.15	1.00	9
1958	.86	.77	1.11	1.00	9
1959	.80	.78	1.03	1.00	9
1960	.81	.78	1.04	1.00	11
1961	.80	.80	1.00	1.00	13
1962	.77	.80	.97	1.00	11
1963	.76	.80	.95	1.00	15
1964	.77	.80	.97	1.00	15
1965	.79	.80	.99	1.00	15
1966	.80	.81	.98	1.00	15
1967	.83	.85	.97	1.00	15
1968	.88	.88	.99	1.00	15
1969	.91	.92	1.00	1.00	15
1970	.95	.96	.99	1.00	15
1971	.98	.99	.99	1.00	15
1972	1.00	1.00	1.00	1.00	18

Table B.11G (continued)

Year	Alternative	Official	Alternative/Official	Weight	Models
1973	1.00	1.07	.93	1.00	17
1974	1.06	1.27	.83	1.00	15
1975	1.35	1.39	.98	1.00	23
1976	1.29	1.44	.89	1.00	26
1977	1.39	1.53	.91	1.00	22
1978	1.47	1.64	.89	1.00	22
1979	1.60	1.82	.88	1.00	18
1980	1.76	1.94	.91	1.00	16
1981	1.77	2.14	.82	1.00	17
1982	1.97	2.30	.86	1.00	18
1983	2.11	2.38	.89	1.00	18

Table B.12   **Comparison of Alternative Price Indexes for PDE with Official Indexes from NIPA, Table 5.6, Row 23, Tractors**

A. Garden Tractors

Year	Sears	PPI	Sears/PPI	Weight	Models
1949	1.24	.66	1.88	.05	1
1950	1.07	.66	1.63	.03	1
1951	1.12	.68	1.64	.03	1
1952	1.11	.71	1.58	.03	1
1953	1.17	.71	1.65	.03	2
1954	1.11	.70	1.58	.03	2
1955	.93	.70	1.34	.03	3
1956	.86	.72	1.19	.03	4
1957	.88	.76	1.17	.03	4
1958	.91	.76	1.20	.03	3
1959	.85	.76	1.12	.03	1
1960	.87	.77	1.13	.04	3
1961	.86	.78	1.11	.04	4
1962	.80	.79	1.02	.04	2
1963	.79	.79	1.00	.05	3
1964	.76	.80	.95	.06	3
1965	.76	.82	.93	.06	2
1966	.77	.83	.92	.07	2
1967	.83	.83	1.00	.08	3
1968	.83	.86	.96	.08	2
1969	.84	.90	.93	.08	2
1970	.87	.95	.92	.08	2
1971	1.00	.99	1.01	.08	1
1972	1.00	1.00	1.00	.08	1
1973	1.00	1.01	.99	.08	2
1974	1.04	1.14	.91	.08	2
1975	1.39	1.28	1.08	.08	2
1976	1.41	1.40	1.00	.08	3
1977	1.41	1.52	.93	.08	7
1978	1.41	1.61	.88	.08	1
1979	1.62	1.72	.94	.08	3
1980	1.47	1.90	.77	.09	5
1981	1.47	2.04	.72	.09	3
1982	1.77	2.17	.81	.09	3
1983	1.77	2.42	.73	.09	1

B. Wheel Tractors

Year	Hedonic	PPI	Hedonic/PPI	Weight	Models
1947	.51	.47	1.09	1.00	17
1948	.62	.52	1.19	.97	17
1949	.75	.55	1.36	.68	14
1950	.66	.56	1.28	.43	17
1951	.82	.59	1.39	.43	18
1952	.84	.60	1.40	.43	18
1953	.79	.60	1.31	.43	19
1954	.75	.59	1.28	.43	15
1955	.64	.58	1.10	.43	8
1956	.68	.60	1.13	.43	10
1957	.70	.63	1.11	.43	6
1958	.77	.66	1.18	.42	10

Table B.12B (continued)

Year	Hedonic	PPI	Hedonic/PPI	Weight	Models
1959	.84	.68	1.24	.42	13
1960	.79	.69	1.14	.42	18
1961	.79	.71	1.12	.42	16
1962	.84	.72	1.16	.41	18
1963	.82	.73	1.11	.41	16
1964	.85	.75	1.14	.40	19
1965	.82	.76	1.07	.40	18
1966	.82	.79	1.04	.40	16
1967	.85	.81	1.05	.39	20
1968	.90	.84	1.07	.39	22
1969	.93	.88	1.05	.39	21
1970	.97	.93	1.05	.39	16
1971	.96	.96	1.00	.39	28
1972	1.00	1.00	1.00	.39	22
1973	1.00	1.02	.98	.40	30
1974	1.05	1.17	.89	.40	25
1975	1.70	1.39	1.22	.39	26
1976	1.78	1.51	1.17	.39	30
1977	1.97	1.65	1.19	.38	12
1978	2.15	1.79	1.20	.38	12
1979	2.43	1.97	1.24	.37	24
1980	2.57	2.26	1.14	.37	24
1981	2.94	2.55	1.15	.37	30
1982	2.99	2.80	1.07	.37	30
1983	2.93	2.97	.99	.37	30

C. Crawler Tractors

Year	Hedonic	PPI	Hedonic/PPI	Weight	Models
1950	.54	.37	1.45	.54	8
1951	.66	.41	1.61	.54	8
1952	.65	.43	1.52	.54	9
1953	.64	.45	1.41	.54	10
1954	.69	.47	1.47	.54	10
1955	.65	.49	1.33	.54	10
1956	.67	.55	1.23	.54	10
1957	.61	.59	1.05	.54	6
1958	.73	.62	1.18	.54	6
1959	.77	.64	1.20	.54	6
1960	.80	.66	1.22	.54	6
1961	.87	.67	1.29	.54	6
1962	.87	.67	1.28	.55	12
1963	.82	.69	1.19	.54	11
1964	.84	.72	1.17	.54	10
1965	.85	.73	1.16	.54	10
1966	.85	.75	1.14	.53	9
1967	.89	.78	1.14	.53	6
1968	.88	.84	1.04	.53	6
1969	.95	.89	1.07	.53	12
1970	1.00	.92	1.08	.53	6
1971	.98	.97	1.02	.53	6
1972	1.00	1.00	1.00	.53	6

(continued)

Table B.12C (continued)

Year	Hedonic	PPI	Hedonic/PPI	Weight	Models
1973	1.05	1.04	1.01	.53	5
1974	1.09	1.23	.89	.53	4
1975	1.29	1.50	.86	.53	2
1976	1.35	1.62	.84	.53	2
1977	1.65	1.76	.94	.53	2
1978	1.69	1.94	.87	.54	10
1979	1.64	2.15	.76	.54	7
1980	1.62	2.39	.68	.54	7
1981	1.68	2.61	.64	.55	8
1982	1.78	2.86	.62	.55	5
1983	1.72	2.96	.58	.55	2

D. Group Average

Year	Alternative	Official	Alternative/Official	Weight	Models
1947	.46	.38	1.18	1.00	17
1948	.55	.43	1.29	1.00	17
1949	.66	.45	1.47	1.00	15
1950	.60	.45	1.33	1.00	26
1951	.74	.49	1.50	1.00	27
1952	.73	.50	1.46	1.00	28
1953	.71	.52	1.36	1.00	31
1954	.73	.53	1.38	1.00	27
1955	.65	.53	1.22	1.00	21
1956	.68	.57	1.18	1.00	24
1957	.65	.61	1.07	1.00	16
1958	.75	.64	1.17	1.00	19
1959	.80	.66	1.21	1.00	20
1960	.80	.68	1.18	1.00	27
1961	.83	.69	1.21	1.00	26
1962	.85	.70	1.21	1.00	32
1963	.82	.71	1.14	1.00	30
1964	.84	.73	1.14	1.00	32
1965	.83	.75	1.11	1.00	30
1966	.83	.77	1.08	1.00	27
1967	.87	.80	1.09	1.00	29
1968	.88	.85	1.05	1.00	30
1969	.93	.89	1.05	1.00	35
1970	.98	.93	1.05	1.00	24
1971	.97	.96	1.01	1.00	35
1972	1.00	1.00	1.00	1.00	29
1973	1.03	1.03	1.00	1.00	37
1974	1.07	1.20	.89	1.00	31
1975	1.45	1.44	1.01	1.00	30
1976	1.51	1.56	.97	1.00	35
1977	1.75	1.70	1.03	1.00	21
1978	1.83	1.85	.99	1.00	23
1979	1.91	2.04	.94	1.00	34
1980	1.92	2.29	.84	1.00	36
1981	2.06	2.53	.81	1.00	41
1982	2.17	2.77	.78	1.00	38
1983	2.12	2.91	.73	1.00	33

Table B.13   **Comparison of Alternative Price Indexes for PDE with Official Indexes from NIPA, Table 5.6, Row 24, Agricultural Machinery, Except Tractors**

A. Tractor-Drawn Plows

Year	Sears	PPI	Sears/PPI	Weight	Models
1948	.34	.41	.83	.18	2
1949	.36	.46	.79	.12	2
1950	.39	.48	.80	.12	3
1951	.42	.54	.77	.12	3
1952	.42	.54	.77	.12	1
1953	.46	.54	.84	.12	1
1954	.49	.56	.87	.12	1
1955	.49	.59	.83	.12	2
1956	.48	.60	.79	.12	2
1957	.49	.63	.78	.12	2
1958	.54	.66	.82	.12	1
1959	.54	.68	.79	.12	2
1960	.34	.70	.48	.12	3
1961	.56	.71	.79	.12	2
1962	.56	.73	.77	.12	1
1963	.56	.75	.75	.12	2
1964	.56	.77	.73	.13	2
1965	.56	.78	.72	.13	2
1966	.58	.80	.72	.13	2
1967	.63	.84	.75	.13	2
1968	.66	.87	.76	.13	1
1969	.70	.90	.78	.13	1
1970	.84	.93	.90	.13	2
1971	.92	.96	.96	.13	2
1972	1.00	1.00	1.00	.13	2
1973	1.04	1.03	1.01	.13	2
1974	1.04	1.22	.85	.13	2
1975	1.53	1.47	1.04	.13	2
1976	1.52	1.63	.93	.12	3
1977	1.49	1.80	.83	.11	4
1978	1.64	1.95	.84	.11	7
1979	1.87	2.16	.86	.10	6
1980	2.31	2.47	.93	.09	5
1981	2.49	2.78	.90	.09	6
1982	3.04	3.04	1.00	.09	5
1983	3.40	3.22	1.05	.09	1

B. Tractor-Drawn Harrows

Year	Sears	PPI	Sears/PPI	Weight	Models
1948	.36	.46	.77	.10	1
1949	.42	.50	.84	.07	1
1950	.39	.52	.74	.06	2
1951	.41	.58	.72	.06	4
1952	.44	.55	.79	.06	1
1953	.44	.55	.80	.06	2
1954	.50	.56	.90	.06	7
1955	.47	.57	.83	.06	5
1956	.45	.59	.77	.06	5
1957	.47	.61	.77	.06	2

(continued)

Table B.13B (continued)

Year	Sears	PPI	Sears/PPI	Weight	Models
1958	.56	.63	.89	.06	3
1959	.56	.66	.85	.07	2
1960	.59	.68	.87	.07	2
1961	.59	.69	.85	.07	1
1962	.59	.71	.83	.07	1
1963	.59	.72	.82	.07	1
1964	.59	.73	.81	.08	1
1965	.66	.75	.88	.08	1
1966	.68	.78	.87	.09	1
1967	.69	.80	.86	.09	2
1968	.72	.82	.88	.09	2
1969	.78	.85	.91	.09	2
1970	.87	.89	.98	.09	2
1971	.93	.92	1.01	.09	2
1972	1.00	1.00	1.00	.09	1
1973	1.00	1.03	.97	.09	1
1974	1.06	1.21	.88	.08	1
1975	1.58	1.46	1.09	.09	1
1976	1.63	1.61	1.01	.09	2
1977	1.63	1.72	.95	.09	2
1978	1.86	1.84	1.01	.09	2
1979	2.13	2.07	1.03	.10	2
1980	2.62	2.40	1.09	.10	2
1981	2.62	2.70	.97	.10	6
1982	3.06	2.83	1.08	.10	4
1983	3.18	3.00	1.06	.10	4

C. Seeders

Year	Sears	PPI	Sears/PPI	Weight	Models
1947	.46	.32	1.43	.22	1
1948	.44	.37	1.18	.10	1
1949	.63	.41	1.52	.07	1
1950	.57	.42	1.35	.06	1
1951	.57	.45	1.26	.06	1
1952	.61	.47	1.30	.06	2
1953	.63	.47	1.33	.06	2
1954	.63	.47	1.33	.06	2
1955	.59	.49	1.22	.06	2
1956	.62	.50	1.23	.06	2
1957	.64	.53	1.22	.06	2
1958	.67	.57	1.18	.06	2
1959	.67	.60	1.13	.07	2
1960	.69	.61	1.12	.07	2
1961	.69	.63	1.10	.07	2
1962	.69	.65	1.05	.07	2
1963	.69	.67	1.03	.07	2
1964	.69	.69	1.00	.08	2
1965	.73	.71	1.02	.08	2
1966	.73	.74	.99	.09	2
1967	.78	.77	1.02	.09	2
1968	.81	.81	.99	.09	2
1969	.89	.85	1.04	.09	4
1970	.92	.87	1.05	.09	4

Table B.13C (continued)

Year	Sears	PPI	Sears/PPI	Weight	Models
1971	.95	.94	1.01	.09	4
1972	1.00	1.00	1.00	.09	2
1973	.99	1.03	.96	.09	2
1974	1.05	1.18	.89	.08	2
1975	1.62	1.37	1.18	.09	1
1976	1.62	1.56	1.04	.09	2
1977	1.62	1.74	.93	.09	1
1978	1.72	1.91	.90	.09	1
1979	1.92	2.07	.93	.10	1
1980	2.22	2.30	.97	.10	1
1981	2.22	2.50	.89	.10	9
1982	2.56	2.66	.96	.10	11
1983	2.55	2.75	.93	.10	8

D. Manure Spreaders

Year	Sears	PPI	Sears/PPI	Weight	Models
1950	.60	.55	1.09	.06	2
1951	.63	.60	1.05	.06	2
1952	.64	.60	1.06	.06	2
1953	.66	.61	1.08	.06	2
1954	.66	.61	1.08	.06	1
1955	.62	.62	1.00	.06	2
1956	.61	.64	.94	.06	2
1957	.71	.68	1.04	.06	2
1958	.73	.71	1.02	.06	2
1959	.73	.74	.99	.07	1
1960	.77	.74	1.04	.07	1
1961	.77	.76	1.02	.07	2
1962	.74	.76	.97	.07	2
1963	.76	.78	.97	.07	2
1964	.78	.79	.99	.08	2
1965	.78	.80	.98	.08	1
1966	.82	.82	1.00	.09	1
1967	.86	.83	1.03	.09	1
1968	.89	.87	1.02	.09	1
1969	.90	.89	1.01	.09	1
1970	.93	.93	1.00	.09	1
1971	.95	.95	1.00	.09	1
1972	1.00	1.00	1.00	.09	1
1973	1.00	1.04	.96	.09	2
1974	1.08	1.15	.94	.08	1
1975	1.53	1.34	1.14	.09	3
1976	1.56	1.40	1.12	.09	10
1977	1.65	1.56	1.06	.09	11
1978	1.81	1.63	1.11	.09	7
1979	2.08	1.82	1.14	.10	10
1980	2.41	2.06	1.17	.10	8
1981	2.45	2.31	1.06	.10	8
1982	2.82	2.45	1.15	.10	11
1983	2.82	2.51	1.12	.10	8

(*continued*)

Table B.13 (continued)

E. Tractor-Drawn Cultivators

Year	Sears	PPI	Sears/PPI	Weight	Models
1949	.44	.44	1.01	.11	2
1950	.43	.44	.96	.10	3
1951	.46	.48	.95	.10	1
1952	.44	.49	.90	.10	1
1953	.48	.49	.97	.10	1
1954	.48	.49	.98	.10	4
1955	.57	.50	1.15	.10	3
1956	.60	.51	1.17	.10	3
1957	.61	.54	1.13	.10	3
1958	.63	.57	1.10	.10	4
1959	.58	.62	.94	.11	3
1960	.58	.64	.90	.11	3
1961	.58	.66	.88	.11	4
1962	.60	.68	.89	.11	2
1963	.60	.70	.86	.11	2
1964	.63	.71	.89	.11	2
1965	.70	.73	.96	.11	2
1966	.73	.76	.96	.11	2
1967	.75	.80	.93	.11	2
1968	.75	.84	.89	.11	2
1969	.76	.88	.86	.11	2
1970	.84	.92	.91	.11	2
1971	.93	.96	.96	.11	2
1972	1.00	1.00	1.00	.11	1
1973	1.00	1.08	.93	.11	1
1974	1.06	1.23	.86	.11	2
1975	1.48	1.44	1.03	.11	1
1976	1.48	1.52	.97	.11	1
1977	1.52	1.61	.94	.10	4
1978	1.81	1.74	1.04	.10	3
1979	2.22	1.86	1.19	.10	2
1980	1.83	2.14	.85	.09	1
1981	2.09	2.47	.85	.09	2
1982	2.22	2.66	.84	.09	2
1983	2.10	2.78	.75	.09	3

F. Sprayers

Year	Sears	PPI	Sears/PPI	Weight	Models
1947	.40	.48	.84	.24	3
1948	.41	.53	.77	.11	3
1949	.43	.55	.78	.07	3
1950	.39	.56	.70	.07	3
1951	.46	.61	.74	.07	3
1952	.51	.63	.80	.07	4
1953	.49	.65	.75	.07	5
1954	.49	.66	.74	.07	4
1955	.50	.66	.75	.07	3
1956	.51	.70	.73	.07	3
1957	.55	.74	.74	.07	3
1958	.57	.75	.77	.07	4

Table B.13F (continued)

Year	Sears	PPI	Sears/PPI	Weight	Models
1959	.62	.75	.82	.07	3
1960	.70	.76	.92	.08	3
1961	.69	.77	.89	.08	2
1962	.70	.77	.90	.08	2
1963	.70	.78	.90	.08	2
1964	.70	.77	.90	.08	2
1965	.70	.77	.90	.07	2
1966	.73	.78	.94	.07	2
1967	.75	.82	.92	.06	2
1968	.76	.88	.86	.06	2
1969	.81	.91	.89	.07	2
1970	.87	.95	.91	.07	2
1971	.89	.96	.93	.07	2
1972	1.00	1.00	1.00	.07	2
1973	1.20	1.04	1.15	.07	2
1974	1.30	1.17	1.11	.07	2
1975	1.54	1.28	1.21	.07	2
1976	1.75	1.39	1.26	.08	1
1977	1.88	1.47	1.28	.08	12
1978	2.05	1.48	1.38	.09	8
1979	2.28	1.55	1.47	.09	6
1980	2.57	1.78	1.45	.10	6
1981	2.67	1.94	1.38	.10	8
1982	2.90	2.11	1.37	.10	9
1983	3.19	2.15	1.48	.10	9

G. Tractor-Mounted Mowers

Year	Sears	PPI	Sears/PPI	Weight	Models
1949	.61	.41	1.49	.37	1
1950	.51	.42	1.22	.36	1
1951	.51	.43	1.17	.36	1
1952	.54	.45	1.21	.36	1
1953	.55	.45	1.21	.36	1
1954	.55	.46	1.20	.36	1
1955	.53	.47	1.13	.36	1
1956	.57	.48	1.19	.36	2
1957	.57	.50	1.13	.36	2
1958	.66	.53	1.23	.35	1
1959	.62	.57	1.09	.33	1
1960	.65	.58	1.12	.32	2
1961	.65	.59	1.10	.31	2
1962	.65	.61	1.08	.29	2
1963	.65	.63	1.04	.27	2
1964	.65	.65	1.00	.26	2
1965	.65	.67	.97	.24	2
1966	.69	.71	.97	.22	2
1967	.71	.75	.94	.22	2
1968	.78	.78	1.00	.23	1
1969	.81	.84	.96	.23	1
1970	.89	.89	1.00	.24	1
1971	.99	.95	1.05	.25	3

(*continued*)

Table B.13G (continued)

Year	Sears	PPI	Sears/PPI	Weight	Models
1972	1.00	1.00	1.00	.25	3
1973	1.11	1.02	1.08	.26	2
1974	1.11	1.12	.99	.27	1
1975	1.51	1.22	1.24	.27	2
1976	1.51	1.25	1.21	.27	4
1977	1.61	1.36	1.18	.27	4
1978	1.63	1.50	1.09	.27	4
1979	1.93	1.70	1.14	.27	4
1980	2.04	1.90	1.08	.26	4
1981	2.04	2.25	.91	.26	6
1982	2.15	2.48	.86	.26	6
1983	2.19	2.60	.84	.26	3

H. Portable Farm Elevators

Year	Sears	PPI	Sears/PPI	Weight	Models
1948	.58	.45	1.30	.13	1
1949	.59	.49	1.21	.09	1
1950	.60	.48	1.25	.08	1
1951	.60	.54	1.10	.08	1
1952	.61	.55	1.10	.08	1
1953	.61	.55	1.10	.08	1
1954	.56	.56	1.01	.08	1
1955	.59	.57	1.04	.08	1
1956	.62	.59	1.05	.08	1
1957	.67	.61	1.10	.08	2
1958	.67	.64	1.05	.09	2
1959	.64	.66	.97	.09	1
1960	.64	.68	.95	.10	2
1961	.64	.69	.93	.10	2
1962	.63	.71	.90	.11	1
1963	.64	.72	.90	.11	2
1964	.81	.73	1.10	.11	2
1965	.81	.75	1.09	.12	2
1966	.85	.77	1.10	.12	2
1967	.88	.80	1.10	.13	2
1968	.88	.83	1.06	.13	2
1969	.87	.87	.99	.13	3
1970	.89	.91	.98	.13	3
1971	.95	.96	.99	.13	3
1972	1.00	1.00	1.00	.13	2
1973	1.04	1.06	.98	.13	2
1974	1.08	1.30	.83	.13	2
1975	1.74	1.60	1.09	.13	2
1976	1.87	1.67	1.12	.13	4
1977	2.17	1.81	1.20	.13	4
1978	2.53	2.01	1.25	.12	4
1979	3.09	2.29	1.35	.12	3
1980	3.57	2.53	1.41	.12	1
1981	3.81	2.78	1.37	.12	1
1982	4.40	2.96	1.49	.12	1
1983	4.76	3.09	1.54	.12	1

Table B.13 (continued)

I. Poultry Brooders

Year	Sears	PPI	Sears/PPI	Weight	Models
1947	.77	.50	1.54	.27	4
1948	.75	.55	1.37	.13	4
1949	.87	.60	1.46	.08	2
1950	.83	.63	1.32	.08	2
1951	.95	.71	1.34	.08	3
1952	.96	.71	1.35	.08	2
1953	.97	.71	1.37	.08	2
1954	.97	.76	1.28	.08	3
1955	.89	.75	1.19	.08	3
1956	.79	.73	1.08	.08	3
1957	.86	.76	1.14	.08	2
1958	.83	.78	1.07	.08	2
1959	.83	.80	1.04	.08	2
1960	.83	.80	1.03	.08	5
1961	.78	.81	.97	.08	5
1962	.81	.82	.98	.08	2
1963	.81	.81	1.00	.08	2
1964	.81	.82	.99	.08	2
1965	.82	.83	.99	.08	2
1966	.83	.84	.99	.08	1
1967	.84	.86	.97	.07	1
1968	.89	.89	1.00	.07	2
1969	.89	.91	.98	.06	3
1970	.94	.94	1.00	.05	3
1971	.96	.98	.98	.05	3
1972	1.00	1.00	1.00	.04	2
1973	1.01	1.02	.99	.04	2
1974	1.06	1.09	.97	.03	2
1975	1.43	1.14	1.25	.03	2
1976	1.55	1.26	1.23	.03	7
1977	1.65	1.34	1.23	.03	7
1978	1.73	1.44	1.21	.03	7
1979	2.14	1.57	1.36	.04	7
1980	2.42	1.73	1.40	.04	6
1981	2.56	1.96	1.31	.04	6
1982	2.85	2.11	1.35	.04	6
1983	3.06	2.17	1.41	.04	6

J. Group Average

Year	Alternative	Official	Alternative/Official	Weight	Models
1947	.50	.38	1.33	1.00	8
1948	.50	.43	1.16	1.00	12
1949	.54	.47	1.16	1.00	13
1950	.50	.48	1.05	1.00	18
1951	.52	.52	1.01	1.00	19
1952	.54	.53	1.03	1.00	15
1953	.56	.53	1.05	1.00	17
1954	.56	.54	1.05	1.00	24

(continued)

Table B.13J (continued)

Year	Alternative	Official	Alternative/Official	Weight	Models
1955	.56	.55	1.02	1.00	22
1956	.57	.56	1.01	1.00	23
1957	.60	.59	1.01	1.00	20
1958	.65	.62	1.04	1.00	21
1959	.63	.65	.97	1.00	17
1960	.61	.66	.92	1.00	23
1961	.65	.68	.96	1.00	22
1962	.65	.69	.94	1.00	15
1963	.65	.71	.93	1.00	17
1964	.68	.72	.94	1.00	17
1965	.69	.74	.94	1.00	16
1966	.72	.77	.94	1.00	15
1967	.75	.80	.94	1.00	16
1968	.78	.83	.94	1.00	15
1969	.81	.87	.93	1.00	19
1970	.88	.91	.97	1.00	20
1971	.95	.95	1.00	1.00	22
1972	1.00	1.00	1.00	1.00	16
1973	1.05	1.04	1.01	1.00	16
1974	1.09	1.19	.92	1.00	15
1975	1.55	1.36	1.14	1.00	16
1976	1.59	1.46	1.09	1.00	34
1977	1.67	1.58	1.06	1.00	49
1978	1.82	1.71	1.06	1.00	43
1979	2.13	1.90	1.12	1.00	41
1980	2.35	2.14	1.10	1.00	54
1981	2.43	2.42	1.00	1.00	52
1982	2.72	2.61	1.04	1.00	55
1983	2.81	2.73	1.03	1.00	43

Table B.14   **Comparison of Alternative Price Indexes for PDE with Official Indexes from NIPA, Table 5.6, Row 25, Construction Machinery, Except Tractors**

A. Post-Hole Diggers

Year	Sears	PPI	Sears/PPI	Weight	Models
1956	.92	.59	1.57	.12	1
1957	.92	.63	1.47	.12	1
1958	.92	.63	1.45	.12	2
1959	.93	.65	1.42	.12	2
1960	.93	.67	1.38	.12	2
1961	.93	.69	1.36	.12	2
1962	.91	.70	1.31	.12	2
1963	.95	.70	1.36	.12	2
1964	.94	.72	1.30	.13	1
1965	.94	.73	1.29	.13	2
1966	.96	.75	1.28	.14	2
1967	.98	.76	1.29	.14	2
1968	.95	.80	1.19	.15	3
1969	.97	.85	1.15	.15	2
1970	.98	.91	1.08	.16	3
1971	1.00	.96	1.04	.16	3
1972	1.00	1.00	1.00	.17	1
1973	1.04	1.05	.99	.17	1
1974	1.04	1.16	.90	.18	1
1975	1.23	1.24	.99	.18	3
1976	1.23	1.47	.84	.17	3
1977	1.23	1.75	.70	.17	2
1978	1.37	1.96	.70	.16	2
1979	1.56	2.11	.74	.15	2
1980	1.82	2.40	.76	.14	2
1981	1.81	2.75	.66	.14	2
1982	2.00	3.11	.64	.14	3
1983	2.10	3.31	.64	.14	3

B. Roto Spaders

Year	Sears	PPI	Sears/PPI	Weight	Models
1948	.96	.46	2.06	.13	1
1949	.95	.48	1.98	.13	1
1950	.95	.49	1.92	.13	1
1951	.95	.53	1.80	.13	1
1952	.94	.53	1.79	.13	1
1953	.94	.54	1.74	.13	1
1954	.94	.55	1.70	.13	1
1955	.87	.56	1.56	.12	1
1956	.92	.59	1.56	.12	3
1957	.95	.63	1.52	.12	3
1958	.95	.63	1.50	.12	3
1959	.85	.65	1.30	.12	1
1960	.89	.67	1.32	.12	2
1961	.81	.69	1.19	.12	2
1962	.82	.70	1.18	.12	4
1963	.82	.70	1.17	.12	3
1964	.81	.72	1.13	.13	4

(continued)

Table B.14B (continued)

Year	Sears	PPI	Sears/PPI	Weight	Models
1965	.82	.73	1.12	.13	4
1966	.83	.75	1.10	.14	5
1967	.85	.76	1.11	.14	2
1968	.88	.80	1.11	.15	4
1969	.98	.85	1.16	.15	6
1970	.98	.91	1.08	.16	6
1971	.98	.96	1.02	.16	6
1972	1.00	1.00	1.00	.17	6
1973	1.03	1.05	.98	.17	6
1974	1.11	1.16	.96	.18	7
1975	1.42	1.24	1.14	.18	5
1976	1.70	1.36	1.26	.17	10
1977	1.69	1.75	.97	.17	5
1978	1.81	1.96	.93	.16	4
1979	2.10	2.11	1.00	.15	4
1980	2.14	2.40	.89	.07	4
1981	2.14	2.75	.78	.00	2

C. Centrifugal Pumps

Year	Sears	PPI	Sears/PPI	Weight	Models
1947	.98	.41	2.40	.16	2
1948	.89	.45	1.98	.13	2
1949	.88	.49	1.77	.13	1
1950	.82	.52	1.59	.13	2
1951	.88	.60	1.47	.13	2
1952	.89	.60	1.50	.13	2
1953	.89	.61	1.46	.13	2
1954	.94	.61	1.54	.13	2
1955	.94	.62	1.52	.12	6
1956	.86	.70	1.22	.12	8
1957	.87	.76	1.14	.12	8
1958	.84	.79	1.06	.12	10
1959	.82	.82	.99	.12	12
1960	.78	.80	.98	.12	12
1961	.78	.79	.99	.12	11
1962	.79	.79	1.00	.12	13
1963	.79	.76	1.04	.12	13
1964	.78	.76	1.03	.13	12
1965	.77	.77	1.01	.13	7
1966	.77	.79	.97	.14	8
1967	.80	.81	.98	.14	8
1968	.80	.82	.97	.15	3
1969	.85	.84	1.01	.15	8
1970	.95	.91	1.05	.16	7
1971	1.00	.97	1.03	.16	5
1972	1.00	1.00	1.00	.17	5
1973	1.00	1.01	.99	.17	5
1974	1.04	1.23	.85	.18	5
1975	1.25	1.42	.88	.18	9
1976	1.35	1.51	.89	.17	9

Table B.14C (continued)

Year	Sears	PPI	Sears/PPI	Weight	Models
1977	1.35	1.63	.83	.17	6
1978	1.45	1.77	.82	.16	6
1979	1.65	1.93	.85	.15	6
1980	1.79	2.13	.84	.14	6
1981	1.96	2.30	.85	.14	6
1982	1.96	2.32	.85	.14	7
1983	2.05	2.31	.89	.14	4

D. Stationary Air Compressors

Year	Sears	PPI	Sears/PPI	Weight	Models
1947	.81	.25	3.29	.16	3
1948	.84	.27	3.08	.13	3
1949	.73	.29	2.53	.13	6
1950	.68	.30	2.29	.13	5
1951	.82	.34	2.41	.13	6
1952	.70	.34	2.05	.13	6
1953	.81	.36	2.28	.13	7
1954	.82	.37	2.24	.13	7
1955	.87	.40	2.16	.12	6
1956	.87	.46	1.89	.12	3
1957	.93	.49	1.91	.12	6
1958	.97	.53	1.85	.12	6
1959	1.05	.57	1.83	.12	6
1960	1.05	.58	1.82	.12	3
1961	1.05	.58	1.83	.12	6
1962	.98	.58	1.70	.12	3
1963	.78	.58	1.33	.12	3
1964	.78	.62	1.27	.13	7
1965	.81	.69	1.19	.13	3
1966	.88	.76	1.17	.14	10
1967	.88	.79	1.11	.14	7
1968	.87	.83	1.05	.15	8
1969	.89	.89	.99	.15	10
1970	.95	.93	1.02	.16	8
1971	1.00	.97	1.03	.16	8
1972	1.00	1.00	1.00	.17	8
1973	1.00	1.04	.97	.17	8
1974	1.02	1.21	.84	.18	11
1975	1.14	1.48	.77	.18	3
1976	1.16	1.52	.77	.17	4
1977	1.21	1.68	.72	.17	3
1978	1.28	1.92	.67	.16	3
1979	1.37	2.13	.64	.15	3
1980	1.41	2.36	.60	.14	3
1981	1.78	2.46	.72	.14	3
1982	1.95	2.53	.77	.14	6
1983	2.11	2.51	.84	.14	3

(continued)

Table B.14 (continued)

E. Portable Concrete Mixers

Year	Sears	PPI	Sears/PPI	Weight	Models
1947	.55	.51	1.09	.56	1
1948	.60	.53	1.12	.47	1
1949	.62	.56	1.12	.47	2
1950	.62	.57	1.08	.47	3
1951	.63	.62	1.01	.47	3
1952	.65	.62	1.04	.47	3
1953	.67	.59	1.14	.47	3
1954	.67	.58	1.16	.47	3
1955	.66	.58	1.14	.44	3
1956	.69	.61	1.12	.42	3
1957	.72	.65	1.12	.42	3
1958	.72	.68	1.06	.41	2
1959	.75	.70	1.07	.41	2
1960	.76	.71	1.07	.41	1
1961	.76	.70	1.09	.40	2
1962	.75	.71	1.06	.40	2
1963	.73	.71	1.03	.39	2
1964	.72	.74	.98	.36	2
1965	.72	.75	.96	.34	2
1966	.74	.78	.95	.32	2
1967	.75	.81	.92	.29	2
1968	.84	.84	.99	.26	2
1969	.86	.87	.99	.23	2
1970	.97	.94	1.03	.20	2
1971	.99	.99	1.00	.18	2
1972	1.00	1.00	1.00	.15	2
1973	1.09	1.04	1.04	.13	2
1974	1.15	1.16	.99	.10	2
1975	1.48	1.23	1.20	.11	3
1976	1.41	1.29	1.09	.14	3
1977	1.62	1.35	1.20	.17	3
1978	1.73	1.38	1.26	.22	3
1979	2.06	1.51	1.37	.27	2
1980	2.19	1.71	1.29	.36	2
1981	2.39	1.71	1.40	.42	2
1982	2.62	1.90	1.38	.42	3
1983	2.88	1.96	1.47	.42	2

F. Differential Chain Hoists

Year	Sears	PPI	Sears/PPI	Weight	Models
1948	.47	.42	1.12	.13	2
1949	.50	.44	1.13	.13	2
1950	.46	.46	1.00	.13	2
1951	.54	.52	1.03	.13	2
1952	.52	.52	.99	.13	2
1953	.54	.55	.99	.13	2
1954	.55	.56	.99	.13	2
1955	.56	.58	.97	.12	2
1956	.56	.62	.91	.12	2
1957	.63	.68	.92	.12	2
1958	.69	.71	.97	.12	2

Table B.14F (continued)

Year	Sears	PPI	Sears/PPI	Weight	Models
1959	.75	.75	.99	.12	2
1960	.77	.76	1.02	.12	2
1961	.77	.76	1.02	.12	2
1962	.79	.76	1.05	.12	2
1963	.76	.76	1.01	.12	2
1964	.76	.76	1.01	.13	2
1965	.76	.76	1.01	.13	2
1966	.76	.78	.97	.14	2
1967	.85	.80	1.06	.14	2
1968	.89	.82	1.08	.15	2
1969	.95	.83	1.15	.15	2
1970	1.00	.89	1.12	.16	2
1971	1.00	.97	1.03	.16	2
1972	1.00	1.00	1.00	.17	2
1973	1.00	1.05	.95	.17	2
1974	1.03	1.18	.88	.18	2
1975	1.29	1.37	.94	.18	2
1976	1.34	1.40	.96	.17	2
1977	1.34	1.50	.89	.17	2
1978	1.56	1.57	1.00	.16	3
1979	1.59	1.67	.96	.15	3
1980	1.69	1.86	.91	.14	3
1981	1.69	2.10	.81	.14	3
1982	1.91	2.22	.86	.14	3
1983	2.10	2.23	.94	.14	3

G. Group Average

Year	Alternative	Official	Alternative/Official	Weight	Models
1947	.69	.42	1.65	1.00	6
1948	.71	.45	1.58	1.00	9
1949	.71	.47	1.51	1.00	12
1950	.69	.49	1.42	1.00	13
1951	.74	.54	1.36	1.00	14
1952	.73	.54	1.34	1.00	14
1953	.76	.54	1.41	1.00	15
1954	.77	.54	1.43	1.00	15
1955	.76	.55	1.39	1.00	18
1956	.77	.59	1.30	1.00	20
1957	.81	.63	1.28	1.00	23
1958	.82	.66	1.24	1.00	25
1959	.84	.69	1.21	1.00	25
1960	.85	.70	1.21	1.00	22
1961	.84	.69	1.21	1.00	25
1962	.83	.70	1.18	1.00	26
1963	.80	.70	1.14	1.00	25
1964	.79	.72	1.10	1.00	28
1965	.79	.74	1.08	1.00	20
1966	.81	.77	1.06	1.00	29
1967	.83	.79	1.06	1.00	23
1968	.87	.82	1.06	1.00	22
1969	.91	.85	1.07	1.00	30

(*continued*)

Table B.14G (continued)

Year	Alternative	Official	Alternative/Official	Weight	Models
1970	.97	.92	1.06	1.00	28
1971	.99	.97	1.03	1.00	26
1972	1.00	1.00	1.00	1.00	24
1973	1.02	1.04	.98	1.00	24
1974	1.06	1.18	.90	1.00	28
1975	1.29	1.33	.97	1.00	25
1976	1.36	1.43	.95	1.00	31
1977	1.39	1.62	.86	1.00	21
1978	1.52	1.76	.86	1.00	21
1979	1.70	1.91	.89	1.00	20
1980	1.82	2.14	.85	1.00	20
1981	1.96	2.28	.86	1.00	18
1982	2.14	2.47	.87	1.00	22
1983	2.31	2.52	.92	1.00	15

Table B.15   **Comparison of Alternative Price Indexes for PDE with Official Indexes from NIPA, Table 5.6, Row 27, Service Industry Machinery**

A. Gas Warm Air Furnaces

Year	Sears	PPI	Sears/PPI	Weight	Models
1951	1.06	1.09	.97	.22	2
1952	1.08	1.06	1.02	.18	1
1953	1.12	1.07	1.04	.15	2
1954	1.12	1.05	1.07	.15	3
1955	1.05	1.04	1.01	.15	2
1956	1.14	1.08	1.06	.15	2
1957	1.14	1.08	1.05	.15	2
1958	1.14	1.05	1.09	.15	2
1959	1.07	1.05	1.03	.14	3
1960	1.08	1.01	1.07	.14	3
1961	1.04	.92	1.14	.13	6
1962	.95	.88	1.08	.13	5
1963	.95	.86	1.11	.12	5
1964	.90	.85	1.05	.12	4
1965	.80	.84	.96	.12	4
1966	.81	.85	.96	.12	4
1967	.81	.85	.95	.11	2
1968	.78	.89	.87	.11	2
1969	.82	.91	.91	.12	2
1970	.83	.97	.86	.12	2
1971	.93	.99	.94	.12	2
1972	1.00	1.00	1.00	.12	2
1973	.98	1.01	.97	.12	2
1974	1.01	1.09	.92	.12	2
1975	1.43	1.21	1.18	.13	4
1976	1.47	1.28	1.15	.13	4
1977	1.47	1.35	1.09	.13	4
1978	1.57	1.43	1.09	.14	4
1979	1.75	1.58	1.11	.14	4
1980	1.80	1.78	1.01	.14	4
1981	2.12	1.99	1.07	.14	4
1982	2.05	2.15	.96	.14	4
1983	2.29	2.21	1.04	.14	4

B. Gas Hot Water Heaters

Year	Sears Hedonic	PPI	Hedonic/PPI	Weight	Models
1947	1.34	.90	1.48	.27	2
1948	1.42	.97	1.46	.20	5
1949	1.45	1.04	1.40	.16	5
1950	1.36	1.03	1.33	.13	5
1951	1.54	1.12	1.38	.10	3
1952	1.64	1.10	1.49	.08	3
1953	1.68	1.08	1.56	.07	4
1954	1.44	1.05	1.37	.07	4
1955	1.38	1.06	1.31	.07	7
1956	1.33	1.05	1.27	.07	7
1957	1.34	1.04	1.29	.07	9
1958	1.25	.99	1.26	.07	6

(*continued*)

Table B.15B (continued)

Year	Sears Hedonic	PPI	Hedonic/PPI	Weight	Models
1959	1.15	.97	1.19	.06	8
1960	1.13	.89	1.28	.06	8
1961	1.05	.81	1.29	.06	8
1962	.96	.80	1.19	.05	6
1963	.96	.82	1.16	.05	6
1964	.94	.80	1.18	.06	6
1965	.87	.80	1.08	.06	4
1966	.89	.82	1.09	.06	6
1967	.87	.80	1.08	.06	6
1968	.82	.81	1.02	.06	10
1969	.89	.84	1.06	.07	11
1970	.90	.91	.99	.07	11
1971	1.00	.95	1.05	.07	12
1972	1.00	1.00	1.00	.06	12
1973	1.01	1.02	.99	.07	11
1974	1.00	1.06	.95	.07	11
1975	1.24	1.22	1.02	.07	13
1976	1.35	1.40	.96	.06	14
1977	1.49	1.43	1.04	.06	20
1978	1.55	1.49	1.04	.05	25
1979	1.71	1.61	1.06	.05	20
1980	1.72	1.76	.98	.04	24
1981	1.72	1.86	.92	.04	19
1982	1.72	1.99	.86	.04	28
1983	1.75	2.08	.84	.04	29

C. Hand Electric Sanders

Year	Sears	PPI	Sears/PPI	Weight	Models
1947	.79	.81	.98	.10	1
1948	.94	.81	1.16	.07	1
1949	1.02	.81	1.25	.06	1
1950	.96	.84	1.15	.05	1
1951	1.02	.91	1.11	.04	1
1952	1.00	.91	1.09	.03	2
1953	1.03	.93	1.11	.03	2
1954	1.04	.96	1.09	.03	2
1955	1.04	1.00	1.05	.03	3
1956	1.08	1.04	1.04	.03	3
1957	1.10	1.04	1.06	.03	3
1958	1.10	1.05	1.05	.03	3
1959	1.04	1.09	.95	.03	3
1960	1.07	1.08	.99	.03	4
1961	1.07	1.02	1.04	.03	4
1962	1.06	1.13	.94	.03	3
1963	.92	1.13	.82	.03	3
1964	.84	1.13	.75	.04	3
1965	.93	1.10	.85	.05	4
1966	.96	1.07	.90	.06	4
1967	.96	1.13	.85	.06	3
1968	.99	1.16	.85	.06	4
1969	1.00	1.14	.88	.06	4
1970	1.00	1.05	.96	.07	3
1971	1.00	1.01	.99	.06	3

Table B.15C (continued)

Year	Sears	PPI	Sears/PPI	Weight	Models
1972	1.00	1.00	1.00	.06	6
1973	.99	1.00	.99	.06	5
1974	.95	1.04	.91	.06	6
1975	1.03	1.16	.88	.06	6
1976	.79	1.19	.67	.07	4
1977	.76	1.24	.61	.07	4
1978	.89	1.36	.65	.07	4
1979	.95	1.43	.67	.08	4
1980	.95	1.54	.62	.08	5
1981	1.10	1.64	.67	.08	2
1982	1.10	1.77	.62	.08	3
1983	1.10	1.81	.61	.08	1

D. Compressors, All Refrigerants Except Ammonia, Open-Type, Over 10 hp

Year	Unit Value	PPI	Unit Value/PPI	Weight	Models
1947	1.64	.34	4.75	.13	9
1948	1.63	.38	4.34	.10	9
1949	1.63	.40	4.03	.08	9
1950	1.53	.41	3.73	.06	9
1951	1.61	.46	3.48	.05	9
1952	1.62	.46	3.51	.04	10
1953	1.59	.48	3.29	.03	10
1954	1.50	.49	3.05	.03	7
1955	1.38	.51	2.70	.03	7
1956	1.41	.57	2.49	.03	10
1957	1.28	.61	2.09	.03	10
1958	1.25	.64	1.96	.03	8
1959	1.21	.67	1.81	.04	8
1960	1.33	.67	1.99	.04	9
1961	1.20	.66	1.80	.04	10
1962	1.12	.66	1.69	.04	10
1963	1.06	.67	1.59	.04	10
1964	1.03	.69	1.50	.04	10
1965	.85	.73	1.16	.03	9
1966	.85	.77	1.11	.03	9
1967	.86	.81	1.06	.03	8
1968	.83	.84	.98	.03	8
1969	.85	.88	.96	.03	14
1970	.88	.93	.96	.03	12
1971	.96	.98	.98	.03	13
1972	1.00	1.00	1.00	.03	13
1973	1.10	1.03	1.07	.03	9
1974	1.29	1.23	1.04	.03	9
1975	1.38	1.51	.91	.03	8
1976	1.47	1.60	.92	.03	8
1977	1.45	1.71	.85	.03	6
1978	1.46	1.84	.79	.03	6
1979	1.59	2.01	.79	.03	7
1980	1.67	2.32	.72	.03	7
1981	1.80	2.62	.69	.03	5
1982	1.89	2.80	.67	.03	5
1983	1.70	2.80	.61	.03	9

(continued)

Table B.15 (continued)

E. Compressors and Compressor Units, Ammonia Refrigerant

Year	Unit Value	PPI	Unit Value/PPI	Weight	Models
1947	.43	.34	1.24	.13	15
1948	.44	.38	1.18	.10	15
1949	.49	.40	1.22	.08	16
1950	.51	.41	1.25	.06	15
1951	.54	.46	1.18	.05	15
1952	.54	.46	1.17	.04	14
1953	.54	.48	1.12	.03	14
1954	.54	.49	1.10	.03	12
1955	.52	.51	1.01	.03	11
1956	.50	.57	.88	.03	13
1957	.53	.61	.87	.03	13
1958	.53	.64	.84	.03	11
1959	.52	.67	.78	.04	10
1960	.58	.67	.87	.04	10
1961	.60	.66	.91	.04	11
1962	.59	.66	.90	.04	11
1963	.61	.67	.92	.04	9
1964	.60	.69	.88	.04	8
1965	.62	.73	.85	.03	8
1966	.63	.77	.82	.03	9
1967	.58	.81	.72	.03	9
1968	.60	.84	.72	.03	9
1969	.60	.88	.68	.03	9
1970	.63	.93	.68	.03	9
1971	.77	.98	.79	.03	10
1972	1.00	1.00	1.00	.03	10
1973	1.21	1.03	1.18	.03	9
1974	1.34	1.23	1.09	.03	4
1975	1.64	1.51	1.09	.03	4
1976	1.77	1.60	1.11	.03	3
1977	1.87	1.71	1.10	.03	3
1978	1.96	1.84	1.06	.03	3
1979	2.11	2.01	1.05	.03	3
1980	2.36	2.32	1.02	.03	3
1981	2.55	2.62	.98	.03	4
1982	2.53	2.80	.90	.03	4
1983	2.66	2.80	.95	.03	4

F. Condensing Units, Air Cooled, Hermetic Type

Year	Unit Value	PPI	Unit Value/PPI	Weight	Models
1947	.72	.34	2.09	.13	4
1948	.72	.38	1.91	.10	4
1949	.66	.40	1.64	.08	4
1950	.68	.41	1.65	.06	4
1951	.70	.46	1.50	.05	4
1952	.71	.46	1.54	.04	5
1953	.67	.48	1.40	.03	7
1954	.80	.49	1.63	.03	6
1955	.80	.51	1.57	.03	6
1956	.84	.57	1.48	.03	9

Table B.15F (continued)

Year	Unit Value	PPI	Unit Value/PPI	Weight	Models
1957	.78	.61	1.28	.03	10
1958	.76	.64	1.19	.03	10
1959	.72	.67	1.07	.04	9
1960	.69	.67	1.03	.04	9
1961	.69	.66	1.05	.04	9
1962	.71	.66	1.07	.04	9
1963	.80	.67	1.21	.04	9
1964	.76	.69	1.11	.04	9
1965	.76	.73	1.04	.03	10
1966	.78	.77	1.01	.03	10
1967	.78	.81	.96	.03	10
1968	.77	.84	.92	.03	9
1969	.79	.88	.89	.03	7
1970	.82	.93	.89	.03	8
1971	.89	.98	.91	.03	9
1972	1.00	1.00	1.00	.03	8
1973	1.14	1.03	1.11	.03	4
1974	1.24	1.23	1.01	.03	6
1975	1.49	1.51	.99	.03	7
1976	1.61	1.60	1.01	.03	7
1977	1.63	1.71	.95	.03	7
1978	1.70	1.84	.93	.03	7
1979	1.77	2.01	.88	.03	7
1980	1.89	2.32	.82	.03	7
1981	2.05	2.62	.78	.03	7
1982	2.22	2.80	.79	.03	7
1983	2.35	2.80	.84	.03	6

G. Condensing Units, Water Cooled, Open Type

Year	Unit Value	PPI	Unit Value/PPI	Weight	Models
1947	.69	.34	1.99	.13	16
1948	.70	.38	1.86	.10	16
1949	.68	.40	1.69	.08	18
1950	.65	.41	1.60	.06	18
1951	.72	.46	1.57	.05	18
1952	.69	.46	1.49	.04	18
1953	.71	.48	1.47	.03	18
1954	.67	.49	1.36	.03	17
1955	.71	.51	1.38	.03	17
1956	.72	.57	1.26	.03	19
1957	.70	.61	1.14	.03	19
1958	.75	.64	1.19	.03	13
1959	.72	.67	1.08	.04	13
1960	.71	.67	1.05	.04	14
1961	.70	.66	1.05	.04	15
1962	.68	.66	1.04	.04	15
1963	.67	.67	1.01	.04	15
1964	.67	.69	.98	.04	15
1965	.67	.73	.92	.03	15
1966	.74	.77	.96	.03	15
1967	.74	.81	.92	.03	14

(*continued*)

Table B.15G (continued)

Year	Unit Value	PPI	Unit Value/PPI	Weight	Models
1968	.75	.84	.89	.03	14
1969	.83	.88	.94	.03	14
1970	.87	.93	.94	.03	15
1971	.88	.98	.90	.03	15
1972	1.00	1.00	1.00	.03	15
1973	1.15	1.03	1.12	.03	15
1974	1.42	1.23	1.15	.03	15
1975	1.52	1.51	1.00	.03	15
1976	1.77	1.60	1.11	.03	6
1977	1.94	1.71	1.14	.03	6
1978	1.98	1.84	1.08	.03	6
1979	2.09	2.01	1.04	.03	6
1980	2.28	2.32	.98	.03	6
1981	2.37	2.62	.90	.03	6
1982	2.52	2.80	.90	.03	6
1983	2.46	2.80	.88	.03	6

H. Condensing Units, Water Cooled, Hermetic Type

Year	Unit Value	PPI	Unit Value/PPI	Weight	Models
1952	.75	.46	1.62	.04	8
1953	.80	.48	1.65	.03	8
1954	.72	.49	1.46	.03	8
1955	.74	.51	1.45	.03	8
1956	.76	.57	1.33	.03	8
1957	.83	.61	1.35	.03	8
1958	.74	.64	1.17	.03	8
1959	.68	.67	1.01	.04	8
1960	.68	.67	1.01	.04	8
1961	.69	.66	1.04	.04	9
1962	.75	.66	1.14	.04	9
1963	.75	.67	1.13	.04	9
1964	.73	.69	1.07	.04	9
1965	.74	.73	1.01	.03	9
1966	.78	.77	1.01	.03	9
1967	.84	.81	1.04	.03	9
1968	.80	.84	.95	.03	9
1969	.82	.88	.93	.03	9
1970	.86	.93	.93	.03	9
1971	.91	.98	.93	.03	9
1972	1.00	1.00	1.00	.03	9
1973	1.04	1.03	1.01	.03	6
1974	1.08	1.23	.88	.03	3
1975	1.59	1.51	1.05	.03	2
1976	1.64	1.60	1.02	.03	4
1977	1.76	1.71	1.03	.03	4
1978	1.79	1.84	.97	.03	4
1979	1.85	2.01	.92	.03	6
1980	2.02	2.32	.87	.03	6
1981	2.15	2.62	.82	.03	6
1982	2.50	2.80	.89	.03	6
1983	2.49	2.80	.89	.03	6

Table B.15 (continued)

I. Automatic Washing Machines

Year	CR	PPI	CR/PPI	Weight	Models
1948	2.04	.94	2.18	.17	4
1949	2.00	.95	2.10	.14	4
1950	1.96	.95	2.06	.11	4
1951	1.89	1.03	1.83	.09	4
1952	1.82	1.02	1.78	.07	3
1953	1.75	1.00	1.75	.06	5
1954	1.69	.99	1.72	.06	5
1955	1.62	.96	1.69	.06	5
1956	1.56	.98	1.59	.06	7
1957	1.49	1.02	1.46	.06	6
1958	1.43	1.01	1.42	.06	7
1959	1.37	1.00	1.37	.06	5
1960	1.31	.99	1.33	.06	5
1961	1.17	.98	1.19	.06	7
1962	1.04	.96	1.08	.06	7
1963	1.01	.95	1.07	.06	6
1964	.99	.95	1.04	.06	6
1965	.99	.93	1.07	.06	6
1966	.98	.93	1.06	.06	9
1967	.98	.94	1.05	.06	8
1968	.97	.96	1.01	.05	10
1969	.96	.97	.99	.05	7
1970	.99	.99	1.00	.04	9
1971	1.00	.99	1.01	.04	10
1972	1.00	1.00	1.00	.03	8
1973	1.00	1.00	1.00	.03	8
1974	.96	1.10	.87	.03	8
1975	1.19	1.24	.96	.03	8
1976	1.25	1.35	.92	.03	10
1977	1.31	1.39	.94	.03	9
1978	1.37	1.45	.95	.03	17
1979	1.44	1.52	.95	.03	18
1980	1.57	1.62	.97	.03	17
1981	1.68	1.73	.97	.03	34
1982	1.72	1.84	.94	.03	30
1983	1.75	1.90	.92	.03	27

J. Electric Clothes Dryers

Year	CR	PPI	CR/PPI	Weight	Models
1951	2.02	.96	2.11	.09	1
1952	2.02	.96	2.11	.07	1
1953	2.02	.95	2.13	.06	1
1954	2.02	.94	2.15	.06	1
1955	1.99	.93	2.14	.06	1
1956	1.96	.95	2.07	.06	1
1957	1.93	.98	1.97	.06	1
1958	1.81	.98	1.85	.06	1
1959	1.70	1.00	1.71	.06	1
1960	1.60	.97	1.65	.06	1

(*continued*)

Table B.15J (continued)

Year	CR	PPI	CR/PPI	Weight	Models
1961	1.50	.95	1.58	.06	1
1962	1.43	.94	1.52	.06	2
1963	1.35	.94	1.44	.06	2
1964	1.28	.93	1.38	.06	2
1965	1.22	.90	1.36	.06	2
1966	1.16	.90	1.28	.06	2
1967	1.13	.92	1.23	.06	1
1968	1.10	.94	1.17	.05	1
1969	1.08	.96	1.12	.05	2
1970	1.05	1.00	1.05	.04	2
1971	1.02	1.01	1.01	.04	2
1972	1.00	1.00	1.00	.03	1
1973	.98	1.02	.97	.03	1
1974	.97	1.11	.87	.03	1
1975	.99	1.24	.80	.03	2
1976	.92	1.35	.68	.03	1
1977	.86	1.41	.61	.03	3
1978	.80	1.48	.54	.03	3
1979	.74	1.58	.47	.03	3
1980	.69	1.76	.39	.03	1
1981	.64	1.90	.34	.03	5
1982	.59	2.05	.29	.03	6
1983	.61	2.14	.29	.03	4

K. Refrigerators

Year	CR	PPI	CR/PPI	Weight	Models
1949	4.19	1.45	2.88	.35	3
1950	3.72	1.47	2.52	.29	6
1951	3.30	1.52	2.17	.22	3
1952	2.91	1.52	1.91	.18	4
1953	2.57	1.53	1.67	.16	9
1954	2.27	1.53	1.48	.16	9
1955	2.15	1.43	1.50	.16	13
1956	2.05	1.39	1.47	.16	10
1957	1.95	1.34	1.46	.16	9
1958	1.88	1.30	1.44	.16	11
1959	1.81	1.28	1.41	.18	9
1960	1.60	1.20	1.33	.19	8
1961	1.48	1.13	1.31	.20	8
1962	1.38	1.09	1.26	.21	11
1963	1.32	1.02	1.28	.22	9
1964	1.26	.99	1.27	.23	10
1965	1.12	.97	1.15	.24	9
1966	1.00	.95	1.05	.26	9
1967	.89	.95	.94	.25	7
1968	.80	.98	.81	.23	9
1969	.86	1.00	.86	.23	21
1970	.92	1.01	.92	.23	26
1971	.96	1.03	.94	.21	22
1972	1.00	1.00	1.00	.19	21
1973	1.04	1.00	1.04	.19	14
1974	1.08	1.08	1.00	.19	13

Table B.15K (continued)

Year	CR	PPI	CR/PPI	Weight	Models
1975	1.13	1.25	.90	.18	18
1976	1.18	1.34	.88	.17	23
1977	1.24	1.40	.88	.16	17
1978	1.29	1.47	.88	.15	20
1979	1.35	1.52	.89	.14	17
1980	1.42	1.62	.88	.13	18
1981	1.48	1.75	.85	.13	26
1982	1.55	1.90	.81	.13	26
1983	1.62	1.97	.82	.13	31

L. Room Air Conditioners

Year	CR	PPI	CR/PPI	Weight	Models
1953	3.56	1.40	2.54	.24	2
1954	3.25	1.40	2.31	.24	4
1955	2.96	1.32	2.24	.24	5
1956	2.70	1.26	2.15	.24	12
1957	2.46	1.21	2.03	.24	12
1958	2.04	1.16	1.75	.23	7
1959	1.69	1.09	1.55	.22	5
1960	1.52	1.06	1.44	.21	7
1961	1.38	1.00	1.38	.20	9
1962	1.35	.99	1.37	.19	9
1963	1.31	.97	1.35	.19	10
1964	1.28	.96	1.33	.18	9
1965	1.25	.91	1.37	.17	8
1966	1.14	.90	1.26	.17	4
1967	1.03	.91	1.13	.15	2
1968	1.02	.93	1.10	.14	11
1969	1.02	.93	1.10	.13	12
1970	1.01	.95	1.06	.13	11
1971	.99	.99	1.00	.11	10
1972	1.00	1.00	1.00	.10	9
1973	1.01	.98	1.02	.09	12
1974	1.03	1.05	.98	.09	12
1975	1.08	1.16	.94	.08	22
1976	1.15	1.15	1.01	.08	22
1977	1.22	1.15	1.06	.08	10
1978	1.29	1.20	1.07	.08	11
1979	1.36	1.26	1.08	.08	18
1980	1.42	1.37	1.03	.08	15
1981	1.48	1.44	1.02	.08	39
1982	1.50	1.50	1.00	.08	49
1983	1.53	1.60	.96	.08	55

(continued)

Table B.15 (continued)

M. Under-Counter Dishwashers

Year	CR	PPI	CR/PPI	Weight	Models
1952	1.62	1.15	1.41	.07	3
1953	1.57	1.16	1.36	.06	5
1954	1.52	1.17	1.30	.06	5
1955	1.47	1.13	1.31	.06	5
1956	1.43	1.12	1.28	.06	7
1957	1.38	1.12	1.24	.06	6
1958	1.34	1.10	1.21	.06	7
1959	1.30	1.10	1.18	.06	5
1960	1.25	1.06	1.18	.06	5
1961	1.22	1.03	1.18	.06	7
1962	1.18	1.02	1.16	.06	7
1963	1.14	1.00	1.14	.06	6
1964	1.11	.99	1.12	.06	6
1965	1.07	.97	1.10	.06	6
1966	1.07	.97	1.10	.06	9
1967	1.07	.98	1.09	.06	8
1968	1.06	.96	1.11	.05	10
1969	1.06	.97	1.09	.05	7
1970	1.05	.98	1.07	.04	9
1971	1.05	1.01	1.04	.04	10
1972	1.00	1.00	1.00	.03	8
1973	.95	1.02	.93	.03	8
1974	.90	1.08	.84	.03	8
1975	.95	1.22	.78	.03	8
1976	1.00	1.26	.79	.03	10
1977	1.05	1.33	.79	.03	9
1978	1.11	1.39	.80	.03	17
1979	1.16	1.47	.79	.03	18
1980	1.22	1.59	.77	.03	17
1981	1.28	1.71	.75	.03	34
1982	1.34	1.83	.73	.03	30
1983	1.40	1.89	.74	.03	27

N. Microwave Ovens

Year	CR	PPI	CR/PPI	Weight	Models
1971	1.06	.98	1.08	.10	2
1972	1.00	1.00	1.00	.10	3
1973	.95	1.03	.92	.10	3
1974	.87	1.11	.79	.10	7
1975	.81	1.25	.64	.11	7
1976	.74	1.33	.56	.11	6
1977	.73	1.41	.52	.11	8
1978	.72	1.47	.49	.11	9
1979	.72	1.55	.46	.11	9
1980	.71	1.70	.42	.11	6
1981	.70	1.63	.43	.12	8
1982	.60	1.57	.38	.12	10
1983	.52	1.56	.33	.12	14

Table B.15 (continued)

O. Commercial Vacuum Cleaners

Year	Sears	PPI	Sears/PPI	Weight	Models
1972	1.00	1.00	1.00	.02	6
1973	1.00	.97	1.03	.02	6
1974	1.00	1.05	.95	.02	6
1975	1.12	1.13	.99	.02	7
1976	1.03	1.18	.87	.03	5
1977	1.13	1.22	.92	.03	4
1978	1.08	1.32	.82	.03	4
1979	1.20	1.36	.88	.03	8
1980	1.10	1.47	.74	.04	3
1981	1.27	1.47	.86	.04	4
1982	1.37	1.46	.94	.04	5
1983	1.56	1.49	1.04	.04	5

P. Automatic Coffee Makers

Year	Sears	PPI	Sears/PPI	Weight	Models
1972	1.00	1.00	1.00	.10	1
1973	1.00	1.01	.99	.10	1
1974	1.00	1.10	.91	.10	1
1975	1.10	1.20	.92	.11	1
1976	.93	1.24	.75	.11	2
1977	.79	1.27	.62	.11	4
1978	.72	1.31	.55	.11	4
1979	.71	1.29	.55	.11	4
1980	.83	1.44	.58	.11	6
1981	.83	1.58	.53	.12	5
1982	.89	1.73	.52	.12	5
1983	.91	1.96	.46	.12	5

Q. Group Average

Year	Alternative	Official	Alternative/Official	Weight	Models
1947	1.94	.89	2.19	1.00	47
1948	2.02	.94	2.14	1.00	54
1949	2.03	.98	2.07	1.00	60
1950	1.91	.99	1.93	1.00	62
1951	1.90	1.06	1.79	1.00	60
1952	1.86	1.05	1.77	1.00	72
1953	1.82	1.06	1.72	1.00	87
1954	1.72	1.06	1.63	1.00	83
1955	1.64	1.03	1.59	1.00	90
1956	1.60	1.04	1.54	1.00	108
1957	1.55	1.04	1.48	1.00	108
1958	1.45	1.03	1.41	1.00	94
1959	1.33	1.02	1.31	1.00	87
1960	1.27	.98	1.29	1.00	91
1961	1.20	.94	1.28	1.00	104
1962	1.14	.92	1.24	1.00	104

(*continued*)

Table B.15Q (continued)

Year	Alternative	Official	Alternative/Official	Weight	Models
1963	1.11	.90	1.23	1.00	99
1964	1.07	.90	1.20	1.00	97
1965	1.01	.89	1.14	1.00	94
1966	.98	.89	1.10	1.00	99
1967	.93	.90	1.03	1.00	87
1968	.90	.93	.97	1.00	106
1969	.92	.94	.97	1.00	119
1970	.94	.97	.97	1.00	126
1971	.97	1.00	.97	1.00	129
1972	1.00	1.00	1.00	1.00	132
1973	1.02	1.01	1.01	1.00	114
1974	1.03	1.10	.94	1.00	112
1975	1.16	1.26	.92	1.00	132
1976	1.15	1.33	.87	1.00	129
1977	1.16	1.39	.84	1.00	118
1978	1.19	1.46	.81	1.00	144
1979	1.25	1.55	.81	1.00	152
1980	1.30	1.71	.76	1.00	145
1981	1.38	1.83	.75	1.00	208
1982	1.39	1.94	.72	1.00	224
1983	1.41	2.01	.70	1.00	233

Table B.16   **Comparison of Alternative Price Indexes for PDE with Official Indexes from NIPA, Table 5.6, Row 28, Electrical Equipment, n.e.c**

A. Tachometers

Year	Sears	PPI	Sears/PPI	Weight	Models
1947	1.41	.38	3.66	.08	2
1948	1.40	.40	3.47	.05	2
1949	1.40	.41	3.44	.05	2
1950	1.36	.42	3.21	.05	1
1951	1.36	.48	2.82	.05	1
1952	1.36	.47	2.88	.05	1
1953	1.24	.49	2.53	.05	1
1954	1.26	.51	2.45	.05	2
1955	1.18	.52	2.28	.05	2
1956	1.18	.54	2.17	.05	1
1957	1.18	.59	1.98	.05	1
1958	1.19	.63	1.89	.05	2
1959	1.19	.65	1.82	.05	1
1960	1.19	.68	1.76	.05	1
1961	1.31	.69	1.91	.05	2
1962	1.31	.70	1.89	.05	2
1963	1.11	.69	1.60	.05	1
1964	1.11	.70	1.60	.05	1
1965	1.00	.70	1.44	.06	1
1966	1.00	.74	1.35	.06	1
1967	.98	.78	1.26	.06	2
1968	.99	.83	1.19	.06	1
1969	.99	.87	1.14	.06	2
1970	.99	.92	1.08	.06	2
1971	1.00	.98	1.02	.06	2
1972	1.00	1.00	1.00	.06	2
1973	1.05	1.01	1.04	.06	2
1974	1.11	1.10	1.01	.06	2
1975	1.26	1.22	1.03	.06	4
1976	1.30	1.30	1.00	.05	2
1977	1.35	1.35	1.00	.05	3
1978	1.35	1.41	.95	.05	2
1979	1.25	1.49	.84	.04	2
1980	1.37	1.59	.86	.04	2
1981	1.56	1.78	.88	.04	1
1982	1.72	1.96	.88	.04	2
1983	1.72	2.06	.83	.04	2

B. Electronic Auto Testers

Year	Sears	PPI	Sears/PPI	Weight	Models
1947	.99	.38	2.58	.08	1
1948	.98	.40	2.43	.05	1
1949	.98	.41	2.40	.05	1
1950	.98	.42	2.32	.05	2
1951	.98	.48	2.04	.05	3
1952	.97	.47	2.06	.05	3
1953	.96	.49	1.96	.05	2
1954	.96	.51	1.87	.05	3

(continued)

Table B.16B (continued)

Year	Sears	PPI	Sears/PPI	Weight	Models
1955	.96	.52	1.85	.05	1
1956	1.13	.54	2.09	.05	3
1957	1.13	.59	1.91	.05	3
1958	1.13	.63	1.80	.05	2
1959	1.05	.65	1.60	.05	2
1960	1.05	.68	1.55	.05	1
1961	1.05	.69	1.53	.05	1
1962	1.05	.70	1.51	.05	1
1963	1.05	.69	1.51	.05	2
1964	.99	.70	1.42	.05	4
1965	.97	.70	1.39	.06	2
1966	.97	.74	1.31	.06	1
1967	.97	.78	1.24	.06	1
1968	.97	.83	1.17	.06	1
1969	.97	.87	1.12	.06	2
1970	.97	.92	1.06	.06	2
1971	1.00	.98	1.02	.06	2
1972	1.00	1.00	1.00	.06	2
1973	1.00	1.01	.99	.06	2
1974	.95	1.10	.86	.06	1
1975	1.23	1.22	1.00	.06	4
1976	1.07	1.30	.83	.05	2
1977	1.21	1.35	.90	.05	1
1978	1.30	1.41	.92	.05	3
1979	1.20	1.49	.81	.04	2
1980	1.01	1.59	.64	.04	1
1981	1.19	1.78	.67	.04	1
1982	1.20	1.96	.62	.04	4
1983	1.32	2.06	.64	.04	3

C. Panel-Type Ammeters

Year	Sears	PPI	Sears/PPI	Weight	Models
1948	.69	.37	1.88	.05	1
1949	.69	.37	1.86	.05	1
1950	.69	.38	1.80	.05	2
1951	.77	.44	1.76	.05	2
1952	.74	.43	1.73	.05	2
1953	.73	.44	1.65	.05	2
1954	.73	.47	1.58	.05	1
1955	.79	.47	1.69	.05	1
1956	.79	.49	1.61	.05	1
1957	.79	.54	1.47	.05	1
1958	.79	.57	1.38	.05	1
1959	.80	.59	1.35	.05	1
1960	.84	.61	1.37	.05	1
1961	.87	.62	1.40	.05	1
1962	.91	.63	1.44	.05	1
1963	.95	.63	1.51	.05	1
1964	.99	.63	1.57	.05	1
1965	.98	.63	1.55	.06	1
1966	.87	.67	1.30	.06	2
1967	.87	.71	1.22	.06	1

Table B.16C (continued)

Year	Sears	PPI	Sears/PPI	Weight	Models
1968	.87	.83	1.05	.06	2
1969	1.00	.89	1.13	.06	1
1970	1.00	.91	1.10	.06	1
1971	1.00	.92	1.09	.06	1
1972	1.00	1.00	1.00	.06	1
1973	1.00	.92	1.09	.06	1
1974	1.04	1.00	1.04	.06	1
1975	1.15	1.11	1.03	.06	1
1976	.94	1.18	.80	.05	0
1977	.94	1.22	.77	.05	0
1978	.94	1.29	.73	.05	0
1979	.94	1.35	.69	.04	0
1980	.94	1.45	.65	.04	0
1981	1.31	1.62	.81	.04	2
1982	1.69	1.78	.95	.04	2
1983	1.88	1.88	1.00	.04	1

D. Replacement Auto Batteries

Year	Sears	PPI	Sears/PPI	Weight	Models
1948	.69	.66	1.05	.56	4
1949	.95	.70	1.36	.56	4
1950	.69	.62	1.10	.56	4
1951	.79	.70	1.13	.55	4
1952	.93	.71	1.32	.55	4
1953	.82	.69	1.19	.55	3
1954	.83	.67	1.25	.55	4
1955	.79	.67	1.18	.55	4
1956	.83	.73	1.15	.55	4
1957	.78	.79	.99	.55	3
1958	.78	.79	.98	.55	7
1959	.75	.81	.93	.55	6
1960	.83	.83	1.00	.55	6
1961	.76	.83	.91	.55	9
1962	.75	.82	.91	.54	8
1963	.74	.81	.91	.54	9
1964	.74	.83	.90	.54	10
1965	.77	.87	.89	.53	8
1966	.78	.88	.88	.53	9
1967	.80	.86	.93	.52	10
1968	.82	.87	.94	.51	9
1969	.88	.89	.99	.51	3
1970	.89	.96	.92	.50	3
1971	1.00	.98	1.02	.48	3
1972	1.00	1.00	1.00	.45	3
1973	1.09	1.01	1.08	.44	3
1974	1.21	1.10	1.10	.42	3
1975	1.51	1.27	1.19	.41	8
1976	1.49	1.27	1.17	.40	8
1977	1.59	1.45	1.10	.39	8
1978	1.70	1.56	1.09	.38	8

(continued)

Table B.16D (continued)

Year	Sears	PPI	Sears/PPI	Weight	Models
1979	1.84	1.88	.98	.37	6
1980	2.61	1.98	1.32	.36	6
1981	2.23	2.08	1.07	.36	5
1982	2.56	2.00	1.28	.36	6
1983	2.63	1.88	1.40	.36	4

E. Fluorescent Lighting Fixtures

Year	Sears	PPI	Sears/PPI	Weight	Models
1947	.72	.49	1.45	.52	2
1948	.67	.52	1.29	.29	2
1949	.72	.54	1.32	.29	2
1950	.63	.57	1.11	.29	2
1951	.66	.63	1.04	.29	1
1952	.72	.64	1.13	.29	2
1953	.72	.65	1.11	.28	2
1954	.69	.66	1.05	.28	2
1955	.68	.70	.97	.28	2
1956	.72	.76	.96	.28	2
1957	.73	.81	.90	.28	2
1958	.73	.84	.87	.28	2
1959	.73	.84	.87	.29	2
1960	.73	.84	.87	.29	2
1961	.73	.93	.79	.29	2
1962	.74	.88	.84	.29	2
1963	.74	.86	.86	.29	2
1964	.74	.86	.86	.28	2
1965	.74	.85	.88	.28	2
1966	.74	.87	.86	.28	2
1967	.75	.88	.85	.27	2
1968	.81	.91	.89	.27	2
1969	.89	.95	.93	.27	2
1970	.95	.99	.96	.26	2
1971	1.00	1.00	1.00	.25	2
1972	1.00	1.00	1.00	.24	6
1973	.99	1.01	.98	.23	5
1974	.95	1.13	.83	.22	2
1975	1.14	1.18	.96	.22	6
1976	1.14	1.19	.96	.21	6
1977	1.14	1.20	.95	.21	3
1978	1.14	1.26	.91	.20	3
1979	1.21	1.44	.84	.20	3
1980	1.38	1.59	.87	.19	3
1981	1.55	1.81	.85	.19	3
1982	1.62	1.94	.83	.19	3
1983	1.62	1.93	.84	.19	3

Table B.16 (continued)

F. Commercial Vacuum Cleaners

Year	Sears	PPI	Sears/PPI	Weight	Models
1972	1.00	1.00	1.00	.07	6
1973	1.00	.97	1.03	.07	6
1974	1.00	1.05	.95	.08	6
1975	1.12	1.13	.99	.10	7
1976	1.03	1.18	.87	.11	5
1977	1.13	1.22	.92	.12	4
1978	1.08	1.32	.82	.14	4
1979	1.20	1.36	.88	.15	8
1980	1.10	1.47	.74	.17	3
1981	1.27	1.47	.86	.18	4
1982	1.37	1.46	.94	.18	5
1983	1.56	1.49	1.04	.18	5

G. Automatic Washing Machines

Year	CR	PPI	CR/PPI	Weight	Models
1948	2.04	.94	2.18	.01	4
1949	2.00	.95	2.10	.01	4
1950	1.96	.95	2.06	.01	4
1951	1.89	1.03	1.83	.01	4
1952	1.82	1.02	1.78	.01	3
1953	1.75	1.00	1.75	.01	5
1954	1.69	.99	1.72	.01	5
1955	1.62	.96	1.69	.01	5
1956	1.56	.98	1.59	.01	7
1957	1.49	1.02	1.46	.01	6
1958	1.43	1.01	1.42	.01	7
1959	1.37	1.00	1.37	.01	5
1960	1.31	.99	1.33	.00	5
1961	1.17	.98	1.19	.00	7
1962	1.04	.96	1.08	.00	7
1963	1.01	.95	1.07	.00	6
1964	.99	.95	1.04	.00	6
1965	.99	.93	1.07	.00	6
1966	.98	.93	1.06	.00	9
1967	.98	.94	1.05	.00	8
1968	.97	.96	1.01	.01	10
1969	.96	.97	.99	.01	7
1970	.99	.99	1.00	.01	9
1971	1.00	.99	1.01	.01	10
1972	1.00	1.00	1.00	.01	8
1973	1.00	1.00	1.00	.01	8
1974	.96	1.10	.87	.01	8
1975	1.19	1.24	.96	.02	8
1976	1.25	1.35	.92	.02	10
1977	1.31	1.39	.94	.02	9
1978	1.37	1.45	.95	.02	17
1979	1.44	1.52	.95	.02	18
1980	1.57	1.62	.97	.03	17
1981	1.68	1.73	.97	.03	34
1982	1.72	1.84	.94	.03	30
1983	1.75	1.90	.92	.03	27

(*continued*)

Table B.16 (continued)

H. Electric Clothes Dryers

Year	CR	PPI	CR/PPI	Weight	Models
1951	2.02	.96	2.11	.01	1
1952	2.02	.96	2.11	.01	1
1953	2.02	.95	2.13	.01	1
1954	2.02	.94	2.15	.01	1
1955	1.99	.93	2.14	.01	1
1956	1.96	.95	2.07	.01	1
1957	1.93	.98	1.97	.01	1
1958	1.81	.98	1.85	.01	1
1959	1.70	1.00	1.71	.01	1
1960	1.60	.97	1.65	.00	1
1961	1.50	.95	1.58	.00	1
1962	1.43	.94	1.52	.00	2
1963	1.35	.94	1.44	.00	2
1964	1.28	.93	1.38	.00	2
1965	1.22	.90	1.36	.00	2
1966	1.16	.90	1.28	.00	2
1967	1.13	.92	1.23	.00	1
1968	1.10	.94	1.17	.01	1
1969	1.08	.96	1.12	.01	2
1970	1.05	1.00	1.05	.01	2
1971	1.02	1.01	1.01	.01	2
1972	1.00	1.00	1.00	.01	1
1973	.98	1.02	.97	.01	1
1974	.97	1.11	.87	.01	1
1975	.99	1.24	.80	.02	2
1976	.92	1.35	.68	.02	1
1977	.86	1.41	.61	.02	3
1978	.80	1.48	.54	.02	3
1979	.74	1.58	.47	.02	3
1980	.69	1.76	.39	.03	1
1981	.64	1.90	.34	.03	5
1982	.59	2.05	.29	.03	6
1983	.61	2.14	.29	.03	4

I. Refrigerators

Year	CR	PPI	CR/PPI	Weight	Models
1949	4.19	1.45	2.88	.01	3
1950	3.72	1.47	2.52	.01	6
1951	3.30	1.52	2.17	.01	3
1952	2.91	1.52	1.91	.01	4
1953	2.57	1.53	1.67	.01	9
1954	2.27	1.53	1.48	.01	9
1955	2.15	1.43	1.50	.01	13
1956	2.05	1.39	1.47	.01	10
1957	1.95	1.34	1.46	.01	9
1958	1.88	1.30	1.44	.01	11
1959	1.81	1.28	1.41	.01	9
1960	1.60	1.20	1.33	.00	8
1961	1.48	1.13	1.31	.00	8
1962	1.38	1.09	1.26	.00	11

Table B.16I (continued)

Year	CR	PPI	CR/PPI	Weight	Models
1963	1.32	1.02	1.28	.00	9
1964	1.26	.99	1.27	.00	10
1965	1.12	.97	1.15	.00	9
1966	1.00	.95	1.05	.00	9
1967	.89	.95	.94	.00	7
1968	.80	.98	.81	.01	9
1969	.86	1.00	.86	.01	21
1970	.92	1.01	.92	.01	26
1971	.96	1.03	.94	.01	22
1972	1.00	1.00	1.00	.01	21
1973	1.04	1.00	1.04	.01	14
1974	1.08	1.08	1.00	.01	13
1975	1.13	1.25	.90	.02	18
1976	1.18	1.34	.88	.02	23
1977	1.24	1.40	.88	.02	17
1978	1.29	1.47	.88	.02	20
1979	1.35	1.52	.89	.02	17
1980	1.42	1.62	.88	.03	18
1981	1.48	1.75	.85	.03	26
1982	1.55	1.90	.81	.03	26
1983	1.62	1.97	.82	.03	31

J. Room Air Conditioners

Year	CR	PPI	CR/PPI	Weight	Models
1953	3.56	1.40	2.54	.01	2
1954	3.25	1.40	2.31	.01	4
1955	2.96	1.32	2.24	.01	5
1956	2.70	1.26	2.15	.01	12
1957	2.46	1.21	2.03	.01	12
1958	2.04	1.16	1.75	.01	7
1959	1.69	1.09	1.55	.01	5
1960	1.52	1.06	1.44	.00	7
1961	1.38	1.00	1.38	.00	9
1962	1.35	.99	1.37	.00	9
1963	1.31	.97	1.35	.00	10
1964	1.28	.96	1.33	.00	9
1965	1.25	.91	1.37	.00	8
1966	1.14	.90	1.26	.00	4
1967	1.03	.91	1.13	.00	2
1968	1.02	.93	1.10	.01	11
1969	1.02	.93	1.10	.01	12
1970	1.01	.95	1.06	.01	11
1971	.99	.99	1.00	.01	10
1972	1.00	1.00	1.00	.01	9
1973	1.01	.98	1.02	.01	12
1974	1.03	1.05	.98	.01	12
1975	1.08	1.16	.94	.02	22
1976	1.15	1.15	1.01	.02	22
1977	1.22	1.15	1.06	.02	10
1978	1.29	1.20	1.07	.02	11
1979	1.36	1.26	1.08	.02	18

(*continued*)

Table B.16J (continued)

Year	CR	PPI	CR/PPI	Weight	Models
1980	1.42	1.37	1.03	.03	15
1981	1.48	1.44	1.02	.03	39
1982	1.50	1.50	1.00	.03	49
1983	1.53	1.60	.96	.03	55

K. Under-Counter Dishwashers

Year	CR	PPI	CR/PPI	Weight	Models
1952	1.62	1.15	1.41	.01	3
1953	1.57	1.16	1.36	.01	5
1954	1.52	1.17	1.30	.01	5
1955	1.47	1.13	1.31	.01	5
1956	1.43	1.12	1.28	.01	7
1957	1.38	1.12	1.24	.01	6
1958	1.34	1.10	1.21	.01	7
1959	1.30	1.10	1.18	.01	5
1960	1.25	1.06	1.18	.00	5
1961	1.22	1.03	1.18	.00	7
1962	1.18	1.02	1.16	.00	7
1963	1.14	1.00	1.14	.00	6
1964	1.11	.99	1.12	.00	6
1965	1.07	.97	1.10	.00	6
1966	1.07	.97	1.10	.00	9
1967	1.07	.98	1.09	.00	8
1968	1.06	.96	1.11	.01	10
1969	1.06	.97	1.09	.01	7
1970	1.05	.98	1.07	.01	9
1971	1.05	1.01	1.04	.01	10
1972	1.00	1.00	1.00	.01	8
1973	.95	1.02	.93	.01	8
1974	.90	1.08	.84	.01	8
1975	.95	1.22	.78	.02	8
1976	1.00	1.26	.79	.02	10
1977	1.05	1.33	.79	.02	9
1978	1.11	1.39	.80	.02	17
1979	1.16	1.47	.79	.02	18
1980	1.22	1.59	.77	.03	17
1981	1.28	1.71	.75	.03	34
1982	1.34	1.83	.73	.03	30
1983	1.40	1.89	.74	.03	27

L. Microwave Ovens

Year	CR	PPI	CR/PPI	Weight	Models
1968	1.25	.90	1.39	.01	0
1969	1.18	.91	1.29	.01	0
1970	1.12	.95	1.18	.01	0
1971	1.06	.98	1.08	.01	2
1972	1.00	1.00	1.00	.01	3
1973	.95	1.03	.92	.01	3
1974	.87	1.11	.79	.01	7
1975	.81	1.25	.64	.02	7

Table B.16L (continued)

Year	*CR*	PPI	*CR*/PPI	Weight	Models
1976	.74	1.33	.56	.02	6
1977	.73	1.41	.52	.02	8
1978	.72	1.47	.49	.02	9
1979	.72	1.55	.46	.02	9
1980	.71	1.70	.42	.03	6
1981	.70	1.63	.43	.03	8
1982	.60	1.57	.38	.03	10
1983	.52	1.56	.33	.03	14

M. Group Average

Year	Alternative	Official	Alternative/Official	Weight	Models
1947	.78	.53	1.47	1.00	5
1948	.76	.58	1.31	1.00	14
1949	.92	.60	1.53	1.00	17
1950	.74	.58	1.28	1.00	21
1951	.81	.65	1.25	1.00	19
1952	.91	.65	1.40	1.00	23
1953	.84	.65	1.30	1.00	32
1954	.84	.64	1.30	1.00	36
1955	.81	.65	1.23	1.00	39
1956	.85	.70	1.21	1.00	48
1957	.82	.76	1.09	1.00	44
1958	.82	.78	1.06	1.00	47
1959	.80	.79	1.02	1.00	37
1960	.85	.80	1.05	1.00	37
1961	.81	.83	.98	1.00	47
1962	.81	.81	.99	1.00	50
1963	.80	.80	1.00	1.00	48
1964	.80	.81	.99	1.00	51
1965	.81	.83	.98	1.00	45
1966	.81	.85	.95	1.00	48
1967	.82	.85	.97	1.00	42
1968	.85	.88	.97	1.00	56
1969	.91	.91	1.00	1.00	59
1970	.93	.96	.97	1.00	67
1971	1.00	.98	1.02	1.00	66
1972	1.00	1.00	1.00	1.00	70
1973	1.04	1.00	1.04	1.00	65
1974	1.08	1.10	.98	1.00	64
1975	1.29	1.22	1.05	1.00	95
1976	1.25	1.25	1.00	1.00	95
1977	1.31	1.34	.98	1.00	75
1978	1.35	1.42	.95	1.00	97
1979	1.42	1.60	.89	1.00	104
1980	1.64	1.71	.95	1.00	89
1981	1.66	1.83	.91	1.00	162
1982	1.81	1.86	.97	1.00	173
1983	1.88	1.84	1.02	1.00	176

Table B.17   Comparison of Alternative Price Indexes for PDE Based on Unit Value Data
                    with Closest Comparable PPI

A. Cast Iron Radiators and Convectors

Year	Unit Value	PPI	Unit Value/PPI	Weight	Models
1947	.35	.30	1.18	.14	1
1948	.42	.37	1.14	.14	1
1949	.45	.40	1.13	.14	1
1950	.45	.40	1.13	.14	1
1951	.51	.44	1.15	.13	1
1952	.54	.45	1.20	.13	1
1953	.56	.48	1.15	.13	1
1954	.59	.50	1.19	.13	1
1955	.57	.51	1.12	.13	1
1956	.60	.53	1.14	.13	1
1957	.59	.56	1.05	.13	1
1958	.61	.57	1.07	.13	1
1959	.60	.59	1.03	.13	1
1960	.60	.59	1.03	.13	1
1961	.63	.59	1.08	.13	1
1962	.66	.60	1.09	.13	1
1963	.64	.62	1.04	.13	1
1964	.66	.64	1.03	.13	1
1965	.65	.64	1.01	.13	1
1966	.66	.67	.97	.13	1
1967	.65	.69	.95	.13	1
1968	.71	.74	.95	.13	1
1969	.86	.78	1.09	.13	6
1970	.81	.94	.86	.13	6
1971	.93	1.00	.93	.13	6
1972	1.00	1.00	1.00	.13	6
1973	1.14	1.01	1.12	.13	6
1974	1.43	1.35	1.06	.13	6
1975	1.84	1.65	1.12	.06	6
1976	1.89	1.76	1.08	.00	6

B. Gasoline Engines, 11 hp and Over

Year	Unit Value	PPI	Unit Value/PPI	Weight	Models
1947	.69	.47	1.48	.14	11
1948	.69	.53	1.30	.14	0
1949	.68	.56	1.23	.14	0
1950	.68	.56	1.21	.14	11
1951	.82	.62	1.33	.13	11
1952	.86	.63	1.35	.13	11
1953	.85	.64	1.33	.13	11
1954	.86	.64	1.36	.13	11
1955	.84	.65	1.30	.13	14
1956	.91	.69	1.32	.13	15
1957	.99	.72	1.37	.13	13
1958	.90	.73	1.22	.13	12
1959	.85	.73	1.16	.13	10
1960	.88	.74	1.19	.13	8
1961	.91	.75	1.21	.13	10
1962	.93	.77	1.21	.13	11

Table B.17B (continued)

Year	Unit Value	PPI	Unit Value/PPI	Weight	Models
1963	.89	.77	1.17	.13	13
1964	.90	.77	1.17	.13	13
1965	.99	.77	1.28	.13	12
1966	.88	.77	1.14	.13	9
1967	.98	.77	1.27	.13	9
1968	1.00	.80	1.24	.13	10
1969	1.01	.86	1.18	.13	11
1970	1.11	.91	1.22	.13	10
1971	1.09	.96	1.13	.13	10
1972	1.00	1.00	1.00	.13	10
1973	.91	1.01	.90	.13	11
1974	1.08	1.18	.91	.13	12
1975	1.19	1.38	.86	.13	10
1976	1.06	1.50	.71	.14	8
1977	1.73	1.60	1.08	.14	5
1978	2.02	1.80	1.12	.14	6
1979	2.20	1.99	1.11	.14	4
1980	2.61	2.26	1.16	.14	7
1981	2.87	2.54	1.13	.14	6
1982	2.91	2.75	1.06	.14	6
1983	3.03	2.85	1.06	.14	6

C. Diesel Engines, Except Automotive

Year	Unit Value	PPI	Unit Value/PPI	Weight	Models
1947	1.34	.37	3.61	.14	20
1948	1.33	.43	3.10	.14	20
1949	1.31	.47	2.81	.14	20
1950	1.29	.48	2.71	.14	20
1951	1.32	.60	2.22	.13	20
1952	1.42	.58	2.44	.13	20
1953	1.45	.59	2.45	.13	19
1954	1.43	.61	2.35	.13	17
1955	1.36	.62	2.19	.13	18
1956	1.36	.68	2.01	.13	19
1957	1.52	.72	2.10	.13	16
1958	1.32	.74	1.79	.13	16
1959	1.26	.75	1.68	.13	18
1960	1.17	.75	1.56	.13	18
1961	1.11	.76	1.47	.13	17
1962	1.07	.76	1.41	.13	17
1963	1.05	.76	1.38	.13	16
1964	.99	.78	1.27	.13	15
1965	.96	.79	1.21	.13	11
1966	.88	.82	1.08	.13	10
1967	.90	.84	1.06	.13	12
1968	.85	.86	.98	.13	12
1969	.85	.89	.96	.13	36
1970	.89	.93	.96	.13	22
1971	.93	.97	.96	.13	22
1972	1.00	1.00	1.00	.13	28
1973	.98	1.03	.96	.13	24

(continued)

Table B.17C (continued)

Year	Unit Value	PPI	Unit Value/PPI	Weight	Models
1974	1.19	1.18	1.01	.13	16
1975	1.39	1.45	.96	.13	11
1976	1.38	1.58	.87	.14	12
1977	1.43	1.69	.85	.14	10
1978	1.58	1.87	.84	.14	10
1979	1.55	2.08	.75	.14	8
1980	1.73	2.34	.74	.14	14
1981	1.89	2.71	.70	.14	12
1982	2.01	2.94	.68	.14	13
1983	2.05	2.99	.69	.14	13

D. Compressors, All Refrigerants Except Ammonia, Open Type, over 10 hp

Year	Unit Value	PPI	Unit Value/PPI	Weight	Models
1947	1.64	.34	4.75	.14	9
1948	1.63	.38	4.34	.14	9
1949	1.63	.40	4.03	.14	9
1950	1.53	.41	3.73	.14	9
1951	1.61	.46	3.48	.13	9
1952	1.62	.46	3.51	.13	10
1953	1.59	.48	3.29	.13	10
1954	1.50	.49	3.05	.13	7
1955	1.38	.51	2.70	.13	7
1956	1.41	.57	2.49	.13	10
1957	1.28	.61	2.09	.13	10
1958	1.25	.64	1.96	.13	8
1959	1.21	.67	1.81	.13	8
1960	1.33	.67	1.99	.13	9
1961	1.20	.66	1.80	.13	10
1962	1.12	.66	1.69	.13	10
1963	1.06	.67	1.59	.13	10
1964	1.03	.69	1.50	.13	10
1965	.85	.73	1.16	.13	9
1966	.85	.77	1.11	.13	9
1967	.86	.81	1.06	.13	8
1968	.83	.84	.98	.13	8
1969	.85	.88	.96	.13	14
1970	.88	.93	.96	.13	12
1971	.96	.98	.98	.13	13
1972	1.00	1.00	1.00	.13	13
1973	1.10	1.03	1.07	.13	9
1974	1.29	1.23	1.04	.13	9
1975	1.38	1.51	.91	.13	8
1976	1.47	1.60	.92	.14	8
1977	1.45	1.71	.85	.14	6
1978	1.46	1.84	.79	.14	6
1979	1.59	2.01	.79	.14	7
1980	1.67	2.32	.72	.14	7
1981	1.80	2.62	.69	.14	5
1982	1.89	2.80	.67	.14	5
1983	1.70	2.80	.61	.14	9

Table B.17 (continued)

E. Compressors and Compressor Units, Ammonia Refrigerant

Year	Unit Value	PPI	Unit Value/PPI	Weight	Models
1947	.43	.34	1.24	.14	15
1948	.44	.38	1.18	.14	15
1949	.49	.40	1.22	.14	16
1950	.51	.41	1.25	.14	15
1951	.54	.46	1.18	.13	15
1952	.54	.46	1.17	.13	14
1953	.54	.48	1.12	.13	14
1954	.54	.49	1.10	.13	12
1955	.52	.51	1.01	.13	11
1956	.50	.57	.88	.13	13
1957	.53	.61	.87	.13	13
1958	.53	.64	.84	.13	11
1959	.52	.67	.78	.13	10
1960	.58	.67	.87	.13	10
1961	.60	.66	.91	.13	11
1962	.59	.66	.90	.13	11
1963	.61	.67	.92	.13	9
1964	.60	.69	.88	.13	8
1965	.62	.73	.85	.13	8
1966	.63	.77	.82	.13	9
1967	.58	.81	.72	.13	9
1968	.60	.84	.72	.13	9
1969	.60	.88	.68	.13	9
1970	.63	.93	.68	.13	9
1971	.77	.98	.79	.13	10
1972	1.00	1.00	1.00	.13	10
1973	1.21	1.03	1.18	.13	9
1974	1.34	1.23	1.09	.13	4
1975	1.64	1.51	1.09	.13	4
1976	1.77	1.60	1.11	.14	3
1977	1.87	1.71	1.10	.14	3
1978	1.96	1.84	1.06	.14	3
1979	2.11	2.01	1.05	.14	3
1980	2.36	2.32	1.02	.14	3
1981	2.55	2.62	.98	.14	4
1982	2.53	2.80	.90	.14	4
1983	2.66	2.80	.95	.14	4

F. Condensing Units, Air Cooled, Hermetic Type

Year	Unit Value	PPI	Unit Value/PPI	Weight	Models
1947	.72	.34	2.09	.14	4
1948	.72	.38	1.91	.14	4
1949	.66	.40	1.64	.14	4
1950	.68	.41	1.65	.14	4
1951	.70	.46	1.50	.13	4
1952	.71	.46	1.54	.13	5
1953	.67	.48	1.40	.13	7
1954	.80	.49	1.63	.13	6
1955	.80	.51	1.57	.13	6

(continued)

Table B.17F (continued)

Year	Unit Value	PPI	Unit Value/PPI	Weight	Models
1956	.84	.57	1.48	.13	9
1957	.78	.61	1.28	.13	10
1958	.76	.64	1.19	.13	10
1959	.72	.67	1.07	.13	9
1960	.69	.67	1.03	.13	9
1961	.69	.66	1.05	.13	9
1962	.71	.66	1.07	.13	9
1963	.80	.67	1.21	.13	9
1964	.76	.69	1.11	.13	9
1965	.76	.73	1.04	.13	10
1966	.78	.77	1.01	.13	10
1967	.78	.81	.96	.13	10
1968	.77	.84	.92	.13	9
1969	.79	.88	.89	.13	7
1970	.82	.93	.89	.13	8
1971	.89	.98	.91	.13	9
1972	1.00	1.00	1.00	.13	8
1973	1.14	1.03	1.11	.13	4
1974	1.24	1.23	1.01	.13	6
1975	1.49	1.51	.99	.13	7
1976	1.61	1.60	1.01	.14	7
1977	1.63	1.71	.95	.14	7
1978	1.70	1.84	.93	.14	7
1979	1.77	2.01	.88	.14	7
1980	1.89	2.32	.82	.14	7
1981	2.05	2.62	.78	.14	7
1982	2.22	2.80	.79	.14	7
1983	2.35	2.80	.84	.14	6

G. Condensing Units, Water Cooled, Open Type

Year	Unit Value	PPI	Unit Value/PPI	Weight	Models
1947	.69	.34	1.99	.14	16
1948	.70	.38	1.86	.14	16
1949	.68	.40	1.69	.14	18
1950	.65	.41	1.60	.14	18
1951	.72	.46	1.57	.13	18
1952	.69	.46	1.49	.13	18
1953	.71	.48	1.47	.13	18
1954	.67	.49	1.36	.13	17
1955	.71	.51	1.38	.13	17
1956	.72	.57	1.26	.13	19
1957	.70	.61	1.14	.13	19
1958	.75	.64	1.19	.13	13
1959	.72	.67	1.08	.13	13
1960	.71	.67	1.05	.13	14
1961	.70	.66	1.05	.13	15
1962	.68	.66	1.04	.13	15
1963	.67	.67	1.01	.13	15
1964	.67	.69	.98	.13	15
1965	.67	.73	.92	.13	15
1966	.74	.77	.96	.13	15
1967	.74	.81	.92	.13	14
1968	.75	.84	.89	.13	14

Table B.17G (continued)

Year	Unit Value	PPI	Unit Value/PPI	Weight	Models
1969	.83	.88	.94	.13	14
1970	.87	.93	.94	.13	15
1971	.88	.98	.90	.13	15
1972	1.00	1.00	1.00	.13	15
1973	1.15	1.03	1.12	.13	15
1974	1.42	1.23	1.15	.13	15
1975	1.52	1.51	1.00	.13	15
1976	1.77	1.60	1.11	.14	6
1977	1.94	1.71	1.14	.14	6
1978	1.98	1.84	1.08	.14	6
1979	2.09	2.01	1.04	.14	6
1980	2.28	2.32	.98	.14	6
1981	2.37	2.62	.90	.14	6
1982	2.52	2.80	.90	.14	6
1983	2.46	2.80	.88	.14	6

H. Condensing Units, Water Cooled, Hermetic Type

Year	Unit Value	PPI	Unit Value/PPI	Weight	Models
1952	.75	.46	1.62	.13	8
1953	.80	.48	1.65	.13	8
1954	.72	.49	1.46	.13	8
1955	.74	.51	1.45	.13	8
1956	.76	.57	1.33	.13	8
1957	.83	.61	1.35	.13	8
1958	.74	.64	1.17	.13	8
1959	.68	.67	1.01	.13	8
1960	.68	.67	1.01	.13	8
1961	.69	.66	1.04	.13	9
1962	.75	.66	1.14	.13	9
1963	.75	.67	1.13	.13	9
1964	.73	.69	1.07	.13	9
1965	.74	.73	1.01	.13	9
1966	.78	.77	1.01	.13	9
1967	.84	.81	1.04	.13	9
1968	.80	.84	.95	.13	9
1969	.82	.88	.93	.13	9
1970	.86	.93	.93	.13	9
1971	.91	.98	.93	.13	9
1972	1.00	1.00	1.00	.13	9
1973	1.04	1.03	1.01	.13	6
1974	1.08	1.23	.88	.13	3
1975	1.59	1.51	1.05	.13	2
1976	1.64	1.60	1.02	.14	4
1977	1.76	1.71	1.03	.14	4
1978	1.79	1.84	.97	.14	4
1979	1.85	2.01	.92	.14	6
1980	2.02	2.32	.87	.14	6
1981	2.15	2.62	.82	.14	6
1982	2.50	2.80	.89	.14	6
1983	2.49	2.80	.89	.14	6

(*continued*)

Table B.17 (continued)

I. Group Average

Year	Alternative	Official	Alternative/Official	Weight	Models
1947	.72	.35	2.05	1.00	76
1948	.75	.40	1.88	1.00	65
1949	.75	.43	1.76	1.00	68
1950	.74	.43	1.72	1.00	78
1951	.81	.49	1.64	1.00	78
1952	.82	.49	1.67	1.00	87
1953	.83	.51	1.62	1.00	88
1954	.83	.52	1.59	1.00	79
1955	.82	.54	1.51	1.00	82
1956	.84	.59	1.42	1.00	94
1957	.85	.63	1.35	1.00	90
1958	.82	.65	1.26	1.00	79
1959	.78	.68	1.16	1.00	77
1960	.79	.68	1.17	1.00	77
1961	.79	.67	1.17	1.00	82
1962	.79	.68	1.17	1.00	83
1963	.79	.68	1.16	1.00	82
1964	.78	.70	1.11	1.00	80
1965	.77	.73	1.05	1.00	75
1966	.77	.76	1.01	1.00	72
1967	.78	.79	.99	1.00	72
1968	.78	.83	.94	1.00	72
1969	.82	.87	.94	1.00	106
1970	.85	.93	.92	1.00	91
1971	.92	.98	.94	1.00	94
1972	1.00	1.00	1.00	1.00	99
1973	1.08	1.02	1.05	1.00	84
1974	1.25	1.23	1.01	1.00	71
1975	1.49	1.50	.99	1.00	63
1976	1.55	1.60	.97	1.00	54
1977	1.73	1.71	1.01	1.00	41
1978	1.83	1.86	.98	1.00	42
1979	1.92	2.04	.94	1.00	41
1980	2.12	2.35	.90	1.00	50
1981	2.28	2.65	.86	1.00	46
1982	2.41	2.85	.85	1.00	47
1983	2.43	2.87	.84	1.00	50

Table B.18   **Summary Table: Comparison of Alternative and Official Price Indexes for PDE**

	1947	1948	1949	1950	1951	1952	1953	1954	1955	1956
Office, computing, and accounting machinery (NIPA table 5.6, row 4):										
Alternative	5.14	5.52	5.46	5.47	5.71	5.56	5.47	5.57	5.63	5.55
Official	.33	.30	.37	.33	.35	.35	.37	.37	.38	.40
Models	1	3	3	4	6	9	12	13	12	10
Weight	.05	.05	.05	.05	.05	.05	.05	.05	.05	.06
Communication equipment (NIPA table 5.6, row 5):										
Alternative	2.81	2.63	2.45	2.25	2.13	1.99	1.66	1.54	1.46	1.57
Official	.66	.67	.66	.68	.70	.69	.66	.67	.67	.69
Models	6	6	8	9	7	10	9	6	8	11
Weight	.06	.05	.05	.06	.07	.07	.07	.06	.07	.07
Fabricated metal products (NIPA table 5.6, row 9):										
Alternative	1.04	1.02	1.06	1.01	1.04	1.02	1.02	1.02	.94	.93
Official	.52	.56	.56	.57	.65	.65	.67	.66	.69	.79
Models	6	24	17	20	23	14	24	23	27	28
Weight	.04	.04	.04	.04	.05	.05	.05	.05	.05	.05
Engines and turbines (NIPA table 5.6, row 10):										
Alternative	1.42	1.41	1.35	1.30	1.27	1.22	1.24	1.25	1.11	1.05
Official	.41	.45	.47	.48	.54	.55	.57	.59	.60	.66
Models	31	39	31	45	48	37	46	42	41	44
Weight	.01	.02	.02	.02	.02	.02	.02	.03	.02	.02
Metalworking machinery (NIPA table 5.6, row 11):										
Alternative	.62	.61	.64	.56	.64	.61	.61	.65	.66	.70
Official	.46	.49	.51	.54	.58	.58	.60	.60	.65	.71
Models	21	21	24	26	28	32	30	33	30	35
Weight	.07	.05	.05	.06	.08	.09	.10	.09	.09	.09
General industrial equipment (NIPA table 5.6, row 13):										
Alternative	.70	.71	.72	.65	.73	.70	.73	.75	.78	.78
Official	.42	.45	.48	.50	.56	.55	.57	.58	.61	.67
Models	12	16	16	16	23	23	27	25	27	24
Weight	.09	.08	.07	.07	.07	.07	.07	.08	.09	.09
Electrical transmission, distribution, and industrial apparatus (NIPA table 5.6, row 14):										
Alternative	1.03	1.04	1.09	1.05	1.13	1.15	1.06	1.08	1.00	1.15
Official	.51	.52	.53	.55	.63	.62	.65	.69	.70	.77
Models	11	13	14	22	23	25	24	57	58	55
Weight	.07	.06	.07	.08	.09	.09	.09	.09	.09	.10
Autos (NIPA table 5.6, row 17):										
Alternative	1.07	1.21	1.01	.98	1.03	1.11	1.09	1.01	1.11	1.07
Official	.53	.60	.65	.65	.78	.88	.71	.80	.74	1.05
Models	48	48	68	78	83	85	78	71	72	78
Weight	.16	.19	.23	.21	.16	.17	.20	.21	.19	.16
Aircraft (NIPA table 5.6, row 18):										
Alternative	4.22	4.23	4.43	5.02	4.85	5.20	5.45	5.81	5.98	6.08
Official	.31	.82	.41	.62	.62	.55	.62	.55	.71	.71
Models	41	63	32	32	20	58	53	56	53	67
Weight	.01	.01	.01	.01	.01	.01	.01	.01	.02	.02
Railroad equipment (NIPA table 5.6, row 20):										
Alternative	.60	.69	.66	.73	.74	.76	.75	.79	.79	.80
Official	.43	.50	.49	.55	.56	.58	.58	.62	.63	.65
Models	10	10	10	10	10	10	10	10	10	10
Weight	.07	.09	.08	.08	.08	.07	.05	.04	.04	.05

(*continued*)

Table B.18 (continued)

	1947	1948	1949	1950	1951	1952	1953	1954	1955	1956
Furniture and fixtures (NIPA table 5.6, row 22):										
Alternative	.70	.67	.70	.66	.69	.77	.76	.75	.74	.80
Official	.47	.50	.52	.54	.60	.60	.62	.63	.65	.71
Models	5	5	6	11	10	10	9	9	9	9
Weight	.06	.05	.05	.06	.06	.06	.06	.06	.07	.06
Tractors (NIPA table 5.6, row 23):										
Alternative	.46	.55	.66	.60	.74	.73	.71	.73	.65	.68
Official	.38	.43	.45	.45	.49	.50	.52	.53	.53	.57
Models	17	17	15	26	27	28	31	27	21	24
Weight	.05	.06	.07	.06	.06	.05	.05	.05	.05	.04
Agricultural machinery, except tractors (NIPA table 5.6, row 24):										
Alternative	.50	.50	.54	.50	.52	.54	.56	.56	.56	.57
Official	.38	.43	.47	.48	.52	.53	.53	.54	.55	.56
Models	8	12	13	18	19	15	17	24	22	23
Weight	.07	.08	.08	.08	.08	.07	.06	.06	.05	.04
Construction machinery, except tractors (NIPA table 5.6, row 25):										
Alternative	.69	.71	.71	.69	.74	.73	.76	.77	.76	.77
Official	.42	.45	.47	.49	.54	.54	.54	.54	.55	.59
Models	6	9	12	13	14	14	15	15	18	20
Weight	.05	.05	.04	.04	.04	.04	.04	.04	.04	.04
Service industry machinery (NIPA table 5.6, row 27):										
Alternative	1.94	2.02	2.03	1.91	1.90	1.86	1.82	1.72	1.64	1.60
Official	.89	.94	.98	.99	1.06	1.05	1.06	1.06	1.03	1.04
Models	47	54	60	62	60	72	87	83	90	108
Weight	.10	.10	.08	.07	.06	.07	.07	.07	.07	.07
Electrical equipment, n.e.c. (NIPA table 5.6, row 28):										
Alternative	.78	.76	.92	.74	.81	.91	.84	.84	.81	.85
Official	.53	.58	.60	.58	.65	.65	.65	.64	.65	.70
Models	5	14	17	21	19	23	32	36	39	48
Weight	.02	.02	.02	.02	.02	.01	.01	.01	.02	.01
Törnqvist index for sixteen included equipment types:										
Alternative	1.11	1.16	1.15	1.09	1.15	1.17	1.14	1.13	1.13	1.15
Official	.51	.56	.58	.60	.67	.68	.66	.69	.69	.78
Alternative/ official	2.17	2.06	1.98	1.83	1.73	1.72	1.72	1.65	1.63	1.48
Implicit deflator for sixteen included equipment types:										
Alternative	.87	.89	.90	.87	.90	.93	.93	.94	.94	.97
Official	.48	.52	.54	.56	.60	.61	.61	.64	.64	.71
Alternative/ official	1.83	1.73	1.67	1.55	1.49	1.52	1.52	1.48	1.46	1.37
Nominal and real—Törnqvist index method—PDE purchases (billions of dollars):										
Nominal	10.6	12.5	11.5	13.0	14.5	14.8	16.4	16.1	17.9	19.6
Real alternative	9.6	10.8	10.0	11.9	12.6	12.7	14.4	14.2	15.8	17.0
Real official	20.7	22.3	19.9	21.8	21.8	21.8	24.7	23.4	25.8	25.1
Nominal and real—implicit deflator method—PDE purchases (billions of dollars):										
Nominal	10.6	12.5	11.5	13.0	14.5	14.8	16.4	16.1	17.9	19.6
Real alternative	12.1	14.0	12.8	15.0	16.1	15.9	17.6	17.1	19.1	20.2
Real official	22.2	24.2	21.4	23.3	24.0	24.2	26.7	25.3	27.8	27.6
Number of observations	275	354	346	413	420	465	504	530	537	594

Table B.18 (continued)

	1957	1958	1959	1960	1961	1962	1963	1964	1965	1966
Office, computing, and accounting machinery (NIPA table 5.6, row 4):										
Alternative	5.50	5.57	4.72	4.28	3.66	3.28	3.09	2.71	2.14	1.75
Official	.41	.41	.40	.46	.51	.51	.62	.69	.71	.74
Models	12	19	13	20	27	14	19	17	32	19
Weight	.07	.07	.06	.07	.06	.06	.07	.07	.07	.08
Communication equipment (NIPA table 5.6, row 5):										
Alternative	1.43	1.21	1.00	1.06	1.04	1.10	.97	.97	.80	.81
Official	.72	.73	.73	.73	.73	.73	.74	.75	.76	.77
Models	12	7	10	9	7	12	10	13	11	11
Weight	.08	.08	.09	.11	.13	.12	.11	.11	.10	.10
Fabricated metal products (NIPA table 5.6, row 9):										
Alternative	.97	1.03	.95	.95	.92	.93	.87	.85	.80	.77
Official	.82	.79	.80	.80	.78	.79	.79	.79	.79	.82
Models	35	29	32	33	35	34	35	39	40	36
Weight	.05	.05	.04	.04	.04	.03	.04	.04	.04	.04
Engines and turbines (NIPA table 5.6, row 10):										
Alternative	1.16	1.16	1.11	1.05	1.03	1.01	.97	.93	.89	.80
Official	.74	.76	.76	.76	.74	.74	.74	.76	.76	.78
Models	45	42	45	43	33	44	45	41	37	29
Weight	.03	.03	.03	.02	.02	.02	.01	.01	.01	.02
Metalworking machinery (NIPA table 5.6, row 11):										
Alternative	.74	.75	.73	.76	.76	.78	.78	.77	.78	.78
Official	.76	.77	.80	.84	.84	.86	.85	.87	.88	.90
Models	38	37	36	37	38	35	37	37	39	36
Weight	.08	.07	.07	.07	.08	.08	.08	.09	.09	.11
General industrial equipment (NIPA table 5.6, row 13):										
Alternative	.83	.85	.87	.87	.87	.86	.82	.81	.81	.82
Official	.72	.74	.76	.76	.76	.75	.75	.76	.77	.80
Models	28	34	36	32	31	31	29	33	24	25
Weight	.09	.09	.09	.09	.09	.09	.09	.09	.09	.09
Electrical transmission, distribution, and industrial apparatus (NIPA table 5.6, row 14):										
Alternative	1.19	1.16	1.10	1.06	.99	.91	.84	.83	.82	.81
Official	.83	.86	.86	.83	.80	.80	.78	.79	.75	.77
Models	54	27	28	25	52	53	53	57	25	26
Weight	.10	.09	.09	.09	.09	.08	.08	.08	.08	.08
Autos (NIPA table 5.6, row 17):										
Alternative	1.06	.90	.96	.96	.99	1.00	1.02	.98	.99	.92
Official	.98	1.07	.94	.92	.95	.91	.93	.91	.87	.90
Models	80	81	82	82	85	89	100	115	127	141
Weight	.15	.16	.17	.17	.17	.17	.15	.15	.14	.12
Aircraft (NIPA table 5.6, row 18):										
Alternative	6.12	5.25	3.06	1.92	1.84	1.83	1.89	1.96	2.01	1.89
Official	.65	.76	.74	.73	.71	.76	.82	.73	.80	.79
Models	96	98	86	117	150	107	64	80	139	185
Weight	.02	.03	.04	.04	.04	.03	.02	.03	.04	.05
Railroad equipment (NIPA table 5.6, row 20):										
Alternative	.89	.97	.84	.93	.89	.88	.94	.90	.88	.88
Official	.73	.80	.70	.79	.76	.76	.82	.80	.79	.80
Models	10	10	10	10	10	10	10	10	10	10
Weight	.05	.03	.03	.03	.03	.04	.04	.05	.05	.05

(*continued*)

Table B.18 (continued)

	1957	1958	1959	1960	1961	1962	1963	1964	1965	1966
Furniture and fixtures (NIPA table 5.6, row 22):										
Alternative	.86	.86	.80	.81	.80	.77	.76	.77	.79	.80
Official	.75	.77	.78	.78	.80	.80	.80	.80	.80	.81
Models	9	9	9	11	13	11	15	15	15	15
Weight	.06	.07	.06	.06	.06	.06	.06	.06	.06	.06
Tractors (NIPA table 5.6, row 23):										
Alternative	.65	.75	.80	.80	.83	.85	.82	.84	.83	.83
Official	.61	.64	.66	.68	.69	.70	.71	.73	.75	.77
Models	16	19	20	27	26	32	30	32	30	27
Weight	.04	.05	.04	.03	.04	.04	.05	.05	.05	.05
Agricultural machinery, except tractors (NIPA table 5.6, row 24):										
Alternative	.60	.65	.63	.61	.65	.65	.65	.68	.69	.72
Official	.59	.62	.65	.66	.68	.69	.71	.72	.74	.77
Models	20	21	17	23	22	15	17	17	16	15
Weight	.05	.06	.05	.05	.05	.06	.06	.05	.05	.05
Construction machinery, except tractors (NIPA table 5.6, row 25):										
Alternative	.81	.82	.84	.85	.84	.83	.80	.79	.79	.81
Official	.63	.66	.69	.70	.69	.70	.70	.72	.74	.77
Models	23	25	25	22	25	26	25	28	20	29
Weight	.04	.05	.04	.04	.04	.04	.05	.05	.05	.05
Service industry machinery (NIPA table 5.6, row 27):										
Alternative	1.55	1.45	1.33	1.27	1.20	1.14	1.11	1.07	1.01	.98
Official	1.04	1.03	1.02	.98	.94	.92	.90	.90	.89	.89
Models	108	94	87	91	104	104	99	97	94	99
Weight	.07	.07	.06	.06	.06	.06	.05	.05	.05	.05
Electrical equipment, n.e.c. (NIPA table 5.6, row 28):										
Alternative	.82	.82	.80	.85	.81	.81	.80	.80	.81	.81
Official	.76	.78	.79	.80	.83	.81	.80	.81	.83	.85
Models	44	47	37	37	47	50	48	51	45	48
Weight	.01	.01	.01	.01	.01	.02	.02	.02	.02	.01
Törnqvist index for sixteen included equipment types:										
Alternative	1.18	1.15	1.08	1.06	1.04	1.03	1.00	.98	.94	.92
Official	.81	.84	.83	.83	.83	.82	.83	.83	.83	.85
Alternative/										
official	1.45	1.37	1.31	1.28	1.26	1.25	1.20	1.18	1.14	1.08
Implicit deflator for sixteen included equipment types:										
Alternative	1.02	1.00	.98	.98	.97	.96	.92	.92	.89	.89
Official	.74	.74	.75	.76	.77	.77	.78	.79	.79	.81
Alternative/										
official	1.39	1.36	1.30	1.29	1.27	1.25	1.18	1.16	1.13	1.10
Nominal and real—Törnqvist index method—PDE purchases (billions of dollars):										
Nominal	21.8	18.7	21.3	22.3	21.7	23.4	25.3	28.4	33.4	38.8
Real										
alternative	18.5	16.3	19.7	21.0	20.9	22.7	25.4	29.0	35.4	42.3
Real										
official	26.9	22.3	25.7	26.9	26.2	28.4	30.4	34.1	40.2	45.6
Nominal and real—implicit deflator method—PDE purchases (billions of dollars):										
Nominal	21.8	18.7	21.3	22.3	21.7	23.4	25.3	28.4	33.4	38.8
Real										
alternative	21.4	18.6	21.8	22.7	22.3	24.4	27.4	31.0	37.3	43.7
Real										
official	29.7	25.3	28.5	29.4	28.3	30.4	32.4	36.0	42.2	47.9
Number of observations										
	630	599	573	619	705	667	636	682	704	751

Table B.18 (continued)

	1967	1968	1969	1970	1971	1972	1973	1974	1975	1976
Office, computing, and accounting machinery: (NIPA table 5.6, row 4):										
Alternative	1.68	1.48	1.33	1.27	1.13	1.00	.92	.87	.81	.70
Official	.80	.80	.88	.98	1.05	1.00	.86	.77	.80	.76
Models	17	16	18	20	12	44	18	25	38	38
Weight	.08	.08	.08	.08	.08	.09	.09	.08	.08	.08
Communication equipment (NIPA table 5.6, row 5):										
Alternative	.78	.79	.80	.86	.94	1.00	.99	1.08	1.09	1.05
Official	.80	.83	.87	.91	.95	1.00	1.04	1.13	1.23	1.31
Models	12	10	8	8	18	25	16	13	19	16
Weight	.11	.11	.13	.14	.13	.12	.13	.13	.13	.13
Fabricated metal products (NIPA table 5.6, row 9):										
Alternative	.80	.80	.89	.94	.97	1.00	1.05	1.10	1.38	1.43
Official	.83	.85	.88	.94	.98	1.00	1.04	1.22	1.34	1.40
Models	38	57	63	71	68	71	64	69	73	73
Weight	.04	.04	.05	.05	.06	.05	.06	.06	.07	.07
Engines and turbines (NIPA table 5.6, row 10):										
Alternative	.84	.83	.89	.98	.98	1.00	1.05	1.22	1.37	1.43
Official	.80	.83	.87	.93	.97	1.00	1.02	1.16	1.42	1.56
Models	37	37	57	48	47	47	48	46	32	33
Weight	.02	.02	.02	.03	.03	.03	.02	.02	.02	.02
Metalworking machinery (NIPA table 5.6, row 11):										
Alternative	.83	.84	.88	.92	.97	1.00	1.02	1.06	1.26	1.39
Official	.93	.96	.98	1.00	.98	1.00	1.04	1.17	1.35	1.43
Models	34	40	42	35	36	41	41	33	36	37
Weight	.11	.10	.10	.09	.08	.08	.09	.09	.09	.09
General industrial equipment (NIPA table 5.6, row 13):										
Alternative	.87	.89	.93	.98	1.00	1.00	1.03	1.06	1.26	1.35
Official	.82	.84	.85	.90	.97	1.00	1.04	1.19	1.41	1.45
Models	22	19	27	24	23	23	22	27	31	30
Weight	.08	.08	.08	.08	.08	.08	.08	.08	.08	.09
Electrical transmission, distribution, and industrial apparatus (NIPA table 5.6, row 14):										
Alternative	.84	.84	.93	.95	.98	1.00	1.00	1.01	1.25	1.26
Official	.80	.85	.88	.93	.98	1.00	1.01	1.13	1.29	1.37
Models	27	26	20	20	20	20	17	17	37	34
Weight	.08	.07	.07	.07	.07	.07	.07	.07	.06	.06
Autos (NIPA table 5.6, row 17):										
Alternative	.90	.93	.88	.94	.99	1.00	.99	.92	1.11	1.22
Official	.92	.91	.94	1.09	1.02	1.00	.98	1.11	1.18	1.15
Models	159	165	162	164	158	178	149	155	175	178
Weight	.13	.13	.12	.12	.14	.13	.11	.10	.11	.12
Aircraft (NIPA table 5.6, row 18):										
Alternative	1.47	1.27	1.24	1.12	1.01	1.00	1.04	1.07	1.13	1.21
Official	.84	.86	.90	.93	.97	1.00	1.05	1.12	1.24	1.41
Models	96	129	230	122	73	95	57	71	83	86
Weight	.07	.07	.05	.04	.03	.04	.04	.03	.03	.03
Railroad equipment (NIPA table 5.6, row 20):										
Alternative	.89	.90	.92	.99	1.02	1.00	1.05	1.17	1.47	1.59
Official	.83	.85	.87	.95	1.00	1.00	1.07⁻	1.22	1.57	1.72
Models	10	10	10	10	10	10	10	10	10	10
Weight	.04	.03	.03	.03	.03	.03	.03	.03	.03	.03

(*continued*)

Table B.18 (continued)

	1967	1968	1969	1970	1971	1972	1973	1974	1975	1976
Furniture and fixtures (NIPA table 5.6, row 22):										
Alternative	.83	.88	.91	.95	.98	1.00	1.00	1.06	1.35	1.29
Official	.85	.88	.92	.96	.99	1.00	1.07	1.27	1.39	1.44
Models	15	15	15	15	15	18	17	15	23	26
Weight	.05	.05	.06	.05	.06	.06	.06	.05	.05	.05
Tractors (NIPA table 5.6, row 23):										
Alternative	.87	.88	.93	.98	.97	1.00	1.03	1.07	1.45	1.51
Official	.80	.85	.89	.93	.96	1.00	1.03	1.20	1.44	1.56
Models	29	30	35	24	35	29	37	31	30	35
Weight	.04	.04	.04	.04	.04	.05	.05	.05	.06	.05
Agricultural machinery, except tractors (NIPA table 5.6, row 24):										
Alternative	.75	.78	.81	.88	.95	1.00	1.05	1.09	1.55	1.59
Official	.80	.83	.87	.91	.95	1.00	1.04	1.19	1.36	1.46
Models	16	15	19	20	22	16	16	15	16	34
Weight	.05	.05	.05	.06	.06	.06	.06	.07	.07	.07
Construction machinery, except tractors (NIPA table 5.6, row 25):										
Alternative	.83	.87	.91	.97	.99	1.00	1.02	1.06	1.29	1.36
Official	.79	.82	.85	.92	.97	1.00	1.04	1.18	1.33	1.43
Models	23	22	30	28	26	24	24	28	25	31
Weight	.05	.05	.05	.05	.05	.06	.06	.06	.05	.06
Service industry machinery (NIPA table 5.6, row 27):										
Alternative	.93	.90	.92	.94	.97	1.00	1.02	1.03	1.16	1.15
Official	.90	.93	.94	.97	1.00	1.00	1.01	1.10	1.26	1.33
Models	87	106	119	126	129	132	114	112	132	129
Weight	.05	.05	.05	.05	.05	.05	.04	.04	.04	.04
Electrical equipment, n.e.c. (NIPA table 5.6, row 28):										
Alternative	.82	.85	.91	.93	1.00	1.00	1.04	1.08	1.29	1.25
Official	.85	.88	.91	.96	.98	1.00	1.00	1.10	1.22	1.25
Models	42	56	59	67	66	70	65	64	95	95
Weight	.01	.01	.01	.01	.02	.02	.02	.02	.02	.02
Törnqvist index for sixteen included equipment types:										
Alternative	.92	.91	.93	.96	.99	1.00	1.01	1.04	1.21	1.24
Official	.88	.90	.93	.98	.99	1.00	1.02	1.13	1.26	1.30
Alternative/										
official	1.05	1.01	1.00	.99	1.00	1.00	.99	.92	.96	.95
Implicit deflator for sixteen included equipment types:										
Alternative	.90	.91	.92	.96	.99	1.00	1.01	1.03	1.21	1.21
Official	.84	.87	.90	.95	.99	1.00	1.01	1.11	1.25	1.29
Alternative/										
official	1.07	1.05	1.03	1.01	1.00	1.00	1.00	.93	.96	.94
Nominal and real—Törnqvist index method—PDE purchases (billions of dollars):										
Nominal	40.4	43.6	48.0	48.9	49.4	55.6	67.4	74.5	76.8	85.2
Real										
alternative	44.0	47.7	51.7	50.8	50.0	55.6	66.9	71.9	63.3	68.8
Real										
official	46.1	48.4	51.7	50.1	49.8	55.6	66.1	66.1	61.1	65.3
Nominal and real—implicit deflator method—PDE purchases (billions of dollars):										
Nominal	40.4	43.6	48.0	48.9	49.4	55.6	67.4	74.5	76.8	85.2
Real										
alternative	44.9	47.8	51.9	50.9	50.1	55.6	66.9	72.0	63.7	70.5
Real										
official	48.1	50.4	53.5	51.4	50.1	55.6	66.6	66.9	61.3	66.2
Number of observations										
	664	753	914	802	758	843	715	731	855	885

Table B.18 (continued)

	1977	1978	1979	1980	1981	1982	1983
Office, computing, and accounting machinery (NIPA table 5.6, row 4):							
Alternative	.66	.62	.51	.43	.36	.30	.24
Official	.73	.71	.68	.60	.57	.55	.45
Models	62	102	83	74	104	111	117
Weight	.09	.09	.10	.11	.13	.14	.14
Communication equipment (NIPA table 5.6, row 5):							
Alternative	1.04	1.03	.94	.82	.85	.88	.76
Official	1.35	1.36	1.39	1.45	1.57	1.71	1.80
Models	16	12	11	13	17	18	9
Weight	.14	.13	.14	.15	.16	.17	.17
Fabricated metal products (NIPA table 5.6, row 9):							
Alternative	1.44	1.49	1.61	2.09	2.16	2.37	2.41
Official	1.48	1.55	1.68	1.93	2.12	2.20	2.29
Models	73	90	87	96	81	97	79
Weight	.06	.06	.06	.06	.06	.05	.05
Engines and turbines (NIPA table 5.6, row 10):							
Alternative	1.56	1.65	1.61	2.29	2.45	2.74	2.75
Official	1.64	1.79	1.95	2.24	2.55	2.73	2.80
Models	22	30	25	38	38	40	33
Weight	.02	.01	.01	.01	.01	.01	.01
Metalworking machinery (NIPA table 5.6, row 11):							
Alternative	1.48	1.55	1.61	1.66	1.90	2.05	2.13
Official	1.52	1.65	1.84	2.07	2.29	2.38	2.39
Models	26	35	35	31	42	39	23
Weight	.09	.09	.09	.10	.09	.08	.08
General industrial equipment (NIPA table 5.6, row 13):							
Alternative	1.29	1.40	1.46	1.55	1.70	1.89	2.01
Official	1.55	1.65	1.77	1.98	2.20	2.32	2.30
Models	19	22	22	19	21	25	17
Weight	.09	.09	.09	.09	.09	.08	.08
Electrical transmission, distribution, and industrial apparatus (NIPA table 5.6, row 14):							
Alternative	1.30	1.36	1.38	1.46	1.89	2.04	2.13
Official	1.41	1.49	1.61	1.81	2.00	2.15	2.24
Models	23	25	23	19	21	25	20
Weight	.06	.06	.06	.06	.06	.06	.06
Autos (NIPA table 5.6, row 17):							
Alternative	1.19	1.28	1.23	1.38	1.52	1.63	1.74
Official	1.15	1.29	1.45	1.75	1.54	1.45	1.40
Models	167	155	151	149	155	124	144
Weight	.12	.10	.08	.08	.08	.09	.09
Aircraft (NIPA table 5.6, row 18):							
Alternative	1.35	1.41	1.42	1.56	1.72	1.78	1.74
Official	1.50	1.65	1.82	2.03	2.23	2.47	2.53
Models	66	81	118	115	75	38	52
Weight	.03	.04	.05	.05	.05	.05	.05
Railroad equipment (NIPA table 5.6, row 20):							
Alternative	1.66	1.77	1.91	2.08	2.29	2.33	2.30
Official	1.85	2.01	2.21	2.43	2.72	2.80	2.80
Models	10	10	10	10	10	10	10
Weight	.03	.03	.04	.03	.02	.01	.01

(continued)

Table B.18 (continued)

	1977	1978	1979	1980	1981	1982	1983
Furniture and fixtures (NIPA table 5.6, row 22):							
Alternative	1.39	1.47	1.60	1.76	1.77	1.97	2.11
Official	1.53	1.64	1.82	1.94	2.14	2.30	2.38
Models	22	22	18	16	17	18	18
Weight	.05	.05	.05	.06	.06	.07	.07
Tractors (NIPA table 5.6, row 23):							
Alternative	1.75	1.83	1.91	1.92	2.06	2.17	2.12
Official	1.70	1.85	2.04	2.29	2.53	2.77	2.91
Models	21	23	34	36	41	38	33
Weight	.05	.05	.05	.04	.04	.03	.03
Agricultural machinery, except tractors (NIPA table 5.6, row 24):							
Alternative	1.67	1.82	2.13	2.35	2.43	2.72	2.81
Official	1.58	1.71	1.90	2.14	2.42	2.61	2.73
Models	49	43	41	34	52	55	43
Weight	.06	.06	.06	.06	.05	.04	.04
Construction machinery, except tractors (NIPA table 5.6, row 25):							
Alternative	1.39	1.52	1.70	1.82	1.96	2.14	2.31
Official	1.62	1.76	1.91	2.14	2.28	2.47	2.52
Models	21	21	20	20	18	22	15
Weight	.06	.07	.06	.05	.05	.04	.04
Service industry machinery (NIPA table 5.6, row 27):							
Alternative	1.16	1.19	1.25	1.30	1.38	1.39	1.41
Official	1.39	1.46	1.55	1.71	1.83	1.94	2.01
Models	118	144	152	145	208	224	233
Weight	.04	.04	.04	.04	.04	.04	.04
Electrical equipment, n.e.c. (NIPA table 5.6, row 28):							
Alternative	1.31	1.35	1.42	1.64	1.66	1.81	1.88
Official	1.34	1.42	1.60	1.71	1.83	1.86	1.84
Models	75	97	104	89	162	173	176
Weight	.02	.02	.02	.02	.03	.03	.03
Törnqvist index for sixteen included equipment types:							
Alternative	1.26	1.31	1.32	1.37	1.43	1.49	1.45
Official	1.36	1.43	1.53	1.66	1.76	1.83	1.82
Alternative/ official	.93	.92	.86	.82	.82	.81	.80
Implicit deflator for sixteen included equipment types:							
Alternative	1.22	1.24	1.21	1.15	1.09	1.02	.84
Official	1.33	1.40	1.48	1.52	1.52	1.52	1.33
Alternative/ official	.91	.89	.82	.75	.72	.67	.63
Nominal and real—Törnqvist index method—PDE purchases (billions of dollars):							
Nominal	105.3	127.5	148.9	156.3	169.9	161.2	170.6
Real alternative	83.6	97.1	112.6	114.5	118.5	108.3	117.9
Real official	77.5	88.9	97.1	94.2	96.7	88.0	93.9
Nominal and real—Implicit deflator method—PDE purchases (billions of dollars):							
Nominal	105.3	127.5	148.9	156.3	169.9	161.2	170.6
Real alternative	86.6	102.6	123.6	136.0	155.2	158.2	203.5
Real official	79.0	91.3	100.9	102.6	111.4	106.0	128.7
Number of observations	790	912	934	904	1,062	1,057	1,022

Notes to Table B.1

A. *10-key adding machines: Sears:* Quality dimensions held constant: ability to multiply and subtract directly, number of columns listed, whether electric, presence of clear key, repeat key, nonadd key, and metal casing. *PPI:* 1947–59, index (old code) 11-53-02, "full keyboard adding machines"; 1960–76, index 11-93-01-07, "electric ten-key adding machine"; 1977–83, index 11-93-01 (note: this comparison should stop when that index disappears). *Weight:* Variable weight on noncomputer systems (see chap. 6) times one-third NIPA weight applied to category 11-93-01, "office and store machines and equipment, calculating and accounting machines."

B. *Cash registers: Sears:* Quality dimensions held constant: whether manual or electric, number of keys, presence of subtotal, correction key, multiplier, tumbler lock, and tape rewind. *PPI:* 1953–59, index 11-93-01, "calculating and accounting machines"; 1960–76, index 11-93-01-06, "electric cash register, electromechanical"; 1977–78, index 11-93-01-11, "POS electrical cash register"; 1979–83, index 11-93-01. *Weight:* Variable weight on noncomputer systems (see chap. 6) times one-third NIPA weight applied to category 11-03-01, "office and store machines and equipment, calculating and accounting machines."

C. *Manual typewriters: Sears:* Quality dimensions held constant; size, whether standard or portable, number of keys, weight. *PPI:* 1948–83, index 11-93-03-13, "manual portable typewriters." *Weight:* Variable weight on noncomputer systems (see chap. 6) times NIPA weight applied to category 11-93-03-13, "portable manual typewriter."

D. *Electric typewriters: Sears:* Quality dimensions held constant: size, type, number of keys, weight. *PPI:* 1958–68, index 11-93-03-12, "standard electric typewriter"; 1969–83, index 11-93-03-14, "portable electric typewriter." *Weight:* Variable weight on noncomputer systems (see chap. 6) times NIPA weight applied to category 11-93-03-12, "standard electric typewriter."

E. *Electronic computing machines: Hedonic index:* See discussion in chap. 6. *BEA index for computer systems:* See discussion in chap. 6. *Weight:* Variable weight on computer systems (see chap. 6).

F. *Electronic calculators: Sears:* Quality dimensions held constant: type of display, presence of constant key, memory, printing. *PPI:* 1970–76, index 11-93-01-03, "electronic nonprinting calculators"; 1977–80, index 11-93-01-05, "electronic printing calculators"; 1981–83, index 11-93-01, "office and store machines and equipment, calculating and accounting machines." *Weight:* Variable weight on noncomputer equipment (see chap. 6) times one-third NIPA weight applied to category 11-93-01, "office and store machines and equipment, calculating and accounting machines."

Coverage calculation: The weights listed above account for 95.5 percent of the total NIPA weight for 1981 in the office, computing, and accounting machinery category.

Notes to Table B.2

A. *Telephone apparatus and equipment: Flamm:* Telephone transmission and switching equipment, see text discussion in chap. 9. *BEA:* AT&T TPI index for "inside plants." *Weight:* 95 percent fixed weight.

B. *Radio receivers: Sears:* Quality dimensions held constant: bands (AM, FM, or both), size of speaker, presence of earphones, type (console, table, or portable). *PPI:*

1947–52, index 12-5, "home electronic equipment"; 1953–72, index 12-51-01-02, "table radio receivers"; 1973–83, index 12-51, "radio receivers." *Weight:* One-third of weight not applied to category 1.

C. *Table television sets: Consumer Reports:* See text discussion in chap. 7. *PPI:* 1947–52, index 12-5, "home electronic equipment"; 1953–83, index 12-52, "television receivers." *Weight:* Two-thirds of weight not applied to category 1.

Coverage calculation: Weights account for 44.52 percent of total 1967 NIPA weight in communication equipment.

Notes to Table B.3

A. *Gas warm air furnaces: Sears:* Quality dimensions held constant: BTU, flue size, motor horsepower, overall exterior size, length of guarantee, and whether manual or automatic control. *PPI:* 1951–83, index 10-62-01-42, "warm air furnaces, steel, forced air, gas." *Weight:* 20 percent of NIPA weight applied to category 10-61, "steam and hot water equipment," table B.3, row 2b.

B. *Gas hot water heaters: Sears:* Based on hedonic regression, see text of chap. 10. *PPI:* 1947–66, index 10-66, "water heaters, domestic"; 1967–83, index 10-66-01-13, "domestic, gas water heater." *Weight:* 20 percent of NIPA weight applied to category 10-61, "steam and hot water equipment," table B.3, row 2b.

C. *Water storage tanks: Sears:* Quality dimensions held constant: presence of insulation, presence of glass or epoxy lining, presence of heavy-gauge steel, presence of built-in anode "against corrosion and electrolysis," working pressure, length of guarantee, capacity, and weight. *PPI:* 1948–80, index 10-72-01-01, "pressure tank, above ground"; 1981–83, index 10-72, "metal tanks." *Weight:* Sum of NIPA weights applied to indexes 10-72-01-01 ("pressure tank, above ground"), 10-72-01-12 ("bulk storage tanks, 6,000 gallons"), and 10-72-01-13 ("bulk storage tanks, 10,000 gallons").

D. *Steam boilers for electricity generation: Hedonic:* Based on hedonic regression, see text of chap. 5. *PPI:* 1948–61, index 10-72-01-01, "pressure tanks, above ground"; 1962–82, index 10-72-01-03, "pressure vessel, 30,000 gallons." *Weight:* NIPA weight applied to index 10-72-01-03, "pressure vessel, 30,000 gallons."

E. *Brass gate valves: Sears:* Quality dimensions held constant: size, pressure, type (globe or gate). *PPI:* 1947–83 index, 11-49-01-02, "gate valve, brass or bronze, 1 inch"; 1983 index, 11-49-02-01 "gates, globes, angles, and checks." *Weight:* Half NIPA weight applied to index 10-49-01, "miscellaneous general purpose equipment, valves, and fittings."

F. *Steel safes: Sears:* Quality dimensions held constant: exterior size, interior size, weight, volume, and type (chest, floor, or wall). *PPI:* 1947–83, index 11-93-05-21, "safes, cabinet-type." *Weight:* Sum of NIPA weights applied to index 10-32-01-11, "barrels, irons and pails, steel barrels, 55 gallons," and index 11-93-05-21, "safe, cabinet-type." In 1981, 6 percent of the combined weight was attributed to the index for barrels and 94 percent to the index for safes.

G. *Cast iron radiators and convectors: Unit value:* See text discussion in chap. 11. *PPI:* 1947–69, index 10-61-01-21, "radiation, 25″ high, cast iron"; 1970–76, index 11-49-01-11, "cast iron flange union." *Weight:* 20 percent of NIPA weight applied to category 10-61, "Steam and hot water equipment," table B.3, row 2b.

H. *PVC piping: Sears:* Quality dimensions held constant: pressure rating, weight, dimensions, whether or not drain pipe. *PPI:* 1967–69, index 10-25-02-52, "copper water tubing, straight lengths"; 1970–78, index 07-21-01-02, "rigid PVC pressure piping"; 1979–83, index 07-21, "plastic construction products." *Weight:* Half NIPA weight applied to index 10-49-01, "miscellaneous general purpose equipment, valves, and fittings."

I. *Electric furnaces: Sears:* Quality dimensions held constant: BTU, flue size, motor horsepower, kilowatts, amps, overall exterior size, length of guarantee, and whether manual or automatic control. *PPI:* 1973–82, index 10-62-01-59, "electric furnaces, forced-air, 10 KW." *Weight:* 20 percent of NIPA weight applied to category 10-61, "steam and hot water equipment," table B.3, row 2b.

J. *Electric hot water heaters: Sears:* Quality dimensions held constant: BTU, size in gallons, number of stages, amp fuses, watts, number of elements, whether in cabinet, presence of power miser, whether glass lined. *PPI:* 1968–83, index 10-66-01-01, "water heaters, domestic." *Weight:* 20 percent of NIPA weight applied to category 10-61, "steam and hot water equipment." table B.3, row 2b.

K. *Prefabricated metal buildings: Sears:* Quality dimensions held constant: weight, inside dimensions, door size, cubic feet, roof type, materials. *PPI:* 1961–81, index 10-74-01-45, "metal buildings, steel, rigid frame"; 1982–83, index 10-79, "prefabricated metal buildings." *Weight:* Half NIPA weight applied to category 10-73, "sheet metal products."

L. *Chain link fencing: Sears:* Quality dimensions held constant: gauge, weight, height, size of mesh, length, type, presence of gate or post. *PPI:* 1955–83, index 10-88-06-13, "chain link fencing." *Weight:* Half NIPA weight applied to category 10-73, "sheet metal products."

Coverage calculation: Weights listed above account for 89.2 percent of total NIPA weight in fabricated metal products category.

Notes to Table B.4

A. *Steam turbine generators: Hedonic:* Based on hedonic regression, see text of chap. 5. *PPI:* 1948–70, index 11-73-02-27, "steam generator set"; 1971–82, index 11-73-02, "generators and generator sets." *Weight:* 40 percent of NIPA weight for engines and turbines is assumed to apply to turbines and 60 percent to internal combustion engines. Thus, the weight attributed to this category is 40 percent of the NIPA weight attributed to category 11-73-02, "generators and generator sets."

B. *Gasoline engines, 11 hp and over: Unit value:* See text discussion in chap. 11. *PPI:* 1947–83, index 11-94-01, "gasoline engines." *Weight:* 60 percent of NIPA weight applied to category 11-94-01, "internal combustion engines—gasoline."

C. *Outboard motors: Sears:* Based on hedonic regression, see text of chap. 10. *PPI:* 1948–83, index 11-94-02-11, "outboard motors, 5–15 hp." *Weight:* 60 percent of NIPA weight applied to category 11-94-02, "internal combustion engines, outboard motors."

D. *Diesel engines, except automotive: Unit value:* See text discussion in chap. 11. *PPI:* 1947–83, index 11-94-03, "diesel engines, other than automotive." *Weight:* 60 percent of NIPA weight applied to category 11-94-03, "diesel engines, other than automotive."

Coverage calculation: The weights listed above account for 83.7 percent of the total NIPA weight in the engines and turbines category.

Notes to Table B.5

A. *Drill presses: Sears:* Quality dimensions held constant: number of speeds, size, horsepower of motor, whether floor or bench model, and chuck capacity. *PPI:* 1947–72, index 11-3, "metalworking machinery and equipment"; 1973–83, index 11-37-12, "drilling machines." *Weight:* One-quarter of NIPA weight applied to index 11-3, "metalworking machinery and equipment."

B. *Metal lathes: Sears:* Quality dimensions held constant: size of swing, size of centers, number of speeds, number of feeds, whether bench or floor model, presence of cabinet, and type of cabinet. *PPI:* 1947–71, index 11-3, "metalworking machinery and equipment"; 1972–83, index 11-37-14, "lathes." *Weight:* One-quarter of NIPA weight applied to index 11-3, "metalworking machinery and equipment."

C. *Free-standing power saws: Sears:* Quality dimensions held constant: whether bench, band, or radial saw, blade size, motor horsepower, maximum cutting depth, number of speeds, whether blade guard, and size of work space. *PPI:* 1947–83, index 11-3, "metalworking machinery and equipment." *Weight:* One-quarter of NIPA weight applied to index 11-3, "metalworking machinery and equipment."

D. *Quarter-inch hand power drills: Sears:* Quality dimensions held constant: load-free rpm, presence of toggle or trigger switch, maximum horsepower, full-load horsepower, and chuck capacity. *PPI:* 1947–83, index 11-32-02-21, "drill ¼ inches"; 1980–83, index 11-32-02, "electrical home utility line." *Weight:* One-fifth of NIPA weight applied to indexes 11-32-01 and 11-32-02, "power driven hand tools."

E. *Half-inch hand power drills: Sears:* Quality dimensions held constant: no-load rpm, full-load horsepower, whether or not reversible, chuck capacity, special type (right-angle), whether toggle or trigger switch. *PPI:* 1947–80, index 11-32-03-02, "drill ½ inch chuck size and over"; 1981–83, index 11-32-03, "electrical industrial line." *Weight:* One-fifth of NIPA weight applied to indexes 11-32-01 and 11-32-02, "power driven hand tools."

F. *Hand power saws: Sears:* Quality dimensions held constant: blade size, cutting depth, free blade speed (rpm), horsepower rating, whether with or without case. *PPI:* 1947–82, index 11-32-02-23, "circular saws"; 1983, index 11-32-02, "electrical home utility line." *Weight:* One-fifth of NIPA weight applied to indexes 11-32-01 and 11-32-02, "power driven hand tools."

G. *Hand power sanders: Sears:* Quality dimensions held constant: belt type, belt width, number of drums, whether with or without case, presence of magnetic power unit, and strokes per minute. *PPI:* 1947–83, index 11-32-02-24, "oscillating, reciprocating and vibrating sanders." *Weight:* One-fifth of NIPA weight applied to indexes 11-32-01 and 11-32-02, "power driven hand tools."

H. *Transformer arc welders: Sears:* Quality dimensions held constant: ampere capacity, maximum input (amperes), fuses (amperes), rod sizes, maximum KVA, maximum KW, number of heats, whether gas engine, whether manual start. *PPI:* 1947–83, index 11-33-01-01, "arc welders, transformer type, A.C.-D.C." *Weight:* One-fifth of NIPA weight applied to indexes 11-32-01 and 11-32-02, "power driven hand tools."

I. *Acetylene welding torches: Sears:* Quality dimensions held constant: length, type, whether twin carbon. *PPI:* 1947–82, index 11-33-04-52, "welding torches, blow type"; 1983, index 11-33-04, "gas welding machines and equipment." *Weight:*

One-third of NIPA weight applied to index 11-32-04, "gas welding machines and equipment."

J. *Acetylene cutting tools: Sears:* Quality dimensions held constant: size, whether with tip, whether wrench included, whether twin-carbon torch. *PPI:* 1947–83, index 11-33-04-53, "cutting tools, blow type." *Weight:* One-third of NIPA weight applied to index 11-32-04, "gas welding machines and equipment."

K. *Acetylene single-stage welding outfits: Sears:* Quality dimensions held constant: hose length and thickness, torch length, hose pressure, miscellaneous equipment included. *PPI:* 1947–83, index 11-33-04-54, "flame cutting machines." *Weight:* One-third of NIPA weight applied to index 11-32-04, "gas welding machines and equipment."

L. *Drill bits: Sears:* Quality dimensions held constant: diameter, length. 1976–83 coverage includes hand and power drills, not just bits. *PPI:* 1947–83, index 11-35-01-03, "twist drills." *Weight:* Half NIPA weight applied to index 11-35-01, "cutting tools and accessories, small cutting tools."

M. *Power saw blades: Sears:* Quality dimensions held constant: gauge, diameter, rpm, type. *PPI:* 1947–82, index 11-35-01-29, "power hack saw blades"; 1983, index 11-35-03, "metalworking power saw blades." *Weight:* Half NIPA weight applied to index 11-35-01, "cutting tools and accessories, small cutting tools."

N. *Micrometer calipers: Sears:* Quality dimensions held constant: type of tip and steel, type of spindle, type of frame, degree of precision, size, whether chrome plated, whether frame with decimal lock and ratchet or frame, miscellaneous detailed quality characteristics. *PPI:* 1947–83, index 11-35-02-42, "micro-meter calipers." *Weight:* One-quarter of NIPA weight applied to index 11-3, "metalworking machinery and equipment."

Coverage calculation: The weights listed above account for 85.7 percent of the total NIPA weight in the metalworking machinery category.

Notes to Table B.6

A. *Stationary air compressors: Sears:* Quality dimensions held constant: horse-power, delivered air (cubic feet per minute), tank size, weight, cutout pressure per square inch, whether electric or gas, and whether two stage. *PPI:* 1947–70, index 11-41-03-03, "stationary air compressors, 75–125 HP"; 1971–83, index 11-41-03-01, "stationary air compressors, 5 HP." *Weight:* Half NIPA weight applied to category 11-41, "pumps, compressors, and equipment."

B. *Centrifugal pumps: Sears:* Quality dimensions held constant: horsepower, performance (gallons per minute at twenty-five-foot lift), whether gas or electric, size of suction pipe, size of discharge pipe, whether self-priming, and whether iron or aluminum. *PPI:* 1947–70, index 11-41-02-08, "centrifugal pumps, 3000 GPM"; 1971–72, index 11-41-02-21, "centrifugal pumps"; 1973–83, index 11-41-02-04, "centrifugal pumps, 90 GPM." *Weight:* Half NIPA weight applied to category 11-41, "pumps, compressors, and equipment."

C. *Differential chain hoists: Sears:* Quality dimensions held constant: ton capacity, lift in feet, and length of chain in feet. *PPI:* 1947–83, index 11-44-04-91, "hand chain hoists, spur gear." *Weight:* NIPA weight applied to category 11-44, "industrial material handling equipment."

D. *Propellor fans: Sears:* Quality dimensions held constant: fan size, weight, number of speeds, cubic feet per minute, size, motor horsepower, mount, whether

V-belt, whether variable speed. *PPI:* 1948–83, index 11-47-01-11, "propellor fans." *Weight:* NIPA weight applied to category 11-47, "fans and blowers, except portable."

E. *Fire extinguishers: Sears:* Quality dimensions held constant: weight, amount of charge, size, rating, type of material, type of metal used in case. *PPI:* 1947–83, index 15-99, "fire extinguishers." *Weight:* NIPA weight applied to category 11-4, "general purpose machinery and equipment."

Coverage calculation: The weights listed above account for 84.0 percent of the total NIPA weight in the general industry machinery category.

Notes to Table B.7

A. *Tachometers: Sears:* Quality dimensions held constant: whether tachometer, dwellmeter, or both, number of cylinders, number of volts, type of dial, scale in rpm, degrees of sweep, and degree of accuracy in percent. *PPI:* 1947–83, index 11-72-01, "electrical (direct meas.) instruments." *Weight:* One-third of NIPA weight applied to index 11-72-01, "electrical (direct meas.) instruments."

B. *Electronic auto tester: Sears:* Quality dimensions held constant: number, types, and characteristics of electric meters. For instance, 1947 model contains regulator-generator tester, double-scale voltmeter (zero to three and zero to fifteen volts), ammeter, five to sixty-five amps), tester for cutouts and lighting circuits. *PPI:* 1947–83, index 11-72-01, "electrical (direct meas.) instruments." *Weight:* One-third of NIPA weight applied to index 11-72-01, "electrical (direct meas.) instruments."

C. *Panel-type ammeters: Sears:* Quality dimensions held constant: negative and positive range, and whether extra oil pressure gauge and water temperature gauge are included. PPI: 1948–83, index 11-72-01, "electrical (direct meas.) instruments." *Weight:* One-third of NIPA weight applied to index 11-72-01, "electrical (direct meas.) instruments."

D. *Fractional horsepower electric motors: Sears:* Quality dimensions held constant: horsepower, whether split phase or capacitor type, whether ball bearing or sleeve, shaft size, and revolutions per minute. *PPI:* 1947–82, an average of indexes 11-73-01-05 and 11-73-01-06, "A.C. fractional horsepower electric motors, with respectively ¼ and ½ horsepower"; 1983, index 11-73-03, "fractional HP motors and generators." *Weight:* NIPA weight applied to indexes 11-73-01-06, -11, -12, -13, and -19, all electric motors of differing horsepower.

E. *Power transformers: Kravis-Lipsey:* See chap. 9 discussion. *PPI:* 1954–64, index 11-74-01-13, "power transformers, 5000 KV." *Weight:* Fixed 35 percent weight of overall category on 1954–64.

F. *Voltage regulators: Sears:* Quality dimensions held constant: whether alternator or generator. *PPI:* 1947–80, index 11-74-01-21, "feeder voltage regulators, 76.2 KVA"; 1981–83, index 11-74, "transformers and power regulators." *Weight:* One-sixth of NIPA weight applied to index 11-74, "transformers and power regulators," on 1954–64, half otherwise.

G. *Fusible-type panelboards: Sears:* Quality dimensions held constant: number of wires and volts. *PPI:* 1950–83, index 11-75-01-01, "panelboards, distribution, fusible." *Weight:* Half NIPA weight applied to index 11-75-01, "switchgear, switchboard etc. equipment, panelboards."

H. *Circuit breaker–type panelboards: Sears:* Quality dimensions held constant: amps of main circuit, number of branch circuit, style of cabinet, and whether circuit breakers are one pole or two pole. *PPI:* 1954–83, index 11-75-01-02, "circuit-breaker-type panelboard." *Weight:* Half NIPA weight applied to index 11-75-01, "switchgear, switchboard, etc. equipment, panelboards."

I. *Indoor safety switches: Sears:* Quality dimensions held constant: whether dual volt, number of amps, and number of plug or cartridge fuses. *PPI:* 1947–83, index 11-75-02-12, "safety switches, a-c, 3 pole, 60 A." *Weight:* Half NIPA weight applied to index 11-75-04, "switchgear, switchboard etc., equipment."

J. *Circuit breakers: Sears:* Quality dimensions held constant: number of poles, and ampere capacity. *PPI:* 1947–83, index 11-73-03-21, "circuit breakers, A.C." *Weight:* NIPA weight applied to index 11-74-03, "switchgear, switchboard etc., equipment, circuit breakers."

K. *Outdoor power switches: Sears:* Quality dimensions held constant: ampere capacity, number of cartridge fuses, number of plug fuses. *PPI:* 1948–64, index 11-75-02-12, "safety switches, A.C., 3 pole, 60 A"; 1965–74, index 11-75-04-51, "disconnect switches, 600 A"; 1975–82, index 11-75-04-53, "bus duct plug in switches, 600 A." *Weight:* Half NIPA weight applied to index 11-75-04, "switchgear, switchboard etc., equipment."

Coverage calculation: The weights listed above account for 63.3 percent of the total NIPA weight in the electrical transmission, distribution, and industrial apparatus category.

Notes to Table B.8

A. *Autos: Alternative index:* See text discussion in chap. 8. *Official:* NIPA implicit deflator for new cars, tables 5.6 and 5.7 of NIPA. *Weight:* This component of PDE contains only one product.

Notes to Table B.9

A. *Aircraft: Alternative index:* See text discussion in chap. 4. *Official:* NIPA implicit deflator, tables 5.6 and 5.7 of NIPA. *Weight:* This component of PDE contains only one product.

Notes to Table B.10

A. *Railroad equipment: Alternative index:* Railroad locomotive and freight cars, see text discussion in chap. 9. *Official:* NIPA implicit deflator for railroad equipment, tables 5.6 and 5.7 of NIPA. *Weight:* This component of PDE contains only one product.

Notes to Table B.11

A. *Typewriter tables: Sears:* Quality dimensions held constant: height, dimensions of top both open and closed, weight, material used for legs and top, number of drawers, utility shelf, brakes, casters with or without elevators. *PPI:* No appropriate index. Substituted index 12-22, "metal commercial furniture," for years 1947–83. *Weight:* Constant weight; 25 percent of December 1973 PPI relative importance of index 12-22-01-01, "metal clerical desk."

B. *Card files: Sears:* Quality dimensions held constant: card size, box size, and number of drawers. *PPI:* No appropriate index. Substituted index 12-22-01-21, "metal filing cabinets," for 1947–78. *Weight:* Constant weight; 25 percent of December 1973 PPI relative importance of index 12-22-01-21, "metal filing cabinet."

C. *Fluorescent lighting fixtures: Sears:* Quality dimensions held constant: all dimensions of fixture, distance from ceiling, number of tubes, watts per light, whether light bulbs are included or not, type of start (regular, rapid, rapid with diffuser). *PPI:* 1947–60, index 12-22, "metal commercial furniture"; 1961–80, index 10-83-01-31, "commercial fluorescent non-air handling lighting fixtures"; 1981–83, index 10-83-03-23, "commercial fluorescent fixtures, recessed, non-air." *Weight:* Constant weight; December 1973 PPI relative importance of all PPI indexes covering commercial fluorescent lighting fixtures: 10-83-01-31, -33, -35, and -37.

D. *Steel desks: Sears:* Quality dimensions held constant: all dimensions of size, number of box drawers, number of file drawers, number of letter drawers, presence of center drawer, finish of top. Minor year-to-year fluctuations in weight do not seem to be reflected in any visible change in desk. *PPI:* 1950–67, index 12-22, "metal commercial furniture"; 1968–77, index 12-22-01-01, "metal clerical desks"; 1977–79, index 12-22, "metal commercial furniture" 1980–83, index 12-22-03-21, "desks and extensions." *Weight:* Constant weight; 75 percent of December 1973 PPI relative importance of index 12-22-01-01, "metal clerical desk."

E. *Filing cabinets: Sears:* Quality dimensions held constant: drawer depth, weight, presence of lock, number of drawers, and whether suspension or nonsuspension type. Minor increases in weight in 1959–60 and 1965–66 are not controlled. *PPI:* 1950–79, index 12-22-01-21, "metal filing cabinet"; 1980–83, index 12-22-02-01, "letter filing cabinets." *Weight:* Constant weight; 75 percent of December 1973 PPI relative importance of index 12-22-01-21, "metal filing cabinet."

F. *Office swivel chairs: Sears:* Quality dimensions held constant: seat size, back size, and weight, whether equipped with adjustable tilt tension. *PPI:* 1949–83, index 12-22-01-11, "swivel office chairs." *Weight:* Constant weight; December 1973 PPI relative importance of index 12-22-01-11, "metal office chair."

Coverage calculation: Half BEA weight is on household furniture, which is inappropriate for PDE. Of the other half, the BEA weight on commercial furniture is 61.2 percent. Of this, the total relative importance in December 1973, accounted for by the PPI indexes used as weights as listed above, is 70.1 percent. Thus, the coverage of this category of PDE is taken to be 61.2 percent times 70.1 percent, or 42.9 percent.

Notes to Table B.12

A. *Garden tractors: Sears:* Quality dimensions held constant: horsepower, whether equipped with or without tires, whether walk-behind or riding model, whether electric or recoil start, number of speeds or transmission type, number of cylinders, capacity of fuel tank, presence of fuel gauge. *PPI:* 1949–83, index 11-11-05-22, "garden tractors, riding type, 8–12 hp." *Weight:* 38 percent of NIPA weight for tractors is assumed to apply to farm tractors and 62 percent to construction tractors. Thus, the weight attributed to this category is 38 percent of the NIPA weight attributed to category 11-11-05, "garden tractors and motor tillers."

B. *Wheel tractors: Hedonic:* See text discussion in chap. 9. *PPI:* 1947–83, index 11-11-01, "tractors, wheel-type, farm"; 1983, index 11-11-02-01, "farm tractors, two-wheel drive." *Weight:* 38 percent of the NIPA weight attributed to category 11-11-01, "tractors, wheel-type, farm."

C. *Crawler tractors: Hedonic:* See text discussion in chap. 9. *PPI:* 1950–83, index 11-28-02, "tractors, other than farm, crawler type." *Weight:* 62 percent of the NIPA weight attributed to the four categories for crawler tractors, 11-28-02-11, -13, -15, and -17.

Coverage calculation: The weights listed above account for 80.2 percent of the total NIPA weight in the tractor category.

Notes to Table B.13

A. *Tractor-drawn plows: Sears:* Quality dimensions held constant: number of bottoms, size, type of hitch, and whether for farm or garden tractor. *PPI:* 1948–83, index 11-12-01, "plows." *Weight:* NIPA weight applied to index 11-12-01, "plows."

B. *Tractor-drawn harrows: Sears:* Quality dimensions held constant: width of cut, disc size, number of blades, tooth type (spring or spike), number of teeth, and number of sections. *PPI:* 1948–82, 11-12-02-13, "disc drawn harrows"; 1983, 11-12-03, "planting and fertilizing machinery." *Weight:* One-third of NIPA weight applied to index 11-12-03, "planting and fertilizing machinery."

C. *Seeders: Sears:* Quality dimensions held constant: capacity, weight, and width, whether heavy-duty, whether electric or PTO. Hand-pushed model 1947–50 and tractor-drawn thereafter. *PPI:* 1947–83, index 11-12-03-22, "drawn corn planters." *Weight:* One-third of NIPA weight applied to index 11-12-03, "planting and fertilizing machinery."

D. *Manure spreaders: Sears:* Quality dimensions held constant: capacity, number of wheels, whether heavy-duty, and whether PTO driven. *PPI:* 1950–83, index 11-12-03-25, "manure spreader, PTO driven." *Weight:* One-third of NIPA weight applied to index 11-12-03, "planting and fertilizing machinery."

E. *Tractor-drawn cultivators: Sears:* Quality dimensions held constant: shank type (spring, stiff, or trip-back), width, number of rows, number of shanks, and size of sweep. *PPI:* 1949–82, index 11-12-04, "cultivators"; 1973–82, index 11-12-04-36, "cultivators, rear-mounted, 4-row." *Weight:* NIPA weight applied to index 11-12-04, "cultivators."

F. *Sprayers: Sears:* Quality dimensions held constant: container capacity, whether hand or tractor driven, number of rows and nozzles, whether tires included, whether pump included, and horsepower of pump. *PPI:* 1947–61, index 11-12-05, "sprayers and dusters"; 1962–82, index 11-12-05-44, "tractor mounted field sprayers"; 1983, index 11-12-05. *Weight:* NIPA weight applied to index 11-12-05, "sprayers and dusters."

G. *Tractor-mounted mowers: Sears:* Quality dimensions held constant: cutting width, whether reel type or rotary type, and number of blades. *PPI:* 1947–83, index 11-12-07-62, "mounted mowers." *Weight:* NIPA weight applied to index 11-12-07, "haying machinery."

H. *Portable farm elevators: Sears:* Quality dimensions held constant: length, whether single or double chain, and whether extendable. *PPI:* 1948–67, index 11-12, "agricultural machinery, except tractors"; 1968–75, index 11-12-09, "farm elevators"; 1976–83, index 11-12-09-81, "farm elevators, portable, double-chain." *Weight:* NIPA weight applied to index 11-12-08, "crop preparation machinery."

I. *Poultry brooders: Sears:* Quality dimensions held constant: capacity, whether gas or electric, number of lamps, type and size of lamps. *PPI:* 1947–77, index 11-13-01-03, "gas poultry brooders"; 1978–83, index 11-13-01, "poultry equipment." *Weight:* NIPA weight applied to index 11-13-01, "poultry equipment."

Coverage calculation: The weights listed above account for 38.8 percent of the total NIPA weight in the agricultural machinery (except tractors) category.

Notes to Table B.14

A. *Post-hole diggers: Sears:* Quality dimensions held constant: augur and shaft size, horsepower, whether one man or two man. *PPI:* 1956–83, index 11-23-01-01, "trenchers." *Weight:* One-fifth of NIPA weight applied to index 11-28-06-01, "tractors other than farm, tractor loader 1¼ and under 2 cubic yards."

B. *Roto spaders: Sears:* Quality dimensions held constant: size of motor, width and depth of cut, diameter and number of tines, number of forward and reverse speeds, and whether rotary mower attachment is possible. *PPI:* 1948–81, index 11-23-01-01, "trenchers." *Weight:* One-fifth of NIPA weight applied to index 11-28-06-01, "tractors other than farm, tractor loader 1¼ and under 2 cubic yards."

C. *Centrifugal pumps: Sears:* Quality dimensions held constant: horsepower, performance (gallons per minute at twenty-five-foot lift), whether gas or electric, size of suction pipe, size of discharge pipe, whether self-priming, and whether iron or aluminum. *PPI:* 1947–70, index 11-41-02-08, "centrifugal pumps, 300 GPM"; 1971–72, index 11-41-01-21, "centrifugal pumps"; 1973–83, index 11-41-02-04, "centrifugal pumps, 90 GPM." *Weight:* One-fifth of NIPA weight applied to index 11-28-06-01, "tractors other than farm, tractor loader 1¼ and under 2 cubic yards."

D. *Stationary air compressors: Sears:* Quality dimensions held constant: horsepower, delivered air (cubic feet per minute), tank size, weight, cutout pressure per square inch, whether electric or gas, and whether two stage. *PPI:* 1947–70, index 11-41-03-03, "stationary air compressors, 75–125 HP"; 1971–83, index 11-41-03-01, "stationary air compressors, 5 HP." *Weight:* One-fifth of NIPA weight applied to index 11-28-06-01, "tractors other than farm, tractor loader 1 ¼ and under 2 cubic yards."

E. *Portable concrete mixers: Sears:* Quality dimensions held constant: drum capacity, batch size, engine size, type of drive, type of fuel, and whether sent from factory or from warehouse. *PPI:* 1947–83, index 11-27-01-11, "portable mixers, 3 ½ cubic feet and over." *Weight:* NIPA weight applied to index 11-23, "construction machinery for mounting."

F. *Differential chain hoists: Sears:* Quality dimensions held constant: ton capacity, lift in feet, and length of chain in feet. *PPI:* 1947–83, index 11-44-94-01, "hand chain hoists, spur gear." *Weight:* One-fifth of NIPA weight applied to index 11-28-06-01, "tractors other than farm, tractor loader 1 ¼ and under 2 cubic yards."

Coverage calculation: The weights listed above account for 19.5 percent of the total NIPA weight in the construction machinery (except tractors) category.

Notes to Table B.15

A. *Gas warm air furnaces: Sears:* Quality dimensions held constant: BTU, flue size, motor horsepower, overall exterior size, length of guarantee, and whether manual or automatic control. *PPI:* 1951–83, index 10-62-01-42, "warm air furnace, steel, forced air, gas, 72-88 MBTU." *Weight:* Half NIPA weight applied to index 10-66, "water heaters, domestic," and one-quarter of NIPA weight applied to index 11-61, "food product machinery."

B. *Gas hot water heaters: Sears:* Based on hedonic regression, see text of chap. 10. *PPI:* 1947–66, index 10-66, "water heaters, domestic"; 1967–83, index 10-66-01-13, "gas water heaters, domestic." *Weight:* Half NIPA weight applied to index 10-66, "water heaters, domestic," and one-quarter of NIPA weight applied to index 11-61, "food product machinery."

C. *Hand electric sanders: Sears:* Quality dimensions held constant: belt type, belt width, number of drums, whether with or without case, presence of magnetic power unit, and strokes per minute. *PPI:* 1947–83, index 11-32-02-24, "orbital sanders." *Weight:* One-fifth of NIPA weight applied to index 11-41, "pumps, compressors, and equipment."

D. *Compressors, all refrigerants except ammonia, open type, over ten horsepower: Unit value:* See text discussion in chap. 11. *PPI:* 1947–83, index 11-41, "pumps, compressors, and equipment." *Weight:* One-fifth of NIPA weight applied to index 11-41, "pumps, compressors, and equipment."

E. *Compressors and compressor units, ammonia refrigerants: Unit value:* See text discussion in chap. 11. *PPI:* 1947–83, index 11-41, "pumps, compressors, and equipment." *Weight:* One-fifth of NIPA weight applied to index 11-41, "pumps, compressors, and equipment."

F. *Condensing units, air cooled, hermetic type: Unit value:* See text discussion in chap. 11. *PPI:* 1947–83, index 11-41, "pumps, compressors, and equipment." *Weight:* One-fifth of NIPA weight applied to index 11-41, "pumps, compressors, and equipment."

G. *Condensing units, water cooled, open type: Unit value:* See text discussion in chap. 11. *PPI:* 1947–83, index 11-41, "pumps, compressors, and equipment." *Weight:* One-fifth of NIPA weight applied to index 11-41, "pumps, compressors, and equipment."

H. *Condensing units, water cooled, hermetic type: Unit value:* See text discussion in chap. 11. *PPI:* 1952–83, index 11-41, "pumps, compressors, and equipment." *Weight:* One-fifth of NIPA weight applied to index 11-41, "pumps, compressors, and equipment."

I. *Automatic washing machines: Consumer Reports:* See text discussion in chap. 7. *PPI:* 1948–83, index 11-41-02-11, "automatic washing machines." *Weight:* Half NIPA weight applied to index 12-41-02, "household appliances, laundry equipment."

J. *Electric clothes dryers: Consumer Reports:* See text discussion in chap. 7. *PPI:* 1951–57, index 12-41-02, "laundry equipment"; 1958–83, index 12-41-02-32, "electric dryers." *Weight:* Half NIPA weight applied to index 12-41-02, "household appliances, laundry equipment."

K. *Refrigerators: Consumer Reports:* See text discussion in chap. 7. *PPI:* 1949–60, index 12-41-03, "refrigeration equipment"; 1961–81, index 12-41-03-36, "refrigerator-freezers"; 1982–83, index 12-41-03. *Weight:* NIPA weight applied to index 12-41-03, "household appliances, refrigeration equipment."

L. *Room air conditioners: Consumer Reports:* See text discussion in chap. 7. *PPI:* 1953–83, index 12-41-04-45, "room air conditioners." *Weight:* NIPA weight applied to index 12-41-03-38, "household appliances, room air conditioners."

M. *Under-counter dishwashers: Consumer Reports:* See text discussion in chap. 7. *PPI:* 1952–66, index 12-41, "major appliances"; 1967–83, index 12-41-04-41, "dishwashers, under-counter." *Weight:* NIPA weight applied to index 12-41-04-41, "dishwashers, under-counter."

N. *Microwave ovens: Consumer Reports:* See text discussion in chap. 7. *PPI:* 1968–78, index 12-41-01, "cooking equipment"; 1979–83, index 12-41-01-21, "portable microwave ovens." *Weight:* One-quarter of NIPA weight applied to index 11-61, "food products machinery."

O. *Commercial vacuum cleaners: Sears:* Quality dimensions held constant: type (upright or canister), suction, attachments, weight. *PPI:* Index 11-68-01-11, "commercial and industrial vacuum cleaners and parts," except 1974–78 and 1980 (index 12-43-01-11) and 1979 and 1981 (index 12-43). *Weight:* NIPA weight applied to index 12-43-01-11, "vacuum cleaner, canister type.")

P. *Automatic coffee makers: Sears:* Quality dimensions held constant: number of cups, brewing time, type of filters, whether automatic timer. *PPI:* 1972–83, index 12-44-01-13, "automatic coffee makers." *Weight:* One-quarter of NIPA weight applied to index 11-61, "food products machinery."

Coverage calculation: The weights listed above account for 94.5 percent of the total NIPA weight for 1981 in the service industry machinery category.

Notes to Table B.16

A. *Tachometers: Sears:* Quality dimensions held constant: whether tachometer, dwellmeter, or both, number of cylinders, number of volts, type of dial, scale in rpm, degrees of sweep, and degree of accuracy in percent. *PPI:* 1947–83, index 11-72-01, "electrical (direct meas.) instruments." *Weight:* One-third of NIPA weight applied to index 12-44, "small electrical appliances."

B. *Electronic auto testers: Sears:* Quality dimensions held constant: number, types, and characteristics of electric meters. For instance, 1947 model contains regulator-generator tester, double-scale voltmeter (0 to 3 and 0 to 15 volts), ammeter (5 to 65 amps), tester for cutouts and lighting circuits. *PPI:* 1947–83, index 11-72-01, "electrical (direct meas.) instruments." *Weight:* One-third of NIPA weight applied to index 12-44, "small electrical appliances."

C. *Panel-type ammeters: Sears:* Quality dimensions held constant: negative and positive range, and whether extra oil pressure gauge and water temperature gauge are included. *PPI:* 1948–83, index 11-72-01, "electrical (direct meas.) instruments." *Weight:* One-third of NIPA weight applied to index 12-44, "small electrical appliances."

D. *Replacement auto batteries: Sears:* Quality dimensions held constant: fillable or presealed, number of cells, amps and volts, length of guarantee. *PPI:* 1948–83, index 11-79-01-01, "storage batteries, automotive, 12-volt, replacement." *Weight:* NIPA weight applied to index 11-79-01, "storage batteries."

E. *Fluorescent lighting fixtures: Sears:* Quality dimensions held constant: all dimensions of fixture, distance from ceiling, number of tubes, watts per light, whether light bubs are included, type of start (regular, rapid, rapid with diffuser). *PPI:* 1947–60, index 12-22, "metal commercial furniture"; 1961–80, index 10-83-01-31, "commercial fluorescent, non-air handling lighting fixtures"; 1981–83, index 10-83-03-23, "commercial fluorescent fixtures, recessed non-air." *Weight:* NIPA weight applied to indexes 10-83, "lighting fixtures," and 10-83-01-23, "lighting fixtures, commercial or residential incandescent, square recessed."

F. *Commercial vacuum cleaners: Sears:* Quality dimensions held constant: type (upright or canister), suction, attachments, weight. *PPI:* 1972–81, index 12-43-01-11, "canister, tank, and all general purpose vacuum"; 1982–83, index 11-68-01-11, "commercial and industrial vacuum cleaners." *Weight:* NIPA weight applied to category 11-43-01-11, "vacuum cleaner, canister type."

G. *Automatic washing machines: Consumer Reports:* See text discussion in chap. 7. *PPI:* 1948–83, index 12-41-02-11, "automatic washing machines." *Weight:* One-sixth of NIPA weight applied to index 12-41, "major household appliances."

H. *Electric clothes dryers: Consumer Reports:* See text discussion in chap. 7. *PPI:* 1951–83, index 12-41-02-32, "electric clothes dryers." *Weight:* One-sixth of NIPA weight applied to index 12-41, "major household appliances."

I. *Refrigerators: Consumer Reports:* See text discussion in chap. 7. *PPI:* 1947–60, index 12-41-03, "refrigeration equipment"; 1961–81, index 12-41-03-36, "refrigerator-freezers"; 1982–83, index 12-41-03. *Weight:* One-sixth of NIPA weight applied to index 12-41, "major household appliances."

J. *Room air conditioners: Consumer Reports:* See text discussion in chap. 7. *PPI:* 1953–83, index 12-41-04-45, "room air conditioners." *Weight:* One-sixth of NIPA weight applied to index 12-41, "major household appliances."

K. *Under-counter dishwashers: Consumer Reports:* See text discussion in chap. 7. *PPI:* 1952–66, index 12-41, "major appliances"; 1967–83, index 12-41-04-41, "undercounter dishwashers." *Weight:* One-sixth of NIPA weight applied to index 12-41, "major household appliances."

L. *Microwave ovens: Consumer Reports:* See text discussion in chap. 7. *PPI:* 1968–78, index 12-41-01, "cooking equipment"; 1979–83, index 12-41-01-21, "portable microwave ovens." *Weight:* One-sixth of NIPA weight applied to index 12-41, "major household appliances."

Coverage calculation: The weights listed above account for 63.3 percent of the total NIPA weight in the electrical equipment, n.e.c., category.

Notes to Table B.18

Total number of products included in this study—110. Number of observations per year on average—692 for 25,605 total observations.

Appendix C

"Secondary" PDE Categories, Annual Listing of Alternative and Official Price Indexes (1972 = 1.00)

List of Tables

Table C.1   **Comparison of Alternative Price Indexes for PDE with Official Indexes from NIPA, Table 5.6, Rows 6 and 7, Instruments and Photocopy**

Year	Alternative	Official	Alternative/Official
1947	1.49	.57	2.63
1948	1.50	.60	2.52
1949	1.51	.61	2.49
1950	1.46	.63	2.35
1951	1.54	.70	2.21
1952	1.55	.69	2.24
1953	1.52	.71	2.16
1954	1.55	.73	2.12
1955	1.55	.75	2.07
1956	1.61	.79	2.04
1957	1.65	.84	1.96
1958	1.66	.86	1.92
1959	1.57	.88	1.79
1960	1.56	.90	1.74
1961	1.56	.91	1.72
1962	1.55	.91	1.71
1963	1.53	.91	1.68
1964	1.52	.91	1.66
1965	1.47	.91	1.61
1966	1.43	.93	1.54
1967	1.43	.95	1.50
1968	1.44	.99	1.46
1969	1.48	1.01	1.46
1970	1.49	1.03	1.45
1971	1.30	1.05	1.24
1972	1.00	1.00	1.00
1973	1.01	1.01	1.00
1974	.97	1.02	.96
1975	.90	1.01	.89
1976	.82	.97	.85
1977	.80	.96	.84
1978	.80	1.00	.80
1979	.75	1.03	.73
1980	.76	1.06	.72
1981	.81	1.11	.73
1982	.86	1.14	.75
1983	.86	1.16	.75

Table C.2   **Comparison of Alternative Price Indexes for PDE with Official Indexes from NIPA, Table 5.6, Row 12, Special Industry Machinery**

Year	Alternative	Official	Alternative/Official
1947	1.21	.66	1.84
1948	1.22	.70	1.75
1949	1.25	.73	1.72
1950	1.18	.76	1.50
1951	1.21	.81	1.49
1952	1.17	.81	1.45
1953	1.16	.82	1.41
1954	1.15	.82	1.40
1955	1.13	.84	1.34
1956	1.14	.88	1.30
1957	1.15	.91	1.26
1958	1.11	.90	1.23
1959	1.06	.92	1.15
1960	1.05	.92	1.14
1961	1.01	.90	1.13
1962	1.00	.90	1.11
1963	.98	.89	1.11
1964	.96	.89	1.08
1965	.93	.89	1.05
1966	.91	.90	1.01
1967	.90	.91	.98
1968	.88	.94	.93
1969	.91	.96	.95
1970	.93	.98	.95
1971	.97	.99	.98
1972	1.00	1.00	1.00
1973	1.02	1.02	1.00
1974	1.04	1.13	.92
1975	1.19	1.29	.93
1976	1.22	1.36	.90
1977	1.25	1.43	.87
1978	1.29	1.52	.85
1979	1.35	1.63	.83
1980	1.40	1.81	.77
1981	1.52	1.96	.78
1982	1.56	2.06	.76
1983	1.60	2.12	.75

Table C.3   **Comparison of Alternative Price Indexes for PDE with Official Indexes from NIPA, Table 5.6, Row 10, Trucks, Buses, and Truck Trailers**

Year	Alternative	Official	Alternative/Official
1947	1.20	.44	2.70
1948	1.27	.51	2.49
1949	1.15	.55	2.09
1950	1.13	.56	2.01
1951	1.16	.69	1.70
1952	1.25	.72	1.75
1953	1.25	.65	1.94
1954	1.20	.70	1.73
1955	1.23	.68	1.81
1956	1.21	.85	1.43
1957	1.27	.84	1.51
1958	1.09	.89	1.22
1959	1.10	.84	1.31
1960	1.06	.83	1.28
1961	1.05	.85	1.23
1962	1.03	.83	1.24
1963	1.03	.84	1.23
1964	.99	.84	1.17
1965	.98	.83	1.18
1966	.90	.86	1.04
1967	.90	.88	1.02
1968	.89	.89	1.01
1969	.87	.91	.95
1970	.91	1.01	.91
1971	.96	1.00	.96
1972	1.00	1.00	1.00
1973	.98	1.00	.98
1974	1.05	1.14	.92
1975	1.24	1.30	.95
1976	1.30	1.35	.96
1977	1.30	1.40	.93
1978	1.42	1.55	.92
1979	1.38	1.73	.80
1980	1.54	2.03	.76
1981	1.70	2.04	.83
1982	1.81	2.06	.88
1983	1.89	2.04	.92

Table C.4   **Comparison of Alternative Price Indexes for PDE with Official Indexes from NIPA, Table 5.6, Row 19, Ships and Boats**

Year	Alternative	Official	Alternative/Official
1947	.82	.47	1.75
1948	.82	.50	1.63
1949	.83	.53	1.58
1950	.80	.54	1.50
1951	.87	.61	1.42
1952	.89	.60	1.47
1953	.88	.62	1.43
1954	.89	.63	1.41
1955	.88	.65	1.36
1956	.91	.70	1.30
1957	.94	.74	1.27
1958	.91	.75	1.21
1959	.88	.76	1.16
1960	.88	.76	1.16
1961	.86	.75	1.15
1962	.86	.75	1.14
1963	.84	.76	1.11
1964	.83	.77	1.08
1965	.83	.77	1.07
1966	.82	.80	1.03
1967	.84	.82	1.03
1968	.84	.85	.99
1969	.89	.88	1.00
1970	.91	.94	.98
1971	.96	.98	.98
1972	1.00	1.00	1.00
1973	1.02	1.02	1.00
1974	1.11	1.19	.93
1975	1.32	1.41	.94
1976	1.38	1.50	.92
1977	1.42	1.57	.90
1978	1.49	1.69	.88
1979	1.59	1.86	.86
1980	1.75	2.09	.84
1981	1.97	2.30	.86
1982	2.12	2.42	.87
1983	2.14	2.46	.87

Table C.5   Comparison of Alternative Price Indexes for PDE with Official Indexes from NIPA, Table 5.6, Row 26, Other Equipment

Year	Alternative	Official	Alternative/Official
1947	.99	.58	1.71
1948	.98	.60	1.64
1949	.99	.61	1.61
1950	.87	.62	1.39
1951	.91	.67	1.35
1952	.95	.70	1.35
1953	.97	.69	1.41
1954	.92	.70	1.33
1955	.85	.70	1.21
1956	.84	.77	1.09
1957	.85	.80	1.06
1958	.85	.82	1.03
1959	.82	.81	1.02
1960	.83	.81	1.02
1961	.83	.85	.98
1962	.80	.83	.97
1963	.80	.83	.97
1964	.78	.83	.94
1965	.79	.84	.94
1966	.78	.85	.92
1967	.82	.86	.95
1968	.84	.88	.95
1969	.87	.92	.94
1970	.91	.98	.93
1971	1.00	1.00	1.00
1972	1.00	1.00	1.00
1973	1.00	1.01	.99
1974	1.00	1.14	.88
1975	1.27	1.24	1.02
1976	1.29	1.30	.99
1977	1.29	1.36	.95
1978	1.31	1.45	.90
1979	1.43	1.60	.89
1980	1.46	1.79	.82
1981	1.53	1.90	.80
1982	1.73	2.00	.86
1983	1.75	2.09	.84

Table C.6   **Comparison of Alternative Price Indexes for PDE with Official Indexes from NIPA, Table 5.6, Row 26, Mining and Oilfield Machinery**

Year	Alternative	Official	Alternative/Official
1947	.69	.42	1.65
1948	.71	.45	1.58
1949	.71	.47	1.51
1950	.69	.49	1.42
1951	.74	.54	1.36
1952	.73	.54	1.34
1953	.76	.54	1.41
1954	.77	.54	1.43
1955	.76	.55	1.39
1956	.77	.59	1.30
1957	.81	.63	1.28
1958	.82	.66	1.24
1959	.84	.69	1.21
1960	.85	.70	1.21
1961	.84	.69	1.21
1962	.83	.70	1.18
1963	.80	.70	1.14
1964	.79	.72	1.10
1965	.79	.74	1.08
1966	.81	.77	1.06
1967	.83	.79	1.06
1968	.87	.82	1.06
1969	.91	.85	1.07
1970	.97	.92	1.06
1971	.99	.97	1.03
1972	1.00	1.00	1.00
1973	1.02	1.04	.98
1974	1.06	1.18	.90
1975	1.29	1.33	.97
1976	1.36	1.43	.95
1977	1.39	1.62	.86
1978	1.52	1.76	.86
1979	1.70	1.91	.89
1980	1.82	2.14	.85
1981	1.96	2.28	.86
1982	2.14	2.47	.87
1983	2.31	2.52	.92

Notes to Table C.1

The photocopy and instruments indexes are proxied using App. B tables in the following steps.

1. A photocopy index is proxied by aggregating all the products (excluding electronic computing machinery) in the office, computing, and accounting machinery industry.

2. An instruments index is proxied by generating a group of subindexes for each of the PPI product categories used in the NIPA to deflate instruments. Each subindex combines alternative indexes and PPIs from App. B tables with equal weights. The subindexes and their product components are as follows: *Instruments:* (1) quarter-inch hand power driven drills; (2) half-inch hand power driven drills; (3) hand electric sanders; (4) transformer arc welders; *Cutting tools and accessories, precision measurement tools:* (1) free-standing power saws; (2) acetylene cutting tools; (3) power saw blades; (4) micrometer calipers; (5) drill bits; *Pumps and compressors:* (1) stationary air compressors; (2) centrifugal pumps; (3) compressors and compressor units, ammonia refrigerant; (4) compressors, all refrigerants except ammonia, open type, over 10 hp; (5) condensing units, air cooled, hermetic type; (6) condensing units, water cooled, open type; (7) condensing units, water cooled, hermetic type; *Electrical direct measurement instruments:* (1) tachometers; (2) electronic auto testers; (3) panel type ammeters; *Metal commercial furniture:* used the entire industry of furniture and fixtures from App. B. *Small electrical appliances:* (1) automatic coffee makers; (2) vacuum cleaners; (3) microwave ovens.

3. The instrument index is weighted with the photocopy index using Törnqvist NIPA nominal investment share.

Notes to Table C.2

The special industry machinery index is proxied by taking the industry group for metalworking machinery and service industry machinery from App. B and aggregating the two together with equal weights.

Notes to Table C.3

The trucks, buses, and truck trailers index is generated from an unweighted average of the following indexes from App. B: (1) autos; (2) diesel engines, except automotive.

Notes to Table C.4

The ships and boats index is generated by first creating six subgroups of indexes, which are then aggregated with 1967 NIPA weights. The group indexes and the product indexes that compose them are as follows: *Fabricated metal products* (App. B); *Pumps, compressors, and general purpose machinery and equipment:* (1) stationary air compressors; (2) centrifugal pumps; (3) compressors and compressor units, ammonia refrigerant; (4) compressors, all refrigerants except ammonia, open type, over 10 hp; (5) condensing units, air cooled, hermetic type; (6) condensing units, water cooled, open type; (7) condensing units, water cooled, hermetic type; (8) fire extinguishers; *Steam and hot water equipment:* (1) gas hot water heaters; (2) water storage tank; (3) brass gate valves; (4) PVC piping; (5) radiator and convectors; (6) electric hot water heaters; *Electrical machinery and equipment, selected items:*

(1) panel-type ammeters; (2) fractional horsepower electric motors; (3) voltage regulators; (4) fusible-type panel boards; (5) circuit breaker-type panelboards; (6) indoor safety switches; (7) circuit breakers; (8) outdoor power switches; *Engines and turbines:* (1) gasoline engines; (2) outboard motors; *Diesel engines, except automotive.*

Notes to Table C.5

The other equipment index is created by aggregating, using NIPA 1967 weights, the following indexes: (1) fluorescent light fixtures; (2) furniture and fixtures (App. B); (3) autos; (4) batteries; (5) fire extinguishers; (6) garden tractors.

Notes to Table C.6

The mining and oilfield machinery index is proxied by the construction machinery index from App. B.

References

Books and Articles

Alexander, Arthur J., and Bridger M. Mitchell. 1984. *Measuring technological change of heterogeneous products*. Rand Report R–3107–NSF. Santa Monica, Calif.: Rand, May.

Archibald, Robert B., and William S. Reece. 1979. Partial subindexes of input prices: The case of computer services. *Southern Economic Journal* 46(October):528–40.

Bailey, Elizabeth E., David R. Graham, and Daniel P. Kaplan. 1985. *Deregulating the airlines*. Cambridge, Mass.: MIT Press.

Baily, Martin N., and Robert J. Gordon. 1988. Measurement issues, the productivity slowdown, and the explosion of computer power. *Brookings Papers on Economic Activity* 19, no. 2:347–420.

Bain, Edward C. 1986. Scrubber scrapper. *Fortune* (April 14):63–64.

Barger, E. L., J. B. Liljedahl, W. M. Carleton, and E.G. McKibben. 1963. *Tractors and their power units*. New York: Wiley.

Barmash, Isadore. 1977. Sears in a switch to newspapers. *New York Times* (September 7):57.

———. 1988. Sears changes catalog operation. *New York Times,* 20 June, 36.

Barzel, Yoram. 1964. The production function and technical change in the steam-power industry. *Journal of Political Economy* 70 (April):133–50.

Berndt, Ernst R., and David O. Wood. 1975. Technology, prices, and the derived demand for energy. *Review of Economics and Statistics* 56 (August):259–68.

———. 1979. Engineering and econometric interpretations of energy-capital complementarity. *American Economic Review* 69 (June):342–54.

Billingsley, James R. 1973. Values of vertical integration in the Bell System. Address given at the sixth annual Seminar on Economics of Public Utilities, Oshkosh, Wis., 8 March. (Also published as a brochure by the Bell System.)

Brand, Horst. 1973. Productivity in telephone communications. *Monthly Labor Review* 96, no. 11 (November):3–9.

Brand, Horst, and Clyde Huffstutler. 1984. Productivity in making air conditioners, refrigeration equipment, and furnaces. *Monthly Labor Review* 107 (December): 11–17.

Bresnahan, Timothy F. 1986. Measuring the spillovers from technical advance:

Mainframe computers in financial services. *American Economic Review* 76 (September):742–55.

Bresnahan, Timothy F., and Peter C. Reiss. 1985. Dealer and manufacturer margins. *Rand Journal of Economics* 16, no. 2 (Summer):253–68.

Brock, Gerald W. 1979. A study of prices and market shares in the computer mainframe industry: Comment. *Journal of Business* 52 (January):119–34.

Burstein, Meyer L. 1960. The demand for household refrigeration in the United States. In *The demand for durable goods,* ed. A. C. Harberger, 99–145. Chicago: University of Chicago Press.

———. 1961. Measurement of quality changes in consumer durables. *Manchester School* 29 (September):267–79.

Bushe, Dennis M. 1981. An empirical analysis of production and technology using heterogeneous capital: thermal electric power generation. Ph.D. diss., New York University, October.

Callahan, Joseph M. 1976. 1977 roominess index. *Automotive Industries* (October 1):32–34.

Cartwright, David W. 1986. Improved deflation of purchases of computers. *Survey of Current Business* 66 (March):7–10.

Cartwright, David W., and Scott D. Smith. 1988. Deflators for purchases of computers in GNP: Revised and extended estimates, 1983–88. *Survey of Current Business* 68 (November):22–23.

Chow, Gregory C. 1967. Technological change and the demand for computers. *American Economic Review* 57 (December):1117–30.

Christensen, Laurits R., and William H. Greene. 1976. Economies of scale in U.S. electric power generation. *Journal of Political Economy* 84, no. 4 (August):655–76.

Clorety, J. A., Jr. 1970. Measuring changes in industrial prices. *Monthly Labor Review* 93 (November):34.

Cole, Rosanne, Y. C. Chen, Joan A. Barquin-Stolleman, Ellen Dulberger, Nurhan Helvecian, and James H. Hodge. 1986. Quality-adjusted price indexes for computer processors and selected peripheral equipment. *Survey of Current Business* 66 (January):41–50.

Consumer appliances: The real cost. N.d. Pamphlet issued by the Massachusetts Institute of Technology Center for Policy Alternatives with the Charles Stark Draper Laboratory, Inc., and Sponsored by the National Science Foundation.

Cooper, R. B., Jr. 1978. Get the Johnny Carson Show before it's bleeped. *TV Guide* (October 21):33–36.

Court, A. T. 1939. Hedonic price indexes with automotive examples. In *The dynamics of automobile demand,* 99–117. Detroit: General Motors.

Cowing, Thomas D. 1970. Technical change in steam electric generation: An engineering approach. Ph.D. diss., University of California, Berkeley.

Cowing, Thomas D., and Kerry V. Smith. 1978. The estimation of a production technology: A survey of econometric analyses of steam-electric generation. *Land Economics* 54, no. 2 (May):156–86.

Cowling, K., and J. Cubbin. 1972. Hedonic price indexes for U.K. cars. *Economic Journal* 82 (September):963–78.

Crandall, Robert W., Howard K. Gruenspecht, Theodore K. Keeler, and Lester B. Lave. 1976. *Regulating the automobile.* Washington, D.C.: Brookings.

Dean, Charles R., and Horace J. DePodwin. 1961. Product variation and price indexes: A case study of electrical apparatus. *Proceedings of the American Statistical Association* (December):271–85.

deMénil, George. 1969. Vintage production functions, monopolistic competition, and price determination. Typescript, Princeton University Economics Department.

Denison, Edward F. 1957. Theoretical aspects of quality change, capital consumption, and net capital formation. In *Problems of capital formation,* ed. Franco Modigliani, Studies in Income and Wealth, no. 19, 215–36. Princeton: Princeton University Press, for NBER.

———. 1967. *Why growth rates differ.* Washington, D.C.: Brookings.

———. 1971. Welfare measurement and the GNP. *Survey of Current Business* 51:1–8.

———. 1972. Some major issues in productivity analysis: An examination of estimates by Jorgenson and Griliches. *Survey of Current Business* 52, no. 5, pt.2:37–63 and Final comments: 95–110.

———. 1985. *Trends in American economic growth, 1929–1982.* Washington, D.C.: Brookings.

———. 1989. *Estimates of productivity change by industry.* Washington, D.C.: Brookings.

Dhrymes, Phoebus J. 1971. Price and quality changes in consumer capital goods: An empirical study. In *Price indexes and quality change,* ed. Zvi Griliches, 88–149. Cambridge, Mass.: Harvard University Press.

Diewert, Erwin. 1976. Exact and superlative index numbers. *Journal of Econometrics* 4:115–45.

———. 1989a. Fisher ideal output, input, and productivity indexes revisited. Discussion paper no. 89–07. University of British Columbia, February.

———. 1989b. The measurement of productivity. Discussion paper no. 89–04. University of British Columbia, January.

Douglas, James W., and James C. Miller III. 1974. Economic regulation of domestic air transport. Washington, D.C.: Brookings.

Dulberger, Ellen. 1989. The application of a hedonic model to a quality-adjusted price index for computer processors. In *Technology and capital formation,* ed. Dale W. Jorgenson and Ralph Landau, 37–75. Cambridge, Mass.: MIT Press.

Early, John F., and James H. Sinclair. 1983. Quality adjustment in the producer price indexes. In *The U.S. national income and product accounts: Selected topics,* Studies in Income and Wealth, vol. 47, ed. Murray F. Foss, 107–42. Chicago: University of Chicago Press, for NBER.

Einstein, Marcus E., and James C. Franklin. 1986. Computer manufacturing enters a new era of growth. *Monthly Labor Review* 109 (September):9–16.

Ellinghaus, William M. 1970. The Bell System's role in data communications. *Bell Telephone Magazine* (November–December):28–31.

Emmet, Boris, and John E. Jeuck. 1950. *Catalogues and counters: A history of Sears, Roebuck and Company.* Chicago: University of Chicago Press.

Faltermayer, Edmund. 1979. Nuclear power after Three-Mile Island. *Fortune* (May 7): 115–22.

Fantel, Hans. 1984. Television 101: Basic buying. *Esquire* (October):46.

———. 1986. The competition for a sharper image comes up against realistic limits. *New York Times,* 2 November, sec. H, 32.

Fettig, Lyle P. 1963a. Adjusting farm tractor prices for quality changes, 1950–62. *Journal of Farm Economics* 45 (August):599–611.

———. 1963b. Price indexes for new farm tractors in the postwar period. Ph.D. diss., University of Chicago, March.

Fisher, Franklin M., John J. McGowan, and Joan E. Greenwood. 1983. *Folded, spindled, and mutilated: Economic analysis and U.S. vs. IBM.* Cambridge, Mass.: MIT Press.

Fisher, Franklin M., James W. McKie, and Richard B. Mancke. 1983. *IBM and the U.S. data processing industry.* New York: Praeger.

Fisher, Franklin M., and Karl Shell. 1972. *The economic theory of price indices.* New York: Academic.

Flamm, Kenneth. 1987. *Targeting the computer: Government support and international competition.* Washington, D.C.: Brookings.

―――. 1988. Economic dimensions of technological advance in communications: A comparison with computers. Working paper. Brookings Institution, March.

―――. 1989. Technological advance and costs: Computers versus communications. In *Changing the rules: Technological change, international competition, and regulation in communications,* ed. R. W. Crandall and K. Flamm, 13–61. Washington, D.C.: Brookings.

Flueck, J. 1961. A study in validity: BLA wholesale price quotations. In *The price statistics of the federal government,* General Series 73, 419–58. New York: National Bureau of Economic Research.

Foss, Murray F., ed. 1983. *The U.S. national income and product accounts: Selected topics.* Studies in Income and Wealth no. 47. Chicago: University of Chicago Press, for NBER.

Gavett, Thomas W. 1967. Quality and a pure price index. *Monthly Labor Review* 90, no. 3:16–20.

Gilbert, Milton. 1961. The problem of quality change and index numbers. *Monthly Labor Review* 85:992–97.

Gollop, Frank M., and Mark J. Roberts. 1983. Environmental regulations and productivity growth: The case of fossil-fueled electric power generation. *Journal of Political Economy* 91 (August):654–74.

Gordon, Robert A. 1961. Differential changes in the prices of consumers' and capital goods. *American Economic Review* 51 (December):937–57.

Gordon, Robert J. 1968. The disappearance of productivity change. Discussion paper no. 38. Harvard Institute for Economic Research.

―――. 1970. Adjusting investment deflators for changes in quality. *Proceedings of the American Statistical Association: Business and Economics Statistics Section,* 174–83.

―――. 1971a. Inflation in recession and recovery. *Brookings Papers on Economic Activity* 2, no. 1:105–66.

―――. 1971b. Measurement bias in price indexes for capital goods. *Review of Income and Wealth,* ser. 17, no. 2 (June):121–74.

―――. 1971c. A rare event. *Survey of Current Business* 51 (July):83–86.

―――. 1974. *The measurement of durable goods prices.* Draft of monograph. New York: National Bureau of Economic Research.

―――. 1975. The impact of aggregate demand on prices. *Brookings Papers on Economic Activity* 6, no. 3:613–62.

―――. 1983. Energy efficiency, user-cost change, and the measurement of durable goods prices. In *The U.S. national income and product accounts: Selected topics,* Studies in Income and Wealth, vol. 47, ed. Murray F. Foss, 205–53. Chicago: University of Chicago Press, for NBER.

―――. 1985. The productivity slowdown in the steam-electric generating industry. Working paper, Northwestern University Economics Department.

―――. 1989. The postwar evolution of computer prices. In *Technology and capital formation,* ed. Dale W. Jorgenson and Ralph Landau, 77–125. Cambridge, Mass.: MIT Press.

Griliches, Zvi. 1961. Hedonic price indexes for automobiles: An econometric analysis of quality change. In *The price statistics of the federal government,* General Series 73, 173–96. New York: National Bureau of Economic Research.

―――. 1964. Notes on the measurement of price and quality changes. In *Models of income determination,* Conference on Research in Income and Wealth, no. 28, 381–404. Princeton, N.J.: Princeton University Press, for NBER.

_____. 1967. Hedonic price indexes revisited: Some notes on the state of the art. *Proceedings of the American Statistical Association,* 324–32. (A revised version appears in *Price indexes and quality change,* ed. Zvi Griliches, 3–15. Cambridge, Mass.: Harvard University Press, 1971.)

_____. 1971. *Price indexes and quality change.* Cambridge, Mass.: Harvard University Press.

_____. 1979. Issues in assessing the contribution of research and development to productivity growth. *Bell Journal of Economics* 10, no. 1 (October):92–116.

_____. 1980. R&D and the productivity slowdown. *American Economic Review Papers and Proceedings* 70:343–48.

Grosch, Herbert R. 1953. High speed arithmetic: The digital computer as a research tool. *Journal of the Optical Society of America* 43 (April).

Hall, Robert E. 1971. The measurement of quality change from vintage price data. In *Price indexes and quality change,* ed. Zvi Griliches, 240–71. Cambridge, Mass.: Harvard University Press.

Hall, Robert E., and Dale W. Jorgenson. 1967. Tax policy and investment behavior. *American Economic Review* 57 (June):391–414.

Hausman, Jerry A., and Paul L. Joskow. 1981. Evaluating the costs and benefits of appliance efficiency standards. Discussion paper no. 13. MIT Energy Laboratory, December.

Hendrickson, Robert. 1979. *The grand emporiums: The illustrated history of America's great department stores.* New York: Stein & Day.

Hogarty, Thomas F. 1972. Hedonic price indexes for automobiles: A new approach. Working paper. Virginia Polytechnic Institute.

Holusha, John. 1989. The next refrigerator may take a step back. *New York Times* (national ed.), 4 March, 17.

Hoover, Ethel D. 1961. The CPI and problems of quality change. *Monthly Labor Review* 85:1175–85.

Horsley, A., and G. M. P. Swann. 1983. A time series of computer price functions. *Oxford Bulletin of Economic Statistics* 45 (November):339–56.

Hudson, E. A., and Dale W. Jorgenson. 1974. U.S. energy policy and economic growth, 1975–2000. *Bell Journal of Economics and Management Science* 5 (Autumn):461–514.

Hunt, Michael S. 1975. Trade associations and self-regulation: Major home appliances. In *Regulating the product: Quality and variety,* ed. Richard E. Caves and Marc J. Roberts, 39–55. Cambridge, Mass.: Ballinger.

Jaffe, Sidney A. 1959. The consumer price index—technical questions and practical answers. *Proceedings of the American Statistical Association: Business and Economic Statistics Section,* 191–97.

Jaszi, George. 1964. Comment. In *Models of income determination,* Conference on Research in Income and Wealth, no. 28, 404–9. Princeton, N.J.: Princeton University Press, for NBER.

_____. 1971. An economic accountant's ledger. *Survey of Current Business* 51 (July):183–227.

Jorgenson, Dale W. 1966. The embodiment hypothesis. *Journal of Political Economy* 74 (February):1–17.

Jorgenson, Dale W., and Zvi Griliches. 1967. The explanation of productivity change. *Review of Economic Studies* 34 (July):249–83.

_____. 1972. Issues in growth accounting: A reply to Edward F. Denison. *Survey of Current Business* 52, no. 5, pt. 2 (May):65–94.

Joskow, Paul L., and Nancy L. Rose. 1985. The effects of technological change, experience, and environmental regulation on the construction cost of coal-burning generating units. *Rand Journal of Economics* 16, no. 1 (Spring):1–27.

Joskow, Paul L., and Richard Schmalensee. 1983. *Markets for power: An analysis of electric utility regulation.* Cambridge, Mass.: MIT Press.

Jung, A. F. 1959. Price variations among automobile dealers in Chicago, Illinois. *Journal of Business,* 32, no. 4:315–26.

———. 1960. Compact car prices in major cities. *Journal of Business* 33, no. 3: 252–57.

Kahn, James A. 1981. The adjustment of the used automobile market to gasoline price shocks: An asset approach. Honors A.B. thesis, Harvard University, March.

Katz, Donald R. 1987. *The big store: Inside the crisis and revolution at Sears.* New York: Viking.

Kelejian, Harry H., and Robert V. Nicoletti. 1974. The rental price of computers: An attribute approach. New York University. Typescript.

Kirchmayer, L. K., A. G. Mellor, J. F. O'Marn, and J. R. Stevenson. 1955. An investigation of the economic size of steam-electric generating units. *American Institute of Electrical Engineers Transactions, Part III, Power Apparatus and Systems* 74 (August):600–614.

Kleinfield, N. R. 1974. For makers of color-TV sets, this year was a black one. *Wall Street Journal,* 4 December, 38.

Knight, K. E. 1966. Changes in computer performance. *Datamation* 12:40–54.

———. 1983. A functional and structural measurement of technology. Paper prepared for the Workshop on Technology Measurement, Dayton, Ohio, October.

Komiya, Ryutaro. 1962. Technological progress and the production function in the United States steam power industry. *Review of Economics and Statistics* 44 (May):156–66.

Kravis, Irving, and Robert E. Lipsey. 1971. *Price competitiveness in world trade.* New York: National Bureau of Economic Research.

Lancaster, Kelvin J. 1971. *Consumer demand: A new approach.* New York: Columbia University Press.

Lichtenberg, Frank R., and Zvi Griliches. 1989. Errors of measurement in output deflators. *Journal of Business and Economic Statistics* 7 (January):1–9.

Lucas, R. E. B. 1975. Hedonic price function. *Economic Inquiry* 13, no. 2:157–78.

McAllister, H. E. 1961. Statistical factors affecting the stability of the wholesale and consumers' price indexes. In *The price statistics of the federal government,* General Series 73, 373–418. New York: National Bureau of Economic Research.

McElheny, Victor K. 1974. Scientists say refrigerators, for 20% more, could be made to run for 50% less. *New York Times* (national ed.), 19 June 1974, 39.

———. 1976. Computer switching of long distance telephone calls put in operation by A.T.&T. *New York Times,* 18 January, 37.

Maddison, Angus. 1987. Growth and slowdown in advanced capitalist economies: Techniques of quantitative assessment. *Journal of Economic Literature* 25 (June):649–98.

Means, Gardiner C. 1935. *Industrial prices and their relative inflexibility.* 74th Cong., 1st sess. S. Doc. 13.

———. 1972. The administered-price thesis reconfirmed. *American Economic Review* 62 (June):292–306.

Michaels, Robert J. 1979. Hedonic prices and the structure of the digital computer industry. *Journal of Industrial Economics* 27 (March):263–74.

Miller, Bryan W. 1980. An extension of the Chow study of technological change and the demand for computers. Undergraduate diss. submitted for A.B. degree, Princeton University, 11 April.

Mills, Frederick C. 1936. Price data and problems of price research. *Econometrica* 4 (October):289–309.

Moore, F. T. 1959. Economics of scale: Some statistical evidence. *Quarterly Journal of Economics* 73 (May):232–45.

Muellbauer, J. N. J. 1971a. Testing the "Cagan-Hall" and the "hedonic" hypotheses. Paper presented to the summer meeting of the Econometric Society, Boulder, Colo., 27 August.

———. 1971b. The theory of "true" input price indices. Economic research paper no. 17. University of Warwick, July.

———. 1974. Household production theory, quality, and the "hedonic technique." *American Economic Review* 64 (March):977–94.

Musgrave, John C. 1986. Fixed reproducible tangible wealth in the United States: Revised estimates. *Survey of Current Business* (January):51–75.

Nadiri, M. Ishaq, and Mark A. Schankerman. 1981. The structure of production, technological change, and the rate of growth of total factor productivity in the U.S. Bell System. In *Productivity measurement in regulated industries,* ed. T. G. Cowing and R. E. Stevenson, 219–47. New York: Academic.

National Bureau of Economic Research. 1961. *The price statistics of the federal government.* General Series 73. New York: National Bureau of Economic Research.

Nerlove, Marc. 1963. Returns to scale in electricity supply. In *Measurement in economics,* ed. C. Christ, 167–98. Stanford, Calif.: Stanford University Press.

Nordhaus, William D. 1982. Economic policy in the face of declining productivity growth. *European Economic Review* 18, nos. 1/2:131–57.

Ohta, Makoto. 1975. Production technologies of the U.S. boiler and turbogenerator industries and hedonic price indexes for their products: A cost function approach. *Journal of Political Economy* 83 (February):1–26.

Ohta, Makoto, and Zvi Griliches. 1976. Automobile prices revisited: Extensions on the hedonic hypothesis. In *Household production and consumption,* ed. N. E. Terleckyj, 325–90. New York: National Bureau of Economic Research.

———. 1986. Automobiles prices and quality: Did the gasoline price increase change consumer tastes in the U.S.? *Journal of Business and Economic Statistics* 4, no. 2 (April 1986):187–98.

Oliner, Stephen D. 1988. Capital and the slowdown of growth in the United States: A review. Working paper no. 87. Economic Activity Section, Division of Research and Statistics, Board of Governors of the Federal Reserve System, July.

Parks, Richard W. 1974. The demand and supply of durable goods and durability. *American Economic Review* 64:37–55.

Phister, Montgomery. 1979. *Data processing technology and economics.* 2d ed. Santa Monica, Calif.: DEC.

Pollak, Robert A. 1971. The theory of the cost of living index. Working paper no. 11. Bureau of Labor Statistics, U.S. Department of Labor.

Prewitt, Edward. 1988. Cleaning up the king of kilowatts. *Fortune* (June 6):180.

Ratchford, Brian T., and Gary T. Ford. 1976. A study of prices and market shares in the computer mainframe industry. *Journal of Business* 49 (April):194–218.

Rees, Albert. 1961a. Alternative retail price indexes for selected nondurable goods, 1947–59. In *The price statistics of the federal government,* General Series 73, 137–72. New York: National Bureau of Economic Research.

———. 1961b. *Real wages in manufacturing, 1890–1914.* Princeton, N.J.: Princeton University Press, for NBER.

Rice, R. B. 1946. Progress report on diesel developments. *Proceedings of the 18th National Conference, Oil and Gas Power Division,* American Society of Mechanical Engineers, Milwaukee, Wis., 12–15 June.

Rosen, Sherwin. 1974. Hedonic prices and implicit markets: Product differentiation in pure competition. *Journal of Political Economy* 82 (January/February):34–49.

Rosenberg, Nathan, and L. E. Birdzell, Jr. 1986. *How the West grew rich*. New York: Basic.

Ruist, Erik. 1968. Index Numbers: (I Theoretical Aspects). *International Encyclopedia of the Social Sciences,* ed. David Sills, 7, 154–59. New York: Macmillan.

Rymes, Thomas K. 1971. *On concepts of capital and technical change*. Cambridge: Cambridge University Press.

Salpukas, Agis. 1978. Machine tools: Uproar over a bottleneck. *New York Times,* 26 February, sec. F-1, 12.

Samuelson, Paul A., and S. Swamy. 1974. Invariant economic index numbers and canonical duality: Survey and synthesis. *American Economic Review* 64:566–93.

Schultz, Theodore W. 1974. Lingering doubts about economics. Paper presented at the meetings of American Economic Association and the History of Economics Society, 30 December.

Searle, A. D. 1964. Capital goods pricing. In *Measuring the nation's wealth,* 358–59. Princeton, N.J.: Princeton University Press, for NBER.

Searle, A. D., Chairman. 1970. Report on criteria for choice of unit values or prices in deflators: Report of the Subcommittee on Prices to the Interagency Committee on Measurement of Real Output. Washington, D.C.: Bureau of the Budget.

Sharpe, William F. 1969. *The economics of the computer*. New York: Columbia University Press.

Snyder, David, and Peter D. Waldstein. 1988. Sears: Why the last big store must transform itself, or die. *Crain's Chicago Business,* 11 July 1988, 15–32.

Sobotka, Stephen P. 1959. *Prices of used commercial aircraft, 1959–65*. Northwestern University Transportation Center, February.

Solow, Robert M. 1957. Technical change and the aggregate production function. *Review of Economics and Statistics* 39 (August):312–20.

———. 1960. Investment and technical progress. In *Mathematical methods in the social sciences, 1959,* ed. K. J. Arrow, S. Karlin, and P. Suppes. Stanford, Calif.: Stanford University Press.

Stigler, George. 1947. The kinky oligopoly demand curve and rigid prices. *Journal of Political Economy* 55 (October):432–49.

Stigler, George, and James K. Kindahl. 1970. *The behavior of industrial prices*. New York: National Bureau of Economic Research.

Stoneman, P. 1978. Merger and technological progressiveness: The case of the British computer industry. *Applied Economics* 10:125–40.

Stotz, Margaret S. 1966. Introductory prices of 1966 automobile models. *Monthly Labor Review* 89, no. 2:178–81.

Straszheim, Mahlon R. 1969. *The international airline industry*. Washington, D.C.: Brookings.

Taylor, C. F. 1962. Engine design for progress. *Proceedings of the 34th National Conference, Oil and Gas Power Division,* American Society of Mechanical Engineers, Washington, D.C., 15–19 April.

Törnqvist, Leo. 1936. The Bank of Finland's consumption price index. *Bank of Finland Monthly Bulletin* 10:1–8.

———. 1937. Finland's Banks konsumtionsprisindex. *Nordisk tidskrift for teknisk okonomi* 8:79–83.

Triplett, Jack E. 1969. Automobiles and hedonic quality measurement. *Journal of Political Economy* 77 (May/June):408–17.

———. 1971a. Determining the effects of quality change on the CPI. *Monthly Labor Review* 94 (May):27–32.

———. 1971b. Quality bias in price indexes and new methods of quality measurement. In *Price indexes and quality change,* ed. Zvi Griliches, 183–214. Cambridge, Mass.: Harvard University Press.

_____. 1975. The measurement of inflation: A survey of research on the accuracy of price indexes. In *Analysis of inflation,* ed. Paul H. Earl, 19–82. Lexington, Mass.: Lexington.

_____. 1983a. Comment. In *The U.S. national income and product account: Selected topics,* Studies in Income and Wealth, vol. 47, ed. Murray F. Foss, 253–65. Chicago: University of Chicago Press, for NBER.

_____. 1983b. Concepts of quality in input and output price measures: A resolution of the user-value resource-cost debate. In *The U.S. national income and product account: Selected topics,* Studies in Income and Wealth, vol. 47, ed. Murray F. Foss, 296–311. Chicago: University of Chicago Press, for NBER.

_____. 1986. The economic interpretation of hedonic models. *Survey of Current Business* 66 (January):36–40.

_____. 1988. Price index research and its influence on data: A historical review. Paper presented to fiftieth anniversary conference of the Conference on Research in Income and Wealth, Washington, D.C., 12 May.

_____. 1989. Price and technological change in a capital good: A survey of research on computers. In *Technology and capital formation,* ed. Dale W. Jorgenson and Ralph Landau, 127–213. Cambridge, Mass.: MIT Press.

Triplett, Jack E., and Richard J. McDonald. 1977. Assessing the quality error in output measures: The case of refrigerators. *Review of Income and Wealth* 23 (June):127–56.

Urquhart, John. 1985. Telephone companies adapt to changing needs for space. *Wall Street Journal,* 13 November, 29.

Weaver, Paul H. 1975. Behind the great scrubber fracas. *Fortune* (February):106–14.

Weil, Gordon L. 1977. *Sears, Roebuck, U.S.A.: The great American catalog store and how it grew.* New York: Stein & Day.

White, Lawrence J. 1982. *The regulation of air pollutant emissions from motor vehicles.* Washington, D.C.: American Enterprise Institute.

Wilcox, James A. 1984. Automobile fuel efficiency: Measurement and explanation. *Economic Inquiry* 22 (July):375–85.

Wills, Hugh. 1978. Estimation of a vintage capital model for electricity generating. *Review of Economic Studies* 45, no. 141 (October):495–510.

Worthy, James C. 1984. *Shaping an institution: Robert E. Wood and Sears, Roebuck.* Urbana: University of Illinois Press.

Young, Allan H. 1989a. Alternative measures of real GNP. *Survey of Current Business* 69 (April):27–34.

_____. 1989b. BEA's measurement of computer output. *Survey of Current Business* 69 (July):108–15.

Young, David. 1979. Electro-motive looks at orders, recalls good old days. *Chicago Tribune,* 18 July, sec. 4, 1, 3.

_____. 1983. Rail cars roll steadily toward standardization. *Chicago Tribune,* 29 May, sec. 5, 1–2.

Zweig, Jason. 1988. It was a matter of economics. *Forbes,* 22 February, 106–8.

Institutional and Government Publications

Aerospace Facts and Figures, various issues.
Automotive News 1971 Almanac Issue.
Aviation Week and Space Technology, 17 December 1984.
Avmark. 1984. *Sales of used commercial aircraft, 1970–83.* Arlington, Va.
Avmark Newsletter, various issues.
Consumer Reports, 1947–87, various issues.

Consumers' Union. 1986. I'll buy that: 50 small wonders and big deals that revolutionized the lives of consumers. In *A 50-year retrospective by the editors of "Consumers Reports."* Mt. Vernon, N.Y.: Consumers Union.

Edison Electric Institute. 1984. *Statistical Yearbook of the Electric Utility Industry/1983,* no. 51. Washington, D.C.: Edison Electric Institute, December.

National Association of Automobile Dealers. *NADA official used car guide.* McLean, Va.

National Market Reports. *Red book: Official used car valuations.* Chicago.

United Airlines. 1983. *Great seats in the friendly skies.* Brochure, July.

U.S. Bureau of the Census. 1947–83. *Current Industrial Reports,* various issues.

U.S. Civil Aeronautics Board. *Aircraft operating cost and performance report* (July).

————. Form 41, Schedule B–43, various years.

————. 1977. A price index for air frames and engines, 1957–76. Mimeograph release, June.

U.S. Department of Energy. 1983. *Thermal-electric plant construction cost and annual production expenses—1980.* Washington, D.C.,: Energy Information Administration, June.

————. 1984. *Financial statistics of selected electric utilities, 1983 annual.* Washington, D.C.: Energy Information Administration, October.

————. 1985. *Historical plant cost and annual production expenses for selected electric plants, 1983.* Washington, D.C.: Energy Information Administration.

————. 1987. *Historical plant cost and annual production expenses for selected electric plants, 1985.* Washington, D.C.: Energy Information Administration.

U.S. Executive Office of the President. Council on Wage and Price Stability. 1977. *The wholesale price index: Review and evaluation.* Washington, D.C., June.

U.S. Federal Power Commission. 1969. *Steam electric plant construction cost and annual production expenses, twenty-second annual supplement.* Washington, D.C.

Index